THE SIXTIES

The Daily Telegraph

THE SIXTIES

A CHRONICLE
OF THE DECADE

edited and introduced by
DAVID HOLLOWAY

researched by
DIANA HEFFER
& DAVID WARD

foreword by
W. F. DEEDES

SIMON & SCHUSTER
London . Sydney . New York . Tokyo . Singapore . Toronto

First published in Great Britain by
SIMON & SCHUSTER LIMITED 1992
under the licence of Telegraph books.

A Paramount Communications Company

© 1992, The Daily Telegraph plc.

Simon & Schuster Limited
West Garden Place
Kendal Street
London W2 2AQ

Simon & Schuster Sydney Australia Pty Limited

A CIP catalogue record for this book is available from The British Library
ISBN 0 - 671 - 71159 - 8

Picture credits: Pictures on pages 19, 21, 27, 32, 47, 50, 51, 60, 85, 87, 112: Topham.
Pictures on pages 14, 15, 23, 68, 82, 110, 116, 133, 139, 152, 154: Hulton Deutsch Collection.

Phototypeset by Imaging Business
Printed and bound in Great Britain by Butler & Tanner, Frome and London.

CONTENTS

INTRODUCTION

Like its companion volume for the 1950s, *The Sixties* does not pretend to be a systematic history of the decade. It is a scrapbook or, if you like, a tapestry of the years 1960 to 1969 as they were reflected in one newspaper. Much has been curtailed but nothing has been altered. Only in the short introductions to each year has any hindsight been allowed. It is more than likely that many of those whose contributions to *The Daily Telegraph* are printed here would not now agree with the views that they expressed then. This does not matter because the purpose of this book is to show what people did and thought during the 1960s.

Very few of the events during the decade were covered in a single item. For instance, the Vietnam war dragged on throughout the period. It has not been possible to present a detailed account of it or any other continuing affair. My policy has been to choose a single moment and let it stand for the whole. The same guidelines apply to, say, the major crimes: the moors murders; the great train robbery, the escape of the spy George Blake.

All the major happenings, I hope, have been covered in one way or another, sometimes on the news pages and at others in leading articles or merely by a picture. To have restricted the selection merely to those stories which dominated the front page would have overbalanced the book, so many smaller items have been included to show how people dressed and ate, what they thought about the new plays and books, who were the popular sporting stars.

Decades are neat divisions of time but history has a tendency to be untidy. The 1960s are no exception. You could argue that the youth culture which took up so much newspaper space began in the middle 1960s and culminated in the student riots of 1967 and 1968. The murder of John F. Kennedy in 1963 brought an end to the hopes of a new frontier which his election of 1960 had foreshadowed. A new era in British politics began with the election of Harold Wilson's Labour government in 1964. By the end of the decade, it might have been struggling with an increasingly difficult economic situation, but there was no hint that it would be turned out of office in the general election of 1970. Only in the race to put a man into space did the decade prove a neat division: Yuri Gagarin completed the first manned flight in 1961 while in 1969 Americans became the first men to walk on the moon. While one year might contain more momentous events than another, within these pages exactly the same space has been given to each year. The division between news, features, the arts, obituaries and sport is maintained throughout.

*

The preparation of a book of this kind is essentially a team effort. I am solely responsible for what is included and am acutely aware of how much, because of restrictions of space, has been omitted. My thanks must go, first, to Bill (Lord) Deedes for writing the Foreword in his inimitable way. I joined *The Daily Telegraph* in 1960. He had already then been on the staff of the paper (and the *Morning Post* which amalgamated with the *Telegraph* in 1937) for some thirty years, and, happily, is still there.

Diana Heffer and David Ward have not only done wonders in searching the files but have with magnificent serendipity produced many items of news which I had forgotten and took place when they were both children. At Simon & Schuster, Sian Parkhouse has kept a firm but kindly eye on my endeavours and Fenella Smart, with Jo Beerts of The Imaging Business, has turned the messy, gummed pages I had prepared into this handsome volume. My last thanks, as always, are to Sally who tolerated our home almost disappearing under green plastic box after green plastic box of cuttings and a dining-room table permanently sticky from my efforts with scissors and paste. Few wives would have done so, and so uncomplainingly.

David Holloway, July 1992

The Daily Telegraph

FOREWORD

My instructions were specific. "Beat", 16, our young visitor from Austria, would travel to London with me and come to *The Daily Telegraph* office in Fleet Street. Thence he would be directed to St Paul's Cathedral up Ludgate Hill (which his mother desired him to see) returning in time for lunch. At 2 p.m. we became anxious. By 4 p.m. we were alarmed. "Beat" had never seen London before. At 4.30 p.m. he came back, delighted with himself. He had been buying gear in Carnaby Street.

London was swinging. It was the mid-60s. To visit London from Europe and not to see Carnaby Street was unthinkable. For the young there was a touch of magic in the air, which seems elusive now … I asked Anne Allport, who now works for CARE, the international relief organisation, to try spontaneously to recapture it.

"I was 16 in 1960, and I can't think of a better time for being 16. We were completely irresponsible, and having an absolutely whale of a time. There was this feeling that London was the centre of the universe – and I suppose that was why it was particularly great, being in London, because it was where it was at - and it really was. It was dancing … it was music … it was drinking … it was Mary Quant ….

"But men started to think about how they should dress as well, which was quite amazing. No one had thought about men and fashion until then. But it was all part of the same thing, that London was the creative place to be, and people just had a wonderful time. We had everything to go for . . ."

"Such as?"

"Well, we were there. We just felt we were liberating ourselves from our parents' generation, who'd all been rather gloomy after the war. And there was a new kind of moral framework in place, because people were starting to use contraceptives and I suppose that sort of eased the way … and there was the influx of music, partly from America, but there was a great creative emphasis for music in this country. And you just felt as if you could do everything … Whereas I think people now don't feel that, you don't get that feeling coming off them … that life's great, and that they've got other things to look forward to …

"And the other thing that I think did happen … class barriers somewhat started to break down. So there was this strange idea that if you came from the north or had a cockney background, you were flavour of the month. It was a kind of inverted snobbery, which was brilliant. So you would go to parties and you'd find that you might be dancing with a peer or you might be dancing with a barrow boy, and I can actually remember a party where I did both. I had one at either end of the room, and it was great … And I was somewhere in the middle, but to have the two extremes …!"

"The money went round?"

"Yes, and we were all certain we were going to get jobs. It never occured to us that we wouldn't get jobs. No one ever said, 'if you get a job', as people do now. It was just 'what shall I do with this wonderful range of opportunities?' We didn't have a huge amount of money, but we had a lot more than our parents ever had – to spend on consumer goodies. There didn't seem to be a problem …"

Malcolm Muggeridge, then 60-something, saw it differently. After declaring that his election as Rector of Edinburgh University by students was due exclusively "to the telly", he went on to complain that education had become a sort of mumbo-jumbo or cure-all for the ills of a godless and decomposing society. Whether it was juvenile deliquency, high-school pregnancies or drug addiction among Brownies, he said, the solution offered was always the same – more education.

The so-called "permissive" morality of those times, he thought, would reach its apogee. "When birth pills are handed out with free orange juice, and consenting adults wear special ties and blazers, and abortion and divorce – those two contemporary panaceas for all matrimonial ills – are freely available on the public health, then at last, with the suicide rate up to Scandinavian proportions and the psychiatric wards bursting at the seams, it will be realised that this path, even from the shallow point of view of the pursuit of happiness, is a disastrous cul-de-sac."

Malcolm in his 60s (though not averse to young company) and Allport at 16 saw the world through totally different spectacles: "The curtain," he insisted, "indeed is falling if it has not already fallen on all the Utopian hopes which have prevailed so strongly for a century or more. I personally rejoice that it should be so because I know that then, desperately looking into the mystery of things, we shall once again understand that fulfilment must be sought through the spirit, not the body or the mind, and will be realised, if at all, elsewhere than in this world of time and space."

There were few interruptions during this address, at the conclusion of which Malcolm Muggeridge was loudly applauded and cheered.

There is a clue to be found, perhaps, to these apparently stark contradictions, and it lies in the words – "we just felt we were liberating ourselves from our parents' generation, who'd all been rather gloomy after the war." Many of us had been gloomy after the war – and for a long time afterwards. Muggeridge, like Evelyn Waugh, saw the outcome of the war as some kind of betrayal by the West to a godless Soviet Union, and partly on that account began to write off the chances of Western civilisation.

And those who had arrived with the "baby boom" of the late 1940s experienced a childhood of rationing and austerity which extended well into the '50s. Butter was rationed until April 1954, meat until July 1954, coal until 1958. Recovery moved like an iceberg. Resettlement was difficult. The human loss in 1939—45 was lighter than the First World War, but the physical damage in this country much heavier. Round many family hearths in those years there was a marked absence of joyfulness.

Furthermore, this had lasted a long time. My salad days had come in the 1930s, and I recall vividly the struggle through the Great Depression, with unemployment on every street corner. Barely had we emerged from that than new spectres arose in Europe. Their shadows grew longer and had finally engulfed us before the '30s were ended. Five years of war; five years of recovery under a Labour government not averse to using austerity as an instrument of social justice; then an uncertain period of convalescence. For young men there was National Service from 1948 until 1960.

After three such decades of mixed constraints and apprehensions, small wonder the young were ready to break out and start throwing their caps over windmills. Macmillan helped to set them off, perhaps, with his speech to a Conservative rally at Bradford in July 1957: "Let us be frank about it, most of our people have never had it so good …"

The world itself seemed ready for new adventures. In January 1960 it learned that John Kennedy would run for President. In July he won the nomination from Senator Johnson. The Eisenhower era, the era of war heroes as national leaders, was fading. Nixon, who had finished level with Kennedy in a drab black-and-white television debate, ran Kennedy close – to 120,000 votes. A biting cold wind and a snow-covered Capitol Hill marked Kennedy's inauguration. But there a mark was set on the spirit of those times.

We may see it differently now, but at that time John Kennedy caught the ears of young and old with his promise of a different and a better world. "For the world is changing. The old era is ending. The old ways will not do … The problems are not all solved and the battles are not all won – and we stand today on the edge of a New Frontier – the frontier of the 1960s – a frontier of unknown opportunities and perils – a frontier of unfulfilled hopes and threats …

"Can a nation organised and governed such as ours endure? That is the real question. Have we the nerve and the will? Can we carry through in an age where we will witness not only new breakthroughs in weapons of destruction – but also a race for the mastery of the sky and the rain, the ocean and the tides, the far side of space and the inside of men's minds?"

In the Los Angeles Coliseum that Friday evening, eighty thousand cheered their hearts out at those words. In many parts of the world, Kennedy's words stirred other hearts as well.

The New Frontier … In London, the decision was taken that Britain must bid to join the Common Market. Both Russia and the United States were reaching into outer space. Early in 1961, Americans put Ham, a chimp, into space; the Russians followed with a brace of dogs. In April their Major Yuri Gagarin became the first man to fly in space. Not until February 1962 did John Glenn become the first American to orbit the earth. In 1965 major Ed White of America was walking through space. Finally, in 1969, Neil Armstrong, commander of Apollo II, took "one small step for man, one giant leap for mankind" by walking on the moon.

In South Africa, as the decade opened, Macmillan declared, "The wind of change is blowing through this continent and, whether we like it or not, this growth of national consciousness is a political fact." Six weeks later, as if to underscore his words, police opened fire in the black township of Sharpeville in the Transvaal. In the massacre, 56 Africans died and 162 were injured.

The growth of national consciousness to which Macmillan referred took widely different forms. In the Congo, Belgian authority collapsed and a bloody civil war began. Somalia was created, Nigeria won independence, Dr Banda – still with us – won his first election in Malawi. Early in 1960, 15 new African nations were admitted to the United Nations. Later, in Nigeria, the agony of Biafra roused furious antagonisms. Here, as the decade opened, there were other signs of a change in style. At Westminster an Act of Parliament was passed to curb Teddy Boys. Hitchcock's *Pyscho* opened to applause. Clark Gable, pre-war symbol of American manhood on the screen, died. The B.B.C. dropped Children's Hour. The first Mothercare opened in Kingston. *The News Chronicle* and its Liberal sympathies vanished into the belly of the *Daily Mail*. Nye Bevan, Labour's most exciting orator of the century, died. The three millionth Mini came off the production lines. Yves St. Laurent, at 21, set up his own couture house in Paris. Early in 1962 an Essex school boy – later to grow into Essex Man – claimed to break the world's record by dancing the Twist non-stop for 33 hours. From Liverpool, the Beatles burst forth.

What lit the sky of cultural freedom, and glowed for a long time, was a decision by Penguin Books to publish an unexpurgated version of D.H. Lawrence's *Lady Chatterley's Lover*. The first run of 200,000 copies sold out on the first day of publication. A prosecution was expected, duly took place and lived wholly up to expectations. To some it symbolised a crusade against censorship; to others, it was opening the sluice gates. The trial was historic, for it led to a form of cultural trench warfare in this country which has been raging ever since.

Here, politically, there were also faint ominous signs of a change in style. Macmillan, whose expansive methods had won for the Tories a third consecutive victory in 1959, had become known as "Supermac", with all the ill omens that carries for a British Prime Minister. *Private Eye* had arrived. Irreverence was in the air. By the Spring of 1962 political restiveness was making itself acutely felt, famously through a by-election at Orpington, where a Government majority of 14,760 in 1959 was turned into a Liberal one of 7,855.

The Sunday Telegraph (also new to the scene) had remarked of Macmillan a month earlier that "those who wish him to remain, and they are the majority, believe that he should revitalise the Administration by carrying out a bold and ruthless reconstruction." The Prime Minister took that in. Discussion centred on when it should be done. Early autumn is usually a good time, but a Commonwealth Conference in September – primarily to discuss the Common Market – made that difficult. The decision therefore lay between July, always a feverish parliamentary month, and August.

I read in the *Daily Mail* of July 12 that Macmillan was about to swoop – though without strong personal interest. I had found ministerial office 1954—57 a useful but unappealing experience and, at that time, singularly ill-paid; and so had retired from office when Macmillan took over from Eden. My first intimation that something odd was happening came on the evening of July 13. We were fitting together an unusually dull Peterborough column at 135 Fleet Street, when a private secretary at No. 10 rang to ask if I would visit the Prime Minister.

It was Friday July 13, and those who are tiresomely superstitious about such dates can take heart from what followed. In truth most of the seven Cabinet Ministers who were sacked had signified their willingness, even their desire, to go at a time convenient to the Prime Minister. But haste, induced by a newspaper leak, proved ruinous. What had been intended as a move to revive the morale of Macmillan's party bore the appearance of a singularly graceless operation. I recall a painful dinner at the House of Commons with Selwyn Lloyd, sacked Chancellor of the Exchequer, while a third party strove to overcome his reluctance to accept Macmillan's consolation prize of a CH. In the following week, the Queen held one of her Garden Parties at Buckingham Palace. The fallen and their successors paraded the garden with their spouses and greeted each other stiffly. It was not a happy afternoon. Nor was it a happy portent.

My duties as a Minister without Portfolio seemed nebulous, but the immediately tangible one was to set in motion a campaign to inform the public about life in the European Community, towards which destiny pointed. This was fun, not least because we had strictly to keep within an offside rule, which was that Government money could never be spent on propaganda, only on information.

I set up a joint committee of senior Treasury and Foreign Office officials, and persuaded parliamentary chums to form a steering committee. We busied ourselves with producing numerous reassuring facts about every aspect of life in Europe. Millions of these fact sheets were then distributed through the nation's voluntary organisations, ranging from the National Farmers Union to the National Union of Women. This was boy's work compared with that of Ted Heath, who was trying to negotiate our entry into Europe, but it gave us a sense of mission. It seemed to me also that women were going to count for much more. So we set up a committee representing every principal woman's organisation in the country, which met at the Treasury once a month to raise pertinent questions about Europe. Officials had to turn up and answer questions on the spot. A pity it died.

Public opinion here was moving towards Europe anyway, but by the end of 1962 I flattered myself that our Boy Scout movement had contributed a nudge in the right direction. The Prime Minister expressed satisfaction. Then, in mid-January 1963, President de Gaulle of France declared for his own reasons that we were unfitted to join the European Community. In retrospect, de Gaulle's decision was a heavy blow, from which in my judgement Macmillan's government never fully recovered. A main objective was removed. We lost momentum.

It was a gloomy time in politics. Hugh Gaitskell died suddenly. Political satire took off with the B.B.C.'s *That Was the Week That Was* – to think that David Frost has lived so long! Amid indignant noises, the B.B.C. declared that the public was six to four in favour. Millicent Martin, star of the show, told a male companion to button up his flies. It was a good summing up.

Governments are like sailing ships. They need wind in the mainsail to keep moving. When becalmed, all sorts of noisome objects creep on board.

> *The very deep did rot: O Christ!*
> *That ever this should be!*
> *Yea, slimy things did crawl with legs*
> *Upon the slimy sea.*

Late in 1962, a 38-year old Admiralty clerk, William Vassall, had been found guilty of spying and sent to jail for 18 years. It was about the time the world was holding its breath over Russian missiles in Cuba, but the Vassall affair rivalled that for the front pages. Correspondence between Vassall and a junior Minister in the Admiralty, Tam Galbraith, was held to be compromising. Although the Vassall tribunal subsequently cleared all Ministers of impropriety, Galbraith was called on to resign. Early in 1963 a *Daily Sketch* journalist was jailed for refusing to reveal sources to the tribunal. A month later, two *Daily Mail* reporters went the same way. Newspapers, as I had reason to know, became resentful – to put it mildly.

Against this unpromising background, the Profumo affair unfolded. Played over and over again ever since, its details do not have to be recited here; but there are footnotes to add. The circumstances in which the drama developed were calculated to produce not so much conspiracy as tragedy. By chance, I was sitting late one night on the Government front bench with Henry Brooke, Home Secretary. Both of us heard the allegations of Labour M.P.s.

It was a Thursday. So the House would meet at 11 a.m. next day instead of 2.30 p.m.; a statement would be sought and there was precious little time to prepare one. Jack Profumo, whose doorstep was picketed by reporters, had prudently taken a sleeping pill and retired to bed. So did others of us, only to be awoken at 2 a.m. and summoned to the Chief Whip's office at the House for further discussions. We then cross-examined a somnolent Jack Profumo. Those who can lay their hand on their heart and declare that in such bizarre circumstances they would unfailingly have told the truth, the whole truth and nothing but the truth are entitled to condemn him. Eventually I took Peter (Lord) Rawlinson off to my room where I kept a typewriter and typed out his statement.

It was, *The Times* declared at the time, a Moral Question and 30 years later it has indeed turned into a Morality Tale, though not as *The Times* then perceived it. Those who felt able to pass the first test must now ask themselves two further questions. Are they positive that the last 30 years of their life has been spent as rewardingly and selflessly as Jack Profumo's at Toynbee Hall, the East London settlement? Are they also sure that they would have had the strength of mind to take that road of self-redemption in the first place? If the answer to all three questions is yes, I salute them. In the long run Jack Profumo has acted more honourably than the riff-raff who have lined their pockets with regurgitations of this story, or the newspaper proprietors who did most of the lining.

But I digress. There were other profoundly depressing political developments in 1963. Early one November evening we learned that President Kennedy was dead, murdered in Dallas, an event which echoes on to this day. President Johnson took office and inherited the Vietnam war. The Beeching axe fell about some 2,000 railway stations and 67,000 jobs. His mission had been conceived by his Minister and admirer, Ernest Marples, as a progressive stroke for the Government. It was seen quite otherwise by railway travellers. It became known that Kim Philby was the Third Man. Rachman, a slum landlord and racketeer, made a rod for the Government's back, and ultimately for the backs of landlords and their tenants. The trial of Stephen Ward kept the scandal pot boiling. The Great Train Robbery netted £2.6 million and left a coshed engine driver impaired for life. It was perhaps the right moment for an ageing Winston Churchill to declare that he would not be seeking future election.

The Central African Federation, designed to bring what was then Northern Rhodesia (Zambia), Southern Rhodesia (Zimbabwe) and Nyasaland (Malawi) into a partnership with Sir Roy Welensky at its head collapsed irretrievably. Another ship sunk. I thought mournfully of the high hopes some of us had entertained for this arrangement; particularly after engineers had brilliantly harnessed the Zambesi at the Kariba dam, which was to provide power for all the region.

Many more, however, had mourned the death by her own hand a year previously of Marilyn Monroe, a shining figure of the '60s, who had earned her studio £70 million: "Everybody is always tugging at you … They would all like sort of a chunk of you." Elsewhere, culture was looking up, or at least forward. Robbins on Higher Education called for a massive extension of higher education. The second of Ian Fleming's James Bond adventures appeared on the screen in 1963 and there was promise of all 12 adventures going into production. The B.B.C. scrapped the panel game *What's My Line?* Beatlemania took a firm grip on this country and stormed the United States; they starred at a Royal Command Performance. By mid-1964 they had become Britain's most popular tourist attraction. In the last days of 1963, France lost her "little sparrow", Edith Piaf, who sand *Je ne regrette rien*. She caught the spirit of the times.

I have never doubted that Macmillan's sudden prostate attack in October 1963, which changed the course of politics, was primarily pyschosomatic. Stress hits politicians – and most people – where they are physically most vulnerable. Alec Home was chosen to succeed him because, whatever people

say, after some months of rattling scandal he looked the cleanest man on board.

Taking into account the impact which Harold Wilson was beginning to make with "the white heat of this scientific revolution", Home did the Conservative party astonishingly well. But for his own homeland, where the Tory vote collapsed, he might have scored a fourth Tory victory on the lines of John Major's in 1992.

Decades are imperfect measurements. In one sense a fresh decade opened in this country in 1964 with the advent of Harold Wilson's first Labour Government. It produced landmarks of its own: a monumental row with Ian Smith's Rhodesia, which roared on for the best part of 15 years; the abolition of capital punishment; a National Plan (which was stillborn); breathtesting of motorists; and measures aimed at improving increasingly strained race relations in this country.

I took an irresponsible fancy to Ian Smith, whose obstinacy was widely deplored in this country – except by those who enjoyed seeing Harold Wilson discountenanced. Wilson's declaration in early 1966 that sanctions "might well bring the rebellion to an end within a matter of weeks rather than months" was to create much mirth. During many visits to Rhodesia in the ensuing years, I came to the conclusion that a country does not discover its character until it has its back hard to the wall. Smith's rebellious and for a time successful drive for self-sufficiency fairly shone alongside much of what we see in Africa now.

By the end of 1966, London had become widely recognised as "the swinging city". "In a decade dominated by youth," *Time* magazine declared, "London has burst into bloom. It swings, it is the scene." Carnaby Street was the place to buy clothes – for both sexes. Twiggy, a cockney of 17 and weighing 6½ stone, became a gleam in many eyes. And there was Mary Quant in King's Road, which offered its own brand of magic: clothes, music, restaurants, the scene …

There was of course a debit side to all this. "Pot" was in vogue, and so were some of its ugly sisters. About this time, I was approached by two former public servants who wanted to create an Institute for the Study of Drug Addiction. We set about it. I am happy to know that it now flourishes under the patronage of the Princess of Wales. Through work with various bodies and travel in America during the next seven or eight years, I formed certain heretical conclusions about dangerous drugs. The world has turned its face away from war, because modern war has produced unacceptable casualties. It will only turn away from drugs when they, too, produce unacceptable casualties.

At the close of 1969, Brian Jones, the Rolling Stones' former guitarist, died (according to the coroner) of "alcohol and drugs". To mark this event, the Stones played to 250,000 people in Hyde Park. Mick Jagger, clad in white, delivered a eulogy to Brian Jones, intoning the lines of Shelley's *Adonais*. All were enraptured. We have not, yet, moved on much from there.

Odd things happened in the Universities. At one, where I delivered a lunch-time talk, they introduced me to a tramp whom the students had installed as a member of the university. They cherished him as a symbol of social injustice. An evening visit to Essex University, then exotically described as "the university without rules", produced extraordinary scenes. The meeting itself was broken up by transvestites with musical instruments and loo paper. After we had called it a day, the local M.P. and myself were stalked round the campus by a bunch of sportsmen who felt the evening's entertainment had been cut short and were spoiling for a fight. The Dean of Studies, blue round the gills with fright, declared he dare not intervene. We left, uninjured, in a badly damaged car. It made a good piece for *The Sunday Telegraph* – "In the Eye of the Student Storm" – which Essex University at the time was silly enough to resent.

It was not atypical of the expanding and radical university scene, which made any visit by a right-wing speaker something of an adventure. The London School of Economics in 1969 exploded with rage at the appointment of a new Director and had temporarily to be closed. This was playground behaviour in comparison with Germany and France. Student leader Daniel "The Red" Cohn-Bendit of Germany (deported by France in April 1969) had few peers but many imitators. In his memoirs, *Time and Chance*, Jim Callaghan, Home Secretary during the difficult years of 1967—70, has put the thing in fair proportion:

Young people in many countries chafed under the materialism and social norms of their elders, searching for new values and standards in questions such as racialism, civil rights, nationalism and sex. There was a fear of nuclear war – that this might be the last generation in history. Fortified by gurus such as Professor Herbert Marcuse, German students declared that they had no confidence in parliamentary democracy and were "taking democracy into the streets". In France a long build-up of student unrest led them to boycott their examinations and to occupy Sorbonne with a defiant declaration that it was open to all workers.

What kept this scene steadily burning was America's war in Vietnam. From August 1964 the Americans became heavily embroiled. In Washington both Houses voted almost unanimously to give President Johnson the powers he sought. By early 1965 American war planes were pounding Vietnam and protests arose in Europe over the growing scale of American commitment. In June 1965, American troops were in action for the first time. President Johnson predicted that the situation would get worse. It did.

Bertrand Russell tore up his Labour party card in protest against British support for America. Early in 1966 America launched its heaviest offensive with 8,000 troops. Thenceforth on the land and in the air America's commitment and casualties cast ever longer shadows over the homes of America's young men. The war produced ugly stains, such as the infamous massacre of Mylai which led to the court martial of Lt William Calley. By January 1969, America counted 33,641 dead, many casualties which would never fully recover and a host of broken marriages.

For the young in Europe and America, it was a *cause célèbre*. A demonstration in London in July 1968, aimed at the United States Embassy in Grosvenor Square, was insufficiently policed and led to ugly scenes. The Home Secretary was warned that this was merely a rehearsal for a much bigger action planned for the autumn. He was urged to ban the march, but much to his credit refused on the grounds that it would present victory to the extremists. The Cabinet accepted this advice. Some of us apprehensively took up positions on the route to witness this advent of the revolution. In the event, though some 250,000 marched, a colossal police presence contained the violent elements. It proved to be the last main event of its kind.

There were three political events in the 1960s, all of totally different character, which have had repercussions to this day. The first was a Private Members' Bill to reform the abortion law which David Steel, later Leader of the Liberal party, brought forward in 1966. It reached the statute book as the Medical Termination of Pregnancy Act a year later. In the Standing Committee which dealt with the Bill, of which I was a member, its provisions occupied months of anguished discussion, and rightly so.

The second event was an outburst of tyranny in East Africa in 1967–68 which provoked tens of thousands of Asians, who were U.K. passport holders, to seek asylum in this country. The Labour Government's Home Secretary, Jim Callaghan, took the view, "We have a responsibility to our own people at home as well as to a million holders of British passports abroad." So restraints on entry were rushed through Parliament and applied, principally by a quota system which provided 1,500 work vouchers a year and an entitlement to bring wives and children.

The third and most serious event came in the late summer of 1969, when Ulster burst into flames, first in Londonderry and then in Belfast. I was convalescing from a minor operation when I received an urgent call from a colleague in the Commons, Mr. Robin Chichester-Clark, brother of Ulster's Prime Minister (later, Lord Moyola). He begged me as chairman of the party's Home Affairs committee to travel to Belfast immediately. We need witnesses, he said.

Gun battles in the Falls Road and the Shankill Road made an inspection of the scene an uncomfortable experience. Snipers were busy. Cars and houses were being attacked with petrol bombs. British troops were being rushed to a fresh duty from which they have not since been relieved. Meanwhile, the Royal Ulster Constabulary patrolled with armoured cars carrying heavy machine guns. I ran into Sir Robert Mark, then Commissioner of Police in London. "What possible use are those enormous machine guns!" he exclaimed – to which there was no ready answer. It was

the first of many visits to Ulster, which has endured for the best part of quarter of a century the armed struggle that opened in August 1969.

There were also three symbolic decisions taken in sport during the decade. One came in June 1963 when the last match between Gentlemen and Players was played at Lord's. Thereafter all cricketers entered and left that field by one gate instead of two. It was the 137th match in a sequence which began in 1806. Four years later, the All England Tennis Club at Wimbledon took a similar decision, turning Wimbledon into an open event, for which both amateurs and professionals could enter. Rod Laver and Billie-Jean King became the first winners under the new regime.

The most far-reaching sporting decision turned out to be Mr Vorster's in South Africa. After Basil D'Oliveira – who was not originally picked for the winter tour – had replaced an injured player, South Africa's Prime Minister banned the tour. It was, he declared, "no longer a cricket team but a team of troublemakers for South Africa's separate development policies". He brought down a curtain which it has taken 30 years to raise again.

The greatest national triumph of the decade came in 1966 when by beating Germany 4—2 in the final, England (managed by Alf Ramsay, and captained by West Ham's Bobby Moore) won the World Cup. Ramsay became Sir Alf. A year earlier Stanley Matthews, leaving the field at 50, became the first soccer professional to be knighted. In 1968 Manchester United, recreated by Mat Busby from the ruins of the Munich air crash, won the European cup.

Among individual British champions, Lester Piggott rode his 1000th winner in 1961; Angela Mortimer and Anne Jones became the first British finalists at Wimbledon since 1914; Tony Jacklin became the first British golfer to win an American major in 1968, and a year later won the British Open. The closest event was a five-day Test Match between Australia and the West Indies in 1961. It ended in a tie, the first in Test Match history.

'There is no consensus about the '60s. The pessimist dwells on the break that came about then between the generations; on the hippies, the mods and rockers; on drugs and free love and children out of marriage; and, as he sees it, a start in the breakdown of moral order. There is room also for a totally different view.

"An optimistic decade?" I say to Allport.

"It was not just optimistic, it was brilliant! And I think that condition has petered out, because if you've had such a great time when you're young, by the time you get to my age and you're in the 40s, you don't mind putting something back; and feeling, O.K., now's the time to be serious, and maybe start doing a few things to help other people.

"That's what concerns me about our children's generation – they really haven't had this great time. And that's unfortunate because they have so many things to worry about. There's environmental degradation. They've got Aids to worry about, so that their sex life becomes strained. There's recession, so they don't have huge amounts of money to spend. They're not certain whether they'll get jobs; and if they do, whether they'll hold them.

"So there's a sort of feeling of doom and gloom around at the moment. And I wonder what effect that will have on them by the time they get to their 40s. It will make a different sort of people. And I notice our generation has this hangover from liberal thinking; we really all think that we can do whatever we want to do, and there is this general feeling of irresponsibility, which I think our young people don't have. You can't be irresponsible over anything now, because there are all these dangers hedging you around."

Mary Hopkin, then 18, caught the same note in a song which took her to the top in 1968:

> *Those were the days, my friends,*
> *We thought they'd never end,*
> *We'd sing and dance for ever and a day,*
> *We'd live the life we chose,*
> *We'd fight and never lose,*
> *For we were young, and sure to have our own way . . .*

So was it sunset or sunrise? "Never forget," Rilke said to his wife, as he lay dying, "never forget, life is magnificent!" And in the 1960s, many of our young, now grown men and women, saw it like that. They had the edge over most of us now.

W. F. Deedes

1960

Africa dominated the first year of the decade. As Prime Minister Harold Macmillan told an uneasy Parliamentary assembly in Cape Town: "A Wind of Change is blowing throughout the Continent." In South Africa the police mowed down striking Africans at Sharpeville. Further north, on the ending of Colonial rule by the Belgians, the Congo erupted into civil war with a United Nations force vainly trying to keep order. Further north still, General de Gaulle had to assume special powers as the French settlers in Algeria battled with the local population who had been promised independence. A disastrous earthquake reduced the Moroccan town of Agadir to rubble.

The shooting down of an American U2 "spy" aircraft by the Russians caused a marked cooling of relations between the Kremlin and the West. A planned summit to discuss disarmament was abandoned. When Harold Macmillan was addressing the United Nations on the Cold War, the Soviet leader, Nikita Khrushchev, took off his shoe to hammer on his desk in disagreement. But there was hope that the situation might be eased when John F. Kennedy, by a very narrow margin, defeated Richard Nixon for the Presidency of the United States. Khrushchev sent a message of good will.

In Britain, the political scene was dominated by the problems within the Labour Party. Hugh Gaitskell, the leader of the party, was defeated over the question of nationalisation. The party's most charismatic figure, Aneurin Bevan, died. In an imposition of a credit squeeze the Bank Rate was raised to 6 per cent.

For the first time, the guests who attended the Westminster Abbey wedding of Princess Margaret and Anthony Armstrong-Jones were able to see the proceedings on closed - circuit television. A second son, Prince Andrew, was born to the Queen.

Among those who died during the year were the Countess Mountbatten, the Nobel Prize - winning author Albert Camus and the popular novelist Nevil Shute. The London newspapers, the *News Chronicle* and the *Star*, disappeared in a merger with the *Daily Mail* and the *Evening News*.

At home, an Old Bailey jury found that D. H. Lawrence's *Lady Chatterley's Lover* was not obscene and 200,000 copies of the Penguin paperback were sold within a few days. Francis Chichester accomplished his solo sail across the Atlantic and the eccentric Dr. Barbara Moore completed on foot the thousand miles from John O'Groats to Land's End.

In sport, Anita Londsborough won for Britain the first gold medal in swimming since 1924. England, by winning the one test match for which there was a result, defeated the West Indies in the Caribbean. Later in the year the West Indies and Australia managed to tie their first test match. Burnley won the League Championship.

The Daily Telegraph
and Morning Post
No. 32,834 LONDON, WEDNESDAY, NOVEMBER 9, 1960
Printed in LONDON and MANCHESTER Price 2½d.

SENATOR KENNEDY IS PRESIDENT

7A.M.: NIXON BACKERS ADMIT DEFEAT

BIG SWING FROM TEXAS TO NEW YORK

LEAD OF OVER 1½ m. VOTES

By 7 a.m. to-day supporters of Mr. Richard Nixon, Republican candidate for the United States Presidency, conceded victory for his democratic opponent, Senator Kennedy, in yesterday's election. Mr. Kennedy stood by awaiting Mr. Nixon's formal telegram of congratulation.

Senator Kennedy's biggest successes were to win New York State, Pennsylvania and Texas from the Republicans. He also won Massachusetts, Connecticut, Maryland, Rhode Island, West Virginia, New Jersey, Delaware and Louisiana and retained the Democratic States of N. and S. Carolina and Georgia and Arkansas.

Mr. Nixon retained Oklahoma, Tennessee, Kansas, Indiana, Kentucky, Florida, Maine, Utah, Virginia, Colorado, Iowa, Idaho and Nebraska.

FOUNTAIN HILL RIGHT AGAIN

Fountain Hill, Pennsylvania, which has supported the winner in every Presidential election this century, voted for Senator Kennedy. Figures were 576 to 380.

The position at 2 a.m. (7 a.m. G.M.T.) was:

KENNEDY		***NIXON***	
ELECTORAL VOTES ..	262	ELECTORAL VOTES ..	141
POPULAR VOTES ...	22,908,265	POPULAR VOTES ...	21,085,813

A total of 269 electoral votes was needed to win the Presidency.

	House of Representatives		Senate	
	NEW	OLD	NEW	OLD
DEMOCRATS	149	283	59	66
REPUBLICANS ...	34	154	30	34

Democrats retain the Senate and House. Among the governors elected was Mr. Faubus, Arkansas.

By 6 a.m. G.M.T. Senator Kennedy's popular vote had soared to 20,884,734 to Mr. Nixon's 19,275,555. The New York Herarld Tribune and the Philadelphia Inquirer, which supported Mr. Nixon, conceded that Mr. Kennedy had won.

Senator Kennedy had won 262 electoral votes. Thus, he was only seven short of assured victory.

Mr. Kennedy waits by Sea; Mr. Nixon's Hope for Late Swing; President Flies to Poll - Back Page; Pictures - P16

Voting Strength of the 50 States

The President of the United States is appointed by the Electoral College. This body consists of 537 members, the representation of each of the 50 States being in proportion to its population. A minimum of 269 votes in the Electoral College is required to secure return.

State	Electoral votes	1956 popular vote majority
Alabama	11	DEMOCRATIC
Alaska	3	-
Arizona	4	REPUBLICAN
Arkansas	8	DEMOCRATIC
California	32	REPUBLICAN
Colorado	6	REPUBLICAN
Connecticut	8	REPUBLICAN
Delaware	3	REPUBLICAN
Florida	10	REPUBLICAN
Georgia	12	DEMOCRATIC
Hawaii	3	-
Idaho	4	REPUBLICAN
Illinois	27	REPUBLICAN
Indiana	13	REPUBLICAN
Iowa	10	REPUBLICAN
Kansas	8	REPUBLICAN
Kentucky	10	REPUBLICAN
Louisiana	10	REPUBLICAN
Maine	5	REPUBLICAN
Maryland	9	REPUBLICAN
Massachusetts	16	REPUBLICAN
Michigan	20	REPUBLICAN
Minnesota	11	REPUBLICAN
Mississippi	8	DEMOCRATIC
Missouri	13	DEMOCRATIC
Montana	4	REPUBLICAN
Nebraska	6	REPUBLICAN
Nevada	3	REPUBLICAN
New Hampshire	4	REPUBLICAN
New Jersey	16	REPUBLICAN
New Mexico	4	REPUBLICAN
New York	45	REPUBLICAN
North Carolina	14	DEMOCRATIC
North Dakota	4	REPUBLICAN
Ohio	25	REPUBLICAN
Oklahoma	8	REPUBLICAN
Oregon	6	REPUBLICAN
Pennsylvania	32	REPUBLICAN
Rhode Island	4	REPUBLICAN
South Carolina	8	DEMOCRATIC
South Dakota	4	REPUBLICAN
Tennessee	11	REPUBLICAN
Texas	24	REPUBLICAN
Utah	4	REPUBLICAN
Vermont	3	REPUBLICAN
Virginia	12	REPUBLICAN
Washington	9	REPUBLICAN
West Virginia	8	REPUBLICAN
Wisconsin	12	REPUBLICAN
Wyoming	3	REPUBLICAN

(Alaska became the 49th State in 1958. Hawaii the 50th State last year.)

In 1956 President Eisenhower (Republican) carried 41 States with 457 electoral votes. Mr. Adlai Stevenson (Democratic) carried seven States with 74 electoral votes.

THE YOUNGEST WINNER

From Alex Faulkner, Daily Telegraph Correspondent

NEW YORK, Wednesday.

Mr. Kennedy early to-day became, at 43, the youngest man ever elected United States President, and the first Roman Catholic to win the office.

He had apparently restored the strength of the old Roosevelt coalition. In Chicago, with its large Negro population, his majority was over half a million.

His Roman Catholic religion evidently helped him in New England, where the Roman Catholic population is politically influential. But it hurt him in rural areas of States like Tennessee. The influence of Senator Johnson, who becomes Vice-President, helped in the South.

6 A.M.

Lead Reduced

Although it was being claimed in many quarters that Mr. Kennedy was now bound to win, Mr. Nixon started to catch up with him a little in the popular vote. With returns in from 52 per cent. of the precincts, Mr. Kennedy's total was 20,874,000 and Mr. Nixon's 19,289,000.

This was half a million below Mr. Kennedy's two million lead at an earlier stage. On the basis of votes totalled at this hour Mr. Kennedy had won, or seemed likely to receive, 334 electoral votes and Mr. Nixon 203. By 5 a.m. London time, midnight in New York, Mr. Kennedy's gains had become a victory parade. Despondency set in at Mr. Nixon's Los Angeles hotel in spite of defiant statements that the Republicans were still quietly confident.

4.30 A.M.

Republican Broadcast

Mr. Kennedy was a driving force for a two million vote lead. With returns in from 37 per cent. of the precincts his total was 15,544,000 to Mr. Nixon's 13,755,000.

In spite of this, Senator Thruston Morton, chairman of the Republican National Committee, made a broadcast at this point asserting: "Don't worry - we've got this. Just wait until the great Middle West and the Rocky Mountain states come in."

2 A.M.

Home State Gain

At 2 a.m. London time, Massachusetts appeared to have gone Democratic for Mr. Kennedy. It is his home State and this was no surprise.

At 1.30 a.m. London time, with a small percentage of the total vote counted, a spokesman for Mr. Nixon said: "He remains confident of victory.

"He feels a heavy vote is a very good sign because we have the impression that a heavy vote will be a fair vote for Mr. Nixon. He expects the first results from the eastern states to favour the Democrats because metropolitan areas will report first."

1.30 A.M.

Kennedy Men Confident

With five per cent. of the popular votes reported, Mr. Kennedy increased his lead to 100,000 and seemed to be holding on to it. The popular vote stood at 1,860,000 (52 per cent.) for Mr. Kennedy and 1,749,000 (48 per cent.) for Mr. Nixon.

These figures indicate 210 electoral votes for Mr. Kennedy and 195 for Mr. Nixon. Kennedy supporters began to feel that their candidate was going to win.

The Democrats had won or were leading for 94 seats in the House of Representatives, with 27 going to the Republicans. In the present House the Division is Democrats 283, Republicans 154.

MIDNIGHT

Good Barometer

Early returns from Connecticut, where the polls closed at midnight London time, suggested that a Kennedy blitz was in the making there. Although this State has only eight electoral votes it often provides a good barometer.

'HE'S JUMPING FOR JOY'

KENNEDY REACTION

From Edwin Tetlow

HYANNIS, Mass., Tuesday.

At his home in Hyannis Mr. Kennedy's first comment on the election came just after he had seen the extent of his victory in Connecticut. "Fantastic," he exclaimed - and a member of his house party added that he was "jumping for joy."

Spirits rose steadily in the Democratic candidate's camp as the evening went on. All the news being received in the Great National Guard Armoury being used as election headquarters was good.

JOHN F. KENNEDY on his way to victory in the American presidential election.

MR. WILSON WILL STAND FOR SHADOW CABINET

ASSURANCES OF SUPPORT

By H. B. Boyne
Daily Telegraph Political Correspondent

MR. HAROLD WILSON, defeated last week in the Labour leadership ballot, decided to allow his name to go forward for the Shadow Cabinet. It is believed that he has received sufficient assurances of support to give him a reasonable chance of election.

Even his most virulent critics think he is likely to be among the successful 12, though much lower on the list than is customary. Last year he topped the poll with 167 votes, 18 ahead of Mr. James Callaghan, his nearest rival.

Some good judges believe Mr. Callaghan will top the poll this time and that Mr. Wilson will do well to secure the minimum necessary for election.

Mr. Wilson took more than four days to make up his mind. It can be assumed that he did not reach his decision without a pretty careful counting of heads.

THREE REASONS

"Unity of Party"

He has given his supporters at least three reasons for standing. These are:

1- His object remains as it was when he decided to oppose Mr. Gaitskell: the unity "indeed the survival" of the party. He does not believe this could best be served by "retiring" and giving the impression that he wished to ally himself with "a party within the party."

2- He still believes the only way to resolve the crisis on defence policy is to re-draft the policy statement, rejected at Scarborough, on a basis which could be "accepted with dignity" by Labour M.P.s but which would reflect the Scarborough decisions.

3- He can still best assist in bringing this about by remaining a **(continued on Back Page, Col. 3)**

LATE NEWS

KENNEDY LEAD

(See This Page)

Popular vote returns at 7 a.m.

Kennedy	24,058,164
Nixon	22,330,225

-Reuter.

KENNEDY LEAD IN NIXON HOME STATE

(See This Page)

With 24 per cent. of votes counted in California, at 7 a.m. London time, Mr. Kennedy was still leading there. Mr. Nixon had not taken lead in his home State at any time during the evening.

At this hour returns were in from 62 per cent. of the precincts and Mr. Kennedy had total popular vote of 23,716,000 to Mr. Nixon's total of 21,876,000.

MR. GAITSKELL'S LIMITED GAIN

DEFENCE PLEA TO PARTY EXECUTIVE

By Our Political Correspondent

The international sub-committee of the Labour party's national executive decided last night to advise the executive that nothing should be excluded from the scope of the forthcoming discussions on the party's defence policy.

This was the outcome of an apparently stormy meeting at the House of Commons. It represents a limited success for Mr. Gaitskell.

For if the executive accepts the sub-committee's recommendation, the talks will not be confined to the single issue that the executive is bound to accept the Scarborough decision calling for unilateral renunciation of all nuclear weapons.

The other parties to the discussion will be the "Shadow" Cabinet, on behalf of the Parliamentary Labour party, and the General Council of the Trade Union Congress. Mr. Gaitskell has pledged himself to a campaign to reverse the unilateral decision at next year's party conference.

LEFT WING OVERRULED

He will now be able to claim that the discussions should be based on the official defence policy put forward by the executive at Scarborough, which relied on the United States nuclear deterrent within N.A.T.O.

QUEEN NOT ASKED TO BRUSSELS

BRUSSELS, Tuesday.

Queen Elizabeth II "has been invited to send her representative to the wedding of King Baudouin and Dona Fabiola on Dec. 15," an official source announced here. She has not been invited to go herself.

Sources close to Laeken Palace said to-night that Queen Juliana of the Netherlands and Grand Duchess Charlotte of Luxembourg had been invited as they rule the countries that are partners with Belgium in the three-nation Benelux union.

PROMPT REPLY TO AGGRESSOR

PREMIER'S WARNING ON USING POLARIS

By Our Own Representative

WESTMINSTER, Tuesday.

Consultation between members of the North Atlantic Treaty Organisation on the use of American Polaris submarines firing underwater rockets may be impossible in the case of a sudden attack on the West.

This was the warning which Mr. Macmillan gave the Commons to-day during a prolonged exchange of questions on the control which may be exercised over the use of a British base for the submarines. He explained that the American contribution to the deterrent would include 30 to 50 Polaris submarines, each costing between £50 million and £60 million to build.

The Prime Minister said that for general control Britain would continue to rely on the close co-operation and understanding with the United States which President Eisenhower had recently reaffirmed. A crucial exchange between Mr. Gaitskell, Leader of the Opposition, and the Prime Minister followed.

FATEFUL DECISION

Mr. Gaitskell's opinion was that the fateful decision to use nuclear weapons for the first time should be taken by collective agreement. The Prime Minister's reply was: "At first sight, to say if the enemy attacks one - ourselves, America or our allies with an overwhelming attack of nuclear forces - we are 15 of us - to sit round and see whether we can get into touch before we make the reply - no sir.

"It is a fact, it is a certainty, that if aggression is made against us the reply will be made by anybody who is in a position to make it as soon and as overwhelmingly as possible. That is the deterrent."

BUCHAN OF AUCHMACOY

Daily Telegraph Reporter

The engagement is announced on Page 14 to-day of Mr. David William Sinclair Buchan of Auchmacoy, 31, only son of the late Capt. Stephen Trevor and Lady Olivia Trevor, of Auchmacoy House Aberdeenshire and the Hon. Susan Blanche Fionodbhar Scott-Ellis, 23, second daughter of Lord and Lady Howard de Walden and Seaford of Wondham Manor, Betchworth, Surrey.

The right to the surname Buchan of Auchmacoy was recognised by Lord Lyon King of Arms in 1949. He is heir to the Auchmacoy estate, now held in life rent by his mother, Lady Olivia.

FOOTBALLERS' PAY

It was decided at the Football League's extraordinary meeting at St. Anne's yesterday not to increase the maximum weekly wage of professional footballers from £20. Several minor compensations included the increase of television fees from £2 to 10 guineas.

WORTH
Je Reviens

The Daily Telegraph
and Morning Post
4 A.M.
No. 32,800 LONDON, FRIDAY, SEPTEMBER 30, 1960
Printed in LONDON and MANCHESTER Price 2½d.

EARLYWARM
All Wool Witney
BLANKETS
1669-1960

PREMIER HECKLED BY Mr KHRUSCHEV

SHOUTS & THUMPS AT BIG U.N. SPEECH

Mr. Khruschev rose to his feet shouting in protest and thumping his desk as Mr. Macmillan yesterday answered his accusations against the West in the General Assembly. Startled delegates witnessed the unprecedented spectacle of a United Nations speaker halted by interruptions.

The president rapped for order as the hall rang with shouts in Russian, but the Russian Prime Minister was soon drumming with his fists again, or waving his arms, while he glared around defiantly. Mr. Macmillan, who remained unruffled, had one of the biggest ovations heard in the Assembly. He:

Expressed confidence in the integrity of the Secretary-General, and condemned Russia's call for changes;

Rejected "out-of-date" colonialist slogans used by Mr. Khruschev, and pointed to representatives present of independent Commonwealth nations. Instead of talking of self-determination in Africa, Russia should explain why she had refused this right to East Germans, 2½ million of whom had fled to the West in 12 years.

Proposed that technical experts should prepare an objective report on disarmament measures, as suggested by Denmark.

Appealed for a return to the spirit that "seemed to be at work even a few months ago," so that a new start could be made. The only way was a step-by-step approach.

MEETING WITH MR. KHRUSCHEV

Mr. Macmillan's forthright review was taken as an indication of the line he would pursue at his meeting later last night with Mr. Khruschev, who refused to comment on the speech. Mr. Gromyko, Russian Foreign Minister, said it was "neither new nor useful".

The evening meeting between the two leaders, which began soon after 6 p.m. (11 p.m. B.S.T.), lasted two hours, eight minutes. In some sharp-tempered comments to reporters before Mr. Macmillan arrived Mr. Khruschev said he had "little hope" of achieving anything.

Report of Speech - P29; British Nuclear Ban Inspection Plan and Mr. Khruschev Silent - Back Page; Editorial Comment - P14

SOVIET LEADER'S FURY

From Our Own Correspondent

NEW YORK, Thursday.

Stung by the urbane logic of Mr. Macmillan and determined, it would seem, to destroy the impact of a memorable speech, Mr. Khruschev to-day four times interrupted the Prime Minister's address to the General Assembly. (Report - P27).

Twice he pummelled the desk in front of him to register a tom-tom-like counter to applause. Twice he shouted interjections in a thick and furious voice.

It was a scene which the world's leaders gathered here will never forget. It has never before happened in the history of the United Nations. Never has a speech by a national leader been so molested.

LONG OVATION

Assembly Feeling

Yet all but the most prejudiced were saying in the corridors here afterwards that Mr. Khruschev had not only made a mockery of the dignity of the United Nations, but had thwarted his own purpose. His behaviour swayed the gathering even more forcibly towards Mr. Macmillan and provoked a culminating ovation at least as long and heartfelt as any seen so far during the session.

Mr. Macmillan was cheered and applauded all the way from the speaker's podium to his seat at the distant left-hand side of the great hall. Signor Segani, of Italy, shook his hand as he passed and so did Mr Herter.

UNRUFFLED PREMIER

Beer After Speech

Mr. Macmillan did not once lose his poise. He was so unruffled, indeed, that when the excitement had died he quietly left the chamber and went to the delegates' lounge. There he had one glass of beer and then strolled back to his seat as leader of the United Kingdom delegation.

The story of this emotional morning is best told consecutively. It began with a round of laughter 20 seconds after Mr. Macmillan had walked to the rostrum.

He opened by congratulating Mr. Boland, of Ireland, on his election as President of this year's assembly.

"It gives me particular pleasure that I should be addressing this distinguished assembly under the Presidency of a country to which my own has so many close ties," he said as he turned towards Mr. Boland.

Mr. Macmillan was probably surprised at the speed with which the Assembly seized the background to the remark. Laughter spread round the chamber and caused Mr. Macmillan to halt his delivery.

Thereafter, he went on smoothly, holding his audience with every word. He commended the American proposals for strengthening the United Nations and condemned Mr. Khruschev's as extending the veto and freezing temporary divisions between the Powers.

Mr. Khruschev, listening with his earphone to his left ear, wriggled ominously. Then, as the soft English voice went on, he exploded as he heard the words: "As for the Secretary-General, I would like to associate myself with the wide expression of confidence in his energy, resourcefulness and above all integrity."

Applause, starting with a hand-clap here and there, spread in extent and rose in volume. Mr. Khruschev could stand no more.

He thumped his desk rhythmically with both hands, growing redder and redder in the face as he did so. Rather meekly and with nothing like the ardour of his chief, Mr. Gromyko followed suit.

"LITTLE HOPE" IN TALKS, SAYS SOVIET LEADER

COMMENT BEFORE SEEING PREMIER

From Our Own Correspondent

NEW YORK, Thursday.

Mr. Macmillan arrived at the Russian United Nations delegation's headquarters at 6.11 p.m. (11.11 p.m. B.S.T.) for his talks with Mr. Khruschev.

He was accompanied by the Earl of Home, Foreign Secretary, and Sir Patrick Dean, head of Britain's United Nations delegation. The Russian leader did not go outside the building to greet them, or to bid them farewell when they left two hours and eight minutes later.

Less than an hour before the meeting Mr. Khruschev denounced the British Prime Minister. "I hold out little hope in this meeting with Macmillan," he stated.

He was holding an impromptu news conference in the footpath in front of his Park Avenue quarters. Asked if he thought Mr. Macmillan's speech was constructive, he replied: "No, absolutely not. Nothing. Both his speech and his attitude remind me much of Chamberlain."

ARMS CRITICISM

On disarmament he said Russia was ready to accept Western proposals if the West would accept hers. He would accept every kind of inspection and control, but considered the work of technical committees on disarmament to be a waste of time.

If Mr. Macmillan repeated his United Nations speech, he added, "he is against disarmament, and I know it's hopeless." Addressing American reporters he exclaimed: "Are you so rich that you can afford rockets as well as butter?"

4 Pages of Books

For the first time since the war THE DAILY TELEGRAPH publishes to-day on Pages 18 to 21 four pages of book reviews, of which two pages are devoted to paperback editions of various types.

SPY-PLANE CHARGE

Asked about talks with President Eisenhower, he replied: "You expect me to ask Eisenhower for a meeting? It would be a humiliation to our country."

He believed the President had no say in the making of decisions. He had given him an opportunity to disclaim responsibility for the U-2 spy-plane flight, but he had not taken it.

But he asserted that Russia wanted friendly relations. She had dealt "very leniently" with Powers, the U-2 pilot, Mr. Khruschev said, and contrasted it with the execution of the Rosenbergs by America in 1953.

Questioned about a Russian colonel gaoled for spying in America he replied: "That is different. There will always be spies. We shot one of our own men only two weeks ago who was spying for your Government."

EKCO DISMISS 600 WORKERS

TV SALES DOWN

By Our TV and Radio Correspondent

Six-hundred television production workers, of a total staff of more than 6,000 at the E.K. Cole factory in Southend, will get a week's notice next Friday.

The firm dismissed 200 employees earlier this month, blaming a fall in TV sales caused by credit restrictions. Of these 200, all but 30 were later absorbed in other departments.

Total sets sent by manufacturers to the trade during July was 115,000 compared with 192,000 for the same month in the previous year, a 40 per cent drop. But radio set sales in July were 167,000 compared with 138,000 a 22 per cent increase.

Last year, TV production reached the record figure of 2,800,000 sets. It is likely that this year the total will be down to about two million.

OUTPUT RISE SLACKENS

By An Industrial Correspondent

The rate of increase in Britain's industrial production is slowing down. The Central Statistical Office announced last night that the production index for August, adjusted to take into account holidays and other seasonal factors, is expected to be 121 or 122. (1954 = 100.)

NIKITA KHRUSCHEV shouts in anger as Harold Macmillan addresses the U.N. General Assembly.

ARGENTINA MAY HOLD HITLER'S DEPUTY

BORMANN FINGERPRINT CHECK

From Our Own Correspondent

BUENOS AIRES, Thursday.

A fingerprint check is expected to decide whether a one-armed man being questioned by Argentine police is Hitler's wartime deputy, Martin Bormann, it was learned in Buenos Aires to-day.

A West German Embassy spokesman said: "We have Bormann's fingerprints at our office and these are at the disposal of the Argentine police." He could not say whether the police had approached the Embassy.

The one-armed man, named as Walter Flegel, was detained at the industrial centre of Sarate, about 50 miles north-west of Buenos Aires. Argentine federal police agents acted after receiving an anonymous tip and a photograph.

Press reports from Zarate say Flegel and his wife, Haydee, 30 have lived there in a modest house for the past 13 years and have three girls, aged 12, nine and four months. Flegel apparently entered Argentina illegally.

A police spokesman told reporters that an apparent difference in age between Flegel and Bormann seemed to indicate that they may be two different persons. Flegel claims he is 48: Bormann would now be 60. Pictures found at Flegel's home show an extraordinary resemblance to Bormann.

Bormann was reported to have fled to South America after the war. There were also reports that he had undergone plastic surgery to alter his appearance.

"SOME MISTAKE"

Assurance to Wife

Flegel's slim, brunette, Argentine wife said: "I cannot believe he is Bormann. I have lived with him these 13 years and would have noticed it."

She said she saw her husband twice after his arrest last Friday and he said to her: "There must be some mistake. Stay calm and don't worry."

Senor Alfredo Vitolo, Interior Minister, said at a Press conference: "The arrest of Flegel was made at the request of the Argentine Government." He added that identification was difficult to establish.

MIDAS STATION FOR BRITAIN

"SPACE" WARNING OF ROCKET ATTACK

From RICHARD BRETT-SMITH
Daily Telegraph Defence Correspondent

WASHINGTON, Thursday.

Arrangements are being completed between the United States and Britain to install a Midas satellite tracking and evaluation site at East Kirkbride, near Glasgow.

Midas is a missile detection system using infra-red techniques, which may well eliminate the four- or five-minute early warning problem for Britain. According to well informed sources here it is likely to be confirmed as an operational satellite fairly soon.

The United States Government wants to establish a Midas station in Britain as soon as convenient. Preliminary discussions have already taken place, but no official negotiations, according to State Department officials, are yet under way.

"AGREEMENT SOON"

But one official said to me to-day: "We hope to start negotiations in the near future," American military and political experts expect an agreement soon.

8 BRITONS DIE IN CRASH

COACH HITS REAR OF LOG TRANSPORTER

From Our Own Correspondent

PARIS, Thursday.

Eight British tourists died and 20 were injured, some seriously, in a road crash at Chamblay, in the Jura, on the main road from Switzerland to Dijon to-night. A coach carrying tourists smashed into the rear of a log transporter.

Tree trunks stacked on the vehicle tore into the crowded coach, which was run by Global Tours, Oxford Street. Its passengers, believed to number 34, were a mixed party of British, American and Commonwealth people.

SUN BLINDED DRIVER

The coach was returning from Montreux, Switzerland. Its driver, Percy Smith, 38, of London, was apparently blinded by the setting sun.

Capt. Leslie Daniels, of York, one of the injured, said: "I was thrown from where I was sitting at the back to the front of the bus. When I recovered I saw tree trunks had crashed through the windscreen into people sitting behind the driver."

French police gave the following names of seven who died at the scene of the crash: Percy Smith, the driver, Mr. Harold Leake and his wife, Mrs. Mabel Davidson Leake, Mr. G. Cullen, Mrs. S. M. Kent, Miss W. Marriott and Miss L. Bain. An injured woman died, unidentified in hospital, bringing the deaths to eight.

The crashed vehicles blocked the road, the main highway from Paris to Basle. It will not be re-opened to traffic until to-morrow.

FIRM'S STATEMENT

First Crash in 15 Years

Mrs. Stella Rosenthal, wife of Mr. H.W. Rosenthal, managing director of Global Tours Ltd., said at their home in Alverstone Road, Willesden, late last night: "It is the first serious accident to happen on one of our coach tours for 15 years. The coach was found to have nothing wrong with it mechanically.

"Percy Smith's death was a great personal blow to us. He had driven for the firm for some years and was highly thought of."

PREMIER WARNS SOUTH AFRICA

SUPPORT 'IMPOSSIBLE' FOR SOME POLICIES

REJECTION OF RACIAL SUPERIORITY

From PEREGRINE WORSTHORNE,
Daily Telegraph Special Correspondent

CAPE TOWN, Wednesday.

Mr. Macmillan said to a hushed meeting of the South African Parliament to-day that there were "some aspects of your policies which make it impossible for us to give South Africa our support and encouragement without being false to our own deep convictions about the political destinies of free men."

The Prime Minister sharply differentiated in his speech between British policy on race from that of South Africa. He said:

"It has been our aim, in the countries for which we have borne responsibility, not only to raise the material standards of life, but to create a society which respects the rights of individuals."

In this society "men are given the opportunity to grow to their full stature, and that in our view must include the opportunity of an increasing share in political power and responsibility; a society finally in which individual merit, and individual merit alone, is the criterion for a man's advancement, whether political or economic."

Britain rejected "the idea of any inherent superiority of one race over another."

But having shown, without any equivocation, where Britain stands on the vexed racial question, Mr. Macmillan assured his silent audience that he did not believe "in refusing to trade with people just because you dislike the way they manage their affairs at home. Boycotts will never get you anywhere."

This reassurance brought the only cheers which interrupted the 40-minute speech.

THE WIND OF CHANGE

Mr. Macmillan said:

"As I have travelled through the Union, I have found everywhere, as I expected, a deep preoccupation with what is happening in the rest of the African Continent. I understand and sympathise with your interest in these events, and your anxiety about them.

Ever since the break-up of the Roman Empire, one of the constant facts of political life in Europe has been the emergence of independent nations. They have come into existence over the centuries in different shapes with different forms of Government. But all have been inspired with a keen feeling of nationalism, which has grown as nations have grown.

In the 20th century, and especially since the end of the war, the processes which gave birth to the nation-states of Europe have been repeated all over the world. We have seen the awakening of national consciousness in peoples who have for centuries lived in dependence on some other power.

Fifteen years ago, this movement spread through Asia. Many countries there, of different races and civilisations, pressed their claim to an independent national life.

To-day, the same thing is happening in Africa. The most striking of all the impressions I have formed since I left London a month ago is of the strength of this African national consciousness.

In different places, it may take different forms, but it is happening everywhere. The wind of change is blowing through the Continent."

(February 4)

SOVIET SPACE DOGS FIT AFTER FLIGHT

From DOUGLAS BROWN
Daily Telegraph Special Correspondent

MOSCOW, Sunday.

STRELKA and BALKA, the first dogs to return from a space orbit, are in perfect condition, according to a bulletin issued here to-night. As soon as they were released, they ran to greet and nuzzle people they knew.

The other "biological subjects" in the Soviet satellite also came back in good trim. Mice started nibbling eagerly and an unspecified plant was found to be still in bloom. The biological subjects included rats, fungi, microscopic water plants and seeds.

The two dogs were submitted to a physiological check with such instruments as an electro-cardiograph. They appeared to have suffered no ill-effects at all.

The chief strain on their systems had been caused by rapid deceleration of the rocket as it re-entered the atmosphere.

CHANGE IN HABITS

They were found to be in the same state as during their training, when some space-ship conditions were artificially produced. The only change in their habits seemed to be a preference for sesame hash over salami and pleasure in being given a bath. Otherwise, said the bulletin, they returned to "their usual terrestrial activities."

(August 22)

10 SKELETONS IN 3,800-YEAR-OLD GRAVES NEAR STONEHENGE

Daily Telegraph Reporter

Ten prehistoric skeletons, comprising seven children and three adults, and a cremation, all buried about 3,800 years ago, have been discovered in a small round barrow only 9in in height near Stonehenge. One is the skeleton of a child buried with an earring made from the tusk of a wild boar, a ring on the left hand and a beaker.

This barrow is one of three round barrows in close proximity excavated under the supervision of Miss E. V. W. Field for the Ministry of Works. Of particular interest was a deep grave side by side with that of the child buried with the earring.

This grave was covered with a cairn of flints. In the grave were many fragments of a beaker.

GRAVE'S CORNER POSTS

Two fragments were carefully placed beneath a whetstone which was behind the head of a young man or woman. The grave had four wooden posts at the corners and probably a wooden lid.

The barrow was originally constructed with a large central grave previously explored in the 19th century and with an irregular surrounding ditch.

(July 7)

FRANCIS CHICHESTER, 58, waving from his 12-ton sloop Gipsy Moth III as he entered New York on Thursday after winning the first single-handed sailing race across the Atlantic. His crossing from Plymouth to the Ambrose lightship took 40 days.

ATLANTIC MAN DEFIED LUNG CANCER

RACE RECORD

From Our Own Correspondent

NEW YORK, Friday.

FRANCIS CHICHESTER, 58, after sailing the Atlantic alone in the record time of 40 days "and a bit," as he put it to-day, had his first full night's sleep since leaving Plymouth on June 11.

He confirmed his belief in faith healing. Two years ago Mr. Chichester, seriously ill with lung cancer, was advised that one lung should be removed. He declined the operation although he was given only a few weeks to live.

He said that because he was sailing to windward for practically the whole of the voyage, he covered 4,000 miles instead of the 3,000 he had hoped to sail in 30 days.

He took a dinner jacket for the good of his morale. "But it became so heavily mildewed," he said, "that I abandoned the dressing for dinner idea. In my clothes locker my things were tossed about so much when I ran into hurricane force winds that holes were worn in them."

DAMAGE IN GALE

During a 36-hour gale off Nova Scotia damage was done to a wind-vane and some stanchions were smashed. Mr. Chichester dropped and broke his barometer when he was tossed against the side of the sloop's saloon.

"I began to think all the wind in the world must be coming from New York, but when I was resting or sleeping Miranda did her work well."

"Miranda" is a self-steering device invented by Mr. Chichester. It resembles a big Japanese fan on the end of a staff mounted astern in his 39ft sloop, Gipsy Moth III.

(July 23)

MLLE. BARDOT RECOVERING

FOUND IN COMA FROM DRUGS

From Our Own Correspondent

PARIS, Thursday.

BRIGITTE BARDOT, the French film actress, was stated to be "out of danger" to-day after taking a large dose of sleeping tablets and cutting her wrists late last night. Yesterday was her 26th birthday.

Mme. Mercedes Simon, the actress's secretary, found her in a coma beside a well at the house where they were staying at Cabrolles, near Menton, on the French Riviera.

BRIGITTE BARDOT

A local doctor drove her to a clinic in Nice specialising in nervous diseases. Dr. Namin, the neurologist in charge said that her condition had been extremely serious on arrival, but she respondec to treatment and he hoped that she would make a quick recovery.

Friends said that the actress had been overworking and felt emotionally upset.

There have been many reports that Mlle. Bardot and her second husband, Jacques Charrier, the actor, were separating and seeking a divorce.

Ten days ago in Paris M. Charrier came to blows with Samy Frey, an actor taking part in Mlle. Bardot's latest film, after they had been out together.

M. Charrier was in Bayonne, in South-West France when he heard about his wife. He drove to Nice to-day to be with her.

The couple were married in June last year. They have one child.

(September 30)

CREDIT SQUEEZE TIGHTENED

Bank Rate 6pc: Special Deposits Doubled

By Our Political Correspondent

New measures to restrain the growth of credit and maintain a sound balance in Britian's internal economy were announced yesterday by the Bank of England and Mr. Heathcoat Amory, Chancellor of the Exchequer.

Bank Rate is raised by 1 per cent. to 6 per cent. It was last at this level in May, 1958, having previously been hitched up to 7 per cent., by Mr. Thorneycroft, in the autumn of 1957.

The clearing banks have to lodge a further one per cent. of their total deposits with the Bank of England. This is the second call of one per cent., since April 28. By freezing part of their liquid cash, it further restricts their ability to lend to customers.

STATE SPENDING

Applying The Brake

Concurrently with these checks on the flow of money for private investment, the Government has decided to limit capital expenditure in the public sector for 1961-62 to the current year's level.

It remains to be seen where the brake will be applied. So far, only the principle has been decided.

It will be for the Ministers concerned to work out the details in consultation with the Chancellor. But the programme of approved capital investment for 1960-61 shows that the biggest shares of the £1,675 million mentioned in the Economic Survey went to:

Nationalised electricity, £326 million;
Local authority housing, £285 million;
British Transport commissions, £200 million;
Education, including universities, £132 million;
National Coal Board, £120 million.

On the face of it, these are the services whose plans will have to be most appreciably revised if they are to keep their capital expenditure down to the current level.

(June 24)

MISSILE WRITTEN OFF AS WEAPON

M.P.s in Uproar Over £65m. Blue Streak

BLUE STREAK, which has cost £65 million, has been written off by the Government as a military ballistic missile, but it may serve as a launching vehicle for space satellites. This announcement by Mr. Watkinson, Minister of Defence, caused uproar in the House of Commons yesterday.

Speaking of the need for some other vehicle for British nuclear warheads, he understood America would supply the airborne missile Skybolt to prolong the effectiveness of Britian's V-bombers. In Washington it was stated that America was ready to sell Skybolts, which would not be ready for at least two years, but not warheads.

The Opposition accused the Government of waste on Blue Streak, and when an inquiry and emergency debate were refused a motion of censure was drafted. When Black Rod, Lt.-Gen. Sir Brian Horrocks, interrupted to request attendance in the Lords there was pandemonium. Labour members protested angrily and only three from their front bench went to the Upper House.

Britain's guided stand-off bomb, Blue Steel, is about to go into production, but it is not a ballistic missile. Besides the £65 million cost quoted for Blue Streak there will be £30 million compensation for loss of contracts. A de Havilland spokesman said some redundancy was inevitable among missile workers at Stevenage New Town, Herts. About 2,000 could be affected.

(April 14)

FAILURE OF 'SUMMIT THAT NEVER WAS'

KHRUSCHEV BLAMED FOR FIASCO

At the end of another day of frustrated efforts the "Summit that never was" fizzled out last night without any discussion of the momentous agenda. Mr. Macmillan and President Eisenhower will leave Paris to-morrow, and Mr. Khruschev is also expected to stay till then.

Mr. Khruschev's wrecking tactics are blamed for the collapse. Mr. Macmillan, who gave a lead towards the Summit, is said not to have concealed the serious view he takes of the adverse developments now possible.

The Russian leader, who repeated his demand for a public apology by Mr. Eisenhower over the "spy-plane" incident, said he would stop at East Berlin on his flight home. An East German Communist official said Mr. Khruschev would sign a separate peace treaty only when East-West negotiations on Berlin had foundered.

MEETING BOYCOTTED

An attempt was made by President de Gaulle to convene the Summit conference yesterday afternoon. A police motor-cyclist sped with an invitation to Mr. Khruschev, who had gone to Sezanne, 70 miles out of Paris. He hurried back to the capital, but remained at his Embassy.

The three Western leaders issued a statement noting Mr. Khruschev's absence and adding that "in these circumstances the planned discussions could not take place."

(May 18)

SHOT-DOWN AMERICAN PLANE. The wreckage of an American aircraft which, Mr. Khruschev announced, had been shot down over Russian territory.

RUSSIA SHOOTS DOWN AMERICAN PLANE

President Eisenhower yesterday ordered a "complete inquiry" into the disappearance of an American weather research aircraft from its base in Turkey, after hearing of Mr. Khruschev's announcement that Russia had shot down a United States plane on Sunday.

The Russian leader told the Supreme Soviet in Moscow that the Air Force deliberately destroyed the plane, which was sent with the aim of wrecking the Summit talks. After an American violation of the Soviet air space on April 9 anti-aircraft gunners were warned not to let any further intrusion "go unpunished."

The State Department in Washington said that the last radio communication with the missing aircraft's pilot was that he was having oxygen trouble and was heading back to base at Adana, Turkey. It was assumed that he had inadvertently strayed off course. Senator Styles Bridges, Republican, said that President Eisenhower should refuse to attend this month's Summit meeting unless a satisfactory explanation was given. If the Russians were going "to shoot first and complain later," then Summit prospects were "grim," declared Senator Mansfield, Democratic Whip.

(May 6)

10-YEAR SENTENCE ON POWERS

Sentence of 10 years' detention, three of them to be spent in prison, was passed on Francis Powers, 31-year-old pilot of the American U-2 "spy-plane" in Moscow yesterday. The sentence, which was five years less than the prosecution demanded, was greeted with applause in the crowded Hall of Columns, but Powers remained calm.

It is expected that for the last portion of the sentence, Powers will be transferred to a camp. Immediately after the trial ended he was reunited with his wife, Barbara for the first time since he was captured on May 1. Although sentence is final Mrs. Powers said she would appeal for clemency. Her lawyers said they proposed to petition Mr. Khruschev. Mrs. Powers had been assured she would be allowed to see her husband again.

President Eisenhower "regrets the severity of the sentence" and deplores Russia's propaganda approach, the White House stated.

(August 20)

63 DEAD IN SOUTH AFRICAN RIOTS

Police fire on Mobs in two towns: 191 hurt

From Our Special Correspondent

JOHANNESBURG, Monday.

SHOOTING by South African police on the first day of a campaign by Africans against the pass laws which require them to carry identity cards to-day ended in the deaths of 63 men, women and children. A further 191 were wounded.

The worst outbreak was in the African township of Sharpeville, near Vereeniging, Witwatersrand, where the Treaty ending the Boer War was signed. Seventy-five white police besieged in the police station fired on thousands of demonstrators, killing 56 and wounding 162.

As news of the heavy casualties spread disorders were feared in other areas. To-night police fired on Africans in the township of Langa, near Cape Town, killing six and wounding 30, of whom one died later in hospital.

The crowd were said by an eye-witness to have "gone berserk" after the firing. Several buildings, including the administrative centre, schools and shops, were stated to be on fire.

To-day's demonstrations were organised by the Pan-Africanist Congress, a militant off-shoot of the African National Congress.

It called on its 31,000 members to leave their passes at home and to surrender at police stations. The African National Congress disassociated itself from the campaign.

"UNDER CONTROL"
Premier's Statement

In a statement to Parliament Dr. Verwoerd, Prime Minister, said Mr. Robert Sobukwe, president of the Pan-Africanists, and other leaders of the movement, had been arrested. The position was now under control he said.

(March 22)

CHANNEL TUNNEL START "POSSIBLE IN TWO YEARS"

LEASE TO RAILWAYS PLAN

Daily Telegraph Reporter

If the British and French Governments agreed, work would start within two years on an £80 million twin-system of rail tunnels to link the two countries. This was said yesterday by Mr. L.F.A. d'Erlanger, British spokesman of the group set up to study the possibilities of a cross-Channel link.

The study group favours this twin-tunnel system on technical and financial grounds. Road tunnels, combined road and rail tunnels, and a bridge were also considered. Introducing the report in London yesterday, Mr. d'Erlanger said he thought Government approval might take eight months or a year to get.

After that, it would take about a year to invite and consider tenders. Selective tendering was likely to be adopted.

The report estimates time between London and Paris would be cut to four hours 20 minutes. I asked Mr. d'Erlanger if this included Customs and immigration formalities.

He replied: "We have five years to negotiate about that." The tunnel would take at least five years to build.

£80 MILLION NEEDED
International Company

The study group believes the £80 million needed to build the actual tunnel can be raised without Government help. The tunnel would be leased to the French and British Railways.

It could pay for itself in 35 years. The two Governments would provide for its destruction, should that ever be necessary. If the two Governments agree to a treaty establishing a new international company, it is expected companies and individuals who pioneered modern study of this old dream will have first opportunity of taking part. The existing Channel Tunnel Co. will cease to exist.

Mr. d'Erlanger, its chairman, said he would expect compensation for shareholders.

(April 21)

DOCTORS TOLD TO LIMIT DRUG PRESCRIPTIONS

WEEK'S SUPPLY ONLY

By John Prince
Daily Telegraph Health Services Correspondent

More than 20,000 family doctors in the National Health Service are being asked by the Ministry of Health to limit the drugs they prescribe to a week's supply. This amount can be exceeded in chronic and special cases.

The aim is economy. The pharmaceutical service, it is estimated, will cost nearly £70 million in the current financial year. The Ministry's call for restraint is contained in a letter which is being sent to doctors through local executive councils. These councils administer the practitioner services.

"AVOID PROPRIETARIES"

The request is based on a recommendation by a committee which, under the chairmanship of Sir Harry Hinchliffe, recently considered the cost of prescribing. In a statement last night, the Ministry pointed out that the committee rejected formal restriction of drugs, but suggested that doctors should be asked voluntarily to limit the quantities they prescribed.

The aim is to cut waste and thus help to secure economy without loss of therapeutic efficiency. Doctors are also asked to use official titles in preference to proprietary names. In recent years the proportion of proprietary brands prescribed by doctors has increased steadily.

(February 2)

END OF BRITISH RULE IN CYPRUS

From Ian Colvin, Daily Telegraph Correspondent

NICOSIA, Tuesday Morning.

Cyprus became a republic at midnight. In a brief ceremony in the House of Representatives, Sir Hugh Foot, the withdrawing Governor for Britain, Archbishop Makarios, as President, and Dr. Kutchuk, as Vice-President, signed the already initialled agreements.

They were also signed by diplomatic representatives of Greece and Turkey. About 5,000 young men and a few women formed a dense crowd outside the Chamber as British guns boomed a 21-gun salute.

There was some applause for personalities entering the hall, but no wild enthusiasm. Crowd control was utterly lacking to-night and Sir Hugh Foot and others had to squeeze their way in while Cypriot police looked on apathetically.

The crowd began drifting away along the dark streets half an hour after midnight. An Eoka stay away appeal had helped to keep it small.

There were no bonfires and no dancing. Nothing looked less like a nation marking its new found freedom. All that could be said was that the crowd was mildly inquisitive and good natured.

(August 16)

BEST BITTER UP 1d A PINT

Daily Telegraph Reporter

Trumans are increasing the price of their best bitter by 1d a pint in the London area. Public bar prices will be 1s 7d a pint, with similar increases in other bars.

A spokesman for the brewery said yesterday that apart from certain parts of East Anglia, where public bar prices would go up from 1s 3d to 1s 4d a pint, the increase applied only to the company's 539 houses in the Greater London area.

The increase was being made to help licensees meet the rising costs of running public houses.

There were no reports last night of increases by other brewers with big interests in the London area. But people connected with the trade thought it likely that other firms would follow the lead.

(August 13)

"PLANET" OVER 500,000 MILES FROM EARTH

By Anthony Smith

America's miniature "planet," Pioneer V, passed the half-million mile mark yesterday. Once again the Jodrell Bank radio-telescope had no difficulty in instructing it to transmit or in picking up its transmissions.

Pioneer V is sending out signals from its small transmitter so well that there has been no need for Jodrell Bank to switch on the much larger one. The smaller one has a power of only five watts, while the larger one is 150 watts.

Each time the telescope picks up Pioneer V, it is establishing a record receiving radio signals from a man-made object in space. Each night, when the earth has spun round, the telescope in Hawaii breaks this record and establishes another.

But the Hawaii telescope will not be able to pick up the five-watt transmissions for more than another week. The "Planet" will have moved too far away from the earth, and the job will be up to Jodrell Bank.

(March 15)

ROUND-UP BEFORE DAWN

From Colin Reid, Daily Telegraph Special Correspondent

JOHANNESBURG, Wednesday.

A state of emergency was declared in 80 of the 300 magisterial districts of South Africa to-day. It followed the arrest before dawn of 234 White and non-White political leaders and party organisers.

Those arrested included ex-chief LUTHULI, president of the African National Congress in South Africa, and Dr. TSELE, leader of the Pan African organisation, who announced yesterday that he would intensify the campaign of violence after Monday's day of mourning for the victims of the police shooting.

Among the Europeans were Mr. PETER BROWN, national chairman of the Liberal party; Dr. MEIDNER, Natal chairman; Mr. DERICK MARSH, former chairman in Pietermaritzburg; Mr. JOHN BRINK, chairman in Pretoria; Mr. JOHN LANG, nephew of a former Governor-General; Father MARK NYE; Mrs. HELEN JOSEPH, of the Federation of South African Women; and Miss. HANNAH STANTON, warden of the Tumelong Mission at the African township of Lady Selborne, near Pretoria.

The round-up took place a few hours after Mr. Erasmus, Minister of Justice, had told Parliament that South Africa was on the verge of revolution. Announcing the state of emergency in Parliament this afternoon, Mr. Erasmus said it applied to those districts in which meetings had just been banned under the Riotous Assemblies Act.

DR. VERWOERD'S CLAIM
No Unnecessary Powers

Dr. Verwoerd, the Prime Minister, rose and said the Government did not intend to take any power unnecessary for the handling of the situation.

In Cape Town to-day a force of Africans estimated to number 30,000 marched in a procession more than a mile long from the riotous suburb of Langa to Caledon Square police station in the heart of the capital. Their aim was to demand the release of the arrested African National Congress leaders, Mrs. Mpheta and Mr. Thomas Ngwyna.

In an effort to reach Parliament they jammed two streets from wall to wall. Women wailed from the railings of the Anglican Cathedral near by, where hundreds of Africans worship regularly.

It was on the renewed appeals of one of the Pan African leaders, Mr. Ngkosana, that the crowds eventually dispersed. The situation in Cape Town remains tense.

(March 30)

NARROW DEFEAT OF Mr. GAITSKELL

Brave Speech Fails to Stop Bomb Ban

From Our Political Correspondent

SCARBOROUGH, Wednesday.

DESPITE what many Labour M.P.s hailed as the greatest and most courageous speech of his career, Mr. Gaitskell watched the Labour party "go unilateralist" before his eyes this afternoon.

The warning he gave as leader, in the gravest and most impassioned terms he could command, was thrown back in his teeth

His only consolation was that the majorities in favour of renouncing nuclear weapons, and against the official defence policy of relying on the nuclear deterrent with N.A.T.O., were much narrower than the commitment of trade union block votes had led the conference to expect.

They were, indeed, almost minimal in the context of a total voting strength of about 6,650,000.

UNDER TWO-THIRDS

Constitution Requirements

None of the majorities for the unilateralist policy comes anywhere near the requirements of the party constitution that "no proposal shall be included in the party programme" unless adopted by a majority of at least two-thirds of the votes recorded.

But this is rather beside the point. The party programme is a collection of specific proposals from which items for periodical general election manifestoes are selected.

There is no General Election in sight for three years. In the meantime, the Labour party has proclaimed to the world that its policy is to "go it alone" in renouncing nuclear weapons, even if it should become necessary for Britain to get out of N.A.T.O.

Unless this policy is changed 12 months hence, or at a special conference summoned earlier, it is just as official as was the policy of German rearmament adopted by a narrow majority six years ago.

The only practical effect of Mr. Gaitskell's magnificent advocacy was to swing the uncommitted element of the constituency party's vote. It is claimed that fully 70 per cent of the round million which they wield were cast in his favour.

(October 6)

DR. FISHER'S 65 MINUTES WITH POPE

ROME, Friday.

The Archbishop of Canterbury, Dr. Fisher, paid his courtesy visit to Pope John XXIII at noon to-day. The conversation lasted 65 minutes.

The Pope received Dr. Fisher at the entrance to his private library. They shook hands and entered on a conversation which Dr. Fisher afterwards described as being "as friendly and natural as possible."

The Archbishop's first words were: "Your Holiness, we are making history." The Pope smiled his assent.

ANGLICAN ACCOUNT

A statement was issued later on behalf of the Church of England information office. It read:

His Grace the Archbishop of Canterbury was received by His Holiness the Pope at the Vatican this morning. The Archbishop was able to give his Holiness some of the impressions which he had gained from his recent visit to Jerusalem and Istanbul.

(March 3)

£180,000 GEMS THEFT FROM SOPHIA LOREN

Daily Telegraph Reporter

An international collection of jewellery, provisionally valued at nearly £180,000, was stolen from the temporary Elstree home of Miss Sophia Loren, the Italian film actress, in a five-minute raid on Saturday night. Three members of the staff were on the premises at the time.

Scotland Yard detectives, led by Det. Supt. Eric Shepherd, were yesterday trying to establish how the thief got into the lavishly furnished chalet, known as the Norwegian Barn, which Miss Loren has rented while she is filming at Elstree Studios. It stands in the 43 acres belonging to Edgwarebury Country Club.

MISS SOPHIA LOREN

BLACK CASE

Three Valuable Sets

The thief went straight to Miss Loren's bedroom on the first floor. He forced one locked drawer in a chest of drawers and took a black leather attaché case about 18 inches square.

In the case were all Miss Loren's jewels. They included three very valuable sets consisting of a necklace, earrings and brooch.

The theft is the largest individual robbery in Britain for many years. The last comparable one was the theft in March, 1959, of Lady Docker's jewellry, valued at £150,000, from her car parked in Southampton. It has not yet been found.

(May 30)

A QUEUE FORMED BY A BOOKSTALL set up outside a shop in Leicester Square yesterday waiting for copies of the unexpurgated version of "Lady Chatterley's Lover" to be sold.

"LADY CHATTERLEY" NOT OBSCENE, JURY HOLD

200,000 PENGUIN COPIES SOON

Daily Telegraph Reporter

"LADY Chatterley's Lover" is not obscene. An Old Bailey jury of nine men and three women settled, within three hours yesterday, the 30-year controversy which has raged about D.H. Lawrence's novel.

Their decision means that anyone in Britain can now read the unexpurgated story of the sexual behaviour of the fictitious Lady Chatterley and her gamekeeper lover, Oliver Mellors. Cheers and clapping came from literary figures in the public seats of the famous No. 1 court when the bespectacled foreman of the middle-aged jury announced that Penguin Books Ltd. was not guilty of publishing the book as an obscene article contrary to the Obscene Publications Act 1959.

Last night a spokesman for the Director of Public Prosecutions said: "Whether there is to be an appeal by the Crown is a matter for the Director. At the moment I have no information."

Penguin Books were arranging immediate distribution of 200,000 copies of the 317-page 3s 6d novel. It should be on the bookstalls a week to-day.

Gaily-coloured posters saying "Now you can read it" and "Lady Chatterley Acquitted. Now you can read it" are also ready for distribution. Plans are in hand to reprint 300,000 more copies of the book.

"HAPPY DAY"

Costs About £10,000

After the verdict, Sir Allen Lane, 58, managing director of Penguins, who founded the firm 25 years ago in the disused crypt of Holy Trinity Church, Euston Road, St. Pancras, said: "This is a happy day for me.

It is the end of a 10-year dream to publish this work. To-night I shall have a lively celebration with my wife and family, ending with a dinner party."

Asked about the cost of defending "Lady Chatterley" Sir Allen replied: "I don't think one could get very drunk on the change from £10,000."

The estate of D.H. Lawrence will benefit by £4,166 in royalties on an assumed sale of 500,000 copies based on payment of 2d a copy. It will be more as the sales go above that number.

CROWDED COURT

Costs Refused

Mr. Justice Byrne, who is expected to retire from the bench soon, concluded his summing-up yesterday morning and sent the jury out at 11.58 a.m. They returned to a crowded court at 2.58 p.m.

While they were out, Sir Allen Lane lunched in a public house opposite the court with his solicitor, Mr. Michael Rubinstein, and a fellow director, Mrs. H.V. Kemp. Sir Allen, obviously tense, nibbled a ham sandwich and drank a glass of Portuguese red wine. He was in court when the jury returned.

When Mr. Leslie Boyd, Clerk of the Court, asked the foreman for the verdict he received a two-word reply "Not Guilty." When the cheers and clapping subsided Mr. Gerald Gardiner, Q.C. defending, who gathered 35 experts on literature and Lawrence to speak for "Lady Chatterley", asked for costs.

He said that Mr. Mervyn Griffith-Jones, for the Crown, had said the case had been brought as a test. Costs had been extensive.

The Judge replied: "I don't desire to say any more than this. I will make no order as to costs."

After the hearing one male juror, a toolmaker, commented: "I was not embarrassed by the book. I found some of the passages rather dull, and I was certainly not uneasy about reading it in the same room with the women."

The jurors left in four taxis provided by Penguin Books.

(November 3)

NEWS CHRONICLE CLOSES DOWN

By Our Industrial Staff

THE NEWS CHRONICLE and its stablemate, the London evening paper, the Star, ceased publication last night. As reported in THE DAILY TELEGRAPH yesterday, both papers have been bought by Associated Newspapers Ltd., and will be merged with existing publications.

The News Chronicle, which has always supported the Liberal party, is to be merged with the Conservative Daily Mail. The Star will become part of the London Evening News.

Associated Newspapers Ltd. have paid £1,500,000 for the titles and plant of the two papers. The price includes valuable freehold premises in Bouverie Street, off Fleet Street, but not the News Chronicle printing plant in Manchester.

(October 18)

MOBUTU'S TROOPS ARREST LUMUMBA

EARLY TRIAL PROMISED

From JAMES O'DRISCOLL,
Daily Telegraph Special Correspondent

LEOPOLDVILLE, Friday.

MR. PATRICE LUMUMBA, 35, deposed Prime Minister of the Congo, was arrested by the forces of the Congolese Army C.-in-C., Col. Mobutu, to-day at Port Francqui, 420 miles from Leopoldville. He had been making his way to his last political stronghold, Stanleyville.

He arrived back in the capital to-night by plane with his hands tied behind his back with a piece of rough rope. He was wearing an open-necked white shirt and blue slacks and looked very dejected.

He did not say a word and was roughly bundled on to an open Army lorry. Under heavy escort, he was driven to the military barracks about six miles outside Leopoldville, where Col. Mobutu lives.

FOUR SUPPORTERS

All Under Heavy Guard

With Mr. Lumumba were four of his lieutenants similarly bound with their hands behind their backs, who were captured with him. As the convoy drove through the capital there were cries of "Down with Lumumba."

The fallen leader and his colleagues are to-night held under heavy guard.

Col. Mobutu said to-day that he will be brought to trial before "the judiciary of the country" charged with inciting a revolt in the army "and other crimes against the common law."

STRONGER POSITION

Col. Mobutu's Prestige

The arrest removes Mr. Lumumba from the political scene, at least for the time being, and further clears the way for Col. Mobutu to reopen Parliament early next year.

The colonel, with the Head of State, President Kasavubu, supporting him and his chief opponent out of the way, is now in a stronger position than ever.

The troops who seized Mr. Lumumba first took him quickly to Luluabourg, from where they sent a cable saying that if Col. Mobutu did not take him away by 2 p.m. they would shoot him. Col. Mobutu immediately replied that they were to do no such thing.

Mr. Lumumba was to be kept in safe custody until a plane could be sent from the capital. The colonel later described this threat as "insubordination which no commander could tolerate."

He added with satisfaction: "My troops at Port Francqui called Lumumba a traitor because they believe he has caused a lot of harm. The whole local population booed and shouted 'Judas' and 'traitor' at him. That is a good indication of the situation."

Before Mr. Lumumba was flown from Luluabourg, the local chief of police and his deputy apparently asked for United Nations protection for him. The United Nations, which has a force of Ghanaians there, refused.

Mobutu forces promptly surrounded the local Post Office to prevent any more messages going to the United Nations. Then they surrounded the police station and the two officers are now under arrest.

Colonel Mobutu mentioned this to-night and also the protection Mr. Lumumba received from United Nations forces in Leopoldville before the fallen Prime Minister escaped from the capital in his ill-starred attempt to rally support in the country.

The colonel commented: "If I had not had the United Nations in my way I would have restored order in the Congo long ago."

United Nations headquarters here remained officially aloof from the search for Mr. Lumumba. An official statement said that the United Nations ceased to be responsible for his protection from the moment he left his official residence.

WHITES BEATEN

Officials Stood By

It was revealed in a report issued by the United Nations itself that its officials stood by while 1,000 Europeans in Stanleyville were arrested, beaten and subjected to other indiginities by pro-Lumumba soldiers. The reason for these indignities was an arbitrary order by the Provincial Government that all whites be rounded up for an identity check last Sunday.

(December 3)

DR. MOORE REACHES LAND'S END WITH 35 min. TO SPARE

Daily Telegraph Reporter

Dr. BARBARA MOORE, who is 56, arrived at Land's End, smiling but exhausted, at 11.25 last night. She was 35 minutes inside the time she set herself for the last day of her 23-day 1,000 miles march from John o'Groats.

A crowd of 3,000 to 4,000 was waiting to cheer her. Dr. Moore walked to the signpost, known to millions, which stands on the cliff above the sea. There she posed to have her picture taken.

She shook hands with two policemen, P.c. Anthony Pearce and P.c. Owen Bulford, who walked the last 10 miles from Penzance with her to protect her from the crowds and from cars overtaking to greet her at Land's End.

It was estimated that a larger number of cars than ever before were outside the Land's End Hotel, at which Dr. Moore was to stay the night. At least 1,500 cars were parked near the hotel.

Two police motor cyclists who had been guiding Dr. Moore towards Land's End burnt out their clutches after 15 miles in low gear.

GLASS OF ORANGE JUICE

In her room at the hotel was a large glass of orange juice put there by the manageress, Mrs. L. Young, a lifelong vegetarian. Downstairs was laid a dinner of melon cocktail in orange juice, vegetable soup, salad, pineapple and ice cream.

On a diet consisting mainly of raw vegetables, fruit juices, nuts, honey and milk, laced in the last stages with Cornish cream, the doctor triumphed over blizzard, ice, hail, flood and rain.

She covered from 30 to 50 miles a day, according to local conditions. On an average she walked at about four m.p.h. for 11 hours a day.

She began her last and longest lap, one of about 60 miles, at Bodmin at 5.30 a.m. yesterday. For a time her speed went up to 6 m.p.h.

Dr. Moore hopes to fly back to London from Penzance to-day. She contemplates, as suggested yesterday, walking across the United States. "The roads there are much nicer, with no potholes," she said.

Sisters Not Far Behind

The two Liverpool sisters, Joy Lewis, 22, and Wendy, 18, who left John o'Groats on Jan. 12, reached Tiverton, Devon, at 1.30 p.m. yesterday. They hope to arrive at Land's End tomorrow, the elder sister's birthday.

(February 5)

65 DIE IN DAY OF ALGERIAN RIOTS

FIERCE CASBAH BATTLE

From John Wallis, Daily Telegraph Special Correspondent.

ALGIERS, Sunday

After a day of serious rioting and fighting between Moslems and Europeans which forced the army to intervene, the curfew in the city to-night was advanced from 1 a.m. to 8 p.m. All day long ambulances have been hurrying through the streets carrying dead and wounded from the suburban battlefields. A Government statement said to-night that 61 people had been killed in to-day's rioting.

These were made up of 56 Moslems, four Europeans and one French police officer. The number of injured was not complete. In addition, four Moslems were killed in Oran.

Mr. Morin, Delegate General, to-night appealed for calm and urged people to return to work immediately.

The Army claims that it opened fire only after being fired on by Moslem demonstrators.

To-night rioting broke out in the Casbah between Jews and Moslems, but at midnight the city, under curfew, was calm.

TELEGRAMS CENSORED

British Protest

All telegrams from Algeria will be censored, but it appears that telephone calls for the time being will not undergo censorship. The British Consulate lodged a protest to-night because its telegrams were being held at the post office and not transmitted. These were in diplomatic code.

To-day, in the Algiers suburbs I saw bodies lying tucked away in tiny streets. Many of the wounded had gone home to be treated.

The trouble started last night in the eastern mixed Moslem and European quarter of Belcourt.

After a day of clashes between French youths and the riot police in the city centre, in which two police died of injuries, the Moslems of Belcourt reported to their native affairs officer that they had been attacked and fired on by a group of Europeans.

He told them to go home and remain quiet, but instead the Moslems started breaking windows of European shops. They set fire to a huge warehouse of a leading chain store and looted other European shops.

(December 12)

Gen. De GAULLE GIVEN SPECIAL POWERS

The French Assembly voted early to-day to grant special powers for one year to Gen. de Gaulle's Government, after M. Debré, the Prime Minister, said the nation had faced civil war over the revolt in Algeria. The voting was 449 to 79, a majority of 370.

M. Debré said the powers were necessary so "essential and urgent" measures could be taken to protect the State and administer Algeria. Several amendments were accepted, one of which provides that the special powers cease if the Government is changed or the Assembly dissolved.

All parties except the Communists, some deputies from Algeria, and a right-wing group led by M. Bidault, voted for the Government. The Bill now goes to the Senate, which is expected to approve it today.

In Algiers the barricades were down. But the atmosphere there is bitter, reports OUR SPECIAL CORRESPONDENT, JOHN WALLIS. M. Lagaillarde, the imprisoned insurrection leader, is regarded as a hero by the settlers.

Before the Paris debate President de Gaulle saw party leaders. He told them that he considered a federation in Algeria as the most probable solution of the issue.

The weekly Cabinet Council under Gen. de Gaulle, which usually takes place on Wednesday, was postponed until Friday so that it could be held after the debate. Officials said they did not think that the President would wish to leave for Algiers straight away. He had originally said he would go to Algiers on Friday.

DE GAULLE AIM

Algerian Federation

Gen. de Gaulle yesterday told party leaders that he considered the creation of a federation the most probable solution in Algeria. The President went out of his way to express this opinion when he received 16 party leaders before the debate.

The President thought self-determination would almost certainly lead to the creation of a federal Algerian state, closely linked to France. He went so far as to say that this would have to be arranged by both France and Algeria.

His aim would be to set up a series of states within an Algerian Federation to allow Frenchmen to retain control over important regions. The federation could include predominant French, Arab and Kabyle states

(February 3)

BUSH SHIRTS FOR POLICE IN LONDON

Daily Telegraph Reporter

London policemen will go into shirtsleeve order for the first time next summer. Mr. Butler, Home Secretary, said in the Commons yesterday that bush shirts will be issued in April.

Women police in London have had shirtsleeve order available in hot weather for over 12 months. Mr. Butler said shirtsleeves would be worn in very hot weather at the discretion of Sir Joseph Simpson, Metropolitan Police Commissioner. This is to ensure that the whole force wears the same uniform at all times.

(June 30)

JAPAN TO SEND MORE GOODS TO BRITAIN

TOYS, CAMERAS AND MOPEDS

More Japanese goods will soon be entering Britain following a trade agreement signed yesterday by the Japanese Ambassador, Mr. Katsumi Ohno and the President of the Board of Trade Mr. Maudling. This agreement covers the period up to March next year.

A board of Trade spokesman was unable to say last night whether or not Japan's goods would have a "competitive price". He pointed out, however, that if there was any danger of dumping then action could be taken.

(July 16)

SMOKE AND FLAMES billow from the upper floors of Henderson's, the Liverpool department store. The building was extensively damaged.

11 KILLED IN BIG STORE BLAZE

WOMEN CUSTOMERS & STAFF TRAPPED

Daily Telegraph Reporter

At least 11 people died yesterday in a fire that swept through one of Liverpool's biggest stores, sending about 700 employees and customers fleeing to safety. Firemen searched the debris for further victims up to a late hour, and will resume the task to-day.

At first it was thought that the casualty roll was confined to one man, who fell 90ft to his death, and a number of people injured. But last night, nearly five hours after firemen had begun their fight, the first party able to enter the ruins found 10 bodies.

Eight of the dead were women and two were men. It was stated that they were customers and staff who had been trapped.

Mr. T. Kelly, Liverpool's chief fire officer, who had supervised 100 men in fighting the blaze, said to me: "We have recovered 10 bodies up to now from the top storey, but part of that floor has crashed right through to the basement. It may well be that other bodies will be found among the ruins."

Flames spread like a forest fire through the five-storey store of William Henderson's in Church Street, which is owned by Harrods. Police sealed off the city centre as the extent of the fire became apparent.

RESCUER DIES

Helped Shop Girls

The outbreak was discovered at 2.30 p.m. Four hundred employees and more than 300 customers ran from the building. The first man to die was Colin Murphy, 34, of Turrett Road, Wallasey, a heating engineer working on the premises.

Mr. John Moore, 25, an advertising representative, said he saw Murphy "shepherd five or six shop girls to safety along the narrow passage to the flat roof of a new block. But part of the ledge collapsed and he was cut off.

"He hung on by his fingers while firemen were running up the escape ladder, but he slipped and crashed through the glass and asphalt canopy 90ft below."

A friend of Murphy, John Williams, 25, of Arnold Street, also helped a number of girls on to the narrow ledge and found an escape route.

"PLACE AN INFERNO"

Other Buildings Saved

Mr. T. Kelly, who mobilised 28 fire appliances, said: "I have never seen a fire gain hold so quickly. The whole place was like an inferno." He supervised the rescue of five shop assistants trapped on a narrow fifth-floor ledge.

Damage was provisionally estimated at about £2 million. Stock worth hundreds of thousands of pounds was destroyed. A section in which the fire is believed to have started was opened last Christmas after a £300,000 reconstruction scheme.

Police are investigating reports that the fire began in a cavity below the restaurant on the fourth floor and that it may have been caused by a chip pan.

(June 23)

SCOOTER THAT HOVERS AT 30 m.p.h.

By Our Motoring Correspondent

The world's first hover-scooter was demonstrated at Long Ditton, Surrey, yesterday. It took off from a lawn, three or four inches above the turf, slipped over the bank on to a small lake, and ran above the surface of the water.

It can travel up to eight inches above the water, but normally runs with a three to four-inch cushion of air beneath it. It can travel at walking pace or up to 30 m.p.h.

(November 10)

DEAD SEA SCROLLS FOUND IN ISRAELI CAVE

JERUSALEM, Israel, Sunday.

Fragments of ancient leather scrolls have been found by Israeli archaeologists in eagles' nests inside a cave on a cliff overlooking the Dead Sea. Prof. Yohanan Aharoni, of the Hebrew University, gave the information here to-day.

It is the first discovery of ancient scrolls in the Israeli part of the Judean wilderness. All other Dead Sea scrolls have been found across the border in Jordanian terrority.

Prof. Aharoni said to-day that his finds included two fragments of leather scrolls with script similar to that on scrolls found in the Murabaat caves in Jordan, some 15 miles to the north. The scrolls preserved in eagles' nests were part of a phylactery, a small box carried by Jews to remind them to keep the Law.

ALMOST COMPLETE

Verses from Exodus

One fragment was almost complete, comprising verses One to Ten of Chapter 13 in the Book of Exodus. A second incomplete text contained verses 11 to 16 of the same chapter.

Another discovery was believed to be an ancient letter, not yet deciphered.

The archaeologists had to use ropes to climb to the hidden cave. They found that nomadic Bedouin tribesmen, who in recent years have raided all caves in the Dead Sea region searching for scrolls, had preceded them.

COINS FOUND

Cave as Refuge Theory

But the Bedouins had apparently made only a superficial examination. Prof. Aharoni said coins found in the cave would help to determine the time of its use.

Some of them had the image of Trajan, who died in A.D. 117 about 25 years before the revolt of Shimon Bar Kochba. Two other coins dated from about A.D. 230.

(February 8)

B.B.C. TO STOP 9 O'CLOCK NEWS

AUDIENCE DECLINE

By A Radio Correspondent

The 9 pm news, a daily feature on the B.B.C. Home Service since 1940, is to be no-more. Mr. Hugh Carleton Greene, Director-General of the B.B.C. has decided to have the evening news bulletin at 10p.m. instead. It will be introduced by the chimes of Big Ben.

It is estimated that 750,000 to a million people listen to the nine o'clock news, compared with 2,250,000 three years ago and several million during the war. A B.B.C. spokesman said last night: "With the great pull of television and a declining sound audience you have got to give the listeners what they want when they want it."

(May 12)

M.P.S REJECT PLEA FOR VICE LAW CHANGE

213-99 WOLFENDEN VOTE

By Our Special Correspondent

WESTMINSTER, Wednesday.

Mild applause in the Commons to-night greeted the announcement that a private Member's motion calling on the Government to take early action on the recommendations concerning homosexuality in the Wolfenden Report had been heavily defeated in the division lobby.

The voting (a free vote) on the motion, which supported the proposal that homosexual acts committed in private by consenting adults should no longer constitute a criminal offence, was:

For the motion 99
Against 213
Majority against 114

Mr. Butler, Home Secretary, who intervened towards the end of the debate, made it clear that the Government had no present intention of Legislating on this issue. He felt the debate had shown a great division of opinion.

In reply to suggestions that the law should be left as it was, but its enforcement narrowly limited Mr. Butler replied that this would be an innovation in British practice. It was impossible for him to give instructions to the police.

UNANSWERED QUESTIONS

Armed Forces Exemption

The Home Secretary asked some questions concerning the phrase embodied in the Wolfenden report "consenting adults in private." What, he asked, does "consenting" mean?

Why should the age of consent be 21? Would the Armed Forces be excepted from amending legislation? How was "in private" to be defined?

He confessed that he did not know the answers to these questions.

(June 30)

PLOT TO POISON COL. NASSER

From Ian Colvin
Daily Telegraph Special Correspondent

CAIRO, Wednesday.

A plot to poison President Nasser, involving a Greek waiter named George Stamatiou, was revealed here to-day when it was announced that members of six spy rings were to be tried soon.

Each group was said to have been spying for Israel "our principal enemy without any doubt" an information Department statement said. A series of postcard-size photographs was flourished before correspondents as the smashing of the spy rings was described.

An intelligence agent stood up to answer questions. He said that the arrests had taken place over the past three years. They were revealed now because "the cases are ripe." The trials will begin in public in May.

The poisoning was said to have been intended to take place at the banquet. A second conspirator was named in this case, Nicolas Coys.

DUTCHMAN NAMED

Meew's Goudswaard, a Dutchman described as a principal spy for Israel and two Italians were mentioned in the first case announced.

The second involved a former co-pilot of the Egyptian Airline named Ali Fahmi. The third was the poison case.

The fourth was said to have involved Mohammed Rizk, described as Director of the Personnel Department of the Ford Company in Alexandria.

(April 21)

DIGNITY & SPLENDOUR OF ABBEY CEREMONY

150,000 AT PALACE BREAK THROUGH POLICE CORDON

The newly-married Princess Margaret and her husband, Mr. Antony Armstrong-Jones, were sailing towards the Channel last night in the Royal yacht Britannia for their honeymoon in the Caribbean. They had been nearly an hour late in reaching the ship, partly because crowds on the way slowed their car.

The biggest crowds in London since the Coronation had gathered early in the day swelling the hundreds who had spent all night on the pavements along the route. Sunshine, which brought the warmest day of the year, added an extra sparkle to the scene.

MR. ANTONY ARMSTRONG-JONES AND PRINCESS MARGARET

2,000 IN ABBEY

There were solid masses of people, sometimes 20 deep, waiting to greet first the bridegroom and the best man and then the Queen, Queen Elizabeth the Queen Mother and other members of the Royal family as they drove past. Bursts of cheers welcomed Princess Margaret and Prince Philip as they followed.

Inside the Abbey, decorated with banks of gladioli, irises and tulips in yellow, blue and red, more than 2,000 privileged guests, including the Commonwealth Prime Ministers, watched the procession of royalty and clergy down the nave and the arrival of the bride followed by the dignity and splendour of the Abbey ceremony.

Peals of bells heralded the appearance of Princess Margaret and her husband outside the Abbey at the end of the ceremony. They smiled and waved in reply to the storm of cheers which greeted them all the way to the Palace in their glass coach. There was an equally warm reception for the Queen and Prince Philip.

(July 7)

CONGREGATION SHARE WHOLE CEREMONY

By NORMAN RILEY

Of all the Abbey ceremonies I have been privileged to attend, yesterday's will remain outstanding as the first in which every member of the congregation was able to follow and share every detail, this time of the marriage service of Princess Margaret and Mr. Antony Armstrong-Jones.

Television showed the wedding in full to an international audience estimated at 300 million.

But, better still, every member of the congregation of more than 2,000 was able for the first time at a Royal wedding to see, besides something of the glorious colouring of the ceremonial, all the other detail of the service through 26 closed circuit television screens.

PRINCESS ANNE
20 Minutes Alone

It was possible, always, to see Princess Anne, only nine years old, alone for what seemed a long time even to adults, standing in the middle of the Persian carpet that covered the 13-century porphyry jasper and alabaster paving of the sanctuary.

For at least 20 minutes, a lifetime to a child, she stood her ground, isolated from all the richly robed dignitaries. Occasionally she discreetly edged her weight from one foot to another. On hassocks along the aisle to the sanctuary steps the seven other bridesmaids, aged six to 12, watched in enviable comfort.

THE QUEEN: A SECOND SON IS BORN

Daily Telegraph Reporters

A SON was born to the Queen at Buckingham Palace at 3.30 p.m. yesterday. Prince Philip was told the news immediately and a bulletin was flashed round Britain and the world shortly afterwards.

A notice, handwritten in ink, was hung on the wrought iron gates of the Palace just after 4 p.m. It read:

The Queen was safely delivered of a son at 3.30 p.m. to-day. Her Majesty and the infant Prince are both doing well.

The birth is the first to a reigning sovereign since 1857, when Princess Beatrice, youngest of Queen Victoria's nine children, was born. Both the Prince of Wales and Princess Anne were born when their grandfather, George VI, was reigning.

FATHER IN HIGH SPIRITS

Immediately he was told, Prince Philip went in to see the Queen and the baby, whose weight has yet to be announced. Obviously delighted and in high spirits, he spread the news to members of the Household staff. It is understood that it may be some days before the names of the new Prince are decided.

Prince Philip telephoned Cheam School and told the Prince of Wales that he had a brother. He was given leave of absence and arrived by car at Buckingham Palace at 8.20, using the rear entrance in Lower Grosvenor Place. He went straight in to see his mother and the baby.

Princess Anne had already been in to see the new Prince. Queen Elizabeth the Queen Mother and Princess Margaret arrived at 6.40 and stayed half an hour.

(February 22)

THE WRECKAGE OF A LOTUS racing car which was being driven by Stirling Moss. It crashed at 130 m.p.h. at Francorchamps on Saturday during practice for the Belgian Grand Prix. Two drivers were killed.

2 BRITONS KILLED IN GRAND PRIX

MOSS BREAKS LEGS: WIN BY BRABHAM

From W.A. McKENZIE,
Daily Telegraph Motoring Correspondent

SPA, Belgium, Sunday.

Two British drivers, Chris Bristow, 22, and Alan Stacey, 26, were killed in the Belgian Grand Prix motor race to-day. This followed serious accidents, in yesterday's practice, to Stirling Moss, 30, and Michael Taylor, 25.

The race, won by the Australian Jack Brabham, reigning world champion, at an average of 133.631 m.p.h., was one of the fastest on any road circuit in the history of motor racing. To-day's tragedies will arouse fresh controversy over the future of the sport.

Stacey's death seems almost certainly to have been due to a freak accident. M. Jean Bovy, a senior official of the circuit, confirmed that a bird hit Stacey's face, smashing his goggles.

The body of a bird was found on the track. There were traces of blood and feathers on the goggles.

It was at a spot called the Fountain of the Bird that Stacey, driving his Lotus at nearly 140 m.p.h., crashed. The car left the path, hit a bank and burst into flames. He died in the ambulance.

THROUGH BUSHES
Crash at Fast Bend

Bristow was well up, lying seventh in his Cooper, when, in the 19th lap, he took the long fast bend known as Burneville, near Malmedy, at over 130 m.p.h., accelerated and overtook another car. Then he seemed to lose control. The car shot off the road and somersaulted three times.

MOSS'S CRASH
Two Broken Legs

The accident in which Bristow was killed happened on the bend at which Stirling Moss, in a Lotus, came to grief yesterday. Moss was swinging down the gradient at 140 m.p.h. when a half-shaft to the left-side axle hub broke.

The wheel collapsed, and the car went spinning round like a top, finally crashing into a bank. Moss was thrown violently on to the track.

He fell on his face and knees and lay motionless for some minutes before a doctor could be brought to him.

Moss was taken to the Malmedy Hospital, where he was found to have both legs fractured just below the knee, three broken ribs, a badly cut and broken nose, two black eyes and several superficial cuts.

(June 20)

MR. SHEPPARD CONDEMNS RACIALISM IN CRICKET

Daily Telegraph Reporter

THE Rev. David Sheppard, 31, who has captained Cambridge, Sussex and England, left a sick bed last night to explain his decision not to play cricket against the South Africans this summer. He said: "I believe it is right for me to make a protest against the evil of apartheid being brought into cricket."

He replied to the "many friends" who said politics should be kept out of cricket. He said: "Politics has not been kept out of the game.

"I do not regard cricket in South Africa as non-political. South Africa has never played against the West Indies or India or Pakistan.

"There are about 20,000 non-white cricketers in South Africa. We have no chance of knowing how good they are, because they are not allowed to play in a club side, a province side or a Test side. Politics has been brought into cricket and it is right for me to protest."

Asked about Denis Compton's reported statement, that he was "horrified" at his decision, Mr. Sheppard answered: "I think most cricketers will be horrified. Probably 90 per cent. of them would not agree with me.

"It is terribly easy in cricket to say that we can talk about the game and if there is a running sore underneath we need not discuss it."

(April 8)

PICASSO'S IMPACT ON ART SHOWN BY EXHIBITION

TATE OPENING TO-DAY: CHANCE TO ASSESS MERITS

By Terence Mullaly

The Arts Council's Picasso exhibition, which opens to-day at the Tate Gallery, presents a comprehensive view of the work of the man who more than any other has conditioned the course of art in the 20th century. Little in the visual arts of to-day would be the same if there had been no Picasso.

This is a simple historical fact. It makes it no easier to answer the challenge of this exhibition; namely to determine the merit of particular pictures and the man's whole output.

Many will pass quickly through the rooms at the Tate and will go away angry or jeering. Others will come to worship the master and will have their easy adulation confirmed.

Yet others will leave the exhibition unhappy and perplexed. Unhappy that such great talents should have been so wantonly squandered, and perplexed that throughout his life even while defying both our sensibilities and our intelligence Picasso had succeeded in producing moving things.

NONSENSE WRITTEN

Judgment Difficult

One of the major difficulties in assessing his work is that such a vast amount of nonsense has been written about him. To many he is a god inviolable, and in this connection the catalogue of the present exhibition is far from exemplary. Too many of its entries contain special pleading and not enough factual information.

Yet here is a unique opportunity to assess Picasso's merits. Those who are familiar with the feuds of the art world will know that much has gone on behind the scenes, and that unworthy rivalries have prevented the loan of certain pictures.

Time and time again we are bemused, and, if we exercise our critical faculties, disappointed. Indeed it is difficult to believe that an artist who could produce things as poignant as the masterpieces of his Blue and Rose Periods should court the grotesque with such assiduity.

Yet hardly ever can we dismiss Picasso. Thus his "Las Menimas" series, which fills most of the South Sculptor Gallery, is nothing like as great as the catalogue suggests. But individual things from the series are enormously witty and a picture such as "Seated Woman," of 1927, has a way of lingering in the memory.

Beginning with the almost legendary "Les Demoiselles d'Avignon," of 1906-7, which when it was first shown them shocked Matisse and Braque, but subsequently exercised a profound influence, Picasso has produced a long series of pictures in which hallowed canons are ignored.

(July 6)

JOHN STRIDE AND JUDI DENCH in the title roles in the Old Vic production of Romeo and Juliet which opened last night.

NOT MUCH OF SHAKESPEARE

"ROMEO" LOST IN ELABORATION

By W.A. Darlington

Last evening at the Old Vic was one which began with promise and ended with disappointment.

When the performance of "Romeo and Juliet" was half-way through, I should have called it a very good production, slow and over-elaborate perhaps, but full of feeling and atmosphere. But at the end I could only say that the tragedy had been swallowed up in a welter of over-production.

Franco Zeffirelli, the Italian director responsible for this, has not avoided the pitfall into which nearly all foreign directors of Shakespeare fall - he has not realised how much the poetry matters to an English audience.

He began very well, with a lively brawl in the strong Italian sunlight which promised well for the spirit of the whole production, and until the balcony scene I had no doubts that this was going to be a memorable evening.

YOUNG AND CHARMING

But in that scene, though the lovers - John Stride and Judi Dench - were eager and charming and young, the low lighting and the muted speech raised an uneasy suspicion that Shakespeare was not going to get much consideration. And so it proved.

Every now and then a well-known passage would be given an elaborate treatment. Alec McCowen's Mercutio, for instance, was conducted through the Queen Mab speech with a positive operatic flourish, and took his opportunity with enormous gusto.

In general, however, the beauty of the language was lost.

Towards the end of the play, the stage was kept so dark and the speech at such an intimate pitch that I began to feel that I was intruding on the privacy of the characters. One effect of the brilliantly handled crowd scenes and the wonderfully spirited fighting was to disturb the balance of the play, in which some disconcerting cuts had to be made. This made a total effect of patchiness.

(October 5)

EVELYN WAUGH ON TELEVISION

By A Television and Radio Correspondent

EVELYN WAUGH was seen on television last night in the B.B.C.'s "Face to Face." He admitted publicly for the first time that in his novel, "The Ordeal of Gilbert Pinfold," the ordeal was largely his own.

Mr. John Freeman reminded him of the sinister voices. "The most odious said that Pinfold was a homosexual, a Communist Jew, a parvenu. Were these the kind of hallucinations that you yourself felt?"

Mr. Waugh replied: "Oh yes. Those were the voices exactly." He said he had been rationalising the experience all the time. It was not like losing one's reason; it was the reason working hard on the wrong premises."

LIFE OF SOLITUDE

The novelist was asked why he had changed from mixing in society and writing books about it to a life of absolute solitude in the country. "Were you conscious of a sudden decision to do that?" Mr. Freeman asked.

It happened about eight years ago," said Mr. Waugh, who is 59, "I gradually got bored with society, largely I think through deafness ... if there is a crowd I get dazed. I don't hear because I'm bored: it's not that I'm bored and can't hear."

Mr. Freeman asked him if his country life was not a kind of charade. Mr. Waugh answered: "It's quite true that I haven't the smallest interest in the country in the agricultural or local government sense. The country to me is a place where I can be silent."

He denied that he ever brooded on what might appear to be unjust criticism of his work. The best he could hope for was for the critics to take no notice of him.

(June 26)

ANGRY MAN NOT SEEKING THE TOP

Now it is Arthur Seaton. Henceforth we shall have to be careful to distinguish between the lusty Midlands lathe-operator and the other protesting figures of contemporary mythology: Jim Dixon, Jimmy Porter, Joe Lampton and Billy Liar.

This is not always easy, because young Arthur, who boozes and bulldozes his way through the film of Alan Sillitoe's novel "Saturday Night and Sunday Morning," comes under the inescapable, sweeping label of "young and angry"; and the liberties he takes with his own and other people's lives bear a certain superficial similarity to the actions of these others.

He is perhaps nearest in spirit to Joe Lampton of "Room at the Top." He possesses a similar sexual athleticism and sense of anarchy. He toys with married women with the same veneer of feeling; and he also meets rough justice in the shadows of a fun fair.

DOUBLE LIFE

But Arthur (played with a most plausible authenticity by Albert Finney) is not a social climber. He is content with his wages at the bicycle factory and the excitement of timing a double life.

Of what, then, does he stand in hatred? The book goes some way into this. The film remains vaguer. We leave Arthur hurling a stone at a row of new box houses, a futile gesture against authority and conformity.

The film, directed by Karel Reisz, owes a good deal to its setting: the damp cobbled gloom of the back streets, clanging monotony of factory life, the escape to pub or club and black-and-tan, and the inevitable extra-mural sex life with husband coming in the back door and lover sneaking from the front.

(October 25) F.G.

"OLIVER TWIST" TRANSFORMED

By W.A. Darlington

"OLIVER TWIST" has always been one of the few Dickens novels which could be effectively adapted for the stage. Last night at the New Theatre it maintained its reputation, this time in musical form.

In the old days it made a favourite melodrama.

Many a remote and rat-ridden playhouse has thrilled to the sight of a long-suffering Nancy dragged round the stage by the hair, and has resounded with hisses as a Bill Sykes banged her hard upon the stage with realistic ferocity.

It was not quite like that last night. Lionel Bart had obviously realised that if he was to compose music, lyrics and book for a musical with the cheerful title of "Oliver!" he must lighten the gloom of the Dickensian story noticeably, though not fundamentally.

LOVEABLE OLD MEN

This he has managed very successfully by a simple device. He has transformed Fagin.

Instead of the sinister character which terrified me when I first read the book as a child, he is now a loveable old scoundrel whose tantrums do not in the least alarm the small boys under his charge. They treat him as schoolboys treat a kindly master who has a reputation for responsibility to keep up.

Mr. Bart and his director, Peter Coe, are to be congratulated on providing an evening of lively enjoyment, and on the skill with which they have contrived a transition of mood which might easily have gone wrong.

Among the principals, Keith Hampshire makes an attractive Oliver, though vocally he is overwhelmed. Ron Moody is a great success as the rehabilitated Fagin, and is given some excellent songs. Georgina Brown as Nancy has great vitality, and puts her numbers across with such vigour that one feels that if Sikes had tried out his old hair-dragging tactics he would have found his hands more than full.

(July 1)

MR. PINTER RETURNS TO ENIGMA

GODOT INSPIRED

By Patrick Gibbs

With "The Caretaker," given a first performance at the Arts last night, Harold Pinter after a lapse into clarity for Sunday's television play, returned to enigma, and very successfully, too, success in this context indicating the extent to which the audience is held - and puzzled.

Indeed, had "Waiting for Godot" never been written this piece would be judged to be masterly. As it is, it appeared to be excessively derivative, almost to the point of parody.

Even so, Mr. Pinter is to be admired for having mastered so thoroughly the precarious art of mystifying an audience and entrancing them at the same time.

SIMPLE PLOT

About the plot there is no doubt, for it is simple - two brothers own a dilapidated room. One befriends a tramp, who occupies a spare bed for a short time. He thinks he will get the job as caretaker of the house, but this comes to nothing and he leaves disgusted.

Of action there is little, of conversation much; and it is largely through matter-of-life-and-death earnestness with which these people discuss a series of odd topics that the play exercises its considerable fascination.

Will the tramp get to Sidcup where his references are, not to mention his identity? Why couldn't he get fitted with a pair of shoes at Luton? Why is his host always fiddling with an electric plug instead of putting up the shed in the yard on which he has set his heart? Why is the gas stove disconnected. Could it be symbolically?

Nothing less than admirable acting would have done, and this was provided by Alan Bates and Peter Woodthorpe, who contrasted cleverly the two brothers, and the experienced Donald Pleasence, who made the old tramp very human and disturbing.

(April 28)

NEW OPERA BY BRITTEN

From Martin Cooper

ALDEBURGH, Friday.

BRITTEN'S "A Midsummer Night's Dream," which he conducted before an invited audience in the Jubilee Hall here this evening, is a composite fantasy in which music emphasises rather than obscures the different level of Shakespeare's comedy.

The libretto, prepared by the composer and Peter Pears, preserves an astonishing amount of the original play and uses nothing but Shakespeare's own language.

The fairy world is suggested by a brilliant array of instrumental timbres, by ambiguous harmonies and spell-like or dancing rhythms - in fact the same means, though much extended, as those used by composers from Weber and Mendelssohn to Ravel in his "L'Enfant et les sortileges."

From his fairy voices, however, Britten breaks quite new ground. Besides a high soprano for Titania (Jennifer Vyvyan) he uses a countertenor Oberon (Alfred Deller) and boys for Titania's suite, and these weak and husky tones went far to undoing the intrinsic enchantment of the fairy music itself.

MORTAL DRAMA

The lovers (April Cantelo, Marjorie Thomas, George Maran and Thomas Hemsley) speak the language of mortal drama - the sharply pointed and nervous language characteristic of the composer - and their quartets of dispute and reconciliation contain some of the finest straight music in the opera.

But it is on still another level, the comedy of the Athenian "mechanics," that Britten has been most successful. Led by an excellent Bottom (Owen Brannigan) they conducted their earthy debate with a dry, sad humour which did full justice to Britten's ingenious characterisation.

John Cranko's production, excellent in the comic scenes, somehow fails to convey the magic of the fairy sequences and Puck - spoken and mimed by a son of the famous dancer Massine, was converted into a hoarse voiced, somersaulting minion.

The delicate detail of John Piper's sets could hardly make its full effect on the small stage of the Jubilee Hall.

(June 11)

CRAZY GANG TO BREAK UP AFTER NEARLY 30 YEARS

By Our Theatre Reporter

The Crazy Gang, the company of comedians which for nearly 30 years has been an institution in British entertainment, is to break up. The next show, "Young in Heart," opening at the Victoria Palace on Dec. 21, will be the last.

The average age of the six members is at present 67, but three of them have birthdays later this year and all will have a similar celebration before the run of "Young in Heart" ends. The ages range from Charlie Naughton and Jimmy Gold at 75 to Eddie Gray at 62.

The decision to split up was taken at a board meeting of the Crazy Gang Ltd., under their chairman, Jack Hylton, who will present "Young at Heart," his seventh successive Crazy Gang show at the Victoria Palace. It was unanimous.

Bud Flanagan said yesterday "We tried, first, to arrange one performance nightly instead of the usual two at the Victoria Palace, but that is not possible at the theatre. So someone suggested that we make this our last show and everyone agreed."

(September 13)

YOUNG MEN'S BREEZY REVUE

I don't remember that any Edinburgh Festival has given me a better laugh than the unpretentious late night review now running at the Lyceum here.

It is an entertainment given by four young men whose uniform get-up of dark blue pullovers and white shirts somehow makes them look younger still, so that when the curtain rises we might be in the Prefects' room at any school.

But once they get to work we find they are of a more adult humour than their looks suggest.

They call their show "Beyond the Fringe" and the title has a literal aptness because they themselves are presented by the Edinburgh Festival Society and therefore can claim to have an official backing which the true Fringe production cannot boast.

Together and separately they offer a gloriously inconsequent medley including topical comment, Shakespearian parody, and imitations of types and individuals political and academic.

(August 28) W.A.D.

BRITISH FILM WINS OSCARS

SIMONE SIGNORET, the French actress, was voted the best actress of 1959 at the Acadamy Awards ceremony in Hollywood tonight for her performance in the British film "Room at the Top." It was her first English language picture.

The film, made from John Braine's novel of Yorkshire life, also won an award for Neil Paterson the British writer, for the best screen adaption.

But the 32nd annual awards ceremony, held for the first time while actors and actresses were on strike against the major studios, was really the night of "Ben-Hur." This film won more awards than any other in the history of the Cinema.

(April 6)

POET FACE TO FACE

By WILLIAM PLOMER

Summoned by Bells. By John Betjeman. (Murray 16s.)

Other people write their auto-biographies in prose; John Betjeman has done his in verse - blank verse, varied with rhymed interludes. His uniqueness as a poet derives more from his originality as a person than from innovation in technique.

This new long poem, extremely readable, never difficult, shows how his strength comes from sticking to what he has felt, enjoyed, and believed most intensely. An integrated nature, he seems quite unspoilt by his success as a public personality.

Privacy has gone out, and in some ways this poem is intimate. It is Betjeman face to face and frankly speaking about his early life and secret fears and hopes.

He has an intense feeling for places - English places. Holidays in Cornwall stimulated this London boy, and his sensuous impressions of it are exactly and freshly presented.

"Japanese lanterns lit the sandy paths;
Over the tamarisks the summernight
Heard Melville Gideon on the gramophone."

Trains, and church architecture, and secondhand books mingle with the stirrings of first love and religious faith, and with "the schoolboy sense of an impending doom" at Marlborough.

Oxford enchanted him early and late, and the ghost of Matthew Arnold might approve

"The rowing back, relaxed and slack;
The shipping oars in Godstow shade."

Betjeman joyfully evokes his pursuit of pleasure at Oxford in days when it was not thought odd "to liven breakfast with champagne"; and

" ... while we ate Virginia hams, Contemporaries passed exams."

If anyone feels a little excluded or envious when reading about the high spirits and "...dear private giggles of a private world," he can take comfort from the fact that Betjeman went down without a degree and became a schoolmaster.

(December 2)

IS & WILL BE · WAS · 1855 LONDON

THE DAILY TELEGRAPH

AND

MORNING POST

DAILY TELEGRAPH - - - JUNE 29, 1855
MORNING POST - - - NOVEMBER 2, 1772
[Amalgamated October 1, 1937]

135, Fleet Street, London, E.C.4.

Telephone: Fleet Street 4242

ANSWER TO KHRUSCHEV

MR. KHRUSCHEV was quite right to pound the table and shout abuse at the British Prime Minister yesterday. For in his quiet and seemingly casual way Mr. MACMILLAN delivered some telling blows which sped under the Soviet guard right to the most painful places. The language, moreover, was as simple and direct as the manner was restrained and conciliatory. Perhaps the best tribute to the speech is the final impression it leaves of surprise that the West should have ever feared for the strength of its own case at this General Assembly. Marshalled by the Prime Minister the facts seem to speak with such overwhelming force in defence of the West. Why, for example, should the West have ever imagined that this meeting in New York, in the course of which 15 new independent African States are taking their seats, would provide a suitable platform for anti-colonialist propaganda?

Surely this was an occasion for Britain and France to hold their heads high. By the same token, surely it was an occasion for Mr. KHRUSCHEV to refrain from talking about the past sins of colonialism and to recognise that the old Marxist refrains were no longer relevant. The measure of Mr. MACMILLAN'S skill was that he made it seem so obvious that the East should be on the defensive that it is difficult now to remember how defeatist the West was when the Assembly opened.

(September 20)

GAITSKELL'S LOST LABOUR

KNOWING what was to come, Mr. GAITSKELL met defeat yesterday in advance and with courage. He deserves much more sympathy than he seems to have had during the past few days from those who call themselves his friends and colleagues. Admiration for the man cannot conceal, however, the effect of his leadership. Having lost the support of his party conference on the vital issue of defence - and he may lose again on nationalisation - he has now to face and convince the Parliamentary party. If he wins there, Labour Members of Parliament will be split from their source of support by a gulf which no double-talk can bridge; their only hope, as Sir TOM WILLIAMSON hinted, will be in a political split among the unions themselves on the lines of yesterday's vote. If he loses at Westminster, the Parliamentary party cannot survive; the leadership of the majority will certainly fall into hands less able and less respectable than his own. Either way, the Labour party as it has been is at an end.

Whatever new party of the Left now emerges, under whatever name and whatever leadership, it must be honest with itself. It is double-think that has undone Labour.

(October 6)

BEHIND THE CROWD

In a crowd like that which clashed with the police in St. Pancras on Thursday night those who egg on the hooligans are seldom in the forefront of the fight. No one therefore, expected to see in court yesterday the men really responsible for the worst evening of violence that London has seen for a long while. They are the same men who have persistently misled the public about the real issue in the rents dispute, who have made it necessary to give police protection to the chairman of the local housing management committee, and who have made St. Pancras notorious for the demagogy and violence of its politics. The Home Secretary has been well advised to give the police powers to ban public processions there, unless they have a religious character, in the next three months. He would be well advised to ask as well for a report on the background of this whole affair, the roots of which lie beyond the scope of routine police inquiries.

It is being said in some quarters, as it always is, that the police used unnecessary force both in the evictions and in the street clash. On the face of it that is unlikely. The stage had been carefully set, the events well publicised; disorder can seldom have been more closely scrutinised by the camera and the human eye. The weight of evidence seems to be that this was a very angry crowd, including the well-known London hooligan element, which tried to provoke police violence and then brought broken bottles into the fisticuffs. It is also likely that some bystanders and peaceful demonstrators were hurt. But this does not amount to an outrage or even an offence by the police against the public. On the contrary, if a crowd of this kind had broken loose in Notting Hill and had not been resisted successfully by the police, then there would have been a great outcry - and especially from St. Pancras.

(September 24)

KARIBA AS SYMBOL OF PARTNERSHIP IN AFRICA

The Kariba Dam, which the Queen Mother will open on Tuesday, is not only an outstanding achievement of engineering but a symbol of what can be done by inter-racial co-operation to tame the forces of Nature.

By

W.F. DEEDES, M.P.

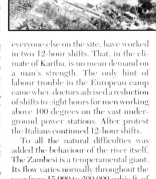

ON a flight between Salisbury and Lusaka there can now be seen, stretching over some 1,500 square miles, what appears to be a flood of disastrous dimensions. In this gigantic basin, the largest man-made lake in the world, are accumulating the waters of the Zambesi River for the Kariba Dam, which Queen Elizabeth the Queen Mother will formally open on Tuesday.

Kariba is a project conceived and achieved on a scale which would have taken the heart of Cecil Rhodes. Its builders have overcome great obstacles, some totally unforeseen. It will supply over 5,000 miles of line electric power to all Rhodesia, from Kitwe in the Copper Belt to Bulawayo. It is a monument not only to engineering skill, but to the work of all races in Africa.

It is just five years since the site was chosen - not without controversy - and the necessary funds, initially £80m. were raised. Kariba was then bush, 100 miles from the nearest town and 50 miles from the nearest road. To this day the nearest railhead is 150 miles away; everything needed has been borne to the site by lorry.

MEN, BEASTS AND NYLONS

A HUGE African population, some thousands of the Tonga tribes had to be moved away to make way for the lake. Game wardens trapped and transported 2,000 wild animals and 500 reptiles. Women surrendered hundreds of pairs of nylon stockings to tie the legs of the beasts painlessly.

A new town was built in 16 months on the heights above Kariba by an English firm to house 10,000 workers, including 8,000 Africans. Roads, sometimes based on elephant tracks, were built and progressively improved until generators, turbines and transformers could move up on 100-ton trailers.

These were preliminaries. The principal task of temporarily taming the Zambesi and building a dam 420 ft. high and 1,900 ft. long fell mainly into the hands of an Italian consortium of four firms.

The Italians, in common with nearly everyone else on the site, have worked in two 12-hour shifts. That, in the climate of Kariba, is no mean demand on a man's strength. The only hint of labour trouble in the European camp came when doctors advised a reduction of shifts to eight hours for men working above 100 degrees on the vast underground power stations. After protest the Italians continued 12-hour shifts.

To all the natural difficulties was added the behaviour of the river itself. The Zambesi is a temperamental giant. Its flow varies normally throughout the year from 15,000 to 200,000 cubic ft. of water per second. It is to even this out and capture some 84p.c. of the annual flow for power that the Kariba lake has been formed.

In 1957 the Zambesi produced what they termed a "once in 500 years flood," some 360,000 cubic ft. of water per second. The phenomenon held up work, but for a miraculously short time. In the following year there came the "once in 10,000 years flood" - a volume of 580,000 cubic ft. a second. It delayed work for six weeks. This year the first main phase of the work finished on time.

The engineer may like to take note that 1,400m cubic feet of concrete went into the dam, that the six floodgates on its face must take a thrust of water of 3,000 tons when the dam is full. The electrician can reflect on a total installed capacity of 1,200m k.w. an ultimate annual output of 8,180m k.w. and 930 miles of single circuit 330 kv steel tower transmission lines connecting Kariba to transforming stations all over the Rhodesia's.

SPORTING PROSPECT

FOR the sportsman, too, there is a wealth of promise. When I flew over the lake yachts were racing. A single boat brought in 133 fish this month. Kariba Lake will soon rival Victoria Falls as a centre for tourists and holiday-makers.

Its waters, now rising above scrub and forest at the rate of four inches a day, will not reach their full height until 1963. Were this dam situated at London Bridge the tail of the lake would be in Exeter.

There is much also at Kariba - in contrast to many schemes of this kind - in which the architect can take pride. The underground transformer hall, 537ft. long, 55ft. wide and 60ft. high, with its curved roof of blue and white, has not only the distinction of size but the rarer distinction of beauty.

A COMMON GOAL

YET none of these attainments conveys the true nature of Kariba's significance. Left to themselves, unseen by civilisation and untouched by politics, the races of the world - some of them hardly less temperamental than the Zambesi by repute - have worked in harmony.

They had a single goal and spared themselves nothing to achieve it, at the cost of 120 lives. Kariba is an exemplar of race relations in Africa.

The future of Central Africa will not be shaped by politics alone, whatever the final shape of Federation. Its natural wealth, though far developed since Rhodes's day, still has about it the space, the possibilities and the grandeur which inspired his life work. Kariba is a reminder of them.

(May 14)

TRACT THAT FAILS

By DAVID HOLLOWAY

NOW that the courts have passed judgment on "Lady Chatterley's Lover" and the churches have preached over it; one further verdict remains - where does the novel stand as a work of literature?

At least some of the crowds who rush to the bookshops this morning to spend 3s 6d for their Penguin will want to know this. The answer must be that "Lady Chatterley" is a failure, albeit an almost brilliant one, but a failure none-the-less.

Let us try to look at the book as if it were brand new, a novel written 32 years ago and just discovered by Penguins. Let us forget the trial, the sermons and the leading articles, and what do we find? A burningly sincere book - there can be no doubt of that.

In it, jostling uneasily, are two moral tracts. One is on the importance of the fulfilment of the individual through love, and the other is on the sapping effect of industrial life on the people of this country.

These two themes do not fit together well and as a result "Lady Chatterley" is an untidy book. The love theme is far more important and it is here that Lawrence was being most revolutionary.

He wanted to release any literary consideration of physical love from romantic evasions, and to discuss it as if it were any other subject. To do this he found it necessary to use words for loving and for the intimate parts of the body that are in the general vocabulary of much of the population of this country. In moderation this device would be a great success, but, like so much of the book, it is overdone. By the mere reiteration of words, the effect is destroyed.

Dialectics in Dialect

It is not easy to quote this language of love, but here is a passage of moderate coarseness that gives something of the flavour. Mellors, the gamekeeper, is talking to his lover, Lady Chatterley: "An if I only lived 10 minutes an' stroked thy arse an' got to know it, I should reckon I'd lived one life, sees ter!"

The moral standpoint of this book has been endlessly discussed. I can only add a personal word. To me it is a far more moral book, in essence, than very many that appear to-day. But its place in the history of literature is far less secure than will be its undoubted niche in the history of law. D.H. Lawrence was a great literary artist, but it is by other books that we shall remember him.

(November 10)

COLOUR TV DRIVE IN U.S.

A big drive to popularise colour television has been launched by the Radio corporation of America in an effort to retrieve a semi-failure on which many millions of dollars have been spent.

It is seven years since I saw an impressive demonstration of colour, at the Waldorf Astoria, and a service was started soon after. Yet the public will not buy because it is claimed that sets have been unreliable.

Now R.C.A. Victor are advertising what the company describes as "simplified colour television." Four "giant steps" are announced.

PRICES REDUCED

They are: A 50 per cent, price reduction for 21-inch sets; an average of four hours' colour show daily; quick, easy tuning with remote control and, biggest attraction of all, a free 90-day R.C.A service including installation and a year's guarantee on all parts, including the picture tube.

(October 17)

END OF THE ARMSTRONG SIDDELEY CAR

The Armstrong Siddeley car, one of the oldest and best known "quality cars" in the British industry, is to go out of production. This was announced by Bristol-Siddeley last night.

(June 10)

LONDON DAY BY DAY

De Gaulle's City Nerves Queen's Deer Record

GEN. de GAULLE was markedly more nervous on his drive to the City yesterday than on that to the Palace when he arrived.

The reason for this, according to his entourage, was that he feared he might make some mistake of protocol at Guildhall. He regarded the nature of the City's reception of him as of historical importance. Its cordiality surprised him.

In fact, I noticed only one minor slip. This was when he rose to speak before the toastmaster called on him. He sat down again so that the correct thing could be done.

Guests near to him observed as he drew out his spectacles to read his speech what thick lenses he now needs. Without them, he has difficulty in seeing anything below eye level.

The Best Heads

The Queen is one of the women who shot five of the best 34 deer in Scotland last season, according to a list in the current issue of the Shooting Times compiled by Mr. G. Kenneth Whitehead.

In order of length but not necessarily of merit - Lady Jane Willoughby comes first with antlers of 35in, at Glenartney, Perth. The other three are Miss Lycett Green at Strathconan, Ross, Mrs. Arthur Strutt at Kingairloch, Argyll, and Lady Anne Bentinck in Caithness.

The Queen's head taken at Balmoral was a 12 point, measuring 27in (left) and 27 15/16 (right). It is described by the author as "a light type of head, with brows bent down, and some damage to top points."

Majestic Vintage

MY recent note on the ancient fellow of an Oxford college who confused the port vintages of 1847 and 1947 had an agreeable sequel last night.

I dined with Lord Furness at his house in Cadogan Place to drink a Quinta do Noval 1847 - one of the most remarkable vintages of the last century.

Under the knowledgeable eye of Col. Ronnie Lambert - a vintage Grenadier in every sense - it had been decanted in the cellars of Chalié Richards that very afternoon. All agreed with him that it delighted both the nose and the palate.

Among Lord Furness's guests was Sir Gilbert Laithwaite, resplendent in the broad blue and red ribbon of the Order of St. Michael and St. George.

He, like his host, was going on to the reception for President de Gaulle, given by the French Ambassador.

The only melancholy thought of the evening was that the President himself should not have shared this vintage.

No Bomb at the "Prom"

On taking my seat at the Albert Hall on Saturday evening about 20 minutes before the start of the last "Prom" of 1960 I was astonished to see that Sir Malcolm Sargent had apparently been arrested.

He stood on the rostrum wearing an overcoat and flanked by helmeted policemen.

There was an undramatic explanation of this curtain-raiser. He had come to warn the audience that they must not display "Ban the Bomb" banners - or any other controversial slogan - in front of the TV cameras.

Sir Malcolm's good-humoured appeal ensured political stability until just before the end of the "Prom". A single banner was raised for a few seconds but instantly dismembered by other members of the audience.

Aerial Mathematics

NOTICE in the duty-free shop at Shannon Airport: "Buy your perfume at Shannon and save up to 150 per cent. on United States prices."

PETERBOROUGH

The Princess Who Kept Her Vow

- that the world would not guess her romance

PRINCESS MARGARET has made her choice. We are all happy that in Antony Armstrong-Jones she has found a man who is so temperamentally suited to her.

"How good that she is marrying someone out of the ordinary rut." That was the comment last night of a friend of Tony Armstrong-Jones (overnight he has become Antony).

"It was a bombshell to us. No one knew anything about their courtship. There was not even a whisper. The way they managed to keep it secret was a real achievement."

But the charming, witty photographer, who worked so hard at his job and took it with the utmost seriousness, nearly gave away the royal secret a day or so ago.

He was arguing at a party when the words ". . . the Queen Mother told me" slipped out. A friend quickly retorted, "Who introduced you to the Queen Mother?" "Oh, the Queen did." he replied.

The Princess was determined to avoid publicity. She never forgot the public curiosity before the Queen's engagement was announced.

Only a week ago the nation was rejoicing at the birth of the Queen's baby, little dreaming that to-day we should be extending our congratulations to her sister.

The Princess's infectious gaiety and spontaneity, her warm nature together with her depth of character make a lovable, complex personality which has won her the public's devotion.

She has strong religious feelings which have influenced her actions in the two major sorrows of her 29 years - her father's death and her "personal message" of renunciation on her parting with Group Captain Peter Townsend.

Her love of the theatre and friendship with many stage people - among them Joyce Grenfell and Danny Kaye - is all part of an artistic nature. She is a talented pianist.

Fashion-conscious, she sets hair, hat and dress styles. Whatever she wears is copied. Young women are particularly quick to follow her numerous changes in hair style, a habit in which she has led the Royal family.

(January 27)

NO MORE TOUGH TEDDYS

WHEN a toy designer sets to work, the last thing he thinks of is the child, "I design for buyers: buyers buy for mothers and aunts: aunts buy for children," a leading soft toy designer told me.

So it's all out for parents appeal at the Toy Fair in Brighton this week, as far as toddlers' toys are concerned.

"Mothers will love these plastic construction kits with nuts and bolts, crazy clowns, and plumbers' tools which all clip together," I was told. "They really keep three to six year olds very quiet."

Doubtless parents will also like the new water colours without water or brushes. There will be no dipping or spilling - just solid paints in plastic tubes.

As for soft toys (by the way expressions are kinder this year - no tough bears), they are made in nylon plush and filled with foam for easy washing.

My favourite is a triple coloured penguin - lemon back, white tummy, blue beak and feet with, of course, the newly fashionable, kind expression.

(February 17)

LINEN MAKES A COMEBACK

IN SPITE OF the tremendous selling power of the drip-dry, non-iron synthetics, women are turning back to the real thing.

Last year it was silk. This year linen is coming into our dress lives again.

At many of the large London stores, the sleeveless, straight resort dress (in linen, of course) is gaining in popularity over the full-skirted pretty-pretty frocks.

Elegant and casual, with comfort and absorbency that only a natural fabric possesses, women are buying dress and jackets in ever increasing numbers.

One example is Givenchy-inspired, a deep saxe blue and will cost 5gns from Harrods next month. A tiny organdie pillbox hat would cost 6gns from the same store.

You can also buy simple and inexpensive linen dresses in gorgeous colours, including brilliant turquoise, soft green and strawberry ice cream shade. Derry and Toms have these for £4 10s to 5½gns.

(April 28)

Airborne Meals Vary So Much

In three weeks I've had the unusual experience of dining four times in the air on a different line each time - and with what different results! What saddened me was to find how badly B.E.A. showed up as a competitor in the dinner stakes.

Flying to Amsterdam, K.L.M. served me with delicious buttered shrimps followed by perfectly cooked chicken with the almost forgotten pre-battery flavour, pleasant cheese and good coffee.

On Lufthansa there was a real beef marrow consommé, excellent grilled veal steak, fruit and coffee. On Pan American Airlines I sampled economy class cramp from lack of leg room with a spacious menu. In fact by having four courses, it transgressed the regulations. I had excellent consommé, good quality smoked salmon, roast pork and its accompaniments, an innocuous mousse and good coffee.

And what did B.E.A. do in the way of dinner flying from Munich to London? No first course. A plateful of soggy chips with a small piece of tough steak; a slice of Swiss roll and a segment of processed cheese followed by very poor coffee. **W.C.**

(January 13)

How Mrs. Sheekey Feeds Her Family on £4 10s a week

HOW can a family of four be well fed when the housekeeping is only £4 to £4 10s a week? Many letters challenging this claim by a clergyman's wife came in after we published a report last month on the financial side of family life on salaries under £1,000 a year.

So we have asked this housewife, Mrs. Barbara Sheekey, of Birchington, Kent, to tell us exactly how she does manage.

She has given us the menus, with costs, she planned for the second week of this month and we shall be publishing them each day this week. At the end, we will show how the total (£4 6s 6d) was made up.

"Since my little girl, now 18 months, has been having 'proper' meals," says Mrs Sheekey, "I've been having £4 10s for housekeeping, an increase of 10s.

"With forethought, I can manage easily on this and have a small sum left for her toilet needs, sewing sundries, birthday cards, my cosmetics, etc.

"I am amazed at the amount of housekeeping money some women spend and listen fascinated in the butcher's to such remarks as, 'My husband wouldn't look at that.' I am thankful for a husband willing to try anything once."

Mrs. Sheekey doesn't stick to the same shops but keeps her eyes open for the best value. She loves bargain hunting.

Obviously she has a good organising sense. "When my husband has no evening engagements, we like to have supper by ourselves at about 7.30 p.m. We then cut out tea, but the children have theirs at the usual time and I make them something like honey sandwiches with an apple and a glass of milk.

"We also have mid-morning coffee and a milk drink at night with biscuits."

And the Sheekeys entertain.

"We like to have friends in to supper sometimes. A typical party menu - which doesn't strain the budget - would be grapefruit cocktail, veal fricassee (made with breast of veal, adding mushrooms and frozen peas and serving in piped potato border) and lemon meringue pie.

I buy frozen foods only for special occasions; we prefer to look forward to fruit and vegetables in season straight from the garden.

We also grow a lot and have a little soft fruit and apples. I also make all my own cakes, jam, marmalade and pickles.

(March 28)

'SUBTLE AROMA' FOR LIPS

THE COSMETIC counters in Paris are filling up with brown lipsticks which are meant to be worn with this spring's new orange and lemon colours.

They are in shades ranging from a pale orange with a mere hint of a brown undertone to a real iced coffee colour that is actually coffee flavoured to give "a subtle aroma to your lips."

But even if your husband or boy friend likes you smelling and tasting of coffee, he won't like your brown tinted lips.

It's an unbecoming shade to the average pink and white English complexion, although the very young will be able to have fun with it.

(January 29)

IT'S THE TOP HEAVY T-LINE

A TOP-HEAVY T-line for spring suits surprised the audience yesterday - the last day of the London fashion shows. The main feature of Ronald Paterson's collection was the way in which he widened the shoulders.

On suits, the cross line of the T extended almost into an epaulette effect, while the downward stroke continued down the jacket, emphasised by the narrow skirt.

He softened this effect with organza scarves draped round the neck. He also widened the shoulders on dresses and achieved a bulkier, wider look on coats.

Colours were daring or subtle - royal and jade were an unusual combination in a wool and Orlon coat; a bronze and green day ensemble had a bright Liberty print hat to match. A similar print was used in a subtler way on a delightful pleated brown chiffon dress.

The natural waist was clearly defined on most cocktail and evening frocks, the skirts soft and flowing in crepe or chiffon, or bell-shaped in a stiffer fabric.

Mad Hatters was an apt title for the breath-taking, enormous brimmed boaters designed by student James Wedge. Some were as wide as the model's shoulders.

Victor Stiebel showed the top-heavy look in a more restrained fashion. A shoulder-wide unpressed pleat gave top fullness to coats, while suits had looser jackets.

Colours and prints for day were restrained - lots of tiny checks, in beige or black and white. But spring blossomed when it came to evening wear. Flowers, large and small, rioted and glowed on shimmering satins and rustling paper taffetas.

Enchanting was a ball-dress in white paper taffeta, and a silver embroidered bodice glittered above a cloud of smoke-brown organza in another gown.

Mattli's collection was exquisite. He returned to the elegant, flattering look seen at the start of the London shows, but he achieved something extra, an international flavour.

There were gently-fitted, hip-length jackets and gay colours - wisteria and white lilac, scarlet, and a delicate grey-green.

Cocktail wear was subtly embroidered. Long evening dresses were slender, the three-quarter length jacket appeared in a pale grey satin over a tube dress.

Paula Davies

(January 22)

THE FORD POPULAR

CHEAP TRANSPORT FOR THE FAMILY

I HAVE been driving the cheapest family car on the British market - the Ford Popular - and am not surprised that there is a considerable waiting list for it.

It is basically the Ford Anglia of a year ago, £75 dearer than the pre-war type Popular which it replaces but £45 cheaper than the 1959 Anglia. At £494, including purchase tax, it is I think, the cheapest full-scale saloon car in the world.

Moreover, since it runs entirely satisfactorily on the cheaper grades of fuel and will cover 30 miles to the gallon at fast routing speeds, it is cheap to run.

There are a number of obvious and sometimes irritating economies - for instance, the lack of a handle for the luggage boot, which is opened by a carriage key kept inside the car, and the absence of sun visors. But a de luxe version is available at an extra £21 which is exceedingly well equipped.

POWER IN PLENTY

The Popular is a comfortable four-seater even for adults and it it is not remarkable for its quietness, the noise is not unduly obtrusive, and the engine is commendably smooth.

There is plenty of power. The absence of a fourth forward gear is sometimes felt, and obliges one to use second gear more than one would like. To change into top before approaching 30 m.p.h. is to sacrifice flexibility, so one tends to stay in second gear in town traffic.

The overall performance however, is good. Through the gears it will reach 40 m.p.h. in 7 sec. and 60 in 35 sec. Fifty-five to 60 m.p.h. is a nice, easy cruising speed on the open road. At full stretch it will just about touch 70. **W.A.M.**

(June 1)

PASTERNAK

POET & AUTHOR OF 'DR ZHIVAGO'

BORIS PASTERNAK, who died last night at his country home 25 miles from Moscow, aged 70, was best known in the West for his novel, "Dr. Zhivago." He was awarded the Nobel Peace Prize for 1958 but declined it after the Soviet Writers' Union had demanded deprivation of his citizenship.

He was ostracised and expelled from the union for "ideological errors" in the book. Russian writers attacked him as a "traitor," "true decadent" and "cold cynic."

In a personal letter, Pasternak begged Mr. Khruschev not to expel him from Russia. "Leaving my motherland would equal death for me," he wrote.

During a visit to London in 1959 Mikhail Sholokhov, the Russian novelist who won his reputation with "Quiet Flows the Don," said "Dr. Zhivago" was a "shapeless" novel that slandered the Russian intelligentsia. He described Pasternak as a little-known writer and said he was "the poet of the old maids."

UNTOUCHED WEALTH

"Dr. Zhivago" which was first published in Rome in 1957, brought Pasternak wealth as well as fame. But he was reported to have said, after being called by the writers' union a traitor who had sold his country for 30 pieces of silver, that he would never touch the royalties.

Pasternak said in February, 1959, that he had decided to dedicate himself to his work and to seek rehabilitation with his writers' union. He had been living quietly in the country, reportedly writing a play about the emancipation of Russian serfs in the 19th century.

He was born in Moscow and studied philology at the Moscow University and later at Marlburg University, Germany. His work first appeared in print in 1912.

LYRIC POETRY
Shakespeare Translations

David Floyd, THE DAILY TELEGRAPH Special Correspondent on Communist Affairs, writes: Boris Pasternak was the greatest master of the Russian language to survive from pre-revolutionary days. His place in the history of Russian literature is ensured primarily by his lyric poetry and his poetic translations of Shakespeare.

But his poetry is difficult to translate and is little known in the West. He lived in great simplicity in the village of Peredelkino, near Moscow. When I visited him there in January last year he told me he had again started to write poetry.

He regretted that he lacked the sense of security necessary for the composition of longer works. More recently he was reported to be writing a play.

WORKS WERE POPULAR

I first met him at a recital of his poetry in Moscow in 1946. His works were then so popular with the young people that they were able to prompt him whenever he forgot a line of his own poems.

He refused to write to the orders of the Communist party. But Stalin spared him, alone of all notable Jewish writers, perhaps because he recognised his great genius.

(May 31)

ANEURIN BEVAN: A STUDY IN AMBITION DENIED

"He was a master of words - and their slave." Such is the judgment of a Parliamentary observer who here traces his political career to its high point and beyond.

ANEURIN BEVAN was a man whose ambition was of a kind that cheated itself of achievement. His ambition was not vulgar. Small shifts of advantage did not concern him.

So little adept was he in plot and stratagem that his opponents in the Labour party learned that they could count on his dashing the cup of success from his own hands by impatient errors of tactics and conduct.

The driving force behind his ambition was a sense of utter superiority over his fellows which showed itself in the superb self-confidence with which he singled out for attack the biggest man in sight.

Bevan's sense of superiority was nourished by his nimble capacity to seize upon and appropriate the ideas in the air around him. He was one of those who knew everything except what is in books. His library scarcely grew with the years. The medium of his inquiring mind was the spoken word.

As he attained prominence, he sought the company of men of mark: not amongst the wealthy or the social elite, but amongst practitioners in ideas - journalists, artists, actors, authors. It was their conversation that he needed to feed his quick, acquisitive brain.

Subjects like history or economics that demanded tenacity of study and ordered thought he never compassed. It was paradox, theory and generalisation that fascinated him.

He was a master of words - and their slave. The brilliance of his language was not a tool of original thought so much as the verbal stimulus that set his mind travelling in grooves of associated ideas. He thought with his tongue.

INSTINCTIVE CHAMPION

IMPATIENCE led him to try to storm his way forward to the position to which he felt entitled in the Labour party faster than any internally democratic party will allow. With impatience went contempt. He was instinctively drawn to the championship of the rank and file workers in the party, who are kept on the job by black-and-white faith in the principles of the party and whose dislike of the enemy is matched by unallayable distrust of leaders who are never sufficiently vigorous.

Bevan's humble origins as a young South Wales miner in a period of depression and unrest deprived him of the opportunity to develop his immense native talents to the full. This filled him with disdain for an unfair system of society, which naturally extended to pale and pusillanimous leaders who compromised with the capitalist and conservative representatives of this system.

He was driven by his very success into spheres ever more remote from the rank and file from whom he drew his strength. He spent only a few months underground in the mines. As he advanced he came to affect not only conversation but food and drink that was beyond the ken of those he championed.

It was not hypocrisy but fear of losing the mainspring of his political being that led him to eschew tails and morning coat whilst sporting the most expensive suits. He felt an essential difference between things better in degree than his followers' and things different in kind.

More and more he had to recreate a relationship that became less real the further he moved from his spiritual anchorage. The terms of abuse that came of themselves off his tongue - "vermin," "desiccated calculating machine" - were a means of re-identifying himself with the forces he relied upon to defeat both the Conservatives and those in the Labour movement who stood in his way.

It was not until his political career had passed its apogee that he began to understand that the highest political leadership is reserved to those who can retain the loyalty of the party conference whilst appealing also to the people at large.

When Bevan achieved Cabinet rank in 1945 he had not resolved the dilemma of a man who had chosen a political path that assured him great power and standing but barred the final heights to him.

ALIEN TASKS

HE was not at ease in office. The study of documents and the weighing of pros and cons were alien to his whole bent. He was not an administrator of the top class who could control the reins of his department. On the other hand he was free of the opposite vice of fidgety interference. His method was to expound to his civil servants the broad lines of what he wanted and then leave them to carry out the policy.

By this means he was able to lay the foundations of a great new structure like the Health Service and to raise the standards of public housing.

He was impatient of subordination and girded against the authority of the inner Cabinet of Bevin, Cripps and Morrison on which Attlee chiefly relied. He sharply resented attempts to keep the mounting costs of the Health Service within bounds and restlessly tried to assert himself in wider fields of policy. It was primarily due to him that, during Morrison's illness, a compromise plan for the public ownership of iron and steel was overset in favour of outright nationalisation.

ANEURIN BEVAN

On Bevin's death he hoped for the Foreign Office or at least the Colonial Office. His transfer to the Ministry of Labour rankled as an obtuse refusal to recognise his ability - the more bitter because Gaitskell shortly afterwards became Chancellor of the Exchequer.

He struck back instinctively and without detailed calculation. His simple impulse was to pull down the temple about his head if only Gaitskell too were crushed.

After fighting a campaign in the Cabinet up to Budget day against the decision to put a charge on teeth and spectacles, he suddenly broadened the field of attack into an onslaught on defence expenditure and resigned.

In the five years after his resignation Bevan was perhaps most in his political element. His stature was great enough to give effective leadership to a rank and file that was disgruntled after six years in office and the depressing setbacks of the 1950 and 1951 elections. They needed a prophet and Bevan offered himself. He gave his name to his followers and was for a time almost an independent force in politics. But it was also in this period that he revealed the weakness of a man who had ambition in such abundance that no room was left for shrewdness.

Bevan set himself to the task that his nature and his past made congenial to him: to marshal the support of the rank-and-file workers in the local parties for a seizure of power within the party.

He mounted his final attack on the citadel in 1956 on the question of the Labour party's attitude towards German re-armament. He could not have chosen a better issue. He rallied to his banner the pacifists, the Zionists, the fellow travellers, those who had bitter memories of the war and a rank and file made more radical by electoral defeat. On this issue he could also count on considerable trade union support that would on almost any other have opposed him.

For a time it seemed touch and go. At the Morecombe Conference Bevan failed by a mere handful of votes to defeat the Executive, due to the last moment switch of a few small trade unions.

But Bevan would have lost either way. His impulsive resignations both in office and Opposition, his electoral irresponsibility, his many rudenesses, had built up a lasting resentment among those who would have been his principal colleagues, the major trade union leaders, the professional party organisers and that solid but inarticulate section of Labour M.P.'s whose confidence must be carried by an established leader.

Bevan had reached the moment of failure to which his career of successes had inevitably led him. He had reached the age when he could no longer calculate on the election after next. He had now to face a choice that came as a shock to him; the choice between risking an electoral defeat that would terminate his own political prospects and working for a victory that would at least ensure him the high office of Foreign Secretary.

He made his choice when he agreed to become "shadow" Foreign Secretary under Gaitskell's leadership. He finally accepted his defeat by a younger man. Having all his life regarded the first place as his right, he now accepted second place.

By his own standards Bevan must be reckoned a failure. But, by any other, his achievements were of the highest order. Despite the electoral damage he did his own party from time to time, his gift for dramatising and personalising politics contributed something to the Labour party without which it would have wanted the colour and emotion that helped to preserve it as a live force in a period in which the two political parties seemed to many to be too little distinguishable.

Bevan's last illness disclosed a degree of public affection, cutting across class and party, that could hardly have been foretold before his operation. He had clearly made an impression on national feeling that is the mark of a man accepted as statesman.

He loved Parliamentary democracy and served it well. He was a true democrat who never quite understood democracy.

(July 7)

ALBERT CAMUS

WRITER & NOBEL PRIZE WINNER

By KENNETH YOUNG

ALBERT CAMUS was certainly the greatest imaginative writer to appear in France since the 1939-45 War. His death yesterday in a motor accident at the age of 46 occurred at a crucial stage in his development and is a severe loss not merely to French but to world literature.

His work had been widely appreciated abroad, as the award of the Nobel Prize in 1957 testifies.

Two of his finest novels, "The Outsider" and "The Plague," as well as a group of pre-war essays, are set in his native Algeria, where he was born at Mondovi, near Constantine.

Camus was brought up in a tenement in Algiers where his mother worked as a charwoman. He won scholarships to the Lycée and to Algiers University, but at the age of 17 suffered the first of a series of attacks of tuberculosis.

He became interested in experimental theatre, in football, in philosophy and in the art of writing, all of which remained his interests to the end.

M. ALBERT CAMUS

WORKER IN RESISTANCE

He was 23 before he set foot in France. During the German occupation he worked in the Resistance there and edited the clandestine paper Combat which continued to occupy him for some years after the war.

Camus never occupied the "ivory tower." But equally he was no party politician. He had flirted with Communism in the 1930s; he rejected it totally in the post-war years, and this led to acrimonious exchanges with Jean-Paul Sartre, with whom his name is often associated.

Unlike Sartre, he brought politics, the death penalty, the North African revolt, to the bar of his own insights and conscience rather than measuring them against dogmatic creeds. "The Myth of Sisyphus," "The Rebel" and such essays as that on the guillotine are moving personal speculations far removed from party politics.

Camus was not essentially a philosopher, not even a philosophical Existentialist. His insight into the nature of the Universe, the feeling of "the absurd" and of the pitiless loneliness of man, run parallel with those of Kierkegaard and Heidegger. But his prime aim was to translate them into literary experiences not philosophical treatises.

WARS AND TORTURES

Born into an era of wars, mass tortures and brain washing Camus sought to express the age of anxiety and to express it in terms of everyday life. As an English critic has correctly said: "Camus, like George Orwell, had the feelings of the common man and the mind of an intellectual."

His success may be measured primarily on his novels, "The Outsider," "The Plague," "The Fall," and his plays "Caligula" and "Cross Purpose." These are profound works of art containing layer upon layer of meaning and capable of sustaining the subtlest analysis.

The development of his thought was awaited with interest all over the world. I believe he had a new novel almost completed, and no doubt there are other unpublished fragments.

After some personal crises and recurrent illness, Camus in latter years had withdrawn into his shell, guarding his time and freedom jealously. But his sudden departure from the scene will be widely lamented.

(January 5)

MR. GILBERT HARDING

TV PERSONALITY NOT "INVENTED"

Daily Telegraph Reporter

GILBERT HARDING, who died yesterday aged 53, will be remembered as the most provocative and, in some ways, enigmatical character who ever found swift fame through broadcasting. He had the power, purveyed most insidiously by television, of exciting his audiences to fierce partisanship.

GILBERT HARDING

Many were angered by the manner of one whom they regarded as Britain's rudest, most over-bearing man. Others dismissed his as a publicity conscious poseur. Others again defended him vigorously as an outspoken intellectual in the Johnsonian tradition.

Those who knew him personally, as I did, realise that Harding was a complex, unhappy character, scholarly but erratic, with the schoolmaster dominant in his mental make up. He did not "invent" the personality that brought him big money and notoriety. The person who appeared in "What's My Line?" on television was the true Harding to the life treating the world as if it consisted entirely of difficult schoolboys.

NEAR BREAKDOWN
"Face to Face"

In the notable television interview with John Freeman in "Face to Face" last September, Harding, near to a breakdown at one point, revealed himself as a "profoundly lonely figure" who would "rather be dead."

He told Freeman: "I'm afraid of dying. I should be very glad to be dead, but I don't look forward to the actual process of dying."

Of the suggestion that he had a first-class mind and was doing work mostly rather below his capacity, Harding said he thought the reputation was largely due to being quiz-master of "Round Britain Quiz" when he knew the answers to erudite questions because they were written down.

His success in broadcasting came because he was something different, and though his forthrightness landed him in many scrapes with the authorities he was always ready to apologise. The criticism that annoyed him most was the suggestion, arising from his bachelor status, that he was a "woman hater." He averred that he was no more critical of women than of British Railways, bad cooking, or noisy children.

Once he lost his temper in "Twenty Questions," attributing it to prolonged mental and physical pressure. The B.B.C. suspended him for several months.

As a panelist in "What's My Line," Harding's observations to challengers frequently brought angry complaints from viewers. Mostly he was unrepentant, but after one incident he stated that "viewers were not wrong in thinking I was a little tiddly."

On one occasion, in which Harding made slighting remarks about the Empire, Sir Ian Jacob, then Director-General of the B.B.C., apologised.

Ill-health had worried Harding constantly during the past few years. It was in reference to this that Harding said in his "Face to Face" interview that when he was very ill he did not wonder if he was going to die. "Afterwards, when people tell you how ill you've been - in my case, at least - I feel, why on earth did they bother? It would have been much better to have let me go.

"That of course, is very mean. I should feel grateful to them."

(November 17)

MACK SENNETT

MACK SENNETT, the film pioneer, who has died in Hollywood, was 76. We think first of the Keystone Cops. It is natural. Those early comic pursuits raised the level of film farce to film art, and they are still very funny.

But there was more to Sennett than an eye for crowd comedy. He was a man of scenario ideas who could recognise genius long before genius was aware of itself.

Born in Denville, Quebec, he toured in musical comedy as a dancer from the age of 17 and then joined the old Biograph company under D.W. Griffith in New York. Sennett stood this for as long as he could.

He worried Griffith with ideas for police comedies and acted with Mary Pickford, who was starting her career. Griffith was unsympathetic, and in 1912 Sennett broke away and formed the Keystone company.

He found immediate success, and two years later when his leading player, Ford Sterling, left to form his own group too, Sennett cast round for a replacement. He finally enticed Chaplin, then in vaudeville and distrustful of the cinema, into films.

"Tillie's Punctured Romance" was the first major result and established Chaplin. E.S.

(November 7)

MISS SYLVIA PANKHURST

A PIONEER SUFFRAGETTE

MISS SYLVIA PANKHURST, who has died aged 79, was the last surviving member of the trio of militant suffragettes whose activities created a storm in the early 1900's; the others were her mother, Mrs. Emmeline Pankhurst, and her sister Christabel, who died in February, 1958.

Sylvia was perhaps the most militant of the three; she was certainly in the public eye as often as any other suffragette, and for longer than most.

Born in Manchester, she was distributing pamphlets and taking collections at political meetings at the age of seven, and by the time she was 10 she was an active assistant to her mother, then a member of the Poor Law Guardians. The poverty and suffering she encountered played an important part in moulding her character.

Her mother enlisted her aid in the women's suffrage campaign in 1905, and she was a pioneer in the formation of the Women's Social and Political Union.

In 1906, when some suffragettes were arrested and charged after attempting to make speeches in the lobby of the House of Commons, she went to the trial and was imprisoned for 14 days for addressing the crowd from the steps of the court. Between then and 1920 she suffered several terms of imprisonment.

"CAT-AND-MOUSE" ACT

In consequence of 13 hunger strikes, she was repeatedly a victim of the "cat-and-mouse" Act, under which prisoners were released until they had recovered their strength, when they were re-arrested.

Few of her sentences were for violence. Her offences usually involved incitement to riot, and she was at one time barred from the precincts of the House of Commons.

She was opposed to the 1914-18 war, and was fined for her speeches against it. But during the war years she worked unceasingly in the East End of London for the betterment of conditions for soldier's dependants and she established several welfare centres for poor mothers and children. In those districts she was idolised.

In 1920 she was sentenced to six months' imprisonment for sedition in connection with articles in a Communist journal.

In her youth she gave every indication of becoming a talented artist. She won scholarships to the Manchester School of Art and to the Royal College of Art, and also studied in Venice. In 1928 she announced the birth of a "eugenic" baby, but declined to reveal the father's name.

A bitter opponent of the Nazis and Fascists, she whole-heartedly supported the 1939-45 war, and in recent years she had championed the cause of Ethiopia. With Lord Horder, she founded the Princess Tsahai Memorial Hospital in Addis Ababa and in 1956 went to live in Ethiopia.

(September 28)

OSCAR HAMMERSTEIN

40 MUSICALS AND 1,000 SONGS

OSCAR HAMMERSTEIN II, who has died aged 65, was the writing half of the American team of Rodgers and Hammerstein. Their musical shows were almost fabulously successful on both sides of the Atlantic.

As a team they began working together in 1943, producing "Oklahoma," which ran for five years in the United States and at Drury Lane had the longest run of any production, running for over three years. It was followed by "Carousel," "South Pacific," "Annie Get Your Gun," and "The King and I."

Their collaboration was probably the most successful writing-composing team of the post-war years. But Hammerstein, as a librettist, author and co-producer, had been for many years a force in the theatrical world.

His first success was in 1920. By 1928 his name was made with "Rose Marie," revived at the Victoria Palace a few hours before he died, "Sunny," "Desert Song," "Showboat" and "New Moon."

His lyrics were written in collaboration with Jerome Kern, Sigmund Romberg and Rudolf Friml, besides Richard Rodgers.

They included such perennial favourites as "Ol' Man River," "Can't Help Loving Dat Man," as well as the song hits from his later musicals. "Some Enchanted Evening," "Oh What a Beautiful Morning," and many more. In all, he contributed to nearly 40 musicals, and wrote about 1,000 songs.

HOLLYWOOD DECADE

Despite his long run of stage successes in what he termed "musical plays," his 10 years in Hollywood in the 1930's were singularly unproductive and few of the musicals on which he worked were hits. One of his major successes was his modern adaptation for America with an all-Negro cast of the opera "Carmen" into "Carmen Jones."

Born into a theatrical family, his grandfather Oscar I built among many others London's Stoll theatre, recently pulled down to make way for the new Royalty Theatre, and his father managed theatres, Oscar II intended to be a lawyer. But a job as assistant stage manager with his uncle Arthur, the producer, started him on his theatrical career.

(April 24)

CONSTANCE SPRY

Mrs. Constance Spry, the flower arrangement and cookery expert, who has died at Winkfield, Windsor, aged 73, was chairman of Constance Spry Ltd. and the Constance Spry Flower School. She was joint principal of the Cordon Bleu Cookery School and Winkfield Place Ltd., girls' finishing school.

Mrs. Spry was adviser to the Ministry of Works on flower decorations for the Coronation in 1953. She was a speaker in THE DAILY TELEGRAPH Flower Arrangement Festival at Harrogate last September and was a member of THE DAILY TELEGRAPH'S former Food and Cookery Brains Trust.

(January 5)

COUNTESS MOUNTBATTEN

COUNTESS MOUNTBATTEN

LAST VICEREINE OF INDIA: SOCIAL WELFARE WORK

COUNTESS MOUNTBATTEN OF BURMA, who has died in North Borneo at the age of 58 while on a tour on behalf of the St. John Ambulance Brigade, was a daughter of the late Lord Mount Temple and a grand-daughter of Sir Ernest Cassel, the financier, from whom she inherited a considerable fortune. She was a godchild of King Edward VII.

In 1922 she married Lieut. Lord Louis Moutbatten, now Admiral of the Fleet Earl Mountbatten, Chief of the Defence Staff. Their wedding was the social event of the year.

As a girl she indulged her craving for adventure by undertaking journeys at which many men would have quailed. She travelled alone across Russia into China, motored across Persia and Iraq, crossed the Andes on mule back. She signed on as the member of the crew of a copra schooner to chart remote Pacific Islands.

She was the first European to travel the entire length of the Burma road into China and the first to fly the Timor sea as a passenger, on the mail route from Australia to London.

In later years she gave unstinted service through welfare organisations. In one war-time period of two and a half months she travelled more than 40,000 miles by air visiting Australian and Indian Red Cross and St. John Ambulance establishments in forward areas in the South East Asian Command.

Lady Mountbatten devoted great energy to welfare work, particularly after the outbreak of the last war. At one time she was connected with more than 60 voluntary associations.

Until 1942 she served as an auxiliary nurse in the East End and at Westminster Hospital. Then, on appointment as Superintendent-in-Chief of the Red Cross and St. John she made a 34,000 miles tour of India and Burma.

Before the surrender of the Japanese in 1945 she travelled 100,000 miles to visit prisoner of war and interned camps in her husband's command in South East Asia. She organised the evacuation of sick and wounded and assisted in the evacuation of 90,000 allied internees.

For these, and other services, Lady Moutbatten was created a Dame Commander of the Royal Victorian Order in 1946. Three years earlier she had been created a C.B.E.

TACT AND DIPLOMACY

Vicereine of India

In 1947 she accompanied her husband to Delhi as the last Vicereine of India. She shared her husband's conviction that partition was the only solution for India's independence.

Her association with India, whose problems and people she knew so well, and her efforts during the difficult days when the country moved towards independence led to a close friendship with Mr. Nehru whose guest she had often been in New Delhi.

Earl Mountbatten was Governor-General of India at the time of Gandhi's assassination. He and Lady Mountbatten attended the ritual Hindu cremation on the banks of the sacred river Jumna in 1948.

Lady Mountbatten had a special love for children. Before leaving England on her latest tour, she said: "As president of the Save the Children Fund I am anxious to see what is being done for the thousands of unfortunate children in Korea."

(February 22)

NEVIL SHUTE

NOVELIST AND AIRMAN

MR. NEVIL SHUTE NORWAY, better known to millions of people as Nevil Shute, who has died aged 60, was a born storyteller. He gained world-wide success with novels that had flying as their main theme.

From boyhood he had been fascinated by aircraft, but his ambition to enter the Royal Flying Corps was frustrated because he was only 14 when the 1914-18 war started, and in 1918 failed medically because of a stammer. When the war ended he went to Balliol and spent the long vacations as an unpaid worker in the de Haviland design office.

On leaving Oxford in 1922 with a degree in engineering he began regular work with the firm. In the course of it he qualified as an "A" licence pilot. In the years that followed he flew practically all types of small aircraft and fequently cruised by air over several countries. His most noteworthy effort was to Australia and back. As a yachtsman he was equally enthusiastic.

In 1924 he left de Haviland's to play a leading part in the construction of the airship R100. As chief calculator he had to overcome many intricate problems to ensure the air-worthiness and specified performance of that remarkable vessel.

OUTSTANDING PLANES

Firm's Products

Shute distinguished himself so much that in the end he was in full charge of the project under the designer Dr. Barnes Wallis. All anxieties disappeared when the great airship, functioning perfectly, flew across the North Altantic and back. In saddening contrast was the disaster that befell its rival, R101, which had been built by the State.

With the abandonment of the airship programme Shute turned to the manufacture of small aircraft. In 1931, possessing limited capital but unlimited optimism, he formed Airspeed.

The company went through a long succession of financial crises but produced aircraft of outstanding merit, such as the Courier, Viceroy and Envoy, and finally the Oxford, which was selected as the R.A.F.'s standard two-seater trainer. No fewer than 8,751 were built.

Shute's connection with Airspeed as joint managing director was severed in April, 1938, and in the following year he joined the R.N.V.R.

When hostilities ceased he had no disturbing thoughts about his future career for he had already begun to profit from his gifts as a novelist.

Shute's own literary urge had started in his early 20s, when he wrote a couple of short stories and a novel without finding a publisher.

His first published novel came as a great surprise to his friends. An even greater surprise was its readability. This book, "Marazan," had been written when he was immersed in all the abstruse calculations attendant on the construction of R100.

NEVIL SHUTE

His second novel, "So Disdained," was written when he was working at even greater pressure on the airship. The third, "Lonely Road," was completed at the time he was battling desperately to prevent his company, Airspeed, from foundering. He did not write anything more for five years because he felt he owed a higher duty to the shareholders and workers.

In 1941 he began again with "Ruined City," and in the years that followed came his long succession of best-sellers. He had always disliked the bustle of the city and the distractions of social life, and a few years after the war made his home in Australia.

He married in 1931 Miss Frances Mary Heaton, and had two daughters.

(January 3)

SIR SPENCER JONES

EX-ASTRONOMER-ROYAL

By Our Science Correspondent

SIR HAROLD SPENCER JONES, the former Astronomer Royal, has died at his home in London. He was 70.

His choice of astronomy for a career went back to when he was at Latymer Upper School, Hammersmith. But astronomers need mathematics, and Sir Harold went on to Jesus College, Cambridge.

His association with the Royal Greenwich Observatory began in 1913, when he was selected by the Astronomer Royal of the time to become Chief Assistant. He spent 10 years in that post, and then became His Majesty's Astronomer at the Cape.

By becoming director of the best equipped observatory in the Southern Hemisphere, and at the age of 33, he had splendid opportunities for work. Little was then known about the stars in the southern skies.

It was while he was at the South African observatory that he became associated with the great international venture that was organised to acquire a better estimate of the sun's distance from the earth.

He became Astronomer Royal in 1933 and continued until five years ago.

WORK ON TIME

Apart from calculating the sun's distance more accurately than before, he also achieved renown for his work on the measurement of time. He was responsible for the introduction of quartz crystal clocks as precision standards.

In 1930 he was elected a Fellow of the Royal Society. He was knighted in 1943. After retiring from the post of Astronomer Royal, he became secretary-general of the International Council of Scientific Unions.

(November 5)

WAY OF THE WORLD

Kiss of Death

Assassins and gunboats being presumably ruled out, how on earth are the Americans to get rid of Castro? I would personally suggest killing him by kindness - the kiss-of-death policy.

From now on no influential American should refer to Castro except in terms of fulsome adulation. He must become "America's staunchest and most loyal ally," a resolute and courageous friend of freedom," "the valiant defender of democratic ideals."

His every action must be applauded as wise, far-sighted and in America's best interest. He must be embarrassed by a constant flood of flattery, gifts and aid, military as well as economic.

If experience is any guide, a mob of anti-American illiterates will soon be foaming at Dr. Castro's door. Whatever emerged from the ensuing chaos, it could hardly be worse than him.

(July 12)

Solidarity

MRS. DUTT-PAUKER, the well-known Hampstead thinker, has had to postpone her plans to join the Algerian International Liberation Army in order to concentrate on more immediate matters. She has just sent off a stirring message of solidarity to the Trinidad bottle-throwers.

"Congratulations on your heart-warming stand against Colonialist oppression," it runs. "Cricket has everywhere become the spearhead of imperialist reaction, just as Lenin said it would. Attempts to impose undemocratic decisions, based on racial discrimination, by umpires who are no more than running dogs of the exploiting class, must be fought by all who care for peace and higher living standards."

Mrs. Dutt-Pauker and her daughter Deirdre, who recently published a successful children's book, "Maisie the Marxist" spent the week-end practising bottle-throwing in the garden, using a dummy colonialist umpire as a target.

They evidently need practice. One of Mrs. Dutt-Pauker's bottles went so wide that it flew through an upstairs window, smashing a signed photograph of Zhdanov which stood on her presentation desk of Outer Mongolian mahogany.

(February 2)

A Perfect Holiday

ONE of the most enterprising of the "mushroom" travel agencies that have been so much in the news lately is "Phonitours" Ltd., of London. This firm specialises in holidays in Spanish railway sidings, but lately it has struck out on a new line.

Mr. and Mrs. Reg Fladd, of Bevindon, and their two children had booked a "Phonitours West of England Farm Holiday" - only £75 a week with everything included - well in advance. When they got to Devonshire they found that the accommodation offered was a broiler-house.

"Mrs. Fladd and the children didn't take to it at all," said Mr. Fladd afterwards. "They kept grumbling that the accommodation was too cramped. And what with all the lights flashing on and off, loudspeakers on all the time and people peering through glass panels at you and working adding-machines, it wasn't at all the restful holiday Mother had hoped for.

"Myself, I enjoyed every minute of it. Comfortable quarters, thermostatic heating, no need to worry about the weather, the very best vitaminised food and water coming through a pipe regular as clockwork - what more could anyone ask on a holiday?

"It was just what the doctor ordered. And if I have my way, we'll be back for more next summer."

(August 16)

What We Stand For

PICASSO'S paintings are, in the view of Mr. Kenneth Baynes, the best possible expression of the positive aspirations of the West: "it is difficult to see how the ideals that I had always hoped we stood for could be better summed up."

The old Colonel's eyes misted over as he finished giving his orders. He could barely see the ring of up-turned faces, grim, haggard and resolute around him.

"Gentlemen," he continued in tones hoarse with emotion, "I need hardly tell you that this will be the hardest battle of all. The Russians are advancing everywhere. Our allies are falling back in disorder. Everything depends on us."

Suddenly he straightened and his voice rang out with a new confidence. "But remember, gentlemen, remember all we are fighting for! Remember this! "- and he pointed to a picture of a woman with two eyes on the same side of her face and wearing instead of a hat a large codfish.. "Our wives! Our mothers! Our sweethearts! Remember them!"

From fifty throats surged the deep response. "We will remember," and then wave upon wave of cheering.

(September 6)

Peter Simple

MISS LONSBROUGH KEEPS STRICTLY TO PLAN

Miss Ferris Recovers from Fifth Position and Finishes Third

From MICHAEL MELFORD

ROME, Sunday.

ANITA LONSBROUGH'S gold medal in the 200 metre breaststroke last night was won after the sort of race which has normally unexcitable middle-aged citizens on their feet shouting like schoolboys. As a tonic and example to others who are to follow it was priceless, as indeed was Elizabeth Ferris's bronze medal in the springboard diving.

Success here is very much a matter of producing your best at the right moment. Miss Lonsbrough not only broke the world record but carried out with wonderful composure and self-discipline what cannot have been an easy plan.

In the previous round on Friday, Wiltrud Urselmann went off at a great pace but, even to an inexpert eye seemed of somewhat suspect stamina over the later stages.

Nevertheless, she was nearly a second and a half faster than the English girl and, with Ada den Haan of Holland, had the added moral advantage of having relieved Miss Lonsbrough of the 200 metres and the 220 yards world records which she set up last year.

It must have needed great patience and restraint to let the German build up an apparently unassailable lead, but Miss Lonsbrough bided her time and swam her out of it over the second 100 metres.

Second Olympic Champion

The new champion, only the second British Olympic swimming champion (after Judy Grinham) that Britain has produced in 36 years, is 19 and is a Huddersfield Corporation clerk in the motor taxation department. She was not in the best of health earlier in the season but has been in great form in recent weeks.

Britain's first medal of the Games and her first in a diving event since Antwerp, in 1920, had been won in the afternoon when Elizabeth Ferris, of Greenford, a 19-year-old medical student at Middlesex Hospital, lived up to the highest hopes and finished third in the springboard.

In the preliminaries on Friday she lay fifth, but yesterday she dived superbly and was beaten only by a German and an American. The news had been kept from her that her father was injured in a street accident, in Cannes, while on his way, with her mother and brother, to watch her dive.

(August 29)

HISTORY MADE AS PATTERSON REGAINS TITLE

From DONALD SAUNDERS

NEW YORK, Monday.

FLOYD PATTERSON, a 25-year-old coloured man from New York, made boxing history at the Polo Grounds here to-night. After one minute and 51 seconds of the fifth round he knocked out Ingmar Johansson of Sweden to become the first former holder of the world heavyweight championship to regain his title.

Patterson's victory was decisive beyond all possible dispute. Several minutes after he had been counted out Johansson was still unconscious.

His stool had to be brought from his corner to the centre of the ring and he was then lifted on to it for further attention from his seconds and a doctor.

Patterson, boxing like a true champion to take three of the first four rounds with speedy punches and brilliant footwork, suddenly unleashed a savage attack at the start of the fifth round.

Patterson continued to take the initiative in the fifth. His left jabs repeatedly rapped Johansson in the face, and then suddenly a fierce left hook sent the champion flying to the floor with his heels flying in the air.

He was up at eight - but Patterson tore after him.

Johansson looked desperately weary as the challenger tried to finish him off. The champion held on grimly, but he could not escape another solid left hook to the chin and was sent sprawling to the canvas.

(June 21)

DON THOMPSON, OF CRANFORD, MIDDX. breasting the tape in the Olympic Stadium in Rome yesterday when he won the 50-kilometre walk and Britain's first athletics gold medal. He set up an Olympic record of 4hr 25min 30sec.

BRITISH GIRLS TRIUMPH IN LAST MATCH

Miss Truman Plays Leading Role in Singles and Doubles

By LANCE TINGAY

THE narrow and exciting British victory over the United States in the Wightman Cup at Wimbledon on Saturday was an event to remember. It was not so much the rarity of success - six wins in 32 contests is a scant ration - as the back-to-the-wall position from which it was achieved.

In the end form worked out well, but only after perils and tensions that brough as much nervous exhaustion to spectators as to the players. When under lengthening shadows the crucial seventh rubber was won by Miss Christine Truman and Mrs. Shirley Brasher against Miss Janet Hopps and Mrs. Dorothy Knode after the agonies of a 0-4 deficit in the first set and one of 2-5 in the second, an afternoon of patriotic anguish ended with Britain home by 4-3.

Not until that first set was secure could Britain see success. America were knocking on the door all the long afternoon and one can only applaud the spirit of the British side in getting first over the threshold

In praising the home victory one should not be over-sanguine about the relative strength of our women compared with the Americans. Their best player, the ambidextrous Mrs. Beverly Fleitz, was absent, and it will not be long before the 17-year-old Miss Karen Hantze, on whom the enforced American gamble barely failed, will become as formidable as any post-war American player, except perhaps Miss Maureen Connolly.

Miss Truman took the honours on Saturday, just as she did in the victory of 1958. She played a gem of a match, reaching her full potential to quell Miss Hantze and she was the main architect of the last doubles win on which everything depended.

Her opening singles win made the score two-all. She won each of her two sets against Miss Hantze on the strength of the one service break in each set. These came in the 12th game of the first and the fourth of the second, but that was just the technicality.

That she was able to turn the key to victory was due to her solid weight of aggressive shot, admirably disciplined and projected with hardly a loose stroke from start to finish. Miss Hantze primarily had her superb service strength, but whereas her main weapon failed, Miss Truman's never looked like doing so.

(June 13)

Saturday's Details

British names First

Miss C.C. Truman bt Miss K.H. Hantze 7-5, 6-3

Miss A.S. Haydon lost to Miss D.R. Hard 5-7, 6-2, 6-1

Miss A. Brasher & Miss Truman bt Miss J.S. Hopps & Mrs D.P. Knode 6-4, 9-7

FRIDAY: Miss Haydon bt Miss Hantze 2-1, 11-9, 6-1. Miss Truman lost to Miss Hard 6-4, 3-6, 4-6. Miss Haydon & Miss Mortimer lost to Miss Hantze & Miss Hard 0-6, 0-6.

NICKLAUS IS GOOD ENOUGH TO LAND "GRAND SLAM"

From LEONARD CRAWLEY

ARDMORE, Philadelphia, Sunday.

The United States won the World Amateur Golf Team Championship for the Eisenhower Trophy here over the Merion Club's course last evening by the overwhelming margin of 42 strokes with a total of 834. Australia, the holders, finished second with 876 and Great Britain and Ireland came next with 881.

America's victory was won by four of perhaps the best amateurs who ever played together in any team. In J. Nicklaus it contained a prodigy the like of whom we have not seen since the glorious days of R.T. Jones Jr.

I suggest Nicklaus is the first man - since Jones made his final bow at Merion 30 years ago - capable of winning the Amateur and Open Championships of Great Britain and the United States.

While it is 10,000-1 against his winning all four championships in the same year, his whole game is so tremendously efficient that there would appear to be nothing to stop him. He has already won the United States Amateur.

Just think of his performance in this Championship: 66, 67, 68, 68 for a total of 269 over a course where Hogan himself won the American Open in 287 10 years ago.

ONE ROUND START

German Extraction

One other comparison of interest is that in four rounds, he beat Dr. Zakaria Taher, of the United Arab Republic, by five strokes before the doctor had embarked on his fourth round.

Nicklaus is 21 years old, married and still at college. As to what is the recipe for producing such a brand of golfer at such an early age I will not even pretend to guess. He is of German extraction, a superbly built middleweight and disguises all his good looks under a hideous crew cut.

His last round of 68 was the best round of all, but for him it was just an exhibition in the certain knowledge that his side was bound to win.

(October 3)

OXFORD'S BROAD BLADES VINDICATED

By A.T.M. DURAND

OXFORD won the 106th Boat Race on Saturday, beating Cambridge by 1¼ lengths in 18mins 59sec. This was their second consecutive victory and although they led from the first stroke the race was one of the most thrilling and desperately contested in history.

It was watched by Princess Margaret, who sat with her fiancé Mr. Antony Armstrong-Jones, cox of the successful Cambridge crew of 1950, in the bows of the Cambridge launch.

In due course Princess Margaret will see a Light Blue win, but she will never see a more courageous Cambridge crew than that of 1960. Nor is Mr. Armstrong-Jones likely to see more curious steering than Oxford's.

Oxford deserved their win, and as always chief credit must go to the president, Rutherford, as the organiser of victory. He himself rowed tirelessly and well in the key position of No. 6.

Cambridge raced magnificently. While it may be invidious to name one man as outstanding I consider that Beveridge deserves it.

But gallant as they were they never in the race looked quite good enough to win or to take full advantage of Oxford's mistakes in steering in the Chiswick and Corney Reaches.

It was Oxford's 47th win. Cambridge have won 58 times, and there was a dead-heat in 1877.

(April 4)

£100,000 FAVOURITE HURT IN DERBY AND SHOT

THOUSANDS of people cheering the 1960 Derby winner, St. Paddy, as he passed the winning post at Epsom yesterday, and millions more watching the race on television, knew nothing of the tragedy which struck down the favourite, Angers.

The French horse, a 2-1 chance, broke his near foreleg as he came down the hill two furlongs before reaching Tattenham Corner. He was destroyed by a veterinary surgeon following immediately behind in a car, even before Lester Piggott got St. Paddy past the post. It is estimated that, before the Derby, the value of Angers was about £100,000.

St. Paddy finished three lengths in front of the Irish-trained Alcaeus, ridden by A. Breasley. This was Sir Victor Sassoon's fourth Derby winner in eight seasons and Piggott's third. Kythnos was third and Auroy fourth. All four were bred in England.

Mr. J. Garrett, the veterinary surgeon who destroyed Angers, said: "I was following the runners in a car, and came upon Angers who had been pulled up and whose jockey had dismounted.

"Angers had multiple fractures to the near foreleg, including the cannon bone, fetlock and pastern. There was no hope of saving the horse and I had to shoot him quickly.

"It is amazing that a horse should get such injuries when galloping. It can be done if the horse is off balance."

(June 2)

D. THOMPSON BREAKS OLYMPIC RECORD

From Our Special Correspondent

ROME, Wednesday.

DON THOMPSON, a 27-year-old insurance clerk from Cranford, Middlesex, to-day gained for Britain her first athletics gold medal of the 17th Olympic Games when he won the 50km. (31 miles) walk in record time - 4hr 25min 30 sec.

The Briton's victory was really won in his bathroom. It was there that for months on end Thompson sealed the door and raised the temperature to a humid 90deg. before going through a vigorous training schedule.

No one in Britain's team could have tried harder to acclimatise himself to the Rome summer and he reaped a worthy reward. Tom Missen, a club-mate from the Metropolitan Walking Club, finished fifth. Britain's third walker, Albert Hohnson (Sheffield) was disqualified for "lifting."

RIDER'S SUCCESS

Another medal, this time a bronze, was gained by 20-year-old David Broome, who finished behind the brothers R. and P. D'Inzeo in the Grand Prix show jumping. Broome, riding Sunsalve, had a bad start in the first round, when he incurred 16 penalty points. But in the afternoon he totalled only seven.

Miss Pat Smythe, on Flanagan, lost all chances of a medal when she hit three obstacles on her second round, losing 12pts for a total of 32. This put her in ninth position.

(September 8)

MOSS WINS GRAND PRIX OF MONACO

From W.A. McKENZIE, Daily Telegraph Motoring Correspondent

MONTE CARLO, Sunday.

STIRLING MOSS driving Lotus-Climax, won the Grand Prix of Monaco here to-day, in one of the most car-wrecking Formula I races in the history of the sport. At the end of the 200 miles race only four of the 16 cars that started were still running.

The rest went out of the race after "shunting" straw bales or walls, or the chief cause, transmission failure. Five of them "motored in" afterwards to finish.

The course, which winds up and down the hilly streets of Monte Carlo, round the yacht-filled harbour, past the Casino and half the chief hotels and restaurants of Monte Carlo, calls for 20 gear changes a lap, 2,000 in the 100-lap contest. It is as exhausting on the driver as on the car.

Moss started off in third place behind Jo Bonnier of Sweden, B.R.M. and Jack Brabham of Australia, Cooper. By the 5th lap Moss had overtaken Brabham, and on the 20th lap had slipped past Boonier to lead the field.

But then the strain on cars and drivers began to tell, and one after another of them was in trouble. Maurice Trintignant, Maserati, was out after eight laps with gearbox fracture, Chris Bristow, Cooper Climax on the 20th and Alan Stacey, Lotus in the 30th.

RESULTS: 1, Moss (Lotus-Climax), time 2hr 53min 45.5sec; 67.5 m.p.h.; 2, Maclaren (Cooper), 2-54-37.6; 3, Hill (Ferrari), 2-54-47.4; 4, Brooks (Cooper) - one lap behind.

(May 20)

BAREFOOT ETHIOPIAN WINS FASTEST MARATHON

THERE have inevitably been some ironical twists of fate in the 1960 Olympic Games but none stranger than that which had a subject of the Emperor Haile Selassie standing proudly under his country's flag by the Arch of Constantine in the heart of Rome, cables Michael Melford.

The last few yards of the marathon were in the Via dei Triomfi, along which conquered kings were forced to walk in procession yoked to the chariots of the victors. But this time, the conquered of less than a quarter of a century ago came in triumph acclaimed by the world.

Abebe Bikila won the fastest-ever Olympic marathon in a few seconds over 2 ¼ hours after a long duel with the Moroccan Rhadi who was with the leaders for a long way in Thursday's 10,000 metres. Abebe came away in the last mile to win by 26sec.

The race in itself was not remarkable but the winner and the setting were. Abebe, who was followed home a few minutes later by a fellow countryman of the same name, is a 28-year-old corporal in the Emperor's bodyguard. He has a Swedish trainer.

Of the three British, O'Gorman was 16th, 8 1/2min behind the winner, Keily was 25th and Kilby 29th. Keily had been with the first two at 15 kilometres but they left him soon after, though at 25 kilometres he was still fifth, 107sec behind them, with O'Gorman ninth.

(September 12)

WEST INDIES FORCE TIE IN AMAZING FINISH

Two Run-outs in Last Over Deny Australia and Make History

From R.A. ROBERTS

BRISBANE, Wednesday.

An historic cricket match flared into a stupendous climax here this evening when Australia lost their last three wickets in the last over and were held to a tie by West Indies. It is the first tie recorded in Test history.

Strong men, heroes themselves of countless Test matches, were on their feet shouting themselves hoarse as Solomon's throw hit the stumps and ran out Meckiff off the seventh ball of Hall's innings with the scores level.

Benaud and Worrell agreed they have never known a greater game. Certainly it was the finest match in my experience.

The light of battle burned brightly throughout, almost blindingly at the climax. Yet not once did the exchanges lose their good humour. It was a match of genuine chivalry as well as gripping entertainment.

The ebb and flow that characterised the game was to the advantage of West Indies in the first two sessions to-day. Hall and Valentine unexpectedly prolonged the West Indies innings by 40 minutes and equally important, by 25 runs. But Australia still looked to have the better chance with 233 needed in 310 minutes and the pitch still playing well.

HALL, WHOSE MAGNIFICENT FAST bowling early in Australia's second innings paved the way to the most exciting finish in test history.

Before lunch, however, Simpson and Harvey were both victims of a Hall altogether more accurate and hostile than in previous spells here. Afterwards he struck deeper by dismissing O'Neill and Favell, while at the other end McDonald was bowled by Worrell.

Half the side were out for 57 and one felt hereabouts that if Hall had adequate fast bowling support, Australia would have been demoralised. With genuine speed at one end only, however, the effort could not be sustained and Australia fought back with characteristic heart and vigour.

Mackay helped to turn the tide before being deceived by Ramadhin's leg-break and Davidson, after a quiet period, reached the fulfilment of a wonderful all-round display. Now his batting, for the second time in the match, revealed high quality. And this time Benaud's was just as good.

At tea, Australia needed 124 in two hours. In the first hour afterwards, instead of playing for safety, Davidson and Benaud added 64 by judicious hitting blended with smart running. Now they were up with the clock and maintained the pace until, with eight minutes left, eight runs were needed.

At this point Benaud called Davidson for a single but Solomon's pickup and aim were too good. So Hall began the last over with Australia six short of victory.

SEVEN DELIVERIES

Unrivalled Excitement

Off the first ball Grout scrambled a leg-bye. Benaud went to hook the next and was caught at the wicket. Six balls left and four to win with two wickets to fall.

Meckiff played his first ball firmly and ran a bye off the next as the fielders went through a series of agonised acrobatics to run him out. Four balls left and three to win.

Grout swung again and the ball went high on the on-side, Hall claimed the catch himself and dropped it. Meckiff pulled the sixth ball high to leg and with Hunte in hot pursuit, the batsman ran two and went through for a third that would have won the match. Hunte's return, however, was fast and true to Alexander and Grout was run out.

All Over - a Tie

So the scores were level with two balls left. Kline came in and played his first ball to mid-wicket.

Meckiff charged down the pitch, but glory be, Solomon for the second time in minutes picked up swiftly and threw down the stumps direct. The small crowd made their voices heard far and wide and they will have something to tell their grandchildren about even if they find it hard to make their story believed.

(December 15)

N. S. BRUCE, OF SCOTLAND, puts up his hands to ward off R. W. D. Marques as the Englishman is brought down by G. K. Smith (Scotland), with P.T. Wright, of England, behind.

PACE & SHARP'S SAGACITY BEWILDER SCOTS

20 Prolific Minutes Give England Grip on Triple Crown

By MICHAEL MELFORD

Scotland ...... 12 pts England .... 21 pts

SPEED, savoir faire and Sharp are three of the best reasons for England's 13th Triple Crown. A remarkable capacity for taking their chances is another, and it was never more evident or important than at Murrayfield on Saturday.

The strong wind, which winning the toss gave England behind them in the first half, had to be used swiftly. The fiery Scottish forwards, and for that matter their 60,000 fervent compatriots, could not be allowed to gather confidence.

For 20 minutes the Scottish forwards, performed well up to expectations having at least an equal share of the play. And in that period England scored 16 points.

Sharp's second attempt at a dropped goal just missed, but nothing else did. His first went over; so did Rutherford's long penalty goal; and in between them so did Rutherford's conversions of two tries scored within six yards and a yard of the touchline. This was opportunism in the grand manner.

To their great credit the Scottish pack lost none of their spirit. Their occupation of enemy territory allowed K.J.F. Scotland to kick three penalty goals, and near the end led to a good orthodox three-quarter try. But by then Phillips and Young, at a speed Scotland could not match, had contrived a brilliant try. Rutherford had converted it - once again from the touchline - and England had moved out of reach.

There was a chance that if Davidson had not dropped the final pass and if Scotland had converted, the score would have been 16-14. The fact that Scotland always had a small chance of recovery added excitement to what was anyhow an eventful and colourful game.

Scottish packs are rarely beaten for want of scrummaging ability. The front row, in which McLeod was winning his 30th successive cap at the age of 27 - and the scrum-half offended Mr. Williams less than England's.

The forwards shoved stoutly and had some possession from the lineout where Kemp had an excellent game. They were quick on the ball in the loose, they backed up well, and in the quicksilver Shillinglaw had a scrum-half of high promise behind them.

These were Scotland's assets. What they lacked was a back row as ubiquitous and constructive as England's and the speed of mind and limb which England's backs possessed.

(March 21)

MANCHESTER CITY END SPURS' GREAT RUN

By DAVID MILLER

Tottenham Hotspur 1
Manchester City 1

All the best things in life sooner or later must come to an end, and at White Hart Lane last night Manchester City drew with fabulous Tottenham Hotspur. So finished Spurs' unparalleled feat of 11 consecutive victories, an achievement that will for long remain a testimony to one of the most brilliant of English teams.

But Spurs are surely destined for greater things. The irony last night was that in none of their previous victories had they made so many rich chances. Yet if one man now put a hand on history it was the magnificent Trautmann, Manchester's goalkeeper.

As Spurs, with devastating skill, scythed their way through Manchester's ranks all through the first half and again near the end, so time after time they were stopped short by this blond, diving, fearless former German paratrooper.

But for him and their own slight hastiness in shooting, Spurs could have been eight up at half-time, instead of just one, and it would have been no injustice.

All through the first half the packed thousands roared and clapped their spontaneous applause, which swelled out of the darkness like wave after wave of a rough sea. For every Spurs move was swift, concise and deadly, and no better football has been played since the Hungarians were here in 1953.

If anyone still doubts that Spurs are approaching that pinnacle of the past, or Real Madrid's pedestal of the present, here was proof.

(October 11)

BURNLEY ARE CHAMPIONS

From DAVID MILLER

MANCHESTER, Monday.

Manchester City 1
Burnley 2

BURNLEY fought their way to their second League Championship, after an interval of 39 years, and a place in the European Cup next season at Maine Road here to-night. In gripping tension that crept through to the skin like a cold wind, they held on for almost an hour to a slender 2-1 lead, and thus robbed Wolves by a single point of a Championship hat-trick and a chance of the elusive Cup League double.

There were but a few glimpses of Burnley the true champions, but what did anything matter but the result? Both Burnley's goals were lucky, as was City's, the winner being scored after half an hour by the tiny outside-right Meredith, who only achieved first team status last month.

A sad looking Mr. Stanley Curtis, hands thrust in pockets, quietly walked away at the finish, the dreams of Wolves shattered by a club with five part-timers among its regulars - Blacklaw, Angus, Miller, Robson, and the injured Connelly.

But many were the moments over the last, interminable half-hour, that Manchester threatened to save Wolves.

Ifs and buts apart, this was a magnificent effort by Burnley. To win or lose all was a frightening challenge, but they met it squarely, including the blow of losing an early lead.

NO GIFT

Pilkington's Burst

It was quickly evident that City were not going to give Burnley an easy time, and a crowd of almost 66,000 seemed right behind them. But within three minutes Burnley were ahead, Left-back Elder found Pilkington; he beat Barnes and Branagan on the outside, cut into the goal line, and his shot flashed in off a surprised Trautmann.

The battle was on, Burnley intent, anxious, always pressing and leaving ominous defensive gaps. Pilkington, Meredith and Pointer cut desperately into City's defence.

Then an agonising moment for right-back Angus. A foul tackle on Colbridge, and Hayes had shot home Barnes's free-kick.

With 21 men in the Manchester half the goal came on the half-hour. A disputed free kick by Cummings bobbed around on the edge of the penalty area, went to Branagan, who violently miskicked, and there was the darting Meredith to speed the ball home.

Twice before and after half-time, Trautmann tipped away thundering drives by Robson. Then the slowly mounting climax; Law bringing Burnley almost to their knees, but Mellroy, superbly holding the ball, delaying. Pointer and the rest chasing and covering until they were ready to drop, and finally the whistle.

(May 3)

KENT DEFEAT WORCESTER BY INNINGS IN A DAY

ON a brute of a wicket at Tunbridge Wells yesterday Kent bowled out Worcestershire twice in two hours 50 minutes for 25 and 61 to win in a day by an innings and 101 runs.

The pitch, brown and grassless, never gave the batsmen a chance and Kent captain, M.C.Cowdrey, afterwards described it as "disgraceful." It is the first County Championship to finish in a day since Lancashire beat Somerset on June 6, 1953, at Bath.

Worcester's first innings total of 25, scored in 75 minutes, is the lowest of the season and only two more than Hampshire's 23 against Derbyshire at Barton in 1958.

It was Kent seam bowlers, Brown and Halfyard, who caused these two collapses yesterday after Worcester had already dismissed their opponents for 187.

Brown took six for 12 in the first innings and Halfyard four for seven. They did most of the damage when Worcester batted again, Brown taking three for 22 and Halfyard five for 20.

Worcester would have fared as badly on their second time out as they did on their first but for a fighting 22 by Broadbent. He apart, Worcester's batsmen had no answer, for a long as the bowlers kept the ball on the stumps, the wicket did not rest.

Five first-class matches have finished in a day since the war and Worcester's first-innings score is their lowest since their 24 against Yorkshire at Huddersfield in 1903. They were, however, dismissed for 25 by Surrey in 1954 and Yorkshire in 1906.

Commendably aggressive batting by the left-hander Jones helped Kent reach 187. Going in with four wickets down for 68, he stayed one hour 35 minutes for 73 before being ninth out at 179.

(June 16)

MANY FAINT AT WIMBLEDON

The Wimbledon lawn tennis championships opened in a heat wave yesterday and many people fainted in a crowd of just under 20,000. J. Drobny, playing as a British subject for the first time, was beaten in the men's singles by the 21-year-old German Wolfgang Stuck in four sets.

(June 21)

ENGLAND'S FIRST SERIES SUCCESS IN W. INDIES

From E.W. SWANTON

PORT OF SPAIN, Trinidad, Thursday.

ENGLAND won the rubber here this morning when by batting on until lunch and beyond they deprived the West Indies of the slightest prospect of winning the Fifth Test match. Nature merely took its course.

It was not an heroic way to achieve history - for, as all now must surely know, England have not hitherto won a series over here. England, however, like the West Indies, were the victims of circumstances.

The latter can be commiserated with in being deprived of three hours' play in this game following two hours in the last. Apart from the loss of five successive tosses one's impression is that providence has not smiled on their efforts, taking the five matches as a whole.

Yet no one who has watched from first to last should be inclined to deny England full credit for their success. Considering the limitations of their bowling it is one of the most remarkable and praiseworthy victories of the recent past.

It is, of course, all the more notable following the wholesale defeat in Australia a year ago.

SELFLESS EFFORT

Fielding Benefits

May and Cowdrey have instilled an emphasis on unselfish team effort and keenness. The results of this have been seen especially in the fielding which overall has been the best I remember by an English side since the tour of F.G. Mann's team to South Africa in 1948-9.

If there is one aspect more than another that has contributed to the result it has been the English rate of scoring which at something over 42 runs per hundred balls has been substantially ahead of the West Indian.

Dexter's arrival has been the chief individual factor in this new approach, and everyone will fervently hope that similar tactics will be applied in the forthcoming series in England against South Africa and Australia.

(April 1)

POLICE-WOMEN MOTOR-CYCLISTS. Three of the women police motor-cyclists undergoing training at the Police Driving School, Hendon. Scotland Yard is training 12 women to ride lightweight machines, the idea being to make a percentage of the women's force in London mobile. If the scheme is successful it will be extended throughout the Metropolitan police area. The women are being issued with special uniforms, including a divided skirt.

MIDGET TELEVISION SET. A portable transistor television set, only slightly larger than a telephone, which has been produced by a Japanese firm. Weighing 12½ lb, it has an 8in screen, 14 channels and an internal battery so that it can be operated out of doors. The receiver will cost about £70 in Japan.

DR. MOORE IN GLENCOE. Dr. Barbara Moore walking through Glencoe yesterday as she continued her journey on foot from John o' Groats to Land's End. She had set out at 6.30 a.m. from Onich, Inverness-shire, after a breakfast of tomato juice and fruit. She stopped for the night in the village of Glencoe.

PREPARING FOR THE LAST LAP. Dr. Barbara Moore eating a salad breakfast early yesterday before setting out from Bodmin, Cornwall, on the last stage of her walk from John o' Groats to Land's End. Also included in the meal were grapefruit, bananas, Cornish cream, honey and hot water and fresh orange juice.

FLY HALF R.A.W. SHARP
(England and Oxford University) in action.

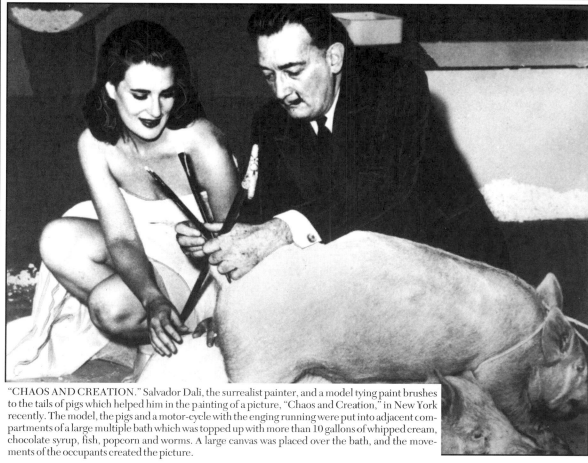

"CHAOS AND CREATION." Salvador Dali, the surrealist painter, and a model tying paint brushes to the tails of pigs which helped him in the painting of a picture, "Chaos and Creation," in New York recently. The model, the pigs and a motor-cycle with the engine running were put into adjacent compartments of a large multiple bath which was topped up with more than 10 gallons of whipped cream, chocolate syrup, fish, popcorn and worms. A large canvas was placed over the bath, and the movements of the occupants created the picture.

1961

This was the year that the first man circled the world in a space capsule. Yuri Gagarin became a household name. This Russian "first" could only be matched by the American success in "bouncing" a man outside the earth's atmosphere. On the ground, the forces of the Soviet Union and the United States faced each other in more dangerous rivalry. The American backing of the Cuban exiles' abortive invasion of their native land strained relationships, as did the building of the Berlin wall.

The new men in the Kremlin and the White House, however, gave promise of an easing of tension. Mr. Khrushchev sent messages of good will to President Kennedy on his inauguration, and the President gave promise of hope on the "New Frontier" that he called for. "Ask not," he said, "what your country can do for you, but what you can do for your country." At the same time, Khrushchev was removing the public manifestations of Stalinism. Even the name of the city where one of the climactic battles of the Second World War was fought: Stalingrad, was changed to Volgograd.

Africa remained a cauldron. The rival forces continued to clash in what was once the Belgian Congo. The presence of United Nations forces could only marginally reduce the tension. Patrice Lumumba, the leader of one of the Congo factions, was murdered. And it was the Congo imbroglio that caused the death in an aircrash of the United Nations General Secretary, Dag Hammarskjeold, as he flew to neutral ground to arrange talks between the warring factions. Algeria remained at civil war and the rebellious French generals threatened Paris with invasion. President de Gaulle called out the tanks to patrol the Champs-Elysées.

In Britain, the country was astonished to find that there were spies in its midst. George Blake, the MI6 officer who had, by the information that he passed to Moscow, compromised the whole of the British undercover presence in Eastern Europe, was given the longest prison sentence in British history, 42 years. In the respectable calm of a north-west London suburb another nest of spies was uncovered.

The agitation calling for the banning of the atomic bomb reached new heights with a mass demonstration in Trafalgar Square where a number of prominent figures were among the more than a thousand arrested. On a more joyful note, the Duke of Kent was married, surprisingly in York Minster rather than in London. A new Archbishop of Canterbury was enthroned.

The world of literature mourned the deaths of Ernest Hemingway, James Thurber and Dashiell Hammett. Those two enduring examples of British eccentricity allied to great achievement, Sir Thomas Beecham and Augustus John, also died, as did the entertainer George Formby and the film star Gary Cooper.

A horse that was given "no hope" by its owner ran away with the Derby. Hampshire was the surprising county champion in a year when the revolutionary idea of a one-day cricket tournament was approved. Tottenham Hotspur managed the double, winning both the Football League and the F.A. Cup. There was an all-British final in the Ladies' Singles at Wimbledon.

The Daily Telegraph

No. 32,964 LONDON, THURSDAY, APRIL 13, 1961

and Morning Post

Printed in LONDON and MANCHESTER Price 3d.

RUSSIAN SPACE MAN SAFELY BACK

PIONEER 89 min. ORBIT OF THE EARTH

SKY "VERY, VERY DARK" AND WORLD "BLUE"

ATTEMPT ON MOON FORECAST: MR. KENNEDY'S PRAISE

MAJOR YURI ALEXEYEVITCH GAGARIN, 27, dubbed "the Columbus of interplanetary space" by Moscow radio, yesterday won for Russia the race to make the first manned space flight. His 4 1/2-ton space ship completed an orbit of the earth in 89.1 minutes, at a height of up to 190 miles, landing safely at the chosen place.

The rocket carrying the space ship Vostok (East) was launched at 9.07 a.m. Moscow time (7.07 BST). Major Gagarin, wearing a space suit and strapped to a couch, could do nothing to control his flight though he had a two-way wireless to operate and instruments to read.

Television enabled scientists to watch Major Gagarin during the flight, while instruments transmitted information about his physical reactions. Braking rockets to bring the ship back to earth were fired 90 minutes after the launching and at 8.55 a.m. BST the major was back on Russian soil.

"I FEEL WELL," ON LANDING

He said on landing: "I feel well. I have no bruises or injuries," Jeremy Wolfenden, Special Correspondent of THE DAILY TELEGRAPH, telephoned from Moscow last night. Mr. Khrushchev, holidaying by the Black Sea, at once telephoned his congratulations to the major. The major said to him: "I could see seas, mountains, big cities, rivers and forests."

Major Gagarin, who is married, with two daughters, is now undergoing a thorough medical examination. He is expected to make a public appearance in Moscow to-morrow.

There were carnival scenes in the Russian capital until well after nightfall yesterday. Students marched with banners, loudspeakers played music and crowds surrounded passing Air Force officers to congratulate them.

After the landing a radio correspondent said the major's first description of the scene he and witnessed from outer space was: "The sky looks very, very dark and the earth bluish."

"EVERYTHING WORKING WELL"

Recordings of the major's messages sent to earth during the flight were also broadcast. They were:

Carrying out observations of the earth. Visibility good. Flight continues well. Can see everything. Flight continues. Everything normal. Everything working well. Feeling well and cheerful. Machine functioning normally.

The space flight lasted a total of 108 minutes, including the climb of the rocket and the return to earth. An official timetable of the flight issued by the Russians has caused some confusion over the vessel's course. It is:

LAUNCHING .... **7.07 B.S.T.**
OVER SOUTH AMERICA **7.22**
OVER AFRICA **8.15**
START DESCENT **8.25**
LANDING **8.55**

Prof. Leonide Sedov, head of Russia's space programme, who is visiting the United States, said in Boston that his country would send a man "to the moon or some planet in the foreseeable future." Mr. Macmillan and President Kennedy both praised the Russian achievement.

NATION HEARS MESSAGES

From JEREMY WOLFENDEN, Daily Telegraph Special Correspondent

MOSCOW, Wednesday.

This morning Russia sent the first man into space, Major Yuri Alexseyevich Gagarin, 27, of the Russian Air Force, flew nearly 200 miles from the earth, stayed in orbit round it for an hour and three quarters, and came safely back to land at the appointed place.

It was about 9 a.m. Moscow time that the rocket carrying Major Gagarin's space ship, named "Vostok" (East), left the ground. Soon afterwards Radio Moscow broke off its programme for the solemn announcement that Major Gagarin was in place.

It added that all the instruments of his ship were functioning perfectly.

An hour later Moscow Radio broadcast a transmission from Major Gagarin, who was then over Latin America. He said that all was well, and that he was not too much troubled by the feeling of weightlessness.

Shortly afterwards another transmission from Major Gagarin was also broadcast. He was now over Africa.

NORMAL LANDING

Braking Rockets

Then the braking rockets were fired to bring the "Cosmonaut," as the Russians call him down out of orbit. And before 11.00 Major Gagarin was back on Russian soil after a flight of one hour and 48 minutes. His first words were:

I wish to report to the Party and Government and personally to Mr. Khrushchev that the landing was normal. I feel well. I have no bruises or injuries. The completion of a flight of a man into space opens magnificent prospects for mankind's conquest of space.

The space ship "Vostok" was described by Tass as weighing just over four and a half tons with Major Gagarin aboard. It took 89.1 minutes to make a full circuit of the earth.

PRESIDENT IS IMPRESSED

"SOME TIME" FOR U.S. TO CATCH UP

From Our Own Correspondent

WASHINGTON, Wednesday.

PRESIDENT KENNEDY to-night described Russia's manned space flight as "a most impressive scientific achievement." It would be "some time" before the United States caught up with Russia in space achievements.

He said at his Press conference that Russia had gained an important advantage by developing large booster rockets. Commenting on a member of Congress's remark that he was tired of America being second, Kennedy said: "Nobody is more tired than I am."

Asked whether he thought the Russian success suggested a danger that the Communist system might prove more durable than the democratic system, he said: "I do not regard the first man in space as a sign of the weakening of the free world."

U.S. ATTEMPT

Some Months Yet

The United States will not be ready to put a man into orbit until late this year. The attempt may not come until early next year. Late this month or early in May an astronaut will make a sub-orbital rocket flight down the Atlantic missile range.

The White House knew immediately when the Russian space ship started to go into orbit. Radar stations, presumably in Northern Turkey and Alaska, picked it up as it soared above the Asian land mass and followed it throughout the flight.

Mr. Kennedy was not informed until 8 a.m. Washington time. Then Mr. Salinger, his Press Secretary, telephoned him. Mr. Salinger said the American tracking information on the space ship "generally was in accord with what the Russians announced as far as the flight was concerned."

Perhaps the longest faces in America today were those of the seven Mercury astronauts in training at Langley research centre, Virginia.

MR. MACMILLAN FLIES HOME

Mr. Macmillan arrived back at London Airport last night from Ottawa in an RAF Comet. He has paid a two-day visit to the Canadian capital.

OUR OTTAWA CORRESPONDENT cabled that the Prime Minister left behind an afterglow of general goodwill and strengthened friendship. His visit brought partial relief on questions affecting Canadian economy, particularly unemployment.

RELENTLESS ARGUMENT IN EICHMANN TRIAL

COMPETENCE OF COURT

From COLIN WELCH, Daily Telegraph Special Correspondent

JERUSALEM, Israel, Wednesday.

It was the prosecution's day to-day in the trial of Adolf Eichmann for the wartime murder of millions of Jews. Relentlessly, for hour after hour, the chief prosecutor, Mr. Gideon Hausner, proclaimed the competence of this court to try Eichmann and the validity of the laws by which he is charged.

Mr. Hausner is Israel's Attorney-General. He cited a wealth of precedents from many other courts in many lands, Germany itself not excluded.

His appearance is reassuring, but authorative, like a bank manager. His pink bald patch, surrounded by a sort of tonsure, glistens in the neon-lights.

QUIET MANNER

Moments of Emotion

His manner is quiet and leisurely, with long pauses while he rustles for documents. He gestures rarely, but fluently and with effect.

But in moments of emotion his hands suddenly flutter out like butterflies, or a long finger shoots forth and wags emphatically at Bench or defence.

He can be eloquent. His voice rises in fiery intensity as he denounces the unpardonable and inexpiable nature of the crimes of which Eichmann is accused.

They were crimes at the time they were committed, he cries, have always been crimes.

STATE AID FOR INDUSTRY

£401m. IN YEAR

By Our Political Correspondent

The extent of Government aid to private industry is shown collectively for the first time in a White Paper published yesterday. It will amount to £401 million in the current financial year, compared with nearly £374 million in 1960-61.

This will include a loan of £30 million to Colvilles for the construction of their new steel strip mill in Scotland, and loans of £40 million to building societies for re-lending to purchasers of pre-1919 houses. Both of these items will be financed "below the line" that is out of Government borrowing.

The White Paper shows that gross Exchequer issues "below the line" are expected to rise by £120 million to £1,089 million this year.

PASSPORT BAN ON BRITONS IN CONGO ARMY

Daily Telegraph Reporter

BRITAIN has taken steps to stop the recruiting of former members of her armed forces as mercenaries for Congolese armies.

Any Briton signing on for a military engagement in the Congo, other than under the United Nations command, will have his passport invalidated or withdrawn. Mr. Heath, the Lord Privy Seal, stated this in a written reply to Sir John Vaughan-Morgan (C., Reigate) yesterday.

Mr. Ian Scott, the British Ambassador in Leopoldville, has been instructed to warn British subjects known to be already serving in Congolese forces that unless they leave the Congo at once their passports will be invalidated.

£140 CONTRACTS

Rhodesian recruits were reported earlier this month to be serving with the forces of Katanga, the Congolese province adjoining N. Rhodesia. They were said to have been given contracts of £140 a month and allowances by President Tshombe, of Katanga.

Passport authorities have been instructed to refuse a passport to any British national applying for one to take up a military engagement in the Congo. Where the passport authorities suspect the applicant, they will ask for a signed declaration that the applicant has no such intention.

TERRORISTS GUN POLICE CARS

From Our Own Correspondent

PARIS, Wednesday

Armed Algerian terrorists attacked a police car in South-West Paris to-night. They wounded the driver with machine-gun fire. Two passers by were hurt by terrorist grenades.

NEW REMAND CENTRES' SITES

ONE "LIKE IMMENSE BATTLESHIP"

By Our Own Representative

WESTMINSTER, Wednesday.

MR. BUTLER, Home Secretary, to-day gave the House of Commons a preview of an all-purpose remand centre "like an immense battleship" at Risley, Lancs.

During a debate on the Criminal Justice Bill he announced that the sites for seven remand centres were already in view. A centre would be opened at Ashford, Middlesex, in July, for the London area.

The remand centres would be in Middlesex, Lancashire, near Durham, near Leeds, near Birmingham, Bristol, Exeter, Cardiff, and, probably, at Winchester.

HANGING AGE STAYS AT 18

COMMONS VOTE

By T.F. LINDSAY, Daily Telegraph Special Correspondent

WESTMINSTER, Wednesday.

It was a field day for Mr. Silverman (Lab., Nelson and Colne) during the debate on the Report stage of the Criminal Justice Bill in the House of Commons to-night.

That meant a long, long slog for Members on both sides of the House whom he led on his route march. But Mr. Silverman was at his best. He put the case for raising the age at which capital punishment should take effect from 18 to 21.

He attacked the present Homicide Act. "No Member of the House of Commons," he said, "believes that the present state of the law is satisfactory."

His case was answered by Mr. Butler, Home Secretary, who was short, swift, and to the point. The Government, he said, remained of the opinion that it is too soon to draw conclusions from the existing Homicide Act.

Secondly, crime statistics were still so high that the clause ought not to be supported. Some young criminals in this age- group had proved to be ringleaders. It was not for sadistic or for brutal reasons that the Government declined to accept the clause.

But the division on the clause was comfortable for the Government: Ayes 144; Noes for the Government 229. there was never a suggestion that the division lobby would, as it were, bring home the bacon.

The Daily Telegraph

and Morning Post

4 A.M.

No. 32,947 LONDON, THURSDAY, MARCH 23, 1961

Printed in LONDON and MANCHESTER Price 2½d.

SPY RING CHIEF GETS 25 YEARS

ALL GUILTY IN NAVAL SECRETS PLOT

LONSDALE TO APPEAL: ADMIRALTY INQUIRY

BRITAIN & U.S. TO TIGHTEN COUNTER-ESPIONAGE

Sentences totalling 95 years were passed by Lord Parker, the Lord Chief Justice, on the five accused in the Old Bailey spy trial yesterday. They were:

GORDON ARNOLD LONSDALE, 37, company director and professional Russian spy: 25 years.

PETER KROGER, 50, and his wife HELEN, 47, whose home at Ruislip was described as the "hub of the spy ring": 20 years.

HARRY HOUGHTON, 55, civil servant at the Admiralty Underwater Weapons Establishment, Portland: 15 years.

ETHEL GEE, 46, Houghton's fiancee, also a civil servant at Portland: 15 years.

All were found guilty, after an eight-day trial, of conspiring to commit breaches of the Official Secrets Act by passing information about the Underwater Weapons Establishment at Portland to "a potential enemy."

"A DANGEROUS CAREER"

Sentence on Lonsdale was given first. A faint smile appeared on his face as the Lord Chief Justice said: "Spying is a dangerous career, and one in which you must be prepared to suffer if and when you are caught."

Later solicitors for Lonsdale said he would appeal against sentence.

Houghton, Gee and Lonsdale were each ordered to pay £1,000 towards the prosecution's costs. The Krogers were ordered to share payment of £1,000, making £4,000 in all.

As a result of disclosures during the case, heads of Western security forces are expected to start soon a "combined operations" plan of counter-espionage. An Admiralty Board of Inquiry is to be convened to investigate the breaches of security at Portland. It will hear evidence in private and report direct to the First Lord.

Questions are likely to be put to the Prime Minister, who is head of security, in the Commons to-day. The Opposition later intend to attack the Government's security arrangements.

LINK WITH U.S. AGENTS

Daily Telegraph Reporter

The Old Bailey was crowded as the Lord Chief Justice passed sentence on the five members of the spy ring yesterday.

GORDON LONSDALE, given 25 years, was a professional Russian spy and the directing mind of the network uncovered in Britain.

Peter Kroger and his wife, Helen, who each received 20 years, were revealed as American citizens who had been associated with Col. Abel, now serving a 30-year term for espionage in America.

Harry Houghton, who went to prison for 15 years, was described by the Judge as "in many ways the most culpable."

LONSDALE'S SMILE

"Spying Dangerous"

Sentence on Lonsdale was given first. As the Judge said to him: "Spying is a dangerous career, and one in which you must be prepared to suffer if and when you are caught," a faint smile appeared on Lonsdale's face.

Peter Kroger, the next to be dealt with, looked white and shaken as he hurried down the steps of the dock. Like Lonsdale, he had been described as a professional spy, different from Lonsdale only in that he was older, and that he was not the directing mind.

Helen Kroger was told that there was nothing to distinguish her from her husband.

KROGERS'S REAL NAME

Morris & Lona Cohen

The sentences on the two Krogers came minutes after Supt. George Smith had stated that they were in fact Morris and Lona Cohen, American citizens of known left-wing views and had left the United States in the year that Julius and Ethel Rosenberg were arrested. The Rosenbergs were executed in the United States in 1953 for spying for Russia.

The Superintendent said that evidence had been found that the Cohens had been associated with a man named Milton, later identified as Col. Rudolf Ivanovitch Abel, head of Russian espionage in America.

Mrs. Kroger smiled faintly as she followed her husband out of the dock, but there were beads of sweat on the forehead of Harry Houghton, the ex-Naval Master-at-Arms, as he walked to his cells.

He had heard the judge tell him that only because it was against the principles of British justice to pass sentence which might involve a man dying in prison had he not been sent down longer.

Ethel Gee, first of the accused named on the charge, was the last sentenced. "It was because people thought you were honest and trustworthy that you were in your position," Lord Parker said to her. "You betrayed that trust."

At the end of the case, Naval Intelligence Officers, American Federal Bureau of Investigation agents and a senior representative of the Royal Canadian Mounted Police were present to hear Lord Parker congratulate the security forces on the work done.

Earlier, Lord Parker had told the Russian spy, his American accomplices, and their two English tools, that the case must be one of the most disgraceful to come before the courts in peace time.

Q.C. DID NOT KNOW

Hushed Court

Supt. Smith revealed that information from the Federal Bureau of Investigation had identified the Krogers as people concerned in both the Rosenberg and Abel cases. This was a fact which Mr. Victor Durand, Q.C., their counsel, did not know until informed by the Attorney-General earlier in the afternoon.

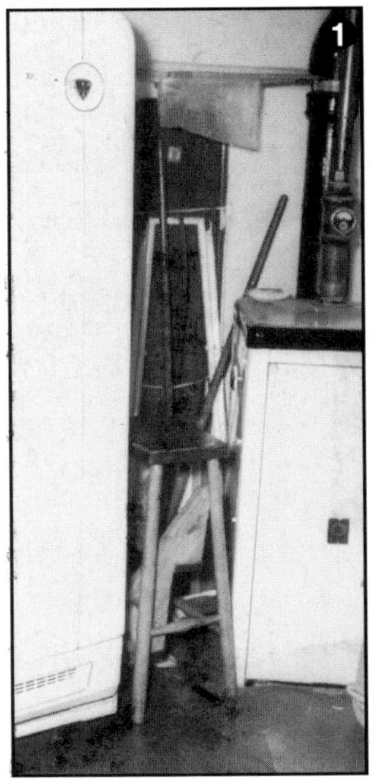

PICTURES TAKEN AT THE KROGERS' Ruislip home and issued by Scotland Yard last night. 1. A refrigerator covering a kitchen trap-door (2.) leading to space in the foundations (3.) where in a cavity (4.) a transmitter and other equipment were hidden. (5.) The loft in which travellers' cheques and dollar bills were found.

COUNTER-SPY PLAN IN WEST

SECURITY SYSTEMS NEED TIGHTENING

By T.A. SANDROCK
Daily Telegraph Scotland Yard Correspondent

Governments of the Western Powers have two major problems following disclosures during the secrets case. Head of security forces are expected to start a "combined operations" plan of counter-espionage. The two problems are:

1 - How to close the loopholes and weaknesses in security systems, and

2 - How to trace the numerous agents who can operate so easily and freely between countries.

Inquiries during the present case by MI5 and Scotland Yard's Special Branch, the American Federal Bureau of Investigation and specialist officers of the Royal Canadian Mounted Police have shown faults in existing counter-espionage methods.

Special Branch officers are expected to show Houghton photographs to-day which may help identify other agents in Britain. The photographs were referred to in court when Houghton's counsel said that Houghton's offered to help police all that he could.

EASE OF TRAVEL

Suspected Persons

It has never been easy to trace unknown spies but the ease with which the Cohens, as persons already suspected by the FBI could move from country to country is itself a condemnation of these methods.

NAVAL INQUIRY IN FEW DAYS

SECRETS CHECK

Daily Telegraph Reporter

Within a few days an Admiralty Board of Inquiry, presided over by an officer of Flag rank, will investigate how the breaches of security at the Portland base were possible. The inquiry will sit in private and will report directly to the First Lord of the Admiralty, Lord Carrington.

Evidence will be given by security officers from the Portland base, and by Capt. George Symonds, director of the under-sea research. It is likely that Capt. N.H.G. Austen, Naval Attaché in Warsaw at the time Houghton served there, will be recalled from retirement to give details of incidents in 1951.

The findings will affect the work of every other secret base in Britain. Army and Airforce as well as Navy. Whatever its findings, some tightening of security seems certain. Senior officers at the Admiralty have been dismayed by the apparent ease with which secrets were stolen.

LABOUR MP QUITS PARTY OVER DEFENCE

MR. GAITSKELL "TOO LEFT"

By H.B. BOYNE, Daily Telegraph Political Correspondent

MR. ALAN BROWN, Labour M.P. for Tottenham, announced yesterday that he had resigned from the party. His reason, almost incredible to political observers, is that Mr. Gaitskell has drifted too far to the Left on defence policy.

"The break is absolute and permanent," Mr. Brown said to me last night. "Defence is a fundamental issue which overrides all others. I simply cannot subscribe to the official defence policy which Mr. Gaitskell now supports."

Mr. Brown's firm stand against the abandonment of Britain's nuclear deterrent may spring from the fact that he is an ex-soldier. During the last war he served with the Bedfordshire and Hertfordshire Regiment, attaining the rank of lieutenant.

A chemist of 47, he succeeded at the last election to the seat formerly held by Sir Frederick Messer, whose views were Left of centre. The contrast in their opinions may have caused some difficulty with his constituency party.

Mr. Gaitskell, I understand, did his utmost to dissuade Mr. Brown when he saw him on Tuesday, but could make no impression. In a letter to the party leader Mr. Brown wrote:

I am bitterly opposed to the implementation of this new policy.

MR. ZILLIACUS SUSPENDED

"SAUCY" LETTER

By An Industrial Correspondent

Mr. Konni Zilliacus, M.P., Gorton, was yesterday suspended from membership of the Labour party. The national executive committee found his explanations for an article he wrote in an East German Communist magazine "unsatisfactory."

Mr. Zilliacus had previously sent a letter of explanation described as "saucy." Later he wrote a second, more conciliatory letter.

At yesterday's meeting Mr. Walter Padley, M.P. (Ogmore) suggested that if action was taken against Mr. Zilliacus, Mr. Woodrow Wyatt should be disciplined. Mr. Wyatt has been asked to appear before the party's officers to discuss articles he wrote for Aims of Industry.

"DETERRENTS" IN ROAD TRAFFIC BILL

By Our Political Correspondent

The theory of the deterrent, as applied to motorists, lies behind the new Road Traffic Bill published yesterday.

Mr. Maples, Transport Minister, feels that motorists fear the loss of their licence most. So for the seven most serious offences, broadly speaking, those which directly endanger life or limb, the courts will have no option but to disqualify for at least 12 months.

The other major feature of the Bill is the higher standard of sobriety it sets for drivers. This will be combined with clinical tests, including the "breath analyser," to ascertain the content of alcohol in the accused's system.

KENNEDY APPEAL FOR JOINT AID

From Our Own Correspondent

WASHINGTON, Wednesday.

President Kennedy is to ask West European countries to give at least one per cent of their gross national products each year in capital for under-developed countries. The proposal will be made at next Monday's meeting in London of the 10-nation Development Assistance Group of the Organisation for Economic Cooperation and Development.

It will be set out by Mr. Ball, Under-Secretary of State, who is preparing the ground in Bonn and Paris this week.

BILL TO KEEP S. AFRICA LINK

STUDY OF PROBLEMS, SAYS PREMIER

By Our Own Representative

WESTMINSTER, Wednesday.

A BILL to make temporary provision for the period from May 31 when South Africa leaves the Commonwealth is to be introduced in Parliament. This was stated in the Commons to-night.

Mr. Macmillan referred to the measure in the opening debate on South Africa. He said practical problems were being studied. Even if South Africa had remained in the Commonwealth the change from Monarchy to a Republic would have required consequential legislation here.

Now it would probably be most convenient to introduce a Bill to make temporary provision. This would maintain existing law for a specified period.

Mr. Gaitskell, Opposition Leader, said if South Africa could have been kept within the Commonwealth it would have been at too great a cost. It could have been disastrous. The purely family tie in the Commonwealth would not be enough for the new nations.

A HAIL AND FAREWELL

ACROSS THE YEARS

By COLIN WELCH, Daily Telegraph Special Correspondent

WESTMINSTER, Wednesday.

With warm eloquence, the Prime Minister paid tribute to "the magnificent patriotism, citzenship and disinterestedness" of South Africa's statesmen.

Racial, religious and political differences, he said, had disappeared "as if by a wave of a magic wand."

He was sanguine enough, he added, to believe that the Union Parliament would in time remove, "by its own gracious and spontaneous act" the colour bar it had seen fit to impose.

British interference in South Africa he deplored as "capricious and spasmodic," often ill-informed, sentimental and detrimental to the interests of the natives themselves.

Yes indeed, he did. But the Prime Minister was Mr. Asquith; the date, Aug. 16, 1909: the occasion, the unification of South Africa.

INTO THE NIGHT

Bidding Farewell

How tragically has the sky darkened since then! Amidst what wreckage of dashed hopes and shattered concord did Mr. Macmillan rise, in the House of Commons to-night, to bid South Africa farewell as she set off alone, grim and defiant into the long, dark night.

He threw no stones at our departing brothers. South Africa's domestic conduct, he implied, would never have been discussed at the Commonwealth Conference had not Dr. Verwoerd given his permission.

CUBANS DETAIN BRITISH CONSUL

From Our Own Correspondent

HAVANA, Wednesday.

The British Consul in Havana, Mr. Frederick Jeffers, and his Vice-Consul, Mr. John MacDonald, were detained for several hours by Dr. Castro's secret police, it was revealed to-day. They were held in a house on a small island about two miles from Havana.

They were sent on Sunday night in search of Mr. John Bruce, a retired British business man, who disappeared from his home in Havana. They found Mr. Bruce, 14 other adults and six children being held by secret police. The three Englishmen were released after the police had telephoned for instructions.

PARIS TAKES GUARD TO REPEL PARATROOPS

FIGHTERS GET ORDERS TO SHOOT: TANKS OUT

Gen. de GAULLE ASSUMES FULL POWERS AGAINST REBELS

EARLY this morning Gen. de Gaulle began organising the defence of Paris against possible airborne attack by the forces of the rebel generals in Algeria. Gen. de Gaulle last night assumed the powers of dictator, provided by the Constitution.

The emergency followed a broadcast warning by M. Debre, the Prime Minister, that rebel planes might try an operation. The Government had information that 1,500 paratroops were ready at Algiers to be dropped or landed in the Paris area this morning. The French News Agency, quoting informed sources said to-day that planes carrying rebel paratroops had taken off from Algiers flying towards France. The report could not be confirmed.

All airfields in Metropolitan France were closed. Buses were requisitioned to block the runways of those around Paris. Air Force fighters were ordered to fire on any plane disobeying orders.

TANKS WITH GUNS LOADED

Soon after midnight the first tanks rumbled into central Paris. Another long convoy of heavy tanks, half-tracks and motorised infantry took up positions near the Elysée Palace. An advance guard of sherman tanks, their heavy guns loaded, was just off the Champs Elysées.

(April 24)

SURRENDER BY REBEL GENERALS

The revolt in Algiers collapsed early to-day. After midnight fighting in Algiers, President de Gaulle announced at 1 a.m. that Gen. Challe, leader of the rebel junta, had sent him a letter of surrender and that all Algeria was again under Government control.

Gen. Salan, another of the junta, who flew from Spain to join the rebels, was at first reported to have committed suicide. This was denied after he had been driven away in a paratroop lorry with Gen. Challe and Gen. Jouhaud to an unknown destination.

News of the rebel's defeat came early to-day from Algiers Radio, which said its station had been occupied by loyal sailors and marines and that rebel paratroopers were pulling out of the city. The radio announced: "Order and Republican law have been restored."

Loyalist troops clashed in the streets and in the Forum with rebel paratroopers. The paratroopers were defeated. Earlier, rebel forces had withdrawn from Oran and Constantine and loyal troops moved in to take over.

FIRING FROM A BALCONY

In Algiers the last stage of the revolt began when loyal forces led by gendarmes in armoured vehicles moved to the centre. With them marched Republican Security Guards, national servicemen and patrols from a Zouave regiment.

(April 26)

TRAFFIC FLOWS BY AS NORMAL whilst tanks mount guard in the French capital.

RUSSIAN BALLET STAR FLEES TO WEST

From Our Own Correspondent

PARIS, Friday.

THE leading male dancer of the Leningrad Kirov Ballet was granted political asylum here to-day after he had been ordered to return to Moscow. He is Rudolf Nureyev, aged 23.

He broke away from two burly Russian officials at Le Bourget Airport and found protection with French police. The rest of the company continued to London, where they are appearing at Covent Garden for four weeks starting on Monday.

An auburn-haired Chilean girl, Miss Clara Saint, who met Nureyev during the Kirov company's three-week run in Paris, was called in to discussions at the airport.

She said she was simply a friend, and denied that Nureyev had decided to stay in Paris because they had become engaged. She did not think she had anything to do with his decision.

APPEAL TO POLICE
"Tough Looking Customers"

Nureyev, compared by one Paris critic with Nijinsky in his heyday, was waiting to go through customs at the airport when he was accosted by two burly Russians.

Described as "very tough looking customers," they told him brusquely that he must return to Moscow immediately, and leave the party going to London.

He refused, then broke away and ran to the nearest policeman shouting: "Protect me, protect me." They took him to their office where the Russian Consul, an attaché and other officials failed to persuade him to change his mind.

(June 17)

LIONESS ELSA FOUND DEAD

HEROINE OF BEST SELLING BOOK

ELSA the lioness, heroine of Joy Adamson's best-selling book "Born Free," has died in Northern Kenya at the age of five. Her body was found in the Ura River area, scene of many of her adventures in the book. Elsa was in the prime of life for lions, which sometimes reach the age of 12. She died from natural causes.

(January 28)

300ft FLATS TO BE HIGHEST IN BRITAIN

Daily Telegraph Reporter

HAMMERSMITH will have the highest blocks of flats in Britain under a plan approved yesterday by London County Council. Two 399ft blocks of 31 storeys will each contain 169 flats.

The borough council's plan was for two blocks of 26 storeys, but the LCC considered these too squat. Building will start when preliminary work on the site has been completed and tenders accepted.

(December 8)

MR. HAMMARSKJOELD DIES IN AIR CRASH

KATANGA PEACE TALK PLANE HITS TREES

MR. HAMMARSKJOELD, 56, United Nations Secretary-General, died in a plane crash early yesterday, near Ndola, North Rhodesia, where he had hoped that peace talks would resolve the Congo chaos that had so long baffled his organisation. President Tshombe of Katanga had been waiting at Ndola since the previous night to meet him.

After a night of conflicting reports about the reason for the Secretary-General's delayed arrival, one of many search planes sighted the smouldering wreckage at the end of a long scar torn through trees. Of the 14 people aboard only one man survived.

The survivor, an American security guard, was badly burned but was able to say that Mr. Hammarskjoeld changed his mind about landing at Ndola and gave another destination, and that later there were explosions in the airliner.

(September 19)

'LONELIEST ISLE' EVACUATED

TRISTAN DA CUNHA VOLCANO ERUPTS

From Our Own Correspondent

CAPE TOWN, Tuesday.

THE ROYAL NAVY frigate Leopard, 2,225 tons, is speeding from Simonstown, South Africa, with food and medical supplies for the 305 inhabitants of Tristan da Cunha. They were evacuated to neighbouring Nightingale Island to-day after the eruption of a volcano believed to have been long extinct.

Evacuation was carried out by two small vessels in stormy seas under a sky darkened by smoke from the volcano. Glowing lava bubbled down the steep slopes of the island, a mountain peak rising 6,760ft out of the South Atlantic.

Since August the island, known as "the world's loneliest," had been shaken by earth tremors of increasing intensity. Rock falls cut off the water supply to the fish-canning plant and huge cracks opened up in the ground.

Then the earth began to heave and bulge. Red-hot lava streamed out of the cracks, threatening to engulf the stone and thatch cottages. Huge fiery bubbles appeared. Sulphurous smoke hung over the island.

Mr. Peter Wheeler, 33, the Administrator, sent a message to Naval H.Q. at Cape Town saying he thought it essential to evacuate Tristan at least temporarily. He said a "bubble of ground" had risen 30ft.

"ALL WELL"
Administrator's Message

To-night Mr. Wheeler radioed from the Tristan: "All are safe and well." He said the evacuees had landed without mishap on Nightingale Island, previously uninhabited, 18 miles from Tristan da Cunha.

(October 11)

MR. KENNEDY IS SWORN IN

EISENHOWER HANDSHAKE

From DENYS SMITH, VINCENT RYDER and DAVID SHEARS, Daily Telegraph Correspondents

WASHINGTON, Friday.

PUTTING his left hand on a family Douai Bible, Mr. Kennedy raised his right hand, and, in a firm, clear voice, to-day took the oath of allegiance as 35th President of the United States.

He stood where Presidents had gone through the same ceremony for more than a hundred years, on a canopied platform in front of the Capitol. The building gleamed and sparkled in the bright sun against a background of a clear blue sky.

Thousands of spectators gathered on Capitol Hill stood in snow and slush, numbed by a bitter north wind. There was a roar of cheers as Mr. Kennedy pronounced the final words "So help me God" and Gen. Eisenhower, now a plain citizen, reached forward to shake his hand.

At 70, Gen. Eisenhower was the oldest man to have served in the presidency. At 43, President Kennedy is the youngest ever elected.

FORTHRIGHT TONE

Crowd Responds Warmly

He delivered his inaugural address in forthright, almost rasping tones. He brought the first laughter and burst of applause with a warning that those who thought they could ride a tiger might finish up inside. It was the only light touch in his speech.

The biggest cheer came when, almost belligerently, he said Americans should not ask what the country should do for them, but what they could do for the country.

With Cuba obviously in their minds, the crowd responded warmly when he said: "Let the rest of the world know that this hemisphere intends to remain master in its own house."

It was a speech bare of promises of easy answers to problems, and free of complacency, but it seemed to be what the crowds wanted to hear. Gen. Eisenhower sat with downcast eyes as Mr. Kennedy appealed to his countrymen to join him in facing the rigours of the "new frontiers."

(January 21)

END OF LCC PROPOSED IN LONDON PLAN

By H.B. BOYNE, Daily Telegraph Political Correspondent

THERE was gnashing of teeth from the Opposition benches in both Houses when the Cabinet announced yesterday its plan for the re-organisation of London's local government.

The scheme involves disappearance in 1965 of London County Council, regarded by Labour as the brightest jewel in its crown.

Lord Morrison of Lambeth, former leader of the LCC, was almost beside himself. Among his choice descriptions of the Government proposals were: "preposterous," "going from foolishness to foolishness," "gerrymandery," "mad," and "idiotic."

He plainly implied that the Government's real idea was to set up a new body on which there would be a reasonable chance of getting a Conservative majority, something the party had failed to achieve in the LCC since 1934.

BILL NEXT SESSION

Re-grouping Boroughs

Legislation implementing Government plan will be one of the major Bills of next session. The principal features, differing in some respects from the unanimous views of the Royal Commission, are creation by merging and regrouping of "London boroughs" with populations of at least 200,000, replacement of the LCC by a "Greater London Council," abolition of the counties of London and Middlesex, and a new central education authority.

The City of London would remain separate with the powers of one of the new "London boroughs." Metropolitan parts of the Home Counties would be incorporated in the Greater London authority. Croydon and East and West Ham would cease to be county boroughs.

(November 30)

Old Bailey Spy Trial

CASE AKIN TO TREASON, SAYS LORD PARKER

"DEATH WOULD BE PENALTY IN OTHER COUNTRIES"

Daily Telegraph Reporter

LORD PARKER, the Lord Chief Justice, sentenced GEORGE BLAKE, 38, a Government official, to a total of 42 years' imprisonment yesterday for his "traitorous conduct" extending over 9 ½ years as a spy for Russia. It is the longest sentence of imprisonment passed this century in a British court against any person on indictment.

Blake, a handsome, tanned man with long brown hair, pleaded guilty to five charges under the Official Secrets Act. He stood with his hands on the dock ledge of No. 1 Court at the Old Bailey with the faint trace of a smile on his lips as he was sentenced.

Then for seven seconds he remained gazing at Lord Parker. He then turned slowly round, taking in the faces at the solicitors' table and the Press seats as though searching for some friendly face. He saw none. Not even his relatives were in court.

So, slowly, he crossed the wooden floor of the dock, escorted by a warder. His legal advisers said later that an appeal was being considered.

Blake, who has confessed to spying for Russia, will not be released from prison until he is at least 66, in 1989, provided he earns full remission for good conduct. If he earned no remission he would be due for release at the age of 80, in 2003.

"AKIN TO TREASON"

Death in Some Lands

Lord Parker told him in passing sentence that his activities, which were akin to treason, were the worst that could be imagined in peacetime. In other countries they would carry the death penalty.

(May 4)

MR. OSBORNE SAYS, 'DAMN YOU, ENGLAND'

LETTER OF HATE

Daily Telegraph Reporter

JOHN OSBORNE, the original angry young man, yesterday made a vitriolic attack on the present British Government and on the leaders of the Opposition. He signed a letter in Tribune, the left-wing weekly, "in sincere and utter hatred." His letter was addressed to "my fellow country-men."

Writing from Valbonne, in France, he says: "This is a letter of hate. It is for you, my countrymen. I mean those men of my country who have defiled it. The men with manic fingers leading the sightless, feeble, betrayed body of my country to its death.

"My hatred for you is almost the only constant satisfaction you have left me. My favourite fantasy is four minutes or so non-commercial viewing as you fry in your democratically elected hot seats in Westminster, preferably with your condoning democratic constituents.

"There is murder in my brain and I carry a knife in my heart for every one of you, Macmillan, and you, Gaitskell, you particularly.

30 YEARS' INSTRUCTION

"I would willingly watch you all die for the West, if only I could keep my own miniscule portion of it, you could all go ahead and die for Berlin, for democracy, to keep out the Red hordes or whatever you like.

"You have instructed me in my hatred for thirty years. You have perfected it, and made it the blunt, obsolete instrument it is now. I only hope it will keep me going. I think it will. I think it may sustain me in the last few months.

"Till then, damn you, England. You're rotting now, and quite soon you'll disappear. My hate will outrun you yet, if only for a few seconds. I wish it could be eternal.

(August 18)

DR. RAMSEY IS ENTHRONED AS 100th PRIMATE

BLESSING TO CROWD OUTSIDE CANTERBURY CATHEDRAL

From NORMAN RILEY

CANTERBURY, Tuesday.

SEATED in the 750-year-old marble throne of St. Augustine, Dr. Arthur Michael Ramsey, 56, the new Archbishop of Canterbury, was to-day vested with all the "Metropolitical rights, dignities, honours, privileges and appurtenances whatsoever" of his office.

It was the 100th time the throne had been used for such an occasion since 1205. It had been brought from its usual place in the Corona or "Becket's Crown," at the extreme east end of the cathedral, for the people in the nave and watching on television to see the climax of the ceremony.

The throne was placed at the top of the steps west of the quire screen. Dr. Ramsey, holding first his pastoral staff and then the Cross of Canterbury, sat like a stern patriarch of old, his cope and mitre of cloth-of-gold, touched with rose-pink and blue aflame in the afternoon sun.

On the border of the cope were embroidered 10 coats of arms of places with which Dr. Ramsey has been associated. He wore the great amethyst ring presented by his former college, Magdalene, Cambridge.

At the end of the ceremony, Dr. Ramsey gave a blessing on the city diocese and province of Canterbury. Emerging from the West Door he smiled on the crowd outside, and asked God to "fill your hearts with all joy and peace."

(June 28)

UNION TO MEET ON COLOUR BAR DISMISSALS

Daily Telegraph Reporter

A PUBLISHER who dismissed 12 workers who refused to work with a coloured man said yesterday: "I am not going to budge from my position. If this situation should arise again I should act in exactly the same way."

The dismissed men worked in a warehouse as drivers, packers and porters and are all members of the National Union of Printing, Bookbinding and Paper Workers. They were employed by Mr. Paul Hamlyn's "Books for Pleasure" publishing group at Greenford, Middx.

The eight other warehouse staff, members of the same union, have remained at work. They have no objections to working with Donald Reid, 21, who comes from Ceylon.

TIME TO CONSIDER

Mr. Hamlyn said that the union had given permission for his firm to engage a man from the local labour exchange as a warehouse porter. He had given the men who objected to working with Reid half an hour to reconsider their decision.

A spokesman of the central branch of the union said yesterday that the union did not have a colour bar and had many coloured members.

(June 3)

BIRTH CONTROL PILLS ON NHS

Birth control pills are available under the National Health Service. This was announced in the Commons yesterday by Mr. Powell, Minister of Health.

Mr. Ridley, Conservative M.P. for Cirencester and Tewkesbury asked if the pills cost up to 17s a month, and if the Minister would publish careful instructions as to when they could be used since this could come to a very large total.

Mr. Powell: It is not for me to indicate to doctors when they should decide for medical reasons to prescribe for their patients.

(December 5)

GOA SURRENDERS TO INDIA INVADERS

INDIAN parachute troops yesterday took over Panjim, capital of Goa, and raised the Indian flag. A surrender was signed, though there were still pockets of Portuguese resistance.

OUR SPECIAL CORRESPONDENTS who entered Goa said that the Indian invaders had overwhelming force, but the Portuguese had not made the most of defensive possibilities. The pro-Indian underground had been little help to the invaders, but after they arrived turned out cheering.

In Lisbon a Government spokesman, quoting a radio message heard in Karachi, declared "fierce fighting" was still going on in Goa yesterday afternoon. The Portuguese Embassy in Paris announced that "hundreds of dead have already been counted."

A Soviet veto in the Security Council blocked a Western demand for a cease fire, and India escaped United Nations criticism. Mr. Stevenson, United States, declared: "We are witnessing the first act in a drama that could end with the death of the United Nations."

(December 20)

THE MILLIONTH MORRIS MINOR

FEAT "UNIQUE"

A million Morris Minors have now rolled off the assembly line. Announcing this yesterday, Morris Motors described production of a million vehicles of common design as "a feat unique in the history of British Industry."

Forty-eight per cent. of the cars were exported. The first Minor came off the Cowley line in October, 1948, and 171,021 were built in the next four years. The Series Two also ran for four years, 322,000 being built. More than 500,000 of the Minor 1,000 have been built since October, 1956.

Morris Motors said: "Throughout this time there has been no fundemental change in body or engineering design." The millionth Minor, finished in pale lilac, was presented last night at Grosvenor House, London, to the National Union of Journalists "to use as they wish in the interests of their benevolent fund".

Mr. J. R. Woodcock, deputy managing director, British Motor Corporation, and deputy chairman, Morris Motors, said it was the first British car to have a production run of a million.

(January 4)

RUSSIANS MAN THEIR TANKS

MOSCOW IN CONTROL

From REGINALD PECK, Daily Telegraph Special Correspondent

BERLIN, Friday.

AMERICAN and Russian tanks faced each other in Berlin tonight for the first time during the crisis. They were separated by about 70 yards at the Friedrichstrasse crossing point.

Seven Russian and six American tanks were counted at the crossing point itself. Three more American tanks and armoured troop carriers and jeeps were in position in the neighbouring Kochstrasse.

The Russian tanks carried green canvas coverings over their markings. They had arrived during the night.

(October 28)

MORE UNIVERSITIES TO BE ESTABLISHED

Daily Telegraph Reporter

Four universities at Canterbury, Colchester, Coventry and a place so far undecided, are to be established. This was announced by Mr. Selwyn Lloyd, Chancellor of the Exchequer, in a written reply in the Commons yesterday.

Their creation has been advised, within the scope of the existing building programme, by the University Grants Committee. No new university is proposed for Scotland.

Mr. Lloyd said that he had authorised the University Grants Committee to enter into discussions with the Promotion Committees in Kent, Essex and Warwickshire.

The new foundations are additional to those already being established at Brighton, Norwich and York. Last January the Chancellor authorised the University Grants Committee to increase the Government-financed university building programmes in 1962 and 1963 from £15 million to £25 million in each year.

MORE STUDENTS

170,000 by Early 1970s

Also, the Committee was authorised to invite the universities to make building plans for 1964 and 1965 on a provisional basis of £30 million in each year. This was to assist them in their task of accommodating the increased number of students who would be coming forward in the second half of the decade.

(May 14)

EPIDEMIC OF DIPTHERIA

By Our Health Services Correspondent

Twenty-five children are in hospital and hundreds of others are being examined because of a diptheria epidemic at Peckham. Nine of the children, aged five to ten, have the disease.

(January 4)

PURCHASE TAX UP 10PC: 4d ON CIGARETTES

DRINKS, PETROL, TV & H.P. TERMS DEARER

INCREASED purchase tax, higher duty on petrol, tobacco, beer and spirits, and a rise in Bank Rate were among the impositions in the "July Budget" introduced yesterday by Mr. Selwyn Lloyd, Chancellor of the Exchequer. Further measures are possible in the autumn if the economy does not respond.

The Chancellor also said the Government could not agree to the size of the proposed pay increases for primary and secondary school teachers provisionally agreed in the Burnham Committee, which would cost £48 million a year.

An Opposition amendment of "no confidence" in the Government's policy was tabled last night.

The Chancellor announced:

PURCHASE TAX: Increase by 10 per cent of existing rate; similar increase on Customs and Excise duties covered by Chancellor's special powers to vary rate, granted in Finance Act; effective from to-day.

1 ½ POINTS ON COST OF LIVING

The extras taxes will add 1 ½ points to the Cost of Living Index, to which the wages of more than two million workers are geared. Cigarettes will go up 4d for 20, an ounce of tobacco 5d and a gallon of petrol 3d.

How the price will go up

	Old Price £	s	d	New Price £	s	d
Cigarettes (packet of 20)		4	2		4	6
Tobacco (per oz.)		5	5½		5	10½
Whisky (bottle)	1	19	0	2	1	6
Wine (bottle)		13	0		13	3
Petrol (gallon)		4	7½		4	10½
Car (A40 de luxe)	650	13	4	669	17	8
Lipstick		6	9		6	11
Washing Machine	59	10	0	60	8	3
Refrigerator	51	9	0	52	5	0
Television Set	67	4	0	68	16	4
Bedroom Suite	100	0	0	100	9	6

The above are typical examples of popular makes and brands

SUBSTANTIAL SUM FROM IMF

BALANCE OF PAYMENTS: "Substantial" drawing on the International Monetary Fund, the amount to be announced shortly.

PUBLIC SPENDING: Postponement or abandonment of "desirable proposals" in services provided by central and local government; considerable cuts in authorisations and loan sanctions to local authorities; "very strict criteria" to be applied to new proposals for industrial assistance next year.

HOUSE PURCHASE: Suspension of 1959 scheme enabling building societies to grant 95 per cent. mortgages for the purchase of pre-1919 houses.

(July 26)

STORM IN COMMONS OVER IMMIGRANTS BILL

AFTER a stormy debate, during which there were Labour shouts of "Colour bar," the House of Commons gave a second reading to the Commonwealth Immigrants Bill last night. In the closing stages the Speaker, Sir Harry Hylton-Foster, had to ask Labour M.P.s to stop singing "Tell me the old, old story."

Three divisions were forced by the Opposition after Mr. Gaitskell, winding up, had asked the Government, even at this last moment to drop this miserable, shameful, shabby Bill."

The House was first divided on the debate closure motion. The closure was carried by 283 votes to 200, a Government majority of 83.

The second Opposition amendment, to refuse a second reading, was defeated by 284 votes to 200, a Government majority of 84. Finally, the opposition to a money resolution connected with the measure was also defeated by 275 votes to 195, a Government majority of 80.

(November 17)

'PAY-ON-REPLY' TELEPHONING

Post Office engineers yesterday demonstrated the new "pay0on-answer" coin boxes in seven telephone kiosks in the centre of Dartford, Kent. Within the next 10 days the remaining 46 local kiosks will have been converted.

The new boxes have no "A" and "B" buttons and pennies cannot be used; only 3d pieces, sixpences and shillings. Money is inserted when the called subscriber has answered which is indicated by a series of "pips".

(May 23)

£140,000 THEFT FROM NATIONAL GALLERY

By JOHN OWEN

GOYA'S painting of the Duke of Wellington, bought for the nation for £140,000 on the eve of its removal to America was stolen from the National Gallery on Monday, the 50th anniversary of the theft of the "Mona Lisa" from the Louvre. A watch is being kept at ports and Interpol is organising searches abroad.

The thief overcame elaborate security precautions, including electronic devices, to remove the picture from its display screen in the main entrance lobby outside Room XIII.

The painting cannot be rolled up, being on wood. It measures 25 ¼in by 20 ½in and is in a frame four inches wide. The time of its disappearance has been narrowed to between 7.40 p.m. and 10.5 p.m., the Gallery having closed at 6 p.m.

Last night, fears for the painting's safe preservation were expressed by Scotland Yard. After consultations with the Gallery Trustees the Yard announced that it was in "a delicate condition."

The missing Goya was not insured and the Government will bear the loss. It is not usual for portraits in national collections to be covered by insurance. The cost of insuring all Government property would be prohibitive.

THIEF'S ENTRY AS VISITOR POLICE THEORY

Police believe that the thief entered the National Gallery with the 5,960 other visitors during the day and went into hiding at closing time.

As soon as officials at the Gallery realised the Goya had vanished, the Gallery was searched from roof to basement in case of a hoax. Shortly before the Gallery opened to the public as usual yesterday Scotland Yard were called in by the Trustees.

Det. Chief Supt. Richard Lewis, Det. Supt. V. Massey and Det. Insp. John MacPherson, led a strong team of detectives. They began the questioning of all members of the staff, seeking first to narrow down the time of theft.

PLACE OF HONOUR

Seen by Thousands

The picture has been on exhibition since Aug. 3, and has been seen by many thousands of British and foreign visitors. It occupied what Scotland Yard described as "the place of honour" at the head of 22 steps in the main lobby.

Hiding places are numerous in the labyrinthine corridors and galleries. It would require many men to make a thorough search for an intruder.

Instead, the night security guard consisted of five men. Their patrol routes took them close to the Goya every 20 minutes, just time enough for the thief to remove the painting from the screen and hope its loss would not be noticed immediately.

(August 23)

PICASSO, 79, AND MODEL MARRY

NICE, Monday.

Pablo Picasso, the 79-year-old Spanish-born painter, was married 11 days ago to his 34-year-old model Jacqueline Roque. This was confirmed to-day by the Mayor of Vallauris, M. Paul Derigon, who performed the ceremony.

On March 2 the couple arrived at the Town Hall in Vallauris, a pottery centre made famous by Picasso, after the staff had left for the night. No banns had been published because of a special Prefectoral dispensation.

The bride was a pottery saleswoman in Vallauris when she met Picasso, and they have been companions for five years. Both have been married before. Picasso's first wife died in February, 1955.

(March 14)

U.S. SPACE MAN SAFELY UP AND DOWN AGAIN

"VERY SMOOTH MISSION"

SPEED OVER 5,000 MPH

From ALEX FAULKNER
Daily Telegraph Special Correspondent

CAPE CANAVERAL, Florida, Friday.

AMERICA'S highest hopes for its first manned space flight were realised to-day when Cdr. Alan Shepard, 37, of the United States Navy, was fired 302 miles in a capsule launched by a Redstone Rocket. The operation was a resounding success from every point of view.

Cdr. Shepard was so little affected by the ordeal that after climbing out of a helicopter on to the deck of the aircraft carrier Lake Champlain, 30,800 tons, he suddenly remembered that he had forgotten his crash helmet and went back to get it.

"Preliminary data," announced officials of Project Mercury in a communiqué which was a masterpiece of understatement, "indicate that the pilot performed satisfactorily during the flight."

15-MINUTE FLIGHT

5,100 m.p.h. Reached

It lasted 15 minutes. In that brief time he went to an altitude of about 115 miles and achieved a speed of approximately 5,100 m.r.h.

And he made a landing which was not only perfect but so near to the aircraft carrier that the helicopter which was to fish him out of the sea was airborne and approaching his impact point before he touched down.

America's first sub-orbital flight with a man on board was an accomplished fact. It was not as impressive obviously, as the Russian manned-orbit of the earth, but a highly satisfactory step forward in the American space programme.

It was carried out in the glare of world publicity and it demonstrated the capabilities of the American space capsule.

President Kennedy spoke to Cdr. Shepard by radio telephone. Then he issued this statement at the White House:

"All America rejoices in this successful flight of astronaut Shepard. This is an historic milestone in our own exploration into space. But America still needs to work with the utmost speed and vigour in the further development of our space programme.

DATA SHARED

Available to World

"To-day's flight should provide incentive to everyone in our nation concerned with this programme to redouble their efforts in this vital field. Important scientific material has been obtained during this flight and this will be made available to the world's scientific community.

"We extend special congratulations to astronaut Shepard and best wishes to his family who lived through this most difficult time with him. Our thanks also go to the other astronauts who worked so hard as a team in this project."

(May 6)

BRITAIN'S EARLIEST MOSAICS FOUND IN SUSSEX "DIG"

Daily Telegraph Reporter

A PALATIAL private residence with rich mosaics, the earliest found in this country, have been uncovered at Fishbourne, near Chichester, Sussex, during the archaeological "dig" which began six weeks ago. The site was noted in May last year when a water main was being laid.

Trial-trenches, dug at Easter, showed that there were large buildings of a very early date, probably extending over most of the five-acre site. Mr. Barry Cunliffe, of Cambridge University, is site director, with Mr. S. Frere, of the Institute of Archaeology, as advisory director.

A.D. 50 OCCUPATION

The 65ft-square courtyard was surrounded by stone columns and several of the capitals have been found. The main entrance was probably flanked by two massive columns, which would explain the varying size of capitals.

An excellent Petworth marble basin, which probably stood in the centre of the courtyard, has been excavated. There are many traces of the earliest occupation, about A.D. 50, and the dating of this period has been particularly successful because of the amount of Samian pottery.

An important find has been the builders' area used during the construction period. This has yielded between 20 and 30 opus sectile, rare flooring tiles, of which previously probably less than half-a-dozen were known in Britain.

(August 28)

INQUIRY ON DECIMAL COINAGE SOON

By Our Own Representative

WESTMINSTER, Tuesday.

THE Government believe that real advantage would follow the adoption of a decimal currency, but before reaching a final decision they consider that there should be a full scale investigation, said Mr. Selwyn Lloyd, Chancellor of the Exchequer, in the House of Commons to-day.

Mr LLOYD, replying to questions by Conservative Members, said the Government had been considering this question in the light of the public interest shown in it, particularly following the joint report of the committees of the British Association and the Association of British Chambers of Commerce.

There should be a full-scale investigation into the best form of decimal currency, the steps by which the change could be brought about, and the cost of the change-over to the economy as a whole.

(December 20)

LUMUMBA KILLED BY VILLAGERS'

"DEATH IN THE BUSH"

From RICHARD BEESTON
Daily Telegraph Special Correspondent
ELISABETHVILLE, Monday.

PATRICE LUMUMBA, former Congo Prime Minister, to-night lies buried in a common unmarked grave beside his two companions, Joseph Okito and Maurice Mpolo, somewhere in South Katanga. And not a single piece of convincing evidence has been produced to refute growing suspicions that they died in Mr. Tshombe's captivity some time before their escape was announced.

In the most cold-blooded Press conference I have ever attended, Mr. Munongo, Katanga Minister of the Interior, and one of the toughest men in the Tshombe Government, stated: "I have gathered you here to announce the death of Lumumba and his accomplices, Okito and Mpolo."

ONE OF THE LAST PICTURES OF MR. LUMUMBA, taken in December.

He then produced to demonstrate "Katanga's good faith" three death certificates dated to-day and signed by a Katanga medical officer, Dr. G. Pieters. They bore simply the name, age and sex of the three men and the laconic phrase, "died in the bush."

Mr. Munongo calmly informed his Press conference that the three men "had been massacred by the inhabitants of a small, unnamed village. They were not severely disfigured and have been identified without any possible doubt."

IMMEDIATE BURIAL
Place "Not Important"

They were buried immediately after their identification and the village where they were alleged to have been killed was paid the £3,000 reward promised by the Government. Earlier, Mr. Munongo had admitted that the reward notices did not make it clear that the fugitives were wanted alive.

The place of burial was "not important," it was also not important why the bodies were buried immediately. "They were criminals in the eyes of every country in the world," said Mr. Munongo.

(February 14)

UN TAKE KATANGA BY FORCE

UNITED NATIONS troops seized the breakaway State of Katanga after widespread fighting yesterday and declared that it was again part of the Congo. But IAN COLVIN, Daily Telgraph Special Correspondent, reported that Katanga forces were fighting back. About 50 Katangese and six United Nations men, including a Swedish major, were killed.

The United Nations claimed it had acted to prevent civil war. Mr. Tshombe, Katanga President, is in hiding, and Mr. Munongo, his Interior Minister, is reported to be fleeing to Northern Rhodesia.

Britain is asking Mr. Hammarskjoeld, United Nations Secretary-General, now in Leopoldville, for explanations of the events in Katanga, of the policies being followed there and about the authority under which they have been undertaken, said a Foreign Office statement last night.

Sir Roy Welensky, Rhodesian Federal Prime Minister, has put Territorials on the alert and sent three companies of White troops and 12 armoured cars to the border "because of the serious threat to our own security." He said the United Nations had acted like a "bull in a china shop."

(September 14)

STALINGRAD NOW VOLGOGRAD

From Our Own Correspondent
MOSCOW, Friday.

Stalingrad, famed for its resistance to the German Armies in World War II, has been renamed. Henceforth it will be knwon as Volgograd, it was announced to-day.

Another city to abandon the name given to it under Stalin's rule is Stalinsk, one of the chief towns of the coal and engineering area of Southern Siberia. It goes back to its traditional name, Novokuznetsk.

Yesterday it was decided that Stalino, a steel town in the Ukraine, would be renamed Donetsk.

(November 12)

Good night... good morning

And how good the morning seems when you've had a really good night's sleep ... restful, energy-building sleep. You feel bright and brimful of vitality, ready to tackle anything the day may bring.

A cup of 'Ovaltine' at bedtime smooths the way to natural, refreshing sleep. And, during sleep, 'Ovaltine' provides concentrated nutriment that helps to build up the energy and vitality you need for the day ahead.

Make delicious 'Ovaltine' the regular bedtime drink for your whole family. There is nothing like it.

OVALTINE
the family drink of today

A HORROR-STRICKEN WOMAN being led away after von Trips's racing car had crashed through the barrier into the crowd yesterday during the Italian Grand Prix.

13 DIE, 20 HURT AT GRAND PRIX

From W.A. McKENZIE,
Daily Telegraph Motoring Correspondent
MONZA, Italy, Sunday.

THIRTEEN spectators were killed and 20 injured when a Ferrari driven by Wolfgang von Trips hurtled into the crowd after a collision with a British Cooper in the Italian Grand Prix here to-day. Von Trips who was leading in the drivers' world championship, died almost instantly.

The crash, one of the worst since the war, occurred a few minutes after the start, at a banked section of the track considered so dangerously fast that British competitors boycotted last year's race. The Ferrari was in collision with a Lotus driven by Jim Clark, Britain.

Von Trips was flung out. His Ferrari and Clark's Lotus thrashed along the wire fences, leaving a trail of debris.

The Ferrari smashed into the wire and ran along it for 50 yards, mowing down closely-crowded spectators, before bouncing back on the track and overturning. The Lotus finished upside down on the opposite side.

Gerald Ashmore, Britain, also in a Lotus, crashed at the same spot almost at the same instant. He was not seriously hurt.

Clark, who appeared none the worse when I saw him told me he was running in von Trips's slipstream when the Ferrari pulled across him "I pulled right over to avoid him. My front wheels touched his back wheels and we both went out of control.

BARON VON TRIPPS

"I hardly know what happened after that. There was a lot of dust, smoke and general mèlée. The details are a blank to me. I know I walked back."

WINNER NOT TOLD
Few Knew

Jack Fairman told me that he passed the spot a few seconds after the accident and had to weave constantly through a hundred yards of debris. There were a car bonnet, wheels and bits of chassis all over the track.

The race was won by Phil Hill, United States, von Trips's team-mate in a Ferrari. Dan Gurney, United States, was second in a Porsche, and Bruce McLaren, New Zealand third in a Cooper.

(September 11)

GOLLIWOG SIGN OF GIRLS' DISHONOUR

From JOHN PRINCE,
Daily Telegraph Health Service Correspondent
SHEFFIELD, Monday.

DEEP concern at the spread of promiscuity and venereal disease among adolescents was expressed at the annual meeting of the British Medical Association in Sheffield to-day.

A special committee, including religious leaders, teachers, social workers and doctors, is to investigate the spread of the disease among adolescents. Two thousand doctors and clergy have been invited to a meeting in Sheffield tomorrow night, arranged by the Churches' Council of Healing.

OTHER "ACHIEVEMENT"
Badge On Chest

The annual meeting to-day urged that recommendations to prevent and control venereal disease should be published with the minimum delay. Germs resistant to penicillin and other antibiotics have emerged.

Dr. R.G. GIBSON, a member of the Council, said: "When some of us were young, in girls' schools it used to be the acme of success to obtain one's lacrosse, swimming or hockey colours. I am told there is a girls' school in England where there is another achievement to be obtained.

"One should have a yellow golliwog pinned to one's chest. If one has this, it indicates to one's fellow pupils that one has lost one's virginity."

(July 18)

SIGNS THAT INVASION HAS FAILED

From Our Own Correspondent
WASHINGTON, Wednesday.

THERE were signs to-night that the invasion of Cuba had failed. Communications between the small force ashore and headquarters outside Cuba ended this afternoon.

A supply ship off shore radioed to the invaders' commander: "Do you want me to evacuate you?" The answer was: "I will never leave this country."

Sabotage and guerrilla activity will doubtless continue. But the exiles' bright hope of overthrowing Dr. Castro quickly had been reduced to the faintest of glimmers to-night.

COST IN PRESTIGE

If the enterprise has been quashed, as seems probable, President Kennedy's Administration must start counting the cost in prestige and diplomatic advantage.

(April 26)

OIL FLOWS FOR A CHIEFTAIN

From STEPHEN BARBER,
Daily Telegraph Special Correspondent
BEIRUT, Tuesday.

AN Arab chieftain flying to London to-day may become one of the richest desert rulers by the end of next year, according to many Middle East oil prospectors.

Sheikh Shakbut Bin Sultan Bin Said, 57, rules Abu Dhabi, a British-protected Persian Gulf state of Trucial Oman. On the island of Das, a mile-long sand spit 60 miles off Abu Dhabi, British drillers have struck oil.

They have found six successive undersea wells and are now drilling for a seventh.

Another potentially productive oilfield has been discovered at Tarif, some 85 miles inland. Oil experts believe the resources there to be even greater than those on Das Island.

Abu Dhabi is fairly floating on oil. "There's no doubt it's a major discovery in the Persian Gulf," said a senior oil company official.

(October 11)

Distress signals

When old age, disability, bereavement or special needs occur amongst sea-farers, distress signals are answered by The Royal Alfred

Pensions, grants & allowances to the aged, widows, and the disabled—and maintenance of our Belvedere Home—involve over £70,000 yearly. We rely on voluntary gifts. Please send a donation to the secretary.

ROYAL ALFRED MERCHANT SEAMEN'S SOCIETY
122, Balham High Road, London, S.W.12 (Est. 1865)
Patron: H.M. The Queen

MORE INVADERS LAND IN CUBA

50,000 ARRESTED IN CASTRO "TERROR"

MORE landings in Cuba were claimed yesterday by the rebels, who said that between 500 and 1,500 men were on their way by sea. The rebels admitted an earlier "grave reverse."

Havana radio said that Dr. Castro was engaged in the "final destruction of criminals." Telephone and cable links between Cuba and the outside world were re-opened last night.

A Swiss diplomat said "the terror has begun against the counter-revolutionaries." About 50,000 arrests were reported. Two more Britons were detained yesterday, making the total six. There have been 29 executions in the past three days. According to an exclusive message to THE DAILY TELEGRAPH, Havana is an armed camp.

President Kennedy would not comment at his weekly Press conference on a report that he had decided to support the Cuba invaders against the advice of Mr. Rusk, Secretary of State. The President is said to have rejected the advice because the Central Intelligence Agency was convinced that Cuba was "ripe for revolt."

(April 22)

BRITAIN APPLIES FOR "SIX" MEMBERSHIP

By WALTER FARR,
Daily Telegraph Common Market Correspondent

BRITAIN formally applied yesterday for membership of the European Common Market with good prospects of joining before the end of next year. All six Common Market governments indicated that they favour rapid negotiations.

France, which earlier was the most hesitant of the Six, is now welcoming the application. Gen. de Gaulle, although expressing concern at some of the special conditions Britain may request, has indicated privately that the way is now open.

M. Couve de Murville, French Foreign Minister, told the National Assembly Foreign Affairs Commission yesterday that France approached the negotiations without any reticence whatsoever.

The negotiations would undoubtedly be difficult and if they failed it would be the beginning of a serious crisis. Their success would transform many aspects of European integration, both political and economic.

(August 11)

SMITH'S TO CLOSE LIBRARIES

103-YEAR SERVICE

W.H. Smith and Son have decided, "with the greatest regret," to close all circulating libraries at their shops and bookstalls on May 27. The service has been operating for 103 years.

After May 27 unexpired subscriptions will be honoured at Boots' libraries so long as they are valid. Alternatively, Smith's will make refunds after Feb. 7.

Smith's said yesterday that the library department had been unprofitable for many years. Since the war, greatly increased funds for public libraries have meant the rapid expansion of a free service. In addition, the vast increase in paperbacks has had a marked effect on reading habits.

The firm, which has alternative work for its library staff, adds: "The stage has now been reached when the continuation of this service can no longer be justified economically or from the point of view of goodwill."

(February 8)

1,314 ARRESTED IN TRAFALGAR SQ.

Canon Collins held: 15,000 marchers

Daily Telegraph Reporters

THERE were violent clashes in and around Trafalgar Square last night when 3,000 police struggled for over seven hours to clear a crowd that reached 15,000 in the biggest "ban-the-bomb" demonstration held in London. At 3.15 a.m. a final total of 1,314 people had been arrested, of whom 658 were bailed.

Among those held were John Osborne, the playwright, Vanessa Redgrave, the actress, Shelagh Delaney, the playwright, Mr. Fenner Brockway, Labour M.P. for Eton and Slough, George Melly, the jazz singer, and Patrick Pottle, acting secretary of the Committee of 100, which organised the demonstration.

Canon Collins, who is chairman of the rival organisation, the Campaign for Nuclear Disarmament, was also arrested. But he protested he was only an observer and was not taking part.

After a loudspeaker statement from the crowd that a march on Parliament Square was planned after midnight, when the emergency police order banning the demonstrators was due to expire, police announced that the order had been extended until midnight to-night.

At midnight when the demonstration had lasted seven hours, there was still a crowd of 1,500 in the square. But soon after police moved in and cleared the square of all but a few cleaners tidying up after the demonstrators.

Working in pairs, hundreds of police seized the nearest people to them and dragged them to a line of waiting coaches.

POLICE VIOLENCE

People Manhandled

This last police effort presented new violence. Some of those seized were making their way quietly out of the square.

When they protested they were thrown to the pavements, dragged forcibly to the vans or coaches and manhandled. These last demonstrators were outnumbered five to one by the police.

John Osborne and Mr. Fenner Brockway were among those arrested after midnight. Mr. Brockway was taken to Bow Street where he was charged with contravening the Commissioner's regulations and bailed to appear at Bow Street on Sept. 28.

STATION CLASH

Crowd Jeers

At midnight dozens more demonstrators were arrested after violent struggles outside Charing Cross Station. The police had tried to clear the Trafalgar Square end of the Strand of all pedestrians.

But when the crowd had been forced back as far as the station entrance they started chanting and jeering, and soon scores of police surged towards them. About 20 were arrested in less than five minutes.

A fresh convoy of police vehicles was brought up to carry the demonstrators away. Mounted police reinforcements were also called in to clear the last strugglers.

As vans filled with arrested demonstrators moved away from the Strand other demonstrators ran into their path and sat down. They were promptly picked up and bundled into the vans and coaches they had stopped.

Soon after 1 a.m. hundreds of police in and around Trafalgar Square formed up into columns and moved off.

(September 18)

SALUTES FROM PASSING AA & RAC PATROLS END

THE traditional salute to members of the AA and RAC from passing road patrols of the two motoring organisations is to be discontinued from to-day in the interest of road safety. This is announced in a joint statement.

The salute will not disappear altogether. A spokesman for the organisations said no patrol would salute vehicles while he was on the move, but would continue to do so when he approached a member or when a member approached him.

"When they are on stand-by at the side of the road, patrols will use their discretion. They will not salute if they consider that to do so would distract the attention of drivers.

The organisations regretted the need to dispense with this courtesy which had been appreciated for over half a century. Interests of road safety were of paramount importance.

"TRAP" WARNINGS

Between 1905, when the AA was formed to combat the actions of the police and patrols were employed to give warning to motorists of speed traps, and the year 1909, the battle between the association and the police grew fiercer.

Patrols, "scouts" as they were then known, were repeatedly prosecuted for obstruction. In 1909 the AA lost a case on appeal, the effect of which made it illegal for patrols to give direct warning of the whereabouts of a speed trap.

The AA's answer was simple, but effective. The salute would in future mean "all is well." No salute meant the opposite.

(November 10)

THE DUKE OF KENT and Miss Katherine Worsley folllowing their marriage.

PROMISE TO OBEY BY DUKE'S BRIDE

PAGEANTRY & SPLENDOUR

Daily Telegraph Reporter

THE marriage of the Duke of Kent, aged 25, and Miss Katharine Worsley, 28, within the mellowed walls of York Minster brought back pageantry and splendour to an ancient city which has not known a Royal wedding for over 600 years.

It also brought one moment of surprise. Puzzled glances were exchanged among the 2,000 guests and probably among millions of television viewers when the bride was heard promising to "obey" her Royal husband.

The Dean of York, Dr. Eric Milner-White, later explained why the Archbishop of York, Dr. Ramsey, who was conducting the service, had introduced the word into the responses.

"OBEY" INTENDED

Couple Asked for it

It had always been intended that it should be used, he said, because the bridal couple had asked for it. "But it did not appear in the service programme because it is impossible to print bits from the two versions together.

"You cannot amalgamate the two. All we did was to add one or two words at the appropriate point."

A good many of the guests who filled the great Minster may not have known that any alteration had taken place for the microphones were not strong enough to carry the responses clearly to all parts of the building.

But it would have taken a much greater incident to mar the splendour and solemnity of the occasion. An occasion graced by a glittering and distinguished assembly, including three Queens, Queen Elizabeth, Queen Elizabeth the Queen Mother and Queen Victoria Eugenie of Spain.

On this day, however, the three Queens were prepared to remain as inconspicuously in the background as possible, leaving the limelight to the young bride and her groom.

(June 29)

43-LETTER ALPHABET TO BE TRIED ON 1,000 CHILDREN

Daily Telegraph Reporter

AN alphabet with 17 letters more than the traditional one will be used to teach 1,000 children who start learning to read in September. The children will be at 24 schools in Staffordshire, Oldham, Lancs and Harrow, Middx.

At least another 1,500 children are expected to join the experiment the following year. Eighty teachers are now attending courses to learn how to spell in the Augmented Roman style as it is called.

The alphabet was devised by Sir James Pitman, in association with the Monotype Corporation. It contains 43 letters, including 24 of the traditional 26. The letters Q and X have been dropped, and 19 others added.

At the University of London Institute of Education yesterday it was said that 14 non-readers in a school at Oldham had learned to read in a fortnight using the new alphabet.

CUTTING LEARNING TIME

Children are helped to recognise the appearance of words because no capital letters are used. Each word had only one pattern, one letter stands for only one sound, and the number of alternative spellings for the basic sounds of the language have been drastically reduced.

It is claimed that the time needed for learning to read can be cut to 50 - 60 per cent. of what it is at present. The majority should be through the scheme by the age of seven, and ready for the transition to the conventional alphabet.

(July 18)

littl red hen
wuns upon a tiem
littl red hen
livd in a barn with her fiev chicks.
a pig, a cat and a duck mæd
thær hœm in the sæm barn.
eech dæ littl red hen
led her chicks out
tω lωk for fωd.
but the pig, the cat and the duck
wωd not lωk for fωd.

SIR LAURENCE MARRIES JOAN PLOWRIGHT

Sir Laurence Olivier and Joan Plowright, the actress, were married to-day at Wilton, Connecticut, by a justice of the peace who confessed later "to his shame" that he did not recognise either.

Mr. Edward S. Rimer, who performed the simple ceremony before only two witnesses said: "It was not until I read the marriage licence that I suddenly realised with a shock whom I was about to marry."

(March 18)

S AFRICA OUT

FAILURE OVER TEA CUPS

By R.H.C. STEED

Daily Telegraph Commonwealth Affairs Correspondent

DECLARING "I feel we are not welcome," Dr. Verwoerd indicated at the Lancaster House conference yesterday afternoon that the long effort to find an honest way to keep South Africa in the Commonwealth was going to be lost. He added sadly that South Africa was becoming an embarrassment rather than a source of strength. He asked for an adjournment and over the tea cups the last effort was made to prevent what was now regarded as inevitable.

When the Prime Ministers re-assembled, he said simply that he had decided it would be better both for South Africa and the Commonwealth if he withdrew his application for continued membership after the republic is proclaimed on May 31. Membership will automatically cease.

The effect of Dr. Verwoerd's decision not to prolong the agony was all the stronger because a formula to keep South Africa in was in sight.

FINAL SPEECHES

Assumptions of Peace

The might-have-been agreement said that South Africa's continued membership when she became a republic had been accepted on constitutional grounds in accordance with precedent. It then gave at length the disapproval that all the other 10 Prime Ministers had expressed of apartheid.

There then followed the arguments that Dr. Verwoerd had put forward in reply. One more redrafting, a few more final alterations to meet minor objections and agreement would have been assured.

The Prime Ministers even made their final speeches, on the assumption that agreement had practically been reached. But as one long statement of mental reservation followed another it became clear that the formula was merely empty words.

A striking aspect of these momentous days is that no Prime Minister has attempted to drive South Africa out of the Commonwealth. All of them have tried hard to find some other solution.

President Nkrumah of Ghana, Tunku Abdul Rahman of Malaya and Mr. Nehru of India, to name only three, stressed the difficulties they would have with public opinion at home if they accepted South Africa but stressed they were prepared to face this if only some progress could be made in its racial policies.

(March 16)

ANASTASIA CLAIM REJECTED

THE claim of Frau Anna Anderson, 61, now living in the Black Forest, to be Anastasia, youngest and only surviving daughter of the last Tsar of Russia was rejected by a Hamburg court to-day. It found she had failed to establish identity.

The court also rejected the counter-claim of Barbara, Duchess of Mecklenburg, the opposing party in the civil action, that Frau Anderson is really Franziska Schanzkowski, a Polish land-worker. It ordered costs of the 3½ years' action to be divided.

These, it is estimated, may be as high as £8,900. Frau Anderson will pay threequarters, the Duchess one quarter. No decision on an appeal has yet been taken.

Frau Anderson has been fighting to establish her claim to the Russian Royal family's millions for 30 years. She claimed to have escaped the murder of the Tsar and his relatives at Sverdlovsk on July 17, 1918.

Frau Anderson, who did not appear in court, had made herself available for questions only for a short period and had answered only a few in a completely inadequate way.

Passing judgment the chairman of the court, Dr. Backen, said Frau Anderson had failed to prove she was identical with Anastasia. Handwriting and anthropological experts' opinions "based on very slender material" were not convincing.

(May 1)

FREE BEER IN WELSH INNS

SUNDAY OPENING DRAWS VISITORS

Daily Telegraph Reporter

Free beer was given yesterday to customers at many of the 3,000 public houses in areas of Wales which voted for Sunday opening last week. Minutes after clocks struck 12 bars began to fill.

In the county boroughs of Cardiff, Swansea, Newport and Merthyr Tydfil and the counties of Glamorgan, Brecon, Flint and Radnor, inn doors were open on Sunday for the first time for 80 years.

They were open too, in Monmouthshire, where they were closed as a wartime measure in 1915.

The doors remained locked, as they have been since 1881, in the eight counties which voted against the change. These were Carmarthen, Pembroke, Cardigan, Montgomery, Merioneth, Caernarvon, Anglesey and Denbigh.

(November 13)

ROBERT BOLT LEAVES GAOL

PLEDGE GIVEN TO AVOID FILM DELAY

Daily Telegraoh Reporter

Mr. Robert Bolt, 39, the playwright, was working on the script of the film "Lawrence of Arabia" yesterday at a secret address outside London following his release from prison on Wednesday because his absence might delay the production.

He had served 14 days of a month's sentence he received for taking part in Ban-the-bomb demonstrations in Trafalgar Square.

(September 29)

POP GOES ANOTHER MUSICAL

By Patrick Gibbs

THE British musical - that graveyard of so many hopes - pops up again this week, after a very decent interval, with The Young Ones (Warner, "U", Monday). It has obviously been designed by the revue writers Peter Myers and Ronald Cass as a vehicle for Cliff Richard.

All starts promisingly with a goodish number sung by young people on their way to their youth club after work at the end of a week.

The camera picks up singers in a splendidly fluid fashion, on a bus, in the street, on a staircase, in a telephone box; and it seems as if the director, Sidney Furie, has learnt at least a little from "An American in Paris" or "On the Town" about the part to be played in musical films by fantasy.

Hopeful Duet

If proceedings at the youth club, with jive and rock, not to mention pop, prove predictable, the duet that follows, called "Nothing's Impossible," between Mr. Richard and his girl (Carole Gray) bring us back, again promisingly, to the sort of invention with which a film can make a good tune seem better.

Though even here, perhaps there is a trace of the theatrical which soon bedevils the production by becoming positively stagey.

Oh, I won't say Mr. Richard doesn't do his stuff, whether singing in the youth club or performing in the theatre, or that several of the songs, from the dozen composers, aren't top-tenish.

But really, his talent hardly enables him to carry a film on his own shoulders; and while the musical support may be strong, the script and dances are woefully weak, so are the performances from a horde of young people, several of whom are set up as comedians.

(December 16)

BACK in the West End for Breakfast at Tiffany's (Plaza "A"). Truman Capote's story seemed ideally suited for a film in the new, off-hand style and Audrey Hepburn just the girl to play Holly Golightly, that amusing tramp living precariously off a pack of wolves.

Alas, Hollywood has done its best to turn what was a delightfully eccentric character-study into a conventional love story. In the process Holly becomes a wayward but essentially virginal "weirdie," with her colourful vocabulary quite appallingly watered down.

Only one scene at a wild party in her flat realises the possibilities of a world hardly explored by the cinema. Somehow a modicum of Mr. Capote's dialogue has been allowed to survive here, and it is put to hilarious use by Martin Balsam as the actors' agent knowledgeable about Holly's past.

"Is she or isn't she?" he asks. "No" is regrettably the answer.

(October 21)

LONDON FOXES IN WILD LIFE SERIES

THE life of the wild creatures to be found among the brick and concrete of London was the theme of the first programme of "Survival," a natural history-with-jazz series introduced last night in Independent television by Aubrey Buxton, a director of Anglia Television.

Mr. Buxton, a Norfolk country gentleman, who produces the series himself, has displayed a shrewd sense of showmanship since he entered television. What he offers is wild life stripped of its sentimentality.

Against a sound track of harsh chords by Johnny Dankworth and his Orchestra, he acts as guide in a succession of out-of-doors conducted tours.

We learn from him about the foxes of London; about the hawks and owls that enjoy the capital's good supply of sparrows; about the dockside rats living in cold storage plants with coats grown doubly thick for the purpose.

(February 2)

BECKET THAT RINGS TRUE

FINE NARRATIVE OF ANOUILH

By W.A. DARLINGTON

IN these days, when so many of our own dramatists are ashamed - or unable - to construct a play, the name of Jean Anouilh on a playbill is a sure promise of fine craftsmanship.

Whether he is in a grave mood or a gay one, you can trust him for impeccable story-telling; and his "Becket" staged at the Aldwych last night in a vigorous translation by Lucienne Hill, is one of his finest feats of the kind.

In drawing his two chief characters the author has made free with history. He drew both Becket and Henry to suit his purpose, working from an outdated and seemingly inaccurate book about the Norman Conquest.

TRANSFORMED ROLES

That was probably all to the play's advantage and this Becket, the clever hedonistic King's man who found himself, to his own surprise, transformed into God's man when Henry forced upon him the Primacy of England, rings dramatically true.

There is very little to choose between the two characters as acting parts. The King and his Chancellor are cast in a very similar mould except for Becket's superior intelligence.

At the Aldwych the similarity is rather too well marked.

I don't mean that I ever actually got mixed up between Christopher Plummer's Henry and Eric Porter's Becket but a stronger contrast of voice, delivery and personality might have helped to dispel a certain sense of monotony.

Peter Hall's handling of the action is impressive.

(July 12)

HANCOCK SOLO SUCCEEDS

By PETER KNIGHT

WITH the opening of his new series on BBC Television last night, Tony Hancock seemed determined to silence those critics who have lamented the break-up of his partnership with Sidney James.

Here was Hancock not only without his partner but appearing alone for 25 minutes without the help of any supporting cast. And just to emphasise his virtuosity, he had boldly chosen to call the series quite simply "Hancock."

Whenever a famous partnership such as this breaks up the inevitable questions follow. Is he as good now as he was before, and how much did he depend on his partner for success?

On last night's evidence he is as good as before. Perhaps the absence of Sidney James slows up the pace of the comedy a little, but this apart Hancock proves that he is good enough to carry the series alone.

"BEDSITTER LAND"

For the new series he has moved to more illustrious surroundings in the "bedsitter land" of Earl's Court. Living alone, he is the frustrated intellectual for ever groping for the dictionary as he grapples with the philosophies of Bertrand Russell.

The coat with the astrakhan collar may have been left behind in Railway Cuttings but basically it is the same Hancock, and few viewers will quarrel with that.

Twenty-five minutes is a long time for one artist to fill the screen, but the boy from East Cheam proved that with or without support he is still the finest comedian television has produced.

(May 27)

MARIA CALLAS IN TV QUARREL

AIRPORT WALK-OUT

Maria Callas, the opera singer, walked out from an Independent Television interview at London Airport last night after being asked only three questions. When asked: "Are you on good terms with Sir Malcolm Sargeant?" she replied: "I am on very good terms with him. In fact I am on very good terms with all conductors".

Then she jumped from her chair, asking "Are you trying to pick a quarrel?

(May 27)

ALBERT FINNEY in the title role of John Osbourne's "Luther"

JAZZ: BY PHILIP LARKIN

Echoes of the Gatsby Era

IN their introduction to an excellent paperback, "Jazz on Record" (Arrow Books, 5s), Charles Fox, Peter Gammond and Alun Morgan lament the capricious attitude of record companies towards the issue and reissue of jazz recordings.

This, they tell us, is miserly and unbalanced, causing a situation in which whole artists, whole epochs are withheld from us. "It is almost as if a book publisher was able to decide that they would suppress half the classics of English literature.."

This is well said. Even the ordinary listener has plenty to complain of, the tired or raucous "name" performances, the jumbling of sessions, the duplication, the deletion. For the expert, who knows what is not issued, the situation must be unbearable.

The problem is to convince the record companies that the issue of jazz as jazz, and not as a poor relation of rock and roll, is commercial, and the only possible answer seems to be to buy such material when it does appear to the best of one's taste and means.

A special obeisance is due, therefore, to Philips for their monumental 4-volume "Thesaurus of Classic Jazz" (BBL 7431-4). This comprises 52 sides made between 1926 and 1930 by New York's leading jazz musicians, and gives a revealing cross-section of a field poorly represented for a long time now.

This is the music of the Jazz Age, but the Jazz Age did not really like jazz. The nearest it got to it was this brand of bright, skilful, melodic, but slightly bloodless music played by the "hot men" of its favourite orchestras - Whiteman's, Goldkette's, Roger Wolfe Kahn's.

Debt to Nichols

These men - Red Nichols, Miff Mole, Adrian Rollini - drew their inspiration from predominantly white originals, the Original Dixieland Jazz Band, the New Orleans Rhythm Kings and Bix Beiderbecke, rather than from the Negroes. In consequence their jazz had a refined, genteel air that suited palates not ready for Armstrong, Ellington and the bands at the Savoy Ballroom.

(February 11)

FINNEY GIVES A FINE STUDY

"LUTHER" STRONG BUT DISJOINTED

By W.A. DARLINGTON

IT seems to have been imagined in some quarters that the recent showing in Paris of John Osborne's "Luther" was the play's "premiere." This was not so.

The play was then on a tour preliminary to London production.

Its premiere was last night at the Royal Court.

It is reported that one or two of the French critics complained that the piece had nothing new to say about Luther. Well, if French playgoers are so well up as all that in the history of the Reformation, their state is the more enviable.

WRITTEN FOR ENGLISH

But the comment lacks point, since the play was written for English audiences.

The average educated Englishman will not pretend, I think, that Martin Luther's complicated life-story is more to him than a page in a text-book, and will be intrigued to learn from Mr. Osborne's pungent account that his single-minded monk, stubborn in mind and will by reason, it seems, of stubborn bowels, reformed the Church almost by accident.

TENSION LACKING

Mr. Osborne gives us glimpses of his hero at salient parts of his life in a series of disjointed scenes.

His dislike of smooth story-telling prevents these scenes from giving us the narrative tension that Luther's career might have provided, but the scenes themselves are strongly drawn and strongly written - too strongly perhaps, for the more squeamish, for the constipation motif, once introduced, is never relinquished.

But he provides, as usual, a central character which gives his leading player something well worth acting, and so gives Albert Finney a chance to show us that he can carry a serious and important play on his shoulders.

Mr. Finney gives a fine study of a completely honest and sincere man fighting against impossible odds and somehow winning through.

A FAULT OF AUTHOR'S

If he does not quite convince us that the man is driven by the force of a deep religious faith, that is not his fault but the author's.

(July 28)

SCALA CHEERS FOR JOAN SUTHERLAND

From MARTIN COOPER

MILAN, Sunday.

JOAN SUTHERLAND scored a triumphal success at La Scala here in a gala performance of Donizetti's "Lucia di Lammermoor."

She was to have sung the title role in the same composer's "Beatrice di Tenda," but disagreements with the conductor Vittorio Gui on the choice of text eventually proved insuperable and the better known work was substituted.

Any disagreement on this count was largely offset by Miss Sutherland's performance, characterised throughout by a firm line and radiant tone. This is matched by an absolute security and a graceful effortlessness in the florid passages with which the work abounds.

If she started the Mad Scene a trifle uncertainly, this may well have been due to a production very different from that to which she is accustomed in London.

SHOWERED WITH FLOWERS

The audience showered the stage with flowers plucked from the gala decorations of the house.

She was admirably supported by a cast including Ettore Bastianini (Enrico), Regolo Romani (Arturo) and Giuseppe Modesti (Bide-the-Bent), but otherwise dominated by Gianni Raimondi (Edgardo).

Here was a voice that warmed noticeably during the evening and a controlled dramatic incisiveness of manner.

(April 17)

BBC CHILDREN'S HOUR TO END

By A TV and Radio Correspondent

CHILDREN'S Hour is to be dropped by the BBC in April after being a regular Home Service feature since 1922. Instead young people are to have their own radio programme nearly two hours every day during the week.

From April 10, "Playtime" will be broadcast daily in the Light Programme between 4.30 and 5.30 p.m. Designed to appeal to young people and adults, it will coincide with schoolchildren arriving home and consist mainly of specially-chosen gramophone records.

Daily programmes between 5 p.m. and 5.55 p.m. in the Home Service will continue to cater for children. "Junior Time" for the very young talks, and such popular features as "Jennings" and "Toytown" will be retained.

(February 8)

CHALLENGING CELLIST AT 16

GRAVITY & POISE OF JACQUELINE DU PRE

By MARTIN COOPER

THIS country has produced very few string players of the first rank, but it may well be that last night's concert at Wigmore Hall revealed a cellist who will reach international rank. At 16 Jacqueline du Pré plays with a technical assurance, a range of tone and a musical understanding that challenge comparison with those of all but the very finest cellists.

Her ability to carry through a phrase to its very end and the gravity and poise of her line-drawing were already remarkable in the finale of a Handel sonata. Her instinctive rubato in the trio of Brahms's E minor sonata only emphasised the vigorous strength of her rhythms in general.

Brahms's last movement demands a greater volume of tone than she could quite muster (not that the duel with the piano is ever a very happy one).

But she brought to the Serenade of Debussy's sonata a mock-rhetorical incisiveness and a gamut of colour from which only the composer's favourite silvery tone was perhaps absent.

(March 3)

Recent Fiction

Bomb in a Bloomsbury Eden

By PETER GREEN

A Severed Head
By IRIS MURDOCH
(CHATTO 18s)

SUBTLE irony, the exquisite intellectual leg-pull, is a dangerous weapon for even the most skilful novelist. There is always the danger that people may miss the point, or, worse, take barbed satire at its literal face value.

Let me make it clear beyond all possible doubt, then, that "A Severed Head" is a wickedly brilliant attack on rationalist ethics, a lethal bomb exploded under the Bloomsbury personal-relationship cult.

At first, indeed, so demure is the narrative, so elegantly deadpan the presentation, one doesn't see what Iris Murdoch is up to. Her hero, Martin Lynch-Gibbon, is a happy, cultured prig, with a good sinecure in the wine business, a smart wife, Antonia, rather older than himself, and a young mistress, Georgie, who lectures at the L.S.E. In his spare time he does a little amateur historical research. He has no religion; hedonism and sweet reason suffice.

The scene being set, Miss Murdoch proceeds to turn this pseudoparadisal enclave upside-down, Antonia suddenly announces she wants to marry her psycho-analyst, Palmer Anderson, on whom Martin turns out to have a mild homosexual fixation, and whose relations with his own sister, the formidable Dr. Honor Klein, will not bear over-close examination. By the time Miss Murdoch is through with her pawns, practically all the men have switched partners at least once, in a weird sort of sexual Musical Chairs.

The moral seems to be that the old Forsterian adage of "Only connect" can lead to disastrous consequences if overdone. All the characters in this modern morality-play are so reasonable, so enlightened. They bear no grudges (they say). They discuss situations like civilised human beings. Yet their whims are random and childish (spiritual nihilism is matched by emotional self-deceit) and their rational façade is constantly being ripped open by hysteria, violence, abortion, attempted suicide.

Miss Murdoch's wit is as sharp and merciless as the Samurai sword with which, Saladin-like, Honor Klein divides handkerchiefs in two. This brilliant satire should set the seal on her deservedly high reputation.

(June 16)

The Prime of Miss Jean Brodie
By MURIEL SPARK
(Macmillan 13s 6d)

SCOTTISH schooldays, in Edinburgh this time, also form the setting of Muriel Spark's new novel "The Prime of Miss Jean Brodie": we shall be lucky if we see a more idiosyncratic piece of fiction this year. Mrs. Spark is *sui generis* with a vengeance, and never takes the easy way out by repeating her earlier successes. The unorthodox, original teacher with a personal touch is a recurrent phenomenon: Mrs. Spark takes one such, and subjects her to a cool, searching, dispassionate analysis.

Miss Brodie is odd, to say the least of it. She has her "set" - Monica, Rose, Eunice, Mary and Sandy - and inculcates all manner of inflammatory and subversive ideas into their heads. The period is the mid-1930s and Miss Brodie has pictures of marching Black-shirts in her room.

And yet, and yet, what splendid yeast Miss Brodie puts into the doughy curriculum of the Marcia Blaine School. It would be hard to assert that the members of her "set" were not, ultimately, the better for her influence, and I fancy Mrs. Spark meant us to feel this.

Her short novel is a miracle of wit and aphorism: every word goes home like a well-aimed arrow.

(November 3)

THE DAILY TELEGRAPH
AND
MORNING POST
DAILY TELEGRAPH - - - JUNE 29, 1855
MORNING POST - - - NOVEMBER 2, 1772
[Amalgamated October 1, 1937]
135, Fleet Street, London, E.C.4.
Telephone: Fleet Street 4242

VERDICT ON EICHMANN

GUILTY - the verdict on EICHMANN was a foregone conclusion. Indeed, in the minds of men he had been tried and condemned long before he was captured and brought to Israel. His activities were known to be what they have now been legally proved to be: they were as much a part of history, as little open to honest doubt, as those of NAPOLEON. EICHMANN could indeed plead superior orders, and has done so. He has described himself as "merely a tool in the hands of higher authorities and in the hands of a merciless fate." But, alas, the prosecution had little difficulty in proving that he remained in the SS of his own free will and choice, that he carried out his duties with a monstrous zeal and relish and that, on occasion, he went far beyond orders from which most men would have shrunk back in horror.

Soon now to be answered, the question still remains, "What are they going to do with him?" It has been suggested that EICHMANN, having served his purpose, should simply be taken back to Argentina and dumped at the very bus stop from which he was spirited away. And certainly his personal fate seems to have become in a sense an irrelevance, a redundant postscript. He cannot very well go free and unpunished: he would hardly survive an hour if he did. Yet the punishment to fit his crimes has not yet been devised.

Most of what his trial was designed to do it has already achieved. It has established to some extent what Mr. BEN-GURION is said to have wanted it to establish: that the State of Israel has claims to represent all Jews throughout the world and to act as the heir and executor of all those who perished in the "Final Solution." The trial has also placed on record for all time as much as will ever be known of what the Jews surrendered under the Nazi tyranny. In doing so it reminds the world of what led to the formation of a Jewish State, of what made such a State seem no longer merely desirable but a desperate necessity.

One thing, perhaps, remains for the trial to do, whether by design or despite itself, and this is to help forwards a German-Jewish reconciliation. If EICHMANN'S death could help to assuage hatred and bitterness, to close the book of the past and enable a fresh start to be made, then he would not die for nothing. And if he is permitted to live, that too will be something for him and us to ponder.

(December 12)

A CASE FOR EUROPE

To join or not to join the Common Market? The debate in Britain has come to be dominated by material and probably inaccurate calculations of possible gain or loss. Our proud title "a nation of shopkeepers" should not be so demeaned. We are not shopkeepers without vision or statesmanship. This is not to say that economic considerations are of scant importance; on the contrary, they are often capable, if overlooked or lightly brushed aside, of exacting the most terrible vengeance and of bringing to naught all the political plans of those who work in their despite. Yet the affairs of nations cannot be conducted prudently on profit and loss alone. This was the main theme of the campaign launched by LORD GLADWYN and an impressive list of all-party colleagues yesterday.

To those who have done most to bring it into being, the Common Market appears a good thing indeed in itself, but not an end in itself. It is rather a means to an end, which is nothing less than the union of Europe on a federal or confederate basis. Recent European history might have been designed to make such an end seem desirable. The two pre-eminent political changes since the Second World War have been the end of American isolationism and the healing of the quarrel between Gaul and Teuton. The Common Market, with us in it, will consolidate these saving mercies.

(May 26)

NEW TOWN LIFE

Life in the New Towns is handicapped by the fact that most people start off as strangers to each other. It was to overcome this and the even greater handicap of having no ready-made community patterns to follow that the idea of the neighbourhood unit was evolved. Yet what the neighbourhood units lack, above all, according to the Ministry of Housing's annual report, is neighbourliness. Have the sociologists and town planners missed the bus in prescribing this particular housing layout? Is the newcomer's initially invigorating experience of having more space, more light and bright architecture after living in drab city streets inevitably to be followed by a sense of loneliness and isolation and what the report calls "New Town blues"?

Much can be done of course, to recreate the sense of social intimacy through the provision of community buildings for cultural, recreational and social activities. But this takes time, and in time people get to know each other anyway.

But that is somewhat beside the point. The new towns, by the very layout of their houses, shops and public places, ought positively to contribute to the feeling that the people belong from the very start to a community. Here the report strikes a sceptical note. The planners may well have over-reached themselves in providing for low-density occupation and the spaciousness of a semi-rural atmosphere. If the intimate life of the city streets is to be recaptured, the planners of the new towns of the future might well find it important to aim at a more truly urban design than they have hitherto accepted.

(August 4)

A BIBLE WITH A NEW IMPACT

By Professor HENRY CHADWICK

The translators of the New English Bible of which the New Testament is published to-day, set out to make it both intelligible and readable. These aims, in the view of the Regius Professor of Divinity at Oxford University, they have brilliantly achieved.

THE appearance of the New Testament in the New English Bible marks the first stage in a great enterprise which began in 1946 on the initiative of the Church of Scotland and was soon entrusted to a Joint Committee, representing the main Christian bodies of the British Isles other than the Roman Catholics.

This Committee appointed four panels of scholars, chosen without regard to denomination, to deal respectively with the Old Testament, the Apocrypha, the New Testament, and the literary style of the whole.

The translators' terms of reference were to produce neither a revision of any existing version (as the 1881 Revisers treated the Authorised Version, or as King James's men treated their predecessors, or even as the American Revised Standard Version of 1946 treated AV and RV); nor a translation of a translation (as Ronald Knox translated St. Jerome's Latin); but a fresh translation of the Apostles, Greek in "the current speech of our own time."

CLOSE TO PARAPHRASE

IT means the abandonment of the principle dear to the 1881 Revisers (though robustly rejected in the AV preface) that the same Greek word should everywhere be rendered by the same English word; this is warmly to be welcomed, though it will inconvenience those whose sole aid to Bible study is a concordance.

More radically, it means jettisoning the Greek word-order and sentence structure. Inevitably, therefore, the translators have sailed close to the wind of paraphrase. In the preface they protest that, free as it is, their work is a "translation in the strict sense and not a paraphrase." The aim is intelligibility and readability. The method has the disadvantage that the NEB is unusable as a student's crib.

The acutest problems are raised by passages charged with Old Testament allusions. There is a tendency to sacrifice the allusion to achieve clarity.

A minor example is Ephesians 6, XV: "Let the shoes on your feet be the gospel of peace, to give you firm footing." A highly controversial instance is the beginning of St. John.

Boldly to begin, "When all things began, the Word already was" is decisive and defensible; but the overtones of Genesis are lost and something of the mystery also.

Certain passages become intelligible for the first time. According to the AV of John 16, X the Paraclete will "convict of righteousness, because I go to the Father and ye see me no more." According to NEB, "your Advocate . . . . will convince them (viz. the world) that right is on my side, by showing that I go to the Father when I pass from your sight." Another instance is the Beatitude (Matt. 5, iii): "How blest are those who know that they are poor."

An interesting detail is the Anglicisation of certain weights, measures times and seasons. The perfume used at the Anointing (Mark 14, V) could have been sold for "thirty pounds" (300 denarii). The talents of the parable become bags of gold. The man who owed 10,000 talents had a debt which "ran into millions." The fourth watch of the night becomes "between three and six in the morning." The wind that shipwrecked St. Paul is not Euroclydon but the "north-easter." The days of unleavened bread become "the Passover season."

DRAMATIC VARIANT

NEW TESTAMENT manuscripts have been so intensively studied in the past century that the translators have been able to work from printed editions. A dramatic variant is followed in Pilate's question (Matt. 27, xvii): "Which would you like me to release to you - Jesus Bar-Abbas or Jesus called Messiah?"

The NEB speaks with intense power, even in the Gospels, where our feelings are most deeply engaged and associations are strongest. It is not, however, the authority of solemn majesty and numinous mystery but rather that of directness and immediacy. The Sermon on the Mount does not come to us in hieratic prose out of the swirling mists, but as a personal confrontation. The impatience with humbug and direct simplicity of the language make the impact inescapable.

This is not to say that there are no regrets. The AV "Solomon in all his glory was not arrayed like one of these" is incomparable. "Splendour" and "attired" do not seem more contemporary; one could understand a change from arrayed to clothed.

There are plenty of lively phrases, but some grate on the ear. The five thousand ate "to their hearts' content"; the prodigal son began "to feel the pinch"; at Nazareth they "fell foul of him." The effect of the discourses in St. John is at some moments banal: "I am the real vine and my Father is the gardener." The reaction to the teaching concerning the bread of life is "This is more than we can stomach!" (John 6, lx). These renderings are accurate enough.

The dialogue with Nicodemus, however, is fresh and alive, without shocks to the reader's sensitivity; and the slight elevation of style in the Lucan canticles is highly successful, the Magnificat being breathtaking. The Beatitudes achieve not only clarity but delicacy.

The initial impression made by the Gospels is that the style, though direct and vigorous, has irritating lapses into cheapness and that "the language of to-day," as here used, is inadequate to the full stature required by the subject. We may not blame the translators (or the literary panel) for the deficiency which merely reflects the debased state of the contemporary usage into which they were instructed to translate the scriptures.

The final verdict must be that the NEB succeeds in its aims. Conservative lovers of the AV will find some things uncongenial; but the evidence is overwhelming that the AV is no longer understood. The NEB is the Bible for the beat generation.

*** "The New English Bible: New Testament." (OUP; CUP, 21s library edition; 8s 6d popular edition.)**

(March 14)

CASH BETTING SHOPS ARE HARD TO FIND

CURB ON ADVERTISING

Daily Telegraph Reporter

The Betting and Gaming Act came into force yesterday, but for the punter who wants the novelty of placing a ready-money bet off the course betting shopd are not easy to find.

Two aching feet bear painful witness to the fact. The shops are there, of course. Finding them is the trouble.

After a tour of Soho I had acquired considerable knowedge of establishments devoted to "strip" shows, including one that boasts intriguingly that the cast is all female. But I failed to find the betting shop that I am assured is there.

The reason is that bookmakers are legally restricted in the manner in which they may advertise their premises. Their name and "Licensed Betting Office" in 3in high letters is all that is permitted.

(May 2)

UNWILLING PEER

Lord Stansgate's arguments have been turned down by the committee of Privileges. In its opinion, he has succeeded to a title which he can neither renounce nor surrender and that is that. It remains for him to present himself again as Labour candidate for South-East Bristol. But his colleagues have to face the risk that, if adopted and subsequently victorious at the poll, he might be replaced on petition by his Conservative opponent. They may wish all the luck in the world to his campaign for "common sense and personal freedom": but not perhaps at such a price.

Few of us, if asked, would sniff at the opportunity of sitting in a place which is even now graced by the Foreign Secretary. This last fact incidentally disposes of any idea that Lord Stansgate's political career must necessarily end with ennoblement, though it may suggest that he belongs to the wrong party. Yet Lord Stansgate is not the first Peer to be dragged upstairs kicking and screaming. Lord Hailsham before him showed a certain reluctance, and there will be others no doubt to come.

All of this is rather disquieting. Our legislature is — or is meant to be — bi-cameral. One of its chambers is the House of Lords, membership of which ought thus to be a real and valued honour, a legitimate aspiration of able, ambitious and active men. Lord Stansgate looks just such a man, yet he plainly regards the House of Lords as no place for him. The fundamental question is this : how well can we manage with a House of Lords which he and his like regard as a graveyard? If the House of Lords were allowed to perform its proper constitutional functions, no one would wish to dodge membership. They would be fighting to get in.

(March 22)

"PIRATE RADIO OFF HOLLAND"

BROADCASTING SHIP

By A Radio Correspondent

A commercial radio station, intending to appeal to British audiences and broadcasting from a ship anchored off the coast of Holland, is due to begin programmes on Feb. 1. Experimental transmissions on a 192-metre wavelength started some weeks ago.

The "pirate" station, an Anglo-Dutch venture is housed in a German-built vessel, Veronica, 457 tons. She is anchored in international waters 5 miles from the shore.

(January 16)

MORE HOSPITALS

MR. ENOCH POWELL does not seem to have let the grass of the Welfare State grow under his feet since his appointment as Minister of Health. Yesterday he announced an impressive programme of hospital building which envisages, as it always ought to have done, long-term plans, generously conceived, with a greater devolution of financial responsibility to the hospital boards. During the next 10-year period, as much as £500m. may be spent on hospital work. As from next month, the maximum cost of individual projects which the hospital boards can undertake without prior ministerial approval will be doubled, from £30,000 to £60,000. And Mr. POWELL has said that during the second five years of the scheme, the boards will not be bound to financial limits in formulating their schemes.

Different circumstances and different responsibilities change a politician's outlook. When he was at the Treasury, Mr POWELL was noted for his Puritanic refusal to countenance increased Government expenditure. His new generosity will be welcome, for hospital building has lagged far behind the requirements of the Health Service. But can the Minister guarantee that the hospitals, once built, will be adequately staffed and serviced? Even in the existing buildings, there have been complaints of dirt and neglect. That is the second, and no less urgent, problem to which the Minister must turn his agile talent for administration.

(January 17)

LONDON DAY BY DAY

Television Ban
The Last Ride

THE Dean of York, Dr. Milner-White, has placed a year's interdict on television in the Minster. It is the result of his experience at the wedding of the Duke of Kent and means that the enthronement later this year of Dr. Coggan as 93rd Archbishop of York will not be seen on any channel.

The Clerk of the Works, Mr. Green, tells me that the ban has nothing to do with the slight damage to the fabric discovered after the wedding.

It is due to the Dean's conviction that television cameras, with their attendant operators and gear, are an undesirable intrusion on a solemn religious occasion. They proved seriously distracting at the wedding.

"I always do this on Trafalgar Day."

Fairwell to Jim

Sir Alexander Robertson has fulfilled forty-two years of servicein the Metropolitan Police.

Yesterday as Deputy Commissioner he led the police on duty at the State Opening of Parliament. To-day he retires, a few weeks before his 65th birthday. His chestnut gelding, Jim, will have a new master.

Sir Alexander's career is singular in that he achieved every rank in the Force from constable to Deputy Commissioner. Not even the Commissioner, Sir Joseph Simpson, held every rank on the way up.

In the Scots Guards in World War I, Robertson became a company sergeant major and won the D.C.M. on the Somme. He joined the Metropolitan Police in 1919.

Rising for John

AUGUSTUS JOHN received one tribute in his youth which it is hard to imagine any British painter receiving nowadays even in maturity. When he moved to Chelsea after the success of his Chenil Gallery exhibition in 1908, he joined the artists frequenting the Café Royal. As he entered art students used to stand up as a mark of respect.

Admittedly, John was easy to recognise, with his red beard and flamboyant dress. But he had scarcely reached 30.

I have never forgotten seeing him years ago on a Welsh mountain, riding a comparatively minute pony to a hillside scattering of the ashes of a friend who shared his passion for the gypsies. If I may so put it, he stole the show.

Farthings Still Money

MANY people and some newspapers seem to be under a misapprehension about farthings.

Yesterday was the first working day since they have ceased to be legal tender but they are still money.

The distinction, I am told, is that a creditor is bound to accept legal tender but may refuse mere money. Scottish banknotes are an analogy.

They are not legal tender in England but if a creditor is willing to accept them they can be used to pay a bill here.

One Can Breathe Again

"FOUND a green budgerigar. She is safe and happy, although a little tired." - Notice outside a house in Hampstead.

PETERBOROUGH

MRS. KENNEDY'S PARIS WARDROBE

AS if to squash for once and for all the rumours that Mrs. Kennedy will take a Givenchy dress with her to Paris this week, Oleg Cassini, her official couturier, yesterday released sketches of clothes he has designed for the visit.

They are a day ensemble of a turquoise and white plaid, sheer wool dress with a matching pale turquoise coat (far left), and two evening dresses.

Left is the gown she will wear at dinner at the Chateau de Versailles on Thursday. Made of pink and white straw lace, it has scalloped detail at the edge of its bateau neckline and hem.

The dress on the right is for President de Gaulle's dinner at the Elysée Palace on Wednesday, the first night of the visit.

It is a one-shouldered dress with a back panel from the side. The white organza over yellow organza is delicately embroidered, with additional jewelled embroidery at the hem and the border of the back panel.

(May 29)

There's an Enchanted-Island Atmosphere in the Luxurious Playgrounds of Beirut

THE enchantment begins at the airport when even the tough-faced Customs officer smiles and says "welcome to Lebanon." To anyone flying in from rain-swept, wintery Britain, Beirut is a dazzling place. It is gay, exotic and extrovert. It lies ringed by pink-mauve mountains with its feet in the sea.

By day it is charged with colour. The hot golden sun beats down on the paprika-coloured earth, the gleaming skyscrapers, lush banana plantations and glossy orange groves. In the warm night air, a thousand lights blaze out festooning the hills around like jewels, while in the city the 300-odd night clubs and bars (in one street I counted 30 within 200 yards of each other) glitter with attractions - anything from the latest Paris chanteuse to Hawaiian singers and Egyptian belly dancers.

Beirut has all the glamour of the East plus the glossy sophistication of the West. You can lunch on superb French food and wines and later shop for a bottle of Dior perfume (cheaper than in Paris) or a Cardin tie. Or you can sip your arak (it tastes like anise) accompanied by mezze (an elaborate, mixed hors d'oeuvre eaten with drinks) and perhaps try - for the fun of it - a hubble-bubble pipe, and afterwards forage the narrow down-town streets for Damascus brocades (£1-34 a yard), turquoise and gold harem rings, embroidered Bedouin head squares, and inlaid wooden boxes.

It is the playground of the Middle East. The rich oil sheikhs sweep into town itching to spend their wealth. They honk through the streets in outsize chromium-encrusted cars.

But you don't have to be a millionaire to enjoy Beirut. Just to relax in the warm sun with a glass of fresh orange juice and watch the fascinating street scene is an adventure.

There is an enchanted-island atmosphere about Beirut. I heard of people who had come for three days and stayed seven years.

Bathing is good. There are golden sands at Jnah, 10 minutes out of Beirut (a taxi will cost you 6s), or the choice of many *plages* right in town - the Sporting Club is one, where you dive into the most transparent water I have ever seen. (Charges for beach facilities and a cabin chair vary from 2s 6d to 4s 6d a day.)

MODERN HOTELS

Hotels, alas, are not cheap, though they are not half as expensive as many people believe. They are all modern and air conditioned. A de-luxe hotel with swimming pool costs £3 10s a day for bed and breakfast, and a first-class hotel - such as Lords just across the road from the beach - £2 a day, while at the excellent second-class Mayflower Hotel you can live comfortably for approximately £2 a day all-in.

BERYL HARTLAND

(January 4)

INTERNATIONAL ROCK AT BATTERSEA

"There's more to teenagers than rock and roll," was the obvious, but serious comment of a young boy at an international teenage party held in Battersea Festival Gardens this week.

"Older people generally think of teenagers as a leather-jacketed, tight-jeaned, side-boarded mob," said David Jacobs, idol of "Juke Box Jury" fans, who was there to see that the 200 young people met each other and enjoyed a happy jiving evening. "The majority are not," he added firmly, "and we're hoping to bring this home to people and perhaps have more of these gatherings in the future."

(June 23)

RUTH BOWLEY asks young secretaries . . .

IS WORKING IN LONDON WORTH WHILE

IN London a fully-qualified secretary can expect a starting salary of £9 to £10, plus luncheon vouchers. An experienced secretary will earn £15 and upwards a week. In the provinces a girl probably begins at £6 and her maximum salary is unlikely to be more than £10. Luncheon vouchers are the exception.

Obviously London offers the big money, but is the higher paid secretary really better off than her country cousin? As the cost of daily travelling to town continues to rise and the rent of furnished accommodation shows no sign of falling, this is the question a number of girls are asking themselves.

Is London, in fact, worth while?

To find the answer to this question I have been checking on the cost of working in London with girls who share flats in Kensington, Hampstead and Chelsea, and with those who live at home and travel some distance to town.

All these girls have been in their jobs at least a year and now have salaries of £11 to £12 a week.

The general opinion seems to be that one cannot live in London on less than £6 a week. To prove this, Robina, a young secretary, who has been in her first job for a year, gave me her weekly budget which I think is typical of many.

She came to London from the country and shares a furnished flat in Hampstead with two other girls. She earns £9 10s a week, after income-tax and insurance have been deducted, and has 15s worth of luncheon vouchers.

All housekeeping costs are shared equally between the three and the girls take it in turn to do the cooking. Robina goes home at most week-ends and though the fare is heavy she reckons she would spend as much on extra food and amusements if she stayed in London.

This is her weekly budget:

	£	s	d
Share of rent	2	18	0
Food in flat	1	0	0
Heating, cooking and lighting		7	6
Laundry (bed linen and towels)		2	0
Lunches (supplement to L.V.'s)		10	0
Fares to and from office		9	2
Fares home at weekends	1	0	0
Total	£6	6	8

This budget leaves Robina with £3 odd a week pocket-money to cover all expenses, including clothes, holidays and hair-do's. (As the standard of dress and appearance at her office is high (much higher, she thinks, than in the provinces) Robina is always stretching her budget.

She shops carefully in the big London stores for clothes, but has her hair done in her home town at week-ends to save paying West End prices. Theatre-going is rationed to once a month, and even entertaining in the flat makes a hole in the budget.

The daily commuter, if she lives fairly near London, is probably better off financially. Susan, who earns in the City about the same as Robina, travels from Woking every day.

Her weekly season is £1 16s 3d. She contributes 30s towards her keep at home and her lunches and fares in town come to £1 a week, leaving her £5 a week pocket money. Certainly she had more to spend on luxuries, but sometimes she is envious of Robina's independence.

(October 18)

CHRISTMAS DAY POST DELIVERY "SUSPENDED"

MR. REGINALD BEVINS, the Postmaster-General, has decided to suspend the Christmas Day delivery this year in England, Wales and Northern Ireland, but the Christmas Eve deliveries will be augmented, the G.P.O. announced yesterday.

The change relates only to this year. But the experience gained will be helpful in deciding what should be done about the Christmas Day delivery in future years.

(September 29)

Go One Better Play an Electric Organ

HAVE you noticed the quiet revolution which is taking place in home entertainment?

Piano sales are up, so are those of sheet music. Cine-photography and colour slides are enjoying tremendous popularity, and at the Radio Show it was the tape recorder people who were looking most pleased with themselves.

Suddenly we have been bitten with an urge to do things. To sit square-eyed and goggle at the television just won't do any longer. Besides, there seems little point in buying a new television set now until the Pilkington committee have decided whether our sets are to have 405 or 625 lines.

If you want to go one better than a piano you can buy an electronic organ. It doesn't take up much more space than a piano and for about £400 you can have one which has as good a tone as a large church organ.

A tape recorder is perhaps the next best thing for those who are musically inclined but can't play an instrument. It offers great scope for experimenting with sound.

Photographer Peter Williams and his friends are still trying to perfect their recordings of Shakespeare recited to an off-beat background of jazz, played on a dulcimer. The result is certainly interesting - if a little odd.

Cinematography and tape recorders can be used in conjunction with one another, though personally I think that it is a bit pompous to record a dialogue to accompany your holiday films.

"Home movies" have now been simplified to the point where you can buy a camera which practically does everything "automatically" except point itself at the subject you want filmed.

ELIZABETH BENN

(September 5)

BAN ON FRILLY PETTICOATS

SCHOOLGIRLS at the Alun Grammar School, Mold, Flintshire, have been told by their headmistress that they must not wear nylons, cosmetics and petticoats in school. They have also been forbidden to dye their hair.

Miss G.M. Parry, the head-mistress, in a letter to parents has given a warning that girls who break the school-dress rules will be sent home.

(October 30)

HARDY AMIES
(NOW DESIGNING FOR MEN)

•

BANISHES BAGGY FLANNELS

Gentlemen, be ready to diet. In his first ready-to-wear collection for men - the latest venture in his ever-growing fashion empire - Hardy Amies, the courtourier, has designed an extra slim tapered line.

Trousers often have plain fronts (single pleats are the maximum) and the legs taper to 17in at the bottom. Not a single pair had turn-ups. "I'm all for that," said one middle-aged businessman. "I'm not", said another, "My teenage sons don't wear turn-ups and I wouldn't dream of dressing like them."

"Away with the baggy flannels," said Mr. Amies, and for casual wear with slim slacks he has designed easy-fitting jackets half-way between a sports jacket and a car coat, to wear over bulky sweaters. He calls them sweater-jackets.

(September 12)

M. ST. LAURENT STARTS ALONE

M. Yves St. Laurent intends to open his own fashion establishment in January. After being called up for military service, he lost his job as chief designer for the House of Dior to M. Marc Bohan.

Now 25, M. St. Laurent hopes that his independent firm will produce clothes for the spring shows next year. He has strong financial backing but refuses to say from whom.

He plans to employ 70 people and to run three workrooms.

(September 22)

DR. C.G. JUNG

WORLD FAMOUS PSYCHOLOGIST

DR. CARL GUSTAV JUNG, who has died aged 85, was the last survivor of the triumvirate of eminent psychologists whose theories and doctrine set the early years of this century throbbing with controversy. The other two were Freud and Adler.

A Swiss, Jung collaborated with Freud for some years, but broke away in 1913 to found his own school of "analytical psychology." Less materialist than Freud, he preached the acceptance of spiritual factors: he also deprecated Freud's insistence that sexual repression was responsible for the bulk of human misery.

"Sex is a playground for lonely scientists," said Jung. "Primitive man had the sex instinct, but he was much more deeply concerned with feeding himself." Once, to gain first-hand information of the life of African tribes, he camped with one for several months in a remote part of Central Africa.

"THE SHADOW"

To Jung we owe the expressions "complex," "extrovert" and "collective unconscious" as a reservoir of common patterns of human experience which continually reappear.

He described pre-existent forms of apprehension as archetypes, all of which affect human thought and behaviour, and sub-divided them into such categories as the "shadow," that side of our personality we dislike and fear, the "anima," the female component of the male psyche, and the "animus," the male component of the female psyche.

The son of a country parson, Carl Gustav Jung was born at Keswyl, in the Canton Thurgau. Educated at Basle, where he secured his medical degree, he specialised for some years in nervous and medical diseases. Psychiatric studies in Paris were followed by employment in a clinic at Zurich and by his association with Freud.

He lectured on psychology at Zurich University from 1905-13, and from 1933-41, when his reputation had become international, he was Professor of Psychology at the Federal Technical University in Zurich. A distinguished classical scholar, he held honorary degrees from eight universities, including Oxford and Harvard.

PROLIFIC WRITER

He was a prolific writer on psychiatry; among his best-known works were "Psychological Types," "Modern Man in Search of a Soul," and "The Relations Between the Ego and the Unconscious."

(June 7)

DASHIELL HAMMETT

DASHIELL HAMMETT, who has died aged 66, was a highly successful writer of detective stories whose name for nearly 30 years has been linked with that of his most successful creation, "The Thin Man." Its publication, in 1934, followed two best-selling previous novels "The Dain Curse" and "Red Harvest."

An immediate success as a novel, it brought him international fame, and earned him a large income when it was filmed, with William Powell as Nick Charles and Myrna Loy as his wife, Nora. This was the basis of a series of "Thin Man" films which, in recent years, also became a television series.

"The Maltese Falcon," and "The Glass Key," the last of his novels, were among his best-known books. He wrote many of the film and radio scripts of his creations but always claimed that the Thin Man bored him.

DETECTIVE EXPERIENCE

Experience as a detective, working for the famous American agency, Pinkerton's, gave him "know how" when he began writing detective stories in 1922. Among one of his cases was that of Roscoe "Fatty" Arbuckle.

After leaving school at 14, Hammett worked as a messenger boy, clerk in an advertising office, time-keeper in a cannery, stevedore, and in other jobs. He served in both world wars.

In 1951, he did two months of a six months' gaol sentence for refusing to disclose who had put up bail for convicted Communists.

(January 11)

THE MAN WHO WAS THE UNITED NATIONS

From IAN BALL
NEW YORK

IT is hard to think of any development that could plunge the United Nations into deeper crisis than Mr. Hammarskjoeld's death at this time. It poses immediate and long-term problems the outcome of which will bring about enormous changes in the character of the United Nations.

It is a tribute to the strength and determination of the man that the "new" United Nations is almost entirely his creation. Admittedly, he did it with the encouragement of the organisation's most powerful political and financial supporter, the United States. But that he achieved even a fraction of what he set out to do is an astonishing accomplishment.

At some point during his first term as Secretary-General - perhaps it was Suez - he decided that the United Nations must be something more than a simple debating society, "a static conference machinery" in his desiccated language. He felt that world events, principally the polarisation of power and the emergence of brash and inexperienced new nations, required the United Nations to develop into a "dynamic instrument of government."

No Testament

IN the turbulent situation his death must bequeath to the organisation, it is difficult to prognosticate. But I feel fairly safe in predicting that the United Nations will not in future be able to intervene in a crisis as positively as it did in the Congo.

Mr. Hammarskjoeld leaves no political will and testament for the organisation. The Russians may or may not come to the formal wake. But once the official period of mourning is past they will have their chance to strike.

In touting his troika plan for the United Nations Executive - a Westerner, a Communist and a neutral each with veto power acting in Mr. Hammarskjoeld's stead - Mr. Khruschev has left the impression among many neutrals that he is willing to bide his time. By this he meant until April 1963, when Mr. Hammarskjoeld's second five-year term as Secretary-General would have expired.

The situation that would have arisen then is suddenly forced on the members. Mr. Khruschev of course, can veto any candidate the West offers. He has already scorned the Asians and Africans with his resumption of atmospheric testing. It seems quite certain that he would be willing to insult the 46 members of the Afro-Asian bloc again by rejecting their candidate for Secretary-General.

For in the absence of a Soviet veto over the post and the Kremlin's insistence on triumvirate control, it would have been left to these African and Asian States to name his successor.

An Indian most likely, but possibly an Egyptian or a Tunisian. Certainly a non-European.

It is ironic that the human factor now plays such a dominant part in legalisms that Mr. Hammarskjoeld erected in New York and around the world. If we try to chart the future we can rule out military intervention by an international force unless it is in effect a Western move carried out under some sort of mandate from 50 or so of the General Assembly's 99 members.

Mr. Hammarskjoeld understood the realities of world politics as well as any statesman alive. When they had no more original ideas American newspaper cartoonists used to fall back on the theme of a distraught-looking Dag on the tightrope between East and West. The cliché had merit though.

Life of Service

WAS Mr. Hammarskjoeld a megalomaniac? Far from it. I feel that few statesmen in history have held such a detached view of the power at their disposal.

Even Mr. Khruschev in denouncing Mr. Hammarskjoeld as a lackey and a wilful tool of the imperialists must privately have had some respect for the dedication and courage of this diffident and remote Swede.

Dag Hammarskjoeld inherited from his father his ideas of a life devoted to public service. From his family background he acquired a special brand of political noblesse oblige, an inbred feeling of being part of an elite. His forebears include a host of Swedish Prime Ministers, generals and archbishops.

DAG HAMMARKSKJOELD
"That he achieved even a fraction of what he set out to do is an astonishing achievement.."

Many aspects of his life as an international civil servant must have been distasteful to a man of such highly cultivated taste and lofty intellect. The inanities of the Congo situation for instance, would have driven to distraction even someone of plodding mentality.

Into the Morning

SOUVENIRS of office, the spears and bark paintings and bongo drums that he collected on his official tours of Africa, are scattered about his New York home, on show presumably in case he was called upon to entertain a representative of one of the donor Governments. How they clashed with his personal tastes we can only imagine.

His interests included modern poetry, particularly T.S. Elliot, the more antiseptic abstract painters, classical music, again limited to a few composers, walking and mountain climbing.

He was a remarkable man, a giant in an assembly of world leaders. Even those who have assailed his policies will sincerely mourn his passing.

(September 19)

GEORGE FORMBY

ONE OF BRITAIN'S GREAT COMEDIANS

THE POLULARITY of George Formby, who has died aged 56, wholly eclipsed that of his father, the Lancashire comedian of the same name who died in 1921.

The younger Formby was in a position to duplicate his music-hall successes in films, on gramophone records and on the radio, and when in 1951, he starred in "Zip Goes a Million" at the Palace Theatre, he established his West End reputation.

He was one of the highest-paid British comedians. In 1950 he earned £35,000 by a seven-week tour of Canada, and his income at the Palace was reputed to be more than £1,500 a week.

Born at Wigan, he was apprenticed at the age of seven to a racing stable at Middleham, Yorkshire, and rode in his first race three years later.

EARLY STAGE NAME

Increasing weight halted his career as a jockey, and, after the death of his father, whose music-hall act he never saw, Formby made his first appearance on the stage under the name of George Hoy.

He reverted to the name of Formby within two years, but his act, consisting of songs to the accompaniment of a ukelele, did not vary. His toothy grin soon became familiar to audiences all over the country.

He refused many lucrative offers, including one from Hollywood, during the 1939-45 War in order to entertain the troops. With his wife, Beryl, as his partner, he was in the first concert party to land in Normandy, and he subsequently toured North Africa, Italy, and India and Burma. Since the war he had visited several Commonwealth countries.

For six successive years he headed a British film box-office popularity poll. Among his films were "No Limit," "Trouble Brewing," "Spare a Copper," and "George in Civvy Street." He appeared in several Royal Command performances.

GEORGE FORMBY

WEAK HEART

Since the war a weak heart had troubled him, causing him to retire more than once from performances. He was playing in pantomime at Bristol when his wife Beryl died at their Lytham St. Annes home on Christmas morning. It was the end of a partnership, begun in 1924, during which he had many times paid tribute to his wife's contribution behind the scenes to his success.

On Feb. 13, less than two months after his wife's death, he made a surprise announcement of his engagement to Miss Pat Howson, a Preston teacher aged 36, whom he had known since her childhood. They planned to be married in May.

(March 7)

MARION DAVIES

MARION DAVIES, the film actress, who has died at the age of 64, was one of the wealthiest women in Hollywood. She lived in the grand manner all her adult life.

When she was one of the world's leading stars of silent pictures over 30 years ago she had an orchestra playing mood music on the set while she was filming. Champagne flowed while she and her friends enjoyed three-hour lunches in her dressing room.

Very early in her career she met Mr. William Randolph Hearst, the publisher, and she became his friend and confidant as well as his protégé. He guided her to stardom and then guided her to wealth.

SPECTACULAR HOME

She lived in a spectacular home called Ocean House which she had built in 1926 for about £1,500,000. It had 55 bathrooms and 37 fireplaces, and at one time had a staff of 32 servants.

(March 9)

GRANDMA MOSES

Grandma Moses, whose full name was Mrs. Anna Mary Robertson Moses, died yesterday aged 101. She was one of the most popular painters in America.

She began to paint at 78, when she could no longer manage tasks like butter-making, cleaning and sewing.

Born on a farm in upper New York state in the same year that Abraham Lincoln was elected president, she left home at the age of 12 to work as a hired girl. She later married a farmer.

On the death of her husband in 1927 their youngest son took over the working of the farm and Grandma Moses began painting without the benefit of any formal training. Her gifts were more than enough to overcome her lack of technical skill.

Her paintings have been exhibited in this country and some of her work is in the Louvre.

(December 14)

SIR THOMAS BEECHAM

A LIFETIME OF MUSICAL GENIUS

SIR THOMAS BEECHAM, who died yesterday, was the elder son of Sir Joseph Beecham, first baronet, the millionaire pill manufacturer. He was born near Liverpool in 1879 and educated at Rossall School and Wadham College, Oxford. He soon became deeply engrossed in music and at the age of 20 he deputised for Richter at a Hallé concert.

His first appearance with the Queen's Hall Orchestra was in 1905, though he had previously toured the London suburbs with the Kelson Truman Opera Company. Later he founded the New Symphony and Beecham Symphony Orchestras. In 1909, at His Majesty's Theatre, came his first venture into opera.

From then until 1920 he spent an immense fortune on a series of brilliant enterprises at Covent Garden, Drury Lane and elsewhere. His name will always be associated with the Russian Ballet and the London debut of Chaliapin. He was knighted in 1916, and in the same year he succeeded to the baronetcy on the death of his father.

From 1920 to 1924 he was involved in the incredible legal tangle resulting from his father's purchase of the Duke of Bedford's Covent Garden Estate, a liability for which Sir Joseph's will made no provision.

FAMILY BUSINESS

For a time Sir Thomas withdrew from the world of music. Eventually the estate and the family business were formed into companies.

Beecham returned to the rostrum and quickly regained his prestige. His grandiose scheme of 1927, the Imperial League of Opera, was a disappointment. In 1932, however, he organised the London Philharmonic Orchestra, and in 1934 he became artistic director at Covent Garden.

In September, 1946, he founded the Royal Philharmonic Orchestra. His memory was prodigious, and his caustic humour made him the hero of many capital anecdotes.

During a tour of America in the spring of last year he was taken ill, but completed the tour and on his return to England conducted concerts at Portsmouth and at the Festival Hall.

But on a visit to Switzerland he suffered a cerebral thrombosis, and had to cancel all engagements.

THREE MARRIAGES

Sir Thomas married, in 1903, Utica, daughter of Dr. Charles Welles, of New York. They had two sons. The marriage was dissolved in 1943.

In the same year he married Betty Humby, the English pianist, daughter of Dr. Morgan Humby, and formerly wife of the Rev. H.C. Thomas. She died in 1958. In August, 1959, he married Miss Shirley Hudson, then 27, administrator of the Royal Philharmonic Orchestra.

The heir to the baronetcy, Mr. Adrian Beecham, the elder son of Sir Thomas's first marriage, was born on Sept. 4, 1904. He is a composer. He married in 1939 Barbara, daughter of the late Edward Cairn. They have two sons and a daughter.

(March 9)

DR. FRANK BUCHMAN

FOUNDER OF MORAL RE-ARMAMENT

AS founder and leader of the Oxford Group, which later became known as the Moral Re-Armament movement, Dr. FRANK BUCHMAN, who has died aged 83, won praise and obloquy in equal measure.

Buchman's principles of "absolute truth, absolute honesty and absolute love," to be practised within the framework of Christianity, received the warm support of some leaders of religious thought. But certain features were whole-heartedly condemned by others. The chief objection was to the practice of public confession.

The Group's activities in the 1939-45 war aroused fresh criticism. Buchman and his followers concentrated on what they termed "morale-building" campaigns in America. Many felt that they could have made a more solid contribution to the war effort. Buchman's apparent pre-war sympathy with Hitler, although doubtless inspired by a detestation of Communism, was also quoted to his discredit.

GROUP REGISTERED

For some years the finances of the movement were something of a mystery. But in 1939 the Group was registered as a public company, and the consequent balance sheets disclosed that the bulk of the income came from donations. Buchman himself always disclaimed interest in finance, but it was noticeable that his activities were usually surrounded by sleek comfort.

DR. FRANK BUCHMAN

Born in Pennsylvania, Frank Buchman received theological training at the Lutheran Seminary, Philadelphia. After founding a hospice and settlement house for poor children, he travelled extensively in Europe and the Near East. From 1909-15 he was in charge of Christian work at Pennsylvania State College.

His visits to Oxford in 1921 and 1922 were followed by a steady growth of the movement. Small meetings in the university developed into house parties in country houses and hotels.

At the Group's headquarters at Caux, Switzerland, assemblies were attended by political leaders, trade unionists and businessmen from many parts of the world. From Caux went teams of "idealogical fighters" to spread the message of Moral Re-Armament.

To meet resentment in Oxford, at the implied association with the university in the Group's registered name, Dr. Buchman made a statement that the Group "did not claim to possess any official connection with the University of Oxford."

(August 9)

MRS. ANGELA THIRKELL

MRS. ANGELA THIRKELL, the novelist, who has died on the eve of her 71st birthday, had written more than 30 novels. Many of them were centred on her favourite country, modern "Barsetshire."

The daughter of the late Prof. J.W. Mackail, she had Sir Edward Burne-Jones for a grandfather and the first Earl Baldwin and Rudyard Kipling as her cousins.

In her only volume of reminiscences "Three Houses" she wrote of them and Sir Edward's homes in London and Rottingdean. She married Mr. J. Campbell McInnes in 1911. The marriage was dissolved in 1917 and she later married Mr. George L. Thirkell.

She worked in Australia for some years, but had been in England since 1930, living recently in Chelsea.

Angela Thirkell never succeeded in creating a place as famous as Barchester, but she did fill the neighbourhood about which she wrote book after book with believable human beings in settings that could easily be recognised by her readers.

She was immensely productive. Her 30 books were all written in 22 years. She did not start publishing her books until she was 40, though she came of a tremendous family of writers and artists, Burne-Jones and Kipling among them. Andrew Lang was her godfather.

Her style was easy to read and made no special demands on her readers. Though her work may be out of fashion now, it could easily in time be accepted as having a genuine period charm, giving as it does a picture of a contented rural England before and during the 1939-45 War.

(January 30)

MR. AUGUSTUS JOHN

COLOURFUL FIGURE

AUGUSTUS JOHN, who has died aged 83, had been for many years one of the most colourful and outstanding figures in British art.

Born at Tenby, Pembrokeshire, in 1878, the son of a solicitor of that town, he was at first intended for his father's profession, but showed instead so marked an inclination towards art that he was allowed in 1894 to enter the Slade School, London University. Before leaving, four years later, he won the prize for composition with "Moses and the Brazen Serpent." Another work which testifies to his student brilliance is "Walpurgis Night," now in the Tate.

In 1899 he first showed in public, with some drawings in the New English Art Club Exhibition at the Old Dudley Gallery. In company with Steer, Orpen and Sickert, he was a leading spirit in the revolt against late Victorian academicism.

But his superb handling of line above all attracted attention, and in 1901 he was appointed for a year as teacher of drawing at Liverpool University. He became an enthusiast for the gipsies' traditions and language, making himself a welcome comrade in their tents and finding among them the subjects of some of his finest work.

CITY'S CRITICISM

Picture of Year

He painted several portraits of Liverpool personalities. That of the Lord Mayor caused a sensation which established him in public notice. The City Council, which had commissioned it, paid its price of £100, but refused to accept it, on the ground that undue prominence was given on the canvas to the Lord Mayor's macebearer, in his flamboyant livery.

EUROPEAN WANDERINGS

Settlement in Chelsea

The following years were closely filled with work and travel. Easily mingling with the life of the people, rather than as a tourist, John wandered through Italy and Spain. At home the caravan was kept busily in use, while Galway and the west coast of Ireland became another haunt.

In 1908 an exhibition at the Chenil Gallery brought universal recognition of his mastery, and next year he settled in Chelsea. Of striking appearance, bearded, long-haired, carrying off gold earrings, sombrero, and an almost operatic dressing of the artist's part with awe-inspiring dignity, he soon became a London figure. Sir S. Rothenstein's "Doll's House" at the Tate, and Orpen's "Café Royal" in the Jeu de Paume in Paris, preserve his appearance in those days.

The Fitzwilliam Museum also possesses the well-known portrait of Mr. Bernard Shaw. Another work became famous by the curious circumstances of its destruction. Shortly after John had painted the first Lord Leverhulme he received back the slashed canvas, minus the head. It transpired that Lord Leverhulme, wishing to store the picture, had preserved the head without caring to save the rest, which was sent back by mistake. Heated letters were exchanged between painter and sitter.

In 1938, after 10 years membership of the Royal Academy, he resigned as a protest against the rejection of Wyndham Lewis's portrait of T.S. Elliot. He rejoined two years later. President of the Royal Society of Portrait Painters, he was invested with the O.M. in 1942.

There are four surviving sons, and two daughters, of Mr. John's marriage to Miss Nettleship. One son is Adml. Sir Caspar John, First Sea Lord.

(November 1)

'FRANK RICHARDS'

Billy Bunter's postal order expected these past 50 years by the Fat Owl of the Remove will never arrive now. Frank Richards, creator of the schoolboy characters of the Gem and the Magnet, died on Christmas Eve after a short illness in a cottage at Kingsgate, Broadstairs. He was 86.

(December 27)

THE MAN WHO SOLD VITALITY

IAN SCOTT-KILVERT reviews the Life and Work of Ernest Hemingway

ERNEST HEMINGWAY, who died yesterday, was one of those authors who became encased in a personal myth so potent that it is difficult to separate the artist from the public personality. Like Byron, he scored a fabulous early success because he created not merely an oeuvre but an attitude, a new costume for Zeitergeist.

As with Byron, too, the ideal of romantic disillusion which he proclaimed demanded a living example, and he combined, as few writers have done, the physique, the appetites, and before long the money to model the life of action which he celebrated. As he says of one of his own heroes, "he sold vitality all his life."

In Hemingway's case the process of glamourisation went further still. The early years of his success coincided with the coming of talking pictures and the tough colloquialism of the Hemingway idiom provided the perfect speed form, enabling him, as one of his critics put it, "to surf-ride to success on the wave of American popular culture."

Mature Talent

HEMINGWAY served his apprenticeship to letters as a newspaperman, always conscious of that peculiarly American craving for the authentic and the candid, determined to strip down description to its essentials, but also to make an art out of the process. The fact that things are missing, pathetically missing, is often the point of his stories and hence of his style.

At any rate, "In Our Time" instantly proclaimed a new and startlingly mature talent in the art of the short story. The effect depended upon juxtaposing the scenes of Nick Adams's apparently healthy, innocent Michigan adolescence with sketches based on Hemingway's journalistic experiences, a scarifying sequence of contemporary atrocities and Goyaesque *desastres de la guerra* reported in dead-pan style.

Blooded in 1918 like Faulkner and Dos Passos, Hemingway had already travelled physically and mentally a lot further than his contemporaries and here, he implied, was a look-behind-the-scenes, a prophetic one as things turned out, at the new world order which the Jazz Age had inherited.

However, it was with his next book, "The Sun Also Rises," that Hemingway really touched the nerve of the times and found himself hailed overnight as the voice of "the lost generation." The first World War, whether or not it had caused all the trouble, was still the great unmentionable subject, only to be handled by suggestion.

In Jake Barnes, the war-mutilated hero, who can only offer love without sex to a heroine only capable of sex without love, who sits in Paris waiting for the rain or escapes it all to fish for trout in Burguete, Hemingway seemed to have created the real-life counterpart of the Fisher-King of "The Waste Land."

Not romantic dissipation, but war, and in particular the onset of death and of fear, made real by fighting and blood-sports, was the subject which permanently fascinated Hemingway. There is little doubt that the mortar-bomb that wounded him in 1918 inflicted a shock from which it took most of his career to recover, death had come so close that afterwards nothing could seem quite so real.

"I felt my soul or something coming right out of my body, like you'd pull a silk handkerchief out of a pocket by one corner. It flew around and then went in again, and I wasn't dead any more." The shattering physical effect of such a wound is described in one of the Nick Adams stories "A Way You'll Never Be."

But Hemingway was also a fatalist who believed that "the world breaks everyone . . . even though afterwards many are strong at the broken places," and thus that whether a man lives his life at peace or at war death and fear will test him sooner or later.

Hence his devotion to bull-fighting, which he extols in "Death in the Afternoon" both as an ordeal of courage and a calculated encounter with death, its rules keeping the odds measured to a hairsbreadth.

Throughout the stories and novels we are constantly confronted with "the Hemingway code." His "fixed" jockeys and prizefighters, beat-up matadors and crooked gamblers are the exemplars of unorthodox honour and courage. They illustrate in action the qualities a man needs to hold onto when life hits him below the belt. But they are mentors rather than heroes, strictly speaking.

In Low Gear

AMONG the heroes most obviously related to the author are those of two of his finest stories, "The Short Happy Life of Francis Macomber" and "The Snows of Kilimanjaro," especially the second, which combines a prophetic vision of death with an artist's day of reckoning with himself.

These stories were succeeded by that impulse towards "engagement" which produced "To Have and to Have Not" and "For Whom the Bell Tolls." The latter is certainly his most ambitious book, but seems to-day, for all its immediate popularity, one of his most uneven, inspired by sentiments which Hemingway never fully assimilated. Somehow the disgust with war and politics expressed in "A Farewell to Arms" rings truer on his lips than the professions of faith in the later novel.

At any rate the books that followed seemed to none the epitaph of Harry Morgan, "No matter how, a man alone ain't got no bloody chance," and to suggest instead that a man may be destroyed but not defeated. "Across the River," in which author and hero have become entangled to the point of incoherence, fails to state this theme very effectively - this is Hemingway in his lowest gear - but in "The Old Man and the Sea" he regains control.

Hemingway's style is probably the most pervasive of any created in the English language of this century. It is essentially a colloquial, non-literary style, stripped of echoes and associations, which tends to disguise the intelligence behind it, concentrates on material objects and eliminates introspection. It reflects the bare and dislocated world of Hemingway's imagination and his characters' peculiar need to hold tight, to feel rather than to think. But it can reflect much more than this.

Consider, for example, "A Clean Well-Lighted Place" in which two waiters bandy the word "nothing": to the one it means just that, to the other nothingness, all the terrors of eternity. This is typical of Hemingway's dialogue, which he has made the very essence of speech, terse but supple, capable of saying everything he wants it to say.

(July 2)

GARY COOPER

LONG SUCCESS DUE TO "NATURALNESS"

GARY COOPER, who has died aged 60, carried off his film roles with a casual air that was deceptive. He believed the secret of his long success on the screen was "naturalness," but regarded his work as serious, and took great pains at it long after he became a star.

Before becoming a film actor he worked as a newspaper cartoonist and an advertising salesman. He arrived in Hollywood in 1925 and his first top role was in "The Virginian" in 1928.

After "The Virginian" he worked hard, being at the studio 16 hours a day, and was sometimes engaged on two films simultaneously. In 1931 his health broke down and he went to Africa for a year.

On his return he was in films such as "A Farewell to Arms," "Lives of a Bengal Lancer," and then began free-lancing. Later he produced some of his own films.

Cooper, who will be remembered chiefly for his success in Western films, spent his formative 'teen-age years in the company of typical Western cowboys. Spending some time on a relative's ranch, he learned to ride and handle horses like any other range-mad youngster.

Born in the State of Montana as Frank James Cooper, he was the son of Henry Cooper, a former British barrister who later became an associate justice of the State Supreme Court of Montana. The boy was at school in England for four years from the age of nine.

Cooper's personality combined easy Western affability with British reserve. His pictures included "Cowboy and the Lady," "Mr. Deeds Goes to Town," "High Noon," and many others. The most recent to be seen in this country was "The Wreck of the Mary Deare."

He married Miss Sandra Shaw, the actress, in 1933. They had a daughter.

PATRICK GIBBS writes: Gary Cooper always appeared to be himself, and very much at ease. He was a constant reminder that six feet of height and good facial features are considerable talents in a film actor; small wonder that when he was doing crowd work in Hollywood in the middle 20s the director should have picked him out for his first featured part.

Nor is it surprising that his first success, one he was to repeat again and again over a span of more than 30 years, was in a Western - "The Virginian." No actor sat a horse better than Cooper, no doubt because he had lived the cowboy life on a ranch before going to college.

But his personality also seemed perfectly suited to portraying those strong silent men of the middle west, and indeed his eyes appeared at their most natural perpetually half closed against a scorching sun or, perhaps, the dust of the trail.

"THE PLAINSMAN"

Best Western

"The Plainsman" of the late 30s, was, I think, perhaps his most accomplished Western though he must have made at least a score. "They came to Cordura," "The Hanging Tree" and "Man of the West" were a late trio, shown here within the last three years, and "High Noon" of a few years earlier was well thought of though to me the star even then seemed somewhat tired.

His career then was past its peak, and recently he had obviously been finding it difficult to sustain parts cast in a romantic relationship to such younger generation actresses as Maria Schell or Audrey Hepburn.

The middle 30s and early 40s were the vintage years, in which he played with equal success in comedy and drama. "Mr. Deeds goes to Town," for instance, and "For whom the Bell Tolls," "Meet John Doe" and "A Farewell to Arms."

VARIETY OF ROLES

Humour When Required

Although never attempting to disguise himself, Gary Cooper managed to get under the surface of a wide variety of characters, to suggest a sense of humour when required and, on occasions, some depth of feeling. He did this with an economy of vocal expression and gesture which might leave the impression that he was essentially a limited actor.

(May 15)

GARY COOPER IN "HIGH NOON", the film which won him his second oscar.

GREATEST SATIRIST SINCE MARK TWAIN

JAMES THURBER, regarded as the greatest American satirist since Mark Twain, has died in hospital in New York, aged 66.

His wit, which took a variety of forms, first convulsed Americans during the years of depression in the 1930's. It was not long before his popularity stood as high, if not higher, in Britain.

For years he enlivened the pages of the "New Yorker" magazine. He reached an even wider public with the film "The Secret Life of Walter Mitty." and with his play "The Male Animal," produced in London in 1949.

CHILDHOOD INJURY

Arrow in Eye

His sight had been steadily deteriorating during the last 10 years, a consequence of an injury sustained in his childhood when his brother accidently shot an arrow into his eye.

In a violent time (he started to write during prohibition) and a sad one (the depression), he made his name by writing about ordinary people against whom the elements rather than the wickedness of man conspired and about a world that was warm-hearted and un-hysterical.

Think of the best of the collections of his humour, "My Life and Hard Times," and what are the stories about "The Day the Dam Broke" (only it didn't). "The Day the Bed fell on Father." "The Night the Ghost got in"?

The titles are enough to remind us of the happy, slightly mad family in Columbus, Ohio, whose neuroses we all share to some extent.

Who has not secretly worried like Thurber's mother that electricity leaked out of unused plug sockets? Who has not been pulled up by a sudden burst of sanity from someone old and apparently full of delusions?

Remember Grandfather demanding the morning after the terrible night when the bed fell: "What were those cops doing tarahooting around the house?" - a terrible moment of sanity that makes the rest of the world seem mad.

JAMES THURBER

But Thurber's writing was far from limited to the world of his youth, even though it was at its best there, "The Secret Life of Walter Mitty" is a tiny master-piece.

But for many people, Thurber was not a humorous writer but a comic artist, above all the creator of a peculiar sort of dog with some vague likeness to a bloodhound but which really and truly can only be described as "The Thurber Dog," though its inventor grew tired of its success.

(November 3)

WAY OF THE WORLD

News of the Devil

I AGREE with those members of the Convocation of Canterbury who want to put the Devil back in the Catechism and throw out the proposed new phrase "all that is wrong."

The dehumanisation of man, the substitution of colourless abstractions for traditional images - "spiritual values" for "soul" and "maladjustment" for "sin" - at once involves the "de-diabolisation" of the Devil.

Anglicans are becoming afraid to use terms which they suspect scientists or scientifically educated persons may not approve of. But if they find it hard to believe in the Devil, I doubt if the Devil is displeased. Quite the contrary.

(January 20)

Split!

IT'S started. Already (writes BRUCE PLUGDEN, Chief "Way of the World" Sports Reporter) there's a split, wide open, gaping, and with jagged edges, between the knock-em-for-six lads and the dour, win-at-all-costs brigade. And it's official - from none other than Aussie skipper Richie Benaud himself.

I got this exclusive, shattering news in an interview yesterday, as Benaud was entering his hotel. "Richie," I said, "is it true that some of your lads don't want this brighter cricket business?"

Benaud stopped. And smiled.

"In other words," I said, "you won't deny that the team is hopelessly utterly, gapingly divided?"

He smiled again. And then came the final shattering confirmation. "So my exclusively-reported rumour of a split is true?" I asked.

And Benaud smiled again and walked into the hotel.

I was the only reporter to report the rumour of a split. Now I am the only reporter to have it confirmed. On Saturday I shall be at Worcester. Watch out, Australia. Even the dressing-room walls have ears.

And watch out all cricket fuddy-duddies and reactionaries everywhere. If I don't come back with another sizzling story from Worcester, my name's not Bruce Plugden.

(April 27)

Sense of Proportion

ANY attempt to call-up reservists or make any other preparations whatever to meet the crisis over Berlin will be resisted to the end by Mr. A. Grudge, the outspoken Labour M.P. for Stretchford North.

"Not a single man should be called up, not a unit moved or a gun loaded while unnecessary expenditure is being incurred by work on Royal dwellings," he said yesterday.

"While fox-hunting and other upper-class sports are being carried on daily, while the wishes of Midland council tenants are flouted, while attempts are made to interfere with trade union elections and the inalienable right of the people to play Bingo all day, it is disgraceful that we should even be thinking of undertaking military adventures against peace-loving foreign nations.

"Leave them alone and they'll leave us alone. The age of gunboat diplomacy is past."

(June 28)

Peter Simple

FA Cup Final

SPURS' WORST SHOWING IS GOOD ENOUGH

Wembley Hoodoo Puts Leicester Attack Out of Balance

By DONALD SAUNDERS

Tottenham Hotspur (0) ...... 2 Leicester City ...... (0) 0
Smith, Dyson 100,000 £49,813

AS Danny Blanchflower accepted the F.A. Challenge Cup from the Duchess of Kent at Wembley on Saturday afternoon, Len Chalmers lay on the treatment table in Leicester's dressing room, receiving attention to a badly injured right leg. That, in essence, is the story of how Spurs achieved the double.

Had Chalmers not been hurt in a clash with Allen after 18 minutes, Blanchflower might not have become the first captain this century to lead his team up the steps of the Royal Box to collect their Cup winners' medals only a week after they had become League champions.

That point will be argued heatedly for a year or two as each Cup Final comes round. Then, when precise details of a disappointing match have been blurred by time, all that will remain clear in the memory is the indisputable fact that Spurs in 1961 created soccer history.

It could be said, with some justification, that they did not on Saturday look worthy of so great an honour. But during a long, exacting season they have sometimes scaled the heights of soccer artistry and never have they been less than efficient.

Does it matter, therefore, that they completed the second half of the double with their poorest performance of the season? Evidently Leicester did not think so.

As Blanchflower and his men ran jubilantly round the pitch with the Cup held high the 10 survivors of Leicester's gallant battle against ever-whelming odds lined up at the tunnel entrance to pay their tribute to their conquerors and a great achievement.

AWKWARD MOMENT
TV Intrusion

What a pity that television, which had taken this memorable occasion into millions of homes, should have been responsible for marring so admirable a climax.

As Blanchflower was about to follow his colleagues through the guard of honour with the Cup he was waylaid by an enterprising interviewer, and by the time the questions had ended the Leicester players, a little embarrassed, had moved on into the darkness of the tunnel.

If only the cameras and microphones had been stationed inside the dressing rooms this discourtesy to an extremely sporting team would have been avoided. But then, this was a match full of "ifs" and "might have beens" as indeed are most Cup Finals.

The first "if" arose after only four minutes, when White, eight yards out, drove the ball wide. Had this golden chance been taken Spurs might have risen to their full majesty and given us a soccer feast to remember.

Instead, they remained taut, nervous and irritatingly defensive, until at last, in the 69th minute, Smith snapped up his now familiar Wembley goal and released the tension.

From then on we saw Spurs as we shall remember them whenever the "Team of the Century" is discussed.

LEICESTER ON TOP
Blanchflower Worried

Between times, however, the honours belonged largely to the sound, sensible men from Filbert Street. When all 11 of them were hale and hearty they looked to be getting the better of a dour, mid-field struggle.

Spurs, - Brown, Baker, Henry, Blanchflower, Norman, M. Mackay; Jones, White, Smith, Allen, Dyson.

Leicester, - Banks; Chalmers, Norman, R. McLintock, King, Appleton; Riley, Walsh, McIlmoyle, Keyworth, Cheesebrough.

Referee - J. Kelly (Chorley).

(May 8)

FOOTBALL LEAGUE GIVE IN: STRIKE IS OFF

By DAVID MILLER

THE football debacle dissolved yesterday, and the way is now clear for the game to advance - revived, firm and with fresh thought. The players have gained their final, and most important, concession. The strike on Saturday is off, League matches are on: the players have won.

At the joint meeting with the Football League and representatives of the Football Association at the Ministry of Labour, agreement was at last reached on the retain and transfer system, the outstanding point of difference.

The alterations bear little difference from those negotiated on Dec. 21. The simplicity, and obviousness, of the new system make the past eight months' squabble seem sadly unnecessary.

Fundamentally the players have been granted the right to change their club, the clubs the right to demand a transfer fee.

Coupled with the concessions given by the League chairmen on Jan. 9 - the removal of the maximum wage from next season and others - the English professional footballer, provided he does not abuse his newfound freedom, is assured of a contented future.

The collective effect of the changes will be to raise the standard of the game, which will bring back the crowds. It will also improve Soccer's social standing and make it an attractive short-term profession for those with skill and brains.

(January 19)

JIMMY HILL IS NEW COVENTRY MANAGER

By L.N. BAILEY

JIMMY HILL, chairman of the Professional Footballers Association and former Fulham inside-forward, was yesterday appointed manager of Coventry City, following the surprise dismissal of Billy Frith.

Mr. Frith loses his job with two and a half years of his contract still to run. With him go the club's two trainers and chief coach. This is the 27th managerial change to be made in League football in little more than a year.

Mr. Hill, who is 33, recently went into partnership with a London sports literary agent, but he is being released from this post. He will also give up his job as chairman of the P.F.A. He says he has signed a five-year contract.

(November 30)

JIMMY GREAVES OF SPURS IN ACTION

GREAVES SIGNS FOR MILAN AT £73,000 FEE

By DONALD SAUNDERS

ONLY drastic and enlightened action by Football League clubs at Friday's extraordinary meeting in London can prevent the Italian League striking a serious blow at British football a fortnight hence.

If English clubs fail to endorse a "new deal" lifting the ceiling of wages and granting players more freedom, the Italians will snap up our best players once a ban on foreign importations has been lifted by their management committee on April 28.

Whatever action is taken on Friday, it will be too late to prevent Jimmy Greaves, one of England's most talented forwards, leaving Chelsea for Milan next season.

Dr. Luigi Scarambone, secretary of the Italian League, confirmed last night that all documents giving Milan first option on Greaves at a transfer fee of £73,000 had been lodged with him. This indicates that Greaves has already signed a contract to join Milan when the Italian rules have been changed.

Dr. Scarambone would not disclose the size of Greaves's signing-on fee, but I estimate it would at least equal the £10,000 John Charles received from Juventus when they paid Leeds £65,000 for his transfer in April, 1957. Greaves's salary would, of course, greatly exceed the £20 a week Chelsea were allowed to pay him.

NO TALKING
Silent Manager

Neither he nor his manager, Mr. Ted Drake, would talk about the matter yesterday. After helping England beat Chelsea 4-3 in a practice game at Stamford Bridge Greaves stated "I can say nothing until Chelsea do."

(April 12)

STIRLING MOSS WINS MONACO GRAND PRIX

From W.A. McKENZIE
Daily Telegraph Motoring Correspondent

MONTE CARLO, Sunday.

THE first of the 1961 world championship series grand prix races goes to a British driver and a British car. Stirling Moss, now 31, won the Grand Prix de Monaco to-day in one of the hardest battles of his career.

Driving the privately-owned Lotus, entered by Rob Walker, he finished 3.6 sec ahead of the leader of a formidable team of factory-entered Ferraris from Italy.

With about 40 b.h.p. above the power of the Lotus they finished in second, third and fourth places. A German Porsche was fifth.

Rave enthusiasts from all parts of Europe came to see this contest. It was the first since the international grand prix formula was changed from an engine limit of 2 ½ litres to 1 ½ litres.

FASTEST EVER

They wanted to know whether the change would slow the sport to the point of ruining it as a great public draw. Instead they found themselves gripped by a needle match for the whole of the 100 laps of this exhausting 1.9 miles "round the houses" circuit.

They found too, the winner averaging 70.5 m.p.h., the highest race average in the 19 years' history of the contest. The race average, in fact, was greater than the record lap of two years ago.

All the British cars, the Lotus, Coopers, and BRMs, were handicapped by the change in the Grand Prix formula. Their sponsors had fought against the change because they had no small engines sufficiently far developed.

On the other hand, the change was ideally suited to the highly developed 1 ½ litre engines of Italy and West Germany.

(May 15)

British Ski Week

TITLE GOES TO PALMER-TOMKINSON

MUERREN, Friday.

CHARLES PALMER-TOMKINSON to-day became 1961 British combined ski champion, clinching the title by winning the downhill - the final event of the week - after finishing third in the slalom on Tuesday.

Palmer-Tomkinson who is at Cirencester Agricultural College, covered the downhill course of 2.3 kilometres (nearly one and a half miles) with a drop of 545 metres (595 yds) and 38 control posts, in 2 min. 7.6 sec.

John Rigby was second in 2:10.9 and the Aga Khan third in 2.11.5.

The first three in the 1961 British combined ski championships were: Palmer-Tomkinson 1.5 pts 1; Robert Skepper 8.91 pts 2; Winston Churchill 10.09 pts 3.

(January 14)

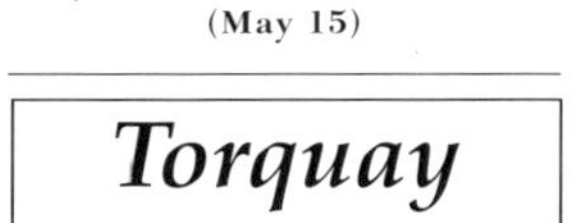

NO HOPE COLT WINS DERBY

OWNER SAID 'DON'T BACK PSIDIUM'

Daily Telegraph Reporter

MRS. ARPAD PLESCH, whose horse Psidium, a 66-1 outsider, won the Derby worth £34,548 at Epsom yesterday, advised her friends not to back the colt. She "didn't think he had a chance."

Psidium, who paid nearly 90-1 on the Tote, was the longest-price-Derby winner since the 100-1 Aboyeur in 1913.

A few minutes after leading the chestnut horse into the winner's enclosure and receiving the £525 Gold Trophy from Lady Rosebery, Hungarian-born Mrs. Plesch, who never bets, said to me: "I must eat my words. It was a splendid victory but I must confess I did not think my horse would be in the first 10."

By her side was her husband, who only had a few pounds on the winner. "I put my money on the Irish horse Neanderthal," he said.

Psidium beat Mme Leon Volterra's Dicta Drake, a 100-8 chance, by two lengths. The judge called on the camera to decide that the French horse took the second place by a neck from Pardao, owned by American Mrs. C.O. Iselin. Women owners took first three places for the first time in the history of the Derby.

The race was a triumph for French jockeys Roger Poincelet and M. Garcia, who took first two places. Poincelet was only asked to ride Psidium a fortnight ago and his mount was confirmed last Sunday at Longchamp by Mrs. Plesch.

The race was watched by the Queen, Queen Elizabeth the Queen Mother, and other members of the Royal Family. It was estimated that more than 250,000 people were on the course.

Mr. Plesch, a Hungarian-born financier who names his horses after botannic plants in his garden in the South of France, said: "Psidium is the Latin name for the guava tree."

(June 1)

Masters Golf

PLAYER WINS BY ONE STROKE

AUGUSTA, Georgia, Monday.

Gary Player of South Africa, won the U.S. Masters Golf Championship here to-day.

He is the first overseas golfer to win the event. His 72 hole total was 280. Plamer, four strokes behind over-night, was second one stroke behind. But Player survived.

Crisp approaches gave him a 2-under-par 34 for the first nine holes as he played two holes ahead of Palmer.

(April 11)

MAGIFICENT PALMER

By LEONARD CRAWLEY

AFTER what he himself described as the four most gruelling rounds he ever played, Arnold Palmer, the great American golfer from Pennsylvania, won the Open Championship at Royal Birkdale on Saturday by a single stroke from D.J. Rees, of South Herts.

Palmer had rounds of 70, 73, 69, 72, for a total of 284. Rees's four rounds were 68, 74, 71, 72, for 285. C. O'Connor, Royal Dublin, tied for third place with N.C. Coles, a playing professional from Coombe Hill, in 288.

K. Nagle, the Australian holder, who played most gallantly in defence of his title, tied with E.C. Brown on 289, and P.W. THOMSON, of Australia, four times winner, finished in 290.

Palmer, by common consent, is the world's greatest golfer to-day, having won almost everything worth winning in the United States. Now at the age of 31, he can look back on the British Open at Royal Birkdale in 1961 as one of his most satisfying triumphs. He beat the appalling weather, he beat a splendid field, and he played the game in the grandest possible manner.

ERROR REPORTED
Self-Inflicted Penalty

Let no one forget that cruel stroke of fate in the bunker at the 17th during the gale in the second round when his ball moved as he was about to strike it. Not only did he mishit it, but he reported himself as having incurred a penalty stroke, and he gaily took seven.

ARNOLD PALMER

It recalled a memorable observation by R.T. Jones in similarly painful circumstances: "There is only one way to play golf."

Though it had been difficult to foresee a British victory before the championship one had some sympathy for our young professionals, who objected strongly to what they had read about the forthcoming "one-horse race."

It happened after all, that the favourite won in what amounted to a photo finish, but no one ever imagined that if a British player was going to finish at the top it would be Rees, now in his 49th year. He has a wonderful record, but the Open has so far avoided him.

He was third at St. Andrews in 1946, third again at Troon in 1950, second at Carnoustie in 1953, second at Royal Birkdale in 1954, and fifth at Muirfield in 1959. When he finished with a glorious three at the last hole on Saturday a shout went up that he will remember for the rest of his days. But by this time Palmer had already won.

(July 17)

BENAUD BOWLS AUSTRALIA TO ASHES VICTORY

England Throw Away Golden Chance By Misjudgment and Poor Batting

Australia beat England by 54 runs, with 20 minutes to spare in the fourth Test to make sure of retaining the Ashes.

From E.W. SWANTON

OLD TRAFFORD, Tuesday.

THE Ashes were won and lost this afternoon in a few overs bowled by Benaud to either side of the tea interval. In four overs before it he had four wickets for nine, in half an hour afterwards two more.

It was fine bowling, and in many ways this has been a magnificent game of cricket. It is better to concentrate on this aspect, rather than to dwell unduly on a glorious English opportunity thrown away by misjudgment and plain poor batting.

At two moments to-day Australia were, in all human probability, a beaten side. First when, after 20 minutes play, they were 334 for nine England needed only the last wicket with the long day stretching before them and a mere 150-odd to get.

Davidson and McKenzie in a last-wicket partnership beyond praise brought their side right back.Yet thanks to Dexter's great batsmanship England, as 4 o'clock approached, needed only 102 runs more at one a minute with nine wickets left. All seemed set fair.

But Dexter left for 76, and the age-old bogey of accurate, teasing leg-spin suddenly knocked this unsound, relatively inexperienced England middle batting right off balance. Australia fielded finely, they took every catch, and suddenly we were left with the prospect of our three fast bowlers needing to hold out for the best part of an hour.

Little did they look like doing so. Trueman stayed for 40 minutes, alternating solid defence with a few safe bits. Then he lost patience, and when all hope of victory had gone aimed a wild swing against a leg-spinner from Simpson - very much as in the first innings - when it had mattered so much less.

DECISIVE FACTORS

Davidson and Benaud

At the end Australia, I daresay, could scarcely believe their luck. With little enough bowling in the first place, and strains to Davidson and Mackay to deplete them, they snatched - thanks to their captain - a game that was three-parts lost.

Davidson this morning and Benaud afterwards, two great cricketers, played the decisive part, and however disappointing it may be to English followers to have got so near and had victory snatched away it is appropriate that Benaud should achieve the ambition of every Australian captain and successfully defend the Ashes in this country.

From first to last on this tour he has sought to play cricket in an enterprising and sporting way. England, indeed, have met him in this, and have contributed - until the last sad phase - no mean part in this fascinating and extraordinary match.

(August 2)

SHACKLETON GIVES HANTS THE CHAMPIONSHIP

Superb Use of Seam on Docile Pitch Breaks Derbyshire Resistance

From A.S.R. WINLAW

BOURNEMOUTH, Friday.

IN an atmosphere of much tension, excitement and then rejoicing, Hampshire became County Champions for the first time in their history by beating Derbyshire here to-day by 40 runs.

There could be no more deserving or fitting player to have brought them the Championship than Shackleton and in a quite magnificent spell of bowling he took six wickets for 39 runs.

He moved the ball away to the slips, brought the ball back, and on the pitch which had hitherto given the seamers no encouragement he bowled a number of really difficult deliveries.

Derbyshire were set to make 252 to win in 193 minutes, and it was obvious that if they were to get them their first four batsmen would have to succeed.

None of them did. Shackleton dismissed all four, and although Taylor and Rhodes batted well at the end, Derbyshire were all out for 111.

48 IN TWO HOURS

Cheering Progress

Hampshire batted until just before one o'clock, and although they lost wickets the runs came quickly and they were able to declare at 263 for eight. In the two hours they scored 48, with the chief contributions coming from Sainsbury and Barnard.

When Derbyshire went in Shackleton had Lee caught behind on the forward stretch from one that lifted from the third over, and immediately after lunch Gibson was lbw.

The breakthrough really came when Shackleton bowled first Oates with one that left him and then Johnson off his pads. This was the important wicket Hampshire wanted. And Derbyshire's shakey middle order never threatened to hold on for long.

Shackleton at this stage had taken four wickets for nine runs. At the other end Wassell again bowled his left-arm spinners with considerable vocation in flight.

Millner, after a nervous start, played a couple of good shots, but Wassell caught and bowled him brilliantly from a drive which hardly rose from the ground.

CAPTAIN'S NOUGHT

Celebrations Near, Then . . .

This made Derbyshire 52 for seven, and Richardson was then bowled without addition. The scene was all set for the celebrations, but there was a short and agreeable breathing space while the wicketkeeper Taylor and Rhodes batted soundly for 40 minutes while adding 52 for the ninth wicket.

Taylor at 19 is certainly a promising prospect as a wicketkeeper and he is the type of player likely to develop with experience into a pretty useful batsman. He swept and pulled very effectively and Ingleby-Mackenzie was committed to give Shackleton his overdue rest after 24 overs.

Sainsbury came on, and Rhodes obligingly hit a long hop straight back to him. Taylor, having made 48, tried to drive Sainsbury for his 50. The ball went in the air for an agonising length of time, but Livingstone held the catch at long-on and history was made.

An enthusiastic scene followed with the Derbyshire players coming from the pavilion to meet the new champions

Ingleby-Mackenzie made a typically humble and charming speech, and Shackleton said it was his greatest and proudest moment - a sentiment loudly and deservedly cheered.

(September 2)

MISS ANGELA MORTIMER proudly holds the Women's trophy after defeating Miss Christine Truman (left) by 4-6, 6-4, 7-5.

SKILL NOT LUCK BRINGS MISS MORTIMER TITLE

By LANCE TINGAY

THE Lawn Tennis Championship ended at Wimbledon on Saturday with Miss Angela Mortimer the first British winner of a singles title for 24 years. What immortality there is in lawn tennis belongs worthily to her.

The quality of her play is simple and enduring. Were this not so she would not have taken the most prized crown at the age of 29, an age when men are reckoned to be one year beyond their peak and women rather more.

Astute court craft and ability to penetrate searchingly against opposition weakness, superb driving control and command of length, these are the merits of Miss Mortimer's lawn tennis. In Wimbledon champions, personality and character are factors that must also be taken into account.

Among lawn tennis players who are usually extroverts rather than otherwise Miss Mortimer is unusually withdrawn and reserved and I am tempted to describe her as a lonely figure. She is also a much loved one.

BRIEF SPEECH

Best of evening

Miss Mortimer, as champion, made one of the speeches at the Wimbledon Ball on Saturday night. It was without a doubt the best of the evening, simple, generous in sentiment, brief and to the point, and it reflected the same qualities that enabled her to raise the prestige of the British women's game to its highest peak for nearly a quarter of a century.

In short, she is a fine champion and I make the point at some length to clear the ground for the question raised in the tense and exciting final, where Miss Mortimer beat Miss Christine Truman 4-6, 6-4, 7-5.

Would Miss Truman now be champion had she not, when within a point of leading 5-3 in the second set fallen awkwardly and lacked mobility for the next six or seven games?

I have seen too many wavering contests between Miss Mortimer and Miss Truman to take for granted that a strong position by one or the other might not be broken. Certainly Miss Truman looked as though she were winning when the sudden net cord, her quick turn and subsequent fall, reduced her power.

In fact, Miss Truman had the cruellest luck. At the same time it would be wrong to regard Miss Mortimer as a lucky winner.

The Champions

(Seeded players in capitals)

MEN'S SINGLES

R. LAVER (Australia) bt C.R. McKINLEY (U.S.), 6-3, 6-1, 6-4

WOMEN'S SINGLES

Miss A. MORTIMER bt Miss C.C. TRUMAN 4-6, 6-4, 7-5

MEN'S DOUBLES

R. EMERSON & N.A. FRASER (Australia) bt R. Hewitt & F. Stolle (Australia) 6-4, 6-8, 6-4, 6-8, 8-6.

WOMEN'S DOUBLES

Miss K Hantze & Miss B. J. Moffitt (U.S.) bt Miss J LEHANE & Miss M. SMITH (Australia) 6-3, 6-4.

MIXED DOUBLES

F. STOLLE & MISS L. TURNER (Australia) bt R.N. HOWE (Australia) & MISS BUDING (Germany) 11-9, 6-2.

(July 10)

KNOCK-OUT COMPETITION WILL START IN 1963

By MICHALE MELFORD

AT a special meeting of the Advisory County Cricket Committee at Lord's yesterday, the counties decided to play a one-day knock-out tournament in 1963 in addition to the Championship programme of 28 three-day matches. This follows the recommendation of the 1961 Cricket Inquiry Committee.

The counties were also invited to vote on a proposal made by the structure sub-committee of the Inquiry Committee that each county should play the others once in a three-day match and on two consecutive days in one-day matches.

This did not originally receive the blessing of the full Inquiry Committee, and it was rejected by the counties yesterday, though only by a narrow margin.

The other main consideration at yesterday's meeting was whether either of these systems could be implemented in 1962, which seems to be an ideal season for experiment.

This also was rejected by a close margin after a long discussion. Everybody seems to have been agreed of the desirability of taking action in 1962, but the difficulties in the way of some counties proved too great.

Yesterday's decision does not attack the main problem with which modern first-class cricket is faced, which is how to cut expenses. It is unlikely to produce any striking profit. Indeed if the weather is against it, it would lose money. Hotel bookings, for example, may have to be kept on for another night, perhaps two.

However, in its knock-out form, one-day cricket will be a novelty and a lively talking point. If skillfully presented, it may well have an initial surprise leading to a lasting prosperity.

(December 21)

DOWNES TAKES WORLD TITLE FROM PENDER

Champion Forced To Retire After Nine Gruelling Rounds

By DONALD SAUNDERS

TERRY DOWNES of Paddington is the new middleweight champion of the world. At Wembley Pool last night, just 10 years and one day since Randolph Turpin took the same title from Sugar Ray Robinson, Downes whipped Paul Pender of Boston into submission in nine gruelling rounds.

The championship changed hands with dramatic suddenness. As the bell ended another hard, close-fought round, Pender sank wearily on to his stool and spoke to his seconds.

They in turn beckoned the referee, Mr. Ike Powell, who was told by Leo Platts, the American's chief "cut man": "I cannot send him out with an eye like that."

The injury to which Mr. Platts referred was a cut on the left eyebrow, which even by British standards could not be called bad. It was the sort of wound that we had been led to believe Americans usually take in their stride.

In the circumstances it is perhaps understandable that Downes should at first have looked completely nonplussed when Mr. Powell signalled the end. Then seconds later, the wonderful truth dawned on him that he was champion of the world, and he jumped for joy before his helpers besieged him.

Certainly Downes had been doing a good demolition job. He had concentrated mainly on the body, with powerful hooks, and was undoubtedly slowing down his opponent. But he had not, in my opinion, completely gained control of the contest.

LEFT JAB

Facial Injuries

Indeed a cut and a deep, ugly bruise under his left eye, a graze on the nose and split and swollen lips made him look the more damaged of the two.

These injuries had been caused by Pender's left jab, a punch thrown with accuracy but not with the fire and frequency of their first clash.

At times I wondered if Downes would ever solve the problem of getting past that left in order to drive home his stamina-sapping punches. He certainly did so more often than in their Boston meeting.

But when he arrived at close quarters the cagey champion sometimes locked him in an embrace that permitted him no exchange of blows.

I wish I could sound more enthusiastic about the enthronement of a Briton as world champion. The fact is however, that I have never seen the holder of a title bow out quite so tamely.

(July 12)

107th Boat Race

CAMBRIDGE COURAGE SEES THEM THROUGH

By A.T.M. DURAND

CAMBRIDGE won the 107th Boat Race against the odds and against a crew which should have beaten them. In commentating on the race it is unhappily necessary to stress the apparent cause of Oxford's failure, so it is only fair to say at once that Cambridge fully deserved their victory.

Cambridge were not a great crew. They had many minor individual faults, and were seldom perfectly together. But they were unquestionably a great-hearted crew, and this for the Boat Race is all-important. In the final test they won quite simply because they lasted the course and Oxford did not.

I have often stressed the excellence of their stroke and seven, Hoffmann and Christian. On Saturday they surpassed themselves, but as we saw only too clearly in the latter part of the race, a first-class stern pair, which Oxford had in Davis and Chester, can do little but display courage if there is a collapse behind them.

In the Cambridge crew there was no collapse. Rather, there was fanatical energy and power, as every man rose splendidly to the occasion.

WELL-EARNED

Praise for Beveridge

To Beveridge, as to every successful president, must go special praise. Very few, even in the other camp, will, I hope, grudge him his outstanding victory. He was much too good a man to go down to history as the first Cambridge Blue in 50 years to lose three Boat Races.

It must have been a day of triumph for Mr. Mays-Smith, the sweeter because it had not always seemed probable. But I am sure he did not rejoice in the manner of his opponents' downfall.

He laid a hoodoo on Oxford. Three times running his crews have won against heavily fancied opposition. In each race an Oxford oarsman failed.

On Saturday when Oxford were leading at Chiswick Steps their No. 6, Cooper, cracked. Though he gallantly managed still to keep time he was a passenger for the rest of the race, so there could be only one result.

Oxford were using their longest oars. Naturally, there is controversy about their wisdom in doing so. I have always regarded these long oars as experimental. Now I believe the experiment to have failed, for even before Cooper cracked the crew appeared to be struggling in the head wind.

(April 3)

MISS RUDOLPH BREAKS WORLD 100m. RECORD

STUTTGART, Wednesday.

WILMA RUDOLPH, the United States triple Olympic gold medalist, broke the world 100 metres record here to-night, clocking 11.2 sec, during an invitation event in the United States v West Germany match. She limped off the track with her face twisted in pain.

Miss Rudolph said that she felt terrible and did not know whether she would be able to run in London on Friday and Saturday. The team doctor, Dr. Hayes, thought after a dressing room examination, however, that Miss Rudolph would be all right within two days.

The listed world record was 11.3 sec which the 21-year-old Tennessee student shared with Russia's Vera Krepkina and Shirley Delahunty, of Australia. But Miss Rudolph also equalled this time in Moscow.

(July 20)

MIDLANDS REVIVAL HOLDS EAST

East ...... 2 Midlands 2

The East, having already been beaten South, North and West had set their hearts on making a clean sweep of all opposition in the women's territorial hockey matches. But they met their match at St. Albans yesterday in a Midlands team which would not be denied.

(February 16)

8ft. CONCRETE WALL GOES UP AT BRANDENBURG GATE

AN ARTIST'S IMPRESSION of the 500ft tower for television and radio telephony which the Post Office propose building at the Museum Telephone Exchange in Howland Street, off Tottenham Court Road.

A VIEW FROM THE REICHSTAG BUILDING of the massive-horseshoe-shaped concrete wall which thousands of East German workmen built during Sunday night at the Brandenburg Gate, the main entrance to East Berlin. The wall, which is six feet thick and more than eight feet high, is strengthened by steel girders. In front of it stood a temporary hardboard screen.

A ROW OF TANKS PARKED in the main road at Warschauer Brucke, in East Berlin, yesterday after the East German authorities had closed the border to stop the mass flight of refugees into the Western sector of the city.

LEFT: A DOUBLE BARBED-WIRE fence dividing the two halves of Berlin, and, beyond it, East Berlin soldiers and labourers at work clearing a site on which a row of houses fromerly stood. The people who had occupied the houses were evicted and the buildings were knocked down to seal off another escape route.

THE MARQUESS OF TAVISTOCK, eldest son of the Duke of Bedford, leaving St. Clement Dane's Church in the Strand yesterday with his bride, Miss Henrietta Tiarks.

ARCHITECTS AND STUDENTS marching along a road near Euston Station yesterday carrying an 18-yard banner demanding "Save the Arch." Plans to demolish the arch have been announced.

1962

The same old troubles carried on. In Algeria the fighting continued, punctuated by occasional cease fires, and the successive revolts of the army officers led to a number of trials. The fact that the leading general, Salan, was not sentenced to death was hailed as a victory by the French settlers in Algeria, who were still trying to hold on to power. The United Nations forces continued to have endless trouble in keeping the warring Congolese factions apart.

The world stood close to global war as the USSR and the United States squared up to each other over the stationing of Russian missiles in Castro's Cuba. The firmness of President Kennedy and the natural caution of Mr. Khruschev led to a slackening of tension as the missiles were shipped home again. The American involvement in what was to become known as the Vietnam War was made public with the news that American "advisers" were carrying out bombing raids on the Communist North Vietnamese. In Mississippi the battle between the blacks and whites over the integration of schools continued while the first black university student received his diploma in Alabama.

In Britain, the effects of the thalidomide drug became known and the long-drawn-out struggle for compensation for the disabled children began. A British civil servant working for the Russians as a spy was sentenced to prison. Revelations at the trial caused the resignation of a British minister, Kenneth Galbraith, who had written affectionate postcards to the spy. The political scene was astonished by the success of Eric Lubbock in winning Orpington for the Liberals in a by-election, overturning a large Conservate majority, and giving rise to a new political figure, "Orpington Man".

Television, watched by ever more Britons, held centre stage. The Pilkington Commission reported its disfavour with ITV but the Government issued a White Paper disagreeing with most of its findings, though giving the go-ahead for BBC colour television. However, potential audiences were magnified by the first satellite transmissions across the Atlantic. Europeans were able to see a live baseball match while Americans could hear the "voice of British television", Richard Dimbleby.

Space rivalry between America and Russia was intensified as the first U.S. rocket orbitted the world three times and the Russians sent up two men into space at the same time.

In Britain the newly consecrated Coventry Cathedral, described as an "honest failure" by *The Daily Telegraph* architectural correspondent, was the setting for the first performance of Benjamin Britten's *War Requiem*, hailed by *The Daily Telegraph* music critic as "a triumph". Sir Laurence Olivier was named as the first head of the National Theatre company, though without a theatre to play in. The dramatic event of the year was Peter Brook's production of King Lear at Stratford-upon-Avon, with Paul Scofield in the leading part.

Among those who died during the year were Eleanor Roosevelt, the mother-figure of American life, and Marilyn Monroe, the glamour figure of her time. The suspicious circumstances surrounding Marilyn's apparent suicide and the possible connection with the Kennedy family were not known until later.

Seven horses fell in a pile-up in the Derby, while 17 managed to complete the Grand National course. Chris Bonington and his partner became the first Britons to climb the North Face of the Eiger.

ASK FOR
Mekay
IMMACULATE SHIRTS

The Daily Telegraph

No. 33,444 LONDON, MONDAY, OCTOBER 29, 1962
and Morning Post
Printed in LONDON and MANCHESTER Price 3d.

DUVAL
8'9 8'9
EMPIRE CREAM SHERRY
PRODUCE OF CYPRUS

RUSSIA TO SHIP HOME CUBA MISSILES

KHRUSCHEV ACCEPTS U.N. SUPERVISION

STATESMANLIKE, SAYS MR. KENNEDY

RUSSIAN missiles in Cuba are to be dismantled, crated up and shipped back to the Soviet Union, Mr. Khruschev announced yesterday. He agreed that this should be done under United Nations supervision.

His message to President Kennedy, broadcast by Moscow Radio, did not repeat his demand that missile bases in Turkey should be removed as a condition of the Russian withdrawal. But it accused the United States of sending a "spy-flight" plane over eastern Siberia yesterday.

Mr. Khruschev added that:

He was anxious to continue talks on general and complete disarmament, and on a nuclear test ban;

Mr. Kuznetsov, Russian First Deputy Foreign Minister, had been sent to New York to assist U Thant, United Nations acting Secretary-General, in negotiations.

U Thant plans to leave New York for Cuba tomorrow to arrange supervision of dismantling by about 50 officers.

U.S. "RECIPROCAL" MEASURES

Mr. Kennedy greeted Mr. Khruschev's decision as "statesmanlike" and an "important and constructive contribution to peace." He said he would approach U Thant about "reciprocal measures" to assure peace in the Caribbean.

In his formal reply to Mr. Khruschev last night the President apologised for the American flight over Siberia. Every precaution would be taken to prevent a recurrence.

The State Department said last night that the blockade was still in effect. No Soviet ships were near.

American officials said Mr. Kennedy had made no "deal" involving either Turkey or Berlin to persuade Mr. Khruschev to withdraw the missiles. There had been several unpublished communications between Washington and Moscow. American military action was very close when Mr. Khruschev made his withdrawal decision.

The British Government welcomed Mr. Khruschev's message warmly, and hailed Mr. Kennedy's diplomatic victory.

CASTRO CALL TO QUIT BASE

Dr. Castro, the Cuban Prime Minister, who was not consulted about the removal of the missiles, demanded in a broadcast yesterday that the United States should abandon its naval base at Guantanamo.

Chou En-lai, Prime Minister of Communist China, said in a telegram to Dr. Castro that the Chinese people would always be "the most reliable and loyal comrades-in-arms of Cuba."

Khruschev Text, Cuba Demands Return of Base, Peking Backs Dr. Castro. Air Photographs Surprise Russians. Missing Pilot Picture and Missiles Round Berlin, Says Senator - Back Page: Missile Picture - P18: London Demonstrations and Picture - P11: Editorial Comment - P10.

'SPY-FLIGHT' ACCUSATION

From JEREMY WOLFENDEN,
Daily Telegraph Special Correspondent

MOSCOW, Sunday.

MR. KHRUSCHEV promised to-day to abandon his missile bases in Cuba. In a message to President Kennedy, he said he had given orders that "the weapons which you call offensive" should be dismantled, crated up and returned to the Soviet Union.

But at the same time he accused the Americans of having again violated Soviet airspace to-day. The message was broadcast by Moscow radio and repeated at intervals for more than an hour.

CONDITION MET
Kennedy pledge

Mr. Khruschev seems now to have met the condition set by President Kennedy which was that the bases should be removed under United Nations supervision before negotiations were started.

He said he was prepared to take this step because Mr. Kennedy had given an assurance that Cuba would not be invaded. Thus the arms were no longer necessary.

But he pointed out that Cuban exiles had fired on Havana from the sea and had attacked merchant ships, including a British cargo vessel. These exiles, he said, must have a base somewhere and the United States, with its ships patrolling the Caribbean, must be able to control them.

He also protested against reconnaissance flights by American aircraft over Cuba. "The violation of Cuban air space by American aircraft could have serious consequences," he said.

NO CROWING OVER KENNEDY VICTORY

Soviet 'contribution to peace'

From Our Own Correspondent

WASHINGTON, Sunday.

PRESIDENT KENNEDY to-day welcomed as "statesmanlike" Mr. Khruschev's decision to withdraw Russian missiles from Cuba. He said "This is an important and constructive contribution to peace."

He would be in touch with U Thant, the United Nations acting Secretary-General, "with respect to reciprocal measures to assure peace in the Caribbean."

The President's special statement was issued while the official text of Mr. Khruschev's message was still being translated. It was followed later in the day by a formal reply.

There was no crowing over Mr. Khruschev's decision though it was evident that Mr. Kennedy had come out on top in a raw contest of power politics.

THE WAY OPEN
Possible Summit

One week, almost to the hour, after Mr. Kennedy was presented with the conclusive intelligence report on the presence of the missiles the position was this:

1 - Russia had agreed to withdraw the missiles, perhaps only days before direct American military action would have been taken against them.

2 - Russia had an assurance that the United States would not invade Cuba as long as it was not an "offensive" military base

U THANT TO GO TO HAVANA

CASTRO INVITATION

From Our Own Correspondent

NEW YORK, Sunday.

U Thant, Acting Secretary-General of the United Nations, has accepted Dr. Castro's invitation to visit Havana. He is expected to leave on Tuesday.

Mr. Vassily Kuznetsov, Russian First Deputy Foreign Minister, and one of the mildest Soviet diplomats, will arrive in New York this evening to take part in the Cuban negotiations. Mr. Khruschev said he was sending him to help in U Thant's "noble efforts aimed at the liquidation of the present dangerous position."

Mr. Adlai Stevenson, chief United States delegate, called on U Thant twice to-day. He delivered a new note from President Kennedy, but refused to disclose the contents.

OBSERVER TEAMS
Missile dismantling

U Thant plans to stay in Cuba only to get Dr. Castro's acceptance of his plan for observer teams to see missile site dismantling is carried out. Then he will leave to obtain Security Council authorisation for the inspection programme.

Dr. Castro's consent will be necessary under the precedent set in the 1956 Suez crisis when it was ruled President Nasser would have to agree to arrangements concerning the United Nations Emergency Force in Egypt. About 50 officers, drawn from States maintaining diplomatic relations with Cuba and in particular not allied with either America or Russia, will be needed to inspect the sites. - NYT Service.

OIL SABOTAGE IN VENEZUELA

CARACAS, Venezuela, Sunday.

Saboteurs, believed to be followers of the Cuban Prime Minister, Dr. Castro, blew up four oil company power stations in Lake Maracaibo, North-West Venezuela, early to-day knocking out one-sixth of Venezuela's oil production.

The bombs destroyed transformer stations of the Creole Petroleum Co., a subsidiary of Standard Oil of New Jersey. A company spokesman said the entire Creole field in the oil-rich Lake was rendered inoperable.

KENNEDY HOPE FOR 'REAL DISARMAMENT'

APOLOGY TO MR. KHRUSCHEV

WASHINGTON, Sunday.

PRESIDENT KENNEDY stated in a personal letter to Mr. Khruschev to-night: "Now, as we step back from danger we can make real progress in disarmament."

The President welcomed Mr. Khruschev's message received earlier in the day, pledging withdrawal of Soviet missile bases in Cuba, as "an important contribution to peace."

"I think that you and I, with our heavy responsibilities for the maintenance of peace, were aware that developments were approaching a point where events could have become unmanageable."

"U-2" REGRETS
Preventing recurrence

President Kennedy expressed regret to Mr. Khruschev that an American plane, he did not say whether it was a U-2, had flown over Soviet territory in the area of the Chukrotka Peninsula.

"I regret this incident and will see to it that every precaution is taken to prevent recurrence."

After saying that the Soviet Union and the United States were stepping back from danger over the Cuban situation, the President said: "I think we should give priority to questions relating to the proliferation of nuclear weapons, on Earth and in outer space, and to the great effort for a nuclear test ban.

"But we should also work hard to see if wider measures of disarmament can be agreed and put into operation at an early date.

"The United States government will be prepared to discuss these questions urgently, and in a constructive spirit, at Geneva or elsewhere."

REPLY "AT ONCE"
Settling crisis

Mr. Kennedy said he was "replying at once" to Mr. Khruschev's broadcast message of Oct. 28, even though the official text had not reached him, "because of the great importance I attach to moving forward promptly to the settlement of the Cuban crisis."

"Mr. Chairman, both of our countries have great unfinished tasks and I know that your people as well as those of the United States can ask for nothing better than to pursue them free from the fear of war." - Reuter.

U.N. CONTROL WELCOMED BY BRITAIN

By Our Diplomatic Staff

THE British Government particularly welcomed Mr. Khruschev's suggestion that missile bases in Cuba could be dismantled under United Nations supervision.

The Earl of Home, Foreign Secretary, kept in close touch with the fast developing situation during the week-end. Mr. Macmillan met him at Admiralty House early yesterday with Mr. Butler, First Secretary of State, Mr. Heath, Lord Privy Seal, and Mr. Thorneycroft, Minister of Defence.

PREMIER'S MESSAGE

At this session the Prime Minister composed his message to Mr. Khruschev. This said:

The essence of the position reached is that once the problem posed by the offensive bases in Cuba has been dealt with under effective United Nations control and the situation in the area normalised, the way would be open for us all to work towards a more general arrangement regarding armaments.

This is an opportunity which we should all seize.

The Russian withdrawal started speculation on possibilities opened up by President Kennedy's firm action and diplomatic victory.

One man who must feel rather left out in the wave of diplomatic activity is Dr. Castro of Cuba. Neither the Americans nor the Russians now seem very much interested in his views.

Over the telephone from Havana he told THE SUNDAY TELEGRAPH that his army and air force stood at maximum alert.

DUCHESS OF KENT ILL

"Minor abdominal operation"

Daily Telegraph reporter

THE Duchess of Kent, who is 29, was admitted to University College Hospital last night. She is to have a "minor abdominal operation" in the next few days, it was learned at Coppins, Iver, Bucks, last night.

The operation will be performed by Sir John Peel, 57, obstetrician to the Queen. Lord Evans 59, the Queen's physician, will be in attendance. They attended the Duchess when she gave birth to her son, the Earl of St. Andrews, on June 26.

The Duke of Kent, who drove his wife to the hospital from Coppins last night, is due to return to regimental duty with the Royal Scots Greys in Hongkong next month. It was announced in the summer that he would be accompanied by the Duchess and their baby.

THE DUCHESS OF KENT

It was understood last night that the Duke's departure for Hongkong would not be unduly postponed.

The Duke and Duchess of Kent returned to London on Oct. 19 after representing the Queen in the Uganda independence celebrations.

The Daily Telegraph

4 A.M.

No. 33353. LONDON, SATURDAY, JULY 14, 1962 — and Morning Post — Printed in LONDON and MANCHESTER Price 2½d.

7 MINISTERS DROPPED FROM CABINET

MR. SELWYN LLOYD A BACK BENCHER

MR. MAUDLING TAKES OVER TREASURY

11 APPOINTED: MR. BUTLER NAMED DEPUTY PREMIER

By H.B. BOYNE,
Daily Telegraph Political Correspondent

ONE of the most drastic Cabinet reconstructions ever undertaken midway through the life of a Government was announced last night by the Prime Minister. It involves a clean sweep of senior Ministers at the Treasury.

Resignations of seven senior members of the Cabinet, including Viscount Kilmuir, Lord Chancellor, and Mr. Selwyn Lloyd, Chancellor of the Exchequer, have been accepted by the Queen on Mr. Macmillan's advice.

To replace them and provide for consequential changes 11 new appointments have been made, including Mr. Maudling as Chancellor, with more to follow. These include six new members of the Cabinet, one of whom, Mr. William Deedes, steps up direct from the back-benches.

For the first time Mr. Butler is named as Deputy Prime Minister. He gives up the Home Office but remains in the Cabinet with the new designation "First Secretary of State."

The Resignations

The seven Ministers who have resigned their posts are:

Viscount KILMUIR, 62, Lord Chancellor.
Mr. SELWYN LLOYD, 57, Chancellor of the Exchequer.
Mr. JOHN MACLAY, 56, Secretary of State for Scotland.
Mr. HAROLD WATKINSON, 52, Minister of Defence.
Lord MILLS, 72, Minister without Portfolio.
Dr. CHARLES HILL, 58, Minister of Housing and Local Government, and Minister for Welsh Affairs.
Sir DAVID ECCLES, 57, Minister of Education.

The Appointments

The appointments, with ages, and names of former holders in brackets are as follows, the salary, in each case except that of the Lord Chancellor, who gets £12,000, being £5,000 and £750 of the Parliamentary salary:

First Secretary of State (new post), **Mr. R.A. BUTLER, 59.**
Home Secretary, Mr. HENRY BROOKE, 59 (Mr. Butler).
Chancellor of the Exchequer, Mr. REGINALD MAUDLING, 45, (Mr. Selwyn Lloyd).
Lord Chancellor, Sir REGINALD MANNINGHAM-BULLER, Q.C., 56, (Viscount Kilmuir).
Secretary of State for Commonwealth Relations and Colonial Secretary (combined post), **Mr. DUNCAN SANDYS, 54,** (Mr. Sandys and Mr. Maudling, Colonial Secretary).
Secretary of State for Scotland, Mr. M.A.C. NOBLE, 49 (Mr. Maclay.
Chief Secretary to the Treasury and Paymaster-General, Mr. J.A. BOYD-CARPENTER, 54, (Mr. Brooke).
Minister of Defence, Mr. PETER THORNEYCROFT, 52, (Mr. Watkinson).
Minister of Housing and Local Government and Minister for Welsh Affairs, Sir KEITH JOSEPH, 44, (Dr. Charles Hill);
Minister Without Portfolio, Mr. WILLIAM DEEDES, 49, (Lord Mills).
Minister of Education, Sir EDWARD BOYLE, 38, (Sir David Eccles).

Two By-elections

To provide for this reconstruction the Prime Minister is risking two by-elections, at Northants South, caused by the appointment of Sir Reginald Manningham-Buller, the former Attorney-General, as Lord Chancellor and at Chippenham, Wilts, through the elevation to the Peerage of Sir David Eccles, former Minister of Education.

The official announcement from Admiralty House said: "Mr. Butler will act as Deputy Prime Minister. He will retain responsibility for the Central African Office and continue to lead the Ministerial Group charged with the oversight of the Common Market negotiations.

"Mr. Sandys will combine the posts of Secretary of State for Commonwealth Relations and Secretary of State for the Colonies."

Six of the new appointments

MR. BUTLER
(First Secretary of State)

MR. BROOKE
(Home Secretary)

SIR REGINALD MANNINGHAM-BULLER
(Lord Chancellor)

MR. DUNCAN SANDYS
(Secretary of State for Commonwealth Relations and Colonial Secretary)

MR. NOBLE
(Secretary of State for Scotland)

MR. BOYD-CARPENTER
(Chief Secretary to the Treasury and Paymaster-General)

MR. MAUDLING (left) Colonial Secretary, who has been appointed Chancellor of the Exchequer in sucession to Mr. Selwyn Lloyd (right), whose resignation from the Cabinet has been accepted by the Queen on the advice of Mr. Macmillan.

POLICIES UNPOPULAR BUT RIGHT, SAYS MR. LLOYD

LETTER TO MR. MACMILLAN

By Our Political Staff

IT is significant that the only exchange of letters published after yesterday's Cabinet resignations is between the Prime Minister and Mr. Selwyn Lloyd, Chancellor of the Exchequer. It is dated only yesterday, and Mr. Lloyd begins his letter with the blunt sentence: "You have told me that you would like me to resign and this I willingly do."

The plain inference is that resignation has in reality been forced upon him, and that the ex-Chancellor feels he is being made the scapegoat for the unpopularity of the Government's income policy.

Mr. Lloyd defends his policy in a letter written from Treasury Chambers. This says:

DEAR PRIME MINISTER,

You have told me that you would like me to resign and this I willingly do. I realise that the policies with which I have been associated have been unpopular.

On the other hand, I believe they have been right and have had a considerable measure of success. In my view our currency is stronger and our economic prospects on a firmer basis than for some time, and we are in a better position to face any difficulties which may come.

NEW DEPARTURES

Incomes policy

I am also glad to have been associated with certain new departures, such as the development of an incomes policy and the creation of the National Economic Development Council.

My primary aim has been to strengthen the country's competitive power and lay the foundation for sound growth.

I know that you are well aware of my concern that these policies should be continued, and also of my anxiety that the growth of public expenditure, so much of it highly desirable in itself, should not outstrip our resources.

I am very grateful to you for the many personal kindnesses which you have shown me.

Yours ever, SELWYN.

PREMIER'S REPLY

Commanded support

To this, Mr. Macmillan replied from Admiralty House yesterday:

DEAR SELWYN,

Thank you very much for your letter. Your courageous policies at the Treasury have always commanded the support of your colleagues. You can rest assured we intend to continue on the path that you have prepared.

I am certain that this is the only way in which we can, in your own words, build growth upon a sound basis. I am sure you realise the need in the present situation for a broad reconstruction of the Government with a view to the future and I am grateful to you for facilitating this.

I am touched by your reference to personal kindnesses. We have worked together for a long time, through many difficulties and I am deeply grateful to you for your friendly support and encouragement.

Yours ever, HAROLD MACMILLAN

CITY WILL BE LOOKING FOR CHANGES

By Our City Editor

IN the City, the change at the helm at the Treasury will not cause any great surprise. Nor, it must be said, will it cause any dropping of spirits.

Though it will be assumed the new Chancellor will follow closely the broad policies espoused by his predecessor, with exports realising high priority, the City will also look for certain changes. It will look for fresh vigour in the pursuit of economic policy and still more for greater cohesion and lucidity.

NEW EMPHASIS

There will also be at least a hope that Mr. Maudling will put such a new emphasis on expansion, as will help to restore the flagging confidence of the business community in economic prospects.

So far as sterling is concerned, the reshuffle should have no adverse repercussions. It can be assumed that there is no intention of attempting to stimulate the economy by methods which would jeopardise the strength of the pound.

In the stockmarkets and in the business community the new look at the Treasury is likely to be regarded as strengthening hopes of better things ahead. But the City will not rush just yet to any firm conclusions.

HEAVY BUYING OF GOLD

By Our City Editor

Keen buying of gold in the London bullion market raised the price yesterday to the highest level since February. After touching \$35.13oz the quotation closed at \$35.12 1/2 compared with \$35.12 on Thursday.

Following its now customary tactics the Bank of England made gold available, thus preventing any sharp rise in price.

Bullion dealers described the buying as "unusually large." Most of the orders came from Continental centres. They were prompted by the news that the Bank of France had switched \$112.5 million of its reserves into gold, thus adding to the heavy drain on America's dwindling gold reserves.

"A POLITICAL MASSACRE"

Labour & Liberals demand election

CALLS for the Government to resign were made last night by Mr. Gaitskell and Mr. Grimond, the Labour and Liberal leaders, after the Ministerial changes were announced.

Mr. Gaitskell spoke of the changes as a "political massacre" which could be interpreted only as a gigantic admission of failure. "Instead of getting rid of his colleagues, the Prime Minister should resign and let the people elect a new Government."

Mr. Grimond said: "The changes are clear confirmation of the total failure of the Government. The logic of the situation is that the whole Government should resign."

"CONFESSION OF FAILURE"

Mr. Wilson, the "Shadow" Foreign Secretary, said at Bristol, "The comprehensiveness of these Cabinet changes is the biggest confession of failure this Government could have made. The men responsible for basic policies in the economic field, in defence, housing and education are gone.

"No reshuffle is worth anything which leaves the present Prime Minister in command. The proper logic of the Government's failure and its repudiation by the electorate would have been to change the pack and replace the present Government by a vigorous Socialist alternative."

U.S. WATCH ON POLICY

DEFENCE CHANGE

From Our Own Correspondent

WASHINGTON, Friday.

Among British Cabinet Ministers dealing regularly with their American counterparts the most striking change in the British reshuffle is the disappearance of Mr. Watkinson as Minister of Defence.

When he was under attack at home recently Mr. McNamara, Secretary for Defence, came to his aid with a strong letter denying that there was any ill feeling between them.

The Kennedy Administration will watch for any changes in British defence policy. It has long urged a speedier build-up of Britain's conventional forces.

MONKEYS GO UP IN BALLOONS

WASHINGTON, Friday.

Four of the largest balloons ever launched will be flown high over Canada, carrying monkeys and hamsters, to determine the effects of cosmic radiation on man. The first two balloons will be launched to-night from near Goose Bay in Labrador.

Travelling on the prevailing easterly winds, the balloons, of 9 million cubic feet capacity, are expected to fly for more than 2,000 miles at an altitude of 128,000ft. The flights, lasting about 55 hours, are expected to end near Edmonton, Alberta - NYT Service.

ADOLF EICHMANN IS HANGED

Final plea rejected: midnight execution

From Our Own Correspondent

TEL AVIV, Friday morning.

ADOLF EICHMANN was hanged at Ramleh Prison near Tel Aviv two minutes before midnight. Just before the noose was put round his neck, he said: "Long live Germany, Long live Argentina, Long live Austria . . . I had to obey the laws of the war and my flag."

He then looked at four journalists who had been chosen to witness the execution. He said to them: "After a short while, gentlemen, we shall meet again, so is the fate of all men. I have been believing in God all my life, and I die a believer in God."

ADOLF EICHMANN standing in his glass bullet-proof dock in the Israeli Supreme Court in Jerusalem yesterday as he heard that his appeal against the death sentence for the mass murder of Jews had been dismissed.

Eichmann, 56, former head of the Gestapo department for Jewish affairs, was sentenced to death for playing "a central and decisive part" in the Nazi extermination of six million European Jews. A Government doctor pronounced him dead at 11.58 p.m.

The Supreme Court, rejecting his appeal, described him as "a fanatical enthusiast" and spoke of his "insatiable blood-thirstiness" in carrying out "these unspeakably horrible crimes to his own gratification and satisfaction of his superiors."

Eichmann was born in the Ruhr in 1906, the son of an evangelical Christian. He was a sales clerk and oil company agent before joining the S.S., the Nazi military and political organisation. Four years later he was appointed head of the Jewish Affairs Department.

TRACKED DOWN
Flowers clue

At the end of the war in 1945 Eichmann vanished and, although variously reported in Latin America, Switzerland and the Middle East was not brought to light until May, 1960. Israeli Intelligence agents tracked him down in Argentina.

He is said to have been given away finally by the fact that he brought flowers for his wife on their wedding anniversary.

Eichmann was kidnapped by Israelis at a bus stop and flown to Israel. Eleven months later, on April 11, 1961, he was put on trial on 15 charges under the Nazis and Nazi Collaborators (Punishment) Law.

(June 1)

WILLIAM JOHN VASSALL, 38-year-old Admiralty clerk, who was sentenced at the Old Bailey yesterday to 18 years imprisonment

18 YEARS' GAOL FOR 'TRAITOROUS TOOL OF RUSSIANS'

Daily Telegraph Reporter

WILLIAM JOHN VASSALL, 38, the Admiralty clerk who said he was blackmailed into spying for Russia, was sent to prison for a total of 18 years at the Old Bailey yesterday. He was described by the prosecution as "a traitorous tool of the Russians."

On a charge that one day in 1955, for purposes prejudicial to the safety or interest of the State, he communicated to another person information which might have been directly or indirectly useful to an enemy, Vassall was sentenced by Lord Parker, Lord Chief Justice, to six years.

He was sentenced to 12 years concurrently each on three other charges under the Official Secrets Act, to run consecutively with the six-year sentence. These were that:

Between Aug. 1, 1956, and May 31, 1957, for purposes prejudicial to the safety or interests of the State, he communicated to another person information which might have been directly or indirectly useful to an enemy.

On Aug. 17 last committed a similar offence; and between Aug 17 and Sept. 12, 1962, for purposes prejudicial to the safety or interest of the State, collected information which might have been directly or indirectly useful to an enemy.

CONFESSION TO POLICE
Statement unacceptable

LORD PARKER said to Vassall, who had pleaded guilty to the four charges: "You have stated in your confession to the police that throughout you had no intention of harming this country. I am unable to accept that.

"A man of your education, experience and intelligence knew full well that this information and these documents would be of assistance to an enemy. I am satisfied that what you did, you did largely for money."

He accepted that when Vassall first started his spying activities in Moscow it was under pressure, but when he returned to England he could have made a clean breast of the matter, and left his Government work where he would not have access to any secret information.

Also, from 1955, Vassall had accepted money for his work to the extent of doubling his £688 a year salary. "I take the view that one of the compelling reasons for what you did was pure selfish greed."

Although the information Vassall passed was of a haphazard character, it was often of a highly secret nature and capable of doing great harm to the country. "You have got to be punished, to an extent that will also be a deterrent to others."

(October 23)

"PIMPERNEL" GAOLED FOR FIVE YEARS

From LESLIE SELBY
Daily Telegraph Special Correspondent

CAPE TOWN, Wednesday.

NELSON MANDELA, the "Black Pimpernel" was sentenced in Pretoria to-day to a total of five years imprisonment. He was found guilty of incitement and leaving South Africa illegally.

Mr. W.A. Van Helsdingen, the magistrate, said Mandela, former secretary of the banned African National Congress, had been the "mouthpiece and master mind" behind a scheme to call a national strike last year. He had acted in a way calculated to lead to tyranny and destruction.

In an emotional last-minute statement, an unrepentant Mandela said his conscience had made it imperative for him to oppose laws which were unjust, immoral and intolerable. "If I had my time over again I would do it again, so would any man who called himself a man."

Mandela pleaded not guilty, but he offered no defence. He did, however, speak at length on how he had devoted his life to the emancipation of his people.

(November 28)

MOSS INJURED IN 110 M.P.H. CRASH

'NOT TO WORRY' MESSAGE

From W.A. McKENZIE,
Daily Telegraph Motoring Correspondent

GOODWOOD, Monday.

STIRLING MOSS, 32, Champion British racing driver, and four times runner-up to the World Champion, crashed here to-day at 110 m.p.h. He was taken to the Royal West Sussex Hospital, Chichester, with what the track medical officers describe as "serious injuries," which included a broken rib, a fractured leg and head injuries.

A late night report to me from the hospital said he was unconscious and being moved to the Atkinson Morley Hospital, Wimbledon, because of head injuries.

HELD IN SEAT
Dazed condition

His Lotus Climax car was so badly smashed in the crash that he was trapped in his seat, and it took the crew of the Goodwood emergency breakdown truck, eight marshals and two doctors half an hour to release his legs from the wreckage.

He was unconscious when the first track marshal reached him, but he regained consciousness and remained in a dazed condition when they took him to hospital.

While he was still trapped he dictated a message to be sent to his mother, Mrs. Aileen Moss, at the White Cloud Farm, Tring, Herts. It said: "I am fine, not to worry, will ring you when I get back."

The accident happened in the chief race of the day, a 42-lap event for this season's 1 ½ litre Formula 1 Grand Prix cars. It turned out to be the fastest race ever held at Goodwood.

(April 24)

OXFORD UNION ADMITS WOMEN

RIGHT TO TAKE PART IN DEBATE

Daily Telegraph Reporter

THE Oxford Union yesterday agreed to admit women to debating membership. So far they have only been allowed as guest speakers.

The Union was the last of Oxford's all-male strongholds. The special poll obtained the regulation two-thirds majority, 730 votes to 307.

The first undergraduates arrived promptly at 9.30 a.m. to vote. All resident members were entitled to a vote.

A number of undergraduates said they had altered their vote from last year. One said: "Over half the members wanted the women in last year and that is good enough for me. I believe in helping democracy to work."

GREETED WITH CHEERS

When the President, Hugh Stephenson, of New College, announced the result at 9 p.m., to about 30 undergraduates in the Union bar he was greeted with cheers. He said he was surprised but delighted by the result.

Wynford Hicks, of Christ Church, who proposed the motion to admit women in a debate last week, said he felt women would maintain or improve the standard of debating. Kedar Malik, of St. Peter's, who had demanded the full poll of members, said: "I still believe women are not equal with men."

(February 17)

BIG ANTI-WALL PROTEST

From REGINAD PECK,
Daily Telegraph Special Correspondent

BERLIN, Monday.

TEAR GAS bombs and water cannon were used by East German border police to-day to scatter West Berliners protesting against the Communist wall on the first anniversary of its construction. At one stage demonstrators numbered more than 1,000.

In the Kreuzberg and Neukoelln suburbs a teargas and stone duel was fought out between East and West. Police on both sides were throwing teargas bombs while civilians on the Western side were hurling bricks and stones from nearby ruins. An estimated total of between 200 and 300 teargas bombs were thrown.

CAR STONED
Wooden cross carried

A Russian car was stoned by angry West Berliners as it drove into the Western sectors to-night and again as it drove out about an hour later. West Berlin police estimated the crowd at the Friedrichstrasse international crossing point where the car crossed at "several hundred strong." But they said none of the three civilians in the car had been injured.

At the Bernauerstrasse a column of about 1,000 West Berliners led by a young man carrying a wooden cross were bombarded by teargas bombs thrown by East Berlin police and drenched by water cannon.

After about half an hour Western police succeeded in sealing off the Bernauerstrasse area. The ugly-looking situation was described by police as "under control."

(August 14)

EDDIE FISHER DENIES RIFT IN MARRIAGE

From Our Own Correspondent

NEW YORK, Friday.

EDDIE FISHER, the singer, held a Press conference in a New York hotel to-day to deny suggestions of an estrangement with his wife, Elizabeth Taylor. He described the suggestions as "preposterous."

Reporters asked him if Miss Taylor, making the film "Cleopatra" in Rome, would subscribe to the denial. He replied: "I think so," and made a telephone call to her.

Afterwards, he said she would not, adding: "You can ask a woman to do something and she doesn't always do it."

"LONG MARRIAGE" FORECAST

Asked about reports of a romance between Miss Taylor and the British actor, Richard Burton, who plays opposite her, Mr. Fisher said: "The only romance is between Cleopatra and Mark Antony and, I might say, a mighty good one."

Recalling that he and his wife recently adopted a child, he said he foresaw a long and happy marriage.

(March 31)

LAST JOURNEYS IN THE TROLLEYBUSES

Daily Telegraph Reporter

THE last 100 of the 1,700 trolley-buses that once ran in London made their final runs last night. The journeys, over seven routes in South-West London, marked the end of the final stage of the replacement of what was once the world's largest trolley bus fleet with Routemaster diesel buses.

The changeover began in 1959 and has been carried out in 14 stages. The trolleybus era ended where it began 31 years ago - at the Fulwell depot, near Twickenham.

The last trolleybus to run in London completed its final journey to Fulwell half an hour after midnight after a 50-minute run from Wimbledon.

Hundreds of drivers and conductors escorted the trolleybus, bedecked with flags and streamers, as Mr. Albert West, 70, Fulwell's oldest driver drove it into the depot. To-day Mr. West, a driver for 41 years, takes out one of the new Routemasters.

(May 9)

3 BREAK OUT OF ALCATRAZ WITH SPOONS

From Our Own Correspondent

NEW YORK, Thursday.

Three prisoners serving long terms for bank robbery vanished from Alcatraz, the island prison in San Francisco bay, early this morning. It is not known whether they escaped to the mainland, drowned in the attempt, or found hiding places in caves that dot the island's waterline.

Prison officials think that the men who broke out to-day used a driftwood raft to navigate the Bay. The escape was a combination of extraordinary patience and ingenuity.

PIPE TUNNEL

Using spoons, they dug over a period of many months through the thick concrete wall of their cells into a pipe tunnel.

(June 13)

LIBERAL VICTORY AT ORPINGTON

7,855 MAJORITY OVER CONSERVATIVE

By H.B. BOYNE,
Daily Telegraph Political Correspondent

THE Orpington by-election result provided a sensation this morning. The Liberals gained their first seat since Torrington four years ago, and converted a Conservative majority of 14,760 into a deficit of 7,855.

The result declared at 12.30 this morning was:

E. LUBBOCK (L.) **22,846**
P. GOLDMAN (C.) **14,991**
A. JINKINSON (Lab.).........................**5,350**
Liberal majority **7,855**

There was no consolation for Labour. Their own candidate's vote was cut by 4,193, and he had the humiliation of losing his deposit.

Nor can either of the major parties contend that the result, because of the size of the poll, is not a trustworthy indicator of current political trends.

Four out of five electors voted: practically the same turnout as at the last General Election. Yesterday's by-election was caused by the appointment of Mr. Donald Sumner (C.) as a County Court judge.

VOTING SWITCH

No apathy

At the General Election the result was:

W.D. SUMNER (C.)......**24,303**
N.J. HART (Lab.)............**9,543**
J.O. GALLOWAY (Lib.) ..**9,092**
C. maj. **14,760**

Yesterday it was not a case of apathy or disgruntled "stayaways," as at Blackpool North. The former Conservative supporters went to the poll all right: for the express purpose of voting Liberal.

Mr. Lubbock is 33 and was brought up and lives at Downe in the constituency. He was educated in Canada and at Balliol. He is the grandson of the late Sir John Lubbock, M.P., and cousin and heir of Lord Avebury. He is married with three children.

Mr. Jo Grimond, the Liberal leader, speaking on Independent Television, was perfectly entitled to claim this as "a wonderful victory."

Lord Aldington, vice-chairman of the Conservative party organisation, agreed that it was "a sensational result." This sort of thing, he added, had happened before. "I am cetain the Conservative party will not be shaken by it. We shall march on and win the next General Election.

It is the first Government seat to be lost since the General Election. With a majority of around 100 in the House Conservatives can argue that the result is an incident, not a disaster.

(March 15)

ERIC LUBBOCK, LIBERAL VICTOR.

U.N. TROOPS SEIZE KATANGA H.Q.

"PEACE" ATTEMPTS FAIL

From Our Own Correspondent
LEOPOLDVILLE, Friday.

UNITED NATIONS troops to-day cleared Katangan roadblocks around Elisabethville and began evacuating United Nations civilians, a spokesman said in Leopoldville. Fighting has been going on in Elisabethville since last night and United Nations troops have captured the Katangan gendarmerie headquarters in the Karavia area of the capital.

Mr. Robert Gardiner, head of United Nations operations in the Congo, said the order to clear the roadblocks was given this afternoon. United Nations soldiers were told to shoot if fired at during the operation.

Shooting by Katangans had been going on for four days, said Mr. Gardiner. A United Nations map revealed that 20 roadblocks manned by Katangans had been set up in Elisabethville in the last two months.

Col. Gunnar Samuelson, a Swedish officer serving with United Nations said Katangans opened fire on United Nations positions near the airport last night. The shooting quickly spread to other parts of the city.

TSHOMBE TOUR

Cease-fire attempts

An hour later President Tshombe of Katanga called on Mr. Eliud Mathu, Kenyan head of the United Nations operations in Elisabethville, and they toured two United Nations roadblocks with Gen. Prem Chand, United Nations commander.

Col. Samuelson said Mr. Tshombe agreed the shooting was being done by the Katangans. He wanted to leave, but was physically restrained by Gen. Chand.

Mr. Tshombe later agreed to give a verbal order for a cease-fire. This was the first of two unsuccessful attempts by the President to halt the fighting.

Firing continued and he made another attempt five hours later. This time he telephoned Gen. Norbert Moke, of the Katangan gendarmerie, and ordered that the shooting be stopped.

But mortar fire was later directed at United Nations forces and six Ethiopians and one Indian were wounded. United Nations troops were then ordered into action against the roadblocks.

(December 29)

THALIDOMIDE FIRM GIVES £250,000 FOR RESEARCH

THE Distillers' Company, which produced and marketed the drug thalidomide under the trade name Distaval for four years, is to set aside £250,000 for research into the incidence and causes of congenital abnormality in human beings.

This was announced by Sir Graham Hayman, the chairman, at the annual general meeting of the company in Edinburgh yesterday. The research will not be carried out by the company. It is proposed to seek the advice of senior members of the medical profession about the best method of using the funds.

Sir Graham said: "I am well aware of the concern felt by a number of shareholders over the tragedies of children who have been born with deformities in circumstances where the company's thalidomide products may appear to be associated with the case.

"I should make it clear from the outset that the company is advised that it has no legal liability in this matter.

"Such information as we have been able to gather indicates that in this country cases of the type with which thalidomide may be associated, still represent a comparatively small proportion of the total number of cases of congenital abnormality.

"There appears to be a notable lack of scientific research in this field and there is quite clearly a need for further study of the incidence and causes of such abnormality."

Commenting on the annual report of the company, Mr. MICHAEL CARR-JONES, chairman of the Society for the Aid of Thalidomide Children, said: "As a parent I feel very bitter and disappointed."

(September 15)

PRINCE'S "GOOD REPORT" AT GORDONSTOUN

THE Prince of Wales, in his first term at Gordonstoun, which he joined in May, has climbed to near the top of his class, it was disclosed yesterday. He is popular with other boys, who call him "Charles." He returned home to London by air yesterday for the summer holidays.

The headmaster, Mr. F.R.G. Chew, said the Prince had joined the choir. He had played cricket and hockey.

"He has done well in his studies," said Mr. Chew. "We do not have a term order, but I can tell you he was very near the top in a class of 28. I know from his examination results that he was well up the class."

The headmaster said that a report showing the Prince's examination results and comments by his house master would be sent to his parents in the same way as reports on all the other boys at the school.

The Prince, who was in Class IIIA last term, will be moving into the fourth form after the summer holidays. He shares a dormitory with 11 other boys.

"I think Prince Charles has settled in jolly well," Mr. Chew added, :"As a new boy he has not yet joined one of the school's services, but he has joined what is called 'the pre-service.'

"The new boys have a general training. This may involve map reading and going over the obstacle course at the school.

"Later they can opt to go into one of the senior services - the fire service, the mountain rescue service, the coast-watchers or the surf sea rescue team.

(July 27)

GOVERNMENT PAY £350,000 TO SAVE LEONARDO

Daily Telegraph Reporter

THE Leonardo cartoon is to be bought for the nation. The Prime Minister announced yesterday in the House of Commons that the Government will provide £350,000 from public funds to make up the balance of the £800,000 purchase price asked for by the Royal Academy.

In four months since the public appeal was started, subscriptions towards the purchase of the charcoal drawing of the Virgin with St. John the Baptist and St. Anne, have topped £450,000. Over 200,000 people have contributed. Yesterday was the last day of the appeal.

In his announcement, Mr. Macmillan said: "The Government have been greatly impressed by the very large number of individual citizens who have contributed towards keeping this great work of art in this country.

"Subject to the approval of Parliament the balance of £350,000 will be found from public funds."

OPPOSITION WELCOME

"Regret" over sale

Mr. Gaitskell, Opposition Leader, said: "Many of us regret that the Royal Academy ever decided to sell this cartoon. It would have been better for them to have accepted a Government grant.

"Nevertheless, public opinion will welcome the grant given by the Government to make up the purchase price."

The Royal Academy decided to sell the picture to meet rising costs. If the £800,000 appeal had failed the cartoon was to be auctioned.

Sir Charles Wheeler, president of the Royal Academy, said last night: "We might have benefited more by a sale by auction than through an appeal. But it has always been the wish of members that the cartoon should stay in this country, and I am naturally pleased at the Government's decision.

(August 1)

MAIDEN FLIGHT FOR 100-SEATER TRIDENT

By JOHN CHAPPELL
Daily Telegraph Air Correspondent

THE first de Havilland Trident jet airliner made its maiden flight successfully yesterday. Mr. J. Cunningham, the de Havilland chief test pilot, took off from the company's airfield at Hatfield, Herts, and flew the plane for 1hr 20min.

On landing he said he was delighted with the plane's performance. During the flight photographs were taken of the Trident from a Canberra bomber and a Meteor fighter. The flight was originally planned for December but was delayed by snow and fog. The second aircraft is due to be ready for flight trials by April or May and a third by the summer. Five Tridents are in various stages of construction.

606 MPH CRUISING SPEED

The Trident is intended to carry up to 100 passengers on short and medium routes from 350 to 2,000 miles. Its most economic operation will be over 1,000 miles. It will have a cruising speed of 606 mph and will be capable of operating from comparatively small airports. It is powered by three Rolls Royce Spey jet engines mounted in the tail. The Spey is the most recent Rolls Royce jet engine to be developed for airline service. There is also a military version.

£30m. BEA ORDER

British European Airways has ordered 24 Tridents costing nearly £30 million with spares and has an option on 12 more. First deliveries are due towards the end of 1963. The Trident has a direct rival in the Boeing 727 jet airliner.

(January 10)

NEGRO STUDENT BARRED AGAIN

From Our Own Correspondent
NEW YORK, Wednesday.

IN four tense minutes to-day James Meredith's third attempt in a week to enrol at the University of Mississippi was thwarted by State officials. Meredith, a Negro, was turned away from the all-white university at Oxford by Mr. Paul Johnson, Mississippi's Deputy Governor.

Behind Mr. Johnson the wide gravel path leading into the university grounds was blocked by three police officers. Meredith was flanked by six Federal marshals and two Justice Department lawyers.

BRIEF SCUFFLE

At one point it seemed that one of the Federal marshals was trying to get through the line of State police and there was a brief scuffle. But no blows were struck.

Mr. Ross Barnett, the Governor of Mississippi, has rejected notice of a court order to appear in New Orleans on Friday to answer a contempt of court charge for failing to comply with an order for Meredith's enrolment.

Battle of wills

OUR WASHINGTON CORRESPONDENT cabled last night: Mr. Robert Kennedy, Attorney-General, is determined to see that the court order for Meredith's enrolment is enforced. He said to-night Federal troops would be used if necessary, but emphasised no firm decision to use troops had yet been reached.

(September 27)

SAAR PIT EXPLOSION DEATH TOLL RISES TO 280

From Reginald Peck,
Daily Telegraph Special Correspondent
SAARBRUKEN, Thursday.

The death toll at the Luisenthal coal mine, Voelklingen, near here, where there was a gas explosion early yesterday, is now 280, with 80 seriously injured in hospital and an estimated 24 still missing underground. About 120 miners, including most of the teenage apprentices on their first underground shift, are believed to have escaped with minor injuries.

Rescue teams reported to-night that they found 24 more bodies in the mine. This is not yet officially confirmed. If it is, the death toll will be 304.

One apprentice, Adolf Welsch, 17, believed at least two of his companions had been killed. He survived only because he was working with Josef Gross and Erich Graeber "roughly a quarter of a mile from the point of the explosion."

BURIED IN DUST

When the heavy "crump" was heard Hans Becker, who had been instructing the apprentices, shouted "Run, it's an explosion." said Welsch. At that instant "we were buried in coaldust and dirt."

A few minutes later the three apprentices and Becker started moving towards the shaft exit. They were soon met by a rescue team.

(February 9)

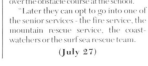

THREE ORBITS AND A SAFE RETURN

COL. GLENN NEARLY 5 HOURS IN SPACE

From ALEX FAULKNER, Daily Telegraph Special Correspondent

CAPE CANAVERAL, Tuesday.

LT. COL. JOHN H. GLENN Jr. landed in the Atlantic Ocean at 7.43 p.m. G.M.T. to-day after three orbits of the earth in the spacecraft Friendship Seven. A crane hauled the capsule on to the destroyer Noa, 2,435 tons, and after mechanics had had trouble with the exit hatch, Col. Glenn exploded it, emerging as a "hale and hearty astronaut."

Col. Glenn landed four hours and 56 minutes after being launched into space from Cape Canaveral. The capsule was plucked from the Atlantic at 8.01 p.m. and within three minutes it was resting on the deck of the destroyer.

The first thing Col. Glenn asked for when he emerged from the spaceship was a glass of iced tea. "It was hot in there," he said.

The astronaut controlled Friendship manually for more than two thirds of the flight. He was in a state of weightlessness for about four hours and 27 minutes of his four hours and 56 minutes flight and spent nine hours in the capsule to-day.

ATLANTIC DESCENT

6 Miles From Ship

The Mercury capsule's three retro-rockets were fired at 7.20 to bring Glenn down into the Atlantic recovery area six miles from the destroyer. He was about 600 miles west of Los Angeles.

Col. Glenn reported the firing of the retro-rockets felt like he was being "sent right back to Hawaii."

As the capsule re-entered the atmosphere, swinging under the parachute. Col. Glenn's voice was heard shouting: "Boy, that was a real fireball."

(February 21)

DJILAS GAOLED FOR 8 YEARS OVER BOOK

From Our Own Correspondent

BELGRADE, Monday.

MILOVAN DJILAS, 51, former Jugoslav Vice-President, was found guilty to-day of disclosing official secrets. He was sentenced to a total of eight years and eight months imprisonment.

Five years of the sentence were for the present charge. The rest was the unserved portion of a previous sentence.

Belgrade District Court rejected a demand that the trial be held in public. Mr. Alexander Atanackovitch, the prosecutor, said security interests demanded that the public should be excluded until the end.

Charges arose from the proposed publication abroad of Mr. Djilas's account of talks with Stalin. He has been accused in the Jugoslav Press of revealing State secrets and damaging Jugoslavia's prestige abroad.

MILOVAN DJILAS

"NOT GUILTY" PLEA

Before the court was closed he said: "I am not guilty. I am here because of my intellectual disobedience.

"I have been defamed in public and I wish to defend myself in public. If the trial is held in secret I shall not answer any questions put by the judge or the prosecutor.

"There is no human or juridical reason why the trial should be secret. The juridical reason does not exist, because part of the book had already been published.

"The human reason is that secrecy would reduce me to a position where I could say nothing."

When the judge ordered that the hearing should be in private the members of the public and correspondents left. Mr. Djilas was allowed to have his wife, his two sisters and his brother in court.

(May 15)

WORST DAY ON WALL ST. SINCE 1929

SELLING on the New York Stock Exchange was heavier to-day than at any time since the Great Depression of 1929-30. The Dow Jones Industrial average dropped by 34.95 to 576.93, the sharpest fall since October, 1929.

The pressure was so great that at the close of the day's trading the ticker tape registering deals was 69 minutes behind. Neither the day's volume nor the Dow Jones fall could be learnt until more than an hour after the last deal.

The New York Times estimated the paper losses on the day's trading totalled £7,428,571,000.

There were two significant facts about the day's trading. One was that for the first time since the present decline began high-class industrials which are the backbone of institutional investment showed losses.

Notable among these was a fall of 10 dollars 12 cents towards the close in American Telephone and Telegraph, the world's biggest corporation.

The other significant factor was that much of the selling was being done by small investors. Some observers in Wall Street said that something approaching panic had developed in this class.

(May 29)

RHODESIANS BAN FLEMING NOVEL

SALISBURY, S. Rhodesia, Friday

A new Ian Fleming novel, "The Spy Who Loved Me," has been banned in the Central African Federation, the Federal Ministry of Home Affairs has announced in Salisbury, Southern Rhodesia.

The ban was imposed because the book contains "passages considered unsuitable for circulation in the Federation," the Ministry said.

(April 14)

CHRIS BONNINGTON, 27, OF HAMPSTEAD and Don Whillans of Lancashire (right) are pictured approaching Brian Nally, 25, of Barnet (upper left).

EIGER CONQUEST BY BRITISH PAIR

From Our Own Correspondent

GENEVA, Friday.

CHRIS BONINGTON, 27 and Ian Clough, 25, to-day became the first Britons to scale the North Face of the Eiger, 13,040ft. As they were nearing the top, the mountain claimed two more victims, one of them feared to be Tom Carruthers, 25, of Glasgow.

The two Briton's successful ascent was the 31st since the North Face, one of the toughest Alpine challenges, was first climbed in 1938. It was one of the four fastest, taking only two days. Ian Clough, who comes from Baildon, Yorks, said to-night: "It was a very enjoyable climb, with no difficulties."

Five weeks ago Chris Bonington, of Hampstead, abandoned an attempt so that he could help rescue Brian Nally, whose companion, Barry Brewster had been killed by a rock fall.

Yesterday Bonington and Clough were the last men to see Carruthers and his Austrian companion.

Two bodies were spotted from the ground this afternoon. Bonington said they must be those of Carruthers and the Austrian, though this will not be confirmed until the bodies are recovered to-morrow.

MOUNTAIN MEETING

Victors travelled faster

The missing men were last seen from the ground at 4 p.m. yesterday, when mist closed in. They are the 24th and 25th victims of the North Face.

Bonington and Clough met Carruthers and the Austrian on the lower part of the face on Wednesday afternoon when both parties set off.

But Bonington and Clough went much faster yesterday and bivouacked on the "Traverse of the Gods" over two thirds of the way up.

Carruthers and the Austrian reached a point above this but apparently fell to a ledge 2,000ft. below.

Bonington and Clough also overtook two Swiss named Jenny and Hausherr, who started a day before them. Bonington and Clough ascended the Spider glacier to-day. Then came the vertical "exit cracks" leading to the summit icefield.

They reached the top at 2 p.m., hidden by mist from watchers below. The Swiss got there at 4.30 p.m.

The Britons made a very fast descent of the normal route down the West-face. They reached the Kleine Scheidegg hotel in less than three hours, and had hot baths.

(September 1)

HYMNS NOT UNDERSTOOD, SAYS ADAM FAITH

DR. COGGAN AGREES CHURCH HAS 'LANGUAGE BARRIER'

By Our TV And Radio Staff

THE Archbishop of York, Dr. Coggan, agreed in a television discussion last night with Adam Faith, the singer, that the church had to simplify the language used in services. The New Testament was now in modern speech and he thought it should be read in churches.

The 30-minute discussion, in BBC Television's religious programme, "Meeting Point," was arranged following the Archbishop's criticisms of Faith. He suggested that the singer placed undue emphasis on sex in his songs.

Faith claimed in the programme last night that young people did not understand hymns because they were not in the language they used daily. But popular songs were, and young people could understand these.

The Archbishop said he would like to see hymns re-written so that they could be more easily understood by young people. Much was already being done, but the Church had to continue to break down the old language barrier.

AN EXPERIMENT

Catechism Revised

Asked by Mr. Ludovic Kennedy, the chairman, if he thought there could be a tremendous re-writing of hymns, the Archbishop said: "I'd be all for it." He had just taken part in an experiment in which the Catechism had been revised so that it could be more easily understood.

To do such a revision it was necessary to learn a certain amount of the "lingo."

Referring to Faith's songs the Archbishop denied that he thought the songs or the enthusiasm shown by young people for them was deplorable.

TEENAGE LOVE

Delicate and Harmless

He said: "I'm one of those who feel that sex is a thoroughly good thing, an instinct implanted by God. I'm not one of those who belong to the generation who thought it was a sort of smutty thing that you only talk about hush-hush."

He did not think that the songs contributed to juvenile delinquency. But there was a danger that too much accent might be put on sex in them.

Defending his songs, Faith said that the most important thing in a teenager's life was love which was what most of his songs were about. The Archbishop agreed with him that teenage love was a very delicate and harmless thing.

(January 29)

TROOPS HURL TEAR GAS AT ADEN RIOTERS

ADEN, Monday.

BRITISH troops threw tear-gas grenades to disperse Arab demonstrators in the bazaar area of Aden tonight. The troops, of the King's Own Scottish Borderers, went into action at the end of a day during which police had made repeated tear-gas and baton charges against battling rioters.

One Arab was killed and three wounded when police opened fire on rioters who set fire to shops. The demonstrators, armed with sticks and stones, were protesting against Britain's proposal to link Aden with the South Arabia Federation as the colony's Legislative Council began debating the federation plan

Demonstrators set fire to the offices of the pro-Federation United National party.

A Government statement to-night said 106 people had been arrested. It added that about 3,000 people had taken part in the demonstration.

BAN IGNORED

March on Council

Several injured demonstrators were taken to hospital, one with a bullet wound in the leg. Fighting began in the bazaar area about an hour before the Council's debate began.

Ignoring the Governor's ban on processions, Arabs tried to march on the Legislative Council. The march was called by the People's Socialist party, which is the political wing of the Aden Trades Union Congress.

In the Legislative Council debate Mr. Mustapha Abdullah Hassan, Independent, claimed the federal scheme tied to Aden "Britain's colonial interests" and deprived the people of South Arabia of "the fruits of their struggle and their legitimate rights." - Reuter.

(September 25)

200m SEE FIRST LIVE TV SHOW FROM U.S.

THE first live television programme from the United States to be seen in Europe was watched by an audience in 16 countries estimated at 200 million last night. Pictures and sound, relayed from the Telstar satellite, were both clear.

The link was made at 7.57 p.m. before President Kennedy was ready to inaugurate the historic programme with a Press conference. So the first live transatlantic pictures were of a baseball match in Chicago.

The return transmission was made at 10.58 p.m., when the Telstar satellite had made another circuit of the earth. Richard Dimbleby linked the contribution from nine European countries, which opened with a view of Big Ben.

The 18-minute programme was seen and heard in millions of American homes. The sound was perfect but the picture was grainy with slight blurring round the edges.

(July 24)

MAN OF 81 LEADS ESCAPE BY TUNNEL

From Our Own Correspondent

BONN, Friday.

A MAN of 81 had led 11 people, almost all elderly, in an escape from East Berlin through a 35-yard tunnel which they dug under the Communist wall. Four were women.

The tunnel, nearly 6ft high, was dug in 16 days within sight of patrolling Communist guards. Asked why the tunnel was so high, the old men said yesterday: "We didn't want our wives to have to crawl. We wanted them to walk unbowed to freedom."

The leader, who lived near the wall at Glienicke for 31 years, first tested the earth in his back yard by pretending to plant a young fir tree. He found the best soil for tunnelling, with the highest sand content, was near his chicken run.

Using picks, spades and a trenching tool from the 1914-18 war, the men started digging.

On May 5, they escaped into Fohnau, West Berlin, one yard beyond the last Communist barbed wire barrier.

(May 19)

NIGHT ON REEF FOR JAYNE MANSFIELD

From Our Own Correspondent

A bedraggled Jayne Mansfield was helped ashore here this morning from a yacht which had picked her up, with her husband, Mickey Hargitay and a friend, after the three had spent a night in swimming costume on a tiny coral reef.

The friend, Mr. Jack Drury, a publicity man, said their hired speedboat overturned during a water-ski trip off Rose Island.

(Februry 9)

LIFE SENTENCE ON EX-GEN. SALAN

Finding of extenuating circumstances

From Our Own Correspondent

PARIS, Wednesday.

EX-GEN. RAOUL SALAN, 62, was saved to-night from the firing squad. He burst into tears when the high military tribunal in Paris surprisingly sentenced him to life imprisonment for leading the Secret Army Organisation. The prosecution had demanded death.

After deliberating for 2 ¾ hours the nine judges convicted Salan of treason but said they had found "extenuating circumstances." As sentence was pronounced people in the public gallery rose and sang the "Marseillaise."

The OAS leader smiled and broke into hysterical laughter with the full realisation that he had escaped the death sentence so widely forecast. His guard half carried him, still laughing, back to his cell.

Shouts of "Algeria Francaise" mingled with the singing in the courtroom as Salan's defence lawyers embraced each other. Salan had earlier wept in the dock when one of his lawyers said that if he was executed, "it is all of us who will be crucified."

The judge did not say what the extenuating circumstances were. M. Gavalda, the Public Prosecutor, had asked for the supreme penalty and all France expected no less.

A few weeks ago ex-Gen. Jouhaud, the OAS deputy commander, was sentenced to death. Jouhaud is still in the condemned cell, but it is difficult to see how a reprieve can now be withheld.

OAS "VICTORY"

Blow to Algeria policy

During Salan's trial it was disclosed that the OAS had threatened to kill the nine judges of the military court if Salan and Jouhaud were executed.

The verdict is bound to be heralded by the Secret Army as a resounding victory. It is a severe blow to President de Gaulle and his Algerian policy. Only last week the President repeated that the crimes being perpetrated in Algeria must be punished.

To-night's decision will also confront the judiciary with a formidable problem when notorious OAS killers such as Roger Degueldre come up for trial.

(May 24)

FOUR BRITONS PRESENTED WITH NOBEL AWARDS

FOUR of this year's six Nobel Prizewinners who received awards from King Gustav Adolf of Sweden in Stockholm Concert Hall to-day, were British. Two of them were: Dr. Max Perutz, 48, Director, Medical Research Council Molecular Research Unit, Cambridge, and Dr. John Cowdray Kendrew, 45, head of the unit's Structural Studies Division.

They shared the Chemistry Prize equally. The two other Britons, Dr. Francis Crick, 46, Cavendish Laboratory, Cambridge; and Dr. Maurice Wilkins, 45, King's College, London, shared the Medicine Prize with an American, Dr. James Dewey Watson, 34, of Cambridge, Mass.

The sixth winner present was the American author, John Steinbeck. He won the Literature award.

King Gustav Adolf handed each of them the Nobel Gold Medal and an illuminated diploma bound in leather. Each prize carries a cash award of £17,740.

The £17,250 for the 1961 Peace Prize, awarded posthumously to Mr. Hammarskjoeld, former United Nations Secretary General, has been returned for use in promoting international understanding.

At a banquet to-night in the City Hall, Mr. Steinbeck said man had taken "God-like power" and become "our greatest hazard and our only hope. Fearful and unprepared, we have assumed lordship over the life and death of the whole world and all living things.

(December 11)

IMMIGRANTS BILL PASSED

By Our Political Staff

THE Government had the surprisingly large majority of 107 on the Third Reading of the controversial Commonwealth Immigrants Bill in the Commons last night.

Since it is believed at least a dozen Conservative M.P.'s abstained, the most obvious explanation is that there could have been 20 Labour abstentions too. Both sides had a two-line Whip only, and many M.P.'s were paired.

Without abstentions on a two-line Whip, the Government would normally expect a majority of about 80. The actual voting figures were 277 for, 170 against.

ABSTAINERS SIT

Of the Conservative abstainers, three sat deliberately in their seats in the chamber during the division. They were Mr. Humphrey Berkeley (Lancaster), Lord Balkiel (Hertford) and Mr. Peter Tapsell (W. Nottingham).

Others known to have abstained were Mr. van Straubenzee (Wokingham) and Mr. Nigel Fisher (Surbiton).

Report of Debate - P22; Unemployed Immigrants - P13

(February 28)

MRS. KENNEDY IN TV TOUR OF WHITE HOUSE

Mrs. Jacqueline Kennedy conducted millions of Americans on a tour of the White House last night. The one-hour programme, was broadcast by the two major television networks, who shared its cost of £35,000.

She explained the changes that have been made in the house's structure and decor since British troops burned it in 1814. She spoke with easy confidence and quiet humour.

With obvious pride she pointed out the pieces she had resurrected from obscurity in odd corners and basements of the White House. These included a pier table that had been used as a work bench.

Many pieces of furniture, and paintings, have come from prized private collections. The donors were given flattering mention by name during the tour. The performance was praised in the Press to-day.

(February 16)

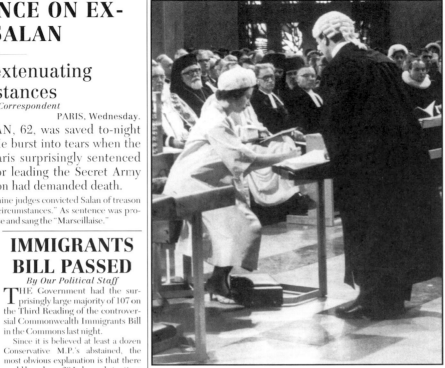

THE QUEEN LEANS FORWARD IN HER PLACE and signs the Sentence of Consecration offered to her by the Registrar during the consecration of Coventry's new cathedral.

QUEEN GOES TO COVENTRY CONSECRATION

From NORMAN RILEY

COVENTRY, Friday.

THE QUEEN, with Princess Margaret and the Earl of Snowdon, attended the consecration of Coventry Cathedral to-day. The Queen signed the Sentence of Consecration at the end of two hours of ceremonies in which there was often a note as new and as dramatic as the conception of the Cathedral itself.

Two observances of great antiquity for such occasions were omitted from the service.

Instead of knocking hard on the closed door of the Cathedral with his pastoral staff and demanding admission, according to tradition, the Bishop Dr. Cuthbert Bardsley, entered to the ring of a trumpet fanfare after crying: "Open the doors. In God's name welcome to you all."

The congregation of 2,000 responded: "In God's name, welcome to you."

The second formality absent was the delivery of the keys to the Bishop on his arrival. Normally a new church is the patron's property, but the new Cathedral church of St. Michael is already vested in the Cathedral Chapter, and the Bishop already has his throne there.

BRILLIANT LIGHTING

Early procession

Through the brilliantly lighted nave, the processions of visiting dignitaries, civic representatives, the diplomatic corps, delegates from other churches at home and abroad, all in their magnificent robes, began nearly an hour before the service proper.

DENMARK'S GIFT

Special music

The Archbishop of Canterbury, Dr. Ramsey, wore his enthronement cope, mitre and stole, of cloth gold, and the Bishop of Coventry was in a cope and mitre of gold silk with appliquèd decorations designed by John Piper.

He carried a staff made of a narwhal tusk, a gift from Denmark. As he entered the Cathedral the Queen, Princess Margaret and Lord Snowdon joined the congregation facing the Great West Window to greet him.

Much of the music throughout the service had been written specially for the occasion. The trumpeters and tympani of the Royal Military School of Music joined in special fanfares.

Dr. Bardsley, in prayer and in every declaration, was in emphatic contrast with the clerical monotone heard on so many similar occasions.

An unusual feature of the service was the co-operation of six Cathedral choirs, from Birmingham, Gloucester, Leicester, Lichfield, Peterborough and Worcester, and the choir of Christ Church, Oxford.

At the consecration of the font, each choir sang beneath one of the carved stone Tablets of the Word a setting by John Hotchkis of the biblical text above them.

(May 26)

"UNDERDOG" CHAPLIN IS PRAISED AT OXFORD

CHARLES SPENCER CHAPLIN, civis Britannicus, better known as Charlie Chaplin, was yesterday made an honorary Doctor of Letters of Oxford University. Grey-haired and dignified, the man who has made generations laugh by his clowning walked solemnly in procession to the Town Hall in Oxford to hear his virtues lauded in Latin.

The Public Orator, Mr. A. N. Bryan-Brown, Vice-Provost of Worcester, recalled Juvenal's lines: "The hardest blow that poverty can deal, is that the poor are laughed at."

But Mr. Chaplin, he said, having endured poverty as a boy, got himself laughed at on purpose and most successfully. As his art matured, he introduced pathos.

"With uncommon sense and magnanimity, he never fears that by surrounding himself with gifted actors he may himself appear less distinguished. In all his films you will find the humour and the generosity of a man who sympathises with the underdog.

"I present to you a 20th-century Roscius, a British citizen, Charles Spencer Chaplin."

(June 28)

U.S. PILOTS ATTACK SOUTH VIET-NAM GUERRILLAS

"SECOND AIR FORCE" IN WAR AGAINST COMMUNISTS

SAIGON, Friday.

HIGHLY placed United States sources have just divulged one of the best kept secrets of the bitter war against the Communist guerrilla force in South Viet-nam. For the past three months, American Air Force pilots have been bombing and firing on the guerrillas.

Flying with Viet-namese co-pilots, the Americans are operating as a second air force in South Viet-nam., according to these sources. They are instructing their Viet-namese co-pilots in the techniques of bombing and attacking in support of ground forces from TA28 fighter trainers and B-26 light bombers.

But the vast majority of the offensive operations in these aircraft are in fact being carried out by Americans.

The Viet-namese Air Force is flying AD-6 fighters and C-47 transports, as well as helicopters. Other helicopter missions are being carried out by three companies of United States Army helicopters. The United States Army is also flying reconnaissance and spotting aircraft.

The American sources say that when the Viet-namese have been trained to carry out these missions efficiently, the United States pilots will stop their combat flying.

OFFICIAL POSITION

No combat missions

The official United States position, stated in Washington and Saigon, has been that American forces are not taking part in combat missions in South Viet-nam, except when their role as advisers brings them under fire. In this case they have instructions to return fire.

(March 10)

THE SUPREME COURT BANS SCHOOL PRAYER

From Our Own Correspondents

WASHINGTON, Monday.

THE United States Supreme Court ruled to-day that recital of an officially-approved prayer in publicly-owned schools was unconstitutional. The decision will affect many thousands of schools.

The daily prayer, adopted by the school authority in New York State, was: Almight God, we acknowledge our dependence upon Thee, and we beg Thy blessings upon us, our teachers and our country.

Jewish Unitarian and non-believing parents objected that it contradicted the constitutional safeguard against an officialy established religion. Speaking for the six-to-one court majority, Mr. Justice Black said that its decision did not indicate hostility to religion or prayer.

(June 26)

SIR OSWALD MOSLEY KICKED & PUNCHED

THERE was mob violence when the British National party and Sir Oswald Mosley's Union Movement held separate public meetings in the East End of London last night.

Sir Oswald himself was kicked and punched as he got out of his car to speak from the back of a lorry at Victoria Park Square, Bethnal Green. He had said only a few words when police told him the meeting must stop.

Late last night Scotland Yard said 43 arrests were made arising from happenings in Victoria Park Square.

People accused included two juveniles, one a girl of 16. The adults were reported to include two women.

Those arrested were charged with possessing offensive weapons, with offences under the Public Order Act, or with using insulting behaviour. They are due to appear at Thames Court to-day.

THE BATTLE OF BALL'S POND RD.

ATTACK ON 40 MEN

Five people were taken to hospital after a crowd of several hundred set on about 40 members of the British National party as the members prepared to hold a meeting at Dalston. A battle took place at Ball's Pond Road.

Later police stated that the incidents in Ball's Pond Road constituted only common assault, and they could take no action. Injured parties were advised to seek remedies in the civil courts.

No police were on the spot at the time, though more than 1,000 were on duty in the East End.

A small number of police were treated for slight injuries after the Union Movement meeting at Bethnal Green.

(September 3)

WATCH FOR £400,000 ART HAUL AT PORTS

Police watched ports and airfields last night after the theft of 35 paintings worth nearly £400,000 from the O'Hana Gallery, Carlos Place, Mayfair, early yesterday. Mr. Jacques O'Hana, 62, owner of the gallery, fears the pictures may be smuggled behind the iron curtain.

Works by Picasso, Renoir, Toulouse Lautrec, Utrillo and Cezanne were among those stolen.

(July 12)

WOMAN JUDGE IN HIGH COURT

Daily Telegraph Reporter

JUDGE ELISABETH LANE, QC, became the first woman judge to sit in the High Court yesterday, when she took her place as a Divorce Commissioner.

She was appointed the first woman county court judge last month, and sat in the High Court in the normal way that all county court judges do. At 10.30 a.m. Judge Lane, to a cry of "silence" from the Usher, took her seat.

Mr. Peter Lewis, due to take a case before her, rose immediately and complimented her, on behalf of male members of the Bar. Speaking of the pleasure it gave them, he said she was making history as the first woman judge to sit in the High Court.

Miss Morgan Gibbon, a woman barrister, also extended a welcome on behalf of the women members of the Bar. She said: "We shall follow your course onwards and upwards with admiration and affectionate regard."

(October 9)

CENTIGRADE'S COOL START

10 DEG. IN SCILLIES

Daily Telegraph Reporter

With the beginning of the Meteorological Office's issue of temperatures in Centigrade as well as Fahrenheit, many parts of England had a sunny day yesterday. Swanage, Dorset, had eight hours' sunshine. A temperature of 10deg. C (50deg. F) was recorded in the Scilly Isles

Temperatures in London remained in the lower 40's, with sun counteracting a cold wind. But by 7 p.m. Gatwick Airport was down to freezing point.

(January 15)

Daily Telegraph and Morning Post, 1962

CHEAPER CARS AND TV SETS

SWEETS, ICE CREAM & SOFT DRINKS TAXED

SPECULATIVE GAINS AS INCOME

AID FOR AGED : DEATH DUTY EASED : SCHEDULE A PLAN

MR. SELWYN LLOYD, Chancellor of the Exchequer, preparing for Britain's entry into the Common Market, proposed in his Budget yesterday cuts in purchase tax, together with some increases. The changes will mean:

CARS: Rate cut from 55 to 45 per cent; equivalent to £34 off a £600 car or £600 off a Rolls-Royce.

RADIO AND TELEVISION SETS: Cut from 55 to 45 per cent; equivalent to £ 5s off £65 television set.

REFRIGERATORS AND WASHING MACHINES: Cut from 27 ½ to 25 per cent; equivalent to about £1 5s off £70 refrigerator.

CARPETS AND CUTLERY: Cut from 13 ¾ to 10 per cent; equivalent to £1 3s off a £50 carpet.

FURNITURE AND CLOTHES (except children's): Raised from 5 ½ to 10 per cent; equivalent to £2 17s 6d on £100 worth of furniture: 12s 6d on £20 suit.

Tax on all goods in 55 per cent range to be 45 per cent; 27 ½ per cent range to be 25 per cent; 13 ¾ per cent and 5 ½ per cent ranges to be "consolidated" at 10 per cent. Effective: To-day. Yield: £576 million in financial year against £585 million at old rate.

Saying that as the father of a small daughter he expected "trouble on the home front," the Chancellor proposed:

ICE-CREAM TAX: Duty of 15 per cent on wholesale value of ice-cream, confectionery, sweets, including chocolate biscuits, and soft drinks. Also 15 per cent on ordinary cider. Effective: May 1. Yield: £30 million this year, £50 million in full year.

The Opposition forced a division on this proposal. But the resolution was carried by 331 votes to 219, a Government majority of 112.

SUGAR PRICE DOWN ½d A LB

BREAKFAST TABLE DUTY: Excise duties on sugar, coffee and cocoa abolished, reducing price of sugar by ½d a pound. Effective to-day. Cost: £15 million.

REVENUE AND EXCISE DUTIES: "July Budget" 10 per cent surcharge abolished. But "consolidation" of duties at existing level will leave most prices, including tobacco, drinks and petrol unchanged.

Duty on light hydro-carbon oil up 1 ½d to 1s 6d a gallon. Pool betting duty up from 30 to 33 per cent. Television advertisement duty up from 10 to 11 per cent.

(April 10)

MR. SELWYN LLOYD, Chancellor of the Exchequer

ANGLO-FRENCH PLANE PACT SIGNED

By Air Cdre, E.M. DONALDSON, Daily Telegraph Air Staff

MR. AMERY, Minister of Aviation, signed an agreement yesterday with the French Ambassador for the development and production of a supersonic airliner. [Mr. Amery's statement—P26.]

The cost of the project, about £160 million, and all work and profits, will be shared. Britain will pay about £9 million a year for the next eight years.

The plane, to be called the Concorde, will be delta-winged and will carry 100 passengers at 1,450 mph. It will be built of light alloy and weigh about 107 tons, less than a Boeing 707. In supersonic flight a steel screen will cover the normal windscreen, and the plane will fly on instruments using a periscope for extra safety.

Two versions, one long-range for Atlantic flights and one medium-range, will be built. Both will be flying by 1966 and in airline service by 1970. Bristol Siddeley engines will be used.

The Concorde will cut the time for the Atlantic crossing from seven and a half to three hours, and that for the Sydney-London flight from 27 to 13 hours. There will be no fares increase.

(November 30)

DR. LUTHER KING GAOLED

DR. MARTIN LUTHER KING and the Rev. Ralph Abernathy, Negro integration leaders of Atlanta, Georgia, were sent to prison for 45 days to-day for holding a street demonstration without a permit. They refused the alternative of paying £62 in fines.

(July 11)

HANRATTY REPRIEVE FAILS

There is to be no reprieve for James Hanratty, 25, A6 murderer. He will be hanged at Bedford prison to-morrow, two days before his mother's birthday.

Hanratty was sentenced to death on Feb. 17 by Mr. Justice Gorman at Bedfordshire Assizes for the capital murder by shooting in a lay-by on the A6 trunk road at Deadman's Hill, near Bedford, of Michael John Gregsten, 36, physicist.

The prosecution alleged that Hanratty also raped and shot Gregsten's companion, Miss Valerie Storie, 23. Miss Storie is now in Stoke Mandeville Hospital, Bucks, recovering from paralysis caused by shot wounds.

The trial lasted 21 days, a record for a murder trial in Britain. Hanratty told the 11-man jury that he was in Liverpool at the time of the shooting.

(April 3)

60 DEATHS FROM LONDON SMOG

Daily Telegraph Reporters

TWENTY-EIGHT deaths attributable to smog occurred in the London area yesterday, making 60 since Monday. Health authorities made emergency plans for treating smog victims.

Fog again covered much of the country and the Automobile Association said that it was the worst for 10 years. Weather forecasters expected it to last for at least another 24 hours.

During yesterday's "black-out" traffic in parts of London was brought to a standstill during the afternoon, with nil visibility on many main roads in the Metropolitan area;

London Airport remained closed, and has had no flights since 7.45 p.m. on Monday;

Most rail services were running late and many trains were cancelled.

The 28 deaths in London yesterday were of people aged between 37 and 86 and comprised 19 men and nine women. Twenty collapsed indoors; six in the street and two at work.

The AA said last night there were two main belts of fog and ice.

One stretched from the Hampshire coast through the Home Counties and London into Middlesex and Hertfordshire. The other reached from the Welsh border and Bristol Channel through the Midlands and into the East Riding.

Fog without the added hazard of ice affected the North Kent and Essex coasts, the area around the Wash, and the Scottish border, Glasgow and the Solway Firth.

GRIM ROAD CONDITIONS
125,000 miles affected

Roads were icy in Somerset, Suffolk and the northern part of Norfolk, the North Riding, Durham and to the south of Edinburgh.

An AA spokesman said: "In London the fog is beginning to waft about and visibility in some areas has improved slightly. In others, however, it has got worse.

"Altogether over 125,000 miles of roads in England and Wales are affected by fog and ice and only 18 counties are complete y clear. The past 48 hours have seen some of the grimmest motoring conditions we are ever likely to get and prospects are that they may get worse before they get better."

(December 6)

JAZZ BAND TOUR

Benny Goodman and his band are due to leave for Moscow next month, but details of his tour are still the subject of negotiation between American and Russian officials. The United States has asked for a nine-city tour while the Russians want to limit it to Moscow and Leningrad.

The Russians are said to be apprehensive about the effect a leading Western jazz band might have in the smaller, less sophisticated cities.

(April 16)

POLICEWOMEN WEARING SMOG MASKS issued yesterday to members of the City force.

ITV SHOCKED BY PILKINGTON

Cheaply sensational & 'excessive violence'

INDEPENDENT television companies were shocked by the criticisms and proposals made by the Pilkington Committee on Broadcasting, in its report published yesterday. The Committee's most important proposals are:

A reorganised Independent Television Authority should plan all programmes and sell advertising time.

Commercial companies should only produce programmes and sell them to the authority.

The B.B.C. should operate a second national television service as soon as possible. Independent television should not be allowed to do so until five years after its reorganisation.

Only one service of local sound broadcasting should be planned. This should be provided by the B.3.C.

SWITCH TO 625 LINES

The present 405-line definition should be changed to the 625-line system in general use on the Continent.

Colour television on the 625-line system should be introduced as soon as possible.

Suggestions for subscription, pay-as-you-view television should be ignored.

The cost of a combined sound and television licence should be increased from £3 to £6. At present there is an additional £1 excise duty, making a total of £4.

"VAPID" AND "PUERILE"

The committee's report, which was unanimous, said the Independent Television service "falls well short of what a good public service of broadcasting should be." Excessive violence was shown, sex was exploited and there was "a preoccupation with the cheaply sensational."

Many mass appeal programmes were "vapid and puerile, their content often derivative, repetitious and lacking in real substance."

Excessive profits made by commercial companies from the use of "a national asset" were sharply criticised.

(June 28)

BBC COLOUR TV SERVICE IN 1964

ULTIMATE rejection of the Pilkington Committee's proposals for fundamental changes in the Independent Television Authority is indicated in the Government's statement of policy for broadcasting, published yesterday. Although the Government has reserved its decision, the tone of the document is a clear pointer.

A firm decision has been taken to authorise the BBC to transmit a second television service on 625 lines. It will contain some programmes in colour. This service should start in London in mid-1964, and the country should have a complete coverage after seven years.

The White Paper also suggests that there may be scope later for a second ITA programme. In fact, a decision is likely to be taken in about two months.

If this was favourable, it is conceivable that the two new programmes could come into operation at about the same time.

On the Government's autumn decisions depends the time table as well as the exact shape of a second ITA programme, the nature of the programme companies and the relationship of the Press to television.

But it is already decided that the BBC Charter and the Television Act are to be renewed for 12 years from July 30, 1964. Legislation will be introduced early next session.

(June 28)

BRITTEN'S FINEST HOUR

LARGE FORCES IN "WAR REQUIEM"

From DONALD MITCHELL
COVENTRY, Wednesday.

THE new work which is perhaps most intimately associated with the peace-making spirit of the Coventry Festival, Britten's "War Requiem," was given its world premiere here to-night in the Cathedral by the Festival Choir, City of Birmingham Symphony Orchestra and Melos Ensemble conducted by Meredith Davies.

Two conductors were in fact involved in the performance of a major work which demands very large forces. Mr. Davies was in charge of the chorus and full orchestra and the composer directed the chamber group.

This novel disposition reflects the brilliantly original plan of the Requiem, which combines the Latin text of the Mass for the dead with nine war poems by Wilfred Owen.

Thus the work reveals a most subtle interplay between a timeless ritual on the one hand and, on the other, living enactments of the condition of war which have all the poignancy, force and terror of immediate experience.

A MASTERPIECE

I must say at once and without reservation that I believe this work to be a masterpiece of the first order. It is certainly one of the finest things that Mr. Britten has yet written and should do much to silence the doubts of those who have thought that his present style of composition concentrated too exclusively on slender sonorities and small, if cumulative, forms.

This astounding Requiem, on the contrary, is built on a very large scale and is unusually rich in elaborate, though always very clear, choral and orchestral textures of a thrilling weight and density.

(May 31)

KINGSLEY AMIS TO QUIT "STUFFY" CAMBRIDGE

KINGSLEY AMIS, 40, the novelist, has resigned his Fellowship at Peterhouse, Cambridge, which he has held since October, 1961, and will leave in September, it was disclosed yesterday. Mr. Amis who is going to Majorca, said he found Cambridge stuffy and that some of the back-biting was indecent.

"I dislike the excessive formality of faculty life; too much dressing up and respectability," he said. "I don't like having to wait for a smoke after dinner until the port has gone round high table twice. Dining out in other colleges as a guest seems to involve an excessive amount of protocol.

"The atmosphere in Peterhouse has always been most friendly. My fellow dons were relaxed, unmalicious and never stooped to backbiting.

"I cannot say the same about the rest of the Cambridge academic world. Some of the backbiting that goes on is positively indecent.

"I shall miss my pupils. They were all very interesting and bright. If I was disappointed by my fellow dons, I was very pleasantly surprised by the intelligence of my pupils at Peterhouse."

PLANS FOR FUTURE

Hope of American post

"When I have escaped from the stuffiness of Cambridge, I shall take my wife and children to Majorca. I stayed there with Robert Graves recently, and I hope that staying in Majorca will be mutually stimulating.

"I hope to finish one uncompleted novel, and I have an idea for a further novel which will be a radical new departure for me." After staying in Majorca for about a year, he plans to seek an academic post in America.

(December 21)

SPIRIT OF "SEVEN PILLARS OF WISDOM" CAPTURED

By PATRICK GIBBS

APPROPRIATELY to its extraordinary subject, David Lean's "Lawrence of Arabia," given a Royal performance at the Odeon, Leicester Square, last night, is an extraordinary film.

Not merely because it lasts, with interval, four hours, but because of the deliberate choice of two different styles, the one to bring the background, the other the hero, into perspective. The first half gives the impression that the author, Robert Bolt, is at pains to perpetuate, indeed extend, the romantic legend which Lawrence himself largely created, and which most people take these days with a pinch of salt.

After a prologue showing Lawrence's death in the motor-cycle accident, and some contradictory interviews with notables after a memorial service at St. Paul's the film moves back to Cairo, 1916, with Lawrence, a junior officer in the Map Room at HQ about to start his association with the Arab Revolt.

SLOW START

Desert splendours

The desert journey by camel to visit Prince Feisal; the birth of the idea of uniting the Arab tribes against the Turks; the meeting and winning over of the important tribal leader, Auda; the first successful combined operation, involving a prodigious march across the Nefud Desert, and taking the port of Akaba from the rear - all these incidents follow the spirit, if not the letter, of the account in "Seven Pillars of Wisdom."

The splendours of the desert scene, rock formations, sky and endless sand, are caught, as in Lawrence's own descriptions, to perfection. That we really feel "the scalding tempest of the sun rays, parching the eyeballs from the glowing sand," is a measure of the wonderful colour photography.

But after the interval the treatment changes with exciting results. The raids on the Hejaz Railway, the key scene of Lawrence's degradation, at Deraa, the massacre at Tallal and the final capture of Damascus are all splendid scenes, but used now to interpret Lawrence's character.

No psychological analysis. No mention, for instance, of sadism, masochism, or latent homosexuality in his nature, revealed to him by the Turkish torture at Deraa; nor of the possibility of impotence, caused by the circumstances of his upbringing in illegitimacy, which is my own contribution to the speculation.

It is enough that some serious emotional disturbance is suggested, followed by disgust with himself and his Arab friends, whose fickleness and cruelty are suggested equally with their more admirable qualities.

It is really with the arrival of Gen. Allenby as the Army Commander that the film turns the corner. The duologues between the General and Lawrence have the cut and thrust of the best theatrical writing, and much is owed to Jack Hawkins, whose Allenby is a completely persuasive portrait.

Very much, too, is owed to Peter O'Toole, whom the film claims to be "introducing" in the part of Lawrence, though we have seen him on our screens before and, of course, on our stages.

(December 11)

POLICEMEN OF CHARACTER

By PETER KNIGHT

AN object-lesson in how to succeed and to fail with television series was given by the BBC last night with the start of their two new programmes, "Z-Cars" and "Compact."

The thin line which separates success from failure is the line which divides the genuine from the false.

From the beginning "Z-Cars" came alive because its characters and situations were genuine and it showed up only too clearly the artificiality which brought failure to "Compact."

"Z-Cars" promises to be one of the most authentic series yet of police at work. Up to now they have usually been either extras in comedy programmes or father-figures patrolling Dock Green.

It is a refreshing change to meet on the screen a policeman who is something more than the symbol of the law. The men here who are to make up the newly-formed crime patrol are as interesting off the beat as on.

FOR A CAPTIVE AUDIENCE

"Compact" is quite obviously designed to attract the already captive audience of the weekly series. Set against the background of a glossy magazine, it seems at first sight to be the usual collection of trivialities drawn from the lives of a none-too-interesting set of characters.

(January 3)

EFFORTLESS THRILLS OF 'LE CORSAIRE'

By A.V. COTON

THE novelty of the evening by the Royal Ballet at Covent Garden on Saturday was a pas de deux from the old Russian ballet "Le Corsaire."

It was rearranged to accommodate the talents of Margot Fonteyn and Rudolf Nureyev.

If a ballet programme of several items lacks a comic or satiric ingredient then for a well-balanced occasion it must provide us with both lyrical or dramatic fare of a high order. Mediocrity of choreography or production spells disappointment, whatever the quality of the dancing.

The excuse for "Le Corsaire" is as a thrilling show of technical exhibitionism. The innate narcissism of ballet dancers is perfectly served by such items - but the price of success is supernormal effortlessness of performance. Any sign of strain brings things down to the level of the classroom.

Fonteyn threw off the smooth phrases of her dancing with a charming elegance which emphasised once again the sheer aristocratic quality of her interpretations on their highest level.

Mr. Nureyev achieved his greatest success so far in this theatre; he bounded and leaped like a demented tiger - though one could fault the admixture of masculine and feminine steps of which his dances were made up.

(November 5)

RETURN OF 'AS YOU LIKE IT' IS WELCOME

By W.A. DARLINGTON

OF the Stratford-on-Avon productions of 1961 the one which lingers most gratefully in the memory is certainly the "As You Like It" of Michael Elliott.

No wonder then that it has been selected for reproduction, with some changes of cast mainly among the smaller parts, at the Aldwych. And no wonder that it received a warm welcome there last night.

It well repays a second visit. Vanessa Redgrave's enchanting and enchanted Rosalind, so many fathoms deep in love, is a piece of acting that one would not willingly lose the chance to see again, and at greater leisure than is possible at a Stratford first night.

Of all the heroines of Shakespeare's comedies, Rosalind depends most on the personality and talent of the actress. Miss Redgrave brings her completely to life.

(January 11)

CRAZY GANG'S GOODBYE

A nostalgic audience filled the Victoria Palace to say farewell to the Crazy gang on Saturday. But few believed that the Gang's 7,994th performance in this theatre was really its last.

(May 21)

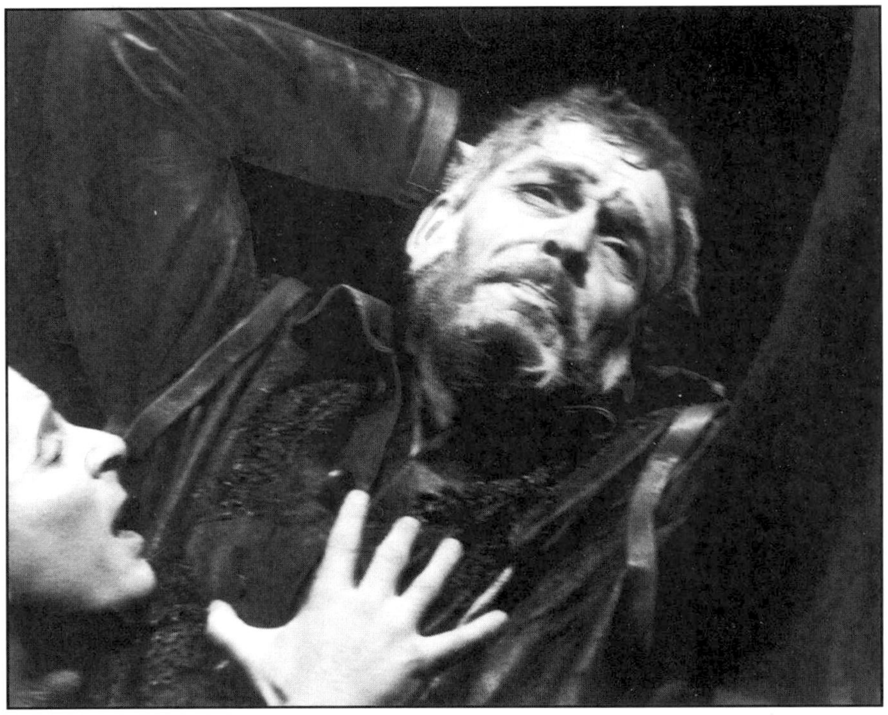

PAUL SCOFIELD AS LEAR and Alec McCowen as the Fool in the Royal Shakespeare Company's new production of "King Lear" at Stratford-upon-Avon.

BACON'S WORKS SHOCK VIEWER

By TERENCE MULLALY

ANY doubts that Francis Bacon is one of the most considerable of living artists are dispelled by the Retrospective Exhibition of his work at the Tate Gallery. It is open from to-day until July 1.

Few contemporary painters can provide an exhibition of 90, mainly large, paintings with their reputations untarnished. Francis Bacon does more than survive. He emerges not only as the creator of haunting images, but also as a master of his craft.

What no one should imagine is that he is the kind of craftsman who brings easy pleasure by creating an illusion of the everyday world. Bacon is not concerned with reality, not the comforting reality of familiar appearances, but the harsh facts of an age living in fear.

Bacon's work shocks. As we move from one obsessive image to another we find no comfort, only a chilling reminder of mankind adrift. It is this that makes his work so profoundly disquieting.

"EMPTINESS" THEME

He is concerned not so much with the shadow of physical destruction and the erosion of institutions, as with the chill in the heart of men. His theme is the emptiness that always haunts man. It is this that gives his work a relevance beyond concrete fears of the moment.

Whether he is painting a series of pictures with a Pope, or a figure in an hotel bedroom, as the ostensible theme, he is concerned, on the one hand with the universal fears and, on the other, with the purely sensual impact he can achieve with oil paint. The one somehow enhances the effect of the other.

The suspicion that if he wanted to, Bacon could bestow simple delights, makes the impact of his work the more devastating. The haunted figure of Van Gogh and the twisted, misshapen creatures cowering before their own fear, shame our pleasure in colour and the manipulation of paint.

(May 24)

SIR L. OLIVIER AS NATIONAL THEATRE HEAD

SIR LAURENCE OLIVIER, 55, is to be the first Director of the National Theatre. He accepted the appointment at a meeting of the National Theatre board yesterday.

He said afterwards: "I shall strive my utmost to lay the foundation of a National Theatre that will finally justify its long wait for existence and be a source of pride to my profession and to the country as a whole."

It is understood that this appointment will not affect the continuance of Sir Laurence's present commitments at Chichester, where he is director of the Festival Theatre at least for the next two years, and that this is agreeable to both organisations.

The appointment will be formally ratified as soon as the National Theatre Board has been officially incorporated under the Companies Act.

NATIONAL THEATRE PLANS

Last month, Mr. Brooke, then Chief Secretary to the Treasury, announced that the Government approved of the setting up of a National Theatre Board.

He announced a scheme which would provide for a theatre on the South Bank near Hungerford Bridge and an opera house adjoining County Hall to replace Sadler's Wells. The Old Vic would be incorporated into the National Theatre.

The scheme would be financed by grants of £1 million from the Government and £1,300,000 from the County Council, and by proceeds of the sale of Sadler's Wells. Annual maintenance grants of £300,000 from the Government and £100,000 from the County Council will also be made.

(August 10)

AN AWESOME LEAR

PAUL SCOFIELD'S VIOLENCE

From W.A. DARLINGTON
STRATFORD-ON-AVON, Tuesday.

VIOLENCE is the keynote of Peter Brook's production of "King Lear" at Stratford-on-Avon tonight and a matching violence is the outstanding quality in Paul Scofield's playing of the King.

There have been many excellent Lears in our time and this one has an assured place among them.

In particular Mr. Scofield succeeds more completely than any of the others that I have seen in making his Lear all of one piece.

Always before I have felt that the opening scene of the play, that in which the kingdom is partitioned in accordance with Lear's daughters' protestations of love, was a weak and even silly opening to be got over somehow before we can come to great tragedy.

UNREASONABLE TYRANT

With Mr. Scofield I do not feel this. His Lear is from the first an unreasonable old tyrant, so used to being obeyed to the letter that he flies into an appalling rage at the least sign of his will being crossed.

He scorns pathos. The nearest he comes to it is that he recognises the danger of his own temperament and knows that its violence may at last send him over the brink into madness.

When in the storm scene his wits do finally founder his strength and authority do not forsake him. They are there still but are no longer under control.

GREAT VOCAL FEAT

This is a tremendous feat, vocally. How Mr. Scofield keeps up that awesome rasping delivery without damage to his vocal chords is his own secret; we can only marvel.

Mr. Brooks's violence is expressed in action. Here is a society only one degree removed from savagery.

(November 7)

'THE ARCHERS' VOTED BEST ON RADIO

FOR the fifth year in succession "The Archers" has been voted the year's best radio programme. Granada's "Coronation Street" was voted the best television programme of 1961, "Ben Hur" the best film, and Stirling Moss, the racing motorist, the outstanding sportsman.

These are the results of THE DAILY TELEGRAPH Gallup Poll. It is the second time a racing driver has won the sportsman of the year award. The late Mike Hawthorn won it in 1958.

(January 1)

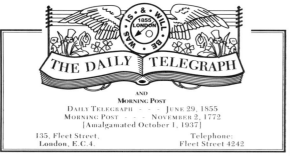

THE DAILY TELEGRAPH

AND
MORNING POST
DAILY TELEGRAPH - - - JUNE 29, 1855
MORNING POST - - - NOVEMBER 2, 1772
[Amalgamated October 1, 1937]
135, Fleet Street, London, E.C.4. Telephone: Fleet Street 4242

CUBAN AFTERMATH

AFTER one week of world-wide alarm and three weeks of relaxed and secret correspondence between President KENNEDY and Mr. KHRUSCHEV, the Cuban crisis has subsided to the point where the American naval blockade can be withdrawn. The Soviet nuclear missiles, duly counted under their tarpaulins, are homeward bound. The Ilyushin jet bombers - antiquated and useless as the ungrateful Dr. CASTRO now declares them to be - are to follow within the month. Yesterday the armed forces of the Soviet Union stood down from their state of alert, and roving submarines were called back to their bases. For good measure, the three American U2 aircraft which were based in Britain to observe the effects of Soviet nuclear tests have likewise gone home.

The major Cuban crisis has left behind it typical problems and large hopes. It is on the former that President KENNEDY continues to concentrate in his exchanges with Mr. KHRUSCHEV - principally on this question of verification, Dr. CASTRO seems to regard it as a one-sided affair, a violation of Cuban sovereignty; but if, as he insists, he feels threatened by the United States, surely the presence of international observers would be his best safeguard. Local solution of the Cuban problem could open the way to wider negotiations with the Soviet Union at which Mr. KENNEDY hinted in his broadcast.

(November 22)

DRUGS AND SAFETY

SINCE the distressing story of Thalidomide was revealed, it has seemed certain that at least the pharmaceutical industry itself would devise fresh methods of ensuring the safety of new drugs. It has now decided to set up a special watchdog committee for this purpose. This will be a useful aid. It is not a substitute, however, for the wider independent organisation which the British Medical Association has suggested. The Minister of Health is taking advice and the Medical Research Council is setting up a committee to review the testing of new drugs. The layman finds it difficult to see why anybody should hesitate to establish a strong central organisation. The old principle of nobody intervening between manufacturer and doctor cannot, as most doctors agree, survive the proliferation of innumerable synthetic drugs of increasing complexity during the past two decades. After all, another old principle — that the first essential of any drug is that it should do no harm to the patient — has not survived either.

Laymen have become uneasily aware that many doctors seem almost as perplexed as they are. Eminent authorities have uttered warnings against anti-coagulants and contraceptive pills. Two doctors in to-days British Medical Journal sound a provisional precautionary note about the use of one group of antibiotics in pregnancy. Many medical men have spoken anxiously of the unknown side-effects of "experimental" drugs. What is "experimental"? Dr. KELSEY, who has been given credit for keeping thalidomide out of America, says that "with many drugs we do not know exactly how they act or even their pattern of metabolism in the body." If that is so, their effect on parts of body cells controlling future growth and heredity must sometimes still remain obscure.

(October 1)

DROWNING ANTIQUITY

ALOOF in their massive dignity, the great figures on the façade of the main Abu Simbel temple await their end. For if nothing is done to save them, they will be submerged in the rising waters of the Nile as soon as the Aswan dam project is complete. An imaginative plan has been put forward by Italian engineers. This is that the temples should be raised bodily, by thousands of tons of concrete pumped in under their foundations. There are, of course, doubts about the feasibility of this plan. The whole site must weigh something like 250,000 tons, and in places the temples are crumbling. Can they be raised above the new water level without substantial damage? The answer is that one cannot know until it has been tried, and since the only alternative is total and irreparable loss, the project is worth trying.

President NASSER'S aim, in pressing ahead with the Aswan dam project, is to improve the deplorable lot of the Egyptian fellaheen. Human lives are, indeed, more important than any marvel. But here is an instance where the life of art is itself threatened with sudden extinction. Do not let it be said of this generation that it floated improbable loans for ephemeral objects and let drown the temples of Abu Simbel.

(July 25)

BEYOND THE SCREEN

SATIRE is an intimate thing between a few gifted artists and small audiences, best sampled at the Fortune Theatre or the Deux Anes. But when it is poured into licensed channels, such as BBC late-night television, it can work like new wine in old bottles. There is, moreover, the temptation, since millions view it, to insert propaganda in the form of satire. This is a reproach that is sure to be levelled against Saturday's programme "That was the week that was." For it guyed cardinals, distorted a film of the Prime Minister to a point beyond ridicule, and made a questionable comment on the judgment in the FELL case.

Obviously wit cannot be processed. Satire eludes, nay it thrives on censorship. Its best subjects are pompousness, hypocrisy and abuse of power. But in a country such as Britain, tolerant to the point of faineance, it may sometimes be easy to overdo the jibe at authority.

(December 10)

The Glory that Was London

Men and Buildings:

By John Betjeman

THE City of London is an English mystery. Behind its gold watch beats a warm heart, but under its silk hat is a shrewd head. The head and heart are often at war, and the former usually wins, hence the modern appearance of the City, with its inhuman cliffs of rent-collecting slabs.

The mystery is ancient and wonderful, and makes the City of London different from anywhere else in England even to-day. Its very government is strange, and has somehow held out against the LCC just as its polite and obliging police force remains independent from the Metropolitan police.

What is the Secondary and High Bailiff of Southwark doing this side of the river, and is the burden of his two duties a strain? What does the City Remembrancer remember? Does the Chief Commoner of the Court of Common Council have more power than the Lord Mayor? These are questions to which I find it rather pleasant not to know the answer, just as in a Gothic cathedral it is satisfying to see through one arch a glimpse of more arches and screens hiding who knows what beyond.

Then there is the mystery of the 82 City Companies, most of which are mediaeval in origin, each with its own ceremonies and feasts when the silver is brought out and glee singers render "Drink to me only" in the cigar smoke of after-dinner repletion. Twelve of these are the Great Companies, but no one explains why the remaining 70 are less great, even though they may have finer halls and larger liveries than the 12 great ones.

Would a man on the court of the Mercers, the chief company, consider it beneath his dignity also to be in the picturesque position of member of the court of the Gold and Silver Wyredrawers, who have no hall, poor things, and are 74th in order of precedence? Finally there are the City churches. Before the fire of London there were more than 100 in the square mile of the city. To-day there are only 35. Eight of these are either not yet open or are awaiting restoration from bomb damage. Eight are mediaeval, 21 are by Sir Christopher Wren, and six are later than Wren and no less magnificent than those by the master. Indeed the interior of St. Mary Woolnoth by Nicholas Hawksmoor, and of St. Botolph, Aldersgate, by an unknown late 18th-century architect, are two of the finest London church interiors.

The City churches almost all do splendid work to-day, and are much used during the week. I can remember the old pre-war days of lazy incumbents living at the seaside, coming up once a week on Sunday, and organising an occasional week-day organ recital. Those days are over, and the Church in the City is coming to life again, with daily services, during the lunch hour.

I have deliberately been so unarchitectural for so long, when writing of the City, because these three elements, its Government, its livery companies and its churches distinguish this ancient place of Roman origin from the rest of London.

You can feel the change as soon as you pass eastward from Temple Bar. You notice it again as you pass out through Aldgate into the oriental mart atmosphere of Whitechapel.

Still a River Port

Imagine the mediaeval City on the wide, slow-flowing Thames, held up by the sluices under London Bridge, with its houses and chapel. There it stands, white-walled in Middlesex fileds, and, once in its gates, the roads are narrow and the alleys narrower still, with the timbered gables nearly touching one another overhead and the smell fearful, and the only places of quiet the numerous little churches and garths.

Crowning everything is old St. Paul's with its spire, the largest cathedral in Christendom. One gets a faint flavour of this City in the churches of St. Bartholomew the Great, St. Helen's and St. Ethelburga's. It was an East Anglian place rather like Norwich.

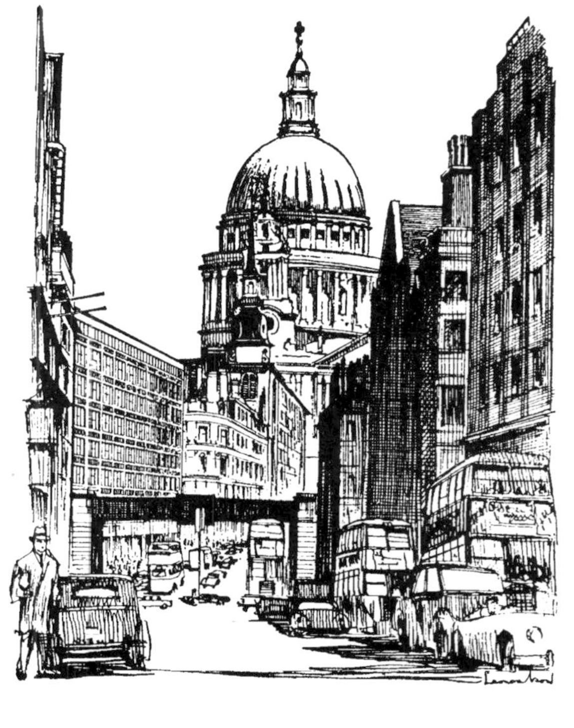

FROM OUTSIDE THE DAILY TELEGRAPH office. The new straight slab on the left ignores the subtle curve of Ludgate Hill climbing to St. Paul's. Both of its windows are out of harmony with its neighbour.

Now see the city rebuilt by Wren and later architects. The walls are breached and handsome red brick houses such as still exist at Spitalfields extend into the meadows. Inside, a forest of Portland stone steeples and lead spires gathers round the mothering dome of Paul's. In the streets merchants still live over their shops and rent box-pews in the parish church. The best Wren interior to survive giving an impression of those times is in St. Mary at Hill, with its wealth of carved woodwork, its sword rests, high pews and marble floor all under a dome supported on four columns.

Now see the Victorian City. The merchants have moved out to big brick houses in Islington, Clapham and Streatham. Many of the churches have been demolished and their sites sold for office and warehouse blocks. Buildings are higher and dwarf the remaining Wren steeples and have even encroached on the building height round St. Paul's.

There is still one place where you can see St. Paul's as Wren meant you to see it, and that is on the north side, where his brick chapter house forms a warm red plinth to the upper stage of the two storeys into which he divided the exterior of his new cathedral.

The old lanes with their shops and chop and coffee houses survive for the precious lunch hours of City clerks, later to go by steam train and knife-board horse-omnibus to greybrick nearer suburbs.

Now see the City of London to-day. The skyline has gone. The alleys are blocked. Hardly a shopping street is left and a few churches and halls stand like museum pieces in cliffs of some of the most undistinguished copybook contemporary ever seen, even in the Middle West of America.

All That is Left

Only around Billingsgate and the doomed Coal Exchange and in a few alleys in the financial quarter and around Guildhall will you find the spirit of even the Victorian City.

Before it is all sacrificed to money and the motor car, see what is left. The old institutions are there, though the people who are "something in the City" to-day mostly commute to Sussex and Surrey and have sold their grandfathers' houses in Streatham and Highbury to the "developer." You could park your car on the new "Route II" in the north of the city were it permissible, for that is the only deserted street in the once glorious City of London.

(March 19)

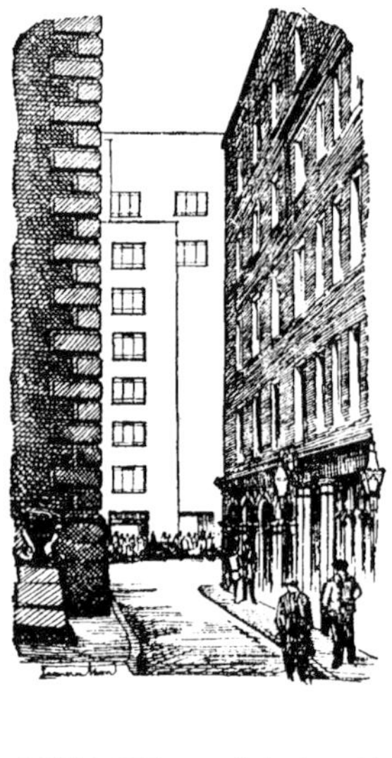

BOW LANE, one of the last old shopping streets in the City, opening onto international nothingness in Cheapside opposite.

£20,000 MIDGET COMPUTER

By A Science Correspondent

An electronic computer the size of a small suitcase is nearing its final testing stages at the Boreham Wood factory of the Elliott Automation Group. It is the first of its kind, robust enough to go in the back of a car and costs about £20,000.

This computer was developed by John Bunt, head of the new mobile computer division of the Boreham Wood factory. Originally designed to fulfill a secret Ministry of Supply specification, it proved so useful that the company has decided to develop it for civilian use.

It will probably take the form of a 2ft black box. Its power consumption will be about 1/2 kilowatt, half the electricity needed to keep a small electric fire going.

It can thus be easily mounted in the back of a Land-Rover.

(February 19)

LONDON DAY BY DAY

Plans for Cambridge Digging up the Bard

PLANS for the development of 48,000 sq. yds. in the historic centre of Cambridge are now well in hand despite fierce opposition from the University.

The 12 University members of the City Council face a powerful consortium of city, county and Jack Cotton interests. His City Centre Properties have acquired three properties on the site including Heffer's Bookshop, bought from Emmanuel College this month, and believe they can acquire more.

Mr. W.L. Waide, county planning officer, has scheduled for comprehensive development a huge site, bounded roughly by Downing Street on the south, St. Andrew's Street on the east, Petty Cury on the north, and Guildhall Street and Corn Exchange Street on the west.

That granted, anything in the area could be made the subject of a compulsory purchase order.

Perils of Interfering

MR. RONALD DUNCAN is the least committed among the five members of the committee formed yesterday by Dr. Francis Carr to urge the opening of Shakespeare's tomb at Stratford.

He told me that he did not favour any particular author for Shakespeare's work. He simply wanted to know the truth.

The risks of taking any stand on the question were illustrated by the fact that Mr. Duncan arrived half an hour late for yesterday's conference, having been delayed at lunch by derisive members of the Garrick Club.

At present the movement has reached deadlock. The Rev. Thomas Bland, Vicar of Holy Trinity, Stratford, will have nothing to do with it.

Dr. Carr hopes to canvass eminent people, re ying "not on popular, but on responsible, support."

In Glass Houses

BECAUSE his customers have continual difficulty in disposing of empties, a wine merchant with customers in the London stockbroker belt is planning to sell wine in brick-shaped bottles.

The idea is that these can eventually be used to build patios, gazebos or even follies.

Treat 'em Rough

IN the Edgware Road yesterday I noticed that the Army Information Office has a colourful recruiting window dominated by a waxwork of the Duke of Cambridge, Commander-in-Chief of the Army from 1856 to 1895.

This seems a curious choice of figure to attract modern recruits. The Duke resisted practically all military reforms until they had become inevitable.

Flogging in the Army was not abolished until 1881, a quarter of a century after he had first assumed command.

On the Tiles

HADDOCK, the handsome honey-coloured cat of the Travellers' Club, has been missing for a week.

He was glimpsed for an instant by the Savage Club a day or two ago in a bedraggled condition.

Though he is not quite such a favourite as the Travellers' last cat, Kipper, who died at the age of 19, members would welcome his return.

Deciding to Decide

"THE decisions which we have to take in both these fields will be dramatic and perhaps decisive."

The Prime Minister in his speech at Llandudno.

PETERBOROUGH

ASCOT MUST LOOK TO ITS LAURELS

THE Derby proved such a fashion warm-up for Ascot that Ascot had better look to its laurels. The Derby dress standard, which has risen notably in the past two years, has now reached that delicate balance between county suits and whirling chiffon - the balance that is one's dream of English good taste.

Navy dominated with grass green a runner-up and yellow a third. Silk suits and silk dress and coat outfits were most women's choice. Under the blazing June sky, women who had chosen wool looked unhappy.

The Queen Mother's ensemble was every whit as chic as Princess Margaret's. She looked fresh and up to the minute in sapphire blue printed chiffon dress and jacket, with her three strands of pearls, ruby-clasped, and a large pearl and diamond brooch. Her hat was a cleanly simple shape- a cloche in sapphire tulle.

Princess Margaret, deep in talk at the Paddock with the Earl of Snowdon about breathing tubes for horses, chose a turquoise wild silk coat and dress. Her Simone Mirman mandarin roque was of turquoise silk, and her handbag matched her bronze calf shoes.

The happiest woman at the Derby was also one of the prettiest and most chic. She was Mme Raymonde Guest, whose husband owns the winner. Her outfit was by Christian Dior.

She was also the coolest woman there, for she and Dior had bargained on a heat wave and her dress was short sleeved, of burnt orange chiffon printed with sage green. Her platter hat had a sage crown, and orange brim.

Serena Sinclair

(June 7)

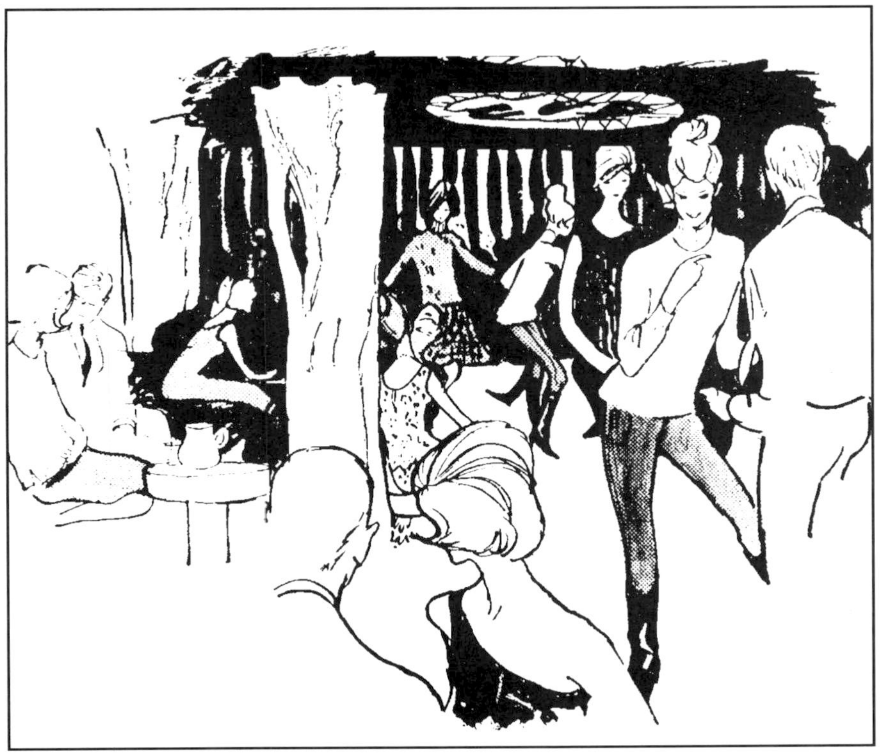

On to a night-club in jeans and jackboots

Report and sketch by BERYL HARTLAND

THERE'S a war going on in London night life, a fashion war of the casual versus the elegant - of sweaters and tweeds versus pearls and the little black dress. There's a mad topsy-turvy look to the night spots.

There are jeans and jackboots worn dancing the Bossa Nova in the new most sophisticated young night places. There are tweed suits worn to a big dinner in Park Lane. It appears you no longer wear what you ought to but what you feel like.

Two new places where you can be as casual as you like in a sweater and skirt, sensational in jeans and jackboots or still dress up if you want to are Brads and The Village - both amusing.

Now six months old, Brads in Duke of York Street, remains as cool and sophisticated as iced vodka in spite of the freedom of dress.

"Young people want to be comfortable," says the proprietor, Lord Ulick Browne, so here men can remove their jackets and ties without a managerial eyebrow being raised.

In the half light of a Jules Verne-ish subterranean grotto the young crowd pulse to the Bossa Nova.

Thirty shillings will make you a member for life and the stereophonic hi-fi pounds out from 10 p.m. to 4 a.m. First drinks are 17s 6d, after that 2s 6d. Hamburgers, frankfurters and hot bacon sandwiches are served for 6s 6d.

Alex Sterling's The Village, in Lower Sloane Street, is friendly, slightly Bohemian and full of life. Climb down the wooden stairs into the candle-lit bar and you find yourself wedged among a stimulating young crowd.

You dance to hi-fi on a small floor set among tables in a pine-panelled room. Open from 6 p.m. - 12.30 (and on Sundays), you can dine here anytime.

The food is simple but freshly cooked and dinner for two costs £2 2s (including a half-bottle of Beaujolais). Carafe wines cost 12s 6d, and bar drinks are pub prices.

Three guineas will make you a member for a year, but it might be very difficult to get membership.

(December 20)

WEEKEND FOOD

After two weeks when prices at the greengrocers moved downwards, the too-good-to-last period has ended. Cauliflowers, tomatoes and cucumbers were all slightly dearer yesterday than a week ago.

English apples continued to be the best buy in fruit. Prices were low - plenty of medium-grade Cox's around 1s 4d lb.

(November 9)

Happy cleaning in the press button age

IF you happen to be a horse I have got good news for you. You have caught up with the Aerosol Age.

For in the first all-aerosol shop in Britain, in London's Edgware Road, I saw sitting between press-button coffee essence and fire extinguishers the newest aid to well-groomed mares - a horse deodorant.

There it was, beside cans to squirt after-shave on many chins, fixative on fingernails, starch on shirt collars and scent behind ears.

I was certain that I heard a horsy laugh somewhere, but perhaps it was the very amused brothers-in-law who have opened Yukan, this aerosol bar which is a do-it-yourselfer's delight.

Mr. Simon Cesar and Mr. E.E.V. de Peyer decided while they were selling their own spray-on enamel they would really be up with the times if they filled the shop with nothing but press-button products.

"Good fun - it's a press-button age," exclaimed monocled Parisian Mr. Cesar. "Good for business," remarked suave Mr. de Peyer, an ex-professional singer, proudly pointing to the glowing shop sign. "I squirted rust preventer on it to-day."

Mr. Cesar, a door-to-door mouthwash salesman before the war, told me: "I did most of my business in East Africa. They were more mouthwash conscious there than here."

A woman came in holding a pet poodle (female). "I'm so afraid to let her loose . . . the dogs you know," she said. Mr. Cesar produced a blue and white can. "It's 5s 9d just press the button and that will do the trick," he advised.

The woman left overjoyed. "Funny" he said, "we've had such a lot of customers coming in for dog deodorants and such things."

I sprayed my spectacles and listened to the story of the man (a bachelor obviously) who rushed in complaining that he kept burning his fried eggs. He went away with a non-sticking vegetable spray and hasn't been seen since.

I hear that you will be spraying clean your gramophone records, your fur coats and your feet before long. Even press button nappy fresheners and tomato hormones are on the way.

Elizabeth Prosser

(March 27)

MORE HOMES TO THE ACRE

DESIGNERS' ANSWER TO LAND SCARCITY

By Our Architectural Reporter

COMPETITION results announced in London yesterday show that private enterprise houses for sale can be designed in attractive layouts at higher densities with more homes to the acre. Estates of this kind are an answer to the growing scarcity of building land.

Clifford-Culpin and Partners, London architects, in their winning design for a 4 ½ acre site in Harlow new town have 15 homes to the acre. The developer will be Laing Housing Co., London.

A husband and wife team of architects, Robert and Elizabeth Mortimer, of Northallerton, Yorks., have 20 homes to the acre in their winning design for a 4 ½ acre site, in Stockport. This will be developed by Hampson and Kemp, Manchester.

£5,000 TOP PRICE

Hitherto the density on most private enterprise estates has been no more than eight to 12 to the acre. In the Harlow design, where it is hoped the selling price of the largest houses will not exceed £5,000 excluding land, there are 58 houses and 12 flats in two and three storey blocks in short terraces and groups.

There will be large pedestrian areas to be grassed and planted with 25ft semi-matured trees. The houses, built in white bricks with panels of dark-grey bricks, will have single pitch roofs covered in aluminium sheeting.

Back gardens will be few but there will be garages and parks for 137 cars. Whole house heating will be installed.

In the Stockport scheme, where the suggested maximum selling price is £3,000, the winning design has 91 dwellings, mostly two and three storey houses and a four-storey block of flats, brick built with tile hung or weather-board panels. Many homes are grouped around mews courts.

ALUMINIUM ROOFS

Low-pitch roofs are covered in aluminium. There are again large grassed and tree-planted areas for pedestrians and ample garages and car parks. Half of the houses have private back gardens.

Using electric under-floor heating and gas-fired warm air heating systems these homes have no fireplaces. The builder faces the problem of overcoming building societies' objections to this.

(January 19)

Victory for winklepicker

BRITAIN'S shoemakers have abandoned the square toe. In so doing they have declared independence from the influence of the great French shoe designers, Roger Vivier and Charles Jourdan, and have hearkened instead to the voice of the customer.

The fact that the customer they're obeying has, in some cases, total lack of taste, doesn't deter them. I saw rows upon rows of winklepickers ready and waiting for autumn delivery to our shops when I toured the big Shoe Exhibition in Harrogate last week.

Some winklepickers are more fierce than others. In the "better class" ranges the point is faintly rounded, given sometimes the intriguing diamond-facetting that the Italians are pushing for autumn. In others the point loomed, stark and savage.

In some shops in Britain it never went out. All the hullabaloo about squares left many shoppers utterly cold. So did the subsequent talk of the successor-to-the-square: the rounded baby toe.

Reptiles are gaining acceptance slowly after waiting in the wings for several years. They will come in, sideways, via trimming on suede and patent court shoes, or in mock-croc shoes which are actually made of calf.

Open-side court shoes, with a strong Italian look, are the news in body-shape. Usually just the outer side of the foot is open, and narrow spaghetti straps bridge the gap. These straps ("worm straps" one maker calls them) dominate the autumn picture. Slingbacks are everywhere. Brown, in all shades, is the colour for autumn.

(April 16)

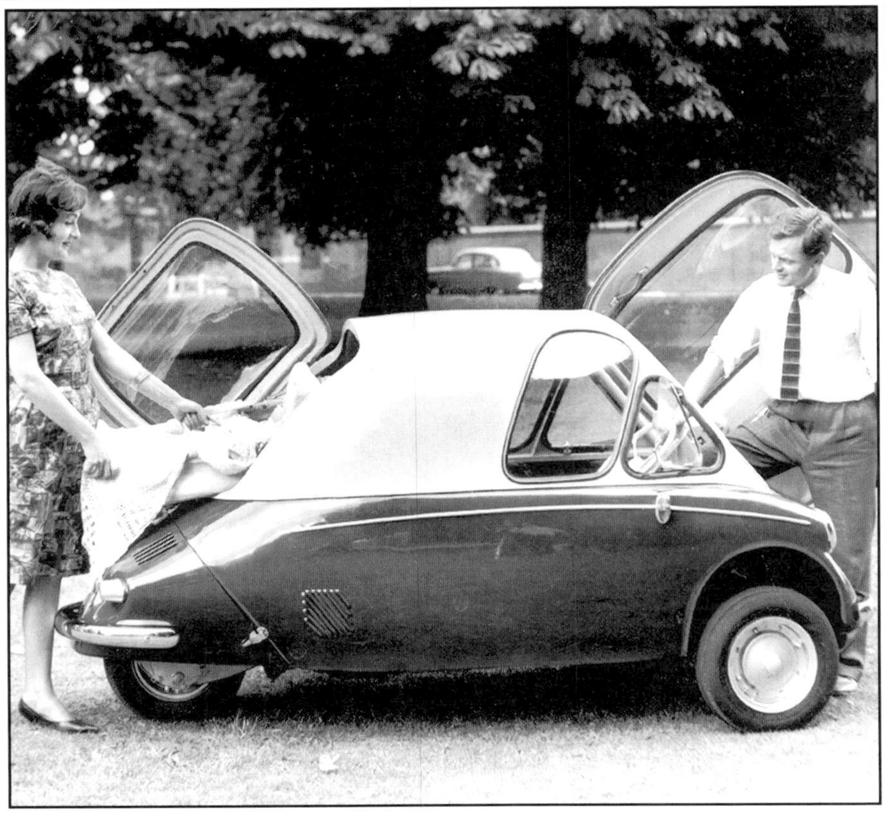

REPORTS from Brussels that Britain is likely to enter the Common Market by the autumn of 1963 lend strength to a wide-spread belief in the motor industry that the purchase tax on cars will shortly be cut again.

At present the tax is 45 per cent of the manufacturer's price. The Common Market aim is a sales tax of up to 20 per cent. British purchase tax would have to come down, probably by stages, to this figure.

The recently introduced Trojan 3-wheel estate van, and its passenger counterpart, is an example of the crippling effect of purchase tax on car sales in the home market.

In estate van trim, shown above, the car retails at £297 10s. As a saloon - with little more than extra window-space to distinguish it from the dual-purpose business and pleasure vehicle - it carries purchase tax and retails at £359 15s.

There would undoubtedly be a very big home market for the saloon version at something between these prices. The 198 c.c. four-stroke engined Trojan car cruises at 45 m.p.h. with a maximum of 55, and the makers claim a petrol consumption of 95 m.p.g.

(July 18)

PRAMS, TOO, ARE STATUS SYMBOLS

ROW upon row of glittering, chrome-plated vehicles shone in swirling, streamlined elegance. The motor show of the parambulator world is on in London at the moment.

Revolving gently on their turntables, in gleaming silver, or subtle two-tone colours, the cream of the pram fraternity stands high above their lesser fellows. To car owners, some of the names will sound familiar, too - Classic, Zephyr, and so on.

Refinements on this year's models are mainly in the colour schemes (squirrel, cornflower, jade) and shapes (shallow with sweeping curves), rather than more useful things like folding and carry-cot type prams which Continental firms make so well.

The glamorous £34 "Markova" pram made by Ballerina, which is lined throughout with quilted, rose-printed plastic is beautiful, but would it be much use in the High Street on a busy morning's shopping?

I discovered, too, that it's not unusual for someone to walk into a shop and peel off £30 or more in notes to pay for a pram, and that sometimes 13gn dolls' prams are bought by the pair.

"The pram is undoubtedly a status symbol," said Mr. V. Tovani, sales manager of another big firm.

Some British manufacturers, make more convenient, easier-to-manage baby carriages, but the majority tell me that the British, as a whole, want the grand stramlined affair. In spite of wanting to be sensible, there is something that draws one to those tall, elegant, inconvenient, oh-so-terribly English prams.

Paula Davies

(January 16)

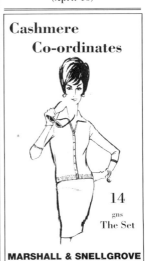

PROF. G.M. TREVELYAN

NO man during the present century did more to encourage the reading and understanding of history than George Macaulay Trevelyan, who has died in Cambridge at the age of 86.

In the tradition of Gibbon, of Carlyle and of his great-uncle Macaulay, he masked great erudition by a graceful literary style. He also brought to his 30 published works the quality of a sensitive imagination by which the past was interpreted and made intelligible in the light of the present.

He was born on Feb. 16, 1876, the third son of Sir George Otto Trevelyan, O.M., nephew and biographer of Macaulay.

One of his earliest memories was of being guarded by a detective as he played in Phoenix Park; his father had been appointed Chief Secretary for Ireland after the assassination of Lord Frederick Cavendish in 1882. Later he was sent to Harrow.

AT CAMBRIDGE
Trinity Fellowship

In 1898 he was elected to a Fellowship at Trinity College, Cambridge, where he had been an undergraduate.

It was as a young Fellow of Trinity that in 1903 he heard Bury deliver that famous dictum which so accurately reflected the spirit of the time. History, declared the new Regius Professor, is "simply a science, no less and no more."

Trevelyan did not disagree with Bury and the German school that the collection and sifting of historical evidence should be scientific in method. But he refused to accept their view that history should be confined to unadorned exchanges between learned men.

To the value of social history he attached particular importance. The sale of half a million copies of his "English Social History" was to give him more than a purely financial satisfaction.

The popularity and diversity of Trevelyan's historical works has sometimes aroused the unjust suspicions of less nimble scholars. From Wycliffe to John Bright, from the Romans to the Edwardians, he was at home in any age and in almost every land.

ITALY'S INSPIRATION
Battlefield Work

Italy he loved almost as deeply as Northumberland. It inspired him to write what is probably his most enduring monument, the trilogy on Garibaldi. Hardly had he finished tramping the Italian battlefields of the past than he was engaged no less adventurously in those of the present, commanding a British Red Cross ambulance unit during World War I.

There followed that brilliant epitome, his "History of England," and the trilogy on the reign of Queen Anne. This was mostly written at Cambridge, where he had been appointed Regius Professor by Stanley Baldwin in 1927.

Like most writers whose works unfold with graceful ease, Trevelyan composed slowly. Each paragraph would usually be transcribed four times before the typing stage.

He was much honoured in his lifetime. His appointment to be Master of Trinity gave him particular pleasure. Like his father, he received the Order of Merit.

His family life was intensely happy. He married in 1904 Janet, daughter of Mrs. Humphrey Ward and a dedicated worker for child welfare. He is survived by a son, C.H. Trevelyan, Fellow of King's and a daughter, Mary, the wife of Dr. John Moorman, Bishop of Ripon since 1959.

(July 23)

V. SACKVILLE-WEST

NOVELIST AND GARDENER

VICTORIA MARY SACKVILLE-WEST, poetress, novelist and gardener, who has died, aged 70, was the wife of Sir Harold Nicolson, whom she married in 1913. She was born at Knole, Sevenoaks, the only child of the third Baron Sackville. She was always known as Vita.

Though she lived with Sir Harold at Sissinghurst Castle, also in Kent, she wrote of Knole in an article in THE DAILY TELEGRAPH in 1948 as her "passionately-loved, personal home." She described running, as a child, about the courtyards, up and down the galleries and discovering secret doors behind the panelling.

She was made a Companion of Honour in 1948. Durham conferred on her a D.Litt. degree in 1950, and she was a Fellow of the Royal Society of Literature. She had two sons, the younger of whom, Mr. Nigel Nicolson, was Conservative M.P. for Bournemouth East and Christchurch from 1952-59.

Everything she ever produced, from a short prose piece about tending a garden to "The Land," the long and often very beautiful eclogue that won her the Hawthornden Prize in 1927, had a touch of distinction, even nobility, in its cadences.

For younger readers her novels "The Edwardians" and "All Passion Spent," written in the early 1930s are perhaps a little too delicate and the style seems rather mannered.

Her non-fiction included much of high quality, particularly in her writing about her own family. But, for many, her greatest distinction was in the short pieces about gardens.

POET OF NATURE
"The hand"

It would not be right to claim Victoria Sackville-West as a major poet, but, as always, it was in nature that she found her truest expression.

In "The Land" she wrote:

"Who has not seen the spring, is blind, is dead.
Better for him that he should coffined lie.
And in that coin his toll to Nature pay
Than live a debtor . . ."

(June 4)

MARILYN MONROE

Hollywood star who became a legend

MARILYN MONROE, who has died aged 36, was probably the best known film actress of this decade. Her legend was created, by her own much-publicised personality, long before she actually played star roles.

In this her radiant looks and in particular her figure coupled with an engaging frankness of speech played no small part. She was known on both sides of the Atlantic for some time before she was accepted.

A highly successful photographer's model by 1947, she made an immediate success in a small role in "The Asphalt Jungle." Her reputation grew in spite of several indifferent films and she played a variety of roles. Among the best known were "Gentlemen Prefer Blondes," "How To Marry a Millionaire," "The Seven Year Itch," "Bus Stop," "Let's Make Love," and "The Misfits," written by Arthur Miller.

Marilyn Monroe was born Norma Jean Mortenson (or Baker) on June 1, 1926, in Los Angeles. She had 12 sets of foster parents and at least one stay in a Los Angeles orphanage.

THREE MARRIAGES
First at 16

Her first marriage at the age of 16 to James Dougherty, a policeman, lasted only a year. She was "discovered" by a photographer while she was working in a paint factory.

In 1953 she was voted the most popular actress in America. In June last, in consequence of her repeated absences from the set of "Something's Got to Give," she was dismissed by Twentieth Century-Fox and the film was abandoned.

In 1954 she married Joe Di-Maggio, a baseball player, but this ended in divorce a year later. She was married for the third time in 1956 to Arthur Miller, the American playwright. He accompanied her on her highly successful visit to England.

Miss Monroe obtained a divorce from Mr. Miller in January, 1961.

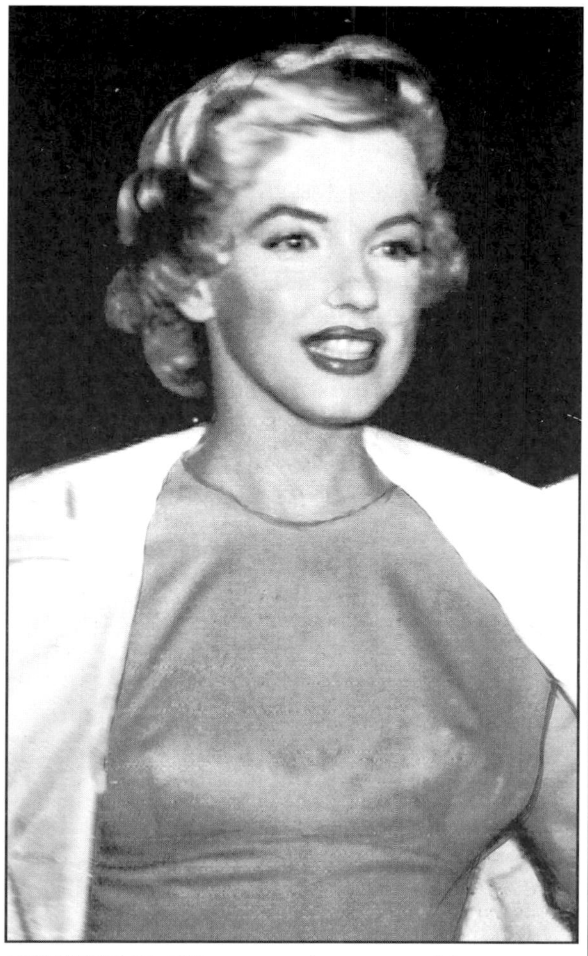

ASPIRATION TO ART
"Cry from the heart"

ERIC SHORTER writes: Time and again Marilyn Monroe said: "I want to be an artist, not a freak." Well, we have heard that somewhere before.

It is the kind of cry from the heart that Hollywood, where so many of the freaks come from, is always putting into the artless mouths of dumb, bosomy blondes and ex-calendar bosomy girls who have been placed under contract but with nothing very artistic to fulfil for the moment.

Well, even as a sex symbol there was more of Miss Monroe than usual. Flesh impact is what Hollywood used to call it, and although the phrase wants subtlety it is more meaningful than the earlier terms "glamour" or "it."

The key is impact, the screen equivalent to stage presence, and this, whether she could act or not, was what Miss Monroe richly possessed.

Meanwhile on the film she remained less expressive; a symbol still. An artiste, yes, but always with that final "e."

Then slowly the gift for comedy came through the shimmering screen presence which our own Dame Edith Sitwell once noted so admiringly. Here, for once, it was a dumb blonde who knew she was dumb, which by definition made her less so.

(August 6)

HERR BRUNO WALTER

GREAT SERVANT OF MUSIC

BRUNO WALTER, the German-born conductor who has died aged 85, specialised in the works of Mozart and Mahler. His first musical experience was in Germany.

He took a post at the Vienna Opera in 1901. Twelve years later he became general music director in Munich.

He paid his first visit to London in 1909. In 1924 he was in charge of the season at Covent Garden.

He was appointed conductor of the Berlin Charlottenburg Opera, in 1925 and took over the Gewandhaus concerts in Liepzig five years later. When Hitler came to power he worked in Austria, and in 1939 he went to the United States.

STERLING QUALITIES
Nobility and Humbleness

DONALD MITCHELL writes: With the death of Bruno Walter the world of music has lost a great servant. His personality offered a rare combination of nobility, integrity and genuine humbleness, and all his music-making bore the impress of these sterling qualities.

He had a markedly personal style of interpretation that was immediately recognisable in the characteristic sound he persuaded from the orchestra. This was never less than extremely beautiful, though one sometimes wished for a show of the muscle that lies beneath even the finest, ripest skin.

He was not fiery and metronomic, like Toscanini, or intellectual, like Furtwangler, or witty and capricious like Beecham. He was, in every sense, a born conductor who was content to use his baton as an instrument to probe the centres of feeling in whatever music he conducted.

It is not surprising, therefore, that he excelled as an interpreter of romantic music. His performances of Brahms, Schubert, Schumann, Strauss and Wagner were all memorable in their way, while of Mahler, whose close friend and disciple he was, he was the most authoritative exponent of his generation.

To all this music he brought passion, warmth and an outstanding technical competence. Orchestras were his willing collaborators, but their compliance should not lead us to underestimate the masterful skill with which he achieved his musical intentions.

(February 19)

PROF. NIELS BOHR

Prof. Niels Bohr, who died yesterday aged 77, was a Nobel Prize winner and one of the great pioneers of the atomic age. He was the first winner of the "Atoms for Peace" award in 1955, and was often described as the father of atomic physics.

Dr. Bohr had many links with Britain. He studied at Cambridge and Manchester under J.J. Thomson and Rutherford, and developed Rutherford's theories on the structure of the atom.

His work, "On the Constitution of Atoms and Molecules," which appeared in 1913 had already won him a wide reputation as a brilliant theoretical physicist. In 1922 he was awarded the Nobel Physics Prize for "services in the investigation of the structure of atoms."

OUR SCIENCE CORRESPONDENT writes. One of the most remarkable events of Bohr's life was his escape from Denmark during the war. From 1940 to 1943 the Germans had let him work on at his Copenhagen laboratory. He appreciated the theoretical possibility of a nuclear bomb, but he did not believe it was practical.

In 1943, when it was thought he was to be arrested, he escaped in a boat to Sweden. Then, fitted into the bomb bay of a Mosquito, he was flown to Scotland.

He was one of the first men to be involved with the political implication of the bomb. He proposed, for instance, to Sir Winston during the war that its secrets should be shared with Russia. But his suggestions were not well received.

(November 19)

G.H. ELLIOTT

G.H. ELLIOTT, the "Chocolate-Coloured Coon," who has died, aged 79, was a link with the old-time music hall who had been a star performer in his own right for nearly 60 years.

He never changed his make-up or his act throughout that period; his audiences resented any attempt to introduce new material.

Among the most popular of the songs he sang were "Lily of Laguna," "Silvery Moon," "Idano" and "Sue! Sue! Sue!" He continued, even at an advanced age, to demonstrate his superb skill at soft-shoe dancing.

Born at Rochdale, Mr. Elliott maintained that he was given his first name because his birth took place in the George and Dragon hotel there.

"LORD FAUNTLEROY"

Taken to America in his childhood, he became a boy soprano, appearing with a minstrel troupe and also in "straight" plays such as "Little Lord Fauntleroy."

He returned to Britain at the age of 11, and pursued this theatrical career in seaside concert parties.

He made his West End debut at the age of 19, and immediately established a reputation that was never to fade.

His burnt-cork make-up (only champagne corks were good enough, he joked) pleasant singing voice and effortless, subtle dancing became familiar to audiences throughout the country.

(November 20)

WILLIAM FAULKNER

WILLIAM FAULKNER, the American portrayer of the Deep South, who has died, aged 64, won the Nobel Prize for Literature in 1949.

His education was sketchy. He left high school before graduation and went to work in his grandfather's bank. His father was a livery stable proprietor who became business manager of Mississippi University.

At 16 he entered the university as a special student but joined the Canadian Air Corps soon after the 1914-18 war started. He was trained in England and spend some time in Oxford.

In 1922 he became university postmaster and then turned to writing. His first book, "Soldier's Pay," was written in six weeks and published in 1926. In 1932, and now a household name in two continents, he went to Hollywood to adapt one of his stories, "To-day We Live."

Besides the Nobel Prize, Faulkner won a Pulitzer Prize in 1954 for "A Fable." His collected stories won the National Book Gold Medal in 1950.

In recent years Faulkner divided his time between Oxford, Miss., and Charlottesville where, since 1957, he had been a writer in residence and lecturer at the University of Virginia. In 1929 he married Mrs. Estelle Oldham Franklin, who survives him.

He transferred to the RAF and when he went to France as an observer was in two crashes. He returned to Mississippi University after the war but left without a degree.

DAVID HOLLOWAY writes: No 20th-century American writer was more revered in his own country than William Faulkner. It was assumed there that the Noble Prize for Literature was his of right, as were the Pulitzer Prize and many other awards.

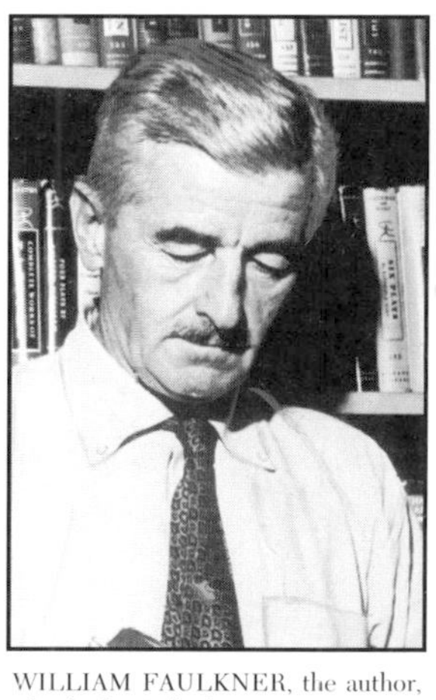

WILLIAM FAULKNER, the author, who died in Oxford, Mississippi, yesterday. He was 64.

Though they might not understand everything he wrote, his fellow-countrymen were sure that Faulkner was a literary genius. And they were probably right, for Faulkner at his best, say in parts of "Sanctuary" or "The Sound and the Fury," could be equalled by few of his contemporaries for his power in conveying emotions or in impressionistic descriptions of Southern life. Yet no whole book was a masterpiece.

(July 8)

MR. HANNEN SWAFFER

For long one of Fleet Street's most arresting and discussed personalities, Mr. Hannen Swaffer, who has died, aged 82, was a pioneer of modern journalism. Twice an editor and for long a dramatic critic, his provocative pen earned him praise and obloquy in equal measure.

(January 17)

LILY ELSIE

Lily Elsie, who has died aged 76, became the toast of London overnight when, as a comparitively unkown actress, she created the part of Sonia in the original London production of "The Merry Widow."

(January 16)

CHARLES LAUGHTON

FAME ON STAGE AND IN FILMS

CHARLES LAUGHTON, who has died aged 63, was an actor of very great ability who only just failed to reach the topmost heights.

As a young Yorkshireman, member of a family of hotel keepers, with no great advantages in the way of looks or physique - he described himself as "fat and ugly" - he showed high promise at the Royal Academy of Dramatic Art, and on the West End stage he soon attracted notice with his pronounced mannerisms and strong "attack."

His Poirot in Agatha Christie's "Alibi" (1928) showed a flair for the eccentric; his unfortunate murder in "Payment Deferred" had a pathos not, as a rule, within his range; his Tony Perelli in "On the Spot" (1930) made him one of the most popular character actors of the day.

Turning to the classics, he played Moliere's Sganarelle in French at the Comedie Francaise, the first appearance of an Englishman at that theatre, Angelo in "Measure for Measure" and the King in "Henry VIII."

Studies in Sadism

It was the screen, though, that made Laughton world famous. His King in Korda's "The Private Life of Henry VIII" was probably the greatest performance of his life, his "Rembrandt" the subtlest.

"The Barretts of Wimpole Street" and "Mutiny on the Bounty" (both studies in sadism) and his sympathetic playing in "Ruggles of Red Gap" (in which he recited Lincoln's Gettysburg address) were also enormously popular. In recent years he toured America with successful readings from the Bible, Shakespeare and Dickens.

Mr. Laughton, at the height of his fame in Hollywood, earned £25,000 a year. In 1950 he became an American citizen. In 1929 he married Elsa Lanchester, the actress.

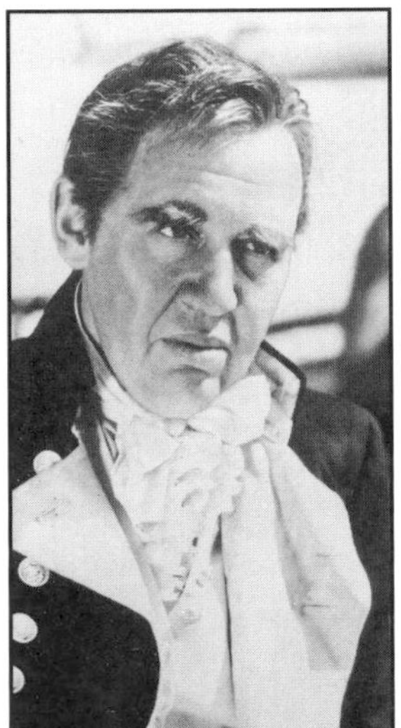

CHARLES LAUGHTON in "Mutiny on the Bounty".

SCREEN CAREER

Notable roles

PATRICK GIBBS writes: It was Hollywood that first realised Charles Laughton's film potentialities. No doubt Paramount, who gave him his first contract, saw him on the New York stage in "Payment Deferred."

In the first film he made for them, which was "The Devil and the Deep," in 1932, he made an immediate impression, playing a submarine commander, his performance quite outshining his co-stars Tallulah Bankhead and Gary Cooper.

He appeared at the top of his form in his last part, that of Senator Cooley in "Advise and Consent," which was shown at the Cannes Festival this year.

(December 17)

MRS. ELEANOR ROOSEVELT

A WOMAN of charm and of great strength of character, Mrs. Eleanor Roosevelt, who has died, aged 78, was one of the few widows of illustrious statesmen to have achieved a distinguished status in her own right.

After the death of President Roosevelt in 1945 she enhanced her already established reputation by embracing with profound and typical earnestness, the causes of peace and of the welfare of humanity. She was appointed a United States representative to the United Nations General Assembly, a post she held until 1953. In March 1961, President Kennedy again nominated her as a representative.

She also became chairman of the U.N. Human Rights Commission, which her own interest and enthusiasm had largely brought into being.

SELFLESS QUALITY

"Most popular American"

Not the least of those characteristics which endeared her to the American public - in 1948 she was voted the most popular living American of either sex - and indeed to people in many parts of the world, was her absolute selflessness.

Most of her earnings from her column, "My Day," which was syndicated to 90 newspapers, and from her many broadcasts and television appearances, were disposed of in a variety of charitable ways.

Her actions were prompted without possible doubt, by devotion to the great ideals she shared with Franklin D. Roosevelt. She was determined that his death would not be the end of them. One American described her, happily, as "the personification of the American conscience."

For many years before the loss of her husband her life had entailed considerable self-sacrifice. He was stricken with infantile paralysis at the age of 40, and many of his relatives and friends considered that his political career should end at once. Fortified by his wife's faith in his future, he stayed on to be four times elected President - a record in American history.

Her autobiography, "On My Own" was published in 1959. At a Foyle's lunch in London to mark its publication, she said Americans lacked understanding of the world, and of the needs, thinking and longing of uncommitted peoples.

Her energy was outstanding. In recent years her day began at 7.30 a.m., and often finished after 1 a.m. She would make 150 speeches in a year and answer 100 letters in a day.

(November 8)

KIRSTEN FLAGSTAD

Kirsten Flagstad, the Wagnerian soprano, who has died in Oslo, aged 67, was born of a family of professional musicians at Hamar, Norway, in 1895. She made her debut in d'Albert's "Tiefland" in 1913.

MARTIN COOPER writes: All her early operatic experience was in Scandinavia, where she sang a great variety of roles, including many in light opera, and it was not until 1933 that she was first heard at Bayreuth.

She sang Sieglinde there the following year. Isolde at the New York Metropolitan in 1935 and Isolde, Brunnhilde and Senta at Covent Garden in 1936-7.

She was in the United States when war broke out and her husband's association with the Quisling party in Norway during the German occupation and her own indiscreet (though according to her autobiography and the findings of a Norwegian Court of Enquiry, wholly innocent) behaviour made her for a time unwelcome in London.

She did not return until 1947. From then until her retirement in 1951 she dominated all the Wagnerian productions at Covent Garden by the power and ease of her singing, her majestic and unhurried phrasing and the tragic dignity of her style.

(December 10)

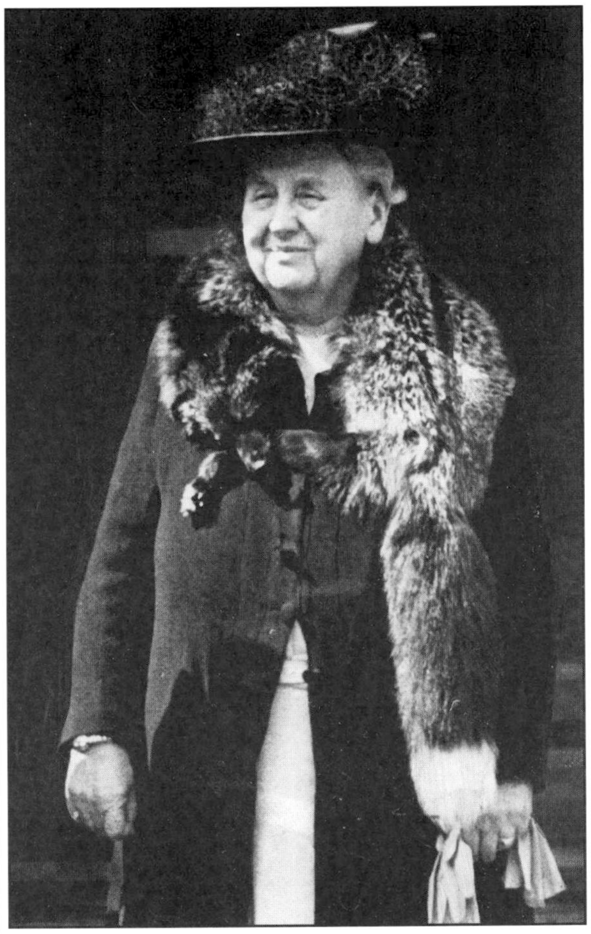

AN INVINCIBLE QUEEN

ENGLAND has not known a more staunch foreign friend or a more welcome guest than WILHELMINA of the Netherlands. By her own request she renounced the supreme royal title when diminished strength persuaded her to transfer her sceptre; but she was of a queenly spirit, and it belongs to her for ever in the sight of history. From her birth she was the symbol of her country's independence, which had been endangered by the absence of an heir to the dynasty; in the hour of mortal peril she became much more than a symbol - an incarnation. It was not for a symbol that the treacherous Nazi onslaught of 1940 took as a major objective the capture of the person of the Queen; a true intuition told them that while she was alive and at liberty their prospect of breaking the spirit of her subjects was hopeless. They failed. After perilous adventures and narrow escapes the Queen found refuge in England.

Knowing that there was still a royal Dutch government though in exile, nerved to endure by the utterances of their undaunted sovereign over the air, the Dutch people put up against the administration of one of the most odious of the gauleiters, a steady and harassing resistance that none of the occupied countries surpassed and few rivalled. Meanwhile a brigade of resolute exiles rallied round their Queen to participate in the campaign of liberation; and when victory came the nation rose to acclaim her as she took her seat to preside over the task of reconstruction. She could see the future secure under a daughter of her own quality before she modestly decided that her work was done.

(November 29)

GLYNDEBOURNE FOUNDER DIES

MR. JOHN CHRISTIE, founder of Glyndebourne opera, died at Glyndebourne last night, aged 79. His health had been failing for some time after an eye operation.

He founded the annual festival of opera in 1934. The first lasted for only a fortnight in a small theatre seating 300 which he built next to his Elizabethan manor house near Lewes.

His wish to help the then languishing cause of opera in England was supported by his wife, Audrey Mildmay, the soprano, whom he married in 1931. She died in 1953.

The first festival was a success. So were those that followed. The stage was enlarged and the seating accommodation doubled by 1937. The theatre was again extended in 1953.

An enterprise that started as the apparently freakish dream of a rich eccentric has set standards of operatic performance that, in their own field, are unsurpassed.

He had a passion for perfection, especially where his favourite Mozart was concerned. No trouble or expense was spared in pursuing that ideal. He saw Glyndebourne grow from a small luxury festival to a company able to compete with all comers in such an international arena as the Edinburgh Festival.

This country owes an enormous debt to John Christie. It is shared in a lesser degree by music lovers all over the world who have benefited directly from the records of Glyndebourne performances and indirectly from the standards set there.

(June 5)

LORD BIRKETT

ONE OF GREATEST CRIMINAL LAWYERS

LORD BIRKETT, of Ulverston, who has died aged 78, was one of the greatest criminal lawyers of his time. For many years, as Sir Norman Birkett, K.C., he filled the place left vacant by the late Sir Edward Marshall-Hall, for whom he was once a junior, as a brilliant advocate for the defence.

He displayed equal brilliance as a Judge for the King's Bench from 1941 until 1950, and then as a Lord Justice of Appeal. He was created a Baron in 1958.

Among the many famous trials with which he was associated as a K.C. were those in which Alfred Rouse and Dr. Buck Ruxton were convicted of murder. Mrs. Pace and Mrs. Hearn, whom he defended, were acquitted of the capital charge, as was Toni Mancini in a Brighton "trunk murder" trial.

Sir Norman was also prominent in the trial of Clarence Hatry. At the height of his career his income was reputed to be more than £30,000 a year.

The man who was to take his place among the great pleaders of the Bar began life in his father's drapery shop in Ulverston, Lancashire.

WIDER HORIZONS

Brilliant Speech

After schooling at Barrow-in-Furness, he helped his father behind the counter; his family were anxious for him to join the business, but he longed for wider horizons, and went up to Emmanual College, Cambridge. President of the Union in 1910, he was called to the Bar of the Inner Temple in 1913.

While devilling for Sir Edward Marshall-Hall, he made his reputation in a case which his senior was unable to complete because of illness. Birkett, after two hours' study, delivered a brilliant closing speech lasting four hours.

As a barrister he defended many cases under the Poor Persons Act. He never knowingly, he said, defended a guilty person, but in several cases he had his own opinion of his client.

He was offered, and refused a judgeship several times before 1941 and while on the Bench wished frequently he were conducting cases "from the floor." The financial sacrifice involved was also quite intimidating.

He broadcast in the early part of the 1939-45 war as "Onlooker," and, with Lord Oaksey, was a British judge at the Nuremberg trials. He was knighted in 1941. In 1948 he sentenced to death George Epton, found guilty of the murder of Mrs. Winifred Mulholland, "the woman in red," in Kensington.

In 1957, he was chairman of the committee which recommended that no evidence obtained by the police by telephone-tapping, on the warrant of the Home Secretary, should be made available outside the public service.

Two years later, he was instrumental, as independent chairman, in bringing to a close the strike of 100,000 workers in the printing industry which affected 1,000 provincial and suburban newspapers.

(February 12)

VIOLINIST OF A SIMPLE STYLE

By MARTIN COOPER

FOR almost two generations the name of Kreisler, who has died aged 86, has been synonymous with violinist among millions of the general public all over the world.

Fritz Kreisler grew up among the last generation of the great Viennese musicians, studying with Bruckner and frequenting the same cafe - nicknamed the "Megalomania" - as Brahms and Hugo Wolf. But profoundly Viennese as he always remained, he early acquired a cosmopolitan outlook.

He must have been the only musician able to boast of having studied with both Bruckner and Delibes, and it is his French rather than his German studies that are to be found reflected in the compositions by which he acquired first fame and then - for a time and in certain circles - notoiety.

His own attitude to these compositions and to his art in general was characteristic of the sunnier, more relaxed atmosphere in which he grew up and of the performing artist for whom the music of all ages is a living lingua franca rather than a scholar's text.

In many of his arrangements and original compositions there is a strong vein of Viennese sentimentality and a frank intention of displaying the characteristic beauties of the instrument with little regard for anything else.

But these bonbons are presented with such artistry and in such an innocent, uncommercial way that they give the simple pleasure at which they aim, without any offence to even severe taste.

(January 30)

WAY OF THE WORLD

Insulting

A GOOD deal of our opposition to joining in a European Union seems to be based on a proposition very insulting to our own country. We are such feeble, miserable people, it implies, that if we do join Europe we shall only be able to play a minor part in it.

Our farmers and industrialists are so lazy and incompetent that they will be unable to stand up to the competition of vigorous Frenchmen, Germans and Italians.

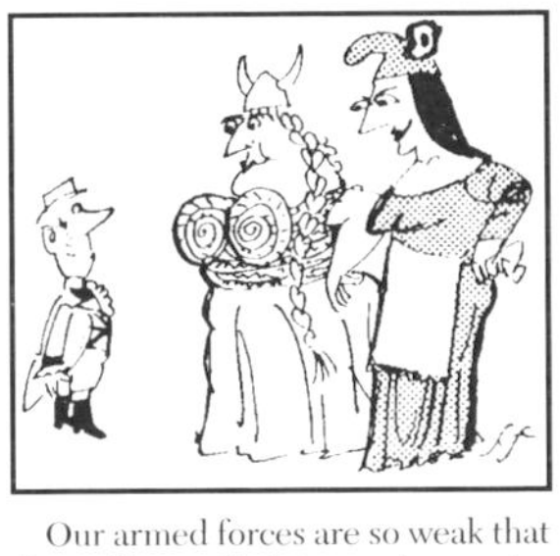

Our armed forces are so weak that they will soon find themselves under the orders of foreign generals, most probably Germans, to be used as unwilling, unreliable second-line troops or camp-followers in new adventures in aggression.

The proposition is not only insulting, but untrue. At any rate, the Europeans themselves do not seem to believe in it. If they did, far from being axious to have us with them, they surely would not take us at any price.

(May 9)

Moo

ANYONE who has not experienced the State education system as part of the normal background of life is "statistically" an eccentric, says a newspaper article. To appoint Sir Edward Boyle, Eton and Christ Church, as Minister of Education is "as absurd as it would be to appoint as Minister of Agriculture a man who knew what a cow looked like only from hearsay."

The ideal choice, I suppose, would be a man who knew what a cow looked like because he'd been one.

(July 24)

Cynicism

CYNICS," says a leading article, "may say that the Russians would be happier to have cheaper bread and meat than intrepid cosmonauts." They might also say, I suppose, that the East Germans would be happier to see the end of the disgusting wall.

Who is the cynic - the man who glorifies the feats of an amoral technology for their own sake, or the man who thinks it better that the ordinary human needs of food and freedom should be satisfied?

For the world at large, Russians included, manned space flight is simply a potential military weapon. For the man in space himself, it is a feat of courage and endurance like the ascent of Everest. But what should we say of an Everest expedition made possible by the planned starvation and imprisonment of whole populations?

(August 14)

H'm

THEY can trace their lineage back to Robert the Bruce . . . they befriended Mrs. Wallis Simpson . . . they hit the world headlines over an ordinary teacup . . . they helped to make Birmingham what it is.

"Few families have such a story to tell as the Cartlands, from great-grandmother Mrs. Polly to granddaughter Lady Lewisham . . ." (advt. in Birmingham Mail).

(May 9)

Peter Simple

ENGLAND LOSE SERIES OF DISILLUSIONMENT

India Win by 128: Two Victories And Rubber For First Time

From P.A. ROBERTS

MADRAS, Monday.

THE series of disillusionment for England followed to the last the pattern established at Calcutta, and India's spin bowlers carried their side to victory by 128 runs soon after lunch here to-day.

So an excited, jubilant India took the rubber in no uncertain fashion by two games to none. It was the first time they have won a series against England, indeed, the first time they have won two matches in one rubber against a senior cricket country.

Calcutta represented a dramatic turning of the tide for them. Until that match they had tasted victory against England only once in 27 Tests. Now they have won two successive matches by an aggregate of something over 300 runs.

It was here at Madras 10 years ago that they halved the rubber against N.D. Howard's team. Now they have proved beyond doubt that under their home conditions, England cannot afford to take the field without their best side against them.

Granted good fortune in the toss - here, as at Calcutta, batting first was vital for the pitch took a progressive amount of spin in direct contrast to those of the first three Tests - India have made more of their opportunities than England.

IMPROVED AS TEAM

Contractor's Leadership

At times they have faltered in the curious unimaginative way we have seen in England but they have improved as a team under the selfless guidance of Contractor.

Their special ability has been to score heavily in the first innings of each match without fail; and England's weakness has been in failing to stop them doing it. As at Calcutta the margin on first innings more or less divided the two teams.

Here this morning with half their wickets already gone England's later order batsmen indicated that a real scrap could have been made of it if either first or second innings had been satisfactorily launched.

For almost an hour Parfitt and Knight made the appearance of a student recumbent in a coffin, draped in MCC colours and conducted in a slock funeral procession around the ground, seem premature.

The ball, however, was turning more to-day and slightly quicker, and it was too much to hope that the "corpse" would have to change his colours.

Durani presently took two wickets which carried his aggregate for the match to 10 and for the series to 23 and after lunch Borde, his partner in India's triumphant progress this past fortnight finished it off.

The Scoreboard

INDIA - First Innings: 428 (Nawab of Palaudi 103, N.J. Contractor 86, F.M. Engineer 65, R.G. Nadkarni 63). Second Innings: 190 (V.L. Mahkekar 85, Lock 6-51).

ENGLAND - First Innings: 281 (M.J.K. Smith 73, Durani 6-105).

Second Innings:

P.E. Richardson, c Jasimba, b Desal	2
R.W. Barber, b Durani	21
K.F. Barrington, lbw b Nadkarni	48
E.R. Dexter, c Nadkarni, b Borde	3
M.J.K. Smith, c Borde, b Durani	15
P.H. Parfitt, c Contractor, b Durani	33
B.R. Knight, c Engineer, b Durani	33
D.A. Allen, c Umrigar, b Borde	21
G.F. Millman, c Contractor, b Prasanna	14
G.A.R. Lock, c Nadkarni, b Borde	11
D.R. Smith, not out	2
Extras (b 2, lb 4)	6
Total	**209**

Fall of wickets: 1-2, 2-32, 3-41, 4-86, 5-90, 6-155, 7-164, 8-194, 9-202

Bowling: Dass: 4-0, 16-1; Umrigar: 6-1, 12-0; Durani: 34-12, 72-4; Borde: 25.3-8, 59-3. Nadkarni: 12-3, 25-1; Prassanna: 11.3-19.

Umpires: S Pan & Dr J. Gopaiskrisha.

(January 16)

'AMATEUR' IS DROPPED FROM CRICKET

THE 17 first-class counties decided at a meeting at Lord's yesterday to abolish the amateur status. In future all players will be called "cricketers."

This decision has to be approved by MCC. It is expected that they will bring it into force at their committee meeting at the end of January.

The ruling will make cricket the only sport, apart from table tennis, in which there is no distinction between professionals and amateurs. One important casualty from this decision will be the Gentlemen and Players match, which was first played in 1806.

Cricketers will, however, still be able to play without receiving payment if they so wish.

Sir Jack Hobbs said yesterday: "It is sad to see the passing of the amateurs, because it signals the end of an era in cricket. They were a great asset to the game, much appreciated by all of us because they were able to come in and play freely, whereas many professionals did not feel they could take chances."

(November 27)

JIM CLARK WINS GRAND PRIX

From W.A. McKENZIE, Daily Telegraph Motoring Correspondent

AINTREE, Sunday.

JIM CLARK, 25, a Berwickshire sheep farmer, scored his second victory in the season's formula I races in the world championship series by winning the Grand Prix of Great Britain at Aintree yesterday. He won the Belgian Grand Prix on June 17 in the same car, a works Lotus.

With no other wins or place awards in the five Grands Prix to date, he now has 18 points, nine for each first place at Spa and Aintree, in the world championship table, and has come up from joint fourth place, with Dan Gurney of America, to second place behind Graham Hill of London.

In fifth place for the championship is John Surtees, ex-world motor cycle racing champion. He finished second here yesterday and now has 13 points.

Clark led the British Grand Prix from start to finish of the 225 miles contest. John Surtees, the only driver to offer any serious competition to the leader, ran with his Lola in second place throughout.

THE RESULTS

The results for the Grand Prix were: 1. J. Clark (Lotus), 2hr 26min 20.8sec, 92.25 mph; 2. J. Surtees (Lola) 2hr 27min 10.0sec; 3. B. McLaren (Cooper), 2hr 28min 05.6sec; 4. G. Hill, (B.R.W.), 2hr 28min 17.6sec; 5. J. Brabham (Lotus), 2hr 26min 41.4sec, one lap short; 6. Tony Maggs (Cooper), 2hr 27min 08.2sec, one lap short.

(July 23)

MOUSE STOPS TEST PLAY

England scored 386 for four on the opening day of the first Test Match against Pakistan at Edgbaston yesterday. M.C. Cowdrey scored 159, E.R. Dexter, the captain, 72, and T.W. Graveney was unbeaten for 96.

A mouse stopped play during the morning session. After scurrying across the pitch and inspecting the wicket, it made off for the boundary.

(June 1)

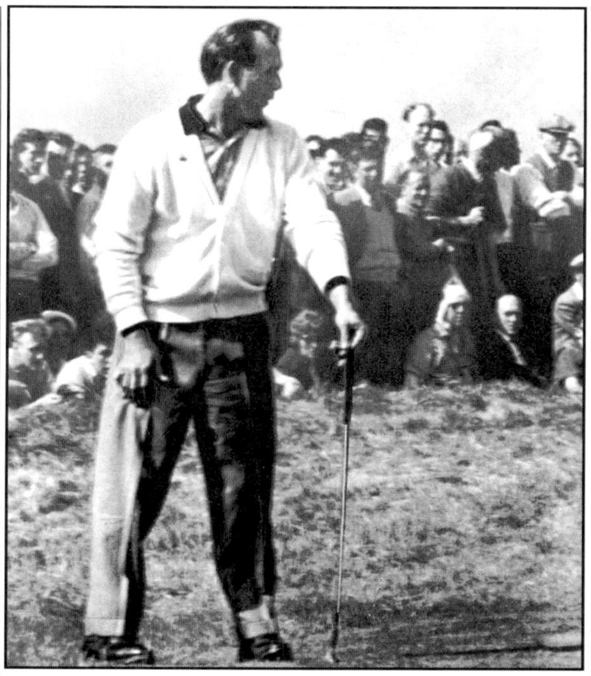

PALMER HOME BY A MILE WITH RECORD 276

Gallant Nagle fights all the way Huggett joint third

From LEONARD CRAWLEY

TROON, Friday.

ARNOLD PALMER, of the United States, won the Open Championship here this evening for the second year in succession and this time in the record total of 276; and he won it by six clear strokes from K.D.G. Nagle, of Australia.

If ever there was a great winner, it was Palmer to-day; and if ever there was a gallant loser it was Nagle, who finished in 282. Nagle won the Centenary Open at St. Andrews in 1960, beating Palmer on the American's first visit to this country by two strokes. So Palmer has again had his revenge.

Nor must we forget that Nagle defending his title a year ago at Royal Birkdale, had a dreadfully unlucky draw in so far as foul weather was concerned, and still finished fifth.

The previous best totals in the Open were by P.W. Thomson at Royal Lytham in 1958 and Nagle at St. Andrews in 1960, each with 278.

Palmer's victory here, as with many others in the long list of Open Championships, was based on a magnificent third round of 67 to beat the record for the course by two strokes but, let no one forget, he did not kill Nagle, with whom he was paired.

Palmer's golf all day was of a brand no other player in the world that I know is capable on a great seaside course running quite fast and distinctly bumpy.

I cannot resist the temptation of pointing out that at about the same hour as the unhappy Gary Player, of South Africa, arrived in New York to-day protesting at the unfairness of Old Troon as the cause of his failure to qualify in the Championship, a far greater golfer triumphed over it with a record score likely to stand for a generation or more.

The American P. Rogers, tied for third place with B.G.C. Huggett, of Romford, in 289, Huggett being the only British player to finish in the first seven. That is a thought which is most depressing to all of us but all due credit to Huggett for a great performance especially in his last round of 69.

(July 14)

THE PORTLY AND ELDERLY ARE SQUEEZED OUT

By Our Bowls Correspondent

THE programme for the EBA National Championship which begin at Mortlake a week on Monday, serve as a useful reminder of two gradual changes which are coming over the game.

Once considered the special province of old men, it is significant that one must go back to 1955 to find anyone over 50 winning the singles championship, the cream of all the events.

Since then it has been won twice by men in their twenties, twice by men in their thirties and twice by men in their forties.

Over those years a second change has been slowly emerging, the greater consistency with which the same players reappear in one way or other of the events at Mortlake. Thus, D.J. Bryant has qualified six years running, T.G. Fleming five, and C. Smith four.

Among the older players E.P.C. Baker four times the singles champion, has survived one or other of his county championships four times in six years and H. Shapland four times in five. These, and others with similar records, are slowly killing the once common claim that luck is all important in bowls.

Both changes have a relationship for both are basically the results of increasing skill. Yet skill on its own is not sufficient, for skill needs ideal conditions if it is to be exploited to the maximum.

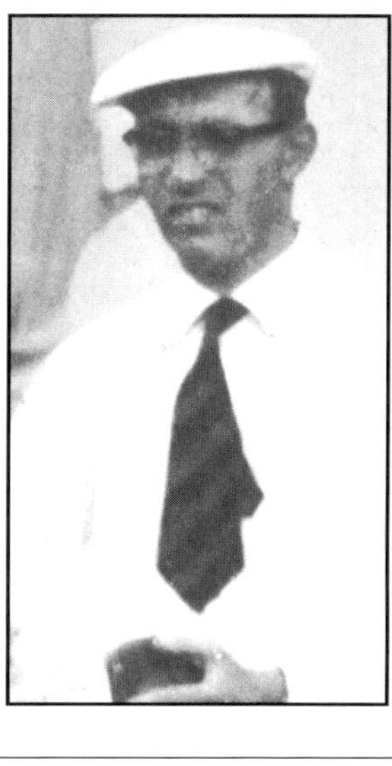

(August 3)

BACKHAND VOLLEY GIVES MRS. SUSMAN TITLE

Court behaviour sets committee difficult problem

By LANCE TINGAY

THE 1962 lawn tennis championships, at Wimbledon, will rank as the meeting where only one player, R. Laver, did what was expected, by becoming the men's singles champion for the second year.

Karen Hantze Susman, the new women's singles champion, was seeded no higher than eighth, the lowest grading ever of the winner, while the Australians R. Hewitt and F. Stolle in the men's doubles, Billie Jean Moffitt and Mrs. Susman in the women's doubles and N. A. Fraser and Margaret du Pont in the mixed, were all graded short of first favourites.

Not for one day was the meeting dull. How could it have been when upsets were constant? Yet, Laver apart, and he is certainly a splendid champion, the best talent seemed to waste rather than fulfil itself.

There was a lot of good lawn tennis but not much that was more than that. Even so, attendances were higher, the total being around 295,000, compared with 282,000 in 1961.

There is some irony in this because on Wednesday the British representative at the meeting of the International Lawn Tennis Federation in Paris will urge that Wimbledon be made open to professionals. Those who oppose the move will stress the unfailing success of Wimbledon with its amateurs.

STILL ONLY 19

Californian crown

What should have been Wimbledon's greatest match, Margaret Smith versus Maria Bueno, never came about. The substitution, Mrs. Susman versus Vera Sukova, in Saturday's final, brought the crown to a Californian.

They fill many places in the role of champion. Mrs. Susman is only 19 and it hardly seems eight years ago that "Teach" Tennant announced she was tutoring an 11-year-old prodigy who she claimed was destined to become champion of Wimbledon.

Mrs. Susman has a disciplined, well tutored game. A hard service, a splendid backhand volley, which was the main means by which she gained her title, and firm ground strokes are welded compactly together.

The final in which she brought down Mrs. Sukova had an element of pathos. No one begrudged Mrs. Susman her title, yet the crowd badly wanted Mrs. Sukova to win.

There is no glamour about the Czech, Mrs Sukova, and certainly no startling clothes. Nor is there much excitement about her game, except on her forehand, which is a splendid stroke.

CHEERY SMILE

Friendly finalist

Mrs. Sukova, aged 30, and an utterly surprising finalist, won the hearts of all by her cheery smile and obvious friendliness. The day before the final she stumbled on the stairs at her hotel and hurt her ankle.

She was by no means lame when she began the match but she lacked full mobility. Even so, she did well and Mrs. Susman won the first set with difficulty at 6-4.

In the second it seemed as if the Czech had measured well her opponent's strength and learned the answer. She built a lead of 3-love which looked commanding. Then, alas! in the sixth game her ankle's weakened strength gave out.

She limped and hopped and struggled against the handicap. She even wrested one more game, painfully hewn out against American aggression by the power of her forehand passing shop. The match, though, was over and Mrs. Susman, herself by no means at ease, was left with what was really merely a formal exercise to establish herself as the champion.

She is a good champion, there can be no doubt of that. She has not yet the ruggedness of Darlene Hard, the athleticism of Miss Smith or the grace of Miss Bueno, but she honours the Wimbledon roll as much as she is honoured by appearing on it.

The Finals

MEN'S SINGLES

R. LAVER (Australia) bt M. Mulligan (Australia) 6-2, 6-2, 6-1

WOMEN'S SINGLES

Mrs. J.R. SUSMAN (U.S.) bt Mrs. V Sukova (Czechoslovakia) 6-4, 6-4

MEN'S DOUBLES

R. HEWITT & F. STOLLE (Australia) bt B. Iovanovic & N. Pille (Jugoslavia) 6-2, 5-7, 6-2, 6-4

WOMEN'S DOUBLES

MISS B.J. MOFFITT & MRS. SUSMAN (U.S.) bt MRS. L.E.G. PRICE & MISS R. SCHUURMAN (S. Africa) 5-7, 6-3, 7-5.

MIXED DOUBLES

N.A. FRASER (Australia) & MRS. W. DU PONT (U.S.) bt R. D. Ralston (U.S.) & Miss A. S. Haydon (G.B.) 2-6, 6-3, 13-11.

(July 9)

SONNY LISTON WINS TITLE IN 2min 6sec

From DONALD SAUNDERS

CHICAGO, Tuesday.

SONNY LISTON became the new heavyweight champion of the world at Comiskey Park here to-night by knocking out Floyd Patterson in only 2min 6sec.

The fight was over almost before it had seemed to begin. Patterson had looked poor as he tried to grab and hold early in the first minute. Then Liston let go with two clubbing rights to the body.

These clearly hurt Patterson and before he could recover he was caught with a right uppercut to the jaw. He seemed to stagger to the ropes and hold on with one arm and was a sitting target for a tremendous left hook to the chin.

Down went the champion, rolling over on to his right side. There was never a hope of his rising. Indeed, he was still lying on his side as the count reached 10. Only then did he stagger upwards and clutch the ropes.

WORRIED VICTOR

Ringside pandemonium

Liston, who has so often been accused of being a merciless opponent promptly walked towards his opponent presumably to inquire if he was badly hurt. But before he could reach the tottering Patterson Liston's seconds surrounded him and went leaping round the ring.

Pandemonium broke out at the ringside as dozens of Liston's supporters tried to reach the ring. The police managed to prevent many of them getting under the ropes but it was fully 10 minutes before the ring was properly cleared.

(September 26)

BRUMEL SETS RECORD

STANFORD, California, Monday.

Valeriy Brumel, of Russia, broke his own world record by half an inch with a leap of 7ft. 5in. but despite this the Russian men received their fourth consecutive defeat from the United States by 128-107.

The Russian women won their match by 66 points to 41. The total attendance for the two-day match was 153,500 - the largest athletics gate in the United States since the 1932 Olympic Games.

(July 24)

MAGNIFICENT SPURS GO DOWN FIGHTING

Benfica score shock goal: Deficit too much to pull back

By DAVID MILLER

Spurs ..... (1) 2 Smith, Blanchflower pen, 65,000
Benfica .... (1) 1 Aguas £25,000
Benfica win 4-3 on aggregate

At the end of a titanic drama, which left the nerves trembling, the throat dry, mighty Tottenham Hotspur, the pride of England, bowed out of the European Cup to the magnificent champions Benfica at White Hart Lane last night.

But they went down still fighting, and as few, surely, could have fought. Never, never was there such a match in England, or for that matter anywhere, said some who have followed this great international game round the globe longer than I. And I could well believe them.

Spurs, if any still need to be told, had their chances - and what chances - to have won; or at least to have forced a play-off.

Yet, like many heroes before them, the slings and arrows over two matches cut too deep into them, left too great a hill to climb. Luck is the greatest ace in football, and it was not dealt to Spurs.

Nor could a soul deny Benfica were deserved winners. Their technique, agility, anticipation were a match and more for Spurs; their hearts and lungs as big. The events tumbled over each other, so desperately, so swiftly, that the whole superlative 90 minutes left the mind spinning.

SAD BLUNDERS
Relentless attacks

In the final reckoning two sad defensive errors in Lisbon and three disputed, dis-allowed goals by Spurs, one last night, were handicaps that finally consumed them. But, oh, the agony as, with strength sapping, they hurled themselves again and again recklessly into attack over the last pulsating half-hour.

If only they could have drawn level, one sensed the whole majestic edifice of Benfica's skill would crumble; highly excitable, they might then have floundered.

Bill Nicholson, Spurs manager, put his normal side in the field, on the strength of Saturday's FA Cup victory. Who is to say he was wrong? But I think, in retrospect, that had Mackay been in attack his dynamic pace and power would have perhaps changed the tide and brought Benfica to panic.

This was a memorable match, and of all the great players on the field more than any it was Mackay's match. At times it seemed he would willingly have played single-handed. No one ever possessed more energy or resilience, more power to come and come again. No one will ever forget his solo efforts in the last quarter of an hour, bringing Pereira to his knees and, with mere seconds to go, hitting the bar.

(April 6)

ENGLAND MEN FALL SHORT IN SKILL AND DEDICATION

From DONALD SAUNDERS

VINA. DEL MAR, Monday.

With their World Cup dreams shattered for another four years, England fly home on Wednesday, empty-handed but perhaps a little wiser. They will not be without company. Also returning are such European giants as Russia, Hungary and Germany.

But that does not alter the fact that it is disappointing to see England fail to move beyond the World Cup quarter-finals. The question as to why they never reached the concluding stages of the competition must be faced.

The simple answer is that the players are still not good enough to match such as the Brazilians. Tactical knowledge has improved in the last four years, but technique of ball control and shooting are below the standard required for success, particularly in these days of defensive football.

This will improve only when the players dedicate themselves to the game at an early age. It is common to see schoolboys, here and in Brazil, spending hours practising ball control so that one day they can become great players like their heroes Pele and Garrincha.

Those days of hero-worship have passed in England. But now that League football is better paid, it is possible that more boys will look to it as a worthwhile career, and be prepared to contribute to it.

It is sad to note that many British professionals are concerned only with what they can get out of the game. It is worse still to see some members of the England party lacking the team pride that is needed of the side if ever to become world class.

World Cup football is a real man's job. One or two over here have not been mature enough to do it.

HINT TO SELECTORS
Leave out players

The selectors would be wise to see that these few players do not wear an England shirt again until they have proved their worthiness of the honour. They have let down themselves, their country, and, worst of all, their colleagues.

(June 12)

ACCRINGTON NO LONGER IN LEAGUE

Accrington Stanley are no longer a Football League club. In fact, their membership ended last Wednesday, the moment their letter of resignation was received at the League's headquarters at St. Annes.

This was made clear by Alan Hardaker, the League secretary, last night. In an official statement he explained that on Sunday the Management Committee had considered the letter of resignation, another letter from the club's secretary seeking permission to withdraw the first one and "all other relevant information."

In addition, Accrington's honorary solicitor, Harry Disley, and a director, George Clarkson, were given a personal hearing.

Mr. Hardaker then added: "In accordance with well established legal precendent, immediately Accrington's resignation was received at the League office it was in operation and the Management Committee had no alternative but to accept it."

Cynics will argue, of course, that the League have hidden behind a legal technicality in order to get rid of a club which had become an embarrassment.

It is, of course, sad to see a town which was among the first to sponsor League football now without a representative in that competition. But once a club can no longer pay its way it clearly cannot expect to remain a member.

(March 13)

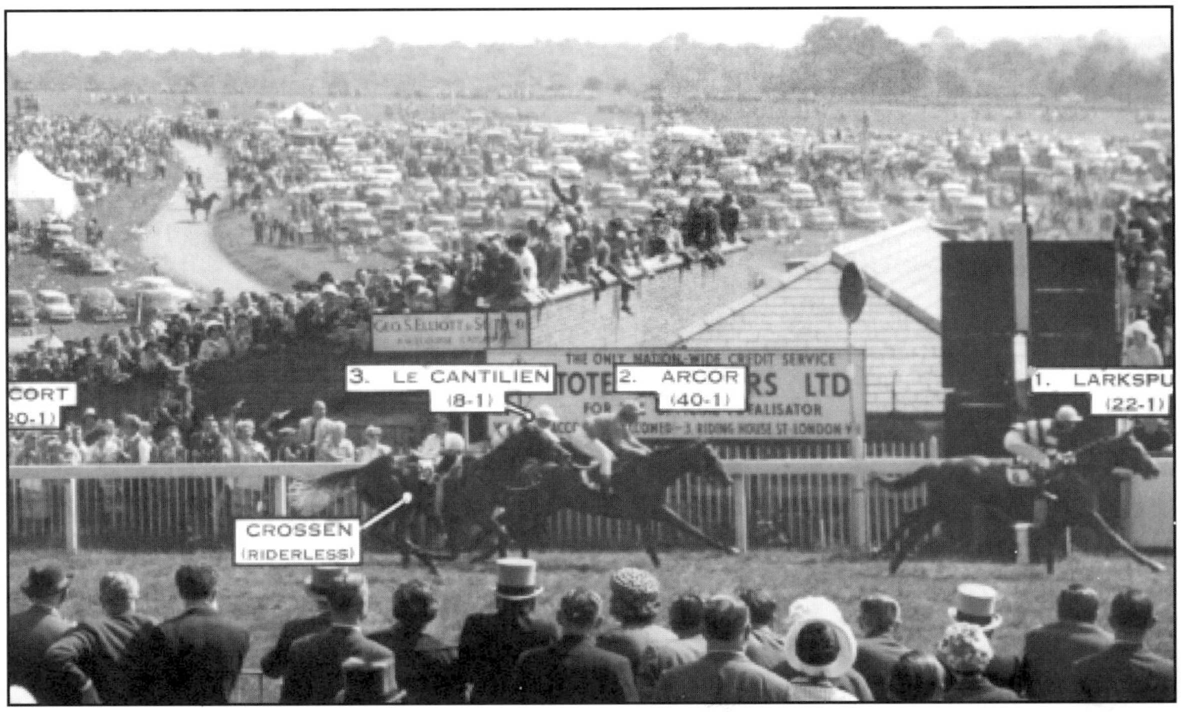

7-HORSE DERBY TUMBLE INQUIRY TO-DAY

FOUR JOCKEYS IN HOSPITAL

By GUY RAIS

Six Derby horses, including the favourite Hethersett, finished riderless at Epsom yesterday. They had been brought down with a seventh horse in a pile-up on the downhill bend towards Tattenham Corner five furlongs from home.

The seventh horse, King Canute II, had to be destroyed on the course. Six jockeys were taken to Epsom & District Hospital for treatment. W.H. CARR, the rider of Hethersett, was detained with head injuries.

Last night the Queen, who was prevented from seeing the Derby through a heavy cold, asked to be kept informed of the progress of Carr, who is the Royal jockey and the other jockeys.

Jockeys treated in hospital were G. LEWIS, S. SMITH, T. GOSLING, W. SINBURN and the French jockey M. LARRAUN, R.P. ELLIOTT, Pindaric's jockey, although shaken, was able to walk back to the stands unaided.

Four jockeys, Carr, Swinburn, S. Smith and Gosling, were detained in hospital. A hospital spokesman said late last night that the condition of all four was satisfactory.

INQUIRY OPENED
Crowd unaware of accident

Immediately after the race the stewards headed by the Duke of Norfolk, the Senior Steward, began an inquiry. It was later announced that the inquiry was postponed until today to enable some of the injured jockeys to give evidence.

Except for those watching the finish along the stands, thousands who thronged both sides of the course had no idea of the trouble that had occurred as the field of 26 thundered around into Tattenham Corner.

The Derby, worth £34,786, was won by Larkspur, American-owned. Irish-trained and ridden by an Australian. It finished two lengths ahead of two of the French runners, Arcor, a 40 to 1 chance, and Le Cantilien, 8 to 1.

Larkspur is owned by Mr. Raymond Guest, 54, a former Senator and farmer, of Virginia, and is trained by Vincent O'Brien in Ireland. The jockey was N. Sellwood.

Mr. Guest is a cousin of Sir Winston Churchill and brother of Mr. Winston Guest, who won the Gimcrack Stakes at York last year.

The race, timed for 3.20 began a few minutes late. The field, led by Romancero, swept up to the mile gate and past the left-hand bend before beginning the descent into Tattenham Corner.

Everything appeared normal but with the closely bunched field just starting to come down the hill at about 35 miles an hour there was disaster. Romulus fell and several horses following behind were unable to avoid Swinburn's mount. Within a split second six others were involved in the melée.

The horses brought down were Pindaric, Changing Times, Hethersett, Persian Fantasy, Grossen and King Canute II. Thousands crowding around the Downs by Tattenham Corner saw horses rolling over on the ground, kicking their legs and trying to rise and their jockeys lying on the ground.

HINT OF TROUBLE
Excitement in stands

The field swept by and the only hint those watching in the stands had of the trouble was the remark by the commentator, describing the race over the public address system, that there was a loose horse among the field.

But when the winner passed the post followed by the riderless horses, who were caught by stable lads waiting by the rails, there was a buzz of excitement.

In its excitement the crowd almost forgot to cheer the winner, but applause greeted the appearance of Larkspur in the winner's enclosure accompanied by Mr. Guest and his wife Caroline.

(June 7)

GIRL SWIMMER TOPS POLL

Women's prowess in swimming earned them the two top places in popularity for sporting achievement in 1962, according to a Gallup Poll survey, just completed, exclusive to The Daily Telegraph.

Linda Ludgrove heads the list, taking the place occupied by Stirling Moss in Gallup's 1961 poll. After her comes Anita Lonsbrough. In answer to the question, "Who do you think has been the outstanding sportsman or woman of 1962?" the following names emerged in order of preference:

1 Linda Ludgrove	Swimmer
2 Anita Lonsbrough	Swimmer
3 Ted Dexter	Cricketer
4 Dorothy Hyman	Athlete
5 Bruce Tulloh	Athlete
6 Brian Phelps	Diver

(December 22)

KILMORE'S VICTORY STIRS BROWN JACK MEMORY

Twelve-year-olds take first three places in National

By HOTSPUR (B.W.R. Curling)

Memories of Brown Jack came flooding back at Aintree on Saturday when Kilmore, who is closely related on his dam's side to the great stayer, won the Grand National in the hands of Fred Winter. Kilmore, bred in Ireland by Mr. G. S. Webb, is out of the mare Brown Image, whose second dam was Querquidella, dam of Brown Jack, winner of 18 races under Jockey Club Rules.

Brown Jack, who won the Queen Alexandra Stakes six times and also the 1928 Champion Hurdle at Cheltenham, kept his zest for racing for an extraordinarily long time and it seems that Kilmore is one of those who keep their form over the years.

Few horses have won the National after having reached the age of 12. The last to do so was Sergeant Murphy in 1923, and he, in fact, scored in his fifth Grand National at the age of 13.

The victory of Kilmore was another triumph for Fred Winter, who had the nerve to ride a waiting race and did not come to the front until between the last two fences though he could have done so earlier. Winter's list of important successes includes two Grand Nationals, three Champion Hurdles, and two Cheltenham Gold Cups.

For Kilmore's trainer, Ryan Price, this was a first Grand National victory. He has previously been regarded as a brilliant trainer of hurdlers rather than as an outstanding trainer of steeplechasers. His Champion Hurdle winners have been Clair Soleil in 1955, Fare Time in 1959, and Eborneezer last year.

17 FINISH
28 survive

It is pleasant to be able to record that 17 of the 32 runners completed the course on Saturday, compared with 14 out of 35 last year, and it is worth noting that 28 were still in the race as they came past the stands for the first time.

This should help silence the critics who are repeatedly saying that the National course is too severe. There is little doubt that the alterations to the fences are a big improvement and have not altered the character of the race.

(April 2)

NOBBLING MENACES NEW FLAT SEASON

By HOTSPUR

The doping scourge seemed at its height during the closing weeks of the 1961 flat racing season and with Lincoln due to open a new Jockey Club season a week hence the Turf authorities must view with dismay the latest activities of the nobblers.

Following last week's attempt to get at the Champion Hurdle favourite Another Flash, The Finn was almost certainly nobbled before Saturday's Monaveen Chase at Hurst Park. Derek Ancil, who trains and rode The Finn, feels there is no doubt that the horse was drugged, but the result of a urine test will not be known until next week.

It is probably significant that both Another Flash and The Finn were hot favourites. There can be no doubt that certain people are withholding information that would clearly be of value to those whose job it is to keep racing clean. The position is most unsatisfactory.

Ancil told me yesterday that The Finn appeared to be all right again apart from cuts and bruises. The trainer first became suspicious that something was wrong when saddling up the horse before the Monaveen Chase.

The Finn crashed through the first fence, unseating his rider, and then galloped loose, only to fall again at the second.

(March 19)

TULLOH LEADS ALL THE WAY

WELLINGTON, Wednesday.

Bruce Tulloh, of Britain, running barefoot, led from start to finish to gain a splendid win in the two miles here to-night.

Tulloh beat Barry Magee, New Zealand's bronze medallist in the 1960 Olympic Marathon, by 150 yards.

(February 8)

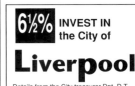

LEFT: CHARLES CHAPLIN on his way to Oxford Town Hall yesterday to receive an honorary degree of Doctor of Letters. The ceremony was held in the Town Hall because the Sheldonian Theatre is being renovated.

RIGHT: THIS IS THE ENTRANCE to a tunnel leading from the basement of a house in Heidelbergerstrasse, here, to communist East Berlin - through which an estimated 35 East Berliners escaped to the West. It was in this tunnel that meat truck driver Heinz Jercha, 28 - who built the tunnel with friends - was shot down by East Berlin police as he returned to lead more refugees to the West after rescuing a young married couple from East Berlin.

A ticket for the P.M.

RIGHT: THE PRIME MINISTER, MR. MACMILLAN, collecting the first ticket from the electronic dispensing machine of the new underground garage beneath Hyde Park. The ticket is stamped with time and date and the motorist pays a cashier when leaving.

Riots in Mississippi

BELOW: A FORCE OF FEDERAL MARSHALLS, who have been ordered to Mississippi because of the integration crisis, lining up at Oxford, the University city, yesterday when they arrived by plane. They wore battle dress and were armed with riot guns.

THE TEMPLES OF ABU SIMBEL. A close-up of the two of the four giant figures of Rameses II which guard the entrance to the Great Temple. The upper portion of the one on the right, ravaged by erosion of the centuries has tumbled and lies at the feet in two massive halves. On the left leg of the statue are Greek inscriptions dating back to Psammetichus II (6th century B.C.).

1963

Without doubt, this was the dramatic year of the decade. Towering over all was the tragedy of the assassination of President John F. Kennedy, followed only days later by the murder of the man believed to be his assassin. In the following decades there have been many theories as to the identity of the assassin, but even as the President's funeral cortège was passing through Washington, there were already rumours of conspiracies.

In America, also, the trouble over the desegregation of schools, universities and other places continued, culminating in the great march through Washington led by the Rev. Martin Luther King. President Kennedy, sympathetic to Negro rights, sent federal troops to Alabama to force the hand of the recalcitrant State Administration.

The scandal involving the cabinet minister John Profumo, who was forced to resign after admitting that he had lied to the House of Commons over his relationship with a call girl, virtually speaking brought down the Government. Three months after the Profumo debate, Harold MacMillan resigned because of ill health, his place being taken by Alec Douglas-Home who was required to renounce his peerage under the procedure made law earlier in the year. Viscount Stansgate (Antony Wedgwood Benn) was the first to avail himself of the procedure.

The "Profumo Affair" flowed over into the courts with the trial and death of Stephen Ward, the artist accused of procuring girls not only for those, like John Profumo, who were in the social circle of Viscount Astor but also for the Soviet Naval Attaché, Capt. Eugene Ivanov. Christine Keeler, the girl at the centre of the affair, was convicted on another charge and was imprisoned.

The whole country was staggered by the effrontery of the "Great Train Robbery" when over £1 million were stolen from a Post Office mobile railway carriage after the driver had been caused to stop by a bogus red signal. This was an event, though wholly unconnected with it, that followed the announcement of the Beeching Plan, a swingeing series of cuts in the routes, schedules and staff of British Rail.

The tall figure of General de Gaulle continued to dominate European politics. Early in the year, he vetoed British entry into the Common Market. As the trouble in Algeria continued, the President found himself the intended victim of an assassination plot. A former prime minister of France, Georges Bidault, implicated in the plot, was forced to flee the country. Yugoslavia suffered a disastrous earthquake at Skopje. Space travel continued with the Soviet team sending up the first woman into orbit and the Americans continued with their less spectacular experiments.

The world was saddened by the death of the reforming Pope John XXIII and also mourned were Hugh Gaitskell, the leader of the Labour Party, Lord Allenbrooke, the Chief of the Imperial General Staff through most of the Second World War, and the pioneer motor manufacturer and philanthropist, Lord Nuffield. The sporting world lost Sir Jack Hobbs, the first professional cricketer to be knighted.

Peter O'Toole played the title role in *Hamlet*, Laurence Olivier's opening production for the still-homeless National Theatre. Beatlemania spread throughout the world. The first one-day cricket competition ended in a victory for Sussex while Henry Cooper knocked down the boastful Cassius Clay before he himself was forced to retire with a cut eye.

Prince Charles on an expedition from his school, Gordonstoun, was spotted by a barmaid ordering a glass of cherry brandy. Princess Anne became the first royal daughter to attend a public school.

The Daily Telegraph
and Morning Post

No. 33776 LONDON, SATURDAY, NOVEMBER 23, 1963
Printed in LONDON and MANCHESTER Price 3d.

PRESIDENT KENNEDY IS ASSASSINATED
Shot in the head in open car on Texas festival drive

MRS. KENNEDY BENDING OVER HER HUSBAND in the back of an open car after he had been shot while they were driving through Dallas, Texas.

FORMER DEFECTOR TO RUSSIA ARRESTED

LYNDON JOHNSON SWORN IN AS NEW PRESIDENT

From STEPHEN BARBER
Daily Telegraph Special Correspondent
DALLAS, Texas, Friday

JOHN FITZGERALD KENNEDY, 46, the 34th President of the United States, died this afternoon within half-an-hour of being shot in the head as he drove through Dallas in an open car. He was on his way to make a speech at a political festival.

The shooting happened as the President's car drove through cheering crowds. Shots rang out and he slumped down in his seat.

Mrs. Jacqueline Kennedy, who was also in the car, jumped up and cried: "Oh, no!" She cradled her husband in her arms as the car sped to nearby Parklands Hospital. Police motor-cyclists with sirens blaring cleared a path through the crowds, and the traffic.

At the hospital President Kennedy was given an immediate blood transfusion and a Roman Catholic priest was called to his bedside to administer the last rites. The President died 25 minutes after being shot.

VICE-PRESIDENT ESCAPES INJURY

Vice-President Lyndon Johnson, 55, who was sworn in later as the new President, was travelling in the car behind President Kennedy's but was unhurt. The Governor of Texas, Mr. John Connally, 46, who was in the President's car, was shot in the chest and head. To-night his condition was described as "serious."

Crowds waiting outside the hospital groaned as priests announced the President's death. Many people collapsed in tears.

Police to-night seized Lee H. Oswald, 24, chairman of a pro-Castro "Fair Play for Cuba" committee. Oswald, wearing a brown shirt, was taken screaming from a cinema. A shot was fired during the arrest. A Dallas policeman had earlier been shot and killed near the cinema.

Oswald of Fort Worth, Texas, a former Marine, defected to the Soviet Union in 1959, and said he had applied for Soviet citizenship. He returned to the United States last year with his Russian wife. Police said he was the prime suspect in the assassination, but had denied all knowledge of the crime. He was later charged with the murder of a policeman.

RIFLE 'SEEN AT WINDOW'

Eye-witnesses reported seeing a rifle being withdrawn from a window in a building overlooking the President's route. A TV reporter said: "A policeman fell to the ground, pulled his pistol and yelled: 'Get down.' It is not known whether Secret Service men in the President's bodyguard returned the assassin's fire.

Police found an Italian-made rifle with telescopic sights in a building nearby. Three spent cartridges were found beside the rifle.

President Kennedy, who was worried by opposition in the Southern States to his Civil Rights Bill, had arrived in Dallas by air during a political tour of Texas. Thousands lined the streets as he drove to the town's Trade Market to speak at a lunch, and the President had the bullet-proof glass top of his car lowered so that he could wave to the crowds.

A woman witness, Mrs. Jean Hill, said in a radio interview that the President and Mrs. Kennedy were looking at a dog in the middle of the road, near an underpass, when the shots rang out. She said: "There were three shots. He grabbed his chest and fell over his seat, and Jackie fell over him."

EMERGENCY OPERATION

The President was unconscious when he arrived at the hospital. Doctors found that the bullet had struck the President's neck, just below the Adam's Apple. There was also a gaping wound in the back of his head. An emergency operation was performed on his throat, to enable him to breathe.

In a corridor Mrs. Kennedy, her clothing stained with her husband's blood, sobbed quietly as doctors fought to save her husband's life. Before it was announced that he was dead, Mrs. Kennedy was led into a private room. She was later stated to be suffering from shock.

About an hour after his death, President Kennedy's body was placed in a bronze coffin to be flown to Washington. His body will lie in state and he will be given a State funeral.

CARS HURTLED PAST

The first that we of the Press knew that anything so terrible had occurred was when we saw the cars hurtle past the Trade Mart auditorium where we had been waiting to hear President Kennedy's speech. Sirens shrieking, the cars raced straight by to the Parkland Hospital, three miles away.

When the President's car reached the hospital his limp body, his wife still clutching his arm, was gently lifted on to a trolley. On the floor of the car, spattered with blood, lay a bouquet of flowers presented to Mrs. Kennedy earlier.

The horror of it all was accentuated by the golden sunshine. As if in Kennedy's honour, a grey drizzle had cleared away upon his arrival at Dallas Airport.

(Continued on Back Page, Co. 4)

WATCHED BY MRS. KENNEDY, Mr. Lyndon Johnson, 55, is sworn in as 35th President of the United States by District Judge Sarah Hughes aboard the Presidential plane at Love Airfield, Dallas, yesterday, within hours of Mr. Kennedy's assassination. In the background is Mrs. Johnson.

JOHNSON TAKES OATH IN AIRCRAFT
From Our Own Correspondent
WASHINGTON, Friday.

MR. LYNDON B. JOHNSON, 55, was sworn-in as the 35th President of the United States at 3.39 p.m. (8.39 p.m. GMT) to-day within hours of President Kennedy's assassination. The new President will serve the remainder of Mr. Kennedy's term, until January, 1965.

The next Presidential election will be in November, 1964. Mr. Johnson took the oath aboard the Presidential plane at Dallas's Love Airfield when he was preparing to fly to Washington to take over the American Government.

He was sworn in by District Judge Sarah Hughes, the first woman judge in the Dallas Federal District. She was crying during the ceremony.

President Johnson promised on arrival in Washington to-night: "I

(Continued on Back Page, Co. 3)

QUEEN'S MESSAGE TO WIDOW

The Queen, who is spending the week-end with Sir Harold and Lady Wernher at Luton Hoo, was informed by telephone of President Kennedy's assassination. She sent the following message to Mrs. Kennedy:

"I am deeply distressed to learn of the tragic death of President Kennedy. My husband joins me in sending our heartfelt and sincere sympathy to you and your family."

'MONSTROUS,' SAYS SIR WINSTON

Sir Winston Churchill issued the following statement: "This monstrous act has taken from us a great statesman and a wise and valiant man. The loss to the United States and to the world is incalculable.

"Those who come after Mr. Kennedy must strive the more to achieve the ideals of world peace and human happiness and dignity to which his presidency was dedicated."

COFFIN IS FLOWN TO WASHINGTON
From VINCENT RYDER and DAVID SHEARS
Daily Telegraph Special Correspondents
WASHINGTON, Friday.

PRESIDENT KENNEDY'S body came home to Washington to-night in a short, sad ceremony. The Air Force Plane No. 1, which carried him to so many places around the world, brought the coffin from Dallas. President Lyndon Johnson travelled with it.

Mrs. Kennedy watched as the coffin was lowered with some difficulty into a Navy ambulance. Mr. Robert Kennedy, Attorney-General and the dead President's brother, jumped from the platform

(Continued on Back Page, Co. 6)

NEW YORKERS WEEP IN THE STREETS

NEW YORK, Friday
NEW YORKERS heard the news in shocked silence. Thousands were returning to their offices from lunch while more poured from skyscraper buildings to drift aimlessly in the streets.

It was as though they emerged from a devastating air raid. Wherever there was a radio or television set a silent crowd gathered.

LATE NEWS

KENNEDY SHOOTING
(See this page)
Washington, Thursday.

Shot which killed Mr. Kennedy fired from the fifth or sixth floor from building in which Oswald was employed as stock clerk, from distance of about 100 yards.

In Dallas, Texas, doctors said the condition of Mr. Connally, the wounded Governor, was "good" after an operation lasting four hours. He had not been told that Mr. Kennedy was dead.

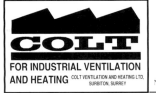

COLT
FOR INDUSTRIAL VENTILATION AND HEATING COLT VENTILATION AND HEATING LTD, SURBITON, SURREY

The Daily Telegraph

4 A.M.
No. 33630, LONDON, THURSDAY, JUNE 6, 1963 — and Morning Post — Printed in LONDON and MANCHESTER Price 3d.

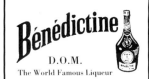

Bénédictine
D.O.M.
The World Famous Liqueur

RESIGNATION OF Mr. PROFUMO

'I misled the House' about Miss Keeler

UNABLE TO REMAIN AS MINISTER OR M.P.

By Our Political Staff

MR. PROFUMO, 48, Secretary for War, has resigned and will give up his seat in the House of Commons. This was disclosed in a statement from Admiralty House last night.

In a letter to the Prime Minister dated Tuesday he admitted "with deep remorse" that in his personal statement to the House on March 22 concerning Miss Christine Keeler, 21, "I misled you and my colleagues and the House."

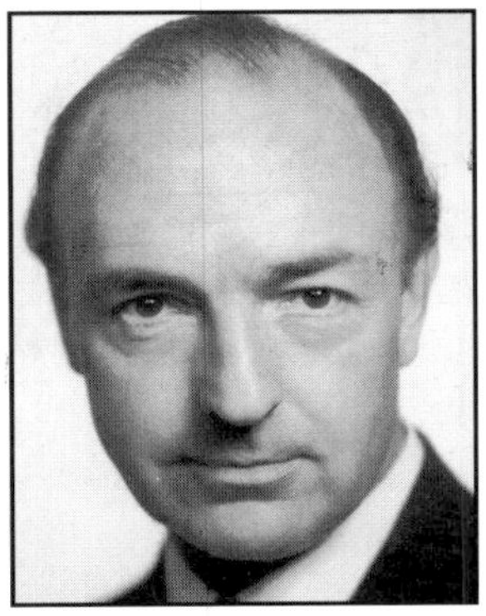

Mr. Profumo

He had come to realise, said Mr. Profumo, "that by this deception I have been guilty of a grave misdemeanour and depite the fact that there is no truth whatever in the other charges [of assisting in the disappearance of a witness and of being involved in some possible breach of security] I cannot remain a member of your Administration nor of the House of Commons."

Mr. Macmillan, in his reply dated yesterday from Ardchattan Priory, Connel, Argyllshire, where he is on holiday, wrote: "This is a great tragedy for you, your family and your friends."

LEFT LONDON
"No idea" of destination

Mr. and Mrs. Profumo, who returned to London on Monday from Italy, where they had spent three days, left London by car for the country at 11 o'clock yesterday morning.

A member of their staff said: "I have no idea what part of the country they have gone to."

As War Minister, Mr. Profumo was included in the London Gazette announcement on Tuesday night of the Queen's periodical appointments to the Army Council. Under the heading of State Intelligence from the Crown Office, the London Gazette stated:

The Queen has been pleased by Letters Patent under the Great Seal bearing date the 1st day of June, 1962, to appoint:

Lieutenant-Colonel the Right Honourable John Dennis Profumo, O.B.E., President.

Then followed the names of the other eight members of the Army Council.

DR. STEPHEN WARD
Letter to Home Secretary

The sequence of events leading up to last night's announcement began early in May when Dr. Stephen Ward, the osteopath, sought an interview with the Prime Minister's Principal Private Secretary, Mr. T.J. Bligh.

Dr. Ward has also written to Mr. Brooke, Home Secretary, and, it is believed, to Mr. Harold Wilson, Leader of the Opposition.

Dr. Ward, it is understood, alleged in each instance that Mr. Profumo's personal statement was in certain respects untrue. This allegation was put to Mr. Profumo on behalf of the Prime Minister.

Mr. Profumo adhered to his statement. But on Tuesday, in the Prime Minister's absence on holiday in Scotland. Mr. Profumo asked to see Mr. Martin Redmayne, the Government Chief Whip.

With them at the interview was Mr. Bligh. To them Mr. Profumo disclosed that in respect of his association with Miss Keeler he had not told the truth in his personal statement.

He declared that he wished to tender his resignation as a Minister and it was also his intention to apply for the Chiltern Hundreds. This painful scene over, Mr. Profumo said that before submitting his formal letter he wished to consult his legal advisers, which he did.

STATEMENT TO M.P.'s
Crowded House listened

Ten weeks have passed since Mr. Profumo rose on one of those rare Parliamentary occasions to make his personal statement. It was an exceptionally crowded House for a Friday.

Mr. Profumo grim and pale, was flanked by Mr. Macmillan and Mr. Macleod, Leader of the House, a gesture of solidarity and trust which is ironical in view of subsequent events. Mr. Profumo was heard with close attention.

LETTER TELLS OF "MY DEEP REMORSE"

THE full text of letters exchanged between Mr. Profumo and Mr. Macmillan were issued from Admiralty House. They read:

3, Chester Terrace
Regent's Park, N.W.1.
June 4, 1963

DEAR PRIME MINISTER,

You will recollect that on March 22, following certain allegations made in Parliament, I made a personal statement.

At that time rumour had charged me with assisting in the disappearance of a witness and with being involved in some possible breach of security.

So serious were these charges that I allowed myself to think that my personal association with that witness, which had also been the subject of rumour, was by comparison of minor importance only.

In my statement I said that there had been no impropriety in this association. To my very deep regret I have to admit that this was not true and that I misled you and my colleagues and the House.

I ask you to understand that I did this to protect, as I thought, my wife and family, who were equally misled, as were my professional advisers.

I have come to realise that, by this deception, I have been guilty of a grave misdemeanour, and despite the fact that there is no truth whatever in the other charges, I cannot remain a member of your administration, nor of the House of Commons.

I cannot tell you of my deep remorse for the embarrassment I have caused to you, to my colleagues in the Government., to my constituents, and to the party which I have served for the past 25 years. - Yours sincerely.

JACK PROFUMO

PREMIER'S REPLY
"Great tragedy for you"

Ardchattan Priory,
Connel, Argyllshire,
June 5, 1963.

DEAR PROFUMO,

The contents of your letter of June 4 have been communicated to me, and I have heard them with deep regret. This is a great tragedy for you, your family, and your friends.

Nevertheless I am sure you will understand that, in the circumstances, I have no alternative but to advise the Queen to accept your resignation. - Yours very sincerely,

HAROLD MACMILLAN

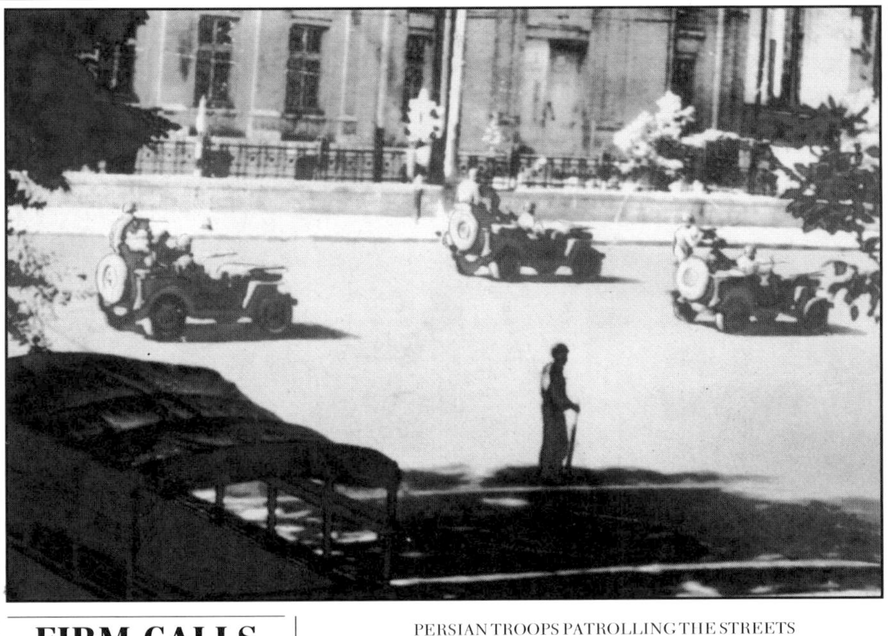

PERSIAN TROOPS PATROLLING THE STREETS of Teheran after yesterday's rioting.

FIRM CALLS IN COUNSEL

HARPER'S HOPE OF RECOUPING LOSS

By Our City Staff

MR. LEONARD MATCHAM, the new chairman of the £7,500,000 Harper Engineering and Electronics group, has told shareholders that counsel is being consulted to see what action, if any, the board can take "in an attempt to recover some of the losses that your company has incurred."

In a statement sent to shareholders he describes the company's problems as arising from some ineffective control in the past. Too many investigations and negotiations are in hand for shareholders to be given a complete review of the various companies in the group.

"We are not positive," he says, "that no other items will come to light that may affect the results shown."

£19,465 IN FEES
Efficiency consultants

For the year to June 30, 1962, the group made a net loss of £505,691, before tax. The auditor's report on the accounts for the year refers to items totalling more than £100,000 for which no adequate or satisfactory information has yet been traced.

One of these items is £19,465 for fees paid to business efficiency consultants.

The accounts of the group show bank indebtedness of £2,873,586. Mr. Matcham tells shareholders that future earnings will "not nearly be sufficient to repay the bank advances." It will be necessary to sell some of the company's assets. Martins Bank is bank to the company.

Mr. Matcham, a certified accountant, says that when he was made chairman he did not realise

(Continued on Back Page, Co. 4)

RAIN HOLDS UP RESCUE

TRAPPED POTHOLERS

From Our Own Correspondent

PARIS, Wednesday.

Oil drums bearing the message "Be patient, we are coming," were sent down the rushing waters of the Foussouble grotto in southern central France to-day to five young potholers trapped in a cave 311ft below.

They were due to return to the surface at mid-day on Monday but sudden heavy storms that morning turned the grotto by which they entered the nine-mile complex of underground caves into a foaming torrent.

Hopes of a rescue rose to-night when the rain stopped. It is believed the potholers are probably in a dry gallery.

The trapped men are Jean Dupont, 21, Emile Cheilletz, 24. Alain Besacier, 24, Bernard Rassy, 27, and Jacques Delacourt, 18.

MARTIAL LAW IN TEHERAN AFTER ANTI-SHAH RIOTS

UNVEILED WOMEN ATTACKED

TEHERAN, Wednesday.

THE Persian Government declared martial law in Teheran to-night after a day of rioting in which 20 people were officially reported killed or injured and Government buildings set on fire. A 10p.m. to 5a.m. curfew was imposed.

Gen. Nassiri, State Police Chief, was appointed Military Governor of the Capital. Steel-helmeted troops with fixed bayonets backed up by tanks and machine-guns to-day swept battling, yelling religious demonstrators from the main streets. An announcement said demonstrators had attacked 10 women for not wearing veils. Unveiling has been permitted in public since 1936.

The riots broke out this morning after the arrest of Rouhollah Khomeini, a Moslem religious leader, his assistant, Seyed Falsafi, and 20 supporters. Police were attacked with knives and clubs. Cars and buildings were set on fire.

The arrests followed demonstrations yesterday against the Shah's programme of reforms, including land reforms and the granting of the vote to women. These reforms are bitterly opposed by the religious Mullahs, who stand to lose both their influence and their income if they are implemented.

NASSER ACCUSED
"Most drastic steps"

The demonstrators this morning were demanding the resignation of the Government, the release of political prisoners and the severance of political ties between Persia and Israel.

The Government to-day accused President Nasser of the United Arab Republic of supporting the anti-Shah elements. The assistant security chief to the Prime Minister, Gen. Pakravan, said the Government had decided to take "the most drastic steps" to restore order.

Large units of troops are guarding the Shah's Imperial Palace and all roads leading to it. Thirty people have been arrested - Reuter & BUP.

CONCLAVE ON JUNE 20

ELECTION OF POPE

From Our Own Correspondent

VATICAN CITY, Wednesday.

The Conclave to elect the new Pope begins on June 20. The Cardinals of the Sacred College will be "walled in" on the evening of June 19.

Vatican masons began to-day the preparations for walling up the doors which give access to the Sistine Chapel from the inner courtyard off the Apostolic Palace. Rooms and makeshift cells are prepared for the participants in the Conclave and for their assistants in the adjoining wing.

AMERICANS TO BUILD 2,000 mph AIRLINER

From Our Own Correspondent

WASHINGTON, Wednesday.

AMERICA is to go ahead with plans for a supersonic airliner that will travel at two to three times the speed of sound. This was announced to-day by President Kennedy at the United States Air Force Academy at Colorado Springs.

His statement came a day after the announcement that Pan American Airways had placed an order worth £24 million for Anglo-French Concorde supersonic airliners. Six members of Congress will go to Paris within a few days to inquire into progress on development of the Concorde.

Development of the American plane is expected to cost at least £357 million. The goal is a 2,000 mph aircraft flying by the end of this decade.

PARTNERSHIP PROGRAMME

Mr. Kennedy said it would mean the birth of an important new programme in commercial aviation. "This country cannot stand still in this area." In his judgment, the Government should go ahead on the development immediately in partnership with private business.

He said the project would be stopped if the designers failed to evolve a plane they considered commercially feasible.

Editorial Comment - P14

PALACE TUSSLE WITH INTRUDER

Daily Telegraph Reporter

Police and a Guardsman last night grappled with an intruder in the forecourt of Buckingham Palace. A witness said: "There was a long struggle between the man, two constables and a Palace Guardsman before he was taken away in a police van."

The man entered the forecourt with his dog and was ordered out by a policeman. He returned with the dog and a struggle ensued before the man was removed.

11 NEW TOWN TYPHOID CASES

Search goes on for source of infection

Daily Telegraph Reporter

ELEVEN cases of typhoid have now been confirmed at Harlow New Town, Essex. Two others are suspected.

As the search for the cause of the outbreak went on last night, health officials said the possibility of "a very few" more cases was not discounted.

All the victims, members of eight different families, come from the Mark Hall neighbourhood. As yet the common link between them has not been discovered.

Dr. Isadore Ash, 54, Harlow's Medical Officer of Health, said last night laboratory tests had shown the "Harlow" type of typhoid fever type "A" was completely different from that which caused the epidemic at Zermatt, the Swiss ski resort.

Dr. Ash said the victims were "fairly comfortable." He added: "I don't think this is a very serious outbreak. I would not recommend mass vaccination because I do not think it necessary. There is no need for panic." Water supply and milk tests in Harlow have proved negative.

THREE STRAINS
Contagion by "carrier"

Our Medical Consultant writes: There are three main strains of typhoid organisms commonly known as typhoid, paratyphoid A and paratyphoid B. They can all cause enteric fever, septicaemia and acute gastroenteritis.

That caused by salmonella paratyphosa A, the technical name for paratyphoid A, is usually shorter in duration, milder and has fewer complications. Contagion may be direct or through food or water or a "carrier," someone who harbours the organism but does not suffer from the disease.

GOLD RESERVE UP £29M.

GILT-EDGED BOUGHT

By Our City Editor

May was another good month for the pound. Britain's gold reserves, which are the central reserves for the whole of the Sterling Area, rose by £29 million. At the end of last month they stood at £1,046 million.

Last month's gain, which followed the April rise of £12 million, exceeded the City's best expectations. It indicates continuing confidence in sterling and a satisfactory underlying payments position for the Sterling Area.

On the Stock Exchange the increase brought in fresh buyers for gilt-edged securities.

City Comment - P2

£5,000 BONDS WIN FOR BOY, 6

Daily Telegraph Reporter

Mark Edward Barratt, six, who has never had any pocket money, was told yesterday that a premium bond birthday present given to him nearly four years ago has won him £5,000.The boy, only son of an electricity board driver, from The Brook, Mapperley, near Ilkeston, Derbyshire, said he would put the winnings in his money box. The £1 bond, No. BS252978, was one of two given to the boy by his mother and his grandmother, Mrs. Sarah Hall, of High Lane East, West Hallam.

£250 prizewinners - P26

LT. GEN. SIR ADRIAN CARTON DE WIART, VC

Lt. Gen. Sir Adrian Carton de Wiart, VC, died yesterday at his home at Killinardrish, Co. Cork. He was 83, (Obituary - P17)

OSWALD MURDERED AT DALLAS POLICE HQ

'I DID IT FOR JACKIE' SAYS CLUB OWNER

From STEPHEN BARBER
Daily Telegraph Special Correspondent

DALLAS, Texas, Sunday.

LEE HARVEY OSWALD, 24, the former Marine charged with the assassination of President Kennedy, was himself murdered to-day.

Millions of Americans saw the shooting, televised "live." It occurred about the time the President's body was on its way to lie in state in the Capitol in Washington.

I was among the crowd of about 50 people who had gathered to watch Oswald being taken from Dallas police headquarters to the County Gaol by armoured car.

A Dallas strip-tease club owner, Jack Rubinstein, 52, known as Jack Ruby, was later charged with murdering Oswald. Police quoted him as saying "I did it for Jackie Kennedy."

Oswald was the first to see his killer coming at him. A film of the shooting showed that he twisted his handcuffed arms to one side as if to protect himself, and made a grimace as if of recognition as Ruby plunged towards him, revolver in hand.

Ruby crouched down and pushed the revolver almost into his ribs and fired a single shot at a range of about nine inches. It was all over in a flash.

ONLOOKERS CHEER
Oswald's cry of agony

Some onlookers cheered when Oswald was shot. The shooting took place in the underground garage of Dallas police headquarters.

Looking pale but calm and flanked by policement, Oswald had just come through some swing-doors into the garage. A cry went up of: "Here he is. It's Oswald."

I heard a voice which I thought was that of a man who did the shooting cry out: "Oswald!" There was a loud report, and a flash lit the ceiling.

Oswald slumped forward with a rasping cry of agony. A policeman beside me shouted: "Oh God, no."

Police and plain-clothes men fell like a rugby pack on both the prisoner and Ruby. Oswald was half-carried, half-dragged back through the swing doors. He made no sound. He died never having admitted that he was the killer of President Kennedy.

Ruby did not struggle and was led wordlessly away in the grasp of police officers. He was taken to the cells Oswald had just left.

Mr. C. A. Droby, Ruby's lawyer, said he would seek a writ of habeas corpus.

(November 25)

ARCHBISHOP OF MILAN IS POPE

From Our Own Correspondent

ROME, Friday.

CARDINAL GIOVANNI BATTISTA MONTINI, who is 65, Archbishop of Milan and formerly Pro-Secretary of State to Pope Pius XII, was elected Pope to-day. He will be known as Pope Paul VI and will be crowned in St. Peter's Basilica on Sunday week.

It is thought probable that the Pope will continue the main lines of the liberal policies of Pope John XXIII, particularly in regard to Christian Unity. But where political issues are involved, he may well adopt a less impetuous tempo.

The 261st successor of St. Peter as Pontiff of the Roman Church, the Pope was born near Brescia and educated in his early years by Jesuits. He entered the priesthood in 1919.

WHITE SMOKE
"Joyful tidings"

The election became known shortly before 11.30 a.m., when the third smoke signal from the Conclave in the Sistine Chapel was seen to be white. A great roar of applause went up from the crowds in St. Peter's Square.

As the white smoke continued to rise from the iron stove pipe, priests in the Apostolic Palace threw open the windows of the papal apartments. This is the traditional confirmation that a Pope has been elected.

(June 22)

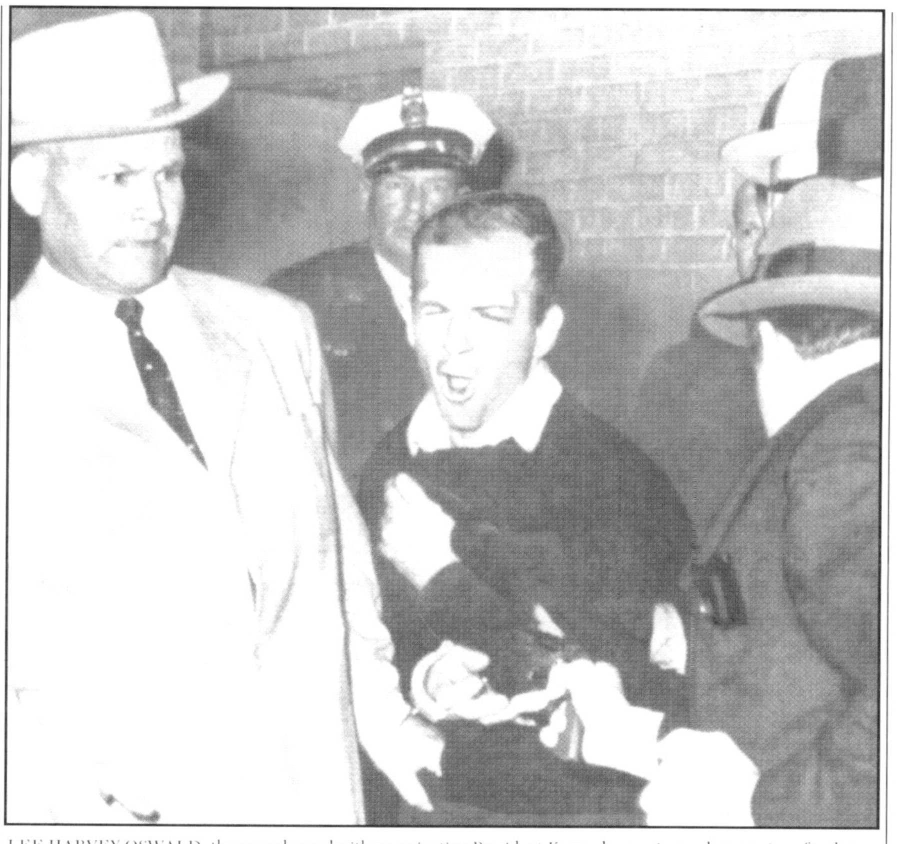

LEE HARVEY OSWALD, the man charged with assassinating President Kennedy, gasping and staggering after being shot at while being led from Dallas police headquarters yesterday. Later Jack Rubinstein, a strip-tease club owner, was charged with his murder.

93 NATIONS HONOUR KENNEDY

WIDOW LEADS MARCH IN SILENT CAPITAL

IN a city silent except for the tap of muffled drums and the tolling of a single bell, President Kennedy was buried yesterday in Arlington National Cemetery, Washington. Later Mrs. Kennedy lit an Eternal Flame that will burn by his grave.

President Kennedy's body was borne on a gun carriage from the Capitol, where it had lain in state, along streets lined with thousands of people. They stood in silence, their heads bowed. Many wept.

Mrs. Kennedy, heavily veiled, and representatives of 93 nations joined the cortège when at the White House. The widow walked behind the coffin for half a mile to St. Matthew's Roman Catholic Cathedral for a Requiem Mass.

(November 26)

WEST BERLIN TRIUMPH FOR MR. KENNEDY

From VINCENT RYDER and BLAKE BAKER,
Daily Telegraph Special Correspondents

BERLIN, Wednesday.

PRESIDENT KENNEDY triumphed to-day when at least 1,250,000 delirious West Berliners gave him the wildest welcome of his political career. A great roar rose from a sea of people before the City Hall when he said, in halting German "Ich bin ein Berliner" [I am a Berliner].

The President made his first visit to the Berlin Wall only two days before the arrival in Berlin of Mr. Khruschev. Although they displayed propaganda placards and photographed him from a distance, the Communists made no attempt to demonstrate against his presence.

After seeing the wall, Mr. Kennedy said to the Berliners: "There are some who say in Europe and elsewhere we can work with the Communists. Let them come to Berlin."

The wall was not only the "most obvious and vivid demonstration of the failures of the Communist system," but "an offence against history and against humanity."

"I do believe in the strength of the great powers working together to preserve the human race. Otherwise we shall be destroyed."

The American shield for the freedom of West Berlin would not be lowered as long as it was needed. But they all had to face realities.

"Reunification will some day be a reality but we all know a police state régime has been imposed on the Eastern sector. Peaceful reunification of Berlin and Germany will not be quick or easy."

(June 27)

PRAYER BEFORE COFFIN

From VINCENT RYDER
Daily Telegraph Special Correspondent

WASHINGTON, Monday.

PRESIDENT KENNEDY was buried to-day on a grassy slope in Arlington National Cemetery, overlooking the American capital. The coffin was lowered into the grave at 8.34 p.m. GMT.

The greatest assembly of national leaders and their representatives that Washington had seen for a generation gathered to pay homage. They did so completely without pomp, and with the unobtrusive sincerity of friends at the funeral of a friend.

FINAL MEMORY
Muffled sounds

What remained in the memory at the end of the day was this quiet dignity and the sounds that had accompanied it: the thud of muffled drums, the plaintive wail of the pipes of the Black Watch, the solemn intoning of the funeral hymn, "Dies Irae," and a bugle sounding "Last Post."

To the cadence of marching feet and muffled drums the coffin was borne back to the White House. There, under a front portico draped in black crepe stood the great assembly of statesmen.

Prince Philip, in Admiral's uniform, Sir Alec Douglas-Home, in mufti with medals on his lapel, President de Gaulle, in his Brigadier's uniform, Emperor Haile Selassie, in Field Marshal's uniform, and a host of others, in uniform, dark suits or Eastern dress, came to attention.

The gun-carriage, drawn by six greys and followed by a riderless horse bearing riding boots reversed in the stirrups, moved slowly up the drive between Servicemen bearing the flags of all 50 States.

Across a square in front of the White House, the bell of St. John's Episcopal church tolled a dirge. As the coffin drew level with the White House portico, a chorus of Naval cadets gently sang "Danny Boy."

Mrs. Kennedy, a black veil over her face, got out of her car. She stood for a moment. Mr. Robert Kennedy on one side of her and Senator Edward Kennedy on the other, until the last notes of the Irish song died away.

The thousands gathered around the White House were so silent that the jingling of the horses' harness, the clop of hooves, and the creaking of the gun-carriage were the only sounds as the procession started on its way to St. Matthew's Cathedral for Requiem Mass.

PROTOCOL ABANDONED
Unstrained dignity

Behind Mrs. Kennedy, the late President's brothers, other members of the family, and President and Mrs. Johnson, the statesmen descended the White House steps to follow on foot, in a group.

A sketchy effort at protocol was abandoned by unspoken consent. There was something very American about the way official stiffness was discarded in favour of an unstrained dignity.

Heads of State led the distinguished crowd. Gen. de Gaulle towering above Queen Frederika of Greece and the Emperor Haile Selassie beside him.

It was Gen. de Gaulle, with characteristic sense of propriety, who announced that he would attend the funeral and inspired other leaders to follow his example, despite the concern of American officials at their ability to cope with such a situation.

SALUTE BY SON
Procession to cemetery

John, the three-year-old son, saluted. It was a gesture others had smiled to see him use in play as he watched his father receive foreign dignitaries at the White House amid military formality.

Senator Edward Kennedy brushed a tear from his eye and he got into his car. The procession went past the Lincoln Memorial, across a bridge over the Potomac River and into Arlington National Cemetery, resting place of thousands of America's war dead.

(November 26)

DRUG TESTERS DISMISSED AT HARVARD

From Our Own Correspondents

NEW YORK, Tuesday.

A professor of clinical psychology at Harvard University who for two years tested the new hallucination-causing drugs on students has been dismissed. An assistant has been "relieved" of his position at Harvard for leaving classes without permission.

The studies conducted by Dr. Richard Alpert and the assistant, Dr. Timothy Laary, involved three experimental drugs, LSD-25, Psilocybin and Mescaline. Among those who have taken the drugs is Aldous Huxley, the novelist, who has hailed their possible benefits.

The university action was reported to-day in the Harvard Crimson, the student newspaper. It quoted Dr. Nathan Pusey, President of Harvard, as saying that Dr. Alpert's dismissal stemmed from his giving drugs to students last spring.

(May 29)

Alcatraz deserted

ALCATRAZ, the famous convict prison known as "The Rock," was deserted to-day. Its last 27 prisoners were shipped to San Francisco for transfer to other goals. The Government decided that the 113-year-old prison would be too costly to repair.

(March 22)

VOLCANIC ISLAND 130ft HIGH

REYKJAVIK, Sunday.

The new island which began rising from the sea bed on Friday following volcanic activity off the south coast of Iceland has now reached a length of 1,500ft and a height of 130ft. Rocks have risen up around it and may constitute a danger to shipping.

The island is three to four miles south-west of the Westman Islands. Volcanic activity continued yesterday and smoke has risen 25,000ft above the new island. - BUP.

(November 18)

BIGGER FLYING SQUAD

Increase to 10 teams from Monday

By T.A. SANDROCK
Daily Telegraph Scotland Yard Correspondent

One of the country's most successful crime fighting units, Scotland Yard's Flying Squad, will have nearly 25 per cent. more detectives from Monday. Plans are in hand also to strengthen the Yard's Criminal Intelligence Bureau.

This was announced yesterday. An extension of the Flying Squad has been expected for some time.

It consists of 80 officers at present, and 19 more will join it from Monday. There will be one detective chief inspector, two inspectors, 10 sergeants and six constables.

The Squad works in teams of eight or nine men. The extra detectives will allow 10 instead of eight teams.

(January 5)

GRANDMOTHER GIVES BIRTH TO QUINS

CARACAS, Sunday.

A GRANDMOTHER, aged 35, gave birth to quintuplet boys in Maracaibo, Venezuela yesterday, it was reported to-day. All are in a satisfactory condition in oxygen tents.

The mother, Senora Ines Cuervo de Prieto, is well. She was taken into hospital on August 2 for special care.

The quintuplets, seven-month babies, weighed between 3lb 1 ½oz and 4lb 2 1/2oz. They have been baptised Robinson, Fernando, Otto, Juan-Jose, and Mario, after the doctors who attended the birth.

(September 9)

MAJORITY DOWN TO 69

PREMIER LIKELY TO RESIGN SOON

MR. MACMILLAN'S majority was cut to 69 in the House of Commons confidence vote last night on the security aspects of the Profumo affair. The Government's nominal majority is 97.

On the Opposition motion to adjourn the House the voting was:

FOR THE GOVERNMENT 321
AGAINST THE GOVERNMENT 252
Government majority.................................69

About 27 Conservative M.P.'s deliberately abstained. This is a serious withdrawal of support from Mr. Macmillan, says our POLITICAL CORRESPONDENT. A broken man, he seemed close to tears after the voting figures were announced.

The only question in the minds of many Conservatives is when the Prime Minister will decide to resign. Next month is considered more likely than during the Summer Recess.

(June 18)

A RAPIER THRUST FOR THE LOST LEADER

By COLIN WELCH
Daily Telegraph Special Correspondent

WESTMINSTER, Monday.

WATCH Wigg, watch Birch: on this day of tremendous tension, with the fate of a Prime Minister in the balance, this was the tip of old hands in the Press gallery.

Mr. Nigel Birch (Conservative, Flint) was certainly worth watching. With an almost Italianate precision he inserted his blade deep into the Prime Minister's vitals. The blade was inscribed with a quotation from Browning's "Lost Leader"... "Never glad confident morning again."

The whole operation was so deftly and neatly done, so quietly and immaculately, that the Prime Minister hardly winced: there was no blood on the carpet, no unseemly uproar.

Yet the fatal words had been spoken: Mr. Birch's Rt. Hon. friend ought to make way for a much younger friend. "Nothing," said Mr. Birch, "could ever be the same again" - nor will it be.

With a dry relish, Mr. Birch quoted Lord Hailsham to the effect that a three-line Whip was no more than a summons to attend. Very well, he had attended, as he asked the Whips to note; how they must have wished he had been less obedient.

MAN OF THE WORLD
Weary, but witty

Alone among the early speakers Mr. Birch gave the impression of being a man of the world. Unlike Mr. Wilson, Leader of the Opposition, he made no reference to the shocked "moral conscience of the nation."

He seemed not "sick at heart," as Mr. Wilson had professed to be, nor did he complain, as did the Prime Minister, of being deeply, bitterly and lastingly wounded. Rather did he seem a shade weary, witty and disillusioned.

Mr. Profumo struck him as being "no cloistered monk," nor a man "to tell the truth in a tight corner." Nor did he imagine Miss Keeler to be "intellectually stimulating"; put the two together, and it was surely improbable that their association would be "purely platonic."

What Mr. Wilson alleged against the Prime Minister was not dishonourable conduct, but a sort of "indolent nonchalance." This was typified in Mr. Wilson's view by the Prime Minister's reference to "a Mr. Stephen Ward" as though this was some unknown person, nothing whatever to do with him.

(June 18)

VOTERS MEET LORD SUTCH

Mr. David Edward Sutch, 22, a singer who is known as "Screaming Lord Sutch," presented himself to the electors here today. He wore an evening dress coat and trousers with black tie, blue and white striped socks and black top hat.

(August 2)

KEELER GETS 9 MONTHS

CHRISTINE KEELER, 21, was sentenced at the Old Bailey yesterday to nine months' imprisonment. She burst into tears as she reached the bottom of the stairs leading from the court to the cells.

She admitted perjury and conspiring to obstruct the course of justice. Wearing a lime-green costume, she looked composed as Sir ANTHONY HAWKE, Recorder of London, said to her:

"I take into consideration that you have been under pressure, under fear and certainly for some time under domination which was not of the best advantage to you."

Mr. JEREMY HUTCHINSON, Q.C., her counsel, in a mitigation plea, said that the late Stephen Ward had fashioned Keeler in a perverted Prof. Higgins way. "Ward is dead," he added. "Profumo is disgraced. And now I know that your lordship will resist the temptation for what I might call society's pound of flesh."

He then quoted Lord Denning: "Let no one judge her too harshly."

(December 7)

DUKE OF ARGYLL GIVEN DECREE

The Duke of Argyll, 59, of Inverary Castle, Argyll, was granted a decree of divorce against the Duchess in the Court of Session in Edinburgh yesterday. This followed 3½ years of litigation.

Lord Wheatley, in a 50,000-word judgment, described the Duchess of Argyll, 49, of Upper Grosvenor Street, Mayfair, as a "completely promiscuous woman whose sexual appetite could be satisfied only with a number of men."

He found the Duchess had committed adultery with three men named in the Duke's petition and an unidentified nude man whose picture, taken from a batch of photographs which the Duke took from her London home, showed the Duchess in the nude "in close proximity to the man."

(May 9)

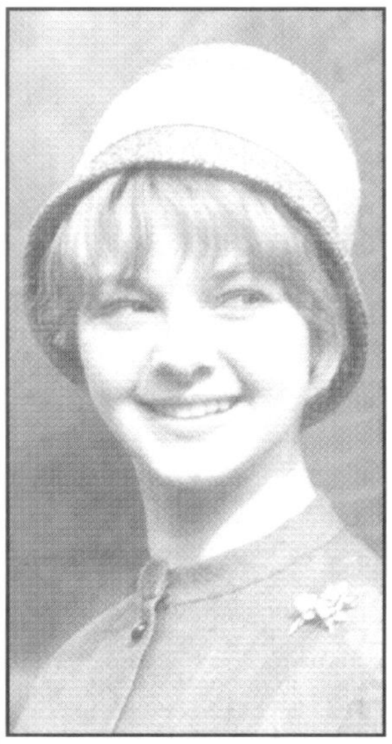

MARILYN RICE-DAVIES

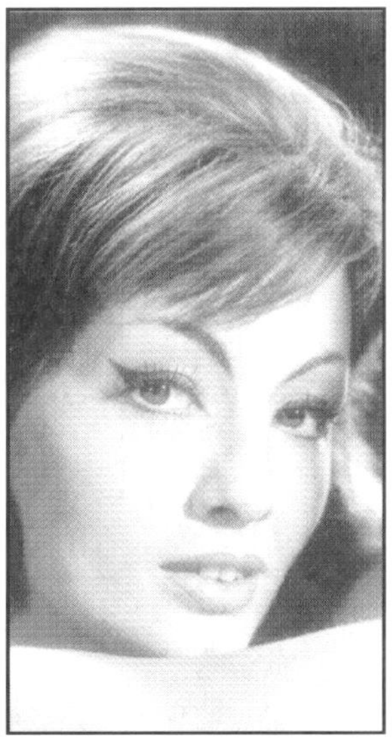

CHRISTINE KEELER

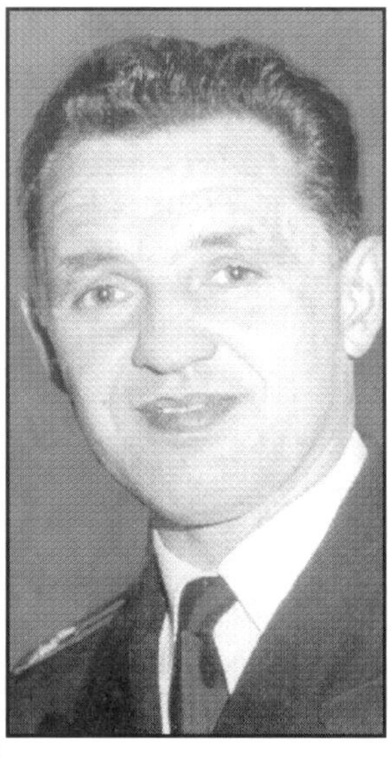

CAPT. EUGENE IVANOV

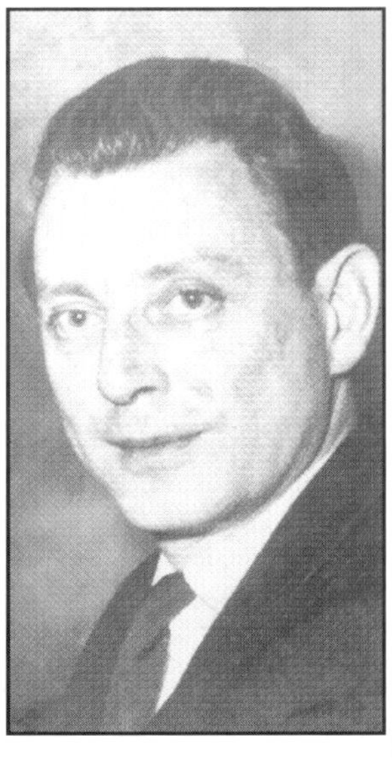

DR. STEPHEN WARD

Ld. ASTOR NAMED BY CHRISTINE & MANDY

Daily Telegraph Reporter

VISCOUNT ASTOR and Mr. Douglas Fairbanks, jnr., were named when the case agains Dr. STEPHEN WARD, 50, osteopath and artist, on vice charges, was opened at Marylebone yesterday. (Report and Pictures - Pp16 and 17.)

MISS MARILYN "MANDY" RICE-DAVIES, 18, claimed that she had sexual intercourse with Lord Astor at the osteopath's former flat at Wimpole Mews, Marylebone. She was answering Mr. MERVYN GRIFFITH-JONES, prosecuting.

Mr. Griffith-Jones had asked her if she had had intercourse with any of the men she met while she was living at the flat last year. When she replied: "With Lord Astor," he interjected: "I don't want you to mention names."

Lord Astor, 56, who lives at Cliveden, Bucks, is the third viscount. He was Conservative M.P. for Fulham East 1935-45 and for Buckinghamshire (Wycombe Division) 1951-52. He is married to Bronwen Pugh, former model. Mr. Fairbanks, the actor, is 53.

"MONEY FOR RENT"
Flat was shared

Miss Rice-Davies said that Lord Astor gave money to pay the rent of Miss Christine Keeler, 21, and herself when they were living at a flat at Comeragh Road, Fulham, in 1960.

Miss Rice-Davies, wearing a black costume with a pink floral hat and a diamond brooch and a pearl bracelet on her left wrist, toyed with a pair of white gloves as she gave evidence.

She said that Dr. Ward had asked her to marry him. He had said that, though he had no money, he had lots of friends and had said: "We have always got Bill [Astor] who can help us."

Mr. GRIFFITH-JONES: Did he mention other men? - Only two men I knew at the time: Lord Astor and Douglas Fairbanks, jnr.

The first mention of Lord Astor was by Miss KEELER when she was asked by Mr. Griffith-Jones who had helped pay the rent of the flat at Comeragh Road. There was a gasp in the crowded courtroom when she named him.

She spoke so softly that her replies were at times inaudible. Twice Mr. JAMES BURGE, for the defence, complained that her replies favourable to Dr. Ward had not been recorded. As she spoke, her replies were repeated into a recording machine.

Mr. Griffith-Jones said that Dr. Ward met Miss Keeler at Murray's Cabaret Club shortly after she came to London in 1958 at the age of 16. He took her to his cottage at Cliveden where intercourse took place and he asked her to marry him, Mr. Griffith-Jones said.

Miss KEELER later denied that she had ever had intercourse with Dr. Ward and described their relationship as "brother and sister." She said she had had sexual intercourse with Mr. Profumo and only once with Capt. Eugene Ivanov (the former Soviet Naval Attaché).

Mr. Profumo had given her presents and money. The money was for her mother.

Miss Keeler said she had received several hundred pounds from a business man, Mr. James Eynan. She had given half of the money to Dr. Ward.

A girl who once worked as a dancer in a Paris night club is expected to be called by the prosecution when the case is resumed to-day. She is Ronna Ricardo, 23, now living in London.

(June 2)

DR. WARD GUILTY ON TWO CHARGES

"GRIEVOUSLY ILL" IN DRUG COMA

Daily Telegraph Reporter

DR. STEPHEN WARD, 50, the osteopath and artist, was convicted at the Old Bailey yesterday of living on the immoral earnings of Christine Keeler and Marilyn Rice-Davies. He was found not guilty of the three other vice charges against him.

When the jury gave their verdict after a retirement of four hours and 20 minutes, Dr. Ward was in a coma in hospital after an overdose of sleeping capsules. He had been found unconscious in a friend's flat in Chelsea yesterday morning.

Mr. JUSTICE MARSHALL postponed sentence until Dr. Ward is fit to attend court. The verdict will be given to him in hospital by his solicitor, Mr. JACK WHEATLEY, who said after the case: "We intend to appeal."

When the jury retired at 2.32 p.m. yesterday Dr. Ward was said to be "grievously ill."

At 8 p.m. a hospital bulletin said: "Dr. Stephen Ward still remains grievously ill. He is, however, showing improved response to treatment so there are increased hopes of recovery."

It was two hours before the eighth and last day of his trial opened that he was found unconscious. By his side was a Nambutal sleeping capsule container with five capsules in it; a half-finished cup of coffee and a burnt-out cigarette.

Also in the flat were several letters and an envelope containing £150 in £5 notes. Mr. Wheatley took possession of the letters.

FIGHT FOR LIFE

The news that Dr. Ward would be unable to attend at the Old Bailey delayed the start of the hearing 42 minutes. By the time Mr. Justice Marshall took his seat at 11.12 a.m., doctors and nurses at St. Stephen's Hospital, Fulham Road, had been fighting two hours and 20 minutes to save the osteopath's life.

After legal arguments, and objections by Dr. Ward's counsel, Mr. James Burge, Mr. Justice Marshall said he would continue his summing-up and the jury would consider its verdict in the absence of the defendant.

Mr. MERVIN GRIFFITH-JONES, prosecuting counsel, asked whether he could apply for a further indictment outstanding against Dr. Ward to go over to the next session for consideration.

JURY DISCHARGED
20-year period

Mr. JAMES BURGE, defending, said he would raise no objection and the JUDGE commented: "I would not consider proceedings on another indictment at this stage at all. I think we have all had enough." The judge then thanked the jury and discharged them from jury service for 20 years.

At 5 p.m. the jury had sent the judge a note seeking advice on the first three charges against Dr. Ward which accused him of living wholly or in part on immoral earnings.

When the jury first retired at 2.33 p.m. the Judge's parting words to them were: "You now have to discharge your own responsible duty. The ball is in your court." So began a four-and-a-half hour wait to bring the trial to an end.

Dr. Ward was released on bail on Tuesday night when the Judge was in the middle of his summing-up. The normal practice is for a defendant, although having been on bail throughout a trial, to be kept in custody overnight when the jury are to be sent out the next day.

The maximum sentence he faces for the offences on which he has been found guilty under the Sexual Offences Act, 1956, is seven years imprisonment.

(August 1)

OVER £1M. HAUL BY RAIL RED SIGNAL GANG

SPLIT-SECOND TIMING

From GUY RAIS

CHEDDINGTON, Bucks, Thursday.

A WORN brown glove and four large torch batteries were all the equipment used by a gang who ambushed a GPO mail train near here early to-day and carried out the biggest and most audacious train robbery in British history.

Late last night Det. Supt. Fewtrell, head of Bucks C.I.D., described the amount taken as "clearly well over £1m."

The gang, armed and masked with balaclavas and scarves and believed to number between eight and 15, operated with split-second timing. They

Tampered with a long-distance signal;

Set another automatic signal on the main line between Leighton Buzzard and Cheddington stations at red;

Stopped the train, known as the Travelling Post Office, split it in two and after coshing the driver and handcuffing him to the co-driver;

Escaped with about 120 mailbags containing over £1 million.

£35,000 REWARD OFFERS

Minister breaks holiday

The GPO described the loss as "very heavy indeed" and said "it may well run into seven figures." Mr. Bevins, the Postmaster General who interrupted a holiday at his home in Liverpool to fly to London to confer with senior officials, offered a reward of £10,000 for information.

AMBER SIGNAL

Brakes applied

The Great Train Robbery began at about 3.10 this morning as the Post Office train, which left Glasgow at 6.50 the previous night for London, had just passed Leighton Buzzard station.

Jack Mills, 58, of Newdigate Street, Crewe, the driver, gently applied the brakes in the cab of his 2,000 hp diesel-electric locomotive No. D326, as he passed an amber signal. This was the first signal the gang tampered with.

As the 12-coach train approached lonely Sears Crossing, about two miles from Cheddington station, Mills saw the signal set at red against him. It was this signal which, two minutes before, had been changed from green to red by some of the gang.

They climbed up to the gantry of the signals, which straddle the main line, and placed the glove over the bright green signal, completely blocking its light. Then they wired four torch batteries bound together with insulation tape, to the bulb of the red signal, lighting it up.

As the train stopped the gang swung into action. Some, armed with picks, who had been hiding beside the track came out of the darkness and began uncoupling the first two coaches. These contained the most valuable registered packages.

ALONE IN CAB

Signal investigation

Other members of the gang climbed into the diesel cab and coshed Mills. He was alone because a few seconds earlier David Whitby, 26, his co-driver, also of Crewe, had stepped down on the track to investigate the danger signal.

As he did so, he saw a man who had been uncoupling the coaches peering out from between the second and third coaches.

Whitby was grabbed by the shoulders by another man who threatened to kill him if he made a noise. He was forced back to the locomotive and put inside with Mills.

Then Mills, suffering from a head injury, was ordered to drive the diesel forward. He did so, leaving the remaining 10 coaches with 70 sorters still inside unaware of what was happening, stranded on the track.

STOPPED ON BRIDGE

Narrow road below

When the two coaches hauled by the diesel reached Sears Crossing, close to the Mentmore Park estate of the Earl of Rosebery, Mills was ordered to stop on Bridego Bridge. This takes the track over a narrow

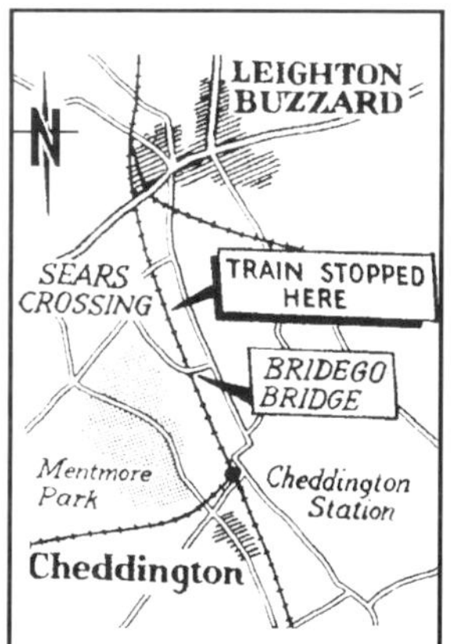

country road about 200 yards from the B488 Leighton Buzzard-Tring road.

Other members of the gang who had been waiting by the bridge climbed up to the padlocked coaches. They had left a piece of white towelling on a stick at the side of the track to tell their confederates where to have the diesel stopped. Some had stolen railwaymen's caps from a hut.

The four GPO men who were inside had realised that they had been ambushed and had barricaded themselves in. The gang, using crowbars, attempted to smash their way through the padlocked doors and the wooden parts of the coach.

Then, watched by Mills and Whitby, who had been handcuffed together and made to sit on the track with a guard on them, the thieves threw nearly 120 mailbags down a 15ft high embankment. A lorry was drawn up by the side of the bridge.

Yard man in charge

Supt. G. McArthur, of Scotland Yard, is leading the hunt in which police all over Britain are helping. He conferred with senior Yard officers before leaving for Cheddington with Brig. Cherry, Chief Constable of Buckinghamshire and Det. Supt. M. Fewtrell, head of the county CID.

(August 9)

SIR WINSTON RETIRING FROM PARLIAMENT

By Our PoliticalCorrespondent

SIR WINSTON CHURCHILL announced last night that he is giving up his seat in the House of Commons. He is 88. On October 1 he completed 60 years as an M.P.

In a letter to Mrs. Doris Moss, chairman of Woodford Conservative Association, dated Tuesday, he wrote:

MY DEAR MRS. MOSS,

I write to tell you that I shall not be able to present myself as a candidate for the next general election.

This is because the accident which I suffered last year has greatly decreased my mobility and it has become difficult for me to attend the House of Commons as I would wish.

(May 2)

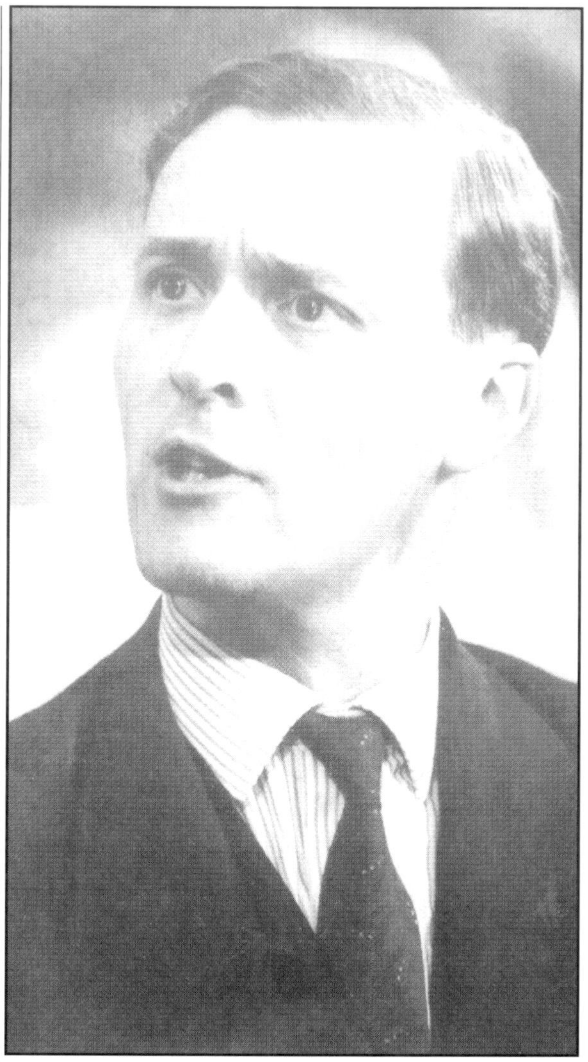

MR. WEDGWOOD BENN

PEERS GET RIGHT TO 'DISCLAIM'

By H.B. BOYNE,
Daily Telegraph Political Correspondent

THE Peerage Bill, which enables hereditary peers to renounce their titles for life and stand for election as commoners, was published yesterday.

Introduced by the Prime Minister, it will have its Second Reading on June 19, two days after the Whitsun recess.

With the Opposition ready to give it a fair wind, there is every likelihood that it will be passed by the beginning of August, when Parliament rises for the Summer. The Government will thus have fulfilled its pledge to change the law in time to allow reluctant peers to stand for the Commons at the next General Election.

With this in view, the Act will come into force on the dissolution of the present Parliament.

There are no surprises in the Bill, except perhaps that it uses the word "disclaimer" for the process of renouncing or surrendering a peerage. An explanatory memorandum says there are "technical reasons" for this.

IRREVOCABLE FOR LIFE

Wife also loses privilege

The Bill makes it clear that a peer's disclaimer is irrevocable for his lifetime. It will divest not only himself but his wife of "all right or interest to or in the peerage, and all titles, rights, offices, privileges and precedence attaching thereto."

A wife whose husband disclaims his peerage will thus become plain "Mrs. So-and-So."

(May 31)

DR. ADENAUER STEPS DOWN IN BUNDESTAG

From Our Own Correspondent

BONN, Tuesday.

Dr. Adenauer, Member for Bonn, returned to-day to the seat in the West German Parliament which he left 14 years and one month ago to become Chancellor. He did so with characteristic good humour, a few shafts at the opposition, and no pathos.

(October 16)

MR. BENN A COMMONER AT LAST

"I am statutorily immunised," said Mr. Wedgwood Benn last night, with understandable satisfaction. "I am the first man in history to be prevented by Act of Parliament from receiving a hereditary peerage."

Mr. Benn attained this distinction about 6 20 p.m. As soon as the Peerage Bill had received the Royal assent in the House of Lords he went to the Crown Office.

Received by Sir George Coldstream, Clerk of the Crown, he produced a document. It was made out in accordance with the new Act and disclaimed his title of Viscount Stansgate.

His signature was witnessed by his wife, who signed "Caroline De Camp Wedgwood Benn."

SEAT RELINQUISHED

As prospective Labour candidate for Bristol South-East, the seat he had to relinquish when his father died two and a half years ago, he has a good chance of becoming an M.P. within a fortnight.

The second peer to lodge an instrument of disclaimer was Lord Altrincham, a Conservative. He reached the Crown Office within 10 minutes of Mr. Benn.

Lord Altrincham will now be know as John Grigg, his family name. Though not yet adopted by a constituency, he hopes in due course to enter the Commons. Before succeeding his father in 1955 he twice contested Oldham West.

(August 1)

RUSSIA'S WOMAN PIONEER IN SPACE

From JEREMY WOLFENDEN,
Daily Telegraph Special Correspondent

MOSCOW, Sunday.

THE first woman in space, a Russian, is circling the earth to-night at a distance of more than 100 miles. She is Valentina Tereshkova, 26, formerly an amateur parachute jumper.

She is 10 miles away from Lt.-Col. Bykovsky's space ship Vostok V, launched on Friday. But the gap is widening. At one time there was only three miles between the two space ships.

There are reports in Moscow to-night that another man will go up to join Miss Tereshkova and Col. Bykovsky in space. His flight, if he goes, is expected to-morrow or on Tuesday.

There is also a suspicion here that Miss Tereshkova was a day late for her rendezvous. A likely time for her to be sent up was 1 p.m. London time yesterday.

At that time the earth's rotation had brought the orbit of Vostok V over the launching pad at Baikonur, in the Central Asian Republic of Kazakhstan.

Moscow Press and television correspondents appear to have been put on the alert for a launching, but the attempt was called off early in the afternoon.

"SIGNED OFF"

Apparently asleep

Valentina "signed off" by radio to-night after six orbits and was now apparently sleeping. Col. Bykovsky had completed his 38th circuit.

Col. Gagarin, the first man in space, writing in Izvestia to-night, said Miss Tereshkova is a quiet, attractive girl with "kind eyes and a good-natured smile."

Jubilant women thronged the Red Square to-day waving hand-painted banners and claiming the right to go into space on the next flight.

A rendezvous in space is regarded by Soviet scientists as a necessary step towards constructing a space station in orbit around the earth. This would be used as a jumping off point for manned voyages towards the moon and towards the other planets.

(June 17)

PALACE WITHDRAWS ITS DENIAL ON PRINCE

HE DID BUY CHERRY BRANDY

Daily Telegraph Reporter

THE Prince of Wales, who is 14, did have a drink in a hotel cocktail bar at Stornoway, Lewis, on Monday. Buckingham Palace yesterday withdrew a denial of reports that he had bought himself a cherry brandy for 2s 6d.

Mr. F.R.G. Chew, headmaster of Gordonstoun, where the Prince is a pupil, said later that boys at the school were forbidden alcoholic drink. He added: "If, after investigation, the reports prove correct I shall consider if disciplinary action is necessary.

"At present, I don't know the full details. I shall be interviewing the boys when they return to school on Sunday." He declined to say what form disciplinary action could take.

He added that the Prince would be treated like any other boy at the school.

PALACE WAS MISLED

P.c.'s phone call

A statement from the Palace said:

In agreement with the headmaster of Gordonstoun, the Press secretary to the Queen wishes it to be known that they were misled by a telephone call from the Metropolitan Police officer with the Prince of Wales concerning a visit to the bar of the Crown Hotel, Stornaway.

It is therefore regretted that the original story was denied and that newspapers were subsequently given incorrect information in answer to their inquiries.

The policeman is P.c. D. Green. He has been attached to the Prince. Under the Licensing (Scotland) Act, 1959, it is an offence for anyone under 18 to buy excisable liquor on licensed premises. People between 16 and 18 can buy only beer, porter, cider or perry for consumption with a meal.

(June 20)

AGREEMENT ON "HOT LINE"

AMERICA and Russia signed the "hot line" agreement in Geneva to-day. The White House and the Kremlin are to be linked "as soon as technically feasible" by a 4,883 mile teleprinter wire and a standby radio circuit.

The Americans think it should be possible to set up this direct link within 60 days from to-day. It would be for use "in time of emergency" to reduce the risk of war by accident, miscalculation or failure of normal communications.

The "hot line" is the first concrete achievement to emerge from the 17-nation disarmament conference in Geneva. This began 15 months ago.

An ordinary commercial cable is to be leased for the teleprinter wire on the route Washington - London - Copenhagen - Stockholm - Helsinki - Moscow. The radio circuit will link Washington and Moscow by way of Tangier.

(June 21)

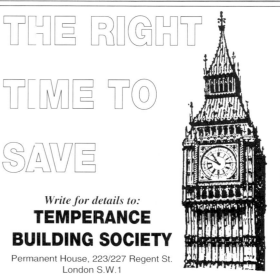

RAILWAYS CUT BY A QUARTER

Dr. Beeching's plan to shut 2,128 stations

By RONALD STEVENS
Daily Telegraph Industrial Correspondent

THE size of the railways will be cut by more than a quarter and 2,128 stations closed if the Railways Board report, published yesterday, is implemented in full. Provisions of the report, much of it written by Dr. Beeching, include:

Withdrawal of passenger services from Scotland north of Inverness, from much of North and Central Wales, and most of the West Country.

Abolition of 290 stopping train services in all parts of the country and "modification" of 71 others.

Elimination by the end of 1965 of extra trains during summer and public holidays.

Introduction of goods "liner trains" consisting of permanently coupled wagons carrying large containers, running between major centres and combining with road vehicles.

Dr. Beeching said yesterday the first closures were likely to take place in the autumn. He expected the reduction in rail jobs to be about 70,000 and forecast fare increases in London of at least 10 p.c.

SCRAPPING OF 8,000 COACHES

Many radical changes in the industry's time-honoured methods and facilities are proposed. They include:

The scrapping of about 8,000 passenger coaches from the present stock of 22,500, and 348,000 goods wagons from a fleet of 848,000.

A reduction in the number of goods depots from 950 to about 100.

Many features of the plan have already been forecast in The Daily Telegraph. Among them are:

"Rationing" of available seats on regular services at holiday time by reservation schemes and higher fares.

The loss of about 70,000 out of 475,000 railwaymen's jobs as a result of closures and new methods. Most of these redundancies will occur in 1964 and 1965, and will be followed by a further reduction in the industry's labour force of about 100,000 by 1970.

NO DISMISSALS
Continuing rundown

It is expected that many of the redundancies will be covered by natural wastage and controlled recruitment, though some men will have to be dismissed. The additional cut of 100,000 will be achieved without dismissals, by continuing the rundown of 25,000 men a year begun in 1962.

The report says that if the whole plan is implemented vigorously "much, though not necessarily all, of the railways' deficit should be eliminated by 1970." Though not yet officially published, last year's deficit was more than £160 million.

(March 28)

2 REPORTERS SENTENCED FOR SILENCE

Daily Telegraph Reporter

TWO reporters, who refused to divulge their sources of information to the Vassall Tribunal, were sentenced in the High Court yesterday to imprisonment for contempt of court. Both are to appeal.

Mr. BRENDAN MUHOLLAND, 29, of the Daily Mail, was sentenced to six months and Mr. REGINALD FOSTER, 58, attached to the Daily Sketch, to three months. The sentences were suspended for five days to allow time to give the sources or to enter an appeal.

Mr. Justice GORMAN ruled that a journalist had no legal immunity, or privilege, for not revealing his sources of information. There was an over-riding public policy: the discovery of truth.

(February 4)

ARABS FORCED RESIGNATION

NORWICH UNION insurance policies were again accepted throughout the world after the resignation of Lord Mancroft, 49, as chairman of the London board, Mr. Martin Chase, Secretary of the Norwich Union Fire Insurance Society, said last night.

A statement by the Norwich Union Insurance Societies said: "The Norwich Union is a mutual organisation with policy holders in all parts of the world. Racial discrimination has never been practised and is not practised to-day.

"Arab interests recently informed the Norwich Union that in view of the association of a member of its London advisory board with certain other business interests, Norwich Union policies would no longer be acceptable."

(December 4)

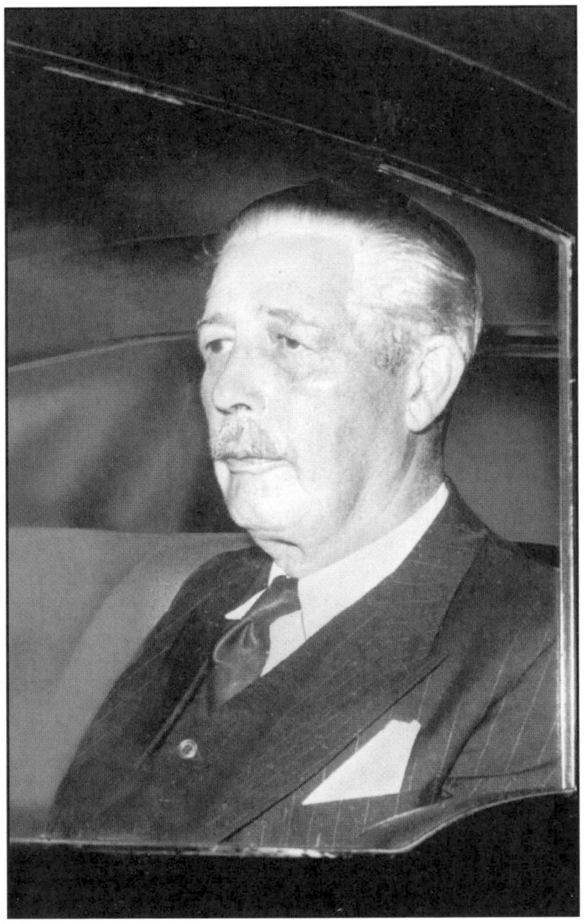

MR. MACMILLAN

HOME CHOSEN BY MACMILLAN

By H.B. BOYNE,
Daily Telegraph Political Correspondent

UNLESS there has been since midnight yet another change in the bewildering struggle for the Conservative party leadership, the man whom Mr. Macmillan will recommend to the Queen to-day as his successor is the Earl of Home, Foreign Secretary.

The choice was made last night, as the Prime Minister lay on his sickbed. It was between Lord Home and Mr. Butler, First Secretary and Deputy Prime Minister.

On what seemed to him satisfactory evidence that Lord Home commanded the widest spread of support at all levels of the party, Mr. Macmillan is reliably reported to have decided in his favour.

Mr. Butler, I was told, is "fighting to the end." There was even talk that he and Viscount Hailsham, another disappointed candidate, might still be induced to combine against Lord Home.

But the chances are that the verdict, once it is made known by the fact that the Queen has sent for Lord Home, will be accepted with good or ill grace by all concerned. The only alternative would be open warfare which could split Government and party from top to bottom.

FINAL ROUND UP
Hailsham eliminated

Lord Home's name came to the fore after a final round up, in Mr. Macmillan's hospital room yesterday afternoon, of assessments from those who have been sounding opinions in all sections of the party.

Lord Hailsham having been eliminated, and support for Mr. Maudling having apparently fallen short of the level required for a decisive expression of the entire party's wishes, he was seen as the sole alternative to Mr. Butler.

The reported consensus in Lord Home's favour probably coincided with Mr. Macmillan's private opinion. There have been suspicions all along that he did not consider Mr. Butler, in the latter's mordant phrase of six years ago, "the best Prime Minister we have."

The upshot is that Mr. Butler is to be blocked, or edged out, by a peer who will have to disclaim his title and win a by-election before he can lead the Government in the Commons.

Lord Home has clearly agreed to submit himself to this process, although the details, I understand, have yet to be worked out.

(October 18)

ROBOT TUBE TRAIN HAS MILE RUN

Daily Telegraph Reporter

LONDON TRANSPORT took a glimpse into the future yesterday when it demonstrated the first automatically controlled Underground train.

If all goes well, one should be in service early next month on the District Line, west of Hammersmith, and full-scale trials may be carried out later on the Hainault-Woodford shuttle service on the Central Line.

The fully automatic system is designed to ensure more regular running of each train and more efficient use of current.

As a passenger on the one-mile demonstration run between Acton Town and South Ealing, I was impressed with the smoothness of the whole operation.

PRESS-BUTTON START

At the press of a button, the train accelerated and then came to a standstill five yards from the "stop" mark.

Mr. Anthony Bull, member of London Transport Board responsible for rail operations and labour relations, said: "We shall not be ready to introduce automatic driving of trains on any substantial scale for some time.

"Nor have we any intention of bringing in driverless trains. We think it necessary that a man should be available to take control or initiate action."

What is foreseen is a central controller for each Underground line who would know continuously the location of any train on his system.

(March 22)

COLLAPSE OF 'SIX' ENTRY TALKS

NEGOTIATIONS for Britain to join the Common Market collapsed yesterday. Mr. Heath, Lord Privy Seal, said in Brussels that they had been "thwarted for political reasons at the will of one man, President de Gaulle".

France broke up the talks because, she said, Britain failed to submit to the "discipline of the Rome treaty and Market rules."

Britain's entry is still supported by France's five Common Market partners. They decided after a meeting with Mr. Heath last night to retaliate against Gen. de Gaulle by cancelling a meeting of the Common Market Council of Ministers in Baden-Baden to discuss France's request that American investment in the Market should be discouraged. Belgium and Holland have threatened to boycott all Council meetings.

"BLACK DAY FOR EUROPE"

The general reaction of the "Five" was summed up by Dr. Erhard, West German Vice-Chancellor, who said "this is a black day for Europe." M. Spaak, Belgian Foreign Minister, said "the European spirit has been badly damaged."

A French spokesman, in an attempt to calm the "Five," said the talks were only suspended, and that President de Gaulle "did not wish to murder the conference."

(January 30)

PLOT TO MURDER GEN DE GAULLE

From Our Own Correspondent

PARIS, Friday

ANOTHER plot to assassinate President de Gaulle was foiled to-day. An Army officer had planned to shoot him, using a rifle with telescopic sights, during his visit to the Paris Military College this morning.

Military intelligence agents and detectives have arrested four people, including three Army captains and a woman teacher of English at the college. This was the seventh attempt on Gen. de Gaulle's life since December, 1960.

Security officers unmasked the plot late yesterday and during the night they searched houses and made the four arrests. But Gen. de Gaulle insisted on carrying out to-day's visit, guarded by armed police who ringed the Military College buildings and watched from rooftops.

A police search through Paris to-day is believed to have brought in other plotters.

The man the police most want is Georges "Cripple" Watin, an Algerian-born engineer said to be the brains behind the plot. He was a leader of the Petit Clamart murder attempt.

After discovery of the plot yesterday a "council of war" was called at the offices of M. Pompidou, Prime Minister. Later police searched the Montparnasse building where Watin was believed to be hiding, but the "Cripple" had escaped.

(February 16)

TOWNS AND VILLAGES CUT OFF BY BLIZZARDS

BLIZZARDS struck many parts of Britain again yesterday after a slight thaw had briefly raised hopes of an end to the 41-day Arctic spell. Many main roads were blocked and many villages cut off.

Conditions were chaotic in Devon, Dorset, Somerset, Gloucester, North Wales, Westmorland and Belfast. The A30 was blocked in at least five places, Exeter was cut off, and roads into Cornwall were blocked.

An AA spokesman said the great fear was that hundreds of drivers could be marooned in their vehicles, nobody knowing of their plight.

Princetown, Devon, was short of food and helicopters continued relief air-drops of supplies. Ilfracombe was plunged into darkness last night when the electricity failed.

SNOW-BOUND TRAINS
Passengers marooned

Fifty railway workmen and two passengers were stranded in a two coach train in a blizzard near Bridestowe on the edge of Dartmoor. At Ashbury, Devon, the 3.13 p.m. from Bude to Okehampton was also hemmed in by snow and six passengers were sheltering for the night at Ashbury station.

Over 100 motorists and lorry drivers stranded on the main Okehampton Exeter road were given shelter in the village of Whiddon Down. The snow was reported to be five feet deep on the road there.

Belfast had its heaviest snowfall in years. Schools and shops were closed early and bus services were cancelled.

The captain and mate of the Dutch cargo boat Grietje, 296 tons, which went on to rocks south of Douglas, Isle of Man in a blizzard early yesterday were rescued later by breeches buoy. The six members of the crew had come ashore.

(February 6)

SNOW CLEARER FOR COUNCIL IS NEW PEER

Death of Earl of Buckinghamshire

Daily Telegraph Reporter

A £10-a-week Southend Corporation workman learned last night that he had succeeded to the title of the Earl of Buckinghamshire, who died in London yesterday aged 56.

He is Mr. Vere Frederick Cecil-Hobart-Hampden, aged 61, of Castleton Road, Southend. He has worked 12 years in the Corporation's Parks Department, and is now working on snow clearance.

"I will still be at work tomorrow," Mr. Hobart-Hampden said, "This makes no difference.

"I am very happy in my life and I shall have to think about this new situation. I don't feel that I want to go to the House of Lords or anything like that.

(January 3)

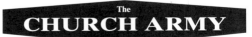

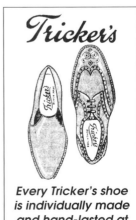

Daily Telegraph and Morning Post, 1963

NEGROES MARCH FOR CIVIL RIGHTS

'Quiet stroll' call to end colour bar

From VINCENT RYDER and DAVID SHEARS
Daily Telegraph Special Correspondents

WASHINGTON, Wednesday.

THE Great Negro March on Washington yesterday turned out to be an orderly, good-humoured stroll around the Lincoln Memorial by the 200,000 Civil Rights demonstrators.

Only two arrests were made. One was of a follower of George Rockwell, the United States Nazi leader. Police hustled him away when he tried to make a speech.

Before the 200,000-strong Civil Rights march in Washington to-day was half over, Mr. Bayard Rustin, deputy organiser and the real moving spirit, spoke of the next move.

He said: "Already one of our objectives has been met. We said we would awaken the conscience of the nation and we have done it."

The next move would be a "counter-filibuster" if opponents in the Senate tried to talk the proposed Civil Rights Bill to death. On every day of this "filibuster" 1,000 Negroes would be brought into Washington to stage a demonstration.

THIRST FOR FREEDOM
No hatred

A great roar of approval met the warning by the Rev. Martin Luther King, the integrationist leader, that America was in for "a rude awakening" if she thought she could go back to business as usual.

"Let us not seek to satisfy our thirst for freedom by drinking from the cup of hatred and bitterness," said Mr. King. Negroes would go on with the struggle until "justice flows like water and righteousness like a stream."

The cheers rolled over the crowd, jammed in front of the Lincoln Memorial and along the shallow reflecting pool.

It was a day of quiet triumph, a mingling of fervent demands with a show of orderly, relaxed calm. Earlier fears of disorder seemed almost laughably out of place.

Personalities in the march included Marlon Brando, Burt Lancaster, Lena Horne, Judy Garland, Sammy Davis, Sidney Poitier and Josephine Baker, who flew from Paris.

For two hours the marchers', numbers swelled around the monument, within sight of the White House and the Capitol, which houses Congress.

They were entertained by singers and by brief speeches from their heroes, Jackie Robinson, the baseball player, and a man who roller-skated all the way from Chicago, and admitted his legs were tired.

NOT NECESSARY
Respectability aim

The organisers expected that this sort of distraction would be necessary to keep tempers under control. They need not have worried. The crowd seemed almost as determined to be respectable as to demand civil rights.

Black suits and dresses predominated. A group of poor Negroes from Parksville, Mississippi, were in well-pressed overalls.

There were clerical collars by the dozen. Clergymen of every denomination joined the demonstration.

(August 29)

KENNEDY 'PRIDE IN MARCH'

President Kennedy said to-night the Great Negro March had advanced "the cause of 20 million Negroes." After meeting for 75 minutes at the White House with the leaders of the demonstration he said: "One cannot help but be impressed with the deep fervour and the quiet dignity of the demonstrators."

It showed their faith and confidence in democracy. "This nation can properly be proud of the demonstration that has occurred here to-day."

In a message for Labour Day next Monday but released to-day to coincide with the march, President Kennedy called on the American people to "accelerate our effort to achieve equal rights for all our citizens."

(August 29)

LONDON HOUSING INQUIRY ORDERED

By Our Political Correspondent

SIR KEITH JOSEPH, Minister of Housing, announced last night that Sir Milner Holland, Q.C., is to be chairman of an independent committee which will conduct a survey of all existing housing in London. This was a guarantee, he claimed, that the survey would be "impartial and thorough."

He was replying to a virulent attack by Mr. Harold Wilson, Leader of the Opposition, on the Government's alleged failure to cope with "Rachmanism" and racketeering.

Mr. Wilson reiterated Labour's pledge to repeal the Rent Act, 1957, and also indicated what a Labour Government would put in its place:

Full security of tenure;

Tribunals to fix rents on appeal by either tenant or landlord;

Parliament to decide what constitutes a reasonable rent, in relation to the rateable value, condition and amenities of the house.

The Holland Committee will be asked to report on the state of housing in London, with special reference to whether rented housing is being used and managed to the best advantage.

The survey will cover publicly-owned houses as well as those owned by private landlords. With this in view, local authorities will be asked to co-operate in the committee's work.

(July 23)

MOB SCENE AT LINCOLN MEMORIAL:
Demonstrators are massed all the way back to the Washington Monument.

MARCHERS CLASH WITH POLICE

LONGEST-EVER COLUMN

Daily Telegraph Reporter

POLICE clashed with militant groups among the 25,000 Aldermaston marchers when they reached Whitehall on the final lap of their four-day trek yesterday. There were 72 arrests in skirmishes between Hyde Park and Trafalgar Square.

Some demonstrators were slightly hurt. One policeman was injured when a bus ran over his foot, and others were scratched and bruised.

One of the 72 arrested, a youth aged 19, was later charged with possessing dangerous drugs on the march. He will appear at Marlborough Street to-day.

Though the column of marchers was the biggest ever, the closing stages of the demonstration were mainly orderly. The breakaway demonstration expected to be made by Committee of 100 followers did not take place.

More than 3,000 police were positioned along the route. Apart from clashes in Hyde Park, Victoria and Whitehall, they were given surprisingly little trouble.

These incidents, largely involving marchers with the Federation of London Anarchists and several Scottish and Irish contingents, created big gaps in the column of marchers. As a result, it took over 2 1/2 hours to pass any point.

CORDON BROKEN
Shouts and screams

In the march towards Whitehall later there were scuffles as some marchers broke through a police cordon, and 12 mounted police were moved in to restore control. There were shouts and screams from some of the women.

Some were knocked over in the crush as the police drove the column back to one side of the road. Further scuffles, in which police helmets were knocked off and other policemen were kicked and bruised, led to about 30 arrests.

Several mounted policemen were nearly unseated in the clashes and others were knocked over. But the police quickly restored order. There were cheers from the marchers as coaches took away those who had been arrested.

(April 16)

JOBLESS FALL BELOW HALF-MILLION MARK

THE number of registered unemployed has fallen below half a million for the first time since September last year. On June 10, 479,675 people were out of work, a drop of 73,948 since May.

Excluding school-leavers and the temporarily stopped, the number of wholly unemployed declined by 51,971. The normal seasonal decrease between May and June is 32,500. This is the third successive month in which the fall has exceeded the normal seasonal amount.

Between April and May the actual drop was 47,000, compared with a normal 23,000 and between March and April it was 75,000, compared with a normal 20,000.

There is, therefore, little doubt that the trend of "real" unemployment is now downwards. Last winter it was rising steadily and was accentuated by the spell of severe weather.

(June 21)

PRINCESS ANNE AT BENENDEN

PRINCESS ANNE, on the first day of her school life, unpacked her belongings in Magnolia dormitory at Benenden School, Kent, last night. The Queen and Princess Anne were received by Miss Elizabeth Clarke, the headmistress.

Most of the 300 girls gathered under the oak trees outside the main entrance to watch the arrival of the Royal new girl. The Princess, wearing the regulation blue school suit and carrying her school hat with the orange band of her house, Guildford, was first out of the car.

(September 21)

MR. WILSON ELECTED AS LABOUR LEADER

By H.B. BOYNE
Daily Telegraph Political Correspondent

MR. HAROLD WILSON, who will be 47 next month, is the Labour party's new leader. He beat Mr. George Brown, 48, by 41 votes. The figures were:

Mr. HAROLD WILSON 144

Mr. GEORGE BROWN 103

One of Mr. Wilson's first statements after his election as chairman and leader was announced to a private meeting of the Parliamentary Labour party last night was that Mr. Brown's future as deputy leader was assured.

Mr. Brown did not actually commit himself to retain his post as deputy leader. He said he would take a few days to think it over.

But he left the strong impression that he will decide in favour of doing so, and Mr. Wilson made it clear that he welcomes this prospect.

"NO HARD FEELINGS"
Call for unity

Everyone admired the "calmness and sportsmanship" as it was described, with which Mr. Brown, who was deputy leader under Mr. Gaitskell, accepted defeat.

Presiding as acting leader, he was the first to congratulate Mr. Wilson, making way for him to take the chair. He did so, according to Labour M.P.'s with "no hard feelings, no hint of pique."

The important thing now, he was reported as saying, was to unite behind the new leader. He would think over his own "personal and political position" during the next few days. He looked forward to frank talks with Mr. Wilson.

(February 15)

'CARICATURE' IN BISHOP'S BOOK, SAYS DR. RAMSEY

THE Archbishop of Canterbury, Dr. Ramsey, said last night that the book "Honest To God," by the Bishop of Woolwich, Dr. Robinson, began with "something very misleading. It is really a caricature of the ordinary Christian's view of God."

Dr. Ramsey was answering questions by Mr. Kenneth Harris in the ATV programme "About Religion." Mr. Harris asked if the image of God as presented by the Church to-day corresponded with the ordinary man's thinking. The Bishop said in his book that it did not and thought our image of God must be modified.

"Do you think he is right?" Mr. HARRIS asked.

THE ARCHBISHOP answered: I think the Bishop of Woolwich's book begins with something very misleading. It is really a caricature of the ordinary Christian's views of God.

When the ordinary Christian speaks of God as being "up there" or of God "being beyond," he does not literally mean that God is in a place beyond the bright blue sky. He's putting in poetic language, which is the only serviceable language we have, that God is supreme.

When the bishop goes on to say that God is "deep down" and we must think of God in depth, I would say that I have always done that. I have always believed, and have always taught all through my time that God is deep down, as well as beyond.

NO QUALIFICATION
Unfavourable opinion

Our Ecclesiastical Correspondent writes:

Dr. Ramsey allowed no qualifying phrase to blur his unfavourable opinion of the Bishop's action in denouncing "the imagery of God held by Christian men, women and children."

A film at which the Archbishop was shown looking before he was interviewed had little relevance to the discussion or the book. Only one of the working people questioned in the street about their religious beliefs had any positive conviction of the existence of a Supreme Being.

(April 1)

BEATLE MANIA AT ROYAL VARIETY SHOW

OVERSPILL OF HIGH SPIRITS

By Our Theatre Reporter

THE Beatle mania hit the Royal Variety Performance in full force at the Prince of Wales Theatre last night. In seven successive Royal shows I have never heard anything approaching the reception given to them by the predominantly middle-aged middle-class audience.

For their "She Loves You" number the audience were already joining in, clapping the rhythm, but by their fourth song, appropriately called "Twist and Shout," the general commotion was incredible.

As it turned out the opening acts of the programme were hardly more than a warm-up for the Beatles. We have had "pop" manias before, but at this show they have generally failed to come off; certainly none has won last night's stupendous applause.

To a classically minded "square" seeing them for the first time they were, to begin with, four strange youngsters with below the fringe haircuts.

Next one noticed the enthusiasm, the absence of any self-pitying moan, and no suggestive wiggling, the curses of the last "pop" crop. They are plainly not just entertainers, but a rallying-point for an overspill of teenage high spirits.

There were, of course, 18 other acts at the performance, of which one remembers, first, the surprising ones. Marlene Dietrich, Max Bygraves, Tommy Steele, Michael Flanders and Donald Swann, Pinky and Perky, Harry Secombe, pleased as one knew they could.

FUNNIEST MOMENT

Dickie Henderson

But a Latin-American juggler Francis Brunn, turned out to be an astonishingly acrobatic magician and Dickie Henderson, in addition to valuable work as "link-man" gave a "relaxed at the bar" impression of Frank Sinatra which was about the funniest moment in the show.

Nadia Nerina and other dancers from the Royal Ballet, closing the first half with the Rose Adagio from "The Sleeping Beauty," reminded us that there are more imaginative things than dreamed of by screaming girls at the stage door.

Tommy Steele was there with his "Half a Sixpence" company and Harry Secombe with the "Pickwick" company, crowded stages which closed the show.

About another set piece, Charlie Drake in a Spanish sketch, one could be more directly critical having seen it, together with a few million other people, on television two nights before, which does take the edge away.

PALACE "DIG"

Steptoe customer

There was the customary friendly dig at Buckingham Palace, this time a sketch specially written for Harry H. Corbett and Wilfrid Brambell as "Steptoe and Son," "totting" without much luck in Birdcage Walk and Downing Street.

Then they move along to the Palace and meet a little boy with a "Beatle" haircut who offers them a polo stick.

(November 5)

LITTLEWOOD WAR SHOW IN WEST END

By W.A. DARLINGTON

IT is not surprising that Joan Littlewood's production "Oh What a Lovely War" has been packing in audiences at Stratford, E.

It is an easy bet that it will continue to pack them in now that it has come to Wyndham's.

As a sermon against war it makes its point completely, by the simple method of presenting the appalling figures of the 1914-1918 struggle as a background to a rough dramatisation of its chief events, presented by a troupe of pierrots.

As a theatrical experience, it moves one in many ways, to feelings strangely mixed.

RAGE AT FOOLISHNESS

It moves one to rage that humanity should have been capable of making a fool of itself on such a scale, and to horror lest it should prove capable of doing so again on an even greater scale.

And yet, mingled with this, there comes a strange exhilaration and a nostalgia. For those who fought in that war and were lucky enough to survive it, this show conjures up memories that are not all painful.

(June 21)

ASHTON TAKES THE HELM

By A.V. COTON

UNOBTRUSIVELY, and without benefit of fanfares of trumpets, Sir Frederick Ashton took over the directorship of the Royal Ballet this week. He succeeds Dame Ninette de Valois, who henceforth concerns herself primarily with the company's school.

There are intriguing possibilities in this situation, for such transfers of authority occur only rarely in any ballet system.

What the Royal Ballet becomes - if it does undergo any obvious change in the next five years - will be what Sir Frederick thinks desirable for the biggest ballet organisation ever created in this country. I suspect that there will be more surprises in store than many ballet people have bargained for.

An original artist in any field is not necessarily a good organiser of that kind of art. Ashton's immense reputation rests securely on his being one of the handful of really significant choreographers of this century.

His work hitherto, and for nearly 40 years, has been to create ballets, to train first-class dancers to perform in them, and to nurture the rising young talents which graduate into the company. He has never had to work on the routing and rather mechanical side of the business of presenting ballet.

(August 17)

CROWD STOPS CLIFF RICHARD

PREMIERE MISSED

Daily Telegraph Reporter

Cliff Richard, 22, the "pop" singer, was "locked out" by his admirers last night from the premiére of his film "Summer Holiday". So many young enthusiasts gathered outside the Warner Theatre, Leicester Square, that police advised him not to try to enter.

Several people were injured in the crush and a girl was taken to hospital. A Warner Pathé spokesman said : "I have never seen anything quite so frenzied. The teenagers got too excited."

Mr. Peter Gormley, Cliff Richard's manager said: "Cliff ended up in a flat nearby watching television instead of his own premiére."

(January 11)

DORIS DAY LEADS POPULARITY POLL

Doris Day, the film actress, has recaptured the position of chief box office attraction. In the annual poll of film exhibitors Miss Day was named as leader of the "Top Ten" Elizabeth Taylor, top of the list last year, has dropped to sixth place.

(January 5)

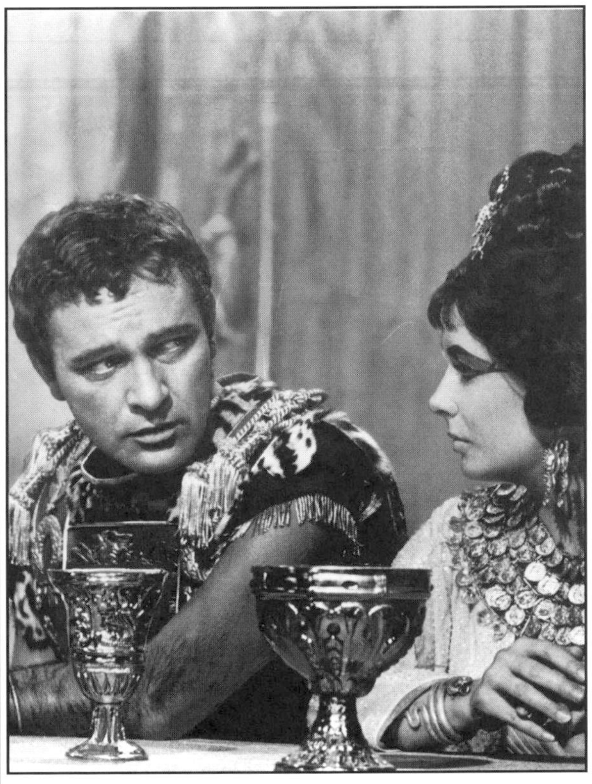

ELIZABETH TAYLOR and RICHARD BURTON in CLEOPATRA.

NATIONAL THEATRE DEBUT GLITTERS WITH STARS

By W.A. DARLINGTON

SO it is over and behind us - the evening so long dreamt of, which 20 years ago seemed doomed never to happen. The first evening, I mean, when you could open your programme and read the words "The National Theatre." There it is in black and white, if not yet in bricks and mortar.

In time to come last night's opening of the full-length "Hamlet" at the Old Vic will be looked on as an historic occasion and we who were privileged to be its audience will be envied.

And indeed there was a sense of occasion in the air, though nothing ceremonious was done to cause it. The play just opened, like any other play.

O'TOOLE'S HAMLET

Passion and tenderness

But almost as soon as the play started the sense of extra quality which a National Theatre exists to achieve, and must achieve to exist, began to make itself felt.

Tiny parts which in an ordinary company have to be given to inexperienced young actors were here being played with an unusual authority, and their lines spoken with an unusual feeling for significance and music.

Peter O'Toole, playing this immense name-part with a passion and tenderness which puts him in the first rank of the Hamlets of our time, had in his supporting cast no fewer than three actors who have themselves won deserved praise in the part.

Most important of these, of course, is Michael Redgrave, now lending to Claudius his extraordinary talent of suggesting charm, ability and wickedness in the same man.

But both John Stride (now Fortinbras) and Richard Hampton (now Bernado) distinguished themselves when they played Hamlet as amateurs. Not since Laurence Olivier produced his film version of the play can he, or any other producer, have had the chance to cast his minor characters so strongly.

As for the major roles, they are all immaculately cast and immaculately played.

Diana Wynyard's Gertrude is a triumph of stupid, good-natured sensuality - comparable with that wonderful performance in the same tone by Laura Cowie which I have never thought could have an equal.

Max Adrian's Polonius, too, is a work of art, solving with precision the problem of seeming a bore without being one.

And for Rosemary Harris's charming, gentle and affectionate Ophelia and Anthony Nicholls's deep-voiced Ghost I can spare only a passing word of appreciation.

(October 16)

IN A SOVIET CAMP

By DAVID FLOYD

One Day in the Life of Ivan Denisovitch.
By Alexander Solzhenitsyn.
Trans. by Ralph Parker. (Gollancz. 18s)

MUCH has already been written about this short story by Alexander Solzhenitsyn since it first appeared in Russian in the Moscow literary journal Novy Mir last November.

It was immediately apparent that it was by far the most striking work to emerge from the Khruschevian "thaw" in Russia. It was also the most typical of the Khruschev period, in that it exposed with greater force than ever before the institution which best summed up the Stalin era - the concentration camp.

There are probably still people outside Russia who doubt whether the forced labour camp was really part of the Soviet régime, and whether the population of the camps reached many millions at their peak. No figures will persuade the doubters. But this story, about one day in the life of one prisoner in one camp, is persuasive.

I think no one could doubt that this is an utterly true account of real experience and real suffering. The author, an officer in the Red Army, spent the first eight post-war years in Stalin's camps.

The book merits publication and translation not only as a social document but also as a work of art. The very fact of its publication in Russia to-day is itself a measure of the distance Soviet society has travelled since Stalin died ten years ago.

This translation by Ralph Parker, the former Daily Worker correspondent in Moscow, leaves much to be desired. He appears, if anything, to have softened the impact of the original. Thus, on P.63 there is a reference to "Gopchik, a Ukrainian lad, pink as a sucking-pig . . ." Mr. Parker has omitted the fact that Solzhenitsyn gave Gopchik's age as 16.

Or take, on p. 49 Ivan Denisovich's reflections on post-war conditions in the collective farms, Solzhenitsyn says: "Half the men never returned from the war at all, and those who did would have nothing to do with the collective farm; they stayed at home and worked on the side."

Mr. Parker translates this as:

"Half the men hadn't come back from the war at all and, among those who had, *were some who cold-shouldered the kolkhoz*." (Emphasis mine)

Why only *some?*

A note on Bendera describes him as "a General in the Soviet Army who betrayed his country in World War II." Bendera was never in the Red Army and was leader of the nationalist partisans in the Western Ukraine.

Another, more accurate, translation has just appeared in America. It is the work of Max Hayward co-translator of "Doctor Zhivago," and Ronald Hingley of St. Antony's College, Oxford.

(February 1)

ELIZABETH TAYLOR IS NO SIREN OF THE NILE

"CLEOPATRA" DISAPPOINTS

From Our Own Correspondent

NEW YORK, Tuesday

WHATEVER else may be said about "Cleopatra," which was shown for the first time in New York to-day, it seems certain that it will not go down in history as the greatest film ever made. When the curtain was rung down after four hours of pageantry, high drama, and passionate love scenes, the Press preview audience gave a few perfunctory claps.

There were many expressions of disappointment. Perhaps we had expected too much. Perhaps the huge expenditure of money, sets on a scale so lavish that their like may never be seen again, and 10,000 extras, do not necessarily produce an artistic triumph.

Rex Harrison is a mature and satisfying Caesar. But Richard Burton is a weak and almost pitiable Mark Antony.

Elizabeth Taylor looks the part, but to many who saw her this afternoon she was no Siren of the Nile. Her voice all too often sounded harsh, and her manner was all too often domineering rather than royal. At times she was a regular shrew.

She was definitely not the Cleopatra to end all Cleopatras, although she was decidedly more dramatic after the interval when Caesar was dead, and Mark Antony was being turned to water by her wiles.

SUPER SPECTACLE

Italian criticism

The Italian correspondents present were the most vociferous in their condemnation of the film as a super spectacle without any deep feeling or understanding.

The London premiere will be on July 31 in aid of the Newspaper Press Fund.

(June 12)

FAREWELL, FAIR LADY

By RONALD HASTINGS

BY the time "My Fair Lady" closes at the Theatre Royal, Drury Lane, on Saturday it will have been seen, in London alone, by 4,325,000 people, 80,000 of whom will have paid for the privilege of standing up. The box office will have taken £3,570,000 for tickets which would stretch end to end for 438 miles, or rather less than the distance the two revolving stages have covered.

From the first day of bookings, which opened seven months before the first night on April 30, 1958, money was accepted for performances nearly three years ahead. Applications for seats came from 65 countries.

The charity preview raised £25,000 and before the first-night 11 other charity performances had been arranged. Advance booking was said at one time to have reached the unprecedented figure of half a million pounds, though the later total from H.M. Tennent was content with a record £250,000.

In London "My Fair Lady" will have run for 2,281 performances, in New York it totalled 2,717. It has also been given in the Argentine, Australia (two companies), New Zealand, South Africa, Mexico, Russia, Germany, Holland, Norway, Sweden, Denmark, Finland and Iceland, with Italy to be added next month.

It is in keeping with this lofty reputation that the London run will end only two performances short of the "Salad Days" record for a musical here, the management pointing out that Drury Lane holds 2,341 people and the Vaudeville, which housed "Salad Days," only 669.

Throughout the world "My Fair Lady" has taken £25 million and the film rights have been sold for £1,950,000. This is far from all, as the London company open in Manchester on Oct. 31 with advance bookings already exceeding a record £135,000.

(October 16)

BELLY DANCE BOOED IN MODERN 'AIDA'

From Our Own Correspondents

NEW YORK, Tuesday.

One of the most glittering evenings in the history of the New York Metropolitan Opera House turned sour last night when the audience hissed and booed in disapproval of a modern dance in a new production of "Aida".

Instead of the traditional performance of the dancing girls in Act Two, Miss Katherine Dunham, who arranged the dance, produced a "ballet" with the emphasis on writhing, modern dance movements.

Large sections of the audience, which included members of New York "Society," booed. In the intermission many people spoke deprecatingly of the "belly dancing."

(October 16)

MARKOVA TO RETIRE

ALICIA MARKOVA, former ballerina of the Vic-Wells Ballet, announced in London yesterday that she will retire from dancing to take up coaching and lecturing.

Born in London in 1910, she began her career at the age of 10 in pantomime. Five years later she was dancing with Diaghileff's Russian Ballet Company as its youngest member ever.

She was an important figure in the early years of both the Ballet Rambert and the Vic-Wells Ballet in the 1930s. She danced regularly and often simultaneously with both.

Miss Markova has a vast experience in ballets of many kinds.

Her knowledge of the 19th century classical ballets will be particularly valuable in her work as a producer and coach.

A.V.C.

(January 2)

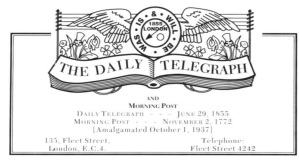

THE DAILY TELEGRAPH
AND
MORNING POST
DAILY TELEGRAPH - - - JUNE 29, 1855
MORNING POST - - - NOVEMBER 2, 1772
[Amalgamated October 1, 1937]
135, Fleet Street, London, E.C.4. Telephone: Fleet Street 4242

MR. PROFUMO RESIGNS

MR. PROFUMO is right to resign from public life and to admit that his public assurance that there had been no impropriety in his private life had been untrue and therefore "a grave misdemeanour." The standards of conduct expected from a Minister and, indeed, from a Member of Parliament must be different from those expected from a private individual. The ordinary citizen may, perhaps, claim that only those of his critics who are without sin should throw stones. But it would not be right that all actions considered legally venial in a private person should be similarly treated as of no account when committed by public men. In the past there may have been cases of excessive censoriousness - the line between morality and priggishness is not always easy to draw. But if all unwritten rules of conduct were abrogated, public characters would be bound to lose in the general respect which they should attract and deserve. For their private reputation is not a matter concerning themselves alone.

That having been said, it is possible to express regret at the ending of a promising career; and to take note of a frankness which was courageous, if belated. It is indeed possible that if confession had come earlier some pain might have been spared to those whom denial was designed to protect. For the deliberate telling of an untruth to the House of Commons is in some ways a greater offence than the incident about which the untruth was told. Nor must this case be taken to reflect any general looseness in the standards of British politics. We are not witnessing a return to Victorian times from a relapse into the morals of the Restoration. The chief feeling must surely include some element of pity for a lapse of a sort which can occur and has occurred in all ages.

(June 6)

SURPRISE CHOICE

AT last the "usual methods of consultation" have produced a result from the arduous process of choosing a new Conservative leader. But it is a most unusual result. The winner is the Foreign Secretary, the 14th Earl of HOME, who would presumably, if he succeeds in forming a Government, take advantage of the Act passed to enable a reluctant Socialist Peer to return to the Commons. It is in some ways sardonic that the only runner who was not very keen to run at all should have carried off the prize.

LORD HOME'S reluctance was quite unfeigned. His political reputation has been made entirely in the Lords; and indeed he made no particular mark in the Commons. His experience in the latter was long in time, but limited in matter - he ended by being Parliamentary Private Secretary to NEVILLE CHAMBERLAIN for two years before the war; and was out of the House after it until a year before succeeding to the peerage. This was not a tremendous training for the political atmosphere to which he now succeeds. Though improving, it is still not redolent of victory. As BALDWIN said at a similar moment, his task evokes prayers rather than congratulations.

(October 19)

TRUTH AND RUMOUR

NOT for half a century has there been such a company of mourners as that which yesterday followed President KENNEDY'S bier to Arlington. It was the world's tribute to the power of the American Presidency and to the goodness and greatness of the man who served humanity in that office. Let us hope that the world's sorrow brought some slight comfort to Mrs. KENNEDY, who, at once regal and pathetic, with courage and resolution beyond even that expected from a First Lady, led the great ones of the earth to pay their homage to her husband. She and the American people will observe how every sentence spoken in the official tributes such as those paid in our own Parliament yesterday has been dominated by the speaker's own personal sorrow and admiration for the dead President.

All this will not still the uneasiness caused by the ghastly deeds of violence and the lapse of the rule of law in Texas. There was only one way in which the Dallas security forces could add one iota to the immeasurable calamity of President KENNEDY'S murder. That was by permitting the alleged murderer to be murdered in his turn. The laxity which allowed this to happen was almost unbelievable. So was the monumental absurdity of the Dallas police chief's statement that the case of President KENNEDY'S murder was "now closed." The killing of OSWALD closed nothing except the main doorway, till then still open, to the whole truth. It opened the door to every sort of rumour and insinuation that evil men can invent to serve their own ends.

(November 2)

THE BEATLES

BY all accounts it seems very hard to dislike the Beatles. They are clean and friendly; the noise they make is happy and extrovert. This is lucky, since we are obviously going to have an earful before their career, be it short or long, ends. Meanwhile, they are borne up on a tumultuous sea of teenage hysteria. Two thousand queued for tickets at Coventry; 4,000 struggled at Newcastle, of whom 100 fainted. On Thursday 1,500 screaming fans brought London Airport and the Prime Minister's car to a standstill as they greeted their heroes. All barriers, social and intellectual, seem to fall before them. They are even said to have a substantial following at the universities.

To hang all sorts of grave reflections on such aberrations is to risk pomposity. Yet who can help wondering what it is all about? This hysteria presumably fills heads and hearts otherwise empty. Nature abhors a vacuum: what will fill it next? Is there not something a bit frightening in whole masses of young people, all apparently so suggestible, so volatile and rudderless? What material here for the maniac's shaping: HITLER would have disapproved, but he could have seen what in other circumstances might be made of it.

Equally disquieting in his way is the educated and sophisticated "pop-fan." Most cultural fads and fashions are fairly absurd. More absurd than most are fashions which, like those of to-day, are largely set from below. Professors, writers, intellectuals, bishops, all take care to be discreetly "with it," fully conversant and in sympathy with all that wells and throbs up from the slums beneath them. The cultural tone of society is normally set by the leisured and moneyed classes. Our teenagers have leisure and money. What sort of cultural tone are they setting?

(November 2)

LORD BEVERIDGE

TWENTY years after he produced his blueprint of the Welfare State, Lord BEVERIDGE'S name remained so completely identified with it that he may have seemed a man of this single monumental achievement. In fact, his zeal never rested - any more than the cost of the Health Service or the concept of National Insurance have rested where that scheme placed them.

In the heyday of planners, he became the vastest planner of them all. The social security he envisaged rested on financial foundations that have proved less secure. He made insufficient allowance for the effects of inflation: for the inner dynamism of medical science, which we now recognise must raise the cost of the best possible health service to the highest figure we are prepared to pay for it. But miscalculations of the planner reflected nothing static in the man.

(March 18)

A RUSH OF SATIRE TO THE HEAD

> *"We are now threatened with a kind of mass-satire in the name of a vague liberalism or of an aimless nihilism"*
>
> *By Michael Wharton*
> *(Peter Simple)*

WE all know by this time (or if we don't, it is not for want of being told) that there is a "boom in satire" in Britain now. The "satire industry" has itself become a subject for satire. A book just published by an eminent classicist, Prof. Gilbert Highet, surveys the historical development, methods and functions of satire in Europe and America from Bion to Mort Sahl (of Indian, Chinese or Australian Aboriginal satire it no doubt wisely says nothing), and asks, without quite answering, the question of what satire is and what it is not.

"The true end of satire," says Dryden, "is the amendment of vices by correction." "Satire," says the novelist Pamela Hansford Johnson, "is cheek," and her husband, the novelist and bureaucrat C. P. Snow, explains: "It is the revenge of those who can't really comprehend the world or cope with it," a definition which, by its firm assumption that those who cope with "the world" and those who comprehend it are the same people, puts every satirist - as well as every artist, every philosopher, every religious teacher and even every "pure" scientist - properly in his place.

Between these two definitions, one lofty, one contemptuous, what is satire? Prof. Highet tries to answer the question by analysing the forms which the satirical impulse has taken in European literature. Here we enter a bewildering maze.

The Origins

Satire is the most vague and elusive of literary forms. The Latin word satura itself (it has nothing to do with satyrs) means a hotchpotch, a medley.

The earliest entertainments called satires in Roman times seem to have been vaudeville shows, usually crude and obscene, in which at first amateur and later professional actors made fun of the ludicrous aspects of contemporary life, lampooned unpopular individuals and generally let themselves go in the grotesquely exaggerated fashion of improvised charades at a drunken party.

"The Anatomy of Satire." By Gilbert Highet. (OUP for Princeton Univ., 30s.)

When Prof. Highet goes on to draw into the net of satire the medieval mock epic of "Reynard the Fox," Cervantes, parts of Shakespeare, Rabelais, Pope, Voltaire, Byron, Dickens, Flaubert, Wyndham Lewis, Aldous Huxley, the science fiction of H.G. Wells, Orwell, Evelyn Waugh, Grock the clown, the wartime impersonator of Field Marshal Montgomery and even C.P. Snow himself, we may begin to wonder whether there is really any such thing as satire at all, whether it is not rather an element which pervades all literature, and perhaps all life.

The satirical impulse clearly has the same root as human laughter itself, however and in whatever remote times it may have originated. Perhaps it is of diabolical origin, an expression of the "spirit which denies." The Snovian view has something to be said for it. Satire is cheek. It is the resource of one who, being impotent to amend evil, escape misfortune or overthrow unjust authority, tries to render them harmless by mockery, that is, by making them appear to be unreal.

The claim of satire to be something more than this, something more than cheek, can be upheld only if it uses laughter in the service of moral judgement. Without this, it is only harmless fun, scurrility or a form of sympathetic magic (Irish bardic satirists were believed to be able to cause boils to break out on the faces of those they mocked, or turn them into rats, by the mere force of their invective).

The true satirist, as opposed to the humorist or the lampoonist, must attack from a firm base of principle, by reference to which he can expose the gap between pretence and reality, the essential material of satire. By reference to the supposed virtues of the old Republic, Juvenal could flay the vices of Imperial Rome. By reference to ideal Reason and Virtue, Swift in "Gulliver's Travels" could savage the whole life of his time, its senseless wars, corrupt politics, preposterous scientific projects, and finally the degraded state of the human race itself.

By reference to that same Reason and Virtue, Pope in the "Dunciad" could elegantly ridicule human stupidity through and through. By reference to the idea of genuine artistic creation, Wyndham Lewis in "The Apes of God" could make the bogus in art expose itself for what it is.

In Opposition

The great satirists of the past were men moved by indignation to mock at stupidity, hypocrisy and vice in the name of intelligence, honesty and virtue. As such they stood in opposition to the mass of their countrymen; they could hardly expect popular acclaim.

To-day we have the great popular success of "Private Eye" and "That Was The Week That Was." What we are now threatened with is a kind of mass-satire in which the whole population can join, giggling uncontrollably and brandishing mass-production plastic rapiers and bludgeons as it thrashes away at the already shaky props which have hitherto supported our lives - patriotism, organised religion and a conventional moral code - in the name at best of a vague, convenient liberalism, at worst of an aimless nihilism.

This mass-satire may seem harmless enough. But it is part of what has been called the "cannibal dance round the idea of Authority," a phenomenon which for reasons yet unknown seems to have appeared in greater force in England than in any other country. It is great fun, but there is no future in it, and if past history is anything to go by, it is liable to be succeeded, when the fashion for it is spent, by some kind of authoritarian, puritanical and even Fascist reaction. If that should happen, the "boom in satire" will be over, but the satirist will go on as best he may, still offering his eternal, necessary "cheek" to those who falsely claim to comprehend and cope with the world.

(February 23)

LONDON DAY BY DAY

ALTHOUGH last night's Royal Academy banquet, which precedes the annual Summer Show, had all the customary political and military trappings, for the first time in my memory Sir Charles Wheeler, President for his seventh year, really had some exciting and concrete news to give.

Not only has last year's sale of the Leonardo cartoon helped to re-embellish Burlington House but the money has also provided funds to put on an unprecedented exhibition next December - "Goya and His Time."

The Prado in Madrid will lend 12 paintings, including both Majas - an unprecedented step. Mr. Sidney Hutchison, my neighbour at last night's dinner and the Academy's librarian, who will take charge of the organisation, tells me the show is to include some 200 paintings and drawings, mainly from overseas.

Last year at the dinner I noted that Sir Charles asked if Britain deserved the Leonardo. Last evening he pointed out that Sotheby's had far higher bids at around £1 1/2m. than the British Government and public paid.

Paris Keeps Pace

THE Musée Grévin, the Madame Tussaud's of Paris, marches with the times. The wax figure of Gen. de Gaulle is now in the foreground talking to Dr. Adenauer. A little way behind de Gaulle on the right the Anglo-Saxons, President Kennedy and Mr. Macmillan, are seen together.

But the British Prime Minister looks forlorn and seems to be totally neglected by Mr. Kennedy, who is deep in conversation with M. Spaak.

Back Room Boy

IN THE SUNDAY TELEGRAPH yesterday was a remarkable photograph of Soviet Embassy staff in London, taken when Capt. Ivanov was assistant naval attaché.

Inconspicuously at the back stands Col. Groshev, a cavalryman and the assistant military attaché. It is he, at any rate since Ivanov's departure, who has been responsible for Soviet intelligence in Britain.

A serious, friendly man, Col. Groshev has stuck close to London during his tour of duty and functioned as the local member of GRU, the Soviet military intelligence system.

Meanwhile, his superior, the affable Maj. Gen. Efimov, continues to deny that his assistants engage in spying.

Gentle Mr. Silverman

A CURIOUS feature of the wary little debate in the Commons yesterday on the motion to record Mr. Profumo's contempt of the House was that Mr. Selwyn Lloyd rose to commend Mr. Sydney Silverman, who could never have expected such an ally.

Deserving Leonardo Forlorn P.M.

But for once he caught the mood of the House better than his pontificating colleagues with his plea that the former War Minister had paid his penalty in full and should not be hounded further.

Earlier, the rumbles of the affair were less gentle. One disturbing incident was when Capt. Sir R. A. Pilkington uttered spirited yet cryptic words on Mr. Macmillan, after the Prime Minister had given a series of negative replies about the habits of political parties in revealing their sources of income.

La Dolce Vita

LORD CHAMPION had cause to air his connoisseurship of fish and chips yesterday during the resumed report stage of the Weights and Measures Bill in the Lords.

He maintained that this combination forms our sole contribution to world gastronimics, and that he can tell the difference between the tang of one paper and another.

"I want to ensure that the retailer of fish gets full weight. I think the Minister should ensure that for the 2s or so I pay for my fish and chips I should get my full whack."

Three years ago Lord Champion, a life peer last year, became the Government-appointed director of the British Sugar Corporation.

PETERBOROUGH

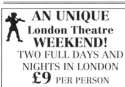

COMPETING FOR THE COUNTRY COTTAGE

By ARTHUR BOWERS
Property Market Correspondent

READERS in quest of peace and quiet often ask me about the possibility of finding a country cottage. Well, let me say at once that there are some about, but most of them can be discovered only by diligent search.

Price and condition vary enormously; those nearest the busiest centres of population are naturally the most costly. They are also the most difficult to find.

There are cottages in villages where mines have been closed down, though the local authority may have already earmarked the sites for redevelopment. But if such cottages are available, even a tiny and fairly derelict example, without services, will cost not less than £200, though small cottages in Devon and Cornwall have gone for £120.

A comparatively run-down building with two or three bedrooms, a cold tap, no drainage and a list of defects to be righted before it can be lived in will be nearer £1,000 to £1,200 in Essex or Hertfordshire, though possibly about £800 might secure one farther from London.

Renovation can cost a great deal, ranging from about £500 on a do-it-yourself basis, to £1,500. Some of the better cottages, still requiring £1,000 or so to be spent on them, make around £2,000.

In the North a cottage, on the whole, is a very modest building; in other parts of the country it can be almost anything. In Somerset, for example, R.B. Taylor & Sons, acting with Edens, the Sherborne land agents, are to offer at auction Chapel Farmhouse, at South Cadbury, Yeovil, with an acre of land.

Georgian House

They describe the property as suitable for renovation, and having the makings "of a truly delightful country cottage residence." The existing accommodation consists of three ground floor rooms, the smallest of which is 13ft by 12ft, with five rooms on the first floor, the smallest being 8ft by 7ft.

These agents are also selling "The Cottage and Annexe" at North Cadbury. In this case the "cottage" is a four-bedroom Georgian house, and the "annexe" provides three more bedrooms. Both have bathrooms.

In the South

In the South, cottage properties "ready to move into" make high prices. For instance, King & Chasemore of Horsham, Sussex, got £9,700 for Rowdell Cottage, a stone-built property with views of Chanctonbury Ring. It has four bedrooms, two bathrooms and stands in about three-quarters of an acre.

A similar price is expected by these agents for Orchard House. Wisborough Green, which has five bedrooms, two reception rooms and a bathroom with about half an acre of garden.

What is described as a converted cottage style residence with a 1 ¼-acre smallholding, known as The Granary at Old Keston, Kent, 14 miles from London, is expected to make more than £10,000. It is a four-bedroom modernised property due for auction by Hampton & Sons.

(October 16)

WHEN A GIRL IS TIRED OF FRILLS

by LOUISE RHOADES

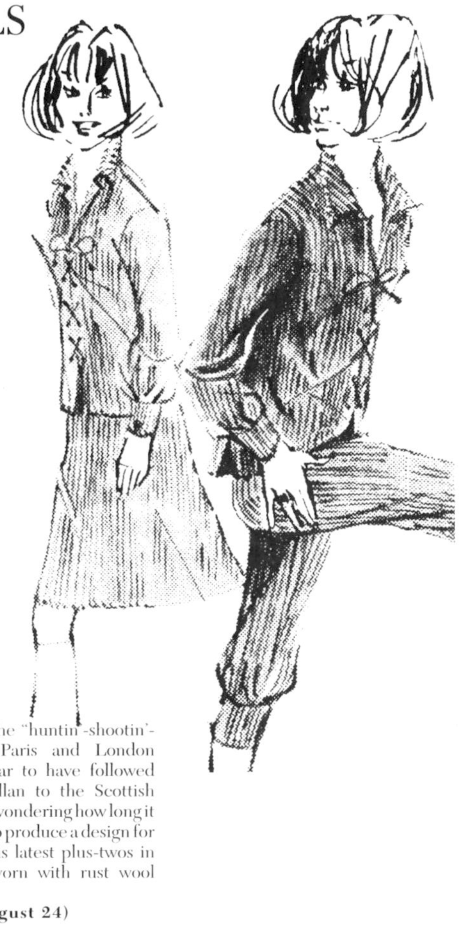

SLACKS, the garment with the shortest history in a woman's wardrobe, has now blossomed into at least 10 variations.

They range from the snug-fitting styles of hipsters, jeans, stretch and ski pants to the looser-fitting bell-bottoms, cigarette styles (straight at the ankle), knickerbockers, plus-twos (a variation of the old plus-fours), culottes and for evening, figure-hugging cat suits. In fact, something for every age.

There are even more if you include shorts such as Bermuda and Jamaican for sports and beach wear.

James Laver, the costume expert, tells me that it was only 20 years ago (during the war) that slacks became part of a woman's life. Many first wore them in factory jobs, and the bus conductresses had them as part of their uniform.

They acquired the taste for the comfort of slacks and chose them as leisure garments from then onwards.

Yet only 50 years ago, society was shocked by daring young women who took the plunge in fashionable resorts such as Brighton in pyjama-style trousers.

Most women wear slacks to relax in. "It is a form of escapism, something completely different. They can be feminine all day long, look enchanting in long evening skirts, but during carefree week-ends they can revolt from comformity to comfort," says a young designer at a leading fashion store.

But it's the KNICKERBOCKER craze that everyone has gone mad about, for it's the "huntin'-shootin'-fishin'" look. Paris and London designers appear to have followed Harold Macmillan to the Scottish Moors and I'm wondering how long it will take them to produce a design for women from his latest plus-twos in tweed check worn with rust wool socks.

(August 24)

A SICK SOCIETY

SINCE the current trend is for being frank, to the point of being tedious, about sex, it was inevitable that sooner or later someone (and who else but an American woman copy-writer?) should write a handbook on "Sex and the Single Girl."*

Helen Gurley Brown, the author, begins by boasting that she married for the first time at 37, and then plunges into what the blurb on the cover describes as a detailed, easy-to-follow blue-print of how to be sexy to every man in eyesight and earshot.

Her aim is to tell single women, presumably from her own experience, how to learn to make the most of life until they meet the man they really want to marry.

Her advice includes, among other things, tips on how to serve "without fidgets" breakfast to an overnight male guest, how to handle the protocol of an affair from beginning to end, and when and how best to extract presents from married lovers.

The only advice she leaves out of this most nauseous of handbooks is what the single girl should do if she finds, after following these tips, she's hoist by her own petard, and is about to become an unmarried mother. Essential advice, we think, in a book which claims to be "not a study on how to get married, but how to stay single - in superlative style."

That a book like this should not only get written, but published as well, seems to us a sympton of a sick society. But there is another side to the coin.

* Published by Frederick Muller at 18s.

(May 24)

WHAT PARENTS SAY ABOUT THE BEATLES . . .

"MANIA or magic?" we asked (on this page last week). Is screaming at the Beatles a safety valve or symptomatic of youth's declining morals?

"Neither," says Mrs. Helen Currie, of Wallington, Surrey. "Couldn't it be that parents and teachers have failed, that the vast majority of youngsters, left to themselves, are lost?"

And this is echoed by Mrs. Alison Lord, of London, E.C.1, who writes: "Long live the Beatles - but may we outlive the need for them - not by decreasing vitality but by finding something better."

Some form of energetic self-expression is needed by young people, most readers were agreed: "If screaming at the Beatles offers an emotional release from this rather grim world, why should we adults presume to criticise?" asks Mrs. C. Phillips, of Basildon, Essex. "It might be better if many parents could go and scream at them rather than at one another or the children."

But where does self-expression end and mass hysteria take over? "Any form of mass hysteria is harmful." writes Mrs. Enid Jones, of London, S.W.9. "Controlled and reasoned action differentiates between humans and the rest of the animal kingdom, between the sane and the mentally afflicted."

Mr. Colin Bolt, of Liverpool, adds: "Oughtn't we - remembering Nuremberg and the '30s - be glad that it is only the Beatles leaving these schoolgirls relaxed and spent?"

Mrs. June Cogdell, of Manor Park, writes: "All that has happened in your correspondent's case is that her pupils have developed a temporary craze, and where is the harm?

"They spend a riotous evening yelling at the Beatles and come away happy, relaxed and on top of the world. How often in a lifetime do we get this wonderful feeling? So seldom that I do not feel this teacher should try to take it away from her pupils."

Where is the harm? A music therapist writes: "The power of music is more potent than political power.

"Subjecting immature young people, especially girls, to long strong doses of crude, coarse, often oversyncopated combinations of sound vibrations can, and obviously does, lead to loss of self-control and low-toned moral behaviour.

"The side and after effects can be seen in the next day's boredom, sullenness and, too often, anti-social behaviour. Music helps to form character. What music? What character?"

£2 goes to readers whose letters have been used

(November 1)

TAHITI TOGA COMES TO TOWN

What better moral-booster just now than a glimpse of Tahiti? It greeted me in a Bond Street shop, where in the lingerie department I found nightdresses, togas, shifts and Muu-muus in rich Polynesian prints of tropical flowers.

The prints, in mixtures of sea blues, emeralds and turquoise, or lime, lemon and orange, were mouth-watering to look at. The Tahiti toga, a new idea, is a long lean garment with deep side slashes. It is elegant enough to wear to a dance although it is really meant for slipping over a nightdress in place of a dressing-gown.

The Muu-muu, in waltz length Polynesian prints, flirts with small frills at the hem. The Tahiti jama with a St Tropez mid-waist top, has knee-length trousers cropped with a frill.

Botany wool polo-necked sweaters for 25s 11d are "disappearing" off the counter at a rate of five a minute in an Oxford Street chain store. Gleeful women with their eye on fashion, warmth and a bargain, are pouncing on the red, black, bottle green, amber and stone sweaters.

(February 2)

PRESENTS PREVIEW

TO EAT

TO his heart through his stomach - and to her heart, well just because she likes good food. Here are just a few of the exciting present ideas in the food stores to give this Christmas:

MARRONS GLACES, In tins, 9s 6d to 29s 6d; Pots of HONEY or (jam) in all shapes and sizes (12s 6d to 22s 6d); natural flower HONEYS in sixes; from Spain - orange blossom, Scotland - heather, Greece - hymethus, 12s 9d; a yard box of a dozen JAMS and MARMALADES, 30s. BRANDY SNIFTERS; four glasses filled with Cheddar in port wine or rum, gorgonzola in brandy and Edam in Sauterne - the glasses you use afterwards, 45s. From California, a wooden barrel of DATES IN BRANDY, 90s. All these from Harrods.

Spode jars of flower HONEY, from 32s 6d; CRYSTALLISED FRUITS, baskets from 35s-4gns - boxes from 14s to 87s 6d; Eight tinned SOUPS in presentation box, includes lobster, scampi, mushroom, minestrone, 36s; RUSSIAN CAVIAR from 46s for a 2oz jar to £15 10s; a Rackful of SPICES, 4gns. PATE DE FOIE GRAS en croute, £5 14s to order. All these from Fortnum and Mason.

TO DRINK

WINE hampers are growing in popularity. First decide if the recipient is to have white, red, rosé or some of all three. A hamper of six bottles, 54s 6d, contains two bottles of red Macon Superieur, and two each of white Burgundy and Bordeaux - Pouilly and Graves de Rions. A 3gn hamper may contain four red and two white wines.

A gold and white box of little quarter bottles of champagne can be an ideal choice for people in hospital. Three bottles of Lanson Black Label cost 29s 6d. All these hampers from Jacksons of Piccadilly.

Those decorative half-gallon white china wine and spirit barrels - replicas of Victorian ones - cost 32s. They have a wooden tap so you can really use them. A china cup to catch the drips cost 8s extra. If you feel you can't very well send an empty barrel, you can have it filled with Tawny Port or Medium Gold Sherry (76s), dry gin (£7 9s) or Scotch (£7 16s). Hedges and Butler of Regent Street will send the barrels to any address in Britain.

Packing and postage costs 3s for an empty barrel and a few shillings more if it is full.

(December 12)

SOON, A WOMAN PRIME MINISTER?

By Constance Noville

We might have expected a regiment of women but only 28 out of the nearly 1,000 eligible turned up for the first mixed session of the Cambridge Union debate this week. It was not a very impressive number to watch one of the last barriers against sex inequality hauled down; not many to lend support in the final breakthrough to the Stock Exchange, the court of Common Council and those few odd bodies where the excuse is still no lavatory accommodation for women.

Numbers don't count so much to-day. Twenty years ago a membership of 28 women out of a possible 1,000 would have been taken as a symptom of anaemia. Now a thin response can be taken as a sign of confidence in the established position of women.

Since 1869 when the first two women's colleges, Girton and Newnham, were founded at Cambridge women have learned to rely on quality — not quantity.

Although individually women may not have recorded many spectacular achievements, their overall impact has been immense. This is no longer a man's world. Men can no longer run industry, fight wars, conduct state affairs, or even venture into outer space without women.

In the House of Commons women's influence has always been far in excess of their numbers. The few have humanised legislation.

If the open doors of the Oxford and now Cambridge Unions are to mean anything more than a symbol of progress they could mean that we now have a training ground for stateswomen as we have had for statesmen for generations.

We might even see, over the blown-up hair-do of an earnest young debater the misty aura of a first woman Prime Minister. This will depend on whether the older universities keep their supremacy as nurseries for leaders in a scientific age.

The entry of women could and should mean a New Look for women public speakers. So far women have failed lamentably on the public platform.

They have produced only one great orator, Lady Violet Bonham Carter, of whom that other great orator, Sir Winston Churchill, wrote: "A gleaming figure capable of dealing with the gravest questions and the largest issues with passion, eloquence and mordant wit."

Note the well chosen "gleaming" — gleamingly feminine.

Women speakers when they gain authority nag and hector. Moreover they ape men. We could do with a new set of gestures, if gestures are necessary; something in which the grace of their hands and arms could be used in place of that sturdy village pump action which so many women speakers adopt.

(November 14)

MISS HUNTER, THE L-DRIVER FINED

Miss Margaret Hunter, 65, who has been described as Britain's most famous learner-driver, was fined £1 at Stockport yesterday for driving while unsupervised. It was said she went on driving after her instructor "baled out" on the A6 road.

Mr. H. Sidebotham, prosecuting, said that although she found herself in a predicament "when her instructor baled out on her, as it were," when she stopped she was one and a fifth miles from where she had been left.

"Her home was in the opposite direction. Her difficulties would merely provide a degree of mitigation."

P.c. S. Smith said that Miss Hunter said to him that at a traffic lights the instructor jumped out of the car and he had shouted "This is lunacy, it is suicide, I am not going another inch with you driving."

(February 5)

POPE JOHN XXIII

POPE JOHN was a man of the most lovable qualities - humble and pious, warmly courteous, hospitable and friendly, serene and hopeful. Other Popes had some or all of these qualities or other qualities just as precious and admirable; yet none was so universally missed as Pope John will be, not only by Roman Catholics but by the whole of the christian world - indeed by the world without qualification. His encyclical, Pacem in Terris, was addressed to "all men of goodwill" by all such men he will be mourned.

The Church of Rome has always claimed to be the Universal Church. Ever since Eastern Orthodoxy broke away, this claim has been belied by fact. With the Reformation, Rome became in appearance but one church among many. It never ceased to assert its supremacy, indeed, but sometimes in language so arrogant and exclusive as to command barely sympathy, let alone assent. Not so Pope John. His language was that of universal charity and understanding: as we are reminded on this page, he spoke not of "heretics" but of our "separate brethren."

It was his fortune - good or bad as one may think it - to be Pope at a time when devout and active Christians of every creed, aware that they were often a minority even in ostensibly Christian States, felt the need not merely to co-operate with each other but also with decent men not necessarily Christians at all. This feeling Pope John most memorably expressed. Almost his last words were: "Let them be one." No man could have done more to make us so.

(June 4)

Ld. BEVERIDGE

LORD BEVERIDGE, who has died aged 84, provided by means of his wartime Report on Social Security, the basis of what he preferred to call the Welfare State.

The present system of comprehensive insurance grew out of the Report, which was instituted by Sir Winston Churchill's Coalition Government in 1941.

He later presided over committees which investigated unemployment, broadcasting and the work of voluntary social services.

Born in Bengal, the son of an Indian civil servant, William Henry Beveridge was educated at Charterhouse and at Balliol. From 1903-05 he was Sub-Warden of Toynbee Hall.

LEADING ARTICLES

Churchill attention won

He became a casual leader-writer on the Morning Post, specialising in social problems, and attracted the attention of Sir Winston Churchill, then President of the Board of Trade.

Sir Winston later made him the first chairman of the Employment Exchanges Committee, an appointment which was to have a profound effect on the rest of his career.

He remained at the Board of Trade until 1916, when he moved to the Ministry of Munitions. He also worked at the Ministry of Food, and was created a K.C.B. in 1919.

Director of the London School of Economics, and a senator of London University from 1919-37, he was chairman of the Unemployment Insurance Statutory Committee from 1934-44.

He was also Master of University College, Oxford, 1937-45.

The "Beveridge Plan," as it was first known, developed from his chairmanship in 1941-42 of the committee on Social Insurance and Allied Services.

(March 18)

LOUIS MACNEICE

Louis MacNeice, who has died, aged 55, made his name as a poet in the 1930s, standing slightly to one side of the politically committed triumvirate of Auden, Day Lewis and Spender.

Though he did not pursue the fashionable flirtation with Communism his senses and sympathies were very much aroused by the decade. His "Autumn Journal" is still considered the most vivid and valuable testement of living through the thirties by a young writer.

(September 4)

THE LIFE AND TESTING-TIMES OF HUGH GAITSKELL

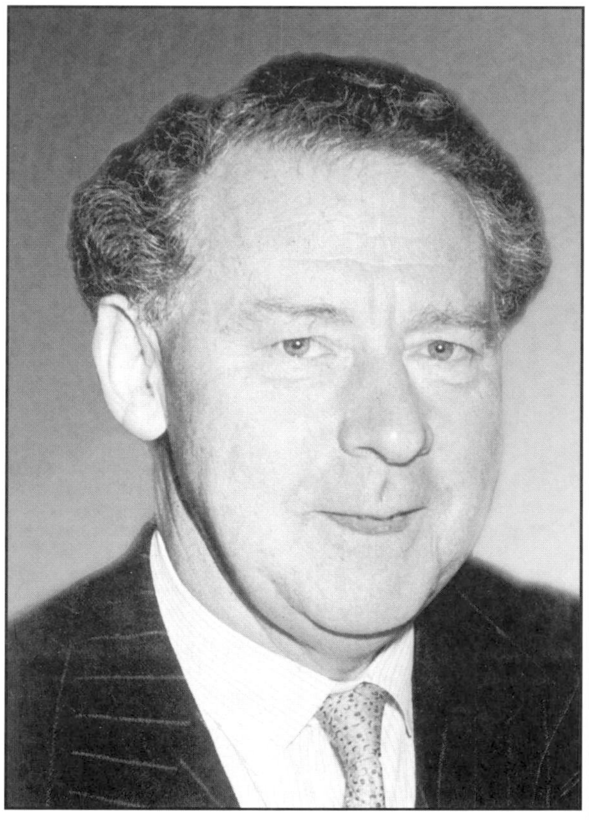

IF Keir Hardie's cloth cap symbolised the rise and purpose of the Labour party before World War I, Hugh Gaitskell embodied perhaps its most significant development after World War II.

He led by Intellect rather than personality. All his early prizes, at Oxford in war-time Whitehall, and at Westminster, were won by exceptional mental capacity and energy.

At 44, within five years of entering Parliament, Gaitskell was Chancellor of the Exchequer. In another five years he was Leader of the Labour party. By any reckoning these were singular attainments. They must be related to the party's post-war history.

Labour had spread its wings in the General Election of 1945. It entered the lists an unknown quantity. It emerged a national party. At the polls and in Parliament it was found to have spanned society. Support had come, sometimes surreptitiously, down surprising social corridors. One was the Senior Common Room.

By 1946 six dons were holding office in Mr. Attlee's first administration. They were, besides Gaitskell, Pakenham, Wilson, Gordon Walker, Jay and Marquand. In such company Gairskell swiftly proved his weight and worth. His ascent, by contemporary standards, was dazzling.

Already, when an undergraduate at New College, Gaitskell had helped the strikers during the General Strike of 1926. His first job as a lecturer in the Workers' Education Association took him to the minefields of Nottinghamshire.

It was an important step. Gaitskell cannot be numbered among those who discovered Socialism in 1945. His political beliefs had respectable roots.

Dalton's Protégé

Back in London he became, at 32, head of the Department of Economics at University College. In 1940 Hugh Dalton, who had an affinity for clever dons with Socialist sympathies and a shrewd eye for young men who could serve him, chose Gaitskell as his private secretary. They worked together first in the Ministry of Economic Warfare, then at the Board of Trade, where Gaitskell was to become a principal assistant secretary.

It is said that, war ended, Gaitskell debated far into one night with Dalton whether to remain where he was or turn to politics. The outcome was his return to South Leeds in the General Election.

He was seriously unwell at the time and did no campaigning on his own account. This illness probably eliminated him from immediate consideration for office. He was a backbencher in the new Labour Government until May, 1946.

After the 1950 General Election, Mr. Attlee created the post of Minister of State for Economic Affairs - it has since lapsed - and gave it to Gaitskell. By October he had succeeded Sir Stafford Cripps, now mortally ill, as Chancellor of the Exchequer.

He appeared to reach his first and only Budget of April, 1951, in relatively calm waters. In a competent speech, lasting 162 minutes, delivered on his 45th birthday, he added 6d to income-tax, doubled the purchase tax on motor cars, and told the nation it would, in future, have to pay half the cost of its false teeth and spectacles.

The cost of National Health, he declared, derisively in the light of later events, must be kept within the sum of £400m. Within the month Bevan and Wilson had left the Government.

Gaitskell was to have four years in Opposition before succeeding to the leadership when Mr. Attlee finally accepted his earldom in December, 1955.

As at most important junctures in his career Gaitskell opened his leadership auspiciously. His speeches were temperate, invariably lucid and sometimes considerable. He inflicted some small wounds on the Government, healed several larger ones within his own party.

He reached the Suez crisis with a gathering reputation for moderation and tactical skill. His first speeches on this enhanced it. One in July was a masterpiece of balanced statement.

The General Election of 1959 plunged Gaitskell into a series of tests which might well have unnerved a party leader of far greater experience. When the Conservatives made electoral history by winning a third time, Gaitskell's first reactions were calm, good-humoured, and in the best British "sporting" tradition. The public applauded him. But a Labour inquest had to be held and the leadership appeared to be in jeopardy.

Clause 4 Compromise

At a week-end conference at Blackpool in November, Gaitskell decided to take an initiative. He called for a revision of the party's 40-year-old constitution. The Left responded with anger and dismay. The sacrosanct Clause 4, demanding the "nationalisation of the means of production, distribution and exchange." was itself in danger.

At Blackpool it was Bevan himself who saved the day in one of the most pacific, though most hard to interpret, speeches which he ever made. "I agree with Hugh," said Bevan. "I agree with Barbara (Mrs. Castle), I agree with myself."

Meanwhile, Gaitskell had been fighting a second, and almost more acrimonious, battle on the party's defence policy. Reinforced by a vote of confidence in June, when the Parliamentary party gave him a majority of 179 to 7, he went to the Scarborough conference in October resolved to oppose the unilateralists led by Frank Cousins, who commanded the formidable card vote of the Transport and General Workers' Union.

Gaitskell's policy was defeated. In one of his best speeches, he declared that he and his friends would "fight, fight, and fight again" to bring the party to a better mind. It was becoming clearer that here was a formidable loser indeed. And, indeed, in October, 1961, the conference reversed its Scarborough decision. The unilateralists were defeated.

In 1962, a third issue arose to cause yet further party divisions. This was the Common Market, to which the Left, uneasily acknowledging the leadership of Harold Wilson, was bitterly opposed, Gaitskell's own faithful deputy leader, George Brown, was equally determined to promote Britain's entry.

At that conference, he almost abandoned the comfort of this position, giving a strong lead to the party's anti-Common Marketeers.

During his years of leadership, the Labour party was never certain whether it required a Lowest Common Multiple or a Highest Common Factor. In declining to be either, Gaitskell saw to it that the party did not fall apart. He also made himself indispensable.

What he failed to achieve was the great, soaring pre-eminence which is only given to a single statesman in each generation. Judging as he did, his own abilities calmly, coldly, and with a rare lack of exaggeration, he hit the mark which he set himself to attain. He sought, and achieved, poise.

(January 19)

ALDOUS HUXLEY

SATIRICAL VIEW OF PROGRESS

ALDOUS HUXLEY, the novelist, philosopher and dramatist, who has died in Hollywood aged 69, had an early ambition to become a doctor. Near-blindness which afflicted him most of his life prevented this.

His mother was related to Matthew Arnold and his father, an editor of the Cornhill Magazine, was the son of T. H. Huxley, the scientist. In Aldous Huxley were united the dominant traditions of Victorian arts and sciences.

He was educated at Eton and Balliol. After a short period of teaching at Eton, which he satirised in "Antic Hay," he turned to writing.

First poems and short stories were published and in 1921 his first novel. "Crome Yellow" was a great success with its satire of society after the 1914-18 war.

WIDER SCOPE

Reputation established

During the 1920s two more considerable novels, again satirical but greater in size and more considerable in scope, "Antic Hay" and "Point Counterpoint," appeared and gave Huxley a reputation as a leading younger novelist.

There was a minor sensation over the frankness, modest by present-day standards, of the writing about sex. But this was nothing compared with the public interest caused by the publication of "Brave New World" in 1932.

In the 1930s Huxley's novel writing grew rarer and he became more interested in political philosophy. He left France where he had been living and settled in the Californian desert where the clear dry air suited his sight.

In 1942 he published "The Art of Seeing" detailing his experiments to improve his sight which brought comfort to many sufferers.

Although since the war Huxley did write a few novels, none of them had the interest of his early work. In recent years much of his writing had been dominated in his awareness of the perils of over-population, which he preached against with all his considerable power.

(November 25)

JACK HOBBS - COMPLETE MASTER OF HIS CRAFT

By E.W. SWANTON

SIR JACK HOBBS, who died on Saturday, aged 81, was the greatest English batsman since W.G. Grace, a supreme master of his craft, and the undisputed head of his profession. Born on Dec. 16, 1882, the son of the groundsman at Jesus College, Cambridge, he made his way to the Oval at the age of 20.

Half a century later, long after his retirement but when his name was still a household word, he accepted the honour of knighthood.

John Berry Hobbs learned his cricket as so many Cambridge men have done before and since, on that sublime stretch between Fenner's and the Town, called Parker's Piece. Tom Hayward was his mentor there, and it was Hobbs's luck, after Hayward had persuaded him to qualify for Surrey, that he should serve his apprenticeship at the Oval as opening partner to that great batsman.

The long span of Hobbs's career made it probable that he would corner most of the aggregate records. Thus no one can match his number of runs, 61,221, any more than they can compete with his 197 centuries. No doubt he was lucky in his opening partners - compared with, say, Hutton. Nevertheless, his figure of 166 stands of a century or more for the first wicket sets an almost unassailable target.

Even more conclusive may seem the consistency of his performances. He averaged just under 50 in England over his whole time, stretching from 1905 to 1934. In Australia his average was 51, in South Africa 68, and in Tests alone it stood at 56.94.

If one summer marked his peak it was perhaps 1925, when, at the age of 42, he scored 3,000 runs, including 16 centuries, and with two hundreds in the match against Somerset at Taunton, first equalled and then surpassed the 126 hundreds made by "W.G."

He was a man of conspicuous personal modesty; but his pride in his position as - in every sense - England's No. 1 gave to his batting an aura of serenity equally communicable to his opponents and to his fellows. No one ever saw Hobbs rattled or in a hurry. And if he was anxious it never showed.

There was a quiet dignity about him which had its roots in mutual respect; for others as for himself.

(December 23)

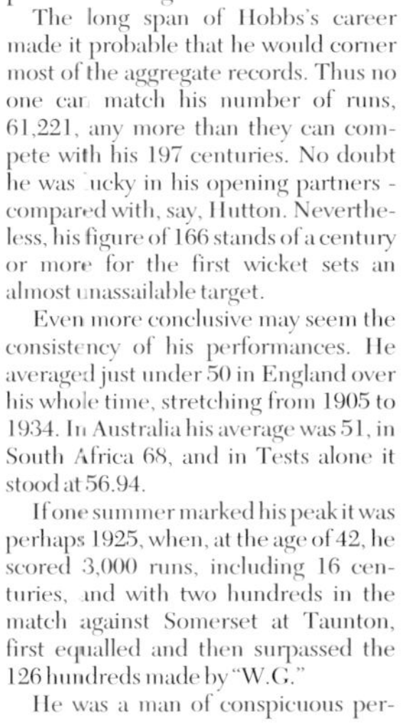

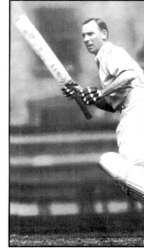

DR. C.S. LEWIS

DR. C.S. LEWIS, the writer, scholar and popular theologian, who has died at his home, would have celebrated his 65th birthday next Friday. Last month ill-health forced him to resign his chair in Medieval and Renaissance English at Cambridge.

Although he had been teaching for many years at Oxford and had written several books it was his popular radio talks on theology in the 1940s that made him a public figure.

"The Screwtape Letters", pastoral theology explained in the paradoxical form of letters from a fairly high-up devil to a junior tempter, were a tremendous success.

Clive Staples Lewis was born in Belfast, the son of a solicitor. He found his preparatory school and his public school misery. After a year he persuaded his father to let him leave Malvern College and go to a tutor.

Under the influence of an unorthodox teacher he progressed rapidly and won a classical scholarship to University College, Oxford.

Before he could take this up he saw service on the Western Front. After the war he returned to Oxford and took a Triple First. In 1925 he was elected a Fellow of Magdalen and remained at Oxford until 1954.

Appeal to children

Apart from his scholarly work and his theological studies, it is as a writer for children that he will be most remembered. In a series of stories he explored for children the world of Narnia, which lay behind a cupboard door.

These stories, like his earlier science fiction, were frankly allegories but had an air of magic about them that found a special response in children's imaginations.

(November 25)

JEAN COCTEAU

LEADER IN MANY FIELDS OF ART

JEAN COCTEAU, the French poet, novelist, dramatist, film director, ballet writer, wit, critic and satirist, who has died, aged 74, was the son of a wealthy lawyer.

Free all his life from financial anxiety, he was at liberty to follow his bent. He started as an infant prodigy, and was hailed in maturity as "the most intelligent man in Europe."

He lived constantly in the limelight and his achievements were constantly acclaimed. Yet it is doubtful whether any of his work will have permanent value, so prodigally did he dissipate his brilliant talents.

He was elected a member of the Academie Francaise and of the Royal Academy of Belgium in 1955. His last film, "Le Testament d'Orphee," made in 1960, was generally recognised to be autobiographical.

In recent years he had joined the group of French artists who took to decorating the interiors of French public buildings. He was made an honorary Doctor of Oxford University in 1956.

(October 12)

ROBERT FROST

Robert Frost, the American poet, has died at the age of 88. Although no such official position has ever existed he was for more than a generation the Poet Laureate of the American people. When President Kennedy wanted a poet to read at his inauguration, it was naturally to Frost that he turned.

As well as one of the best American poets of his time, Frost had a particular claim to the affection of his fellow countrymen because he remained an essentially American poet, writing peerlessly and tirelessly about his own countryside, New England.

While Ezra Pound, T.S.Eliot and Gertrude Stein went to live overseas, Frost remained firmly rooted as an American farmer, although his first book of poems was published in this country when he could find no one to read his verse in the United States.

(January 30)

SIR DAVID LOW, CARTOONIST

SIR DAVID ALEXANDER CECIL LOW, who has died aged 72, was described by Sir Winston Churchill, himself a frequent victim of Low's merciless pen, as "the greatest of modern cartoonists."

For 40 years Low caricatured the outstanding personalities in this country with a pungency, wit and economy of line which were entirely his own.

He seized on idiosyncrasies which his subjects accepted as part of their public image; Sir Winston's cigar, Baldwin's pipe, Herbert Morrison's (now Lord Morrison of Lambeth's) quiff and the late J.H. Thomas's dress suit.

Often, because of Low's highly individual and Left-wing views, his cartoons and captions were biting, but few of those he drew bore him ill-will.

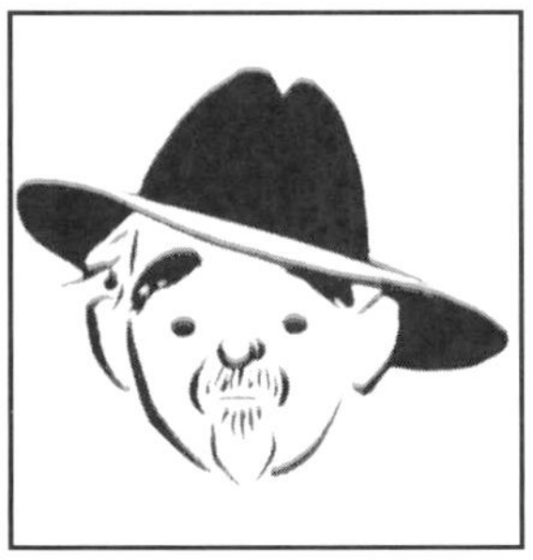

A SELF-PORTRAIT

Banned by Hitler

Exceptions were Hitler and Mussolini, who both banned his work which alternately attacked and ridiculed them long before the war. But Stalin is said to have had a Low cartoon over his mantelpiece.

Two of his satirical creations have become part of the vernacular; Colonel Blimp, the walrus-moustached reactionary, and Buttercup, the ponderous TUC horse, by turns spirited and stubborn.

Of Scottish stock, Low was born in Dunedin, New Zealand, and had his first cartoon published soon after he left school at the age of 11.

He came to London to join the Star in 1919, but eight years later began 23 years' work with the Evening Standard. His views were not those of his paper, but he demanded and was given an almost unprecedented licence.

In 1950 he joined the Daily Herald, but friction over, among other things, the T.U.C. horse led him to move in 1953 to the Manchester Guardian, now the Guardian. He was knighted in 1962 and drew his last cartoon for the Guardian about three months ago.

(September 21)

VISCOUNT ALANBROOKE

C.I.G.S. FROM DUNKIRK TO DEFEAT OF JAPAN

By Lt.-Gen. H.G. MARTIN

FIELD-MARSHAL VISCOUNT ALANBROOKE, wartime CIGS, who died yesterday at his home at Hartley Wintney, Hants, aged 79, belonged to a family which could be traced back to Sir Basil Brooke, Governor of Donegal in the time of Queen Elizabeth I.

Here then was the family setting. Here in Donegal and Fermanagh the Brookes belonged to a dominant minority. They have represented Protestant Ascendancy in this Catholic corner of the north.

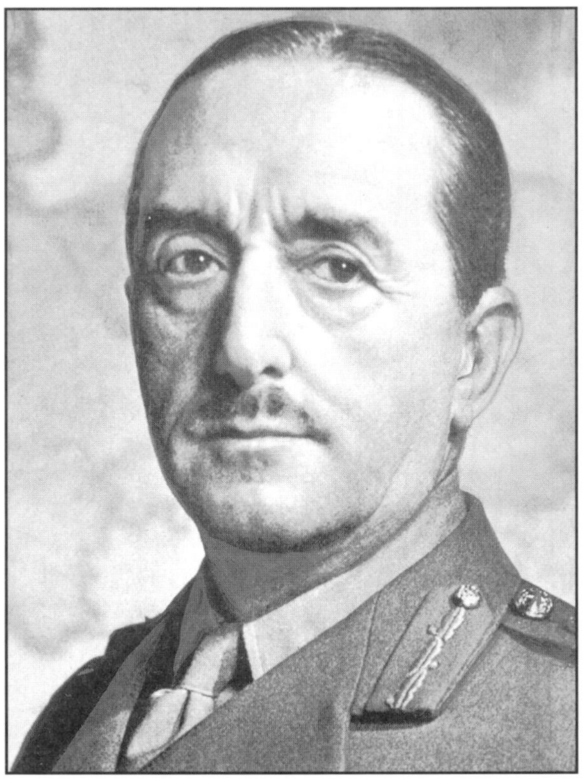

SOLDIERLY VIRTUES
Modicum of intolerance

What qualities do we associate with a dominant minority? Surely, soldierly virtues in the main - firmness of spirit, an alert mind, self-confidence, an inflexible will and a modicum of intolerance.

If we add for good measure a love of field sports and a merry wit, we get precisely the qualities that made Alan Brooke the very great soldier that he was.

From the "Shop" Alan Brooke passed into the Royal Field Artillery and in due course got his jacket in "N" Battery, Royal Horse Artillery in India. In 1914 he went to France.

In the next four years Brooke was to win the D.S.O. and Bar and to be six times mentioned in Despatches. By the end of the First World War he was already numbered among the elect destined for military greatness.

DUNKIRK RETREAT
Brilliant generalship

In the years between the war promotion came steadily while Alan Brooke held a multiplicity of important posts. The outbreak of the Second World War found him C-in-C, Southern Command, and in 1939 he went to France in command of the 2nd Corps.

In May, 1940, he handled his Corps brilliantly, notably in the later stages of the retreat to Dunkirk when, by a display of generalship that finds repeated mention in Mr. Churchill's memoirs, he successfully filled the gap left by the Belgian Army's surrender.

Sent out once more in June 1940, to command the British forces caught in the maelstrom south of the Somme, he soon realised that the position was hopeless.

Thereupon he countermanded all reinforcements: and - by a stroke of almost unbelievable good fortune - succeeded in finding a telephone line still intact by which he could get direct speech with Mr. Churchill.

"After 10 minutes," Mr. Churchill writes, "I was convinced that he was right and we must go. That prompt and resolute decision saved us 150,000 men. He returned to take command of Home Forces.

Less than 18 months later - on Christmas Day, 1941, Brooke became Chief of the Imperial General Staff in place of Field-Marshal Sir John Dill. It would not be true to say that things went smoothly from the first. Mr. Churchill and Brooke were both men of inflexible purpose.

In those desperate days Brooke set himself four objects: To clear North Africa and to reopen the Mediterranean; to knock out Italy; to bring Turkey into the war and so to keep Russia in it; and to prepare the invasion of Western Europe.

Brooke's greatest disappointment was American refusal to keep enough strength in the Mediterranean to exploit the 1943 Italian collapse.

In his hopes of commanding once more in the field, Brooke was to meet with two other and more personal disappointments. On Aug. 4, 1942, as Mr. Churchill recounts, he offered Brooke the Middle East Command in succession to General Auchinleck; but Brooke felt that he must decline.

Again, early in 1943, Mr. Churchill had promised Brooke that he should command "Overlord," the invasion of North-West Europe; but later at Quebec Mr. Churchill felt constrained to propose to Mr. Roosevelt that an American should be appointed instead.

So VE-Day approached at last; no soldier had done more than Brooke to speed its coming.

In June 1946, after holding the appointment of C.I.G.S. for four-and-a-half of the most critical years in our country's history, he handed over to Field-Marshal Montgomery.

He went to civil life with every honour that his King and country could bestow. He was Field-Marshal, Viscount, Knight of the Garter, holder of the Order of Merit, Knight Grand Cross of the Bath.

(June 18)

VISCOUNT NUFFIELD

VISCOUNT NUFFIELD, who has died aged 85, made probably more money, and certainly gave more away, than any other British Industrialist. Considered the English counterpart of the late Henry Ford, he was estimated to have made gifts amounting to more than £27 million, mostly for medical research.

His unparalleled munificence culminated in the establishment in 1943 of the Nuffield Foundation, which he endowed with Ordinary stock in Morris Motors valued at £10 million, with the object of assisting medical, natural and social sciences. In addition, he continued to make many other contributions for the advancement of science and for charitable purposes.

Like so many of the great philanthropists, he was a man of quiet and unassuming mien, who liked to wear old clothes and smoke a briar pipe. He lived without ostentation at Henley-on-Thames and had few interests outside work and the welfare of his fellow-men. He invariably decided personally the allocation of his gifts.

In 1952 he resigned his directorships in the British Motor Corporation, the merger of Austin and Morris interests which took place in the previous year, and in Morris Motors, but continued with his benefactions.

Born at Worcester in 1877 of yeoman stock, William Richard Morris was responsible, more than any other man, for reversing the situation which prevailed in his youth, in which 90 per cent. of the cars on British roads were of American manufacture. His early ambition was to be a surgeon, but as one of a family of seven he was apprenticed at 16 to a cycle manufacturer in Oxford.

Just over £4 he had saved during his apprenticeship was his entire capital when he set up in the cycle business for himself.

His shop was a success from the start, and he enhanced the reputation of his machines by racing them himself. Soon he switched to motorcycles, and by 1910 was designing his first car. It appeared in 1912 in the shape of the first "bull-nosed" Morris from a modest workshop in Cowley.

During the 1914-18 war this was turned over to making mine-sinkers. Peace found him with worn-out machinery and a lost trade while anything on four wheels was fetching fabulous prices. By 1921 Morris was re-established, but the boom in cars was apparently over.

PRICES CUT BY £100

It was that moment that he chose to cut his prices by £100. His rivals scoffed, but he had launched the moderate-priced family car. Four years later output at Cowley had grown from 3,000 cars a year to 48,000 and Morris was making a fortune.

In 1926 the biggest of all American motor concerns tried to buy him out; in his own words, they "flourished a cheque for 11 millions in my face." That same year Morris turned his own business into a public company.

He was created a baronet in 1929 and a baron five years later. In 1938 he was created a viscount.

The tale of his benefactions is world-wide and almost endless. No great hospital appealed to him in vain. During an Empire tour he gave £88,000 to help the crippled children of Australia and New Zealand. In 1936 alone he gave away over £6 million - £2 million to Oxford University for medical research, £2 million for the relief of the distressed areas, and £2,125,000 in shares in trust for his workpeople.

When the 1939-45 war broke out the "Nuffield organisation," comprising the Morris, Wolseley, M.G., Riley, Morris Commercial and Morris Industries export companies, were turned over to war work. From 1945 onwards their enormous and increasing exports contributed to Britain's recovery.

Lord Nuffield personally conducted, in 1948, the negotiations which resulted in the standardisation of parts with his great rivals, Austins, a precursor of the amalgamation.

(August 22)

MR. JOHN SPEDAN LEWIS

Mr. John Spedan Lewis, founder of the John Lewis Partnership, who decided 34 years ago to give all future profits to his workers, has died at his home in Stockbridge, Hants. He was 77.

Soon after inheriting the Oxford Street store of John Lewis and Co. from his father in 1928 he announced his idea of making every employee a partner in the firm.

He formed the John Lewis Partnership in 1929 by a settlement in trust. He completeed the foundation in 1950 by a second settlement, making the consent of the workers necessary to voluntary liquidation. There are now 16,000 partners and the firm's captial is £28,500,000.

(February 23)

EDITH PIAF

Edith Piaf, the French singer who has died, aged 47, was born in Paris. Despite a chequered background and a lurid private life, she became one of the handful of French entertainers who are legends in their own lifetime.

In a remarkably frank autobiography she told how she had been abandoned at the age of two months by her mother, an Italian café singer. She was brought up in Normandy by her paternal grandmother.

By the time she had reached her 15th birthday she was singing in cafés, at fairs and outside circuses. In Paris she tried hard to get on the music-hall stage and succeeded when she was 20.

Her songs achieved international fame and like her personality were tinged with the memories of unhappy childhood. Mme. Piaf had a long history of illnesses, many aggravated by her refusal to take doctors' advice.

In the early 1950s after a road accident in which she broke an arm she became a morphine addict. Her alcoholism which she said dated from frequent doses of red wine to keep her drowsy and well behaved as a child, also took its toll on her health. Her greatest success was a song, "La Vie en Rose"

(October 12)

M. GEORGES BRAQUE

GEORGES BRAQUE, the French artist who has died aged 81, was the founder, with Picasso, of Cubist art.

Born in Paris, the only son of a house painter and decorator, he learned his father's trade, but broke away in 1902 with the determination to become an artist. After study and work in Montmartre he held his first exhibition in 1906.

He fought in the French Army in the First World War, was severely wounded, and temporarily blinded. After a successful operation he resumed painting.

Ballet decor

Diaghilev commissioned him to do the decor for a ballet in 1923, and 10 years later he held his first retrospective exhibition in Basle. Britain's first exhibition of his work was in 1934.

During the Second World War, he stayed in Paris, and after a serious illness was able, in 1953, to complete a series of pictures on the ceilings of the Louvre. His paintings are represented in galleries throughout the world.

Braque's place in the history of art is secure. Whatever the verdict of time as to the merits of his work, his role as a key figure in the evolution of 20th-century art is beyond doubt.

(September 2)

MAX MILLER

CHEEKY CHAPPIE OF MUSIC HALL

MAX MILLER, the comedian who was billed as "the cheeky chappie" has died at his home in Burlington Street, Brighton, after a heart illness. He was 68.

Millions remember Max Miller in florid silk plus-fours. With a wink and a glance halfway between a leer and candid stare, he would launch on the syle of patter which he kept up throughout a lifetime on the stage.

THE HARD WAY

The comedian, whose real name was Thomas Henry Sargent, started in show business the hard way. He joined a circus as a youngster for half-a-crown a week. Later he stowed away on a liner.

He organised concert parties while serving with the Army in the 1914-18 war, and afterwards he obtained his first engagement at the old Shoreditch music hall.

He built up his reputation at variety theatres throughout the country in the next 20 years, reaching the £1,000 a week class and at one stage being the highest paid music hall comedian. He made several films and many appearances on television and radio. Success in the West End was followed by Royal Command performances.

But he had ups and downs during 40 years on the stage. Once he was banned by the B.B.C.

(May 9)

WAY OF THE WORLD

Public and Private

ONE, perhaps the most deplorable, result of the Profumo scandal is that it has let loose a stupendous flood of moral indignation which, following on the recent flood of pseudo-satire, threatens to knock the country permanently off its balance. Already raucous voices are demanding official investigation into the private lives of politicians as a test of their fitness for public office.

The orgy of self-righteousness we will now have to endure for weeks to come will do nothing to improve the moral standards of any single person in this country. That will certainly not be achieved, if at all, by bellowings from the Press or vapourings from party politicians. It is still one thing that people have to do for themselves, even in the Welfare State.

All that this fashion for moralising will achieve is a confusion of ideas in many minds about what politics should be concerned with and what it should not. A highly dangerous confusion; for it is important to realise that it is not the morals of a War Minister, *qua* War Minister, that matter, but his ability to provide an Army that is fit and able to defend the country.

It is by its fitness to govern, not by the morals of one of its Ministers, that the Conservative party should be judged. Once confound the public and the private sphere and we are on the direct road to the totalitarian State.

(June 11)

Lard Talking

ERIC LARD, who has surged to the top these last few years as one of England's greatest writers, tells me he had practically finished his new novel, "Bogmouth," All that remains

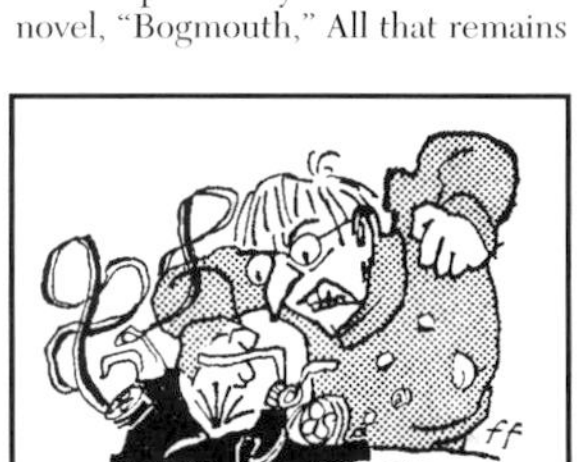

is a little crudifying and insertion of a few extra expletives.

Lard has mellowed a lot since the days when he was an angry, sweatered young controversialist (he drinks champagne now instead of light ale), but he is still a fearless critic of the Establishments ready to sneer witheringly at the Church of England or the Royal Family at the drop of a cheque book.

"I think the one absolutely vital thing, if we are to get anywhere," Lard told me, "is to talk and write about sex and race the whole time, until consciousness of our revolutionary human condition penetrates the minds even of two-year-old children. That is the best way of breaking up the disgusting, Establishment-ridden pattern of life in Britain to-day, with its outmoded morality and middle-class values."

"What do you want to put in its place?" I asked. Lard did not answer; he had caught sight of his own reflection in a mirror and his expression hardened into a ferocious yet complacent smile.

"Bogmouth" is one of his most ambitious works so far, a vast, storm-infested study of racial tension in a seaside town full of beatniks, out of work Negroes, retired people and what Lard wittily calls" — Tories."

(October 17)

He Spared Us This

THE M.P.'s had better be careful going on about Rachman. It was only out of the goodness of his heart that he let them stay in the House of Commons. He could have made twice as much out of it by converting it into a plastic gnomes factory.

(July 23)

Peter Simple

Knock-out Cup Final

SUSSEX WIN COMPLETES CHAPTER OF HISTORY

Worcestershire merit praise for well-balanced approach

By E.W. SWANTON

A NEW chapter of cricket history was given an exciting and altogether worthy climax at Lord's on Saturday. Sussex won the first Knock-out Cup and all credit to them; but credit, too, in fully equal portion for Worcestershire, who over the seven hours of the game fought an even fight and lost finally with a mere over and four balls to go, by 14 runs.

Where so much has been mediocre this summer, and the weather most of all, it is almost miraculous that both the Test series and this experimental competition should have passed off so well.

Often during Saturday's play one feared that the rain or the light or both would necessitate the game dragging on until this morning.

The atmosphere could not have been recaptured. However, though Sussex had a wet ball for their last seven or eight overs and Worcestershire a shocking batting light, the umpires were never called upon to make what would have been an unpalatable and highly unpopular decision.

Perhaps on a cold analysis the luck more or less evened out, for the pitch, which never flattered stroke-making, seemed to grow somewhat easier for batting as it dried. Runs always had to be earned against generally accurate bowling and a uniformly high fielding standard.

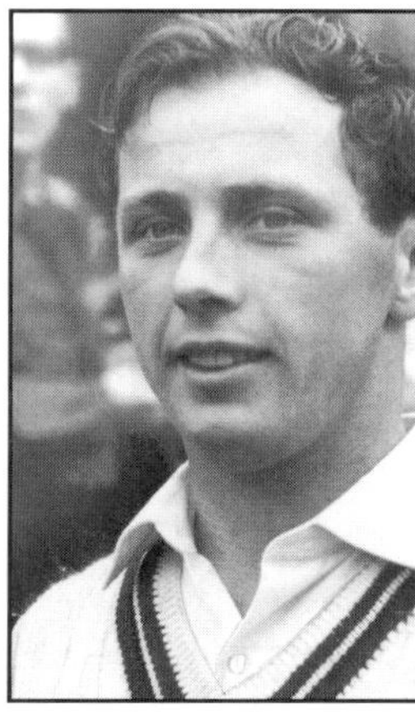

NORMAN GIFFORD

NO GIMMICK

Enjoyable day

In the broad aspect this no doubt is to the good. Nothing is better to see than the ball hit hard and often when the conditions allow; but this "instant cricket" is very far from being a gimmick and there is a place in it for all the arts of cricket, most of which are subtle ones.

That is why the day was so enjoyable, not only for the patriots with their banners and their rosettes "up for the Cup," but for the practising cricketers, past and present, of all ages and types, who seemed to form the bulk of the crowd.

Everyone seemed to be "with it," and the only regret perhaps was that the weather uncertainty decided MCC (reasonably enough) against allowing in the extra 5,000 who could otherwise have been accommodated on the grass.

I say one regret, but it could be remarked by anyone looking objectively on the scene as it reflected county cricket in 1963, that it would have been preferable for victory to have gone to the side with a balanced attack (conspicuously well organised and handled by Kenyon) rather than to a lopsided array of fastish and medium-paced bowlers, all individually admirable, such as enmasse make the modern game so dull and stereotyped to watch.

The Scoreboard

SUSSEX

R.J. Langridge, b. Gifford 34
A.S.M. Oakman, c. Slade, b. Gifford.19
K.G. Suttle, b. Gifford 9
°E.R. Dexter, c. Broadbent, b. Horton .3
†J.H. Parks, b. Slade 57
L.J. Lenham, c. Booth, b. Gifford 7
G.C. Cooper, lbw. b. Slade..................0
N.I. Thomson, lbw. b. Flavell 1
A. Buss, c. Booth, b. Carter 3
J.A. Snow, b. Flavell 10
D.L. Bates, not out..............................3
Extras (b. 9, lb. 10, nb. 3) 22
Total 168
Fall or wickets: 1-62, 2-67, 3-76, 4-98, 5-118, 6-123, 7-134, 8-142, 9-157
Bowling: Flavell 1.2-3-31-2; Carter 12-1 39-1; Slade 11-2 23-2; Gifford 15-4 33-4; Horton 8-1 20-1

WORCESTERSHIRE

°D. Kenyon, lbw. b. Buss 1
M.J. Horton, c. and b. Buss 25
R.G.A. Headley, c. Snow b. Bates 25
I.W. Richardson, c. Dexter, b. Oakman 29
D.W. Richardson, c. Parks b. Thomson......3
R.G. Broadbent, c. Bates b. Snow.....11
§ R. Booth not out 33
D.N.F. Slade, b. Buss..........................3
N. Gifford, b. Snow 0
J. A. Flavell, b. Snow 0
R.G. Carter, run out.................... 2
Extras (b. 8, lb 9, nb. 2)................ 19
Total 154
Fall of wickets: 1-7 2-38, 3-80, 4-91, 5-103, 6-128, 7-132, 8-133, 9-133.
Bowling: Thomson 13-2 2-4 35-1; Buss 15-2 39-3; Oakman 13-4. 17-1; Suttle 5-2 11-0; Bates 9-2 20-1; Snow 8-0 13-3.
Umpires: F.C. Gardner & F.S. Lee

(September 9)

MISS SMITH EARNS FIRST TITLE FOR AUSTRALIA

MARGARET SMITH, the most athletic woman ever to grace the courts, took the women's singles crown in the belated finish to the lawn tennis championships here today. In 50 minutes she beat the American Billie-Jean Moffitt 6-3, 6-4 and an Australian name is now, for the first time, on the roll of singles champions.

In eight days' time Miss Smith will be 21, and her two previous Wimbledons, when she was a failure as a favourite, tends to make one forget how much she has accomplished.

Four times singles champion of Australia, twice champion of Italy, once of France, once of America and now of Wimbledon, this is a record that can be matched with the great players of the past.

No one, though, will think of the doughty Miss Smith in the same context as players like Maureen Connolly or Helen Wills Moody. Althea Gibson and Alice Marble are her predecessors in style, in the adaptation of the masculine technique of service and volley to feminine skill.

The final to-day, which was watched by a full Centre Court and without any sense of anti-climax, must be recorded in masculine terms.

The shots that mattered were service and volley and service returns, for if the bouncing Miss Moffitt is less obviously a trained athlete than Miss Smith, the big guns of lawn tennis are equally as important a part of her technique.

The curious thing about Miss Smith's Wimbledon victory, as was I am told, her winning progress throughout the Australian programme last winter, is that it was taken without her ever playing quite as well as she can.

In to-day's final there were a lot of easy points she cast away for no other reason than her muscles did not obey the dictates of her mind.

(July 9)

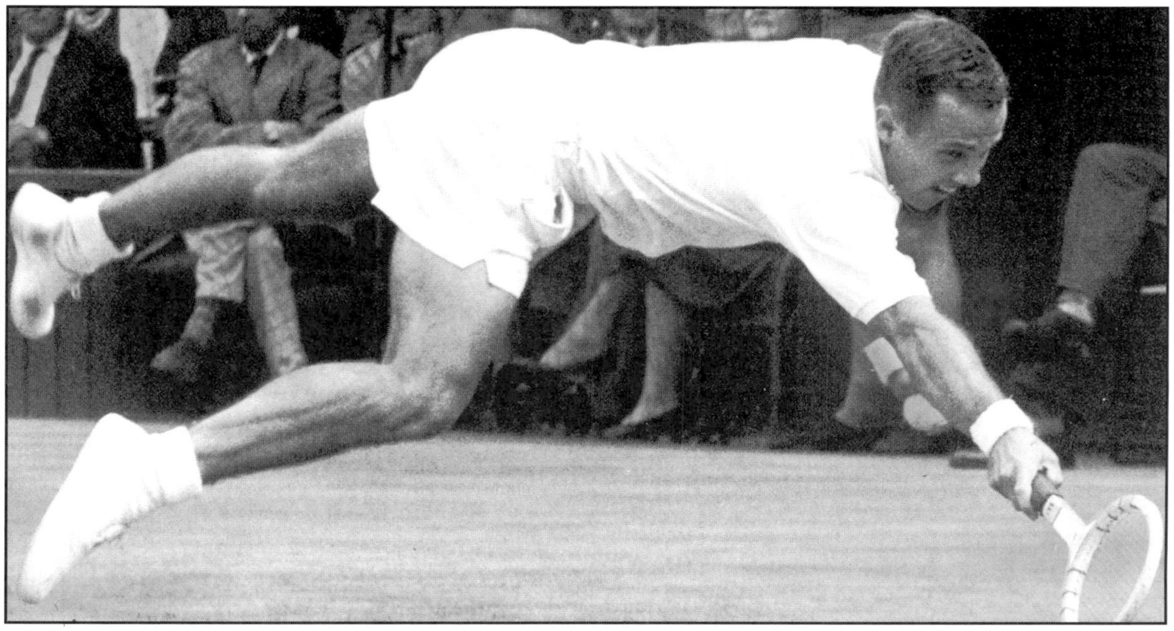

CHUCK MCKINLEY, USA making a full length dive to successfully return a difficult shot from F. Stolle, Australia, during their Men's Single Final match on the Centre Court at Wimbledon, this afternoon.

MCKINLEY'S ACROBATIC SKILLS BEAT STOLLE

From LANCE TINGAY

WIMBLEDON, Friday.

TRADITION was followed and tradition was broken as the flying Missourian, C.R. McKinley, 22, won the men's singles title in the lawn tennis championships to-day by beating F.S. Stolle, of Sydney, 9-7, 6-1, 6-4. Many Americans have preceded McKinley in his distinction, and, in fact, 13 players born in America had won Wimbledon's major title 16 times.

Furthermore, the only two men similarly to have won the singles without the loss of a set (reckoning, of course, from 1922 when the challenge round system was abolished), were Americans, also, J.D. Budge did so in 1938 and M. Trabert in 1955.

McKinley, who was seeded fourth, beat an unseeded man and here, too, tradition was borne out in the unseeded man failing to get a set, though Stolle must be acclaimed as having done as well as any in extending one of the sets to 16 games.

Where McKinley earned himself a distinctive niche in the annals of Wimbledon was in becoming champion without having to meet another seeded player.

Whatever task was set for McKinley by the draw and the seeding committee he accomplished impeccably. There have certainly been greater Wimbledon champions than McKinley but for forthright application of zealous effort he has had few equals, and if energy and acrobatic skill be held as part of a champion's quality he is unique.

McKinley is a student of mathematics at Trinity University, San Antonio, Texas. His facility with figures were, I think, of use to him to-day for there can be no doubt that the greatest contributing cause to his victory was his permutation of service variation.

(July 6)

WEST INDIES 3-1 WIN IS RICHLY DESERVED

From E.W. SWANTON

THE OVAL, Monday.

WEST INDIES cricket to-day had its finest hour since the great victories of 1950. That was a "first time" and so has a special place in history. But in 1950 England were weak. Now whatever faults can be found in Dexter's side he has just returned from fighting a drawn series in Australia.

England have been beaten only twice in nine years in a rubber on their own grounds. The West Indies have won by three matches to one: a richly deserved win and they can fairly claim at this moment, pending the visit of the Australians to their islands in the spring of 1965, that they are the best-equipped and most powerful side in the world.

Frank Worrell leaves the scene to-night a figure of dignity and charm and withal a great leader of whom Barbados, the island of his birth, and Jamaica, that of his adoption, may be equally proud.

I have not known a better series than this in an experience going back now, it is rather sad to think, a quarter of a century. Nor have I known, looking round all the Test-playing countries, a better captain.

If there is one lesson in this game other than the need for an overhaul of English batting technique it is that on the sort of good lasting wickets Test matches ought to be played on the captain needs a complete attack and that, of course, includes a leg-spin bowler.

At the end, the players were engulfed in such a scene of enthusiasm as even the ancient Oval has never known. The England captain needed a good five minutes to force his way through a crowd of thousands.

The gates were closed to-day, which meant that 97,550 people saw the game and paid more than £42,000 for the privilege.

(August 27)

THREE FOOTBALLERS ARE SUSPENDED FOR LIFE

THE Football Association Commission yesterday permanently suspended three players who were recently fined on bribery charges. The Commission was set up to investigate claims of bribery among Football League players.

The men are ESMOND MILLION, goalkeeper, KEITH WILLIAMS, inside forward, of Bristol Rovers and BRIAN PHILLIPS, centre-half, of Mansfield Town. The case arose from a Third Division game between Bristol Rovers and Bradford on April 20.

The penalty imposed by the Commission, sitting in Birmingham, was the maximum. The men are suspended for life from football and football management.

Last month at Doncaster Millison was fined £100 and Williams and Phillips £50 when they pleaded guilty to bribery summonses.

In a statement yesterday Mr. Denis Follows, secretary of the Football Association, said the Commission took a serious view of the situation revealed.

(August 16)

ENGLAND SCALE HEIGHTS AND BEAT THE WORLD

Greaves caps brilliant display by scoring winning goal

By DONALD SAUNDERS

England .... 2, Rest of the World 1
Paine, Greaves Law
£89,000 100,000

ELEVEN English footballers gave the FA the most suitable of 100th birthday presents at Wembley yesterday by scoring a well-merited victory over the greatest 16 players FIFA could gather together from the rest of the soccer world.

A brillian old-fashioned dribble by Charlton which led to a well-taken goal by Greaves three minutes from time clinched England's triumph, just when it seemed that the Rest of the World were going to spoil this memorable occasion by scrambling an undeserved draw.

Let me say at once that this was a better match than I had expected. It might have been even better had FIFA not decided to send on five substitutes in the second half.

Possibly England would not have won had the Rest of the World's first XI played throughout. But the tension, the keen competitive spirit on which top class football thrives, would have been maintained to the end.

MORE EXCITING

Battle of wits

Against that it must be admitted that the game became, at least for Englishmen, more exciting after the interval when Alf Ramsey's men gained ascendancy over opponents who had lost their early rhythm.

For 45 minutes this was an absorbing battle of wits to delight the soccer student. We saw 11 great footballers from all parts of FIFA's far-flung empire trying to blend their superb individual artistry into match-winning harmony while England, not yet themselves as smooth a machine as they would wish, fought equally hard to destroy them.

At half-time the outcome was still in the balance Then, as their colleagues refreshed themselves in the dressing-room, the world's five reserves limbered up on the pitch ready to take over.

Right to the end I hoped FIFA might change their mind and use only 11 players. But as the two teams returned from the tunnel we saw that Yashin, Djalma Santos, Masopust and Eusebio were missing.

ENGLAND - Banks (Leicester); Armfield (Blackpool, capt.); Wilson (Huddersfield); Milne (Liverpool); Norman (Spurs); Moore (West Ham); Paine (Southampton); Greaves, R. Smith (Spurs); Eastman (Arsenal); Charlton (Manchester Utd.).

REST OF THE WORLD - Yashin (Russia); D. Santon (Brazil); Popluhar (Czechoslovakia);Schnelinger (W. Germany); Pluskal, Masopust (Czechoslovakia); Kopa (France); Law (Scotland); D. Stefano (Spain, capt.); Kumble (Portugal); Genta (Spain).

SECOND-HALF SUBSTITUTES - Soskic (Jugoslavia, goal); Eymguirre (Chile, right-back); Baster (Scotland, left-half); Seeler (W. Germany, right-wing); Puskas (Hungary, inside-left).

Referee - R. Davidson (Scotland).

(October 24)

EVERTON FACE EUROPE

NOW that Everton have won the League Championship for the first time since 1939, the city of Liverpool, one of the last English bastions of soccer fanaticism, can look forward to seeing next season the cream of Europe's footballers.

Everton, a businesslike methodical and progressive club, thoroughly deserve their prize. Their consistency on the pitch has been matched by the singleness of purpose shown by their board and their manager.

John Moores, a self-made, rich industrialist, may not be everyone's idea of what the ideal football club chairman should be.

His hard-headed businessman's approach to soccer has from time to time upset those who have been associated rather longer with what they still like to think is a sport.

But Mr. Moore's realistic methods have brought results and must now command respect. Many an industrialist, flirting with the game, has poured thousands of pounds into a club and achieved nothing but disappointment. Mr. Moores has made sure that his money has been wisely spent.

TALENT CORNERED

Assessing players

For this he can thank Harry Catterick, the former Everton player who was called back to Goodison from Sheffield Wednesday, where he had built a reputation as a tough, shrewd team manager.

Mr. Catterick's skilled assessment of a player and Mr. Moores's open cheque-book between them enabled Everton to corner some of the best English, Scottish, Irish and Welsh talent available.

But buying a collection of stars does not guarantee success. Each man must be the right one for a particular job and all must be matured into a team.

Mr. Catterick rarely picked wrongly. Mr. Moores never failed to produce the cheque when his manager explained what position needed strengthening, what player could do it and what the price would be.

(May 13)

CLAY DEFEATS COOPER IN FIFTH - AS PREDICTED

British champion's cut eye sours victory for 'Louisville Lip'

By DONALD SAUNDERS

CASSIUS CLAY, the Louisville Lip, added another accurate prediction to his long list at Wembley Stadium last night, when he stopped Henry Cooper, the British heavyweight champion, in the fifth round, just as he said he would.

But victory did not come in quite the fashion the young American had expected. Tommy Little, the referee, was forced to intervene midway through the round, because blood was streaming from cuts over Cooper's so-often-injured left eye.

And a few minutes earlier, Clay had looked anything but "the greatest" as he landed in an untidy heap on the canvas after taking a left hook flush in the jaw.

The cocksure American, taking one chance too many, had walked into that punch in the dying seconds of the fourth round.

He slumped to the boards and came to a rest with his head against the bottom rope. The roar of the crowd prevented even those of us at the ringside hearing the bell. At all events, Mr. Little continued the count under the new rule, until Clay heaved himself up at five, and walked poker-faced to his corner.

INTERVAL ENIGMA

Escaping the onslaught

What might have happened had the round not ended then no one can say. Clay looked more surprised than hurt, but who knows what might have been the outcome had he been obliged to meet the full fury of Cooper instead of being able to walk to the safety of his stool?

In my view, Clay could have finished this fight in the third or fourth round, but instead kept things going so that he could stupidly hold up his five fingers triumphantly for the cameramen later.

As it happened, he got away with it, but perhaps when tempted henceforth he will remember the end of that fourth round against Cooper, and wonder whether the bell will always toll in his favour.

But let us now turn away from the future and go back over those five memorable rounds.

No one on this blustery, chilly night could accuse Cooper of being worried. The British champion has not for years made so aggressive a start.

He charged forward repeatedly trying to nail the poker-faced Clay with his left hook. Sometimes he got through, sometimes he missed badly, but never could he persuade his opponent that he was a potential menace.

BLOOD TRICKLE

Seconds' work in vain

Then, as Cooper walked back to his corner at the end of the round blood began to trickle from a cut over his left eye. Despite urgent attention during the interval, that trickle changed into a stream early in the third.

Clay, more and more confident with every second, just punched when and where he chose.

I thought it might end in the fourth when Clay once or twice cut loose with both hands. But then the "Louisville Lip" remembered that he was supposed to be the greatest and pranced contemptuously in front of the half-blinded Cooper.

Desperately Cooper let go a left hook and a split second later Clay, now looking like a spanked child, was sitting wide-eyed against the ropes.

But any hopes we had that Clay might have overstepped the mark ended when he walked off to his stool. A minute later he came storming out of his corner, tore into his opponent with both hands, and as blood spurted from perhaps the worst eye injury Cooper has ever suffered, Mr. Little had no alternative but to step between them.

(June 19)

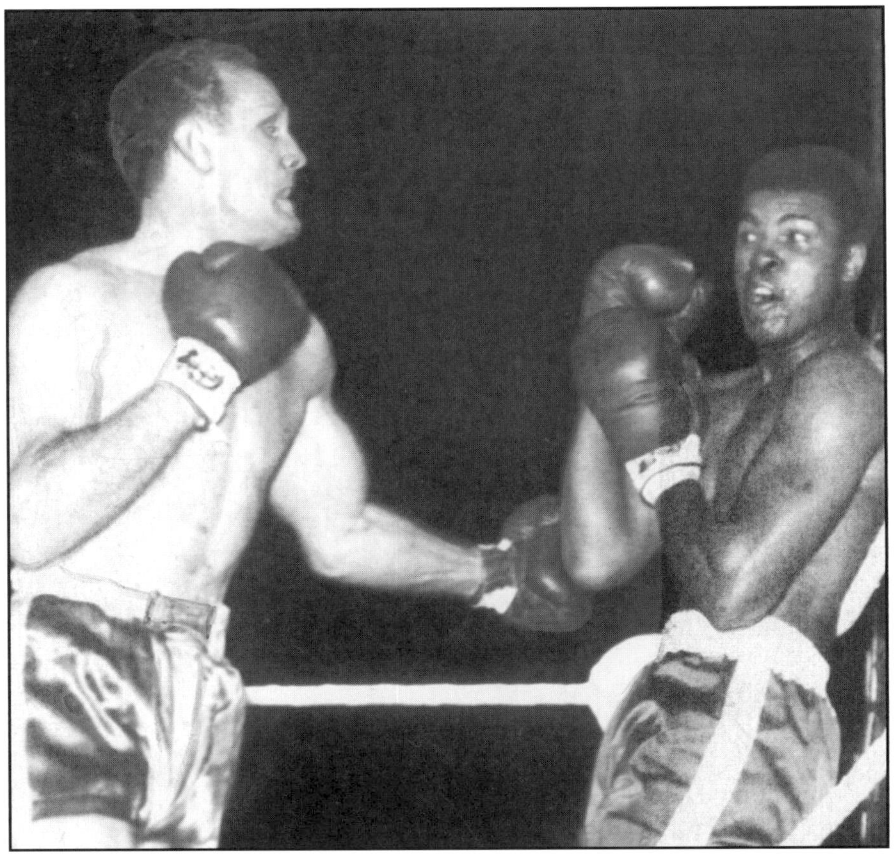

CLAY, IN TROUBLE, covers up on the ropes against Cooper's two-fisted attack in the first round at Wembley last night.

AMERICANS HIT BACK TO SWAMP BRITAIN 20-6

From LEONARD CRAWLEY

ATLANTA, Georgia, Sunday.

THE United States retained the Ryder Cup here this evening by the overall margin of 20 matches to six with six halved in the 15th contest between the two countries.

The British Isles won four matches, lost three and halved one in the morning singles; but in the afternoon play followed very much the same pattern as it had on the first two days and all Britain succeeded in doing was to get one halved match out of eight.

It would be quite wrong to pretend that the hot sunshine in the afternoons had anything to do with the result for the British men were all fit and ready for the fray.

The feature of the morning's play was the defeat of the three greatest American players - Arnold Palmer by Peter Alliss, Julius Boros, the American Open champion, by Harry Weetman, and Dow Finsterwald by Bernard Hunt - all on the last green.

It strikes me that the merit of the Britons' morning victories was that they played their game against players with a colossal reputation and of unquestionably far greater skill.

Each match in its way was a classic, but naturally one chooses the victory of Alliss over Palmer as the best of the day. The two had met in the Ryder Cup match at Royal Lytham two years ago, when they finished all square, after Palmer - if I remember rightly - had holed a bunker shot at the 15th and Alliss had saved himself at the 18th with a pitch and putt.

Alliss to-day finished heroically. Having got an early advantage, Palmer, who has the capacity to produce wonderful figures at exactly the right moment, did so once again, but Alliss refused to let him go.

(October 14)

WORLD 440-YDS RECORD GOES

ADOLPH PLUMMER and Ulis Williams, the American university students who are the biggest threat to Robbie Brightwell in his quest for a gold medal at next year's Olympics in Tokyo, shattered the world 440yds record in Tempe, Arizona, writes James Coote.

Plummer, of New Mexico University, won in 44.9sec. which is four-fifths of a second faster than Glenn Davis's time of 1957, one of the oldest records. Williams, of Arizona State, took second place in 45.6sec.

The world pole vault record was beaten in Modesto, California, for the fifth time this season when Brian Sternberg (Washington University) regained it from John Pennel, the American serviceman, with 16ft 7in, one quarter-of-an-inch higher than the previous best.

(May 27)

JIM CLARK WINS BELGIAN GRAND PRIX

From Our Special Correspondent

FRANCORCHAMPS, Belgium, Sunday.

JIM CLARK, 27, the Scottish farmer, had a remarkable win in the Belgian Grand Prix on the world's fastest race circuit at Francorchamps to-day. The race ended in chaos after a thunderstorm had flooded the circuit.

Clark, in a Lotus Climax, had built up a lead of nearly three minutes over the American Dan Gurney (Brabham Climax) when torrential rain forced the cars to travel at less than half speed. In the confusion Bruce McLaren (Cooper Climax) snatched second place from Gurney.

Only six cars were still running at the end of the race. Clark had lapped every driver except McLaren.

Fifteen minutes before the end Colin Chapman, the Lotus chief and BRM officials appealed to the organisers to terminate the race, leaving the drivers to keep their existing positions.

They pointed out that it had been in progress for 15 minutes longer than the minimum period specified for World Championship Grand Prix under international regulations. But as the rain then eased off the race officials decided to allow the drivers to complete the 32 laps.

(June 10)

BRITAIN ARE CHAMPIONS

DAVIS CUP WIN

By LANCE TINGAY

Btitain became European tennis champions yesterday by beating Sweden 3-2 in the Davis Cup European Zone final at Wimbledon. M.J. Sangster beat U. Schmidt 7-5, 6-2, 9-11, 3-6, 6-3 to clinch the win. Britain won the European Zone final in 1933.

There were 274 games in the tie, the greatest number ever played in the Davis Cup.

Two Inter-Zone finals need to be won before Britain can challenge Australia for the Davis Cup itself. The first of these finals will be against the American Zone winners, expected to be either Mexico or the United States.

(August 6)

SHARP & WILLCOX GIVE ENGLAND TITLE

By TONY GOODRIDGE

England 10pts, Scotland 8

A CROWD of about 70,000 which included the Prime Minister, to whom the teams were introduced before the start, saw England, eight points down after 15 minutes play, beat Scotland in the Calcutta Cup match at Twickenham on Saturday by two goals to a goal and a dropped goal.

So England became outright international champions for the first time since 1958. After this last hardly acquired but intensely exciting victory, the distinction of being champions becomes them well.

In all but the score Scotland must share to the full the honours of this match which did so much to restore one's confidence in the game and those who play it at this high level.

This was a thoroughly satisfying game. The sense of purpose of both sides was always apparent and at no point was a fear of losing allowed to obscure the picture. It was a battle of movement, fast and furious, but splendidly clean and well fought.

That it ran as it did was a credit to those taking part and to the referee, Gwynne Walters, whose feeling for the manner of the game contributed to its success in no small measure.

England's defensive covering has proved itself time and again this season but it surely has not been so tested as it was by Scotland at the start of the game. For 20 minutes they set such a scorching pace that England were at full stretch to keep them in some sort of control.

Then as England began to reply in kind, the position largely righted itself although the Scots, with a splendid tenacity, had England defending for all they were worth again at the end.

Behind the England forwards, the deceptively quick acceleration of Phillips, the ability of Jackson to manoeuvre in the most minute space - sometimes it even seemed in no space at all - was splendid to watch. At stand-off Sharp had a rough trip at the start but then, standing, it seemed, a little deeper his old flair appeared and with it the scoring of a memorable try.

To Willcox at full-back goes every credit. His fielding and touch-finding were immaculate, often under great difficulty and his conversion of the first of the two tries was a magnificent effort into a heavy enough wind almost from the touch line.

Those of the forwards, such as Rogers, Manley and Perry, who always make their presence felt, did so once again and so indeed did Davies, who deputised with great success for T.A. Pargetter. Godwin and Judd amply justified their recall in both tight and loose.

(March 18)

SUPERB OXFORD JUSTIFY TENNANT'S DECISION

By DESMOND HILL

NO man played a greater part in Oxford's victory in the 109th Boat Race than the president, T.W. Tennant, who, seeing victory within reach a fortnight earlier, stood down to ensure that his own loss of form should not prejudice his crew's chance.

Credit, all too seldom paid, must go also to Oxford's finishing coach, Anthony Rowe, who, in three short weeks transformed a sadly bewildered crew into a confident fighting force, which was absolutely right "on the day."

All oarsmen row above their form when their race is won and a tour de force in the cox's seat often passes unnoticed. This would do grave injustice to Strong, whose resolution above Harrods turned possibility into certainty in the space of a few seconds.

"O thou of little faith, wherefore didst thou doubt?" All the evidence of the past three weeks showed that if Oxford could maintain sufficient pressure after the first 1 1/2 miles their greater strength would prevail over a lightweight Cambridge whose timing had always been suspect.

The question remained: what would constitute sufficient pressure? Throughout practice Oxford had been unaccountably slow off the start. Many of their humiliations by their second crew stemmed entirely from this one failing.

Cambridge for all their self-confidence, must have been conscious of their own weaknesses. No boxer, particularly if his strength is suspect, willingly goes the full 13 rounds if he can end the fight with an early knockout. On this early knockout Cambridge staked their all and in seeking it they destroyed themselves. The race was lost and won in the second minute.

(March 25)

DERBY SUCCESS FOR RELKO

Sixth French win since the war

Daily Telegraph Reporter

THE French gained their sixth Derby success since the war at Epsom yesterday when the 5-1 favourite Relko, owned by M. Francois Dupre, 74, a Paris hotel owner, won by six lengths. Relko was the first favourite to win since Crepello in 1957.

The English-trained Merchant Venturer, 18-1, ridden by Greville Starkey was second, with the Irish-trained Ragusa at 25-1, three lengths further away, third. The race, worth £35,338 to the winner, was a triumph for the youngest rider, the French jockey Yves Saint-Martin, 21, who was having his second ride in the Derby.

OWNER'S ILLNESS

Relko, trained at Chantilly by Francois Mather, was led into the winning enclosure by Mme. Anna Dupre. Her husband, who has been suffering from a slight stroke, was unable to fly over, but heard the race over the radio.

Mme. Dupre and Relko's trainer were congratulated by the Queen who saw her own horse Aubusson win the St. James's Stakes.

Carrying the gold trophy worth £500, Mme. Dupre left immediately for Paris. When I asked her if she had had a bet on her horse she replied "No I never bet and neither does my husband."

IN OAKS DOUBLE

Mr. William Hill, the bookmaker said "Relko is coupled in big doubles with Noblesse, which runs in the Oaks on Friday. If the filly wins we stand to lose £51,000."

There was a record Derby Day Tote turnover of £284,665, compared with the previous high figure of £245,046 in 1961.

Mr. Peter Digby, of Ongar, Essex, won £21,000. This was the first prize in the Stock Exchange Derby draw. Mr. Digby had the ticket given to him. He is married and has two young children.

(May 30)

NO-BALLING OF MECKIFF ENDS TEST CAREER

By E.W. SWANTON

THE no-balling of Meckiff at Brisbane, which has certainly brought his Test career to an end, is the most significant happening in the campaign against unfair bowling to which all the Test countries pledged support at the Imperial Cricket Conference of 1960.

He is the first man since to have been no-balled in Test cricket. More than that, he is the first Australian to have been called for throwing in any Test anywhere in the world since the celebrated Jim Phillips made a single call against Ernest Jones at Melbourne in 1898: the second only in their history of 266 Test matches, and, let it be hoped, the last.

The cynic may say that the fact of the umpire and Australia's captain being booed and the bowler carried from the field as if in triumph is an eloquent commentary on the modern spectator attitude to big sport.

The whole affair has certainly done no good to Australia's sporting reputation, but for that matter many in the Lord's crowd made a hero of the unhappy Griffin.

When Lock was no-balled by F. Price at the Oval some of my fellow members of Surrey disgraced themselves by booing the umpire. These embarassing occasions are apt to bring the worst out of many people. As for the Brisbane spectators, they are not greatly renowned for their knowledge of the game.

(December 9)

ABOVE: THE BEATLES "POP" GROUP standing in a crowd of 1,500 which greeted them at London Airport yesterday when they returned from Stockholm.

A DARK CLOUD OF SMOKE HANGING above the volcano of Agung, in Bali, which erupted this week, killing about 1,000 people, according to Indonesian Government officials, and causing the evacuation of 250,000 from the area.

ABOVE: JOHN KENNEDY JNR., who was three yesterday, saluting his father's coffin.

BELOW: RICHARD BURTON, the actor, wearing a patch over his eye yesterday. Mr. Burton suffered a black eye during a fracas at Paddington Station on Saturday as he returned from watching the Wales versus England Rugby international.

LOSING A GRIP ON THINGS is Rohan Kanhai, the West Indies batsman, at Lord's yesterday as he drove a ball from D. Bennett, the Middlesex bowler, but saw his bat go flying into the air as well. Kanhai made four runs before he was out l.b.w. to Bennett.

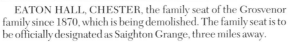

EATON HALL, CHESTER, the family seat of the Grosvenor family since 1870, which is being demolished. The family seat is to be officially designated as Saighton Grange, three miles away.

BELOW: THE GREEK-OWNED CRUISE LINER LAKONIA, 20,238 tons, ablaze in the Atlantic yesterday 180 miles north of Madeira.

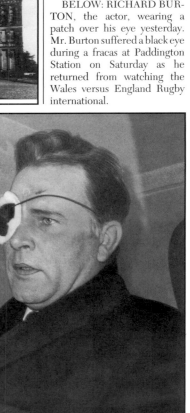

1964

This was the year of the first British television election. It was generally believed that the skull-like head and blank stare through half-glasses of Sir Alec Douglas-Home, the out-going Prime Minister, cost him votes when his performance was compared with that of Harold Wilson, the Labour leader, whose confidence in front of the cameras and general mateyness encouraged voters to believe in him. Even so, it was a close-run thing with the Labour party taking over with a majority of five votes. The new government was immediately faced with a financial crisis. A run on the pound necessitated not only an emergency budget with heavy increases of taxes but the plea for a rescue effort from the International Monetary Fund.

Newspaper editors were, on the night of the general election, faced with a dilemma: should the "lead" of the paper be the prospect of a Labour victory (the actual result would not be clear until the next day) or should it give the main emphasis to the sudden removal of Nikita Khrushchev from office? *The Daily Telegraph* opted for the election but the Russian events shared the front page, both stories being given a three-column headline.

The other problem facing Mr. Wilson was the prospect of Southern Rhodesia, under the leadership of its new Prime Minister Ian Smith, deciding on a Unilateral Declaration of Independence. The first shots of a long-running diplomatic campaign were fired.

By contrast with the British election, Lyndon Johnson was re-elected to the Presidency of the United States in a landslide. His hawkish opponent, Senator Goldwater, who advocated the bombing of North Vietnam cities, was rejected by the electorate, increasingly concerned with the nation's involvement in the fighting in the Far East.

Riots, as they were to continue to be called throughout the rest of the decade, became a fact of life on both sides of the Atlantic. On British bank holidays Mods and Rockers fought bloody battles between themselves, involving ever-increasing numbers of police. The streets of Harlem in New York were full of rampaging mobs. Against the background of these disorders, *The Daily Telegraph* received an unprecedented number of letters; some, perhaps predictably, called for the re-introduction of the birch. By contrast, the House of Commons, in a free vote, passed a private member's bill abolishing the death penalty.

The 400th anniversary of the birth of William Shakespeare was widely celebrated, not least by the 12-hour long presentation on one day of five of the Bard's historical plays under the general title of "The War of the Roses". Laurence Olivier made his debut at the National Theatre, of which he was in charge, in the title role in *Othello*.

Among those who died during the year were Pandit Nehru, the Indian Prime Minister, General Douglas MacArthur, the controversial defender of the Philippines in the Second World War who was a decade later spectacularly fired from his command of the United Nations forces in Korea by President Truman, the newspaper tycoon Lord Beaverbrook and the first woman to take her seat in the House of Commons, Lady Astor.

The Olympic Games in Japan proved the most successful for Great Britain for many a year, including the gold medals in both men's and women's long jump and the first Olympic medal (a silver one) in men's swimming since 1924. Scobie Breasley won his first Epsom Derby at the age of 50.

The Daily Telegraph
and Morning Post

No. 34055 LONDON, SATURDAY, OCTOBER 27, 1964   Printed in LONDON and MANCHESTER Price 3d.

Labour majority of 4

WILSON NAMES SIX IN HIS CABINET

BROWN AS ECONOMIC AFFAIRS CHIEF

GORDON WALKER AT FOREIGN OFFICE

HEALEY FOR DEFENCE

MR. WILSON named six Cabinet Ministers and a Chief Whip last night within a few hours of becoming Prime Minister. Labour's final overall majority in the Commons is expected to be four.

The seven appointed, with their ages and salaries (including their M.P.'s pay) and holders of office in the Conservative Government are:

FIRST SECRETARY OF STATE AND MINISTER FOR ECONOMIC AFFAIRS,
MR. GEORGE BROWN, 50, £5,570   (new post)

FOREIGN SECRETARY,
MR. PATRICK GORDON WALKER, 57, £5,750 (Mr. R.A. Butler)

LORD PRESIDENT OF THE COUNCIL,
MR. HERBERT BOWDEN, 59, £5,750 (Mr Quintin Hogg)
Mr. Bowden will also be Leader of the House

LORD CHANCELLOR,
LORD GARDINER, Q.C., 64, £12,000 (Lord Dilhorne)

CHANCELLOR OF THE EXCHEQUER,
MR. JAMES CALLAGHAN, 52, £5,750 (Mr. Reginald Maudling)

SECRETARY FOR DEFENCE,
MR. DENIS HEALEY, 47, £5,750 (Mr. Thorneycroft)

CHIEF WHIP,
MR. EDWARD WATSON SHORT, 52, £4,500 (Mr. Martin Redmayne)

Lord Gardiner, Mr. Callaghan, Mr. Healey and Mr. Short have all been made Privy Councillors.

Mr. Wilson's salary as Prime Minister and First Lord of the Treasury is £10,000, of which £4,000 is tax free.

COMMONS SEAT NEEDED

A seat in the Commons will have to be found for Mr. Gordon Walker, who was defeated by the Conservative at Smethwick.

State of the parties, with one result (Argyll, expected to stay Conservative) to come:

	Gains	Losses	Seats	Majority over Cons.	Overall Maj.
Conservatives ...	5	61	303	-	-
Labour ...	61	5	317	14	5
Liberals ...	4	2	9	-	-

The Conservative total includes Mr. Speaker who does not vote and stood as an Independent.

FOUR LIBERAL GAINS

Fourteen seats changed hands in yesterday's declarations. Labour gained nine from the Conservatives and lost one, Norfolk South-West, to them. The Labour gains were:

Brighton, Kemptown, Buckingham, Cleveland, Derbyshire South-East, Dover, Ealing North, Epping, King's Lynn and Meriden.

The Liberals gained Bodmin, Ross and Cromarty and Inverness from the Conservatives and Caithness and Sutherland from Independent.

There will be nine Liberal M.P.'s in the new Parliament, two more than in the last one and the highest number since 1950. No other election since the war has given the Liberals more M.P.s than they had at the Dissolution.

MAJORITY ASSURED

Labour had to wait until 4 p.m. for the certainty of an overall majority, when by holding Penistone they secured their 316th seat.

At 3.22 Sir Alec Douglas-Home left 10, Downing Street for Buckingham Palace to tender his resignation as Prime Minister. He left the Palace at 3.42.

Mr. Wilson arrived at the Palace from Transport House at 4.4 in answer to a summons from the Queen. He kissed hands on his appointment as Prime Minister and left for Downing Street at 4.24.

On the steps of No. 10 Mr. Wilson, after pledging that his Government would do everything it could in the country's best interests, began his "first 100 days" with a warning that "We are facing at this time very great problems. But there is nothing we cannot do together."

(Continued on Back Page, Col. 4)

MR. GEORGE BROWN
(First Secretary of State and Minister for Economic Affairs).

MR. PATRICK GORDON WALKER
(Foreign Secretary)

Late marginals fail to follow national swing
PETER PULZER
Tutor in Politics, Christ Church, Oxford, and an authority on elections

THE outcome was uncertain to the last. It was not until the result from Penistone was announced just after 4 p.m. that Labour finally held the 316 seats necessary to form a Government.

Yet in many ways the battle has been fought and won along the lines generally expected. The seats which mattered were the ones considered marginal on the basis of their 1959 majorities.

For all the population movements which have taken place in the past five years, there is only one seat where the result could be said to have been affected by migration, Putney, which was gained by Labour.

VULNERABLE SEATS
Significant deviations

Throughout the spate of declarations, the swing from Conservative to Labour remained very steadily between three and four per cent, and most of the seats that changed hands were precisely those vulnerable to that swing.

The deviations were few; but it was those deviations which made the difference between the present unsatisfactory parliamentary majority of the Labour party and the lead of 25 to 30 which seemed probable during most of Thursday night.

What made the final phase of the count so agonising was that many more of Labour's failures to capture necessary marginals were occurring yesterday - Lowestoft, Maldon, Bedfordshire South and The Wrekin, for instance - too many to compensate for such surprise Labour victories as Brighton Kemptown or Glasgow Pollok.

Moreover, Labour had extremely bad luck in recounts and lost three seats by majorities of 15 or less.

ASSUMPTIONS FAIL
Percentages of swing

Labour's pitch was queered even more by the strong Conservative tide in the Midlands and East Anglia; three of their four captures occurred in those areas.

Nevertheless, it was generally assumed that Labour could not hope for a majority if the swing remained under four per cent., or unless Labour were at least 2.5 per cent. ahead of the Conservatives in votes.

WILSON'S EARLY START ON CABINET-MAKING

MORE MINISTERS TO-DAY
H.B. BOYNE
Daily Telegraph Political Correspondent

SCARCELY pausing for breath after he had accepted the Queen's invitation to form a Government, Mr. Harold Wilson announced last night the first six members of his Cabinet and the new Chief Whip.

The remainder of the Cabinet, which is to be markedly smaller than Sir Alec Douglas-Home's 23, will be made known to-day. Another list, naming all Ministers in charge of departments, Ministers of State, and Under-Secretaries, will follow to-morrow.

Any loose ends will be tied up next week, and the new Government will be fully manned by the time Parliament meets on Tuesday week for the election of a Speaker and the swearing-in of Members.

There are no surprises in the first instalment of Mr. Wilson's speedy Cabinet-making. The appointments earmarked for Mr. Brown, Mr. Gordon Walker, Mr. Bowden, Lord Gardiner, Mr. Callaghan, Mr. Healey and Mr. Short had been freely forecast.

What is set beyond all doubt is the position of Mr. Brown in the Wilson-dominated hierarchy. He is clearly designated as "No. 2" in the Government, and would have been named as Deputy Prime

(Continued on Back Page, Co. 3)

PROBYN CAUGHT AFTER EAST END RAID
Daily Telegraph Scotland Yard Correspondent

Walter "Angel Face" Probyn, on the run after escaping from Dartmoor, was recaptured in the East End of London last night. A strong squad of policemen, some of them armed, laid an ambush and raided a house in Piggot Street, Limehouse.

There was a scuffle when they burst in and shots were fired. Probyn was injured before being overpowered and taken to hospital. His injuries were said to be not serious.

STOCK MARKETS "SEE-SAW"
Daily Telegraph City Staff

FACED with a Labour victory, stock markets opened on a demoralised note yesterday.

But within an hour bargain-hunters appeared and prices began to rally, with steel and property shares recovering most of their early falls.

By the close the fall in the Financial Times index was limited to 5.4 at 359.5.

Trade gap wider

In its preoccupation with the election outcome the City gave less than usual attention to the September overseas trade figures. These showed a further widening of an already ominous gap between exports and imports.

While exports, on a seasonally adjusted basis, fell last month to £346 million compared with the August total of £370 million, imports showed only a small decline from £479 million to £471 million.

The election result and the September trade figures had their repercussions in the foreign exchange market where the £ came under renewed selling pressure. The rate on New York fell 0⅜ cents to 2.78¼.

City Comment - P2

COLE PORTER

Cole Porter, one of America's greatest composers of popular music died shortly before midnight last night in Santa Monica, California, where he underwent a kidney operation on Tuesday. He was 71.

The youngest Premier since Rosebery
Daily Telegraph Reporter

WHEN Mr. Wilson kissed hands on appointment as First Lord of the Treasury yesterday, he became the youngest Prime Minister since the Earl of Rosebery took office in 1894 at the age of 47.

A council school boy from Yorkshire whose career has been a text book of success, has reached the highest office in the country at the age of 48.

Don at 21

He won his way to Jesus College, Oxford, by scholarships, graduated with first class honours in P P E (politics, philosophy and economics) and became a don at 21. He went on to become a Lecturer in Economics and a Fellow of University College before going to the Ministry of Supply during the war.

He was first elected to the Commons in 1945, and went straight to the Front Bench. As President of the Board of Trade in 1947 he was the youngest Cabinet Minister since William Pitt.

He will move to Downing Street from a four-bedroom semi-detached house in Hampstead Garden Suburb.

LABOUR'S FIRST SUSSEX M.P.

A Labour candidate has been returned in Sussex for the first time. Councillor Dennis Hobden, a G.P.O. catering officer, defeated Mr. David James, in Brighton Kemptown by seven votes, the narrowest majority of the election.

Early yesterday morning, after five recounts ending at 2.45 a.m., the weary tellers were back at work for another two recounts. The final figures were: Hobden, 22,308; James, 22,301.

S. AFRICA ARMS HOPE
Daily Telegraph Staff Correspondent

CAPE TOWN, Friday.

Mr. J. J. Fouche, South African Minister of Defence, said to-day that he did not think the Labour win in Britain "would have an adverse effect" on South Africa's buying arms. He mentioned orders valued at £45 million for which she "could turn to other countries."

Gardners
TRANSFORMERS
FOR ELECTRONICS
GARDENERS TRANSFORMERS LIMITED CHRISTCHURCH HANTS

The Daily Telegraph
and Morning Post

4 A.M.

No. 33925. LONDON, TUESDAY, MAY 19, 1964 — Printed in LONDON and MANCHESTER Price 3d.

EXTRA COVER AGAINST INJURY WITH
Britax
TERYLENE SAFETY BELTS

SEASIDE GANGS IN FRESH CLASHES

76 BRIGHTON ARRESTS: MARGATE STABBINGS

GAOL AND FINES FOR 'SAWDUST CAESARS'

BATTLES between gangs of "Mods" and "Rockers" flared up again on the South Coast yesterday. In Brighton 76 youths were arrested after police had driven about 600 "Mods" out of the centre of the town and several people were hurt in beach brawls.

Skirmishes continued in Margate and two youths were stabbed. Fifty-one arrested in Sunday's Margate clashes were described as "little sawdust Caesars" by the magistrate in imposing fines totalling £1,900, four detention sentences and one of imprisonment. One paid his fine by cheque.

On the warmest Whit Monday for ten years thousands of returning motorists choked roads from the coast yesterday. The AA said that 45,000 vehicles an hour were pouring into London at the peak period last night.

Sixty-seven people died on the roads in the first three days of the Whitsun holiday, Lord Chesham, Parliamentary Secretary, Ministry of Transport, told motor racegoers over the Goodwood loudspeaker yesterday. Later provisional figures said that eight people died yesterday, bringing the total to 75 for the four Whit days.

Pictures - P18; Court Report - P23; Brighton Arrests - Back Page; Editorial Comment - P14

GANG VIOLENCE AGAINST A YOUTH on Margate beach yesterday when "Mods" and "Rockers" renewed their battles in South Coast resorts.

4-DAY DEATH TOLL OF 75

Daily Telegraph Reporter

A SHOCKED Lord Chesham, temporarily in charge at the Ministry of Transport, announced the latest Whitsun road death toll of 67 over loudspeakers to the crowd at Goodwood motor races yesterday. "It is unusual, but I want them all to get home alive to-night," he said to me before the broadcast.

Later provisional figures showed that at least eight people died yesterday, bringing the total for the four Whit days to 75.

Lord Chesham said to the crowd: "I suppose it is by no means impossible that someone listening to me now might be dead by to-night and one or two lying seriously injured in hospital.

"Probably it will be at its worst by to-night. Do me a favour, just don't let it be you."

17 SUNDAY DEATHS
Black Monday feared

Seventeen more people died on the roads up to midnight on Sunday. The 67 deaths for the first three days of the Whitsun holidays are more than double the figure for the same period last year and worse is feared when yesterday's casualties are known.

Sunday's total of 17 full deaths compares with eight on Whit Sunday last year and 11 in 1962. Past experience indicates that Monday is one of the worst days of the Whitsun weekend, with so many cars returning home.

Comparative figures for this year and the last two years are:

	1962	1963	1964
Friday	17	12	22
Saturday	21	13	18
Sunday	11	8	17
	49	33	67

TOLERATION URGED
AA "appalled"

Lord Chesham said last night that Sunday's figures and the total for the week-end showed the vital necessity for enormous care and tolerance in the very difficult conditions of the end of the holiday.

The suggestion of introducing stiffer medical requirements for drivers was interesting and would have to be looked at.

The Automobile Association, while "appalled" at the continuing rise in the Whitsun road deaths compared with previous years, drew a small crumb of comfort from the fact that Sunday's casualties were fewer than those in the first two days of the holiday.

ANALYSIS SOUGHT
Accident factors

It suggested this was particularly significant in view of the fact that road traffic on Sunday was the heaviest ever known. The AA called for a close analysis to establish the true factors that combine to cause accidents.

EARLY START HOME AFTER RAIN THREAT

Daily Telegraph Reporter

BECAUSE storms had been forecast, thousands of holidaymakers left resorts for home early yesterday. "It was one of the earliest starts we can recall," an Automobile Association spokesman said.

After the warmest Whit Monday for 10 years, those who left later found congested roads. The AA said that 45,000 vehicles an hour were pouring into London at the peak period last night.

21-MILE JAM
Lake District congestion

The day's biggest queue was reported to be that between Weston-super-Mare and Bristol. Here, there was a 21-mile traffic jam.

One of the biggest traffic jams known in the Lake District developed at the junction of the A6 and A590. It covered 14 miles. The Southern Region put on more than 100 extra trains and the Midland Region 82 additional long-distance trains. At London Airport 11,000 people watched planes bringing back holidaymakers from the Continent and Channel Islands. Incoming passengers totalled 10,000, a quarter of Friday's outflow.

HELICOPTERS IN WATCH ON FRENCH ROADS

PARIS, Monday.

Nearly two dozen helicopters, with doctors on board, were used in "Operation Survival" mounted by French police to-day to cope with the 1,250,000 Parisians returning to the capital after the Whitsun holiday.

A hundred mobile radio units and 50,000 police controlled traffic, and directed the helicopters to accidents. The injured were flown to hospitals where emergency wards were kept open. Official figures to-night of weekend casualties on the roads were 50 dead.

Trippers see Rockers and Mods searched

By JOHN OSMAN

MARGATE, Monday.

TWO youths were stabbed on the sands at Margate to-day and the buffet at the railway station was attacked as violence continued here for the second successive day.

Following the knifings, thousands of trippers watched police on the seafront search opposing "Mods" and "Rockers."

The youths who were stabbed in separate incidents were Michael Fenton, 20, of Streatham, and Michael Stewart, 17, of the Elephant and Castle. Both were released from Margate Hospital after treatment, their wounds being stitched.

BEATEN UP
Dragged from scooter

William John Moore, 17, was dragged from his scooter in the car park of the Dreamland Amusement Park. He was beaten up and was in hospital receiving treatment to-night.

A fourth youth, who did not go to hospital, was also reported to have received a knife gash.

Trouble began, following yesterday's day-long violence, at 8 a.m. About 200 "Mods" with a sprinkling of "Rockers," came in from the beach, where many spent the night, to meet friends arriving in trains from London.

In the station buffet they smashed three windows and tipped over five tables scattering tea, cakes, crockery and customers.

(Continued on Back Page, Col. 5)

£6M. ORDER WON FOR THREE CARGO LINERS

Daily Telegraph Shipping Staff

Orders worth £6 million for three fully refrigerated cargo liners of 10,000 tons deadweight have been won by the Sunderland shipyard of Bartram and Sons only a month after extending their berths to enable them to build bigger ships.

The orders are from New Zealand Shipping Co. "It means that during the past two years, when orders for ships have been extremely difficult to obtain, we have won orders for 10 ships worth more than £13½ million." Mr. C. McFetrich, a director and secretary of Bartrams, said.

NEUTRALIST FORCES IN LAOS DEFEATED

'CRITICAL,' SAYS PREMIER

Daily Telegraph Diplomatic Staff

INTENSE diplomatic activity is going on behind the scenes in an effort to stave off a new South-east Asian crisis arising from the breakdown, under Communist military attack, of the neutralist forces in Laos.

Reports from Vientiane indicate that the moderate forces of Prince Souvanna Phouma, the Prime Minister, have been almost entirely eliminated, at any rate in the Muong Phanh area in the Plain of Jars. The Prince told a Press conference in Vientiane that the situation was critical.

Pathet Lao and North Vietnamese troops had completely "submerged" the neutralist positions.

The capture of the town of Thathom was proclaimed to-day by the Pathet Lao radio. The town is 90 miles north-east of Vientiane.

Should the Communists continue successfully in their attack, it will undoubtedly mean the end of Prince Souvanna's efforts towards reintegration of the warring factions in his country and the establishment of a united, independent, and neutral Laos.

APPEAL TO PATHET LAO
Britain and Russia

The effect of this would be that Laos would almost inevitably become a part of the anti-guerrilla war which the United States is supporting in South Vietnam.

Yesterday it was stated in Vientiane that Britain, Russia and the International Control Commission were trying to send a delegation to Khang Khay, Central Laos. This would ask Prince Souphanouvong, the Pathet Lao leader, to stop the fighting.

Britain and Russia were co-chairman of the 1962 Geneva con-

(Continued on Back Page, Col. 5)

EXTRA AID FOR S. VIET-NAM SOUGHT

Daily Telegraph Staff Correspondent

WASHINGTON, Monday.

President Johnson to-day asked Congress to add over £44 million to the budget for military and economic aid to South Viet-nam. The House Foreign Affairs Committee immediately called for a hearing on the matter. Congress considers the extra appropriations are necessary.

BACK FROM HOLIDAY TO MANSION FIRE

Daily Telegraph Reporter

A FAMILY returned from holiday in Nice yesterday to find their house at Landhurst, Hartfield, Sussex, on fire. Part of the mansion was destroyed including a child's bedroom.

The fire was at the home of Mr. J. McArthur Rank, nephew of Lord Rank. The alarm was raised by Mrs. Moira Rank's secretary, Mrs. Daphne Hordall.

Mrs. Rank, who returned from holiday with two of her three children, Caroline, 20, and Camilla, 11, said: "The fire was in one half of what we call the nursery wing, which has three storeys. The roof collapsed on one side and three bathrooms and five bedrooms were destroyed. We think the fire started in the boiler room.

PIRATE RADIO PROTEST BY BELGIUM

Daily Telegraph Television and Radio Correspondent

Belgium, which has a law against pirate radio ships, has protested to the British Post Office about interference with their broadcasting service caused by the broadcasts of Radio Caroline off Felixstowe.

The two stations affected are low power Brussels transmitters.

France is expected to protest against interference from the other pirate, Atlanta, with a group of eight synchronised low-power stations.

'Arms without delay' promise by Khruschev

CAIRO, Monday.

MR. KHRUSCHEV said to President Nasser and other Egyptian leaders at a banquet in Cairo tonight: "There will be no delay over arms if they are needed."

Mr. Khruschev made the remark while expressing appreciation for the award of Egypt's highest military order, the Star of Military Honour, to Marshal Andrei Grechko, Soviet First Deputy Defence Minister, who is accompanying Mr. Khruschev on his visit to Egypt.

Aden bases

Mr. Khruschev said: "Undoubtedly the nation which liberated itself from imperialism needs very strong armies to defend its independence.

"The geographical position of the United Arab Republic is a tempting one for aggression. There are still remnants of imperialism, that is, the presence of bases like those in Aden and Cyprus.

"They are there to preserve imperialistic positions in the area. The United Arab Republic will not stand idle but will repulse any aggression against her. We wish her success in her actions."

Khruschev tired

Mr. Khruschev is "very tired" and changes have been made in the programme of his Egyptian tour. A Soviet Embassy spokesman said to-day the programme for to-morrow was being changed. But the Egyptian Information Department said the Port Said visit would go ahead as planned.

Khruschev-Nasser Talks - P21

ISRAEL SEEKS FACTS ON ATTACK BY KHRUSCHEV

Daily Telegraph Correspondent

JERUSALEM, Israel, Monday.

Mrs. Golda Meir, the Israeli Foreign Minister, to-day summoned the Russian Ambassador and asked him to explain the anti-Israeli remarks claimed to have been made by Mr. Khruschev in Egypt.

According to a Cairo report Mr. Khruschev said that he considered Israel to be a menace not only to the Arabs but the whole world.

The report added that Russia and Egypt would serve Israel with an ultimatum to execute the United Nations resolutions on Palestine and discontinue the river Jordan scheme. If Israel did not comply Russia would sever diplomatic relations with her.

6d ON PETROL & 6d ON INCOME TAX

INSURANCE STAMPS UP 5S. 3D. A WEEK

AN increase of 6d in the standard rate of income tax from April 6 next year and an extra 6d a gallon on petrol from six o'clock last night were proposed by Mr. Callaghan, Chancellor of the Exchequer, introducing his autumn Budget yesterday.

The Chancellor also announced increased National Insurance benefits and contributions, effective from March 29 next year, and gave notice of capital gains and corporation taxes to be introduced in the spring. He proposed:

INCOME TAX: Standard rate to rise by 6d to 8s 6d from April 6, 1965. Reduced rates on first £300 of individuals' taxable incomes after personal allowances not affected. Estimated yield in full financial year £122 million.

PETROL DUTY: Increase of 6d a gallon on petrol, light hydro-carbon oils and diesel oil for road vehicles. Effective last night. Yield in 1964-65, £32 million. In full year £93 million. Measure will add one-fifth of a point to the cost of living index which now stands at 107.8.

NATIONAL INSURANCE: Contributions to rise from March 29, 1965, as follows:

EMPLOYED MAN: 2s a week. EMPLOYER: 3s 3d a week
EMPLOYED WOMAN: 1s 9d a week. EMPLOYER: 2s 10d a week.

£6 10s FOR MARRIED COUPLES

PENSION INCREASES: National Insurance and associated benefits to go up from March 29:

SINGLE PEOPLE: By 12s 6d to £4 a week
MARRIED COUPLE: By 21s to £6 10s a week
"TEN SHILLING WIDOWS": By £1 to 30s a week. Affects some 83,000 women married before July 5, 1948, and not eligible for benefits under 1948 Act.

Earnings rule for all widows to be abolished. War pensions and industrial injury benefits to be increased, by £1 to £6 15s for 100 per cent. disability. National Assistance rates up by 12s 6d for single people and 21s for married couples.

The Chancellor also proposed legislation to give effect to the 15 per cent. imports levy and tax incentives to exporters, including rebates on petrol and vehicle licence duty, announced on Oct. 26. Books and periodicals, ships of 80 tons or more and large aircraft exempt from levy.

In a full year the tax changes will produce £415 million, comprising £122 million from income tax, £93 million from petrol duty and £200 million from imports levy. National Insurance and National Assistance improvements, with abolition of prescription charges, will cost £130 million.

Mr. Callaghan said that allowing for the import charges, export rebate and increased petrol duty, the overall deficit next April might now be between £400 and £450 million, against Mr. Maudling's estimated £790 million.

(November 12)

AFTER A JOURNEY of 243,665 miles lasting three days, the United States Ranger VII kept its appointed rendezvous with the moon at 2.25 p.m. yesterday and sent back to the earth the first close-up pictures of the lunar surface.

FIRST CLOSE-UPS OF THE MOON

VINCENT RYDER
Daily Telegraph Staff Correspondent
WASHINGTON, Friday.

MANKIND was given its first close look at the moon to-day. America's Ranger VII spacecraft sent a stream of "superb" pictures in the 13 minutes before it crashed into the moon's surface at 2.25 BST. It landed less than 10 miles from its target after a 243,665 mile journey.

Jubilant scientists at Goldstone tracking station, California, were first to see the pictures. The earliest quick prints looked "exceptionally good," said Mr. Harris Schurmier, manager of the project. The Russian Lunik III took pictures of the moon from 40,000 miles in 1959.

Ranger's six television cameras were still working in the split second before the spacecraft hurtled into the Sea of Clouds at more than 4,000 m.p.h. Altogether the 4,000 pictures cost America about £71 million, mostly spent on previous attempts.

Ranger VII is the fourth man-made object to reach the moon. Of the others, two were American and one Russian.

Until to-day, man had been able to discern nothing smaller on the moon than a quarter of a mile in diameter, and that only in uncertain fashion through telescopes.

Final pictures taken by Ranger are expected to cover an area of a third of a square mile. They should make it possible to see rocks and holes the size of small cars.

1,100-MILE "SHOTS"
Sea of Clouds mystery

The first pictures were taken from a distance of 1,100 miles. Scientists hoped to learn whether the surface in the Sea of Clouds, misnamed by old astronomers deceived by poor telescopes, was a thick layer of dust, a boulderstrewn plain or a smooth, level area.

This will affect the design of the Apollo spacecraft which will carry the first Americans to the moon, probably in 1969 or 1970.

The National Aeronautics and Space Agency refused to be rushed into issuing the first pictures for publication. "We are going to process them with tender, loving care," said Dr. William Pickering, director of the Jet Propulsion Laboratory, which directed the operation.

Ranger did everything asked of it from its launching from Cape Kennedy, Florida, until it hit the moon 68 hours later. Tension mounted in the final minutes as reports on its progress were relayed simultaneously to Washington and to the Jet Propulsion Laboratory headquarters in Pasadena, California.

(August 1)

DOCTORS WATCH FOR DANGER DRUG TABLETS

By Our Health Services Correspondent

Doctors in Britain are on the watch for a new and dangerous drug tablet, thought to be imported, which can cause serious, though temporary, mental trouble, including distressing hallucinations.

The tablets are believed to be a solid form of LSD, lysergic acid diethylemide. They can be obtained in certain clubs and public houses in London and other big cities.

LSD and similar drugs, such as mescaline, have not yet been subjected to any control. At least one death has been reported from self-experimentation with LSD which, it is claimed, heightens the taker's appreciation of life.

The *British Medical Journal* refers to LSD experiments on himself by the late Aldous Huxley, the author. "It is unfortunate," the Journal says, "that he appears to have made the experimental self-dosing with such drugs respectable and slightly daring."

(March 28)

KHRUSCHEV RESIGNS HIS TWO TOP JOBS

JEREMY WOLFENDEN
Daily Telegraph Staff Correspondent
MOSCOW, Thursday.

MR. KHRUSCHEV to-day stepped down from the posts of Prime Minister and First Secretary of the Russian Communist party. He was the first Russian leader to give up the post without a struggle.

Mr. Khruschev said that his decision was due to "increasing age and degenerating health." He is over 70, and he has made a number of exhausting trips abroad in recent months.

At a meeting yesterday of the Central Committee of the Communist party, Leonid Brezhnev, aged 58, a Ukrainian, was elected the new First Secretary of the Communist party. He is the man groomed for the post by Mr. Khruschev himself.

At another meeting to-day, Mr. Alexei Kosygin, formerly First Deputy Prime Minister, took over Mr. Khruschev's post as Prime Minister. He is a 60-year-old economist who has grown in the service first of Stalin and then of Mr. Khruschev.

KHRUSCHEV ERA
Importance for Russia

This is the end of the Khruschev years, which were in their way as important for Russia as the "New Frontier" was for the United States.

For the first time a ruler of Russia, let alone of Communist Russia, went among with the masses and used their own language.

The effect may not always have been what Mr. Khruschev wanted. Many Russians could not stomach this kind of familiarity. Equally Mr. Khruschev sometimes got annoyed with the type of criticism which he received.

The decision to resign seems to have been taken very suddenly, even within the last two days.

Mr. Khruschev was expecting to spend the next month in seclusion in the South, preparing his report for the Central Committee meeting next month, and his campaign against the Chinese Communists.

Whether there was any ideological pressure behind his decision is still not known and will not be known for weeks or months.

But is seems most likely that he had some sudden illness which confirmed his decision to quit.

Recently both Russians and Westerners have been afraid that Mr. Khruschev, with a strenuous 70 years behind him, was driving himself too hard. He was indulging in long and wearing foreign tours which clearly sapped his strength.

The party newspaper Pravda indicated to-day that the party will continue to carry out policies of de-Stallinisation and economic improvements under its new leadership.

(October 16)

Admiralty's flag lowered for last time

By Our Naval Correspondent

THE famous Admiralty flag, which has flown over the Admiralty building in Whitehall since the place was built nearly 240 years ago, was lowered for the last time last night. The Admiralty loses its identity by being merged into the new Defence organisation.

Henceforth the big crimson flag with the gold fouled anchor will rarely be seen. Subservient to the Royal Standard, it will be flown only when the Queen, as Lord High Admiral, is visiting H M ships.

As a signalman slowly lowered the flag on its tall staff above the imposing Admiralty entrace to Horse Guards Parade, the ceremony was watched from a dais by dignatories surrendering their title of Lords Commissioners of the Admiralty.

(April 1)

THREE 'TOPLESS' WOMEN GUILTY OF INDECENCY

WOMEN who wear topless dresses in public are guilty of an act of indecency, it was laid down at Bow Street yesterday when three women were found guilty in the first topless dress cases in Britain.

All three were given conditional discharges for a year because they were test cases. But Mr. A. BABINGTON, the magistrate, gave a warning that the position of any future offenders might be "somewhat different."

Mrs. DIANA GORTON, 28, a Buckinghamshire housewife who was allowed not to disclose her address, pleaded not guilty to a summons under an L C C by-law of 1900 alleging she committed an act of indecency to the annoyance of "residents and passengers" at Westminster Bridge on July 3.

A street photographer, Mr. LEONARD WINTER, 70, of Union Road, South Lambeth, said he had seen nothing like it in his 38 years of taking photographs on the bridge.

He said the woman, wearing a plaid shawl, was walking to the bridge with her husband and a photographer. "Her husband pulled the shawl off her shoulders. She was topless. Nothing on top." The photographer in the party took eight close-up pictures.

In evidence, Mrs. GORTON said she had not wanted to do anything indecent. "I merely wanted to be a trend-setter."

Two sisters, VALERIE MITCHELL, 21, and MARION MITCHELL, 24, cabaret singers, of Holland Park Avenue, Notting Hill, also pleaded not guilty to a similar summons.

Defending, Mr. BASIL WIGODER said the girls were trying to "create an entry." Because the incident was only momentary and at night, he submitted it did not constitute indecency.

Finding them guilty, Mr. BABINGTON said: "I think a considerable number of people would be annoyed by the sight of a woman in a topless dress. I find that what you did constitutes an act of indecency."

(August 22)

PIRATE RADIO SHIPS JOIN FORCES

By Our TV and Radio Correspondent

Caroline and Atlanta, the two pirate radio ships operating off the East Anglian coast in the region of Felixstowe, have agreed to amalgamate. Both will operate under the title and call sign of Caroline.

Mr. Roman O'Rahilly, the managing director of Planet Productions, the agency for booking air time on Radio Caroline, said that the original Caroline would be going north, to anchor off the Isle of Man.

The reason, he said, was "the tremendous public response to commercial radio in the north." Caroline would sail via the Channel this weekend broadcasting as she goes.

(July 3)

SAUD DEPOSED BY HIS BROTHER

Daily Telegraph Correspondent
AMMAN, Monday.

King Hussein of Jordan was the first Arab monarch to congratulate King Feisal of Saudi Arabia on his succession to-day. The announcement that the ailing King Saud, 62, had been replaced by his brother, Crown Prince Feisal, 59, was made by Mecca radio.

(November 3)

BLACKMAIL, SAYS RHODESIA

REPLY TO WILSON ON TREASON WARNING

DAVID ADAMSON
Daily Telegraph Staff Correspondent
SALISBURY, Rhodesia, Tuesday.

RHODESIA will declare independence unilaterally only if Britain withdraws her support in the United Nations or attempts to interfere in the country's internal affairs, said Mr. Smith, the Prime Minister, in the Assembly to-day. In no circumstances would his Government seize independence without consulting the people.

He repeated once again that he would not consider a massive "yes" at the independence referendum on Thursday week as a mandate for a unilateral declaration.

This was his reply to the British statement on the consequences of unconstitutional action. The statement came over the local radio stations this morning with the force of an ultimatum threatening war.

For the first time the European population was brought face to face with the consequences of a unilateral declaration. Few seemed to like it.

Mr. Smith described the statement as an attempt at blackmail and intimidation. A letter from Mr. Wilson which he received over the week-end had asked for a "categorical assurance forthwith" that he would not declare independence.

"I treated it exactly as any other decent Rhodesian would have done," he said. Waving a sheaf of British official letters marked "secret" in red, he complained once again about British breaches of etiquette in making public her communications to him.

He wondered whether it was worth going to London after the referendum for talks on the crisis with Mr. Wilson and his Government. They had been "exceedingly impetuous."

Mr. Smith accused them of giving way to the African Nationalists, whose leaders, Mr. Nkomo and the Rev. Ndabaningi Sithole are in gaol in Rhodesia.

BOYCOTT DISMISSED
South Africa quoted

Mr. Smith declared that an African Government in exile would not succeed. It would not represent anyone. As for the threat of an economic boycott, when in history had one succeeded? South Africa was a good example of the failure of that sort of pressure.

"I should like to say to the people of Britain, that if we should be driven to a unilateral declaration at any time it will be the recent action of the new British Government which has driven us.

"Surely it is time these people realised that we Rhodesians have had enough of this sort of behaviour. Who can blame us when one sees what has happened in the rest of Africa to the north of us."

(October 28)

21-GUN SALUTE AS QUEEN OPENS FORTH BRIDGE

Daily Telegraph Reporter

A 21-GUN salute was fired by ships anchored in the Forth yesterday as the Queen opened the £20 million Forth Road Bridge before a crowd of 100,000 people.

It was Scotland's most exciting and spectacular occasion since the Queen's accession to the Throne and her State visit to Edinburgh. During her opening speech yesterday the Queen spoke of the "great benefit" the bridge would bring to Scottish economy.

Until a short time before the ceremony a thick sea mist threatened to play havoc with the carefully-planned arrangements. A mass fly-past by Lightning fighters had to be cancelled because of the low cloud base.

CROWDED RIVER
25 Naval ships

From dawn the river was a mass of small craft. They surrounded the 25 anchored Naval ships.

In her speech the Queen emphasised the immense economic and commercial value of this link between the Lothians and the Kingdom of Fife.

She said: "The flow of private and commercial traffic which it will make possible is bound to have a most stimulating effect throughout this part of Scotland and I am certain that it will bring great benefits to the economy of the whole of Scotland."

The opening of the bridge was greeted by the 21-gun salute and 120 rockets were fired from the parapets of the 74-year-old railway bridge a mile down river.

The Royal party then drove across the bridge's one-and-a-half mile dual carriageway to the north bank, where they were received by the Earl of Elgin, Lord Lieutenant of Fife. The Queen inspected the elaborate system of approach roads on the north side.

(September 5)

40 MICROPHONES IN U.S. EMBASSY

DAVID SHEARS
Daily Telegraph Staff Correspondent
WASHINGTON, Tuesday.

MORE than 40 secret microphones have been found by American security officers in the walls of the American Embassy in Moscow, the State Department disclosed to-day.

It said Mr. Foy Kohler, the United States Ambassador in Moscow, delivered a strong protest to the Russian Government to-day. The microphones were apparently placed in the building before the United States Government leased it from Russia in May, 1953.

"It must be assumed that at least some of them were in operating condition when discovered," the department said. They were embedded eight to 10in. in the walls.

A review was being made to determine whether there have been any significant compromise of secret information.

Ever since the building was first occupied by American diplomats, security men have used various devices to try to track down the microphones they were sure must exist.

But all such searches proved unavailing. Finally last February the security men decided to start tearing down walls. The first room chosen for this drastic treament yielded a hidden microphone.

From then on the technicians followed the wiring network to the other hidden devices.

The microphones were displayed at the Press conference at which to-day's disclosures were made. One, little bigger than a cigar box, was detected by a dog belonging to an American diplomat.

HIGH-PITCHED WHINE
Painful to dog

It gave off a high-pitched whine inaudible to human ears, but excruciatingly painful to a dog. Security experts believe the microphones in the top three floors of the 16-storey building were capable of picking up conversations at 10 to 15ft range.

(May 20)

'FANNY HILL' IS OBSCENE

Daily Telegraph Reporter

"FANNY HILL," the 18th-century novel by John Cleland, was judged to be an obscene publication at Bow Street yesterday.

Sir ROBERT BLUNDELL, the Chief Metropolitan Magistrate, ordered that 171 copies of the book seized in a bookshop in Tottenham Court Road should be forfeited. The decision that the book is obscene applies only to the Metropolitan area.

The seized copies were part of a 100,000 print of a paper-back edition selling at 3s 6d. Eighty two thousand were distributed to booksellers. Those still in the booksellers' hands are expected to be returned to the publishers, Mayflower Books.

The prosecution was brought by the Director of Public Prosecutions against Mr. R. GOLD, of G. Gold and Sons. The publishers appeared as interveners and, in effect, conducted the defence.

The costs of the Bow Street proceedings, including legal fees, may well reach £5,000 or even £6,000, according to Mr. L. V. Fennelly, managing director of Mayflower Books. An appeal is being considered.

(February 11)

THE 'SUN' TAKES OVER FROM 'DAILY HERALD'

The last issue of the Daily Herald founded by a group of Socialists in 1912 and taken over by the Labour party officially in 1923, was published yesterday. The Trades Union Congress sold its 49 per cent. interest to the International Publishing Corporation for £75,000 in February.

A front-page statement declares that the Sun is "politically free, and will not automatically support or censure any party or any Government."

(September 15)

AFRICANS DEMONSTRATE AT MANDELA TRIAL

EIGHT MEN FOUND GUILTY

LESLIE BEILBY
Daily Telegraph Staff Correspondent
CAPE TOWN, Thursday.

A CHANTING crowd of Africans demonstrated outside the Palace of Justice in Pretoria to-day when eight of the nine accused in the Rivonia sabotage trial were found guilty on various counts.

Under the watchful eye of scores of police, the Africans marched up and down shouting slogans, raising their fists and crying "Amandla nga weto" (Strength is ours). At one time it looked as if their mood might become dangerous, but the moment passed.

In readiness for any trouble, the police were out in force and road blocks were set up outside Pretoria. Cars were stopped and checked.

TROOPS STAND BY
Fear of violence

Prominent among the crowd was Mrs. Walter Sisulu, wife of one of the accused. She led the Africans in singing "Nkosi Sikelele Africa," the anthem which has become associated with African nationalism.

Inside the court the nine accused of plotting to overthrow the Government by sabotage and guerrilla warfare remained impassive when Mr. Justice de Wet delivered his judgment.

NELSON MANDELA, 46, former head of the African National Congress was found guilty on all four counts against him. He faced two counts of sabotage and two under the Suppression of Communism and General Laws Amendments Acts.

WALTER SISULU, 52, former Secretary-General of the African National Congress; DENNIS GOLDBERG, 33, a white man; GOVAN MBEKI, a former African journalist; RAYMOND MAHLABA, 44, ELIAS MOTSOALEDI, 39, and ANDREW MLANGENI, 38, were also found guilty on these four counts.

(June 12)

POPE IN 'SUMMIT' WITH PATRIARCH

From ANTHONY MANN
Daily Telegraph Special Correspondent
JERUSALEM, Sunday.

WITH a symbolic "kiss of peace" the Pope and the Patriarch Athenagoras, head of the Eastern Orthodox Church met in Jerusalem to-night. They set a seal on an attempt towards greater understanding between their two Churches.

The two leaders embraced during their historic encounter lasting 29 minutes.

The kiss came as Patriarch Athenagoras entered a reception room at the Roman Catholic Apostolic Delegation on the Mount of Olives, where the Pontiff awaited him.

In a 500-word address, the Pope said: "Doubtless on the one side and on the other the roads which lead to union may be long and sown with difficulties. But these two paths converge towards one another and eventually reach the sources of the Gospel.

"Is it not then a happy augury that to-day's meeting takes place in that land where Christ founded his Church and shed his blood for her?"

POPE IN ISRAEL
Border opened

Earlier Pope Paul, who appeared relaxed and unwearied to-day despite the fatigues of yesterday, followed the footsteps of Our Lord on the soil of Israel.

There were further scenes of enthusiasm on the route from Jerusalem to the crossing point specially opened for him on the Arab-Israeli traceline.

These resulted in President Shazar of Israel being kept waiting one hour, 16 minutes in the open at Megiddo, overlooking the Plain of Esdraelon, the Armageddon of Biblical tradition.

Jordanian security and police authorities at Nablus, Jenin and other points were apparently unable to restrain the throngs and ensure the prompt arrival of the Pontiff in Israel.

The old Nablus-Nazareth road, which has been closed by ferro-concrete obstacles and barbed wire for 16 years, was opened for the Pope's passage. United Nations truce troops, in blue berets, had been responsible for clearing the barriers.

Jordanian troops manned the crossing point silently from 7 a.m. Fifteen yards away the Israeli chief of protocol and officials of the Ministry of Religions were in readiness.

There was visible irritation in Israel as it became apparent that the delicate and tightly packed programme of the Pope's precious 12 hours on Israeli soil would be dislocated by a failure of the Jordanian authorities to get him to the truceline by the agreed time.

(January 6)

SOTHEBY'S BUY PARKE-BERNET

SOTHEBY'S, the London auctioneers, has gained control of New York's leading auction house, the Parke-Bernet Galleries, it was announced to-day.

A four-hour meeting of shareholders agreed in principle that the controlling interest should be sold to Sotheby's.

A statement issued by Parke-Bernet said: "It is Sotheby's intention to preserve the identity of Parke-Bernet.

"Parke-Bernet and Sotheby's feel that the combined resources and international prestige of their organisations will ensure that the best possible results are obtained in the New York and London markets.

(July 15)

Daily Telegraph and Morning Post, 1964

185 MAJORITY TO END HANGING

•

WILSON VOTES FOR SILVERMAN'S BILL

ROWLAND SUMMERSCALES
Daily Telegraph Political Staff

THE House of Commons last night decided by a majority of 185 that hanging should end in Britain.

The division figures of 355-170, on a free vote, were an even bigger victory for the abolitionists than had been predicted. The decisive moment came a few minutes before 11.15.

Sir Geoffrey de Freitas and Mr. Chataway, Labour and Conservative tellers for the division, which technically was on an amendment against the Abolition Bill's second reading, forced their way through M.P.'s crowding the Bar of the House and walked to the table with the figures.

In a hushed and crowded chamber, Sir Geoffrey announced the result. There was a moment of disbelief, then an outbreak of cheering.

Across the gangway Labour Members stretched hands to congratulate Mr. Sydney Silverman, Labour M.P. for Nelson and Colne, for whom the result meant a noteworthy triumph after years of effort.

WILSON'S SUPPORT
Conservative backing

The Prime Minister was one of the members of the Government voting for abolition. With him were a number of members of the former Conservative Administration.

They included Mr. BROOKE, former Home Secretary, Sir HUGH LUCAS-TOOTH, a former Parliamentary Secretary at the Home Office, Mr. MACLEOD, SIR DEREK WALKER-SMITH, Miss PIKE, Mr. PETER THOMAS.

(December 22)

£107,000 STAR OF INDIA GEM THEFT

FRANK TAYLOR
Daily Telegraph Staff
Correspondent
NEW YORK, Friday.

THE Star of India, the world's largest blue sapphire, and the De Lond Star Ruby were among 22 precious stones worth over £107,000 stolen from the New York Museum of Natural History last night.

The thieves smashed three display cases in the J.P. Morgan collection on the fourth floor to get the gems. None of the cases has a burglar alarm. The theft was discovered at 10 a.m. to-day by a museum guard.

Museum officials said the gems were not insured, but may be covered by a blanket policy on the museum collections.

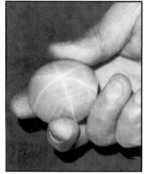

The Star of India, of 563.35 carats, and the Star Ruby, of 100 carats were both said to be worth about £35,000. Independent experts said this estimate was incredibly low. The Star of India is so big it could not have a market value.

The stones are so well known that they could not be sold intact. They would have to be recut.

The thieves broke in through a window on the park side of the building. Poor lighting and trees and bushes gave them plenty of cover.

(October 31)

NEW YORKERS FIGHT TO SEE THE BEATLES

From Our Own Correspondent
NEW YORK, Friday.

TWO hours of bedlam engulfed Kennedy International Airport to-day when the Beatles arrived from London for a ten-day tour. More than 5,000 teenagers greeted them.

Looking fairly fresh after their flight, the pop group were escorted through Customs and immigration by a solid ring of Port Authority men. At the Customs hundreds of young people hammered on the glass partitions.

Chant of Welcome

Police had to clear them away for fear someone would be pushed through the glass. The teenagers chanted "Welcome to Beatlesville" and sang snatches of Beatle songs.

Veteran reporters said they had never seen anything like this chaotic 20-minute Press conference at which photographers and television men fought and scrambled to get pictures.

(February 8)

MR. SYDNEY SILVERMAN

SCHOOLS CLOSED IN TYPHOID CITY

Daily Telegraph Reporter

ALL schools in Aberdeen will be closed from Monday. This was announced just before midnight last night as a "second wave" of infections brought the number of confirmed cases of typhoid in the city to 136 with 36 suspected cases.

Dr. Ian MacQueen, Aberdeen's Medical Officer of Health, said that the closure of the schools indicated the seriousness with which the typhoid outbreak was being treated.

He advised parents to keep their children at home. "We do not want children mixing with others in the streets," he said.

The first death in the outbreak occurred in Aberdeen City Hospital last night. The victim was an elderly woman.

Dr. Alexander Duncan, the hospital's Medical Superintendent, said that she had been suffering from "two other fairly serious complaints" as well as typhoid.

Earlier yesterday Dr. MacQueen said that the tin of corned beef blamed for the outbreak may have been 13 years old.

It was thought that the beef was part of a consignment imported from South America and bought by the Ministry of Food. The corned beef had presumably been released by the Ministry although this was not certain.

The 78-bed Tor-Na-Dee hospital on the outskirts of Aberdeen, is being evacuated to take typhoid victims, and will be ready for them to-day.

MINISTRY STOCKPILE
"Regularly examined"

A Ministry of Agriculture spokesman said last night that the Ministry did have a stockpile of corned beef. This was regularly examined by public inspectors and from time to time surplus stocks were disposed of through the trade.

"No stocks were released unless the inspectors were satisfied with their condition."

Dr. MacQueen's statements were being investigated. "We cannot say just where this tin came from," the spokesman added. "Some of the corned beef released could be quite old."

(May 30)

Later Bank Holiday in August

Daily Telegraph Reporter

AUGUST Bank Holiday will be the last Monday of the month next year and in 1966. The Government's decision to make this experiment was announced in the Commons yesterday by Mr. Heath, Secretary for Industry.

If it is decided to make the arrangement permanent after 1966, the present Whitsuntide Bank Holiday may also be replaced by a fixed Spring holiday on the last Monday in May. The Government wants to ease holiday congestion.

(March 5)

RECORD LEAPS 19 PLACES TO TOP OF CHART

Daily Telegraph Reporter

In only their second week in the Top 50 of the popular record chart, The Animals, from Newcastle Upon Tyne, displace the American singer, Roy Orbison, from the No. 1 spot, with their record, "House of the Rising Sun." It was 19th last week.

Orbison's "It's Over" drops to No. 2 after two weeks of heading the hit parade. Straight into the Top Ten this week goes "It's All Over Now" by the Rolling Stones, while "Hold Me" by P. J. Proby is up from No. 14 to No. 3.

(June 30)

500 DEATHS FEARED IN PERU SOCCER RIOT

LIMA, Peru, Monday.

DOCTORS and police are still not certain how many people died in yesterday's riot during a football international at the National Stadium in Lima. The official death roll was given as 263, but police said 350 had died and some reports said the final figure would be nearer 500.

Medical teams worked all night tending almost 1,000 people injured in the riot, which began when the Uruguayan referee disallowed a goal by Peru during a match with Argentina, who were leading 1-0. Spectators tried to invade the pitch, and were met with tear-gas bombs thrown by police.

A youth who was at the match said that the crowd, caught between the tear-gas and the steel netting which protects the field, smashed their way through the netting.

"The police tried to beat them back with clubs," he said, "When the police used their dogs to hold them back I saw one dog literally torn to pieces by the infuriated mob."

Other sections of the crowd of 40,000 panicked and charged towards the exits, only to find the gates shut and locked. Hundreds of spectators, many of them women and children, were crushed and trampled on by the mob trying to get out of the stadium.

(May 26)

MISS TAYLOR AND BURTON MARRIED

From Our Own Correspondent
NEW YORK, Sunday.

ELIZABETH Taylor, 32, and Richard Burton, 38, were married this afternoon in Montreal, their publicity director announced.

Miss Taylor wore a daffodil yellow chiffon dress in the Empire style made for her by her personal designer, Irene Sharaff. Her hair was dressed with hyacinth and lily of the valley in a chignon coil.

A friend of Richard Burton's, Mr. Robert Wilson, was best man. Miss Taylor declined to comment after the wedding. Burton said: "Elizabeth Taylor and I are very, very happy."

(March 16)

3 CITIES TO STOP LONDON "CHOKING"

By Our Political Staff

The Government has accepted the objects of a 20-year plan to solve London's expansion problems. It will involve the biggest planning operation in the free world.

The plan, to house, employ and transport an increased population of 3½ million, will mean three new cities in the Southampton-Portsmouth, Hants, Bletchley, Bucks and Newbury, Berks, areas.

Six large expansions are proposed at Ashford, Kent; Ipswich, Suffolk; Northampton and Peterborough, Northants; Swindon, Wilts, and Stansted, Essex.

(March 20)

JOHNSON WINS

•

New York victory by Robert Kennedy

Daily Telegraph Staff Correspondents
NEW YORK, Wednesday.

PRESIDENT JOHNSON won an overwhelming victory in the American Presidential Election to-day. His victory became certain at 3.11 a.m. GMT when he carried his home State of Texas to give him a majority of Electoral College votes.

The Democrats also retained control of the Senate and seem assured of a bigger majority in the House of Representatives. They were romping home in the race for the State governorships.

Mr. Robert Kennedy, the late President's younger brother, won his costly and bitterly fought Senate seat battle in New York with Senator Kenneth Keating.

His brother, Mr. Edward Kennedy, won a Senate contest in Massachusetts.

Twenty Republican strongholds fell to Mr. Johnson: New Hampshire, Maine, Vermont, Oklahoma, Ohio, Indiana, Wisconsin, Kansas, Colorado, Iowa, Virginia, Kentucky, Florida, Tennessee, Oregon, Utah, Montana, Washington, Nebraska and California with 40 electoral votes, the biggest after New York.

Ohio was one of the four major States Senator Goldwater had said he needed to win, along with some smaller ones, to gain the Presidency. By 1 a.m. GMT National Broadcasting Company computers were forecasting one of the biggest wins of the century for Mr. Johnson.

In what the network's commentator Walter Cronkite called "this amazing landslide" the President had about 60.6 per cent. of the popular vote.

Only two other Presidential candidates in American history passed the 60 per cent. mark. They were Mr. Harding, Republican, in 1920, and Mr. Roosevelt, Democrat, in 1936 who had 60.8.

More than anything else, the result across most of the country was a massive rejection of Mr. Goldwater himself, with some other Republicans suffering the consequences by having to fight for their political lives in Congressional and Governorship races where they might otherwise have had an easier time.

(November 4)

115 NATIONS' FLAGS FLY FOR SHAKESPEARE

Daily Telegraph Reporter

THE flags of 115 nations flew at Stratford-on-Avon yesterday to celebrate the fourth centenary of the birth of William Shakespeare, on St. George's Day, 1564. Prince Philip spent more than six hours in the town after arriving by helicopter.

Crowds lined the route in April sunshine and showers as Prince Philip and the official entourage visited the new Shakespeare Centre and the birthplace next door. Then the party crossed the River Avon to the birthday lunch for 750 guests in the Festival Pavilion.

The Queen, in a message read at the lunch by the Earl of Avon, said: "The treasure of Shakespeare's legacy to our nation and to the world at large is beyond estimation.

"He saw through all windows and he had in abundance the two great gifts of humanity, the gifts of laughter and compassion."

After lunch Prince Philip opened and toured the £250,000 Shakespeare Exhibition before recrossing the river to attend a special performance of 'King Henry IV, Part 1," at the Royal Shakespeare Theatre.

Earlier in the day crowds began to assemble outside the main post office to buy the commemorative set of five Shakespeare stamps for the first day cover. Queues remained along the pavement for most of the day.

HEROINES SEEN TO-DAY
Ld. David Cecil's theory

Other tributes to Shakespeare were paid at ceremonies in Oxford, London and Guildford. At Oxford, Lord David Cecil, Goldsmiths' Professor of English at the university, addressed the Oxford Preservation Trust's memorial ceremony at Lincoln College.

He said the English ideal of an attractive woman was "very largely Shakespeare's creation." His heroines could be seen in life to-day. "Through life imitating literature, possibly Englishwomen are what they are partly because of the heroines of Shakespeare."

(April 24)

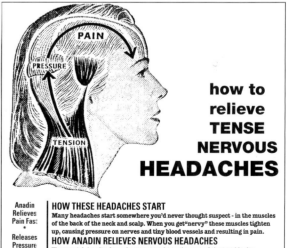

7 IN TRAIN CASE GET 30 YEARS

'Sordid crime of vast greed,' says Judge

By T.A. SANDROCK
Daily Telegraph Scotland Yard Correspondent

TWELVE members of the Great Train Robbery gang were sentenced at Aylesbury yesterday to 307 years in gaol. [Report - p23.] This was the highest total of prison terms ever imposed at a criminal trial in Britain.

The judge, Mr. Justice Edmund Davies, described the mail train raid in Buckinghamshire last August, when £2½ million was stolen, as "a crime which in its impudence and enormity, was the first of its kind in this country."

He added: "I propose to do all in my power to ensure that it will also be the last of its kind. This was nothing less than a sordid crime of violence, inspired by vast greed."

Seven of the men were gaoled for 30 years, four for between 20 and 25 years, and one for three years. Most of them showed no emotion as they were sentenced.

When Leonard Field was sentenced to 25 years his mother shouted: "He is innocent." As officials led her from the public gallery Field, 31, replied: "Never mind mum. I am only a young man."

NOTICE OF APPEAL

More wanted men

Ten of the men have given notice of appeal against conviction

Yesterday's sentences have by no means ended the case. There are still as many men again to be caught, and more than £2 million in cash to be recovered.

The identities of some of the men being sought are known to the police, but others have not been established Special efforts are being made to trace some of the "smaller fry" who may give a lead to the missing money.

The heavy sentences imposed yesterday could mean that part of the stolen money will rot before the criminals leave prison. In any case bank note design will change, and Britain may even have decimal currency by the time they are released.

Police will keep up the pressure to trace both the men and the money. At Aylesbury Police H.Q. and Scotland Yard, the glow of success has been dulled by the fact that half the gang and most of the money are missing.

One of the police secrets in the case which can now be disclosed is of the discovery at Leatherslade Farm, the gang's hideout, of several suits of denims, the Army fatigue dress.

These bore Special Air Service shoulder flashes. The gang wore them on the raid so that if the alarm was given more quickly than was anticipated after the robbery, they could pose as an Army unit on night manoeuvres.

The vehicles they used included two Land Rovers and an ex-Army truck. Had such a "unit" been stopped on its way to the hideout in the early hours after the raid, the chances are the bluff would have worked.

(April 17)

MAIL RAID ESCAPER ON RUN

Daily Telegraph Reporter

CHARLES FREDERICK WILSON, one of the masterminds behind the Great Train Robbery, is to-day the most wanted man in Britain after his daring escape from Birmingham's Winson Green prison. For Wilson, 32, the "quiet criminal", knows where most of the £2,500,000 proceeds from the 12-months old robbery is hidden.

Wilson, gaoled for 30 years, is believed to be the "treasurer" of the robbery gang. He was sentenced at Aylesbury Assizes on April 16 last.

Yesterday's gaolbreak had the identical ingredients that made the robbery the crime of the century; militarily meticulous in its planning, audacious in its execution.

Three men broke into the turreted, grey-walled prison to release Wilson in the early hours of the morning, one year and four days to the minute after the Great Train Robbery. They achieved the almost impossible, for Wilson was under special watch as a potential escaper.

This meant he was in a specially strengthened cell, once occupied by the Russian spy, Gordon Lonsdale, and under regular surveillance through the night. His accomplices must have had a master key to enter the prison buildings and a cell key to release Wilson, once inside the block.

(August 13)

ROLLING STONES FANS RIOT

Five thousand fans of the Rolling Stones pop group went berserk last night after guitarist Keith Richards aimed a kick at a fan on stage. Dozens of police had to be called in to quell a near-riot as hundreds of youths poured on to the stage. The group ran for safety.

Then the fans wrecked the stage in the Empress Ballroom at Blackpool and smashed the group's equipment, worth £2,000. Keith Richards said afterwards: "Some youths kept spitting at us. I lost my temper and tried to kick one. He just went mad."

(July 25)

RONALD ARTHUR BIGGS, a carpenter, of Redhill, Surrey, who after a separate trial was found guilty at Buckinghamshire Assizes yesterday of two charges arising out of the Great Train Robbery.

HUSBAND OF DAME MARGOT SHOT

SCOTT FRANCIS
Daily Telegraph Correspondent

PANAMA CITY, Monday.

DR. ROBERTO ARIAS, 46, the Panamanian diplomat and husband of Dame Margot Fonteyn, the British ballerina, was shot three times and seriously wounded in his car in Panama City to-day.

He was taken to San Tomas Hospital, and given an immediate blood transfusion. One bullet was reported to have pierced his lung and a doctor described his condition as "very bad."

Police said the shooting, in a suburban street, followed an argument between Dr. Arias and a political colleague. Dr. Arias, a former Panamanian Ambassador to Britain and the son of a former President of Panama, was elected to Panama's National Assembly last month.

The man with whom he was said to have been arguing was Alberto Jimenez, an alternate candidate in last month's elections. Police said Jimenez had disappeared.

Each deputy in the National Assembly has an alternate who takes his place in the chamber when he cannot be there himself. The votes for alternates have not yet been counted.

CROWDS GATHER

National Guard called

Crowds gathered outside San Tomas Hospital as news of the shooting spread. National Guardsmen were called in to hold them in check and screen everyone entering the hospital. An appeal was made for blood donors.

Only this morning Dr. Arias visited my office and chatted cheerfully for quite a time. He did not seem to have a worry in the world.

He was obviously delighted at his election as a deputy and inquired anxiously whether I had cabled the news to The Daily Telegraph. He laughed at the reports that he was planning to leave Panama.

Dr. Arias was Panamanian Ambassador in London from 1955 to 1958, when he resigned. In 1959 he was accused of leading an unsuccessful armed revolt against President de la Guardia.

He was forced to take refuge for two months in the Brazilian Embassy in Panama City. Eventually he was granted safe conduct out of the country.

Dame Margot, 45, whom he married in February, 1955, was also arrested in Panama City at the time of the 1959 revolt. After 24 hours in prison she was asked to leave the country.

Dr. Arias was reappointed Ambassador in London in 1960 following a change of Government in Panama but resigned again in 1962 for personal reasons.

To-day's shooting shocked Panamanian politicians. Senor Pepe Erhman, a fellow candidate in the recent elections, said: "We have no idea why this should have happened. Arias and Jimenez were good friends."

(June 9)

AVERAGE WAGE NOW £16 14s 11d A WEEK

Manual workers' earnings rose again last year. According to Ministry of Labour figures issued yesterday, earnings of 6,500,000 workers averaged £16 14s 11d a week in the second pay week in October. In April the average was £16 3s 1d.

The rise between April and October represented a 3.7 per cent. increase. In October earnings were 5.6 per cent. higher than a year earlier and 42.1 per cent. higher than in April 1956.

Average hours worked in October were 47.6 a week. This compares with 46.9 in April, 47.0 in October, 1962, and 48.6 in April, 1956.

(January 21)

CANDLELIGHT DEFEAT AT TV CENTRE

By Our Television Staff

The long-awaited, much publicised opening of the BBC-2 service was put off until to-night when at 9.45 last night BBC executives, meeting by candlelight at Television Centre, decided the situation was "hopeless" because of the power failure.

For two hours programmes had been re-timed with the hope of power being restored. The first casualty was "Kiss Me Kate," the 90-minute spectacular musical which will now be broadcast to-night.

As compensation for the viewers it was decided to put on a News programme from Alexandra Palace at 10p.m.

(April 21)

ENGINEERS AS 'BRAIN DRAIN' MAJORITY

MANY CHEMISTS

From Our Own Correspondent

WASHINGTON, Wednesday.

BRITAIN is America's second largest outside source of scientific and engineering talent after Canada. Other European countries are far behind Britain.

Of the total of 912 British "scientists and engineers" who entered America as permanent immigrants in the 12 months ending in June last year, more than two thirds were engineers.

The National Science Foundation gave this breakdown of the British contingent: 626 engineers, 147 chemists, 82 physicists, 18 mathematicians, 15 biologists, 10 agricultural scientists, six geologists and eight other natural scientists.

Twice as many Canadians

Officials of the foundation lack data as to how many of the total took up teaching and pure research work and how many entered American industry.

Canada provided roughly twice as many scientists and engineers to America as Britain. West Germany supplied only half the British figure and France about a tenth.

(February 13)

BRITISH WOMAN WINS NOBEL PRIZE

AN Oxford woman scientist, Prof. Dorothy Crowfoot-Hodgkin, aged 54, has been awarded the 1964 Nobel Prize for Chemistry. It is worth just over £18,750 tax free.

Prof. Crowfoot-Hodgkin is Fellow of Somerville College and Oxford University Reader in X-ray Crystallography. She is married, with two sons and a daughter, and is also a grandmother.

Her husband is Dr. Thomas Hodgkin, chairman of Ghana University's Institute for African Research. She is at present in Ghana with him.

Prof. Crowfoot-Hodgkin is best known for her work in finding the structures of penicillin and later, vitamin B12, a liver extract used in fighting pernicious anaemia.

She is only the third woman to win the prize. The others were Mme. Marie Curie in 1911, and her daughter, Irene Joliot-Curie, in 1935.

(October 30)

ITA CURB ON CIGARETTE ADVERTISING

L. Marsland Gander
Daily Telegraph Radio and television Correspondent

Advertisements which suggest that it is safer to smoke one brand or type of cigarette than another are to be banned by the Independent Television Authority. This is one of the new provisions in a revised Code of Advertising Standards and Practices issued yesterday.

Other prohibitions are:

Advertisements which play on fear;

Abuses of trick photography producing misleading effects:

"Bait and Switch" advertising by tricksters who try to exploit a cheap and sometimes non-existant article to press inquirers into something much more expensive.

Films scrutinised

The new rules, introduced yesterday by Lord Hill, chairman of ITA, codify provision of the new Television Act. Under this, it is the authority's job to take a day-to-day part in seeing that the rules are obeyed.

The authority's advertising control staff now see the scripts of most advertisements and also join with the programme companies in viewing the finished films before acceptance.

(June 3)

57 escape to West in tunnel

BLAKE BAKER
Daily Telegraph Staff Correspondent

BERLIN, Monday.

FIFTY-SEVEN refugees have escaped through a tunnel under the Communist wall to West Berlin. Shooting broke out at the Eastern end as the last of the 57 crawled through early to-day.

Two cars and a motor-cycle carrying three Communist security men and four border guards arrived at the opening of the tunnel in a courtyard off the Strelitzerstrasse, East Berlin, shortly after the last of the refugees had passed through it after mid-night to-day.

A number of shots from Communist machine-pistols were then heard. Later the official East German news agency ADN announced that a border guard had been killed by "several aimed shots from armed bandits" who had dug the tunnel with the connivance of West Berlin police.

31 women in group

None of the 23 men, 31 women and three children who escaped was hit by the Communist shots, although one received grazes.

At the Western end of the tunnel, which was dug from a disused bakery, block and pulley gear was installed to lift out each refugee. Later the bakery tunnel exit was sealed.

Another party of 14 East Germans escaped during the week-end through Communist minefields and across the inter-zonal border to Lower Saxony.

(October 6)

'Pirate' radio disturbs PO ships service

Daily Telegraph Reporter

TEST broadcasts from Radio Caroline, the "pirate" radio ship, have been causing "fairly serious" disruption of the North Foreland radio station's ship-to-shore communications, the GPO said last night.

Yesterday the radio ship took up its proposed transmitting position outside the three-mile limit off Felixstowe, Suffolk. North Foreland, a GPO station between Margate and Broadstairs, on the Kent coast, handles heavy communications traffic with ships in the Straits of Dover.

Successful test

Earlier yesterday the station aboard the 763-ton former passenger ship Carstone announced that its test transmissions over the week-end had been so successful that commercial broadcasting would begin officially in a fortnight.

A GPO spokesman said: "The pirate station is outside our territorial waters. Nevertheless, this type of broadcast is contrary to international regulations."

(March 30)

HOFFA SENTENCED TO 8 YEARS

From Our Own Correspondent

NEW YORK, Thursday.

James Hoffa, 51, president of the Teamsters' (lorry drivers) Union, was sentenced in Chattanooga, Tennessee, to-day to eight years' imprisonment for trying to bribe a jury hearing conspiracy charges against him. He was also fined £3,500.

The sentence could mean, eventually, the loss of his job as leader of the world's biggest union. He gave notice of appeal and was released on bail.

(March 13)

$3,000M TO SAVE THE POUND

NEW CREDITS BY 11 CENTRAL BANKS

FRANCIS WHITMORE
Daily Telegraph City Editor

THE battle to save the pound, still raging fiercely in the world's foreign exchange markets yesterday, took a surprise turn last night.

Well after business hours in London, but while New York dealings were in progress, arrangements were announced to make $3,000 million (£1,071 million) available to support the pound.

As a result of negotiations conducted by the Bank of England, the central banks of Austria, Belgium, Canada, France, Germany, Italy, Japan, the Netherlands, Sweden, Switzerland and the United States are taking part, as is also the Bank for International Settlements.

Included in the total is a loan of $250 million from the Export-Import Bank of the United States.

These new credits are separate from the existing Central Bank credits which have been heavily drawn on in the support of sterling in recent months and which will shortly be due for repayment.

The new credits, which are available immediately, need not be repaid for three years.

The existing credits which include an outstanding short-term debt to the Federal Reserve Bank of New York, will be repaid from Britain's stand-by credit of $1,000 million (£357 million) which Mr. Callaghan has intimated will be drawn next week.

All the indications are that practically the whole of the IMF drawing is already earmarked to repaying these short-term debts.

Within the hour, the announcement of the rescue operation had a favourable effect. "The pressure on sterling has evaporated completely," said a New York spokesman for the Foreign Exchange department of the First National City Bank. "Speculators who were pouring sterling on to the market now are buying it back."

By close of dealings the sterling rate to the United States dollar had risen in New York to 2.79.15. The opening quotation had been 2.78.60 and dealers said it was maintained at that level only through the support being provided by the Bank of England.

SEVERE PRESSURE
Strengthening defences

With selling pressure on the pound still severe despite Monday's Bank Rate leap to 7 per cent. it has become clear that fresh support would need to be mobilised to stop the rot. The new $3,000 million arrangements are designed to strengthen the defences on such a scale as to make it plain to the world that the pound is not to be devalued.

The hope is that this will, in turn, stem the speculative and other selling which has latterly involved a heavy drain on the reserves.

Mr. John Hambro, chairman of Hambro's Bank, the world's biggest merchant bank and one of the leading foreign exchange dealers in London, said the arrangement "shows the solidarity of the central banks of Europe behind the pound and will certainly see us through what, after all, was only a temporary crisis without permanent damage."

(November 26)

BEECHING GOING

MR. FRASER, Minister of Transport, confirmed in the Commons yesterday that Dr. Beeching will not, after all, advise the Government on achieving greater co-ordination of road, rail and inland water transport.

He will leave his £24,000-a-year post as chairman of the British Railways Board in the next six months, to return to Imperial Chemical Industries. Mr. Fraser gave M.P.'s the strong impression that he is inclined to take on the transport integration study himself.

His aim is to complete the task "long before the end of 1965" as chairman of a small "Steering group" of well-informed people unconnected with the Ministry.

CLEAR IMPLICATION
Survey in consultation

The Minister stopped short of saying that Dr. Beeching had rejected the job because the Government was unwilling to give him a free hand.

But he went far towards doing so when he explained that it would not be practicable for Dr. Beeching to "carry out the sort of study the Government wants in the way we think it should be done."

The clear implication was that the Government thought Dr. Beeching ought to carry out his survey in consultation with transport interests, representing both management and unions, and that he preferred to work alone.

So they agreed to differ, with "no hard feelings."

(December 24)

3 BODIES IN CIVIL RIGHTS HUNT FOUND

WASHINGTON, Tuesday.

THREE bodies have been found in graves at the site of a dam near Philadelphia, Mississippi, where three Civil Rights workers disappeared six weeks ago.

This was announced to-night by the Federal Bureau of Investigation. The bodies were about six miles from the town, in a wooded area where the three young men were last seen.

The Civil Rights workers, two Whites and a Mississippi Negro, were Andrew Goodman, 20, of New York; Michael Schwerner, 24, also of New York, and James Chaney, 22, of Meridian, Mississippi.

(August 5)

MR. GREVILLE WYNNE reunited with his wife, Sheila, and son, Andrew, outside their home in Upper Cheyne Row, Chelsea, yesterday.

WYNNE BACK AND 'OVERJOYED'

Daily Telegraph Reporters

MR. GREVILLE WYNNE, the 45-year-old British businessman gaoled as a spy by the Russians, was re-united with his wife and elder son Andrew 12, outside their Chelsea home yesterday.

The couple embraced, then ran arm-in-arm into the house. Asked how he felt after his 18-month ordeal, Mr. Wynne said: "I feel as I look. So you can judge for yourself."

Mr. Wynne, who lost nearly three stones in weight during his 17 months in Russian prisons, was flown home after being exchanged at a Berlin border checkpoint early yesterday for Gordon Lonsdale, the Russian spy gaoled for 25 years in Britain in 1961.

Mr. Wynne's release followed reports that his health was deteriorating. He was examined by a London doctor, Dr. E.C.A. Bott, two hours after arriving home. Dr. Bott said "Mr. Wynne is as well as can be expected. He is in very good heart."

Mr. Wynne had a celebration dinner and drank champagne with his family and friends last night while a policeman stood guard outside his house. He went to bed early.

Meanwhile Lonsdale, 40, whose real name is Conon Molody, was somewhere behind the Iron Curtain. Lonsdale was the master spy of the Portland espionage ring.

THIN AND STRAINED
Silent on treatment

After the Berlin exchange, Mr. Wynne was flown to Northolt Airport in an RAF Transport Command plane. First aboard when the plane landed was a Foreign Office official, closely followed by public relations officers from the Ministry of Defence and the Ministry of Civil Aviation.

Looking thin and strained, Mr. Wynne came out of the aircraft and posed for pictures at the top of the steps. He was wearing a well-cut grey suit, with a Nottingham University tie, and a lightweight blue raincoat.

He would not speak to reporters about the treatment he had received in Russia, apart from saying that the three meals a day he was offered in prison did not agree with him.

He was the only Englishman in a Russian prison on a spying charge. It was obviously good public relations, if nothing else, to get him back.

Mr. Wynne was managing director of Mobile Exhibitions Ltd., a firm he formed for the purpose of promoting trade behind the Iron Curtain. It was while he was in Hungary organising a stand showing British machinery at the Budapest trade fair that he was arrested.

(April 23)

TSR-2 FLIGHT CONFIRMS ALL EXPECTATIONS

AIR CDRE. E.M. DONALDSON
Daily Telegraph Air Correspondent

THE most advanced aircraft in the world, the TSR-2, has flown and it is the product of British designers and constructors. It behaved beautifully at Boscombe Down yesterday and did all that was expected of it.

Mr. Beamont, the pilot, who also tested the Canberra, bomber and Lightning fighter, had no difficulties in controlling it and the fantastic 70,000-lb thrust of its Bristol Siddeley Olympus engines. This thrust is equivalent at 600 mph of 140,000 horsepower.

Some "experts" have been saying the TSR-2 is two years late. It is not late. It has made its first flight at the time predicted four years ago when it was ordered.

From ordering to a first flight in four years is incredible for even a more simple plane. But this aircraft can take off from a 600-yard field fully loaded with nuclear bombs.

TREETOP FLIGHT
Deadly accuracy

It is then capable of flying at treetop level to Moscow to deliver them. The whole flight there and back is done automatically with deadly accuracy regardless of weather.

Its radar, the most advanced in the world, not only navigates, but looks ahead for obstacles. This information is fed through computers and the TSR-2 turns slightly this way and that and climbs and dives.

The wing design is also revolutionary. It gives the pilot a specially smooth ride and makes possible speeds from 100 mph to two-and-a-quarter times the speed of sound.

(September 28)

ITALY EXPELS 'MAN IN TRUNK' DIPLOMATS

Daily Telegraph Staff Correspondent

ROME, Wednesday.

THE Egyptian Ambassador in Italy, Mr. Naguib Hashim, to-day presented "abject apologies" to the Italian Foreign Ministry for the "gross breach of diplomatic privilege" by two members of his staff who tried to send a man to Cairo by air last night locked in a trunk marked as diplomatic baggage.

The diplomats Mr. Abdel Moneim el-Neklawy and Mr. Selim Osman el-Sayed, both First Secretaries, were expelled by the Italian Government. They left for home by air to-night.

The man in the trunk was found bound and gagged and with his hair dyed blond.

The Italian police learned from Jerusalem to-night that he was a 28-year-old Israeli army deserter named Mordecai Benm Masuud-Lok.

He had given the name of Josef Yussuf Dahan, but later admitted that this was fictitious. He feared reprisals against his family.

ON BOTH SIDES
Trip "for punishment"

Dr. Salvatore Luongo, head of Rome's "Flying Squad," told me the impression gained is that the man worked as an agent for both the Egyptians and the Israeli. He was discovered as a double agent and was to be sent to Cairo for punishment.

Rome police laboratories discovered that the trunk used by the diplomats was manufactured in Perugia, Central Italy, by a small firm on orders of "Arab gentlemen." The trunk was fitted with straps, a stool and a helmet-like piece of metal to protect the head.

It had been used before. Two different sets of human hair were found on the inside of the helmet.

There were also other indications that the trunk was used before. Customs officials on the airport recognised it as having been handled by them several times.

The Fome newspaper Il Messagero quoted an airport official as exclaiming when the trunk was found: "So its true they are shipping them this way."

The Egyptian Embassy in Rome said in a statement that it was "completely in the dark" about the contents of the trunk. "The two Embassy Secretaries declare that the diplomatic suitcase in question is not the suitcase sent by the Embassy."

(November 19)

POLICE CHARGE RIOTING HARLEM NEGROES

SHOTS FIRED OVER CROWD

FRANK TAYLOR
Daily Telegraph Staff Correspondent

NEW YORK, Sunday.

SHOTS were fired into the air by police to-night as racial violence flared afresh in Harlem, where night-long rioting yesterday and early to-day left at least one person dead and scores injured.

Riot squads charged into the crowd. The outbreak took place outside an undertaker's chapel where services had started for a Negro boy, aged 15, who was fatally shot last Thursday by a white policeman.

Three days of simmering resentment over the boy's death had erupted into bloody rioting in Harlem last night. Thousands of Negroes raced through the streets hurling bottles and bricks at policemen, smashing shop windows and harassing white people.

Early to-day, six and a half hours after the trouble began, 500 police had brought the situation under control. In the process one Negro was killed, 32 people were arrested, and 17 civilians and 12 police injured.

UNDER SIEGE
Bricks & dustbin lids

At the height of the fighting 125th Street, the heart of Harlem and the street where some of the toughest gangs in New York history have made their homes in the past, was under siege.

Police "paddy wagons" and patrol cars were at every junction. Hundreds of Negroes held police at bay by throwing bricks and dustbin lids from rooftops.

The police repeatedly fired their revolvers over the heads of the crowd.

The disturbances started with a demonstration in front of the police station at West 123rd Street protesting against the killing on Thursday of James Powell, 15, by Lt. Thomas Gilligan. Mr. Gilligan fired three shots at the boy, who he said was attacking him with a knife.

Shortly before the demonstration hundreds of mourners filed past the boy's coffin at an undertaker's in Seventh Avenue, Harlem.

The boy's mother, Mrs. Annie Powell, was weeping and became hysterical when she saw the coffin.

Gradually the crowd in the street increased. Negroes began to shout: "Killers, killers," as police reinforcements arrived.

Bricks, bottles, including one or two Molotov cocktails, and other objects began to rain down on the police from the roofs of tenements.

Policemen were issued with steel helmets. The transport authorities ordered its own police to guard all Underground station entrances, fearing that trains might be attacked. All buses were re-routed to avoid the seething streets.

A police spokesman said that a Negro, Michael Coates, 35, was killed by police bullets after he refused an order to stop throwing bricks from a roof. Another man was shot and wounded "while he was looting a shop." Two other people were hit by stray bullets.

By morning the police began to gain control. Negroes with blood streaming from head and face wounds drifted away to their homes. Policemen with cuts and bruises returned to their stations.

Both white and Negro police work in Harlem. Where possible a white and a Negro policeman normally patrol the streets together.

(July 20)

£200 FINES IN "CLIP JOINT" BILL

As from next April, anyone who conducts a "clip joint" or "near beer" establishment in Soho or elsewhere will face a fine of £200 and three months' imprisonment if he touts for custom or fleeces his customers. This is the effect of the Refreshment Houses Bill, published yesterday.

(June 12)

MUCH TO ENJOY IN "A HARD DAY'S NIGHT"

ANOTHER BEATLES SUCCESS

By PATRICK GIBBS

WITH their first feature film "A Hard Day's Night" at the London Pavilion, the Beatles have repeated their success of night club, theatre and television. They are much helped by the humour of Alun Owen's script, tactful handling by the director, Richard Lester, and the support of half a dozen useful players.

The script, although it provides an effective enough vehicle, is hardly original, being essentially one of those backstage pieces so familiar in musical films; though this time it is the television studio that provides the show business background.

The Beatles are shown in what is presumably a typical day, starting with a train journey to a West Country city where they are to make a television appearance in the evening, preceded by the usual rehearsals.

Throughout, Mr. Owen exploits the Beatles cleverly in their public image, which is to personify a defiance of convention.

Perhaps the stuffy "old boy" type (Richard Vernon), who shares their carriage much to his disgust, is rather an obvious caricature; so is the precious, if not exquisite television producer (Victor Spinetti), who is driven desperate at rehearsal.

Wisely these roles are kept minor, which is more than can be said of the roguish old relation, (Wilfred Brambell) taken along for the trip, who becomes tiresome both in the writing and the playing.

The Beatles' long-suffering manager (Norman Rossington) is better company, the plot being largely concerned with their escapes from his surveillance.

These give rise to escapades in a dance hall and gambling saloon, with the pursuit of young girls a constant and sometimes amusing hazard.

Most effective of these digressions is when the Beatles are caught indulging in horse-play in some playing fields, the director emphasising the surrealistic quality of the scene with vertical shots in both accelerated and slow motion.

Actors they may not be, but personalities they certainly remain, engagingly provocative and wonderfully photogenic. They also display the ability to make much of a good line, so that Mr. Owen's jokes against the conventional couched in saucy dialect, seldom miss the mark.

EXPECTED SONGS

Studio context

The Beatles also, need I add, fill the air with the sort of noises with which they are associated, the film being well punctuated with the expected songs.

Most are given in a studio context, but just a few - and there might well have been more - take their part in the narrative, as when they sing in a luggage van or when running down a fire escape.

There are also girls, to decorate, to pursue and, of course, to scream. Not perhaps a very filmic film but a very potent concoction.

(July 7)

EXOTIC EPIC PLAY BY SHAFFER

By ERIC SHORTER

AFTER the neatly conventional, smooth and sensitive style of his earlier plays, Peter Shaffer has suddenly gone all epic, and exotic epic at that. The result is very strange and rich and quite enjoyable but ultimately unsatisfying.

"The Royal Hunt of the Sun," with which the National Theatre begins its Chichester season, is at once a dramatised documentary on Spain's conquest of the Inca empire and the study of a man's immortal longings.

And the two themes do not always coalesce into an effectively dramatic whole.

As a documentary, the play vividly recreates the gentle sun worship and well ordered life of 16th century Peru, ruled over by a benevolent despot who supposes himself born of the sun.

But as a picture of a lonely, ageing general who seeks a faith which will give life meaning, the chronicle fails to catch theatrical fire until it is half over.

But when Mr. Shaffer at last fastens on his theme of the old soldier searching for a soul to go marching on, the evening really gathers emotional weight. Colin Blakely, as the general, and Robert Stephens, as his prisoner, rise admirably to the occasion.

There are some solid supporting performances from Michael Turner and Robert Lang as the narrator among others; and the production by John Dexter and Desmond O'Donovan is highly atmospheric.

(July 8)

CHAGALL CEILING IN PARIS OPERA

The Paris Opera's new ceiling, painted by Marc Chagall, was shown to the press this morning. Covering 240sq yards, the painting depicts musicians and a dance of opera characters.

Chagall refused any fee for his work. The artist said to-day he was offering it as "a gift in gratitude to France and the school of Paris, without which there would be no colour or liberty."

(September 22)

PERFECTION IN 'MY FAIR LADY' FILM

"MY FAIR LADY,"one of the greatest musical shows Broadway has seen, returned to Broadway this afternoon as one of the the loveliest and most entertaining films ever shown there.

The occasion was the world Press premiere of a picture that has cost £6 million and achieves perfection in its class. The world premiere takes place here to-morrow, but London will have to wait until Jan. 21.

With such actors and actresses as Audrey Hepburn, Rex Harrison, Stanley Holloway, Wilfrid Hyde-White and Gladys Cooper at his command, George Cukor has succeeded beyond hope in making the screen version in every way as delightful as the one so many people have already seen on the stage. But to-day the first applause as the credit lines appeared was for the man who started it all, George Bernard Shaw. The latest metamorphosis of his "Pygmalion" would have given him, one imagines, nothing but pleasure.

Beaton triumph

For Cecil Beaton, who designed the stunning costumes, scenery and the production as a whole, the film is a triumph.

If there was disappointment among the devotees of the original stage version when it was decided to pass over Julie Andrews, they will be mollified when they see Audrey Hepburn in her place.

She has caught and sharpened marvellously the picture of the little Cockney flower girl. Rex Harrison, giving his 1,007th performance as Prof. Henry Higgins, has brought everything to perfection.

(October 21)

NO AWARD OF 3 PULITZER PRIZES

No awards were made for drama, fiction or music in the Pulitzer Prize lists, published to-day. These are generally the most controversial. A spokesman would give no explanation.

Two awards were made for news coverage of the assasination of President Kennedy. Robert Jackson of the Dallas Times Herald won the prize for an outstanding example of news photography for his photograph of the shooting of Lee Harvey Oswald by Jack Ruby.

(May 5)

LAURENCE OLIVIER AS OTHELLO

'TOM JONES' WINS OSCAR FOR BEST FILM

From Our Own Correspondent

NEW YORK, Tuesday.

The British comedy "Tom Jones" won an Oscar as the best film of the year and took three other Academy Awards at a ceremony in Santa Monica, California, last night. It was the first British film to win this award since "Hamlet" in 1948.

Tony Richardson took the Oscar for best director, for "Tom Jones." Margaret Rutherford, 72, won the best supporting actress award for her role as the bewildered dowager in "The V.I.P.'s."

"Tom Jones" also gained awards for the best substantially original musical score and the best screenplay adapted from another medium. It had been nominated for 10 awards.

FIRST NEGRO

Poitier "best actor"

The best actor award went to a Negro for the first time in the 36-year history of the awards. Sidney Poitier, 37, won it for his role as a hymn-singing Baptist who helps Roman Catholic nuns build a church in "Lilies of the Field." Albert Finney had been strongly backed for his performance in "Tom Jones."

The best actress award was taken by American actress Patricia Neal, for her part as the slatternly housewife in the modern Western "Hud." Miss Neal lives in England and was unable to attend because she is expecting a baby.

Melvyn Douglas's portrayal of the patriarch father in "Hud" won the best supporting actor award. A third Oscar was for black-and-white photography.

BEST FOREIGN FILM

Fellini's "8 ½"

The Oscar for the best foreign film of the year went to "8 ½". Federico Fellini's introspective view of life as seen through a film director's eyes. It had not been nominated for the best film award.

"Cleopatra," at £14,285,000 the costliest film ever made, won Oscars for art direction, cinematography, costume design,and special effects. It had been nominated for nine awards.

(April 15)

A REVOLTING LODGER'S SWAY

By W.A. Darlington

NOT for a long time have I disliked a play so much as I disliked Joe Orton's "Entertaining Mr. Sloane" at the Arts last night.

In its backhanded way, this is a compliment. If an equally nasty play had been ineptly written or ineffectively acted, I should have been able to dismiss it with contempt. But I can't despise this one because it comes to life; I feel as if snakes had been writhing round my feet.

Mr. Sloane, who comes as a lodger to the Kemp household, is nastiness personified; but he exercises a ghastly attraction over the younger Kemps, brother and sister. His writ does not run with old Kemp, their father, who detests Sloane at sight and thinks he has seen him before somewhere.

Hushed-up murder

The climax comes five months later when Sloane, trying to coerce the old man to keep quiet about what he knows, assaults him so brutally that he dies.

Neither brother nor sister has any thought but to hush up the murder, treat it as an accident.

Madge Ryan gives a scarifying picture of an ageing woman besotted over a young thug and Dudley Sutton as Sloane and Peter Vaughan as the scarcely less brutal Ed Kemp go relentlessly through with their jobs.

Charles Lamb as old Kemp stands apart from the general degradation. Producer, Patrick Dromgoole.

(May 7)

OTHELLO WHO ROARS BUT NEVER RANTS

OLIVIER'S DEPTH

By ERIC SHORTER

TO say that Laurence Olivier's performance of Othello at the National Theatre is the finest of our time is not perhaps to say very much, since our age is scarcely notable for Othellos.

Indeed as Ellen Terry observed, it does not suit the English temperament, and the playgoer's memory must go back at least to Frederick Valk before recollecting a more generally exciting performance, and Valk, remember, was a Czech.

This is what we miss in Olivier's beautifully controlled and deeply felt performance.

Syllabic perfection

Olivier roars without ever ranting in his fit of wrath and jealousy, and he also gives us every syllable of the verse. Indeed it may be doubted if we have ever heard quite so much of Othello before.

But when it comes to the truly torrential passion, the role remains just beyond the reach of even this, our most powerful actor. We are not swept along helplessly at the pity of it all though we are often deeply moved and generally kept on the edge of our seats.

Of how many Othellos can that be said? Indeed how many of them have ever had so total a grip on the part as Olivier at the National?

Masochism implied

While the seeds of jealousy are being sown by Frank Finlay's parade ground, matter-of-fact Iago with his devilish fantasies, a hint of masochistic pleasure is implied in Othello's growing suspicions.

In any case, Olivier's mastery of the verse and his ever-present sense of irony make this Moor a continuously exciting performance. It is never stronger than in its moments of pathos when he sees his tragedy approaching in the innocent eyes of Maggie Smith's unusually intelligent Desdemona.

Mr. Finlay's Iago is distinguished in both its respect for the Moor and in not raising a laugh all night. A refreshingly non-intellectual interpretation and none the worse for that.

Elsewhere John Dexter's production does not always quite rise to the occasion. It drags somewhat towards the end and there is too much gonging at the start.

(April 22)

12HOURS OF SHAKESPEARE IN ONE DAY

By W.A. DARLINGTON

ACCORDING to the seating plan, the capacity of the Aldwych Theatre is approximately 1,012. I must therefore share with 1,011 other people (approx.) the record in London playgoing established there on Saturday for all the seats in the house were sold.

It was indeed a formidable record. "The Wars of the Roses" a rearrangement by Peter Hall and John Barton of four Shakespeare histories, consists of three plays each 3 ½ hours long counting an interval. (On Saturday the whole sequence was presented, the performance extending over 12 ½ hours.)

More than that really. Those of us who arrived a little early for the 10.30 a.m. kick-off found that guards had already taken up a silent vigil on the stage over the coffin of Henry V, so that the play was already in being. And the final curtain fell at 10.45 p.m.

WORTH THE EFFORT

Startling sense of continuity

An ordeal, both for actors and audience. But in the opinion of the half-dozen spectators for whom I can personally answer; it was worth the effort; and if vigorous applause is anything to go by the other 1,006 (approx.) thought so too.

The sense of continuity that it gives to go straight on from the Henry VI trilogy to "King Richard III" is startling. Although Shakespeare obviously did not design it to fit on, it does so extraordinarily neatly.

The full-day performance is to be given twice more during the present Aldwych season. I advise all playgoers with the necessary stamina and enthusiasm not to miss the chance to see it.

The acting and production in these plays were noticed last year when the sequence was first staged at Stratford-on-Avon.

But to see it again in a single day is to realise more completely than before what a fine piece of work is Peggy Ashcroft's study of Queen Margaret in her career from vivid ambitious youth to embittered and disappointed age.

There are other fine performances notably David Warner's as that ineffectual angel Henry VI. But to mention all who deserve it would be invidious unless I committed myself to a mere catalogue.

(January 13)

EXHIBITION AN AFFRONT TO MODERN ART

By TERENCE MULLALY

"THE New Generation" is the challenging title of the eagerly-awaited exhibition at the Whitechapel Art Gallery. Now that the exhibition is open it is seen to be remarkable in two ways.

The first concerns the idea behind it and the rewards being offered. Not only is the Peter Stuyvesant Foundation subsidising the exhibition, but it is also offering travel grants to, and buying one work by, six of the 12 young artists represented.

This is patronage of an imaginative kind. Unfortunately, those entrusted with selection of artists and their works have failed lamentably.

Here we have the second remarkable point about the exhibition. It is an affront, with few parallels, to what is serious contemporary British art.

Indeed there have been few comparable examples in the whole troubled history of modern art of so wilful and narrow an exposition of a partisan point of view. Of taste and judgment there is no evidence.

Little purpose would be served by describing the works on view. Most are very large, and if few are quite as empty as the pictures by Paul Huxley, who needs a canvas measuring 68in x 68in to put on it four rudamentary shapes, all are aesthetically barren.

Only four of these artists, Patrick Caulfield, David Hockney, Peter Phillips, with his poster-like pictures of mechanical objects, makes any worthwhile impact on the mind.

(April 2)

CLIFF RICHARD AGAIN MOST POPULAR STAR

Cliff Richard, the "pop" singer,is named as the year's most popular star for the second year running by the London Bureau of the New York Motion Picture Herald. It is on the strength of the film, "Summer Holiday," the second most popular film.

The James Bond thriller "From Russia with Love" was the most popular film of 1963. Sean Connery who played Ian Fleming's secret service agent, climbed from tenth in 1962 to become the fourth most popular star.

Their successes were decided by a box-office survey among about 2,300 cinemas. Epic films "Cleopatra," "How the West was Won" and "Lawrence of Arabia," which played at selected cinemas, were not included.

Top stars, in order, were: Cliff Richard, Peter Sellers, Elvis Presley, Sean Connery, Hayley Mills, Elizabeth Taylor, Marlon Brando, Albert Finney, Dirk Bogarde and Norman Wisdom.

(January 3)

THE DAILY TELEGRAPH
AND
MORNING POST
DAILY TELEGRAPH - - - JUNE 29, 1855
MORNING POST - - - NOVEMBER 2, 1772
[Amalgamated October 1, 1937]
135, Fleet Street, London, E.C.4.
Telephone: Fleet Street 4242

ROPE'S END

ABOLITIONISTS naturally and rightly rejoice at Monday's vote in the House of Commons. But the vote itself, and the nature of the Bill, now present the Lords and the people with some Parliamentary and judicial points which still merit discussion. In the first place, the majority on Monday night was not such as to support the forecasts of those who believed that some 60 per cent. of Conservative M.P.s were firmly in favour of abolition. Public opinion polls, too, have consistently shown a strong majority for retention throughout the country, Mr. SILVERMAN and others rightly argued that M.P.s are representatives, not deputies, and that this country is not governed by plebiscites. But if they press this view too hard, they will only weaken their case against the "unrepresentative" Lords, should the latter go against the Bill.

It can still be regarded as probable that this time the Lords will not wish to frustrate the free vote of the Commons. Should they do so, it might be for a number of reasons, of which the least admirable would be for Conservative Peers to scan the Commons division lists and find in them some kind of party political mandate. But retentionism, as a doctrine, is still held by many Peers with high moral conviction, and these may argue that they more truly represent the national will.

Many speakers in Monday's debate showed an inclination to strengthen the effect of the life sentence in order to compensate for the loss of capital punishment as the unique deterrent. This discussion has never been, and cannot be, clear cut. In principle, it seems best for abolitionists to accept the loss of a certain amount of deterrence in order to secure a greater moral good for the nation.

(December 23)

MARGINAL MAJORITY

IF Mr. Wilson had been asked to describe in advance the circumstances in which he would like to ascend to political power, the last thing that he would have envisaged would have been a journey to Buckingham Palace backed by a Parliamentary majority of four, to the accompaniment of the resignation of Mr. KHRUSCHEV and the explosion of a Chinese nuclear bomb, with some poor export trade figures thrown in for seasoning. Even the minute majority of 1950 was an easy burden in comparison, since Ministers were well experienced in office and in any case had more or less run out of new ideas. The trials of such a majority are much greater when Ministers are trying to concentrate on learning their business and discovering how they are going to try to implement the electoral promises they have made. Labour's room for Parliamentary manoeuvre will be minimal. Even the loss of a vote for the period necessary to find a seat for Mr. GORDON WALKER will be hard to spare. We will at any rate hear no more of the idea of making a Labour member Speaker.

None the less, even with this majority it is possible to govern, and the thoughts that were expressed in this column in the later editions yesterday remain valid. Above all, we shall hope to see less of Mr. WILSON the demagogue of recent weeks, and more of the man who was one of Labour's most businesslike Ministers 15 years ago. With no wealth of talent wherefrom to find his own Ministers now, he faces a load of troubles. The Board of Trade figures published yesterday are a reminder that the expected rise in exports has still not happened. Some realism has got to be injected into policies.

With such a narrow majority, and with at least an occasional prospective need for Liberal support, Mr. WILSON may well be content to defer some of the most controversial and complicated measures, though even here a question mark hangs over steel nationalisation. We must hope that he will defer any crucial change in nuclear policy or in any of the present international defence engagements.

(October 17)

AN AWFUL TENNER

For the first time since 1945 a Bank of England note for £10 is put in circulation to-morrow. The illustration on another page will extinguish any sanguine expectation of a return to the old elegant and dignified design, with its austere copperplate inscription upon the fine white paper which the classic Victorian novelists, with Homeric fixity of epithet, invariably described as "crisp". All that survives of that stately pattern is the legend, over the signature of the Chief Cashier, to the effect that "I promise to pay the Bearer on Demand" the sum named on the face of the note; a vestigal remnant long emptied of any meaning, since we are only paid out with more paper.

On turning his trophy over, however, the fortunate earner of £10 finds an original contribution to art. The study of the curate's little daughter as Britannia in the parish pageant has been removed to the front, and so reduced in size that at first glance it had been mercifully overlooked. In its place is set a quadruped which is neither the leopard of England nor the lion of Scotland, but an amiable hybrid of vaguely Assyrian aspect, its tresses coiffed in the style popularised in Ptolemaic Egypt by Miss Elizabeth Taylor. It grins like a dog and seems prepared to run about the City. Insecurely clasped in what heralds would blazon as the creature's dexter paw, an instrument between a skewer and a paperknife is no doubt a parable of some mystery rightly withheld from the impecunious multitude. Without seeking to comprehend, however, the multitude will no doubt endeavour to collect specimens of this work of art as abundantly as may be.

(February 20)

Hazardous Hunt for North Sea Oil

By WILLIAM RANDOLPH

BRITAIN'S adherence to the Continental Shelf Convention, which confers on each nation mineral rights in the seabed as far as the shelf extends from its coasts, is expected to precipitate one of the greatest gambles the oil industry has ever undertaken.

Capital of the order of several million pounds will be sunk, almost literally, in an attempt to raise the oil which may lie beneath those grey, wind-swept waters.

What are the prospects of success? Exploration in Holland led four years ago to the discovery at Slochteren of a gasfield now known to be Europe's largest. On the British side small quantities of natural gas have been found on the Yorkshire coast. Since then intensive surveying by ship and aircraft has suggested that the same gas-yielding formation lies under much of the sea between. During the summer, at selected points on both sides, drills will put this conjecture to the test.

All major oil companies have entered the search, in various groupings which have so far shown more evidence of collaboration than rivalry. The seismic and magnetometer surveys, for instance, have been carried out by specialist exploration companies acting jointly for nearly all comers. The same joint approach may be used to obtain the special weather forecasts and other services which will be needed if - as is almost certain to happen eventually - drilling extends far from protective coasts.

The early drilling will probably be within territorial waters, where concessions are held by B P and the French Coastal Oil on the British side and by N A M (a Shell/Esso group) and American Caltex on the Dutch. Other groups have interests in German, Danish and Norwegian waters. Beyond the territorial fringe on the British side Shell have surveyed 30,000 square miles for themselves, Esso and B P between Lowestoft and the Forth, while Pan-American jointly with the Gas Council are exploring off Norfolk, Lincolnshire and Yorkshire. American companies are operating still further off-shore.

The Prize

If oil or gas is discovered in any quantity, especially in the area (totalling nearly half the North Sea) over which Britain will exercise mineral rights, it can scarcely fail to have a heartening effect on our economy. Even if not, the search seems likely to bring welcome employment to British shipyards and foundries. Although some off-shore rigs are coming from America, not all are suitable for North Sea conditions. Rigs for the early inshore drilling will probably be available. If the search is pursued to the outer depths, special equipment will be needed.

Off-shore oil rigs are of two kinds; one a platform whose four legs incorporate a jacking device which allows them to rest on the seabed while raising it a safe distance above the water; the other a floating barge. The first can operate only in fairly shallow water, can continue drilling in almost any weather, but is exceedingly vulnerable when moving (some were lost in the Persian Gulf before special weather services were introduced); the second can operate at greater depths, can move more easily, but may have to stop drilling in heavy seas.

The North Sea will provide scope for both, but the platform type will predominate at first. Caltex brought one across the Atlantic (it was damaged en route) a few weeks ago. At Kiel a German/American group are building a 55 ½m. platform, 233ft long, with six legs 33ft in diameter, incorporating special winter features and able to accommodate a crew of 50. A Canadian group, Place Oil and Gas, are considering building a rig specially for use in the Wash.

The cost of these operations is going to be enormous.

But the glittering prize - oil-hungry Europe, with ever increasing consumption, fed from its own doorstep - is one on which oil men throughout the world have their eyes firmly fixed.

(May 14)

Self-lighting cigarettes in court case

A High Court judge was asked yesterday to decide whether a self-lighting cigarette could also be classified as a match.

Mr. Malcolm Morris, Q.C., for the Autolite Cigarette Company, lit one of the cigarettes in court by striking the top against the packet. He took a puff and handed it to a solicitor to be extinguished.

"Would you like to finish it?" asked Mr. Justice Marshall, smiling.

Mr. Morris: Your Lordship is very kind, but I feel it would be trespassing too much on your Lordship's generosity.

Mr. Morris said that self-lighting cigarettes were soon to be manufactured in Britain.

(October 9)

DIPLOMATIC SERVICES TO MERGE

By MICHAEL HILTON
Daily Telegraph Diplomatic Correspondent

THE Government has accepted recommendations for the creation of a unified system for British representation abroad, without distinction between Commonwealth and foreign countries.

The Queen has given her approval for the new service. It will be called "Her Majesty's Diplomatic Service."

The new service will come into effect on Jan. 1, 1965. Sir Harold Caccia, at present Permanent Under-Secretary at the Foreign Office, will be appointed first Head of the Diplomatic Service.

Sir Alec Douglas-Home announced the Government's decision in the House of Commons yesterday. The change was recommended in the report, published yesterday, of a committee under the chairmanship of Lord Plowden.

Also accepted are recommendations for improved allowances for overseas service.

(February 28)

MODS AND ROCKERS

The recent outbreaks of violence between Mods and Rockers have brought the largest number of letters for several years on a single subject to The Daily Telegraph, a selection of which we print here.

(May 24)

Modern pressures produce 'gaping, blank minds'

SIR I write this after arriving home from a week-end visit to Brighton, where I went with a few friends, all of us aged 19 or 20. Having witnessed first hand the pathetic play of the Mods and Rockers, we returned feeling uneasy, shocked and bewildered.

I am very surprised at my easy-going self for having felt the need to write this letter, always having been an unheeding drifter in many respects. However, the idiot Mods and Rockers tantrums have upset me more than I would have deemed possible. The fact that so many people of my age should exhibit such gaping, blank minds scares me.

The most sickening aspect of the attacks was the furtiveness and the creeping cowardice. I felt there was something festering and sinister in that. I hope someone will help me to comprehend what influences hold these people so rigidly and blindly. Not having studied sociology or psychology, I am worried about not being able to see their motivations. I feel thankfully, completely alien to them, but they are as close to my position in society as anyone.

One noticed how, all the time, they would look to one another for support. This need for support was shown when two or three Rockers walked through huge, straggling masses of Mods. They walked through calmly and safely until they were well clear of the mob. Each Mod knew what the precedent was and looked round anxiously at the others in case they were not playing their part. Then, seeing each other react, the reassured mob shflled tentatively forward until, finding themselves of one accord, they burst into a headlong pursuit.

As they rushed past me I kept looking at their faces, trying to find a guiding light. Most of them were expressionless, concentrating only upon the act of running behind someone else; other faces showed elation. Human bodies devoid of intelligence and retaining or perhaps regaining, the animal instinct. They caught the quarry and swarmed over him, fighting to get a kick at him, to fulfil their purpose and impress the appropriate people. Suddenly when the quarry was mastered and limp on the ground, they would all turn and flee in a pack.

None of these troublemakers came from grammar schools, or if they did they left at 15. Between 15 and 20 a person develops individuality of thought and an active, intelligent constructiveness, but only in the right sort of situation. The rapid bombardment of pressures in the world to-day is too great to allow this otherwise.

RODNEY ADDINGTON
London, N.W.9

'Church and State' not to blame

Sir - It is pointless to pretend that "Church and State" are responsible for the contemporary social malaise which has just exploded into the news. For years the Press, radio, television and literature have been the vehicles by which agnosticism and hedonism have been placed in the homes and the minds of our countrymen, and the authority and influence of the Christian Church has been constantly eroded. How dare the Press now turn to lay blame for the results of this wickedness upon the Church? Parents and schoolmasters are indeed partially responsible for what has happened. Both have failed, in most cases, to teach Christian precept, and - above all - to set Christian example.

Yours faithfully
(Rev.) BRIAN STOWE
Bushey, Herts.

Pilot experiment for birch urged

Sir - It would probably be found that in any resort where the magistrates introduced three or four strokes of the birch for the worst offenders in the juvenile hooligan riots the whole thing would cease miraculously, almost as effectively as the Act of a few years ago cleared the streets of prostitutes, because it contained a real penalty.

At any rate it is worth trying a "pilot" experiment at this stage of despair in high places.

Let some one bench of magistrates, say at Margate or Brighton, try it for a few months *pour encourager les autres*, and let everyone in the country see what happens and draw what morals there may be.

Yours faithfully,
R.P. VALLANCE,
London, W.1.

LONDON DAY BY DAY

THE first British bank to enter hire purchase, the National Commercial Bank of Scotland, has now added a double first to its record of innovation.

Its new partnership with the City house of Schroder's in a jointly-owned Scottish merchant bank is a unique move for a clearing bank, but will probably create less controversy than the decision to open a "ladies only" - both staff and customers - branch in Edinburgh's Princes Street.

Mr. Ian Macdonald, the former Glasgow professor who is the bank's chairman, is almost coy but gallant about this, and no doubt women will enjoy the new "comforts."

On the other hand, they will still be unable to cash cheques in that arid hour when all Scottish banks close for lunch.

Conscience as an Ally

DR. MARTIN LUTHER KING, the Negro civil rights leader, spent nearly three hours at St. Paul's Cathedral yesterday.

After his 40-minute Evensong address he crossed to the Chapter House for a Press conference chaired by his friend Canon Collins.

Dr. King, who is on his way to Oslo to receive the Nobel Peace prize, now describes himself as a "pragmatic pacifist." Solutions to the world's problems must be achieved by non-violent methods.

But he admits it is always easier to run a non-violent campaign when you have a potential ally in the conscience of your opponents.

"We're conducting an un-biased public opinion poll on the legislation of commercial radio."

60 Years Publishing

AT 79, Sir Stanley Unwin yesterday arrived punctually at his offices in Museum Street and celebrated 60 years in publishing with his standard complaint that the post was not yet in.

He spend much of his customary 9-6 day working on a new book about the Swedish match king Ivor Krueger, whose enterprises collapsed in the 1930s - though not before Sir Stanley had sold his shares.

He joined his uncle's firm, T. Fisher Unwin, Ltd., in 1904 and the following year found an excuse to visit Dublin and two of the most distinguished authors on their list, W.B. Yeats and George Moore.

Ladies Only
King in Pulpit

Well, You Try

A WORRIED Kensington executive tells me he has been asked, for business purposes, to decode the following from the 1960 Road Traffic Act schedule dealing with cases in which a carrier's licence is not required.

"12. The use of a vehicle for any purpose specified in regulations or the use of a vehicle of any class or description specified in regulations for any purpose or for any purpose so specified."

My correspondent wonders whether he should just chance it.

PETERBOROUGH

PARIS IS OUT OF DATE!

SERENA SINCLAIR

Say these three young designers whose clothes British women are buying

THREE top fashion designers - all women whose clothes are sold in Britain - don't give a hoot what Paris couture shows the world. Spring Collections may come and go, but these three independents dare to ignore the Paris message. They plough their own way - and successfully, too. They have created an entirely new way of looking.

The Paris message isn't everything for lots of buyers, either. They make good money in selling the clothes of these three designers.

The three young women are Mary Quant, Jean Muir (of Jane and Jane) and a French-women on a mutual wavelength - Emmanuelle Khanh.

MARY QUANT

"Paris collection stories? Can't - won't read them. It bothers me. Perhaps it's a reaction from my six years with Jaeger, when we visited the Paris collections, took copious notes, read all the fashion writers. Now I want to be quite free of influence.

"Anyway, the couture is desperately out of date." So says tiny, deceptively gentle Miss Muir, a waif with a will of iron.

Mary Quant made her name first of all for clothes totally unlike the Paris ones, clothes that made a decisive statement about her generation and its world. She's kept this up, though there are some who feel the wheel's come full circle, that Paris has come round to her way of thinking and designing.

"We've done our collections so far ahead that Paris can't really make much difference to us. Oh yes - I look at the pictures, out of curiosity. But the nicest thing about Paris Collections for me is the week-end there with all those good parties!"

Emmanualle Khanh's emancipation is more praiseworthy, more remarkable, for she actually lives in the rue St. Honoré, in the hotbed of it all. Having once modelled for Givenchy she broke away to become a designer. She claims Paris clothes are stultifying. "The couture is dead."

(January 13)

FOLK WEAVE TWEED WITH HOME WEAVE LOOK BY MARY QUANT

WAISTCOAT AND TROUSERS IN ONE FOR MEN

OVERCOATS and suits to match; lacy edges to collars; a gleaming look for evening wear; bright scarlet jerseys; and the "Combo" from Merseyside. These were some of the highlights of a men's fashion parade yesterday.

The parade was to mark the opening of the International Men's and Boys' Wear Exhibition at Earl's Court. The exhibition will remain open until Friday.

The "Combo" was described as the "new Mersey look." It is a waistcoat and trousers in one, with a round scoop neckline worn over a striped shirt with white collar.

The commentator announced each male model by his Christian name; "Ken shows us the jacket with the Henley stripe," or "Rodney wears the anorak."

Some shirts had lurex stripes. One was in silver lamé. An evening suit was in a deep iridescent black and red shade.

But the shirt with the "novelty edging" to collars and cuffs, the one with the lacy look, was in plain white poplin. A little novelty goes a long way.

The "jacket with the Henley stripe" was collarless in bold black and white vertical stripe. It was worn with a polo jersey.

There was a hat to fit any size. It had a stretchable nylon-knitted base. Most of the hats had tiny brims.

COLLARLESS JACKET

Vertical stripes

Far, far removed from Prof. Higgins were some of the cardigans. Scarlet was a favourite colour. There was a black cardigan with a "pony skin" front of printed brushed Acrilan.

But for the "squares" there were bowlers, rolled umbrellas and a British "warm" of impeccable cut.

(February 25)

TROUSER SUITS 'HIDEOUS,' SAYS HARTNELL

MR. NORMAN HARTNELL, the Queen's dressmaker, speaking of the latest trouser suits for women, told a Brighton audience yesterday: "There are limits to this monstrously hideous fashion."

"The female form in ice-cold marble is beautiful. It is not so attractive wobbling about inside tweed trousers," he said.

He admitted that he had seen some reasonable trouser suits worn by attractive young ladies. But his advice was "Haunches are better hidden. If you are going to wear trousers have a jacket long enough to hide that danger area where you sit down."

Midseason preview

He had just watched a "keyhole" preview of mid-season clothes by some of the members of the London Fashion House Group in a final presentation by The Sunday Telegraph.

The day and evening clothes he had designed for the Queen's visit to Canada this month were delivered to Buckingham Palace on Thursday night ready packed to be flown to Canada. But Mr. Hartnell declined to be drawn about these.

The trouser suits included a brilliant double-breated fuchsia-check tweed by Strelitz, and a dashing Susan Small outfit with strap-top trousers and matching jacket in green and white overcheck.

(October 3)

LET'S PUT THE FUN BACK INTO SHOPPING

Is the supermarket a boon or just a glass palace where Big Brother is watching every impulse-buy?

Virginia Waite ... Hitting Out for the Housewife

"Stop rationalising the glass palaces and let us get on with the fun of shopping." So said a housewife in between washing her husband's shirts, baking a cake and flying out to the shop — a small independent grocer — for the sugar she'd forgotten.

What did she mean? "Glass Palaces" referred to supermarkets, and although she accepts that they have their advantages, she doesn't like the idea of being used as a pawn in big financial stakes.

She has the feeling that behind the the palaces there are men pigeon-holing and docketing her, working out by maps, diagrams and computers which counters she will go to, what to-and-fro moves she will make, how long she will spend in the supermarket.

Big business, in the form of supermarkets, is attempting to de-humanise her, to put her under a microscope and analyse her actions. Many housewives find supermarkets and self-service stores fun. But others resent this surreptious interference.

"I feel as though I'm being watched by a sort of 'Big Brother'," said one housewife. "I feel bemused among the piles of baked beans and tinned carrots, I regret the lack of someone to consult (if only to say 'good morning') and I hate the queueing at the cashier's desk."

Her comments are backed up in a survey by the British Market Research Bureau entitled "Shopping in Surburbia" and dealing with the housewife and the supermarket. It also pin-points the surprising number of housewives who DON'T use supermarkets. In a given area, for instance, one in five had never set foot inside one.

But, paradoxically, the housewife with the "Big Brother" feelings DID use a supermarket, though only for branded goods. "I still yearn for the little old shops and feel I can't desert my family grocer," she told me.

What worried her about supermarkets was their coldness and lack of personality, their clinical gangways, their endless neatly stacked piles of cans.

The worst hate of all (and the biggest barrier to success as far as the supermarkets themselves are concerned) is the pre-packaged perishable goods.

"My feelings are probably quite illogical," said one housewife, "but somehow those wrapped lamb chops and slabs of cheese look manufactured and unattractive. I fear they might not be fresh and wonder how long they've been wrapped. I also worry about not being able to see the bottom lamb chop."

So much for the disadvantages. But apart from the excitement of trading stamps, housewives DO like supermarkets in some ways. They like the fun of going round making their own selections, the delight of pitting their wits against other shopkeepers by getting something at cut price.

They also find supermarkets attractive for reasons which have nothing whatsoever to do with the goods they sell. "They're fun, tremendous fun, to look around," said a housewife, "and when I take my baby for her daily airing I often walk to the supermarket instead of to the park."

Both comments reveal the changing pattern of shopping. They also reveal the fact that we don't go shopping just to buy a dozen eggs and 1lb bacon. We go often for company, often for colour, often for an outing away from home.

The male brains behind supermarkets and self-service stores are busy working out logical processes for making shopping easier (and presumably more lucrative for them). The only trouble is that housewives are illogical — and many like it that way.

"Shopping is an essential part of one's life and I thoroughly enjoy it," said one housewife. "I do hope that enjoyment isn't going to be forcibly removed by this automation and analysis of shops and shopping habits.

(January 8)

Hiring a disc jockey for your party

Nicola Hemingway

If your daughter is coming out this season you are bound to come up against the problems of giving a dance or party. Most people agree that it's the music that makes the party swing.

But large dances which cannot be contained between the four walls of a room often suffer from having a splendid source of music in the main room but a rather inadequate supply in the other. Dancing off the beat to muffled strains can hardly be called satisfactory.

A juke box looks so ugly and is subject to a first-come-first-served approach, and the workings of a tape recorder baffle many.

The answer could well be a mobile discotheque service which provides the latest in audio equipment, over 200 records and a disc jockey into the bargain for 25gns a party. (To hire a good band can cost you up to £140).

Robert Morrison, who runs the only mobile discotheque in England, tries to create a nightclub atmosphere on the lines of the permanent discotheque clubs like the Garrison and Annabel's in London, with a selection of modern music including most of the top twenty and some foreign records.

(March 13)

HOW MUCH LONGER WILL LONG HAIR GO?

THE Beatles started it, the Stones took it a stage farther and now Britain's teenage boys are carrying it beyond a joke; the cult of long hair.

It comes to something when a 14-year-old Dalkeith schoolboy, Owen Holmes, has to sit in a girls' class because he won't get his hair cut.

We could stomach it if long hair went with the sartorial elegance of the Stuarts, but when it is accompanied by shapeless jerkins and grubby, baggy jeans the whole effect is, frankly, ghastly.

And the astonishing thing is that these young men with the luscious curls of shoulder-length hair would punch you on the nose if you dared to call them effeminate.

Girls I spoke to said they wouldn't be seen dead with a boy whose hair rivalled theirs in length.

Barbers, not unnaturally, are showing some concern about it all. They would be out of business if the craze spread to other age groups.

Some have doubled their prices for boys with Beatle cuts; others are charging so much an inch for cutting hair and some in despair are directing their long-haired clients to women's hairdressers.

The Beatles and the Rolling Stones have a lot to answer for.

ANN STEELE

(September 2)

And why not a woman right at the top?

THERE is no earthly reason why a woman shouldn't be Prime Minister one day, according to Mrs. Barbara Castle, Minister of Overseas Development.

That idea, perhaps preposterous itself, seems to be the most natural thing in the world, coming from Britain's dynamic highly intelligent and only woman Cabinet Minister.

Over the tea cups in her office yesterday afternoon she said with great conviction: "Of course I can see a woman as P.M. if she is the best person for the job. I wouldn't mind having half the Cabinet women. But not all," she added with a smile, "I couldn't bear the exclusive company of women.."

The devastating thing about Barbara, who is 53, is that she is entirely feminine as well as entirely efficient, in a mainly man's world.

She is the living proof that it can happen. It may be very rare, but blue stockings go with blue eyes, burnished copper hair and high heels.

Women in the past, she believes, have just not had a chance to show their worth. Harold Wilson has made "a very cunning move" in choosing several women for office and will get the women of the country on his side.

"Women have failed to achieve high office in the past," she says, "half because of lack of opportunity and half because of defeatism on their own part."

She laughed, "In the 1955 election we thought I was out on one count. My husband was absolutely panic-sticken at the thought of my becoming a housewife."

She believes there should be help to get women going again when they have been at home for a long time. There should be far greater facilities for training middle-aged women in new careers.

GERDA PAUL

(October 23)

NANCY LADY ASTOR

WIT AND COURAGE ADDED COLOUR TO POLITICS

NANCY VISCOUNTESS ASTOR, widow of the second Viscount, who has died aged 84, was the first woman M.P. to take her seat in the House of Commons. She represented the Sutton Division of Plymouth from 1919-45.

Lady Astor was American-born, the last survivor of five beautiful sisters who were known in their youth as the "Gibson Girls." She married the late Viscount Astor in 1906.

NANCY VISCOUNTESS ASTOR

Since her marriage she had identified herself closely with the country of her adoption, although she never failed to express pride in her Virginian antecedents.

Nancy Astor's vigorous provocative nature found abundant opportunity for expression in the course of her 25 years at Westminster. She was elected as a Conservative, but sat where her fancy dictated in the House.

CHURCHILL TARGET

Wit and courage

With characteristic independence she criticised members of her own party as freely as those of any other. Two of her favourite targets at one time were the then Mr. Churchill and Mr. David, later Lord, Kirkwood.

Her challenging interpolations brought her to the notice of the Speaker on several occasions, but it was generally conceded that her wit, incisiveness and courage added considerable colour to the political life of the country.

She disposed of pre-1939 allegations that she ran a pro-German "Cliveden set" - a reference to house-parties at her beautiful home at Taplow, Bucks - by revealing that she had never even met many of the politicians and diplomats with whom her name was associated.

She was one of the closest friends of Bernard Shaw.

INCISIVE VIEWS

Women's pay

Her views on all subjects were incisive and more frequently controversial than not. "We have got to make the world safe for men." she said once. "They have made it darned unsafe for us. The country has been in danger for 2,000 years - ever since men began to rule it alone."

Lower pay for women she described as a "great dishonesty."

Lady Astor also once denounced this "modern strip-tease age," and said only educated men and women could put things right.

"We have got to stop paying too much attention to the common man. It is the uncommon people who have achieved things. Although, as one of the common people myself, I like the common people, it is the uncommon people that I follow.

Lady Astor once advocated abolition of the hereditary peerage to get rid of snobbishness. "You have women who in their own right cannot sit in the House of Lords," she said, "but any old mumbo-jumbo can sit there."

On at least one occasion she made a speech which had international repercussions. This was in 1942, when she declared that the Russians were fighting not for us, but for themselves.

Goebbels made great use of the speech for propaganda purposes, and the Russians protested. Lady Astor subsequently claimed her words had been misinterpreted.

LLOYD GEORGE SPONSOR

Row over painting

Even her introduction to Parliament provoked a storm. She had as sponsor Mr. Lloyd George and Lord Balfour, and five years later a painting of the scene by Charles Sims was presented to Parliament and hung on a staircase.

Protests at living politicians being so honoured led to the withdrawal of the picture and to the rule that portraits could not be hung at Westminster until 10 years after the death of the subject.

Nancy Witcher Langhorne married as her first husband Robert Gould Shaw, from whom she obtained a divorce in 1903. He died in 1930. There are four sons and a daughter of her marriage to Viscount Astor, who died in 1952.

(May 4)

AUTHORESS OF 'PEYTON PLACE' DIES

MRS. GRACE METALIOUS, authoress of the controversial novel "Peyton Place," died in a Boston hospital to-day from a chronic liver complaint. She was 38.

The novel caused a storm in the New Hampshire town of Gilmanton when it was published in 1956. Residents accused her of basing the sexually frank book on their own lives. Her husband, George, was reported to have been dismissed from his job as headmaster of the local grammar school.

Mrs. Metalious denied the allegations and said: "To a majority of people who live here it is a dirty book. People suddenly decided George was not the type to teach their sweet, innocent children." Sales of the book reached 7,000,000 copies.

Libel suits settled

Two libel suits brought against the authoress for £100,000 were settled out of court. Mrs. Metalious sold the film rights for £178,000.

It would not be fair, though, to dismiss her purely as someone who wrote to titillate. Mrs. Metalious was an immensely competent craftsman, and showed in her last novel, "No Adam in Eden," that she could write with only minor erotic trimmings.

(February 26)

Prof. Haldane scientist of repute

PROF. J.B.S. HALDANE, who has died in India aged 72, was one of the most brilliant and controversial scientists of our time. He was a distinguished biologist and expert on genetics research.

He was once regarded as the British Communist party's prize capture, but broke away from it after a scientific split between East and West following the publication of the Lysenko theory in genetics.

Prof. Haldane will always be remembered for his outstanding work concerning diving, and finding its limiting physiological factors. He ruthlessly used himself as guinea pig for these dangerous and exhausting tests.

From his knowledge of the behaviour of the human body under such conditions, he calculated "diving tables" which lay down the permitted rate of ascent of a diver and give the times at which he must stop so that the dissolved nitrogen in his blood can be released.

(December 2)

LORD BEAVERBROOK, CHAMPION OF IMPERIAL CAUSES

THE death of Lord Beaverbrook yesterday at the age of 85 removes from British life a forceful and original man who exercised a considerable political influence in the war-time Cabinet and, before and since, through the newspapers under his control.

LORD BEAVERBROOK

William Maxwell Aitken, or "Max" as he was known throughout life to his friends, was born at Maple, Ontario, Canada, on May 25, 1879. He was the third son of the Rev. William Aitken, a Presbyterian minister, and one of a family of ten.

He went to school in Newcastle, New Brunswick, to which the family had moved. Later he studied law at Chatham, in the same province, and started business in Halifax, Nova Scotia.

Then, at the age of 20, he began a run of remarkable success. In 10 years he became a millionaire.

In 1910 he formed a "merger" of all the Canadian cement mills. This brought him an immense fortune at one stroke. He became the target of a Press campaign, but the Cement Trust was successful and its finance was sound.

Aitken then transferred his activities to England, where he found a political situation well suited to his adventurous temperament and to his new ambitions.

MET BONAR LAW

Visits to Britain

He had visited this country on several occasions selling bonds and securities to City houses. In the course of one of these visits he saw Mr. Bonar Law at his flat in Whitehall Court, and he invested in one of Aitken's companies.

When Aitken arrived in England he found that Mr. Bonar Law had become Unionist party leader.

In December 1910, Aitken captured Ashton-under-Lyne from the Liberals fighting as an uncompromising Imperialist. He was knighted in the following year.

On the arrival of the first Canadian contingent early in the 1914-18 war he was officially attached to it as Canadian Government Representative.

Returning to London he was appointed Chairman of the War Office Films Committee and Lieutenant-Colonel in charge of the Canadian War Records. Then in 1918, on Bonar Law's recommendation, he was invited to join the Government as Minister of Information and Chancellor of the Duchy of Lancaster.

Ill-health compelled his resignation before the year was out. He had received a baronetcy in July, 1916, and a peerage followed six months later.

Probably Lord Beaverbrook had more to do than anyone else with Bonar Law's decision to support the motion for the break-up of the Lloyd George Coalition at the famous Carlton Club meeting in 1922. After a few months of office Bonar Law was smitten with fatal illness and resigned.

Mr. Baldwin then succeeded and the purely political career of Lord Beaverbrook was suspended.

TURN TO NEWSPAPERS

Political propaganda

He turned to the field of newspaper proprietorship. Henceforth he used his newspapers to further his political principles, varied with occasional appearances on the public platform when his crusade of the moment required.

He was no stranger to Fleet Street. He had owned the now defunct Globe during its decline, but had disposed of this before acquiring, in 1913, his first holding in the Daily Express. During the war his control was intermittent, but in 1918 he assumed full charge. The circulation of the Daily Express was then about 350,000. It is now well over four million. Lord Beaverbrook proceeded to found the Sunday Express; and in 1923 he completed the triad he desired by purchasing the Evening Standard.

When Lord Beaverbrook took up a subject or a principle he let it dominate his mind. He was not content to inspire articles in his papers; he wrote them himself and he wrote with zeal and sincerity. If he had a first article of faith it was his faith in the British Empire. Every Imperial cause found in him an eager supporter.

Yet his Empire Free Trade policy and his United Empire party failed to attract any really formidable support in Britain or in the Dominions.

Not more successful were his crusade in favour of isolation - based on the slogan: "Choose between Europe and the Empire" - his call for the repudiation of the Locarno treaties, and his campaign in favour of Britain's quitting the League of Nations.

The best-remembered of all similar errors of judgment was the continued asserveration throughout the crises of 1938 and 1939: "There will be no war." But when the war did come Lord Beaverbrook came into his own in the sphere of national politics.

It was in May, 1940, when Britian faced the supreme ordeal of the war, that Mr. Churchill appointed Lord Beaverbrook as the first Minister of Aircraft Production. In the days that followed Dunkirk and the collapse of France - and seemed the prelude to invasion - the post was vital.

His ruthless energy and resource carried him through all difficulties. He adopted extraordinary measures; he used unconventional methods; inevitably he made many enemies in the process. But he obtained results. As one colleague said: "He swept like Genghis Khan through every department," Mr. Churchill declared that this drive had "worked magic."

He entered the War Cabinet. After a short spell as Minister of State with supply duties in the Defence Committee, he was appointed Minister of Supply. The interlocking problems of aid to Russia and aid from the United States confronted him.

In August, 1941, he accompanied Mr. Churchill to the "Atlantic Charter" meeting with President Roosevelt. From there he went on to Washington. In September he headed the British mission to the Moscow supply conference.

Throughout these vital exchanges Lord Beaverbrook made adroit use of his gift for propaganda no less than his talent for negotiation. It is on record that during his tenure of the Ministry of Supply our production of tanks was doubled in six months.

On Feb. 4, 1942, he became Minister of War Production, being succeeded by Sir Andrew Duncan, but 15 days later, on the reconstruction of the War Cabinet, he relinquished his new post.

His last Ministerial office was that of Lord Privy Seal, which he held from 1943 to 1945. For some time during that period he was in charge of plans for civil aviation.

The General Election of 1945 brought his newspapers into great prominence - particularly in regard to the issue of the higher command of the Socialists - but he later repudiated any suggestion that he had determined the strategy of the Conservative party.

In May, 1947, he was installed as Chancellor of the University of New Brunswick. There he had endowed scholarships for postgraduate study at London University, and had contributed lavish financial aid. He had been Hon. Life Chancellor since 1954.

When Lord Beaverbrook entered his 86th year last month a younger Canadian newspaper proprietor, Lord Thomson of Fleet, gave a party for 658 at the Dorchester. There were tributes from the Duke of Windsor, Mr. Lester Pearson, Viscount Rothermere and Sir Winston Churchill.

He married, in 1906, Gladys, second daughter of the late Brig. Gen. Charles William Drury, of Halifax, Nova Scotia. She died in 1927. In 1963 Lord Beaverbrook married the widow of Sir James Dunn. He leaves, by his first marriage, a son and a daughter.

(June 10)

BEHAN, STAGE IRISHMAN IN REAL LIFE

BRENDAN BEHAN, the Irish paywright, author and poet, who has died aged 41, was one of the most extraordinary literary characters of all time.

From the moment he achieved prominence with the production of his first play, "The Quare Fellow," in 1956, he was rarely out of the news.

His drinking excesses put him in hospital, in Ireland, England, Canada, and the United States more times than he would have cared to count. They landed him in gaol, mostly for one-night stays, in five different countries.

Each attempt to go "on the wagon" was followed by another wild bout of drinking.

Educated in a convent, he left school at 14 and joined the IRA, an organisation outlawed by the Eire Government. At the age of 16 he received a Borstal sentence of three years for illegal activities in Liverpool.

Expelled from Britain later, he returned to Ireland and in 1942 was sentenced by a military court to 14 years imprisonment for shooting at police officers.

The eight years he spent in prison, provided the material for "The Quare Fellow." His period in Borstal inspired the novel "Borstal Boy."

Although "The Quare Fellow" was enthusiastically received by the critics it was a television appearance, during which, as he admitted later, he was drunk which made his name known over-night throughout Britain. A successful West End run for the play firmly established him.

(March 21)

COLE PORTER

30 MUSICALS AND 10 FILMS

COLE PORTER, the American song-writer, who died late on Thursday night, aged 71, was possibly the most widely quoted man this century. Certainly his output of songs that captured the public imagination was prodigious.

Miss Otis, Argentines without means, and the young woman whose heart belonged to daddy, must be familiar figures to millions of people all over the world.

He composed often with breathtaking rapidity, in cafés and at noisy parties, in aircraft and cars, between courses at dinner. On a world tour in 1934 he wrote the score for the Broadway musical "Jubilee" including one of his greatest successes, "Begin the Beguine."

He himself said he worked on the lyrics of a song while waiting for help to come when a fall from his horse in 1938 agonisingly crushed both legs.

INHERITED MILLIONS

In Foreign Legion

Always well-to-do, he inherited several million dollars while still a young man. His early experiences might well have induced him to adopt the wealthy man's traditional habits of benefaction or dissoluteness according to temperament.

For although tunes are said to have poured from him when he was only 10 years old, his first assault on Broadway with "See America First" in 1916, while a student at the Harvard Music School, was a flop.

Frustrated, he joined the French Foreign Legion, transferred to the French Army when the United States entered the war and was awarded the Croix de Guerre. After the war he studied at the Schola Cantorum, Paris, where Vincent d'Indy was one of his tutors.

Years of effort and disappointment followed until his breakthrough came in 1928 with the Broadway production of "Paris."

After that Broadway success followed success almost every year, sometimes twice a year, for more than 20 years - in all some 30 stage shows and 10 films, including "Anything Goes," "Dubarry Was a Lady," "Kiss Me Kate," and "Silk Stockings."

But the last few years for this egregious man, whose comprehensive range of interests were once proverbial, had been solitary. Through his accident, he was in intermittent pain for years. He endured more than 30 operations, including the amputation of his right leg. Childless, the death of his wife in 1954 left him alone.

(October 17)

MISOGYNIST OF OXFORD DIES

ONE of the last of the woman-haters at Oxford University, Mr. Christopher Thomas Atkinson, Emeritus, Fellow of Exeter College, died yesterday in St. Luke's Home, Oxford. He was 89.

Known as "Atters," Mr. Atkinson was a Fellow of Exeter from 1898 until he retired in 1941. He was a military historian.

He was, perhaps, better known for the strategy he employed to keep women undergraduates away from his lectures. He managed this successfully even after the university authorities had ruled that they should be allowed to attend.

According to one story, he informed one persistent young woman that as he had got wet cycling into Oxford, he proposed to take off his trousers. She fled.

His hatred of women was equalled only by his hatred of reference books. But he lavished affection on his dog, a surly beast of which everyone went in awe, and on Magdalen, which he always referred to as "The College."

At the time of King Edward VIII's abdication, his sole comment was: "He's let the College down."

(February 19)

GEN. DOUGLAS MacARTHUR

CONTROVERSIAL SOLDIER ADMIRED AND ABUSED

THERE have been few more controversial figures in military history than General of the Army Douglas MacArthur, who has died aged 84. He won praise and obloquy in equal measure.

To his admirers in America, who were vociferous in their devotion, he was the militarily omniscient hero of Bataan and Corregidor, and the architect of victory in the South-West Pacific; they blamed the vacillations of politicians for his failures.

GEN. DOUGLAS MacARTHUR

"Bombastic blunderer" and "would-be Mikado" - a reference to what some considered his despotic control of occupied Japan - were terms used by his detractors.

His conduct of the Korean campaign, from the command of which he was dismissed in 1951 by Mr. Truman, provided his critics with a great deal of ammunition. He appeared to have been taken completely unawares by the invasion of South Korea; subsequently his strategy and misplaced optimism frequently created unease and puzzled British military authorities.

MacArthur's personal courage was never in doubt; impeccably dressed, invariably unarmed, he displayed it in all his campaigns.

But the buoyancy, ascribed by many to egotism - which caused him to make such incautious utterances as the "home by Christmas" message to the troops in Korea in 1950 - aroused misgivings at times even among his admirers.

His handsome appearance, the rakish angle of his cap, and his willingness to pose for photographers long ago earned him the title of "the picture-postcard general" from the cynics.

RECALL IN 1941

Philippines campaign

But, called from retirement in 1941 to lead the American forces in the Philippines against overwhelming odds, he gave a superb display of doggedness and craft. He subsequently proved more than a match for the Japanese in guile and in aggressive tactics.

The son of a lieutenant-general of Scottish descent, Douglas MacArthur was born at Little Rock Barracks, Arkansas, in 1880. He graduated from West Point in 1903, and was twice wounded in the 1914-18 war, in which he rose to brigadier-general.

MacArthur decided to meet trouble half-way. He ferried troops and supplies by air to Port Moresby, and not only fought and defeated the Japanese but chased them back over the mountains. He established footholds in western New Britain and the northern Solomons and seized the Admiralty Islands. The threat to Australia was removed, and was not to recur.

In 1944 he returned to the Philippines, as he had pledged himself to do when he slipped away in the darkness two years before.

But this time, at the head of a great armada, he swept away the opposition. The Japanese suffered more than 423,000 casualties, of whom 300,000 were killed, in a campaign which lasted for 250 days.

On the unconditional surrender of Japan MacArthur was appointed Supreme Allied Commander to direct the occupation of the country.

He was twice married. His second wife, formerly Miss Jean Faircloth, whom he married in 1937, survives him, with a son.

(April 6)

NEHRU: A NATION WITHOUT AN HEIR

By Martin Moore

JAWAHARLAL NEHRU was a man of contrasts and contradictions. They sprang perhaps from the mingled, but unblended, elements of East and West in his education.

Barristers of the Inner Temple were common enough in India; but the product of Harrow and Trinity College, Cambridge, was an incongruous figure in the entourage of Gandhi. He became, in his own words, "a queer mixture, out of place everywhere, at home nowhere."

He certainly was not at home in the spiritual climate of Gandhism, "I dislike violence intensely," Nehru wrote in his autobiography, "yet I am full of violence myself and, consciously or unconsciously, am often attempting to coerce others." When power came to him, the coercion was frequently conscious and deliberate.

The passionate opponent of Fascism and Nazism had himself the stuff of which dictators are made. Nine times imprisoned by the British for political agitation, he clapped Communists into gaol when they attempted the same methods against his own Government.

Nehru was a man of much charm and a warm humanity of manner. His cultivated background had made him an easy conversationalist on a wide range of affairs, a facility which he perfected during 16 years of unbroken leadership at home and multitudinous activity as elder statesman of the Afro-Asian group.

If his economics were more theoretical than practical, and if he had a rather airy head for figures such as were involved in India's vast planning and foreign aid requirements, he was nevertheless a shrewd manipulator of men. He was a politician to his delicate finger-tips.

Nehru's family, though long settled in Allahabad, were Kashmiri Brahmins - an origin which helps to explain the passionate intransigence of his attitude when the Kashmir dispute brought India and Pakistan to the brink of war. "I love Kashmir like a woman, he once said."

His father, Motilal Nehru, was a rich barrister. The story that he habitually sent his linen to be laundered in Paris may not have been true, but it is indicative of the atmosphere of wealthy refinement into which Jawaharlal was born on Nov. 14, 1889, and to which he returned after his aristocratic English education.

But not for long. Young Nehru became a convert not only to Gandhi's nationalist movement, but to the Gandhian way of life. Dressed in homespun, he moved out of his father's house to live in a hut in the garden.

In 1940 Nehru was arrested for the eighth time, for making anti-war speeches. When Japan entered the war in the following December he was released, but his attitude was that India would co-operate in repelling the Asian aggressor only if independence was first conceded.

After the failure of the Cripps Mission he supported the Congress "Quit India" campaign. "We shall fight the British Government to the last." he declared. Faced with this challenge, and with the enemy at the gates, the Government had no choice but to rearrest Nehru, Gandhi and the other Congress leaders.

In June, 1945, Nehru was released. The next two years were occupied by tortuous negotiations about the form and timing of India's promised independence, with Nehru pressing ever more urgently for British withdrawal and stubbornly resisting the Moslem demand for a separate State. In August, 1946, he was asked to form an interim Government; and after accepting at last the separation of Pakistan he became Prime Minister of the Dominion of India at midnight on Aug. 14, 1947.

Confronted with the enormous tasks of strengthening India's economy, repelling the recurrent threat of famine and combating communalism, Nehru was never too preoccupied to make pronouncements on whatever disputes happened to be engaging the outside world.

His loyalty to the Mahatma was far from uncritical. "Gandhi," he said, "is the great peasant, with the peasant's outlook on affairs, and with the peasant's blindness to some aspects of life."

The thread on which these contradictions were strung and reconciled was Nehru's single-minded determination to achieve independence for India; to mould it into a secular State, based on a socialised economy; and to attain for his country (and himself) a rather vaguely conceived moral leadership in Asia and the world.

For these aims he was ready to sacrifice a life of luxury and his own liberty, just as he was prepared to risk the bloodbath which followed the premature withdrawal of British control.

Nehru's own outlook was that of Western industrial Socialism. While declaring that he was "not a Communist in the accepted sense," he confessed himself strongly attracted towards Marxism as "the only reasonable and scientific explanation of history."

Finally, ageing and weary, Nehru had to compromise his own most consistently cherished principle of non-alignment, when India herself became a victim of aggression and a Chinese army swept across the North-East frontier in October, 1962.

Since it was still impossible to act tough, his fighting speeches made no impression on the Chinese - but they won tremendous acclaim from his own countrymen, at a time when there was a good deal of murmuring against him for his "softness."

The same process, in reverse, was observable in Nehru's handling of the Goa issue. From the first he was determined to incorporate the Portuguese enclave. He hoped, or professed to hope, that this could be achieved by peaceful means.

But when at length he resolved to strike, his patience reached a well timed exhaustion.

At home, a nationalistic triumph against Goa was well calculated to offset humiliation in the Himalayas and to win patriotic votes in the coming elections.

These, in February, 1962, confirmed Congress for the third time as the only possible source of Government. As Congress is more than a political party, so Nehru was more than a party leader.

This was manifest in his most critical hour, when the Chinese attack exposed India's military unpreparedness and political miscalculation. If the blame rested squarely on Nehru, so did the sole hope of galvanising national resistance. There was nobody else; a Chamberlain had to become a Churchill in the same man.

That Nehru could attempt, and while the crisis lasted achieve, such a transformation was the measure of his ascendancy. At home and abroad, he was identified with the nation itself, and to this status he has left no heir.

(May 28)

Ian Fleming, creator of James Bond

IAN LANCASTER FLEMING, the writer, who has died, aged 56, made his name with his novels of espionage in which the character of his hero, James Bond became synonymous with danger, luxurious living and women.

As author he was a best-seller with his blend, in his novels, of sex, sadism and snobbery plus the swift, and almost unbelievable, adventures of a secret agent. But he also found time for serious investigation of reputed treasure caches of the past.

A journalist, he was with Reuters from 1929-33 and later was with a firm of merchant bankers. From 1935 he was a member of a firm of stockbrokers until 1939. During the 1939-45 war, he became personal assistant to the Director of Naval Intelligence.

UNDERWATER FISHING

Expert knowledge

From 1945 until 1959 he was foreign manager of Kamsley, later Thomson Newspapers. An underwater fishing expert, he used his knowledge for one of his novels.

He made his home after the war in London and Jamaica, lending his Jamaican house to Sir Anthony Eden for his convalescence after the illness which led to his retirement as Prime Minister.

He married in 1952 Anne, Viscountess Rothermere, whose marriage to Viscount Rothermere was dissolved in February, 1952. In the suit Mr. Fleming was cited as co-respondent. He leaves a widow and one son.

One of his novels, "Thunderball," was the subject of a High Court action which was settled last year. As a result of the action, a film producer, Kevin McClory, was given the film rights to the novel.

In 1961 Mr. Fleming had a coronary thrombosis, which his doctors said was due to heavy smoking. They advised him to reduce his cigarette smoking from 60 to 20 a day.

Last May he spent a fortnight in the King Edward VII Hospital for Officers, Marylebone, suffering from "general fatigue." Over the past 12 years he produced 12 Bond books. He had just completed the 13th "The Man with the Golden Gun."

The latest Bond film, "Gold finger," is due for release in October. His publishers have the manuscripts of two children's books, with a hero named "Chitty-Chitty-Bang-Bang," based on a 1920 racing car driven by Count Louis Zborowski.

Mr. Fleming turned himself into a limited company, Gildrose Productions Ltd. He sold 51 per cent. of the company to Booker Bros. a City investment group.

(August 13)

'Dumb' Harpo Marx Dies at 75

Daily Telegraph Reporter

Harpo Marx, who has died in Hollywood, aged 75, was the "dumb" member of the Marx Brothers whose eccentric, quick-fire comedy in films earned them immense popularity and a fortune.

Harpo was the blonde-chasing member of the team. Instead of speech he used an old taxi horn, honking two blasts for "Yes" and one blast for "No". He used a wild blond wig and a harp, which he played with skill.

The Marx Brothers, Chico, who died in 1961, Groucho, Harpo, Zeppo and Gummo, made their name in the Broadway show "I'll Say She Is." Their first film was "The Coconuts." At the height of their careers the brothers earned about £7,000 a week.

(September 30)

Eddie Cantor

EDDIE CANTOR, the American comedian, who has died aged 72, was one of the highest-paid artists on films, stage and radio in the inter-war years. Despite a weak heart, he continued to earn enormous sums on television.

He made several visits to Britain, but his reputation was founded mainly on his films. He made such pictures as "The Kid from Spain," "Roman Scandals," "Whoopee" with its famous "Whoopee" song, and "Kid Millions." His "pop-eyes" and sophisticated humour won him great popularity.

Cantor's real name was Edward Itzkowitz. He acted in his youth as "Little Arthur," a juggler's clumsy assistant. For a time he was a singing waiter in a Coney Island Beer garden, with Jimmy Durante accompanying him on the piano.

He lost a fortune in the Wall Street crash, but wrote a humourous book about it called "Caught Short." He made another fortune working in films for Sam Goldwyn.

At one time in the 30's he was reputed to earn £50,000 a picture, plus a percentage of the takings.

(October 12)

DAME EDITH SITWELL, A FLAMBOYANT ASCETIC

DAME EDITH SITWELL, who has died aged 77, was an original poet and her quality was widely recognised. But she became a familiar figure to millions who had never read a line of her verse.

This was because of her striking, not to say dramatic, public personality. When quite young, she adopted a vaguely Tudor style of dress consisting of wimpole, floor-brushing skirt and saucer-size ornaments.

At the time her dress caused an astonished American to remark: "She's Gothic enough to hang bells on." Nevertheless it suited her aquiline features, straight fair hair and somewhat hieratic bearing.

In public she could be relied upon for something quotable, if occasionally rather outré. She could also be tart; particularly with those who ventured to criticise her work - she admitted to "Lacking the virtue of patience with maliciously stupid people."

On the other hand she was generous in praise and help to young writers; as early as 1938 she was canvassing the genius of the then almost unknown Dylan Thomas.

Some are mannered perhaps, but many have a sharp beauty and a genuine poetic "inscape." Such are the collections called "Bucolic Comedies," "Facade" and "Marine" (so curiously reminiscent of Raoul Dufy's water colours).

After the war, she wrote "The Shadow of Cain" and "The Canticle of the Rose," in which she speaks like a seer borne down by sorrow for mankind.

These are considered by many to be her greatest work; others hesitate over their sometimes allusive imagery and abstractions. But of their originality and individuality there is no doubt.

(December 1)

PHYLLIS DIXEY

PHYLLIS DIXEY, who made her name during the 1939-45 war years as "the girl the Lord Chamberlain banned," died yesterday at her home at Epsom. She was 50.

In her revue "Picadilly to Dixie" at the Phoenix Theatre, she appeared in several daring poses, one in the nude.

She took over the Whitehall Theatre in 1944, but gave up the lease three years later, and in 1949 her company, Phyllis Dixey Ltd., went into voluntary liquidation.

After 16 years of appearing in nude shows, Miss Dixey decided, in 1956, to give up her act. Her husband, Mr. Jack Tracey, said at the time that she would return to straight acting or comedy.

(June 3)

WAY OF THE WORLD

B.A. (Bingo)

TO break the "stranglehold" which it is alleged Oxford and Cambridge exert on Britain's university system, Mr. Brian Jackson suggests in Where? the journal of the Advisory Centre for Education, that places at those universities should be allotted "by ballot."

This, he points out, "would cut out the whole complex of interviews, scholarship examinations and choosing the college man."

But why stop there? Why not allot all university places by ballot? Why not, come to that university degrees?

This, after all, would not only cut out the whole complex of study, examinations and marking of papers, but banish for ever the demons of ability and application which have always made it so difficult to evolve a truly egalitarian system of education in this country.

Mind you, it would also destroy the rest of us along with our educational system - but, after all, isn't that the whole idea?

(January 7)

Cultural Aggression

I HAVE not heard any broadcasts from the pirate radio ship Caroline. But I assume they are not musically of a high order. This seems a terrible wasted opportunity.

Were I rich I would buy a pirate radio ship, man it with a crew of musicians, poets and philosophers and anchor it in international waters, jamming other stations and deluging the British public day and night with non-stop broadcasts of chamber-music and Wagnerian opera and with talks on Holderlin and Kierkegaard.

The ship would have to be heavily armed. There would be constant danger of a punitive expedition, organised by the TTT or Terrible Television Tribesmen, headed by the Grand Moron himself, putting out in boats from Canvey Island, boarding the ship and massacring the crew to the last man.

(April 10)

Sense of Occasion

FAR from ignoring the quarter-centenary of Shakespeare's birth, the GPI Television Network is to enter completely into the spirit of the thing. Shakespeare will, in fact, colour almost every programme from now on. For the rest of this year all announcers will appear in doublet, ruff and hose; the news and even the weather reports will be compiled and read in blank verse or sonnet form.

The GPI Festival will wind up with a debate between Stretchford and Oxford Universities on Stretchford's motion "That this house believes that Shakespeare's works should be adapted in Basic English versions so that the beauty of his language may be available to all, irrespective of class, colour or creed."

(March 18)

Peter Simple

AMERICA'S CUP 4-0 DEFEAT FOR SOVEREIGN

DAVID THORPE
Daily Telegraph Yachting Correspondent

OFF NEWPORT, Rhode Island, Monday.

BRITAIN'S 19th America's Cup challenge was contemptuously turned away here to-day for good. The New York Yacht Club's Constellation secured the necessary four victories by defeating the Royal Thames Yacht Club's Sovereign by 15 min 40 sec in their final race.

Sovereign out-Sceptred the 1958 challenger Sceptre by losing her four races by the staggering average margin of 12 min 2 sec in the series.

For Britain Sovereign's defeat has been the worst since Bunkers Hill. The Stars and Stripes fly proudly while the Union Jack droops as never before over Newport to-night.

BAD START
Line crossed too soon

Peter Scott, Sovereign's helmsman got off to a bad start, crossing the line three seconds early and being recalled. This meant Constellation had a 51 sec lead even before the race had got properly under way.

Constellation was outfooting and outpointing her. She reached the weather mark 4 min 47 sec ahead and set her pale blue spinnaker for the reach. Sovereign, a half mile astern did a beautiful hoisting of her parachute and began a long futile chase.

The challenger changed her blue chute for a red and white candy striped sail but lost 34 sec. On the next spinnaker reach she tired of the candy stripe and set a red chute but it was a poor change and she lost a further 62 sec.

WIND DROPS
10-foot swell

The wind dropped slightly but the giant 10-foot swell kept rolling in as they rounded again the America's Cup buoy to begin the last but one beat.

The American yacht by the windward mark, had added 7 min 3 sec to her lead and had Sovereign a mile astern.

Under spinnakers they headed for the lee mark. The last turning buoy of the 1964 America's Cup series.

Sovereign lost the first race last Tuesday, by 5 min 34 sec, the second race, two days later, by 20 min 24 sec and Saturday's third race, by 6 min 33 sec.

(September 22)

A SMILING ANN PACKER (55), winning the 800 metres in a world record time from Maryvonne Dupureur (45), Ann Chamberlain (151) and N. Szabo (107) in Tokyo yesterday.

OLYMPIC 'GOLD' FOR MARY RAND

By DONALD SAUNDERS

TOKYO, Wednesday.

MARY RAND, who is 24, earned Britain's first Gold Medal of the 1964 Olympics at the National Stadium in Tokyo this evening when she won the women's long jump championship.

Mrs. Rand, whose performance was watched by her husband, a former international sculler, is the first British woman athlete to become an Olympic champion.

Her victory is the only success achieved in a field event by any Briton since Timothy Ahearne won the triple jump in the 1908 Games in London.

World record

With her best jump of 22ft 2in. Mrs. Rand shattered the world record of the Russian, Tatyana Shchelkanova, who finished in third place.

She is now among the favourites for the women's pentathlon, which begins on Friday, and is in the sprint relay team.

This is likely to be her last season in international athletics because she wants to spend more time with her family. She has a two-year-old daughter, and lives at Henley-on-Thames.

(October 15)

ANN PACKER INSPIRED BY FIANCE'S DEFEAT

GOLD MEDAL AND WORLD RECORD IN LAST RACE

By JAMES COOTE

TOKYO, Tuesday.

THE defeat of Robbie Brightwell in the 400 metres yesterday inspired Ann Packer, his fiancée, to win a gold medal and set a world record in the 800 metres at the National Stadium here to-day.

At 3.5p.m. yesterday, immediately after Brightwell had finished fourth, Miss Packer, already the silver medallist in the women's 400 metres, vowed that she would win the 800 metres.

Until that moment Miss Packer had been prepared to run as well as she could in this event. She qualified only at the last minute and was selected on condition that she did not let it interfere with her 400 metres training.

She had no idea of tactics of pace setting or how to avoid getting boxed in. She had run her first two-lap race at Leyton in May. This final was only the seventh time she had covered a competitive 800 metres ... and it would be her last individual race.

Though Miss Packer came here with a fair time she lacked until yesterday the motive that is necessary to win a gold medal. To-day, just before going on the track, she was overjoyed to see Brightwell cross the winning line first in a 4 x 400 metres relay semi-final.

RECORD NEEDED
French danger

She went to the start ready to win but not knowing how fast she would need to travel. Marise Chamberlain, of New Zealand, who finished third, had no such inhibitions. Runner-up to Dixie Willis when she set a world record of 2 min 1.2sec in 1962, she knew it would take a world record, but thought that Maryvonne Dupureur, the French champion, would be the one to do it.

Miss Dupureur and Nagy Szabo, of Hungary, were the front runners by the time the first 120 metres had been covered. Antje Gleichfeld, a German, strode confidently behind in their wake and in sixth and seventh positions were Miss Packer and Anne Smith, the other British competitor.

The French girl had a fractional lead at the end of the first lap which she covered in an amazing 58.6sec. Miss Packer was half a second behind and looking easy, but Miss Smith was out of the running.

Soon after entering the back straight Miss Supureur attempted to break away but gained little advantage. Behind the action was becoming really live. Miss Chamberlain, who wanted to delay her finish, was just to the outside of Miss Packer, who tried every way to get through.

Finally, in desperation, she slackened her pace, swung out and then, to the delight of the British crowd, moved steadily through the field.

RAPID ACCELERATION
Fatigue tells

From sixth, to fifth, to fourth, on she travelled, accelerating all the while. The unfortunate French girl her head wobbling from side to side in fatigue, could not hold on and to her despair had to watch Miss Packer striding nearer and nearer the finish and the gold medal that she had thought would be her own.

Miss Packer's time of 2min 1.1sec beat Miss Willis's record by a tenth of a second and is 4.2sec faster than she has done before.

What a pity that Miss Packer will never be seen in action again after this trip. I am convinced she could bring the time lower than the ultimate of 1min 57sec she forecast for this race.

Sin Kim Dan, of North Korea, who did not compete here because of political squabbles, has covered the same distance in 1min 59.1sec. but this mark has not been accepted because it was set at an unratified meeting.

(October 21)

DAVIES OUTJUMPS THEM ALL TO LAND 'GOLD'

By JAMES COOTE

TOKYO, Sunday.

LYNN DAVIES, whose first sporting steps were taken among the slag heaps of Nantymoel, spent the longest 20 seconds of his life seated, with eyes closed, on a damp bench in the National Stadium here to-night before learning he had won a coveted gold medal.

On a wet, miserable day Davies outjumped the 1960 Olympic champion, Ralph Boston, from the United States, and Igor Ter-Ovanesyan, of Russia, who have monopolised the world rankings these past four years, and in so doing set a British record.

His was not Britain's only success in a week-end of medal winning that has never been surpassed. Paul Nihill, from London, to-day battled his way through the soggy streets of Tokyo to take second place in the 50 kms walk, completing the distance six minutes faster than he has ever done before.

It was also a "Silver day" for Britain in yesterday's sun shine, with Maurice Herriott, of Birmingham, taking second place in the steeplechase, with Ann Packer only inches from a first place in the 400 metres and with Mary Rand, already a "golden" girl adding a pentathlon silver to her collection.

It is, I think, fair to say that Davies' victory over two jumpers who have frequently cleared greater distances is the outstanding athletics achievement of the Games so far. Although he came with the chance of a bronze medal, it was impossible to give him much more than that, because he is still only 22 and lacks the experience of many of his rivals.

How, then, could this young Welshman who only just qualified with his last jump this morning after he had found he placed his run-up mark 2 feet short, beat the world? Because he was the strongest of them all and because the conditions we experienced here to-day suited him down to the very tips of his spikes.

Under the aegis of Ron Pickering, national coach for Wales, to whom Davies gave much of the credit, he has been lifting an immense poundage to increase the power of his thighs. How this paid off became apparent to-day when on a soft run-up Boston and Ter-Ovanesyan could never reach the 27-foot plus marks to which they are accustomed.

SILVER FOR NIHILL
Record beaten

Nihill has one of the most interesting background stories of all the athletes here. He used to box as an amateur but switched to cross-country running and became a performer of some repute. Then, after an operation for the removal of a knee-cap, he switched to walking.

To-day he had a battle royal with the Italian favourite, Abdon Pamich, whom Don Thompson beat out of first place in Rome. "Everything went according to plan," said Nihill. "I was not worried when Agapov, of Russia, hared off at the start, but I realised the pace would be very fast."

(October 19)

McGREGOR JUST SHORT OF GOLDEN TOUCH

By PAT BESFORD

TOKYO, Monday.

BOBBY McGREGOR, of Falkirk, to-night became the first British man for more than half a century to win an individual Olympic swimming medal. It was a silver in the 100 metres freestyle, the prestige event of the whole swimming Games.

Every man here would give his right arm to be fast enough to win it; McGregor came within inches, and it was his misfortune on this day of days that there existed a swimmer even greater than himself.

Don Schollander, of the United States, the world recordholder for 200 and 400 metres, took this title with a final five-yard spurt which carried him past the 20-year-old Scot, who had led from the start.

McGregor, in lane two, shot away at the gun and was leading at the turn which he reached in his target time of 25sec to Schollander's 25.6. He hit his turn to perfection, and stormed back up the bath still leading.

After the long years of waiting for a British success, the months of conjecture that must have strained McGregor's nerves to breaking point, and the anxieties of yesterday's heats and semi-finals for the huge British contingent here, the tension seemed unbearable.

The Falkirk boy was still just ahead with five yards to go, but by then the American, in lane five, was closing fast. And at the finish it was Schollander's arm that shot forward to touch one tenth ahead in an Olympic record of 53.4.

(October 13)

SOUTH AFRICA BANNED FROM OLYMPIC GAMES

LAUSANNE, Tuesday.

The International Olympics Committee announced in Lausanne to-day that South Africa had been barred from the 18th Olympic Games in Tokyo because she had refused to dissociate herself from apartheid in sport.

During the Winter Olympics in Innsbruck in January the committee withdrew South Africa's invitation to the Games. It ruled that she could compete only if she publicly renounced racial discrimination in sport.

At Lausanne in June South Africa was given another 50 days to make the declaration. But Mr. Frank Braun, president of the South African Olympic Committee, has replied that South Africa will not change her attitude. - Reuter.

(August 19)

MATTHEWS TAKES GOLD IN 20KM WALK

On a day in which the standard of performances was astounding there was no greater event for Britain than the 20 kilometres walk. Matthews's victory for the small British contingent here in the National Stadium overshadowed even Bob Hayes's classic 100 metres victory, Al Oerter's third successive gold medal in the discus and the high jumping of Iolanda Balas that brought her another gold medal.

At too irregular intervals news was posted on the electronic signboard at one end of the stadium of Matthews's progress. At the five-kilometre mark he was only one second ahead of Ronald Zinn, of the United States, who had set a cracking pace. So fast was it that Matthews later said that he wondered briefly if he would flag at the end.

But he need not have worried. He went out ahead and none of the opposition dared stay up for risk of being "pulled" for lifting. By halfway Dieter Lindner, of Germany, had moved into second place, a position he was to keep until the finish, and was 24 seconds behind.

This was a procession led by Matthews whose feet, shod with the dirty old black shoes that he wore to win his European gold medal in Belgrade, pattered a regular rhythm on the Tokyo streets.

The wait seemed immeasurable but then in came Matthews as relaxed as if he had been on a Sunday afternoon stroll. Round the track he strode, completing the last 400 metres blowing kisses and waving to the cheering crowd.

(October 16)

LONG BREAKS OWN WORLD SHOT RECORD

By A Special Correspondent

Dallas Long, of the United States, moved further away from the rest of the American shot putters, when he broke his own world record by the surprising distance of 7¼ in at Fresno, California on Saturday.

Competing in the West Coast Relays, Long threw 66ft 7¼ in with his second attempt to become the first man over the magic 66ft barrier and to bring within sight of reality the 67ft mark.

His ratified world record is 65ft 10¼ in which he set in May 1962; it was only within the past few weeks Long had thrown 65ft 11¼ in, a mark which is still to be ratified.

(May 11)

12 MORE EVENTS PROPOSED

Twelve more events will be added to the Olympic swimming programme if proposals agreed at yesterday's congress of the Federation Internationale de Natation Amateur are accepted by the International Olympic Committee, cables **Pat Besford**.

The suggested events for men are the 100 metres backstroke, 100m breaststroke and 100m butterfly, two 200m freestyle and 200m individual medley and 800m freestyle. The last three events are also put forward for women plus the 200m backstroke and 200m butterfly and 100m breast-stroke.

(October 20)

ENGLAND SCORE 611 IN THE FORMAL DRAW

BARRINGTON (256) ADDS FINAL IRONIC TOUCH

By E.W. SWANTON

OLD TRAFFORD, Tuesday.

ENGLAND nearly batted out the day, but not quite, and as a final touch of irony in a game that had been full enough of it they were required to field for five minutes this evening before the proceedings could legally be concluded.

So with Barrington bowling to Simpson ended one of the more extraordinary contests in the long history of Anglo-Australian Test matches, not with a bang or a whimper, but just a yawn.

Barrington went on to-day with prodigious application to make a further 103, 256 in all, and richly earned the gratitude of his fellow-players for keeping them in the pavilion rather than exercising themselves pointlessly in the field.

He did not bat quite as long as Simpson, so that his innings rates for length as the fourth longest in Test cricket and, in magnitude, as the third highest for England against Australia. All Hammond's four double-hundreds were passed in turn; only Sir Leonard Hutton and R.E. Foster now stand above him in the books.

Little less remarkable as a physical feat was Veivers' 95.1 overs, only 17 balls fewer than Ramadhin delivered against England in that still more remarkable match at Edgbaston seven years ago. Veivers to-day bowled every over, 55 in all, at the upwind end, his labours stretching over five and a quarter hours. No doubt, this is some grisly kind of record.

McKenzie, too, bowled 60 overs and with far greater reward; seven wickets, in fact, for 153, which brings his bag for the series to 23.

FORMAL COURSE

Fight concluded

The fight, as a fight, having been concluded by the excellent stand between Dexter and Barrington yesterday, to-day's cricket pursued a formal course, inevitably boring, and with what small interest still lingering focused on personal performances and the consideration whether or not England would top Australia's score.

It will occasionally happen in the best-regulated circles that the ball is utterly mastered, and bowling is a complete drudgery. Yesterday I mentioned the Old Trafford Test of 1934. Much more recently there was the Bridgetown Test of 1960 when as the result of the best part of 30 hours play England made 482 and 71 for no wicket, the West Indies 563 for eight declared.

Test scoreboard

AUSTRALIA - First Innings

W.M. Lawry, run out 106
°R.B. Simpson, c Parks, b Price.......311
I.R. Redpath, lbw, b Cartwright........19
N.C. O'Neill, b Price........................47
P.J. Burge, c Price, b Cartwright.......34
B.C. Booth, c & b Price....................98
T.R. Velvers, c Edrich, b Rumsey......22
#A.T.W. Grout, c Dexter, b Rumsey...0
G.D. McKenzie, not out.....................0
Extras (b1, lb 9, nb 9).......................19
Total (8 wkts. dec.).........................656
Fall of wickets: 1-201, 2-211, 3-318, 4-383, 5-601, 7-652. 8-656

BOWLING

	O.	M.	R.	W.
Rumsey	35.5	4	99	2
Price	45	4	183	3
Cartwright	77	32	118	2
Titmus	44	14	100	0
Dexter	4	0	12	0
Mortimore	49	13	122	0
Boycott	1	0	3	0

Did not bat: N.J.N. Hawke, G.E. Corling.

Second Innings

W.M. Lawry, not out..........................0
°R.B. Simpson, not out.......................4
Total (no wkt.)..................................4

BOWLING

	O.	M.	R.	W.
Barrington	1	0	4	0
Titmus	1	1	0	0

ENGLAND - First Innings

G. Boycott, b McKenzie....................58
J.H. Edrich, c Redpath, b McKenzie..6
°E.R. Dexter, b Velivers..................174
K.F. Barrington, lbw, b McKenzie...256
P.H. Parfitt, c Grout, b McKenzie....12
°J.M. Parks, c Hawke, b Velivers......60
F.J. Titmus, c Simpson, b McKenzie...9
J.B. Mortimore, c Burge, b McKenzie..12
T.W. Cartwright, b McKenzie............4
J.S.E. Price, b Velivers.......................1
F.E. Rumsey, not out..........................3
Extras (b 5, lb 11)............................16
Total...611
Fall of wickets: 1-15, 2-126, 3-372, 4-417, 5-560, 6-589, 7-594, 8-602, 9-607.

BOWLING

	O.	M.	R.	W.
McKenzie	60	15	153	7
Corling	46	11	96	0
Hawke	63	28	95	0
Simpson	19	4	59	0
Velivers	95.1	36	155	3
O'Neill	10	6	37	0

Umpires: J.S. Buller & W.F. Price.
1ST TEST (Trent Bridge) drawn
2ND (Lord's) drawn.
3RD (Leeds), Australia won by 7 wkts.
5TH (The Oval), August 13-18.

(July 29)

NEW ZEALANDERS REDUCE BARBARIANS TO SIZE

Barbarians ... 3pts New Zealanders ... 36

THIS inimitable code of football produced its second great spectacle in successive weeks in the All Blacks' final performance on Saturday. After Twickenham, Cardiff.

In the last half of the last game of their tour Wilson Whineray's side excelled themselves to the extent of an exhibition of combined handling that has not been equalled since the 1951-2 Springboks on a more sinister occasion pulverised Scotland at Murrayfield.

South Africa 44, Scotland nil, was the score that day, and Scotland, it was said, were "lucky to get nil."

Saturday's effort was far from being such a rout but it could be said that the Barbarians were lucky to get three, since their goal came from a mark which was superbly dropped from 45 yards by I.J. Clarke against his own countrymen. It might be described as an "own goal."

The fortunes of the day were decided in the first five minutes of the second half wherein the All Blacks were presented with two peculiarly soft tries. At the change-over the score had been 6-3 and, with both sides trying to run with the ball, despite the greasy going, there had been little hint of one of them utterly submerging the other.

The All Blacks seemed conscious of the Barbarians' famous defeat of the Springboks here three years ago.

The two tries, however, one caused by lax defence at a scrum on the goal-line, the other a fluffed Barbarian pass actually behind the line, altered everything. Goals from each brought the score to 16-3. The result was assured.

Now, said Whineray and his men, "We'll show 'em," and indeed they did, in one breathtaking set piece after another, with six, seven or even more men handling the ball in perfect cohesion, all with a finely developed positional sense.

(February 17)

SANTA CLAUS SWOOPS TO DERBY TRIUMPH

By HOTSPUR (B.W.R. Curling)

EPSOM, Wednesday.

SCOBIE BREASLEY, at the 13th time of asking and at the age of 50, won the Derby to-day on the favourite Santa Claus. The winner was sold as a foal for only 800 gns. and resold as a yearling for 400 gns. more.

Like another celebrated champion jockey, Sir Gordon Richards, Breasley has taken a long time to win the Derby. To-day, as many expected, he rode a waiting race and came from a long way back to catch and beat the Chester Vase winner Indiana in the last 50 yards.

The winning margin was a length. The 100-1 chances Dilettante II (a further two lengths away) and Anselmo, both prepared for the race in Ireland by Paddy Prendergast, were third and fourth, with Crete, the Prendergast first-string, sixth.

After the 2,000 Guineas it was good to see a colt English-bred and English-owned winning the most valuable race ever run in Europe.

Santa Claus's breeder, Dr. F.A. Smorfitt, lives in Warwickshire and acts as a course doctor at two or three Midlands meetings and has always been keen on hunting and horses.

His trainer Mickie Rogers, is one of the few Englishmen training in Ireland - there are many Irishmen training in England!

ONCIDIUM FLOPS

Beaten in straight

The disappointment of the race was Oncidium, who came round Tattenham Corner leading on the rails, but was beaten more than a quarter of a mile from home, while Indiana, who had twice this season finished well behind Oncidium, was only caught up the final hill by Santa Claus.

(June 4)

LISTON BEAT BY CLAY AFTER SIX ROUNDS

From DONALD SAUNDERS

MIAMI BEACH, Tuesday.

CASSIUS CLAY pulled off one of the greatest surprises in the history of boxing at the Convention Hall here to-night when as a 7 to 1 underdog he took the world heavyweight title from Sonny Liston, the man so many had thought to be invincible.

Liston retired at the end of the sixth round with a shoulder so badly injured that he was unable to continue.

At the time one judge had Clay leading on points, the other thought Liston was in front. The referee scored them even.

So Clay, the brashest, most talkative young man boxing has seen for many a day, kept his promise to take the title.

Whether he would have won the title but for Liston's injury no one can say. But certainly up to then he had boxed at great speed and with considerable skill to keep out of trouble. He had also opened a cut under Liston's left eye and had made the champion look slow and old.

Liston went straight into attack but Clay made him miss three times with jabs before countering.

Liston, his pride shattered that he, the Iron Man, had been forced to quit, stood sadly in his corner shaking his head. And to add to his misery he had to listen to the crowd's boos as he made his way to the dressing room.

(January 26)

MISS BLUNDELL IN FINAL

Heather Blundell, 22, of Australia is within one match of completing a hatrick of title victories in the British women's squash rackets championship.

She reached the final at the Lansdowne club, London, last night with a 9-4, 7-9, 9-1, 9-3 win over Anna Craven Smith, of Wolverhampton, the British No. 3.

By taking a game Miss Craven Smith spoiled Miss Blundell's record of not dropping a game in the three years she has competed in the championship.

In the final to-morrow Miss Blundell plays Mrs. Fran Marshall (Abbeydale) the British No. One.

(February 21)

LAW AND BEST PUT END TO CHELSEA'S RUN

By BRYON BUTLER

Chelsea ... 0

Manchester United ... 2

CHELSEA were found wanting for the first time this season at Stamford Bridge last night. But if there was pain for them in defeat there was no disgrace.

Manchester United, a team of flickering and unpredictable brilliance, rose as always, to the big occasion.

A young side who think football and work at their football like no other in the land were beaten by a team studded with players to whom the graces and subtleties of the game come as naturally as breathing. It was as simple as that.

Chelsea are good, perhaps good enough to win the championship. But they do not have talents such as Law, Best, and when he is in the mood, Charlton; nor do they yet have the composure or experience to stifle such genius.

It was Best, 18, a lean little chap with an unruly mop of dark hair, who did as much as anyone to win the night. He was rarely where the book says a left winger should be.

MIS-HIT BACK-PASS

McCreadie's dejection

He was at inside-right, for example, when McCreadie mis-hit a short back-pass after 32 minutes. Best had the ball past Bonetti in a twinkling as poor McCreadie slumped on one knee, head bowed.

It was Best again who paved the way for the second goal in the 82nd minute. He centred from the left, Bonetti palmed the ball up and behind him and Law, who had been hovering with intent, leaped high to nod the ball into the net.

(October 1)

Lightning kills Spur's John White

JOHN WHITE, Tottenham Hotspur's 27-year-old Scottish International footballer, was killed by lightning on a golf course at Enfield Middx. yesterday.

He was found under an oak tree near the first fairway on the Crews Hill course.

He was seen by other golfers sitting under the tree with a sheet of newspaper wrapped round his legs. There was a sudden flash of lightning followed by a clap of thunder.

(July 22)

FA PROMISE WAR ON HOOLIGANISM

By BRYON BUTLER

THE echoes of a Saturday afternoon of hooliganism on the terraces and wretched sportsmanship on the field rattled loudly through Soccer's corridors of power yesterday. Promises were made which will have to be kept.

They were promises made with the image in mind of Ken Stokes, 44, a referee from Newark, suspending the game between Everton and Leeds at Goodison Park for 10 minutes - an action unprecedented in League football.

They were promises made in the knowledge that 26 players have been sent off in the past 12 weeks - the worst start made to a season in the 76-year history of the League.

"We must make soccer fit for people to watch," said Denis Follows, secretary of the Football Association. "The whole question will be discussed at a full meeting of the F.A. Disciplinary Committee early in December."

Mr. Follows said stiffer penalties were "the first and most obvious remedy ... We have got to show players and clubs that we will not stand for this at any cost. And I say clubs with good reason."

"The clubs themselves must accept much of the blame. They employ and pay the players."

It is anything but coincidence, of course, that sportsmanship has counted for less in Soccer since the wage ceiling was removed and crowd and position bonuses were introduced.

Everton's players, for example, are paid £2 per 1,000 over 32,000 if they are in the top six, only £1 per 1,000 if seventh or below. A single point can be worth an extra £20 a week. Players feel they cannot afford to lose.

But this, of course, is only part of the problem facing the game. Too many players with limited talent are earning too much money for doing too little. It is a condition which plays havoc with whatever sense of proportion they possess; and now they feel that the game owes them a living.

Such comment does much less than justice to the many dedicated players there are in League football. But they and, more important, the game itself are judged by the deeds of the miscreants.

The effects of all this can be read in declining gates at League matches. In 1948-49 the aggregate League attendance was 41,271,414. Last season it was 28,535,022 ... just about the pre-war level.

(November 9)

Surtees wins world driving championship

Daily Telegraph Correspondent

MEXICO CITY, Sunday.

JOHN SURTEES, 30, of Britain, took the world championship title from Jim Clark, also of Britain, when he came second in the Grand Prix in Mexico City to-day.

Clark, 27, was winning until the last lap of the 65-lap race. Half-way through this his Lotus sprang an oil leak.

Dan Gurney, of California, won the race in a Brabham, Lorenzo Bandini of Italy, in a Ferrari, was third.

Bandini's gesture

The six points earned by Surtees gave him a total of 40. Graham Hill was struck in the tail by Bandini in the 31st lap and retired with a broken exhaust.

Bandini, Surtees's team mate, allowed Surtees to pass him in the final lap to make up the points needed to win the championship.

Clark told correspondents after the race: "It has been a season of it. It is all in the jampot."

He was awarded fifth place for finishing 64 laps. This put him in front of Pedro Rodriguez of Mexico, in a Ferrari, who finished fifth. Mike Spence of Britain was fourth in a Lotus.

(October 26)

BRITAIN'S FIRST COLOURED POLICEMAN, Astley Lloyd Blair, 27, photgraphed after he had taken the oath of allegiance before the Gloucester City Magistrates yesterday. With him is Insp. K. Moss of the Gloucestershire Constabulary.

THE POPE, IN A SYMBOLIC ACTION OF SYMPATHY to the poor of the world, lays the triple papal crown on the altar at St. Peter's Basilica yesterday when he decided to auction the crown and distribute the proceeds to the poor.

ALONG THE GARDEN PATH to his country cottage at Elstead, Surrey, Peter Sellers carries his bride to the reception. On Saturday he flies to the United States to start a film while Miss Eklund remains in England, also to make a film.

THE NEW RED AND WHITE maple leaf flag of Canada being held by M.P.'s from Quebec as they sang "O Canada" inside the Parliament building in Ottawa early yesterday.

MR. WILLIAM WILLIS, 71, being congratulated after completing a 10,000-mile lone crossing of the Pacific in a metal raft, "Age Unlimited." His voyage from Peru ended on a beach 800 miles north of Brisbane.

This was the year in which Space became almost crowded. Both the Russians and the Americans achieved meetings between their astronauts as they circled the Earth and, for the first time, men emerged from their capsules to "swim" in Space.

On the ground, events were less awe-inspiring. India and Pakistan went to war over Kashmir. General Franco, pressing the Spanish claims to Gibraltar, enforced a landward siege of the Rock. Ian Smith, the new prime minister of Southern Rhodesia, after much huffing and puffing issued his unilateral declaration of independence from the Commonwealth. Immediately, the British Government imposed sanctions. American forces became ever more deeply involved in the war in Vietnam. U.S. bombers, contrary to President Johnson's earlier assurances, began bombing North Vietnamese territory.

In Britain Harold Wilson maintained his Government with a tiny majority. In one vote, over the proposed Corporation Tax, there was an actual tie after which the Speaker used his casting vote, as tradition demanded, in favour of the Government. A political era came to an end with the death of Sir Winston Churchill. As his state funeral wound through London, first by road and then by water, more than half the population of the country watched the event on television. Sir Alec Douglas Home, unsurprisingly, resigned the leadership of the Conservative Party, to be replaced, surprisingly, by Edward Heath rather than the better fancied Reginald Maudling.

After many years of debate, in a free vote, both the House of Commons and the House of Lords passed a bill ending hanging. Barely had the Royal Assent been given than the country was shocked by the revelation of the Moors murders. Ronald Biggs, one of the great train robbers, escaped from prison to evade capture from then on. Goldie, the London Zoo's golden eagle, twice escaped from its cage but each time was lured back after a happy spree in Regent's Park.

London, although it was yet to receive the title, was beginning to "swing". Carnaby Street became a Mecca. The Beatles were made M.B.E.s, an award which made a few crusty elderly persons return their similar awards in outrage. For the first time the dreaded "F" word was used on television by the most swinging of theatre critics, Ken Tynan. A galère of beat poets took over the Royal Albert Hall for a chaotic reading and the Marquess of Bath introduced a pride of lions into his Longleat estate as a tourist attraction.

In America the civil riots agitation continued, bursting into extreme violence in Watts, a suburb of Los Angeles, where looting and shooting lasted for several days. Malcolm X, the extremist Negro leader, was shot dead by a fellow Black in New York. Much of New York state and areas bordering it were hit by a blackout which stranded people in underground railways as well as in their highrise apartments, and in some cases actually in the lifts carrying them up and down. A sequel to this event occurred nine months later when there was a sudden increase in the birth rate. Those unable to watch TV had gone to bed early.

In addition to that of Sir Winston, the deaths were announced of the great humanitarian Albert Schweitzer, and the politicians Herbert Morrison and Adlai Stevenson. The world of writing lost T.S. Eliot and W. Somerset Maugham.

Substitutes were used on the soccer field for the first time to the disgust of some traditionalists, while football was honoured with its first knight, the peerless Stanley Matthews.

FB The name to specify in heating and ventilating equipment **Fenton Byrn** West Molesey, Surrey Tel : Molesey 7777

The Daily Telegraph
and Morning Post

No. 34138 LONDON, MONDAY, JANUARY 25, 1965   Printed in LONDON and MANCHESTER Price 3d.

SIR WINSTON CHURCHILL DEAD

At his grandson's wedding in 1964

Peaceful end with wife & family at bedside

STATE FUNERAL ON SATURDAY

QUEEN'S MESSAGE: WHOLE WORLD IS POORER
By NORMAN RILEY

SIR WINSTON CHURCHILL died yesterday shortly after eight o'clock in the morning. A bulletin of 18 laconic words signalled, to the world he helped save from catastrophe, finis, in peace and without pain, to more than half a century's valiant, turbulent years.

The bulletin, issued from Sir Winston's London home, 28, Hyde Park Gate, was the 20th since it was announced last Friday week that he had had a stroke. Signed by Lord Moran, 82, his personal physician and friend, it said:

Shortly after 8 a.m. this morning, Sunday, January 24th, Sir Winston Churchill died at his London home.

Signed: MORAN

Sir Winston was 90 on Nov. 30. When the end came, members of his family were at the bedside. They included Lady Churchill, who is 79, his only son, Mr. Randolph Churchill, and his two daughters, Mrs. Mary Soames and Miss Sarah Churchill. It was the 70th anniversary of the death of Sir Winston's father, Lord Randolph Churchill.

By arrangement with the family, the bulletin was telephoned to news agencies with universal coverage. Within seconds, messages were reaching London expressing sorrow at Sir Winston's passing and paying tributes to his leadership during "the finest hour." They were being handed in at the house in hourly batches throughout the day.

Memorial to Sir Winston in colour

A MEMORIAL tribute to Sir Winston Spencer Churchill, in full colour, will be published in The Daily Telegraph on Wednesday.

Comprising 24 pages, it will be a special extra number of Weekend Telegraph, and will be distributed free with every copy of the paper.

This pictorial record of Sir Winston's life, with a specially written profile by Andre Maurois, is an historic document which all will wish to retain as a memorial to the greatest Englishman.

LAST HOURS IN ROOM OF MEMORIES
Daily Telegraph Reporter

SIR WINSTON CHURCHILL died in a room with a large picture of the Houses of Parliament above his head, at his London home in Hyde Park Gate.

Lady Churchill and Sir Winston's three surviving children and other members of his family were at his bedside.

In contrast to scenes during the early days of Sir Winston's illness, with crowds anxiously waiting for news at the top of the quiet Kensington cul-de-sac, there was only a handful of journalists in the street when the death occurred a little after 8 a.m.

But within half an hour of the announcement over the BBC, silent crowds began to gather to pay final homage to the memory of Britain's greatest leader.

FAMILY PICTURES
Treasured photographs

The room in which Sir Winston had been lying for the past 10 days was converted into a bedroom four years ago after he fell and injured his back following his 86th birthday.

He moved some of his most treasured photographs and paintings into the room. There were oils of his father, his grandfather, the 7th Duke and other members of the Marlborough family.

(Continued on Back Page, Co. 6)

MANY-SIDED GENIUS

One of the first to be told of the death was the Queen. In an immediate message to Lady Churchill, Her Majesty said:

The news of Sir Winston's death causes inexpressible grief to me and my husband. We send our deepest sympathy to you and to your family.

The whole world is the poorer by the loss of his many-sided genius, while the survival of this country and the sister nations of the Commonwealth, in the face of the greatest danger that has ever threatened them, will be a perpetual memorial to his leadership, his vision and his indomitable courage.

Signed: ELIZABETH R.

WESTMINISTER HALL CEREMONY

The Prime Minister, in a statement from 10, Downing Street, said that the Queen will ask subject to resolutions receiving House of Commons approval to-day, for a three-day lying-in-state in Westminster Hall from Wednesday, before a State funeral service in St. Paul's Cathedral next Saturday.

Representatives of foreign and Commonwealth Governments are being invited to the funeral, which the Queen is expected to attend. This is the first time since 1898, when Gladstone was accorded a State funeral, that any British citizen out of uniform has been so honoured.

"HE IS NOW AT PEACE"

As flags the world over flew at half-mast in mourning, Mr. Wilson epitomised the universal feeling. "He will be mourned all over the world by all who owe so much to him," said the Prime Minister. "He is now at peace after a life in which he created history and which will be remembered as long as history is read."

Sir Alec Douglas-Home, Leader of the Opposition, said it was Sir Winston "above all others, with his passionate hatred of evil, who rallied the nation against tyranny, and who, by his will-power and courage, swung the balance of war from defeat to victory."

To Mr. Grimond, leader of the Liberal party, he was "the largest human being of our time, the greatest man of action that this nation has ever produced."

(Continued on Back Page, Co. 6).

The Queen leads nation in mourning
Daily Telegraph Reporter

THE QUEEN led a nation in mourning yesterday. The news of Sir Winston's death was telephoned to her at Sandringham at breakfast time.

Later, at morning service in the small local church, she knelt with Prince Philip, Queen Elizabeth the Queen Mother, estate workers and their wives, in silent memory.

In a special prayer, the Rector of Sandringham, the Rev. Patrick Ashton, said: "For 10 days now this great Englishman has been in the prayers and thoughts of millions.

"All that is left for us now is to thank God for his example, for his courage and his leadership."

The service was relayed to a crowd of about 500 outside, many of whom joined in the prayers. The Queen looked sad as she left afterwards.

HALF-MAST FLAGS
Royal command

She is expected to return to London on Wednesday. On her command all flags on public buildings were flown at half-mast yesterday and all will be at half-mast from 8 a.m. to sunset to-day.

From the Houses of Parliament, from Westminster Abbey, from naval stations and lightships, from Sir Winston's old school, Harrow, from the embassies of Kensington Palace Gardens, from public buildings and private homes, the flags spelled their sad message.

STATE BELL
"Great Tom" tolls

So did the bells. At St. Paul's, where the funeral service is to be held, instead of the normal peal the State bell, "Great Tom" was tolled at intervals of one minute.

St. Paul's and Westminster Abbey headed the nation's churches in prayers and minutes of silence.

The 650 boys at Harrow School attended a special service. At St. Martin's Parish Church, Bladon, where Sir Winston will be buried, a congregation of 33 said prayers for the repose of his soul.

> *"I know what it's like to be a log: reluctant to be consumed but yielding in the end to persuasion."*

Sir Winston said these words recently as he gazed into a log fire.

SOLEMN PROCESSION TO ST. PAUL'S

DETAILS EXPECTED TO-DAY
Daily Telegraph Reporter

SIR WINSTON CHURCHILL will be honoured with the first State funeral for a civilian since that of Gladstone in May, 1898. After three days of lying-in-state in Westminster Hall his body will be borne in solemn procession to the funeral service in St. Paul's Cathedral.

Historians noted yesterday that although Gladstone had expressed a strong desire for a "very simple" burial near his home at Hawarden, Flintshire, his family agreed to Government urging that he be interred in Westminster Abbey among such famous statesmen as Palmerston and Pitt.

The Earl Marshal, the Duke of Norfolk, is in charge of the funeral arrangements for Sir Winston. When the Queen has given her approval to Parliament for a State funeral, the details will be announced, probably to-day.

FAMILY'S WISHES
"Former Naval Person"

Provisional arrangements have been made, subject to royal approval and, of course, to the wishes of Lady Churchill and members of Sir Winston's family.

These include, it is understood, a funeral procession from Westminster Hall next Saturday, along Whitehall to Trafalgar Square, the Strand, Fleet Street and Ludgate Hill.

Here an alternative has been suggested so that the route would include Admiralty Arch as a fitting tribute to a man whose affection for the Royal Navy was so great.

(Continued on Back Page, Col. 3)

THREE-DAY LYING IN STATE
Daily Telegraph Reporter

DR. RAMSEY, Archbishop of Canterbury, is expected to receive Sir Winston Churchill's bier when it arrives at Westminster Hall to-morrow night. Plans are being made for Dr. Ramsey to lead the nation's prayers in a broadcast service at the bier's side.

The hours during which the hall will be open to the public from Wednesday to Friday are expected to be announced to-morrow.

The public lying-in-state of Queen Mary, the most recent at Westminster Hall began at 4.10 p.m. on March 29, 1953, and ended at 3.05 a.m. on March 31.

Crush barriers were being erected in Bridge Street nearby last night as part of the preparation for the crowds.

Taste the difference
CINZANO
THE BIANCO

The Daily Telegraph

4 A.M.

No. 34387. LONDON, FRIDAY, NOVEMBER 12, 1965 — and Morning Post — Printed in LONDON and MANCHESTER Price 4d.

a small deposit secures any article
'IMPACT'
EVO-STIK

SWIFT SANCTIONS ON REBEL RHODESIA

BRITAIN'S REPLY TO BREAKAWAY

SMITH PUTS COUNTRY ON WAR FOOTING

BRITAIN yesterday outlawed the Rhodesian Government. This was Mr. Wilson's swift answer to Rhodesia's seizure of independence, announced in a broadcast by Mr. Ian Smith.

Five hours before Mr. Smith made his proclamation, Mr. Wilson, who had been up almost all night, made a final effort by telephone to stop him going over the brink.

The Prime Minister is reported to have said: "I cannot understand why a man of your stature allows himself to be surrounded and kicked around by the bunch of thugs you have now."

GOVERNOR HAD TO SIGN

It became clear to Mr. Wilson that a breakaway was imminent when he learned that Sir Humphrey Gibbs, the Governor of Rhodesia, had been constrained to sign orders transferring some of his powers to members of Mr. Smith's Government.

An Enabling Bill to be passed on Monday will empower the Government to revoke that part of the Constitution under which the Governor had to assign these powers.

'HELL-BENT' ON ILLEGAL ACTION

Mr. Wilson told a hushed Commons that the Rhodesian Government had been "hell-bent on illegal and self-destroying action."

Sir Humphrey Gibbs had informed Mr. Smith and his Ministers that because of their rebellion against the Crown they had ceased to hold office. It was the duty of British subjects in Rhodesia to remain loyal to the Crown and to recognise the British Government's authority.

Mr. Wilson said Britain would have no dealings with the rebel Government. The British High Commissioner in Salisbury was being withdrawn and the Rhodesian High Commissioner in London was being asked to leave.

TOBACCO IMPORTS BAN

Parliament, which is to debate Rhodesia to-day, is to be asked on Monday to approve a Bill imposing the following sanctions:

Imports of Rhodesian tobacco and sugar to be banned.

Exports of arms and spare parts to cease.

Rhodesia to be removed from sterling area, to lose Commonwealth preference and to receive no more British aid.

Special exchange control restrictions to be applied, exports of British capital to Rhodesia to stop and Rhodesia to be barred from London capital market.

No further cover from Exports Credits Guarantee Department for export to Rhodesia.

REGENT TO BE APPOINTED

Mr. Smith's Government put Rhodesia on a war footing last night when the Government assumed wide emergency economic power including the power to impose rationing. Press and broadcasting censorship prevented people from learning of Britain's reprisals, but Mr. Wilson's broadcast last night reached those with short-wave radios.

The new constitution states that if the Queen does not appoint a Governor-General, on the advice of the Rhodesian Government, within 14 days, a "regent" will be appointed. His role will be that of a constitutional president.

In Zambia, Rhodesia's land-locked northern neighbour, President Kaunda announced last night that his Government is imposing emergency powers to combat any possible Rhodesian action.

SECURITY COUNCIL TODAY

Mr. Stewart, Foreign Secretary, flew to New York last night for a meeting of the United Nations Security Council today. The meeting was called by Britain, because, as Mr. Wilson explained to Conservative interrupters in the Commons, "if we don't somebody else will."

The General Assembly, by 107 votes to two, called on Britain to take measures, including force, against Rhodesia. South Africa and Portugal voted against, France abstained, and Britain did not take part.

Last appeal by Wilson ignored

H.B. BOYNE
Daily Telegraph Political Correspondent

THE Prime Minister's statement to the Commons yesterday [Pg 26 and 27] outlawed the rebel "Government" in Rhodesia and replaced it, in effect, by a Wilson Government in exile.

Behind the statement lay a night-long story of fruitless efforts to dissuade Mr. Ian Smith from an act of treason.

These culminated in a 16-minute telephone conversation which began at 6 a.m. Even then, five hours before the proclamation, Mr. Smith did not disclose that a unilateral declaration of independence had been decided upon.

Mr. Wilson had the impression throughout that he was being forced into it, against his own will and judgment, by pressures within his Cabinet.

His personal preference, it seemed, was for a Royal Commission to test the acceptability of the 1961 Constitution as a basis for independence.

The Prime Minister, who still thinks Mr. Smith stands head and shoulders above anyone else in the Rhodesian Front he created, tried in vain to convince him that he was big enough to go to the Governor, Sir Humphrey Gibbs, and say he wanted to form a new Government.

"A great many people of goodwill would swing in behind you," Mr. Wilson is reported to have urged him. "I cannot understand why a man of your stature allows himself to be surrounded and kicked around by the bunch of thugs you have now."

Apparently Mr. Smith took no particular exception to this description of some of his colleagues, whom Mr. Wilson referred to in the Commons later as "small and frightened men."

(Continued on Back Page, Col. 4)

U.N. ASSEMBLY URGES USE OF FORCE

Daily Telegraph Staff Correspondent
NEW YORK, Thursday.

The United Nations General Assembly tonight adopted by 107 votes to two a resolution condemning Rhodesia's seizure of independence and calling on Britain to implement previous resolutions urging the use of force. South Africa and Portugal voted against, France abstained and Britain took no part in the vote.

Stewart flies out

Mr. Stewart, Foreign Secretary, flew to New York last night for today's Security Council meeting. Before leaving London Airport he said United Nations military intervention would be inappropriate and unwise.

S. AFRICA KEEPS NORMAL TIES

Daily Telegraph Staff Correspondent
JOHANNESBURG, Thursday.

Dr. Verwoerd, South African Prime Minister, declared tonight that his country will continue normal relations with Rhodesia.

Mr. John Gaunt, Rhodesian diplomatic representative in Pretoria, said he "knew" that "all South Africans" would support Rhodesia. Sir De Villiers Graaff, Leader of the Opposition United party, called at the party congress in Bloemfontein today for immediate de facto recognition of Rhodesia's independence.

Sir Patrick Renison

Sir Patrick Renison, former Governor of Kenya, died yesterday in the King Edward VII Hospital for Officers, Marylebone, following an operation. He was 54.

MR. SMITH, WATCHED BY MEMBERS OF HIS CABINET, signing Rhodesia's proclamation of independence in Salisbury yesterday.

SMITH GETS POWER TO IMPOSE RATIONING

PETROL CUTS DEMAND

DAVID ADAMSON
Daily Telegraph Staff Correspondent
SALISBURY, Rhodesia, Thursday.

Rhodesia was put on what amounted to a war footing tonight. The Government assumed wide powers over the economy, including the introduction of rationing if necessary.

Car owners, which means the whole European population, and a considerable number of Africans, were urged to cut down petrol consumption. Business was threatened with even further disruption by the announcement that all import licences granted since control was introduced six days ago have been cancelled.

Licence holders will have to apply again, as more stringent controls have been introduced. Export control is being introduced from tomorrow to conserve essential supplies and exporters will have to obtain licences.

Mr. Wrathall, Minister of Finance, spoke of the "need for stern discipline" in a statement tonight.

"We trust that normal trading and financial relations will continue. But we must be prepared to meet a situation in which sanctions of an aggressive character may be taken against Rhodesia.

"If the need should arise, we must be ready to endure a situation of real hardship for some time ahead."

Holiday travel allowances are cut to £100 a year and the automatic allocation of business allowances discontinued. A severe check on would-be emigrants from Rhodesia has been imposed.

(Continued on Back Page, Col. 6)

GRIM WILSON TALKS OF 'SMALL MEN'

Daily Telegraph Reporter

IN a television broadcast to the nation last night MR. WILSON said of Rhodesia: "The world has taken a step backwards today by the action of a group of small and frightened men.

"It is now our task, without rancour, to take measures which will bring the Rhodesian people back from this dangerous path into which they have been led. I do not know what the dark consequences of this action will be."

Grim and serious, the Prime Minister referred to Rhodesia's part in the 1939-45 war. "It is a terrible commentary that men with a heroic record are now destroying in their own country the very values they fought for."

Punitive measures opposed

Speaking after Mr. Wilson, Mr. HEATH, leader of the Opposition, agreed that the Rhodesian Government of Mr. Smith was now invalid. But they did not favour punitive measures purely for the sake of being punitive.

Mr. Grimond said later that there would be no point in Britain's trying to enforce ineffective sanctions. The whole situation was one of extreme delicacy.

WHITE TROOPS ON BORDER, SAYS KAUNDA

Daily Telegraph Correspondent
LUSAKA, Thursday.

President Kaunda of Zambia tonight announced emergency powers to combat any Rhodesian action. They include the imposition of curfews, control of Zambians returning from abroad and the acquisition of land buildings, vehicles, foodstuffs and medical supplies.

In a nation-wide broadcast, he disclosed that two battalions of white Rhodesian troops had been moved along the Zambian river.

If Zambia were invaded "we will not hesitate to meet force with force," Zambia was determined to see that Mr. Smith's "act of rebellion is brought to an end."

LORD CHUTER-EDE

Lord Chuter-Ede, the former Labour Home Secretary, died in a nursing home at Ewell, Surrey, yesterday, aged 83. He had been unwell for some time.

PRICE WARNING ON CIGARETTES

Daily Telegraph Commercial Correspondent

Tobacco companies are planning gradually to reduce the proportion of Rhodesian tobacco in cigarettes, now amounting to about one-third. Present stock will last 18 months, but the Carreras group gave warning last night of possible price increases because replacement stock will cost more.

WILLEY TAKEN ILL

Mr. Fred Willey, 55, Minister of Land and Natural Resources, was taken ill in the Commons last night and had some difficulty in finishing his speech.

Tightening the financial screw

Daily Telegraph City Staff

NEW orders made under the Exchange Control Act have far-reaching effects.

They exclude Rhodesia from the sterling area, control its sterling balances and future transactions with Britain, and reduce the Rhodesian pound to the status of a minor foreign currency.

A spokesman for the Bank of England said yesterday that a recent return from the Bank of Rhodesia showed that the country has about £24.2 million of all foreign assets made up of £3 1/2 million in gold and about £20.7 million in all other items.

This suggests that Rhodesia's sterling balances held by Britain must be well under the estimate of around £23 million that has been put around recently.

SPECIAL CATEGORY
Effect on Rhodesians

The new rules put Rhodesia into a novel and special category which leaves room for further tightening of the screw.

They also exclude residents of Rhodesia, their accounts and securities, from certain general exemptions and permissions that apply to residents of all other countries outside the sterling area.

The question now is how severely the controls, which will apply to all transactions between residents of the United Kingdom and residents of Rhodesia, will be enforced.

Payments by British residents to residents of Rhodesia may be made only in sterling to the sterling accounts of residents of Rhodesia with banks in Britain.

(Continued on Back Page, Col. 3)

'LEAVE BRITAIN' ORDER TO HIGH COMMISSIONER

Daily Telegraph Commonwealth Affairs Correspondent

Brig. Andrew Skeen, Rhodesian High Commissioner in London, was told by Britain yesterday that he no longer represents his Government in London. He was asked to leave London by tomorrow.

A letter from Mr. Bottomley, Commonwealth Secretary, told him that in the absence of any statement from him declaring his opposition to unilateral action he was no longer acceptable.

JET BURNS WITH 88 ABOARD

SALT LAKE CITY, Friday.

A Boeing 727 jet airliner with 88 people aboard burst into flames on landing at Salt Lake City, Utah, last night. There were 21 known survivors. Another Boeing 727 crashed earlier this week near Cincinatti, killing 58. - Reuter.

Daily Telegraph and Morning Post, 1965

FOUR AMERICANS MEET IN SPACE

FLIGHT INFORMATION AT 10FT. APART

ALEX FAULKNER
Daily Telegraph Staff Correspondent
CAPE KENNEDY, Wednesday.

AMERICA'S two Gemini spacecraft made history today by achieving the first rendezvous in orbit. They successfully steered to within six to 10 feet of each other.

The meeting, 185 miles above the Mariana Islands in the Pacific, came at 7.27 p.m. GMT, five hours 50 minutes after the faultless launching of Gemini VI from Cape Kennedy.

Gemini VI was 1,200 miles from Gemini VII when it arrived in orbit. The two spacecraft, flying at 17,500 mph gradually closed together during a 103,000-mile chase.

Then the unidentified voice of one of the four astronauts shouted: "We did it." Flags were unfurled at Manned Spacecraft Centre in Houston, Texas, and scientists stood and cheered.

FOUR-HOUR FLIGHT

The United States had beaten Russia in achieving one of the most complicated manoeuvres in the race to the moon. President Johnson said they had moved man "one step higher on the stairway to the moon."

After flying together almost four hours the spaceships parted at 11.20 GMT in preparation for Gemini VI to splash down in the Atlantic 900 miles east of Miami at 3.29 this afternoon. Gemini VII is to be brought down at 9 a.m. on Saturday after a record 14-day flight.

During the joint flight the astronauts, Walter Schirra and Thomas Stafford in Gemini VI, and Frank Borman and James Lovell, who have been orbiting in Gemini VII for 12 days, chatted and gave technical information.

Mission Control said that the actual reporting of rendezvous, which was only one minute late, was done by Stafford in "the calmest voice we have ever heard." Borman was heard to remark: "We have company tonight." Schirra said the meeting was "sure big deal."

Over Madagascar the two crews reported that they could see each other clearly. Schirra said to Gemini VII: "You guys sure have big beards." Lovell said he could see Schirra's lips moving. The reply to that was "I'm chewing gum."

(December 16)

CAPT. WALTER SHIRRA, 42

CDR. JAMES LOVELL, 37.

MAJOR THOMAS STAFFORD, 35.

LT-COL FRANK BORMAN, 37.

10,000 CYCLONE DEATHS IN EAST PAKISTAN

About 10,000 people died in the cyclone which hit East Pakistan last Wednesday, reports received in Karachi said to-day. Over five million have been rendered homeless.

Official figures stated that there were 1,400 deaths but in the Barisal district alone about 1,000 people are known to have died. In one sub-division there were 262 deaths. About 33,000 cattle perished.

The entire local fleet of the Pakistan International Airlines was damaged disrupting internal services. Road rail and telecommunication systems, were knocked out but they were repaired with lightning speed because of the threat from India.

(May 17)

German suitor of Princess Beatrix

Daily Telegraph Correspondent
THE HAGUE, Thursday.

A WEST German diplomat, Herr Klaus von Amsberg, 38, from Bad Godesberg, is the suitor of Crown Princess Beatrix of the Netherlands, it is reported in The Hague.

There have been no official announcements because the Dutch Court feels that so far there is not much more than a romance, and definitely no engagement.

Princess Beatrix, who is 27, and Herr von Amsberg met at a ski-ing party in Gstaad, Switzerland, in February.

The Dutch Cabinet will meet on Friday to discuss the matter.

(May 7)

LIMIT ON ALCOHOL IN DRIVER'S BLOOD

Daily Telegraph Reporter

MR. FRASER, Minister of Transport, told the Commons yesterday that he hopes to introduce a Bill this year dealing with drink and driving. It will set a limit on the amount of alcohol allowed in the blood.

Mr. Fraser said: "The present law is so highly unsatisfactory that the Government has decided we should amend it and introduce a statutory limit of alcohol in the blood, provided it can be administered fairly. We think it can."

There was ample evidence that the concentration of alcohol in the blood was the best objective test of impaired ability to drive and that a level would be fixed which would be fair.

A number of questions had still to be studied before it would be possible to draft a satisfactory law, but if the Parliamentary timetable permitted it might be possible to introduce the Bill this year.

On the Minister's "firm promise," a Conservative backbencher withdrew a Private Member's Bill which would have made it an offence for anyone with more than a prescribed amount of alcohol in his blood to be in charge of a motor vehicle.

BMA WELCOME

"Best method"

The British Medical Association welcomed Mr. Fraser's statement last night. A spokesman said: "We believe that analysis of the concentration of alcohol in the body affords the best available scientific evidence of impairment of the ability to drive properly due to alcohol."

Mr. Cecil Orr, secretary of the Automobile Association, said last night that the AA was opposed to legislation based on conviction for content. "The difficulties are almost insuperable."

The AA thought that the 1962 Act, making it an offence for a person to drive when his ability was impaired by drink or drugs, was adequate to deal with the problem given proper enforcement. There was no reason to suppose it was ineffective.

(June 19)

PARATROOPS IN FIRST U.S. OFFENSIVE

FRANK ROBERTSON
Daily Telegraph Staff Correspondent
SAIGON, Tuesday.

AMERICAN troops have switched to the offensive in South Vietnam. In a joint operation with Government forces they overran networks of trenches and tunnels in a Viet Cong stronghold 30 miles east of Saigon.

Their objective was a wide area in Zone D, an important Viet Cong stronghold. But only light contact was made with the guerrillas in an area of dense jungle and deep swamp infested with leeches.

Most of the 173rd Airborne Brigade and a large Government force were flown into the area yesterday by 130 helicopters operating from Bien Hoa, a military air base 12 miles from Saigon.

About 1,200 Americans and 800 South Vietnamese troops are believed to be in action. A United States spokesman declined to say whether an American was in overall command for the first time.

But the action appears to mark the beginning of regular commitment of American troops in an offensive role.

(June 30)

PLANES STRAFE DOMINICAN REBELS

Daily Telegraph Staff Correspondent
NEW YORK, Monday

At least eight people, including a six-year-old child, were killed in Santo Domingo, capital of the Dominican Republic, to-day as Army rebels fought with forces loyal to the overthrown junta of Senor Donald Reid Cabral.

The rebels, who want to bring back from exile the former president Juan Bosch, were opposed for the second day by a strong faction of the Air Force and one Army general with 1,500 men and 30 tanks.

(April 27)

78 ARRESTS NEAR U.S. EMBASSY

Seventy-eight people are to appear in magistrates' courts to-day after a two-day non-stop demonstration near the United States Embassy in Grosvenor Square, organised by the British Council for Peace in Vietnam and the Campaign for Nuclear Disarmament.

Fifteen arrested yesterday when police closed the square will appear at Marlborough Street.

(October 18)

HEATH WILL LEAD THE TORIES

H.B. BOYNE
Daily Telegraph Political Correspondent

MR. EDWARD HEATH, 49, is to all intents and purposes the new Leader of the Conservative Opposition in the Commons. A formal declaration will be made at 11.30 a.m. today.

Mr. Reginald Maudling, 48, whom Mr. Heath yesterday defeated by 17 votes in the first ballot for the Conservative party leadership, had no hesitation in conceding victory. He also made it known that he will serve in any required capacity under Mr. Heath's leadership.

Mr. Enoch Powell, 53, the third candidate, also announced his withdrawal from the contest. So did Mr. Peter Thorneycroft, 56, who had previously reserved his position.

ONE NAME IN BALLOT BOX

This makes it inconceivable that a second ballot will be necessary. No other candidate would have the slightest chance of collecting a respectable tally of votes, much less of succeeding.

So Mr. Heath's will be the only nomination in the box when it is opened today by Sir William Anstruther-Gray, Chairman of the 1922 Committee. All that remains is to declare him elected.

Mr. Maudling, unruffled as ever, yielded to his rival with this statement: Mr Heath has obtained an overall majority on the first ballot.

I am grateful to all the friends who have supported me, but I have no doubt at all that in the interests of the party I should not contest another ballot.

I hope to have the opportunity of working under Mr. Heath's leadership to defeat the present Government as soon as possible.

298 M.P.s IN POLL

Majority of two votes

The result of the ballot, in which 298 Conservative M.P.s voted, was:

MR. HEATH 150
MR. MAUDLING 133
MR. POWELL....................15

Mr. Heath thus had an overall majority of two, though not the lead of 45 required under the rules to dispense with a second ballot.

The figures, announced to members of the 1922 Committee just before 2.15 p.m. were telephoned to Mr. Maudling who was lunching at his bank in the City. As soon as he heard them he was clear that he ought to withdraw.

As a mark of goodwill, it is confidently expected that Mr. Maudling will now propose Mr. Heath's nomination afresh, and that Mr. Powell will second it. But the rule precluding any disclosure of proposer's or seconder's names is being strictly observed.

Mr. Maudling frankly confessed to friends that the result was a surprise to him. During the four and a half days since Sir Alec Douglas-Home announced his resignation he had felt all along that things were going well for him.

(July 28)

M.P.S PASS BILL TO END HANGING

By T.F. LINDSAY
WESTMINSTER, Thursday.

LACKING only the formality of the Royal Assent, the Murder (Abolition of Death Penalty) Bill, is now all but law. It sank on to the Statute Book this afternoon in an atmosphere of weariness hardly consonant with a great historic occasion.

The Commons were debating the three amendments made to the Bill in the Lords. Only the first of these aroused real controversy.

This was the provision that, in a murder case, the trial judge should have a statutory right to recommend to the Home Secretary the minimum period which his sentence of "life imprisonment" ought in fact to imply. Almost every Member who spoke, on both sides of the House, criticised this amendment.

"Poor compromise"

It was called a "disappointing compromise," "a pretty poor amendment," something which could do "no harm, but no good."

Only Sir Frank Soskice, Home Secretary, and Mr. Silverman (Lab., Nelson and Colne), promoter of the Bill strongly urged that it should be accepted.

On the other side were Mr. Brooke, former Home Secretary. Mr. Thorneycroft, Shadow Home Secretary, Sir John Hobson, former Attorney-General, and Mr. Paget (Lab., Northampton). Indeed a formidable array.

(October 29)

BEATLES GET £171,000 U.S. OFFER

Ian Ball
Daily Telegraph Staff Correspondent
NEW YORK, Monday.

The Beatles were offered a new American contract today which could bring them $480,000 (£171,000) for two nights' appearances in New York next summer.

Mr. Sid Bernstein, the impressario who organised the Beatles' concert in a New York stadium last night, asked the group to make another visit after seeing the reception they received from a capacity audience of 55,600 almost hysterical teenagers.

Prices Increased

He said: "I have offered the boys a guarantee of $250,000 (£89,000) against 60 per cent. of the takings, whichever is the larger.

"I want them to do two concerts on consecutive nights next summer. Ticket prices will be increased so the total receipts could reach $800,000 of which the boys would take $480,000.

(August 17)

First Aston Martin with four seats

By W. A. McKenzie
Daily Telegraph Motoring Correspondent

Two new Aston Martin cars, a saloon and a convertible, are announced today by the David Brown organisation. The DB6 saloon is the makers' first car with seating for four adults.

It has more head, body and leg room than any Aston Martin previously built and a new body design to provide greater road adhesion and safety at speed. It is capable of more than 150 mph.

The convertible, the Volante, differs from its predecessor in styling with divided wrap-round bumpers front and back.

France has become the best export market for the British Motor Corporation's high performance Mini Cooper saloons. B.M.C. has six major distributors and 400 service points throughout the country.

(September 29)

RUSSIAN BAN ON SOCCER TEAM 'DRUNKS'

Daily Telegraph Staff Correspondent
MOSCOW, Tuesday.

A series of scandals rocket Soviet soccer today as its national team left by air for World Cup ties against Wales and Denmark. The Soviet Football Federation announced that eight first division players had been banned for life for being "incorrigible drunks."

(October 13)

13 LOST AS OIL RIG SINKS IN N. SEA

2 LEGS OF DRILLING PLATFORM COLLAPSE

Daily Telegraph Reporter

BRITISH PETROLEUM'S giant oil rig, Sea Gem, capsized and sank in rough weather in the North Sea yesterday. Four of the 32 on board were known last night to be dead and nine were missing.

Nineteen survivors were rescued from life rafts and the icy sea by the British ship Baltrover, 2,179 tons and an RAF helicopter. Three are seriously injured.

When the Baltrover landed all 19 at Hull last night, one man from the Sea Gem said that he saw two of the drilling platform's ten legs give way.

A spokesman for B.P. said that the exact cause of the sinking would not be known until an inquiry had been held.

Divers will go down tomorrow to see if the rig, which had beaten 20 other oil groups in the race for North Sea gas, is recoverable.

The £2,500,000 rig capsized 40 miles east of the Humber after being lashed by 30-knot winds and 20ft waves. The first news of the disaster came when the Baltrover radioed:

"Oil rig Sea Gem has just collapsed and sinking. Am sending a boat across to her. Require further assistance."

The boat from the Baltrover, which was returning from Poland to her home port of Hull, picked up 20 men, one of whom was dead and three injured.

It is believed that no SOS message was sent from Sea Gem, which was equipped with radio and telex.

FLOATING RAFTS

Dinghies in sea

The RAF helicopter from Leconfield, Yorks, winched three men from the water. Two were landed on the Baltrover and the third was flown to hospital, where he died last night.

Sgt. Lee Smith, the pilot, said last night: "The scene was chaotic. There were barrels floating around in the water and we saw several empty life rafts and dinghies floating about.

"We saw several bodies in the water and at least two of the men were definitely dead. It was a question of looking for survivors. There was no point in picking up the people who were dead."

Flt. Lt. John Hill, 35, who navigated the helicopter, said: "All we could see above water was a corner of one of the legs, and there was wreckage everywhere. Men were clinging to bits of wreckage, and we saw that two were dead and had to leave them."

A BP official said: "This would have been tragic at any time, but it seems even worse at Christmas. Sea Gem had done extremely well in the North Sea.

"Ours is the only company to have had a real success in the search for gas, and for this to happen now is absolutely disastrous."

The loss would cost "a great deal of money." But the company's first concern was for the men. After that it would have to "shop around for another rig."

(December 28)

Dr. King and his 10,000 end their march

LESLIE BEILBY
Daily Telegraph Staff Correspondent
MONTGOMERY, Alabama, Thursday.

NEARLY 10,000 Civil Rights workers marched into Montgomery to-day like a victorious army entering a conquered city.

Led by Dr. Martin Luther King, they streamed through the streets to end the five-day march from Selma at the steps of the State Capitol, where they will try to present a petition on Negro grievances to governor Wallace. He has refused to meet a delegation.

The crowd swelled until it numbered nearly 20,000. Army helicopters hovered overhead. Roads surrounding the Capitol were filled with lorry-loads of troops.

Some way to go

Dr. King spoke to the crowd from a rostrum in the square. He described the trek as "one of the great marches in the history of America." Segregation was on its death bed in Alabama, but there was still some way to go.

"Our aim is not to humiliate and defeat the white man, but to win his friendship and understanding." The meeting broke up peacefully after nearly four hours.

This morning's march began at St. Jude Roman Catholic Centre on the outskirts of Montgomery.

The 300 Civil Rights workers Black and White, who had marched the whole way from Selma, were joined by thousands who poured in from many parts of the United States.

(March 26)

SHORT DRESS CHANGES TAX RULES

Daily Telegraph Reporter

ABOVE-THE-KNEE dresses in the style made famous by Jean Shrimpton, the fashion model, have forced the Customs and Excise Commissioners to change their regulations.

Up until now, length has been used in the regulations to distinguish between women's dresses, on which purchase tax of 10 per cent. of the wholesale value must be paid, and children's frocks which are tax free.

But with hemlines still rising, officials have been afraid that some traders might try to sell women's dresses as children's, thus evading purchase tax.

Bust measurement

To prevent this, a bust measurement has been added to the regulations governing the size of tax-free dresses. From Jan. 1 a dress will not be exempt from purchase tax if it is more than 38in long or 36in round the chest, or marked for any bust size more than 32in or hip size more than 35in.

(November 6)

SOVIET SPACE STATION ON WAY TO MOON

THE Soviet Union launched an automatic space station. Lunar V, in the direction of the moon today. It is unmanned.

It was launched by multi-stage rocket - as part of the programme of studies of outer space. There was no further information on the purpose of the shot, the fifth in a series which has generally disappointed Russian scientists.

The announcement said the station's systems were functioning well. It was first put in an orbit of the earth and then automatically sent on its way towards the moon.

(May 10)

COLONEL TELLS POP GROUP TO GET HAIR CUT

The six Ricochets, a British pop music group, sacrificed their shoulder-length hair to fulfill a booking to-day at an American air base near Madrid. Col. Richard Hughes, commander of the Strategic Air Command base at Torrejon, refused to allow them in the camp until their hair was cut.

(April 19)

MRS. MARY WHITEHOUSE, co-founder of the "Clean-Up TV" campaign and Major James Dance, Conservative M.P. for Bromsgrove, during yesterday's Press conference.

FRANCO BLOCKS FRESH FOOD FOR GIBRALTAR

HAROLD SIEVE
Daily Telegraph Staff Correspondent
GIBRALTAR, Sunday.

GEN. FRANCO is now tightening his naval blockade of Gibraltar in an effort to cut off the colony's fresh food supply. The Spanish coastguard flotilla patrolling the area has been increased.

This latest ploy in the campaign against the Rock followed a decision to bring in Moroccan fresh fruit and vegetables from Tangier. Not only were they cheaper but also helped to demonstrate Gibraltar's resolve to carry on even if Spanish supplies were barred from crossing the frontier.

An enterprising Moroccan, in collaboration with an English businessman here, Mr. Robert Benson, started recently to ship goods across the Straits in 30-ton motor-driven "faluchos."

The Spaniards quickly reinforced their anti-smuggling fleet at Algeciras. Its strength was raised from four to 12 fast 100-ton launches.

The vessels, mainly former German E-boats armed with machine-guns, have succeeded in intercepting some of these food ships. Taken into Algeciras for "examination for contraband," they have been detained long enough to allow the food aboard to perish.

Others returning from Gibraltar empty have been held up on the same anti-smuggling pretext for 48 hours. That has been sufficient to turn the operation into an economic loss for the operators.

Finally, the regular Gibraltar-Tangier ferry has been brought into service to bring over perishable foodstuffs. These are being snapped up on arrival by the patriotic Gibraltarians while the Spanish imports on the market place are being neglected.

The ferry normally carries 70 cars a day to Morocco with twice that number at the height of the summer tourist season. The Spanish frontier restrictions have cut the number to a mere 10 to 14 a day.

(February 8)

BRITISH UNITED PIONEER ROUT TO LENINGRAD

An agreement between British United Airways and Aeroflot, the Russian airline, to operate what was said to be the first air service between London and Leningrad was announced last night.

(February 26)

LORD BATH TO STOCK HIS PARK WITH 50 LIONS

Daily Telegraph Reporter

FIFTY lions are being imported from Africa by the Marquess of Bath in his latest venture to attract visitors to his family home at Longleat, near Warminster, Wilts. Work started yesterday on making a nature reserve in 96 acres of parkland through which the lions will roam freely.

Lord Bath has gone into partnership with Mr. James Chipperfield, of the circus family, in forming a company, Lions of Longleat, to promote the project.

Visitors will be charged £1 a car to drive through, and for others special mini buses will be provided. Lord Bath is recruiting about 10 game wardens to patrol the area with rifles.

No open cars will be allowed and notices will warn visitors not to feed the animals or get out of their cars.

The fences will be 12ft high with a 3ft extension arm. Lord Bath was given planning permission subject to his being responsible for all safety precautions.

Lord Bath said that in making the roads care was being taken not to uproot the trees laid out by Capability Brown, the designer of Longleat gardens and parkland.

Fighting danger

London Zoo has eight lions in Regent's Park and another two at Whipsnade. Keepers there seemed to think Lord Bath was not getting so much a pride of lions as an "ostentation."

(August 10)

'CLEAN UP BBC' GROUP FORMED

INQUIRY SOUGHT INTO FINANCES

L. MARSLAND GANDER
Daily Telegraph Television and Radio Correspondent

NEW demands for the cleansing of BBC television programmes were formulated yesterday by Mrs. Mary Whitehouse, co-founder of the "Clean Up TV" campaign, when she announced the formation of a National Viewers and Listeners Association.

The association, she said, would strive for:

The appointment of a full-time chairman of the BBC Board of Governors, with the same powers as Lord Hill, chairman of the ITA.

A separate secretariat for the Board. At present "all letters go in by the same door and out through the same postbag."

Regular reports to the nation to "build up confidence and understanding" and a public inquiry into the finances of the BBC, because "there is a developing conviction that a proportion of its revenue is being spent in ways detrimental to the public interest."

Crucifix Incident

Mrs. Whitehouse quoted as "the latest example of BBC bad taste and irresponsibility" an incident in the BBC 3 programme when a crucifix was used as a pipe rack.

The association wanted to establish that viewers' opinions should be made public, not ignored, patronised or ridiculed.

"We do not say we are always right but we have a right to be heard. If the BBC try to ridicule the views of half a million people what else will they ridicule in the same way?

"Mr. Huw Wheldon (Controller of Programmes) referred to us as the lunatic fringe. 'Swizzlewick' was an attack on this campaign. The little men in TV will destroy anything for the expression of their own egos."

Mrs. Whitehouse said that the "Clean Up TV" campaign had 425,000 signatories. There were 5,000 regular subscribers, 1,000 of whom had already contributed £250 to VALA.

(November 30)

Man & woman accused of moor murder

Daily Telegraph Reporter

A MAN and a woman were charged at Hyde, Cheshire, yesterday with the murder of LESLEY ANN DOWNEY, aged 10, whose body was found buried in peat on the Pennine moors six days ago.

The man, IAN BRADY, 26, stock clerk, appeared on remand, accused of murdering EDWARD EVANS, 17, of Addison Street, Ardwick, Manchester, at a house in Wardle Brook Avenue, Hattersley, Hyde.

The woman, MYRA HINDLEY, 23, shorthand-typist, also appeared on remand on a charge of harbouring and assisting Brady knowing that he had murdered Evans. The new charge says that they murdered Lesley Ann Downey in Cheshire between Dec. 26, 1964 and last Saturday.

Separate appearances

Brady and Hindley made separate appearances during a seven-minute hearing in the crowded courtroom. They were remanded in custody for a week and granted legal aid. No addresses were given in court.

Supt. ROBERT TALBOT said that Lesley Ann Downey left her home in Charnley Walk, Ancoats, Manchester, at about 4 p.m. on Boxing Day to go to a fairground in Hulme Hall Lane.

She had not been seen since. Her body was found after an extensive search of the moors near the Greenfield to Holmfirth Road on Saturday.

(October 22)

TWO PRESIDENTS OPEN TUNNEL

JOHN WALLIS
Daily Telegraph Staff Correspondent
COURMAYEUR, Friday.

THE seven-mile tunnel under Mont Blanc was opened today by President de Gaulle and President Saragat. The longest road tunnel in the world, it was begun over six years ago.

Smiling and outwardly happy, the Presidents opened the seven-mile tunnel in rain at Chamonix, and in bright sunshine at Courmayeur on the Italian side of Mont Blanc.

The two leaders, who were together 4½ hours, made no progress in solving the difficulties between their two countries on the future of Europe and the crisis in the Common Market.

"While both are playing the brotherly ties between the two nations, they both agreed politely to disagree." a French report said.

Both Presidents spoke glowingly in public speeches of Franco-Italian friendship, but made no attempt to conceal the differences that existed.

Less cordial

Signor Fanfani and M. Couve de Murville, French Foreign Minister, were much less cordial.

Signor Fanfani, acting as President of the Foreign Ministers Council of the Common Market, announced his intention of calling a Ministerial meeting, already unanimously approved, on July 26. The French made it clear they would not attend.

President Saragat told President de Gaulle at the Italian end of the tunnel that the tunnel would reinforce "the desire for unity among all nations on the Continent."

(July 17)

Daily Telegraph and Morning Post, 1965

RIOT CITY CALLS IN TROOPS

LOS ANGELES BUILDINGS LOOTED AND FIRED

Daily Telegraph Staff Correspondent

NEW YORK, Friday.

NATIONAL GUARD troops were ordered into Los Angeles tonight as 5,000 Negroes wrecked, looted and started fires unchecked in the third and worst day of rioting in the area known as the "Black Ghetto."

Throughout the day an arson-minded mob ran wild through the Negro community of Watts, putting the torch to more than half a dozen buildings. Brick-hurling rioters turned back many fire engines. Massed police units got others through, mostly too late.

A police spokesman said: "We simply do not have the men or equipment to control this situation. Looters are entirely out of hand. Many are helping themselves to guns and ammunition from looted stores. There have been many cases of our men and helicopters being shot at.

A helicopter televising the scene swooped low over building after building going up in flames, with no fire equipment in sight. Little knots of people stood around and watched.

The helicopter, saying it was under rifle and pistol fire from the ground, suddenly soared and darted among the towering columns of black smoke visible throughout the Los Angeles basin.

One fire completely consumed a furniture store covering two-thirds of a city block. Another ruined a large supermarket.

SHOPS DESERTED
Police H.Q. besieged

Most white shop owners abandoned their premises, leaving them easy prey for marauders. Hundreds had windows smashed, and were then looted.

An angry crowd even gathered outside the 77th Street police head-quarters. All doors except the front one were bolted, and armed guards were placed outside.

Rioters ripped up streets for pieces of asphalt to throw at police, fire engines and cars containing whites.

The latest figure for arrests was given as 125. Since the riots started on Wednesday night more than 100 police vehicles have been damaged and 76 commercial buildings wrecked or attacked by looters.

Dick Gregory, the Negro comedian, who was shot in the leg in last night's rioting, told a Press conference today that "the sight of the police uniform, a symbol of injustice to the Negro," was causing the continued rioting.

"The uniform of the Los Angeles police has the same image to the Negro community that the British uniform did to the colonials."

Civil rights leaders have long predicted a race explosion in Los Angeles, but when it came with sudden violence on Wednesday night it took authorities by surpise.

The Negro population, accounting for nearly 400,000 of the city's 2,500,000, has not previously reacted to the civil rights drive in the violent manner of Southern towns, Philadelphia and New York.

But police and Negro leaders believe the Watts rioting is the result of deep-seated frustrations, of dissatisfaction with appalling housing conditions and lack of proper schooling.

AIRLESS TENEMENTS
Temperature 100 deg.

The present heat wave, with temperatures approaching 100 degrees, is making life in overcrowded, airless tenement buildings almost unbearable.

When police arrested a Negro for drunken driving on Wednesday night there were hundreds of hostile witnesses. The streets were jammed with Negroes trying to get what relief they could from the humid night.

The "Black Ghetto" has the highest population density of just over 27 people per acre, compared with the average for Greater Los Angeles of 7.4. Its residents are 98 per cent Negro.

(August 14)

AMERICAN HELD 'AFTER BURNING CALL-UP CARD'

Daily Telegraph Staff Correspondent

NEW YORK, Monday.

A university graduate, David Miller, 22, who was said to have set fire publicly to his Army call-up card during demonstrations against the Vietnam war, was arrested in New Hampshire by six agents of the Federal Bureau of Investigation today.

Miller, of Syracuse, New York, was the first person to be charged under a law signed by President Johnson in August prohibiting destruction of draft cards. Miller faces a maximum penalty of $10,000 (£3,570) and five years gaol.

(October 19)

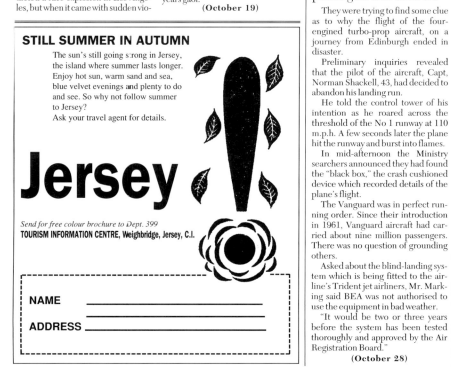

THE JAPANESE DAIHATSU Compagno Berlina Saloon.

JAPAN INVADES BRITISH CAR MARKET

EVERY POSSIBLE 'EXTRA'

JOHN LANGLEY
Daily Telegraph Motoring Staff

JAPAN is trying to break into the British car market by supplying cars with nearly every possible "extra" included at the standard price. The first of the Japanese invaders went on sale yesterday.

It is the two-door four-seater Daihatsu Compagno Berlina saloon, with a 797cc engine, smaller than a Mini's and costing £799 including import duty and £141 purchase tax.

"Extras" in the standard specification range from a built-in radio to "anti-glare glass."

They include fully reclining front seats, a cigarette lighter, whitewall tyres, wheel trims, an electric clock, two fog lamps and a reversing light, wing mirrors, locking petrol cap and electrically-operated windscreen washers.

Stainless steel bumpers are fitted and an AC generating plant is used instead of a dynamo to keep the battery fully charged even in heavy traffic. An estate car version is available without some of the special equipment at £789, including £139 tax.

The manufacturers claim that the car will do up to 60 miles to a gallon of petrol and that it has a top speed around 80 mph. If these figures are accurate, they will be the envy of most British and European manufacturers.

(May 26)

SEARCH FOR CLUES IN VANGUARD WRECK

Daily Telegraph Reporter

MINISTRY OF AVIATION officials yesterday began investigating the wreckage of the BEA Vanguard airliner which crashed in fog in the early hours of the morning at London Airport, killing 30 passengers and six crew.

They were trying to find some clue as to why the flight of the four-engined turbo-prop aircraft, on a journey from Edinburgh ended in disaster.

Preliminary inquiries revealed that the pilot of the aircraft, Capt, Norman Shackell, 43, had decided to abandon his landing run.

He told the control tower of his intention as he roared across the threshold of the No 1 runway at 110 m.p.h. A few seconds later the plane hit the runway and burst into flames.

In mid-afternoon the Ministry searchers announced they had found the "black box," the crash cushioned device which recorded details of the plane's flight.

The Vanguard was in perfect running order. Since their introduction in 1961, Vanguard aircraft had carried about nine million passengers. There was no question of grounding others.

Asked about the blind-landing system which is being fitted to the airline's Trident jet airliners, Mr. Marking said BEA was not authorised to use the equipment in bad weather.

"It would be two or three years before the system has been tested thoroughly and approved by the Air Registration Board."

(October 28)

GUEVARA FINDS 'NEW FIELDS OF BATTLE'

VINCENT RYDER
Daily Telegraph Staff Correspondent

WASHINGTON, Monday.

THE fate of Senor Ernesto "Che" Guevara, once Dr. Castro's closest partner, remained a mystery today despite the Cuban Prime Minister's announcement at a rally in Havana last night that he had left the island for "new fields of battle against imperialism."

Dr. Castro read what he said was a handwritten letter from Senor Guevara delivered on April 1. According to this, he said: "I have fulfilled the part of my duty that bound me to the revolution in your territory."

He was giving up his Cuban citizenship, his Ministry in the Government and his rank of Major. He was leaving his wife and children in Cuba under the care of the Government.

Economic role

The uncompromising revolutionary, now 37, was born in Argentina, became a doctor and was mixed up in revolutionary movements in several Latin American countries before throwing in his lot with Dr. Catro. He became chief economic organiser when the revolution succeeded.

(October 5)

WILSON SAVED BY CASTING VOTE

H.B. BOYNE
Daily Telegraph Political Correspondent

THE Government plumbed the depths of humiliation in the Commons last night. On the first Opposition amendment against the new Corporation Tax, designed to postpone its operation for a year, it could do no better than register a tie.

With the eight Liberals present supporting the Opposition, the figures were 281 a side.

As luck would have it, the Member temporarily in the chair when the result of the division was announced was a Conservative, Sir Herbert Butcher. (Holland-with-Boston). True to conventional procedure, he gave his casting vote in favour of retaining in the Finance Bill the words which the amendment would have struck out.

This saved the Government from defeat.

Amid Conservative jubilation and defiant jeers from the Government benches, Mr. Heath, Shadow Chancellor, moved the adjournment of the debate.

He called in vain for a statement of the Government's intentions from the Prime Minister, who had been in the House a few minutes earlier and had taken part in the division.

"TRY AGAIN"
Reply to Heath

In Mr Wilson's absence Mr. Callaghan, Chancellor of the Exchequer, met Mr. Heath's challenge by arguing that there was plenty of time ahead to get on with the Bill. The Opposition, he said, "can try their luck again and see if they are as successful next time as this time."

The Chancellor's evident confidence was justified. When the House divided on Mr. Heath's motion the Government had a majority of five, the figures being 284 to 279.

As before, the eight Liberals voted with the Conservatives, their two other M.P.s being "paired" with Labour.

This raised two questions. Why did the Government fail to muster its full strength in the first Division? And why were the Conservatives two "light" in the second?

CHAPTER OF ACCIDENTS
"Technical failure"

The answers revealed a chapter of accidents Three Labour M.P.s including two Ministers, were in the building but did not reach the division in time for the first vote. Two Conservative M.P.s missed the second because of an alleged "technical failure" of the division bells.

This explanation was received with some scepticism by Liberals. "The Tories appear to be keeping Labour in power." said Mr. Hooson (Lib. Montgomery). "Everyone knew there would be a second vote in a matter of minutes, and yet there were two missing."

As Conservatives see it, the inci- dent was a stark demonstration of the fact that the Government is trying to run Parliament and the country "on a razor's edge."

The last time a casting vote had to be used in the House was on May 1, 1950, when Major James Milner, Deputy Speaker, now Lord Milner, used it to uphold the second Attlee Government against a Conservative motion to reduce the Ministry of Transport estimates.

(June 3)

ARGENTINA AGAIN CLAIMS ISLES

Daily Telegraph United Nations Correspondent

NEW YORK, Monday.

Speaking in the United Nations General Assembly today Senor Zavala Ortiz, Argentine Foreign Minister, pressed his country's claim to the Falkland Islands. He said Britain exercised an "illegal administration over the islands, an integral part of Argentine soil occupied by violence."

He denied the right of the Falklands to self-determination. Those who "occupied" the islands "had been sent there by Britain."

(September 28)

WHISKY 4s UP CIGARETTES 6d

EXPENSES LUNCH FOR EXPORT ONLY

CIGARETTES, tobacco, wines, spirits and beer cost more from to-day as a result of the Budget introduced yesterday by Mr. Callaghan, Chancellor of the Exchequer.

In the first full Labour Budget since 1951 the Chancellor imposed stringent curbs on business expenses, increased Road Fund duty and announced the cancellation of the TSR-2 project. Seeking increased tax revenue of £164 million in 1965-66 and £217 million in 1966-67, he proposed:

TOBACCO DUTY: Rates increased by 10s a lb., putting 6d on packet of 20 cigarettes selling for 4s 11d, 5d on most other kinds and 4d on small filter-tipped brands selling for 3s 2d. Effective to-day. Yield in full year £75 million.

SPIRITS: Duty raised by £1 14s 6d a gallon, equivalent to 4s on bottle of whisky or gin. Effective to-day. Yield in full year £19 ½ million.

WINES: Increase of 6s a gallon on fortified wines and 3s on table wines, equivalent to 1s a bottle and 6d a bottle respectively. Effective to-day. Yield in full year £6 ½ million.

BEER: Duty raised by 1d a pint. Effective to-day. Yield in full year £26 million.

Up Goes The Cost

		Old	New
Whisky		£2.4s 6d	£2.8s 6d
Gin		£2.2s 9d	£2.6s 9d
Cigarettes	(20 plain or king sized tipped)	4s 11d	5s 5d
"	(20 tipped)	4s 2d	4s 7d
"	(20 small tipped)	3s 2d	3s 6d
Small cigars	(pkt of 5)	4s 4d	4s 7d
Pipe tobacco	(1 oz)	6s 0d	6s 7d
Car licence		£15	£17.10s

BUSINESS EXPENSES: Spending on business entertainment, except where overseas buyers are involved, will not be allowed as an expense for tax relief from to-day. The initial allowance of 30 per cent. on firms' cars is withdrawn.

CAPITAL GAINS TAX: Levied on gains realised on all assets, at flat rate of 30 per cent. for 1965-66 on assets held for more than a year, with following principal exceptions:

Owner-occupied houses;

Goods and chattels realised for not more than £1,000.

Yield expected to reach £125 million in full year.

HOLIDAY TRAVEL: Amounts of foreign currency provided for travel abroad to be entered on passports as curb on "misuse" of facilities. Anyone requiring more than £250 must satisfy Bank of England that funds are required for genuine travel expenses.

(April 7)

GOLDIE, THE ZOO'S GOLDEN EAGLE, perching in a tree in Regent's Park yesterday after escaping for a second time. Goldie first escaped last March, when he was free for 12 days.

GOLDIE NO MATCH FOR KEEPERS' WILES

DAWN CAPTURE IN PARK
By KATHLEEN WELSH

GOLDIE, the golden eagle which achieved international fame in 12 days of freedom from the London Zoo, was recaptured yesterday. He was caught by Mr. Joe McCorry, deputy head keeper of birds of prey at the Zoo, without even the help of a snare.

His capture was a triumph for the bird psychology of the experts. He was caught on one of their food lures, a dead rabbit, as they had predicted from the first that he would be, when he grew hungry enough to take it.

He was captured when they had said he would be, in the early morning, before sightseers were around to distract him.

RABBIT RUSE

Last picnic in Park

At 5.45 a.m. Mr. McCorry and Mr. Ernest Scrivener, head keeper, entered the Park, and with Mr. Michael Chester, an RSPCA official, laid out their rabbit on a football pitch near Goldie's favourite haunt, the wild fowl sanctuary. They tied a rope to it only to make it move and appear alive.

An hour and a half later Goldie swooped from a tree to dig his talons in his last picnic in the Park. Mr. McCorry gave him a minute or two, then walked quietly up and seized his legs.

Mr. McCorry had no apprehensions about catching Goldie with his hands. "Eagles don't bite," he said.

Like most recaptured prisoners, Goldie was given a good meal on his return to captivity, the remains of the rabbit, followed by a second course of raw beef. Then he went back, slightly subdued, to rejoin his mate Regina in their private aviary. It was not an ardent reunion.

WORLD FAME

Goldie's fame spread world wide. Broadcasting networks telephoned from Canada, America, New Zealand, Australia, and Japan, as well as Europe, asking for information about him.

Numbers of visitors to the Zoo last Sunday showed a big increase on the corresponding Sunday a year ago. Figures last Sunday were 6,500 compared with 3,700 a year ago. A Zoo spokesman said: "We attribute some of the increase to Goldie."

(March 11)

Beatles MBE protests mount

Daily Telegraph Reporter

CAPT. DAVID EVAN REES, 70, who became an OBE in 1941, in recognition of 44 years sea service, is to return his insignia in protest against the Beatles being made MBEs.

The captain of Grangetown, Cardiff, was torpedoed in the North Sea and off Nova Scotia. He said yesterday he felt the award to the Beatles took value from the Order.

On Monday, it was stated that MBE insignia was being returned in protest by Mr. Hector Dupuis, former Canadian M.P., and by Mr. Paul Pearson, of Haywards Heath, Sussex, former RAF squadron leader.

Last night Mr. James Berg, 52, deputy headmaster of Wishmore Cross School, Bagshot, Surrey, announced he was returning his insignia. He was made an MBE as a warrant officer first class when serving with Anti-Aircraft Command in London.

'Losing standards'

Mr. Berg said: "I have been proud to wear my decoration since 1942 when it was pinned on my chest by King George VI. But now the whole thing has become debased."

A coastguard, Mr. George Read, 51, of Hartland, Devon, who became an OBE for his part in rescuing nine sailors, said yesterday: "I am so disgusted with the Beatles being made MBEs that I am considering sending my insignia back."

Our Political Staff writes: Return of awards is not uncommon and protest letters are received at 10, Downing Street after most Honours Lists. But the award to the Beatles has sparked off the largest number of protests for some time.

Members of the Orders cannot resign. They can always claim back their insignia.

(June 16)

MALCOLM X SHOT DEAD
LESLIE BEILBY
Daily Telegraph Staff Correspondent

NEW YORK, Sunday.

AN assassin's bullets to-day ended the life of Malcolm X, the Negro nationalist leader, who had preached a doctrine of violence in the fight for Negro rights.

He was shot four times as he rose to address a rally of 400 of his followers in the Audubon ballroom in Harlem. The words "Brothers and sisters" had just faded from his lips when eight to 10 shots rang out.

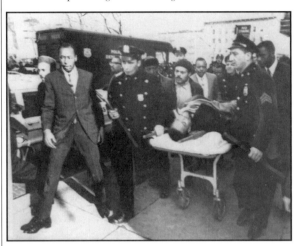

MALCOLM X, THE AMERICAN NEGRO LEADER, being carried unconscious from the Audubon ballroom in Harlem yesterday after he had been shot. He died in hospital.

Malcolm X, who was 39, was hit in the chest and face and died later in hospital. Three Negroes have been detained and police are seeking two others.

Pandemonium broke out in the ballroom as Malcolm X pitched forward on to the stage. People screamed and ran for the exits and a woman yelled: "They've shot Malcolm X."

In the mêlée some of his followers seized two Negroes and, pinning them to the floor, began kicking and punching them. Police had to fight to release them before arresting them.

A third man ran out of the ballroom into the arms of a policeman and was also detained. Another, carrying a pistol, fled from the ballroom pursued by a dozen men.

WOUND IN LEG

The three Negroes being detained are Thomas Hagan, who has a bullet wound in the leg and is in Bellevue Hospital, where he is being guarded by 12 policemen, Willie Harris and William Parker.

Police said Hagan, 22, had a pistol and four unspent bullets in his pocket. Two other men were slightly wounded in the shooting.

After the shooting, members of Malcolm X's organisation of Afro-American Unity ran to put their leader on a stretcher on which he was taken to the Vanderbilt Clinic of the Columbia-Presbyterian Medical Centre nearby.

He was taken to the emergency operating room shortly after 3 p.m. but died about 50 minutes later.

A police spokesman blamed the assassination on the bitter feud between Malcolm X's supporters and the Black Muslim organisation. Malcolm X broke with the Black Muslims over a year ago.

He has been in fear of assassination ever since. Members of the Black Muslims denied any knowledge of to-day's crime however. "We don't know anything," one said.

(February 22)

WHITE MAN IS GAOLED FOR NEGRO MURDER
Daily Telegraph Staff Correspondent

NEW YORK, Thursday.

An all-white jury in Anniston, Alabama, tonight convicted Hubert Damon Strange, 25, also white, of the murder of Willie Brewster, 38, a Negro, last July. Strange was sentenced to 10 years' imprisonment.

Brewster, a foundry worker, was shot as he drove along a road near Anniston. The jury took nine hours to reach a verdict.

(December 3)

Main line plan saves £50m, says Beeching
RONALD STEVENS
Daily Telegraph Industrial Correspondent

DR. BEECHING, chairman of the Railways Board, said yesterday that between £50 million and £100 million a year would be saved by selective rather than comprehensive use of the main trunk routes.

He was commenting on the Board's report, published yesterday, on trunk route development.

Of the main lines excluded from the development proposals, Dr. Beeching said that some would wither away, and some would be maintained at a lower standard as freight or feeder lines. Others would be converted from double to single track.

Railmen's jobs

He offered no estimate of the likely effect of the proposals on railwaymen's jobs.

But he did not think they would "cause railwaymen to wonder about their jobs any more than they wonder now. They will help to remove uncertainty, rather than create greater unease."

Dr. Beeching said that he was "quite satisfied" with Mr. Fraser's reaction to the report. "My hope is that we shall reach agreed decisions about the problem so that we can take action and put our house in order as quickly as possible."

The report has already been submitted to Mr. Fraser, Minister of Transport, and will be considered by Lord Hinton, his new adviser on transport planning.

(February 17)

AUSTRALIA TO SEND 1,000 MEN TO VIET-NAM
Daily Telegraph Correspondent

SYDNEY, Thursday.

An Australian infantry battalion of about 1,000 men will fight alongside American troops in the defence of South Viet-nam. The unit is the 1st Bn., Royal Australian Regiment.

Sir Robert Menzies, Prime Minister, announcing the decision, read a letter from President Johnson saying that he was "delighted."

New Zealand force

Our Correspondent in Wellington, New Zealand, cabled last night: The 16th Field Artillery Regiment of the New Zealand Army may be sent at any time to join forces in South-East Asia.

(April 30)

INDIAN ARMY DRIVES FOR LAHORE

'BOMBERS ATTACK BASE'

VICTOR ANANT
Daily Telegraph Correspondent

NEW DELHI, Monday.

INDIA invaded West Pakistan yesterday "to forestall an attack on the Punjab." Within hours Pakistan had dropped paratroops behind the Indian lines and claimed to have destroyed 22 Indian fighters.

Indian troops in brigade strength were tonight reported to be moving towards Lahore, about 20 miles from the border at Wagah. Lahore is symbolically important as West Pakistan's traditional Islamic and cultural centre.

The Indian Air Force attacked "military installations, a goods train carrying military supplies and an oil tanker train near Lahore."

PARATROOPS' ROLE

Attack on installations

Pakistani paratroops were dropped tonight behind Indian lines in the Punjab. They jumped in small groups near Patiala an air defence radar installation, more than 100 miles behind Indian lines, and near Pathankot, a railhead for Kashmir, apparently to damage installations.

Other New Delhi reports say that Pakistani bombers attacked the Indian military base at Jamnagar in the Kathiawar peninsula tonight. The planes were also reported to have bombed Jamnagar airport but the extent of the damage in both places was not stated.

The Defence Minister, was wildly cheered three times this morning in the Indian Lower House of Parliament when he made the announcement of India's attack. He said the action was to forestall Pakistan's next move to attack across the Punjab border.

Mr. Shastri, Indian Prime Minister, told the Congress Parliamentary party executive today that there is now "a full scale war" between India and Pakistan. Mr. Shastri said that it may be "a prolonged affair."

He added: "Pakistan's desire to annex Kashmir has to be ended once and for all. There may be ups and downs but there should be no doubt that the ultimate success would be ours."

Meanwhile, it was reported that the village of Jaurian, in Kashmir, was "in flames." Pakistani troops in the Chhamb sector were said to be retreating.

Five Pakistani tanks were claimed to have been damaged. No Indian planes were damaged and all returned safely from their sorties this morning it was stated in New Dehli.

The Indian move across the Punjab borders caught the Pakistanis by surprise. A second front was expected along the border with East Pakistan or farther north, near Sialkot.

British residents in Amritsar and the border areas have been asked to stay away from the operational front.

(September 7)

£1,000 FINE FOR INCITING RACE HATRED

Daily Telegraph Political Correspondent

SIR FRANK SOSKICE, Home Secretary, introduced in the Commons yesterday his long-awaited Bill to "prohibit discrimination on racial grounds in places of public resort" and to "penalise incitement to racial hatred."

The first of these offences, new to British criminal law, is punishable by a fine of £50, or £100 if repeated. A person convicted of an offence in the second category can be sent to prison for two years and fined £1,000.

The penalties will seem salutary enough to Labour M.P.s who have been pressing for years for legislation of this kind.

Under the Bill, the offence of discrimination can be committed only by a proprietor, manager or employee of a "place of public resort." It is defined as discriminating "on the ground of colour, race, or ethnic or national origins," against any person seeking access facilities or services.

Places of public resort are carefully catalogued. They include hotels, restaurants, public houses, theatres, cinemas, dance halls, sports grounds, all forms of public transport,and any other "place of public entertainment or recreation."

But shops are excluded from the Bill's provisions, so are private hotels, lodgings or boarding houses where terms of accommodation are individually agreed rather than subject to a common tariff for allcomers.

There is no mention of the clubs which refuse membership to Jews or coloured people, nor of employers who deny them jobs. And it will still be possible for independent schools to practise racial discrimination in selecting their pupils.

(April 8)

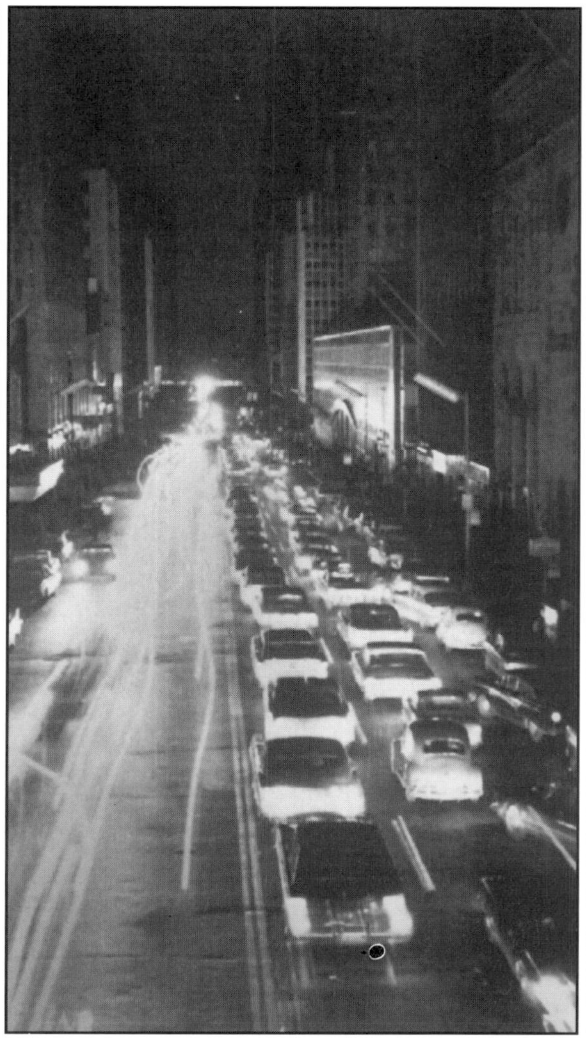

CAR HEADLIGHTS providing the only source of light in a darkened New York street.

AMERICAN SEABOARD HIT BY BLACKOUT

NEW YORK IN DARKNESS: TRAFFIC CHAOS

ALEX FAULKNER
Daily Telegraph Staff Correspondent

NEW YORK, Tuesday.

A LARGE area of the United States and parts of Canada were paralysed by a power blackout tonight. It struck New York as office workers were on their way home.

The area affected stretched as far afield as Boston and inland to Buffalo. Ottawa and Toronto were also hit by the blackout, caused by a break in a line at a switching station on the Niagara power system.The blackout stranded 150,000 people in subway trains for nearly two hours, cut television and radio, trapped people in lifts and halted all flights at Kennedy International and La Guardia airports.

There were reports of looting in many places. Police declared a state of emergency in some cities.

The worst hit city appeared to be Rochester, in New York State, where police fought a crowd of hundreds in an area which is largely Negro. Shop windows were smashed and looted.

REPORT TO PRESIDENT

Power line repairs

Mr. Buford Ellington, Director of the Office of Emergency Planning, reported to President Johnson, that power line workers expected to finish repairs so that power could be restored to the North-East of America by 10 p.m., after four and a half hours of blackout.

Power was eventually restored in Massachusetts, most of Connecticut, Toronto, Ottawa and Buffalo. In all 80,000 square miles, populated by nearly 30 million had been hit.

Police emergency squads were rushed to a prison near Boston when rioting broke out.

New York newspapers, restaurants, theatres and night clubs were dislocated. Crowds descended in hordes on hotels to stay overnight because they could not get home.

People began camping in the lobbies. Many stayed in their offices unable to get down from their skyscrapers because lifts had broken down.

(November 10)

All an adult needs to eat 'for 1s a day'

By GERDA PAUL

AN adult could get all the nourishment he needed from vegetable stew and dumplings for 1s a day, Mr. D. S. Miller, research nutritionist of London University, said in Leeds yesterday.

The challenge became irresistible when he also gave the recipe for the stew: carrots (1d) and cabbage (½d). Eightpence for flour and 2d for lard for the dumplings. Total 11 ½d.

I decided to make it a lunch for four. But first I had to get the co-operation of my greengrocer in Earls Court.

I bought two-thirds of a pound of carrots, at 10d a lb, and one-fifth of a pound of spring greens (no cabbage) at 10d a lb.

The flour was easy. I bought four lb at 9 ½d a lb, and ½ lb of lard for 10d, subtracting the appropriate amounts from each item later, to stick to Mr. Miller's budget.

Only 13 dumplings, one person's portion, would fit into the pressure cooker with the vegetables. When they were done, they looked like a mound of tennis balls covered with bits of seaweed.

But when we tasted it, we decided that the Miller meal was not so bad considering the price.

Mrs. Elizabeth Porisini, from upstairs, said that the stew was too watery, and flavourless, but if you were very hungry you could enjoy it.

(April 24)

TRAIN ROBBER IN GAOL BREAK

T.A. SANDROCK and JOHN WEEKS
Daily Telegraph Scotland Yard Staff

ONE of the Great Train Robbers escaped from Wandsworth, a maximum security prison, yesterday. He is Ronald Arthur Biggs, 35, serving a 30-year sentence for armed robbery and conspiracy.

Biggs and three other men got away while at exercise in the prison yard in an operation planned as meticulously as the one which freed another train robber, Charles Wilson, from Winson Green Prison, Birmingham, last August. Wilson is still at large.

The four men climbed the 20ft prison wall by a rope ladder and a tubular steel ladder thrown down by one of an armed "rescue" gang. They dropped on to a pantechnicon van beside the wall.

A considerable amount of work had been done to convert the van for the escape.

It had been painted red, a quarter of the roof had been cut away, and a wooden platform built inside the van.

The men jumped through the hole in the roof onto the platform built inside the van and then dropped to the floor. They ran to two cars and were driven off.

THREE ACCOMPLICES

Old Bailey sentences

The men who escaped with Biggs were:

ERIC FLOWER, serving 12 years for armed robbery, a joint sentence imposed at Hants Assizes in July, 1964, and the Old Bailey in December, 1964;

ROBERT ANDERSON, serving 12 years for burglary, shop breaking, larceny and conspiracy, who was sentenced at the Old Bailey on May 12;

PATRICK DOYLE alias ANTHONY JENKINS, serving four years' imprisonment and sentenced at the Old Bailey in June, 1964.

BIGGS, who is 6ft tall, is of medium build with dark brown curly hair, grey eyes and an oval face.

One who saw the escape was Mr. Peter Head, who lives in Heathfield Square. He saw three men in prison clothing near the pantechnicon and ran back into his house looking for a weapon.

He armed himself with a spanner and ran from his house, but the driver of one of the cars started going towards him, holding what Mr. Head described as a shotgun or a rifle.

He ordered Mr. Head back into his house and he obeyed. He then watched through a hole in a shed and saw the man with the weapon get back into the car and pull a mask over his face.

Biggs of Alpine Road, Redhill, Surrey, is one of seven conspirators in the Great Train Robbery, who were sentenced to 30 years' imprisonment at Buckinghamshire Assizes last year.

He is married with two young sons. Before the robbery he was a partner in a carpentry business.

He had nine previous convictions, including robbery, burglary and housebreaking. He escaped from Borstal and deserted from the RAF.

In the neat, semi-detached house in Alpine Road where the Biggs family lived the present occupant, Mrs. Barbara Ottaway, said she had no knowledge of the present whereabouts of Mrs. Biggs and her two young children.

Mrs. Biggs left the house just before Christmas. It was partly furnished and she had lived there for five years with her husband and her son, Michael, aged five.

Her second son was born there just over two years ago. The house, one of a terrace in a quiet road facing a sports ground, was sold this Spring.

(July 9)

Mixed college launched at Cambridge

Daily Telegraph Reporter

UNIVERSITY COLLEGE, the first at Cambridge to admit both men and women, was officially launched yesterday. The college, which will be for graduates only, has elected its first 30 Fellows, of whom two are women.

But it is unlikely that any members of the college, Fellows or otherwise, will move into Bredon House, a late Victorian family house in the west of Cambridge which the university has given to the college for its use, until next March.

The university, which founded the college by the creation of a trust between the university and five individual trustees, has also promised to give £192,000 to the college over the next ten years.

Bridges foresaw need

The need for a graduate college was foreseen in the Bridges Report on Cambridge in 1962. Many Cambridge dons have also recognised the need for a graduate college to cater for the needs of those senior members without a college post or Fellowship.

Until last year there could not have been a mixed college in Cambridge because a university statute, now repealed, said colleges should consist of either men or women.

(October 14)

'BEATLE' HAIR IS DANGER IN FACTORIES

LEGISLATION which compels women factory workers to wear hair nets should be extended to men with "Beatle" hair styles, says Dr. Alan J. Byron, of the Royal Hospital, Sheffield, to-day.

A new type of industrial accident, he writes in the British Medical Journal, had resulted from young men's long hair. Much of it was torn away, and sometimes the scalp, too, because it became inextricably entangled in moving machinery.

He cites a case history, a boy of 17 with hair of average length 9in. He is employed as a machinist at a cutlery firm.

His hair became entangled with a rapidly revolving lathe. As his head was pulled towards the machine, he violently jerked it away and a substantial wedge of hair, measuring 5in by 2in was torn away, but no scalp was removed with it.

(January 15)

PRINCE OF WALES HAS 5 'O' LEVELS

THE PRINCE OF WALES, who was 16 last November, gained five Ordinary level passes in the General Certificate of Education examination four months previously. The passes were in English language, English literature, history, Latin and French.

This examination was the one conducted by the Oxford and Cambridge Schools Examination Board, which is taken by boys at Gordonstoun where the Prince has been a pupil since May, 1962. More than 140 Gordonstoun boys appear in the list of successful candidates.

(January 28)

£300,00 FIRE PUMP HAS TEST IN NEW YORK

The world's most powerful fire pump, built for the New York Fire Department, had its first fire trial in Brooklyn yesterday. The pump is powered by a British-made Deltic diesel engine of the type used in locomotives.

(August 14)

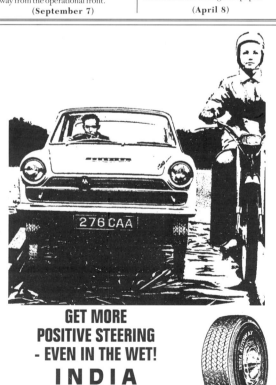

'BEAT' POETS TAKE OVER THE ALBERT HALL

A 'PLANET-CHANT CARNIVAL'

Daily Telegraph Reporter

ALLEN GINSBERG, the American "beat" poet, sat on the steps of the Albert Memorial in London yesterday under the sculptured figures of Dante, Homer, Milton and Shakespeare and read from a yellow foolscap sheet:

International poetry incarnation! World declaration of hot peace shower! Spontaneous planet-chant carnival! Mental cosmonaut poet epiphany!

A Press conference was taking place, much to the surprise of a passing park-keeper. The words came from the programme note of the peotry reading in which Mr. Ginsberg is taking part at the Albert Hall to-morrow.

It was hammered out at a round-table conference of the participating poets from six or seven countries.

"NOBODY'S CRAZY"

Declaration of joy

"What about punctuation?" I asked. "Use exclamation marks," said Mr. Ginsberg, and went on to the finale:

Self evident for real naked come the words! Global synthesis habitual for this eternity! Nobody's crazy! Immortal forever!

I asked: "What does it mean?" Mr. Ginsberg replied "It's a declaration of joy!"

One of the organisers, Mr. John Esam, a New Zealander, said: "It is a completely spontaneous affair.

"So many poets turned up in London we said it would be a good idea to have an international poetry congress. "Let's take the Albert Hall," said somebody, and somebody went out and hired it.

"We have not got a set programme and there is no fixed time. It depends on the audience and the poets as to what is created."

Mr. Ginsberg's contribution may include his "Howl," famous after its clashes with American censorship. He has not made up his mind yet.

CASTRO FIGHTER

Sounds-only Dane

Poets to take part include Pablo Fernandez, a Cuban who fought for President Castro. Simon Vinkenoog from Holland, Anselm Hollo from Finland, Pablo Neruda from Chile, several other Americans and Ernst Jandl, a Dane who composes his poetry in sounds rather than words.

English contributions will come from Alan Sillitoe, author of "Saturday Night and Sunday Morning," from Alexander Trocchi, whose "Cain's Book" has been taken before the courts, and from Bruce Lacey, who appeared in the West End not long ago in "An Evening of British Rubbish."

(June 10)

POETS OF OUR TIME

By WALTER ALLEN

For the Union Dead. By Robert Lowell. (Faber. 15s)

A LATE flowering of the New England spirit, Robert Lowell shows in his new poems all the qualities of his earlier work, a preoccupation with historic New England places and persons, Jonathan Edwards, Hawthorne, Melville, the fascination exercised on him by the sea, and the agonised self-confrontation of a mind at once sceptical and Christian.

His is bedrock poetry, poetry stripped to the bone. There is nothing superfluous. His words have the hardness of pebbles, his images the singularity and weight of natural objects.

In "For the Union Dead" he ranges from New York, Boston and the New England seaboard to Italy and South America. If there is no poem here as immediately striking as his early "The Quaker Graveyard at Nantucket" it is mainly, I think, because his verse has become even more compact, more naked and intransigent in its utterance.

Memory of Aquarium

Even so, I doubt if he has ever written anything finer than the title poem, "For the Union Dead." It begins with a childhood memory of the Boston of to-day and develops into a scrutiny of American experience - indeed of universal experience - since the Civil War. It ends:

The Aquarium is gone. Everywhere, giant finned cars nose forward like fish; a savage servility slides by on grease.

(March 11)

TRAP FOR THE INNOCENT

W.A. DARLINGTON

IN his title, "The Killing of Sister George," Frank Marcus lays a little trap for the innocent playgoer.

Sister George is killed all right, but no murder is committed. She is not a human being, but a character in a BBC serial.

She has to be slaughtered because June Buckridge (Beryl Reid), the actress who plays her, has been misbehaving.

Though a national favourite, and identified by the general public with the radio character, she must be disciplined.

And so Sister George has to die in a street accident and be given a funeral.

That situation, and June's reactions to it, provide the main structure of Mr. Marcus's play; but a good deal of attention is paid to the questionable relationship between her and a young woman known as "Childie," who shares her flat.

However, the evening's chief interest consists not so much in the play as in the acting.

Miss Reid herself, hitherto known in London only as a revue actress, gives an excellent account of June in her various moods; and of course, comedy is in her very bones.

Eileen Atkins plays the enigmatic "Childie" with an air of complete understanding.

Lally Bowers gives a perfect study of a slightly over-refined lady from the higher ranks of the BBC. And Margaret Courtenay fills in corners as a fortune-teller from the flat below. Director, Val May.

(June 18)

'Quiet Flows Don' author Nobel winner

Mikhail Sholokhov, 60, Russian author of "And Quiet Flows the Don," was awarded this year's Nobel Prize for Literature today.

The Swedich Academy said it was honouring Mr. Sholokhov for the "artistic power and integrity with which, in his epic 'And Quiet Flows the Don' he gave artistic expression to a historic phase in the history of the Russian people." The novel was first published in 1928 and in English in 1934.

Mr. Sholokhov is the second Russian to win the Literature Prize since its inception in 1901. It was awarded in 1958 to Boris Pasternak who first accepted it and then, under pressure from the Soviet authorities because he refused to accept their dictates in literature, declined it.

(October 16)

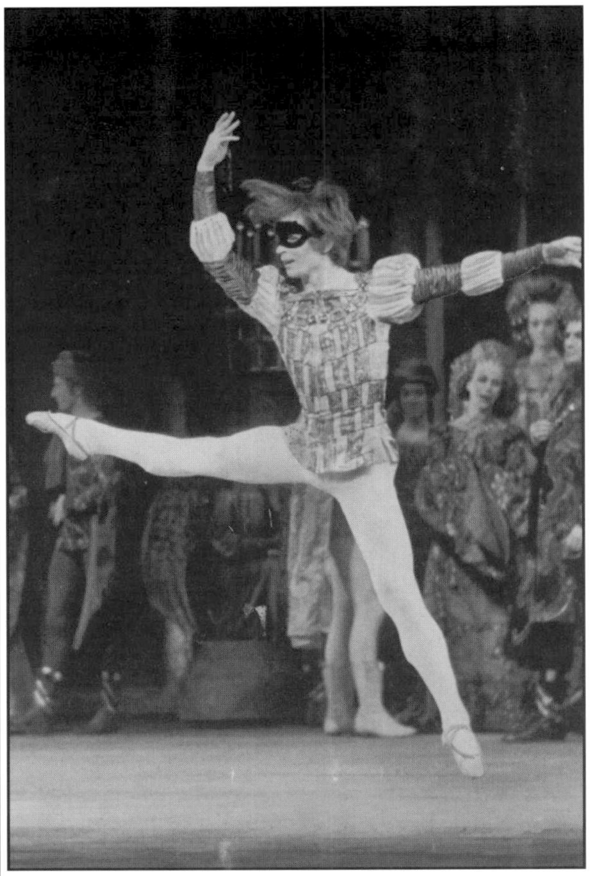

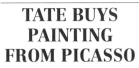

RUDOLPH NUREYEV REHEARSING AT COVENT GARDEN for "Romeo and Juliet," which he danced last night with Dame Margot Fonteyn.

TATE BUYS PAINTING FROM PICASSO

THREE DANCERS'

By TERENCE MULLALY

PICASSO'S "The Three Dancers," a key picture in the development of 20th century art, has been bought by the Tate Gallery direct from the artist for an undisclosed sum.

The acquisition of this large painting has been possible only because of the Tate's Special Treasury Purchase Grant of £50,000 a year for five years. This is specifically earmarked for foreign works painted between 1900 and 1950.

There are no precedents for the public sale of an immediately comparable Picasso. But if this picture had appeared at auction I would have expected it to fetch substantially over £50,000.

That Picasso has been prepared to part with a painting of such importance for the understanding of the evolution of his work is a triumph for the Tate. It dates from 1925 and had an immediate effect in artistic circles, and in particular upon the Surrealists.

(February 13)

ITV COMPANIES RESTYLE POP SHOWS

Daily Telegraph Television Correspondent

Changes in pop music programmes, moving away from the long-haired beatnik style, were announced yesterday by Independent television companies. They follow the decision of Rediffusion, the London week-day contractors, to end "Ready, Steady, Go."

The ABC programme "Thank Your Lucky Stars," on Saturday evenings, will, from Oct. 2, go out at a later time. It will last slightly longer at 45 minutes.

Television Wales and West's teenage show "Discs-A-Gogo" which has been running for four years, will continue until Christmas. It will then be replaced by a new show called "Now."

(September 6)

Outrageous & gruesomely funny play

By ERIC SHORTER

"YOU'RE getting demented," observed a graceless son to his elderly father in Harold Pinter's new play "The Homecoming" at the Aldwych.

He says it soon after the curtain has risen on the largest and greyest and murkiest lounge hall to have been depicted on the London stage since lounge halls first began.

And as the piece wends its hypnotically outrageous, gruesomely funny way towards its unedifying conclusion, we relish the onesidedness of that statement.

For they are all demented in this North London patriarchy which is so unexpectedly visited by a long-lost and successful son with his wife, who stays remarkably on as a sort of mother-prostitute figure.

Why she comes to prefer this squalid household to her own family life on the American campus, whither her husband returns alone with shoulders shrugged, must remain Mr. Pinter's secret and the subject of much speculation. It looks like reversion to type.

Breathtaking nastiness

But in telling us how and in setting out the circumstances for the ultimate, breathtaking nastiness of his play, this author has never put his art to more absorbing, hilarious or stylish purpose.

The play blithely plumbs the depths of human degradation and is assuredly not for all tastes.

But the quality of its language, the variety of its mood, the tension of the dialogue (or rather interlocking monologues), the feeling for cockney idiom and the cool confidence with which the play unfurls its sordid theme are a constant source of pleasure.

Peter Hall's production is a model of timing, which is to say, well-timed pauses; the company, led by Paul Rogers in cloth cap and slippers as the tyrannical, stick-wielding widower, meets most of the play's exacting demands.

As a change from Shakespearian kings, Ian Holm is a flamboyantly cockney pimp.John Normington as the uncle with a family secret acts with pale precision and Vivien Merchant and Michael Bryant are the visiting couple who set the cat among the quintessential Pinter pigeons.

(June 4)

Royal Ballet given 43 curtain calls

By A.V. COTON

THE Royal Ballet took 43 curtain calls lasting 34 minutes last night.Constructing a ballet on a familiar work of literature is a common practice.

The test of success is that the choreographer shall create an effective paraphrase, or a fresh illumination, of the original. He can never expect to amplify the material into something larger than the author created.

Kenneth Macmillan's full-length "Romeo and Juliet" staged by the Royal Ballet at Covent Garden last night is a considerable achievement. It can be reckoned one of the most sumptuous adventures in English ballet since 1945.

The achievement is mainly of solid craftsmanship and organisation. Prokofiev's score and the décor of Nicholas Georgiadis are splendid supporters of the choreographer's aims.

Clash in mixture

Mr. Macmillan's invention is finely exciting in some scenes, meagre in others. He creates brilliant solo and ensemble dances then mingles them with episodes notably lacking in inspiration.

Shakespeare's plot has been a little shaken about to fit the ballet into three acts and three hours.

Dame Margot Fonteyn as Juliet and Rudolf Nureyev as Romeo perform together like a pair of finely adjusted instruments. But the score that they played largely compelled them to present much the same personalities that they have often projected in partnership.

She covered the wider range of feeling and brought to the final scenes great pathos. He was throughtout, Nureyev-Romeo rather than Romeo.

(February 10)

M.P. 'SHOCKED' BY WORD IN BBC SHOW

Daily Telegraph Television Staff

AN M.P., who says he was shocked by the use of a four-letter word in the television programme "BBC-3" on Saturday night is to try to get the incident raised in the Commons.

Brig. Terence Clarke, Conservative M.P. for Portsmouth West is to table a question to Mr. Wedgwood Benn, Postmaster General.

Hundreds of protesting viewers telephoned the BBC on Saturday night and early yesterday morning after the word was used by Mr. Kenneth Tynan, literary manager of the National Theatre, in a discussion on censorship with the American writer Miss Mary McCarthy.

Mr. Tynan was asked by the compere Mr. Robert Robinson if he would go so far as to allow a play to be put on at the National Theatre in which sexual intercourse took place on the stage.

He said that he would and added: "I doubt if there are any rational people to whom the word .... would be particularly diabolical, revolting or totally forbidden."

Mr. Huw Wheldon, Controller of Programmes, BBC, said: "When I heard it I was surprised but I was not appalled. It was quite germane to the discussion that was taking place. I thought it was a responsible discussion and a reasonable one."

Mrs. Mary Whitehouse, co-founder of the Clean-Up TV Campaign, said last night that she would write to the Queen asking her to use her influence with the BBC governors to prevent a repetition.

(November 15)

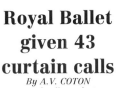

SCENE ENDED IN DEAD SILENCE

By W.A. DARLINGTON

IT is common knowledge that the Royal Court has become a club to evade the censor's ban on John Osborne's "A Patriot for Me." Last night's audience, then, consisted of members and guests.

It was a curious evening in the main, the play is a straightforward and unsensational account of the downfall of an Austrian officer, Colonel Alfred Redl (a historical character) who was discovered just before the Great War to have sold military secrets to the Russians.

We are shown how the Russians selected him early in his career as a potential victim for blackmail. He is a brilliant young man, but vulnerable.

He has expensive tastes, no money but his pay, no background. Also, he is a homosexual; and among his many indiscretions is a visit to a transvesites' ball.

Dragged-in air

It is here that the censor stepped in and no wonder. The scene is played with unpleasant cleverness and is sometimes funny in a nasty way. But it is out of key with the rest of the play, and has a dragged-in air.

There was a certain amount of teeheeing when the curtain rose on a stage-full of men dressed as women, but this died away. The scene ended in dead and I think shamed silence.

After this lapse the play never seemed to recover its former momentum and the applause at the end was persistent rather than enthusiastic.

Good acting

There was some good acting, though. Maximilian Schell was admirable as the Colonel, Jill Bennett as the beautiful spy of tradition was the most effective, Clive Morton and Sebastian Shaw were in strong support.

(July 1)

15 curtain calls for Callas

Daily Telegraph Theatre Correspondent

MARIA CALLAS, smiling but obviously tired, drove from the Royal Opera House, Covent Garden at midnight after receiving tumultuous applause for her performance in the gala presentation of "Tosca" last night.

She took 15 curtain calls during the evening, eight at the end of the second act and seven at the end of the performance.

Mme. Callas, with Tito Gobbi and the other principals, was presented to the Queen, Prince Philip and Queen Elizabeth the Queen Mother. Afterwards Mme. Callas said: "It was one of those evenings that were born well."

"Maria sang beautifully"

Tito Gobbi said: "I could tell from the start it was going to go well. The audience was wonderful. Maria was singing beautifully."

The performance was in aid of the Royal Opera House Benevolent Fund. Mme. Callas, who last week cancelled three out of four appearances at Covent Garden for health reasons, did not rehearse today, though "very well," said Mr. Sander Gorlinsky, her manager."

(July 6)

Sprightly jazz by Louis Armstrong

Although well above the normal pensionable age for jazz men Louis Armstrong remains indestructibly sprightly.

At the Odeon, Hammersmith, last night he demonstrated his genius for clear-cut economical expression and relaxed but compelling swing.

It is true that he is getting a bit short of breath and has lost some of the old fullness of tone but he played with enough of the authority which made him the most respected trumpet palyer jazz has ever known.

(May 31)

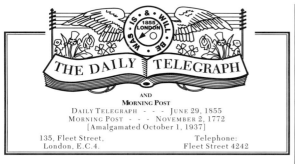

THE DAILY TELEGRAPH
AND
MORNING POST
DAILY TELEGRAPH - - - JUNE 29, 1855
MORNING POST - - - NOVEMBER 2, 1772
[Amalgamated October 1, 1937]
135, Fleet Street, London, E.C.4.
Telephone: Fleet Street 4242

FAREWELL

THERE are few, high or low, eloquent or not, who have not tried this week in some way to express the gratitude, the love, the admiration that they feel for WINSTON CHURCHILL. It has not been easy for anyone to say things that are new or original in expressing the feelings that are shared by all. The old exploits have been recalled; the famous sayings repeated; the precious little anecdotes re-told. We are all conscious of the inadequacy of what we say. But at such a time words, like flowers, lose nothing of their freshness or sincerity by repetition. We may be sure that the broken, murmured phrases of gratitude and grief from the hundreds of thousands coming out from Westminster Hall would have been no less welcome to WINSTON CHURCHILL himself than the eloquent tributes of Prime Ministers and Presidents. He identified himself with the ordinary people of Britain as they have identified themselves - this week more unmistakably than ever - with him. Their tributes have come more easily because they have been expressions of affection, loyalty and sympathy rather than of distant praise.

To-day we bid him farewell. There is not one of us who does not feel that we are bidding farewell also to a part of our own past; not one of us who does not know that we owe to him our past, our present and our future, that Britain, in the worst dangers that ever confronted her, was inseparable from his leadership. There can scarcely be one who dares to think what Britain might be if he had not lived. But not Britain alone. At St. Paul's to-day will be Kings and Princes, Presidents and Chancellors, Ministers and Marshals. Many of them would dare as little to think what their world would have been, or the world that their peoples have to live in, had it not been for the brave and steadfast heart that inspired courage and unity in his own country and for the ringing voice that lifted up men's spirits in so many others. Freedom, which knows no national frontiers, is paying its homage to-day to one of her greatest servants.

(January 30)

NEW LEADER

Mr. HEATH has been chosen leader of the Conservative party and thus, perhaps, next Prime Minister of this country. The machinery which chose him was till now untested. If it has thus passed its first test with flying colours, this must be partly due to its own merits. Partly, however, it is due to the quick good sense, generosity and selflessness of the runner-up, Mr. MAUDLING, to his immediate realisation that the welfare, unity and will of the party must come above any personal ambition. This was no ruthless and unprincipled struggle for power. From Sir ALEC DOUGLAS-HOME'S resignation on, it has been an almost perfect example of how men may put other interests above their own and differ without losing sight of what unites them.

On the personal plane, the vote has been for toughness and pugnacity, for absolute commitment and political professionalism. Mr. WILSON as Prime Minister will find himself confronted with an opponent intellectually at least his equal and in rigourous consistency far his superior. The vote seems also to have a further meaning within the party. The hitherto dominant Tory philosophy of one nation has sometimes tended to conceive the national interest as something including and compounded out of all sectional interests. Mr. HEATH by contrast, has always been conscious of the potential clash between the general and the particular; in his dauntless efforts to force Britain's entry into Europe and, more successful, to abolish resale price maintenance, as in his philosophy as a whole, we may see a man dedicated to the triumph of the general good over all that thwarts and denies it.

Mr. HEATH is the choice of those who know him best and are thus best qualified to judge. It remains for him to make himself known to the country as a whole and to prove that his supporters were right. He has some way to go here — further than Mr. MAUDLING would have had. Yet he should not find it too difficult. It is hard to believe that television or other means of communication will obscure his gifts of character, intelligence and authority.

He must lose no time, with the loyal support of his colleagues in impressing those gifts upon the public.

(July 28)

HONOURS SWITCHED ON

MR. WILSON'S second list of honours shows that new creations of hereditary dignities are most unlikely while Labour is in office. The House of Lords will be enriched by a selection for personal ennoblement which, among its six names, balances learning, science and industrial eminence - the Provost of King's, the President of the College of Surgeons and Dr. BEECHING.

All forms of service to the State are now acknowledged to deserve these graduated expressions of the Sovereign's favour; it is not wholly impossible to try to rank them in approximate order of value. It is much more difficult with those whose service is not to the State but to the Muses - a sisterhood that has acquired in modern times some curious adoptive members. Dame BARBARA HEPWORTH enters the second class of the Order of the British Empire; the Beatles are ranked three classes lower. How is the grading calculated?The placing of the four young men seems to depend on the reason for honouring them. Is it economic? If so, they have earned more foreign currency for the nation than any of those more generously honoured for export achievements in recent years, and the MBE would seem a meagre acknowledgment. The same might be said if the award depended on the number of people to whom they have given pleasure. Is the disproportion of honour intended to express a judgment of the relative status of "pop" entertainment? But then arises the further question, how the Beatles, the masters of their art, if art it is, are equated in the Order with, say, the head of the typing pool in a Government office. Should arts, letters and sports have a separate Order of their own?

(June 12)

BEHIND THE CLUMSY TERROR IN ADEN

By ERIC DOWNTON

IT all revives bleak memories of Palestine, Cyprus and Kenya.

The sneak attacks; the seeming political impasse; the guns and guards and barbed wire; finger-on-trigger patrols prowling the cluttered streets in squat trucks. Special Branch police officers with pistols tucked into their sports shirts and slacks - after five months of intermittent Cairo-backed terrorism among the barren rocks of Aden it looks as though the security situation here will get worse before it improves.

Grenades and bazookas have been used in more than 40 anti-British attacks. A 16-year-old English girl and three Servicemen have been killed, over 40 Service personnel wounded. A distinguished Adeni police officer was murdered on a busy street, several Arab civilians have been killed and a number injured.

A repellent aspect of this "Arab nationalist" terrorism is that so far it has been mainly directed at women and children. Only the terrorists' extraordinary technical inefficiency with timing devices and detonators, particularly when performing such heroic feats as leaving bombs in buses crowded with children and women, has saved the British garrison here from some very ugly incidents.

This terrorism is mainly the work of the "National Liberation Front." Probably it is being quietly assisted - certainly it is not being actively opposed - by Aden's bigger political parties, the People's Socialist party and the South Arabian League, and the Aden Trades Union Congress, which is closely affiliated with the PSP.

The "National Liberation Front" is simultaneously attacking on another flank, organising armed uprisings by tribesmen in the States of the South Arabian Federation, stiffened by subversive infiltration from the Yemen on a considerable scale. The Front has its headquarters in Cairo, is primed with Egyptian money and armed and instructed by the Egyptian Army and intelligence service.

Arab Backing

All members of the Arab League including Jordan, which continues to be looked on by London as a friendly State, have given formal pledges of support for the "liberation" struggle in South Arabia. It is reported to have become clear, however, during meetings just held in Cairo of the League's Committee for South Arabia that most Arab States are not happy about putting up cash and kind for the campaign so long as it is monopolised by Egypt.

Ironically Kuwait, whose Ruler owes his survival in the face of Iraqi aggressive designs a few years ago to British military aid based on Aden, is said by Egyptian officials to have subscribed several million pounds from its vast oil wealth for anti-British operations in Aden and South Arabia.

More irony: despite the Arab League's strident demands for instant independence for Aden, the Adeni nationalists are in no hurry to be rid of the British presence.

They want a definite promise of independence but with the event phased conveniently to give them time to strengthen themselves politically against the Sultanates of the South Arabian Federation.

The Adeni politicians have a very lively fear that the Federal Army may try to seize power in the wake of British withdrawal. If Britain offered to give up political control here tomorrow the Adenis would see in the move a British plot to hand over to the Sultans. With military coups a normal part of Arab politics they could hardly expect outside intervention in their favour.

Adeni politicians also know that the majority of their followers directly or indirectly owe their livelihood to the British base. Before committing themselves to specific demands for removal of the base they want assurances from other Arab States and Russia of adequate compensation.

So far the general relationship between Briton and Arab here remains good. This condition could quickly change if professional Cairo-trained killers take over more activities from the half-hearted, bumbling amateurs.

The political problem, which forms the immediate backdrop to the day-by-day terrorism, is becoming more complex. The new Chief Minister, Mr. Abdul-Qawee Mackawee, hews very close to the Cairo line.

In handling the Aden problem there is certainly room for a more flexible approach by the British authorities to the local political scene. Firmness in security need not inhibit reasonable encouragement of political development.

What is very much needed is a strong unambiguous statement by the British Government that it intends to retain the Aden base for the next five or ten years despite all the emotion-charged winds blowing down from the Arab lands.

(March 30)

GIBRALTAR COLD WAR

RELATIONS between the Spanish Government and Gibraltar have from time to time approached a state of cold war. Here the facts of geography combine with history to give the Spaniards an almost effortless means of advertising their claims to the sovereignty of the Rock. By the slightest pressure, amounting to no more than obstructive customs and passport controls, it is possible to disrupt the flow of workpeople, tourists and goods across the narrow passageway between the two territories. What happens there can be taken as the touchstone of Anglo-Spanish relations, but it is not normally expected that the Madrid Government will press action to the point of seriously prejudicing national self-interest.

That the Government yesterday should have cut off the supply of oxygen for Gibraltar's hospitals - an uncharacteristic and unchivalrous act in itself - is an indication of the state of tension. This accompanies tightened border controls, interfering not only with the transit of workers to and from Gibraltar but also the tourist traffic. It is highly unlikely that the Spanish Government will want to prejudice the rich harvest of the coming summer tourist season. Events will tell. Had the British Government been less eager to snub the Spanish authorities over the prospective purchase of frigates and the subsequent withdrawal from joint naval exercises, its previous diplomatic *démarches* might have met the position. Now nothing short of a strong protest is called for.

(February 6)

THE SUPREMO RETIRES

Earl MOUNTBATTEN, who retired yesterday, had as dazzling, varied and successful a career as any of the Great Captains of history. He combined personal courage, a dash and style in leadership that became legendary and the imagination of the innovator.

After a diversion as Britain's last great Pro-Consul in India he resumed his climb to the top of the Navy ladder and finally, as Chief of the Defence Staff, applied himself in the manner of the contemporary top executive to the reorganisation of Britain's defence machinery.

In an earlier century - in many countries even in this century - a man of so much ability, so much dash and courage, such an aura of leadership, and with so marked a strain of egotism, might have carved out an empire for himself as a politico-military conquistador. MOUNTBATTEN, however, was well attuned to his times. He could make mistakes; some of his judgments and decisions have been controversial. But his services to his country have been great and distinguished.

(July 17)

CONTINETAL ROAD SIGNS FOX BRITONS

Lack of knowledge of the Continetal road signs now in widespread use in Britain presents a "problem of alarming dimensions" according to a survey by Mass-Observation, the market research firm.

A report on the survey, published today, says that only 59 per. cent. of motorists correctly identified the "no overtaking" sign, a black car and a red car in a red circle.

A mere 16 per. cent. knew that a red circle enclosing a car with a motor cyclist shown above meant "all motor vehicle prohibited."

(December 6)

1440 map of America published

Dr. ANTHONY MICHAELIS
Daily Telegraph Science Correspondent

THE only known map of America of 1440, 50 years before the continent's discovery by Columbus, is published today in England and America.

It appears in a book called "The Vinland Map and the Tartar Relation," published by the Yale University Press. Vinland was the name given to America by the Vikings because of its wild grapes.

The book's authors are Mr. R. A. Skelton, Superintendent of the Map Room of the British Museum; Dr. Thomas Marston, Curator of Medieval and Renaissance Literature at the Yale Library; and Mr. George Painter, Assistant Keeper of Printed Books at the British Museum.

EXTREME ACCURACY

Greenland drawing

The map's representation of Greenland is extremely accurate and to the west there is a large island labelled "Vinland, discovered by Bjarni and Leif in company." Above is a long Latin inscription, part of which reads:

"By God's will, after a long voyage from the island of Greenland to the south toward the most distant remaining parts of the western ocean sea, sailing southward amidst the ice, the companions Bjarni and Leif Eriksson discovered a new land, extremely fertile and even having vines, the which island they named Vinland."

Compared with a modern map the northern sea passage to the inland lake is reminiscent of the Hudson's Bay and the Hudson Strait, whereas the southern inlet resembles closely the St. Lawrence. Although the map first came to light in 1957, attached to an unknown manuscript giving an account of a medieval expedition, it required eight years of painstaking research to establish its authenticity.

(October 11)

SIAMESE CAT CREST FOR LORD SNOW

Lord Snow, Parliamentary Secretary, Ministry of Technology, who became a life peer last October, has had a coat of arms designed for him by the College of Arms. In heraldic terms it is: "Arms: azure semy of snow crystals proper. Crest: on a wreath argent and azure a telescope fesswise between two pens in saltire proper. Supporters: on either side a Siamese cat proper."

(February 23)

LONDON DAY BY DAY

Wheldon's Art Chance
Dr. King as Peacemaker

HUW WHELDON, originator of the BBC's cultural "Monitor" feature and now Controller of Television Programmes, has a fine chance to be true to his principles, if he cares to take it.

This arises out of the charge by Humphrey Brooke, the Royal Academy's secretary, that the BBC's neglect of art since commercial TV became a rival is largely responsible for the public indifference to such exhibitions as the Mellon one just ended.

Its attendance, 47,195, is the worst Burlington House has known since the war - and less than a tenth of the numbers attracted there in the 1930s, when TV did not exist.

Mr. Brooke told me yesterday that the BBC has publicised only six Academy shows and ITV only one. With the rise of ITV, the BBC gradually abandoned Burlington House and attendances began to slump.

"Monitor" has covered only a single Academy event: the 1958-9 show of Soviet art. Commerical TV, which in Mr. Brooke's view has reduced the BBC's standards and had a devastating effect on British cultural life, had then been going for three years.

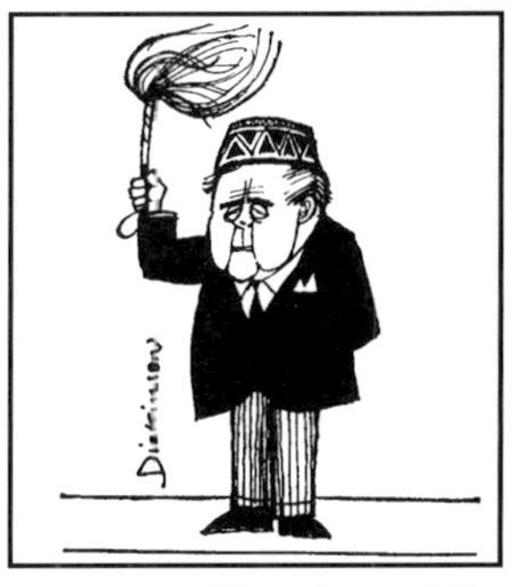

Brisk Business

DR. KING, the new Speaker, is clearly going to make his own distinctive contribution to sharpening Parliamentary procedure.

He took the House through Question Hour yesterday at a brisk enough pace to catch the Government front bench on the hop. For the last two of 53 questions addressed to 10 different Ministers the Treasury failed to put in an appearance.

This is the sort of mishap which gives Chief Whips nightmares. The Government Whip on duty is responsible for assembling all Ministers likely to be reached. "We are sorry," said Mr. George Brown, not without ribald comment from the Opposition.

Fifty-six questions in 55 minutes yesterday represented a marked increase in productivity and there is every sign that it will be sustained.

Computer Composition

SOME unaccustomed sounds will be heard in Wigmore Hall when Lejaren Hiller's "Machine Music" has its first performance here at to-night's Macnaghten Concert.

The pianist rises to blow a tin whistle and push around a toy trolley with built-in glockenspiel, and a balloon is exploded in the front stalls. Four brake drums are among the vast battery of percussion instuments.

Hiller, a young American composer who is Associate Professor of Music at Illinois University, has also written, among other works, a "Computer Cantata" based on material supplied by an IBM 7090 computer.

New From Madeira

THOUGH Madeira wines have lost much of the popularity they enjoyed here in the 19th century, a revival has been proceeding recently and yesterday a new kind was introduced at the Casa Portugal in Lower Regent Street.

This, Ribeiro Dry, comes via Winefare Ltd. from the 165-year-old Funchal shippers Henriques and Henriques. Their chairman, Senhor Alberto Jardim, is the father of Senhor Miguel Jardim, the Portuguese Commerical Attaché in London.

Ribeiro is a blend of Sercial, which some palates tend to find a little harsh on its own, with two other grapes. The result is a light, softer aperitif wine, best drunk chilled.

From the Portuguese point of view the launching comes at a very favourable moment. This year's Madeira vintage is considered the best for over a decade.

Above Board

CUSTOMER in a London restaurant, pointing to one piece on the cheeseboard at the end of his dinner, "Is that Wensleydale?"

Waitress: "Oh no, sir, it's all today's."

PETERBOROUGH

Carnaby Street village - Mecca for the switched-on people

By BERYL HARTLAND

Do you want to express yourself? Want a 1930-style bathing suit (the latest craze), a pair of the tightest, sleekest slacks for 49s 6d. some art nouveau cuff-links or a belt made in one hour?

Or a 1908 gramophone - sure proof you're a trendsetter - or a chest with "Bless Our Home" splashed across it? You'll find them all and more in and around Carnaby Street.

There is nothing quite like it anywhere. It has the garish enticement of a bazaar, with its 100 yards of wide-open doors, bright colours and non-stop pop music spilling into the crowded street.

"It is like a village" says Mr. Canter of Cranks, the interesting salad restaurant bang in the middle of all the furore. Yes, like a village, but what a village!

All down its narrow length the boutiques jostle each other, as tightly packed as beach huts at Brighton. You hardly know whether you are shopping in His Clothes. Male, W.1 or Domino Male.

But does it really matter? Seeing that they are all owned by the same man.

Only a few years ago it was a dreary thread of a street straggling along a stone's throw behind Regent Street. Now it is the Mecca of the men, and girls too, who want one-step-ahead clothes and ideas, offering terrific choice of sharp, well-cut gear at fair prices.

To walk along the street is an eye-opener, all ages and types mill along the narrow pavements.

You can bump into people, as I did, such as Mick Jagger buying a sports jacket and Gerald McCann, the dress designer, carrying away a 1930-style swim suit.

The Duke of Bedford, Peter Sellers, Lord Snowdon shop at John Stephen's boutiques, Marlene Dietrich buys her trousers there. Jo Grimond, Cilla Black and Sean Connery are regulars at Vince's, the man who opened the first boutique 11 years ago.

(May 28)

YOU, TOO, CAN BE AN AVENGER IN THIS JUMPSUIT

By SERENA SINCLAIR

Thrown anyone over your shoulder lately? The only thing to wear - in autumn 1965 - for such violent activity is a lace jumpsuit with flared trouser legs. Who says so? Patrick Macnee, star of "The Avengers" who will be thrown, bruised and charmed by the show's new leading lady, Diana Rigg, when the latest series starts on Oct. 20.

What's more, you can buy it, and other clothes worn in the show, in shops all over the country. Chanelle, for example, have ordered a white PVC redingote, while Woollands 31 Shop went for the lace jumpsuit.

Miss Rigg, a lithe redhead of 5ft 8in with, says her co-star, "curves in all the right places," wears a white lace-over-pink jumpsuit in the series for sultry, seductive violence.

She shows her navel, too - in a gleaming turquoise lamé outfit of hipsters, bra and cardigan. "It's impudent, erotic - I like it," says Macnee, immaculate himself in an amber-and-green tweed suit with covered buttons.

She switches into a white PVC raincoat, very skinny, flared, with gilt buckle over the midriff, for the outdoor shots in English countryside.

They used to tell people appearing on TV never to wear black or white. Yet nearly all of the "Avengers" fashions, shown to store buyers in London yesterday, were of black with white - inspired by Courreges and Op Art.

Tailored clothes by Reginald Bernstein will stalk the windows of many shops, including Marshall and Snelgrove of Manchester and Chanelle.

(August 25)

10-DAY HOLIDAY AT £16 FOR AVERAGE BRITON

The traditional British seaside holiday retained it popularity and attracted three-quarters of all holidaymakers last year, a British Travel Association survey disclosed yesterday. This was in spite of the continued increase in travel abroad.

Nearly 20 million people spent an average of 10 days on the beaches of Britain in 1964. Each spent an average of £16.

Thirty-one million went away on holiday and spent a total of £675 million, £20 million more than in the previous year.

The number going abroad increased from 4,500,000 in 1963 to 4,600,000. Their expenditure rose from £225 million to £245 million.

July and August are easily the most popular months, at home and abroad. Of those holidaying in Britain one in five headed for the south-west to keep it at the top of the "most popular holiday region" league.

London with four per cent. of 1964's holidaymakers was at the bottom just behind the Midlands and the East, both with seven per cent.

Abroad, Spain and Italy were the most popular destinations for Britons; France, Switzerland and Germany were next in that order.

At home one in five stayed with friends or relatives and nearly half in hotels or boarding houses. More than half went by car with the rest divided equally between bus or coach and train.

(March 17)

CANING OF BOY WAS PROPER SAYS JUDGE

Daily Telegraph Reporter

A judge said yesterday that a schoolboy of 14 given three strokes of the cane was properly punished.

His father was ordered to pay the costs of a case heard at Slough county court on Dec. 21 when judgment was deferred.

Judge Duveen ruled against Mr. JOSEPH DALY, 38, the boy's father, a factory worker. He claimed damages from Mr. Leslie Marchant, headmaster of Warren Field comprehensive school, Britwell, Slough.

Evidence was given for the defence at the earlier hearing that the boy had been seen fighting in class and was rude to a woman teacher. Mr. Daly, of Woodford Way, Britwell, said after the case that he would appeal.

(January 9)

BATHROOM-KITCHEN UNIT SAVES TWO WEEKS

HENRY BATE
Daily Telegraph Architectural Reporter

A new phase in the use of factory methods for the rapid erection of homes was demonstrated yesterday on an estate of owner-occupier flats at Weybridge, Surrey.

A factory-built unit consisting of the complete bathroom and the plumbing and equipment for the kitchen was lowered into position by crane.

The 1 ton unit is then ready for connection to main services, saving two or three weeks in completion time. Prices are similar to those for traditional work, but mass production is expected to cut costs.

This system can provide an improved standard of finish as satisfactory standards can be obtained more easily in the factory than by on-site work. The units are being installed in a three-storey brickbuilt block of traditional flats priced at £4,925 leasehold.

They are being made in a London factory by McAlpine's for delivery to sites within 100 miles of London. The firm plans to develop the design for two-storey houses built by conventional or industrialised methods.

(May 13)

SHOES FOR ASCOT

Right now hundreds of women are worrying about what shoes to wear to Ascot. You may well think them mad, for what is noticed in all that scrum except the hat that floats above it? But morale is all, and for women who want to feel they look chic about the feet, the news is: spectator shoes, ties and flowers.

Revival of the spectator shoe, that great favourite of the forties, is strong at Edward Rayne, the Queen's shoemaker. His customers are liking it in grey flannel with the black patent toecap and heel (81/2 gn). Deep sandy beige calf gets that Chanel look with its black calf toecap, in Leonards's shoe at 59s 11d.

The holey look comforts Ascot feet — beige or black nylon, 69s 11d, Lotus. Flowery print pink cotton slingback, 59s 11d at Saxone.

(June 4)

TIP-UP CAR AIMS TO SOLVE PARKING

Daily Telegraph Motoring Staff

A single-seater "commuter's" car which can be parked by tipping it up on its tail is being developed in Britain to beat congestion in towns. When parked, it will occupy just over a square yard. It will be 8ft long, 2ft shorter than a Mini, and will be powered by a 250 cc motor-cycle engine mounted behind the rear wheels.

The driver gets out by raising the roof canopy. The car can be easily pivoted on to its tail, resting on aluminium "buffers."

The project is being sponsored by a consortium of businessmen including Mr. Ian Winterbottom, former Labour M.P. for Nottingham Central. The car has been designed by Mr. Dennis Adams, designer of the Marcos sports car, at Bradford on Avon, Wilts.

Like the Marcos, the car will be of lightweight construction with a glass fibre body on a box chassis of marine plywood. The wooden chassis of the Marcos was developed originally from techniques used in the Mosquito aircraft.

Because of its light weight, the car should have excellent acceleration and a top speed of nearly 70 m.p.h.

"We believe the businessman who will buy this type of vehicle wants a comfortable four wheeler with adequate performance rather than a glorified bubble-car," Mr. John Thorpe, 32, one of the sponsors said yesterday.

"What we are aiming at is to produce a motorised train seat. We hope to sell the fully equipped de luxe model at £350, together with a cheaper standard model.

(January 23)

CRASH ROLL BAR

"BUFFERS" FOR VERTICAL PARKING

A DRAWING OF A 250CC single-seater car designed to solve parking problems. It stands on its tail and in this position occupies only about a square yard of space.

Dangerous Customers

By F. J. Salfeld

To discover why English food, though generally better than it was, is still less good than it might be, lunch and dine in a different place each week or two and study your fellow guests. You will find that where the cooking is poor the customer is to blame as much as the cook.

An autumn tour such as I have just made to the Lakes and back to London is enough to confirm two dangerous failings in the bulk of one's countrymen. The first is that they seem subconsciously to regard their bellies as improper organs, best ignored; the second that they are pathologically reluctant to make themselves even faintly conspicuous by sending a dull course back.

In a pre-war essay Harold Nicolson blamed this indifference on the large British breakfast. Races taking good breakfasts, he said, had bad lunches and dinners, and he saw no hope for Anglo-Saxon cooking until we started the day on rusks and coffee and abandoned afternoon tea altogether. This view seems to me unnecessarily pessimistic. A more reasonable solution, surely, is a hearty breakfast, a light lunch, no tea and an elegant dinner eaten not so much for volume as for flavour.

I tried this programme and must admit that it involved a great deal of effort. Outside large towns decent eating places are still hard to find. Thus the common alternatives are a too-large lunch at a hotel—more hotels should imitate Trust Houses and the Lygon Arms at Broadway by offering a smaller menu at a lower price—or a probably frustrating search around cafés with one thing in common: complete lack of imagination. Egg and chips, sausage and chips, pie and chips, fish and chips—that is the pattern. About the coffee it is kindest not to speak.

These passionately monotonous premises must be half-empty then? Not at all. Many of them are bulging in the middle of the day. If their stuff is not what customers want, it is undoubtedly what they endure.

(October 7)

Do You Remember Lillet? The Refreshing Aperitif

LILLET
SERVE VERY COLD

DR. ALBERT SCHWEITZER

GENIUS AND SAINT

As intellectual and artistic activities grow ever more specialised, the universal genius becomes increasingly rare. As material success becomes more sought after and admired than moral excellence, and as churches become ever larger and more efficiently organised, saints seem to be, if not fewer, yet harder to identify.

In Dr. SCHWEITZER the attributes of both were combined, sustained by energy and courage of an equally outstanding order, and dedicated to the practical service of the humblest of his fellow men in one of the most primitive parts of Africa.

Few men have ever rendered such great and varied services to their epoch over so long a life span. His theological, philosophical and musicological works, as also his virtuosity as an organist, would each have won any man the highest international reputation. His philosophy of "reverence for life" enriched and vindicated by practical experience is an invaluable corrective in a civilisation increasingly dominated by impersonal science and technology. It is doubtful whether any doctor can claim personally to have brought healing to so many people who would otherwise have been entirely neglected. His accumulated experience of, and contribution to, tropical medicine must surely have been unrivalled. His insistence on "African conditions" for his African patients, intended as a deliberate psychological contribution to therapy, vindicated itself in its environment and has produced valuable ideas for more sophisticated conditions.

Yet perhaps Dr. SCHWEITZER'S greatest service to his age was his sorely needed inspiration and example. He renounced the world of fame and riches that lay at his feet. Yet his was not the negative renunciation of the self-absorbed ascetic or hermit. Everything about SCHWEITZER'S philosophy and way of life was practical and positive. How many men and women offered their services as a result of his example cannot be assessed; nor how much more material assistance flowed out from such a man and such services, it is mean to complain that he was an autocrat in the hospital and leper colony he built, and to the thousands of Africans to whose service he dedicated his life.

(September 6)

HERBERT MORRISON

ALTHOUGH he twice came within striking distance of becoming leader of the Labour party, it is not for political success, in the party-Parliamentarian sense, that the late Lord MORRISON will chiefly be remembered.

His lifelong devotion to Socialism was not backed by the special talents that might have ensured his emergence as a leader, first perhaps of a caucus, and ultimately of his party. Neither his oratory, which was cosy rather than dominating, nor his presence, which was friendly rather than impressive, marked him out as a potential Prime Minister. Yet - and this is perhaps the greater achievement - he served his country, and particularly the London which he so dearly loved, in an unforgettable manner.

He was the architect of the Labour majority in the London County Council, which has endured for three decades. This unshakable supremacy was exercised in no mean or partisan spirit. MORRISON'S "County Hall" principles induced him to force through the London Traffic Bill of 1931 in the teeth of strong trade union opposition. Twenty years later, the Festival of Britain and the development of the South Bank further illustrated his enterprise and his vision.

These were the achievements of a great administrator. Indeed, it was in administration that MORRISON was often at his happiest and his most able. As Home Secretary in 1940, he was primarily responsible for civil defence, and countless families are grateful for the shelters which bore his name. Those were days of improvisation, but it requires a man of courage and determination to improvise successfully. Courage, too, was necessary to administer humanely the 18B regulation for the internment of the politically dangerous - notably, for instance, to release Sir OSWALD MOSLEY, whose health was affected by confinement. For a man who could accomplish these things, the corridors of the Foreign Office were altogether too slippery, the green benches of the Commons and the red benches of the Lords not invariably comfortable. Yet his memory will endure while London river slips quietly past County Hall and the Palace of Westminster to the sea.

(March 8)

JEANNETTE MACDONALD

MISS JEANNETTE MacDONALD, star of many Hollywood musical films in the thirties, died in the Methodist Hospital, Houston, Texas, to-day, two days after admission for a heart operation. She was 57.

She was married to Gene Raymond, the actor, for over 27 years.

Miss MacDonald's partnership with Nelson Eddy lasted through many productions. Among her most successful films were "The Merry Widow," "The Vagabond King," "Naughty Marietta," "New Moon," "The Firefly," "Love Me To-night," "One Hour With You," and "Rose Marie."

She made her first appearance on the stage in the chorus of a New York revue in January, 1920. She started her screen career in 1929 in "The Love Parade."

In 1931 she made a personal appearance at the Dominion Theatre, London.

(January 15)

Jack Hylton, bandleader, dies at 72

By Charles Graves

Mr. Jack Hylton, who died yesterday aged 72, will be chiefly remembered for raising the status of the British dance orchestra to the same kind of pinnacle previously enjoyed only by leading American bands, such as Paul Whiteman's.

In this capacity he toured Europe and the United States, his band being the first British one ever to be heard on a national hook-up. It says much for his reputation that American bands fought tooth and nail to stop him playing in America.

He did not reach the West End of London until 1923 when he became pianist at the Queen's Hall roof night club.

Here, seeing that improvised jazz was going to be superseded by properly arranged melodies, he made a series of recordings for HMV and with his band toured Europe. The success of radio caused him to present on stage such broadcast favourites as "Palace of Varieties" and "In Town Tonight."

Last year Mr. Hylton formed a new company, which presented the musical, "Camelot," at Drury Lane.

(January 30)

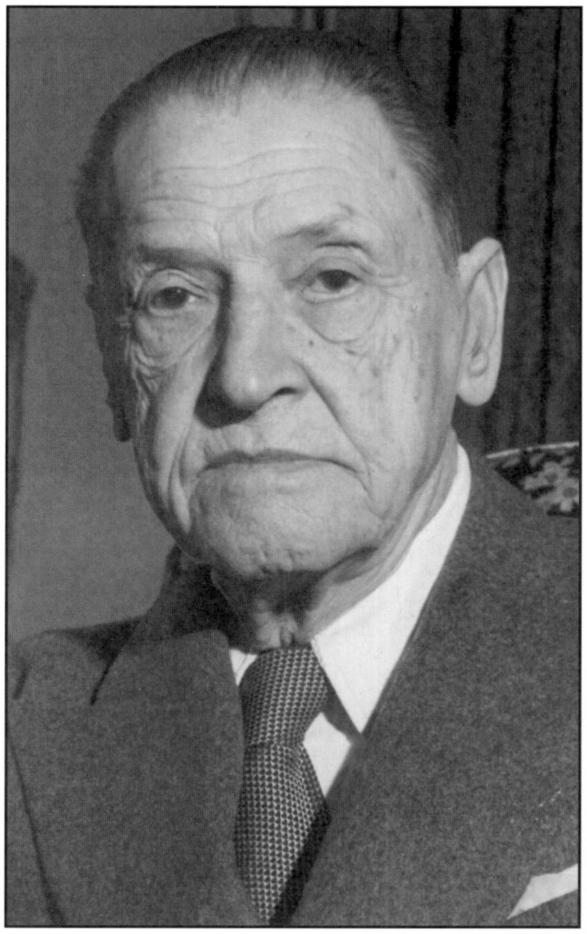

SOMERSET MAUGHAM, who has died in a hospital in Nice. He was 91.

SOMERSET MAUGHAM

SOMERSET MAUGHAM, who has died aged 91, after a long and colourful life and a distinguished career as author and playwright, regarded death as a new adventure.

Wearied by age and saddened by his failing sight and hearing, he said on his 90th birthday: "There are moments when I have so palpitating an eagerness for death that I could fly to it as to the arms of a lover."

Death, he said, gave him the same passionate thrill as years ago life had given him. "I am drunk with the thought of it.

"It seems to me to offer the final and absolute freedom." When he awoke on his 91st birthday in January, his first comment was: "Oh hell, another birthday."

80 MILLION SALES

Highest paid author

Maugham, who earned an average of £100 a year for 10 years at the beginning of his career, became one of the highest paid of British authors. Early last year more than 80 million copies of his books had been sold.

His prodigious output included the best sellers. "The Moon and Sixpence," 1919. "Cakes and Ale," 1930. "The Razor's Edge," 1944, and numerous stories of life in India, Malaya and the South Seas. He maintained that "Of Human Bondage," published in 1915, was the only one which was any good.

Among his best plays were "Caesar's Wife." "The Constant Wife," "The Circle," "Sheppey" and "For Services Rendered."

"The Sacred Flame," written in 1929, was severely criticised by some as "the most immoral play ever produced in London." Others hailed it as the finest of all his productions.

The son of a former solicitor to the British Embassy in Paris, William Somerset Maugham was educated at King's School, Canterbury, and Heidelberg University. In compliance with the wishes of his parents he studied and qualified in medicine at St. Thomas's Hospital.

But like Conan Doyle, A.J. Cronin and others, he forsook medicine for authorship. It was this success in 1897 of his first novel, "Liza of Lambeth," prompted by his experiences as a medical student, that determined his career.

Nonetheless 10 lean years followed his abandonment of medicine for a life of letters. "Often I had not enough to eat," he said. Then came the lucky break.

A play had to be taken off suddenly at the Court Theatre. Maugham persuaded the management to try "Lady Frederick" and it ran for a year.

The playwright who was to see four of his plays running simultaneously in London, was established.

There followed years of success in which he achieved worldwide fame and came to be regarded as the wealthiest author yet. By mid-century, about 25 million copies of his books had been published and sales of "The Razor's Edge" had reached 2,500,000.

SECRET SERVICE

During the 1914-18 War, he served with an ambulance unit and then, using his ability to speak five languages, worked for the British Secret Service. His experiences resulted in some of his most exciting stories such as "Ashenden."

He gave his services free to the Ministry of Information in the 1939-45 war. When France fell in June, 1940, he escaped to England in a coal boat.

Later he went to the United States where he stayed until 1946, living in a New York hotel and in a cottage at Charleston, Carolina, built for him by his publisher.

After the war he returned to his huge villa at Cap Ferrat in the South of France. It had been occupied by the Germans and Italians, bombarded by the RAF and the British fleet and looted.

Maugham, whose elder brother was the first Lord Chancellor, married Syrie, the daughter of Dr. Barnardo in 1916. They were divorced in 1929 and she died in 1955.

He criticised her fiercely and described in detail the turbulent years leading up to their divorce in an autobiography, "Looking Back," which remains unpublished as a book. Extracts from the manuscripts were serialised by the Sunday Express in 1962 and in America.

(December 16)

CRICKET WORLD SHOCKED BY HAMMOND'S DEATH

By E.W. SWANTON

THE death of Walter Hammond at 62, came as a shock to those who, coming back from the MCC South African tour, reported how wonderfully he seemed to have recovered from a grievous car accident a few years ago.

There has been nothing like the calm serenity of Hammond advancing to the crease, and surveying the field after taking guard. If he made a duck he did so like an emperor, but of course, ducks were not his speciality.

Between 1927 and 1947 (six years being lost by war) he made more runs in Test cricket than any other man: 7,249, averaging 58, and including more hundreds (22) than anyone bar Sir Donald Bradman.

With 110 Test catches, most of them in the slips where he scarcely had a superior, he far and away heads the field. He was also a more than usually useful change bowler, of about the pace of Maurice Tate, with, as might be supposed, an action that mirrored all the virtues.

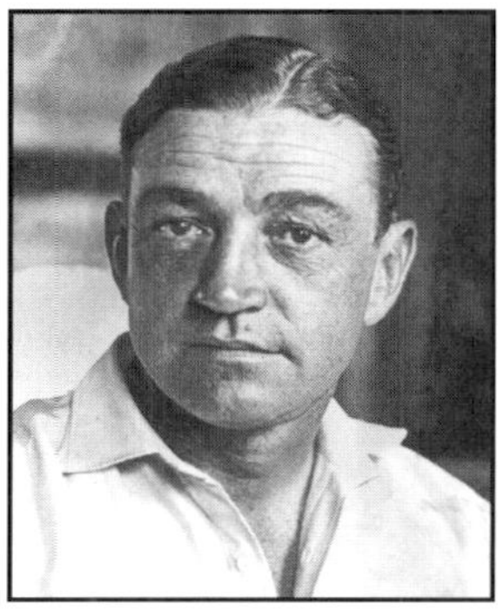

HAMMOND at the height of his career.

The basis of his batting was the massive power of his driving, straight and to the off, but he used every stroke, except the hook to fast bowling. O'Reilly aimed to peg him by attacking his legs, but this only curbed his speed of scoring. He averaged 51 against Australia.

In Test cricket he never played better than in his first Australian tour under A.P.F. Chapman when he scored the record aggregate of 905 with an average of 113. But the innings that will specially be remembered by English followers will be his masterful 240 against Australia at Lords in 1938.

His first-class record was as imposing as his figures in Tests. With 50,493 runs to his name he had a higher aggregate than all save Hobbs, Woolley, Hendren, Mead and Grace, all of whose careers were substantially longer.

His centuries, numbering 167, have been bettered only by Hobbs and Hendren. Only two men, Woolley and Grace, held more than his 819 catches. No one exceeded his 78 in a season, or his 10 in a match, achieved in 1928.

ONE FLAW?

His captaincy

Was there then no flaw, no Achilles heel, in this truly wonderful cricketer? Technically his batting was only less than excellent against the fastest bowling. He could be discomposed by a Constantine or a Larwood, although the innings which greatly helped to bring him to fame was one of much splendour against MacDonald at Old Trafford.

The only limitation concerns his captaincy. On changing status from professional to amateur in 1938 he became captain both of his county and of England, but in Test cricket at any rate, the glamour that surrounded his own cricket found no reflection in his leadership.

(July 3)

ED MURROW

EDWARD R. MURROW, the American radio and television commentator, who has died aged 57, initially established his international reputation as a reporter of the Battle of Britain for the Columbia Broadcasting System.

American listeners heard his trenchant and moving accounts of the bombardment to the background of the battle itself.

"This" he would announce in resonant tones, "is London." and frequently, if a raid was in progress, he continued as anti-aircraft guns went into action and bombs rained on the Metropolis.

On his return to New York, he featured in the documentary series "See it now" and "Person to Person."

At the height of his career Murrow was reputed to earn £100,000 a year. At the invitation of President Kennedy, he became in 1961 director of the United States Information Agency. He resigned this post in January, 1964, after he had had an operation for lung cancer.

Last month he was appointed an honorary Knight Commander of the Order of the British Empire in recognition of outstanding services in furthering Anglo-American friendship and understanding.

(April 28)

Nat 'King' Cole, singer and pianist

NAT "KING" COLE, who died yesterday at Santa Monica, California, aged 45, was one of America's most popular artists. His throaty baritone earned him the nickname of "The Sound."

The Negro vocalist's husky rendering of such songs as "Nature Boy," "Mona Lisa," "Too Young," "Rambling Rose." "Unforgettable" and "Somewhere along the Way" eventually became the foundation of a show business empire, Nat King Cole Incorporated. He also owned a film production company.

Born Nathaniel Adams Coles in Montgomery, Alabama, Nat "King" Cole (he dropped the "s" from the family name) was the son of a Baptist minister, the Rev. Edward Coles, and his wife, Perlina.

While a student in Chicago he organised his own band. In 1936 he went on tour with the "Shuffle Along" Negro revue. After the show broke up in Hollywood in 1937 he worked as piano soloist in small night clubs until he formed the original King Cole trio, with Oscar Moore, guitar, and Wesley Prince, bass.

The "King" title was given to Cole one night when a club manager asked him to wear a gold paper crown.

Starting with "The Christmas Song," recorded in August, 1946, Cole began to add string sections to augment his trio for his vocal records. By 1950 he was a major figure on the popular music scene, his jazz associations were almost forgotten and the "King Cole Trio" name was dropped.

(February 16)

DAVID SELZNICK

David Oliver Selznick, the American film producer and winner in sucessive years of the Motion Picture Academy award for the best production of the year, died in a Hollywood Hospital today after a heart attack. He was 63.

He was one of Hollywood's most prolific producers. His Academy Award films were "Gone With the Wind," his most successful production and "Rebecca."

(June 23)

CLARA BOW

Clara Bow, who has died in Culver City, Los Angeles, aged 60, was the red-haired, roguish-eyed first "It" girl of the silent screen in the 1920s. Helena Rubinstein, in "Just for Luck," wrote of her "heart-shaped mouth." Miss Bow got the name "It Girl" from the novelist, Elinor Glyn.

(September 28)

RICHARD DIMBLEBY

By L. MARSLAND GANDER
Daily Telegraph TV and Radio Correspondent

RICHARD DIMBLEBY, who died aged 52, was in a class apart among the new breed of television screen personalities. He became a national figure, almost an institution.

His driving ambition, energy and journalistic versatility matched his massive frame.

Thoroughness of preparation was one secret of his 30 years' success as a radio and television commentator, anchor man and reporter.

He earned the reputation of one whose fluent command of words never deserted him, one who never "fluffed" and who could extemporise in any emergency. Thus on one occasion when a hasty word escaped from him over the air, it became national news. Though some accused him of pomposity his descriptions of State and Royal occasions were models of felicitous expression.

I can think of no one who more successfully overcame a physical handicap of excessive weight, for his 16-stone plus tended to eclipse the screen, yet did not deter him from undertaking many "stunts" that called for daring and agility.

He was a glutton for work and revelled in his marathon all-night stints at election time. In "Who's Who" he proclaimed himself as "broadcaster, author, newspaper director, editor and film producer."

Newspaper enterprise was in his blood. His father, Fred J. Dimbleby, was Daily Mail political correspondent and, incidentally, adviser to Lloyd George, and the family owned the Richmond Times.

NEWSPAPER POSTS
First radio reporter

Richard himself, at 18, went into the family business, then to the Southern Daily Echo and the Hampshire Advertiser. By 1935 he had become News Editor of the Advertisers' Weekly.

In 1936, at his own suggestion, he was engaged by the BBC to be the first radio reporter who "would go down in submarines and up in aeroplanes."

Later he became the first and best known of the BBC war reporters, covering 14 theatres of war and flying on 20 operational sorties with the RAF, including the first 1,000 bomber raid.

He first televised in 1946 as a commentator at the Victory Parade and it was soon apparent that he had found his metier. His colourful flowing phrases imbued with due homage were apt to each event.

On sound radio Mr. Dimbleby's programmes included the long-running "Down Your Way" and "Twenty Questions." In recent years he had become most familiar in his role of anchor man of the BBC magazine "Panorama."

(December 23)

Farouk dies after collapse in restaurant

EX-KING FAROUK of Egypt died early to-day at a Rome hospital after collapsing in a restaurant. He was 45.

He was dining at the Ile de France restaurant with a woman when he collapsed on the table.

Ex-King Farouk was the first and last king of an independent Egypt since the days of the pharaohs. He had lived in Rome since he was forced to leave Cairo after the Egyptian revolution 12 years ago.

It was then said that he had a fortune of up to £90m., but recently there have been reports that he was near poverty.

He was less to blame personally for the steady deterioration in Anglo-Egyptian relations than some of his Ministers — he could not altogether escape responsibility for a situation which brought Egypt to the verge of war with Britain long before the Suez affair. –BUP.

(March 18)

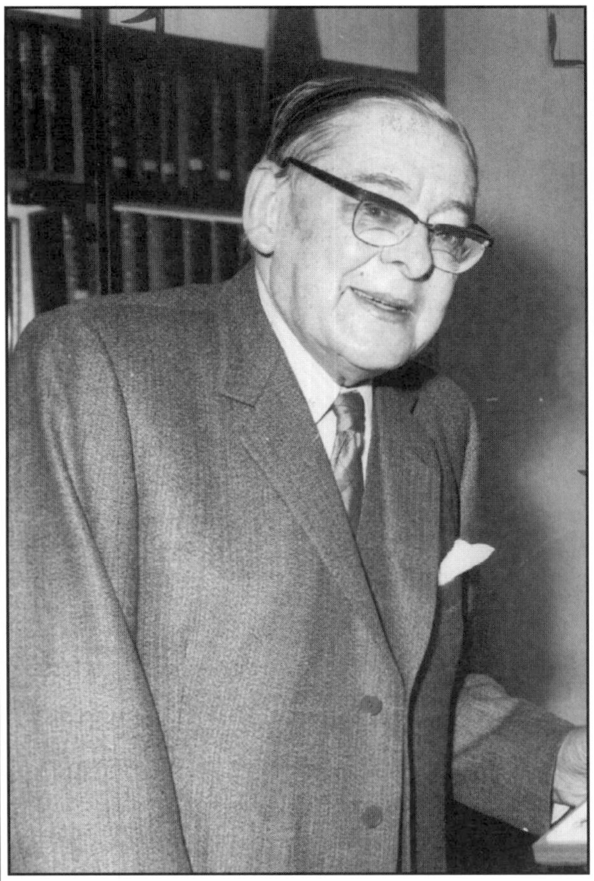

T.S. ELIOT, POET AND PLAYWRIGHT

THOMAS STEARNS ELIOT has died aged 76. He was awarded the O.M., and the Nobel Prize for Literature, in 1948. Last year he was presented with the American Medal of Freedom, America's highest civilian honour.

Of American birth - he came from St. Louis, Missouri, but was of unmistakably European culture, he adopted British nationality in 1927. He was the first American writer since Henry James to do so.

BONAMY DOBREE writes: By the death of T.S. Eliot, his own generation and that immediately succeeding it have lost the poet who seemed the most surely, and with the greatest power, to speak what they felt.

In the chaotic but by no means despairing years that followed World War I, he contrived to connect the grim actualities, the strivings, the farcical nonsense and the ironical betrayal of hopes, with tradition and with something beyond the immediate.

JUVENILE WORK
Little magazines

His juvenile work, though individual enough, began from 1909 to creep into little magazines. In 1917, however, "Prufrock," already a characteristic poem startled a slightly wider audience into attention, an audience further enlarged by the collection "ara Vos Prec," published in 1920.

A good deal of what Eliot was to stand for later was implicit in those works, written in the disturbing manner that became familiar to the reading public with the appearance in 1922 of "The Waste Land," which established Eliot's commanding position as renovator.

It was easy enough for the timid, the conventional, those wedded to older modes, to dismiss Eliot as an outrageous young poet, wishing to scandalise. The juxtaposition of the sordid and the magnificent, the conversational tone unexpectedly dovetailing with powerful utterance of which nobody could deny the poetic quality, was to some profoundly disturbing; but to others it was a glorious vindication of the right of poetry to treat any and every subject.

Moreover, the technique was superb; here, beyond question, was a master of the world.

"The Waste Land," with its violent contrasts, its horror, and its beauty, all comprised within a firm structure, determines a landmark in English poetry.

It achieved what the "Lyrical Ballads" of Wordsworth and Coleridge had triumphantly done 120 years earlier in freeing poetic expression from old shackles, to enable it once more to give voice to the feelings of multitudes of men. It took great poetry out of the hot-house.

To many of Eliot's readers, indeed, he seemed too erudite; but those who read him, and they were increasing in number, came to find that the allusions stirred the imagination, and ceased to perplex the mind or to interfere with the force of the poetry. But still it could not be seen where he was going.

Then in 1930 there appeared his first specifically Christian poem. "Ash Wednesday," the movement and imagery of which made something more compelling even than "The Waste Land." With this poem Eliot's work attained another dimension.

By now he had won unchallenged pre-eminence in the literary world. Not only his volumes of poetry and prose but also the creation of that substantial and always fresh magazine, the Criterion, made him the most influential author or the day.

(January 5)

JUDY HOLLIDAY

JUDY HOLLIDAY, the actress, who won an "Oscar" for her performance in the film "Born Yesterday," died in a New York hospital to-day. She was 41.

Miss Holliday had been ill for several years and in 1961 underwent an operation for cancer. Her last appearance was two years ago, on Broadway, in "Hot Spot."

She became a star by accident in 1946 when Jean Arthur, the lead in the stage version of "Born Yesterday," was taken ill before the show opened in Philadelphia. Judy Holliday played the role of Billie Dawn on Broadway for four years.

Miss Holliday was born in New York, her real name being Judith Tuvim.

She made her screen debut in "Something for the Boys." She also appeared in "Adam's Rib," "The Marrying Kind," "Phffft" and "Solid Gold Cadillac."

She married David Oppenheim, a musician, in 1948 and they had a son. The marriage was dissolved in 1957.

(June 8)

ADLAI STEVENSON, U.S. AMBASSADOR TO U.N.

MR. ADLAI EWING STEVENSON, who has died aged 65, was the unsuccessful Democratic candidate for the United States Presidency against Gen. Eisenhower in 1952 and 1956.

After Mr. Kennedy's election, many Democrats supported Mr. Stevenson for appointment as Secretary of State. But the then President chose him instead to be Ambassador to the United Nations, a post for which he was well trained.

Through his extensive travels he knew the leaders of many countries and was familiar with their problems.

Stevenson was a fervent believer in the international organisation. An often quoted remark was that if the United Nations did not exist it would have had to be invented because it was essential to the preservation of world peace.

In his post at the United Nations he often had to defend the United States against accusations from the Soviet block countries.

He may sometimes have found himself in a slightly awkward position in his dealings with the State Department, being in the anomalous position of ambassador and a member of the Cabinet at the same time. But he enjoyed the full confidence of the Presidents whom he served.

Few politicians in the United States had more devoted followers than did Stevenson. The fact that he twice met defeat as the Democratic candidate for the Presidency failed to depress his admirers who wanted him nominated again.

They argued that he lost in 1952 and 1956 to Gen. Eisenhower because the General was an extraordinarily popular candidate with an extraordinarily popular appeal as a great war figure.

Mr. Stevenson's campaign against Gen. Eisenhower in 1956 looks in retrospect, like a foretaste of President Johnson's Great Society. In domestic affairs, he advocated an increase in farm income and medical aid for the elderly and the poor.

In foreign affairs he spoke out for an end to the testing of hydrogen bombs, and denounced the administration's "erratic" and "vacillating" handling of the Suez Canal crisis which broke out during the election campaign.

Stevenson was born in Los Angeles, California, of a well-to-do family. He once said: "It is true that politics is the art of compromise. I've had a good start.

"My mother was a Republican and a Unitarian. My father was a Democrat and a Presbyterian. I ended up in his party and her Church."

His grandfather, after whom he was named, was Vice-President of the United States under President Grover, Cleveland from 1893 to 1897. His father was a newspaper executive.

After leaving Princeton University, Mr. Stevenson entered journalism before becoming a lawyer. He took a keen interest in foreign affairs, and in 1939 became energetic in the advocacy of American aid in the fight against the Nazis.

Shortly afterwards he became assistant secretary to Mr. Knox, Secretary of the Navy. In that capacity he took part in a tour of American bases in the Pacific after the attack on Pearl Harbour and later visited many other countries.

In 1946 he was senior adviser to the United States delegation at the first assembly of the United Nations in London.

When he returned to Chicago in 1947 he was picked as Democratic candidate for the Governorship of Illinois and was elected by a record margin of 572,000 votes.

By what he called "plain talk, hard work and prairie horse sense," he carried out far-reaching reforms. Every month he broadcast by radio a report on the progress that was being made.

(July 15)

MME HELENA RUBINSTEIN

Mme HELENA RUBINSTEIN, who has died in New York aged 94, was the founder and president of Helena Rubinstein Inc., which sold beauty to women all over the world.

She was born in Cracow, Poland, and became a medical student, but the smell of antiseptics made her dizzy. When, at 18, her proposed marriage to a medical student was vetoed she went to Australia to visit an uncle.

She took with her some jars of face cream, made from an old family recipe. She always maintained that the principal ingredient was water-lily leaf juice. Australian women, their faces dried and roughened by the climate, borrowed some of her cream.

Realising that she was spending most of her time advising women, she opened her own salon in Melbourne. In 1906 she started in London.

VIRGINIA WAITE writes: During the First World War when Helena Rubinstein went to America women secretly used rouge on their lips so that their husbands would not accuse them of being "hussies". This and chalk-white rice powder was too drab for "Madame."

Later her constant cry was for skin care. Recently a skin moisturiser appeared on the market which was developed in France eight years ago. Helena Rubinstein did not use much make-up, but she used this moisturiser.

(April 12)

Le CORBUSIER, ARCHITECT

LE CORBUSIER, who has died aged 77, was probably the most controversial architect of his age. His real name was Charles-Edouard Jeanneret.

Born in Switzerland and a naturalised Frenchman, he had at least as many critics as admirers and many copyists. His work, which won him international recognition, earned for him the description of "high priest" of modern architecture.

His "concept for living" the Unite d'Habitation in Marseilles, built between 1945 and 1950, was a block of flats to meet his own ideal of a functional, self-sufficient community. It provided the living-space, light and sunshine in which he believed.

The building, erected on giant concrete legs, was regarded either as a masterpiece or as a rabbit warren.

"Mad egg boxes" was one description of his tall, isolated, concrete buildings, surrounded by greenery and set down uncompromisingly and uninhibitedly.

Young architects came from all over the world to study his methods. But, apart from his work in France, his best known achievement is Chandigarh, the new capital of Punjab, which he was commissioned to plan for 35,000 people.

DESIGN AT 17
Few tapestries

Le Corbusier designed his first building at the age of 17. He studied architecture at his local school of arts and crafts and later worked as a draughtsman in Vienna before moving to Paris in 1908.

Among the most famous, apart from his "radiant cities," the first built in Marseilles, was the chapel at Ronchamp and his new concept on a monastery at La Tourette.

His ideas were not easily accepted and he was often accused of arrogance. In his book on his own work, his waspish comments reflected the slights from which he had suffered in the past.

But he died knowing that over the world thousands of imitators were inspired by his ideas and ultra-modern designs for living.

(August 28)

VICE-ADML MUSELIER

Vice-Adml. Emile Muselier, who has died aged 83, rallied the Free French Naval forces to Gen. de Gaulle in London in July, 1940, after the fall of France. He chose the Cross of Lorraine as their emblem.

He began his naval service in 1899 and after a distinguished career commanded the French 2nd Cruiser Division in 1937. Shortly before the outbreak of war he was put in charge of the Fleet at Marseilles.

(September 3)

WAY OF THE WORLD

Blazing Crosses

THE repulsive morons who put fiery crosses at coloured people's doors in England have no importance in themselves. Their importance lies only in their propaganda value to the ideologues and agitators on the Left, who, however repulsive, are unfortunately not morons by any means.

What better opportunity could they have of exploiting the feelings of those who feel a decent sympathy for persecuted people? What better opportunity of lumping all their opponents together as uneducated and malevolent idiots?

What better opportunity of shaming-those who cannot see why our society should be turned upside down in violence and confusion for the sake of an experiment in the Brotherhood of Man, to further the general aims of Revolution?

For the progressive advocates of this experiment every blazing cross at a poor Indian's door should, whether they admit it or not, be a cause of deep joy and satisfaction.

(June 15)

Nature Notes
By "REDSHANK"

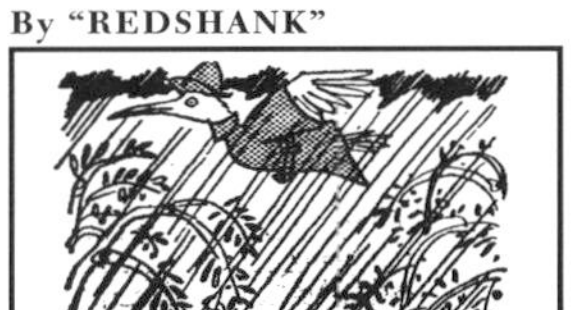

LOOKING out of my study window yesterday at the rain falling steadily from overcast skies, I began reflecting on how the bad weather affects the creatures of field and woodland as they go about their lawful occasions.

Most of them, instead of grumbling and moping, seem to ignore it quite cheerfully, setting an example to us all. The dotterel, in other ways also an anomaly in the feathered world, is one of the few who react in a quasi-human way.

Old Josh Elbow, an amateur naturalist and a veritable raging inferno of nature lore, has made half a dozen miniature machintoshes out of old Army gas-capes and has already persuaded two or three bittern to wear them. But his attempt to supply miniature umbrellas to the local badger population has had no success with cautious and conservative Old Brock.

(August 3)

Get Cracking - Now!
roars JACK MORON

"I'M hopping mad." Yesterday Prof. Reg Burst, top endothermologist and man of the people, kicked moodily at a zinc-lined computer in his Stretchford University laboratory and told me he was hopping mad.

"It's up to the Government whether I decide to work in Britain or America." Prof. Burst, latest victim of the brain drain explosion, told me it was up to the Government whether he decided to work in Britain or America.

No wonder Prof. Burst is hopping mad. No wonder he is thinking of shaking the dust of Britain from his feet and going to live in a country where science is taken seriously.

(March 20)

Peter Simple

SUBSTITUTES THREATEN 11-A-SIDE GAME

FA CHIEF EXPECTS LESS USE OF NEW RULE

By DONALD SAUNDERS

WITH 14 out of 90 clubs replacing injured players during the opening matches, the Football League's substitute rule has lost any chance it had of being quietly integrated into the English soccer scene.

Fifteen-and-a-half per cent. is a somewhat higher figure than the authorities expected on the first day of the season, and one which will be pounced on with glee by opponents of the new move.

I suggest, however, that it is far too early to reach firm conclusions about an experiment that is intended to be tested over nine months.

Joe Mears, chairman of the FA, believes that for some time yet managers will tend to employ the new rule the moment a player is injured, but with experience may decide that it is often wiser to delay substitution.

I am inclined to agree with him. After all, this is the first new toy League club managers have been given for years, and it is scarcely surprising that some of them are itching to play with it.

EXPERIENCE TELLS

Highbury boos

Significantly, in the First Division, where the most experienced managerial talent is to be found, only one substitute was used. I understand that Stoke's manager, Tony Waddington, sent on 12th man Bebbington eight minutes from the end of the Highbury game against Arsenal, only when it became clear that the captain Viollet, was handicapped by a damaged ankle.

Like several of the other 13 switches, this one was booed. That does not surprise me. Most home supporters will be as vehemently opposed to substitutions by the visitors as they have for years been to the award of penalties against their own teams.

Nevertheless, a certain uneasiness will be felt during the next few weeks by all who have the interests of League soccer at heart. If managers continue to use substitutes with the alacrity and at the high percentage of the opening day, some of us are seriously going to wonder whether the League have inadvertently put an end to 11 a-side soccer.

(August 23)

RIOT AFTER CHELSEA GAME

By BRYON BUTLER

ROME, Wednesday

AN angry crowd smashed the windows of a military-escorted coach in which Chelsea football team and officials were travelling after an explosive Inter-Cities Fairs Cup match in Rome tonight.

Two Chelsea players, J. Boyle and E. McCreadie, were struck in the face by missiles thrown from the terraces during the game, against A.S. Roma, and Mr. Joe Mears and Tommy Docherty, Chelsea manager, were narrowly missed.

Hundreds of policemen struggled to hold back a crowd of thousands outside the Flaminio Stadium as the Chelsea coach left the ground. There were four vehicles carrying military riot squads in front and four behind.

"Simply terrifying"

The coach had gone only 20 yards before the bombardment started. Three windows were smashed before the coach, horn blowing and quickly accelerating to 60 m.p.h. was out of range. Police made several arrests.

Mr. Docherty said: "Rough play on the field is one thing. Missiles being thrown from the terraces is yet another. But what happened afterwards was simply terrifying.

Chelsea, who won the first leg at Samford Bridge 4-1, drew 0-0 and now go into the second round, the draw for which is being made tomorrow in Basle.

(October 7)

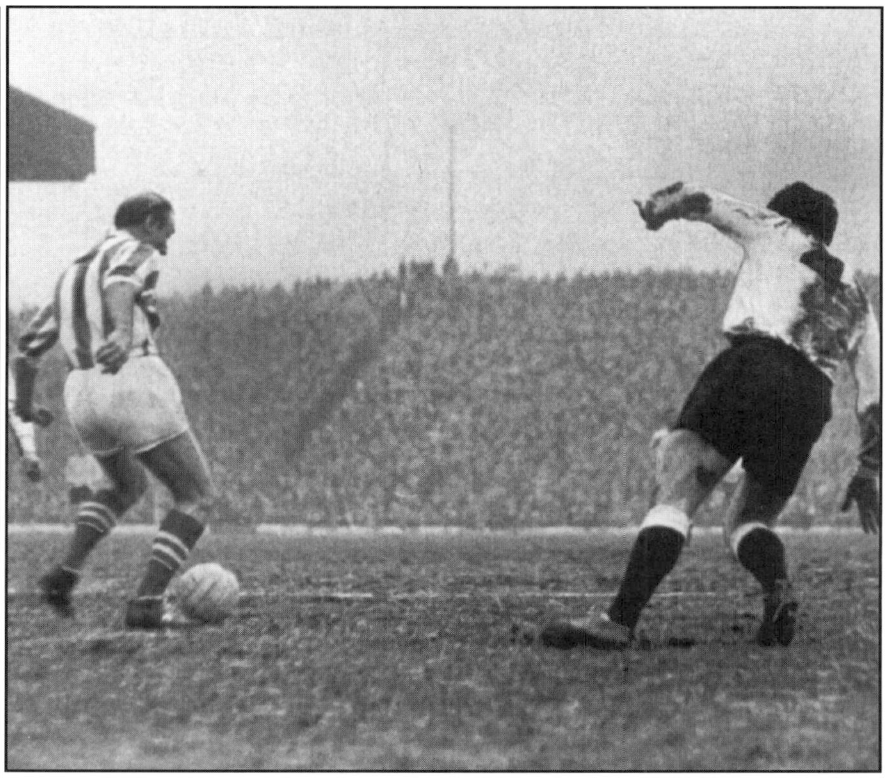

MATTHEWS NIPS THROUGH A GAP between Brown (No. 4) and Langley, who has Leggat backing him up.

MATTHEWS: FIRST GENTLEMAN OF SOCCER

By DONALD SAUNDERS

STANLEY MATTHEWS, professional soccer's first knight, has been the first gentleman of Association Football for most of the 32 years during which he has graced the pitches of the world.

Since his unique career began in a Second Division match at Bury in February 1932, the "old maestro" the "wizard of dribble" - call him what you will - has made many lasting contributions to the game he loves.

None of his services to soccer, perhaps, has been of greater importance than his earning of a knighthood at this moment. He has been honoured at a time when soccer in England is passing through the blackest period of its 101 years.

Misconduct on the pitch, misbehaviour on the terraces, public wrangling between the FA and club managers . . . all have dragged the good name of football through the mud that now disfigures the green turf on which the season began so optimistically last August.

A Precedent

This morning's announcement that a professional footballer is for the first time to be dubbed a knight will not remove all the clinging mud.

But it may serve as a reminder of the high standards of sportsmanship English soccer once attained and as an inspiration to those who wish to regain that enviable reputation.

(January 1)

276 mph give Campbell speed double

Daily Telegraph Correspondent

PERTH, Western Australia, Thursday.

LESS than nine hours before his deadline, the end of 1964, Donald Campbell broke his own water speed record to-day and became the first man to set up land and water speed records in the same year.

He raised the water record to 276.33 mph in a "last chance" attempt.

Fulfilment of his 10-year ambition to bring off the "double" in the same year came on the 16th anniversary of the death of his father, Sir Malcolm Campbell, who once held both records.

Donald Campbell's 276.33 mph was set up in two runs on Lake Dumbleyung, Western Australia in his jet boat Bluebird. His previous record was 260.35 mph on Coniston in 1959.

Last July he attained 403.1 mph on Lake Eyre Salt Flat, Central Australia, in his gas turbine car Bluebird, and this was recognised as the land record.

Hope nearly gone

This afternoon he touched 286.3 mph on his first run. Then the engine had a "flame-out."

On the second run he thought he was failing and he called over the radio: "What's my bloody speed?" It was 269 mph over the measured kilometre and he gave a whoop of joy as he heard the timekeepers shout: "He's got it."

(January 1)

CLAY BEAT LISTON IN 60 SECONDS

LEWISTON, Maine, Tuesday.

CASSIUS CLAY retained the heavyweight championship of the world at St. Dominic's Arena here to-night when he knocked out Sonny Liston in the first round with just about the first hard punch thrown throughout the brief encounter.

Liston, once known as the Iron Man, lasted exactly one minute of a sensational contest. He was floored by a short, right to the jaw, went down in a heap, and was unable to beat the count. At eight he tried to get up, but stumbled back, while the referee, Jersey Joe Walcott, temprarily lost control of the situation.

Walcott at first stood staring helplessly towards the time-keeper. Then he hurried across the ring to find out whether the full count had been tolled. Meanwhile Clay went hammering away with both hands at a man he had already beaten.

Walcott rushed back across the ring to restrain him and then, realising that he had won so easily, Clay jumped for joy and raised his arms in triumph.

It was the fastest recorded knockout in the history of the world heavyweight championship.

(May 26)

WORLD CHAMPION SIMPSON

TOMMY SIMPSON, the Durham-born cyclist who in September became the first Briton to win the 162-mile world professional road race championship, has been elected Sportsman of the Year in the annual Sports Writers' Association poll.

Simpson has hardly been out of the news since he packed his bags and left his Yorkshire home near Doncaster for the Continent just over six years ago. In this time he has consistently made British cycling history, culminating in his world title triumph in San Sebastian.

This achieved, he has gained the confidence that makes the complete rider and having been named "animator-in-chief" of the Paris-Tours race, he went on to win the season's last classic, the Tour of Lombardy.

(October 15)

SEALEY'S GOALS CLINCH WEST HAM TRIUMPH

By BRYON BUTLER

West Ham ... 2 TSV Munich 1860 ... 0

RON GREENWOOD'S team brought the European Cup-winners' Cup back to England and back to London at Wembley last night. Two goals in 90 seconds by Alan Sealey, mid-way through the second half, were too much for the brave, virile but finally outplayed Munich.

This was a magnificent climax to three years of passionate work and clear thinking by West Ham. But, more than that, it was a triumph for football itself.

West Ham's rise out of the wastes of mediocrity to the same dizzy heights achieved by the 1963 Spurs owes nothing to damp, safety first tactics or to "traditional" English theories.

West Ham have travelled far to see and learn. They have believed in themselves and their ideals. And, last night, they got their just reward.

But the crowd, too, made its contribution to this memorable night. More people (100,000) paid more money (£76,000) than ever before to watch a floodlight match in England.

Yet there was another difference. This was a crowd of genuine football supporters, who cared passionately about the teams and about the game . . . a happy contrast from much of the crowd that attends the FA Cup Final each May.

"I'm forever blowing bubbles" they sang when West Ham took the lead. Then came "Sea-ley, Sea-ley" - a moving tribute to West Ham's right-winger, a player who has rarely been sure of his first-team place.

Munich? It takes two teams to make such a match as this. They were hard, industrious, mobile, fast, and, during moments in the first half, looked more than capable of becoming the first German club to win a major European trophy.

(May 20)

Never a night or a knight like this

By Byron Butler

The match between an International XI and Sir Stanley Matthews's XI was a fitting farewell to Soccer's own knight at Stoke yesterday evening.

We saw the incomparable left foot of Puskas score two superb goals and di Stefano darting explosively through the middle

The international XI won 6-4 with goals by Puskas (2), Van den Boer, Masopust, Kubula and Henderson. But if they won they did not dominate, and Sir Stanley's side replied with goals by Douglas (2), Greaves and Ritchie.

And then it was all over. Players of a dozen nations linked arms in the centre of the field, the sound of Auld Lang Syne filled the air and then Sir Stanley was chaired off the ground as a crowd of 34,450 sang "For he's a jolly good fellow." There will never be another like him.

(April 29)

TROPHY REMAINS WITH UNITED STATES

By LEONARD CRAWLEY

UNITED STATES professionals gained their 13th victory in the Ryder Cup match at Royal Birkdale on Saturday by 18 matches to 11 with three halved. It had been a gruelling time for both sides.

Three days of foursomes, four-ball matches and singles, each with two matches a day over 18 holes, is a test of stamina both physical and mental which only the toughest can endure.

Most of the 32 matches were very close, and the balance in favour of the Americans showed itself in an advantage of one to two shots per round. This grows proportionately over the more exacting test of strokeplay round by round over 72 holes.

Once again an American side, admirably handled and presented by a great golfer - this time Byron Nelson - showed their extraordinary capacity to finish strongly under pressure. Their spirit is invincible and we salute them with profound sincerity.

No one could fail to recognise the performance of Peter Alliss, who won five out of six matches during the three days. He was the outstanding British player.

His father, Percy, of incomparable skill 30 years ago, must be feeling contented in his home at Ferndown today.

The Americans again showed how easy it is to come from - in a matter of hours - the big ball which must be struck accurately, to the little one which can be mishit straight far too often.

In the three days of this thrilling spectacle when one was hoping against hope that we could hang on against the formidable enemy, a brassie shot by Alliss stands out.

And so does the awful four-footer which Alliss holed to beat Billy Casper at the 18th on Saturday morning. He stood up to the putt twice and returned to base as it were; yet at the third address he struck it in.

SUPERB SECOND

Long and tortuous

The largest crowds inevitably assemble round the last green, where the excitements of the day boiled over, and it was before one of these vast audiences on Friday afternoon that Alliss, with that superb long second shot, had wrested from the long and tortuous 18th the only three it was obliged to surrender until the superlative stroke by Arnold Palmer 24 hours later which secured the Ryder Cup.

It was against the irrepressible Palmer himself that Alliss's shot was played, and it brought victory to the Englishman and Christy O'Connor over Palmer and Dave Marr by two holes in the second series of four-ball matches. No doubt the great man stored it away as something that would require to be attended to later.

(October 11)

12-YR-OLD KAREN MUIR SETS WORLD RECORD

By PAT BESFORD

BLACKPOOL, Tuesday.

KAREN YVETTE MUIR, 12 years, 10 months and 27 days old, today broke the world 110yds backstroke record with a time of 68.7sec. No one so young has broken a world record in any sport governed by the rule of absolute measurement.

This achievement, set in a heat of the National Girls' Championships, slashes eight-tenths of a second off the mark made by Linda Ludgrove, of Britain, only 17 days ago.

Unbelieving, almost, was this slender South African, tears trickling down her cheeks, as continuous cheers from the watch-clutching crowd, the like of which I have never heard here, reverberated through the Derby Bath even before her rivals had finished, before the result and her official time were announced.

ENGLISH COACH

This fair-haired swimming wonder from Griqueland, is coached by a young Englishman, Frank Gray, from Watford, who left for South Africa about five years ago.

(August 11)

CLARK REGAINS WORLD DRIVERS' TITLE

W.A. McKENZIE

Daily Telegraph Motoring Correspondent

NURBURGRING, Sunday.

JIM CLARK, won the Grad Prix of Germany at Nurburgring today in the fastest contest ever held on this 14-mile Eifel mountains' circuit.

It was his sixth grand prix victory this season, all those he has competed in, which is a record. He is also now assured of the Drivers' World Championship, which cannot be taken from him in the remaining races of the series.

He took the world title from Graham Hill at the end of the 1963 season, then, a year later, lost it to John Surtees.

His win today also consolidates the lead of the Lotus concern, whose cars he drives, for the manufacturers' world championship.

The speed of the race, coupled with the punishing nature of the course, brought early troubles to the cars. Of the 19 starters, only eight cars finished.

Clark won at an average speed of 99.79 m.p.h., nearly 1 1/2 m.p.h. above the previous lap speed record. He beat Graham Hill, BRM by 15.9 seconds, and the American Dan Gurney, in a Brabham, by 21.4 secs.

World championship placings: Clark, 54 points; Hill, 32; Stewart, 25; Surtees, 17; Gurney, 9; McLaren, 8.

(August 2)

Third Test-Second Day

EDRICH HITS NINTH 300 IN TEST HISTORY

New Zealand made 100 for five in reply to England's total of 546 for four declared.

By E.W. SWANTON

HEADINGLEY, Friday.

THE TEST today went the way that was foreshadowed by the events of yesterday. Edrich, by taking his score from 194 to 310 before England's declaration, made his imprint on history, after which New Zealand's batting suffered the sort of reaction that a surfeit of runs not infrequently induces among those who have fielded out to them.

Reid gave his side heart so long as he was there, and batted quite admirably, but no one else played with distinction against a competent English attack.

Perhaps the most interesting aspect of this was the bowling of Larter, who maintained a useful pace and control over two spells of little short of an hour each. The only criticism of him was that his length was rather too full.

Anyone so tall ought to consider the shortish ball a regular (though not an over-used) item of his equipment. Larter errs on the side of almost never testing a batsman's hooking powers, or making him worry about his ribs.

The England innings was allowed to proceed for all but a further three hours and a half before, on Edrich reaching his 300, Smith brought it to a merciful close. Of the two periods, that before lunch was notable for some more very adequate bowling by New Zealand with the new ball that was taken first thing, the second for a final hammering by Edrich.

He had been restrained this morning, while few runs had been coming at the other end. This afternoon he ended with a barrage of crisp strokes that brought him 71 more runs in 85 minutes. The purple moment came in an over from the luckless young Yuile wherein Edrich hit successive balls for 4, 6, 6, 4.

The sixes were fine swinging hits that pitched a long way over the boundary to the off-side of the screen. When Smith called off the chase it was time to take stock of what Edrich had achieved.

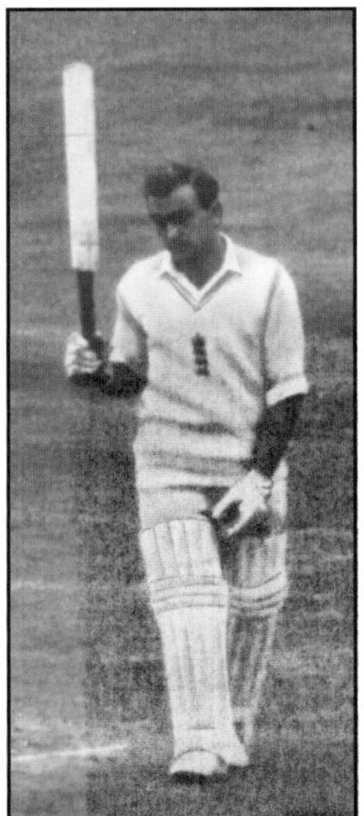

His 310 was the ninth treble century in Test matches, and the fourth by an Englishman: Hutton, Hammond, and Sandham have preceeded him. It was the third such score at Headingley, the others having been made, need it be said, in more momentous circumstances by Bradman.

A not uninteresting little subsidiary "record" is that no one apparently has ever before hit so many boundaries in a Test match: Edrich's tally was five sixes and 52 fours.

So far as his wonderful run of scores goes his total in nine innings is now 1,311, his average 218. When on earth will the luck turn?

The scoreboard

ENGLAND - First Innings

R.W. Barber, c. Ward, b. Taylor....13
J.H. Edrich, not out....310
K.F. Barrington, c. Ward, b. Motz 163
M.C. Cowdrey, b. Taylor....13
P.H. Parfitt, b. Collings....32
°M.J.K. Smith, not out....2
Extras (b 4, lb 8, nb 1)....13
Total (4 wkts dec)....546
Fall of wickets: 1-13, 2-382, 3-407, 4-516.

BOWLING

	O	M.	R.	W.
Motz	41	8	140	1
Taylor	40	8	140	2
Collings	32	7	87	1
Yuile	17	5	80	0
Morgan	6	0	28	0
Pollard	11	2	46	0
Congdon	4	0	12	0

Did not bat: °J.M. Parks, R. Illingworth, F.J. Titmus, F.E. Rumsey, J.D.F. Larter.

NEW ZEALAND - First Innings

G.T. Dowling, c. Parks, b. Larter....5
B.E. Congdon, c. Parks, b. Rumsey.13
B.W. Sinclair, c. Smith, b. Larter..13
°J.R. Reid, lbw, b Illingworth....1
V. Pollard, not out....12
B.W. Yuile, not out....0
Extras (b 1, w 1)....2
Total (5 wkts)....100
Fall of wickets: 1-15, 2-19, 3-53, 4-61, 5-100.

BOWLING

	O.	M.	R.	W.
Rumsey	13	3	40	1
Larter	14	4	24	2
Illingworth	11	4	26	2
Titmus	2	1	8	0

To bat: B.R. Taylor, R.C. Motz, °J.T. Ward, R.O. Collings.
Umpires: J.F. Crapp & C.S. Elliott.

(July 10)

TRUEMAN SUSPENDED BY YORKSHIRE

Daily Telegraph Reporter

FOR the second time this season and the third time in recent years, Freddie Trueman, 34, is in trouble with the Yorkshire Cricket Club.

He has been suspended for one match by the committee following incidents in the recent Roses match with Lancashire at Sheffield.

Interview sought

Trueman said last night: "I have asked for a personal interview with the Yorkshire president, Sir William Worsley. I shall talk over the whole question of my future with my wife when I get home tonight.

"As I see it the committee's statement accuses me of not trying. The incident in the Lancashire match occurred when I was given half the leg side field to look after when I had just finished a long bowling stint.

"I asked the captain for another man and the committee must have thought I was gesturing dissent."

Earlier in the season Trueman was reprimanded for breach of contract concerning the publication of articles in his name. Three years ago he was reprimanded by the committee after being sent home from Taunton for arriving late for the start of the match with Somerset.

(August 13)

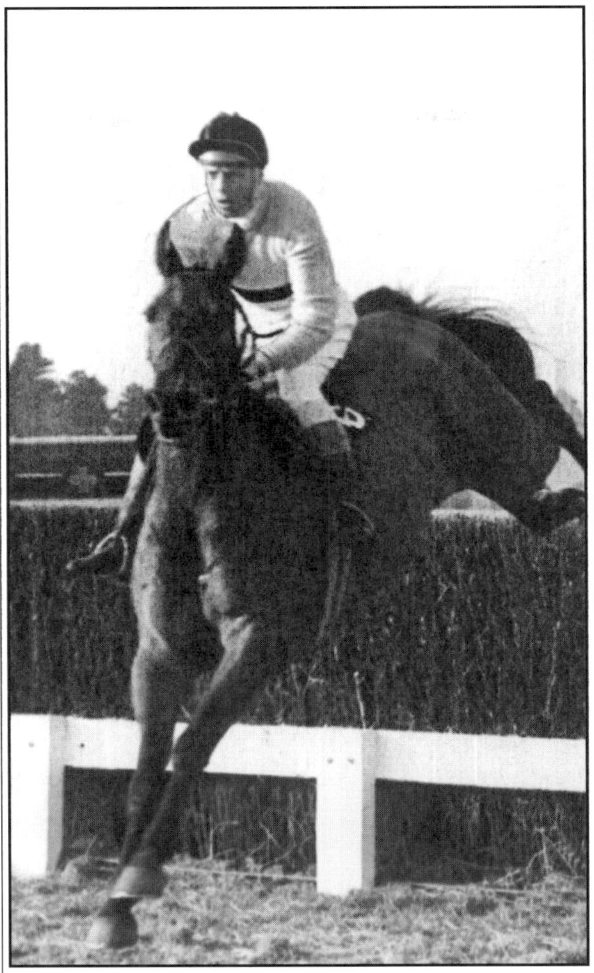

ARKLE RUNS AWAY FROM GALLANT MILL HOUSE

By HOTSPUR (Peter Scott)

CHELTENHAM, Thursday.

ANNE, DUCHESS OF WESTMINSTER'S Arkle broke one record, equalled another and set a time that seemingly only he can better when winning his second Cheltenham Gold Cup with complete authority here this afternoon.

Arkle's 20-length margin over Mill House has been equalled in this race only by Easter Hero, both in 1929 and 1930, but Easter Hero had no rival of Mill House's calibre to beat.

Arkle's earnings from 19 steeplechase and hurdle victories now stand at £36,818. Team Spirit's old record of £29,495 for English and Irish National Hunt racing is thus eclipsed.

Arkle returned 6 min 41⅕sec. against 6min 45⅘sec a year ago when he had 75 yards farther to run. Jockey Pat Taaffe believes he is a much better horse now and few will quarrel with that.

Poor Mill House, so much superior to any other long-distance chaser yet fated to compete with a superb racing machine, invincible on anything like fair and level terms.

Mill House certainly never looked better or brighter in himself than today. Arkle was away from his fences like a flash but Mill House matched him until the English horse's first mistake at the 16th jump.

ANOTHER ERROR
Jockey "knew his fate"

Another followed three fences later and Willie Robinson said afterwards that he knew his fate then for Arkle was still going as easily as could be.

Between the final two fences Taaffe decided that the "match" had lasted long enough and Arkle accelerated into a lead of some eight lengths as they came into the last. Here, said Taaffe he made his biggest leap of the whole race and the gap back to Mill House more than doubled at the run in as Arkle galloped mercilessly on.

Thirty lengths behind Mill House came the Australian farmer Mr. Bill Roycroft on his Tokyo Olympic Games star Stoney Crossing. It was Stoney Crossing's first steeplechase anywhere and he fully earned cheers that eclipsed those for many of the meeting's winners.

(March 2)

SEA BIRD II TOYS WITH DERBY RIVALS

THE Derby prize went to an overseas stable for the 10th time in 20 years and France scored her seventh victory in that period when M. Jean Ternynck's Sea Bird II coasted home from Irish-trained Meadow Court here this afternoon.

Backed down to 7-4 from his overnight price of 5-2, Sea Bird II started the hottest favourite since Crepello in 1957. He was among the last away but soon took a place in the first 10.

Pat Glennon produced him to challenge up the centre of the course, Sea Bird II freewheeled past I Say 350 yards from home and held off Lester Piggott on Meadow Court by two lengths.

I Say finished third, a further length and a half away.

The French colt was hanging left towards the far rails in the last 100 yards but certainly not through distress. He would have found several more lengths had it been necessary and must rank as one of the better recent Derby winners.

Sea Bird II's only defeat in six races came when he failed to catch his stable-companion Grey Dawn in the Grand Criterium last October. Sea Bird is entered for the Grand Prix de Saint-Cloud and King George VI and Queen Elizabeth Stakes at Ascot next month, but future plans will not be settled for a few days.

(June 3)

EMERSON OVERWHELMS OFF-FORM STOLLE

ONE-SIDED SINGLES FINAL LASTS ONLY 67 MIN

By LANCE TINGAY

WIMBLEDON, Friday.

AT the age of 28 the wiry Queenslander, R. Emerson, every inch a skilled athlete, is men singles champion of Wimbledon for the second year. It was all one-sided brevity on the Centre Court today and Emerson overwhelmed his doubles partner, F.S. Stolle, by 6-2, 6-4, 6-4 in 67 minutes.

Emerson thus joins two other Australians, R. Laver, the champion of 1961 and 1962, and L.A. Hoad, the champion of 1956 and 1957, in taking the title two years running. The record of Stolle is more distinctive, but he certainly would not want to have it.

Poor Stolle! He and the German, G. von Cramm, now have in common the undesired record of having played, and lost, in the final three years running.

Von Cramm's years in this situation of sublime failure, were 1935-1937, when he lost twice to F. J. Perry and once to J.D. Budge. From 1884-1886 H.F. Lawford failed in the challenge round against W. Renshaw.

But what of the triumphant Emerson? The second Wimbledon title he so ably picked up today makes his tally of important championships up to nine singles, and, if doubles be included, to 24.

One cannot, then, dispute his status as a good player, though whether he would be able to hold his own with the leading professionals like Laver and K.R. Rosewall is, in my opinion, doubtful. But I am sure Emerson is a better player than a year ago.

His service is more sure, especially his second delivery. His forehand is a sounder stroke. He always was mercurial on the court, and he has certainly lost nothing of his dashing speed of foot.

The Finals

MEN'S SINGLES
R. EMERSON (Austalia) bt. F.S. STOLLE (Australia), 6-2, 6-4, 6-4.
WOMEN'S SINGLES
MISS M. SMITH (Australia) bt. MISS M. E. BUENO (Brazil), 6-4, 7-5.
MEN'S DOUBLES
J.D. NEWCOMBE & A. D. ROCHE (Australia) bt. K.N. FLETCHER & R.A.J. HEWITT (Australia), 7-5, 6-3, 6-4.
WOMEN'S DOUBLES
MISS M. E. BUENO (Brazil) & MISS B.J. MOFFITT (U.S.) bt. Miss F. DURR & Miss J. LIEFFRIG (France), 6-2, 7-5.
MIXED DOUBLES
K.N. FLETCHER & MISS M. SMITH (Australia) bt. A.D. ROCHE & Miss J.A.M. TEGART (Australia), 12-10, 6-3.

Stolle today was a shadowy representation of what he could have been. His return of service was inadequate, to say the least, his volleying skill a travesty of what he can really do in the forecourt.

(July 3)

OXFORD WASTE THEIR PACK'S HARD WORK

By Tony Goodridge

Oxford ....5pts Cambridge.........5

After all the months of intensive training, scheming and plotting, the University Match at Twickenham yesterday ended with Oxford and Cambridge each scoring a goal, Cambridge close on half-time and Oxford in the second half.

A drawn game suggests excitement, and this one lacked none of that, but it also gives a hint of frustration and thoughts of what might have happened if only this or that had been done.

It also has a certain rarity value. Of the 84 games played in the history of the event this was only the 13th to be drawn, and the first since 1953 when Oxford scored a penalty goal and a try to Cambridge's two penalty goals.

Craig and Gibson had been contempories at Campbell College and yesterday's result may in part be attributed to the certain familiarity that the rival captain's inevitably had of each other's thinking.

FORWARD POLICY
Dark Blue Tactics

In any event Oxford had to make certain through their forwards that Gibson would be denied enough of the ball with which to confound them with his own particular talents.

In this Oxford may be said to have succeeded for, while they by no means accquired a monpoly from the scrum, their heeling was generally quicker and cleaner and Waldron, Craig and Brewer were rather more effective than Cambridge at the line-out, although on occasions Morrison and Martin jumped well.

The significant outcome of all this was that the game produced scarcely a threequarter movement of distinction. Cambridge were sufficiently contained near the scrum and this precluded Gibson bringing Kitchin and Jolliffe much into the game.

Oxford seemed to have no such valid excuse. They had opportunities that were allowed to go begging.

Read's over-obsession with kicking also seemed to be costly and he rarely made any effort to bring his three-quarters into play as the result of a passing movement.

The Cambridge forwards came out of the game with considerable credit and Rees, in particular, had a fine game in the general run of forward play. They had at their heels Hamp-Ferguson passing well, spoiling effectively and above all kicking astutely.

They could not, however, manage to assert themselves with sufficient authority to allow Gibson that bit of freedom which was so essential to Cambridge's needs.

Near the interval Gibbs, taking an overhead pass and splendidly supported by Doyle, Jolliffe and Carter, set up another Cambridge attack. An offside spoilt this but shortly after a superb weaving run by Gibson from another reverse pass by Hamp-Ferguson brought play once more to the Oxford line.

Gibson could not break the cover but managed to pass to Drake, who had the inevitable Rees with him to score. Gethin converted splendidly from a wide angle.

Maybe Oxford need not, or should not have been behind at the interval but since they were they took prompt steps to rectify the position. A good move between Hiller and Coker ended on the Cambridge line and a moment later a loose ball was kicked through by Oxford, and Gabitass gathered a rebound and scored a try near the posts that Gould converted.

(December 8)

FANS STORM PALACE AS BEATLES GET MBES

ABOVE: A POLICEMAN, under pressure from the crowd, almost loses his helmet.

RIGHT: POLICE AND VOLUNTEERS searching the Etherow Valley, near Wood-head, Cheshire, yesterday following information that a number of bodies may be buried there. Over 100 men and 12 dogs carried out the search of Pennine moorland in heavy rain. Nothing was found.

Detectives from Lancashire, Cheshire and Manchester are trying to find a link between eight people, including three children, who have vanished from the Manchester area during the past three or four years.

ABOVE: CAPT. CHRISTOPHER OWEN, 25, who as aide-de-camp to the Rhodesian Governor resigned his commission rather than leave him, hauling down the standard at Government House, Salisbury, at sunset. He said it would be raised in the morning.

BELOW: PHOTOGRAPHER DAVID BAILEY, wearing sweater and slacks, pictured when he married 21-year-old French actress Catherine Deneuve, at St. Pancras Town Hall Register Office, London this morning. David Bailey was at one time thought to be marrying top model Jean Shrimpton, whom he helped to launch.

U.S. Marines go ashore in Viet-nam

United States Marines wading ashore on a South Viet-nam beach near Da Nang during the week-end.

1966

It was a year of triumph and disaster. In the summer, when far from the favourites, England's footballers defeated Germany's to win the World Cup. Two months later, the world was saddened when 84 children at their desks in the village school at Aberfan in Wales were killed as a hill of mining waste, loosened by the rain, poured down upon them.

Time magazine declared London to be a "swinging city" and the centre of the new culture as exemplified by the Beatles and the fashion styles of Mary Quant and her contemporaries. As the Beatles had done in the previous year, Mary Quant appeared on the birthday honours list. Some American radio stations banned Beatles' records because of a flip remark by John Lennon that he and the other members of his group were "greater than Christ."

In Britain, in a spring election, Harold Wilson was able to turn his minute Commons majority into a substantial one of over 90. It was not an easy year for the Government, though. By the end of the year, difficult economic conditions and large demands for wage increases led to a freeze on wages and prices before the end of the year. This was accompanied by Cabinet resignations and a general air of dissatisfaction exemplified by the election of the first Welsh Nationalist MP who overturned a Labour majority in his constituency of more than 9,000 votes.

The Home Secretary announced plans for the amalgamation of a number of the smaller police forces in Great Britain, giving as a reason the rise in the crime figures and the horror of the nation at the revelations at the trial of the "Moors Murderers" and at the shooting of three policemen in London. A Texas gunman killed 12 as he shot indiscriminately inside a university building. The spy, George Blake, was helped to escape from Wormwood Scrubbs prison and made his way safely to Moscow hidden in a camper van driven by British sympathisers while the police were watching airports and harbours thinking he might be shipped out as diplomatic baggage by the Soviet Embassy in London.

The Vietnam war dragged on with ever higher casualties. The situation in East Africa continued unstable. The trouble between the Nigerians and the secessionist Biafrans continued while the first prime minister of an independent African country, Ghana, formerly a British colony, was ousted in a coup. In South Africa the prime minister, Dr Verwoerd, was assassinated in the Parliament building. The Indian prime minister, Dr Shashtri, died whilst on a good will mission to the Soviet Union and was succeeded by Mrs Indira Gandhi. The shooting of a Civil Rights marcher worsened the situation in the Southern states of America where the row over segregation continued. An Argentinian invasion of the Falklands Islands was frustrated when the small party of extremists who had hi-jacked a plane were quickly rounded up by Royal Marines, backed by armed islanders. Many works of art were lost as heavy floods hit Italy, Florence bearing the brunt of the damage.

The novelists Evelyn Waugh and C.S. Forester died as did the creator of Mickey Mouse, Walt Disney. Those two great stalwarts of American comedy, Buster Keaton and Sophie Tucker, also died.

England's success in the World Cup was not equalled by the country's cricketers who were badly beaten by the West Indies team led by Gary Sobers. Arkle, the greatest National Hunt horse of his time, ended his career after pulling up lame at the end of a race. A woman, after a long legal battle, was awarded the right to train horses under her own name.

83 DEAD, 46 ENTOMBED IN WELSH AVALANCHE

ENGULFED IN A SEA OF MUD

Rain-soaked coal tip hits school

88 CHILDREN SAFE: 'DISASTER AREA'

AT least 83 people, mostly children, are dead, and 46 were still entombed early today on the hillside at Aberfan, near Merthyr Tydfil, after a rain-soaked coal tip avalanched on Pantglas infants' school, a farm and a row of houses yesterday morning. Eighty-eight children are safe and 36 are in hospital.

Laughter, then shouts & screams

Daily Telegraph Reporter

ONE of the children to get out of the school, Dilys Pope, aged 10, later gave this description of what happened when the avalanche of slag struck the building:

We were in Standard IV and laughing and talking among ourselves waiting for our teacher to call the register.

We heard a noise, and we saw all stuff flying about. The room seemed to be flying around. The desks were falling over and the children were shouting and screaming. We couldn't see anything but then the dust began to go away.

My leg was caught in a desk and could not move and my arm was hurting.

The children were lying all over the place. The teacher (Mr. H. Williams) was also on the floor. His leg was caught. He managed to free himself and he smashed the window in the door with a stone.

I climbed out and went round through the hall and then out through the window.

I opened the classroom window and some of the children came out that way. There were stones everywhere. The teacher got some of the children out and he told us to go home.

Another of the lucky ones was Alan Morgan, 14, of Aberfan Road. He was late for school and when he got there a teacher

Continued on Back Page, Col. 3.

STUDENT SAYS SORRY FOR TV INTERRUPTION

Daily Telegraph Reporter

A student at the College of Technology, Kingston-on-Thames, who interrupted the 5.55 p.m. Independent Television News bulletin last night with an appeal for a students' charity rag, later apologised "most sincerely."

The student, Anthony Knight, 20, of Colwyn Bay, North Wales, appeared on screens just after the newscaster, Peter Snow, had completed a report on the Aberfan disaster. Sound and vision were cut off for several seconds.

Knight said last night that he did not know of the disaster at the time of his interruption.

Mr. S.O. Davies, Labour M.P. for Merthyr Tydfil, said that debris from a local colliery was still being tipped on the slag heap when the disaster happened.

Last night the village was declared a disaster area. Mr. Thomas Griffiths, Merthyr's Chief Constable, said later that the slag heap was now under control. Many homes had been evacuated.

RESCUERS INJURED

Among those brought out alive and taken to hospital was the headmistress, Miss Ann Jennings, 64. The body of the deputy head-teacher, Mr. D. Beynon, was found with five little children in his arms, all dead. Several rescuers were injured.

The Prime Minister and the Secretary for Wales, Mr. Cledwyn Hughes, were among those who flew to the disaster area. Mr. Wilson has given Mr. Hughes "military style powers" to deal with the situation and has promised a high-level inquiry.

The Queen and the Prince of Wales sent messages of sympathy and Prince Philip is flying to the scene today.

There have been long-standing complaints about the danger of the coal tip, which belongs to the 92-year-old Merthyr Vale colliery.

All-night rescue work

By GERDA PAUL

ABERFAN, Glamorgan, Friday night.

RESCUE work was going on all through the night at the stricken village of Aberfan. It will go on all tomorrow and the next day, and the next day if necessary, to bring out all those trapped in the black slag and slime.

There was little hope for the waiting, watching village. Women cried at their doorways, others wandered the streets. Every door was open, everyone man woman or child, was helping.

Earlier, as the bulldozers got to work, human bucket-chains were formed by villagers and relatives, to help clear away the rubble. Every so often there would be silence, when it was thought that someone had been found beneath the wreckage.

SCHOOL BUS DELAYED

Because of early morning fog, 50 children from the neighbouring village of Mount Pleasant escaped the tragedy. Their school bus was delayed and they arrived at the school 10 minutes late, and just after the landslide had occurred.

The mother of one of them, Mrs. Olwyn Morris, said: "If there had been no fog, my boy Joel, 14, would have been in the school. He ran home crying and told me what had happened."

Another parent, Mrs. Joan Jones, of Aberfan, said: "My daughter Joyce, 7, would have been in the school if she had not been in hospital for an operation. For the first time, I am glad she was ill."

The farmhouse in the path of the landslide is owned by Mr. Douglas Lewis. He and his wife, Gladys, had gone shopping. His mother-in-law and their two young children, aged 13 and 11, who remained behind, are among the missing.

A row of six houses opposite the school and another seven in adjoining Moy Street disappeared. Five teachers in the junior school and a few children in the neighbouring senior school, which was also damaged, are unaccounted for.

(Continued on Back Page, Col. 4)

Full inquiry promised by Wilson

Daily Telegraph Reporter

MR. WILSON said last night that there would be a high-level inquiry "as soon as possible," into the cause of the Aberfan disaster.

He was speaking in Merthyr Tydfil after visiting the village. He had flown from Liverpool, he said "to make absolutely sure that the Secretary for State for Wales, Mr. Hughes, had all the backing he needed in everything that needed to be done."

Mr. Wilson, who had walked through ankle-deep mud to the school, added: "I don't think any of us can find words to describe this tragedy." All the necessary powers in the name of the Government had been given to the rescuers.

Earlier in the day, during a tour of Wigan, he had a 30-minute telephone conversation with Mr. Hughes and before he left Liverpool he said he had given Mr. Hughes "military style powers" to deal with the situation.

"Scene of desolation"

At the scene of the disaster Mr. Hughes was joined by Mr. Marsh, Minister of Power, and Mr. H. S. Stephenson, Chief Inspector of Mines, who had flown from London.

Late last night Mr. Callaghan, Chancellor of the Exchequer, who had been speaking in Cardiff, arrived at the village with his wife Audrey. "It is a scene of indescribable desolation," he said.

WARNING ABOUT TIP TWO YEARS AGO

Daily Telegraph Reporter

MERTHYR TYDFIL'S borough planning committee was told in January 1964 that if the tip moved "it could threaten the whole school." The warning came from Councillor Mrs. Gwyneth Williams, who has since died.

She asked that the National Coal Board should carry out an investigation into the tip's condition. The committee rejected the idea.

People living in Moy Road, Aberfan, said yesterday they had noticed the tip beginning to move at 8 p.m. on Thursday.

Mr. David John Evans of Aberfan, a tram maintenance worker at the Merthyr Vale Colliery, was on top of the 500ft high tip when part of it collapsed yesterday.

He went there after reports that the tip had moved during

Continued on Back Page, Col. 6

'GREAT SORROW' SAYS HEATH

Mr. Heath, Opposition leader, sent a message to Merthyr's mayor which said: "It is with the greatest sorrow and distress that I have learned of the tragic disaster today at Aberfan. I would be grateful if you would express my deepest sympathy to the members of the families who have suffered such grievous loss."

Stewart shocks CBI

R.F.D. GREEN Daily Telegraph Commercial Correspondent

MR. STEWART, Minister for Economic Affairs, yesterday introduced an order prohibiting laundries and dry cleaners from raising most of their prices without Government consent. It takes effect on Monday.

The decision enraged leaders of the Confederation of British Industry, who heard of the order on their way to discuss with Mr. Stewart voluntary co-operation in the period after the freeze. They told him there was no point in holding the discussion.

The delegation, led by Mr. John Davies, director-general, left Mr. Stewart's office after accusing him of "a severe breach of faith." In particular, they complained bitterly of a lack of proper consultations.

Q.C. FOR ADEN ON 'TORTURE' INQUIRY

MICHAEL HILTON Daily Telegraph Diplomatic Correspondent

Mr. Roderic Bowen, Q.C., former Liberal M.P. for Cardigan, has accepted the invitation of Mr. Brown, Foreign Secretary, to visit Aden as personal representative.

He will examine the procedures for arrest, interrogation and detention of suspected terrorists.

This follows allegations of torture of detainees made by Dr. Salahadin Rastgeldi, a member of the Swedish executive of Amnesty International, who visited Aden.

Mr. Bowen came to the rescue of Mr. Wilson's majority of three last October by agreeing to become Deputy Chairman of the Ways and Means Committee and Deputy Speaker, after the death of the Speaker, Sir Harry Hylton-Foster. He lost his seat at the last election.

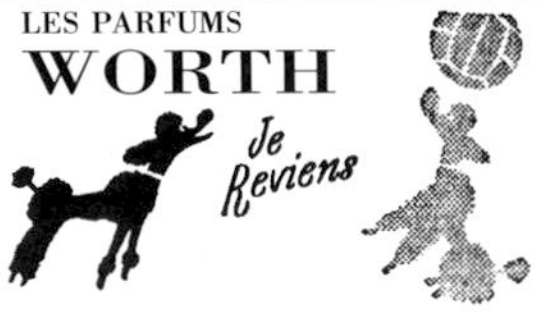

The Daily Telegraph
4 A.M.
No. 34658. LONDON, WEDNESDAY, SEPTEMBER 28, 1966
and Morning Post
Printed in LONDON and MANCHESTER Price 4d.

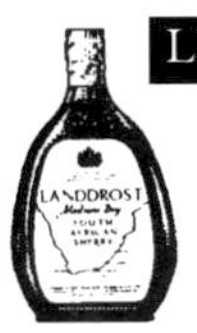

WILSON WARNING OF LONG SQUEEZE

'No easing until we pay our way'

CALLAGHAN SEES 'HEALTHY SURPLUS'

MICHAEL JONES
Daily Telegraph Industrial Staff

THE Prime Minister warned delegates to his National Productivity Conference in London yesterday that there could be no general easing of the current economic squeeze until "we are paying our way and seen to be paying our way."

"I cannot forecast today when the dis-inflationary process will have worked itself out to the extent necessary to permit any general reflation," he said. [Report - P23.]

Mr. Callaghan, Chancellor of the Exchequer, however, made this forecast to the International Monetary Fund and World Bank in Washington: "We can now be confident that Britain will move out of deficit and that, taking 1967 as a whole, Britain will enjoy a healthy surplus in her balance of payments overall." [Report - P21.]

Mr. Brown, Foreign Secretary, questioned in his constituency at Belper about the BMC redundancies, said: "I tell you quite frankly, I have some doubts as to whether it needs all the people it has.

"What I do know is that in the West and East Midlands, and my Division straddles them both, we have eight jobs for every person available. And I do not want any more people in BMC than are necessary for BMC to produce cars they can sell, and to a large extent sell abroad."

New equipment under-used

Mr. Wilson, who was addressing 80 representatives of management, the trade unions and Government departments attending the one-day conference at Lancaster House, criticised British industrial performance, defended his economic policy and called for increased investment.

His strongest attack was reserved for the misuse of industrial resources. Over "too wide an area of industry" new equipment was under-used.

Equally, "a very wide sector" of industry was failing to get anything like the true potential of its existing machinery "whether through unimaginative management, timid management or through out-dated working practices and manning schedules."

UNIONS WARNED

Redeployment "essential"

In a renewed warning to the unions, he said that the redeployment of labour was essential "however had, however painful this is." Because of this, the Government had had to ask for "the release of labour rather than the spreading of work."

Mr. Wilson's speech was seen last night as his most uncompromising commitment so far to a policy of continued and unconditional deflation

He dwelt on the way Britain had "lagged behind" its international rivals in its level of industrial investment, the yield produced by that investment, the sophistication of newly installed plant and machinery and the use of new technology in industry.

GLOOMY VIEW

Oratorical style

The view of British industry presented to the invited delegates was distinctly gloomy. Although Mr. Wilson began his speech by saying that the conference was not an occasion for speeches, delegates also noted that the Prime Minister has not abandoned his heavily oratorical style.

Mr. Wilson's main aim appeared to be to urge industry to step up its investment programme while the Government was creating "room for manoeuvre in the economy" through the redeployment of labour.

One of the discussion papers presented by NEDC experts proposed a campaign to persuade firms to aim at raising industrial productivity by at least 10 per. cent. within the next 12 months.

£1M. LESS PROFIT TO CHEMISTS

Daily Telegraph Reporter

THE 13,000 National Health Service chemists in England and Wales have been making too much profit on prescriptions. Now they have agreed to accept a cut of almost 1d a prescription.

Disclosing this last night, the Ministry of Health said the saving on prescriptions would be nearly £1m a year. The new rates start on Saturday.

The Ministry said that retrospective reviews were agreed between the Ministry and the chemists' representatives at the time of the last settlement in 1964.

These have shown that "factors which could not have been allowed for at the time had led to significant variations from the forecast estimates on which payments for 1964 and 1965 have been based."

Profit "too high"

"These payments resulted in a rate of profit per prescription higher than had been intended," the statement said. In 1964 the overpayment was £244,000 and in 1965 it totalled £859,000.

The main "unforeseeable factor" was the abolition of prescription charges in 1965, which meant that chemists were called upon to dispense thousands more prescriptions, thus cutting the cost of each one in relation to his general costs and overheads.

Though costs have increased this month with the introduction of selective employment tax the chemists agreed the reduction was necessary to allow the previous overpayment to be offset.

Prescriptions dispensed by chemists rose from 208,122,000 in 1964 to 249,804,000 in 1965 with the cost increasing from £105,593,000 to £128,762,000.

SMALLER RISE IN CHRYSLER AND FORD PRICES

Daily Telegraph Staff Correspondent

NEW YORK, Friday.

The Ford Motor Company and the Chrysler Corporation today rescinded part of theprice increases announced last week for 1967 models to remain in competition with General Motors, the giant of Detroit's "Big Three." General motors had announced smaller price increases.

Ford has cut its planned increase from $113 (£40) to $56 (£23 11s) and Chrysler from $92 (£33) to $64 (£22 17s). The General Motors increase averaged $54 (£19 5s).

BMC lays off 9,000 workers

Daily Telegraph Reporter

ABOUT 9,000 workers at British Motor Corporation factories in the Birmingham area were laid off yesterday and nearly all assembly at the BMC Longbridge plant in Birmingham was stopped at the end of last night's shift.

The hold-up is due to an official strike of delivery drivers employed by the Longbridge group of delivery agents in protest against 300 of the drivers being declared redundant because of the 22 per cent. cutback in BMC production.

The delivery drivers ferry cars from BMC assembly factories to ports and distributors. Their strike resulted in 7,500 being sent home from Longbridge yesterday; 580 were idle at Nuffield Metal Products and 533 at Morris Commercial Cars.

The effect will be felt at all BMC plants in Birmingham, Coventry, Oxford, Llanelli and Bathgate. By next week about 50,000 workers will be idle.

Space found for Minis

A night shift of about 1,020 men continued work at Longbridge on Mini and Princess 1100 production lines because more storage space had been found for the cars. Another 14,000 working on engine production at the plant will be laid off later this week.

Among 4,000 who will lose their jobs at Longbridge are 500 old age pensioners who will be retired.

The Ministry of Labour yesterday called the Longbridge group of delivery agents to its Midlands headquarters so that a report could be sent to Mr. Gunter, Minister of Labour.

This was in preparation for his meeting today with representatives of the Transport and General Workers Union, who have made the strike of the delivery drivers official.

Already BMC have 38,600 workers on short time and are to declare some 10 to 11 per cent. of their 108,000 labour force redundant on Nov. 4.

Drivers 'used as puppets'

Daily Telegraph Reporter

AN official of the Transport and General Workers' Union, to which the 748 striking car delivery drivers belong, said last night the men were being "used as puppets."

Many of the drivers do not agree with the strike. Others cannot understand BMC's redundancy decisions.

Mr. Frederick Hill, union branch secretary, said that a week ago he had delivered an A40 to an Eastbourne garage. "The proprietor told me he had waited nine months for it. What sense is there in that?

"BMC say they are getting too few orders and that this justifies redundancies. But this cannot be true. As agents get rid of cars BMC are not restocking the agencies."

BMC "SABOTAGE"

Country's economy

Another union official accused BMC of sabotaging the country's economy. "This is a measure to get rid of the payroll tax and to take the squeeze off hire purchase," he said. His attitude was reflected by many other BMC workmen.

The firms affected by the strike and the numbers they employ are:

Auto Car Conveying Company	237
Carringtons	72
Car and Commercial	55
Barnetts	125
Dealers Deliveries	53
Auto Delivery Services	43
MVT	34
Tessel	12
Car Care	6
Challenor	7
Safe Car	5
Safety	6

The total, including two companies in Liverpool employing a total of 93, is 748 men. Of these redundancy notices were received by 333.

The drivers' union is allowing transporters to take export work to Birmingham stations and is also permitting Austin's transporters to deliver cars from the company to storage depots.

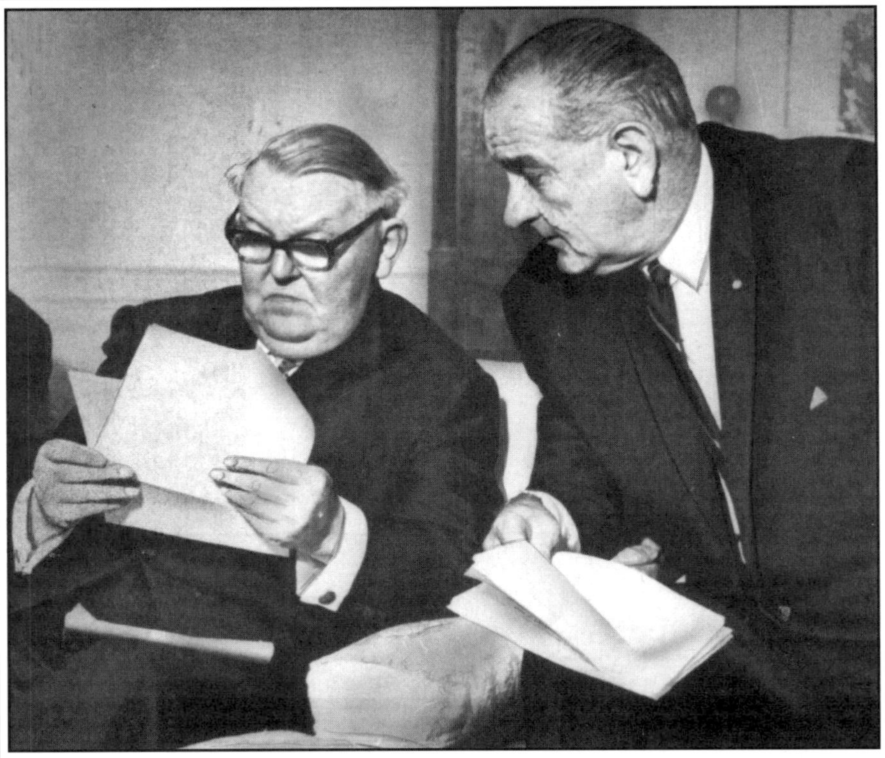

PRESIDENT JOHNSON AND DR. ERHARD, West German Chancellor, concluding their two days of talks at the White House yesterday.

CUTS & REPAIR SAVING IN RHINE ARMY

BONN OFFER ONLY £31½M

Daily Telegraph Defence Staff

The Government clearly indicated yesterday its determination to cut Britain's forces if the West German Government is not prepared to give greater assistance with the costs.

Bonn has moved only a small way towards bridging the annual foreign exchange cost. The Germans have now increased their offer from £27 million to £31.5 million, but this is only about 40 per. cent. of the £47 million the British Army of the Rhine will still cost in foreign exchange after projected economies have been made.

Both NATO and the Western European Union have already been informed that when Britain decides to withdraw forces from Germany they will be consulted about how this can be done in a way least damaging to the alliance.Meanwhile a new committee, from within the Army Department of the Ministry of Defence, has been given the task of recommending the size and composition of the army in the 1970s, when on grounds of economy the total manpower ceiling is expected to be reduced to 165,000. The committee is to visit the Rhine Army next week.

Projected economies in the Rhine Army include reduction of war maintenance reserves to about 10 days, to match the capacity of NATO forces for effective defence. This will enable the stockpiles at Antwerp and

Continued on Back Page, Col. 5

BRITISH FRIGATE TO LEAVE SOUTH AFRICA

Daily Telegraph Naval Correspondent

As part of the Government's economy measures in overseas spending, the Royal Navy is to reduce its permanent presence in South Africa. Details are being worked out, within the framework of the Simonstown Agreement, for the withdrawal of the frigate Puma, 2,300 tons.

She is the only frigate on the South Atlantic and South American station and would be replaced by periodical visits by frigates and submarines based in Britain. This is considered important for the anti-submarine training of ships of the South African Navy.

This may be followed by the return to England of Vice-Adml. J. M. D. Gray, C-in-C, and his staff, at present based at Wynberg, Cape Province.

56-YEAR-OLD YACHT IN DISTRESS

Daily Telegraph Reporter

The 56-year-old steam yacht Norian, 64 tons, which put to sea against advice that she was not suitable for an Atlantic crossing, was in trouble 20 miles south west of the Eddystone lighthouse last night.

The distress call received by Land's End Radio said the 62ft yacht with six people aboard had broken down and was "rolling badly" in heavy seas.

At midnight there was a muddle over salvage rights. The Norian's American owner, Mr. Chadwell O'Connor, 52, refused to accept a tow from a Dutch trawler.

A Falmouth tug urged the yacht not to accept a tow from the Plymouth lifeboat. Plymouth Lifeboat Association's secretary said: "It looks as if the Norian's crew don't know what to do for the best."

The Norian sailed from Plymouth on Monday on an 8,600 mile voyage via Panama to Los Angeles. Local experts advised Mr. O'Connor that the yacht was too narrow-beamed and top-heavy for an Atlantic crossing. Mr. O'Connor considered that adjustments to her trim had made her "stable enough" and she behaved well on trials.

U.S. AIDS INDONESIA

WASHINGTON, Tuesday.

America is to resume aid to Indonesia, it was announced today at the end of a five-day Washington visit by Mr. Malik, Indonesian Foreign Minister. Tomorrow Indonesia will be readmitted to the United Nations, which she left in January, 1965, in protest against Malaysia's admission to the Security Council.

Johnson for Manila talks on Vietnam

Vincent Ryder
Daily Telegraph Staff Correspondent

WASHINGTON, Tuesday.

President Johnson will visit the Philippines next month for a conference, propably on Oct. 18, of countries giving military aid to South Vietnam, it was announced today.

He is expected also to visit Australia, New Zealand and South Korea. It will be his first lengthy tour abroad since becoming President, almost three years ago.

Mr. Johnson is not likely to go to South Vietnam. A visit would create political turmoil in Saigon and require massive, and embarrasing security precautions.

Australia, New Zealand, South Korea, the Philippines and Thailand, the countries supporting Saigon, will be represented at the Manila conference by their political leaders.

Policy unchanged

While it will not mark any change in Vietnam policy, the conference will support Mr. Johnson's contention that the United States is not isolated in Asia in fighting the war.

Mr. Johnson who, in protocol terms, is heavily in arrears in returning visits by other statesmen, has yet to visit Europe as President. Last night he told Dr. Erhard, the West German Chancellor, that he would do his best to accept an invitation to Bonn next spring.

Vietnam War News —P20

'MOST LIKELY THE PUFFIN'

Daily Telegraph Reporter

An upturned boat seen in mid-Atlantic on Sept. 16 is "extremely likely" to be the Puffin, missing with two British rowers aboard, said Mr. Colin Mudie, the boat's designer, last night. The Puffin was sighted from 200 yards by Capt. R. I. Heys, master of the Ocean Monarch, 13,581 tons.

Mr. Mudie said on Independent Television News: "The attitude in which the master saw her floating is the attitude the Puffin would lie if overwhelmed. I am extremely worried that she may have been overwhelmed by Hurricane Faith."

The rowers, Mr. David Johnstone, 35, of Farnham, Surrey, and Mr. John Hoare, 28, of Leicester, set out in May from America for England. They have not been seen since Aug. 11.

Overall majority of 98

WILSON CLAIMS CLEAR MANDATE

13 LOSSES ON TORY FRONT BENCH

WITH only Argyll to be declared today, Mr. Wilson last night had, in his own words, "a clear mandate," a majority of 98 overall and of 111 over the Tories. The state of the parties was:

	SEATS	GAINS	LOSSES
LABOUR	363	49	1
CONSERVATIVES	252	-	51
LIBERALS	12	4	2
REPUBLICAN LABOUR	1	1	0
THE SPEAKER	1	-	-

Soon after his return to Downing Street the Prime Minister had talks with his Foreign Secretary, Mr. Stewart, and then called a meeting of his chief Ministers, including Mr. Callaghan, Chancellor of the Exchequer, and Mr. Brown, First Secretary.

The toll of Tory losses included 13 Front Bench spokesmen. Among prominent casualties were Mr. Soames, foreign affairs, Sir Martin Redmayne, transport, and Mr. Thorneycroft, home affairs.

CHAMPAGNE FOR LIBERALS

The Conservatives retained Peterborough by a majority of three, after seven recounts. The Liberals were two up, gaining Cornwall North and Aberdeenshire W., and one down, losing Caithness to Labour, Lord Byers, party chairman, has sent each winning Liberal a bottle of champagne, Liberal representation now goes up from 10 to 12.

Mr. Heath, dignified and good-humoured in defeat, promised party workers a "vigorous" Opposition. The campaign they had fought had been "absolutely right."

(April 12)

'ANTI-SOVIET' WRITERS GET LONG TERMS

JOHN MILLER
Daily Telegraph Staff Correspondent
MOSCOW, Monday.

THE Russian writers ANDREI SINYAVSKY and YULI DANIEL were sentenced to long terms in a labour camp today for "slandering the Soviet State." Sinyavsky got seven years, the maximum sentence, and Daniel five.

The verdict, against which there is no appeal, was announced after a four-day closed trial in Moscow. The two men, both aged 40, had pleaded not guilty.

Their harsh sentences appeared to confirm reports that they had stubbornly refused to concede having committed any crime.

The charges were based on their novels smuggled to the West and published under assumed names.

The single gesture of leniency was that the court did not meet the prosecutor's request for long periods of exile for both men after they had completed their sentences.

The Soviet Press has so far suppressed details of the defence and the final court plea by Sinyavsky, a teacher of world literature, who used the pseudonym Abram Tertz.

Daniel, a translator, known in the West as Nikolai Arzhak, addressed the court today for nearly an hour.

To-day's proceedings in the three-storey yellow courtroom near Moscow's zoo lasted nearly four hours.

Outside, a group of 20 sympathisers of Sinyavsky and Daniel paced up and down throughout the day in the bitter cold. About 100 young hand-picked Communists were also present to argue the Soviet case with Western correspondents.

(February 15)

up with the lark and down with a smile to

CALIFORNIA PRUNES

for breakfast

Hint to wives: Wrap California Prunes in bacon rashers. Cook under grill or in hot oven.

ISLANDERS KEEP WATCH AS INVADERS SHIVER

Daily Telegraph Correspondent
PORT STANLEY, Falkland Islands, Thursday.

THE Argentine nationalist "army" which invaded Port Stanley, capital of the British-owned Falkland Islands, yesterday, stood shivering on the racecourse there today hemmed in by a local Defence Force cordon.

The 20 nationalists are members of the Right-wing extremist "Condor" group which claims the Falklands, on the edge of the Antarctic, as part of Argentina. They landed after capturing an Argentine DC-4 airliner and forcing the pilot to fly to Port Stanley.

A young blonde woman appears to be their leader. The only woman in the "army" she is believed to be Maria Cristina Verrier, a playwright.

A six-man detachment of Royal Marines is backing about 150 armed islanders who last night took shifts on guard around the floodlit airliner. The invaders, armed with rifles, played records through the night to keep their spirits up.

It was reported from Buenos Aires today that two Argentine Air Force planes with police on board had taken off for Rio Gallegosi, Southern Argentina, for an eventual flight to the Falklands.

It was not clear whether their task would be to take home the airliner's crew and 26 passengers not involved in the operation, or to arrest the invaders.

(September 30)

ABSE WINS SEX BILL APPROVAL

By ANDREW ALEXANDER
WESTMINSTER, Tuesday.

BY 244 votes to 100, the Commons today permitted Mr. Leo Abse (Lab., Pontypool) to bring in, under the 10-minute rule, a homosexual law reform Bill.

The vote followed a short but, oddly enough, merry debate which had the House guffawing freely. The amusement was provided not by Mr. Abse or his Bill but by the ingenious fervour of his opponent, Sir Cyril Osborne (C., Louth).

Mr. Abse, short, dapper and bespectacled, is not without considerable Celtic fervour himself but he was at one with the mood of most Members when he spoke.

DEEP INDIGNATION

Slight smiles

He described the Bill as no condonation of homosexuality since it increased the penalties for offences against those under 21. But it was an attempt to make the law logical and to show understanding for adults. There were special provisions to keep the law unchanged for the Forces.

Sir Cyril rose and many Members permitted themselves slight smiles. Deep indignation is Sir Cyril's forte.

The complication about Sir Cyril's argument is that at one moment he seemed to argue that homosexuality is so catching that only draconian measures will check it. The next, he seems certain that it is so widely detested as to be almost non-existent.

(July 6)

FOOD PRICES 'WILL KEEP GOING UP'

Daily Telegraph Reporter

The housewife's weekly grocery bill costs her 1s in the pound more each year, according to today's issue of the Grocer.

Food prices will continue to rise as wages and overheads chase selling and production costs. But the increase will not be startling

There may well be some periods of cheaper food as commodities such as bacon, butter, cheese and eggs fall in price momentarily due to special market or seasonal conditions.

During the last seven weeks 1,000 items have gone up. Today's latest lists show 91 are higher compared with 250 last week.

These include sausages, canned meat and fish and mincemeat. There are 10 decreases on poultry, biscuits and canned fruit.

The National Federation of Wholesale Grocers said yesterday that the December index of wholesale prices showed eggs up 27.8 points to 175.9, the highest in nine years. The index stood at 114.8 points, 5.8 higher than a year ago, for all groceries and provisions.

(January 15)

CHANGE TO DECIMAL MONEY IN 1971

H.B. BOYNE
Daily Telegraph Political Correspondent

A FIRM decision to change to decimal currency in February, 1971, was the surprise packet unfolded yesterday by Mr. Callaghan, Chancellor of the Exchequer.

It was the "momentous and historic" feature of an electioneering trailer in which Mr. Callaghan disclosed box-office aspects of the Budget he hopes to introduce next month.

One of the most effective flourishes, in which M.P.s discern the hand of Mr. Wilson, was to assert that new taxes on betting and gambling will meet the cost of new mortgage-interest reliefs for owner-occupiers.

CALLAGHAN'S PROPOSALS

The main proposals of a statement which exceeded in scope many a full-scale Budget were:

NATIONAL SAVINGS: From March 28 a new £1 certificate, worth 25s if held for five years, will be on sale. The rate of interest will be £4 11s 3d tax-free, equal to 7¾ per cent. subject to income tax.

MORTGAGES: New and existing owner-occupiers will have the option of claiming tax relief on mortgage interest payments, if liable, or benefiting by a 2½ per cent. reduction on the prevailing rate of interest, subject to a minimum of 4 per cent.

The difference will be made up to the building society by the Government. Arrangements for the Government to guarantee the "last slice" of mortgages taken out by people of modest means are also to be discussed with the building societies.

CARS: There is to be no "differential" tax for this year at least.

BETTING: A tax of 2½ per cent of the stake money, 6d in the £, is to be imposed on all forms of betting except football pools and fixed-odds football coupons, which already pay 25 per cent. At dog tracks this will replace the existing duty on the "tote" and bookmakers' licence duty.

(March 2)

EX-BUA CHIEF STARTING OWN AIRLINE

Air Cdre. E.M. DONALDSON
Daily Telegraph Air Correspondent

MR. FREDDIE LAKER, 43, who made British United Airways into Britain's largest independent airline, is to start an all-jet airline catering for the package holiday trade, he announced in London last night. His wife, Joan, and himself will be sole directors of the company, Laker Airways.

He has purchased three British Aircraft Corporation One-Eleven 75-seater airliners at a cost of £4 million. The money was raised from City banks.

To start operations, Mr. Laker is spending £211,500 of his own money. No Government aid will be sought.

Mr. Laker started in the airline business with his £40 RAF gratuity in 1946. He is now reported to have a personal fortune of more than £1 million.

Mr. Laker told me: "The inclusive holiday trade by air is about to explode. I will make possible cheaper and longer holidays by efficiency and speedier travel."

Laker jets will be hired to travel organisations, rather than chartered for individual flights. In the winter they will serve the sunshine spots and winter sports areas.

No one will travel in a propeller-driven plane after 1968 if Mr. Laker can help it. His planes will be painted in his horse-racing colours of red, black and white.

(February 9)

Submarine recovers H-bomb

Reginald Peck
Daily Telegraph Staff Correspondent
PALOMARES, South-East Spain, Monday.

Observers at Villaricos, southern Spain, have little doubt that the hydrogen bomb missing since an American bomber crashed on Jan. 17, was recovered from the sea today.

Cpl. Young, the American chief Press officer refused to confirm or deny this. He said he would make a statement tomorrow.

Activity by the deep-diving American submarine Aluminaut was watched from the shore. Towards nightfall the submarine's mother ship, Plymouth Rock, 5,880 tons, moved out to sea escorted by destroyers.

The entire operation is believed to have cost the Americans about $35 million (£12 million). A total of 16 naval vessels has been involved.

Wreckage of the American Globemaster plane carrying vehicles and supplies for the search, which disappeared on Saturday on a flight from Seville, was found today on Mount Mulhacen, 11,600ft, in the Sierra Nevada range. All eight aboard were dead.

(February 15)

BEATLES WILL STILL TOUR, SAYS EPSTEIN

CHRISTOPHER MUNNION
Daily Telegraph Staff Correspondent
NEW YORK, Friday.

MR. BRIAN EPSTEIN, the Beatles' manager, said today that the group would go ahead with their American tour later this month. Earlier he had talks to assess the "ban-the-Beatles" campaign.

Radio stations throughout America most of them in the Southern "Bible Belt" States are broadcasting appeals to teenagers to collect Beatles' records and souvenirs for bonfires.

The campaign started in Birmingham, Alabama, when a station manager read an article in the teenage magazine Datebook, in which John Lennon was quoted as saying: "Christianity will go. It will vanish and shrink … We are more popular than Jesus now; I don't know which will go first - rock 'n roll or Christianity."

More than 40 radio stations had joined the campaign when a worried-looking Mr. Epstein, who had curtailed his holiday, flew into Kennedy Airport last night.

When an American reporter asked him if he thought the Beatles were more popular than Jesus, he snapped "Of course not."

One radio station in Fort Knox, Kentucky, which has never before played a Beatles' record, today began broadcasting one of the group's records every half-hour.

(August 6)

SUSSEX DOWNS NAMED AS BEAUTY AREA

The Sussex Downs area from Beachy Head to the Hampshire border has been designated an Area of Outstanding Beauty under an order by the National Parks Commission, confirmed by Mr. Crossman, Minister of Housing and Local Government.

(April 15)

BRADY & HINDLEY GET LIFE SENTENCES

'COLD-BLOODED MURDERS'

Daily Telegraph Reporter

IAN BRADY, 28, and MYRA HINDLEY, 23 were both sentenced to life imprisonment at the "Bodies on the Moors" trial at Chester Assizes yesterday after being found guilty of murder.

The jury found Brady guilty of murdering EDWARD EVANS, 17, LESLEY ANN DOWNEY, 10, and JOHN KILBRIDE, 12. HINDLEY was found guilty of the Evans and Downey murders but not guilty of the Kilbride murder.

Hindley was also found guilty of harbouring Brady, knowing he had murdered Kilbridge.

Brady was sentenced to life imprisonment concurrently on all three charges.

Hindley was sentenced to life imprisonment concurrently on the charges of murdering Evans and Downey. She was sentenced to seven years on the harbouring charge to run concurrently.

Mr. Justice FENTON ATKINSON said to Brady: "These were three calculated, cruel, cold-blooded murders. In your case I pass the only sentence which the law now allows, which is three concurrent sentences of life imprisonment."

He said to Hindley: "You have been found guilty of two equally horrible murders."

Brady and Hindley, both of Wardle Brook Avenue, Hattersley Cheshire, said nothing on being sentenced. Hindley swayed a little and closed her eyes. A woman prison officer took her arm and led her away.

The JUDGE commented: "It should be said here that these matters clearly were only brought to light by police investigation of the utmost skill."

(May 7)

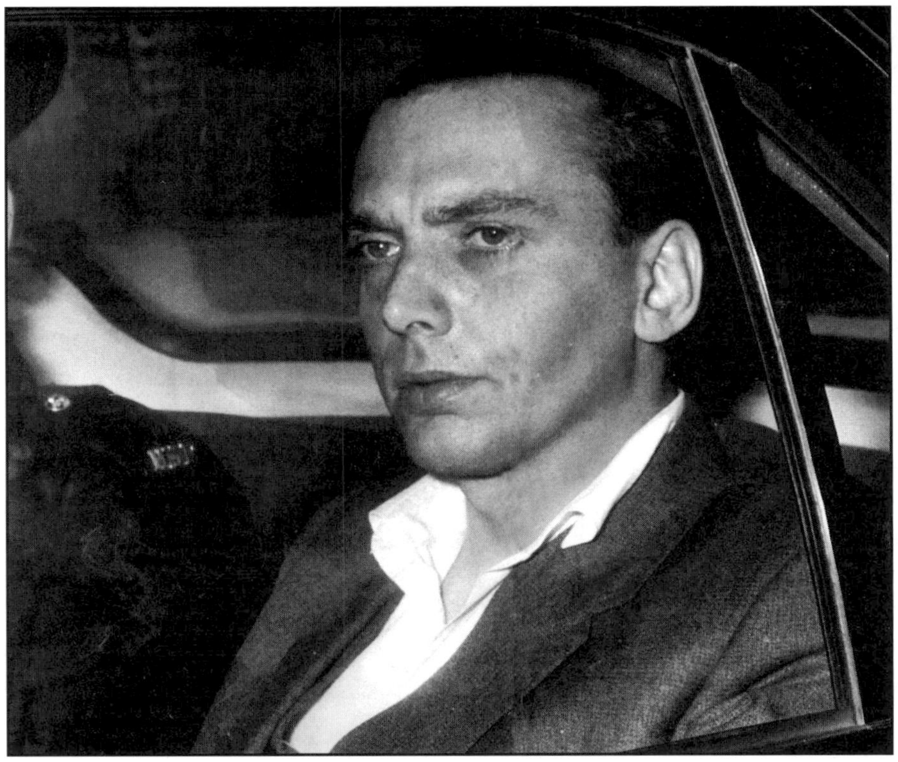

IAN BRADY AND (below) Myra Hindley, who were sentenced to life imprisonment yesterday at Chester Assizes.

£57m damage to Florence art works

Daily Telegraph Correspondent

ROME, Tuesday.

FLOODS caused damage totalling 100,000 million lire (£57,470,000) to the art treasures of Florence. Signor Giovanni Elkan, Under-Secretary to the Italian Education Ministry, said today.

More than 600 paintings were damaged and "Crucifixion" by Cimabue (1240-1302) was completely ruined. Signor Elkan said 2,000 million lire (£1,149,000) was needed immediately to restore many of the damaged paintings.

A hundred art experts and monks were converging on Florence from Rome, Bologna, Genoa, and Pisa to help in the restoration work. An appeal for international help has been issued by a committee comprising Florence museum officials and professors.

Manuscripts ruined

More than 1,000 manuscripts and books of incalculable historical value in the National Library in Florence were partly destroyed. Hundreds of thousands of other books of lesser value were soaked and covered with mud.

The Italian Cabinet met twice today to forge a national plan to aid victims of the floods which ravaged one-third of the country. Government officials feared the damage could amount to £893 million.

The Pope made a personal gift of 50 million lire (£28,736) for flood victims. He authorised clergy to sell votive objects to raise funds.

Meanwhile, alarm lessened in the Po delta and the Venice lagoon where volunteers worked overtime on filling breaches in the dykes. Sunshine and calm weather gave a breathing space in which to secure the fragile sea and river defence.

(November 9)

BONN CURBS ON STARFIGHTERS AFTER CRASHES

PETER SCHMITT
Daily Telegraph Staff Correspondent

BONN, Sunday.

WEST-GERMANY has imposed restrictions on its 700 American - designed F-104G Starfighters after the 61st plane of this type crashed earlier this month, killing the 35th pilot since 1961.

Flying under 500ft and at the weekend has been forbidden. Night flying will be permitted only twice a week and there will be no flights over the sea.

The pilot who died after the 61st Starfighter crash baled out into the sea. He is believed to have been drowned as his equipment for the sea was out of order.

British task

The sea-flying restrictions mean that practically all Luftwaffe's seas reconnaissance planes in Northern Germany are grounded leaving the main task to British reconnaissance Lightnings.

NATO has promised to respect the German need for restrictions which would be lifted automatically if Germany were involved in fighting a Communist attack.

(July 25)

AA MEMBERSHIP TO COST EXTRA GUINEA

The annual AA subscription will go up from two to three guineas from next January. It has been unchanged since the AA was formed in 1905.

Lord Fraser of Allander, honorary treasurer, said at the association's annual meeting in London yesterday that the increase was "inescapable." A surplus of £68,000 in 1964 had changed to a deficit of £188,000 last year.

(June 2)

V.C. FOR GURKHA

The Victoria Cross has been awarded to a Ghurka, Lance-Cpl. Rambahadur Limbu, 26, for 20 minutes of outstanding bravery during a hill battle against Indonesian irregulars in Sarawak in November.

The citation says that his actions "reached a zenith of determined, premeditated valour which must count among the most notable on record." He is now waiting to fly to London, for the Queen has said that it is her personal wish to invest him with the VC at Buckingham Palace.

Cpl. Rambahadur was in command of an ifantry light-machine-gun section when his company of the 10th Princess Mary's Own Gurkha Rifles attacked a strong, well-entrenched enemy hill position.

(April 23)

Worshipper of Nazis and his willing pupil

By T.A. SANDROCK and ROLAND GRIBBEN

IAN BRADY, who during phases in his life was known at times as "The Undertaker" and "Dracula," was the product of Glasgow's Gorbals area, an illegitimate child. He idolised Hitler, Nazism and horror.

He delighted in reading about perversions and was so convinced of his own superiority that he thought he could dictate to Fate. Perhaps he believed he had such influence when he met Myra Hindley.

She became a willing and efficient pupil to this teacher, whose textbooks were on murder, torture and sexual perversions.

Brady went through three phases in his life showing viciousness as a child, then a period of retraction within himself and finally the demented philosophy which led him to the dock.

THREE PHASES

Hindley's life

Hindley's life also followed a three-phase pattern, but her story might well have been very different if the "million-to-one-chance" that brought them together in 1961, when she was 18, had not materialised.

A war-time baby from a Manchester slum area, her association with Brady brought out and developed an inhuman streak. This changed her from a young woman with natural maternal instincts into a sadist who took pleasure in watching a child being subjected to vile practices before being murdered.

Her phases of life went through a reasonably normal childhood until she saw a child drown. Then came a phase of religious fervour before the complete degradation as the more than willing tool of Brady.

It ended with her accepting the Nazi "ideals," the philosophy of the Marquis de Sade, posing for pornographic photographs and choosing the infamous Irma Grese, female "Beast of Belsen," as her "heroine" and even carrying Grese's photograph with her.

Brady was born in a Glasgow maternity hospital on Jan. 2, 1938, the son of Margaret Stewart, a tea-room waitress. He was soon sent to foster parents, Mr. and Mrs. Sloan, with whom he lived in Camden Street, Hutchesontown.

When he was 11, he moved with his foster parents from the dingy tenement to spacious, airy surroundings on a new estate at Pollock.

In 1951 he appeared in Glasgow Sheriff Court on charges of housebreaking and attempted theft. He was put on probation for two years. In July, 1952, he was admonished on charges of housebreaking and theft in Govan Court.

Then came nine charges of housebreaking and theft for which he received two years' probation, a condition of the order being that he went to live with his mother in Manchester. He was still only 15 years old.

CHANGED NAME

'Slipped back to crime'

He changed his name to Brady and found work with his stepfather while living at Cuttell Street, Gorton, but he slipped back to crime. In December 1955, he appeared on a theft charge and was sent to Quarter Sessions for sentence. He was sent to Borstal.

Between school leaving and joining Millwards in 1961, Hindley had several boy friends but her closest attachment was with Ronald Sinclair, formerly of Dalkeith Street, Gorton to whom she became engaged.

She then revealed an interest in Germany and obtained application forms for joining the Naafi so that she could go there. This was before she met Brady. When she met him she gave up the idea and "set her cap" at Brady.

He had already lost most of his friends at the firm because of his "Hitler was right" and "Britain is decadent" attitudes.

The change in Hindley became marked and noticeable. Her emotionless reaction to murder and the indulging in degrading practices show how complete was the change. Her one stable emotion was love of her dog Puppet.

Brady, too, had now become completely perverted. He still thought he was better than everyone and that no could or dare laugh at him.

(May 7)

COLOURED P.c. RECRUITED IN COVENTRY

Britain's first regular coloured policeman was sworn in yesterday to the Coventry force. He is P.c. Mohamed Yusuf Daar, 23, a factory worker until last Friday at nearly double his starting pay in the police.

P.c. Daar, who was born in Nairobi, Kenya, and speaks six languages, was sworn in before Mr. Ron Blake, a local magistrate. He said later: "This has been a wonderful day for me."

(March 16)

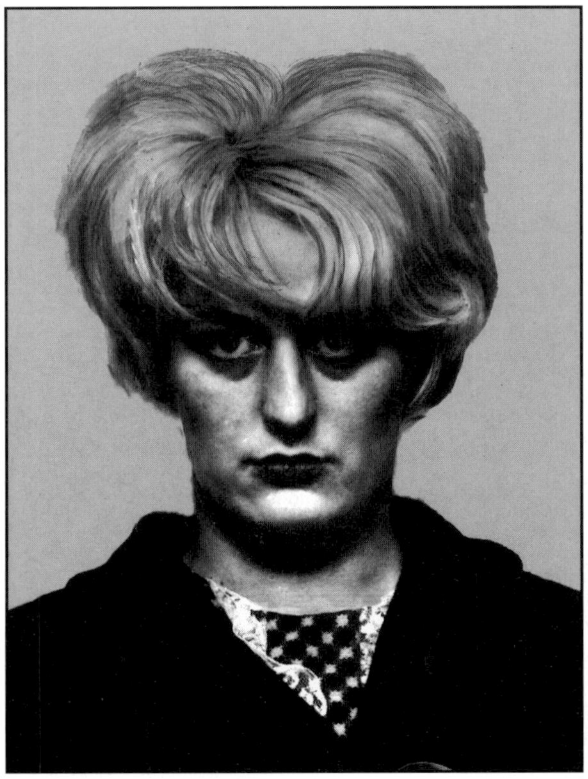

PAISLEY WANTS TO BECOME NORTHERN IRELAND M.P.

Daily Telegraph Reporter

THE Rev. IAN PAISLEY, Moderator of the small Free Presbyterian Church and extremist Ulster Protestant leader disclosed his political aspirations in Belfast yesterday at a rally of about 1,000 people at the Ulster Hall. He said he hoped to be elected to the Northern Ireland Parliament.

He was later arrested because he had refused to be bound over on charges of unlawful assembly arising from disturbances in Belfast on June 6. In his address Mr. Paisley attacked the Ulster Unionist Government.

He said: "The Prime Minister, Capt. Terence O'Neill has attacked us from behind the privilege of the House of Commons. Let me tell you the day is coming when I will be in the House of Commons."

For some seconds there was silence but as the audience realised the implications they broke into cheers, whistles, flagwaving and foot-stamping for several minutes. It was the first time he has publicly said he was interested in becoming an Ulster M.P.

In his address, which he called "Why I Choose Gaol," Mr. Paisley said only he, the Rev. John Wylie and the Rev. Ivan Foster would not sign the bail bond imposed on them by the magistrates after being found guilty of unlawful assembly.

"We choose not to sign so as to focus attention on the fact that there are two sets of laws in this country. One set is for the O'Neillites who can beat up a clergyman and be fined £3, and the other is for people who protest against Romanist tendencies in a Protestant country and are put under rule of bail.

"The politicians say that by going to gaol I am trying to become a martyr, but I want to nail that lie this morning."

Mrs. Paisley said at the meeting that yesterday her sister, who was looking after the Paisleys' children, was threatened.

(July 21)

VOLUNTEER FORCE BAN IN ULSTER

Daily Telegraph Reporter

CAPT. TERENCE O'NEILL, Prime Minister of Northern Ireland, yesterday outlawed the Ulster Volunteer Force, an extreme Protestant group. "It is an unlawful association under the Special Powers Act," he told the Ulster Commons.

He had interrupted a visit to France to fly back and make a statement on recent disturbances in Belfast.

"I do not think the House would expect me to describe in detail the terrible events of Sunday morning. It is enough to say that four young men were wantonly and wickedly attacked, leaving one dead and only one uninjured. Since then, police activity has been intense."

"Dangerous conspiracy"

Information which had come to hand in the last few days made it clear that the safety of law-abiding citizens was threatened by a dangerous conspiracy.

Capt. O'Neill referred to the authentic and original Volunteer Force, the basis of the 36 Ulster Division, almost wiped out at the 1916 Battle of the Somme.

"Let no one imagine that there is any connection whatever between the two bodies." he said.

(June 29)

QUEEN MOTHER 'DOING WELL'

Daily Telegraph Reporter

Queen Elizabeth the Queen Mother, who returned to Clarence House at about 9.30p.m. on Wednesday following her abdominal operation on Dec. 10, was stated yesterday to be getting on well, and walking about a little.

The Queen, Prince Philip and their children are leaving Windsor Castle today for Sandringham, where they will spend most of January.

(December 27)

SPY HUNT WATCH ON RED SHIPS

BLAKE USED LADDER OF KNITTING NEEDLES

T.A. SANDROCK
Daily Telegraph Scotland Yard Correspondent

A SPECIAL watch for George Blake, 44, the double agent who escaped from Wormwood Scrubs on Saturday evening, was being kept last night on eight Communist cargo ships in London docks.

The docks police, and Special Branch men keeping Iron Curtain embassies and their staff under surveillance, were told to look out for any attempt to ship out a large packing case with "diplomatic bag" protection.

A watch was also being kept on all ports and airports and on the homes of Blake's mother and his former friends. But there was a strong feeling that Blake, serving 42 years for spying for Russia, was taken out of the country almost immediately he escaped.

Two clues, 10 pairs of size 13 knitting needles and a pot of pink chrysanthemums, may give police a lead to the men who helped him.

HOME-MADE LADDER
Reinforced rungs

The 20 steel needles were used to reinforce each of the 20 rungs of the home-made ladder which Blake used to scale the outer prison wall.

The pot of chrysanthemums wrapped in green paper of F. Meyer Ltd., a florist with branches in West London, was found outside the wall in Artillery Row, a narrow lane, at a point where the rope ladder hung down inside.

Police think that the flowers, which were fresh, were used to mark the escape point. Alternatively an accomplice may have posed as a flower seller.

Blake's escape, between 5.30 p.m. and 7 p.m. was described to me yesterday as "shattering" to the security system. It is expected to have international implications.

The ladder, made of clothes line type rope, was not secured to the top of the wall in any way. Assuming it was held from outside while Blake climbed it, police are then faced with the problem of how he got down into Artillery Lane.

All possibilities, including the use of a large van as in the escape of Ronald Biggs, the train robber, from Wandsworth Prison, are being examined.

(October 24)

SWINGING LONDON 'CITY OF DECADE'

ALEX FAULKNER
Daily Telegraph Staff Correspondent
NEW YORK, Monday.

LONDON is the city of this decade, the place to go, the place that is making its influence felt most widely in foreign countries, says Time magazine today of what it calls "The swinging city."

In a decade dominated by youth, the magazine states, London has burst into bloom. It swings; it is the scene.

"Switched on"

"This spring, as never before in modern times, London is switched on. Ancient elegance and new opulence are all tangled in a dazzling blur of op and pop.

"In a once sedate world of faded splendour, everything new, uninhibited and kinky is blooming at the top of London life.

"London is not keeping the good news to itself. It is exporting its plays, its films, its fads, its styles, people.

"It is also the place to go. It has become the latest Mecca for Parisians who are tired of Paris. The new vitality of the city amazes both its visitors and inhabitants.

"Britain has lost an empire and lightened a pound and in the process it has also recovered a lightness of heart lost during the weighty centuries of world leadership."

(April 12)

MORAN BOOK 'FALSE SLANT ON HISTORY'

Daily Telegraph TV and Radio Staff

LORD MORAN'S book on Sir Winston Churchill was criticised yesterday by Mr. A. Montague Browne, Sir Winston's secretary, as giving a "false slant on history."

It purported to give an accurate day-to-day account of Sir Winston, but the dates mentioned showed it was a false picture. He doubted whether Sir Winston would have approved the book.

Mr. Brown was being interviewed in "The World at One" in the BBC Home Service.

"I'm not suggesting that Lord Moran intends to mislead," he went on, "but the picture of the sick man whose powers were failing as long ago as 1943 is to me absurd."

"Politics not discussed"

Lord Moran saw Sir Winston when he was ill. Sir Winston no more discussed politics nor strategy with him than he discussed his health with the Chiefs of Staff.

Referring to the family's bruised feelings, he said this was one of the aspects of the book that disturbed him most.

"I leave out the medical aspect; that's for Lord Moran's professional colleagues. But if he had written his memoirs and shown them to the family I am sure this trouble could have been avoided. Nobody would have sought to censor them."

Lord Moran had said that Sir Winston authorised him to publish the book, but no one knew of this, including Lady Spencer-Churchill, Sir Winston's private office and his advisers.

(June 11)

BARCELONA POLICE CLUB PRIESTS

Daily Telegraph Correspondent
BARCELONA, Wednesday.

A protest march by about 150 priests and members of religious orders outside police headquarters at Barcelona this afternoon was broken up by truncheon charges.

Ten priests are reported to have received head injuries. A number were also kicked. Parties of priests who took refuge in two churches were besieged for some time before being allowed to leave unmolested.

The priests held a 45-minute meeting at Barcelona Cathedral before marching to present a letter protesting against the alleged ill-treatment of a university student.

Twice they refused to obey orders to disperse. Several were arrested and freed later.

Tonight Roman Catholics are preparing a demand for the ex-communication of police involved.

Eighteen professors at Barcelona University have been suspended without pay while the authorities investigate their part in recent student unrest. The university was closed on April 27.

(May 12)

TALLEST TREE

Dr. Paul Zinke, a California University professor of forestry, claims to have discovered the world's tallest tree, a 369ft, 3in Redwood in Humboldt State Park, California. The record has been held by a 367ft. 8in Howard Libbey tree in Redwood Creek, Humboldt County.

(August 18)

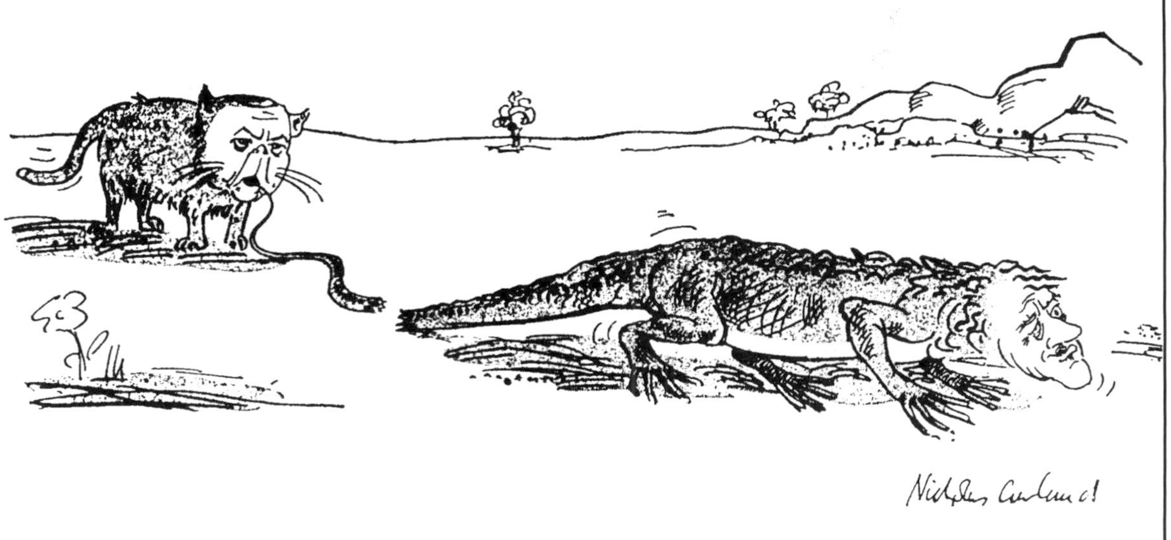

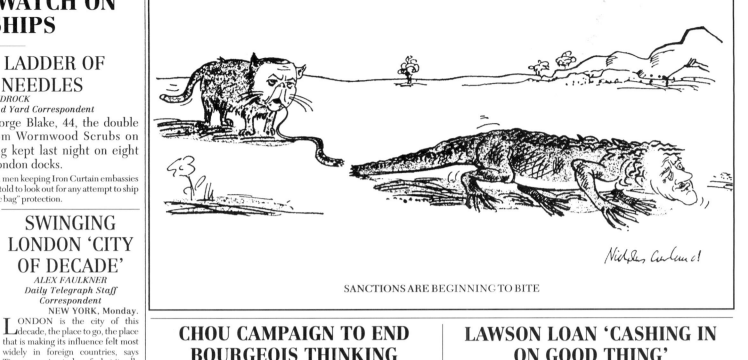

SANCTIONS ARE BEGINNING TO BITE

CHOU CAMPAIGN TO END BOURGEOIS THINKING

STEPHEN CONSTANT
Daily Telegraph Communist Affairs Staff

COMMUNIST China's Prime Minister, Chou En-lai, in a speech over the weekend, launched a massive, nationwide political campaign to eradicate all vestiges of "bourgeois" thinking among China's writers, artists and intellectuals.

He told a mass rally in Peking that a "social-cultural revolution of great historic significance" was being launched in China. He called for a fierce and protracted struggle to wipe out "bourgeois ideology" in all cultural fields.

Chou En-lai's speech followed the publication in china of an abject piece of "self criticism" by Kuo Mo-jo, 75, China's leading intellectual and holder of important official positions.

TEARS OF SHAME
No value in work

In a speech to the standing committee of the National Peoples' Congress (the Chinese "Parliament"), of which he is the vice-president, Kuo Mo-jo said that though he had written several million words, all his work should be burned.

It had "no value at all" by the standards of today and tears of shame were "running over his stomach."

The drive against intellectuals has already resulted in 160,000 of them being sent by the authorities to work in farms, factories, mines or in the armed forces. The figure will presumably increase as the campaign gathers momentum.

This process is officially described as "tempering." The impetus for the campaign comes from Mao Tse-tung's dictum: "If you want the masses to understand you, if you want to be one of the masses, you must make up your mind to undergo a long and even painful process of tempering."

The regime's propaganda against intellectuals is anxious to put over the idea that scholarship, talent or even genius are of no value unless they accurately reflect the "thinking of Mao Tse-tung."

Marshal Chen Yi, Foreign Minister, recently emphasised the unimportance of artists who are not 100 per cent. politically reliable when he praised a novel written by a 35-year-old member of the Chinese armed forces, an amateur.

Of it, he said: "This shows that creative writing is not something mystic and that if only we undertake to arm ourselves with the thinking of Mao Tse-tung, even though we are not professional writers and have little or no writing experience, we shall still be able to complete good literary work.

(May 2)

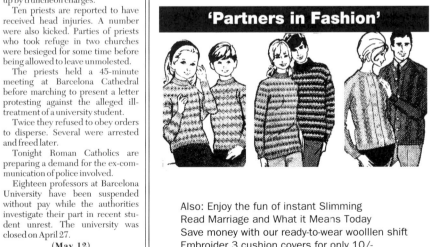

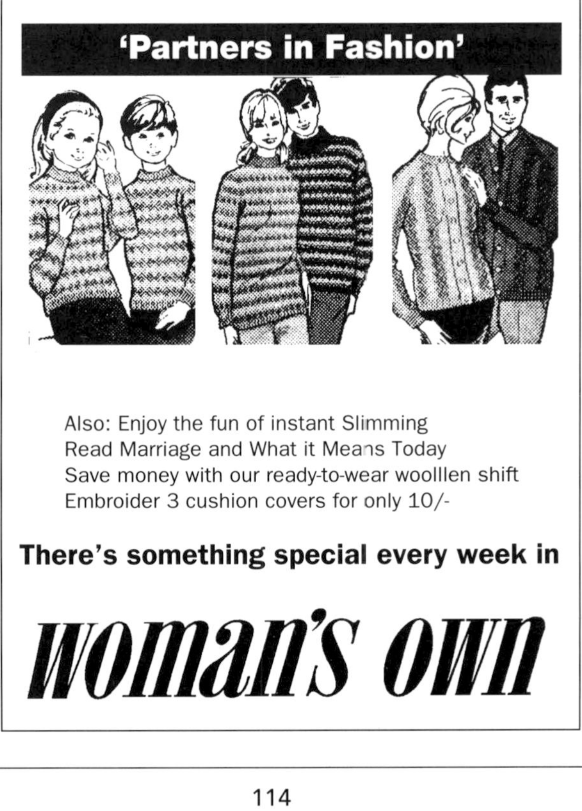
'Partners in Fashion'
Also: Enjoy the fun of instant Slimming
Read Marriage and What it Means Today
Save money with our ready-to-wear woolllen shift
Embroider 3 cushion covers for only 10/-
There's something special every week in
woman's own

LAWSON LOAN 'CASHING IN ON GOOD THING'

Daily Telegraph Reporter

MR. NIGEL LAWSON, editor of the Spectator, was attacked by a woman Conservative member of the Kensington and Chelsea Council last night for having applied for the £20,000 loan which the council granted him to help buy 24, Hyde Park Gate.

Councillor Mrs. DIANA PAUL said in the council chamber that people who applied for this type of loan were acting contrary to the spirit of local authority loans.

"The malaise of the era is cashing in on a good thing. It depresses me."

She was speaking during a debate on the council's mortgage policy which has been suspended because of the "credit squeeze."

"CEILING" URGED
Labour plea

Councillor JOHN BALDWIN, chairman of the Housing Committee, said an upper limit on house loans would have to be considered. Labour members of the Conservative-controlled council urged a £10,000 ceiling.

Mrs. PAUL complained that in many cases people looking for a local authority loan were the first to support private enterprise all down the line.

Local authority loans were intended for people who could not find the money in other ways.

(January 12)

M.P.S ANGRY AT TV IN COMMONS

Daily Telegraph Political Staff

TELEVISION'S peep at the Commons yesterday brought a reaction of anger from Conservative and Labour M.P.s when the House met again in the afternoon after the State opening ceremony.

Senior Backbenchers on both sides lost no time in protesting about the way in which the decision to allow cameras into the Chamber for the first time had been taken.

Most of the criticism is aimed at the Commons Services Committee, which handles domestic issues, and party whips. The critics are saying that the committee should not have recommended Dr. King, the Speaker, to permit proceedings to be televised without a resolution by the House.

Shinwell "surprised"

In a protest in the Chamber, after cameras and rows of lights had been removed during the lunch break. Mr. Shinwell, Labour M.P. for Easington, said he had been surprised to learn from the newspapers that permission had been given.

As the Conservative Whips were consulted and gave their blessing, the issue is now turning into a Backbenchers against Frontbenchers battle.

Members who are complaining include Sir Gerald Nabarro (C., South Worcestershire); Sir Harmar Nicholls (C., Peterborough); Mr. William Hamilton (Lab., West Fife) and Mr. van Straubenzee (C., Wokingham).

(April 22)

Cavern closed but melody lingered on

Daily Telegraph Reporter

ABOUT 100 teenagers barricaded themselves in The Cavern Club, Liverpool, yesterday, by blocking a stairway with chairs, The Cavern is the club where the Beatles first started.

The teenagers were opposing a move to close the club after a receiving order for £1,500 had been made against the owner of the club, Mr. Ray McFall, 38, in Liverpool County Court by Mr. Registrar, J. Tegid Jones.

When the Official Receiver went to the club, many of the teenagers who had been in the underground premises since the previous afternoon were still dancing to beat groups pounding out the Mersey sound from the little stage. They said they would not leave until carried out.

Eventually three policemen talked with officials from the Official Receiver's office and a start was made clearing the furniture blocking the narrow stone stairs.

They found it impossible however, to get through the last few feet. After half an hour entry was made through a back door.

After an appeal to the teenagers to leave quietly they all streamed out and the Official Receiver took over the remainder of the Cavern property.

(March 1)

ALABAMA WIN FOR MRS. WALLACE

The primary election in Alabama has made it clear that the newly-enfranchised Negroes still lack the power or the will to put moderates into office in any appreciable numbers.

Mrs. Lurleen Wallace, 39, wife of the retiring segregationalist Governor, Mr. George Wallace, defeated nine other candidates for the Democratic Party nomination for the election of Governor in November.

About 235,000 Negroes were on the electoral roll, representing 20 per cent. of the total. They turned out in large numbers but Whites produced a massive vote.

(May 5)

GEMINI DAMAGED IN SATELLITE LINK-UP

FROGMEN PARACHUTE TO RESCUE

ALEX FAULKNER
Daily Telegraph Staff Correspondent
CAPE KENNEDY, Wednesday.

TWO American astronauts made an emergency splash-down in the Pacific tonight after their Gemini-8 spacecraft completed the first link-up in space with another satellite.

The astronauts, Mr. Neil Armstrong, 35, and Major David Scott, 33, of the United States Air Force, were ordered to return when they reported that the main thruster rockets were not working properly after ending their link-up with an Agena satellite.

The spacecraft landed about 500 miles east of Okinawa, in the west Pacific, instead of in the Atlantic, south of Bermuda. The nearest vessel was the destroyer Leonard F. Mason, 2,425 tons about 160 miles away.

Other aircraft and ships were steaming toward the splash-down, weather was reported clear in the area. Waves were reported about three feet high but choppy.

Gemini control said the capsule was riding on the water "upright and quite normal."

Mr. John Hodge, 36, British-born flight director, made the decision to end the flight for the sake of the astronauts' safety after a feverish conference at mission control.

This flight, the first American one to be cut short because of a major emergency, had proceeded perfectly up to the link-up. The Agena was launched from Cape Kennedy exactly on time at 10 a.m.(3 p.m. GMT).

PERFECT LAUNCHING

Gemini-8 was launched "to the second," 110 minutes later. Communications were reported to be better than any other flight.

The spacecraft was placed in an almost-perfect eggshaped orbit ranging from an altitude of about 99 miles to about 168 miles. The Agena achieved a very nearly perfect circular orbit 185 miles up.

The manoeuvre was completed after Gemini had "chased" Agena for 120,000 miles and almost five times round the earth. The two craft flew in formation before the docking, made 6 1/2 hours after Gemini's launching.

As Gemini's nose was eased gently into Agena's collar, latches were closed into place to secure the two craft as they orbited the earth at about 17,500 m.p.h.

The flight was to have continued till Saturday. Gemini-8 and Agena were to stay locked together while the astronauts slept.

(March 17)

NO STARCH IN UNIFORMS FOR NURSES

Starch is likely to be dropped from nurses uniforms following prizegiving in London yesterday for winners of a competition to design a uniform on the assumption that it would normally be worn without cap or apron.

The winning entries featured knee-length, shirt-necked dresses and jackets in Terylene and cotton and Crimplene. First prize of 100gn went to Miss Chris Smith, 20, of Kingston College of Art.

(November 9)

PRIVATE EYE 'CANNOT AFFORD £5,000 DAMAGES'

Mr. Peter Cook, one of the defendants in the Private Eye libel case, said last night that the magazine could not afford to pay the £5,000 damages and £3,000 costs awarded in the High Court yesterday to Lord Russell of Liverpool.

Mr. A.P. Rushton, managing director of Pressdram Ltd., owners of Private Eye, said: "We have not got anything like £5,000. We will have to consider very seriously how we're going to get it." Mr. Richard Ingrams, the editor, said: "The atmosphere is full of gloom."

(February 4)

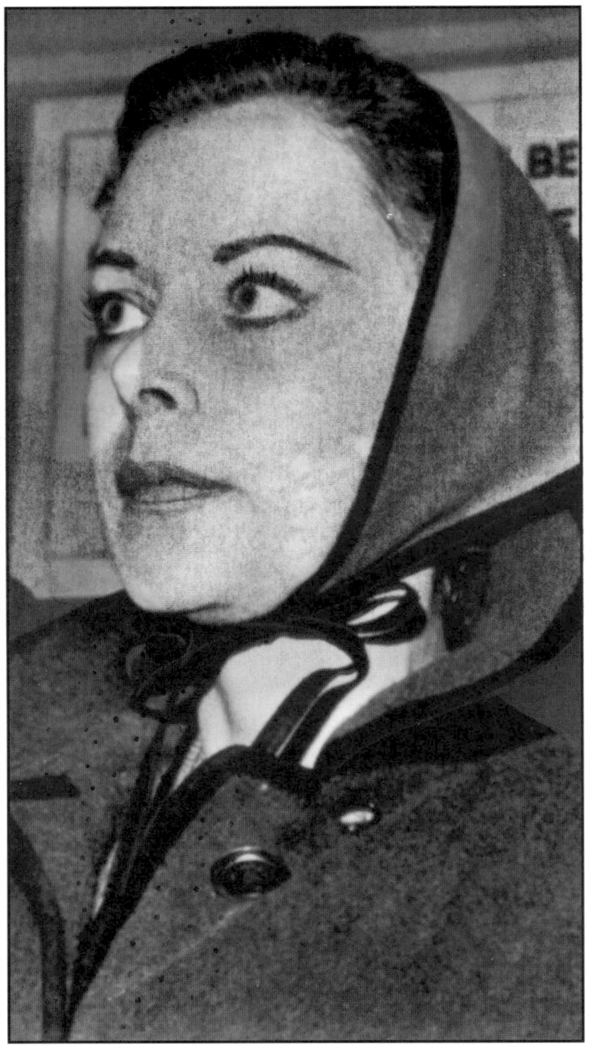

HEDY LAMARR

Hedy Lamarr on £30 theft charge

HEDY LAMARR, 51, the Vienna-born film actress, being released on bail from a Los Angeles gaol yesterday after she had been charged with stealing from a store clothing, a necklace and other items worth $86 (£30).

She was said to have been carrying cheques and personal valuables worth at lease $14,000 (£4,998) when she was arrested.

A lawyer who helped to obtain her release on bail said: "She had been shopping in the store with a friend and I am thoroughly convinced this is all a matter of a misunderstanding."

Miss Lamarr divorced Mr. Lewis W. Boles, her sixth husband, last June. He was ordered to pay her alimony of $1,250 (£446) a month, plus half of his gross income over $15,000 (£5,355) for two years.

(January 27)

Mob stones house in Belfast

Daily Telegraph Reporter

A MOB of about 2,000 people threw stones and bottles at a house in Belfast last night. It was one of several disturbances at the end of a day of celebrations to mark the 50th anniversary of the Easter Rising.

The trouble began when three girls aged about 20 wearing miniature Republican tricolours were chased by members of a Protestant parade which was entering Carlisle Circus.

One of the girls, who ran to police for protection, was taken into a house in Denmark Street. Howling with anger the mob broke all the windows. The crowd dispersed when 200 policemen arrived and sealed off the street.

In another incident police at a Royal Ulster Constabulary barracks at the junction of Falls Road and Glen Road, Belfast, rushed out when an explosion shook the area.

(April 18)

Man & his dog find World Cup

T.A. SANDROCK
Daily Telegraph Scotland Yard Correspondent

THE World Cup was found by a man exercising his dog last night. It was lying undamaged in the gateway of his home in Beulah Hill, Norwood.

Mr. David Corbett, 26, a Thames lighterman, found the trophy in the front garden as he left his ground floor flat with his mongrel dog, "Pickles" to go for a Sunday evening walk.

"I was about to put the lead on Pickles when I noticed he was sniffing at something near the path," he said. "I looked down and saw a bundle. I picked it up and saw it was wrapped in newspaper."

"I couldn't believe it for a few minutes, then I got into the car and drove to Gypsy Hill police station. Pickles saw it first - he found it, the little darling."

Intensive police inquiries which had gone on since Friday had failed to trace the cup, the Jules Rimet Trophy.

During the weekend Mr. Mears disclosed that he had been approached to "ransom" the trophy. A man phoned the Chelsea club, asked for him by name and was given his number.

The caller said Mr. Mears would receive a parcel the next day and that he should follow the instructions which would come with it. After the parcel arrived, there was a telephone call instructing Mr. Mears to put a message in a London evening paper.

It was arranged that when the man telephoned after the advertisement had appeared he would be told Mr. Mears could not keep the appointment but a friend of his would come. A detective was to take his place at the meeting, arranged for last Friday.

Later extensive police inquiries were made which resulted in a man being arrested and charged early on Saturday morning with being concerned in the theft of the World Cup. He appeared in court and was remanded.

(March 28)

RHODESIA 'MAY NOW BE REPUBLIC'

JOHN BULLOCH
Daily Telegraph Staff Correspondent
SALISBURY, Rhodesia, Thursday.

RHODESIA must become a republic following Britain's application to the United Nations for mandatory sanctions and she may already be one, Mr. Ian Smith said today.

He added that he was waiting for the opinion of his legal advisers to see if a referendum was necessary, or whether the British action had resulted in Rhodesia "automatically" becoming a republic.

Mr. Smith was speaking at a Press conference in Salisbury from which a number of local journalists and overseas correspondents were excluded.

He complained that the "ultimatum" given him aboard the Tiger meant he and his Cabinet had to give a quick verdict on a hasty and ill prepared document. Mr. Wilson, he said, "had the air of a hunted man" and had to do certain things by a certain time.

Mr. Smith said he was waiting for advice from legal and constitutional experts before taking the next step. If possible he would hold a referendum of everyone entitled to vote.

The question on whether or not the country should stay in the Commonwealth would be included, but he thought the decision had already been made for Rhodesia.

"If I am correct, this embarrassing decision, an agonising one for many Rhodesians, may be something we do not have to face up to. This is something Mr. Wilson has done for us."

(December 23)

RONALD REAGAN CANDIDATE FOR GOVERNORSHIP

Daily Telegraph Staff Correspondent
NEW YORK, Wednesday.

Ronald Reagan, 55, veteran of 50 films, was chosen by California's Republican voters as their candidate for the State's Governorship in next November's election. He defeated Mr. George Christopher, former mayor of San Francisco, by more than two to one.

On the Democratic side, Governor Edmund Brown, 61, who is seeking a third term, defeated Mr. Samuel Yorty, mayor of Los Angeles, but he only just managed to win his party's nomination. "I like a tough fight," he said philosophically today.

Mr. Reagan has been a film actor nearly 30 years. Politically he is close to the former Senator Goldwater, but not aggressively.

(June 9)

MARY QUANT MADE OBE IN BIRTHDAY HONOURS

Daily Telegraph Reporter

PETER SELLERS, 40, the actor, is made a CBE and Mary Quant, the Chelsea fashion designer, becomes an OBE in the Queen's Birthday Honours List published today. New Knights include Mr. Joe Richards, President of the Football League.

Six new life peers are created, including Dame Evelyn Sharp, 63, who was the first woman to become a Permanent Secretary, at the Ministry of Housing. They bring a total of life peerages since they were instituted to 124.

Other life peers are Prof. Ritchie Calder, 59, Professor of International Relations at Edinburgh University and a former Fleet Street journalist; Mr. John Cooper, 58, general secretary, National Union of General and Municipal Workers, and Sir John Hunt, leader of the Everest expedition, for services to youth.

The New Zealand detective story writer Ngaio Marsh, of Christchurch, becomes a D.B.E.

(June 11)

POLICE DOGS CAN DETECT MARIJUANA

METROPOLITAN police dog trainers have succeeded in teaching two Labradors to forget the scent of men and pick up only the scent of canabis, better known as marijuana.

They passed their final tests by working with the Yard's Drug Squad on five cases, and in each they found hidden and even buried drugs.

The two Labradors, Pytch, aged 20 months, and Rupert, just over four years old, were selected by Chief Insp. Morphy, the senior instructor at the school, from 10 of the best "scent" dogs in the Metropolitan Police district.

(March 9)

SHELL FINDS OIL IN MUSCAT

Daily Telegraph Reporter

Shell has struck oil in the Trucial State of Muscat and Oman.

The company hopes to be shipping out 10 million tons of crude oil a year by the end of next year and up to 15 million tons by 1970.

Shell, which has been short of crude oil recently, is spending £25 million on a 156-mile pipe-line to carry the oil overland.

It is also providing a port for tankers up to 165,000 tons.

(February 28)

BIG VOTE FOR ABORTION LAW REFORM

By ANDREW ALEXANDER
WESTMINSTER, Friday.

A PRIVATE Member's Bill to ease the laws on abortion was given a second reading today after an amendment for its rejection was defeated by a staggering 223 votes to 29, a majority of 194.

The size of the vote drew murmurs of surprise from the House and provoked a well-satisfied smile from the Bill's sponsor, Mr. David Steel (Lib., Roxburgh, Selkirk and Peebles), who, at 28, is one of the youngest M.P.s in the Commons.

The debate itself was impressive in its earnestness and standard of argument, as many Members were constantly pointing out. Emotionalism rarely broke through and some of the credit for that must go to Mr. Steel, who called for a restrained discussion of the issues and set an example in an strikingly cogent and well-thought-out speech.

Mr. Roy Jenkins, Home Secretary, spoke up for the Bill, in a personal capacity. The Government's view, he said, was entirely neutral. Like a number of other speakers, he emphasised that the present situation gave rise to one law for the rich and another for the poor.

The position was arbitrary and unsatisfactory.

The last spokesman against the Bill was Mr. St. John Stevas (C., Chelmsford) who described the Bill as barbarous.

But members present, one of the largest gatherings on a Friday for a long time, would have none of it. When it came to the vote, the result, though not the scale of it, was a foregone conclusion.

(July 23)

DOCTORS TO GET £1,000 RISE

BMA ATTACK: 'BITTER DISAPPOINTMENT

JOHN PRINCE
Daily Telegraph Health Services Correspondent

PAY rises, ranging from 10 per cent. to 35 per cent. are to be given by the Government to family doctors, hospital doctors and dentists.

The average salary of the country's 23,000 general practitioners will rise from £3,000 a year to £4,000. Half of the £28 million increase will be paid at once, the remainder next year.

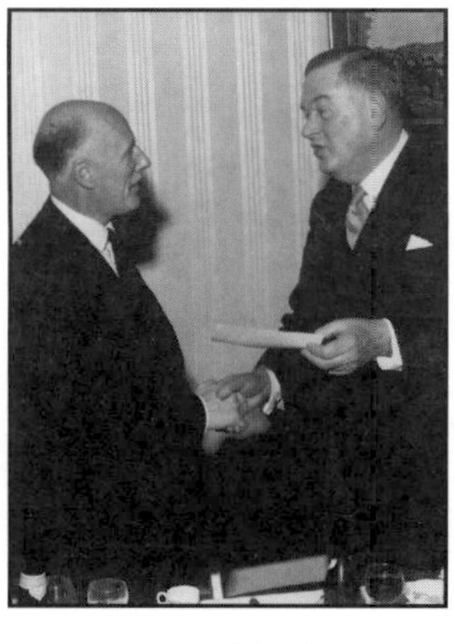

MR. STEVENSON (left) and Mr. Moore

Dentists and hospital doctors will get immediately the full rises recommended in the report of the Review Body on Doctors' and Dentists' Remuneration, published yesterday. Examples of the new pay for hospital staff, with the old in brackets, are:

CONSULTANTS: £3,200 - £4,885 (£2,910 - £4,445)

REGISTRARS: £1,650 - £2,050 (£1,425 - £1,595)

HOUSE OFFICERS: £1,100 - £1,300 (£770 - £940)

The family doctors' new pay structure, coupled with help towards better surgeries and employment of secretaries and nurses, could make for a renaissance of general practice.

BASIC ALLOWANCE
Extra for over-65s

There will be a new basic practice allowance of £1,000 a year, plus a fee of £1 for each patient or £1 8s where the patient is over 65 years of age plus 2s 6d for each patient on the doctor's list in excess of 1,000.

But the Prime Minister's announcement in the Commons that the full increase will be delayed for a year will displease many doctors. More tough bargaining lies ahead.

Dr. Derek Stevenson, secretary of the British Medical Association, said last night that the delay would "come to family doctors as a bitter and unexpected disappointment." His personal view was that the reaction would be one of anger.

(May 5)

25,000 join U.S. march last stage

THE three-week-old Mississippi "March Against Fear" for Civil Rights swept 25,000-strong into Jackson, the State capital tonight.

The marchers, mainly Negroes, but including many whites, converged for a mass rally outside the State Capitol in Jackson. Steel-helmeted State troopers with guns and gas ringed the building.

Demonstrators tore Confederate flags from the hands of startled segregationists.

A sizeable contingent of military police and National Guard moved unostentatiously into nearby barrack areas yesterday.

Meredith's protest

Dr. Martin Luther King, the moderate Civil Rights leader, and the Hollywood stars Marlon Brando, Burt Lancaster, Sammy Davis Junior, and Tony Franciosa, and the comedian Dick Gregory were in the march.

James Meredith, the Negro who started the march alone to encourage Mississippi Negroes to register to vote and was shot down by a segregationist, rejoined the demonstration. For two miles he defied doctors' orders not to walk, but then because of pain he rode in a car at the head of the march.

(June 27)

MENZIES GIVES UP AUSTRALIAN PREMIERSHIP

Daily Telegraph Correspondent
SYDNEY, Thursday.

Sir Robert Menzies, 71, today announced his retirement as Australian Prime Minister after a record 16-year term. He is also expected to resign his seat in Parliament.

The official resignation will be tendered to Lord Casey, the Governor-General, this afternoon. Sir Robert's successor, Mr. Harold Holt, 57, Federal Treasurer, is not expected to be sworn in until Tuesday to meet constitutional requirements.

The retirement of Senator Shane Paltridge, 56, Defence Minister and Government Leader in the Senate was announced yesterday. He has entered a Perth hospital, where he is seriously ill with chest cancer.

(January 20)

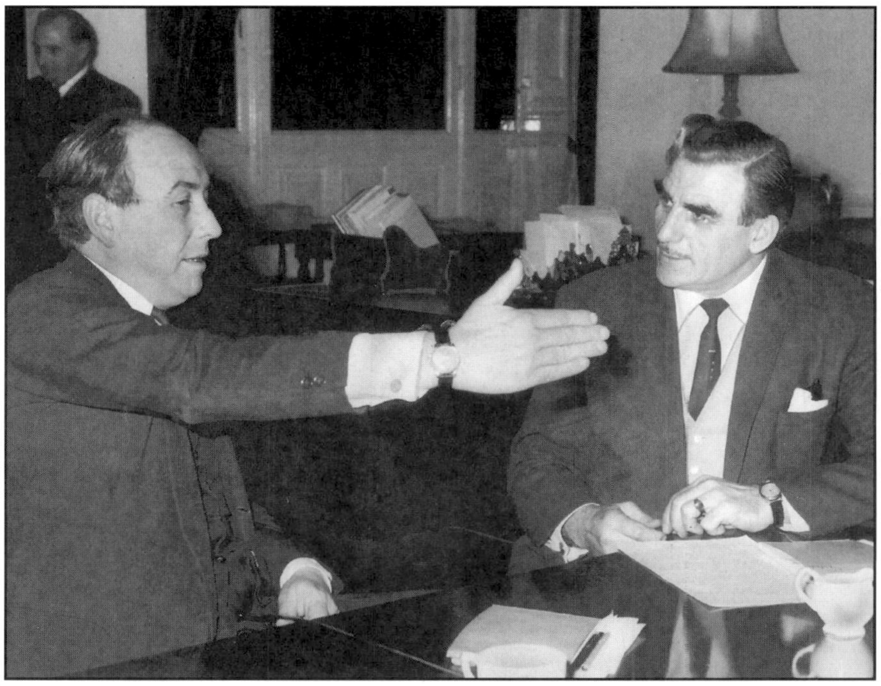

MR. JENKINS, HOME SECRETARY, explaining a point to Mr. Reginald Webb, chairman of the Police Federation, who led a deputation yesterday to discuss police manpower and efficiency. Mr. Jenkins agreed to set up an inquiry to be conducted by the Police Advisory Board.

JENKINS WILL 'AXE' 68 POLICE FORCES

Daily Telegraph Political Staff

A DRASTIC reorganisation of the police forces of England and Wales was announced in the Commons yesterday by Mr. Jenkins, Home Secretary.

Its general effect is that, either voluntarily or compulsorily, the number of forces will be reduced from 117 to 49 - a cut of 68. Provincial English police forces, which now range in size from 111 to 3,900 will be revised to between 663 and 6,700.

Mr. Jenkins intends to act with urgency. He hopes that as many as possible of the voluntary schemes will operate from April 1 next year.

Even where compulsion is necessary, the final target date is April 1, 1968. Examples of the suggested reorganisation are amalgamations of:

Twelve county borough police areas with LANCASHIRE;

Seven police areas with the WEST RIDING;

Five authorities in the THAMES VALLEY (Oxford City, Oxfordshire, Reading Berkshire and Buckinghamshire);

DEVON, PLYMOUTH and CORNWALL;

Four separate forces in WALES instead of 12.

The background to the Government's plan is that since 1961 the number of indictable offences has risen from 806,900 to more than a million in 1964 and a further increase is expected in last year's figures.

(May 19)

SNIPER IS SHOT DEAD AFTER 14 KILLINGS

IAN BALL
Daily Telegraph Staff Correspondent
NEW YORK, Monday.

A FORMER Marine killed his wife and mother, then shot dead 12 other people from the 26th floor observation room of the University of Texas in Austin today. Thirty-four people were wounded.

Fire engines and police using rifles with telescopic lenses ringed the tower as more than 100 bullets whined into the grounds. Ambulances were brought from all parts of Austin, and an armoured van was called in to pick up the wounded lying on lawns and footpaths.

After a siege lasting an hour and a half, police announced that the sniper was dead. A white flag appeared on the tower, then a man was dragged struggling from the building. Police said he died from bullet wounds on the way to hospital.

He was named as Charles Whitman, 24, an architectural engineering student at the University. Police said he was armed with a sporting rifle, two other rifles and a 38 pistol.

The shooting started at noon and was cruelly accurate, even at distances up to 500 yards. Most of those taken to hospital had been shot in the stomach and were in a critical condition.

As doctors were fighting to save the lives of some of the wounded, police forced an entry to Whitman's home. There they found the bodies of his wife and mother, apparently shot before the University massacre began.

The sniper frequently changed his firing position from one side of the slender tower to another. At times he fired in staccato bursts at other times there were single shots, about 30 seconds apart.

(August 2)

Anti-war film puts case for deterrent

Brig. W.F.K. THOMPSON
Daily Telegraph Military Correspondent

THE National Film Theatre was picketed by a small party of CND supporters yesterday when the BBC gave a private showing of their film "The War Game" by Peter Watkins.

This is the film which has stirred great controversy since the BBC's decision that it was unsuitable to be shown on television.

Before the film was shown, Mr. Kenneth Adam, Director of Television, assured us that the Governors of the BBC had taken their decision "carefully, reluctantly, I hope responsibly, I know independently."

After seeing the film I believe that on balance they were right.

Facing the facts, as the CND banners urged us, the first half of the film was, I think unintentionally, the strongest case for maintaining the nuclear deterrent I have yet seen.

If the message of the film is what it seemed to be, that Civil Defence is not worthwhile, we must presume that all should be so left.

(February 9)

HP curbs: £50 foreign holidays

A SIX-MONTH standstill on wages and dividends was announced by Mr. Wilson yesterday in his economic crisis statement to the House of Commons.

It will be followed by a further six months of severe restraint. Prices will also be "frozen" for 12 months.

In the first instance the Government would rely on workers and employers to observe the "freeze" voluntarily, but the Prices and Income Bill would be strengthened to ensure that "the selfish do not benefit."

Salaries and directors' fees subject to individual negotiation will also be affected. Companies will be required to supply details of them.

The Prime Minister's decision that "a time has come to call a halt" to inflationary wage increases had an immediate effect on foreign exchange markets. The pound rallied.

Other points in Mr. Wilson's austerity package deal, the effect of which will be to reduce demand on the domestic economy by £500 million and to save £150 million in overseas payments, are:

HIRE PURCHASE: Minimum deposit on cars, motor-cycles and caravans was raised at midnight from 25 to 40 per cent. and the repayment period cut from 27 months to 24 months. Deposit on domestic goods raised from 25 per cent. to 33 ⅓ per cent., but the repayment period remains at 24 months.

TRAVEL ALLOWANCE: Starting on Nov. 1 the basic allowance will be cut from £250 to £50 for persons going outside the sterling area. The £50 will have to cover all the cost of hotels and travel, except for fares paid for in sterling in Britain.

(July 21)

BOMB BLOWS UP DUBLIN MONUMENT

Daily Telegraph Reporter

The 134-ft high Nelson's Column in O'Connell Street, Dublin, was blown-up early today.

The granite column, similar to that in Trafalgar Square, and a tourist attraction, was blown in half by the explosion. Tons of rubble were strewn across the road.

Police, working by searchlight, closed O'Connell Street to traffic until engineers could inspect the remains of the pillar and see if it was safe.

The explosives are thought to have been hidden on the winding staircase inside the column. One policeman said it was a "professional job."

(March 8)

LABOUR OUSTED AT CARMARTHEN

H.B. BOYNE
Daily Telegraph Political Correspondent

IN a staggering anti-Government swing, the Welsh Nationalists have captured with a majority of nearly 2,500 Carmarthen, the seat which Labour had held by more than 9,000 only three and a half months ago.

After perhaps the most depressing day of his Prime Ministry, Mr. Wilson must have felt he was really up against it when he learned the by-election result early this morning.

The result declared early today, with General Election figures in italics, was:-

G. EVANS
(Welsh party) **16,179** *7,416*
G.P. DAVIES
(Lab.) **13,743** *21,221*
H. DAVIES
(Lib.) **8,650** *11,988*
S. DAY (C.) **2,934** *5,338*
Welsh party maj. **2,436**

The only consolation for the Government is that the Conservative lost his deposit by an even greater margin than at the General Election. But Carmarthen, so far as Conservatives are concerned, was never more than a token fight.

The uncomfortable fact, from Mr. Wilson's viewpoint, is that there are 167 constituencies which Labour holds with majorities smaller, expressed as percentages, than was Carmarthen's.

While none of them, probably, is in any danger from Plaid Cymru, the Carmarthen result proves that all are vulnerable to a change of heart away from Labour.

It can no longer be argued with such conviction that the electorate everywhere is still in the mood to "give the Government a chance."

Hundreds of cheering men and women gathered in Carmarthen for the result. Many cried openly and hugged each other when the result was made known.

(July 15)

Mrs. Gandhi's peace pledge as Premier

Rawle Knox
Daily Telegraph Staff Correspondent
NEW DELHI, Wednesday.

MRS. INDIRA GANDHI, 48-year-old daughter of Mr. Nehru and newly elected Prime Minister of India, pledged tonight that she would "strive to create what my father used to call a climate of peace."

She told reporters that she would honour the Tashkent agreement with Pakistan signed by Mr. Shastri, her predecessor. When asked if she planned an early India-Pakistan "summit" conference, she said: "Not at the moment."

Mrs. Gandhi beat Mr. Morarji Desai, 69, former Finance Minister, by 355 votes to 199 in the contest within the ruling Congress party members of the two Houses of Parliament.

Report to President

Crowds gathered outside Parliament House, where the election was held, cheered her wildly as she went to the President's House to report. She will not become Prime Minister until she submits her Cabinet to the President.

Mr. Desai pledged his full co-operation with Mrs. Gandhi.

"Skilled for job"

Sanjay Gandhi, 19, son of Mrs. Gandhi, who is studying in Crewe, said last night: "I am sure she has the stamina and political skill to do the job properly. But I also know that at times she would like to be living a simple, ordinary life."

(January 20)

£25,000 BOND PRIZE

The third £25,000 Premium Savings Bond prize, announced at the start of the 111th draw yesterday was won by number IZP 995067 one of a £500 block. Winning numbers for the £5,000, £1,000 and £500 prizes are given on page 15.

(August 2)

Impassioned, skilful plea for peace

By ERIC SHORTER

"US" at the Aldwych is an elaborately unambiguous soapbox drama: an impassioned plea by Peter Brook and others for an end to the war in Vietnam and, by implication, to the nastiness in human nature.

It is quite the most unusual entertainment in London and will not be missed by any playgoer who is interested in the art of what is called Didactic Theatre. But it is also often boring, obvious, and sometimes pandering to a particular kind of audience of whom it finally makes amusing fun.

The message can be taken as read. Presumably we all hate horror. What cannot be taken as read. is the astonishing skill, variety, force and pungency with which much of it is noisily delivered.

Is there any director more adept than Mr. Brook in achieving such compelling pregnant silences on stage? Was ever London audience more politely confused than by the agonised moans of half the cast with their heads in paper bags, groping their way, blindly down to the stalls to see what we would do?

Did ever a show end more embarrassingly as the company stands accusingly silent on stage awaiting or daring our diffident departure? It was Kenneth Tynan who last night fortunately gave the signal, but who will be there tomorrow?

And even if it all seems irksomely solemn, there is a notable vigour and freshness in the stage pictures; particularly Sally Jacobs' vast rubbery symbolic corpse draped over the proscenium arch and once solemnly lowered.

(October 14)

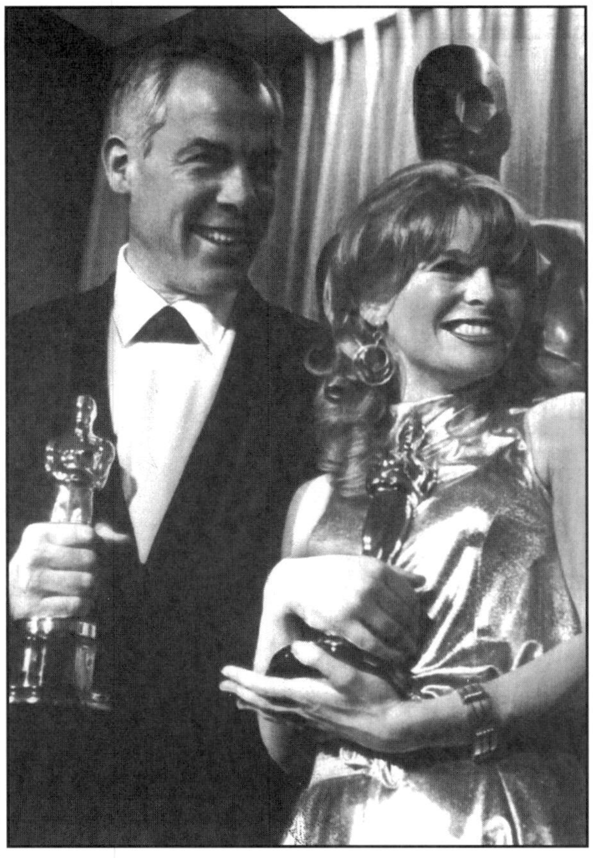

LEE MARVIN AND JULIE CHRISTIE with their Oscar academy awards after the Hollywood presentation. They won the best actor and actress awards respectively for "Cat Ballou" and "Darling."

ZHIVAGO'S WASTED YEARS

By PATRICK GIBBS

SO often has a film based on a well-known novel or play born little resemblance to the original that it would seem that producers buy copyrights largely for publicity value of a good title.

Regrettably this appears to have been the case with the film of Doctor Zhivago (Empire "A"), with which it seems almost an impertinence to connect the name of the author, Boris Pasternak.

I say "regrettably" because we have here not just any old bestseller but what has been generally acknowledged to be that rarity, the great contemporary novel - perhaps (in Edmund Wilson's opinion) one of the great novels of all times.

The tallest possible order for any film-maker and, not surprisingly, it turns out to be far beyond the capabilities of the producer, Carlo Ponti, most of whose recent films have been lighthearted comedies for such players as Marcello Mastroianni and Sophia Loren.

Potted Pasternak

Certainly the director, David Lean, and adaptor, Robert Bolt, have done satisfying work in the past, collaborating, for instance, on "Lawrence of Arabia." Here Mr. Lean seems to be more inspired by the scene than the text, making something both spectacular and significant of "the vast countryside glowering under revolution and war," especially in the snowbound rigours of winter. But in more intimate scenes he is given nothing very satisfactory to work on by Mr. Bolt, whose version of the novel is very much potted Pasternak.

Presumably to avoid having two casts, Mr. Bolt has dispensed with these childhoods pretty well entirely; and at least one important episode in which Zhivago sees Lara for the first time after the attempted suicide of her mother and realises she is Komarovsky's mistress loses much of its effect through Zhivago being a grown man rather than a boy.

Even so, these early Moscow scenes in which the young Lara is seduced by her mother's middle-aged protector are the most effective in the whole film, partly because neither of these characters needs the elaborate introduction others require if they are to be understood, but largely because the players concerned, Julie Christie and Rod Steiger, seem perfectly to understand the characters they are portraying.

If other players give just the opposite impression, not they but Mr. Bolt is to blame for having wiped out their childhoods.

As for the famous passages of dialogue, they are missing, too, and anyone hoping to hear in this context those brave words "the great misfortune, the root of all evil to come, was the loss of faith in the value of personal opinions," will be in for a disappointment.

In fact the novel's comment, that it is the individual who is important rather than the system is not only dimished but, as I interpret the final scene, actually perverted.

No Compensation

While we do certainly see the disrupting affect on people's lives of the revolution, especially during the savage civil war, the final scene with its background of a splendid Soviet-made dam and introduction of a nice Communist youth to look after Zhivago's and Lara's daughter suggests that the end has, indeed, justified the means whereas the novel makes clear that to Pasternak nothing that later happened could compensate for the miseries imposed on people by Communism.

Compared with this monstrous misrepresentation what Mr. Bolt does with a balaaika handed to Zhivago after his mother's death; what Mr. Lean does with a field of daffodils which grows conveniently outside the lovers' hideout in the Urals; and what the composer, Maurice Jarre, does with what will doubtless be called the "Lara" theme, can be judged as merely harmless lapses of taste.

(April 29)

Recent Fiction

Love-Hate under the Raj

ANY book of importance, said a literate philosopher, should be re-read immediately. Lack of time prevents me from re-reading Paul Scott's "The Jewel in the Crown" just now, but I know that closer acquaintance will enhance my high opinion of it. Its proper place on any book shelf is beside "A Passage to India."

An English girl falls in love with an Anglicised Indian. She is raped one evening in a deserted garden. Her friend is among those arrested. What is the truth? How did it come about? The questions ripple outwards until all India is in our mind, and the total experience of the English presence in India.

Mr. Scott is concerned, as Mr. Forster was, with what a character in this novel calls the "area of dangerous fallibility" - the no-man's land between intention and realisation, where abstraction becomes reality, and rationality is hopelessly distorted by the reason of the heart. He is no less pre-occupied than the old master with the Anglo-Indian love-hate relationship and the fragility of liberal

The Jewel in the Crown.
By Paul Scott. Heinemann. 30s.)

Last Exit to Brooklyn.
By Hubert Selby, Jnr.
(Calder & Bovars. 20s.)

attitudes. But his theme is pursued at a time (1942) when the Raj is tottering, and the subtleties of personal relations are jarred into disorder by huge social convulsions.

What is the truth? Mr. Scott asks. What, in fact, is Truth? To come at his answer he has had to find a method of portraying the epic movements of the time in terms of fully realised individuals - a technique of reconciling within a coherent whole the delicacy of a miniature and the boldness of a vast panoramic canvas. I.H.

(July 28)

IT'S a hard life for the brutally honest author who writes a book about the dregs of modern society. If he escapes the clutches of the ban-it-and-burn-it brigade, it is only to be quietly smothered by the we-don't-stock-it boys.

Thus I understand that one of our leading booksellers is refusing to stock Hubert Selby Jr.'s "Last Exit to Brooklyn.," though I believe it will obtain the book for customers shameless enough to order it. As a result, one of the most important novels to come out of America in recent years has been virtually relegated to little back-street bookshops, to rub shoulders with horror comics and grubby sex manuals.

Admittedly, this novel is not the ideal birthday present for a maiden aunt; it contains the alltime record number of obscenities per page, and it occasionally made me feel physically sick.

But unless we are smugly determined to ignore the pitiful but dangerous uncivilisation, we need a Selby to depict the sub-strata of modern society as much as the Victorian age needed Dickens and Mayhew. What is remarkable about "Last Exit to Brooklyn" is that it is not simply masterly reportage but attains a truly tragic stature.

(February 10) R.B.

Oscar for Julie Christie

A TEARFUL, gasping Julie Christie was awarded last night the Hollywood Oscar for the best actress of 1965.

Shaking with joy and able only to splutter out her thanks, she fell into the arms of Rex Harrison when he handed her the award. She won her Oscar for her portrayal of the amoral London model girl in "Darling."

Miss Christie, 25, last Thursday, created a small sensation at the ceremony in Santa Monica, California, by wearing a gold lamé trouser outfit, the first time a woman had accepted an Oscar in anything but evening gown.

"Darling," a relatively low-budget film, won two other awards. Frederick Raphael was given an Oscar for best screenplay written directly for the screen and Miss Julie Harris won the award for best costume design for a black-and-white film.

"The sound of Music," in which Julie Andrews, winner of last year's best actress award, has the starring role, was selected as the best film of 1965. Lee Marvin, who played the drunk in "Cat Ballou," a spoof on Westerns, won the Oscar for best actor.

(April 20)

ACADEMY HAS BLOODLESS REVOLUTION

By GERDA PAUL

THE Royal Academy has undergone a bloodless revolution. Gone is the system of having rows and rows of respectable, conventional pictures, with modern, daring stuff banished to one gallery like naughty children.

At this year's summer exhibition which opens to the public tomorrow the two are merged for the first time.

Abstracts and semi-abstracts more numerous than ever before hang side by side with the portraits of aldermen in robes, the "old school" landscapes, and other "straight" stuff in every one of the galleries.

One feels that modern art at last has arrived, that it is accepted into the social circle.

BRATBY MURAL
"Feeding the 5,000"

Some of the modern works are not only sincere but distinctly religious. John Bratby, with his huge mural "Feeding of the Five Thousand" is again likely to be the most talked about artist.

The painting has 35 figures in modern dress, himself among them as Christ, a great many fishes, a clump of irises and huge rocks like ice floes.

Less striking, but even more controversial, is Anthony Green's "Black Crucifix," a scene of men and women in drab underclothing milling about against a black cross.

The portrait of the Queen as Air Commodore-in-Chief, Royal Air Force Regiment, by Huseph Riddle, 53, a member of the Royal Society of Portrait Painters, is very like her. Sir Charles Wheeler said he thought it an extremely good portrait.

Mr. Riddle, a former fighter pilot, was commissioned to do it by the RAF Regiment. The Queen gave him about half a dozen sittings at the Palace, and he said she was "absolutely charming."

(May 6)

PLAY'S PLEA FOR HOMELESS FAMILIES

By SYLVIA CLAYTON

"CATHY Come Home," shown last night on BBC1 was not a television play but a fierce propaganda poster signalling the distress of the homeless. The author, Jeremy Sandford, claimed that every incident described was authentic.

He followed the painful downhill journey of a young couple who began their married life full of hope and gaiety and ended it as casualties of the Welfare State, separated from their children.

After an accident cut the husband's earnings, the couple lived with unfriendly relatives, were evicted from squalid tenements, were driven out of a caravan site, and finally found unhappy refuge in a bleak, rat-ridden hostel.

I should have preferred to see a problem of this magnitude treated as a full-scale documentary investigation rather than a tragic individual love story, but the suffering of decent, bewildered people was powerfully conveyed.

Tony Garnett and Kenneth Loach directed a vivid, noisy, sometimes over-emphatic production, which showed with compassion the raw degradations of hostel life. A large cast, headed by Carol White and Ray Brooks as the young couple, showed once again how strongly the technique of naturalistic acting has developed on television.

(November 17)

NOVEL EARNS $2m BEFORE PUBLICATION

A FORTNIGHT before publication of the book, "In Cold Blood," Truman Capote, the author, has received $2 million (£714,000) in magazine, book and film payments. This is about $14 (£5) a word.

Mr. Capote calls his book "the non-fiction novel." It has taken six years to write and is the result of "playing with the idea of a book that would synthesise fictional techniques with journalism."

He said today: "Considering the work and all the years of training that went into that book, it is not a very fantastic bonanza. When you average it out over six years, and consider the taxes, any small-time Wall Street operator gets at least that much."

The story tells of the murder of a couple, their son and daughter in a small Kansas town, of the criminals who killed them, and the detectives who solved the crime.

(January 1)

SEIZED BOOK WILL STAY ON SALE, SAYS PUBLISHER

Daily Telegraph Reporter

MR. JOHN CALDER, publisher of "Last Exit to Brooklyn," which a magistrate at Marlborough Street decided on Saturday would "tend to deprave and corrupt," said yesterday that he intended to keep the book on sale in Britain.

The magistrate, Mr. Leo Gradwell, ordered that three copies of the book, seized from the premises of Calder and Boyars in Brewer Street, Soho, should be destroyed.

The books were seized under Section 3 of the Obscene Publications Act, 1959, after an information had been laid by Sir Cyril Black, Conservative M.P. for Wimbledon.

Mr. Calder said the only effect of the decision was the destruction of the three copies. They would continue to sell the book within the jurisdiction of the Marlborough Street court and elsewhere.

"Psychological warfare"

It was "purely psychological warfare." They were expecting a sustained attack on the book and other proceedings for seizure to be brought under Section 3.

He would prefer action by the Director of Public Prosecutions under Section 2 of the Act, when the defendant can opt for trial by jury, to a series of attacks under Section 3.

Giving his ruling on Saturday, Mr. Gradwell said that "Last Exit to Brooklyn" by the American author, Hubert Selby, junior, would certainly, taken as a whole, tend to "deprave and corrupt. I cannot think in spite of the evidence I have heard that it can be justified by literary merit."

(December 12)

BOB DYLAN IS BARRACKED AFTER SONGS

Incredibly, although up to £10 was being offered for £1 tickets for Bob Dylan's concert at the Albert Hall last night, barracking broke out among a section of the audience. It followed a series of noisy songs, most of whose words were incomprehensible, in which Dylan was accompanied by a quite ordinary rhythm group.

He won over the main body of the audience with a typical stroke. "Oh, come on," he said with coaxing irony. "These are all protest songs."

This apparent call to stand up and be counted checked a dangerous situation but after that whole rows sat with scarcely a sign of applause at the end of numbers.

(May 27)

BEATLES STAY ON TOP FOR FOUR WEEKS

The Beatles head the Melody Maker's Top Ten records for the fourth successive week with "We Can Work It Out," and "Day Tripper." Spencer Davis's "Keep On Running," fourth last week, is now second, in place of Ken Dodd's "The River," now third.

(January 4)

Dr. Who is chosen

The BBC has chosen Patrick Troughton to play the part of Dr. Who in its children's television serial, in place of William Hartnell.

When "Dr. Who" returns on Sunday week Mr. Hartnell will still be playing the name part. The switch in actors, which will be one of the surprises of the serial story, will not take place until November.

(September 2)

"TWANG!!' TO CLOSE AFTER £80,000 LOSS

Daily Telegraph reporter

The Lionel Bart musical "Twang!!" is to end its run at the Shaftesbury Theatre today fortnight. Notices giving the statutory 14 days' notice were posted last night.

Mr. Bart, 34, told the 50-strong cast that the show was a financial flop. It has lost about £80,000 since it opened in London on Dec. 20.

(January 15)

BBC SERIES COCKNEY IN ITS HUMOUR

BBC television's new comedy series "Till Death Us Do Part," an offshoot of its Comedy Playhouse, is a well recognisable chip from the Steptoe mould, written by Johnny Speight. It leans heavily on the love-hate relations of different generations each with their own bias against the other.

(June 7)

WAS · IS · & · WILL · BE
1855 LONDON
THE DAILY TELEGRAPH
AND
MORNING POST
DAILY TELEGRAPH - - - JUNE 29, 1855
MORNING POST - - - NOVEMBER 2, 1772
[Amalgamated October 1, 1937]
135, Fleet Street, London, E.C.4.
Telephone: Fleet Street 4242

FREEZE FOR ALL

IF the Government's proposals for reducing public spending are vague, its ideas about freezing wages and prices seem to be vaguer. Mr. WILSON'S statement called for a standstill of wages and other incomes for six months followed by a further six months of severe restraint. He also made a call for a halt in price rises for a year, with some exceptions such as those made inevitable by increases in taxation. There is little indication so far that much more will be involved in the first place than a renewal of Ministerial exhortation.

MR. WILSON mentioned that the Prices and Incomes Bill will also be strengthened in some unspecified way. To go by past experience the wooliness of his statement indicated the vacuity of policy thinking. How are we to interpret the statement that, where commitments exist to increase pay or reduce hours, these are to be deferred for six months? There will no doubt be cases of employers back-dating pay increases. It is not clear that such retroactive settlements need be caught by the freeze. The potential loopholes are legion. It will be interesting to see whether some exception will be made in favour of the staff of Transport House, who were due for rises of the order of 40 per cent. - the final decision being ironically delayed until the very day of the statement.

It is well-nigh certain that one way or another earnings will rise. The principle of voluntary wage restraint is not only unworkable but invidious as well. The patriots will get nothing, the self-seekers will get all. The swollen bureaucracy of the Prices and Incomes Board may indeed hold down prices rather more effectively. Yet this will defeat the main end of Government policy, which is to restrain home demand and thus reduce imports. It is rather quaint that what are rather imprecisely called the "gnomes" seem to be in favour of the freeze, however little they would think of applying it in their own countries.

(July 2)

ULTIMATE CORRUPTION

AVARICE, fear, lust, jealousy, revenge - the common motives for murder are so related to the temptations to which all human flesh is subject that few sensitive spirits can exclude moments of sympathy and pity for the prisoner in the dock. The terrible fascination exerted by the "Moors" trial over the public mind throughout this country and far beyond reflects the sense that here has broken into the human life we know a thing utterly inhuman, that we have had a glimpse of naked evil, unashamed. Nevertheless these two pitiless child-killers are not satanic creatures from another world, but examples of human nature reduced to extreme corruption; and the evidence has indicated something of the process of their descent into depravity.

"Sadism" is cruelty rooted in sexual perversion, or exercised as a stimulant to perverted erotic sensation. In this case the actual works of the Marquis DE SADE, with much else of a similar tendency, were the drugs with which IAN BRADY and MYRA HINDLEY poisoned their minds. Other malign figures exercised a spell upon them: they appear to have soaked themselves in the mythology of HITLER and the bestial Nazi crimes against humanity. Our generation has reacted strongly against the principle of literary censorship, and a single dreadful example is not a ground for repudiating the belief in the free circulation of ideas, even those most repellent to the normal mind. Nevertheless this appalling case is a salutary reminder that the printed word can deepen depravity which other things, including horror films, may have started. It is a case not to be forgotten in discussion of issues affecting the exposure of susceptible minds to corrupting influences.

(May 7)

CHANGING TIMES

During its long and distinguished history, the Times newspaper has gone through many strange vicissitudes. Last night, however, was a turning point: subject to the Board of Trade's permission, yet to be granted, it ceased to be an independent newspaper. Perhaps this had to be: finance may have dictated it. If so, there is no point in weeping for what cannot be helped.

The group it seeks to join, moreover, is of a peculiarly loose and tolerant sort. At its head sits LORD THOMSON, who has never concealed the fact that he runs newspapers not to make propaganda, or for any higher or lower public purpose, but simply for gain. DR. JOHNSON once remarked that a man was seldom so innocently employed as in making money and LORD THOMSON'S record supports him. The newspapers of the Thomson Organisation cannot be called independent, but they do enjoy many of the priviliges of independence.

(October 1)

HOMOSEXUALITY

MR. HUMPHRY BERKELEY'S Sexual Offences Bill, which aims to legalise homosexual behaviour between consenting adults in private, was yesterday given a second reading by the Commons. Of M.P.s, 164 voted in its favour, 107 against. This division almost exactly reproduces feeling in the country, in which, according to the polls, 63 per. cent. of those asked approve the substance of the measure. This disposes of one hoary argument against it — that public opinion is not yet ripe.

What will the Bill achieve if passed? It will remind people afresh of the valuable but often blurred distinction between sin and crime; it will end a law equally disreputable for being largely unenforceable and often cruel where enforced; it will lift a great fear from many people, no more sinful than most of their neighbours; it will cut the blackmailers income; not least it will end a controversy which has become unseemly and disproportionate, and rob homosexuality of the false glamour which always attaches to persecuted minorities.

(February 12)

The Marks of Britain's Decadence

By ANTHONY LEJEUNE

AN intelligent young woman recently returned to Britain after working in America told me the other day that seeing this country again with fresh eyes had profoundly shocked her. "I really think," she said, "that Britain has become the most decadent nation in the Western world."

The only unusual thing about this comment was that it came from an Englishwoman; from a candid American or European it would not have been in the least remarkable.

Anyone who has travelled abroad during the past few years, or who talks often to foreigners visiting Britain, must be aware that there are, to put it mildly, aspects of the contemporary British scene which have not merely surprised the outside world but which increasingly provoke its contempt and derision.

That deep-rooted changes have taken place is clear. To call them symptoms of decadence may be facile as an explanation, but has a disturbing ring of truth. They certainly deserve harder scrutiny, a more critical examination than we generally find it comfortable to give them.

One of the first things which strikes anybody from overseas, trivial in itself, perhaps, but spectacular and not without significance, is the physical appearance of many young people: the extraordinary long hair of the boys, the unkemptness of the girls, the weirdness of their clothes. We may laugh at these extravagances of juvenile fashion, or shrug them off as unimportant: we may even laugh at the censorious foreigners who disapprove of them: but the fact remains that most foreigners do disapprove of them, and the keenest disapproval is expressed by visitors from those countries which are furthest from being, in any sense, decadent.

London has been described by several journalists lately as having become "the fashion centre of the world." What they mean is not what such a compliment would once have meant - that London tailoring is unmatched in the quality of its workmanship., in its durability and in its classic good taste: but that the most extreme of juvenile fashions originate and proliferate here. Britain also has the dubious international distinction of being hailed as the Mecca of pop music, not just the home of the Beatles and Rolling Stones but spiritual home of the whole tribe.

"Fashion Centre"

Modern British fashions, whether in clothes or music or speech of manners, no longer percolate down from an upper class; on the contrary, the upper classes now adopt them from the lower. And the level at which they are created is often very low, not merely in a social sense, but in terms of quality and talent.

All these changes and many more are summed up in the current boast that London, which used to be staid and stuffy, has become a "swinging" city. It cannot be wholly a coincidence that the new swinging London is also a city in which crime and drug taking have increased at an alarming rate. Britain's juvenile delinquents may still seem innocuous compared with the dangerous young animals who prowl the streets of some foreign cities, but our non-delinquent juveniles have established a collective image which is as bad as any in the world. To comprehend this image in its full horror one has only to look at the BBC's television programme, "A Whole Scene Going." In which the male compere can be distinguished from his female colleague, it has been helpfully pointed out, because his hair is longer and parted in the middle.

What is so horrifying is not that some teenagers should enjoy such a programme but that the BBC should produce it. Similarly, obscenities on the Eamonn Andrews Show or in the BBC's satire programmes do not matter in themselves; what matters is that people who think such remarks, in public, normal or amusing should be invited as guests and admired as celebrities.

The culture or sub-culture to which these phenomena belong is essentially rootless and feverish. One degenerate form of it, known as "pop culture," has actually been defined by its admirers as being consciously ephemeral. It is, nevertheless, powerful and pervasive; so pervasive that many of its natural opponents have given up the struggle.

No one, however, can merely withdraw and get on with his own business, because one of the characteristic trends of modern Britain has been the movement toward collectivism, making independence and self-sufficiency almost impossible, treating the desire for them as though it were a vice rather than a virtue.

The result is plain to see; a nation which has lost its pride and its confidence, though not its complacency; which has lost the will to play a strong role in the world; a nation in which envy and mass bribery are the currency of domestic politics; a nation chronically in debt, living behind crumbling facades which it can no longer afford to maintain.

"Decadence" is an imprecise, but not a meaningless word; it refers to a state of mind which really does overtake nations and individuals. Its manifestations are well enough known to be diagnostically useful.

In art, for example, they are the effects of a jaded palate; extravagance of taste, a sophisticated yearning for the primitive, impatience with straightforward quality; a desire to shock and increasing difficulty in doing so; an accelerating turnover of fashions. In philosophy and in the conversation of intellectuals there will be comparable symptoms. The wider symptoms will be a breaking down of discipline, of traditional structures, of established values, and their replacement with a blend of carelessness and anxiety, of cynicism and credulity.

These symptoms were present during Rome's decline.

(April 12)

CHINA'S FLOWERS DROOP

VIA OVICIPITIUM DURA EST - the way of the egghead is hard. It certainly is in China. Times have changed since Chairman MAO upheld the cause of intellectual freedom under which the proverbial thousand flowers should bloom. Now China's intellectuals from the highest to lowest are on the run. They are being chased from the cloisters to the factories, mines and barracks where they are to be "tempered" in the white heat of Peking's "social-cultural revolution." If anything further was needed to convince the lesser intelligentsia that their future is no bed of roses, that has been provided by the latest abject statement of KUO MO-JO. For he is China's leading intellectual and he has just publicly eaten the millions of words he has produced in the past, calling them verbiage fit only for the fire.

The roots of present intolerance are to be found in the anxieties of old men. China's political establishment is the oldest in the world. It is also more cut off from outside influences and more absorbed in its own fantasies than any other ruling class. Chairman MAO is apparently obsessed with the fear that he will share the fate of STALIN, that his political heirs will not respect his memory but revile it, will not keep faith with the principles of the revolution but follow some new ideological heresy. These worries grow more morbid as evidence mounts of the failure of the regime's policies. So the old men are in a hurry to brainwash their successors. In turn there have been campaigns against the armed forces, the bureaucracy, and now the scholars. In attacking the latter the regime is opposing the ancient tradition of the mandarin. Chairman MAO is himself a distinguished classical Chinese scholar and poet, and Premier CHOU EN-LAI went to the Sorbonne.

(May 2)

Union Jack clothes shock Americans

The "instant patriotism" of clothes shown in New York this week by the Associated Fashion Designers of London amused many young Americans but shocked officials of various patriotic organisations which campaign against improper use of the American flag.

The American groups had a purely academic interest in the show since it was the Union Jack, not the Stars and Stripes, that was employed by the designer. But they gave notice that any use of the American flag in imported styles would provoke the sternest possible reaction.

(February 26)

Last stand of the Old Contemptibles

Daily Telegraph Reporter

A STRONG gust of wind caught the Old Contemptibles' branch standards lined up on the steps of St. Paul's Cathedral yesterday.

The bearers struggled manfully. But some of the more frail bent like reeds and two of the standards tumbled to the ground.

"Can't hardly hold them up, can they, just as well they're making it the last one." said a young man in the watching crowd, not unsympathetically.

"It was the last national parade of the Old Contemptibles, veterans of the 1914-18 war. As Mr. W.D. Goss, their organiser, told me: "Hardly anyone is under 70, and you can't go on. We decided this would be the parade of parades."

Gleaming medals

And so, in spite of the frailties, it was. More than a thousand took part, three times as many as last year. Rows of medals gleaming on their civilian suits, their bowlers, homburgs and caps at a smart angle, the "Chums" rallied in the City near the Bank, and marched to the Cathedral.

Luckily the rain cleared in time, and umbrellas and mackintoshes were tucked under swinging arms.

At their head came the Band of the Grenadier Guards, and the President of the Old Contemptibles' Association. Lt.-Gen. Sir Edmond Schreiber. In the ranks of men who fought the terrible battles in France and Belgium were three V.C.s, Brigadier G.R. Roupell, the Rev. G.H. Woolley, and Mr. S.J. Bent.

The cathedral was crowded. Many old soldiers who had been unable to march in procession came in leaning on sticks. A few blind men were led, and there were some in wheelchairs.

Afterwards the Duchess of Gloucester and the Ambassadors of Belgium and France took the salute from a temporary base halfway down Ludgate Hill.

To the tune of "Tipperary" the old soldiers swung into their last march.

(May 23)

WILLIAM THE CONQUEROR NOT FORGIVEN

The tiny Normandy commune of Veauville has refused to join in this year's celebrations marking the ninth centenary of William the Conqueror's landing in England. William imposed a heavy tax on the place to help subsidise his expedition, and he has never been forgiven for it.

(February 5)

LONDON DAY BY DAY

MR. ENOCH POWELL'S remarkable speech on defence yesterday occupied exactly one hour and a quarter. To maintain a sustained argument and the attention of the whole House for so long is for a member of the Opposition, a rare feat.

On the Government side his audience was small but select. Soon after he had risen the Prime Minister arrived, followed by Mr. Brown. Like Mr. Healey, the Chancellor of the Exchequer was present throughout.

In fairness to Mr. Wilson it must be said that he took in good part and without attempting to interrrupt Mr. Powell's final passages assailing his speech on the Navy to the electors of Plymouth in 1964.

It recalled a gesture by Winston Churchill when Aneurin Bevan, making as Mr. Powell made yesterday one of the memorable speeches of his career, began a direct attack on him as Leader of the Opposition. "Don't spoil a good speech now," murmured Churchill.

Neck and Neck

READING Conservative Association may be cutting things a bit fine with the special constituency tie it is putting on sale today. The dark blue tie is exbroidered with the figure "X," for Mr. Peter Emery's 10-vote majority at the last General Election.

The agent, Bryan Edgell, tells me that only 200 will be sold, so the tie should be fairly exclusive. But only Mr. Wilson can decide how soon it may be out of date.

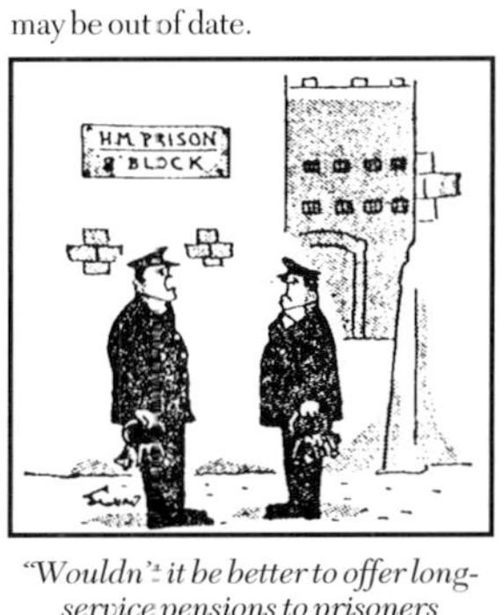

"Wouldn't it be better to offer long-service pensions to prisoners rather than us?"

Blowtorch Blue

"FASHION'S an awful thing to live with," said Miss Mary Quant at the Foyle's Dorchester lunch yesterday to mark the publication by Cassell's of her book "Quant by Quant." Everyone expected a good clothes designer to be also good at writing and making speeches.

Diffidently, she explained she couldn't spell, never had any clothes of her own, and sometimes moved giant rhubarbs into her home because her admirers thought them smarter than flowers.

She was introduced by Cecil Beaton who said: "She's made fashion fun," Her ideas, like clothes in "blow-torch blue and entrail purple," had been just waiting to be thought of. He was grateful to have been invited to "a posh nosh-up" - but Miss Quant was too nervous to eat anything.

Powell's Big Offensive
Fashion Becomes Fun

Crossfire on BBC

IT seems a nice point whether Mrs. Avril Fox, chairman of Cosmo (Freedom for TV) Group or her rival Mrs. Mary Whitehouse, leader of the National Viewers' and Listeners' Association is going to worry the BBC most.

Mrs. Fox, a progressive, stands for freedom on BBC and deplores the passing of BBC-3. Mrs. Whitehouse's views are tolerably well known.

They are pretty evenly matched and, to judge from past experience, their antagonisms should prove immensely beneficial to recruiting on both sides.

Shades of Gowers

"Thank you for your letter in respect of your car. The lack of attention was due to the writer's absence of illness. However, we are progressing your claim...." — From a Kent car distributor's letter to a Bromley customer.

Cost of Living

A colleague making his first visit had New York life summed up for him by a cab-driver's warning: "Don't go down to West Side, buddy: they'll kill you for a dollar there. And don't go down the subway either. Down there they kill you for pleasure."

PETERBOROUGH

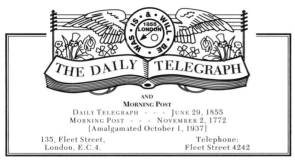

HOW'S LONDON LOOKING?

One of the Continent's top fashion artists says: 'Just marvellous'

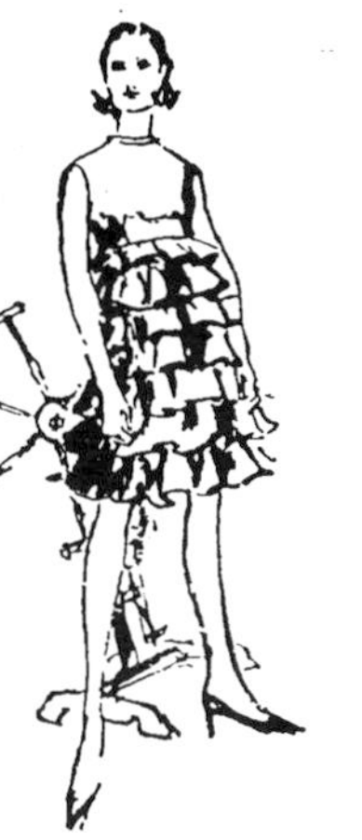

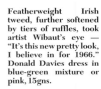

Featherweight Irish tweed, further softened by tiers of ruffles, took artist Wibaut's eye — "It's this new pretty look, I believe in for 1966." Donald Davies dress in blue-green mixture or pink, 15gns.

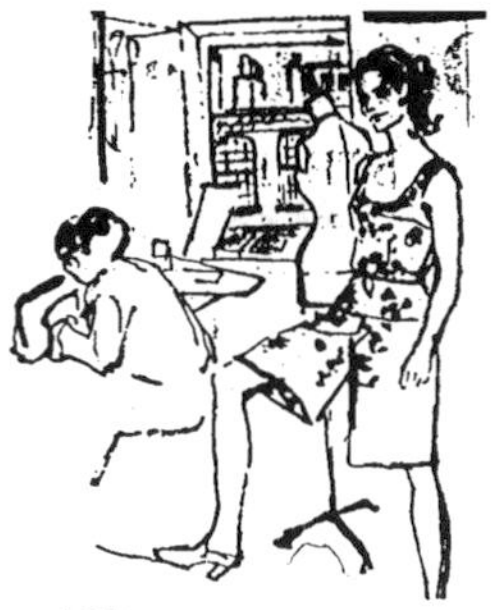

Resort special: cool Liberty lawn in black and white print, fully-lined, camisole top and matching culotte (above), by Dara and Shi for 11 ½ gns. Overplaid of red on black on bunny trench-coat (right), by Calman Links Furs.

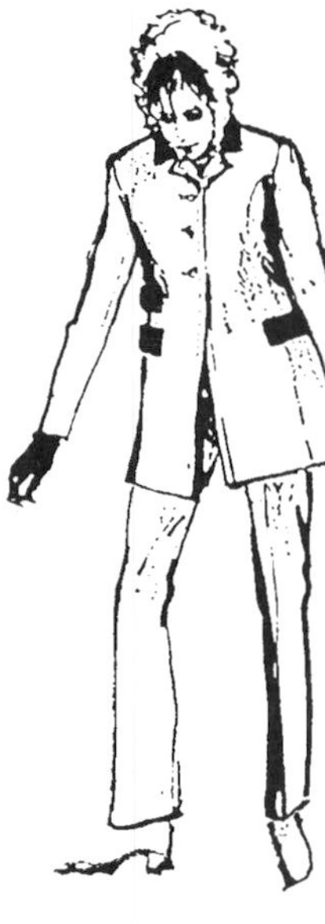

Rich-looking herringbone, with prissy little-boy Chesterfield velevet collar and pocket flaps, makes way-out trouser suit called "Christopher Robin" by Tuffin and Foale. Suit is 21gns; optional skirt 5 ½ gns.

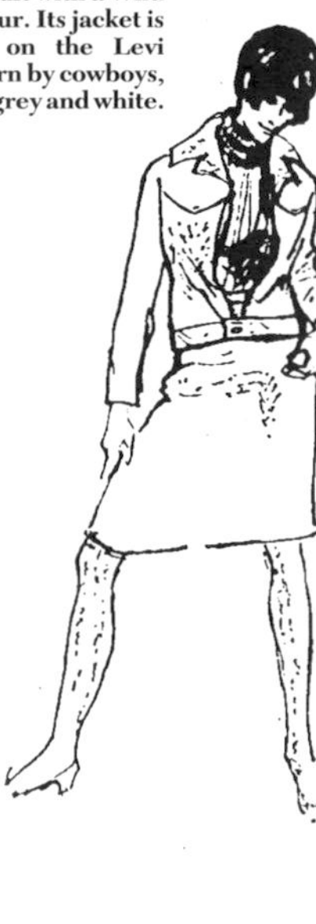

Herringbone gets used in a far-from-city-like way by designer Ossie Clark for Woollands 21 Shop in a suit with a Wild West flavour. Its jacket is modelled on the Levi jackets worn by cowboys, 15gns., in grey and white.

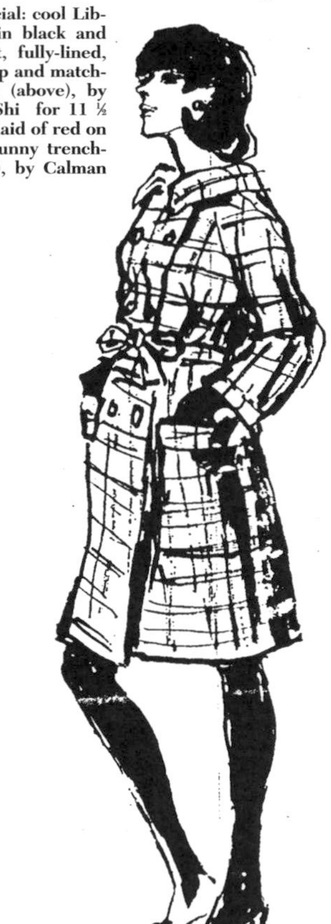

Sketches by CONSTANCE WIBAUT

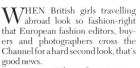

When British girls travelling abroad look so fashion-right that European fashion editors, buyers and photographers cross the Channel for a hard second look, that's good news.

Constance Wibaut, from Amsterdam, one of the Continent's top fashion writers and artists, found her curiosity mounting every time she covered the Paris Collections for her publication.

"Your British model girls in their own clothes looked as fabulous as the stuff in the salons. I simply had to come over and see this new London Look."

So artist Wibaut, on her first visit in five years, rambled round the back streets and the glossy shops with me. What struck her most were our superb natural fabrics - the pure fine cottons, the herringbone tweeds from Scotland, handwoven sheer wools from Ireland - used in dashing new cuts, elegant lounging and party wear.

Would the live-wire London clothes go in Holland? "How I wish it! We need them dreadfully," she said. "Our young follow French ready-to-wear now, but they would love these."

SERENA SINCLAIR

(January 5)

Where to dine well and keep some change

By CLAIRE BUTLER

What are the prospects for tourists dining out without overspending in this year of rising prices?

I can report that the choice of restaurants in London and Brighton, where you can enjoy an evening of good food, a glass of wine and conversation in an attractive *milieu* for under 25s a head, is improving.

First, a bright spot in Chelsea. Peter Evans, the man behind some of the best of our "eating houses" as he calls them, has provided an appealing meeting place for the Sloane Square set in the King's Road. The atmosphere is stimulating and you can dine for around 23s to 25s a head, including a glass of wine.

Your decor, by David Hicks, is bright, cheerful and colourful "pop" art: dramatic, vivid walls with large elliptical slices of orange or green, purple or blue, intersected with triangles of contrasting colours.

On Sunday evenings when the King's Road is the most open and lively street in London, this eating house, which serves good honest grills (of British meat) jacket potatoes and always some fresh vegetables, is full of lively diners who have either been kept by their work in London or are just back from the country.

Not all dining-out follows this happy mood. Visits to some tourist restaurants can cost you £2 10s to £3 a head for indifferent food, in which the deep freeze plays too large a part, and overpriced wines. This type of restaurant often has unusual decor for which you pay heavily.

So it was a great treat to find in Mayfair an honest, pleasant place with absolutely no chi-chi. In Massey's Chophouse in South Audley Street, the Edwardian decor, pleasant bar and watchful service enhanced the good fare - grills cooked over charcoal, jacket potatoes and delicious salads.

"When I get to Brighton I'm going to put my feet up," vowed Mrs. Gwen Brampton, whose husband owned and ran the Magic Carpet Inn in Chelsea for 20 years.

She rebelled against the machine existence of London, felt that for both their sakes she must go out for fresh air and relaxation.

They have not relaxed yet! They have opened a charming Magic Carpet restaurant in Preston Street, Brighton, and sold the Chelsea place. Lunchers and diners will enjoy reasonably priced specialities such as Boeuf Strogonoff for around 12s 6d.

(April 11)

Billy Graham wide of mark over Chelsea

By KENNETH CLARKE

Dr. Billy Graham, it appears, could not have been wider of the mark when he talked at the end of his London crusade of a religious revival blossoming among the mini-skirts and long-hairs of Chelsea.

Along the King's Road the wearers of mini-skirts and other more startling apparel debunked the evangelist's enthusiasm.

Miss Andrea Farr, 18, a film actress, said she had been brought up in a religious home but regarded Dr. Graham as "a typical American" selling the church like soapflakes.

Debates at parties

Religion I found was well debated at parties, along with sex and politics, but it is very difficult to find anyone who actually goes to church.

Mr. Jim Page, a young musician, said: "This crusading may appeal to those who have been brought up on Christianity, but it's not for us. Zen-Buddhism is more like it for young, thinking people. It opens the mind."

(July 7)

FRANK SINATRA 'TO MARRY MIA FARROW'

Frank Sinatra's engagement to the Actress, Mia Farrow, 21, who plays Alison McKenzie in the "Peyton Place" television series, was announced by Miss Farrow's mother, Maureed O'Sullivan, in New York today.

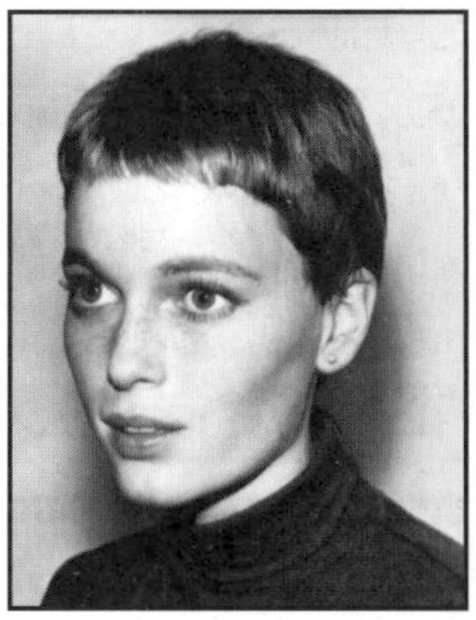

Mr. Sinatra who is 50, and Miss Farrow will marry in the United States between Thanksgiving, Nov. 24, and Christmas, Miss O'Sullivan said. Mr. Sinatra would be making a film "The Naked Runner" in England until October.

(July 14)

PARTY FASHIONS, WITH FRILLS

Pass me the smelling salts . . . the girls by night are looking as wildly romantic as 19th-century heroines, writes BERYL HARTLAND.

I blithely went to a party in my pared-down short dress and found nearly everybody else gathering up their long ruffled skirts.

I felt practically scalped with my short hair as concoctions of curls and flowers trembled enchantingly on heads and locks tumbled on to milky shoulders, Tom Jones style.

All around me the girls awoke nostalgia with ruffles, ribbons, lockets, waists, bosoms and even patches on the cheek. You could almost smell the lavender.

And the men too, are dressing in the same period style and look as though, at the drop of a handkerchief, it could be pistols for two at dawn.

Are ties on the way out for evening?

Could be - the party men were Byronic, with dark swept-back locks, open-necked shirts and velvet collars, or had hair clubbed into a velvet bow and frothing lace ruffles.

(December 29)

No 'Morning Glory' from Woolworth's

Daily Telegraph Reporter

The sale of "Morning Glory" flower seeds has been banned in all Woolworth's stores until the results are known of an investigation by the Pharmaceutical Society on reports that young people are using the seed to make an hallucination drug.

A spokesman for Woolworth's said last night: "We are not saying there is anything wrong with the seeds. It is purely a precautionary measure until we find out if, in fact, they are dangerous.

(March 22)

Dandy look of 1692 back in fashion

By NORMAN RILEY

To the Dorchester hostelrie in Parke Lane this day to see what sorte of morning gownes, peruiques and cloake-coates our equals will wear in 1966.

There did find nothing in all good conscience which our worthiest friends of good cloth do not already wear in this year of 1692.

A tailor with a regular, virtuous and learned conversation about his trade, S.A. Lynne, Esqr., did say to me: "Of great distinction in 1966 anno domini will be high buttoning, slim waisted jackets with a pronounced flare and close fitting trousers which flow off slightly at the ankle."

For a rout there are long white garments called "dinner jackets" with black trousers, each leg having such a broad white braid the length of it.

(February 25)

If you're a trend setter

Do you know any teenager who isn't wearing gypsy hoop earrings? The new enamel or plastic ones in brilliant sugar colours to match one's dress are pulling crowds into the stores. They give a necessary feminine touch to a girl whose hair is cropped shorter than her escort's.

Prettiest hoop earrings in London are the oval ones of tortoiseshell discovered by fashion buyer Judy McMinn in an antique shop.

Do you know that the beautiful colours (revivals both) we'll be wearing next autumn are brick (copper, terracotta) and purple. The Italians are making their most handsome suits and coats in brick, and our own knitwear people say the shade will be in all the shops come August.

(April 4)

Butcher wants cash not credit card

It comes as a shock when a banker talks about doing away with money. But that is more or less what Mr. John Thomson, chairman of Barclays, did in Northampton recently.

He was referring to the spread of interest in credit cards, and spoke of a cashless society in which people will carry around the minimum of cash—and the maximum of credit-granting certificates.

A straw in the wind, which ordinary bank customers will have seen, is the notice in branches asking them to accept the higher £5 and £10 notes, and not to insist on new notes.

Although credit cards sound sophisticated to most Britons, they have been commonplace for years in the United States. The best-known names are American Express and Diners' Club, both of which ask a membership fee of between £3 3s and £3 12s, and demand that the holder has a yearly income of at least £2,000. These cards can be shown at shops, hotels, and other establishments registered as members of the organisation, and allow the holder unlimited credit in his own country, provided he settles up later.

Over 1 ½ million people carry American Express cards, and about 40,000 have Diners' Club cards.

Many women will already be familiar with the kind of card issued by these and other companies if they have an account ticket for one of the larger London West End stores.

Like these, credit cards are small, and save the bother of filling in a cheque.

In this they have the advantage over cheque cards, now available from almost any bank. These idenify the owner of a cheque book, and make it possible for him to get cash at any branch of the issuing bank.

Andrew Lumsden

(July 11)

17pc OF DIRECTORS GET OVER £10,000 A YEAR

R.F.D. GREEN
Daily Telegraph Commercial Correspondent

Seventeen per cent. of members of the Institute of Directors are paid more than £10,000 a year according to a survey carried out by the Institute.

Only 11 per cent. of the directors earned less than £3,000 a year. High incomes are not confined either to older men or to those working for large companies.

More than a quarter of the directors under 40 had a total annual income over £10,000.

The survey figures in full are:

Total personal taxable income

Under £3,000	**£5,000 - £7,000**
11 per cent.	23 per cent
£3,000 - £5,000	**£7,000 - £10,000**
33 per cent.	16 per cent.
Over £10,000	
17 per cent.	

The survey, which is based on information supplied by 2,400 of the 42,000 members of the Institute, is not a representative cross-section of company directors. Nearly two-thirds of the replies came from chairmen or managing directors.

(April 9)

WALLS RAISE ICE CREAM PRICES

Prices of five lines of Walls ice cream go up today. Letters to retailers, sent earlier this week, blame the increases on higher purchase tax.

Walls which has about 100 ice cream lines, is recommending these higher prices: Orange Sparkle, Gaytime Tub and chocolate bars (from 8d to 9d); Neopolitan Family Sweet (from 2s to 2s 3d a block); sterile liquid mix, used by retailers to manufacture soft ice cream, up by 3d a gallon.

(August 12)

WALT DISNEY, CREATOR OF ENCHANTED WORLD

WALT DISNEY, who has died aged 65, made screen history by opening up an enchanted world of fantasy with animated cartoons which delighted young and old all over the world.

His animal character, Mickey Mouse, became perhaps the most internationally popular hero that show business had ever known.

He gave fairy tales new lustre in feature-length cartoons in colour, the first of which ever made was his "Snow White and the Seven Dwarfs."

Disney was not the inventor of the animated cartoon, but he raised it to the level of a new form of art worthy of serious criticism.

Though he later turned his energies to live-action adventure films and nature study films Disney's reputation rested on his cartoons and the animal stars born of his imagination.

Mickey Mouse had popular partners, including Minnie Mouse, Pluto and particularly Donald Duck, who eventually displaced him as a star, but he remained Disney's supremely original character.

On D-Day in the 1939-45 war "Mickey Mouse" was the password at Allied Supreme Headquarters in Europe.

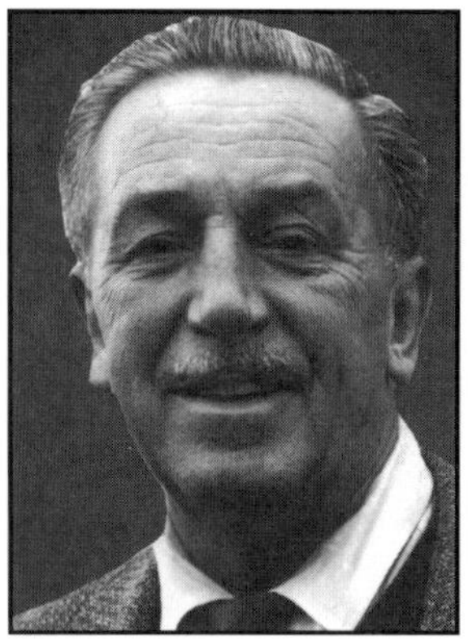

WALT DISNEY

The Disney productions grew into a considerable industry employing thousands of draughtsmen, technicians and other workers in a studio city at Burbank, California.

Apart from cartoons and live films, Walt Disney also made series and features for television and owned publishing and recording companies as well as factories turning out toys and other by-products of his success.

EARLY EXPERIMENTS

Partnership with brother

Walter Elias Disney was born in Chicago, the son of an Irish-Canadian contractor and builder and of a German-American mother, Flora Call.

At 15 he had a short interlude in trade when he sold magazines, sweets and peanuts in trains between Chicago and Kansas City.

When the United States entered the 1914-18 war he went to France, though not yet 17, with the American Red Cross to drive an ambulance

Back in Kansas at the end of the war, he was for a time an advertising artist before becoming a cartoonist for a local slide company. There he gained his first experience of cartoon films and he started experimenting with friends in an unused garage.

A short cartoon, "Little Red Riding Hood," was the result and Disney formed his own company.

In 1923 he went to Hollywood, where he formed a partnership with his brother, Roy, who was to look after the affairs of the Disney Studio.

Soon the Mickey series, in which Disney provided Mickey's voice himself, gained world wide popularity.

It was shortly before the 1939-45 war that Disney produced the first feature-length cartoon, "Snow White and the Seven Dwarfs." Before long the whole world was singing its songs.

Its success led the Disney organisation to move from Hollywood to a great new plant at Burbank, in the San Fernando Valley.

Then followed "Ferdinand the Bull" (1939), "Pinocchio" and "Fantasia" (1940), and such favourites as "Dumbo" (1941) and "Bambi" (1942).

During the 1939-45 war Disney was busy with training and educational films, and afterwards started directing coloured nature films, such as "Seal Island," "Beaver Valley" and "The Living Desert."

AMUSEMENT PARK

"Disneyland" attractions

In 1955 he opened "Disneyland," an amusement park near Los Angeles, which drew millions of people annually.

Disney held many Academy and other awards. In 1925 he married his secretary and assistant, Lilian Marie Bounds. They had two daughters.

(December 16)

Lenny Bruce

LENNY BRUCE, comedian and satirist, who brought "sick" humour into fashion in America and shocked night-club audiences by using four-letter words, was found dead last night in his Hollywood home. He was 40.

Police said that drug-taking equipment was beside his partly-dressed body. A post mortem examination is being made. Police believe that an overdose of drugs caused his death.

Towards the end of his career, he had spent almost as much time in court as he did on the stage. He was arrested several times for using drugs or uttering obscenities. He was deported from Britain three years ago.

(August 5)

Elizabeth Arden

ELIZABETH ARDEN, who has died in New York, was the founder of the modern beauty parlour. As such she deserved the thanks of all women and girls in the Western world.

Her beauty treatments were sold in the harems of Saudi-Arabia. More remarkably, her lipsticks made a great hit in Russia. Her Maine Chance beauty farm in Arizona was the prototype of all similar establishments.

Many years ago she was offered £5 million for her business, but refused indignantly. One of her best-known scents was Blue Grass, named after the Kentucky paddocks where she kept her racing stables, a perfect example of the way in which she integrated her pleasure and business interests.

(October 19)

Sister Rowe, midwife to the Queen

SISTER Helen Maude Rowe, who has died aged 71, was midwife to the Queen. A gentle but firm woman, she was present at the births of all four Royal Children.

The arrival of Sister Rowe at Buckingham Palace became a customary prelude to a Royal birth. But the crowds who took this to be a significant signal not infrequently had a long wait before the official bulletin announcing the new baby was posted on the palace railings.

Sister Rowe, who lived in Eastbourne, was remarkably active until overtaken by her recent illness. She trained as a nurse at King's College Hospital, London, from 1917 to 1920, and it soon became evident she had marked ability.

She is recalled with affection by many who successfully sought her services. Lady Dartmouth regarded her as "one of the family."

Sister Rowe had her own rules, but would not lay down rules for new mothers. "There are no hard and fast rules which will turn a woman into a successful mother," she said. "What is right for one baby may not be right for another."

(January 11)

EVELYN WAUGH, AUTHOR OF HIGH MERIT

MR. EVELYN ARTHUR ST. JOHN WAUGH, the novelist, who has died, aged 62, was a prolific writer of high literary merit. He had produced books since 1928. "Vile Bodies," of 1930, and "Put out More Flags," 1942 were outstanding examples of his talent.

Among his last published works was his autobiographical "A Little Learning." A projected history of the Crusades was abandoned recently. He was a brilliant writer of war novels.

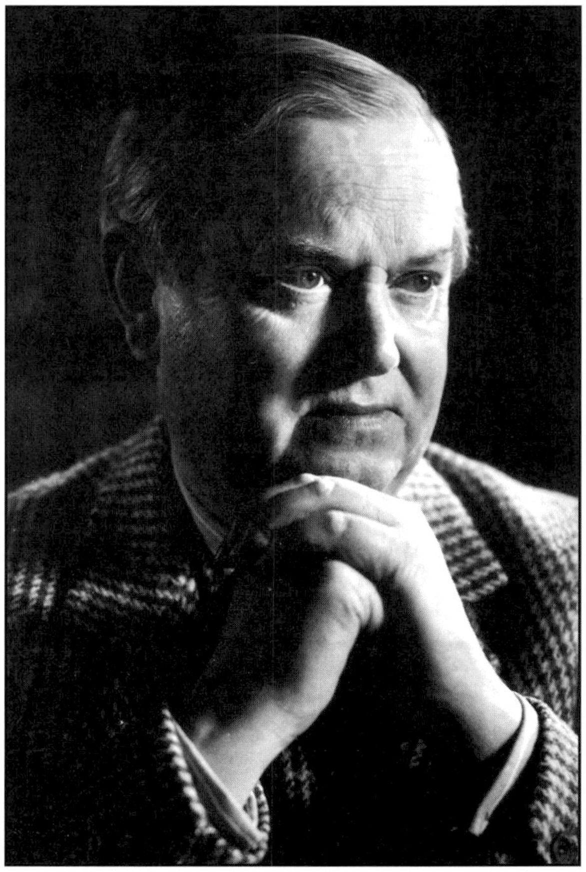

EVELYN WAUGH

His trilogy of the Second World War, "Men At Arms," "Officers and Gentlemen," and "Unconditional Surrender," was last year printed as a single volume under the title "Sword of Honour."

If literary style were the test of a novelist, then undoubtedly Evelyn Waugh was the finest novelist of the last 30 years. He was a superb literary craftsman; even the least sympathetic of his work was splendidly contrived.

His distaste for the age he lived in and his championing of the virtues of the ancient Roman Catholic landed families may have dismayed the readers of his later books, but he never lost the power to create the great comic characters with which he first made his name.

Captain Grimes, the rogue schoolmaster of "Decline and Fall," and Basil Seal, the cad, were perhaps the best known, but Apthorpe, the ancient captain of "Officers and Gentlemen," published 10 years ago, was perhaps his masterpiece.

Light-hearted satire

At first Waugh's satire was entirely light-hearted: "Decline and Fall" was followed by "Vile Bodies," both of which dealt with the bright young things of the 1920s.

Soon after he was to show that he was capable of something deeper with perhaps the best of all his novels, "A handful of Dust," with its terrifying ending of the hero being condenmed for ever more to read Dickens to a madman deep in the South American jungle.

Other novels like "Brideshead Revisited" and the last war trilogy, were perhaps more technically accomplished but they lacked the unity of feeling of "A Handful of Dust" and were tainted by Waugh's later doctrinaire tone.

Waugh had a great distaste for personal publicity and took pleasure in plaguing those who sought to interview him.

When he did submit to cross-questioning, he preferred to show himself as a benign "old buffer" - his own description - far more aged than his years. Fortunately this apparent tiredness of spirit was never obvious in his writing.

It is indeed difficult to say of any of one's contemporaries that here is a man whose writing will live, but one can feel confident that Capt. Grimes, Margot Metroland, Cpl-Maj. Ludovic and the rest will join the great gallery of satirical figures that will please generations yet unborn.

(April 11)

BUSTER KEATON

BUSTER KEATON, who has died in Hollywood, aged 70, was one of the greatest clowns of the silent screen. He made his name as the comic who never laughed.

As a slapstick comedian, famous for his baggy trousers and straw hat, as well as his "frozen" face, Keaton became one of the highest paid stars of silent films. But during his career he spent several fortunes.

Born at Piqua, Kansas, he was christened Joseph Francis. He is said to have received his nickname from Houdini, the magician, who, seeing young Keaton fall downstairs without hurting himself, exclaimed: "What a buster!"

He first appeared with Roscoe ("Fatty") Arbuckle, who started him in films in "The Butcher's Boy." In the early twenties he made feature films, including "The General" and "The Navigator," which are still regarded as classics of their kind.

He never made a popular success in talking pictures and between the wars worked as a script writer. After the war he staged a come-back on television and did provincial tours of Britain. He had a small part in Chaplin's "Limelight."

Mrs. Eleanor Keaton, formerly a dancer, his wife of 25 years, was at his bedside when he died. He left two sons by a previous wife. Natalie Talmadge, one of the three famous Talmadge sisters.

(February 2)

Mr. Shastri, Premier of India

MR. LAL BAHADUR SHASTRI, who has died aged 61, succeeded Mr. Nehru, as India's Prime Minister, in 1964. Shortly afterwards he sufferd a mild heart attack and he was advised that it would be unwise to attend the Commonwealth Prime Ministers' conference.

He resigned as Minister for Home Affairs to devote himself to the strengthening of the Congress party structure. In January, 1964 as a result of Mr. Nehru's illness, he rejoined the Cabinet as Minister without Portfolio. It was assumed that he was Mr. Nehru's putative successor.

Mr. Shastri had worked with Mr. Nehru nearly all his political life. He joined the Congress party when he was 17, and at 31 became the youngest party secretary Congress had ever had. He had never been out of India, except to Nepal.

After his election as Prime Minister, Mr. Shastri said "our main enemies" were poverty and unemployment.

Within a few months Mr. Shastri was confronted with the explosive situation over the dispute in the Rann of Kutch on the India-West Pakistan border.

KASHMIR BATTLE

"Meet force with force"

By August last year India claimed Pakistan had infiltrated into Kashmir. Mr. Shastri told the Indian Parliament that force would be met by force.

By the end of the month Indian and Pakistani tanks and planes were in conflict. Both countries were prepared to face a long and bitter war.

With the news that Indian troops had marched into Pakistan, Mr. Wilson intervened to send an urgent "stop the fighting" plea to President Ayub and Mr. Shastri.

The move was unsuccessful, but on Sept. 23 Mr. Shastri said that India had accepted the Security Council's demand for a ceasefire after assurances had been received that Pakistan had also accepted it.

Five feet two inches in height, he was known as the "Sparrow from Allahabad." While for all practical purposes Mr. Nehru was a British product, Mr. Shastri, a Sanskrit scholar, was completely Indian. He was a firm anti-Communist with a strong belief in the value of the Commonwealth

He came from Mr. Nehru's home State of Uttar Pradesh. His father was a school teacher who later became a Government official. When Mr. Shastri was only a year and a half old his father died and he, with his two sisters, was brought up by his maternal grandfather.

He went to the Harish Chandra School in Varanasi until he was 17. He was then drawn into Gandhi's non co-operation movement.

When Kashi Vidyapeeth was formed as one of the national universities he resumed his studies, and graduated as a "Shastri" equivalent to BA, with philosophy as his principal subject. He had been called Mr. Shastri ever since.

(January 11)

Margery Allingham

MARGERY ALLINGHAM, one of the most popular and successful English writers of detective stories, died in hospital at Colchester yesterday at the age of 61.

Apart from the ingenuity of the plots, her crime stories, particularly those she wrote just before and just after the Second World War, were notable for the good humour of their writing.

Her detective who was known as Albert Campion, although his real name was never revealed as other than Rudolph K., the younger son of a peer, began as a minor character in "The Crime at Black Dudley."

After a few lightly written almost Bulldog Drummondish adventures Campion settled down to be a more conventional sleuth in her best books "Fashion in Shrouds." "Dancers in Mourning" and "Flowers for the Judge."

(July 1)

Dr. Hewlett Johnson, the 'Red Dean'

FEW ecclesiastics of modern times have earned such notoriety as Dr. Hewlett Johnson, Dean of Canterbury from 1931 to 1963, who has died in the Kent and Canterbury Hospital, aged 92.

The "Red Dean" as he was called, made frequent journeys about the world as an apostle of Marxism. In this he professed to see the practical application of the Christian faith.

As Dean of Canterbury, people abroad constantly took him to be a person of greater consequence than he was, and often indeed confused him with the Archbishop.

In appearance he was almost a caricature of a dean. The bald head, the mass of white locks above either ear, the constant smile, the suave and polite manner would have done credit to a stage character.

In his personal relations he was a man of great charm and a delighful host.

FIRST MOSCOW VISIT

Stalin Prize award

He first visited Moscow in 1938. In 1951 he was awarded the Stalin Peace Prize of 100,000 roubles (about £9,000) and a gold medal.

One of Stalin's warmest admirers during the dictator's lifetime, he had preserved an enigmatic silence since Mr. Khruschev's revelations.

His ability to reconcile the irreconcilable opposites of Christianity with Godless Marxism was a clear indication that his tenets would have strained the tolerance of even the broadest churchman.

Though he had been appointed in 1931, on the recommendation of Mr. Ramsay MacDonald, he held office technically under letters patent of the Crown. It was somewhat doubtful whether he had technically gone far enough to enable the Prime Minister to petition the Crown for their revocation.

Popular demand for his dismissal grew when, during the Korean war and following a visit to China, he supported the allegation that United Nations' aircraft had dropped containers of germ-carrying insects. No action, however, was taken.

The Archbishop of Canterbury, Dr. Ramsey, said on Saturday: "Disagreeing, as I did, with some of his views, I held in regard his many-sided gifts and his keen human sympathy."

(October 24)

Capt. George Pitt-Rivers, Anthropologist

CAPT. GEORGE HENRY LANE FOX PITT-RIVERS, who has died, aged 76, was a notable anthropologist, who owned what was widely regarded as the finest private museum in England.

His controversial views on a variety of subjects expressed his unorthodox character and may have been responsible for his detention under the Defence Regulations in June, 1940.

His remarkable career began with his service in the First (Royal) Dragoons during the 1914-18 war, when he was severely wounded. In 1920 he became private secretary and ADC to Lord Forster, Governor-General of Australia, whose daughter Emily he had married in 1915.

Then he threw himself enthusiastically into the study of anthropology, which led him to live for several years practically as a native among the people of the Melanesian islands, and established his reputation as an authority upon the subject.

He was equally interested in eugenics and psychology. His lecture to the Eugenics Society in 1927 on "The Failure of monogamous marriage" did not escape criticism.

(June 18)

DR. H. VERWOERD, SOUTH AFRICAN PREMIER

DR. VERWOERD, Prime Minister of South Africa, who was assassinated yesterday, aged 64, was the chief architect of apartheid, aiming at complete segregation of the races.

He will also go down in history as the man under whose government the South African people chose to become a Republic and found it impossible to stay in the Commonwealth.

Hendrik Frensch Verwoerd was born in Holland. When he was aged one his parents emigrated to South Africa and settled in Brandfort, Orange Free State.

He went to the Milton Boys' High School in Bulawayo, Southern Rhodesia, where his father moved after becoming a Dutch Reformed Church Minister.

Appointed Professor of Applied Psychology at Stellenbosch in 1928, he became Professor of Sociology and Social Work, a post which, he said, introduced him to politics.

He came into prominence in South Africa in 1936 when he led a small group of Stellenbosch professors in a protest against the admission to South Africa of Jewish refugees from Germany.

During the last war he spoke through his newspaper for the anti-war section of the Afrikaner people and sued the rival Johannesburg Star for libel in asserting that his "spiritual home was nearer to Berchtesgaden" than South Africa. He lost his case.

Meanwhile, he had begun to play an active part in politics. He worked hard for the victory that the Nationalists won at the first post-war general election in 1948.

SEAT IN SENATE

Ministerial appointment

Later in the year, after South Africa's first Nationalist Government was formed under the late Dr. Malan, he ran successfully for the Senate and in 1950 entered the Government as Minister for Native Affairs.

One of his first actions as Minister was to put a summary finish to a dispute between the Government and the Natives' Representative Council, by abolishing the Council.

To replace it Dr. Verwoerd laid the foundation for the establishment of Native Tribal Councils in Native areas under the Bantu Authorities Act.

At a party caucus after the death of Mr. Strijdom three months later he was elected leader of the Nationalists over both the acting Prime Minister, Mr. Swart, and the Minister of the Interior, Dr. Donges.

On becoming Prime Minister Dr. Verwoerd, in a broadcast to the nation, announced that he would devote all his energies to the establishment of a republic, which he said was the only way to bring about unity between the English-speaking and Afrikaans-speaking people of the Union.

In 1960, Dr. Verwoerd announced in the House of Assembly that legislation would be introduced during the session to provide for the holding of a referendum on whether the Union should become a Republic.

Soon afterwards politics took a violent turn with mass arrests, shootings, declaration of a state of emergency and finally an attempt on the Prime Minister's life.

PEAK OF POWER

Hammarskjoeld visit

In 1961, the year of the declaration of the South African Republic, Dr. Verwoerd was at the summit of his power.

In January, he had talks with the then Secretary-General of the United Nations. Mr. Hammarskjoeld, who flew to South Africa from New York and spent a week in the country investigating South Africa's race policies.

Two months later Dr. Verwoerd flew to London to play a leading role in the crucial meeting of the Commonwealth Prime Ministers' Conference that led to South Africa's withdrawal from the Commonwealth.

Though the decision was received with dismay by the opposition United Party, Nationalists hailed it as the only one possible in the circumstances and on his return gave him a hero's welcome.

Since then he had been content to allow the spotlight to fall more and more often on his younger colleagues, in particular on his Minister of Justice, Mr. B.J. Vorster, architect of the 90-day detention clause and other legislation ruthlessly designed to maintain and advance apartheid in the face of growing pressures from without and within.

But behind the scenes Dr. Verwoerd had remained firmly in control, just as, in the country at large, he had been seen by English-speaking as well as Afrikaner voters as white South Africa's natural leader in the circumstances of the day.

(September 7)

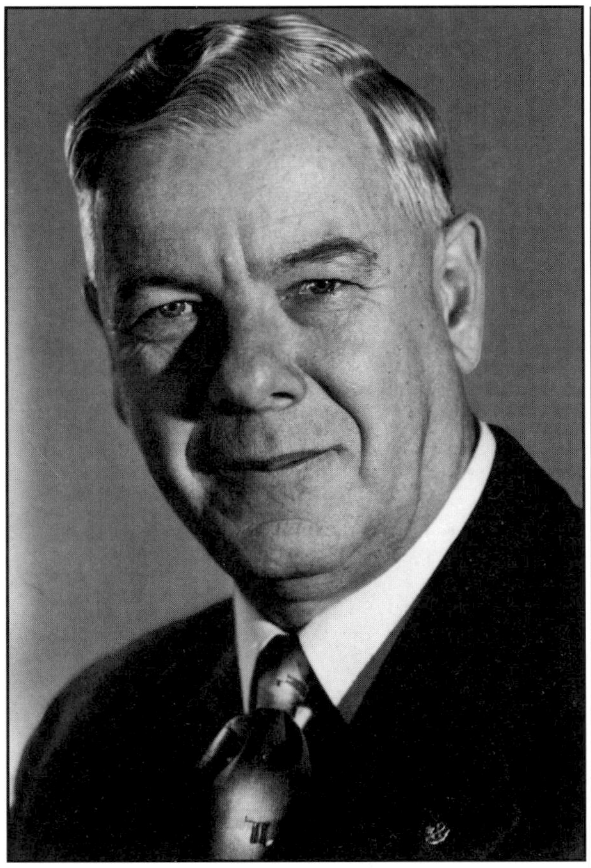

Adml. NIMITZ, STRATEGIST

FLEET ADML. CHESTER WILLIAM NIMITZ, who had died aged 80, was one of the United States most distinguished Naval commanders. He was a far-sighted strategist and a supreme exponent of amphibious warfare on an unprecedented scale.

Succeeding Adml. Kimmel in 1941, after the Japanese attack on Pearl Harbour, as C-in-C, United States Pacific Fleet and Pacific Ocean Areas, he fought his way through from Pearl Harbour to the very coast of Japan.

His command complemented the South-west Pacific area commanded by Gen. MacArthur. Under the direction of Nimitz and his subordinates were fought the battles of Midway, the Solomons, the Gilbert Islands, the Marshalls, Marianas, Palaus, Philippines, Iwo Juma and Okinawa.

WASHINGTON TRIBUTE

Address to Congress

He took part for the United States in the Japanese surrender aboard his flagship, the Missouri in Tokyo Bay in September, 1945. In Washington in the following month thousands cheered the victorious admiral as he drove through the city. President Truman pinned the Gold Star on his breast.

Adml. Nimitz was a man of deeds rather than words, but he assured his countrymen in 1942: "Your Fleet is busy." After the Midway Island battle he said in his communiqué: "Perhaps we will be forgiven if we claim we are about midway to our objective!" This pun on the name of the island delighted the American people.

Born in Fredericksburg, Texas, Adml. Nimitz graduated from the United States Naval Academy, Annapolis, in 1905. He spent a large part of his subsequent career under water. In 1918 he served as chief of staff to the commander of the United States Atlantic submarine force.

Although he commanded a battleship division in 1938-39 he retained a proper degree of the submarine man's disrespect for the big ships. Asked once why a battleship was called a "she," he replied: "Because it costs so much to keep one in paint and powder."

(February 21)

Sir Ernest Gowers, foe of 'officialese'

SIR ERNEST ARTHUR GOWERS, who has died at Midhurst, Sussex, aged 85, was a distinguished civil servant who had presided over many official committees of inquiry.

He also told civil servants and others how to write good English instead of "officialese."

Capital punishment, the preservation of historic homes, the employment of women in the Foreign Service, foot-and-mouth disease and conditions of shop and office workers were among the problems he investigated.

Sir Ernest was educated at Rugby and Clare College, Cambridge, and entered the Civil Service in 1903. He was called to the Bar of the Inner Temple in 1906. One of his earlier appointments was that of principal private secretary to Mr. Lloyd George as Chancellor of the Exchequer.

Wartime post

During the 1939-45 war he was Regional Commissioner for Civil Defence, London Region. From 1947 to 1950 he was chairman of the Harlow New Town Development Corporation, and from 1948 to 1957 of the National Hospitals for Nervous Diseases.

In his book, "A Life for a Life?" published in 1956, Sir Ernest told how, after serving on the Royal Commission on Capital Punishment he became convinced that the abolitionists were right in their conclusions. His "Plain Words," 1948, written at Treasury request primarily to curb verbosity in the Civil Service, became a best seller. He also wrote "ABC of Plain Words," 1951, and "The Complete Plain Words," 1954. Last year his revision of Fowler's "Modern English Usage" was published. It became a best seller.

Sir Ernest advised the simple word instead of the pompous phrase. Instead of "in the contemplated eventuality" he preferred "if so." But he was not against new forms of speech, and once said: "The talk of the present generation must be allowed the catchwords of today if it is to be lifelike."

(April 18)

Turpin-rags to riches to rags

By DONALD SAUNDERS

RANDOLPH TURPIN, 37, the former world middle weight boxing champion, was found shot dead in a bedroom over his wife's transport café in Leamington Spa yesterday afternoon. A gun lay by his side.

Turpin was born in a Leamington Spa back street, earned a fortune with his fists by the time he was 24, lost most of it before he was 30, and died a few weeks short of his 38th birthday in another Leamington back street.

He was certainly the greatest of post-war British champions at any weight, and possibly the finest middleweight ever produced by this country.

A magnificent physical specimen, he possessed remarkably quick reflexes, was a better-than-average boxer and could punch harder than many British heavyweights.

GREATEST MOMENT

Outpointed Robinson

His greatest moment came nine months later when he pulled off one of the biggest surprises in modern boxing by clearly outpointing Sugar Ray Robinson in a world title bout in London.

The following September, a crowd of 61,370 paid 767,326 dollars (£277,400 - still a record for a non-heavyweight fight) to see the return match at the New York Polo Grounds.

In the 10th round Turpin seemed to be within sight of victory, with the referee clearly concerned about a bad cut over Robinson's eye.

Moments later the young Briton was on the floor and although he regained his feet at nine his 64-day reign as world champion was ended shortly after by the referee's intervention.

Thereafter, he moved into the light-heavyweight division, winning and relinquishing the British title twice before retiring in 1958.

By then much of the £250,000 he was estimated to have earned in purse money had been dissipated on such flamboyant gestures as the purchase of a castle in North Wales, other unsuccessful investments, and assistance to the many "friends" who flocked round him.

In an effort to increase his now meagre earnings, this once great boxer fought in fairground booths, unlicensed promotions, and briefly in the wrestling ring.

The public sadly turned their backs on him. They preferred to remember Rudolph Turpin as the eager young fighter who once had outboxed Sugar Ray Robinson, reputed to be the greatest of them all.

(May 18)

Montgomery Clift dies in his sleep

NEW YORK, Sunday.

Montgomery Clift, the film actor, died in his sleep yesterday in his New York home. Doctors said he had had a heart attack. He was 45.

Clift, a bachelor, had recently finished filming "The Defectors" in Munich.

(July 25)

GIACOMETTI

ALBERTO GIACOMETTI, who has died at Chur, Switzerland, aged 64, was one of the leading sculptors of the century and a notable painter and draughtsman. He also wrote poetry.

He is known for his variations upon single themes and above all will be remembered for his long, attenuated figures.

Although more familiar as a sculptor than a painter, some critics have found his paintings and drawings more satisfying. His most familiar sculptures are immensely tall, thin, rigidly upright human figures.

They vary widely in scale, some being only a few inches high, while others are larger than life size. Many such figures made the Arts Council's Giacometti Exhibition at the Tate Gallery in 1965 somewhat repetitious.

Giacometti was born in the Italian-speaking area of Switzerland. His father was Giovanni Giacometti, who in his day was a celebrated landscape painter.

The young Alberto produced his first sculpture in 1914. In 1919 he attended the Ecole des Arts et Metiers at Geneva.

Since the 20's he had spent most of his life in Paris, although from 1940-45 he lived in Geneva. His work is in all leading museums of modern art, including the Tate Gallery.

(January 13)

FORESTER, CREATOR OF HORNBLOWER

MR. C.S. FORESTER, who has died at Fullerton, California, aged 66, was the author of the best-selling Hornblower series. Horatio Hornblower was a doughty sea warrior who confounded Britain's enemies in the days of sail.

Readers got the impression that Forester must at least have sailed in windjammers. In fact, he never did. He declared that all his information about the management of ships in sail came from an old Admiralty manual, which he picked up in a second-hand bookshop in Portsmouth.

In his "Second World War." Sir Winston Churchill wrote: "Oliver Lyttelton [now Viscount Chandos], Minister of State in Cairo, had given me 'Capt. Hornblower, R.N, which I found vastly entertaining. When a chance came I sent him a message, 'I find Hornblower admirable.'

"This caused perturbation in the Middle East Headquarters, where it was imagined that 'Hornblower' was the code-word for some special operation of which they had not been told."

(April 4)

BERT THOMAS

Bert Thomas, who drew the 1914-18 war cartoon, "Arf a Mo' Kaiser," died yesterday at his home in Bayswater. He was 83.

(September 7)

Sophie Tucker

THE abounding verve of Sophie Tucker, the American singer, established her as a music-hall favourite on both sides of the Atlantic.

Miss Tucker first appeared in London more than 40 years ago. She rendered facetiously philosophical songs such as "Nobody Loves a Fat Girl" and "Life Begins at Forty" in a powerful voice. Her patter was designed closely to fit the label "red hot momma," which was fastened on her in middle age.

Among her most popular numbers was "Some of These Days." This became her signature tune.

Few of her contemporaries could hold a sophisticated London audience spell-bound, as she could, with a lengthy and emotional number sung throughout in Yiddish.

Miss Tucker was born in Russia on Jan. 13, 1888. She added four years to her age when she started in New York cabarets as a girl of 16. The "stolen" years made a mystery of the singer-comedienne's real age for the rest of her life.

In 1934 she had one of her proudest moments with a performance in London before King George V and Queen Mary. She cocked her head towards the Royal Box and waved, "Hi yah King."

(February 11)

WAY OF THE WORLD

Ould Daddah Knows

THAT revered figure, President Ould Daddah of Mauritania, has just given further proof of his paternal wisdom. After the killing of six people in a demonstration against compulsory Arabic in secondary schools, he has banned all public discussion of the country's "racial problems."

He would have a short way with our own Board of Race Relations, and with all the other agencies which are springing up in thousands all over the country to make the new racial-problematological industry one of the most flourishing and expanding parts of our economy.

One word from Ould Daddah and the incessant public and private jabbering about racial probems would falter and die. After a little while we might even find, to our surprise, that the racial problems themselves had died with it.

Hundreds of thousands of professional and amateur sociologists would be out of a job. But Ould Daddah would find them suitable work to do - such as digging holes in the sands of Mauritania and filling them in again.

(February 25)

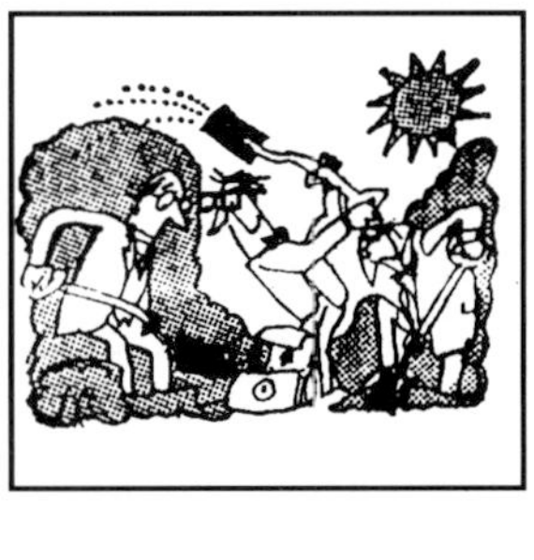

What's On in London

LONDON Suet Centre, Regent Street, W.1. Exhibition: "Suet Dumplings through the Ages." Open 9.30-6, until April 10; admission 2s 6d; children 1s 6d, coach-parties by arrangement.

Lecture: "Aspects of the Swedish Music-hall, 1885-1890," by Dr. Bengt Grundqvist, Boeotian Hall, daily, 7.30-11.45. Admission 7s 6d all seats bookable.

Friday March 25, at 2.30 p.m., underwater organ recital by Dr. J.S. Strachan-Forbes, MRCVS, at St. Botolph's, Grimsgate, E.C.2. Admission free, waterproof clothing provided.

N.S. Gokhale Memorial Hall, Gower Street. Demonstration of dental extraction by Lemmonsodhayana Yoga by Prof. Prem Chand Anagram, BA, of Madras. Daily 11.30, 2.30, 5.30, 8.30. Sandwiches, lantern-slides.

(March 22)

March of Freedom

A SPECIAL court for "economic crimes," which can impose the death penalty, has been set up in Algeria. This brings a country which not long ago groaned under the yoke of Western colonialism into line with the advanced, enlightened countries of the East.

Are you satisfied, heroic fighters of the FLN? And are you satisfied, heroic if remoter fighters of the Left-wing Press, who poured out your moral indignation so unstintingly that Algeria might be free?

(July 19)

Peter Simple

ENGLAND TWICE FIGHT BACK FOR GREATEST TRIUMPH

By DONALD SAUNDERS

England ... (1) 4 West Germany ... (1) 2

(After extra time, Score 90 minutes 2-2)

Hurst 3	**Haller**
Peters	**Weber**

AT WEMBLEY, 93,000.

NOW the Jules Rimet trophy is safely in England's keeping for the next four years, Alf Ramsey and his world champions can at last put up their feet and briefly enjoy the privileges due to all-conquering heroes.

Their repite from the strain and toil of modern competitive football will be short. By Saturday fortnight, the 22 players, who for eight weeks have devoted all their waking hours towards the cause of World Cup victory, must be prepared to meet the demands of a gruelling nine-months League programme.

Mr. Ramsey could extend his holiday indefinitely if he chose. He has handsomely accomplished the task he undertook three and a half years ago. To quit at the top is his undeniable right; the temptation to do so must be almost overwhelming.

But I think he will carry on. While the vast crowd were ecstatically chanting his name from the stands and terraces of Wembley, after Saturday's 4-2 victory over West Germany, he hinted that a visit to the 1970 finals is among possibilites he will contemplate, during his first real break from work since 1963.

"Everybody is concerned about what I am going to do" said England's manager, with the enigmatic smile that has disconcerted so many experienced interrogators in recent years.

RAMSEY'S VIEW

Another World Cup

"I haven't thought about it," he assured his listeners, before adding, again with that smile: "There's another World Cup in Mexico in 1970. That would be nice."

The task facing English soccer during the next four years is even more testing than the one just completed.

Prestige must be upheld, at home and abroad, the flag must be shown, no matter how great the risk and the trophy must be defended on foreign soil against the determined onslaught of the rest of the world.

All this can be accomplished only by footballers of ability, character, intelligence, spirit and superb physical condition. Mr. Ramsey has found one such squad. Soon he, or his successor, must begin the heartbreaking process of dismantling and rebuilding it.

Meanwhile, let me, a Welshman pay tribute to 11 Englishmen and 11 West Germans for their noble contribution to the sagging prestige of international sport, during the most exciting final the World Cup competition has produced in 36 years.

They did not approach the heights scaled for the first and only time by Pele, Didi, Vava and Garrincha in Stockholm eight years ago. I have no doubt that England and West Germany would have been too powerful, well-drilled and persistent for the Brazilian champions of 1962.

At Wembley on Saturday these well-matched finalists provided a virile exhibition that sent the most knowledgeable into ecstacies, and a nod of approval from the professors and persuaded even the romantics to cease their sighing over the premature departure of Brazil.

For two hours, that strained the emotions of all who watched, both teams played with dogged persistence, supreme courage and methodical efficiency, qualities that amply compensated for the absence of Latin artistry.

It took a man of character and judgment to lead England back into the game after Wilson, making his first mistake of the tournament, had nodded the ball down to the feet of Haller who promptly slammed it past the unsighted Banks.

In that dreadful 12th minute, Moore, who was yesterday named the world's top footballer, rose calmly, quietly, but firmly to the occasion, England's captain, noting that West Germany, perhaps unwisely, were employing the normally enterprising Beckenbauer to shadow Bobby Charlton, decided he could and should risk playing a more attacking role.

Though Moore's move forward caused some anxiety behind him, it helped produce the pressure that ultimately relaxed the Germans' grip in mid-field.

Within six minutes England were level. Hurst racing 10 yards to head on a free-kick from Moore, while the Germans mistakenly kept close watch on the Charlton brothers.

SKILL AND PURPOSE

Powerful trio

For the remainder of the first half two determined sides fought for control with skill and purpose and I was not the only spectator who feared that Held, Haller and Seeler were going to win the battle for West Germany.

After the break England's forwards found their touch. Passes from Bobby Charlton, Peters and Stiles, more regularly reached their destination and Ball, Hurst and Hunt thrust deeply into enemy territory.

Now it was the Germans' turn to call on their courage, and their plea was not in vain. Tenaciously they fought to deprive England of possession and 30 seconds from the end of normal time they snatched the equaliser.

There was, it is true, an element of luck about their goal. The Swiss referee, Gottfried Dienst, somewhat harshly awarded a free kick when Jack Charlton climbed above Held to clear. Moreover, Haller seemed to handle Emmerich's shot before Weber popped the ball into the net.

Mr. Dienst signalled a goal, and seconds later the end of the first 90 minutes.

As his troops flopped disconsolately to the turf, trying to absorb this blow, Mr. Ramsey moved among them, assuring them with a smile here, a pat on the back there, that England would still win the Cup.

They believed him and, inspired by the calm authority of Moore, and young Ball's tremendous energy, they again took control.

With three minutes of the first period remaining, Hurst thumped a cross from Ball straight at goal and Tilkowski pushed it against the underside of the bar, whence it rebounded to the turf. The Germans will forever claim the ball did not cross the line. The Russian linesman, Tofic Bakhramov ruled otherwise.

Even now these plucky Germans did not give in. During the second period of extra time they forced their leaden legs forward in a desperate effort to overcome opponents they realised were as close to the point of exhaustion as they were.

But England refused to be robbed of their well-deserved prize twice in the same match.

With the referee looking at his watch, Hurst trundled on to a through pass and drove home a goal that earned him the distinction of becoming the first player to score three times in a World Cup Final, and confirmed England as undisputed champions.

(August 1)

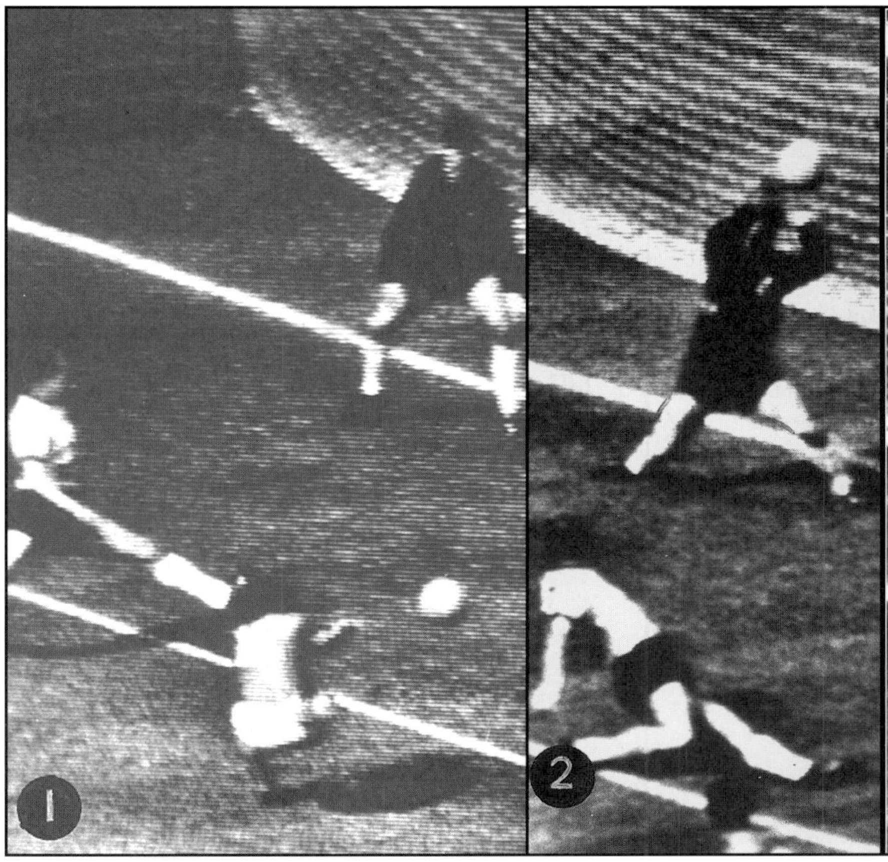

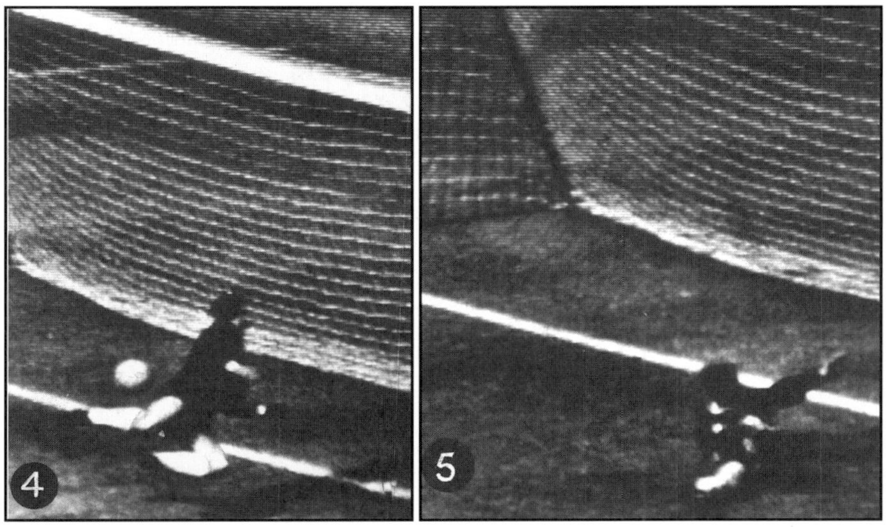

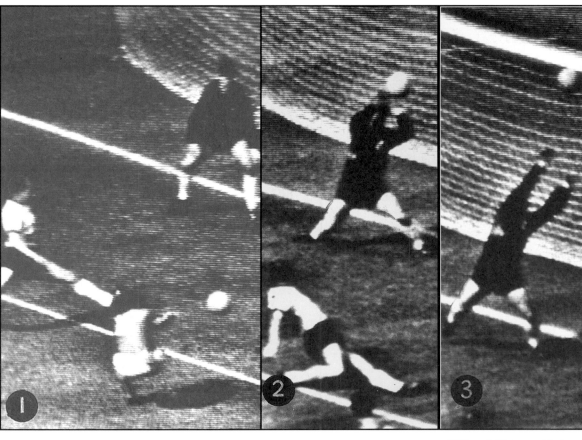

ENGLAND'S CONTROVERSIAL THIRD GOAL. (1) Hurst shoots. (2) Tilkowski gets his hands to the ball, and (3) pushes it against the underside of the crossbar. (4) The ball rebounds behind the goalkeeper and (5) spins back out of goal.

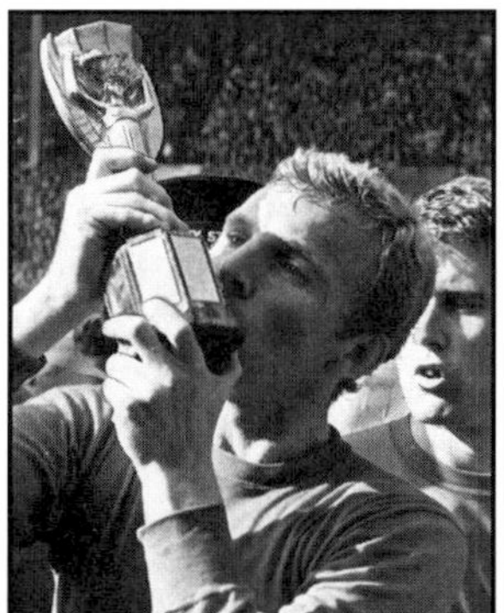

BOBBY MOORE, the England Captain.

PLAYER PRODUCES BEST GOLF OF CAREER

By LEONARD CRAWLEY

PLAYING the finest golf of his career, Gary Player of South Africa won the Piccadilly World Match-Play tournament and £5,000 at Wentworth on Saturday. In the 36-hole final he beat Jack Nicklaus, of the United States, by six and four.

To beat Arnold Palmer and Nicklaus in successive rounds is a tremendous feat. In shooting terms, some right and left! In years to come Player may well look back upon this tournament as his greatest triumph.

For six rounds he played with a sustained brilliance never surpassed in this country. It showed him to be armed to the teeth - the complete modern golfer.

When he pulled up on Saturday he looked as though he could have gone on for a month. Twos were his jokers and he produced eight of them in the tournament.

I have the greatest admiration for Nicklaus, both as a man and as a golfer. On all types of courses over a period I would put my money on him against any player in the world. But, alas, his disagreement on Saturday with the referee. Col. Anthony Duncan, at the ninth hole, disturbed the atmosphere of a great occasion and it is my guess that no one lost more by this than Nicklaus himself.

His wild hook from the ninth tee in the morning put the ball in a ditch - a bad stroke which was probably a psychological mistake, since he had been talking about this very ditch at dinner the night before.

Nicklaus asked for a ruling from Duncan and was allowed a drop under a penalty of one stroke. The drop was an unfortunate one and, noticing a large advertisement board 60 yards away, he asked for another drop and the answer was no.

It is not a question of who was right, for in the rules of golf it is quite clearly stated that in match play the referee's decision is final and so it is in the printed local rules for this championship. Therefore Duncan is a very eminent golfer and there is no greater authority on the rules of golf today. His generous gesture in handing over to Gerald Micklem, the only other person so complete in his knowledge of the rules and so lucid in his explanation of them, is somewhat ironical.

Thank heaven my good friend young Jack did not jump from the frying pan into the fire, for it would have burned furiously.

(October 10)

AMERICAN, 19, BREAKS WORLD MILE RECORD

BERKELEY, California, Sunday.

Jim Ryun, 19, an American student from Wichita, Kansas, set a world record for the mile today at Berkeley, California. His time was 3min 51.3sec.

The previous record was 3min 53.6sec by Michel Jazy of France in June last year. Ryun was running in the all-American Athletics meeting at the University of California Stadium.

REUTER.

(July 18)

Nothing is in sight to beat Toria

By A Special Correspondent

CASTLE BAY, Barra.

Only eight boats had arrived at the second Round Britain race port of call here this evening, and another stage victory for Derek Kelsall's trimaran Toria seems inevitable

None of the other seven crews already grabbing their 48 hours' rest have beaten Toria's time of two days, 21 hr 18 min for the 450-mile passage from Crosshaven.

(July 11)

Cooper talks of another Clay fight

Daily Telegraph Reporter

NURSES and patients leaned out of ward windows overlooking the central gardens at Guy's Hospital, London, yesterday to give Henry Cooper a special round of applause.

Cooper, who failed to wrest the world heavyweight championship title from Cassius Clay on Saturday because of a severe cut over his left eye, had come to Guy's to have the wound stitched.

Cooper will get £50,000 for last Saturday's fight. Clay, who flies back to America tomorrow, receives £100,000. A provisional gross figure for the fight would exceed £400,000, the promoters said yesterday.

Was Cooper punched or butted in the first minute of the sixth round? The greengrocer-boxer had no doubt. "It was most definitely a clash of heads. This cut was not caused by Clay's fist. He came in and caught me with his head."

Cassius Clay, or Muhammad Ali, as he insists on being called since embracing Islam, hotly denied that Cooper's cut was caused by "a clash of heads."

Speaking at a Press conference at the Piccadilly Hotel yesterday. Clay said the cut was as a result of "a solid snap right-hand blow." He said that anyone watching that part of the bout in slow motion on the film now being shown at 150 cinemas throughout the country could see this for themselves.

(May 23)

BRITON WINS WORLD TITLE FIGHT

Daily Telegraph Reporter

WALTER McGOWAN of Hamilton became the world flyweight champion when he outpointed Salvatore Burruni of Sardinia over 15 rounds at Wembley last night.

McGowan finished the contest with a bad cut over his right eye but it did not prevent him from an almost total supremacy over the 33-year-old champion.

McGowan, 23, is the ninth Briton to have won the title and the fourth Scot. The last time it was won by a Briton was in 1950 by Terry Allen.

Burruni said after the fight that McGowan was a worthy champion.

(June 15)

WEST INDIES ROUND OFF THREE GREAT YEARS

VERSATILE SOBERS AGAIN DECISIVE FACTOR

West Indies beat England by an innings and 55 runs.

By E.W. SWANTON

HEADINGLEY, Monday.

THE overwhelming victory of the West Indies here this afternoon brings their exploits of the last few years to a wonderful climax. Since 1963, they have beaten England in two rubbers, Australia in one, and this is easily the most comprehensive success of the three.

The West Indies have, perhaps, owed more to Sobers than any Test side have ever owed to any one player, let alone any captain. He has scored 641 runs in the four games, taken 17 wickets, and held a bagful of catches.

He has not lost a tactical trick, and has taken a good many that were by no means obvious.

The captain has held the centre of the stage from first to last, and to some extent has eclipsed the other stars in his distinguished side. But that this has been a notable team effort, nevertheless was always clear enough from the West Indies performance in the field.

The disparity between the sides in this department is even more pronounced than in the other two, and that is saying a good deal.

ILL LUCK WITH TOSS

But England outmatched

The plain fact is that England have been outmatched. No doubt if some of the four tosses had gone the other way - and especially the one at Old Trafford - things would have taken a different course, but the result must have been the same.

There is no disgrace in losing to a side of such calibre, but the manner of today's defeat, to take one instance, was indeed disappointing and it was sad to see the crowd making for home in the early afternoon sunshine.

Several hundred, and as many Yorkshiremen as West Indians, delayed their departure for an hour or so, thronging the front of the players' pavilion and calling for the victors, who obliged on the balcony.

Sobers was applauded afresh when he made a special appearance on the announcement that he had won the special Horlicks Award for the best bowling of the match as well as the best batting.

This £400 brings his tally for these particular prizes to £800, which - as in the case of those Englishmen who have won awards - is I understand, divided among the team.

BENIGN PITCH

Hall's teeth drawn

England today had as fair a chance of bringing about a recovery as could have been hoped for. The pitch played as benignly as ever and though Hall as usual spared no effort he could not recapture the divine spark that fired his bowling on Saturday.

Nor was Griffith ever very formidable, which meant that the burden had to be shouldered mostly by Sobers and Gibbs. Sobers himself bowled in his faster style for the first 80 minutes, and took the first two wickets of the day, those of d'Oliveira and Barber. Then Gibbs relieved him and demolished the middle and tail.

The innings of most consequence was played by Barber. Once or twice he seemed hypnotised by the length ball outside the off stump and he is a little too inclined to offer hostages to fortune in that direction. But at least this springs from the desire to look for runs and to get on top.

Milburn, pursuing the same theme, made 42 in 36 minutes coming in at No. 7 when, with the board showing 128 for five, the issue was almost decided. Milburn hit seven fours and picked up a good length ball from Gibbs and lifted it on to the players' pavilion at square leg.

Unfortunately Milburn then took some of the gloss off his performance by sweeping Gibbs, now bowling round the wicket, and losing his middle stump.

Apart from these two it was a case of everyone making a few and looking quite composed about it before falling to a lapse either of judgment or of technique, or both. This was the aspect today that made the second innings so depressing from the English point of view.

TEST AVERAGES

ENGLAND - Batting

	M	I	NO	R	H'st	Ave.
T.W.Graveney	4	7	1	459	165	76.50
C.Milburn	4	8	2	316	126*	52.66
B.d'Oliviera	4	6	0	256	88	42.66
R.W.Barber	2	3	0	97	55	32.33
M.C.Cowdrey	4	8	0	252	96	31.50
G.Boycott	4	7	0	186	71	26.57
J.M.Parks	4	8	0	181	91	22.62
I.A.Snow	3	5	2	62	59*	20.66
K.Higgs	5	8	0	147	63	18.37
W.E.Russell	2	4	0	61	26	15.25
K.Barrington	2	4	0	59	30	14.75
F.J.Titmus	3	5	0	61	22	12.20
D.E. Underwood	2	4	2	22	12*	11.00
R.Hillingworth	2	3	0	7	4	2.33
I.J.Jones	2	3	3	0	0*	—

Played in one match: J.T.Murray 112, J.H.Edrich 35, D.L.Amiss 17, D.B. Close 4, M.J.K.Smith 5&6, D.A. Allen 37 &1, D.J.Brown 14&10, B.R.Knight 6.

*Not out.

Bowling

	O	M	R	W	Ave
Higgs	236.4	49	611	24	25.46
Close	12	3	28	1	28.00
Barber	51.1	7	182	6	30.33
Snow	138.5	29	451	12	37.58
Titmus	81	20	190	5	38.00
d'Oliveira	160	48	329	8	41.12
Illingworth	63	24	165	4	41.25
Knight	51	3	169	4	42.25
Allen	31.1	8	104	2	52.00
Underwood	69	25	172	1	172.00
Jones	75	11	259	1	259.00
Brown	28	4	84	0	—

WEST INDIES — Batting

	M	I	NO	R	H'st	Ave
G.S.Sobers	5	8	1	722	174	103.14
S.M.Nurse	5	8	0	501	137	62.62
B.F.Butcher	5	8	1	420	209*	60.00
R.B.Kanhal	5	8	0	324	104	40.50
D.Holford	5	8	2	227	105*	37.83
C.C.Hunte	5	8	0	243	135	30.37
P.Lashley	2	3	0	81	49	27.00
W.W.Hall	5	6	2	69	30*	17.25
C.C.Griffith	5	6	1	82	30	16.40
E.D. McMorris	2	3	0	26	14	8.66
L.R.Gibbs	5	6	3	22	12	7.33
D.W.Allan	2	2	0	14	13	7.00
J.L.Hendricks	3	4	1	11	9*	3.66

Played in one match: M.C.Carew 2&0.

Bowling

	O	M	R	W	Ave
Gibbs	273.4	103	520	21	24.76
Sobers	269.4	68	545	20	27.25
Hall	175.3	35	555	18	30.83
Griffith	144.3	27	438	14	31.28
Holford	90.5	13	302	5	60.40

Also bowled: Lashley 3-2-1-1: Carew 3-0-11-1: Hunte 13-2-4-10.

(August 9)

Brabham wins championship

JACK BRABHAM, 40, of Australia today became the fist man to win the racing driver's world championship in a car of his own construction. He was standing in the pits here at the time.

Brabham's third world championship was clinched on the 32nd lap of the Italian Grand Prix. His car had been wheeled away with engine trouble when he was leading the race after only eight laps of the 68-lap event.

It was on lap 32 that John Surtees, the only other driver who could beat him pulled into the pit and retired his Cooper-Maserati with a severe petrol leak.

(September 25)

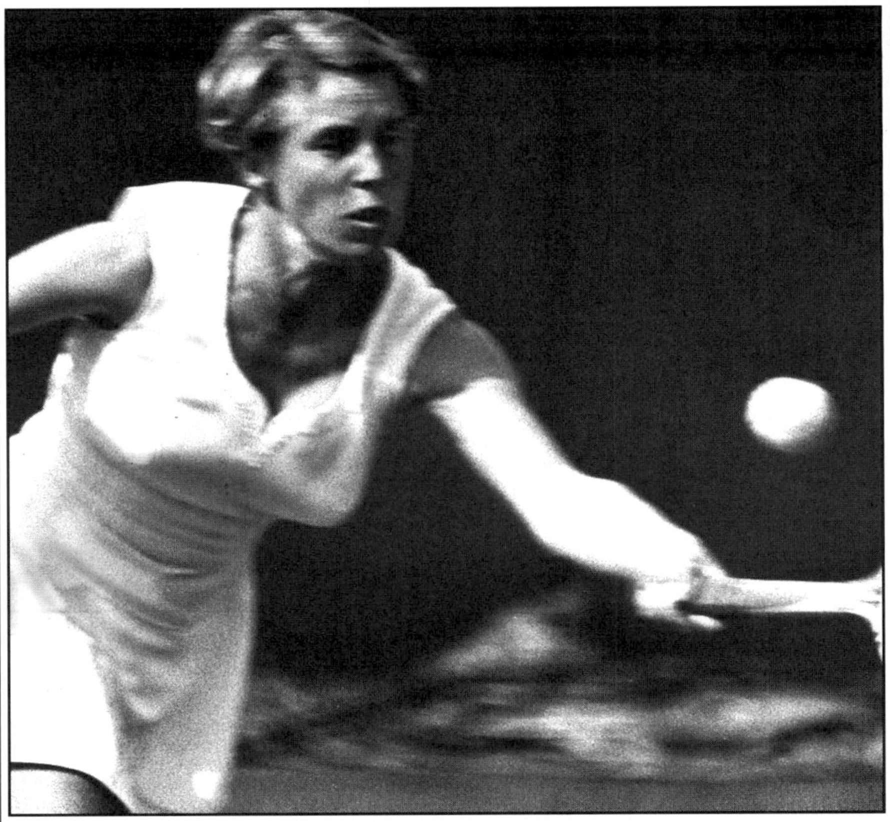

MRS. ANN JONES, whose thrilling victory over the United States joint No. 1 Miss Nancy Richey brought her the French hard court championship to add to her Italian championship.

MRS. JONES WINS TOP HARD COURT TITLE

By LANCE TINGAY

ANN JONES, already champion of Italy, is again champion of France. She battled through to a thrilling and memorable victory this afternoon over the Texan Nancy Richey, the United States joint No. 1, by 6-3, 6-1, to take the world's most coveted hard court title which she previously won in 1961.

A. Roche also made an Italo-Franco double. This brilliant New South Wales left-hander, who is 21, won the men's singles final against the Hungarian I. Gulyas 6-1, 6-4, 7-5, despite an injured ankle which delayed the match for 24 hours and for which he had a pain-killing injection.

The bare record of Mrs. Jones's final win, 6-3, 6-1, looks one-sided. It was anything but that, for there was hardly a rally not rigorously contested, and it took 78 minutes to play.

This was no spectacular victory, more a matter of brain than brawn. On Friday Miss Richey lambasted the world's No. 1, Margaret Smith, from the court, because Miss Smith tried to match pace for pace and drive for drive. Mrs. Jones did not make the same mistake.

She took up against Miss Richey just where she left off in the Wightman Cup in Cleveland, Ohio, last autumn. Then, on a rather faster court, she won by playing a looped ball down the middle of the court, and the contest today could have been a continuation.

HUMILIATING SCORE

Infinity of pains

The top-spin looped forehand of Mrs. Jones down this court took her opposition on the backhand and not only spiked Miss Richey's guns but almost stifled her into defeat. She was left with nothing but what on paper looked a humiliating score for an infinity of pains.

To win by inducing error on the other side requires patience and strong tactical sense. Mrs. Jones has all this, and the ability to play all the stops in the game as well. Her drop shots were a delight and often outright winners. Many times Miss Richey had to scamper up court and then scamper back again to retrieve the lob.

(June 6)

STEWART IN BRM WINS AT MONACO

JACKIE STEWART, the young Scots driver, won the Monaco Grand Prix to-day. It was the first championship race under the new three litre formula, but Stewart was driving a two-litre BRM which lost its fifth gear.

(May 23)

EMERSON WIN KEEPS TROPHY IN AUSTRALIA

AUSTRALIA successfully completed their defence of the Davis Cup yesterday, defeating India 4-1 in the challenge round in Melbourne, reports Reuter.

Australia gained a 2-0 lead on the opening day, Roy Emerson and Fred Stolle both winning their singles matches in straight sets, and although Ramanathan Krishnan and Jaideep Mukherjea won the doubles for India on Tuesday, the Australians completed a clean sweep of the singles by winning both matches yesterday.

Emerson took only 95 minutes yesterday to beat Krishnan 6-0, 6-2, 10-8 and give Australia a winning lead. With the pressure off, Mukherjea played tenacious and sometimes brilliant tennis in a two-and-a-half-hour battle against Stolle, who eventually won by 7-5,6-8,6-3,5-7,6-3.

It was a fine performance by Mukherjea, whom Australian team manager, Harry Hopman, acclaimed as a player with a big future. Though he was unable to match Stolle's power. Mukherjea volleyed crisply and hit his passing shots accurately and fully extended his experienced rival.

Krishnan, slow about court and with a vulnerable second service, was never really in the match against Emerson. But they met when the humidity caused over 300 cases of heat exhaustion among the 8,500 spectators. Conditions were better for the second match, with a strong wind springing up.

Since Brazil eliminated the United States in an inter-zone final, the Australians were confident they would retain the Davis Cup.

(December 29)

WOMAN WINS RIGHT TO TRAINER'S LICENCE

Daily Telegraph Reporter

MRS. FLORENCE NAGLE, 70, won her 20-year fight against the Jockey Club Stewards yesterday and became the first woman in Britain to be granted a licence to train racehorses for "flat" racing.

Her challenge to the unwritten rule of the male-controlled Jockey Club that no woman should hold a trainer's licence ended in the High Court. The Jockey Club agreed to grant her a trainer's licence, provided she expressly acknowledged that the licence was granted in the exercise of the Stewards' absolute and unfettered discretion.

The terms of settlement were agreed by Mrs. Nagle and the Jockey Club before Mr. Justice SACHS.

Mrs. NAGLE, who trains horses near Petworth, Sussex, sued Viscount ALLENDALE, of Hexham, Northumberland, and Sir RANDLE GUY GEILDEN, of Minster Lovell, Oxon, on their own behalf and on behalf of the Stewards and all other members of the Jockey Club.

In February three Appeal Court judges allowed Mrs. Nagle's appeal from a decision of Mr. Justice JOHN STEPHENSON striking out the statement of claim in her action. She was told she could argue her case in the High Court.

Mrs. Nagle's legal fight cost her more than £1,000. Outside the court, she said: "I am very happy. It is not a glamorous profession for a woman."

For more than 20 years, Mrs. Nagle has trained a stable of about 14 horses with her head lad holding the trainer's licence. She had on previous occasions been refused a trainer's licence by the Jockey Club.

(July 29)

CASSIUS CLAY IS GRANTED DIVORCE

Cassius Clay, world heavyweight boxing champion and a member of the Black Muslims, was granted a divorce at Miami today from his wife, Sonji. She will receive an allowance of $150,000 (£53,000) in monthly installments of $15,000.

Giving evidence in his divorce suit against her, he said that he spent seven hours a day before their marriage instructing her in Black Muslim beliefs. He stressed that his wife should wear modest clothing at all times.

(January 7)

LIONS FORWARDS INSPIRE STORMING RECOVERY

By TONY GOODRIDGE

Australia ...8 pts. British Isles ... 11

IN a magnificently sustained storming finish the British Isles, 8-0 down shortly after the interval, struck back so successfully that they won the first International of their tour at the Sydney cricket ground by a goal, a penalty goal.

It was not, as might have been supposed, the greater penetration of the Lions backs that turned the scales because they rarely got moving smoothly in a collective sense at all but the fitness and the ability to keep going together of the forwards that brought home the spoils.

The Lions had not, in fact, cut a very distinguished figure during the first half for the spoiling of the Australian back row, Davis, Shepherd and Guerassimoff, was fast and incisive.

Crittle was jumping and reaching the ball in the line-out faster and more constructively than anyone else. Moreover, Catchpole was playing a sound and intelligent game at scrumhalf.

The Lions during this half did not suggest much in the way of a manufactured score but once Stuart Watkins almost hobbled over for a try before he was caught by Cardy and Rutherford, Watkins and Weston all had attempts to kick penalty goals.

The Lions, too, made things more difficult for themselves just after the interval when they failed to retire the requisite distance at a penalty and made Ruebner's kick at goal that much easier.

But that was as far as they were prepared to go and from thereon a gaily coloured crowd of 42,000 were held fascinated as the Lions began their way back.

Rutherford began it by kicking a penalty goal which really gave the needed spur. The difference was only five points now and after a few encouraging runs by the backs McLoughlin broke from the front of a line-out.

Kennedy was in attendance and McLoughlin was still there in the end in support of Murphy who actually scored the try which was finely converted by Rutherford.

Then with the scores level some five minutes from the end the Lions forwards were back in full support of McLoughlin who again had moved down the touchline with Williams, Kennedy, Pask and Murphy. They passed with bewildering speed as they continually drove onward to the line and a try scored by Kennedy.

AUSTRALIA - P. Ryan; G. Ruened (N.S.W.) R. Trivett (Queensland), B. Ellwood, A. Cardy; P. Hawthorne, K. Catchpole; A.R. Miller, P. Johnson, J. Thornett (capt.) P. Crittle, R. Heming (NSW) J. Guerassimoff (Queensland), D. Shepherd, G. Davis (NSW)

BRITISH ISLES - D. Rutherford, (England); S.J. Watkins, D.K. Jones (Wales), D. Watkins (Wales), R.M. Young; R.J. McLoughlin, K.W. Kennedy (Ireland), D. Williams (Wales), M.J. Campbell-Lamerton (Scotland, capt.), B. Price (Wales), J.W. Telfer (Scotland), A.E.I. Park (Wales), N.A.A. Murphy (Ireland).

Referee - K. Crowe (Queensland).

(May 30)

Arkle hurt and may never race again

By JOHN LAWRENCE

ARKLE may never run again. The news issued from Kempton Park last night, cast a pall of sadness far beyond the narrow confines of National Hunt racing.

Running yesterday in the King George VI Chase, which he won last year and for which he started a red-hot favourite, Arkle was beaten into second place by the 10-1 outsider, Dormant.

He hobbled, dead lame, away from the unsaddling enclosure, travelled back by horse box to the racecourse stables and was immediately examined by two official vets.

(December 28)

ABOVE: POPE PAUL AND THE ARCHBISHOP OF CANTERBURY, Dr. Ramsey, embracing when they met in the Vatican's Sistine Chapel yesterday. Watching them is Bishop Willebrands, of the Secretariat of Christian Unity.

BELOW: A SMOKE BOMB EXPLODING behind the wedding coach of Crown Princess Beatrix of the Netherlands and Herr Claus von Amsberg in Amsterdam yesterday.

ST. MARKS SQUARE turned into a lagoon after the sea walls guarding Venice had been breached. On the left is the Doge's Palace and in the background is the Church of St. George.

A new leading role

MR. RONALD REAGAN, the former actor who has just been elected as the new Republican Governor of California pictured with his wife Nancy.

JAMES MEREDITH, 32, the American Civil Rights worker, crawling for cover after he had been shot near Hernando, Mississippi, when taking part in a march from Memphis, Tennessee, into his home State. Other marchers are hiding behind the car.

The flower children may have congregated for a love-in at Woburn but the bloom of the 1960s was beginning to fade. The economic situation in Britain became acute as the Labour Government was forced to devalue the pound. President de Gaulle said a firm "Non" to the renewed British application to join the Common Market. The oil tanker Torrey Canyon hit the rocks off the Cornish coast and its contents pouring from the damaged ship threatened the beaches of south-west England. In a desperate effort to limit the damage the RAF was despatched to bomb the wreck.

In China the rampaging Red Guards set fire to part of the British Embassy in Peking, roughing up members of the staff. The Reuter's correspondent in the city was put under house arrest. In a bizarre incident in London, Chinese diplomats armed with sticks and a gun rushed from their embassy to attack the police guarding their building.

Israel swept to victory in the 6-Day War, securing its frontiers and extending its territory. For once the Americans and Russians were in accord at the United Nations in arranging a peace between Israel and her Arab neighbours. President Nasser of Egypt, whose forces had been humbled by the Israelis, resigned. The coup by the "Generals" in Greece forced King Constantine into exile. The forces of the Nigerian Government invaded the breakaway province of Biafra, the beginning of a long and bloody war. More and more American forces were drawn into the war in Vietnam while the protests against the war spread to London where a mob fought with the police outside the American Embassy. Cassius Clay, who had changed his name to Mohammed Ali on joining the Black Muslims, was first stripped of his World heavyweight title and then imprisoned for refusing to be drafted into the army.

As the British defence secretary announced the withdrawal of troops from most of the Far and Middle East, the rioting continued in Aden up to the moment when independence was granted to the Republic of South Yemen and the last British servicemen pulled out. Che Guevara, not yet the potent symbol of rebellious youth that he was to become, was reported dead in Bolivia.

Dr. Christian Barnard performed the first successful heart transplant operation. Sad to say, a few weeks later the patient was to die when his body rejected the new organ. Sir Francis Chichester, knighted at Greenwich by the Queen in the same place where Elizabeth I had dubbed Sir Francis Drake, returned from his single-handed journey round the world. Donald Campbell was killed as he tried once again to break the world water-speed record.

Two senior statesmen, Earl Attlee and Konrad Adenauer, died during the year while two entertainers of a different kind, Sir Malcolm Sargent and Vivien Leigh, took their last bows. The Poet Laureate John Masefield and the war poet Siegfried Sassoon also died.

Tony Jacklin, in winning the Dunlop Masters tournament, became the man to watch in golf. After an incredible pile up of horses in the second circuit of the Grand National course, Foinavon, an outsider, was able to slip through to win the race.

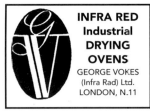

The Daily Telegraph
and Morning Post
No. 34872 LONDON, SATURDAY, JUNE 8, 1967
Printed in LONDON and MANCHESTER
4d.

UN calls for 9 pm cease-fire: War goes on

EGYPT DEFEATED, SAYS ISRAEL

Army near Canal: Jericho falls

THE United Nations Security Council approved unanimously a Russian resolution calling for cease-fire in the Middle East by 9 o'clock last night, but the war went on. The Israelis claimed to have won the battle for Sinai and to have routed the Jordanian Army. Gen. Yitzhak Rabin, Israeli Chief of Staff said: "The Egyptians are defeated."

Israel announced that she had captured: The whole of the Sinai peninsula up to near the Suez Canal.

Sharm El Sheikh, the Egyptian fortress controlling the Strait of Tiran.

Most of Jordan west of the River Jordan, including Jericho. The Old City of Jerusalem.

Gen. Rabin said that all Egypt's efforts "are aimed at withdrawing behind the Suez Canal, and we are taking care of that. The whole area is in our hands."

Israel has thus achieved in little over 50 hours her two main purposes in the war: the crippling of Egypt's Russian-equipped Army and the lifting of the Aqaba blockade.

TIRAN PARACHUTE DROP

Sharm El Sheikh was captured yesterday by one section of the three-pronged tank attack in Sinai and by paratroops dropped on Ras Nasrani nearby.

The remainder of the Israeli Army was driving towards three points on the Suez Canal: Qantara in the north, Ismailia in the centre, and Port Tewfik in the south. Gen. Moshe Dayan, Minister of Defence, said they had no intention of going to the canal, but one report said troops had arrived opposite Ismailia. The Egyptian commander in Gaza officially surrendered unconditionally.

The Israelis said that by far the bitterest opposition of the war was put up by the Jordanian Army, most of which was taken prisoner. Jordan admitted that "certain areas" had been occupied and the Prime Minister, Saad Juma, agreed to the cease-fire.

A report from Rome last night said that an aircraft carrying King Hussein of Jordan was expected to arrive to refuel on its way to London. Mr. Medhit Juma, Jordanian Ambassador in London, said the king was still at the head of his army.

JERUSALEM 'OURS FOREVER'

Thousands of exultant Jews poured into the old city of Jerusalem yesterday afternoon after the last bitter resistance by Jordanian troops had ended. In the shadow of the Wailing Wall, Gen. Dayan declared: "We earnestly stretch our hands to our Arab brethren in peace, but we have returned to Jerusalem never to part from her again."

Mr. Abba Eban, Israeli Foreign Minister, told the Security Council last night that Israel would cease fire if the Arabs would, and "if there is no cease-fire at this moment it is because the United Arab Republic and Syria have not accepted, and Jordan is not in a position to carry it out." Russia said she would cut off diplomatic relations if Israel did not cease fire.

Egypt, Syria and Iraq all rejected the cease-fire yesterday. Syria said its Army had invaded Israel and was chasing the Israelis towards Nazareth. Saudi Arabia and Bahrain cut off oil to Britain and America, and the Lebanon severed diplomatic relations.

CARRIER INSPECTION OFFER

Mr. Brown, Foreign Secretary, told MPs that Britain welcomed the Security Council cease-fire resolution. It was "much in their own interests" for Egypt and Iraq to accept quickly. "It is now very clear the military struggle has been going in the favour of Israel."

To nail Egypt's lie that British and American aircraft had intervened on Israel's behalf, Britain was ready to join the United States in her offer for United Nations observers to visit any warships or air bases.

Britain's 24-hour arms embargo, which expired yesterday afternoon, is being continued, says Our Diplomatic Correspondent. But it is under continuous review, and will be lifted soon, possibly today, if Russia and America fail to impose a ban.

MP'S FOUR POINTS ON PEACE

H.B. BOYNE
Political Correspondent.

BECAUSE practically everyone now assumes that Israel has already "seen off" President Nasser, the main topic among MPs last night became the need to ensure that a fair and equitable long-term settlement is reached.

There is a noticeable measure of agreement between Government and Opposition about the principles on which a lasting peace in the Middle East should be founded. These are:

1 - Recognition by all the Arab countries of Israel's right to independent existence, secure within her frontiers and free to develop her international trade;

2 - Guaranteed free passage for all shipping, including Israel's through the Suez Canal and the Tiran Strait to and from the head of the Gulf of Aqaba;

3 - A plan for speedy and humane resettlement of the Palestinian Arab refugees;

4 - A United Nations peace-keeping "presence" along all Israel's frontiers, on the Israeli as well as the Arab side.

REFORMED U N
Heath's suggestion

Ministers would probably agree with Mr. Heath's suggestion, in his speech at the Conservative women's conference, that the United Nations' secretariat must be reformed and strengthened, so that U N peace-keeping operations should "never again be brought to nothing overnight at the whim of a single State."

But they would find it difficult to go as far as the Conservative Leader in appearing to advocate Anglo-American action outside the U N if necessary.

"If Britain and American are to be successful in preventing an

Continued on Back Page, Col. 3

'BUILD A NEW PEACE' AIM BY JOHNSON

Daily Telegraph Staff Correspondent
WASHINGTON, Wednesday.

President Johnson, announcing an effort "to build a new peace" in the Middle East, set up a special advisory committee today. It matches in form, and partly in membership, the "Executive Committee" set up by President Kennedy to handle the 1962 Cuban missile crisis.

His statement that America would work inside and outside the United Nations clearly implies that an attempt will be made to work directly with Russia. The hope would be to end the use of the Middle East as an arena for rivalry between the two Powers.

PROTEST TO CHINA

By Our Diplomatic Staff

Britain delivered a strong protest to China last night for her failure to protect the British mission in Peking from a rioting mob. The Chinese acting Chargé d'Affaires, Shen Ping, who was called to the Foreign Office to see Mr. Rodgers, Parliamentary Secretary, rejected the protest.

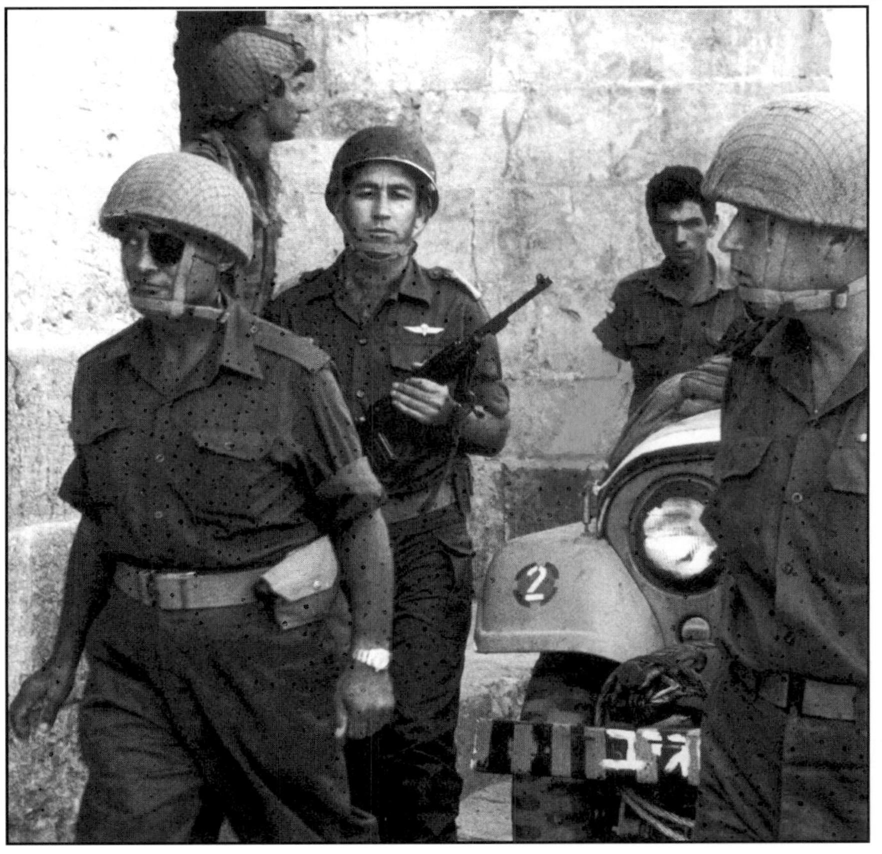

GEN. MOSHE DAYAN (centre), Israeli Defence Minister, with his troops yesterday at the Wailing Wall in the Jordanian sector of Jerusalem.

U.N. sets cease-fire deadline

GEOFFREY MYERS
United Nations Correspondent
NEW YORK, Wednesday.

AT a new emergency meeting today, the United Nations Security Council unanimously called for a cease-fire to be made effective in the Middle East by 9 p.m. BST today.

It adopted a resolution presented by Mr. Fedorenko, the Soviet representative, who asked for an urgent meeting to enforce the cease-fire call which the Council made last night.

This had called upon all Governments concerned as a first step to take measures for a cease-fire and for a cessation of all military activities in the area.

FIGHTING GOES ON
Russia blames Israel

Mr. Fedorenko, presenting today's resolution, said that Israel, which was responsible for the aggression in the Middle East, was continuing the fighting. Russia decisively and categorically condemned the completely unjustified aggression of Israel against the Arabs.

The situation in the area was menacing, and the Security Council without any delay should demand a cease-fire.

Mr. Fedorenko was in such a hurry to get the new ceasefire call that in his original draft he had demanded it to become effective at 1600 hours GMT, which would have been roughly an hour before the Council met at 1 p.m. New York time.

CEASE-FIRE CALL
Jordan accepts

In a report on the Middle East fighting U Thant, United Nations Secretary-General said that he had received a cable from Jordan saying that it had accepted the Security Council's call for a cease-fire. U Thant informed the Government of Israel of the cable.

U Thant reported that an Irish officer of the United Nations truce supervision organisation was killed early today.

The death of a Brazilian officer of the United Nations peace-keeping force was officially confirmed. In the Indian contingent of the force nine men had been killed, 20 wounded and 12 were missing.

NO WESTERN AID
Eban assurance

After today's Security Council vote. Mr. Eban, Israeli Foreign Minister, said that his country had not received one single ounce of help from the United States or from Britain in repelling the Arab "aggression."

All governments should have recognised the cease-fire call and taken measures to implement it.

Continued on Back Page, Col. 5

EXULTANT JEWS FLOCK TO WAILING WALL

BOOBY TRAPS EXPLODE

By DAVID LOSHAK
JERUSALEM, Wednesday.

THOUSANDS of exultant Jews streamed in triumphant procession to the Wailing Wall in the Old City of Jerusalem this afternoon, and for the first time for 20 years prayed at the historic shrine.

There were scenes of near-riot as Jews thronged through the Mandelbaum Gate into the Old City after Israeli troops and tanks had completed occupation of the Jordanian half of Jerusalem. Among those who went to pray at the Wailing Wall were Mr. Eshkol, the Israeli Prime Minister, Gen. Dayan, Defence Minister, and Gen. Rabin, Army Chief of staff.

Gen. Shlomo Goren, chief chaplain to the Israeli Army, blew the Shofar, the traditional Jewish trumpet sounded to herald religious events and holy days.

Extreme Orthodox Hassidic Jews and others wearing prayer shawls came to the Wailing Wall, despite the explosions of booby traps.

At one stage soldiers and police struggled with thousands round the Mandelbaum Gate as the crowds threatened to get out of control. Only the explosion of a mine caused them to go back.

Continued on Back Page, Col. 4

Police called to cope with volunteers

Daily Telegraph Reporter

POLICE were sent to Heathrow airport last night to help control hundreds of people trying to get seats on the first flight to Israel for three days. Many had spent the past two nights at the airport in the hope of flying to Tel Aviv to assist in the war work.

Scores of young volunteers recruited by the Jewish Agency tried to force their way to the El Al desk seeking tickets. There were 162 seats available on the 707 jet.

Priority was given to medical students and technicians. A few places were available for youngsters who had volunteered to work on Kibbutzim.

Airline staff made repeated calls for order over the public address system but finally police assistance was needed at the Oceanic Terminal. The flight will leave from Gatwick because of noise-control regulations.

PRICE RISE ON STOCK EXCHANGE

By Our City Staff

THERE was a marked move for the better in London stock markets yesterday and equity prices often closed above the levels prevailing at the time of the outbreak of the Arab-Israeli war.

London operators followed the overnight lead from Wall Street and all the main investment sections enjoyed the presence of buyers. British funds staged a good recovery.

The Financial Times ordinary share index had its biggest rise for over two years and closed 8.1 higher at 344.5, or 4.9 above the figure of 339.6 prior to Monday's Middle East fighting.

More City Comment - P2

'TORTURE' TRIAL VERDICTS

Charles William Richardson, 33, was found guilty on nine counts by the "torture" trial jury at the Old Bailey yesterday. Four of the other seven were also found guilty on various charges. Sentences will be pronounced today.

Hussein 'for London' mystery

Daily Telegraph Reporter

THERE was speculation last night on the whereabouts of King Hussein after the Italian Defence Ministry said the King's plane would be landing in Rome during the night for refuelling on its way to London.

But Mr. Juma, Jordanian Ambassador in London, said: "The King is still in Jordan and at the head of the Army. His morale is very high and he is doing his job. Everything is in order."

FIRST OF ALL...
RSL
Rawlings & Sons (London) Ltd., Waterloo, S.E.1.
South African Sherry

The Daily Telegraph
and Morning Post
4d.
No. 35013. LONDON, MONDAY, NOVEMBER 20, 1967
Printed in LONDON and MANCHESTER Price 4d.

MAKE TISSOT YOUR WATCHWORD
T
TISSOT
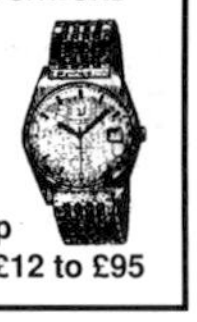
the finest watchmanship
your money can buy— £12 to £95

£ devalued 14.3pc...Bank Rate 8 pc...Higher Corporation Tax...Car H.P. curb

WILSON SEES WAY TO BOOM IN 1969

DE GAULLE OPPOSES FULL $3,000M LOAN AID

DESPITE the fact that it is a complete reversal of the policy to which the Government has been pledged for the past three years, the Prime Minister seems convinced that he can "sell" the 14.3 per cent. devaluation of the pound, announced on Saturday, to the Labour party and the country.

He sees it as the key to an economic expansion in which the Government can "put Britain first," with no more need to worry about the effect on reserves of speculation against sterling.

This was the note on which Mr. Wilson ended his Ministerial broadcast to the nation last night. Stressing the chance which devaluation gave to "break out from the straitjacket" of past years, he added: "We're on our own now. It means Britain first."

PAYMENTS SURPLUS TARGET

The Government hopes, says Our Political Correspondent, that the economic recovery in the wake of devaluation will be shaping towards boom conditions in 1969, with the balance of payments in substantial surplus.

The Conservatives are to vote against a Government motion asking the Commons to approve Mr. Callaghan's devaluation statement in a two-day debate tomorrow and Wednesday. Business in the House of Lords is being rearranged to allow for a debate tomorrow.

FRENCH OBJECTIONS

The French Government indicated last night that it would support the International Monetary Fund's $1,400 million standby loan requested by Britain. But President de Gaulle feels that Britain has not yet given sufficient assurances to justify France supporting the projected additional loan of $1,600 million from the Central Banks which would have made a total of $3,000 million.

Finance Ministers of the Common Market meeting in Paris last night similarly agreed to support the $1,400 million loan, but failed to agree on the second course. West Germany's contribution to the loan will be $200 million.

The United States discount rate - equivalent to Bank Rate - has been increased from 4 to 4 ½ per cent. in response to Britain's devaluation. Canadian Bank Rate is being raised from five to six per cent. from today.

CALLAGHAN'S REMEDIES

The crisis measures announced by Mr. Callaghan, Chancellor of the Exchequer, in a statement issued at 9.30 p.m. on Saturday were:

DEVALUATION of the pound by 14.3 per cent., cutting the exchange rate from $2.80 to $2.40;

BANK RATE raised to 8 per cent., with a directive to banks to limit advances except to exporters and priority borrowers;

HIRE-PURCHASE regulations on cars tightened, with a minimim deposit of 33 ⅓ per cent. and a maximum repayment period of 27 months against the present 25 per cent. and 36 months;

CORPORATION TAX to be increased at the next Budget from 40 to 42 ½ per cent., and a "strict watch" on dividends;

SELECTIVE EMPLOYMENT TAX premiums for manufacturers to be withdrawn, except in development areas, saving over £100 million;

EXPORT REBATES to be abolished, saving nearly £100 million a year;

DEFENCE SPENDING to be cut by over £100 million next year;

PUBLIC EXPENDITURE, including nationalised industries' capital expenditure, to be reduced by £100 million.

One effect of the increase in Bank Rate to 8 per cent. will be that overdrafts will be more expensive. The building societies have not yet decided whether they will put up the interest rates on house loans.

B A O R PAY HIT

The proposed £100 million saving in the defence budget will be achieved by cuts in re-equipment programmes for the Services rather than major changes in overseas deployment. The pay packets of 61,000 British soldiers and airmen in Germany, who are paid in marks, will be lowered by 14.3 per cent. Local allowances may be adjusted when prices settle.

HOLIDAYS IN SPAIN NO DEARER

SPAIN last night devalued the peseta from 60 to the dollar to 70, thus restoring it to the old rate of 168 to the £. Holidays in Spain for Britons will thus be no dearer.

Eleven other countries had earlier followed Britain's devaluation lead. They are: Denmark (7.9 p.c.), Egypt, Fiji, Hongkong, Ireland, Israel, Jugoslavia, Malta, Nepal, Bermuda, and Guyana.

Announcements that they would not devalue came from: The United States, Japan, Switzerland, Norway, Sweden, the Common Market countries, Greece, Russia, India, Brunai, Singapore, Malaysia, Rhodesia, Turkey, Iraq, Kuwait, Saudi Arabia, Libya, Bahrain, Austria, Zambia, Finland, Libya and South Africa.

New Zealand was expected to devalue, while Australia, Portugal, Malawi and Jordan had still to decide.

Dearer Holidays Abroad - P20

DEARER BEEF AND BREAD LIKELY

By Our Business Staff

PRICES will certainly start to climb in the weeks ahead, but devaluation will only be one cause. Others include normal seasonal factors and the epidemic of foot-and-mouth desease.

On a Treasury estimate, prices will go up by a maximum of 3 p.c. or about 7d in the pound, because of devaluation.

The final increase in the shopping bill may well be less than that. It all depends on how many countries, particularly those exporting food, follow Britain's devaluation.

Both Denmark and Ireland promptly announced that they would follow Britain's lead. Britain is the main customer of both for meat and dairy produce, so that there should be no exceptional price increases for pork, bacon and butter.

Britain is also a vitally important market for New Zealand, particularly lamb and butter. The pressure on its Government will therefore be strong to follow Britain. If it yields the British housewife will benefit.

Sharp rise

Beef prices will rise sharply if the Argentine does not follow the devaluation. The foot-and-mouth disease outbreak will also put pressure on prices.

Beef is likely to go up by about 2d to 3d a pound. Poultry and eggs are unlikely to be affected by devaluation.

Bread will almost certainly go up by ½d to 1d a loaf, since about 30 p.c. of our wheat is imported and paid for in dollars. This will be the most rapid price response to devaluation.

Petrol and oil prices should not be affected to a very large degree. Crude oil imports will probably go up. A Shell spokesman said: "Petrol prices seem certain to rise but it is impossible to say when."

The tobacco import bill could rise sharply to near the £100 million a year mark. The Rhodesian situation has meant buying dearer supplies from America.

After the last devaluation in 1949 prices rose by only 2 p.c. overall, but food went up by 4 p.c.

BANK & STOCK EXCHANGES SHUT

Banks and Stock Exchanges will be closed throughout Britain and Northern Ireland today because of devaluation. Bank staffs should still report for duty.

£500m aim in payment surplus

KENNETH FLEET
City Editor

DEVALUATION is only one, admittedly the most important, of the measures the Government is taking to bring about an improvement of £500 million in the balance of payments.

In order to tide sterling over the awkward post-devaluation phase in the world's foreign exchange markets Bank Rate is now 8 p.c. instead of 6 ½ p.c., and a loan of $1,400 million is being negotiated at the International Monetary Fund.

Foreign bankers in the "Paris Club" of the 10 richest countries are expected by the Treasury to make available $1,600 million of short-term credits. The French Government, which alone of the Europeans refused until the last moment to undertake not to devalue the franc, is also resisting on this front.

France has not agreed to put up any part of the loan and is still endeavouring to persuade her Common Market colleagues to hold back until firmer assurances are given.

If as the Government evidently hopes 8 p.c. bank rate is temporary, the inevitable rise in other domestic interest rates would also prove short lived. Bank overdrafts for tomorrow, if you have one (getting one may be impossible), start around 10 p.c. and the bank deposit is 6 p.c.

Building societies will not hurry to raise their borrowing and mortgage lending rates in the belief that bank rate will soon come down.

The Government's second set of measures include stiffer hire purchase terms for cars, a strict limit on bank lending except to "priority customers," a £200 million cutback in defence and nationalised industries' spending and a near £200 millions saving in Selective Employment Tax and export rebates.

IMPORT SAVINGS

Shift of resources

The Government's intention is emphatically "to shift the use of resources to exports and import saving," not to deflate and depress the economy.

The official Whitehall view is that unemployment is already moving firmly down. Even without the stimulus to industry devaluation is expected to bring, the level of unemployment in sight for the spring is put around 1.8 p.c. of the working population.

It is now patent that the Government is contemplating with electoral relish a much lower rate towards the end of next year.

Although pious utterances have already been made about not letting the competitive advantages of devaluation get lost in higher wages and salaries, it is significant that the Government intends no statutory tightening - certainly no return to the 1966 freeze - of its defences against claims for higher wages.

PRICE RISES

"Genuine" cases

On the other hand it is prepared to see "genuine" price increases following the rise in certain import prices that devaluation brings in its train.

The Treasury has estimated that the cost of living may go up as a result of devaluation by about 2 ½-3 p.c. - that is between 6d and 7 ½d in every £ spent by the householder.

The impact of ordinary domestic spending is limited by the decision to devalue of countries like

Continued on Back Page, Col. 4

WILSON'S CAR THEFT PUZZLES THE YARD

Scotland Yard CID and Special Branch were trying all yesterday to solve the mystery of devaluation night, how someone managed to steal one of the Prime Minister's official cars right under police noses in Downing Street.

The Humber Imperial was driven away between 11.30 p.m. Saturday and 12.20 a.m. Sunday. Crowds were still about. The car was recovered an hour and a half later at Heathrow Airport.

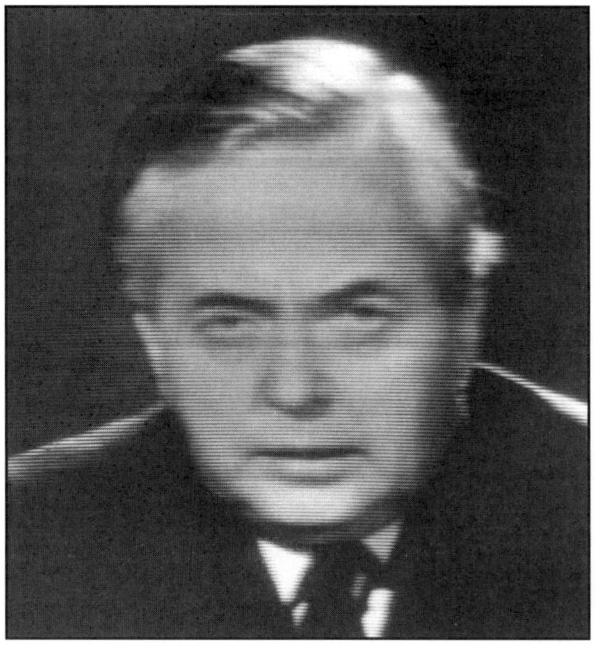

MR. WILSON SPEAKING ON TELEVISION LAST NIGHT.

RECOVERY BY SPRING, THEN A SURPLUS

WILSON'S ROSY PICTURE

H.B. BOYNE
Political Correspondent

IN the Government's view, the economic recovery touched off by devaluation will be well under way by next spring. By the autumn it will be shaping towards boom conditions in 1969.

Unemployment will have long ceased to be a problem, and the Government's chief concern will be to ensure that inflationary tendencies are offset. It is part of this rosy picture that the balance of payments will be in substantial surplus during 1969.

Mr. Wilson is looking forward to having "freedom of manoeuvre." He undoubtedly sees this in electoral terms.

In other words, he hopes to be in a position to stage an election any time from the spring of 1969 onwards. He is confident that the voters, their wallets lined with devalued pounds resulting from overtime on export orders, will be happy to return the Government that has performed the "economic miracle."

IMMEDIATE TASK

Party confidence

Nothing, however, is further from Mr. Wilson's thoughts than the idea of being forced into an election in the near future. So his immediate task is to placate the Parliamentary Labour party and secure an impressive vote of confidence for devaluation in the Commons this week.

Mr. Callaghan, Chancellor of the Exchequer, is to make a statement in the Commons this afternoon, amplifying the one he issued through the Treasury on Saturday night.

He will be closely questioned by Labour MPs on "the steps that will be needed to protect the most vulnerable sections of the community from hardship resulting from the change in the exchange rate."

VEIL LIFTED

Rents reference

Mr. Wilson lifted one corner of this veil in his broadcast, by mentioning a Government decision to refer "certain council rent increases" to the Prices and Incomes Board.

It has also been made clear that there will be no reintroduction of Health Service charges and no slowing down of housing, school or hospital building. The Chancellor has been discussing social welfare provisions with Mrs. Hart, Minister of Social Security, but not with a view to cutting them. The intention is rather to ensure that extra help goes where it is needed.

Coninued on Back Page, Col. 3

BBC ACCUSED OF 'MUZZLE' ON TORIES

NORMAN HARE
Television Staff

THE Conservative Central Office yesterday accused the BBC of a deliberate attempt to muzzle the Opposition view of the financial crisis.

The Chancellor of the Exchequer and Mr. Macleod, Shadow Chancellor, had been invited to take part in the radio programme "The World This Weekend." When Mr. Callaghan turned it down the BBC withdrew their invitation to Mr. Macleod.

A Central Office spokesman commented: "The BBC have informed the Opposition that their spokesmen are not to be allowed to express their views on devaluation on TV or radio today. We are asking for the right to reply to Mr. Wilson's broadcast."

Shadow Cabinet incensed

Members of the Shadow Cabinet were incensed by the BBC decision, which they understood to have been taken by Sir Hugh Greene, the Director General.

What mainly worries them is the thought that the Government can keep the Opposition off TV and radio simply by rejecting an invitation for one of its own spokesmen to appear.

A BBC spokesman said last night that in the last 24 hours statements by the Opposition had been fully covered.

EGG WELCOMES CALLAGHAN

Mr. Callaghan, Chancellor of the Exchequer, was booed by part of a 500 crowd when he arrived back at No. 11 Downing Street yesterday. An egg landed in the road after he had entered his official residence.

DOCKERS STAY OUT

The unofficial London docks dispute, now in its seventh week, goes on. A noisy meeting of 2,000 dockers yesterday twice refused to vote on a union recommendation for a return to work to allow negotiations to begin.

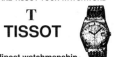

RED GUARD MOB BURN BRITISH CHANCERY

RADIO CUT: 'THEY'RE COMING IN...'

JOHN RIDLEY
Diplomatic Staff

THE main chancery building of the British Legation in Peking was burned down last night by a howling mob of Red Guards. Furniture was thrown out of the windows of the residence of the Chargé d'Affaires opposite and smashed.

The Foreign Office said the chancery was "a write-off," but all the members of the Legation were safely lodged in other embassies. Some had been mishandled, but none seriously hurt.

After a day of anti-British demonstrations, the Foreign Office lost contact with the Mission when a wireless operator interrupted a message to tap out:

"They're coming in . . ." Then there was silence.

Radio contact had still not been re-established late last night, and the only message received by the Foreign Office was from a friendly foreign mission.

The mob of Red Guards broke into the chancery shortly after the expiration of Peking's 48-hour ultimatum to Britain challenging her policy in Hongkong.

A report that the building had been set on fire was confirmed in London later through a friendly diplomatic mission in Peking, which stepped in when the British communications were cut off.

Flames were seen coming from the residence of Mr. Donald Hopson, 52, the Chargé d'Affaires, according to a French report, but his house was stated not to have been destroyed.

A vast crowd assembled and prevented any contact with the diplomatic mission. Fire engines later appeared. According to French sources, Red Guards roamed the streets looking for Britons.

Four members of the mission's staff were reported to have been manhandled by the mob. Reports received by the Foreign Office said that all the British staff were "safe."

(August 23)

BROWN CENSURES CHINA DIPLOMATS

THE Foreign Office last night accused Chinese diplomats of deliberately provoking yesterday's pitched battle outside the Chinese Mission in London, during which three policemen and eight Chinese were wounded.

All demonstrations and gatherings near the Chinese Legation in Portland Place, Marylebone, were banned by Scotland Yard last night following yesterday's bloody running battle between police and diplomats in the mews behind the legation.

At one stage during the incident one member of the Legation staff produced a heavy automatic pistol. Police Supt. Michael Keen put his arm in front of the man and ordered him to stop.

One report said that Shen Ping, China's acting Chargé d'Affaires was believed to have been among the mass of struggling fighters.

The cause of the trouble was a Special Branch police car parked outside the garage beside the Legation's rear entrance in Devonshire Close, an attractive mews cul-de-sac.

At first the Chinese objected to the car's position and asked for it to be moved. Then about 10 of them clustered around it, refusing to let it leave until they had received an apology for an "insult" to Chairman Mao.

This apparently concerned a Mao badge, which the Chinese alleged had been taken by one of the occupants of the car.

A police inspector repeatedly asked them to get out of the way so that the car could be moved, but the Chinese refused to do so. Still demanding an apology, they screamed abuse at the police and hammered on the car's bonnet.

Police reinforcements moved up, and several constables tried to pull the Chinese bodily from the car. From my viewpoint a few yards away, bedlam and confusion then broke out.

More Chinese bringing the total to about 30, rushed out from the Legation, wielding staves, iron bars, clubs and axes and attacked the police. The police closed in.

As helmets rolled on the cobblestones and the melee surged to and fro, I saw a young policewoman and a policeman struggling to restrain a Chinese whose face was streaming with blood.

(August 30)

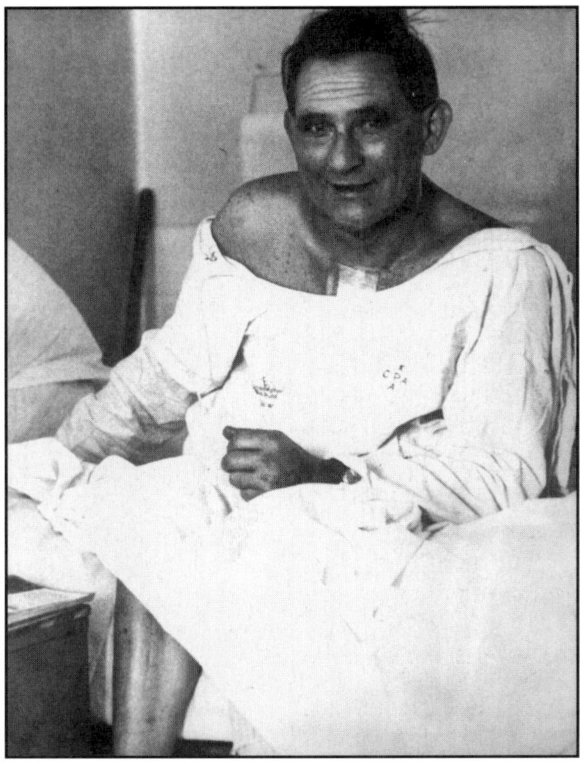

MR. LOUIS WASHKANSKY

GIRL'S HEART GIVES DYING MAN LIFE

HISTORIC TRANSPLANT: PATIENT 'DOING WELL'

From Our Correspondent
CAPE TOWN, Sunday.

A MAN aged 56, who last night was dying from cardiac failure, is today "doing well" after the transplanting of the heart of a young woman killed in a road accident.

The six-hour operation, the first human heart transplant in history, was conducted in Groote Schuur Hospital, Cape Town, by a team of 30 doctors and nurses led by Prof. Christian Barnard, Professor of Cardio-thoracic Surgery at the University of Cape Town.

The patient, Mr. Louis Washkansky, a wholesale grocer, has fully recovered consciousness. His new heart is working normally.

He was admitted to hospital a month ago in "a very bad state of heart failure." Surgeons realised that a transplant was the only hope, even if it was a remote one.

"WITHOUT HESITATION"
Proposal accepted

The proposal was put to Mr. Washkansky. He accepted "without hesitation."

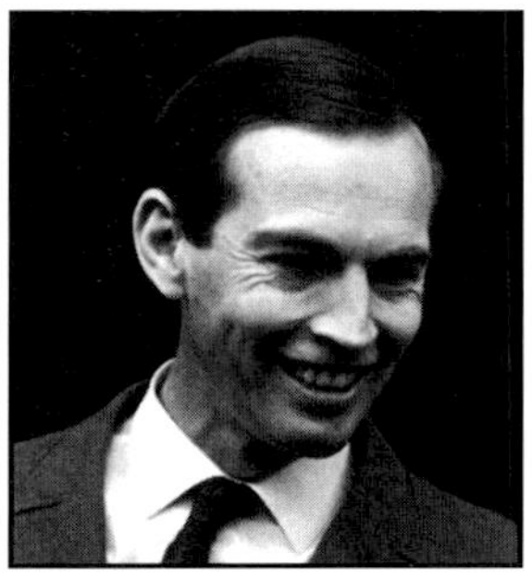

PROF. CHRISTIAN BARNARD

A lookout was kept for a suitable heart from any person who had just died. The team nearly operated two weeks ago, but the heart - from a car crash victim - was found to be damaged.

Last night Miss Denise Darvall, 25, a bank clerk, was brought in dying after a road accident in which her mother was killed.

Realising that they could not save his daughter's life the doctors asked the father whether he would agree to her heart being transplanted. He did so.

As the operation neared its end the transplanted heart was for a fraction of a second given an electric shock to start it working. It sprang to life immediately.

Prof. Barnard said tonight that the next few days would be vital. "The transplant was not really a problem, but the question of tissue rejection is the important one."

(December 4)

BRUSSELS STORE FIRE TOLL 319

Daily Telegraph Correspondent
BRUSSELS, Tuesday

A TOTAL of 319 people is believed to have died in yesterday's fire which destroyed the Brussels department store L'Innovation.

M. Bolle, the store's manager, said tonight that 281 people were missing, 28 hours after the fire began. Only 38 bodies have been recovered so far, 14 of them unidentified.

Fires still smouldered today within the store which, with the stock, was insured for £6 million, some of it with London firms. Neighbouring buildings were still burning.

Police are investigating the possibility of arson. They said that the fire broke out in two different parts of the store apparently simultaneously.

The store was holding an American week One theory being investigated is that the fire was started by anti-American elements who demonstrated last week outside the store against American policy in Vietnam.

(May 24)

CAMBRIDGE GIRL GRADUATE DEAD IN ROOM

Police inquiring into the death of a 22-year-old woman graduate at Cambridge were working on the theory yesterday that she had been upset by studying too much Greek tragedy.

Miss Linden Janette Sewell was found dead on Sunday night. She was surrounded by piles of books of Greek tragedy in her flat in Claredon Street, Cambridge. One of the books was still open at her bedside. Near the book were a number of pills and a letter.

(May 30)

CHICHESTER HOME IN TRIUMPH

By GUY RAIS and JOHN OWEN
PLYMOUTH, Sunday.

SIR FRANCIS CHICHESTER's epic voyage around the world, totalling 28,500 miles, ended at 8.56 tonight when a gun was fired from a yacht as Gipsy Moth IV crossed the finishing line at Plymouth.

The arrival was marked by tumultuous scenes, as, surrounded by hundreds of small craft, he steered a course inside the Sound helped by craft of the Royal Navy.

As he passed the breakwater a Revenue launch unobtrusively drew alongside and passed a bulky package of official documents requiring a declaration from Sir Francis that he was not carrying dutiable goods and was free from infection.

Before reaching the comparative safety of the Sound he repeatedly used his loud hailer to warn the accompanying small boats to keep clear. Even when he had reached the Sound he waved his arms to keep them away.

Shortly after Sir Francis entered the relatively calm harbour sea, Lady Chichester and their son, Giles, went aboard.

For several minutes the family had their own quiet reunion before the Customs launch arrived. Two bottles of champagne were taken on board.

SAILS LOWERED
Lady Chichester at helm

Soon fire tenders opened up their sprays as a sign of greeting and celebration.

Lady Chichester in peaked yachting cap and cherry-red sweater, stood by her husband in the cockpit and watched the huge jets of water.

Sir Francis, bespectacled, his blue-peaked yachting cap held on by a strap, acknowledged the cheers of the crowd but continued to supervise the lowering of the mainsail with the number 142 across the top.

Crowds in the boats around him began cheering and Sir Francis waved continually. Lady Chichester took over the steering of Gipsy Moth as the yacht approached her berth.

Slowly Gipsy Moth, all sails stowed, nudged her way for the last half-mile across the Sound towards the jetty of the Royal Western Yacht Club where Sir Francis came ashore, leaving the yacht for the first time for 119 days.

(May 29)

ISRAEL TO ANNEX GAZA STRIP

THE Gaza Strip is to be annexed by Israel, Gen. Moshe Dayan, Israel's Defence Minister, announced tonight.

Annexation steps begin at once. From next week residents in the strip will be granted permits to enter Israel and regular transport with Israel will be introduced.

Inhabitants will be allowed to visit the West bank of the Jordan where many have family roots.

(July 6)

£30-a-week pirates get BBC jobs

Norman Hare, Radio Staff

Seventeen disc jockeys who have been employed by pirate radio stations have been given contracts to work on BBC radio.

More than half of those who will play records on Radio One, the new BBC popular music service, will be former pirates. The BBC are thought to be paying them more than the average wage of £30 that they were earning on the pirate stations.

They include Tony Blackburn, Pete Brady, Keith Skues, Mike Raven and John Peel.

Jazz fans will get more of their kind of music on Radio One.

Mr. Robin Scott, controller of the Light programme, said last night: "We went out to get the best men as Radio One disc jockeys. We chose them for professional reasons but we shall be encouraging new people to come along."

(September 5)

Majority verdicts legal in October

By Our Political Staff

MAJORITY verdicts can be brought in by juries in criminal cases after September this year. This is one effect of a Home Office Order making operative nearly all the provisions of the Criminal Justice Bill by Oct. 1 next year.

Restrictions on reporting committal for trial proceedings start on Jan. 1. Possessing a shotgun without a certificate will be prohibited on May 1.

Former prisoners

Other provisions, apart from majority verdicts, coming into force this year on Oct. 1 are:

Ex-prisoners disqualified from serving on juries in criminal cases;

Preventive detention and corrective training abolished.

Setting up of local review committee and appointment of the Parole Board, so that the release-on-licence scheme can start in April;

Corporal punishment abolished in prisons.

On Jan. 1 restrictions will be introduced on magistrates' courts' powers to refuse bail. There are also provisions for suspended sentences; power to increase fines for many offences; and further restrictions on sending fined defaulters to prison.

From April 1, the licence scheme will enable selected prisoners to be released early, when they have reached a peak in their prison training and are no risk to the public.

(August 22)

FEDERAL TROOPS 'SEIZE BIAFRA CAPTIAL'

LAGOS, Wednesday.

The Nigerian Federal military Government said in Lagos tonight that Federal forces had captured Enugu, capital of the breakaway State of Biafra.

A Federal announcement said that mopping-up operations were continuing in the city.

Mr. James Parker, Deputy-British High Commissioner in Enugu, has left the city with Mr. Robert Barnard, American Consul.

(October 5)

Record Price of £190,000 for Picasso

By Terence Mullaly

A Blue Period Picasso was sold for £190,000, a world record price for the work of a living artist, at Sotheby's yesterday.

It was sent to the sale anonymously and bought by Mr. David Mann, of the Bodley Gallery, New York.

This staggering price placed the final seal of that 20th Century God, money, upon the unique position Picasso occupies in his own time.

The picture, which dates from 1902, was painted in Barcelona. Yesterday it provided the centre of attraction in one of the most remarkable sales ever held by Sotheby's, that home of great sales.

The total for only 87 Impressionist and modern paintings and pieces of sculpture was £1,058,200. Their sale in under two hours by Mr. Peter Wilson, Sotheby's chairman, produced a record for a sale of this sort held in Europe.

(April 27)

5 MINISTERS TO FIGHT OIL

10 MILES A DAY FLOW ON SUSSEX & KENT

Daily Telegraph Reporter

AS the tanker Torrey Canyon was breaking up in heavy seas on Seven Stones reef last night, with oil still gushing from her, five Government Ministers took charge of the battle against what Mr. Foley, Under-Secretary for the Navy, described as "the greatest peace-time menace to Britain's shores."

Mr. Foley told a Press conference that the tanker was "a menace and a threat to Britain. Given the extra oil now floating off Cornwall, all the extra men and equipment in the world could not deal with this problem."

As he spoke, oil from the stricken vessel, now in three pieces, was fouling beaches along more than 100 miles of Cornwall's coast. Westerly winds, it was thought, will move it 10 miles a day, threatening the whole of the South and South-East coast.

Salvage attempts on the tanker, which still has 60,000 tons of oil on board, have been delayed by the weather. More than 30,000 tons have escaped since the break-up.

A flotilla of small ships involving 4,000 men, has been spraying detergent on the oil. On the shore, 2,000 soldiers and Royal Marines, aided by civilians, have been fighting the battle.

Each of the five Ministers involved in the fight to save the South Coast will head a team of experts. South Coast areas for which Ministers will be responsible include Sussex and Kent.

This was decided yesterday by the Standing Emergency Committee, which met in London under Mr. Jenkins, Home Secretary. He said neither financial nor legal considerations would influence them in dealing with the disaster. Mr. Foley would still be responsible for off-shore operations.

The Home Secretary said it would be better for people to keep away, as they were only complicating matters.

While detergent would continue to be employed in an effort to break up the oil at sea, an experiment was to be started at Devonport involving the burning of oil on the beach and the large scale movement of sand and earth from the beaches.

Naval headquarters at Plymouth said later: "It was not a success. To ignite the oil, it had to be heated to a terrific temperature. The light oil burnt off and the rest just went out, leaving a soggy, tarry mess worse than before."

Mr. Jenkins said that pumping oil out of the tanker would require calm weather and even then it would be hazardous. Immediate arrangements were being made for pumping if there was the possibility of the weather improving.

The tanker was outside British waters. But this had not been the governing factor as to what they had or had not been able to do.

Twenty-five foam rubber booms had already been placed across estuaries and harbour mouths. Seventy-five more were on their way to the South coast. Already about £700,000 had been spent in fighting the oil.

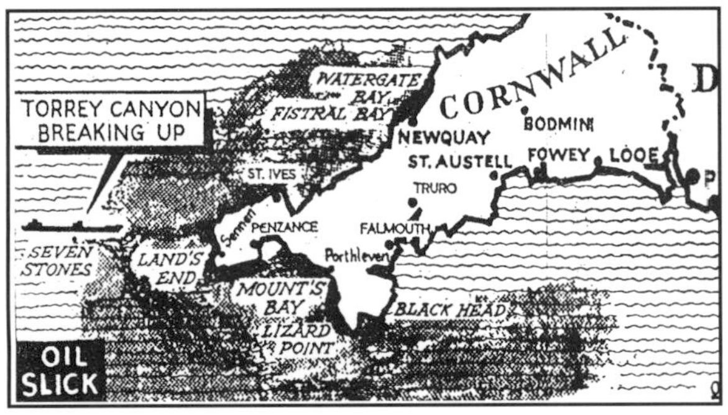

(March 28)

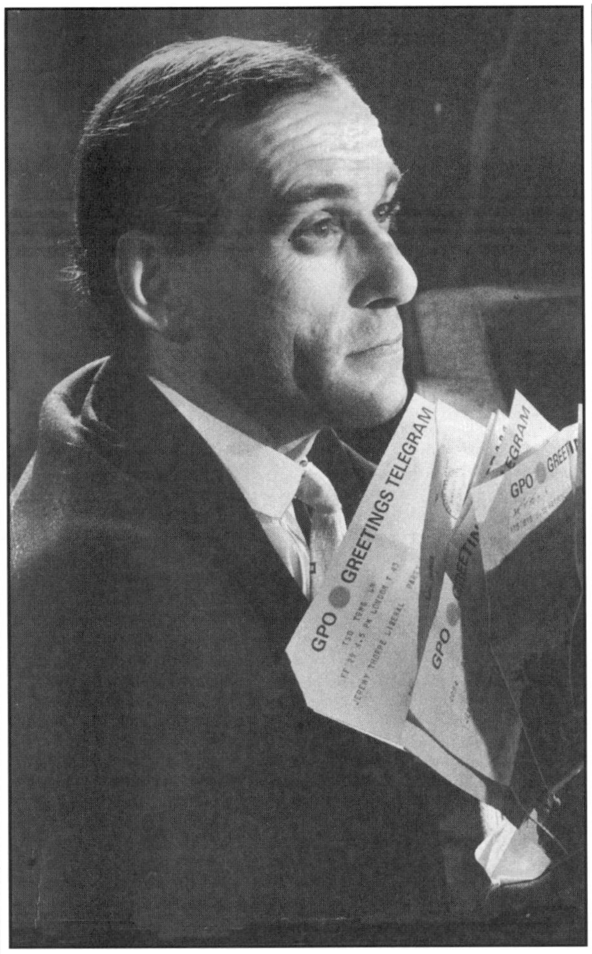

MR. JEREMY THORPE, 37, the new Liberal party leader, holding congratulatory telgrams after his election at the party headquarters yesterday.

JEREMY THORPE LEADS LIBERALS

H.B. BOYNE
Daily Telegraph Political Correspondent

MR. JEREMY THORPE, an extrovert Old Etonian of 37 with outstanding talent as a mimic and a television "personality," is the new leader of the Liberal party. The feeling at Westminster last night was that under his command the party will move to the left.

An even more determined challenge for Labour votes than under Mr. Grimond is expected. Having no need of Liberal support in this Parliament, the Government would have preferred to see a Right-wing Leader in the hope that he would draw votes from Conservatives at the next election.

By the same token, the Opposition are happy to find the Liberal Left in the ascendant, because they have nothing to lose in that direction.

Of the 12 Liberal M.P.s six, including himself, voted for Mr. Thorpe and three each for Mr. Eric Lubbock, 38, M.P. for Orpington, and Mr. Emlyn Hooson, 41, M.P. for Montgomery.

This meant that there was no "bottom" candidate to eliminate.

Thus the procedure of the alternative vote, by which second preferences are transferred to one of the remaining candidates, could not be brought into play.

At their own request, Mr. Lubbock and Mr. Hooson had a hurried consultation with Mr. Thorpe in private. The upshot was an agreement to withdraw their candidatures in his favour.

The resentment of many Liberals in the country over the manner in which the election had been "rushed" by the M.P.s, within 24 hours of Mr. Grimond's resignation, was made very clear.

The main complaint was that there had been insufficient time for party opinion at large to be consulted about the leadership.

(January 19)

DAUGHTER OF STALIN 'FLEES TO WEST'

SVETLANA STALIN, 41, daughter of the late Soviet leader Joseph Stalin, has defected to the West through the American Embassy in India, it was reported in Washington tonight.

She was said to have applied for asylum at the Embassy recently, and to be now in Rome. The American State Department declined all comment on the report, which was first circulated by the American Mutual Radio network. But a statement by the Department is expected tomorrow.

Svetlana was born in 1925, but little has been heard of her since Stalin's death in 1953.

Her mother, Nadzehda Alliluyeva, Stalin's second wife, died in 1932. There have been reports that she either killed herself or was murdered because she objected to the harshness of Stalin's regime.

Svetlana was trained as a philologist. In 1951 she married Mikhaill Kaganovich, son of Lazar Kaganovich, former Soviet Deputy Prime Minister, whose sister was Stalin's third wife. - Reuter.

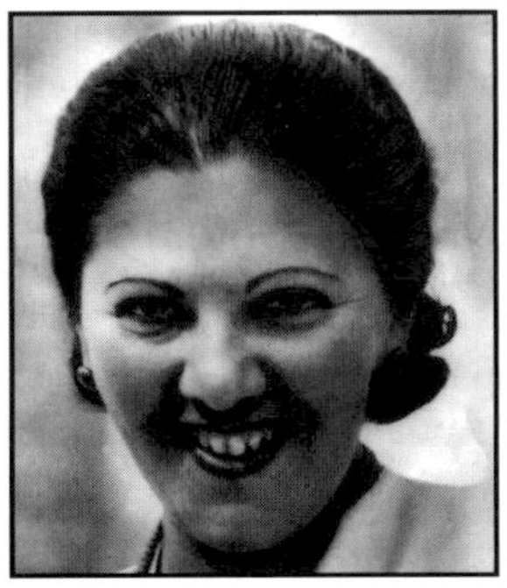

(March 10)

BRITISH FORCES CUT BY 20p.c.

RICHARD COX
Defence Correspondent

A 20 PER CENT. cut in the size of Britain's forces and a complete withdrawal from Singapore and Malaysia by the mid-1970s were announced by the Government yesterday.

It is made abundantly clear in the Supplementary Statement on the Defence White Paper that henceforward Britain is to be primarily a European power, with her forces aligned to the defence of Europe within the structure of NATO.

These decisions, which complete the process of reassessing Britain's military role begun by last year's Defence Review, are intended to lead to a defence budget of £2,200 million in 1970-71 and of £2,100 million in the mid-70s.

The 1967-68 defence estimates were £2,205 million. As the average rise in the cost of living is 3 per cent., the mid-1970s estimate represents a considerable saving.

Strong factors in the decision were the pressing need to reduce overseas expenditure and the disappointingly slow growth of the British economy.

Despite the cuts already made Britain's defence budget still takes 6.5 per cent. of the gross national product, the same figure as it did under the Conservatives.

Mr. Healey, Defence Secretary, forecast yesterday that by the mid-1970s it will be down to five per cent. In financial terms he is aiming for a defence budget of £2,200 million in 1970-71 and of £2,100 million in the mid-1970s.

The withdrawal from the Far East will not affect Hongkong, where the 7,000-man garrison remains.

The pullout from Singapore and Malaysia involves reducing the present 85,000 Servicemen and civilians to 45,000 by 1971. Of this 45,000 some 25,000 will be servicemen, including Gurkhas.

(July 19)

Long live free Quebec, cries de Gaulle

MONTREAL, Monday.

PRESIDENT DE GAULLE drove triumphantly into Montreal tonight to a riotous welcome from Canada's largest city. He electrified a large crowd outside the City Hall by shouting "Long live free Quebec."

Hundreds of Quebec separatists in the crowd drowned the Canadian national anthem "O Canada" with loud booing as Gen. de Gaulle stood to attention.

"Be own masters"

He reached Montreal after a 170-mile tour from Quebec City. At each stop he exhorted French-Canadians to take their destiny in their own hands and become their own masters.

He ended his Montreal speech: "Vive le Quebec. Vive Quebec libre." [The slogan of those who would separate French-speaking Quebec from the rest of Canada.]

Shouts of "Down with the Queen" came from the crowd outside the City Hall. - Reuter and UPI.

(July 25)

MISS PARKER'S ESTATE FOR LUTHER KING

Daily Telegraph Staff Correspondent

NEW YORK, Monday.

Dr. Martin Luther King, the Civil Rights leader, has been left the bulk of the estate of Miss Dorothy Parker, the poet and satirist, who died on June 7, aged 73. The total value of her estate is yet to be determined. The will was filed today in Manhatan Surrogates Court.

It directed that Dr. King should inherit "cash and negotiable securities, if any." The rest of the estate — copyrights, royalties and contract rights — is to be placed in trust, income from which goes to Dr. King for life.

(June 27)

Savundra's TV clash with Frost

Daily Telegraph Reporter

DR. EMIL SAVUNDRA denied during an extraordinary scene on television last night that he had any moral responsibility to people who had policies with the Fire, Auto and Marine insurance company.

The company failed last year with liabilities of £2,310,000 and an estimated deficiency of £1,400,000.

After being confronted by two women widowed in road accidents, he threw his hands in the air and said: "I sold out. I have no legal responsibility and no moral responsibility."

He was speaking on ITVs "The Frost Progamme," and when members of the audience tried to interrupt, he called: "I do not want to cross swords with the peasants."

Both Dr. Savundra and Frost were glaring at each other, their faces a few inches apart.

Mr. FROST: "What did you create?"

Dr. SAVUNDRA: "I created the greatest thing that insurance in Britain had known."

Mr. FROST: "This is what horrifies me. You can hand over a company and say that absolves you from moral responsibility."

D. SAVUNDRA: "For the simple reason that the man who took over was the managing director of the company from the day it was formed. He had run the company all that time."

Mr. FROST: "You have either to be stupid or dishonest."

Dr. SAVUNDRA: "Neither. You have surely delegated responsibility and authority yourself. When you delegate, you delegate totally and fully."

Asked about affairs of the Merchants Finance Trust, Dr. Savundra agreed that he had borrowed more than £300,000. He had not got the money now. The loan had been taken over completely by Mr. Walker.

After the broadcast, Dr. Savundra was escorted by police from ITVs Wembley Park studios to his car. As he was driven away with his wife and two children, a small crowd of people booed him.

(February 4)

£10,000 PEARL FOUND IN TAY MUSSEL BED

A pearl which could be worth £10,000, half an inch in diameter and weighing 34½ grains, has been taken from River Tay mussel beds. It has been bought from Mr. Bill Abernathy, 35, of Coupar-Angus, Scotland's only professional pearl fisher, by Perth jewellers, A. and G. Cairncross.

A partner of the firm, Mr. James Caincross, said yesterday: "The pearl is almost literally priceless. I don't believe we will ever be able to match it, for it is a once-in-a-lifetime find." The Abernathy family have supplied pearls to Perth jewellers for a century.

Mr. A.J.Hardwick, head of the jewellery department of Asprey and Co. the Bond Street jewellers, said last night: "If the quality claimed for it is correct it is quite exceptional and could be worth up to £10,000.

(August 18)

DE GAULLE SHUTS BRITAIN OUT

DEVALUATION STORM THREATENS $

By ANTHONY MANN

PARIS, Monday.

PRESIDENT DE GAULLE today flatly rejected any early negotiation over British entry into the Common Market. He sharply warned his five European partners against trying to force his hand.

At his twice-yearly Press conference, he said he was "not prepared to begin a negotiation with Britain which would destroy the partnership of which France is a member." On the contrary, in face of American pressure, he thought it necessary to tighten the rules of Community.

After a sarcastic review "in five Acts" of Britain's changing attitude to the Common Market, the General suggested that she had discovered an interest in Europe only when she thought that membership would help her to solve her economic problems and to go on playing a leading part in European affairs.

The General, who spoke for 92 minutes to an audience of 1,000 in the Elysée, denounced America for her "deplorable" payments deficit and inflation.

France "has had nothing whatever to do with the storms which have forced devaluation of sterling and which are now threatening the dollar."

It was "possible that these storms will ultimately lead to restoration of the international monetary system which is founded on the immutability, the impartiality and the universality which are the privileges of gold."

Britain regarded Europe as a means to get others to share her burdens, "to save her substance, and to give her back a dominant role."

"This is only salutary for Britain, and satisfactory for Europe, provided that the British people, like those it wants to join, is ready to submit to the fundamental changes that would be necessary to restore its own equilibrium."

Before the British could join the Continental nations "there must be a radical transformation of Great Britain."

(November 28)

47 ARRESTS IN BATTLE OUTSIDE U.S. EMBASSY

Daily Telegraph Reporter

THIRTY-EIGHT policemen were injured yesterday as thousands of demonstrators protesting against the Vietnam war tried to break through a police cordon around the American Embassy in Grosvenor Square, Mayfair.

Most were treated at police stations, but seven - a sergeant and six constables - need hospital treatment, including stitches to wounds. Forty-seven of the demonstrators were arrested and will appear in court today.

Spurred on by small groups of militant extremists, 3,000 people got into the gardens in the centre of Grosvenor Square. Fireworks, sods of earth, bottles and abuse were hurled at the police.

The clash coincided with anti-Vietnam war demonstrations outside the Pentagon in Washington in which 400 arrests were made.

An attempt to break the cordon appeared to be made when a Mini car, "dressed" as a tank, came forward and seemed to be breaking the police ranks. But reinforcements were summoned and the car's disguise torn from it.

Traffic in the area from Oxford Street to Piccadilly Circus was brought to a standstill as police reinforcements were brought in. Later Oxford Street was again blocked when the demonstrators moved out.

One innocent victim of the demonstration appeared to be a hot dog stall which got caught in the rush of demonstrators being pushed along Brook Street and eventually wound up in the square with the mustard intact, but no sign of the hot dogs.

Police handling of the crowd varied from extreme restraint to what appeared to be unreasonably rough behaviour, although this was undoubtedly provoked. Police were booed each time they made an arrest, but there were no jeers for those who struck policemen.

(October 23)

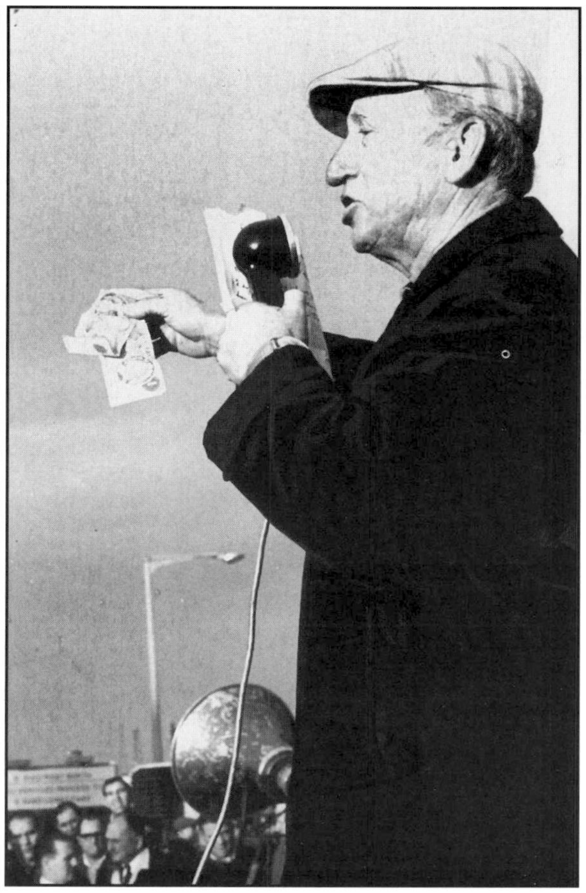

JACK DASH collects strike fund contributions.

DOCKERS PELT UNION LEADERS WITH EGGS

Daily Telegraph Reporter

MR. JACK DASH, the 60-year-old Communist, unofficial leader of London's dockers, emerged triumphant and more firmly in power at the strikebound Royal group of docks yesterday.

Three thousand men howled down leaders of the Transport and General Workers' and Stevedores' and Dockers' unions and pelted them with eggs as they appealed for a return to work. After the officials left without calling for a show of hands, Mr. Dash took control of the dock-gate meeting.

Later he headed a 200-strong march on Downing Street, where he handed in a petition to the Prime Minister.

While Mr. Dash was busy planning further unofficial strike meetings at London and Sheerness, London Port authorities stated last night that 7,002 men were absent from the London docks; 4,776 at the Royal group where 24 ships are idle.

More than 16,000 dockers, or one in every four, are now involved, mostly in London and on Merseyside.

The dispute is over clauses in the decasualisation agreement which, say the strikers, the employers are using to get around the "continuity rule."

Under the old rule, which the London strikers want restored, dockers stayed on a ship until loading or unloading was completed. By the new agreement, they may be transferred to other ships as work demands to maintain efficiency and spread earnings.

(October 17)

GUEVARA KILLED IN BOLIVIA

ERNESTO "Che" Guevara, the former Cuban leader, was identified in Vallegrande today as one of three guerrillas killed by troops in south-east Bolivia yesterday.

Two other guerrillas were wounded and captured. Four Government soldiers were killed and four wounded.

The Bolivian Government had said that Guevara, 39, the former righthand man of Dr. Fidel Castro, Cuban Prime Minister, was organising the seven-month-old outbreak of guerrilla activity here.

Argentinian-born Guevara disappeared from Cuba two and a half years ago. His whereabouts have been a mystery since then.

Regis Debray, the French writer, who is on trial in Bolivia accused of aiding the guerrillas, told reporters last week that he had seen Guevara earlier this year during his stay with the guerrillas. - Reuter.

(October 10)

Terrifying bungling ineptitude

THE National Coal Board is blamed for the Aberfan disaster by the three-man tribunal led by Lord Justice Edmund Davies in its report published yesterday.

The other main findings and the recommendations of the inquiry are:

1 - The basic cause of the disaster was a total absence of tipping policy;

2 - The disaster could and should have been prevented;

3 - A National Tip Safety Committee should be appointed;

4 - A Standard Code of Practice is needed;

5 - Local authorities should have more control over tips;

6 - The law on tips and their safety needs strengthening.

The tribunal criticises:

The National Coal Board for its failure to provide a tipping policy; for failing to heed clear warnings, and for wasting the tribunal's time in stubbornly refusing for so long to accept the blame;

Lord Robens, chairman of the Coal Board, for "inconsistent" evidence and for a television interview at Aberfan two days after the disaster when he said it was impossible to know there was a spring in the heart of the tip.

'Not villains'

Refusing to brand those responsible, villains, the tribunal comments:

The Aberfan disaster is a terrifying tale of bungling ineptitude by many men charged with tasks for which they were totally unfitted, of failure to heed clear warnings and of total lack of direction from above.

Not villains, but decent men led astray by foolishness or by ignorance or by both in combination are responsible for what happened in Aberfan.

(August 4)

U.S. SPACEMEN DIE IN FIRE

THE entire three-man crew of the Apollo I spacecraft was killed in a rehearsal today when fire swept the Saturn rocket on its launch pad at Cape Kennedy, Florida.

The three, Virgil Grissom, Edward White and Roger Chaffee, were due to blast off into space on Feb. 21. Today technicians and astronauts had started the first of a series of tests leading up to the first Apollo mission.

Lt. Cdr. Chaffee, 31, had never flown in space. Col. Grissom, 39, Air Force, was the first American to make two flights Lt. Col. White, 35, Air Force, made America's first space walk. They were all in the capsule on top of the rocket.

At first the National Aeronautics and Space Administration said only one unidentified astronaut was dead. Later they said: "We lost the entire prime crew."

The Apollo I crew were to have spent up to 14 days orbiting the Earth to test the spacecraft's operation. A manned Apollo spacecraft has never been orbited although the craft has gone up unmanned. The spacecraft is almost an exact copy of the type due to carry three astronauts to the moon before 1970.

The fires occurred while the astronauts were in the spacecraft during the countdown of a simulated flight test. The accident occurred at 6.31 p.m., 10 minutes prior to the planned simulated lift-off.

The spacecraft was located 218ft above the launch pad and was mated to the uprated Saturn 1B launch vehicle.

Hatches on the spacecraft were closed. Emergency crews were hampered by dense smoke in removing the hatches.

An unknown number of launch crew workers were treated for smoke inhalation at the Cape Kennedy dispensary. The crew entered the spacecraft at 3 p.m. Minor difficulties had been encountered during the count, with the environmental control and communication systems.

One report said the fire was in the main engine section of the spacecraft housing the main engine, control systems and oxygen supplies.

3-MONTH DELAY

Stand-by crew

Our Science Correspondent writes: The disaster will delay American plans by only three months. Other similar spacecraft and launching rockets are known to be in the process of manufacture and will replace the one destroyed. There is a back-up crew standing by.

Apollo was due to be launched on Feb. 21 as the first of the near Earth orbital spacecraft to test both astronauts and the components of the capsule. One of these was a fuel cell based on the invention by a British engineer, Mr. F. Bacon.

(January 28)

FIVE-YEAR SENTENCE ON CASSIUS CLAY

CASSIUS CLAY, deposed world heavyweight boxing champion, was sentenced to five years' gaol in Houston, Texas, tonight immediately after an all-white jury had found him guilty of refusing his induction into the Army.

Normally there would have been a pre-sentence investigation by the judge, but Clay, in a surprise move, asked that this be waived. "I'd appreciate it if the Court will do it now, give me my sentence now, instead of waiting and stalling for time."

A fine of $10,000 (£3,570) was also imposed. The sentence is the maximum for the charge.

Clay, 25, who calls himself Muhammed Ali, claims exemption on the ground that he is a Black Muslim minister. He also challenged the legality of his one-A-classification.

During the two-day hearing, Clay did not go into the witness box, and showed little emotion during evidence by four defence and four Government witnesses.

When the word "guilty" was heard from the jury foreman, Clay lowered his eyes, leaned over, and coughed faintly.

Clay had earlier said that, as a coloured man, he could not fight against the coloured people of Asia in Vietnam. He also opposed a system which denied Negroes fair representation on the draft boards.

Clay is still recognised by the British Boxing Board of Control as world champion, in spite of his being officially stripped of the title in America.

(June 21)

P.J. PROBY OWES £52,000 INCOME TAX

Daily Telegraph Reporter

The pop singer, P.J.Proby, 28, born in Texas, was detained by immigration officers at Heathrow Airport yesterday for more than four hours because of confusion over a work permit. He had flown in from the United States.

Proby, who filed a bankruptcy petition in Los Angeles two days ago, was given permission to enter Britain after undertaking not to work. He was admitted as a tourist and is staying at the May Fair Hotel.

He said yesterday that he had debts of £180,000 and assets of £174.

(February 10)

ELVIS PRESLEY MARRIES

NEW YORK, Monday.

Elvis Presley, 32, married Miss Priscilla Ann Beaulieu, 22, today in a Las Vegas hotel. The ceremony, attended by a small group of relatives and friends, was conducted by a Justice of the State Supreme Court.

Mr. Presley, once the darling of pop music enthusiasts, met Miss Beaulieu while he was on Army duty in Wiesbaden in 1959. She is the daughter of Lt.-Col. Joseph Beaulieu and grew up in the singer's home town, Memphis, Tennessee.

(May 2)

NEGRO IN HIGH COURT

Mr. Thurgood Marshall, 58, a leading civil rights lawyer, was named today by President Johnson as the first negro to serve in the Supreme Court. He has been Solicitor-General since 1964 and replaces Mr. Justice Clark, 67, who retired yesterday.

The President said:"I believe it is the right thing to do," and that it was the proper time to nominate a Negro to the Nation's highest court. Mr. Marshall, grandson of a slave from the Congo, built his reputation as a lawyer defending civil-rights cases.

(July 14)

JOAN BAEZ GAOLED

Joan Baez, the folk singer, and her mother, aged 54, were sentenced to 45 days imprisonment today for taking part in yesterday's anti-Vietnam demonstration outside the Oakland induction centre.

(December 21)

Bomb hoax at local radio debut

A bomb scare, fog, and optimistic speeches marked the opening yesterday by Mr. Short, Postmaster-General, of BBC Radio Leicester, first of the new local stations. A woman telephoned the station manager and the police about the "bomb." But nothing happened.

(November 9)

JUNTA 'DEPOSES' GREEK KING

'FLEEING FROM VILLAGE TO VILLAGE'

This pooled dispatch from Athens reached London last night

KING CONSTANTINE, 27, gambled his throne today in an attempt to overthrow the eight-month-old military régime and restore Greece to democracy. The Athens Junta claimed that the counter-revolution had been crushed.

"Constantine is trying to flee the country, hiding from village to village."

Other reports - necessarily unconfirmed - said that the Greek fleet was on its way to Crete, which was said to have sided with the King.

KING'S SUPPORT
'Air Force pledge'

It was also reported that the 28th Tactical Air Force at Larisa, in central Greece, as well as the Tanagra airbase some 60 miles North-West of Athens had joined the King's counter coup.

From the local radio station in Larisa he issued a proclamation announcing the formation of a new Government led by Mr. Petros Garoufalias, the former Defence Minister, and urging countrymen to rally behind him.

Meanwhile, the Junta, having taken a firm grip on the capital and having deployed its forces to defend the classical approaches to Athens from the north, proclaimed its determination to oppose "by force of arms" the counter coup into which "King Constantine was led by common adventurers motivated by foolish ambitions."

INEVITABLE CLASH
Greece split in two

JOHN WALLIS telephoned from Rome last night: After eight months of an uneasy alliance, King Constantine of the Hellenes and the Junta of colonels came into open opposition today, dividing Greece geographically, into at least two or three camps. This clash was inevitable.

An armed forces broadcast from the King's headquarters in Larisa said the King had dismissed five Ministers of the Junta. They are Brig. Gen. Pattakos (Interior), Col. George Papadopoulos (Minister to the Prime Minister's office), Mr. Makarezos (Economic), Lt. Gen. Zoitakis, and Brig. Patillis.

Tension in Athens mounted today with the first broadcast by King Constantine. Calling for the people of Greece to unite behind him to overthrow the Junta, he said: "A spirit of revenge will not prevail. But I will not accept any disobedience from now on and it will be crushed mercilessly. There will be no compromise."

In Athens the military régime ringed key buildings with troops and tanks.

Tonight the Junta deprived King Constantine of his royal authority. They named as Viceroy Lt.-Gen. Zoitakis.

Athens Central Armed Forces Radio said that a new Government had been formed under Col. Papadopoulos.

(December 16)

BRIAN EPSTEIN IS FOUND DEAD

Daily Telegraph Reporter

BRIAN EPSTEIN, 32, the man who discovered and managed the Beatles, was found dead in his locked bedroom yesterday afternoon in his £31,500 house in Chapel Street, Belgravia.

A spokesman at Scotland Yard said last night: "As far as we are concerned there are no suspicious circumstances. We will not know about an inquest until there has been a pathologist's report. The coroner will then decide on whether to hold an inquest."

Commander J. Lawlor, one of two senior Yard officers called to the house, said: "It was a sudden death."

The Beatles, who were in Bangor for five days of meditation with an Indian mystic, made immediate arrangements to return to London. Paul McCartney, looking pale and distressed, said as he left that the death was "a great shock."

John Lennon said: "I do not know where we would have been today without Brian. It is difficult to think of future plans at this stage."

YOGI CULT
Initiation expected

Lennon, who was still waiting at midnight with the other two Beatles for a car to take them to London, added that they had expected Mr. Epstein in Bangor today to be initiated into the cult of the Maharishi Yogi.

"The Maharishi told us not to become overwhelmed by grief. Fortunately I have lost only a few people who were very close to me. This is one of those occasions. I feel my course of meditation here has helped me to overcome my grief more easily than before."

Mr. Epstein, the eldest son of a Liverpool Jewish family, was a failure at school and went into the family furniture shop in Liverpool as a £5 a week salesman when he was 15.

Later he opened his own record shop. In 1962 he got several inquiries about an unknown Liverpool group, the Beatles. He found them singing for £3 15s a night in the Cavern Club, a disused warehouse, and offered to become their manager.

Within less than two years Mr. Epstein and each of the Beatles was worth more than £1 million. Among other stars who joined his "stable" were Cilla Black, Gerry and the Pacemakers, and Billy J. Kramer.

(August 28)

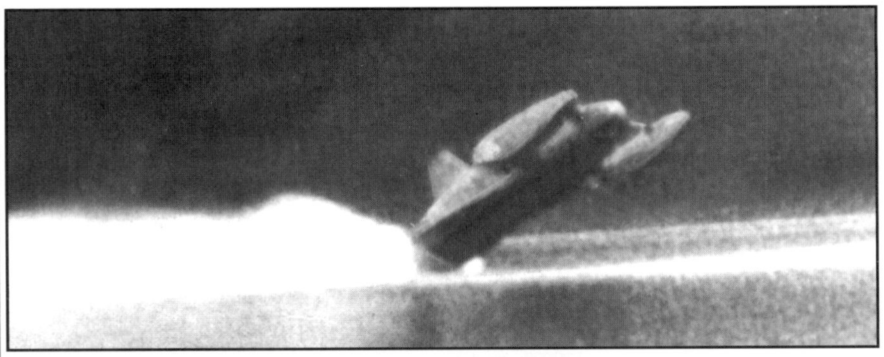

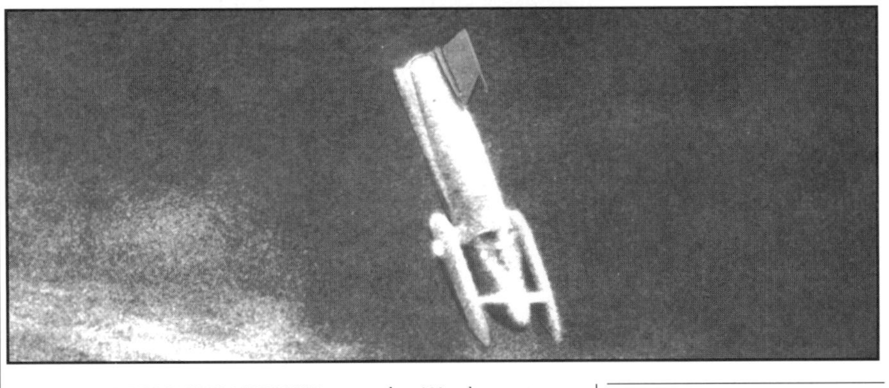

BLUEBIRD BECOMING AIRBORNE at more than 300mph to start a complete backward somersault before plunging into Coniston Water.

CAMPBELL DIES IN SIGHT OF RECORD

BLUEBIRD SOMERSAULTS AT OVER 300 MPH

Daily Telegraph Reporters

FROGMEN halted their search last night for the body of Donald Campbell, 45, after his jet-powered Bluebird had leapt into the air, somersaulted and plunged into Coniston Water when he was within a fraction of a second of beating his own water speed record of 276.33 mph.

Naval divers will resume the search this morning in an attempt to recover Bluebird, which lies in about 120ft of water. Campbell's helmet, shoes, oxygen mask and teddy bear mascot were found at the spot where the boat plunged.

His wife Tonia, the cabaret singer, flew to Coniston yesterday, accompanied by a doctor friend of the family. Prince Philip sent her a personal message of sympathy from Sandringham.

Eye witnesses say Campbell was travelling at more than 300 mph on the second of the two runs required for record attempts when the accident happened.

He was only about 150 yards, a fraction of a second in time, from the end of the measured kilometre over which his speed was recorded.

"SHE'S GOING"
Last words on radio

Onlookers saw Bluebird rear up almost on her tail. She soared nearly 60ft into the air and turned a back somersault.

Over the radio, Campbell said: "She's going - she's going. I'm almost on my back."

Then the boat hurtled downwards and hit the water like a bomb, sending up a huge explosion of spray.

One eye-witness said: "Bluebird became airborne quite gracefully. It seemed that if she had fully recovered an even keel she would have continued on her course."

Because he had not completed the two runs required, Campbell cannot be credited posthumously with the record.

TEDDY BEAR MASCOT
Card game "omen"

Campbell, described by his friends as very superstitious, always took with him "Mr. Whoppitt," the teddy bear wearing Bluebird overalls, which his wife gave him.

Playing patience on the night before his death, Campbell turned up the Ace of Spades followed by the Queen. He said: "Mary Queen of Scots turned up the same combination and from it she knew she was going to be beheaded.

"I know that one of my family is going to get the chop. I pray God it will not be me."

(January 5)

MANY JOIN IN MURIEL SPARK OBE PROTEST

Daily Telegraph Reporter

The Society of Authors yesterday supported women novelists who protested at the announcement of "such a low award as the OBE" to Muriel Spark, the novelist, in the New Year's Honours List. Dame Rebecca West said that as a DBE, she had been "deeply embarrassed."

Pamela Hansford Johnson, novelist wife of Lord Snow, said: "I am a great admirer of Mrs. Spark. It does seem to me that a writer of her calibre ought not to be offered an award which is less than those given to people in the field of sport."

(January 6)

TWO VIYELLA COTTON MILLS SHUT

Daily Telegraph Reporter

Viyella International, one of the textile industry's "big four," announced yesterday that it is to close two cotton mills, employing nearly 2,000 workers in Wigan and at Littleborough, near Rochdale, Lancs. The £40 million group closed four other mills in the past six months.

The mills are Eckersley's in Wigan and Clegg and Hall's Shore Mill at Littleborough. Mr. Joe Hyman, 44, Viyella's chairman, said the closures were part of the group's rationalisation policy to make the fullest use of modernised factories.

Immediate reaction from Lancashire cotton workers was a threat to join the growing ranks of union members stopping their contribution to the Labour party's political levy.

(February 21)

'PRIVACY' IS KEY WORD IN SEX BILL

By Our Legal Correspondent

THE activities of homosexuals are unlikely to become any more noticeable than they are now, after the Bill legalising homosexual acts between consenting adults in private reaches the Statute Book as is expected later this summer.

Legal homosexual acts will have to take place strictly in private such as in the flat of one of the men, and if a third person is present the act becomes illegal. Both parties must be 21 or over.

Apart from the general rule that any legal homosexual act must be in private, the Bill includes a clause banning acts in lavatories to which the public have access.

Decency law "effective"

In the Commons, several MPs claimed that "in private" should be more closely defined, but the unsuccessful amendments were tabled to cover acts committed in public parks and woodland. The Government attitude has been that the courts should be left to interpret the phrase.

Procuring a person to commit an act with a third man is punishable by up to two years' imprisonment. It is already an offence under the Sexual Offences Act, 1956, for a man persistently to solicit or importune in a public place for "immoral purposes."

(July 5)

TEA BREAKS PART OF WEEK'S WORK

THE Industrial Court agreed with a trade union yesterday that a 10-minute afternoon tea break is part of the normal working week.

The court was asked by Mr. Gunter, Minister of Labour, to make a ruling on a dispute over the status of the tea break between Japiada Products, a leather firm, of Radcliffe, Lancs, and the Amalgamated Society of Leather Workers.

Its findings will strengthen the trade union view that tea-breaks accepted by any company as part of the normal routine are in fact officially part of the basic hours.

Common Practice

In its submission to the court the union said that it was common practice in the leather industry to have a morning and afternoon break. Unlike lunchbreaks, they were accepted as part of the normal working week.

(February 29)

ALL NIGHT SIT IN BY LSE STUDENTS

Daily Telegraph Reporter

WORK at the London School of Economics was halted yesterday by more than 500 students staging a sit-down in protest against the suspension till the end of the summer term of two student leaders.

The two students, David Adelstein, 20, president of the student's union, and Marshall Bloom, 22, president of the graduate students' association, were suspended for disobeying Sir Sydney Caine, the Director, and holding a meeting on Jan. 31, when a porter died after a heart attack.

Students decided at an orderly meeting yesterday afternoon when the three-month suspensions were announced to boycott the School until the sentences were rescinded and to start the sit-down. Their protest is supported by some staff members.

The 500 students, chanting and shouting sat down in the entrance hall and corridors of the Houghton Street building.

At midnight 276 students, including girls, were taking part in the all-night sit-in behind table barricades across the entrance doors which had been locked open.

BARRIER REMOVED
Exit only

Early today the students were persuaded by a senior member of the staff to remove the barricades. The doors were shut and some students were allowed to leave, but not to return.

The students said Mr. Peter Archer, Labour MP for Rowley, Regis and Tipton, had agreed to see Mr. Crosland, Education Minister, today to ask him to lift the suspensions pending a public inquiry.

Pickets were organised to allow into the School today only those students prepared to support them. Other groups will move round the School to persuade students to join in boycotting lessons and tutorials until the suspensions are rescinded.

The meeting called on Jan. 31 was to consider "direct action" against the appointment of Dr. Walter Adams, who is 60, former Principal of the University College of Rhodesia, to succeed Sir Sydney, who is 64, in October.

ALLOWED TO STAY
Director at barricades

Sir Sydney Caine arrived at the School at 10.10 p.m., 20 minutes before the school was due to close. The students allowed him into the building when he said he wanted to speak to them.

He said they could remain in the building all night if they wanted without molestation. He said the two suspended students could appeal and "will get as fair a hearing as they have received already."

Sir Sydney told the students that he knew there was a great deal of feeling among them. But any appeal would not be affected favourably by such a demonstration.

At the end of his three-minute appearance students burst out cheering and jeering.

(March 14)

HELICOPTERS HUNT BOSTON STRANGLER

Helicopters and bloodhounds were taking part in a huge manhunt today for Albert DeSalvo, 35, self-proclaimed "Boston Strangler," who escaped last night from a Bridgewater, Massachusetts, lunatic asylum. He took two other patients with him.

DeSalvo's lawyer, Mr. F. Lee Bailey, has said that DeSalvo admitted killing 13 women in the Boston area between June, 1962, and January, 1964. The lawyer described him recently as "a completely uncontrollable vegetable walking around in a human body."

(February 25)

40 KILLED IN RAIL CRASH

Daily Telegraph Reporters

FORTY passengers were killed and at least 55 injured in a train crash near Hither Green station last night. Ten coaches of the 7.43 p.m. Hastings to Charing Cross train overturned and many people were trapped in the wreckage.

The crash occurred on the bridge spanning St. Mildred's Road, Hither Green, only about a mile from the scene of the Lewisham train disaster on Dec. 4, 1957, in which 90 people were killed and 175 injured.

The first two coaches of the 12-coach diesel electric train which was travelling at about 50 mph broke away from the rest and ran on, intact, to Hither Green station, a quarter of a mile away. The remaining coaches jack-knifed.

Teams of doctors from Guy's Hospital and Lewisham Hospital clambered among the wreckage to give blood transfusions and administer oxygen to seriously injured victims. More than 120 firemen and large numbers of ambulancemen and police worked to free those trapped in the wreckage.

FIREMEN IN TEARS

The scene at the crash was unbelievable. Coaches were overturned on the tracks and the train veered crazily on the edge of a 20ft high embankment. A railway spokesman said most of the dead were in the third coach.

Passers by who rushed in to help stood helpless. Some wept. A man trapped under the second coach, although seriously injured, talked to his rescuers as they battled to cut him free. Battered, bloodstained luggage and personal belongings lay strewn over the track.

Hardened police officers and firemen were seen with tears streaming down their faces as they pulled out the terribly injured body of a man. Shortly after, a child's body was pulled out of one of the wrecked carriages.

(November 6)

FOOT & MOUTH CONTROL EXTENDS TO SCOTLAND

THE whole of Scotland became a controlled area at midnight in the latest move by the Ministry of Agriculture to check the foot-and-mouth epidemic.

The effect of the order, which makes the whole of Britain except Northern Ireland, a giant controlled area, will be to forbid movement of animals except under licence. England and Wales were made a controlled area last Saturday.

Britain's worst epidemic of the century resulted in another 59 outbreaks yesterday, bringing the total to 963. More than 170,000 animals have been slaughtered since the epidemic began a month ago.

Yesterday's outbreaks were in Cheshire, Shropshire, Flint, Denbigh and Montgomery. One Shropshire farmer lost his herd of 320 cattle and 750 sheep.

A National Farmers' Union spokesman said last night: "We would like to see next month's Royal Smithfield Show called off, though it is confined to machinery and carcases."

The Kent branch of the National Farmer's Union is today placing pads of straw and other materials soaked in disinfectant on major roads leading into the county. Motorists are asked to slow down at barriers marked with warning signs.

(November 25)

'Boy's Own Paper' closes after 88 years

Daily Telegraph Reporter

THE Boy's Own Paper, possibly the world's best-known magazine for boys, is to close. The British Printing Corporation announced yesterday, the 88th anniversary of the paper's first publication, that its last issue would appear next month.

A spokesman for the corporation said that although the paper had been "a faithful friend to generations of boys, marked changes have made its continuation impossible."

In its heyday, in the 1890's, the Boy's Own Paper had a weekly circulation of 190,000. This declined to its latest figure of 24,000 at a price of 2s monthly.

Among the magazine's famous contributors were R.M. Ballantyne, G.A. Henty, Conan Doyle, Algernon Blackwood and Talbot Baines Reed. Perhaps the most famous figure in its adventure stories, serials and "yarns" was Sexton Blake, the detective.

(January 11)

First giant hovercraft 'winched out'

John Petty
Shipping Correspondent

COWES, Thursday.

British invention and technology achieved one of its great post-war moments here today when the world's first giant hovercraft emerged for the first time from the hangar where the Princess flying boats were built nearly 20 years ago.

The craft is as big as a 600-seat cinema, and able to carry 800 passengers.

The £1,750,000 SR. N4 craft consolidates Britain's world lead in hovercraft and may open the way to export orders worth more than the combined total of the aircraft and shipbuilding industries.

The 130ft-long white and yellow craft was winched out of the hangar along three sets of tramlines. It will stand out in the open as systems are checked and fitments added before taking the water in January.

It will make its debut on the English Channel in February or March and will undergo exhaustive tests before going into service with Seaspeed, the British Railways hovercraft subsidiary, between Dover and Boulogne in August.

Fitting out the SR. N4, which is 77ft wide and 42ft high, starts immediately with the fixing of the 7ft high "skirt" of plastic covered nylon weave which will contain the air cushion.

(October 27)

POPE CREATES 27 CARDINALS AT CONSISTORY

The Pope created 27 new cardinals at a consistory today. There are now 118 members of the Sacred College, a record number. His choice has surprised some observers, who had expected younger men and more from developing countries.

Instead there are 20 Europeans and four Americans. Only three of the new cardinals are from developing countries, two from Latin America and one from Indonesia.

The oldest is Archbishop Fasolino of Santa Fe, Argentina, who is 80. The youngest is Archbishop Bengsch of Berlin, who is 45. The average age is about 61.

(June 27)

COMMONS FIRST MORNING SITTING

The House of Commons will hold its first morning sitting on Wednesday, beginning at the "unParliamentary" hour of 10 a.m. Despite this early start, there is no guarantee that M.P.s will get home to bed in good time.

Business for the normal sitting, starting about 3.30 p.m., is the second reading of the Consolidated Fund Bill.

(January 27)

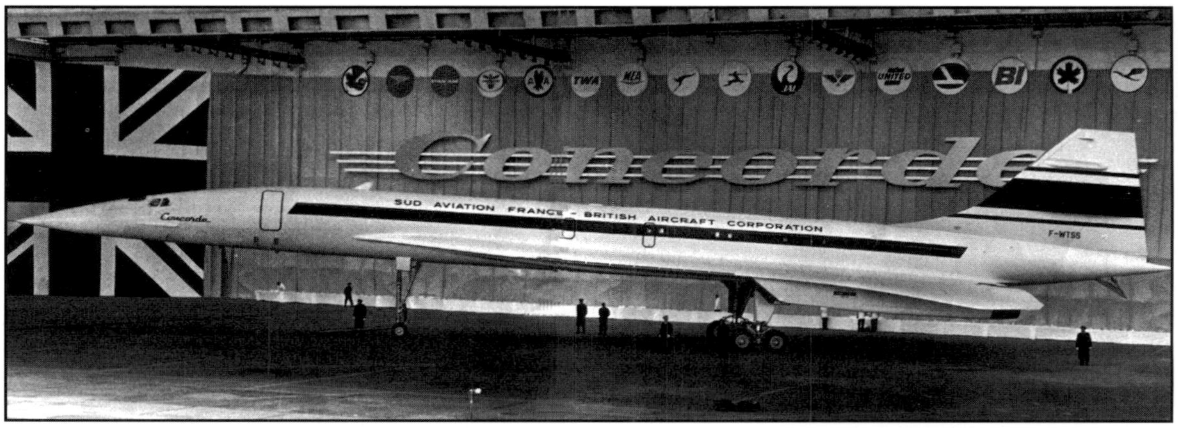

THE ANGLO-FRENCH CONCORDE SUPERSONIC AIRLINER standing in a hangar at Toulouse before it was rolled out yesterday.

BENN YIELDS ON CONCORDE

Air Cdre. E.M. DONALDSON
Air Correspondent

TOULOUSE, Monday.

THE gleaming white prototype of the Anglo-French Concorde, the world's first supersonic airliner, was formally rolled out of its hangar at Toulouse, in the South of France, today.

The main surprise of the ceremony, which puts the Concorde five years ahead of its American rivals, was an announcement by Mr. Benn, Minister of Technology, that Britain had decided to follow France in spelling Concorde with a final "e."

He said that as there had been complete failure to agree on the subject, he had decided to resolve it himself. From today Britain would add an "e" which stood for "excellence, for England, for Europe and for the Entente."

The announcement startled British technicians, who recalled that the first Concorde could not have been made without the Bristol-Siddeley Olympus engine.

Also the Concorde's aerodynamics were evolved in the main by British scientists at Farnborough and the British Aircraft Corporation factory at Filton, Bristol, between 1956 and 1960, long before French participation.

BOAC ORDERS

"We will be first"

Sir Giles Guthrie, chairman of BOAC which is to receive eight of the first 24 Concordes built, said he was determined the corporation would be first into service with the airliner.

The Concorde would make three-hour transatlantic crossings twice in each direction every day of its working life. It would get to Sydney in 18 hours instead of the present 30 hours.

"Humiliating defeat"

Two Conservative MPs, Mr. Ronald Ball (South Bucks) and Mr. William Deedes (Ashford), last night tabled a Commons motion on the final "e" in Concorde. It "notes with interest the Minister of Technology's attempt to be spry about his latest humiliating defeat at the hands of General de Gaulle and the French aircraft industry."

(December 12)

GAOL SENTENCES ON JAGGER & RICHARD

By GUY RAIS

TWO members of the Rolling Stones "pop" group were gaoled on drug charges at West Sussex Quarter Sessions, Chichester, yesterday. MICK JAGGER, 23, leader of the group was sentenced to three months and KEITH RICHARD, 23, guitarist, to one year.

There were cries of "Oh" and "No" from teenagers in the crowded public gallery as the jury found Richard guilty of allowing his house in West Wittering, Sussex, to be used for the smoking of Indian hemp. ROBERT FRASER, 29, art gallery director, was gaoled for six months for possessing heroin.

Jagger, who was found in possession of four tablets of an Italian-made drug, almost broke down and put his head in his hands as he was sentenced. He stumbled out of the dock almost in tears.

Hundreds of teenagers and schoolchildren waited at the back entrance of the court building to catch a glimpse of the two Rolling Stones before they were driven to prisons in London. But they left handcuffed from the front entrance of the building.

There is no official prison regulation that hair lengths of prisoners should conform to a set length, but it will be at the discretion of prison governors whether or not their hair should be cut.

They can order this to be done if they consider it is unhygenic or untidy.

The Rolling Stones group will not break up as a result of the two members going to prison. A spokesman said that the three other members would remain together and wait for Richard and Jaggar to return. They have no further bookings.

(June 30)

18 BRITONS SHOT IN ADEN MUTINY

By CHRISTOPHER MUNNION

SEVENTEEN British soldiers and one British civilian were shot dead today and 26 Britons wounded as an internal insurrection in the South Arabian Army developed rapidly into a large-scale mutiny within the armed Aden police.

Four Arabs, including two police officers, were also killed and many wounded in confused and indiscriminate crossfire which spread from the Khormaksar airfield area to the Crater suburb.

Eight British soldiers in two Land-Rovers were shot dead by a machine gunner on a rooftop at one South Arabian Army barracks. In Crater, armed police released 500 prisoners in the main gaol, and terrorists fired on British troops from rooftops with bazookas and automatic rifles, and threw grenades.

A British helicopter crashed after being hit by automatic fire, injuring the three Servicemen on board.

Crater was sealed off and civilians fled. One European said "It is complete and terrible chaos. There are bullets, bodies, and blood everywhere."

(June 21)

U.S. FACING WORST RIOT SEASON

HOT AND HUMID

By IAN BALL

NEW YORK, Monday.

NEGRO and white leaders across America were prepared today to acknowledge that the present "long hot summer" will probably exceed in violence the bloody summer of 1965 which saw the Watts ghetto in Los Angeles go up in flames.

The Watts riots lasted four days. Before 14,000 National Guardsmen restored order, 34 people were dead, 1,032 injured and more than 4,000 under arrest. Damage was estimated at $50 million (£18 million).

Since that time there have been about 45 serious racial clashes. Most during June, July and August when hot, muggy weather is the rule in densely populated areas of the north.

Calm after storm

With the exception of Detroit, the weekend trouble spots were returning to normal today.

Calm was restored in the Puerto Rican ghetto - within-a-ghetto called Spanish Harlem. A thousand police reinforcements were sent to the Area to disperse stone-throwing, window-smashing mobs in the second outbreak there in 24 hours.

The immediate cause of the renewed outburst seems to be intervention by the elite Tactical Police Force, a riot squad.

In Cairo, Illinois, renewed racial strife seemed to have been averted when city officials promised to try to find more jobs for Negroes. When about 30 Negroes applied today at the city's largest factory they were told that there were no openings at present.

Police in New Britain, Connecticut, which has had two nights of disturbances, were confident that they had the situation in hand today.

Negro leaders there have complained that coloured families were roughly treated by the State Highway Department, which recently informed many residents that they had 30 days in which to leave their homes to make way for a road to be built through the heart of the Negro area.

(July 25)

Queen gives her name to Cunard liner

JOHN PETTY
Shipping Correspondent

CLYDEBANK, Wednesday.

BELLOWING sirens mingled with cheering from 100,000 people as the Queen bestowed the name Queen Elizabeth II on the £29 million Cunard liner launched at the John Brown shipyard at Clydebank today.

From a platform high against the bulbous ram bow of the 58,000-ton liner, the Queen, with Prince Philip and Princess Margaret by her side, pressed the launching button and a bottle of champagne shattered against the bows.

Long seconds passed with apparently nothing happening. But the ship was moving imperceptibly all the time.

Mr. George H. Parker, the shipyard director, gave her a symbolic push with his left hand and the 963ft-long liner gathered speed to reach 22 mph - seven mph faster than the Queen Elizabeth at her launching in September, 1938.

Two-foot wave

It was like seeing a 13 storey building, 130ft high and as long as three football pitches, hurtling down a crowd-lined road.

As the vast bulk entered the water a two-foot high wave was pushed across the Clyde towards the mouth of the River Cart.

Then, as her stern came up in the water, the yacht-like bow dipped, almost as though she was dropping a curtsy to the Queen. The Queen Elizabeth II was afloat.

(September 21)

£2,000M GAMBLING TOTAL IN BRITAIN

Latest Customs and Excise figures indicate that the people of Britain gamble almost £2,000 million a year. This is nearly enough to meet the annual defence budget.

(December 19)

NEW ATTEMPT BY SHEILA SCOTT

Twelve months after her record solo flight round the world, Miss Sheila Scott, 39, plans to set off again. She told a Press conference at the Royal Aero Club in London yesterday she would attempt to better Amy Johnson's 78 hours 28 minutes from London to Cape Town.

(June 14)

TWO CHARACTERS IN A DREADFUL LIMBO

By W.A. DARLINGTON

WHAT do Rosencrantz and Guildenstern do when they are not taking part in the play of "Hamlet?" It's a fair question, and there might be quite an interesting answer to it even if it were asked and answered in conditions of straight realism.

But that wouldn't do at all for Tom Stoppard, whose "Rosencrantz and Guildenstern are Dead" opened at the Old Vic last night under the production of Derek Goldby.

He does not regard them as human beings at all, and he says they are dead even before his play begins because for him they have never been alive, and are scarcely alive even to themselves.

Except when they are taking their parts in Shakespeare's play - and even so they never fully understand what they are up to - they live in a sort of dreadful limbo, apparently an anteroom in the castle, where they pass the time tossing coins and nattering.

Well, it is all very clever, I dare say, but it happens to be the kind of play that I don't enjoy and would in fact much rather read than see on the stage. It is the kind of play, too, that one might enjoy more at a second hearing, if only the first time through hadn't left such a strong feeling that once is enough.

John Stride (Rosencrantz) and Edward Petherbridge (Guildenstern) carry the play firmly on their shoulders and are funny when they get the chance (which happens quite often). Graham Crowden is impressive as the Player, and John McEnery gives an effective impression of Hamlet.

(April 12)

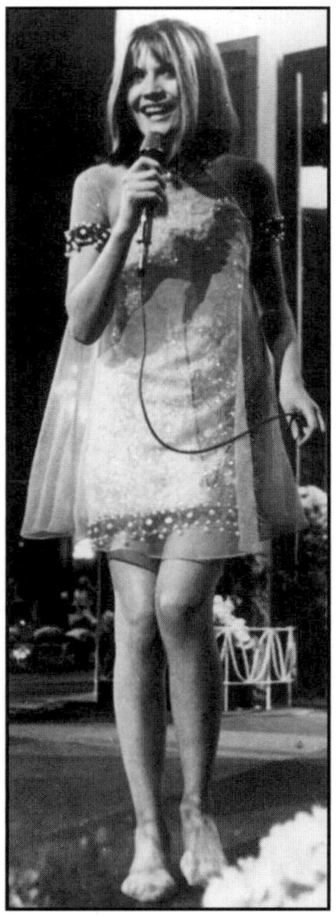

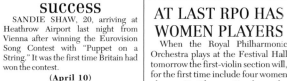

Home after song contest success

SANDIE SHAW, 20, arriving at Heathrow Airport last night from Vienna after winning the Eurovision Song Contest with "Puppet on a String." It was the first time Britain had won the contest.

(April 10)

POPS

Sargeant Pepper's Lonely Hearts Club Band. The Beatles.

This continues the Beatles' tradition of musical improvement. It has moments of great beauty, force and humour which make one wonder what the group might ultimately achieve.

The variety of orchestration makes the instrumentals of "Revolver" sound meagre, which they certainly were not. In fact, their intriguing sounds, although never painfully detailed as in "Strawberry Fields Forever," help, together with the surprisingly audible and sometimes very neat lyrics, to obscure the mediocrity of a few of the melodies, such as "For the Benefit of Mr. Kite" and "Fixing a Hole."

There are some very good songs, however, "She's Leaving Home" is a beautiful ditty, reminiscent of "Eleanor Rigby," suitably scored for strings.

Hugh Parry

(June 24)

Stockhausen heard to advantage

By MARTIN COOPER

STOCKHAUSEN and Boulez are without doubt the two most influential figures in the music of the last 10 years.

But, whereas in this country we have been given plenty of opportunity to become acquainted with Boulez's work, both as composer and conductor, Stockhausen's music is much less well known.

The performance of his "Gruppen" at the Albert Hall last night had the unusual advantage of numbering Pierre Boulez among the three conductors who control the dialogue, contrasts, echoes, contradictions and convolutions of the three orchestral "groups" which give the work its name.

Anyone placed outside the triangle formed by these three bodies of performers must be counted, quite literally, as a biased listener and it would be interesting to compare three performances of the work from three different vantage points, each giving preference to a different group.

The acoustic effect of the music was certainly enhanced by the sight of the elaborate, and apparently precise, mechanism required to produce what to the ear appeared for the most part completely random sounds, often attractive in themselves, but strictly speaking unintelligible.

(September 6)

AT LAST RPO HAS WOMEN PLAYERS

When the Royal Philharmonic Orchestra plays at the Festival Hall tomorrow the first-violin section will, for the first time include four women players. Sir Thomas Beecham, the founder, would have strongly disapproved.

Apart from Cherry Isherwood, the harpist, women have been kept out of the orchestra ever since it started nearly 21 years ago. The decision to change Sir Thomas's rule was made some months ago, and the four violinists were successful at auditions.

(March 30)

'SAN FRANCISCO' RISES TO No. 1

Scott McKenzie's record "San Francisco" is No. 1 in this week's Melody Maker top ten. It replaces the Beatles' "All You Need Is Love," which drops to second place. Dave Davies' "Death Of A Clown" rises from fourth to third position.

Other positions, with last week's placings in brackets are: 4 (3), "It Must Be Him", Vicki Carr: 5(8); "I'll Never Fall In Love Again"; Tom Jones; 6(10), "Up Up And Away", Johnny Mann Singers; 7(9), "I Was Made To Love Her", Stevie Wonder.

(August 8)

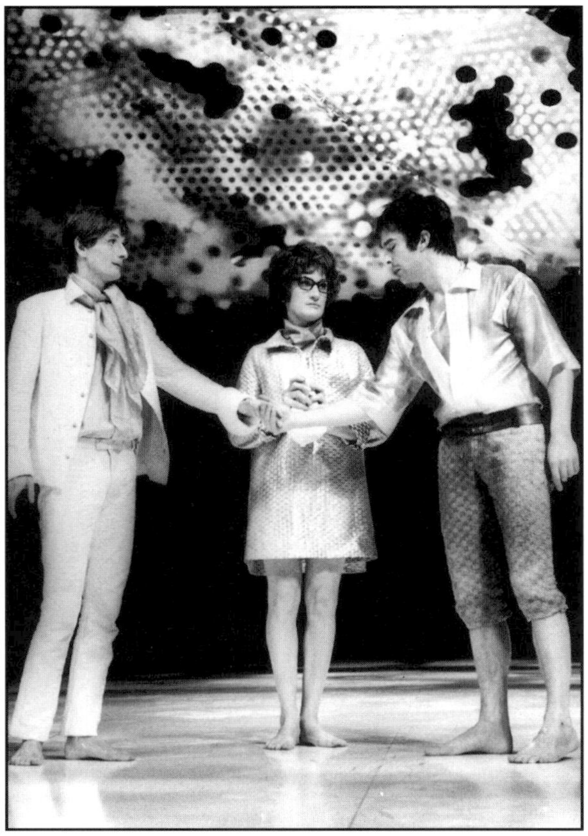

EXPERIMENT COMES OFF BRILLIANTLY

By W.A. DARLINGTON

EVER since the National Theatre announced its all-male production of "As You Like It" I have been trying to think out what point or purpose this experiment would serve, without success.

Since I could neither think of a good reason for myself nor find one in the advance publicity which I read in the papers, I came to the conclusion that my only sensible course was to dismiss all such speculation from my mind, present myself at the Old Vic with a virgin surface and see what impression the production made, and how it came off.

Well, it has come off brilliantly, Rosalind and Celia had not been on the stage five minutes last night before I had accepted them completely. Ronald Pickup, in his character as Rosalind, was no more expecting us to take him for a woman than Dorothy Tutin, in her scenes as Ganymede in a recent production of the same play, expected us to take her for a man.

In other words, it does not matter which sex the player of Rosalind belongs to, so long as he or she can act well enough to make us think first of the character and only secondarily of the player - which is anyhow the best test I know of a good actor.

Mr. Pickup is to be sincerely congratulated then, on the tact and delicacy with which he presented Shakespeare's enchanting heroine. Occasionally, when he overdid the mincing walk which goes with long skirts we had an impulse to giggle, just as we had if Miss Tutin ever overdid the long strides which went with her male get-up.

The other three actors who played women - and had not Mr. Pickup's chance to get back into male clothes - were all successful in their different ways.

Charles Kay's sophisticated Celia was of immense supporting value, always in the picture yet never ostentatious; Richard Kay's Phebe was so feminine in voice and gesture that he might have been a woman; Antony Hopkins's Audrey was a pantomime dame in embryo.

(October 4)

'MAN FOR ALL SEASONS' WINS SIX OSCARS

BRITAIN again dominated the Film Academy awards ceremonies in Hollywood last night, capturing Oscars for the best film, the best actor and the best actress. The winning film, "A Man for All Seasons," the screen version of Robert Bolt's stage play about Sir Thomas More, won six Oscars.

Paul Scofield, 45, named best actor for his portrayal of Sir Thomas in the all-British film, was in bed at his home in Sussex when the award was made. It was accepted for him by Wendy Hiller.

Elizabeth Taylor, 35, who was chosen best actress for her explosive role as a drunken wife in "Who's Afraid of Virginia Woolf?" also missed the ceremonies. She is completing a film in Nice. Her Oscar, her second, was accepted by Anne Bancroft.

(April 12)

TRIUMPHANT 'FORSYTE SAGA' SERIAL ENDS

By SEAN DAY-LEWIS

After a habit-forming six months' run on BBC-2 television, "The Forsyte Saga" reached its swan song on Saturday, just as yet another BBC sound radio adaptation of John Galsworthy's story, in 48 weekly instalments, is about to start.

In the final television episode, to be repeated tomorrow, Soames duly receives his unlikely death blow from his prize Goya, and after a discreetly cut mutual roll in the long grass of Robin Hill, Jon returns guiltily to his pale wife and his cousin Fleur returns sadly to her pale husband.

The death of Soames, so symmetrical and full of irony, is more acceptable as novel than as dramatic technique but was so excellently acted as to jerk tears in all the copious measure intended.

Looking back the early episodes were most effective just as the early books are most satisfying, really because Galsworthy gave the old Forsytes more depth, variety and, in his Victoria nostalgia, some grandeur.

Donald Wilson's dramatisation and production has been a considerable achievement, the dialogue often a real improvement on the book and the domestic and rural scenes mostly excellent in observation and period atmosphere.

(July 3)

AREN'T MEN BEASTS?

By Anthony Smith

The Naked Ape. By Desmond Morris (Cape. 30s)

THE earnings from "The Naked Ape" topped the £100,000 mark even before publication day. Therefore, confronted by such formidable success, the cynics amongst us immediately muttered that sex must be involved. Clever cynics that we undoubtedly are, we were right once again. However, it is not just sex; Desmond Morris has also exploited a brilliant idea.

This is to write about man as if he were an animal, and use scientific terms in matter-of-fact fashion as if the species under discussion were a herring gull, stickleback or 9-banded armadillo. Hence the title: man is just another ape - the only naked one.

Dr. Morris does indeed get on to sex very early in the book. Chapter two is entitled "Sex" just as baldly as the ape in question is naked. The scientific language enables this author to be blunt about the subject in a way that no poets, novelists, etc., would ever dream of.

Not all the book is about sex, merely a fifth of it. The other chapters are devoted to rearing, exploration, fighting, feeding, comfort, and animals, this last being the only chapter which describes man's attitude to species other than his own. These chapters are all full of odd bits of information.

I am still astounded at the £100,000, and still like the notion of treating man in animal fashion. Dr. Morris has exploited the idea skilfully. He writes simply: he mixes the cultures easily; he deserves success, and one is happy to admit in one's more generous moments that he deserves quite a lot of that money.

(October 12)

ANGUS WILSON'S PASSING SHOW

No Laughing Matter. By Angus Wilson (Secker & Warburg. 2 gns.)

THERE is in my mind no doubt that Angus Wilson is the most considerable British novelist to emerge since the second world war. But I have always felt that he must prove it, and that he never has. The promise was infinite, but the performance, except in the first two sets of short stories, has never quite equalled it.

This is perhaps because he has always seemed to shy away from the big book. Even "The Old Men at the Zoo," which was large in size, somehow lacked essential stature. Now with "No laughing Matter," he has produced a big book: this is undeniable, and it is very nearly an extremely successful one. Had it kept the promise of its beginning it would have been the greatest novel for many years. As it is, it is just infinitely better than most.

The book has two themes: at one level it is the story of the interrelated lives of a family of six children all born in the 20 years before the first world war, and at a second it is the story of England itself, for between 1912 and the present day the six suffer and enjoy most of the experiences of their generation.

This is no ordinary family saga remorselessly moving forward; Mr. Wilson varies his techniques by dropping into dialogue, written in the dramatic style of the period he is dealing with. He includes long passages from Margaret's stories and even Quentin's political diatribes. The hefty structure of the book is not always quite under control and Mr. Wilson's sureness of touch seems to have left him by the end, but there is no denying this is a big book. D. H.

(October 5)

At the Jerusalem. By Paul Bailey. (Cape. 21s)

OLD age wears an uglier mask in Paul Bailey's first novel "At the Jerusalem." This is the story of the widowed Mrs. Gadny, whose stepson places her in a shabby old women's home called The Jerusalem. She spends her first night in the converted workhouse crying to herself, and the matron tells the nurses with unconscious irony. "She thinks she's come to an institution. Use velvet paws."

Velvet paws or no, Mrs. Gadny is convinced that she has been "disposed of" like old rubbish, and cannot reconcile herself to her new home. Sickened by the squalid sights and smells around her, wounded by the spiteful back-biting of her neighbours, she takes refuge first in her memories, and then in total withdrawal. At the end of the book she is removed to a mental hospital, an irrecoverable wreck.

It would be difficult to praise this short novel too highly. Sensitive, but unsentimental, it is all the more moving for its quiet restraint. R.B.

(June 1)

HUMANITY IN BRONZES BY ELISABETH FRINK

By TERENCE MULLALY

ELISABETH FRINK is very much a sculptor of our time. Veering between savage strength and the enigmatic, she has always spoken a language that has seemed relevant. Now, with six bronzes in her latest exhibition at the Waddington Galleries, Cork Street, she adds to relevance a new element.

There is about these particular heads a sense of inevitability, a suggestion of timeless qualities that lifts them beyond illustration or the category of exercises in the handling of a challenging material. The heads are mounted in lonely strength in two parallel rows. In one these heads are unadorned, in the other they wear goggles.

Both series are chunky, heavy of jaw, massive of feature. There is no grace here, no elegance, or charm, but, one suddenly perceives the fact, there is much humanity.

Superficially there is little difference between individual heads of the two series. In fact, the variations although subtle are decisive.

(December 11)

PALLADIUM SHOW AGAIN AT TOP

Daily Telegraph Television Staff

The most popular programme on television in the week ending May 7 was again the London Palladium Show, according to figures issued by Television Audience Measurement. It was seen in 8,250,000 homes.

The BBC had four programmes in the Top Twenty list — "Frost Report" at 10, the "Benny Hill Show" at 12, and "Z Cars" and "Tomorrow's World" equal at 17.

The Top Ten programmes for the week were: 1, The London Palladium Show; 2, Cinema; 3, "No Hiding Place; 4, "Coronation Street" (Monday); 5, "Take Your Pick"; 6, equal, "Market in Honey Lane" and "Mr Rose"; 8, "The Seven Deadly Virtues"; 9, "Coronation Street" (Wednesday); 10, "Frost Report."

(May 13)

'WHITER SHADE OF PALE' HEADS TOP TEN

Procol Harum's record, "A Whiter Shade of Pale," has taken over first place in the Melody Maker Top Ten from the Tremeloes' "Silence is Golden."

(June 6)

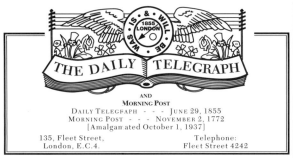

THE DAILY TELEGRAPH
AND
MORNING POST
DAILY TELEGRAPH - - - JUNE 29, 1855
MORNING POST - - - NOVEMBER 2, 1772
[Amalgamated October 1, 1937]
135, Fleet Street, London, E.C.4. Telephone: Fleet Street 4242

STILL NO CONFIDENCE

WHATEVER may be the ultimate consequences of Mr. WILSON'S devaluation of the pound, let it be humbly recognised that devaluation is an action to which a measure of disgrace always properly attaches. Mr. CALLAGHAN himself has called it a breach of faith, in which honour is devalued as well as money. Certainly, it involves the abandonment of those who have entrusted this country with the keeping of their money as well as of those under-developed nations who have first been promised extravagant aid and are now deprived of a large part of its real value. If it does not raise the price of food, petrol and tobacco and of many manufactured goods, it will have failed in its purpose. If it is to work at all it must inevitably hit those "vulnerable sections of the community" whom Mr. CALLAGHAN has announced his intention of protecting. The proper demeanour for a Government whose policy is in ruins and whose pledges have been dishonoured on all sides is one of penitence. By contrast, the boastful and over-confident tone adopted by the Prime Minister in his broadcast last night came near to being a breach of taste. It will increase rather than reduce the public anger, already seen in Downing Street, against a leader who has forfeited respect. This is not only a proud nation, as Mr. WILSON called it, but an angry one.

This crisis is not the fault either of the British people or of the bankers who, if anything, have erred on the side of failing to demand the positive reforms which can alone provide the security for their advances. Whether it or something like it would have happened had the Tories been in power is an irrelevant speculation. What is certain is that it is now the Opposition's duty not merely to urge the public to accept such necessary burdens as any policy for recovery must impose; it is also its duty to insist that these burdens should be so distributed as to foster, not sterilise, production.

The Government which continues to stifle those energies has yet no title to trust. Devaluation is not in fact, as Mr. WILSON implied, a panacea. At best it merely buys time for self-reform, room for manoeuvre. The Government will be judged by the use it makes of this time, this room. The first signs, alas, are far from encouraging.

(November 20)

FALLEN COLOSSUS

No tears need be shed over the fall of President NASSER. He was a wild and dangerous man to have ruling a land like Egypt. Arabs who resisted his assumption of a divine right to lead them were imprisoned, assassinated, bombed into submission. His narcotic was the dream of Arab unity; his catchword, the Arab revolution. It seems extraordinary that a colossus fallen from such a height should be able to appoint his successor. It is far more probable that ZAKARIA MOHIEDDIN was imposed upon him by the Egyptian Army. The new President, though a founder member of the Revolutionary Council, is said to be a practical man who long held misgivings about Col. NASSER'S conduct of policy.

What can Britain do at this time to protect her interests in the Middle East? Little indeed, at a time when Arab States are losing their heads and blaming it on us. British Ambassadors, and even consuls, are being expelled from Syria, Iraq and the Lebanon. How can Britain use her good offices in such conditions? She can do nothing on her own to allay the Israeli-Arab dispute. President MOHIEDDIN will have to enter direct talks with Israel, which holds the big cards. Britain should also beware of becoming involved in United Nations initiatives, in wordy resolutions, or movements to send back the United Nations Emergency Force - the umbrella which was taken away when it started to rain. Britain's best policy today is to maintain a watchful silence.

(June 10)

CHINESE BRIGANDAGE

COMMUNIST CHINA has hitherto been fairly tolerant towards those journalists whom she has admitted through the bamboo curtain. Yesterday's attack by Red Guards in Peking on the car of Mr. DAVID OANCIA, whose dispatches from China appear in this newspaper, is a flagrant and regrettable departure from civilised behaviour. He and his Swedish and Norwegian companions were on their normal eyewitness duties when the mob of guardists jumped on their car and systematically wrecked it. How is there to be accurate reporting of events in China if such treatment is condoned? Far from disavowing such hooliganism, the Foreign Ministry spokesman in Peking described it as "fully justified." Police and troops looked on. A bad advertisement indeed for the "great cultural revolution."

An even more sinister act is the detention in his home of Mr. ANTHONY GREY, Reuter's correspondent in Peking. This appears to be a reprisal for the sentence properly imposed on a New China News Agency man by a Hongkong court for subversive activities there. Diplomatic Notes appear useless. The New China News Agency man in London might well be given a taste of the same inconvenience as Mr. GREY. Reprisals in kind are the only language that China understands in her present hysteria. In Hongkong Britain must stand firm, and the firmer the better, in the knowledge that 85 per cent. of the people want to live in peace under the British flag. Any show of weakness or hesitation there could have the worst consequences.

(July 25)

When the Flowers Open Up

By GERDA PAUL

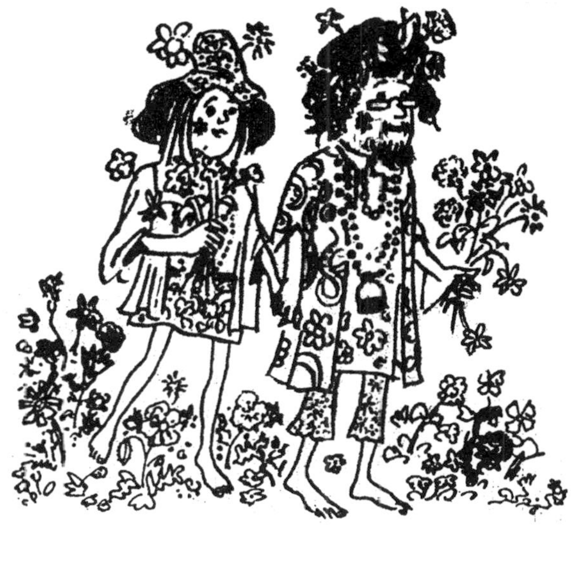

PICKING my way through the Flowers, I thought how easy it was for older people to become angry or to mock. "Layabouts. Drug addicts. A short course in the Army ..."

In a way, they look so manifestly, touchingly absurd in their floral furtrimmed garments, beads round their necks, tinny bells jangling, sickly sweet joss sticks smouldering between their teeth and all those flowers in their unkempt hair. The girls are half-drowned Ophelias, loosely, longly, garbed, whole hedgerows tangled in their reedy dank hair. The young men are painted Red Indians, or genii, or Afghan shepherds, peering through or over improbable Mr. Pickwick specs.

There they sit or sprawl, among the garbage of a week-end's picknicking, listening to a continuous blast of amplified pop.

But are the Flowers layabouts, drug-taking louts? A little nature study seemed only fair.

Going from one group to another, squatting with them on the grass, I have to admit that I could not find any who were not in jobs, or between jobs, or studying at university or technical colleges. The San Francisco hippies may be kept by rich parents but our Flower Children, at least those I talked to, are certainly not. As for drugs, some admitted to having had marijuana, or LSD, but very few said they were on them now. Hardly any drank, or smoked ordinary cigarettes.

What do they want? It depends on whether they are real or fringe Flowers. One learns not to generalise. The real ones, in my definition, are kindly, earnest, most often intelligent. They want love, they want peace, they want freedom from convention and from bitter inhibition.

They generalise far too much about the older generations, of course, and who's responsible for all those wars and this rotten, old world. (But so do older generations generalise about the young, and how the country's going to the dogs; with less excuse, because we should know better.)

There were superior ones, lofty Chelsea Flower Show breeds, young intellectuals, inbred, self-sufficient groups of boys and girls, who pleasantly but fairly plainly indicated that I should mind my own business.

There were also boisterous, sturdy, bomb-site and cottage-garden border flowers. Among them was a group of jolly lads from the Midlands all in full gear. They'd been drinking beer and were in high, but by no means unpleasant, spirits, working hard, as a team, building a bonfire of dead branches, "to liven things up a bit." With them was a slightly older man, in "plain clothes." He uttered the surprising words: "Don't you get it? It's what you find in the Army, the pleasure of doing something together, with your mates."

He wouldn't agree that drugs, to the weak, could be as dangerous as drink; nor that it might be cant to suggest that there was a physical road to Heaven. "No, the drugs help you, they show you the way."

His friend, whose long brown curls peeped from under a Harpo Marx hat, wore a "defraction disc" symbolising the third eye, he said, on his forehead. He showed me a book by an American author, bought in Charing Cross Road. The key was that God was in you. A new spiritual age was coming. "It's great, it's all so true."

The boy who said he worked in a Rut (it turned out to be a factory) had a cardboard flower stuck over the right-hand lens of his dark glasses. He was suspicious when I asked if he could see properly. "You making fun of me?" he wanted to know. I told him I wasn't really laughing at him, but the clothes were all meant to be a bit of fun, weren't they? He broke into a reluctant grin, rather gruffly handed me a ragged carnation, which, because I was touched, I carried for hours.

Fringe Flowers were the four young men in one of the Pop groups. From the Home Counties, they had the right Indian gear and Liverpool accents - "You've got to, to get on." They didn't take drugs, they were too busy trying to get to the top.

(September 2)

FIGHT FOR LIFE

So the valiant struggle to save the life of Mr. WASHKANSKY has failed. This will be a cause of sadness to millions of people the world over, who have watched the battle day by day with compassionate interest. Essentially the same drama - the fight to save a life - has been enacted countless times before, and arouses in those who witness it essentially the same emotions as those experienced by Mr. WASHKANSKY'S world public in the last three weeks.

As Prof. BARNARD, the surgeon in charge of the case has insisted, the claims of scientific inquiry were from the first subordinate to those of healing. The aim was to keep a patient alive and to restore him, for as long as possible, to the enjoyment of health.

There can be no doubt, however, that in the process the cause of medical science has greatly benefited. It seems that the heart transplantation itself was, in the surgical sense, a complete success, and that Mr. WASHKANSKY'S body did not in fact reject the new organ. The trouble, which had always been foreseen, was that action taken to prevent this rejection gravely weakened the patient's resistance to invading germs. The risk was calculated and in future it may prove possible to reduce it. In suitable cases, the operation will and ought to be attempted again.

Mr. WASHKANSKY'S own strong personality (his courage and sportsmanship have won just admiration) was certainly not altered by the acquisition of a new heart. There is no justification, either, for the apprehension that doctors will soon be put in the position of having daily to decide who should live and who should die. The human body still presents many mysteries which are not in sight of conquest. In seeking to unravel them, medical men will not be inhibited by confused sentiments and ill-conceived philosophical scruples.

(December 22)

DEGREE COURSES BY TV

Daily Telegraph Reporter

BRITAIN is to get its "University of the Air" by the autumn of 1970, Miss Jennie Lee, Minister for the Arts, announced at a Press conference in London yesterday.

A new university institution is to be created which will provide courses leading to degrees and other qualifications by a combination of television, radio correspondence, tutorials, short residential courses and local audio-visual centres.

Miss Lee has appointed a planning committee presided over by Sir Peter Venables, Vice-Chancellor of the University of Aston, Birmingham.

Their task is to work out a comprehensive plan for the university in line with the 1966 White Paper, and to prepare a draft charter and statutes.

The capital cost of starting the university is expected to be less than £1 million. Running costs are estimated at between £3 million and £4 million annually. Tutors will be recruited regionally.

Television programmes may cost £2 million a year. This cost, said Miss Lee, would be static and would remain however many students there were.

TUTORS FOR ALL

Fees not decided

Students would receive books, correspondence courses and paperbacks. Each would be advised by a tutor.

The university, "The Open University" Miss Lee prefers to call it, is to be grant-aided by the Department of Education and Science. It will not fall within the University Grants Committee system.

As agreed with the BBC, television programmes are being provided on BBC 2 and the cost will come from the university's funds.

It was intended that the university would be a degree-taking body in its own right, setting its own examinations.

(September 19)

Birth-Control clinics to advise singles

The 681 clinics of the Family Planning Association will from today be free to give birth-control advice and contraceptives to all over 16 who seek them, whether they are married or not.

Hitherto, the association has limited its advice to the single to couples about to marry.

(October 6)

LONDON DAY BY DAY

"Oui, mais..."
Slim likeness

AFEW months ago M. Giscard d'Estaing, replaced as Minister of Finance by M. Debré, formulated as his attitude to Gaullism "Yes, but..." and later the President commented that "You cannot govern with buts."

Now it seems this is precisely what he will have to do. With a minute Government majority, Giscard controls at least 45 votes, possibly more, and is better able to influence policy than M. Lecanuet's Opposition group of 30.

Two or three Giscardians at least are expected to be in the new Cabinet, though their leader is reported not to be seeking fresh office. He wants to concentrate on consolidating his party-within-a-party. It might take over the Gaullist heritage some day.

Painted by Friends

LORD SLIM'S portrait which is being unveiled by Gen. Sir Frank Messervy at Sandhurst tomorrow night is a remarkable tribute to the affection the field-marshal has inspired.

Leonard Boden was commissioned to paint it last year to commemorate Lord Slim's 75th birthday, and the picture is being presented to the National Army Museum.

An appeal brought subscriptions from two British regiments in which he served, 36 Indian Army officers' associations, 24 branches of the Burma Star Association and four businesses he is now associated with.

More than 250 of the subscribers will be at the unveiling, when Field-Marshal Sir Gerald Templer will accept the portrait on behalf of the Army Museum's council.

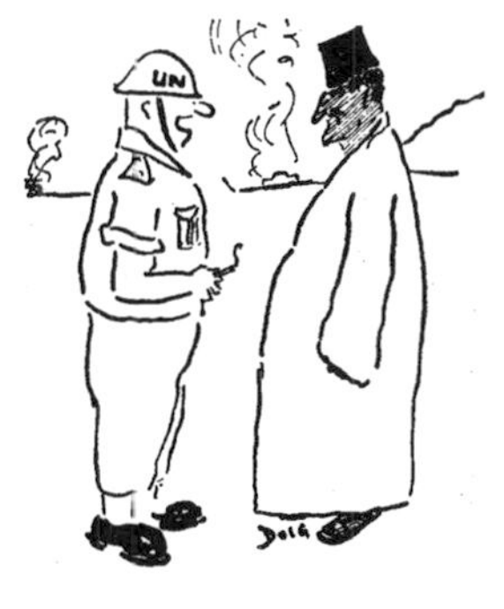

"Anything doing while we've been away?"

Wait for It

CONTINENT-BOUND holiday makers were pretty critical yesterday of the organisation - or lack of it - at Heathrow.

In the crowded departure lounge at breakfast time there was only one assistant at the buffet and the flight announcements were made so loudly that passengers were half-deafened.

A colleague who eventually boarded a Rome plane was then told there would be an hour's delay owing to an electrical fault. "At this rate," remarked another traveller, "shall we ever get into Europe?"

Americanised Billions

Incidentally, Mr. Callaghan's statement referred to 1.4 and to three billion dollars. This, I believe is the first Treasury use of billion in the American sense of a thousand million instead of the English, a million million.

Let us hope, for clarity's sake, that it will be the last. We don't really have to carry the special relationship to these lengths.

Not Classic, But Useful

"Above all a Riesling year" was the verdict of Mr. Austin Hasslacher, Deinhard's chairman, at their Bakers' Hall tasting yesterday of the unprecedented total of nearly 70 German 1966 Moselle and Rhine wines, 11 from their own estates.

They promise not a classic but a very useful vintage, better balanced and thus longer living than the '64s, and reasonably priced. Charges are scarcely up on 1964.

Nowadays wines are drunk younger than in former times, and Mr. Hasslacher thinks the cheaper Moselles can be tried this autumn and the better ones and lower-quality Rhine wines next spring.

But the best Rhine '66s should be allowed 18 months or so in bottle, which means patience until the autumn of 1968 or the spring of 1969.

Thought for Today

"MAO TSE-TUNG for Poet Laureate" - Suggestion chalked in large letters on the bridge over the canal at the top of Ladbroke Grove.

PETERBOROUGH

TWIGGY

By ANN STEELE

IN "Pygmalion" Professor Higgins and Eliza Doolittle came from vastly different backgrounds. Now it isn't necessary to leap the class barriers to effect a transformation in a girl's life - as Nigel Davies has demonstrated in the celebrated case of Lesley Hornby.

Under his guidance, ex-schoolgirl Lesley has blossomed forth as Twiggy, the girl tipped to oust The Shrimp in the 1967 model stakes.

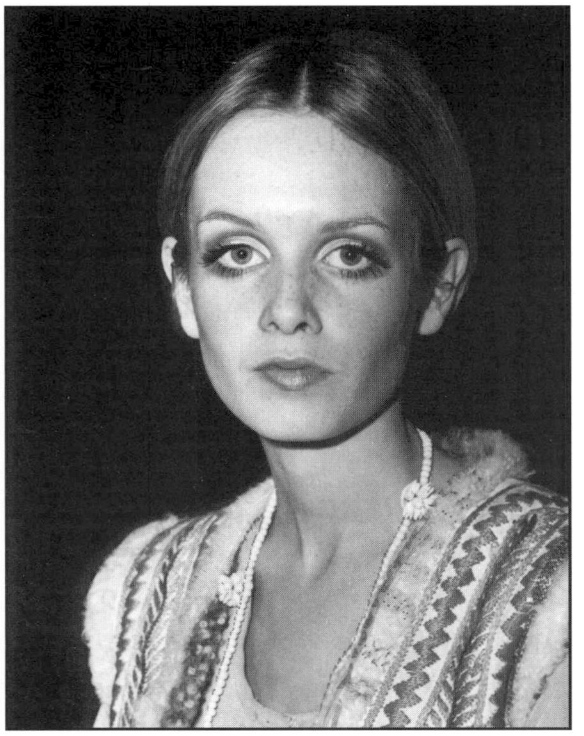

Nigel Davies changed her name because he saw her, in his words, as "the mini-queen of a new social aristocracy."

To take his own place in this aristocracy he also changed his name. For Nigel Davies from Bow now read Justin de Villeneuve, of Chelsea.

"It's more elegant," explained the 27-year-old one-time hairdressing assistant to Vidal Sassoon who is now full-time manager of Twiggy Enterprises Limited.

Like the proverbial pools winner, Twiggy, 17, has not let it change her life at all.

She still lives in the same suburban semi-detached with Mum and Dad, chairman and managing director of Twiggy Enterprises. She still prefers to stay at home and watch the telly in the evenings instead of going to cocktail parties. "I hate the 'in' places. I hate people staring at me and asking silly questions. I never know what to answer," she says.

She still goes to bed at 10 p.m. She doesn't smoke. She doesn't drink. And flying terrifies her.

When she was 15 and doing a Saturday hairdressing job to earn an extra pound a week pocket money, she met Nigel Davies.

"I saw the potential there, but it took two years to really get her launched," says Mr. de Villeneuve.

Twiggy left school last March.

Since then she has done things that, as a fifth former at Kilburn and Brondesbury Grammar School, she would not have thought possible in her wildest dreams. She has hob-nobbed with celebrities, turned down film offers and has just cut her first disc.

"It is not sloppy or sentimental - nothing fantastic. Just a nice little ballad," she says shyly. "Nonsense," butts in Mr. de Villeneuve, "Twiggy's got a great voice."

Twiggy acquired the improbable name because of her lanky legs (she's 5ft 6in tall and weighs only 6 ½ stone). From earning £1 on Saturdays at 15 she now commands 10 guineas an appearance.

The record is being launched with a reception at Claridge's this month. "I have never been there," she says with awe. "Though I managed to get into the Savoy one evening for dinner dressed in orange corduroy trews and T-shirt."

As a schoolgirl the farthest she travelled was to the Isle of Wight. Now she's been to Tunisia, Italy and flies to Paris every other week.

What has this girl got? She looks like a child of 12. Enormous eyes. An extraordinary face. A waif who can look like a star.

"She's also got personality," her manager insists earnestly. "She has brought reality to the model world and to hundreds of youngsters who hope to follow in her footsteps. A few years ago, unless you came from the right social background, you were out. Now it is a disadvantage to have a highclass accent."

Twiggy's voice is definitely Cockney - that is, when she airs her views.

Normally she is content to listen to Justin. He goes everywhere with her. "Without him I would never have got this far."

Her Dad looks after the financial side of the business and allows his daughter £10 a week spending money. Outside on the pavement stands the only status symbol so far: a gleaming white £3,500 Ford Mustang.

"Twiggy can't drive but she will learn," says Justin. Meantime he acts as chauffeur.

(January 4)

New 100mph Sunbeam Rapier

By Our Motoring Staff

A completely new 100mph Sunbeam Rapier was announced yesterday to complete the Rootes "new deal" for 1968. It has an attractive, fastback body and there is no loss of headroom in the back or lack of space because of the styling.

The car seats four to five people. The two-door body is pillarless so that windows down the Rapier will provide open-air motoring with a roof on. Volume production is just starting and the first Rapiers will be available at home in December.

The price of £1,200 including £225 purchase tax seems remarkably low in view of the car's appearance and specification.

The Rapier is powered by the well-proved 1,725 cc Rootes engine which has twin carburettors, producing 94 bhp at 5,200 rpm. Overdrive on top and third gears is a standard fitting. A top speed of 102 mph is claimed together with a creditable 0 to 60 mph acceleration in just over 12sec.

Consumption of 30 mpg

The exceptionally low drag factor due to the design means that a petrol consumption figure of around 30 mpg may be expected.

As always with Rootes cars, the Rapier is well appointed and beautifully finished. Special attention has been paid to soundproofing. There is a split propellershaft with a rubber-housed centre bearing to counteract vibration. Engine vibration is also reduced by hydraulic damper.

There is glass fibre and polyester padding under the bonnet and bootlid and foam and felt padding is also placed under the carpets, around the gearbox tunnel and between the head lining and roof panel. The underside of the car is coated with bituminous sound-deadening compound.

The individual reclining front seats are fitted with a positive lock to prevent them tipping forward in an emergency or under severe braking.

Anti-burst doors

Safety features include anti-burst door locks, special rims on the wheels to hold tyres in place in the event of a blowout and a toughened windscreen.

Sunbeam Rapier:

Price £1,200, inc. £225 p.t.

Automatic transmission £43 extra; Seat belts £8 extra

Engine 1,725 cc, four cylinder, 94 bhp at 5,200 rpm.

The instruments include, besides the usual speedometer, rev counter and gauges, an electric transitorised clock working from a battery independent of the car's electrical supply.

(October 10)

How to get your maxi coat

WANT to wear a maxi coat? Now that icy winds are blowing and knees are a-blueing, lots of women are keen. Fashion's biggest guessing game is: where can the maxi coat be found?

Oddly enough, not at the places you'd normally expect. Not at Wallis, at Fenwick or at Jaeger. Why? The first two were scared; Young Jaeger sold out, don't plan to make any more.

Miss Selfridge love the maxi coat. In on Thursday; a batch of black or brown gabardine maxi coats, very Victorian, waisted and with velvet trimming, for 17gns.

Dickins and Jones and Fifth Avenue will have, in a fortnight, a new batch of Harbro's maxi coats. There are just a few blacks and browns in Dickins now.

A racy looking herringbone maxi is on sale at Peter Robinson's made by Sheraton and costing 13 ½ gns. Liberty's are getting Donegal maxis by Cojana at the end of the week.

Galeries Lafayette have, predictably, a beauty in from France in rose wool at £27 15s and a good buy in an Alexon wool maxi coat (lilac or red) at just £13 15s.

(November 27)

ROYAL OPERA HOUSE PUTS UP PRICES

THE Royal Opera House, Covent Garden, is to raise its seat prices by an average of nine per cent. from April 17. The main burden of the increases will be carried by the more expensive seats.

For the amphitheatre, seating over 800, there is to be no change in the prices, which are from 5s to £1 7s 6d. Prices of some side seats in the balcony stalls will also remain the same.

Stalls prices will go up by about 12 per cent. The highest increase will be for a stall seat at one of the more expensive performances, £4 10s instead of £4. A grand-tier seat at an expensive performance will cost £5, against £4 12s 6d now.

Throughout April there will be some performances for which the old prices will still operate. These will be of works already in the repertoire.

Covent Garden wanted to raise all prices last Autumn, but permission was refused because of the financial "freeze."

(February 28)

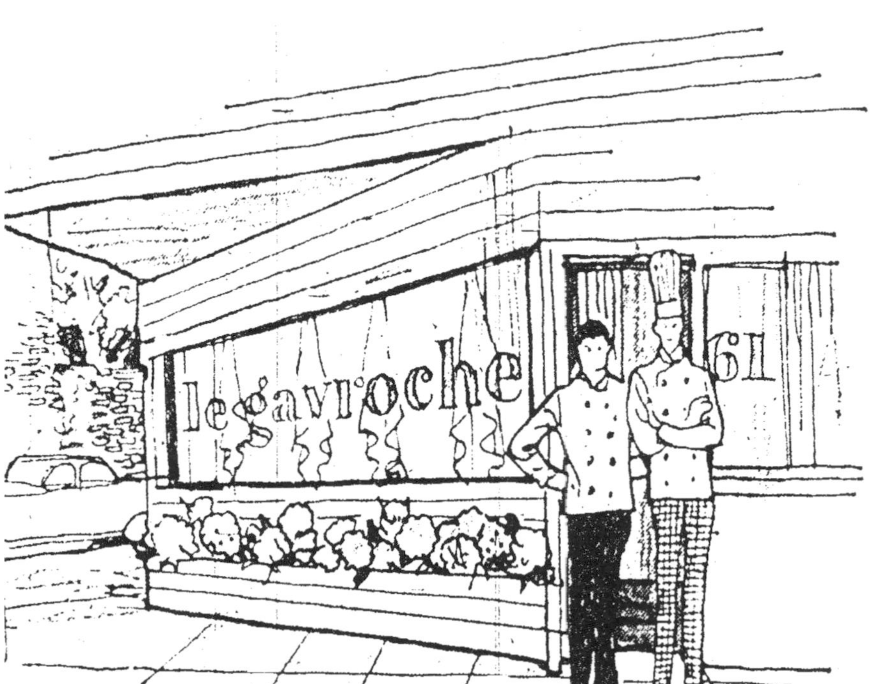

Men are catching on to the cape

Men wearing capes are quite a common sight these days in the King's Road, Chelsea. Some buy their capes second-hand in the Portobello Road or the antique supermarket in the King's Road. Others buy them new at the girls' shops: Fenwick's report that theirs are frequently snapped up by men.

Artist Ivan Ripley told me that two years ago when he was in Munich capes for men seemed very fashionable; with them the men wore flat, wide-brimmed matador hats.

But that's not to say the girls haven't gone overboard about capes, too. And a few weeks ago in Paris, both Lanvin and Cardin gave their approval to the caped look.

(February 20)

ENID BLYTON BOOK BAN IN CAPE TOWN

THE Cape Town city librarian has banned the works of Enid Blyton, the children's author, from his shelves.

The librarian, Mr. G.H. Vermeulem, said he did not like the way the books are written. Children portrayed in them were impertinent to their parents, he said.

Mr. George Greenfield, Miss Blyton's agent, commented yesterday: "Miss Blyton writes very readable and realistic stories and does not try to make out that her children are little angels.

"Children in actual life do say rude things to their elders."

(October 5)

FIVE POUNDS TAKES TWO TO FRANCE

BERYL HARTLAND'S latest discovery

WITH London the target for so many talents, it had to happen; two brilliant young French chefs - who have often cooked for royalty and heads of state - have crossed the Channel to open a restaurant in Chelsea that is as French as the tricolor.

Le Gavroche in Lower Sloane Street is so new the paint is hardly dry on the walls, but the two young brothers Roux, Albert, 31, and Michel, 27, are old in the knowledge of their art.

After training in Paris, dark stocky Albert worked for the French Embassy in London and later with Major Peter Cazalet, at whose house the Queen Mother has often dined. Michel (first time in England), slim, fair and speaking no English, was chef in Paris to Mlle. Cecile de Rothschild. He has already won awards galore for his cooking.

If your idea of a good dinner out goes no further than smoked salmon and scampi the Gavroche is not for you, but if you appreciate real French food as it is cooked in France anybody worth his gourmet salt should at least try a meal there.

Inside you could be eating in the heart of Paris, surrounded by solid comfort and large snowy-clothed tables. In true French fashion it is the food that counts here, not the decor.

Albert and Michel take week-about turns cooking their specialities; while one is in the kitchen the other, in crisp chef's outfit, is taking orders, suggesting dishes ("you are going to taste the turbot, not only the sauce") or deftly cutting a sliver of paté for you to sample.

But after four weeks' experience of the British public's way of life and eating, how do these young French perfectionists feel?

Last week I found them more than faintly disillusioned. Many of the customers don't know or care much what they are eating they told me.

There was a man who argued the French dressing was wrong and wanted sugar in his; there are the people who regularly cry out for English mustard with French dishes and there was the customer who insisted his thick juicy veal escalope be changed for a flaccid piece beaten so thin you could see through it.

Dinner for two at the Gavroche will cost you around £5-£6 and there is a small, excellent wine list. Among the specialities I have tasted are the Souglé Suisse, a delicate twice-cooked cheese concoction, and Omelette Rothschild, a delicious if rich sweet.

(May 25)

LONDON'S HAIR LINE

However much the fashion world may be waiting with baited breath to see what Rome and Paris do in the next two weeks at the spring fashion shows, the world lead in hair styling now comes from London.

And last night the man who has largely helped us to win this place, Vidal Sassoon, launched his Greek god "look" for 1967. His famous geometric cut is still with us, but shorter than ever, and softly permed into curls that lie close to the head.

(January 12)

EARL ATTLEE

RT. HON. AND GALLANT

THIS has been called an age of small men and great events; but even in such an age a man must possess exceptional qualities to be twice Prime Minister of Britain. At first sight these qualities were not strikingly apparent in Lord ATTLEE. One of his opponents in a sardonic moment once described him as "a sheep in sheep's clothing," meaning that it was hard to recognise the leader of the Left in so unobtrusive and dim a character. Nevertheless, the great qualities - though perhaps more negative than positive - were there. Nobody ever accused him of insincerity. He was a man of character such as, rightly or wrongly, the British are apt to prefer to a man of brilliance.

Looked at objectively, of course, his career was a mass of contradictions. The gallant if undistinguished soldier of the First World War turned pacifist; the denouncer in equally virulent terms of the Fascist and Nazi dictators and of British rearmament; the man who in manner was as mild as milk, and yet had a curious streak of ruthlessness when any colleague got at cross-purposes with him. His strength was that nobody could believe that such a man could stray into extreme courses. Yet it will probably be found, when the fully-informed history of his career is written, that he had in fact the persistence of a fanatic in pursuit of the theories to which he had been converted.

(October 9)

KONRAD ADENAUER

GERMANY'S ARCHITECT

AFTER clinging to the last faint spark of life with characteristic tenacity for a week, KONRAD ADENAUER died yesterday in his beloved Rhineland in the house where, an age ago, he had scorned HITLER and cultivated roses. By the time, in 1963, he retired from office he had restored in 14 years, in more senses than one, what HITLER had destroyed in 12. It is an achievement that gives him a unique claim to the gratitude of the German people, of Europe and of the whole world.

It would be unfair to ADENAUER and to the German people to see their achievement only in terms of the Economic Miracle, as if the status that the Federal Republic now enjoys were no more than a projection of this. When at the age of 73 he set about clearing up after Gotterdammerung, he provided scope and stimulus not only for the German virtue of industriousness, but also for democratic aspirations and idealism. These have found stable and creditable expression in the political life of the country and in Europeanism.

ADENAUER showed skill and toughness in exploiting Russia's westward pressure to Germany's advantage in her relations with the West. Yet the identity of interests on which this policy was based on both sides has proved valid, and Germany has been a good ally. Despite all pressures at home and abroad, he steadfastly rejected reunification on Russian terms. No doubt he was autocratic. Yet in his era shocked and divided Germany needed a father figure.

(April 20)

BOMBARDIER BILLY WELLS

BOMBARDIER BILLY WELLS, one of the best known of British heavyweight boxing champions, died suddenly at his home in Ealing, Middlesex, yesterday. He would have been 80 in August.

Until last November when the present champion, Henry Cooper, surpassed his record, Wells had been the longest reigning British heavyweight champion. He won the title in 1911 and kept it for seven years 303 days.

His career was also one of the most colourful and varied in British boxing. In the words of A.F. Bettinson, who helped stage many of his early fights at the National Sporting Club, "He had it in him to sweep the board, but flattered to deceive.

Wells was superbly endowed physically. His defeats by Carpentier led to the coinage of the phrase of "horizontal British heavyweight."

He left boxing to go into music hall and films, and played alongside Helen Vinson in the "King of the Damned" in 1935.

(June 16)

LAST MANCHU EMPEROR DIES IN PEKING

Henry Pu Yi, last of the Manchu Emperors of China, has died in Peking, aged 61, it was reported from Peking yesterday. "Four times an Emperor, but only once alive" was how he once described himself. One of his last acts was to write his memoirs for the Communist Government's historical commission.

Deposed, briefly restored, deposed again, made a puppet Emperor by the Japanese in Manchuria, captured and imprisoned by the Russians and later by the Chinese, he was given an amnesty in 1959. Until 1961 he worked in Peking's botanical gardens.

He became Emperor first in 1908 at the age of two, but was forced to abdicate in 1912 when Dr. Sun Yat-sen set up the republic. He was Emperor again in 1917, for under two weeks, when counter-revolutionary elements tried to restore the Manchu dynasty.

(October 19)

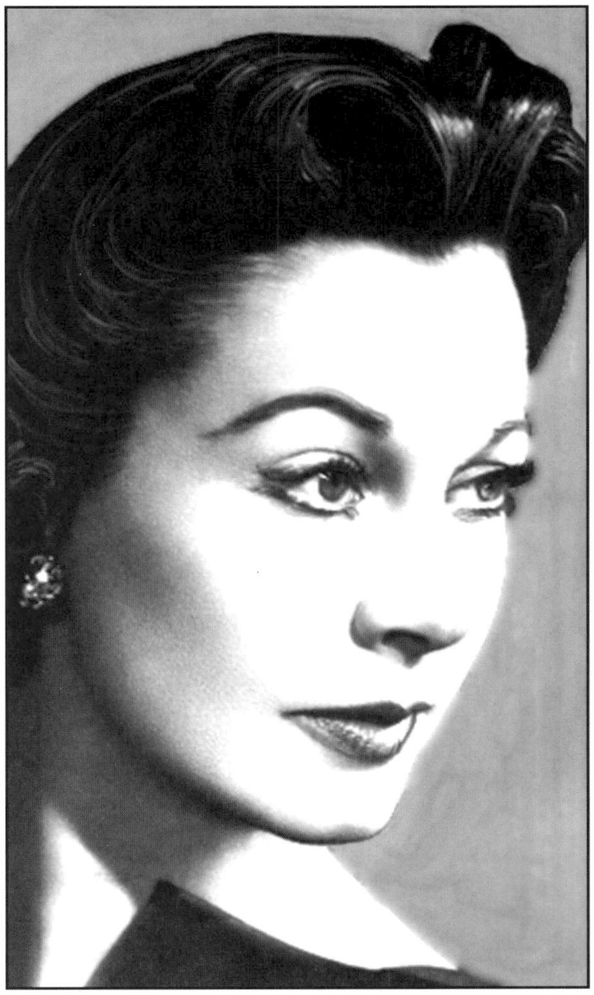

SIR MALCOLM SARGENT, CONDUCTOR AND WIT

SIR MALCOLM SARGENT died yesterday at his home in Albert Hall Mansions, next door to the Albert Hall where for 20 years he had conducted the Promenade Concerts. He was 72.

A spokesman at the Albert Hall said last night: "He was the best-loved British musician of his time. His death is a sad blow, and for many the 'Proms' will never be quite the same again."

Sir John Barbirolli, 67, conductor-in-chief of the Hallé Orchestra, said: "I will always think of Sir Malcolm as a gay cavalier."

Malcolm Sargent had been one of the great personalities in English musical life for almost five decades and recently the most popular and effective ambassador of English music all over the world.

Like many English musicians of his generation, he started as an organist, but he first showed the true nature of his gifts when, at the age of 26, he conducted a work of his own at (prophetically enough) a Queen's Hall Promenade Concert. The foundations of what were to be the great musical enthusiasms of his life were all laid before 1930.

INSTINCT AND EMOTION

A brave man

Children's concerts meant the early discovery of another special gift, which was to be used with spectacular success later in the Robert Mayer series; and his lifelong devotion to the Savoy operas found its first expression in 1926, when he conducted a London season of the D'Oyly Carte Opera Company.

Two years later began his long association with the Royal Choral Society, while the Courtauld-Sargent concerts established his name as an often brilliantly effective conductor of purely orchestral music.

But it was as a choral trainer and conductor that he won his greatest successes, especially in later years with the Huddersfield Choir.

Although he succeeded Sir Adrian Boult as conductor of the BBC Symphony Orchestra in 1950, Sargent's most characteristic successes in the years since the war were not so much in this country - where his chief work was done during the Promenade season - as in travelling all over the world as an ambassador of British music and a propagandist for the English composers of the older generation - Wlgar, Hoist, Vaughan Williams and Walton.

The consciousness of being out of sympathy with the new forces in English musical life made him sensitive and, we may suppose, unhappy but not bitter, since he was aware of being a much-praised conductor from Moscow to Houston.

Sargent was a singularly brave man, who had much to contend with in precarious physical health. His charm and gaiety often hid these circumstances from his critics, who were all too aware of his obvious weaknesses, which were in most cases the little vanities that often go with greatness.

(October 4)

SIR VICTOR GOLLANCZ

SIR VICTOR GOLLANCZ, who has died in London, aged 73, was the head of an internationally celebrated and controversial British publishing house and an author in his own right. But he will be remembered by his host of admirers principally as a humanitarian.

He was described by the late John Strachey in contradictory epithets as "Capitalist and Socialist; man of the world and latter day saint; Jew and Christian, rationalist and theologian; rebel and traditionalist."

His bright yellow dust-covers stand out on any bookshelf. Among his discoveries were A.J. Cronin, Daphne Du Maurier and Kingsley Amis.

In recent years he became increasingly concerned with religious questions which he dealt with in a series of impressive anthologies. In 1955-56 he was chairman of the National Campaign for the Abolition of Capital Punishment, and later joint chairman.

(February 9)

Vivien Leigh, actress of classic beauty

VIVIEN LEIGH, actress of screen and stage, who has died in London, aged 53, was hailed at an early age as a new and brilliant star in the theatrical firmament.

Her husband was Herbert Leigh Holman, by whose second name she became known professionally. The marriage lasted eight years before it ended in divorce. They had one daughter.

She then married Mr. (later Sir) Laurence Olivier. In 1960 they were divorced on her petition.

It is seldom that an unknown actress achieves fame on her first stage appearances, but Vivien did exactly that.

At the Q theatre in February 1935, she was in "The Green Sash," and at the Ambassadors in the same year as Henriette in "The Mask of Virtue" she was greeted as "the most remarkable theatrical discovery for years." Sir Alexander Korda immediately gave her a £50,000 film contract.

Slim and dainty, with a small oval face and grey-green eyes set widely apart which seemed for ever to be contemplating something far away, she possessed a piquant charm which was not the least of her attractions.

"GONE WITH THE WIND"

Oscar awards

But the role which made her name familiar throughout the world came in 1939, when she appeared as Scarlett O'Hara in the American film version of "Gone with the Wind."

This performance won Vivien an Oscar, which was followed by a second one in 1952 for her "A Streetcar named Desire."

As one commentator put it: "Not many actresses have both the authority which can command the stage and the gifts of beauty and charm which make the film star. Vivien Leigh is at home in both worlds."

ERIC SHORTER writes: It is easier for a camel to pass through the eye of a needle than for an actress rich in beauty to enter the kingdom of critical heaven, especially when that beauty is as distinguished, fine and classical as Vivien Leigh's.

To make her task more difficult, she married and acted in partnership with the man who is now accepted as our greatest actor. It is well known that the wives of eminently great actors are apt to seem overshadowed.

Whatever real talent Vivien Leigh possessed, she had to overcome the prejudice of those who suspected her looks and supposed that her art was heavily dependent on Olivier. Among connoisseurs of acting she never overcame it, but she still proved a gifted actress in her own right.

(July 10)

Harold Holt

Mr. Harold Edward Holt, Australia's Prime Minister, who was missing presumed drowned, yesterday, aged 59, had the formidable task of succeeding Sir Robert Menzies on his retirement in January, 1966, after leading the nation for an unbroken second term of 16 years.

Renowned for his social and sporting qualities as much as for his claims as a long-serving and widely experienced politician, Mr. Holt tackled his role with energy and fearlessness.

(December 18)

'SOUL SINGER ' OTIS REDDING

Otis Redding, the Negro known as the "king of the soul singers," was one of seven people killed yesterday in a private plane crash near Madison, Wisconsin. Two bodies have been recovered.

Redding, who was 26, was flying with four members of his troupe, his valet, and the pilot of his personal plane. The pilot was attempting an instrument landing in fog and light drizzle when the plane crashed into a lake.

(December 12)

Siegfried Sassoon

By CHARLES GRAVES

SIEGFRIED SASSOON, who has died at Heytesbury House, Warminster, Wilts, aged 80, was the original angry young man, yet lived to be awarded the Queen's Gold Medal for poetry, not to mention the CBE and the Hawthornden Prize.

His first slim volume of poems was published in 1917 as a result of his war-time experiences with the Royal Welsh Fusiliers, a regiment in which Robert Graves also served. It was followed by a further collection of poems immortalised by:

Good morning, good morning, the general said,
When we met him last week on our way to the line,
Now the soldiers he smiled at are most of them dead,
And we're cursing his staff for incompetent swine.
He's a cheery old card, grunted Harry and Jack,
As they slogged up to Arras with rifle and pack,
But he did for them both by his plan of attack.

He was educated at Marlborough and Clare College, Cambridge, hunted with the Southdown, won a number of points-to-point and joined the Sussex Yeomanry on Aug. 3, 1914, transferring soon afterwards to the Royal Welsh Fusiliers, where he met and compared notes with Robert Graves in the trenches.

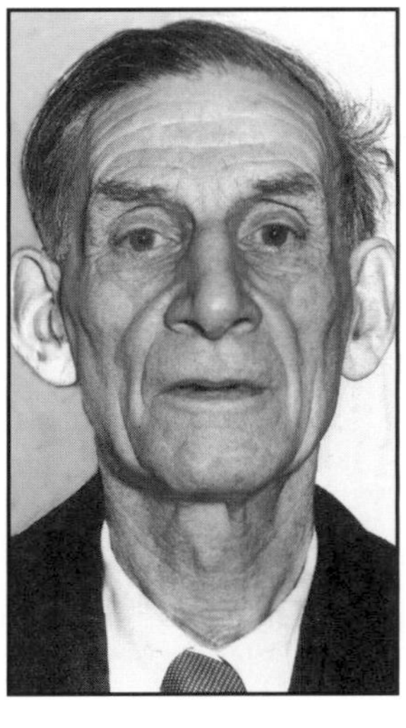

SIEGFRIED SASSOON

Sassoon, with a profile as elegant as that of Ivor Novello, proved to be a real fighting man, completely regardless of danger and won the sobriquet of "Mad Jack."

On one occasion, single-handed, he captured a complete line of trenches. He received the M.C.

Wounded three times, he joined the anti-war movement started by the Nation while on sick leave, and refused to return to France.

Thanks to Robert Graves, who continued to be his close friend for some years, he was put into a mental home under the famous Dr. W.H. Rivers, instead of being court-martialled. Incidentally, he threw his Military Cross into the water.

Siegfried Sassoon was best known to the public at large for his series of autobiographical and semi-autobiographical works.

Outstanding among these were "Memoirs of a Fox-Hunting Man" (1928). "Memoirs of an Infantry Officer" (1930), serialised in The Daily Telegraph, and "Siegfried's Journey" (1945)

In "Sequences" (1957) he developed a contemplative, intellectual, religious vein. In 1957 he had become a Roman Catholic.

(September 4)

RENE MAGRITTE.

In Brussels, aged 68. Surrealist painter; studied in Brussels and successively influenced by cubist, futurist and expressionist movements; active member surrealist school in Paris, 1927-30.

(August 17)

Playwright & flat-mate found dead

JOE ORTON, 34, the playwright, whose play "Loot" has run almost 400 performances at the Criterion Theatre was found dead yesterday with severe head injuries in his bed-sitting room in Noel Road, Islington.

His room-mate Kenneth Leith Halliwell, 41, a freelance writer, was also found dead, probably from an overdose of drugs. The two had shared the room for eight years.

Police are satisfied that no one else was involved and are treating the case as murder and suicide. Orton was found on a bed clothed only in a pyjama jacket. Halliwell was lying naked on the floor. Police took possession of some small bottles.

A preliminary post mortem, conducted by Dr. F. Camps indicated that Orton had been attacked with a hammer found near the bed.

Examination of the room suggests that Halliwell carried out the attack and that the first blow, police believe, stunned Orton sufficiently to prevent him moving.

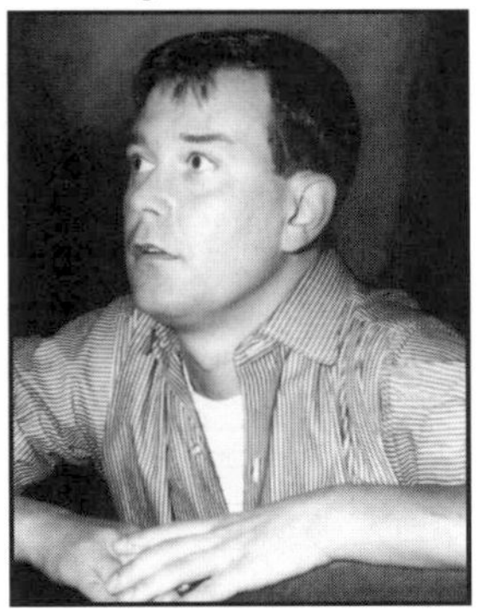

There appeared to have been several blows struck while he lay unconscious.

ERIC SHORTER writes: Joe Orton's talent did not suit all tastes. It specialised somewhat in unsavoury matters and did not disdain those themes for which the so-called dirty drama was attacked. But his feeling for language and theatrical situation - a genteel elegance of phrase in the most sordid circumstances - gave to his writing an incongruous dimension and curious ersatz flavour. Whether he was an imminent major playwright seems doubtful.

"Entertaining Mr. Sloane" was a lively, eneven but promising start, and "Loot" struck me as fulfilling that promise in the careful control of its black-farcical chaos. He was nothing if not a stylist and ashrewd observer of life in certain sections of society; and if "Loot" seemed likely to be his only line of writing, he will be missed by many playgoers with a taste for sardonic comedy.

(August 10)

WOODY GUTHRIE

Woody Guthrie, who died yesterday in New York, aged 55, was one of America's most celebrated folk singers and guitarists.

His songs in the recorded "Dust Bowl Ballads" were produced in 1940, when his talents were particularly impressive. One of his best-known was "This Land is Your Land."

Guthrie had suffered for 15 years from Huntington's chorea, an hereditary disease from which his mother died.

(October 4)

'INVISIBLE MAN CLAUDE RAINS DIES'

Claude Rains, London-born star of many films including H.G.Wells's "Invisible Man", died yesterday in hospital at Laconia, New Hampshire. He was 76.

Cause of death was given as abdominal bleeding and shock. His long career of screen charcter studies culminated in "Lawrence of Arabia."In "The Invisible Man," he was never seen after the beginning until he materialised in the final scenes.

(May 31)

John Masefield, poet laureate

WHEN John Masefield, O.M., who died yesterday aged 88, was chosen by Mr. Ramsay MacDonald in 1930 to succeed Robert Bridges in the Poet Laureateship, the contrast between the two poets was widely remarked on.

Bridges was a severe, restrained classicist, while Masefield was regarded as expansive and romantic. But even then he was regarded as a very definite force in literature.

Although Masefield was always reticent about his early days, it is known that he was born on June 1, 1878 at Ledbury, Herefordshire, within sight of the Malvern Hills.

He went to King's School, Warwick, until at 14 he joined the training ship H.M.S. Conway. After winning prizes for seamanship he signed as an apprentice on board a sailing ship bound around Cape Horn to Chile.

He was so seasick on the voyage that he returned by streamer and never served again in a sailing vessel.

After qualifying as a merchant officer he was appointed sixth officer in the White Star liner Adriatic, but on arrival in New York he resigned his commission and renounced life on the sea.

For a time he lived a vagrant life in America, doing odd jobs on farms and finally returning to New York, where he worked as a potman in a Greenwich Village bar.

What little leisure he had during these years in America was spent in reading. The purchase of a copy of Chaucer's works, read by candlelight in his room, determined him to be a poet. For this purpose he returned to England.

POEM OF SEA

Royal occasions

His literary career began in 1902 with the publication of "Salt Water Ballads," One of the poems in this work was "I must go down to the seas again."

Success did not come for some time, however, and although he published further volumes of poetry and experimented with plays like "Nan," "The Campden Wonder," and "Pompey the Great," and with novels like "Captain Margaret," he did not find his true medium until the publication of a series of tales in verse, beginning in 1911 with "The Everlasting Mercy."

This work offended many people by its bluntness and realism, but attracted more by the beauty of its lyrical passages. It is the story of the reclamation of a drunken poacher, which moves from ugliness to great beauty.

This was followed by perhaps his best-known poem of the sea "Dauber," and "The Daffodil Fields," "Sard Harker," although written in prose, seemed to take its inspiration from poetry and is believed by some critics to be his best novel.

Other types of works by Masefield have been boys' adventure stories, "The Nine Days Wonder," a diary of Dunkirk written in prose after interviewing survivors, and a number of poems written on Royal occasions.

The Poet Laureate received the Order of Merit in 1935. Three years later he received the Hanseatic Shakespeare Prize worth £830 from Hamburg University.

In 1961 Masefield became one of the first Companions of Literature. He was awarded the 1961 William Foyle Poetry Prize of £250 for "The Bluebells and Other Verses."

(May 13)

Death at 83 of Arthur Ransome

Arthur Ransome, one of the best-loved loved writers of books for children of this century, has died in hospital in Manchester after a long illness. He was 83.

When he was in his late 40s, a breakdown in health forced him to leave a successful career as a foreign correspondent to live in a cottage in the Lake District.

(June 6)

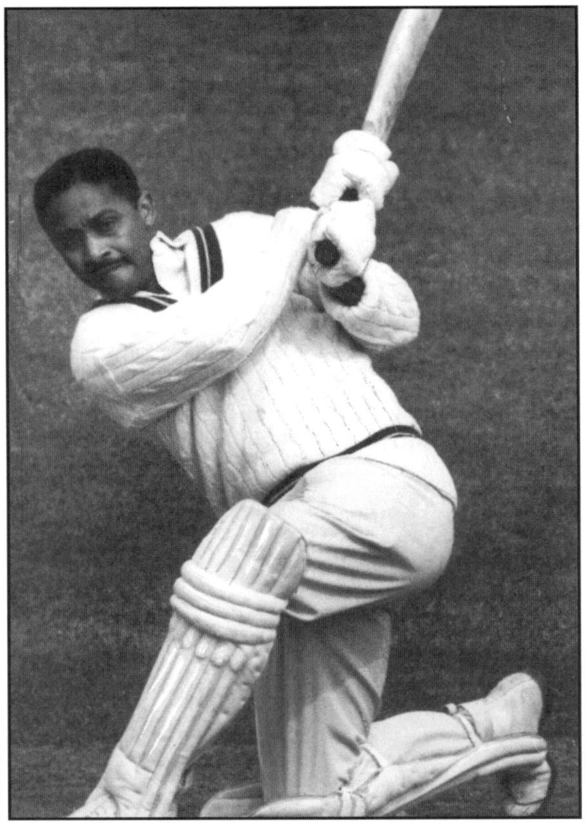

SIR FRANK WORRELL - A GREAT ALL-ROUNDER

By E.W. SWANTON

SIR FRANK MORTIMER MAGLINNE WORRELL, who has died with such tragic suddenness at the age of 42, will be remembered as a cricketer of the highest attainments, as a great captain and not least as an outstanding citizen of the West Indies.

Born in Barbados on Aug. 1, 1924, his cricket came to light in the war years. He made 308 not out against Trinidad at the age of 19.

When the West Indies re-entered the Test scene in 1948 he was a natural choice along with the other members of the trinity of "Ws" from the same island, Clyde Walcott and Everton Weekes.

Thereafter, the achievements in concert of these three are legendary. Walcott and Weekes had, however, retired from Test cricket when at the age of 36 Worrell was faced with his sternest trial.

In 1960 he assumed the captaincy of the West Indies in Australia for what turned out to be in all respects the best, as well as the most exciting, series of modern times. The climax of it was a motercade through the Melbourne streets amid a cheering throng of half a million people. Three years later he led the West Indies to their famous 1963 success in England.

Worrell was a magnificent cricketer, as elegant a batsman as ever walked to the wicket, and on his day a dangerous bowler, but it was as a leader of serene temperament who commanded the loyalty and affection of his men to an extraordinary degree that his name will shine with a special lustre in the game's history.

It was, of course, his high personal qualities which gave him such a valuable influence with young people.

In the developing countries of the West Indies he seemed to have a special part to play and I believe nothing was more certain than that a Governor-Generalship would have been offered him had he lived to full maturity.

(March 14)

Spencer Tracy

SPENCER TRACY, the veteran American actor, who has died in Hollywood, aged 67, combined rugged strength with sensitivity, and without effort managed to dominate the majority of the many films in which he appeared.

By virtue of his outstanding talent, and the leading roles he played for more than 30 years, he was regarded as something of a "grand old man" in Hollywood. He was also held up as something of an object lesson to aspiring young artists.

He twice won the Academy of Motion Picture Arts and Science award for the best actor. The first time was in 1937 for his portrayal of a Portuguese fisherman in "Captains Courageous."

PATRICK GIBBS writes: Spencer Tracy's performances became so rewarding as his career drew to a close that one was inclined to think of him as an actor who improved with middle age.

This is to do him an injustice, for he was from the very start a finished artist, owing something, no doubt, to stage experience on Broadway and in stock companies.

(June 12)

MARSHAL OF THE RAF LORD TEDDER

MARSHAL of the Royal Air Force Lord Tedder, who has died aged 76, was wartime deputy supreme commander under Gen. Eisenhower.

The 1939-45 war was about half-way through when it was suddenly realised generally that Arthur William Tedder, of the RAF, had become one of the greatest Allied leaders in the field.

Exciting adventures as a fighter pilot had nothing to do with it; his fame came as a result of the extraordinary skill with which he had directed the air effort in the battle of El Alamein, and the conquests that followed.

They were, however, to be only the prelude to even greater victories.

In 1914 he was given a cadetship in the Colonial Service and sent to Fiji. When the 1914-18 war broke out he hurried home at his own expense to take a commission in the Dorset Regt.

While training he injured his knee so seriously that he was told he would not be of any further use in infantry.

Thereupon, though his leg was in a splint, he managed to enter the Royal Flying Corps. He went "solo" on the same day that he received his first lesson in the air.

The ability he showed in various capacities attracted Lord Trenchard's attention and led to quick promotion.

Between the wars Tedder progressed so considerably that by 1938 he had become Director-General of Research and Development, Air Ministry. In November 1940, he was appointed Deputy Air C-in-C, Middle East. Six months later he was in full control of air warfare that had helped so materially to bring the Germans to defeat in the Desert, North Africa, Sicily and Italy.

NORMANDY INVASION

Eisenhower's request

When the plans for the invasion of Normandy were being prepared one of the first requests from his firm admirer. Gen. Eisenhower, was that Tedder should be his deputy in the Supreme Command.

There were to be acrimonious disputes over the particular methods, for political or economic reasons, but Tedder's view's never failed to command the maximum respect.

After the war he was created a Baron and appointed Chief of the Air Staff. In 1950 he was installed as Chancellor of Cambridge University. He also became vice-chairman of the BBC Board of Governors from 1951 to 1954 and joined important business concerns.

(June 3)

Oppenheimer, 'father' of atom bomb

DR. J. ROBERT OPPENHEIMER, who has died at Princeton, New Jersey, aged 62, was sometimes called "the father of the atomic bomb."

He was director of the science laboratories at Los Alamos, New Mexico, while the first atomic bomb was being developed between 1943, and 1945. Later he came under a cloud of distrust.

The Atomic Energy Commission barred him from the secrets he had helped to unlock because of his alleged association with Communists.

The same Commission in 1963, awarded him the Enrico Fermi Award, worth £17,850, for his outstanding contributions to theoretical physics and his scientific and administrative leadership."

Dr. Oppenheimer was against development of the hydrogen bomb. The "security risk" label was attached to him in the subsequent controversy on whether the hydrogen bomb should be made.

Our Science Correspondent writes: With the death of Robert Oppenheimer America has lost her greatest scientist, the physicist who worked out the theoretical details of making the first atomic bomb and then supervised its complex construction.

He has been compared with Galileo, not only for his brilliant contribution to science, but also for fighting the established authorities for his scientific beliefs.

(February 20)

Dr. Mossadeq

Dr. Mossadeq, the former Persian Prime Minister, who died in Teheran yesterday, aged 87, was one of the most remarkable figures in the post-war international scene.

A man of eccentric, arrogant and intractable character, he yet captured, and for a long time held, the imagination of his fellow-countrymen by his passionate and persistant campaign against alien interference in the affairs of Persia.

(March 6)

WAY OF THE WORLD

Timely

IN view of the present troubles in the race relations industry, one of Britain's key industrial growth-points, the appearance of a new pamphlet from H.M. Stationery Office, "Race Relations in the Race Relations Industry" is most timely.

As the pamphlet points out, there is a growing tendency towards discrimination against white people in this industry, and a danger that coloured antiracialists, West Indian, Indian, Pakistani and so on, may themselves divide on racial lines.

On the credit side, no complaints of racial discrimiation in the race relations industry have yet been referred to the Race Relations Board. But it can be argued that if race relations in the race relations industry become largely confined to relations between people of the same race, no great degree of racial integration will be achieved.

One solution to the problem, the pamphlet suggests, would be to set up a Higher Race Relations Board concerned with race relations in the race relations industry (of which the present Race Relations Board is of course a part).

Another solution, which might have an even more beneficial effect not only on relations between races but also between people in general, would be to allow the race relations industry to run down altogether, absorbing its redundant workers in other sectors of progressive industry.

(December 12)

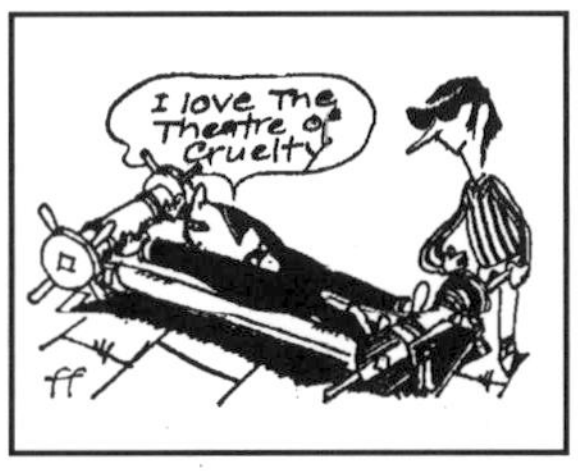

Shapes of Dread

MY hopes that the Committee on play censorship would recommend strengthening the powers of the Lord Chamberlain, giving him the right not only to ban plays without explanation but to close down theatres and place actors, producers, critics, audiences and all other people connected with the theatre under arrest at his discretion have been disappointed.

Instead the Committee recommends that what it absurdly calls the "anachronistic powers" of the Lord Chamberlain should be abolished. New licence will thus be given to the theatre to extend even further its deadly grip on every part of our national life.

Let no one imagine that the theatre will now be satisfied. The report, I notice, says that managements should still be free to refuse to put on plays whenever they think fit; that critics should still be allowed to describe plays in whatever terms they choose; and - most extraordinary of all - that the public should still be free to refuse to attend plays or to walk out if they do not like them.

How long are these poor remaining freedoms likely to last? With the Lord Chamberlain and his blessedly anachronistic powers (here as so often, anachronism is the safeguard of liberty) out of the way, it will not be long before the Left-wing theatrical Establishment, that chosen instrument of Compulsory Socialist Culture, has absolute sway.

Theatre managers will be tortured to compel them to put on some favoured propaganda play; critics will sit gagged and muffled at their typewriters and will write whatever they are told to write about it; the public will be rounded up in batches and forced to watch it at gun-point, or be shot "while trying to escape."

It will be too late then to regret the mild rule of the Lord Chamberlain. But if I am not languishing in Tynan's dungeons, and am still free to speak at all, I will try not to say "I told you so."

(June 22)

Peter Simple

BOYCOTT DROPPED AS DISCIPLINARY MOVE

AMISS & BROWN COME IN: BARRINGTON WILL OPEN

By E.W. SWANTON

THE bringing in of Amiss and Brown to the England team for the Lord's Test on Thursday, welcome though both of these young players will be, is of course, heavily overshadowed as a news item by the dropping of a man who has just taken out his bat for an innings of 246.

The official explanation of the dropping of Boycott says that it is a disciplinary measure for one match, in accordance with the policy laid down over the past two years.

Thus has this earnest, introverted cricketer been reminded in the starkest manner that the England selectors will not tolerate the brand of batting with which he made the first day at Headingley such a weariness to the flesh.

If it be argued for Boycott as it should be, that he came into the game badly out of form, it is a fair answer surely that while his first two hours may have been acceptable on those grounds the last four were not.

If there were difficulties in the wicket, or if partners had been coming and going at the other end, a score of 106 in six hours might just have been justifiable. But these factors did not apply.

The only assumption that seems necessary to win the approval of this watcher and critic is that either at lunch, when he made 25, or at tea when he was 62, or at both intervals, the captain made it clear that he expected a higher rate of progress. I suppose that Close asked for it and did not get in.

There are many angles from which the selectors' decision will be discussed. For instance, it can be said with complete truth that such an innings could only have been contemplated in the context of a five-day match.

(June 19)

ASIF WINS GLORY WITH OLD-FASHIONED 146

England beat Pakistan by eight wickets to win the series 2-0 with one match, drawn.

By E.W. SWANTON

OVAL, Monday.

SOMETHING on the grand scale was required to give a worthy curtain to this summer's Test cricket. At 12.30 p.m. such a thought seemed futile indeed. Three hours later Asif Iqbal, the young Pakistani all-rounder, had achieved it.

His innings of 146 here today, begun with the board showing 53 for seven and ending on the stroke of the tea interval after the innings defeat had been averted and a new world record established for the ninth wicket in Test matches, was an effort to warm the heart.

It was an innings also to revive the spirits of critics and followers, underlining as it did their belief in the value of a style of play which our modern player-theorists tell us is oldfashioned, and in the more "scientific" conditions of today, so called, impossible of achievement.

Asif was magnificent. He begins with a backlift that is high and open, he leans into the ball as he comes forward, and when he plays back he gives himself room by making ground towards the stumps and hits the ball a crisp blow, generally with the bat in or near the vertical plane.

Intikhab, the more experienced man and a good bat in his own right, played the perfect second-string innings, falling only once or twice into a rashness that brought from his partner an apparently admonitory word.

The England captaincy, the bowling and fielding stood up tolerably well to the onslaught, though at times the out-cricket looked somewhat ragged and uninspired. The dynamism was flowing this time from the opposite direction.

(August 29)

ROYAL PALACE SWEEPS TO DERBY VICTORY

By HOTSPUR (Peter Scott)

EPSOM, Wednesday.

MR. H.J. JOEL'S Royal Palace proved a most worthy Derby favourite here today, achieving his owner-breeder's lifetime ambition after a fairly-run race in which two other English-trained horses, Ribocco and Dart Board chased him home.

Royal Palace went into a clear lead with more than two furlongs to run and from that point only Ribocco offered the slightest danger. The pair of them had been Derby favourites when betting opened last autumn.

Ribocco, redeeming himself after three disappointing spring races, came wide for his challenge and drew almost level with about a furlong left.

Then George Moore produced the whip on Royal Palace and Lester Piggott, riding Ribocco, saw the mount, who might have been his, pull away once more to give Moore his greatest-ever triumph and his third successive English classic.

Whatever the faults of Piggott's partnership with Ribocco in the past, nobody could have ridden a more tender, coaxing race than did the champion on this little bay horse today.

With so much at stake the temptation to drive Ribocco for all he was worth must have been well-nigh unbearable. Piggott resisted it, and Ribocco who has shown marked dislike for such forcing tactics, returned the kindness by giving all he had.

It was not enough. In Royal Palace he met an emphatically better horse and one who is surely destined now, barring accidents, to win the Triple Crown.

(June 8)

SOUTH AFRICA CRUSH FRANCE 26-3

South Africa, who had lost eight of her previous nine internationals, defeated France 26-3 after leading 18-3 at half-time, reports Reuter from Durban.

South Africa won by four goals, a try and a penalty to a try, Henry de Villiers, the new full-back, kicking 11 points.

(July 17)

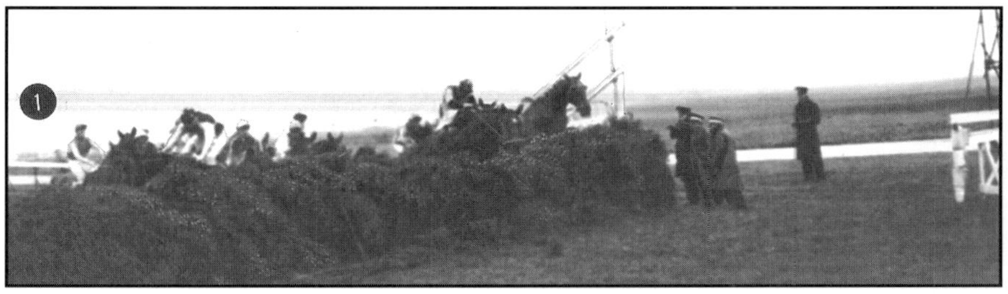

FENCE NO. 23 IN SATURDAY'S AMAZING Grand National, and the chaotic pile-up begins.

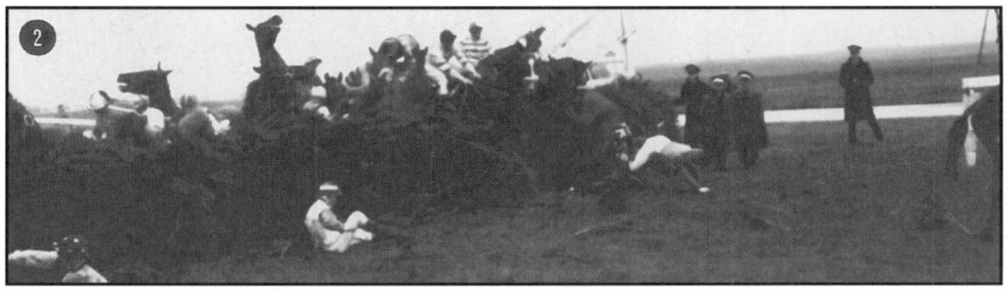

JOCKEYS HURLED OVER and through the thron fence as their mounts are bought to a sudden halt.

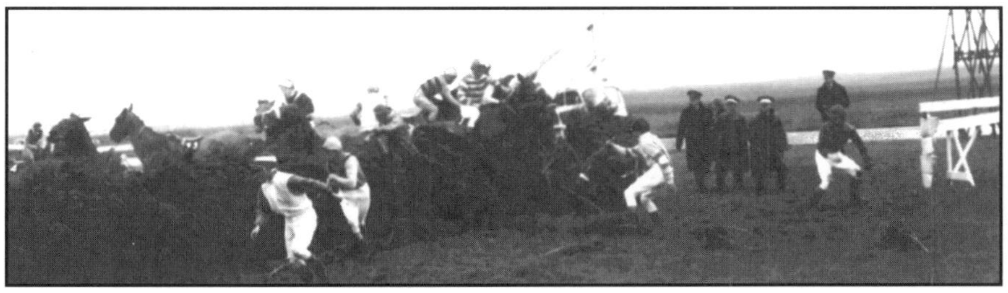

WITH THE PILE-UP still continuing, Mr. Lawrence dashes round the fence to find his mount.

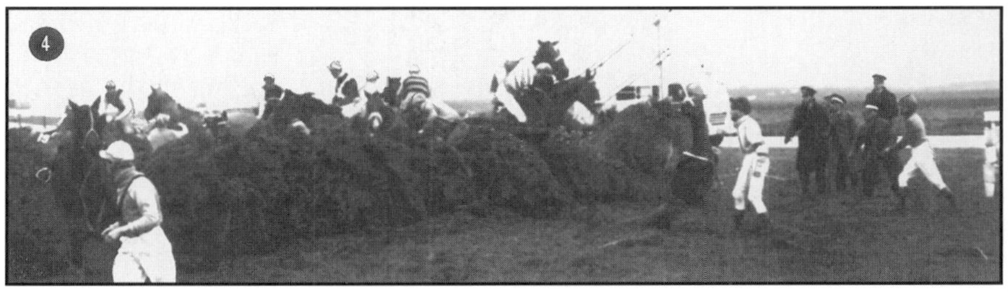

HORSES STILL JAM THE take-off side as Mellor makes off in search of The Fossa.

TIGHTER QUALIFICATION NEEDED FOR NATIONAL

By HOTSPUR (Peter Scott)

FOINAVON'S Grand National, in which 26 horses were either brought down or to a halt at the 23rd fence, must eclipse even 1951 - with its ragged start and first fence pile-up - as the most chaotic since Easter Hero's day.

Easter Hero was still in the race with a good chance when his mishap at the Canal Turn in 1928 caused such havoc behind. On Saturday the culprits were two riderless horses.

Few people hope that Foinavon will go down as the last Grand National winner but even if the race stays at Aintree there must be changes and they must come soon.

Most important among them in my view are tighter qualifications for entry, more pronounced breaks to the inside railing to encourage riderless horses off the course, and comprehensive television coverage for spectators.

There is no Grand National fence further from the stands than that which provided this year's havoc and thus the bulk of race-goers had only a hazy idea of the momentous happenings shown so clearly to those who stayed home and watched TV.

The relayed commentary could not everywhere be clearly heard and, although the stewards filled in some gaps with an official statement, most visitors left Aintree insufficiently informed, besides being wet and out of pocket.

Popham Down, brought down at the first fence, soon galloped riderless up to the leaders. He and another loose horse headed the field when they refused and began the turmoil.

It is by no means always the forlorn hopes that do the damage but numbers increase the chaos of incidents like this, and one can hardly eliminate the better-class entries. Foinavon had not managed to win any of his 23 races for the past two seasons and had often failed in poor company. Such a record can only serve to encourage others with similarly slim prospects.

I realise that tighter qualifications to enter would be bitterly opposed by a number of experienced racing men and that they would sometimes eliminate deserving cases, but the line must be drawn somewhere.

(April 10)

YORKSHIRE TRIUMPH

By HENRY CALTHORPE

SUPERB off-spin bowling on a turning wicket by Illingworth, who took 14 for 64 in the day, brought Yorkshire to their third championship title in five years and to a two-day victory over Gloucestershire here by an innings and 76.

In the first innings, when Gloucester were all out for 134, Illingworth took seven for 58, and then, when they followed on 175 behind and were out for 99, he had the remarkable figures of seven for six in 13 overs. All his wickets were taken after lunch.

Illingworth bowled 36 overs with complete control of length and line, and clever variation of flight and pace, and this victory was another demonstration of the all-round professional competence which has taken Yorkshire to their 30th title.

(September 8)

SOBERS SIGNS FOR NOTTS. AT £250 A GAME

Garfield Sobers, 31, the West Indies Test captain and the world's greatest all round cricketer, will play for Nottinghamshire in next season's county championship. He has signed a three-year contract and will captain the side.

He will be paid on a match basis, probably at £250 a match. This would amount to over £7,000 a year if he played in all matches.

(December 14)

TIDEWAY SHOW THEIR POWER

The Tideway Scullers finished first, second and fifth in the Head of the River from Mortlake to Putney on Saturday, confirming not only their own pre-eminence among clubs but also the high standard of the Boat Race crews, for their first boat was very little faster than Cambridge, writes Desmond Hill.

Six crews broke 19 minutes and then came Emanuel School, almost repeating last year's extraordinary performance, a tired Isis and a disappointing Nautilus (Midlands). Radley (10th) were the second fastest school, ahead of Molesey veterans, Nottingham & Union and Durham University, the last two winning the Jackson and UAU trophies.

(March 27)

McGREGOR IN TOKYO TEAM

Bobby McGregor, the European 100 metres champion and Olympic silver medallist, was yesterday named with three other men and six women — all internationals — for the British team for the World Student Games in Tokyo next month.

(July 14)

JACKLIN'S HISTORIC 64 BRINGS DUE REWARD

By GEOFFREY COUSINS

THE rise of Tony Jacklin, 23, to the eminence he achieved in winning the Dunlop Masters' tournament at Sandwich on Saturday has been rapid and impressive. Indeed, he has risen from champion assistant to Master golfer in two years.

The manner of his latest victory, by three strokes with an aggregate of 274 for 72 holes, left no doubt about the determination with which he is tackling his climb to the top.

Jacklin is full of drive. He has the physique for the job, has developed a very sound method and is developing not only a personality but also a gift for creating drama.

Success on Saturday did not depend on the holing of his tee shot at the 16th on the Royal St. George's links, but that ace enabled him to beat the 33-year-old record for the course.

His 64 is likely to have an historic value at least equal to that of the 65 which helped Henry Cotton to win his first Open championship at Sandwich in 1934.

DEDICATED PLAYER

Gained in experience

Jacklin is dedicated to getting as much fame and fortune as he can from a game which offers so many rich rewards. His performances in North America this year have enlarged his experience and enriched his pocket. Now, as Master golfer, he can face next month's Ryder Cup match in Texas with confidence.

Jacklin has not qualified for the rich Alcan tournament at St. Andrews on Oct. 5-8. The right to play, so far as competitors on the British circuit were concerned, was determined by performances in this country and in selective events.

The seven chosen are Malcolm Gregson and Tommy Horton, who finished first and second in the 1967 order of merit, Peter Alliss, Peter Butler, David Thomas, Brian Barnes and O'Connor.

(September 18)

Briton dies in Tour de France

From Our Correspondent

CARPENTRAS, Southern France, Thursday.

TOMMY SIMPSON, the British professional cyclist, collapsed while racing on the Ventoux Mountain in to-day's stage of the Tour de France. He died in hospital at Avignon where he was taken by a police helicopter.

Simpson, aged 29, had kept with members of the leading group of riders, including the race leader, Roger Pingeon of France, until three miles from the summit of the 5,750ft mountain, known as the "Giant of Provence."

The Englishman then dropped back and was seen to be pedalling with extreme difficulty. Eventually he fell by the roadside.

Second fall

The British team car, driven by Ken Ryall, a cycle dealer of Twickenham, was immediately behind and Harry Hall a mechanic, went to help Simpson.

Simpson said he wanted to continue, remounted and rode a further half-mile under the scorching sun - temperatures were in the 90s. He fell again and when the Tour doctor arrived within a minute or so Simpson was unconscious.

Tommy Simpson was the most successful road racing cyclist Britain had produced, winning the world professional road championship in 1965. His other victories included the "Bordeaux-Paris," "Tour of Flanders," "Milan-San Remo" and the "Tour of Lombardy" classic races.

(July 14)

FANTASTIC CELTIC MAKE HISTORY

INTER MILAN'S DEFENCE TORN TO SHREDS

By BYRON BUTLER

LISBON, Thursday.

Inter Milan ...... 1 Celtic 2

THE European Cup, like the World Cup, has come home. Celtic tonight became the first British club to win the world's toughest club competition because brilliantly, emphatically, they overcame the toughest defence in the world.

Inter Milan converted a penalty after six minutes, and then wretchedly tried to hang on to their lead. They succeeded for an hour. Play was confined to the Italians' half of the field, and every person who respected football poured down resentment on to their heads.

But Celtic proved themselves magnificent competitors, and in the second half they succeeded in breaking the unbreakable.

Goals by Gemmell (62nd minute) and Chalmers (84th) gave them the European Cup to add to the Scottish League Championship, Scottish Cup, Scottish League Cup and Glasgow Cup.

The final whistle acted like a starting pistol. An army of Celtic supporters - about 8,000 of them - whooped their way off the terraces and just as the Scots had done at Wembley, swarmed like ants on to the pitch. Fifty thousand other spectators stood transfixed.

It was a precious moment, for this was the cup that even such sides as Manchester United and Blanchflower's Spurs failed to win. But not only that, it meant defeat, and probably shame, for a club whose influence on football is wholly bad.

True, Inter were without Suarez and Jair, and might even conceivably have had their sights on a replay on Saturday in the hope that one or both would be fit.

But Inter's philosophy, their play-acting their time-wasting and irritable temper, lost them thousands of would-be friends.

It meant, of course, that Celtic's problems were halved. They were able to ignore the fact that most sides are asked to prevent goals as well as score them.

Inter's defence is no ordinary one. It employs up to 10 men, and is a devious, complex immensely physical thing in which everything and everybody are sacrificed in the cause of survival.

They failed this time because they could do nothing to relieve the pressure, and because in Celtic they had opponents who more than matched them for class, and strength, and persistence.

The pity of it all was that Inter were given the one encouragement they most needed - an early goal, and that a penalty. Craig made a messy attempt at tackling Cappellini, and the referee was quick enough to award a penalty from his position 40 yards away. Mazzola shot to the left, Simpson dived to the right.

Inter promptly retreated into their shell, and the pattern of the match was irredeemably established. Celtic often took the Italians' defence apart, but always there was wood, or an arm or a leg to baulk them.

Auld hit the bar, Gemmell, too, saw a long, diagonal centre drift on to the bar, and Simpson apart, everybody hurled themselves at the wall.

Equaliser at last

But after an hour, in which Inter's grip seemed to become tighter and in which even Scottish supporters were beginning to lose steam Gemmell, that most aggressive full-back, got the equaliser. His right-foot shot from 20 yards was powerful enough to have carried two or three Interplayers into the net.

Even so, extra time, and even a replay, seemed more than just a possibility, Sarti, Inter's goalkeeper, had one of those days that men in his job get perhaps twice in a lifetime. He made three or four saves that were so good they were outrageous.

(May 26th)

PROFESSIONAL SOCCER WINS ITS ACCOLADE

By DONALD SAUNDERS

THE prominent appearance of Sir Alfred Ramsey and Bobby Moore, OBE, in the New Year's Honours List emphasises that professional soccer is now accepted as a highly respectable and important part of British life.

Professional football, of course, has been officially recognised before. But this is the first time a manager has been knighted or a young player appointed to the Order of the British Empire.

The last barriers of prejudice, unconsciously supported though they may have been, against our national winter game were swept away when England, managed by Ramsey and captained by Moore, won the World Cup last July.

Few will argue that this achievement was not worthy of honour and even fewer will suggest that the manager who built the team and the captain who led it were not the correct persons to receive the awards.

If their triumph did nothing else, it brightened an otherwise grim summer for millions of people whose knowledge of soccer had hitherto not extended beyond the list of teams appearing on their pools coupon.

As England progressed faltering through the early rounds, then won an ill-tempered quarter-final, entertaining semi-final and agonising final, one sensed a feeling of what soccer's new knight would call "togetherness" that, perhaps, no sport had given this country before.

This did not last long, of course, and few of the millions of new enthusiasts who were glued to their television sets in July have been found this season in the stands or on the terraces of football grounds.

Meanwhile, they may be a little more tolerant of those irritating Saturday afternoon traffic jams and perhaps, less scornful of the noisy hordes who stand shivering beneath their funny woollen hats and gaudy scarves to watch 22 overpaid young men kick a ball about.

(January 2)

PETER AND RON SPRINGETT SWAP CLUBS

Peter Springett, the England Under-23 goalkeeper, will join Sheffield Wednesday today for a fee of £40,000, and his elder brother, Ron Springett, the former England goalkeeper, will return to QPR to replace him at a fee of £16,000.

Negotiations were completed at Loftus Road yesterday.

(May 22)

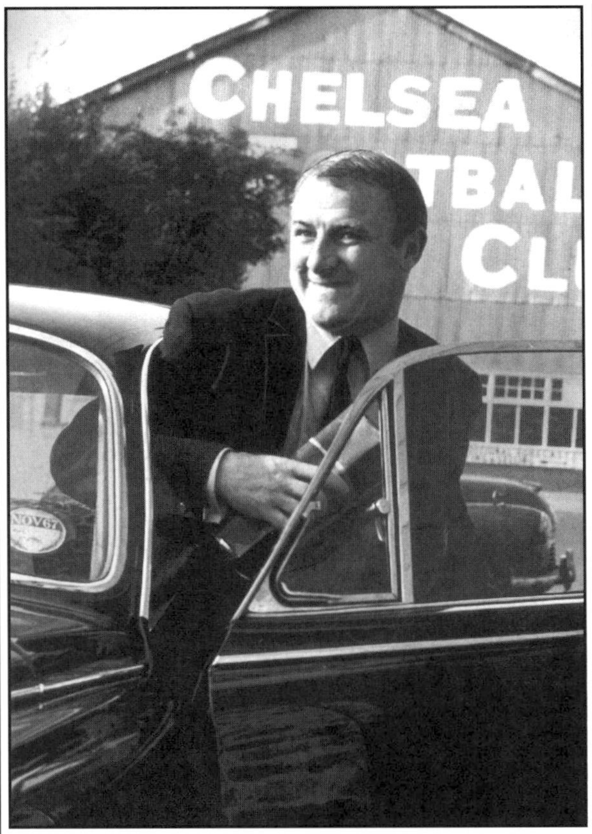

DOCHERTY QUITS AFTER FA BAN

By DONALD SAUNDERS

TOMMY DOCHERTY, 38, one of the most controversial figures in post-war British soccer, resigned yesterday as Chelsea manager a few hours after being suspended for 28 days from Monday by the Football Association.

The suspension is for alleged misconduct, including being involved in an incident with a referee during Chelsea's tour of Bermuda in June. He will be unable to attend a soccer match even as a paying spectator for the four weeks.

The suspension evidently came as a shock to Mr. Docherty, and played an important part in his decision. A short statement issued last night said his reasons for leaving Stamford Bridge were "purely personal."

He said: "I came to my decision over a period of time.

"The sudden and totally unexpected news . . . persuaded me that this was as good a moment as any for myself and the club to make a fresh start."

The Chelsea Board took much the same view. Meeting yesterday afternoon they accepted his resignation, gave him "a substantial golden handshake" and appointed Ron Suart, the assistant manager, temporarily.

Mr. Charles Pratt, Chelsea's chairman, emphasised that there had been "no row." He said: "We shook hands with Tommy and had a farewell drink."

So ended Mr. Docherty's five-year term as manager at Stamford Bridge, during which he has been largely responsible for the transformation of Chelsea from a music-hall joke to one of the Football League's leading clubs.

(October 7)

WATKINS TURNS PRO FOR RECORD £13,000

By JOHN REASON

DAVID WATKINS, the British Lions, Wales and Newport outside-half, has turned professional. He signed for the Salford Rugby League club yesterday. The fee was reported to be £13,000, which comfortably exceeds the £10,000 Bradford Northern paid for Terry Price, and is therefore a record.

Watkins was expected to be named as captain of Wales for the match against New Zealand at Cardiff on No. 11.

He was captain of Wales last year, he captained the British Lions in New Zealand when M.J. Campbell-Lamerton was injured, he was captain at Newport, and altogether he won 22 Welsh caps.

Two days ago his new club signed Bob Prosser from St. Helens. Prosser is the Coventry Welshman who played scrum-half with Watkins at Newport before turning professional.

It had been reported that he had been offered £15,000 to turn professional, and I asked him how on earth a player at his stage of his career could turn down a sum like that. "It's a lot of money," he said.

Watkins must have realised that this value to the Rugby League was likely to decline. He was sensitive about the suggestions that J. Dawes might be a strong candidate for the captaincy of Wales.

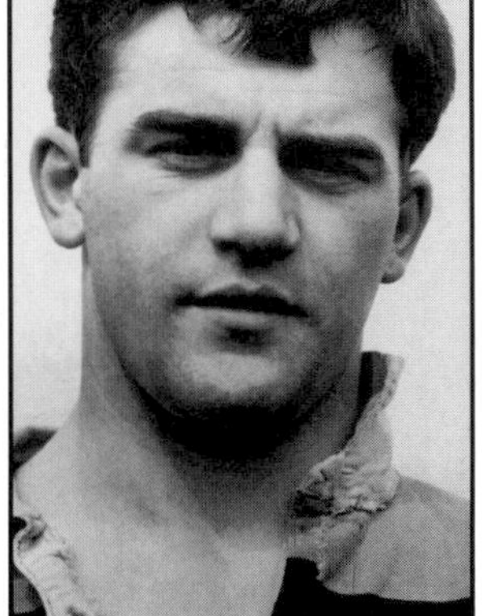

(October 20)

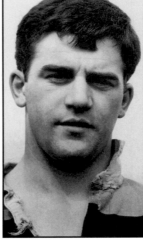

COOPER CLAIMS THIRD LONSDALE BELT

By DONALD SAUNDERS

HENRY COOPER became the first owner of three Lonsdale Belts at Wembley Pool last night when he stopped his fellow Londoner, Billy Walker, in the sixth round to retain the British heavyweight championship for the eighth time.

It is ironic, perhaps, that Cooper, who has so often been obliged to struggle under the handicap of injured eyes, should have moved into boxing's history book because his opponent had been badly cut over the right eyebrow.

The end of a much harder battle than any of us had expected came 40 seconds from the end of the sixth round, when the referee, George Smith, ordered the boxers to stop fighting. He examined Walker's wound and promptly indicated that it was all over.

Walker and his brother manager, George, protested briefly. Then the challenger swallowed his disappointment and walked over to congratulate his conqueror. Cooper patted him on the shoulder sympathetically and said: "I know how you feel." It is a pity of course, that a contest of historic importance to British boxing should have ended somewhat inconclusively.

It seemed to me, however, that Cooper was in any case destined to remain champion. Though he had to weather one or two unexpectedly fierce storms early on, he appeared to be in control of a weakening challenger when Mr. Smith intervened.

Let me emphasise, however, that while it lasted this was a good honest fight, worthy of the highly-respected title that was at stake.

(November 8)

BRITAIN ENDS TENNIS PROS AND AMATEURS

By LANCE TINGAY

BRITISH lawn tennis yesterday abolished the amateur-professional distinction. From April 22 next there will in Britain be just "players" and the 1968 Wimbledon championships will be open to professionals.

The annual general meeting of the Lawn Tennis Association in London voted for the reform, with only five of about 400 votes cast against. The move is in direct defiance of the ruling of the world's governing body, the International Lawn Tennis Federation.

The Federation's management committee declared some days ago that Britain would be suspended if she took her threatened action.

The next meeting of the management committee is on April 20-21. By then reform proposals from their own special committee should be in front of them.

The Australian delegate at yesterday's meeting, Ben Barnett, former Test cricketer, gave a warning of the dire consequences of the British action. "Australian players will be barred from coming to Britain."

Sir Robert Fraser, Association treasurer, said there was no cause to worry about financial repercussions.

(December 15)

BANDINI HURT IN MONACO GRAND PRIX

By Courtenay Edwards

MONTE CARLO, Sunday.

Lorenzo Bandini, 31, the leader of Italy's Ferrari Grand Prix team, lies gravely ill in hospital tonight with severe burns following a crash in his three-litre Ferrari in the Monaco Grand Prix.

While lying second behind Denis Hulme, who went on to win, the handsome young Italian crashed into the chicane—an artificial corner—at the bottom of the hill leading from the tunnel to the harbour.

Hulme, a New Zealander, was driving a Brabham.

About 50,000 spectators watched in horror as Bandini's car rolled over, spilling petrol and setting fire to the straw bales lining the route. Bandini was trapped under the blazing car and he was badly burnt when pulled free after four minutes.

He was placed aboard a firefloat which had gone to the scene and was taken across the harbour to an ambulance. Flames from the straw leapt many feet into the air and a pall of smoke spread slowly over the town and harbour.

Prince Rainier and Princess Grace were among those who saw the accident. It happened with 12 of the 100 laps to go. Bandini was then only 15 seconds behind Hulme.

(May 8)

BRITAIN OWES MUCH TO GINA HATHORN

By ALAN SMITH

SESTRIERE, Tuesday.

LAST week a nervous, attractive and far-from-robust English girl made ski-ing history. In the slalom at Grindelwald, Gina Hathorn beat all but the world champion, Annie Famose, and left ski racing all the better for being shaken out of its rut.

Unlike many of her Continental rivals, Gina is no "tough, sexless hulk." Not even particularly athletic by nature, out of uniform she looks as if she would be more at home at a Buckingham Palace garden party.

The influence of three men, and her own determination that if she is going to race at all she will do it well, are responsible for her rise to fame. And the first of these, both chronologically and in order of importance, is Carlo Muhlbauer.

When Gina first started to train for racing as a diminutive nine-year-old in St. Moritz. it was Muhlbauer who set her on the right road. At the same time he lavished upon her the care and attention that gave her the feeling of security she so much needs.

"Go all out," were his instructions. "Fall rather than go slowly." And this is what is happening, not merely to Gina Hathorn, but to the rest of the team, too, all burning with determination, furious when they do not do quite as well as they could.

Perhaps next season's Olympics will be the end of Gina's racing. She says she finds the pre-season training increasingly hard to take, yet admits that holiday ski-ing is "deadly dull," and has no plans for her future when she does give up.

(January 18)

LEFT: THE £29 MILLION SHIP failed to move when the Queen pressed the buttton to release the giant triggers holding her on the slipway. Then the liner began imperceptibly to move and, gathering speed, made a perfect launching.

A Beatlemobile

A ROLLS-ROYCE PHANTOM V owned by John Lennon, of the Beatles, has taken on the appearance of a Romany caravan. The coachwork, which was originally black, has been sprayed yellow and adorned with flowers and the signs of the zodiac.

THE TOREY CANYON, 61,263 tons, on fire after running aground on the Seven Stones reef, off Land's End.

New knight of the sea sails home

LEFT: SIR FRANCIS CHICHESTER looking very fit at his Press conference in Plymouth Guildhall.

GYPSY MOTH IV crossing the finishing line at Plymouth last night.

STEEL-HELMETED BRITISH TROOPS wearing respirators in Aden yesterday after tear-gas was used against demonstrators.

This was the year when the flower children grew thorns. The streets in many countries on both sides of the Atlantic were full of students and others protesting against their courses of study and against the Vietnam war. Names like Daniel Cohn-Bendit and Tariq Ali became familiar to newspaper readers. Paris was almost in a state of siege as the mobs processed. Grosvenor Square in London was for a few hours a battleground. The Democratic Convention in Chicago to choose a presidential candidate became the scene of bloody conflict between anti-Vietnam protestors and the police and National Guard.

The Western world saw a glimmer of hope when Dubcek in the spring of the year seemed to be leading Czechoslovakia away from Communist tyranny but by the summer the Soviet government had sent tanks to Prague and the embryo democratic government was crushed. The war in Vietnam became fiercer, as exemplified by a Vietcong guerilla attack on the Vietnamese capital Saigon. The civil war in Nigeria dragged on with growing suffering for the separatist Biafrans.

In the United States Robert Kennedy, like his brother, was assasinated by an extremist and Martin Luther King was shot from a passing car by a murderer who escaped to London before he was caught and returned to the United States. Riots followed in many American cities. Richard Nixon, campaigning on a platform which included the ending of the war in Vietnam, narrowly won the American presidency.

The Labour government in Britain faced an increasingly difficult economic situation. Divisions in the Cabinet led to the resignation of George Brown. A speech by Enoch Powell, urging the repatriation of African and West Indian immigrants, led to his expulsion from the shadow cabinet by Edward Heath. The increasing number of Indians arriving from Kenya led to cross-party agreement to the passing of an immigration bill limiting the numbers of hopeful migrants. At the same time, there were plans announced to reduce the voting age to 18. Decimal coinage was introduced and, for the fist time, a two-tier post came into operation.

Theatrical censorship was ended and on the day after the Lord Chamberlain's powers were removed, the musical *Hair*, featuring for the first time on a public stage performers moving around without clothes, opened. This was the last production reviewed by *The Daily Telegraph's* long-serving dramatic critic, W. A. Darlington. He did not enjoy it.

The much loved Princess Marina, widow of the Duke of Kent who was killed on active service during the Second World War, died. So did the combative and litigious son of Sir Winston Churchill, Randolph. Sir Harold Nicolson, writer, politician, husband of Vita Sackville-West, was among the literary figures who died during the year. The Nobel prize-winning American novelist, John Steinbeck was another.

The turbulent atmosphere of the year was echoed on the sporting field. Some of the American runners who won medals at the Olympic Games held in Mexico City gave the black power salute as their national anthem was played. A riot over an umpiring decision led to the suspension of a test match between the West Indies and England. On a happier note, Bobby Charlton of Manchester United set a goal scoring record for England.

The Daily Telegraph
and Morning Post

No. 35181. LONDON, THURSDAY, JUNE 6, 1968   Printed in LONDON and MANCHESTER   5d.

Brain damage - critical 36 hours

ROBERT KENNEDY SHOT: 'EXTREMELY GRAVE'

BULLET REMOVED: 'FAILURE TO IMPROVE'

By DAVID ADAMSON
LOS ANGELES, Wednesday.

SENATOR ROBERT KENNEDY clung to life today in the Good Samaritan hospital, Los Angeles, breathing with the aid of a resuscitator. His condition, after he was shot early today by a gunman in the Embassy ballroom of the Ambassador Hotel, was described as "extremely grave." He is 42.

Five other people were wounded by the gunman. Tonight Sirhan Sirhan, 24, an immigrant from Jordan, was accused of attempting to murder Senator Kennedy. When overpowered at the scene of the shooting he was said to have shouted: "I did it for my country."

The Senator has frequently expressed support for Israel. Today was the anniversary of the Arab-Israeli six-day war.

Whether Senator Kennedy lives - or, perhaps almost as important, with what degree of physical impairment or brain damage he survives - may be decided according to the doctors, within the next 12 to 36 hours.

SPECIALISTS CONCERN

The team of specialists were concerned tonight over his continuing failure to show improvement in the post-operative period. A statement issued at 1 a.m. London time, said his condition was "extremely critical as to life."

An earlier bulletin said:

The result of a series of tests undertaken by the medical team treating Senator Robert Kennedy are inconclusive and do not show measurable improvement in Senator Kennedy's condition.

His condition remains extremely critical. His life forces - pulse, temperature, blood pressure and heart - remain good and he continues to show ability to breathe on his own, although his breathing remains assisted by a resuscitator.

Mr. Frank Mankiewicz, a Kennedy aide, said Senator Kennedy was being fed intravenously and had not regained consciousness. Dr. Henry Cuneo, one of the surgeons who operated on the Senator, said tonight he "might not make it."

PRE-DAWN OPERATION

For three hours before dawn a team of six neural surgeons had worked to extract the larger part of a bullet and several pieces of bone from where they had lodged in or near the brain stem.

Another bullet, which entered in a slanting direction through his shoulder was left in the Senator's neck, where it was not causing harm.

The examination showed that a third bullet had grazed his forehead. The bullet which caused the most serious injury entered through the right mastoid area indicating that the Senator was turning away from his assailant when he was shot.

BLOOD FLOW DANGER

It stopped in an area which controls many physical functions such as breathing, the heart, arm and leg and other muscular functions.

There is a danger that the blood flow to the brain has been affected, but despite some bleeding the doctors found no evidence that the reasoning functions of the brain have been harmed.

The arrested man, Sirhan Sirhan, was born on March 19, 1944, in Jordan, and was admitted to the United States as a permanent resident in 1957.

Shooting in ballroom

IT was shortly before midnight when Senator Kennedy arrived to deliver his victory speech in the Embassy ballroom of the Ambassador Hotel, his headquarters for the Californian primary elections, in which he defeated Senator McCarthy, his chief opponent for the Democratic Presidential nomination, by 50 per cent. poll to 20 per cent.

The crowd of Kennedy workers and television and newspaper men had waited for four hours under the hot and glaring television camera lamps.

(Continued on Back Page, Col. 4)

SIRHAN SIRHAN, 24, A NATIVE OF JORDAN, being taken from the Ambassador Hotel in Los Angeles after the shooting.

Suspect called bitter Arab revolutionary

LOS ANGELES, Wednesday.

THE man charged with shooting Senator Kennedy was described as a "revolutionary" today by the man for whom he worked in Pasadena, California. He was named as Sirhan Sirhan, 24, a native of Jordan who has lived in the Old City of Jerusalem.

He was born in Jordan on March 19, 1944, and admitted to the United States as a permanent resident on Jan. 12, 1957. His name in Arabic means "wanderer."

He was described as combining bitterness over the Arab defeat in the war last June with a refusal to accept any authority. Identification was made by two of his three brothers in Pasadena after he refused for hours to answer questions about his identity or his motives.

An obvious clue to his motives lies in his shouted declaration immediately after the shooting: "I did it for my country. I love my country."

Senator Kennedy has frequently stated his support for the Israelis. During the primary campaigns, he recommended maintaining arms supplies to Israel as a deterrent to an Arab attack.

SECRET HEARING
Heavy guard

Sirhan was arraigned in secret on six charges of assault with intent to murder, one charge for each person hit. He was taken under heavy guard to the central gaol.

The accused, who is in a maximum security block, was treated for a broken finger and a sprained ankle sustained during the struggle after the shooting this morning.

A 0.22 calibre pistol confiscated by police was traced to Los Angeles and San Francisco, but a three-year gap remains in the history of its ownership.

Sirhan also had four $100 (about £40) notes and some foreign currency. According to Mr. Yorty, Mayor of Los Angeles, a notebook was recovered from Shirhan's rooms containing "a direct reference to the necessity to assassinate Mr. Kennedy before June 5."

The fact that Sirhan was carrying the money produced suggestions that he may have been a hired gunman. Mr. Clark, Attorney-General, said, however, that there was no evidence of a conspiracy.

In Sirhan's pocket was a newspaper cutting critical of the Kennedy family.
Continued on Back Page, Col. 3

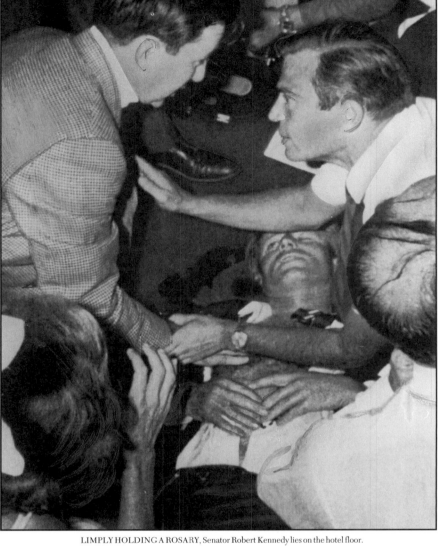
LIMPLY HOLDING A ROSARY, Senator Robert Kennedy lies on the hotel floor.

2 SURGEONS 'FEARFUL OF OUTCOME'

By HENRY MILLER
NEW YORK, Wednesday.

DR. LAWRENCE POOL, Professor of Neurology at the Columbia Presbyterian Medical Centre in New York, said today that the bullet wound to Senator Robert Kennedy's brain was much more serious than was at first thought.

He had learned this from Dr. Henry Cuneo, the chief surgeon at the Los Angeles hospital where the operation was performed.

"There is serious damage to the extreme back of the head on the right side, but what is more dangerous is the damage to the mid-brain which connects the brain to the rest of the body.

"Critical area"

"This part of the brain affects not only the motion of the arms and legs, but eye movements, face movements and practically all body functions. It is a very critical area, and that is why I fear the outcome may be extremely tragic."

Dr. Pool said that if Senator Kennedy made a complete recovery, there was no reason why his intellectual capacity should be impaired, but this was not true of all of his life functions such as heart rate and breathing.

Several major arteries had been severed and the brain had suffered an extensive loss of blood and oxygen. The Senator had also suffered injury to his spinal cord.

Both Dr. Pool and Dr. Cuneo were greatly fearful of the outcome, both in terms of Senator Kennedy living, and of his being

BRITAIN WILL DRAW £580M

OFFICIALS of the International Monetary Fund prepared today to arrange a "package" of foreign currencies on which Britain can draw $1,400 million (£583 million) under stand-by arrangements which officials in London said would be used almost immediately.

JOHNSON SAYS VIOLENCE MUST STOP

CAMPAIGNS SUSPENDED

By VINCENT RYDER
WASHINGTON, Wednesday.

AMERICANS "must put an end to violence and to the preachings of violence," President Johnson said tonight in a televised speech to the nation.

He was appointing a commission of distinguished citizens to inquire into the "tragic phenomena" of violence, reflected by the shooting in Los Angeles of Senator Robert Kennedy - an event which "shocked and dismayed" him. Dr. Milton Eisenhower, brother of the former President, will head the commission.

"Tonight, this nation once again faces the consequences of lawlessness, hatred and intrigue. Let us, for God's sake, resolve to live under the law.

"What inspired the attack is not known. What is known is that Senator Kennedy has been senselessly and horribly stilled. The outcome is still in the balance: we pray to God that He will spare Robert Kennedy."

America was not a country sick or bereft of a sense of direction, Mr. Johnson said in the 7½-minute speech. Though 200 million Americans did not strike down the Senator - any more than they had shot President Kennedy or Dr. Martin Luther King - they could not escape responsibility for such attacks.

'SOBER TIME'
Stop gun sales plea

It was a sober time for this great democracy. "What makes possible such murder and violence?"

As if to answer his own question, the President urged Congress to "bring the insane traffic in guns to a halt" by passing meaningful controls.

Other members of the Presidential commission include Mgr. Terence Cooke, Roman Catholic Archbishop of New York; Mrs. Patricia Harris, former Ambassador to Luxembourg Mr. Eric Heffer, the dock worker-philosopher of San Francisco; Senator Philip Harris, Democrat of Michigan; and Mr. Hale Boggs, Democratic member of Congress from Louisiana.

The Presidential election campaign came to an abrupt halt earlier today amid shock at the shooting. All the other candidates, Democratic and Republican, announced an indefinite suspension of all political activity.

Senator Eugene McCarthy flew from Los Angeles to Washington to confer with President Johnson, Vice-President Humphrey - the other Democratic candidate - senior aides of Senator Kennedy and other political leaders. They will consider how to deal with the election campaign.

There are obvious objections to campaigning while Senator Kennedy's life hangs in the balance. Even if he recovers it is questionable whether he will be fit to campaign this year.

Despite the flow of sympathy today, it is equally questionable whether the American public would, in November, be willing to vote into office a man who had recently suffered such an injury.

The other candidates of both parties are burdened with a share of the sudden responsibility of seeing the country through a shock to its self-confidence.

The Daily Telegraph 4d.
No. 35246. LONDON, WEDNESDAY, AUGUST 21, 1968 and Morning Post Printed in LONDON and MANCHESTER

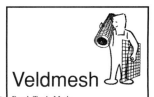

2 a.m. invasion warning

RUSSIANS MARCHING ON PRAGUE

'Do not resist' call to Czechs

RUSSIAN troops invaded Czechoslovakia early today. Prague Radio announced at 2 a.m. that Soviet forces had started to cross the borders from East Germany, Poland and Russia.

The broadcast, first reported by Associated Press, said that the invasion started at 11 o'clock last night. A later report from United Press International said that Polish and East German troops were also taking part.

Prague Radio said in broadcasts repeated every ten minutes that the Czechoslovak Army and People's Militia had not been called out to defend the country.

It appealed to the Czech people to remain calm and not to resist, and for all Communist officials to remain in their jobs.

There was no indication if Mr. Dubcek, the Czech leader, and his liberal colleagues had been overthrown by Stalinists in a "palace revolution" and the Russian troops called in.

VIOLATING BASIC RIGHTS

But Prague Radio did say that the Russians were moving into the country without the knowledge of Mr. Svoboda, the Czechoslovak President, Mr. Smkovsky, the Chairman of the National Assembly, or of Mr. Dubcek, First Secretary of the Communist party.

The broadcast said the Presidium of the Czechoslovak Communist party appealed to all people of Czechoslovakia not to resist the advancing troops. The National Assembly and the Communist party central committee had been called to discuss the situation.

"This procedure goes against basic rights of States and relations between Socialist countries."

Reports from Prague said that there was unusual activity at Prague airport with jet fighters apparently landing. Aircraft could be heard over the city throughout the night.

In London, it was announced that the Prime Minister and Foreign Secretary would be returning to London from holiday first thing this morning.

JOHNSON CALLS TALKS

In Chicago, Mr. Dean Rusk, American Secretary of State, cut short an appearance before a Democratic party committee to check the accuracy of reports of the Russian invasion.

Mr. Rusk hurried from the witness stand when the text of the Prague Radio broadcast was read to a hushed gathering. "I think I'd better go and see what this is all about," he said, brushing reporters aside and leaving the room.

Soon afterwards it was announced that President Johnson had called an emergency meeting of the National Security Council, which advises him on security matters.

Reports from Vienna said that travel to Czechoslovakia from the West had been barred since early this morning. The Austrian Interior Ministry said today that from midnight travel to Hungary from Austria had also been closed.

TANKS AT BRATISLAVA

An official of the Ministry said tanks were blocking the bridge at Bratislava. He said he had been told by Austrian travellers, who were still allowed to pass the Czechoslovak checkpoint, that the tank soldiers ordered them to go back to Austria. Shortly after, travel was also blocked at the checkpoint.

American State Department sources said early this morning that reports from the American Embassy in Prague confirmed that Soviet, Polish and East German troops had crossed the Czechoslovak border.

The sources said they had no information on the strength of the forces. They noted that so far no Hungarian troop movements were reported, and it appeared safe to assume that Hungary abstained from action.

WILSON CUTS HIS HOLIDAY

MR. WILSON and Mr. Stewart, Foreign Secretary, are cutting short their holidays and returning to London today in view of the Czech crisis.

A spokesman at 10 Downing Street said early today: "The Prime Minister got the news of the development in Czechoslovakia in the early hours. He has spoken to the Foreign Secretary."

The spokesman added: "We are expecting the Prime Minister to arrive at 10, Downing Street, this morning.

"It is thought that he will fly from the Isles of Scilly at the crack of dawn."

EDITOR IN ATTACK ON 'REFORMERS'

By REGINALD PECK

PRAGUE, Tuesday.

MR. OLDRICH SVETSKA, editor of the Czech official party organ, Rude Pravo, and "conservative" member of the party, Presidium, wrote a cold-war-style leader in his paper earlier today. He criticised "liberal reformers" and appeared to be doing his best to aid the Kremlin in its new nerve war on his country.

Mr. Svetska wanted to know in particular what it was that "the workers" stood to gain from the new trend in Czechoslovakia towards Press freedom and intellectualism.

He wrote also of leaflets alleged to have "appeared" in the Moravian industrial town of Brno. According to Mr. Svetka, the unnamed authors of the leaflets called on the workers to post them on their factory gates.

If they did not do so they would suffer the fate that the leaflets demanded for the Czech militia. This was disbandment or "death."

Party Congress

Mr. Svetska's leader was seen in Prague as a late attempt to influence the Slovak party Congress which opens in Bratislava next Monday. The Slovak Congress will be the curtain raiser to the national Congress which opens in Prague on Sept. 9.

Czech comment in Prague on Mr. Svetska's article was "He is an old hand at the cold-war game and should not be taken too seriously."

Mr. Jiri Duben, 45, head of the works council of the factory of the Praga works in Prague, which makes car gear boxes, denied today that he was now living in "mortal terror" because he had put his signature to a letter of loyalty to Russia.

Reactionary forces

The claim had been made in Pravda, the Russian Communist newspaper, which had said that since signing the letter with other workmen, Mr. Duben had been the victim of "a frenetic campaign unleashed by reactionary forces."

In the letter, written while Russian troops were in Czechoslovakia, the 60 signatories objected to the way the Czech Press was calling for a departure of the Russians. The Russians should go in their own time, or, if pressure were brought, it should be by the Government, not the Press.

SOVIET CHIEFS 'IN EMERGENCY TALKS'

Daily Telegraph Staff Correspondent

MOSCOW, Tuesday.

Speculation in Moscow that the Central Committee of the Russian Communist Party had been called into urgent session coincided today with warnings in the Russian Press that elements in Czechoslovakia were thinking of entering into a partnership with Bonn.

Johnson summons advisers

By VINCENT RYDER

WASHINGTON, Tuesday.

WITHIN minutes of reports reaching Washington that Russian, Polish and East German troops had started moving into Czechoslovakia, President Johnson sent out emergency messages for his National Security Council to meet him at the White House.

The council consists of his senior, military, diplomatic and Intelligence officials.

Mr. Rusk, secretary of State, had just finished addressing the Democratic party committee drafting the manifesto for presentation to next week's convention. He drove straight from the Washington hotel where the meeting was taking place to the White House.

Whistles of dismay

At the democratic party meeting in Washington, there were gasps and whistles of dismay when the chairman, Mr. Hale Boggs, announced the news.

Mr. Rusk, who had just finished a prepared speech and was waiting to answer questions said: "I think I ought to go and see what this is all about." He left immediately.

At 10 p.m. (3 a.m. BST) the Czech Ambassador in Washington said he had not yet received any reports from his Government on what was happening.

CONCORDE HAS OFFICIAL TEST ON RUNWAY

Daily Telegraph Staff Correspondent

PARIS, Tuesday.

The prototype Concorde 001 Anglo-French supersonic airliner underwent its first official runway test on the specially constructed runway at the Sud Aviation works at Toulouse today.

After reaching 35 mph the test pilot, M. Andre Turcat, said the test had been carried out under extremely satisfactory conditions. During the coming days, he hoped, further tests with speeds of up to 120 mph would be made.

NEWMARKET CONTRACT WON FROM BBC

By Our TV Staff

Independent Television yesterday signed a two-year contract to cover all racing from Newmarket for the next two years, outbidding BBC which had offered to renew its contract. The ITV companies will pay a total of £14,000 for the contract which begins next year.

It was negotiated by ITV Sport, a central unit set up by the Independent Television Authority, to negotiate sports coverage on behalf of all the companies.

The contract will give ITV coverage of the 1,000 and 2,000 Guineas, and the autumn double - the Cesarewitch and the Cambridgeshire from Newmarket. They already have exclusive coverage of the Oaks and the St. Leger, but share the Derby with the BBC.

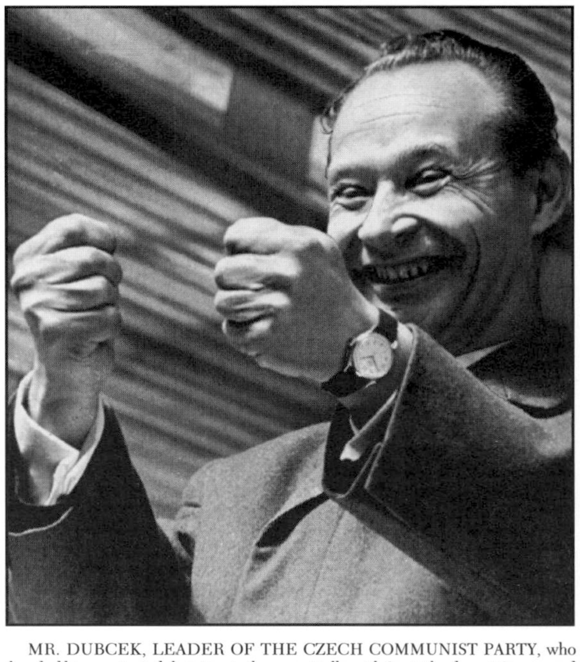

MR. DUBCEK, LEADER OF THE CZECH COMMUNIST PARTY, who headed his country's delegation in the recent talks with Soviet leaders at Cierna-nad Tisou, a village on the Czech border with Russia.

INTER-CITY RAILWAY FARES GOING UP

POLICY OF 'SELECTION'

Daily Telegraph Reporter

A POLICY of selective fares increases on inter-city routes - instead of the rate-per-mile basis - is to be introduced by British Railways on Sept. 8. Widespread fares increases in the London area and Home Counties take effect simultaneously.

Generally, the larger of the selective increases fall on routes where passengers have little choice but to travel by rail. Other factors considered are frequency, speed and reliability of services.

Several years of market research by the passenger and commercial departments determined the extent of the selective rises.

Extensive use of market research techniques is in keeping with British Railways' attempts over the last few years to modernise its image.

It also reflects the Prices and Incomes Board report on fares which urged the railways to be more flexible. Last year the Railways' loss was £153 million. The new fare increases are expected to yield £6 million a year.

Examples of inter-city fares increases, second class, single, are:

Newcastle-London from 72s to 78s.

Brighton-London 14s to 15s

Ashford-Cannon Street 15s to 16s 6d.

Ipswich-Liverpool Street 18s 9d to 20s.

Some of the smallest increases are on routes between Scotland and London.

"MODERN METHODS"

Concessions continue

A railways spokesman said last night that it was the first time since nationalisation that the principle of a standard rate-per-mile arrangement had been abandoned. The decision was in line with the railways awareness of commercial competition.

He stressed that since 1965 there had been only minor adjustments.

Continued on Back Page, Col. 6

5,000 TROOPS FOR CHICAGO

From Our Correspondent

NEW YORK, Tuesday.

More than 7,500 United States Army troops, have been given intensive riot-control training in case serious disturbances break out in Chicago during the Democratic convention next week.

Mr. Samuel Shapiro, the Governor of Illinois, who is a Democrat, has ordered more than 5,000 National Guardsmen for duty in the city during the convention.

EISENHOWER IS OFFERED 20 HEARTS

Daily Telegraph Staff Correspondent

WASHINGTON, Tuesday.

AT least 20 healthy Americans have offered to have their hearts transplanted into Gen. Eisenhower, the Walter Reed Army Hospital, Washington, said today.

"Four or five would-be donors have telephoned every day since the General had his last heart attack," said a spokesman after doctors had stated that Gen. Eisenhower's condition remained grave.

The General's doctors have given "careful consideration" to a transplant. They rejected the idea because of the General's age, 77, and other "major medical considerations."

His weakened condition would make it very difficult for him to withstand the complications and high risk of infection.

Family consulted

The family was consulted by the doctors and presumably accepted their views. It is not known whether the matter ever reached the stage of surgeons who have performed the operation being asked for their opinions.

A bulletin today said the General was "resting comfortably" despite occasional heart spasms.

The former President's condition remains critical.

Mr. Nixon, Republican Presidential candidate, interrupted his campaign today to visit the General.

LIVING COST 5 P.C. UP

By Our Business Staff

The retail price index, the Employment and Productivity Department's official measure of the cost of living, shows prices rising more than 5 per cent. during the year up to July 16.

MARTIN LUTHER KING SHOT DEAD

By IAN BALL

NEW YORK, Thursday.

DR. MARTIN LUTHER KING, 39, the 1964 Nobel Peace Prize winner, and America's most respected Civil Rights leader, was assassinated tonight as he stood on the balcony of his hotel in the centre of Memphis, Tennessee. A single shot apparently fired from a passing car, struck him in the neck and chin.

"Martin Luther King is dead," said a police official about an hour after the Civil Rights leader had been taken by ambulance to a Memphis hospital.

Riot-equipped police were rushed to the hotel and sealed off a large area of the Memphis business section. Two men were arrested several hundred yards from the hotel. Police would not say whether they were suspected of murdering Dr. King or whether they were implicated in the killing.

Police broadcast a bulletin instructing all units to look for a young white man. He was seen running from the scene and police said he dropped a weapon.

"He didn't say a word. He didn't move," said one of Dr. King's key assistants, the Rev. Andrew Young.

HARLEM GRIEF-STRICKEN

He and Negro leaders throughout America were grief stricken at the murder of a well-loved public figure.

There was horror and public grief as the news spread through New York's Harlem. Men and women stood with heads bowed as they listened to the news in the street and in restaurants and bars. Many wept openly.

Dr. King was with the Rev. Jesse Jackson and other members of his Southern Christian Leadership Conference in the hotel room preparing to eat dinner. Dr. King stepped out on to the balcony of the second floor room to get some evening air.

"He had just bent over," said the Rev. Jesse Jackson. "If he had been standing up he would not have been hit in the face."

Others who were with Dr. King said that moments before they stepped out on to the balcony he had talked about a meeting in Memphis tonight. "Be sure to sing 'Blessed Lord' tonight and sing it well," were his last words before he was shot.

Dr. King had been the subject of repeated assassination threats over the past 10 years. There were at least two serious attempts on his life.

Two years ago a knife was hurled at him while he was speaking in Chicago's Marquette Park. In January, 1957 a bomb placed on the porch at his home in Montgomery failed to explode. The fuse burned out just before reaching the explosive - 12 sticks of dynamite bundled together.

In January, 1965, the Negro leader was punched and kicked in the groin as he registered at a previously all-white hotel in Selma, Alabama.

(April 3)

OBSCENITY LAW 'PERPLEXES' APPEAL JUDGES

The publishers of "Last Exit to Brooklyn" had their conviction for publishing an obscene article quashed by three Appeal Court judges yesterday because the trial judge had failed adequately to direct the Old Bailey jury. The £100 fine and order to pay £500 costs were also set aside.

Giving judgement Lord Justice Salmon, Mr. Justice Geoffrey Lane and Mr. Justice Fisher admitted they were "perplexed" over the meaning of the Obscene Publications Act, 1959.

Mr. John Calder, a director of Calder and Boyars Ltd., of Brewer Street, Soho, publishers of the book, said last night: "Publishers and writers can now breathe a little more easily. But we would still like to know the exact meaning of the law on obscenity."

(August 1)

TURBAN BAN ON BUS CREWS STAYS

Sikh bus crews in Wolverhampton will still not be allowed to wear turbans or beards, the transport committee decided last night. About 140 Sikhs, half the bus staff, have threatened to strike if the decision is not reversed.

The Rev. Jeffrey Spratling, a member of the Wolverhampton Council for Racial Harmony, said last night: "The decision is completely absurd."

(March 7)

SIR ALEC AND LADY ROSE raising glasses of champagne on the balcony of their greengrocer's shop in Southsea yesterday after the announcement that the round-the-world yachtsman had been awarded a knighthood.

ALEC ROSE KNIGHTED FOR WORLD VOYAGE

CHAMPAGNE CELEBRATION

By GUY RAIS

ALEC ROSE, 59, the lone, round-the-world yachtsman, returned to his greengrocer's shop after a haircut in Portsmouth yesterday and was greeted by the Lord Mayor with the words: "Alec, you have been knighted."

But the news came as no surprise to Mr. Rose, still in a daze after his welcome home ceremony on Thursday. He had been told 24 hours earlier that he had been recommended for a knighthood. Only the timing caught him unawares.

Like the K.B.E. conferred on Sir Francis Chichester last year, after he had reached Sydney on his round the world voyage, the award of Knight Bachelor to Mr. Rose was made on the recommendation of the Prime Minister.

A Naval officer was told to inform Mr. Rose of it when he stepped ashore at Portsmouth.

Mr. Rose's award is evidently regarded as closing the chapter. It would be a mistake to assume that anyone else who sails round the world will be knighted.

(July 6)

'New-style' leader for Canada

By David Adamson

CANADA'S Liberal party rejected the old political figures last night. In a near-frenzy of hero worship it swept into power a 46-year-old French Canadian from Quebec.

The new party leader - and the next Prime Minister - is Mr. Pierre Elliott Trudeau, Justice Minister in the Cabinet of the retiring Prime Minister, Mr. Pearson.

A new-style almost casual politician, Mr. Trudeau's success owes more to television and the Press than to ambition. To some extent his popularity is due to the fact that half the Canadian population is under 30 and searching for something new.

He is both a French Canadian and a champion of the federal system. Keeping the secession-minded province of Quebec within the federal framework will be his chief task as Prime Minister.

A wealthy bachelor, Mr. Trudeau's aura is a curious mixture of Left Bank and James Bond. His background is that of university professor and Left-wing journalist, but he has a well publicised taste for sports cars and he enjoys the society of pretty women.

(April 8)

Bill to reform grounds for divorce

By Our Political Staff

THE irretrievable breakdown of marriage would become the only ground for divorce under the Divorce Bill, a private Member's measure, published yesterday.

Mr. Leo Abse, Labour MP for Pontypool, one of its sponsors, said he hoped the Bill would become law by the autumn.

Breakdown of marriage would be established by proving one or more of five sets of facts:

That the parties have lived apart for at least two years and that neither party objects to the divorce.

Even though one partner objected to a divorce, that the couple had lived apart for at lease five years.

That one of the parties had behaved in such a way that the other could not reasonably be expected to live with him or her.

That the petitioner had been deserted by the other partner for two years.

That one party had committed adultery and the other found it intolerable to live with him or her.

(January 16)

LIFE DETENTION GIRL, 11, IN REMAND CENTRE

Mary Bell, 11, sentenced to life detention at Newcastle Assizes yesterday, is now in a remand centre "while the question of her future detention is under consideration," a Home Office spokesman said last night. She was found guilty of the manslaughter of two small boys.

"The question of her release from detention will be considered in the same way as the care of any person sentenced to life imprisonment," the Home Office said.

(December 18)

5D ON CIGARETTES & PETROL

BANK LOANS CURB: PURCHASE TAX UP

WITHIN 30 minutes of flying back to London from the Bonn financial crisis talks yesterday Mr. Jenkins, Chancellor of the Exchequer, announced in the Commons tax increases of £250 million to deflate the British economy. Changes announced were:

PETROL: Up 5d a gallon. Duty now 4s 4d a gallon.

TOBACCO: Up to 5d on a packet of 20 cigarettes.

DRINKS: 4s on a bottle of spirits; most beers up 1d a pint. But the Brewers' Society said some beers would go up by 2d a pint.

CARS, FURNITURE DEARER

PURCHASE TAX: All four categories go up. New rates with former rates in brackets are:

13 ¾ per cent. (12 ½ per cent.): Including furniture, clothing and carpets;

22 per cent. (20 per cent.): Including soft drinks, ice cream and sweets;

36 ⅔ per cent. (33 ⅓ per cent.): Including washing machines, cars, refrigerators and television sets;

55 per cent. (50 per cent.): Including furs, jewellery, records, cameras and photographic equipment.

BANK LOANS: Tightening in granting of loans, particularly finance for consumer spending. Banks may have to ask for repayment of some outstanding credit. Clearing banks are being asked to reduce their lending ceiling by next March to 98 per cent. of November, 1967, level. This would mean £100 million reduction in non-fixed rate lending to private sector.

MR. JENKINS said that the measures were "undoubtedly harsh." He expected that they would raise the cost of living by about one per cent. immediately and that by the end of next year this would be "somewhat higher."

(November 23)

23 pc ROAD DEATH FALL SINCE BREATH TESTS

By Our Motoring Staff

ROAD deaths fell by 23 per cent. and total casualties by 16 per cent. during the last three months of 1967, the Ministry of Transport said yesterday. Breath tests came into operation on Oct. 9.

December's casualties were the lowest for the month since 1958 when there was half as much traffic. There were 36 per cent. fewer road deaths at Christmas with 30 per cent. fewer people being seriously injured.

In the first nine months of the year, according to the Ministry, the reduction in casualties was only two per cent.

However in October, November and December total casualties fell by 16,474 or 16 per cent., compared with the same period in 1966. There were 579 fewer road deaths, a reduction of 23 per cent.

More traffic

Serious casualties were down by 17 per cent. and slight injury cases 15 per cent. In the three months traffic was estimated to have increased by two per cent.

During 1967 as a whole personal injury accidents fell by five per cent. from 291,725 to 276,942, while traffic is thought to have increased by four per cent. over 1966.

Deaths totalled 7,319, a fall of 666 or 8 per cent.

(March 22)

BEATLES ARRIVE AT YOGI'S HQ

Daily Telegraph Staff Correspondent

NEW DELHI, Friday.

Two of the Beatles, John Lennon and George Harrison, arrived today at the Maharishi Mahesh Yogi's academy at Rishikesh in the Himalayan foothills to begin a two month course in transcendental meditation. Their wives are with them.

There are already 60 Europeans and Americans at the academy, including Mia Farrow, wife of Frank Sinatra.

(February 17)

INQUIRY INTO FLATS CRASH

THREE DEAD AS NEW BLOCK CRUMBLES

By GUY RAIS

AN immediate full-scale inquiry into the collapse of a wing of a 22-storey block of flats in Canning Town, East London, in which at least three people died, was announced in the Commons yesterday by Mr. Callaghan, Home Secretary.

Besides the two men and a woman who were found dead in the wreckage, another woman was still missing last night, and three more women were detained in hospital.

Many families living in the new 220ft block in Butchers Road, Custom House, Newham, said last night that they would not return there "even if we are told it is safe."

Disaster struck the flats at 5.52 a.m. as most of the 250 residents, many of them elderly and living alone, were asleep. In the next five minutes, the south-east corner fell to the ground, leaving a gaping hole.

Residents described hearing two explosions before furniture and masonry crashed on to the forecourt. The explosion shook homes in a wide area.

The top seven one-bedroomed flats were demolished, and their combined weight swept away the sitting rooms of all 15 flats underneath. The bedrooms of these 15, where most tenants were still asleep, were left intact.

POINT OF EXPLOSION

Thrown to floor

Miss Ivy Hodge, 56, of Flat No. 90 on the 18th floor, told me last night in Poplar Hospital, where she was "comfortable" with burns to her face, arms and right leg, of an explosion in her flat that experts believe may have caused the disaster.

With gauze covering burns on her face, she said to me in a whisper: "I got up to make a cup of tea about 6 a.m.. I remember going into the kitchen and filling the kettle, but then all I can remember is being thrown to the ground.

"I managed to get to the door of what was left of my flat, and I was helped downstairs. I don't remember anything else."

Asked if she had struck a match, Miss Hodge said: "I don't think so."

Firemen and rescue workers were on the scene within minutes. The corner of the block gaped open like a wound. Furniture perched precariously against sagging walls, and carpets and bits of curtains were hanging from the rubble on all floors.

Cranes with steel hawsers began lifting huge slabs of masonry inch by inch to prevent further falls, while firemen and police tunnelled into the wreckage to search for survivors.

A young policeman who helped in the rescue operations told me last night: "While I was at the flats, a man of about 30 who lived there said that a gas leak had been reported to the local board the previous night."

A Gas Board spokesman commented: "Gas leaks take absolute priority, and if one had been officially reported there is no chance of it having been overlooked."

(May 17)

GOODBYE TO LION ON EGGS

THE "Lion" stamp on eggs sold through the Egg Marketing Board is to disappear almost immediately. This follows an announcement in the Commons yesterday by Mr. Cledwyn Hughes, Minister of Agriculture.

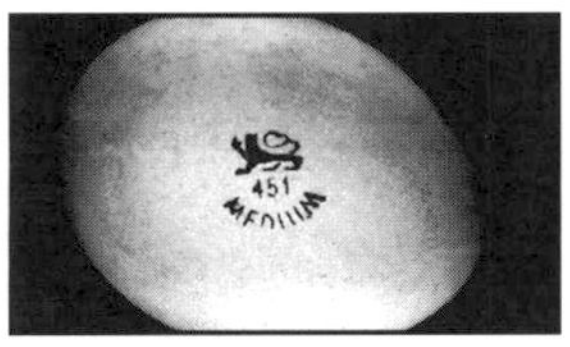

Mr. Hughes, in a written answer, said a Statutory Order was being laid before Parliament that day to remove the obligation to stamp subsidised eggs with effect from next Monday.

Up to now eggs eligible for the subsidy have had to be stamped indicating whether they are large, standard, medium or small, and must also carry the packing station code number.

(December 20)

LAW TODAY TO BAN MISLEADING TRADE CLAIMS

Shoppers are protected from sharp traders and misleading advertisements under the Trade Descriptions Act, which comes into force today.

For the first time traders and manufacturers giving materially false information, orally or in writing, about goods and services will be liable to criminal prosecution. They face an unlimited fine and up to two years' imprisonment.

The task of enforcing the Act falls on already overworked local weights and measures inspectors. A shopper who suffers from a false description which leads to prosecution will normally still have to rely on being able to bring a civil action to recover compensation.

(November 30)

ACT ABOLISHING CENSOR GIVEN ROYAL ASSENT

Royal assent was given yesterday to the Theatres Act, 1968, which abolishes the powers of the Lord Chamberlain to censor stage plays.

The section of the Act abolishing censorship will come into force on Sept. 26, at the same time as provisions making it a criminal offence to present or direct an obscene performance of a play in public or private.

The only exceptions are performances in a private house on a domestic occasion, and rehearsals and plays performed to make a record, broadcast or film.

Local authorities will replace the Lord Chamberlain as the theatre licensing authority.

(July 27)

CUNARDER MAKES LAST TRIP

Daily Telegraph Reporter

THE 143 crew who are to stay aboard the Queen Elizabeth for the next six months are to be visited by their wives and children at the liner's new home in Florida.

The liner is to be used temporarily as a floating restaurant and will probably house aircraft crews for the winter season.

The crew heard the news shortly before the liner left Southampton yesterday on her last voyage. The men's families will be flown to Florida by the liner's new owners, the Queen Elizabeth Corp. next spring and will stay for two or three weeks.

The Queen Elizabeth, 83,000 tons, cast off in darkness watched by about 100 people, who were reinforced by the band which had played her in from her last commercial voyage.

(December 30)

"DRY' STATUS ENDS

After almost 50 years as a "dry" town, Kirkintilloch, Dunbartonshire, voted 5,293-4,858 last night in favour of a return of licensed premises. The town was the last "dry" burgh in Scotland.

(December 11)

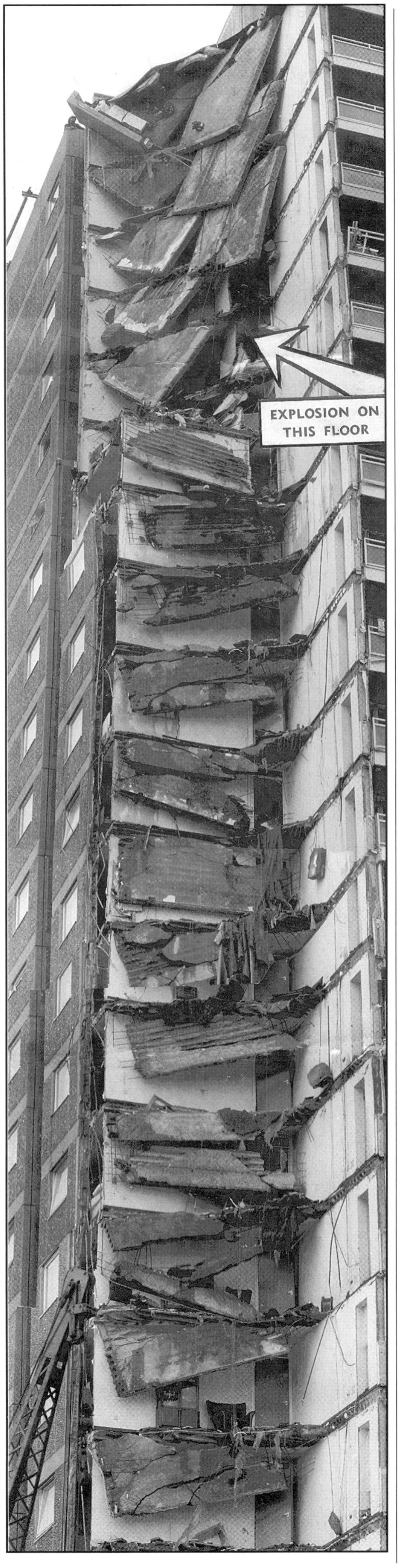

TROOPS CLASH WITH CHICAGO MARCHERS

By DOMINICK HARROD

CHICAGO, Thursday.

NATIONAL Guardsmen and demonstrators clashed this afternoon in Chicago, less than 24 hours after the violent confrontation between police and demonstrators last night in which 300 people, including Mr. James Auchincloss, half-brother of Mrs. Jacqueline Kennedy, were hurt. Another 300 were arrested.

A large crowd set out after a rally in front of the Conrad Hilton Hotel, moving southwards. They were met by Guardsmen in jeeps equipped with barbed wire frames. The demonstrators withdrew to continue their rally in the southern section of Grant Park.

An investigation of behaviour by both police and demonstrators last night is to be carried out by Mr. Thomas Foran, the United States Attorney (Federal prosecutor), in Chicago.

It was a night hard to believe in the light of this morning.

Hard to believe but for the rows of National Guardsmen still standing guard outside my hotel, and but for a dull ache in my left leg, a personal memento of the Battle of Michigan Avenue.

Mr. James Conlisk, Superintendent of Police, defended his men.

"The force used was the force necessary to repel the mob."

Last night, I was a member of that "mob" into which the police charged with flailing batons outside the Conrad Hilton hotel.

A well-dressed 20-year-old Chicago girl who happened to be on the scene was run down from behind by a plainclothes policeman, from whom she was running, obeying his yell to "move on."

As his baton hit her shoulder, and she fell, Mr. Winston Churchill, reporting for the Evening News, and Mr. Auchincloss, working for the National Broadcasting Company, ran towards her.

As she rose, and I was moving towards the mêlée, the plainclothes man darted away across the avenue towards parked police vans.

At that instant, a motorcyle policeman hurtled along the road, screeching to a noisy standstill a yard from us, one wheel against the curb, before turning and roaring off across the street again.

Within minutes, Mr. Churchill, Mr. Auchincloss, Mr. Stephen Barber, correspondent of The Sunday Telegraph, and I were picking ourselves up after another charge, this time on foot, and comparing baton bruises on heads, wrists and thighs.

Our personal adventure was typical of the scene up and down Michigan Avenue for at least three hours.

The demonstrators maintained their courage. At every police charge, leaders of the by now fragmented rally called out: "Walk, walk - don't run."

"MOVE ON"

Rifles and gas

It was difficult not to run, however. The police were walking slowly along the street in a broken line and then, at about 15 yards distance, breaking into individual chases, yelling: "Move on, get out, run - move!"

To fall was no guarantee against being hit. Policemen often dragged those who had stumbled to their feet, only to hit out, and yell at them again.

(August 30)

VICTORY FOR WELSH SUNDAY DRINKERS

Daily Telegraph Reporter

THE Welsh referendum on Sunday drinking ended yesterday in victory for the supporters of seven-day opening. Three former "dry" counties, Montgomeryshire, Denbighshire and Pembrokeshire went "wet."

Eight other counties and county boroughs voted to continue "wet." Five counties decided to remain "dry," but by reduced majorities.

Mr. David Baird-Murray, chairman of the Wales and Monmouthshire Seven-Day Opening Council, said: "The result shows that a referendum every seven years is a waste of public money and unjustified by public opinion.

"We hope there will be amending legislation allowing the opening of licensed premises for ever."

The results were:

"WET"	Merthyr Tydfil
Monmouthshire	Swansea
Glamorgan	Brecknockshire
Radnorshire.	"DRY"
Flintshire	Merioneth
Montgomeryshire	Cardiganshire
Denbighshire	Carmarthenshire
Pembrokeshire	Caernarvonshire
Cardiff	Anglesey.

(November 8)

WORD NEGRO RESENTED BY 'BLACKS'

THE word Negro is now eschewed by almost all the younger and more militant members of that race, according to a survey published today.

It is also disliked by White people anxious not to give offence. Mr. John Lindsay, Mayor of New York, seldom uses the word, and usually substitutes "black."

Mr. Rap Brown, the Negro leader, has said: "The largest newspaper in Harlem, the Amsterdam News, uses the term "Afro-American." Dr. Ralph Bunche, United Nations Under-Secretary, a Negro, uses "black" as often as "Negro," "Afram" is favoured in some quarters.

(February 27)

MEDICINE CHARGES RETURN

By JOHN PRINCE
Health Correspondent

AFTER more than three years of free medicines. National Health Service patients will from today be asked to pay 2s 6d an item on prescriptions from their family doctors.

There was no last-minute rush for free medicines, said doctors. The probable reasons were that this is the season of least sickness, and that more than 20 million people in England and Wales - over 40 per cent. of the population - will be exempt from the charge.

They are children under 15, people of 65 and over, expectant and nursing mothers who hold an exemption certificate issued by a local executive council and people with a similar certificate who have illnesses requiring prolonged treatment.

Bitter opposition

The charge is introduced amid bitter opposition, including that from many Labour MPs and the Pharmaceutical Society.

Mr. Robinson, Minister of Health, defends it as a regrettable necessity. Without it, the hospital building programme would have to be cut.

Medicines prescribed by general practitioners and in hospitals cost about £190 million a year. Mr. Robinson hopes to save £25 million by the charge. Running costs of the scheme are estimated at £250,000.

(June 10)

TWO-YEAR GAOL SENTENCE ON Dr. SPOCK

Dr. Benjamin Spock, 65, the baby care specialist, was sentenced to two years in prison and fined 5,000 dollars (£2,083) in Boston today for conspiracy to aid, abet and counsel young men to avoid conscription.

Sentences of two years imprisonment and fines were imposed on his three co-defendants.

(July 11)

5,000 MARCHERS CRY 'TELL TRUTH'

DUBCEK APPEALS FOR ACCEPTANCE

FIVE thousand angry Prague citizens, 25 abreast, marched from Wenceslas Square to the National Assembly building last night as a wave of fury swept Czechoslovakia at the failure of the country's leaders to achieve immediate withdrawal by Russia.

As they chanted "We don't want to live on our knees," and "We want to know the whole truth," Russian troops, who had withdrawn from main thoroughfares earlier, rushed into the square before the Assembly building.

The Russians appeared about to open fire when an Assembly Deputy persuaded the crowd to disperse by telling them: "The Assembly will not endorse any agreement that is against our freedom to speak and to write, or against our sovereignty. The Assembly does not agree with the Moscow communiqué."

Reducing democracy

MR. DUBCEK, who was arrested by the Russians a week ago yesterday, broke down and wept several times last night as he made a 26-minute broadcast to the nation.

He said: "I have heard about the distrust in the results of the Moscow talks and the promised withdrawal of troops. I must warn you against this point of view.

"It is easy to bandy such words about. But we must weigh them against further loss of life and material destruction, which already is great enough."

His voice breaking, Mr. Dubcek added: "We will have to take some temporary measures which will reduce the degree of democracy which we already have, but I beg you to realise the time we are living in." He appealed to the people to support the Government in their efforts to return the country to normal conditions and secure the withdrawal of the Russians.

The Czechoslovak Communist party's central committee announced late last night that it had received details of the Moscow communiqué "with bitterness and was overcome with emotion. We are yielding to superior force, but we shall never renounce the demand for sovereignty and freedom."

(August 24)

10,000 STUDENTS IN PARIS RIOT

By ANNE SINGTON

PARIS, Monday.

THE worst street fighting since the Liberation of Paris in 1944 shook the Left Bank tonight as students and police fought for control of the Boulevard St. Germain.

Smashed cars and overturned buses used as barricades littered the street, while riot police charged again and again, trying to force some 10,000 students into side streets.

As they were bombarded with tear gas grenades the students, at least half of them mini-skirted girls, replied with bricks, cobbles, firecrackers and chairs snatched from cafes. The heavy pall of smoke from the grenades and street fires, together with reports from the tear gas guns, added to the illusions that this was Paris in August 1944.

The Boulevard St. Germain, main artery of the student quarter, was totally blocked when 1,500 rioters overturned two buses and pushed them across the road. Several other buses were abandoned by drivers and passengers.

"COMMANDO SQUADS"
Police ambushed

By 11.30 p.m. the authorities reported that well over 150 people had been injured, some seriously during clashes. Student "commando squads" ambushed police whose helicopters were circling overhead.

Water cannon, a new police weapon, were brought in, but within minutes students had smashed the vehicles' windscreens, forcing the drivers to flee.

Fighting had raged all day. The Sorbonne students were protesting against university conditions and against last week's closure of the Faculty of Letters in suburban Nanterre.

They were also protesting against alleged police violence during previous demonstrations on Friday over the Nanterre decision which followed persistent student rioting there.

Demonstrators were joined tonight by a contingent of university professors who this afternoon sent a delegation to demand the resignation of the Rector of the Sorbonne. It is estimated that tomorrow four university professors out of five will be on strike.

M. Maurice Grimaud, the Prefect of Police, said one demonstrator, hit directly by a tear-gas bomb, may lose an eye.

There were violent clashes at the Place Maubert and in the Boulevard St. Germain, in the heart of the Latin Quarter, where students tore up paving stones to use as weapons, and built barricades from vehicles and street gratings.

Police at first succeeded in driving back demonstrators at the Sorbonne, where Daniel Cohn-Bendit, Left-wing student ringleader, appeared this morning before a university disciplinary council.

At one point several thousand students were driven across the Seine by pursuing police. They continued their march through the Opera district, on the Right Bank, before crossing back to the student quarter.

(May 7)

London Docks closure makes 1,300 jobless

PLANS to close London Docks by next September, as well as to sell the adjacent St. Katharine Docks to the Greater London Council for £1½ million, are to be announced by the Port of London Authority today.

Jobs of about 1,300 employees are affected. Mr. Dudley Perkins, the Authority's director-general, broke the news to them last night.

Port officers will begin talks with customers today on switching trade and shipping lines to the other four dock systems on the Thames.

London Docks, planned in 1797 and now covering 102 acres of Shadwell and Wapping, have become outdated and are losing £1 million a year. St. Katharine Docks, covering 25 acres, are likely to become a housing site.

London Docks have a declining business with small ships. Some trade is likely to be diverted to Surrey Commercial Docks, which have lost much timber trade to Tilbury, where larger ships can be accommodated.

(January 23)

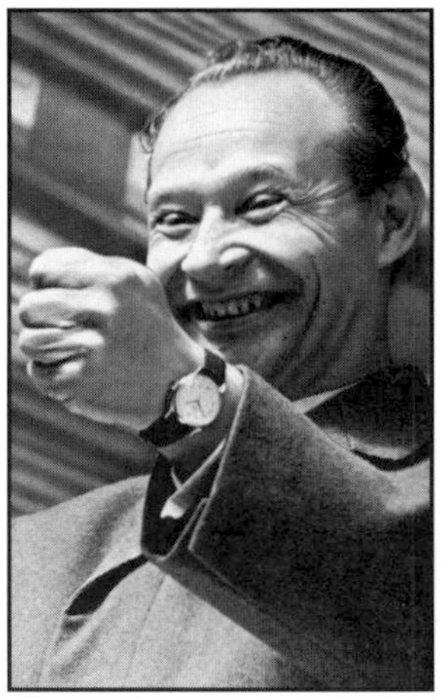

MR. DUBCEK

SUCCESSOR TO SALAZAR TAKES OVER

By JOHN SMALLDON

LISBON, Thursday.

PRESIDENT TOMAZ of Portugal announced tonight that Prof. Marcelo Caetano, 62, is taking over from Dr. Salazar, 79, as the first new Prime Minister the country has known for 36 years.

In a televised speech the President said the illness of Dr. Salazar, who is still in a coma ten days after a brain haemorrhage, had posed a grave problem.

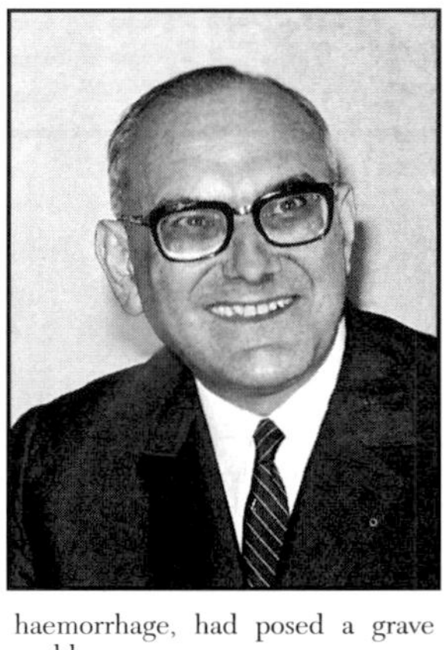

"It is no longer feasible, in the higher interests of Portugal, at the present moment to postpone a decision any further." Even if Dr. Salazar survived there was no hope of him being able to carry out his duties.

Speaking with emotion, he said he knew that Dr. Salazar did not wish to die in office, and he released him from his post.

(September 27)

DEARER BREAD LIKELY AFTER 14s PAY RISE

By Our Industrial Correspondent

Bread is likely to be dearer next year following the approval last night by Mrs. Castle, Secretary for Employment, of pay rises for 40,000 bakery workers, and other cost increases.

The present price of a standard 1¾lb loaf is 1s 7d. Under the pay deal, men will receive 14s 11d a week more from Dec. 1 and women 13s 4d from March 2.

Previous rates for the workers, who are those employed by wholesale and multiple bakeries, ranged from £13 9s 6d to £16 2s 7d a week for men and from £9 6s 6d to £11 8s 4d for women.

(December 5)

GROUCHO RETIRES

Daily Telegraph Staff Correspondent

NEW YORK, Monday.

Groucho Marx, 72, is retiring as a professional entertainer. He will devote the rest of his life to fighting injustices by means of non-commercial radio and television programmes. The comedian said today: "I'm the last of the angry old men."

(January 16)

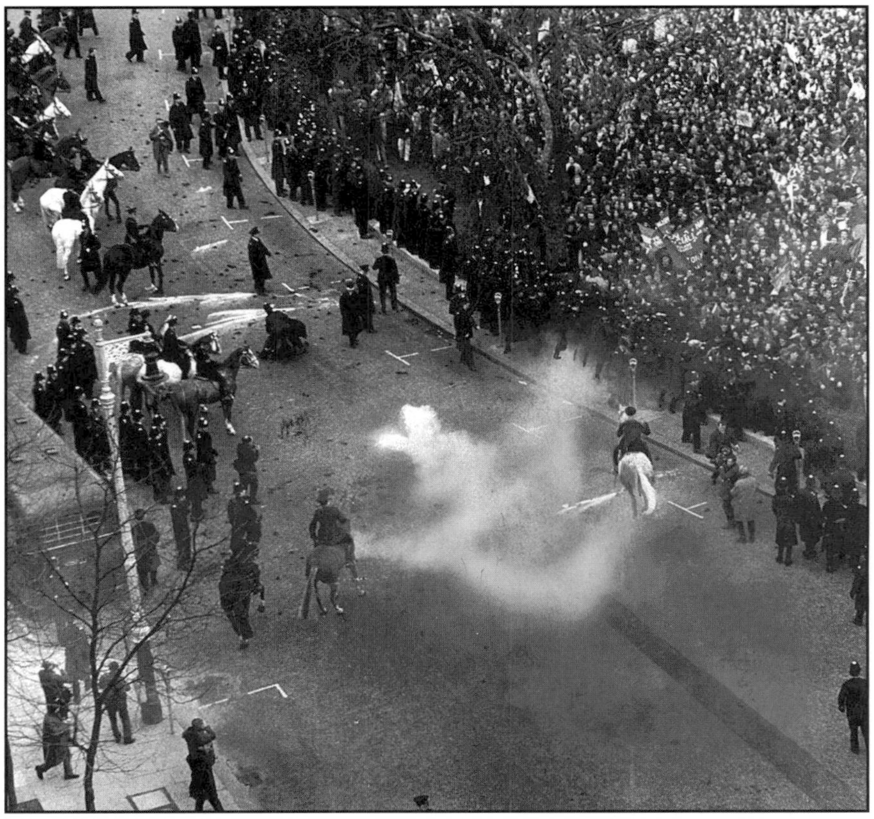

A SMOKE BOMB EXPLODING IN FRONT OF MOUNTED POLICE guarding the American Embassy against anti-Vietnam war demonstrators yesterday.

MUGGERIDGE QUITS UNIVERSITY POST

Daily Telegraph Reporter

MR. MALCOLM MUGGERIDGE announced from the pulpit of St. Giles Cathedral, Edinburgh, last night that he is to resign as Rector of Edinburgh University over the question of making the contraceptive pill available to all students.

He took this unprecedented course in an address at a service to mark the start of a new term. Mr. Muggeridge's action follows an open letter printed in the current edition of Edinburgh University's newspaper, Student.

It called on him to resign if he did not agree with the Students' Representative Council's resolution that the contraceptive pill be available on request to all students.

Mr. Muggeridge condemned the students' craving for "the old slob's escapes of dope and bed."

Education seemed to have become a sort of mumbo-jumbo or cure-all for the ills of a decaying and Godless society.

"No doubt we shall go on raising the school age, multiplying and enlarging our universities, increasing public expenditure on education, until juvenile delinquency, beats and drug addicts, and general intimations of illiteracy multiply so alarmingly that at last, the whole process is called into question.

"In the same sort of way, the so-called 'permissive' morality of our time, will, I am sure, reach its apogee.

"When birth pills are handed out with the free orange juice and consenting adults wear special ties and blazers, and abortion and divorce . . . are freely available on the public health, then at last, with the suicide rate up to Scandinavian proportions and the psychiatric wards bursting at the seams, it will be realised that this path ... is a disastrous cul-de-sac."

After the service Prof. Michael Swann, principal of Edinburgh University, said: "I have nothing to say on the matter. I may make a statement tomorrow."

Mr. Muggeridge, who will be 65 in March, was installed as Rector for a three-year-term last February. Early in December he threatened to resign if the students supported legalisation of drug-taking.

(January 15th)

TRIUMPH FOR LAW AND ORDER

39 arrested in Grosvenor Sq

Daily Telegraph Reporter

FOR three hectic hours, a 12-deep cordon of police stood firm in Grosvenor Square yesterday as 5,000 anti-Vietnam war demonstrators tried to force their way to the American Embassy.

Four major charges were hurled against the defensive lines, but banner-poles, fireworks and coins, which were the anarchists' ammunition, failed to upset either the cordon or the patience of the police.

Finally the disappointed militant demonstrators gave up and withdrew in bedgraggled defeat. The Oct. 27 protest faded with the autumn daylight, having failed to live up to the dire predictions made for it.

It is estimated that at the peak of the Grosvenor Square battle more than 1,000 police were facing 5,000 demonstrators.

Some 300 slogan-screaming anarchists spear-headed the attacks, thrusting banner poles lance-like into the policemen's faces, but not once did it look remotely possible that they would break through. The nearest they came to the embassy was 20 yards.

Demonstration day began with Central London looking as if it were under siege. Police were guarding public and Government buildings, and many shops on the route had boarded up their windows.

Hours before the march was due to begin demonstrators converged on the assembly point on the Embankment near Charing Cross.

Banners proclaimed contingents from most universities from Edinburgh to Brighton. There were also many groups of overseas students, African, American, Greek, Indian and German.

At two o'clock and with Tariq Ali, a leader of the Vietnam Solidarity Campaign, at the head, the march set off along the Embankment.

The spirit of the mile-long crocodile of marchers was more in keeping with a carnival than a vicious political demonstration. It was like some massive bohemian Sunday school outing.

Young bearded parents wheeled children in push-chairs under banners which ranged from "Lords of Anarchy," "Hands off Vietnam," "Smith Must Go" to "Camden Town demands American withdrawal."

At Trafalgar Square about 3,000 of the estimated 30,000 marchers broke off for Grosvenor Square. Tariq Ali found his position at the head of the main march challenged by a group of about 50 youths who mustered under a large North Vietnamese flag.

At the Cenotaph a demonstrator climbed the memorial and hung a black flag near to the Union Jack. It was quickly taken down by the police.

The demonstrators destroyed several wreaths which earlier in the day had been placed around the base of the memorial to mark the anniversaries of several battles.

Meanwhile the breakaway group at Trafalgar Square were being urged on to Grosvenor Square by Edward Davoren, 28, Irishman and liaison officer of the Maoist Revolutionary Socialist Student Federation, and two other Maoists, Nick Bateson and Henderson Brooks.

With their way to the American Embassy blocked, the leaders decided that their best bet was a gesture against United States imperialism. Mr. Davoren pulled an American flag from his pocket and decided they would burn it. But nobody had a light.

Eventually one of their supporters produced a box of matches. The flag had just started to go up in flames and the crowd were cheering when a police inspector stamped out the fire.

It ended with a song

Despite all the secret plans and the hours of provocation the massive police cordon was still firmly in control to win the battle of Grosvenor Square.

There were some good points too, from the demonstrators. Students running a first-aid service helped a young policeman who had a head injury. As they drove him away in a mini-car, the advancing hordes banged on top of the car.

It all ended with good-humoured exchanges between the small crowd of demonstrators left in Grosvenor Square and the police.

Just before the crowd finally dispersed the police linked arms and sang "Auld Lang Syne" to cheers from the crowd.

(October 28)

HEATH SACKS POWELL FOR RACE SPEECH

By ROWLAND SUMMERSCALES
Political Staff

MR. ENOCH POWELL, who on Saturday said Britain must be "mad, literally mad, as a nation" to allow 50,000 dependants of immigrants into the country each year, was last night removed from the Shadow Cabinet.

Mr. Heath, Leader of the Opposition, made the announcement after urgent consultations with Mr. Whitelaw, Opposition Chief Whip. He said he had told Mr. Powell he considered his Birmingham speech to have been "racialist in tone and liable to exacerbate racial tensions."

"The Conservative party is utterly opposed to racialism and discrimination of a racial or religious kind," he said. Mr. Heath also announced that Mr. Maudling, deputy leader, will become Shadow Minister of Defence, in Mr. Powell's place.

Sir Alec Douglas-Home will take over responsibility for Commonwealth affairs in addition to foreign affairs. He said from his Berwickshire home that he had told Mr. Heath he would do so temporarily "until something permanent was arranged."

Mr. Heath acted swiftly after reading reports of Mr. Powell's speech, which came as a complete surprise to him. He could only conclude that it was a deliberately timed exercise, which, whatever its aim, struck directly at his authority.

"CAREFUL" WORDS
Not to be misunderstood

Mr. Powell said on ITV last night that he chose the words of his speech "very carefully indeed." He added: "I didn't wish to be misunderstood, and I believe there is no room for misunderstanding."

Questioned about the effect of his speech on the Conservative party Mr. Powell said: "I was speaking to the official line."

In Wolverhampton last night, Mrs. Powell said: "My husband has gone to bed. He will write to Mr. Heath tomorrow and has no further comment to make."

Mr. Powell is not the kind of man to regret his actions. That he contemplated the possibility of dismissal is shown by the final words of his speech: "All I know is that to see, and not to speak, would be the great betrayal."

The two men have clashed before. The outcome was not explained, but it has always been understood that Mr. Powell would never accept as a condition of membership of the Shadow Cabinet, an obligation of silence on issues on which he felt deeply.

Even Labour MPs who will accuse Mr. Powell of bidding for votes, and moderate Conservative MPs who are outraged by Mr. Powell's speech, are uneasily aware that it may represent mass opinion in the country.

Mr. Powell has sometimes been an embarrassment in the Shadow Cabinet in the past and Mr. Heath had suffered the inconvenience. This time he decided Mr. Powell had gone too far.

(April 22)

RIOT ALERT FOR 2,000 U.S. POLICE

By MABEL ELLIOTT
NEW YORK, Monday.

LOS ANGELES authorities ordered 2,000 police officers to stand by today to avert any further racial violence in the Watts district, where three Negroes were killed and 45 wounded during a gun battle last night.

One man has been charged with the attempted murder of two officers and a large part of the slum, in which live most of the city's 335,000 Negroes, has been cordoned off.

With memories of the 1965 riots in which 34 lives were lost and more than £16 million of property was destroyed, a senior police official said today: "It is better to over-react and control the situation than run the risk of it getting out of hand."

Jazz festival

Last night's violence began with a barrage of bricks and bottles after a Watts Festival of Art - exhibits, films and jazz - to commemorate the third anniversary of the riots.

The disorder quickly turned into an outburst of arson and shooting with negroes firing at each other. Six policemen were among the injured.

The real violence apparently started as police arrested a Negro woman on a drunken driving charge. As she was hauled kicking and screaming into a police car, Negroes fanned out yelling "police brutality."

Firemen were forced to dodge sniper fire as they fought fires deliberately started by young Negroes.

(August 13)

'PELICANS' TO REPLACE X-CROSSINGS

A new type of pedestrian road crossing, the "Pelican," is to replace the experimental X-way crossings. Like the X-way, it will be controlled by push button, but it will not be so complicated.

For drivers, Pelicans will be the same as ordinary traffic signals except that a flashing amber light will show where red-and-amber shows on ordinary traffic signals.

(July 23)

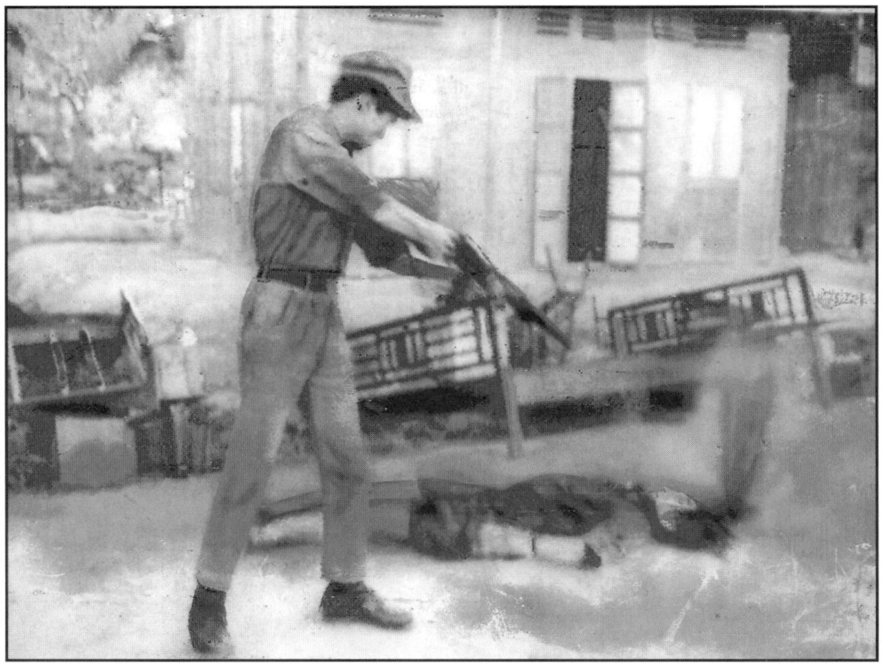

BULLETS FROM A VIETNAMESE SOLIDER'S RIFLE kicking up the dust beside the head of a wounded Viet Cong.

VIET CONG BATTLE INSIDE SAIGON

SAIGON, Wednesday.

VIET CONG suicide squads, dressed in South Vietnamese Government uniforms, launched a rocket and mortar attack on the centre of Saigon early today and seized part of the American Embassy. Six hours later, at 9 a.m., American troops regained control of the building.

At least 10 helicopters landed on the roof of the eight-storey building and the troops swarmed out to subdue the Viet Cong who had held out against military police. At least 10 Americans and 30 guerrillas were believed killed in the fighting in the city.

President Thieu's palace was also attacked by a Viet Cong force which was later reported to be holed up in a building nearby. Besides Saigon, the guerrillas mounted fresh assaults on nine cities throughout the country, including Can Tho, in the Mekong Delta.

In Saigon another Viet Cong target was the Government radio station, which went off the air early today.

American living quarters, the South Vietnamese Navy HQ and the Philippines Embassy also came under fire. There was fighting around Tan son Nhut air base, outside Saigon.

DA NANG ATTACK
30 aircraft hit

Several of the other cities attacked had already suffered Viet Cong assaults early yesterday as inhabitants were celetrating the Lunar New Year.

At Da Nang air base, the Americans' biggest in Vietnam, 30 aircraft, including helicopters, were destroyed or damaged.

In Ban Me Thuot, a province capital in the Central Highlands about 160 miles north-east of Saigon, the Viet Cong attacked with riot gas. Communist bazooka teams reached the city centre.

The Viet Cong reached the perimeter of a South Vietnamese army headquarters compound but did not penetrate it.

In the fighting throughout the country more than 500 Viet Cong and North Vietnamese were reported killed. American casualties were said to be comparatively light.

Hanoi Radio said the attacks had been launched to "punish" the Americans for calling off the Lunar New Year truce.

(January 31)

LIZ TAYLOR BUYS £127,000 DIAMOND

Elizabeth Taylor paid a world record price for a diamond ring, $305,000 (£127,000) for the 33.19 carat Krupp diamond at a Parke-Bernet auction in New York today. The emerald cut stone is one of the most perfect in the world.

(May 17)

20 KILLED BY HURRICANE IN SCOTLAND

AT least 22 people were killed yesterday in the hurricane that swept across the north of the British Isles, 20 of them in Scotland and two in Ulster, and hundreds of people were made homeless.

Gusts which reached 120 mph cut a swathe of devastation in Scotland 17 miles long and 15 miles deep. Winds touched 134 mph, the highest confirmed wind speed since records began, at Great Dun Fell, Westmorland.

Late last night weathermen said another gale force wind with gusts up to force eight - gale pitch, was expected to hit North-West Scotland later today.

The dredger Cessnock capsized and sank 300 yards off Princess Pier, Greenock, and three Glasgow men were drowned.

Police in Glasgow, where nine people were killed, described the conditions as "worse than the blitz." Two died in Edinburgh, and a man and a woman were killed in Greenock. More than 100 were injured and nearly 700 made homeless.

The gales wrecked tenements, brought hundreds of chimneys and trees crashing, wrecking cars and blocking roads.

(January 16)

MAJOR WHO 'CUT OFF' OWN LEG SATISFACTORY

Major Rowland Bowen, 52, who is thought to have amputated his own leg, was "very satisfactory" in Princess Alice Hospital, Eastbourne yesterday. The acting hospitable secretary said that the major had been visited by his brother.

A cricket historian and life long member of the MCC, Major Bowen is employed by the Ministry of Defence. It is thought he cut off his own right leg below the knee to prove that the operation could be performed painlessly.

(September 9)

DECISION DASHES HOPES

Daily Telegraph Reporter

THE POPE'S decision, announced yesterday has dashed the hopes of many of Britain's 5,000,000 Roman Catholics that some easement of the Church's teaching on birth control would be made. But while many Roman Catholics expressed disappointment Archbishop Roberts, the Jesuit, was more critical.

He said the Popes had always maintained the law on contraception was a Divine Law.

"If I cannot agree with that, I think it is honest for me to say so," he said. "I have said it. Protestants have been discussing this for 50 years and are almost unanimous in saying contraception is not forbidden by Divine Law.

"The majority of the Pope's own experts have said so. The surprising thing is that he has, in fact, endorsed the minority view expressed by four people only and has disregarded not only the numbers but the views of the other experts in all the other departments."

IRISH SUPPORT
"No snap decision"

Cardinal Heenan, Archbishop of Westminster, said: "This is clear enough; this is no snap decision." Dr. McQuaid, Archbishop of Dublin, said: "I gratefully welcome this reaffirmation."

Mr. Norman St. John-Stevas, Conservative MP for Chelmsford who is a Roman Catholic, said the debate would go on within the Church. The encyclical might ask for obedience but it could not command intellectual consent.

(July 30)

STONEHOUSE LEADS 5d POST RALLY

Daily Telegraph Reporter

A MORALE-BOOSTING message was sent to all postal workers yesterday by Mr. John Stonehouse, Postmaster-General, on the eve of the introduction of the controversial two-tier letter service.

He told them they had been under fire in recent weeks "because we have been brave enough to introduce a new and different system. Now the challenge is with us all. I ask you all to meet this challenge. Be proud of our fine postal service and speed the mails."

Mr. Stonehouse said that the new letter service - with its 4d or 5d choice - was the biggest change in 100 years.

With the 5d first-class service, the aim was to increase the present proportion of 18 fully-paid letters out of 20 delivered the day after posting to 19 out of 20.

But the signs are that the 4d second-class service is going to be heavily burdened while many large business and industrial concerns will practically boycott the 5d rate.

(September 14)

GEN. GOWON AGREES TO 10-DAY AIRLIFT INTO BIAFRA

By CHRISTOPHER MUNNION
LAGOS, Tuesday.

THE Federal Nigerian Government agreed in Lagos today to allow International Red Cross planes to fly relief supplies from the Spanish island of Fernando Poo into Biafra for 10 days, beginning on Thursday.

The supplies will be transported in four DC4 and one DC6 aircraft, donated by the Swiss and Scandinavian Governments. They will be flown to the Biafran-controlled airstrip of Uli-Ihiala, in jungle country about 35 miles north-west of the Ibo town of Owerri.

The flights from Fernando Poo, where 3,500 tons of relief supplies have built up during the 16-month-old civil war, will take place in daylight, between 8 a.m. and 4 p.m.

Today's agreement, the first of its kind between the Federal Government and the Red Cross since the war began, came after a secret flight from the island to Lagos by Dr. Auguste Lindt, Swiss Red Cross co-ordinator.

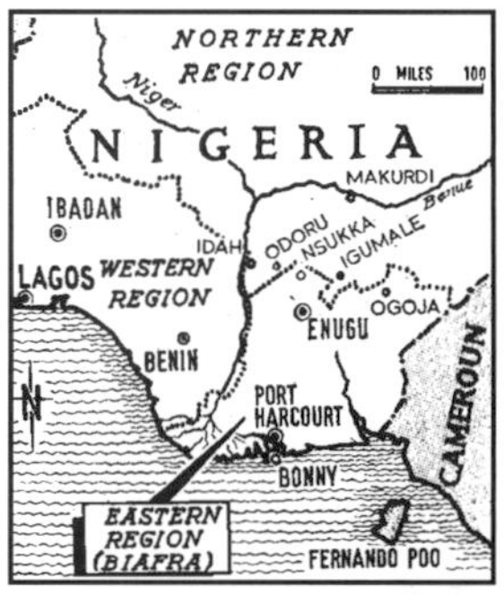

ASSURANCE TO GOWON
Escort discounted

Dr. Lindt met Gen. Gowon, the Federal leader, today with Dr. Fritz Real, Swiss Ambassador to Nigeria. The Swiss doctor assured the general the Red Cross wanted to co-operate.

It had never been the intention of the organisation to bring in supplies to the country under armed escort "as that would be contrary to the principles of the International Red Cross."

A Federal statement described the flights as "an emergency measure." It said that the Red Cross would also "use its influence and take steps," to make it possible to ship relief material through a land corridor, south of the captured Biafran capital of Enugu, to Awgu or along other agreed corridors.

Red Cross relief operations in Federal-held areas are being stepped up immediately. Two DC4 transport planes will airlift 800 tons of food to Enugu and Calabar, while 500 tons will be sent by rail to Oturkpo for onward delivery.

The Federal offensive continued today. Fighting was still reported in Aba, largest of the three main towns held by Biafra.

(September 4)

Motorway to have 'hotel of 70's'

Britain's first combined motorway hotel, service area and recreational centre — designed to cater for the motorist in the 70's— opens this month at Selby Fork, near Leeds.

It was built by Ross Services Division of the Ross Group at a cost of £750,000.

The hotel, shaped like a letter T, has a heated indoor swimming pool, nine-hole minature golf course, exhibition and conference rooms, children's playground and a private heliport, in the 20-acre grounds. It will offer a 24-hour service in the grill room for passing motorists.

Single rooms will cost from £3 14s a night, with double rooms from £5 10s. There will be reductions for children.

(March 17)

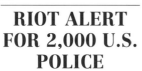

Success a long time coming

By VINCENT RYDER
WASHINGTON, Wednesday.

MR. NIXON was elected 37th President of the United States today after one of the closest contests in American history. He scraped home by a tiny margin after long hours when a deadlock seemed imminent.

Mr. Nixon's Vice-President will be Governor Spiro Agnew of Maryland. Both will take office on Jan. 20, putting the Republicans in the White House for the first time since Gen. Eisenhower left in 1960.

It was just after noon (6 p.m. BST) when his Democratic rival Vice-President Hubert Humphrey sadly conceded defeat. The last polls had closed more than 12 hours earlier.

Mr. Nixon's triumph came eight years after his narrow defeat by Senator John Kennedy, in the Presidential race, and six years after he was defeated in a contest for the Governorship of California after which he petulantly announced he was finished with politics.

Ironically, it was a narrow success in California that averted a deadlock in the Electoral College.

PULLING TOGETHER
Search for peace

The victor told cheering supporters in the ballroom of New York's Waldorf-Astoria hotel this afternoon that a great object of his Administration would be to bring the country together.

His would be an open Administration - "Open to men and women, critics as well as supporters." He would try to "bridge the gap between the generations and the races."

(November 7)

BARROW BOYS REFUSE NEW COINS

Daily Telegraph Reporter

LONDON'S usually sharp-witted barrow traders seemed rather less smart than usual yesterday, the day the first two decimal coins, 10p and 5p, became legal tender. Only a third to whom I offered a 10p piece, equivalent to 2s was really willing to accept it.

I gave one to an Oxford Street barrow boy as payment for 2s worth of bananas. He pocketed it with scarcely a glance, apparently taking it for a florin.

I asked if he had noticed what I gave him. He fished it out and looked at it. "Oh" he said smoothly, "Can you give me four sixpences darling?"

As I obliged, I asked if he did not trust the new currency, "No, not yet," he said, adding diplomatically, "and I could do with the change."

The same 10p piece was offered to another barrow boy selling oranges, he looked at it hard. "What's that?" he asked, "I don't want that."

An alert driver leaned from his stationary van beside the stall and called: "I know what it is. I'll have it. How much is it?"

He nipped smartly from the van, handed me a florin, and grabbed the 10p.

I asked the trader if he did not trust the new coins. "No I don't. I work for a guv'nor, and if I give him a lot of funny looking coins, he'll say, 'What's this?'"

Collectors who want souvenir sets of five, will find them on sale through banks and post offices in May or June. They will consist of 10p, 5p and three copper coins, half a new penny, a new penny, and two new pence, which will not be legal tender until 1971.

(April 24)

PRINCE CHARLES LEARNS POTTERY

The Prince of Wales has joined a night school class of housewives, secretaries and bank clerks at Cambridge College of Arts and Technology to learn pottery making.

Prince Charles, a keen potter at Gordonstoun, has attended the class four times.

(March 14)

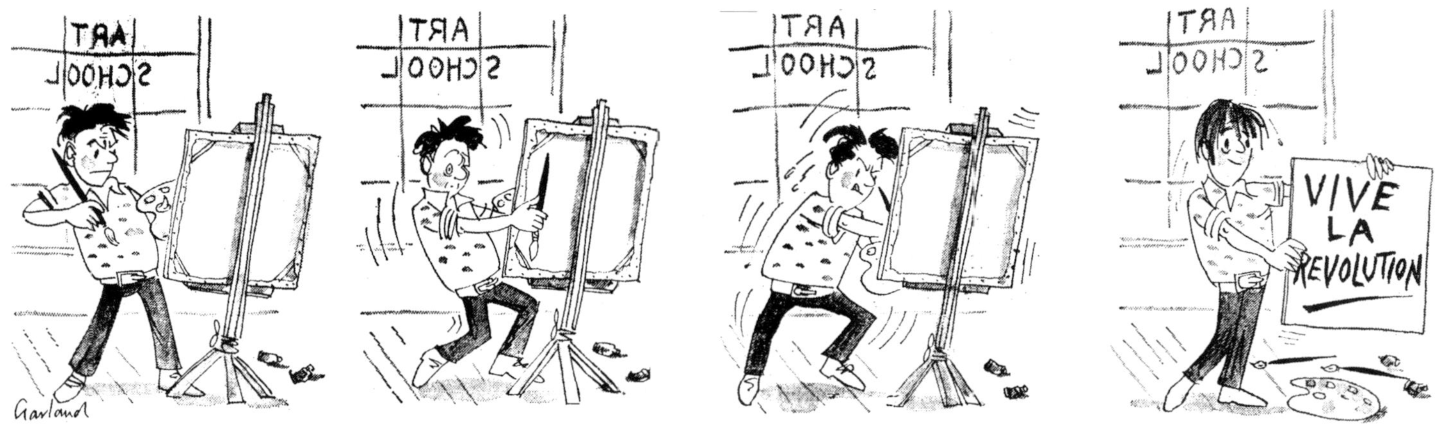

BILL TO GIVE 18-YEAR-OLDS VOTE BY 1970

By ANDREW ALEXANDER
WESTMINSTER, Monday.

A BILL to reduce the voting age to 18, to increase candidates' permitted expenses and extend polling hours was promised in the Commons today by Mr. Callaghan, Home Secretary. The Government is also to consider methods of registration so that party labels can be included on ballot forms.

At the same time Mr. Callaghan firmly declined to legislate against the publication of opinion polls and betting odds 72 hours before Parliamentary elections, as recommended by the Speaker's conference on electoral reform.

The Bill is to be introduced in the forthcoming session so that 18-year-olds can be on the electoral register by February, 1970, and entitled to vote from then on. The extra hour for polling will mean that voting will take place from 7 a.m. until 10 p.m. instead of 9 p.m.

The new expense limits will raise permissible expenses for Parliamentary candidates by £300 making the maxima £1,250 in county constituencies and £1,125 in boroughs.

Mr. Callaghan was introducing a debate on the report of the Speaker's conference which had recommended votes at 20 and the limited ban on opinion polls and betting odds.

His plan met with a mixed reception, Mr. Hogg, Shadow Home Secretary, was doubtful about the value of lowering the voting age, even though he supported most of the recommendations of the Latey Committee for making 18 the age of majority.

But that, he stressed was purely his personal opinion.

(October 15)

FRESH VIOLENCE IN LONDONDERRY

Daily Telegraph Reporter

STEEL-HELMETED police riot squads last night dispersed angry demonstrators in Londonderry after hours of bloody street fighting in the second day of violence over alleged discrimination against Northern Ireland's Roman Catholic minority.

Twelve people were taken to hospital in the rioting which lasted for more than four hours. This brought the number injured in the weekend riots to nearly 100. Twenty-seven men and two women have been arrested.

Petrol bombs were hurled at police and makeshift barricades of heavy timber were thrown across a main street to block armoured police patrols. Crowds estimated at 800 stormed two police strongpoints at the entrance to the Catholic area of the city, but baton-swinging police forced them back.

Hundreds of shop windows were smashed and broken glass and other debris littered the streets.

Police using Land Rovers and armoured water wagons with high pressure hoses charged the crowds in an effort to keep the demonstrators from reaching the city centre.

The trouble began on Saturday with a march organised by a committee drawn from the Londonderry Labour Party and a "housing action group." It was claimed by its sponsors to be "non-sectarian."

Mr. Gerard Fitt, who sits at Westminster as Republican Labour MP for West Belfast had his head stitched after a clash with police.

Mr. Fitt said: "A policeman hit me on the head and as I was falling he hit me again. As I was lying on the stretcher I saw young boys, 17, 18 and 19, being brutally assaulted by the police.

(October 7)

WESTMINSTER & NATPRO IN £2,930M MERGER

By John Cavill and Clifford German
City Staff

National Provincial Bank and Westminster Bank are merging to form Britain's biggest banking group with deposits totalling £2,930 million and nearly 4½ million customers.

The announcement of the biggest banking merger in British history was made on the 16th floor of National Provincial's skyscraper headquarters in the City yesterday after 10 days of talks.

The City had been expecting a statement that Martins Bank was being taken over. It was taken by surprise and in hectic after hours dealing bank share prices rose sharply.

At a joint Press conference with Mr. Duncan Stirling, 68, Westminster's chairman, Mr. David Robarts, 62, chairman of National Provincial, said: "This is not a take over. We are merging.

"We think that this is in the best interests of all the people concerned – our shareholders, staff and customers."

The new giant bank will be top of Btitain's Big Five, displacing Barclays. While the Bank of England has been informed of the merger plans they have yet to be approved by the Board of Trade.

(January 27)

QUICK CURB ON IMMIGRANTS

By H.B. BOYNE
Political Correspondent

BY next Thursday evening the Government hopes to have on the Statute Book a new law restricting the entry of Commonwealth immigrants with British passports.

They are to be subject to a quota of 1,500 work vouchers a year. Allowing for an average of three or four dependants for each voucher holder, the total entry might thus be between 6,000 and 7,500 annually.

This compares with 13,600 from East Africa, mainly Kenya, last year, since when the influx has risen to 2,294 in January and at least 2,500 in the first three weeks of this month.

The Government's decision to bring a new legislation at top speed was announced yesterday by Mr. Callaghan, Home Secretary, after a three-hour meeting of the Cabinet.

It has the ready support of the Conservative Opposition, which indeed had pointed the way with a policy statement by Mr. Heath the night before.

PUBLICATION TODAY
1962 Act amendment

The Immigration Bill, which amends the Commonwealth Immigrants Act, 1962, will be published today. It will have its Second Reading in the Commons on Tuesday, and will pass through committee, report and Third Reading in that House on Wednesday.

The intention is that the Lords should complete all stages of the Bill on Thursday, so that it will receive the Royal Assent the same evening.

(February 23)

FILM MAKER SHOT IN NEW YORK

Daily Telegraph Staff Correspondent
NEW YORK, Monday.

ANDY WARHOL, 36, the so-called underground film maker, was shot in the abdomen and seriously wounded today in his New York office. Police are searching for a woman who appeared in one of his "pop" films.

Mr. Mario Amaya, 30, the American art critic and author who operates a gallery in London, was also shot but was released after treatment.

Mr. Warhol, one of the most prominent figures in the pop art scene in the United States, made his name with his painting of a tin of Campbell's soup.

(June 4)

EARTHQUAKE DEATH TOLL UP TO 20,000

By DAVID HARRIS
TEHERAN, Monday.

AS fresh earth tremors shook Eastern Persia today, the official death toll from Saturday's and yesterday's two earthquakes was put at 11,000, but it is believed to be more than 20,000, and the true figure may never be known.

At least 100 towns and villages have been devastated, 100,000 stunned, weeping people made homeless, and another 50,000 injured in the worst earthquake in Persia's history. Already rescue workers have buried 10,000 bodies.

Government rescue teams digging frantically in mud and ruins said today that the twin shocks had flattened 1,300 square miles of North-Eastern Persia "like an atom bomb."

Today's aftershocks shook the few still standing buildings but the growing army of rescuers ignored the danger in the race to find survivors.

Graveyards and hospitals are overflowing, and mass burial ceremonies have been held in dozens of villages and towns. Survivors are still being dug out of mud and rubble after being buried for more than 48 hours. Bodies, wrapped in white Moslem shrouds, stood in lines awaiting burial.

More than 5,000 people, from cabinet ministers to foreign tourists, queued to give blood. Thousands of medical students and doctors joined rescue teams from the Red Lion and Sun, Persia's Red Cross organisation.

TOWN FLATTENED
60 die at hospital

The township of Ferdows, badly hit on Saturday, was completely flattened yesterday. Two thousand more people were killed including some 60 survivors from Saturday's shock, who were trapped in an emergency field hospital.

(September 3)

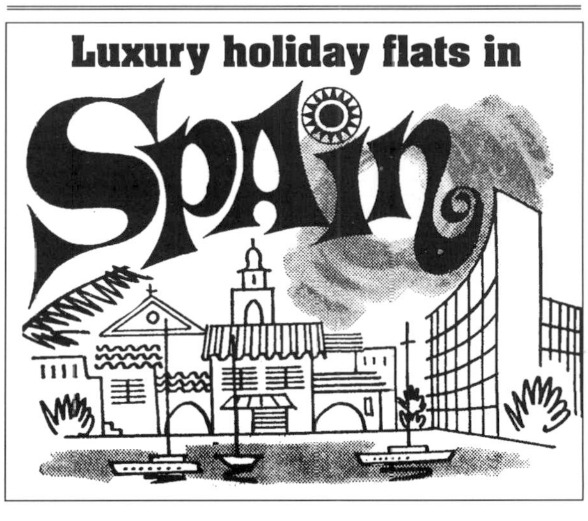

PRINCE PRAISES 'NO PAY' GIRLS

Daily Telegraph Reporter

PRINCE PHILIP said yesterday that the decision by five typists to work an extra half-hour a day for Britain without pay was "the most heartening news I have heard in 1967."

In a telegram to the girls' firm, Colt Heating and Ventilation, of Surbiton, Surrey, Prince Philip added: "If we all go into 1968 with that spirit we shall certainly lick our problems and put this country well on its feet again. Good luck and keep up the good work."

Employees at two Portsmouth firms, both in the Cope Allman group, have joined the "work for Britain" movement.

Ten engineers and three office workers at Greeneco will do an extra half-hour for no pay, and 40 factory workers at Aluminium (Portsmouth) have also agreed on an extra half hour.

Colt will send to firms joining the campaign thousands of lapel buttons bearing a Union Jack and the words "I'm backing Britain." Colt's Amalgamated Engineering Union workers at Havant, about half the 500 employees there, will consider today whether to join the scheme.

(January 1)

COLONY'S END 'IN SIGHT'

By MICHAEL FIELD
PORT STANLEY, Falkland Islands, Thursday.

LORD CHALFONT wound up his visit to the Falkland Islands today with a final meeting with the Executive Council, the colony's governing body.

He was loudly applauded at a public meeting in the town hall last night as islanders read out their questions, some of which were quite barbed. Generally, Lord Chalfont, Minister of State at the Foreign and Commonwealth Office, has carried the day. One local official, however, asked: "Can he really be satisfied that he has been applauded too much?"

He answered his own question: "Doesn't it mean they simply haven't understood that whatever we want, it means the end of the colony is in sight?"

Lord Chalfont had told his audience of 500 that they should think carefully about their future and when they say they want to be British they should be quite sure they know what this means today and not think of Britain as she was in 1900.

(November 29)

ARTHUR FOUND ON DOORSTEP

By Our Crime Correspondent

Arthur, the television cat, was found last night. Mr. T.D. de Gray, television agent for Mr. Toneye Manning called police to his home in King's Gardens, Kilburn, where he said Arthur had been left in a box on his doorstep.

He found the box, he added, after someone had knocked on the door. Earlier Mr. Manning, an actor, was committed to prison for contempt of a High Court order that Arthur should be given back to Spillers, the pet-food manufacturers, pending an action over ownership.

(March 1)

Vitality plus a desire to flout standards

By W.A. DARLINGTON

LAST night at the Shaftesbury, in the middle of the first act of "Hair," somebody - I think one of the performers, who were running about all over the place - handed me a yellow paper on which was printed a cabbalistic design in red.

This, when more closely examined in the lights of the interval, proved to bear the words "Be-in Be-in Be-in Yip Yip Yip Yip Yip Yip Yip."

Well, if that was intended as advice I needed it, for I have seldom been more out of anything as I was of this production. Obviously I am the wrong age for it and possibly the wrong nationality. For this is the youth of America expressing itself in very American terms.

To me the whole evening was a complete bore. It was noisy, it was ugly, and quite desperately unfunny.

It tried hard. A young man took off his trousers and handed them to somebody in the front row of the stalls and my reaction was very much what Queen Victoria's might have been.

As for the much-discussed nudes, there were some bare-looking skins at one point in the shadows at the back of the stage, but if that's all it amounts to some people are going to be very disappointed.

Some people obviously were disappointed for one reason or another, for the piece had what is usually called a mixed reception - cheers and boos. It is very much that kind of show; it will please the King's Road and upset the respectable suburbs.

Since I find it personally uninviting, let me at least try to weigh up the reason for the cheers.

The company have enormous vitality and a great sense of rhythm, and their concerted dancing carried them along very effectively. This, added to their infantile desire to flout established standards and be shockingly outspoken, may earn them a success. But I doubt it.

(September 28)

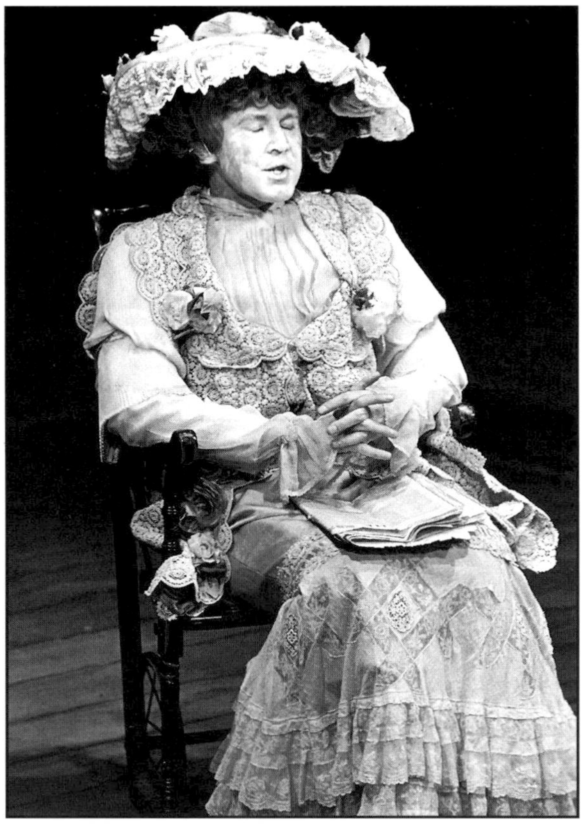

GRANDES DAMES: Alan Bennett in his own play "40 Years On" at the Apollo

Brilliant first play's survey of history

By JOHN BARBER

THE new play-cum-revue "40 Years On" at the Apollo Theatre is both a funny-satirical and a melancholy-nostalgic survey of English social life in the past half-century.

As might be expected of Alan Bennett, who wrote it and plays in it, the wit is affectionate, dry, smutty, donnish and penetrating - rather in the manner of his contributions to "Beyond the Fringe." By any odds it is a remarkable first play.

Its structure is complex. The claustrophobic scene throughout is the assembly hall of a public school, significantly named Albion House, on parents' day. Here with many interruptions, boys and masters perform disconnected sketches written by the new liberal-minded headmaster. Much of the material outrages the retiring head, played by John Gielgud.

These playlets move back and forth down the years, from the Boer War to VE Day, with many lark-about interruptions from a score of youngsters brilliantly drilled by Patrick Garland, the director.

Gielgud dominates all with an unexpected caricature of a mincing pedant, his noble features blurred so as to mimic a fussed and fatuous egghead. From the great mandarin of the theatre, a delicious comic creation.

It all builds into a potted history of England in comic strip. Alan Bennett stars in some of the funnier episodes; as a Wildean dowager; as an excruciatingly embarrassed sex-instructor; and as a man's man straight out of "Sapper."

One recalls Coward's "Cavalcade," which was a more spectacular and less bookish blend of story, song and fierce patriotism. For through all this show's sniggers and cocking of snooks a mood rises like a miasma; of regret for lost ideals, and of bitterness for today's shoddy standards.

(November 1)

£5,000 for best British novel

A £5,000 prize for the best British novel, by far the largest literary award in Britain, was announced yesterday by the Publishers Association and Booker McConnell. It will be open to writers in Britain, Ireland, the Commonwealth and South Africa.

Announcing the Booker Prize for Fiction at the Café Royal yesterday, Mr. Peter de Sautoy, chairman of the Publishers Association, said that it was "an exciting and important day for British books - by which I mean British authors and publishers."

It is hoped that the prize will attract as much publicity as the Prix Goncourt in France which is directly worth less than £5 but which enormously stimulates sales of the winning book.

A short list of about six possible winners will be released six weeks before the final decision is made, with the intention of stimulating the sort of public speculation - if not intrigue - which is so fashionable with the Prix Goncourt in France.

The first panel of judges consists of Dame Rebecca West, Stephen Spender, Prof. Frank Kermode and David Farrer. The chairman will be W.L. Webb, literary editor of the Guardian.

Booker McConnell have guaranteed the prize for the next seven years.

(October 4)

Images of our Time

By TERENCE MULLALY

ANDY WARHOL has done a lot of things. They have helped to make him, for the really with-it people, a cult high priest of the moment.

This is not surprising, for some of his activities are remarkable, like making a six-hour film about people asleep, in which nothing happens, or being the presiding spirit behind a Lower East Side club that is not only way-out and fashionable, but is actually enjoyable. But then, that is in New York!

Now Warhol of the dark glasses, the capitalist beatnik, has his first one-man show in London, and this is the oddest thing of all that he has done. New York, Los Angeles, Buenos Aires, Milan, Turin, Stockholm, Hamburg, he has had exhibitions in them all, and not in psychedelic nightclubs, and they seemed acceptable. Not so London.

Nor does Bruton Place, where his one-man show is at the new Rowan Gallery, appear the most suitable setting. There is little to prepare the visitor for Warhol in this quiet mews, a stone's throw from Bond Street, where the garage doors are opened while the Rolls Royces are washed down.

The end of Bruton Place from which the approach to the Rowan Gallery had really better not be made is Berkeley Square. The old grace has gone, but there is still enough of proportion, and shade from the centre of the square, where everything is placed just right.

This first London one-man show is no underground exhibition. It consists of 22 heads, all much larger than life-size. Twelve are of men wanted by the New York police, ten of Marilyn Monroe. At once Warhol plays a disconcerting little joke. The heads of the wanted men look like blown-up photographs, those of Marilyn clumsy paintings. It turns out to be the other way round; the wanted men are paintings, the heads of Marilyn prints.

In both series Warhol is at pains to deny all those little niceties of painterliness and craftsmanship, all those respectful references to the long-hallowed, that provide comfort.

(March 16)

Satire on Dunkirk spirit

By SEAN DAY-LEWIS

WHAT was the Dunkirk spirit so often invoked since by politicians with bad news? Partly, no doubt, the nervous sense of humour of "Dad's Army," a new comedy series by Jimmy Perry and David Croft which opened on BBC-1 television last night.

The series revolves around a unit of the Local Defence Volunteers, later to be known as the Home Guard, formed in 1940 to help with the defence of a small South Coast town against Hitler's impending invasion.

There was an excellent start with the recent "Back Britain" movement and some symbolic Union Jacks and swastikas. As the Walmington volunteers assembled, Messrs. Perry and Croft showed a real gift for satire.

The result was often funny, particularly in the sequence where the new recruits were each greeted by the self-appointed commanding officer (Arthur Lowe excellent here) and signed on. But at other times the humour was laboured.

Much trouble has been taken to get the documentary details right, and the inevitable voices of Vera Lynn and Bud Flanagan were to be heard. But were German tanks so heavily armed and were "Itma" catch-phrases in such general use as early as 1940?

(August 1)

Colin Davis to succeed Georg Solti

COLIN DAVIS, 41, is to succeed Georg Solti as music director at the Royal Opera House, Covent Garden, in 1971.

Mr. Solti, 56, will leave at the end of the summer, Mr. Davis taking up his duties in the autumn of 1971.

In the Royal Opera House's report for 1967-68 the directors state: "If we are to be able to meet inescapable increases in our costs we are bound to look for further increases in our revenue, both from public funds and from house receipts."

Despite a £1,150,000 grant from the Arts Council the excess of expenditure over income was £11,439, less than 0.5 per cent. of total expenditure.

The idea of reducing the numbers employed was rejected as it gave no scope for significant savings. To cut back the number of international singers would be "A disastrous mistake," as Covent Garden was now a great international opera house.

(December 20)

150,000 GREET ENA SHARPLES

A crowd believed to be 150,000 strong blocked the streets of Adelaide tonight when Violet Carson, Ena Sharples of the television serial "Coronation Street," arrived by road from Melbourne. Rose petals were thrown before her car and bouquets thrust at her.

(March 11)

BUDDY RICH'S BAND EXCELS

The present moment in time seems auspicious for a prediction that big bands are on their way back into jazz. The Don Ellis Orchestra created a seismic tremor when it visited Britain in August and this month the Buddy Rich Big Band has been doing the same.

His new band, fierce and hard-working, bears the stamp of these early great swing bands. The mawkish sentiment to which many of them were prone has been stripped away. The band is a pared-down, streamlined version of all the music Rich himself has been associated with in the past.

(October 7)

MORECAMBE & WISE RETURN IN COLOUR

After 13 years' absence, Morecambe and Wise returned to BBC television last night. They had the laughter of the millions who watched them regularly on ITV and put them to the top of the ratings to restore any confidence they lost when their previous BBC series flopped.

They also had colour, which will be vital in any intention they have of becoming international TV stars, with the sale of this BBC-2 series abroad.

(September 3)

'Light Brigade' as a social disaster

By PATRICK GIBBS

AS with so many films on historical subjects so with Tony Richardson's "The Charge of the Light Brigade;" it may well be more conducive to enjoyment to forget anything one happens to know.

Perhaps I should not have read some time ago Cecil Woodham-Smith's wonderfully well-organised account of events leading to the Battle of Balaclava in "The Reason Why" - which is mentioned in the credits as providing only "additional source material."

Having done so, I found myself comparing the construction of Charles Wood's script unfavourably.

But not immediately. For its first half the film provides a pictorial feast with a view of mid-Victorian England divided sharply into two classes, rich and poor, that seems to owe more to Disraeli's novel "Sybil" than to history; and indeed the fictional element is strong.

Indeed, with the action moving from England to the Crimea the film seems to find itself in difficulties of exposition to which the parodies of political cartoons of the period introduced at this stage draw attention rather than provide a solution.

The battle itself I found especially disappointing because here is a field in which the film director can easily do better than the writer.

As it is, the camera fails to make clear the all-important difference in fields of view between Cardigan at the head of the Light Brigade in the valley and Raglan on the heights 600ft above.

So Cardigan's or rather Lucan's mistaking the guns that they were ordered to attack goes pretty well unexplained - they couldn't see them, whereas Raglan could - and while the charge itself is caught with much realism (though I missed the guns to right and left) it loses much interest and excitement, to my mind, from being viewed in general terms as a social rather than military disaster.

(April 13)

A Diseased Society

By David Floyd

Cancer Ward, Part 1.
By Alexander Solzhenitsyn.
(Bodley Head. 30s)

Alexander Solzhenitsyn first became known to readers in the west through the appearance in 1967 of his "One Day in the Life of Ivan Denisovich." Because that was primarily an exposure of the evils of the Stalinist prison camp system, and because Khruschev, the great "de-Staliniser" was still in power, "Ivan Denisovich" appeared first in Russian.

Solzhenitsyn has not been so fortunate with this later work, "Cancer Ward," written since 1960 and completed last year. Though it was accepted for publication in Tvardovsky's Novy Mir and even reached the stage of being set in type, it was never published in Russia.

In "Cancer Ward" Solzhenitsyn takes a much broader canvas than he did with "Ivan Denisovich." His subject is the whole of contemporary Soviet society and the people who compose it. It is set in the year 1954 or 1955 — a period of maximum uncertainty in the Soviet Union, when Stalin was already dead but before the course of events in the post-Stalin era had begun to take shape.

The cancer ward itself is a device for presenting people close to death and conscious of their mortality and so more prone to reveal their true selves. It serves also as a symbol for the diseased body politic of Soviet Russia itself. In this setting Solzhenitsyn paints a series of highly realistic portraits, of which the most striking and damning is that of Rusanov, the Party official, in whose nasty, mean character so much of "Soviet life" becomes visible.

(September 19)

Spain Wins Eurovision Song Contest

Spain won the Eurovision Song Contest, televised from the Albert Hall on Saturday night, in a photo-finish with the United Kingdom, which came second. Only one vote separated the leaders and there was a dead heat when the moment came for the last of the international juries, Jugoslavia, to give its verdict.

To increase the suspense the Jugoslavs made a mistake and registered 11 votes instead of 10. When this was sorted out Spain was the winner with 29 points against 28 for Britain and Cliff Richard's spirited onslaught on "Congratulations."

(April 8)

Sex pictures to illustrate new Bible

Anyone complaining about the violence and sex portrayed in an exhibition of pictures in a gallery in Dover Street, Piccadilly, must be referred straight back to the Bible.

For the 650 works, commissioned by the Oxford University Press from 22 artists are for its new edition of the Old Testament.

John Bratby, of "kitchen sink" and sunflower fame, makes no bones about depicting accurately the lines from Job: "Man is borne of woman. He cometh forth like a flower." He makes it a sunflower, of course.

(October 5)

Beatles find their film feet

AT last the Beatles have found their film form. The secret seems to be to keep them off screen. They do not appear in "The Beatles Yellow Submarine" until the very last minute and their appearance is not very funny. But the film itself is.

Not since Disney's "Snow White" or "Make Mine Music" has a full-length animated film cartoon come upon us with such surprising skill and charm and freshness as this inventive little epic.

Naturally, the Beatles are heard. They sing quite a few songs, several of which are new; and their voices, with those flat Liverpudlian vowels, contribute vitally to the fantasy.

But they themselves are only drawn - and very cleverly drawn - as creatures in a weird and witty world of Lewis Carroll-type doings; and as animated figures, each with his droning voice, they are able to enter more wholeheartedly into the wilder extravaganza.

The Beatles' spirit is here, if not the flesh; their good-natured gusto, their kindly curiosity, their sympathy with their fellow men and their lack of pretentiousness are all summed up here with gaiety.

One of the richer moments in a well to-do film comes when the definitive intellectual, The Nowhere Man, joins their adventures. These have to do with a grotesquely conducted war between a nation which likes music, happiness and love and a nation which hates all three. That is, Pepperland v The Blue Meanies.

(July 17)

John Lennon's wife granted decree

Mrs. Cynthia Lennon, wife of John Lennon, 28, the Beatle, was granted a decree nisi in the Divorce Court yesterday because of her husband's adultery with Yoko Ono Cox, the Japanese artist.

(November 9)

THE DAILY TELEGRAPH
AND
MORNING POST
DAILY TELEGRAPH - - - JUNE 29, 1855
MORNING POST - - - NOVEMBER 2, 1772
[Amalgamated October 1, 1937]
135, Fleet Street, London, E.C.4.
Telephone: Fleet Street 4242

FRANCE IN ERUPTION

AN intellectual and economic revolt has gripped France. To the mutiny of the students and the swiftly spreading strikes may be added a host of obscure grievances that have erupted all over French life. Television, the Opera Comique and the Cannes Film Festival are all infected in varying degree. Niggardly State salaries, repressed wage claims, censorship and discrimination are the sores long endured. When President DE GAULLE left for Rumania a week ago, patrician government seemed to have lost its imperturbable front, to have faltered and been found out. The mess to which he returns is far worse than that which he left behind to his Ministers. For whatever reasons, he hesitates to talk to the nation. He has instead held something like a conseil de guerre. The upshot is to be "reforms but not fouling the bed." A fine de Gaullesque sentiment. Unfortunately, the bed is already fouled.

President DE GAULLE is remembered by the British chiefly as the stern old man who has repeatedly refused them entry into the Common Market. How are the mighty reduced in size! But to wish him to be swept away in this sort of violence and hysteria is to think like the Trotskyists, the anarchists and the Communist Revolutionary Youth. No good would come from that to France, to Europe or to Britain. Frenchmen will rally to him again, rather than accept the prospect of total anarchy. The reforms, however, will have to come in many walks of life. They will affect niggling censorship, bureaucracy, police methods and patronage. But meanwhile there must be a real attempt to restore order.

(May 20)

ENOCH'S LOGIC

MR. POWELL'S speech was very carefully worded. It is the duty of his critics to read it just as carefully, and to note precisely what he did not say, as well as what he did. In particular, we must note that he called for a programme of repatriation of immigrants which was not only organised, financed and subsidised but also voluntary. We must not therefore accuse him of directly advocating compulsory repatriation.

Yet we are entitled to ask him a question. What if his voluntary policy were to be put into effect and did not have any significant effect? Would he just shrug his shoulders, shut up and give up? This would surely be the wise and humane course. Yet how could such a course be reconciled with the extreme or even disproportionate importance which he attaches to the presence here of immigrants, who cause, in his view problems not to be endured or passively watched? His own logic should lead him to the advocacy, in circumstances by no means remote or improbable, of a measure of compulsory repatriation.

There are people, who think it a mistake to have admitted so many immigrants, who would think it worse than a mistake now to deny, as Mr. POWELL seeks to deny, what we have solemnly promised - the entry of their wives and families. There are things other than the presence of immigrants which cannot be endured or passively watched.

(November 18)

SPONGING ON THE STATE

MR. CROSSMAN may find that he has stirred up a hornet's nest. He says that the man living by choice on social security payments is "not doing anything morally or legally wrong. He is fully taking his rights as a citizen." Already Sir FREDERIC BENNETT has said that he will ask the Prime Minister for an explanation when the Commons reassembles. And recent polls have suggested an increasing public impatience with people who will not work and are, in effect, subsidised by their fellow citizens.

Nevertheless, it is essential to distinguish between what Mr. CROSSMAN actually said and what he ought to have said. This is, indeed, not a moral issue. We take the world as we find it and every citizen has the right to maximise his income - whether it be from the State or from elsewhere - just as he has the undoubted right to minimise his tax bill. A widower, say, with six children may actually be doing the best by his family by staying at home and minding the house.

Yet all this is in a sense beside the point and it is a great shame that Mr. CROSSMAN never really got to the point. For surely it is the duty of the State to create conditions in which it pays people to work.

(September 7)

SICK FASHIONS

VIETNAM is not forgotten. The dying soldiers, the maimed children, the political prisoners in the last agonies of torture — all can take solace from the fact that their sufferings are being elegantly commemorated in the expensive Paris salon of M. YVES ST. LAURENT, one of the most high-minded of contemporary fashion designers. This year he has decreed that his clients should wear black in mourning and, no doubt, in vicarious penitence for the tribulatins of the Vietnamese. The sacrement is to be honoured in innumerable creations suitable for all occasions (anyway M. ST. LAURENT also decrees that no occasion differs from another). It is to be delicately blended with other fantasies of perennial appeal — as in a transparent black chiffon "cat-suit" on which a few ostrich feathers perform the traditional function of the fig leaf.

M. ST. LAURENT, of course, is not breaking new ground in using his art as a vehicle of social and political commentary. Throughout the ages couturiers have delighted in such exercises which lend "significance" (and maybe even "importance" as well) to a profession which the vulgar might otherwise be tempted to despise as trivial or even unmanly. Such devices for reconciling complacency with a reputation for concern are often welcome to the rich. To others they must seem like mocking and insolent parodies of the human condition.

(July 9)

MR. NIXON AND THE NEW AMERICA

By VINCENT RYDER

WASHINGTON.

AS almost anybody will tell you, the United States is going to hell on roller skates today, just as it was 10 years before that and has been at regular intervals for almost 200 years.

Ten years ago, if I recall correctly, the trouble was a bovine admass of a people guided by organisation men in grey flannel suits, saddled with an apathetic younger generation, and the lot led by political dullards; the bland leading the bland.

But that was long ago. Now America is deemed heading for perdition because everybody is in revolt against something, almost all organisations are in disrepute and the country feels it has been led into a mess by a politician in the White House who was too clever by half.

The puzzle about Mr. Nixon is whether he has settled for administrative competence or has some sense of the social forces running loose in America and intends to play a positive role in re-ordering the country to conform with new ideas. It is not the same country or the same world that it was when he was Vice-President under Eisenhower.

Patriotism is questioned, money-making is a practice but no longer an ideal, Communism is no longer regarded as some invisible poison gas that will seep through the keyhole if you don't watch out, the bottom of the social heap is heaving and simple praise of the American way of life tempts derision.

No group has more emphatically turned against the old assumptions than the children of white, middle-class America. Some of their parents agree with them but a lot more do not and a lot of working people who have managed to do quite well share the resentment at all this new uncertainty. These are the "forgotten Americans" Mr. Nixon appealed to in his election campaign and they are people who will see his Cabinet as a decently representative bunch of people.

Perhaps Mr. Nixon has guessed that most Americans want peace and quiet while they sort themselves out and perhaps he is right. Whether he can keep things peaceful and quiet is another matter. At least in his choice of a corporation lawyer as Attorney-General he has not gone for the kind of door-busting, headcracking man that the angriest Americans, those who voted for George Wallace, would have liked.

In a difficult exercise, Mr. Nixon may manage to harness a new mood that is building up in the country: for reform but against chaos.

Even among people who feel that serious changes in American attitudes are inevitable and desirable - and they include people who a decade ago would have been pillars of authority and respectability - there is a feeling that too much attention has been hogged by self-publicists and pseudo-leaders in the ghettos and the universities.

There was a telling moment the other day at San Francisco State College when Prof. Hayakawa, a renowned expert in semantics and the meaning of words, tore the wiring out of loudspeakers being used by student rebels. There may be a lot more of that sort of thing in the next few months.

There is one thing that Mr. Nixon can do that will satisfy the great majority of Americans, at least until the diplomatic bill has to be paid. That is to wind up the Vietnam war as soon as possible.

He has left himself fairly free of commitments on terms on which to negotiate, but it must be as obvious to North Vietnam as to anybody else that it would now be politically impossible to work up American support for continuing the war on a large scale if negotiations went badly.

It is equally clear that for a long time Americans will not support another Vietnam war or anything that looks remotely like dragging them into one.

There are uncertainties on every side in American foreign policy under Mr. Nixon, apart from the central fact that the mood of his country will not allow him to take risks, such as a strong attitude on the Nigerian war, and will make him think more than twice before responding to challenges to American influence in Europe, the Middle East and Asia.

What he would like to do is to arrive at an understanding with Russia that would avoid direct confrontations, see Britain move into a unifying Western Europe, keep the lid on the Middle East for four years in Asia that would end unilateral American responsibilities.

The chances of everybody else in the world co-operating are not very great. It is pretty much what President Johnson wanted to do and we know how far he got.

(December 14)

Military Apathy in Vietnam

By CLARE HOLLINGWORTH

SAIGON

"WE thought you were the ice cream coming in," the American corporal shouted in a disappointed tone above the roar of the helicopter engines as we landed at the old French fort - a hilltop landing zone commanding Highway Nine between Khe Sanh and the Laotian frontier.

Living conditions are austere here, but the role of these air mobile forces is interesting and varied.

The men told me they rarely listened to the news; when they had radios they tuned them to pop music and when their newspaper, the Stars and Stripes, arrived, five or six days after publication, they looked first at the cartoons - Dick Tracey and Denis the Menace - and then turned to the sports pages.

The lack of interest in the course of the war is in strong contrast to that of American troops in World War II. Men were then deeply interested in why and how they were fighting; this is not so today. Of course, there are many exceptions, and the soldiers in the Northern Tactical Area - the Air Cavalry and the Marines - naturally have a higher morale than the troops around Saigon or on the line of communications, where almost every sentence opens with the number of months, weeks and days - sometimes even hours - they must serve in Vietnam before the blissful moment when they leave for "Stateside."

Hawkish Set

However, there is among every group of officers and NCO's - especially among the Marines - a hawkish set who would like to bomb more villages, burn more forests and napalm more mountain-sides. They resent criticism and the fact that the public in the United States is not 100 per cent. behind the war. They are bitter, too, that Britain is not an ally. The doves tend to talk in whispers away from the crowd; they are often youthful intellectuals and supporters of Bobby Kennedy.

Among the soldiers everywhere there is widespread cynicism and a majority appear to believe President Johnson delivered his "Neither-seek-nor-accept" speech as part of a well planned campaign to get back to the White House.

It is most unlikely that the Americans will mount any more serious operation than the routine searches for arms which have been in progress under a variety of names for the past three years, until the peace talks have taken place or the prospect abandoned.

(April 18)

PREFABS HERE FOR YEARS

The prefab, that familiar utility stop-gap bungalow introduced to relieve the acute housing shortage at the end of the war, is likely to remain for some years to come, some housing officials say.

Many authorities still have sizeable numbers of prefabs, despite the fact that in the immediate post-war period it was widely believed that the prefab was "not here to stay."

The optimists thought it would have a short life of about ten years. But today there are still something like 40,000 of them, many 23 years old, in England and Wales.

(November 25)

MEN FORCE WOMAN BUS DRIVER OUT

A Corporation's busmen yesterday voted to "bar" a woman from driving their town's buses. But she beat them by earlier quitting her job because of insults she says she received from her workmates.

For 18 months Miss Brenda Armstrong, 30, has been a conductress on Great Yarmouth's buses. Last week she qualified to drive double-decker buses and heard other busmen say they would strike if she got behind a steering wheel.

(July 1)

Heat jams Tower Bridge

Daily Telegraph Reporter

THE South-East roasted in the hottest day for seven years yesterday. But other parts of Britain battled against heavy flooding, which blocked roads and storms with hailstones as big as gold balls.

In London even Tower Bridge found it too hot to work. It was opened up to let a ship through. The metal expanded several inches and one arm of the bridge would not slot into place.

Police closed it to traffic for more than two hours during the rush-hour last night as firemen played hoses on the metal in an effort to cool it. Capt. Charles Gosling, the Bridgemaster, said: "I don't think this has happened in the last 20 years."

At Wimbledon, St. John Ambulance Brigade dealt with a record 550 cases, mostly of heat exhaustion and sunburn.

In Central London, temperatures rose steadily throughout the day; Compared with Sunday the figures were:

	3p.m.	6p.m.	8p.m.	10p.m.	1a.m.
Y'day	89F	84F	81F	77F	72F
	(32C)	(29C)	(27C)	(25C)	(22C)
Sun.	77F	77F	77F	75F	72F
	(25C)	(25C)	(25C)	(24C)	(22C)

At Heathrow Airport the temperature reached 90.5F (32.5C).

There were cries of "No!" from the Conservative benches in the Commons when Labour M.P.s wanted to adjourn or remove their jackets.

Girls walk out

Workers in several factories walked out because of the heat, including 30 girls at the Turkish Delight department of Frys factory near Bristol. The chocolate began to melt.

The day began with cars and houses covered in a fine dust, said to be sand carried from the Sahara and Southern Spain.

Then came hailstones, hailstones "the size of golf balls" were reported from Minehead in Somerset. They damaged cars.

Torrential rain brought floods, especially in Yorkshire and Lancashire and the West of England. Again enormous hailstones were reported three and a half inches in diameter, at Burnley.

(July 2)

CARS GO FREE IN BR MINI-TOURS

The cheap mini-tour tickets which British Rail are making available for passengers with cars to the Continent, starting today and returning up to Tuesday, involve no payment for the car. The return fare of £20 16s represents the fare for four adults or two adults and four children.

(August 30)

LONDON DAY BY DAY

JOHN BETJEMAN who has edited the Shell county guides either solely or jointly since 1934, has resigned because Shell insisted on deletions from the latest one.

This, as I mentioned on Monday when Faber published it, covers Northamptonshire and the Soke of Peterborough. It was written by Lady Juliet Smith, Lord Birkenhead's daughter, and I quoted her comment that the great opportunities offered by the post-war upsurge of building had been "tragically wasted" and the aesthetic standards of most new housing estates were "extraordinarily low."

But Shell drew the line at her categorising individual buildings as ugly, for fear of causing offence in the county. Such delicacy seems to me curious, considering how much frank condemnation of modern architecture is printed nowadays.

Biters -

DANIEL COHN-BENDIT, the Nanterre university student leader, became a victim yesterday of his own revolt. Arriving at Orly to board a plane for Berlin he was pained to learn that all flights were cancelled.

But for an extra £12 10s he was told, he could take a bus to Brussels and fly from there "Too expensive for me," said the rebel, and went away in a huff.

- Bit

French and foreign journalists returning to Paris after de Gaulle's visit to Rumania took part above the Tyrolean Alps in a unique trade union meeting.

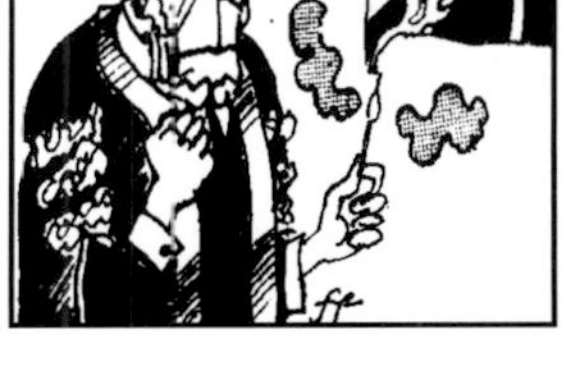

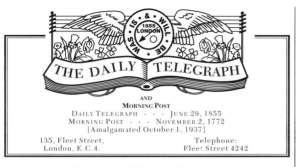

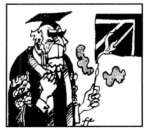

Their pilot suggested that Orly should be asked to let the plane land there to show solidarity with the strikers. This was carried by 23 votes to nine, the foreign Press not being allowed to vote.

Unfortunately, Orly control said no and the plane had to land at Basle. Its passengers reached Paris nearly two days after the President - and a little disenchanted with solidarity in an all-night bus ride.

Betjeman and Shell Part: Thrifty Rebel

The Rape of Bloomsbury

THOSE who love Bloomsbury, as architecturally civilised a region as any captial city can show, had better take a last look at it before its unique character is finally eroded.

Rugby School failed in its assault on Great Ormond Street, but the larger part of four streets and a mews between there and Gray's Inn Road are now to be pulled down to make way for a GLC school.

London is thus losing more fine Georgian houses with many handsome details - doorways, staircases, railings and so on. They certainly needed attention but they need not have been allowed to deteriorate.

Perhaps the saddest part of this massacre is that it is being carried out in the name of education, the process begun years ago by London University further to the west.

PETERBOROUGH

In the boutiques of Rome: real beauty and bright ideas

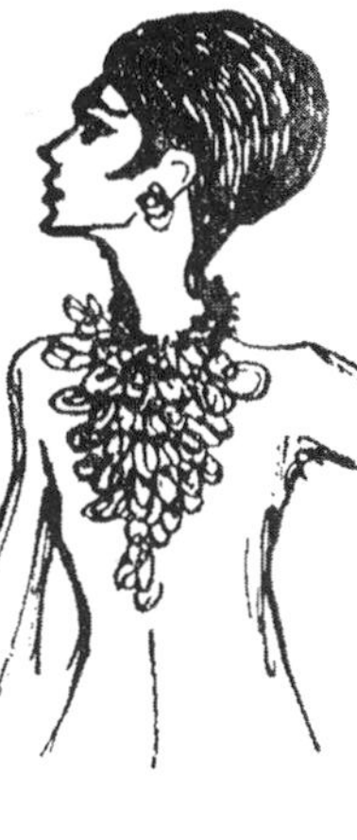

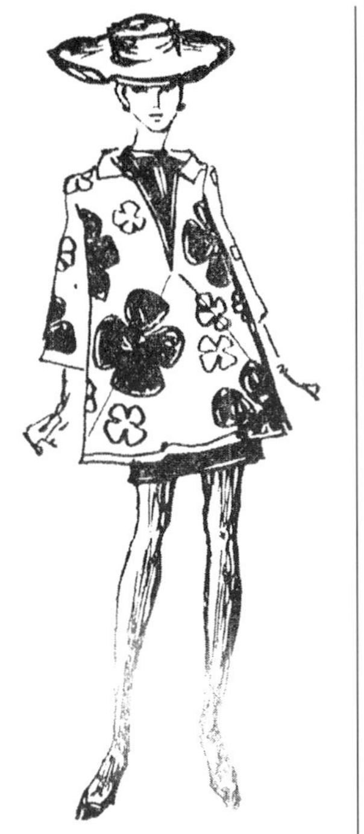

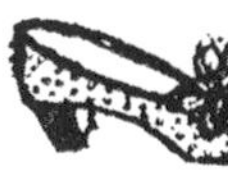

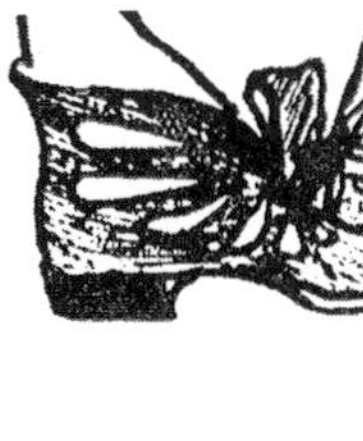

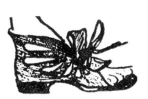

ROME'S boutiques offer as much beauty and news as her couture and many women prefer to shop or lift ideas from them.

La Mendola perched enviably on top of the Spanish Steps draws wealthy tourists as well as Roman elegants and was started there four years ago by two talented Americans, Michael La Mendola and Jack Savage.

Debenhams have started to buy dresses to copy from them. Accessory ideas are worth trying too, such as a stretch knit evening shoe sewn all over with crystal beads with nodding bouquet of crystal loops over the toe.

New winner is a V-shaped necklace, a solid triangle bristling with crystal bead loops and opaque circles like Smarties. This sets you back 50,000 lire and looks terrific on a plain yellow crepe evening dress.

Man's sandal in rustic leather with cut-outs and ankle lacing recalls imperial Rome.

Newest men's beach shirts are skinny and hug the body, an effect emphasised by hand-printed stripes to give an illusion of slimness.

(January 15)

Power flowers

IT may be bouquet garni for the boys (great new menswear colour being bayleaf), but for women it's just plain bouquet. Flowers are back in a big way and I do mean big.

The spring sensation is going to be the flower-printed gaberdine from the trendsetting Nattier fabric firm in Turin used in Riva's nine-tenths tunic coat over navy dress, sketched above.

Those pressed flat flowers look like a steal from a child's colouring book and Nattier call them "naive flowers." They come in red, navy and curry on a white ground for some of the prettiest coats and suits in Italy. First seen this weekend they'll be blooming here all week at the shows and again in Paris.

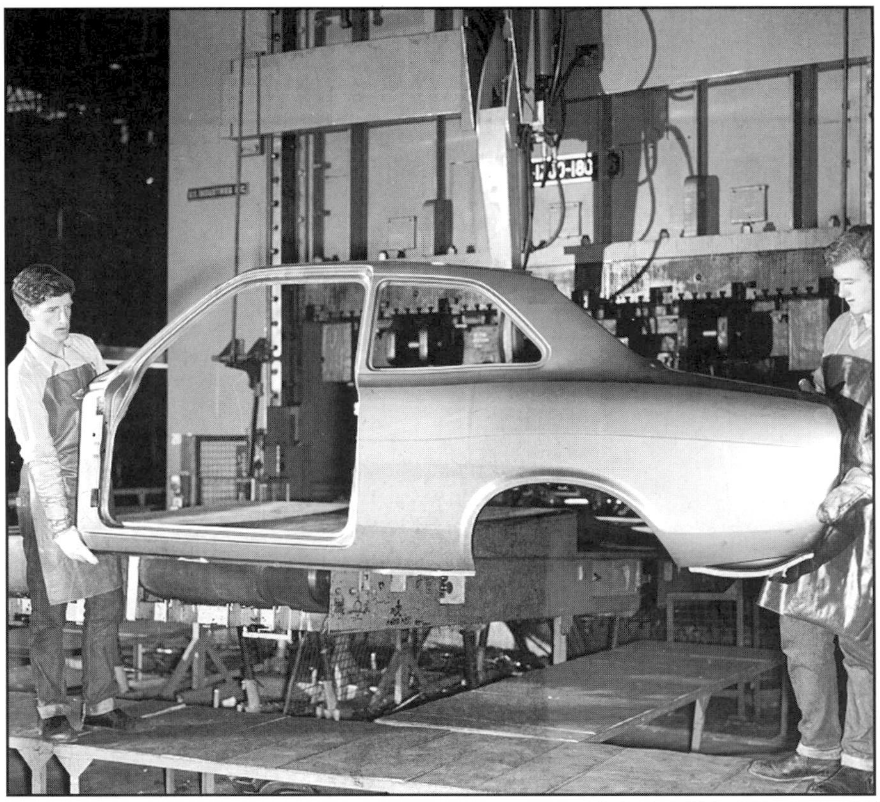

Escort Takes Over from Anglia

By JOHN LANGLEY

THE year's first important model change from a British manufacturer comes out today from Ford, with a range of small cars named Escort. It replaces the Anglia series and marks the disappearance of a model name associated with Ford for 28 years.

Like its predecessors, the Escort is a basically conventional two-door saloon, but it offers a choice of four engines, with extra performance, more room and new refinement at most competitive prices.

Advanced production techniques have been introduced at the Halewood plant, near Liverpool, where all Escorts will be made to make the new models particularly suitable for assembly overseas - for example, the body sides are pressed out as a single unit. Escorts will be assembled at the German Ford plant in Ghent, Belgium, to reduce the effects of the Common Market tariff barriers.

Ford say they have designed the Escort to continue basically unchanged as an international car far into the 1970s. One of the most interesting aspects of the new range is that it reinforces the trend away from the production of really small cars by British manufacturers.

BMC with its Minis, and Rootes with the Imp are left to fight it out in the smallest car category. On the face of it, this seems a considerable gamble by Ford, as Britain's second largest manufacturer.

The Ford reasoning is that for a relatively modest increase in original cost, their bigger small car can offer much better value in terms of accommodation and performance, without seriously increasing operating costs. This, the Ford planners say, is what the bulk of the public wants.

The most obvious target of the Escort is Vauxhall's Viva, the car which was the British industry's success story of 1967. It is remarkably similar in concept to the Viva, although the broad design of the Escort was settled some 18 months before the new-type Vauxhall went into production. It will also compete with the BMC 1100-1300 models and the Triumph Heralds.

FORD ESCORT PRICES (including delivery charges);

Escort de luxe (1100) £635 including £118 purchase tax; Escort Super (1100) £666 including £124 tax; Escort 1300 Super £691 including £129 tax; Escort GT £765 including £143 tax; Escort Twin Cam £1,080 including £201 tax.

Engines: 1,098 cc. 4 cylinder, 49.5 (net) bhp; 1,298 cc. 4 cylinder; 59.5 (net) bhp; (GT version, 71 bhp net).

(January 17)

Those matador pants are dandy - if you can stop breathing!

CREEPING up the King's Road the other day in a pair of pink slacks that belonged to the greyhound I share a flat with - I was searching for a pair of my own - it struck me that there is nothing more elusive than trousers which are a perfect fit.

I realise that there are girls shaped like greyhounds and girls shaped more like basset hounds, and expecting both to fit into the same pair of slacks with the same success is lunacy. But to judge by some slacks I've tried on, only a strange moon creature would find them at all possible.

Trousers which end way above our ankles do nothing for the leggy look we seek, nor do trousers with such deep-cut seats that they must have been made for Humpty Dumpty. And haven't we all met pairs which don't seem to allow for the fact that thighs have flesh on them?

"Then why bother with trousers at all, if they don't seem to do much for you - nasty, unfeminine things anyway," I can hear the stalwart anti-trouser brigade crying out in triumph.

I reply that slacks are an integral part of my lazy weekend kit, that when I go on holiday I am sometimes careless enough to acquire sun-satiated fiery legs which I must cover up Short of wearing ankle-length skirts, trousers seem to be the only answer - and for boats, planes, trains, hectic walking or idle pubbing they are often the most useful things to wear.

On this particular shopping spree I visited 10 shops before I lighted on a pair that pleased me. I found them in an unlikely man's shop at unexpected expense.

While trouser suits are having quite a quiet summer (the exceptions: styles with short nipped-in battledress jackets or matching waistcoats) rails of independent trousers have become much more exciting and the signs are that this will continue into winter, especially in evening separates. Simon Massey, for example, have about six different black crepe trousers to go with their black crepe waistcoats and jackets.

The newest trouser shape is high-waisted, matador-pants style. But unless you happen to be a lean, low-waisted girl, I should treat them with caution; they demand a silhouette free of a midriff bulge or an excess of bottom and even then it's best if you don't bend or sit, and keep your breathing shallow. Still, they do look good on the right girl.

Also popular this summer: Oxford bags with turnups, and trousers with buttoned matelot panels in the front. But anything goes as long as they are cut straight or flaring.

NICOLA HEMINGWAY

(July 23)

IN AFGHANISTAN: SEARCH FOR 'TRUTH'

"OUT, OUT,' shouted the receptionist to my guests at Spinzar Hotel, Kabul. And I got my first taste of the hippie invasion of Afghanistan.

After a nine-hour bus journey from Peshawar, West Pakistan, I was waiting in the foyer for two boys, both far from being hippies, who had travelled with me. I'd asked them over from their "dry" hotel for a drink before dinner.

Bathed, hair washed, beards trimmed after our dusty trip in scorching heat - 112 degrees - they had changed into immaculately clean blue tunic-style shirts with one line of embroidery, bought during their travels. One wore clean jeans, the other shorts. To the hotel, this dress meant "hippie."

In vain I said that they were dressed just like my own strictly non-hippie sons, dressed like any other young people travelling light in a hot climate. Foiled and thirsty, we went off to the Khyber Restaurant, patronised by both tourists and hippies.

An Afghan Government official tells me that his country is now planning further restrictions to keep out the long-haired drug addicts who often become beggars in the streets of Kabul.

"We insist that they must have enough money to maintain themselves before we give them visas valid for one month only, after which time all must report to the police. But once they are in, they hide their money, or spend it all at once. Then what are we to do?"

Some end up in gaol, guilty of smuggling offences. Some sell themselves or their girlfriends, particularly easy if they are blonds. Some are repatriated.

At the British Embassy I heard of the young girls who come to Kabul, searching for religious truth, or drugs - or both - but all claiming to be escapees from the materialist West.

Nearly all come from upper- and upper-middle-class families. Daddy is usually busy making money. Mummy in, say, Majorca. Neither parent seems to care that daughter is slowly killing herself in Kabul.

And sometimes not all that slowly. With poor food, dirty needles and syringes, the addict's life expectation is short.

Since prying journalists are not welcome, I went there claiming to be searching for a fictitious nephew. A dazed-looking British boy said I could look round for him. In the shady garden a transistor radio was playing Beatles' music.

Sitting on ancient bamboo chairs or cross-legged on the ground were about 30 young men and women.

All were long-haired, some wearing jeans and shirts, a few in dirty white robes with beads and bracelets. The girls were dirtier than the men, their hair matted.

They talked very little to each other. A hookah was passed round, most taking a pull at it, and the sickly sweet smell of hashish rose in the evening air.

Paula Walton

(August 2)

WOMEN MAY BE CUSTOMS OFFICERS

Women Customs officers are likely to be appointed in the future as a result of reorganisation proposals now under discussion by the Customs and Excise Department.

Until now women have never been recruited among the 5,000 Customs officers or the 3,500 preventive officers, although 25 women clerks have been employed as women search officers when women travellers are referred for investigation.

(May 20)

BIG RISE IN COWBOY BOOT SALES

NEW YORK, Monday.

A BIG increase in the sale of cowboy boots was reported today by the Wall street Journal. They are being ordered from firms in Texas not only by authentic cowboys but also by stockbrokers, actors and politicians.

Because of their growing popularity, they are now being mass produced. Custom-made boots cost at least £40 but some, decorated with precious stones, are worth £500 and more.

The Tony Lama Company of El Paso says that its sales have increased from about £400,000 a year 10 years ago to £2,500,000 a year. Sam Lucchese, of San Antonio, has among his customers Governor Winthrop Rockfeller of Arkansas, Gregory Peck, John Wayne, Bob Hope and Zsa Zsa Gabor.

But he has lost President Johnson because Mr. Lucchese disclosed Mr. Johnson's peculiar foot measurements, explaining: "When a shoe is big enough in one place, it's too small in another place. It's like having a size 12 in the front part of the foot and a size 11 in the back."

(April 16th)

'INSULTED' MISS SPAIN QUITS COMPETITION

Miss Spain, Senorita Maria Amparo Lorenzo, 19, withdrew last night from the "Miss World" contest because, she claimed, her neighbour, Miss Gibraltar, had "insulted" her and her country.

Mr. Claude Berr, European organiser, said that Miss Gibraltar, Sandra Sanguinetti, 18, had, according to the Spanish Press, said she was glad Spain had an entrant to oppose her as that indicated they recognised Gibraltar was not Spanish territory, but British.

The televising of a parade of the girls in national costume was put back for an hour. But Miss Spain refused to be coaxed from her hotel room. "This is a national scandal," she said.

(November 12)

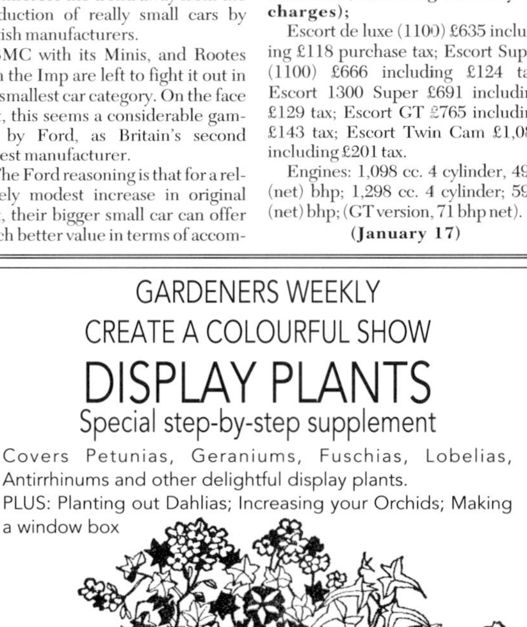

Helen Keller beat deafness and blindness

MISS HELEN KELLER, who died at Westport, Connecticut, on Saturday, aged 87, was one of the world's most remarkable women. Mark Twain described her as one of the two most interesting characters of the 19th century, the other being Napoleon.

Despite total blindness and deafness, with consequent dumbness, in infancy, she lived to become a cultured and charming personality. She worked unselfishly all her life for her afflicted fellow-creatures.

Although she lived for so long in a darkened and silent world of ideas and ideals, based only on touch, taste and smell, she graduated from college with a B.A. degree, could read four languages and was a distinguished author.

She "listened" by placing her hand gently on the throat or lips of the speaker and while she could speak slowly and gutterally she usually preferred to transmit her thoughts by the quick flutterings of her fingers.

Her other senses became more highly developed with the passage of time. She could eventually recognise what part of London or New York she was in by the distinctive odours and "smell" the trade of people introduced to her such as farmers painters, or mechanics.

She learned to feel vibrations through her feet. Sitting in a hotel lounge, she liked to assess the character and personality of passers-by by their manner of walking. In the words of one of her friends, she demonstrated the "almost illimitable power," of the human will.

LOVING COMPANION

Miss Sullivan's work

When she was six her parents engaged a young woman, Miss Anne Sullivan, in an attempt to train her. Thus began a loving companionship which lasted for 50 years, although at first the terribly handicapped child was completely intractable.

Miss Sullivan finally attracted her interest by teaching her the names of objects which she touched in the manual alphabet. From this she graduated to Braille and then to writing. At the age of 10 she learned how to speak orally although at this, not unnaturally, she was never completely successful.

Miss Sullivan remained her constant guide and companion through school and college, patiently interpreting by means of the manual alphabet the various lectures and the contents of textbooks.

In 1914 another girl, Miss Polly Thompson, had joined her as helper, and when Miss Sullivan, who became Mrs. Macy, herself began to suffer from failing eyesight, Miss Thompson assumed the role of visual and oral interpreter. She died in 1960. Miss Sullivan had died in 1936.

TRAVELLED WIDELY

Trips to Europe

Miss Keller, who was associated with many organisations concerned with the welfare of the deaf and blind, travelled widely in her efforts on behalf of her fellow-sufferers, even when she was over 70.

She made several trips to Europe, during which she met the late King George V and Queen Mary. In 1946 she had a long audience with the Queen, now Queen Elizabeth the Queen Mother. In 1955 she met Sir Winston Churchill.

In 1965 Helen Keller was named one of the 10 greatest living American women for the Women's Hall of Fame at the New York World's Fair.

(June 3)

YOUSSEF BEIDAS

Mr. Youssef Beidas, founder of the Intra Bank, Beirut, died in Lucerne, Switzerland, yesterday, aged 66. Last May he was transferred to a clinic for an operation and recently had a relapse.

Intra, one of the Middle East's biggest banks, closed its doors in October, 1966, after running out of cash to meet large withdrawals. It later reopened.

(November 3)

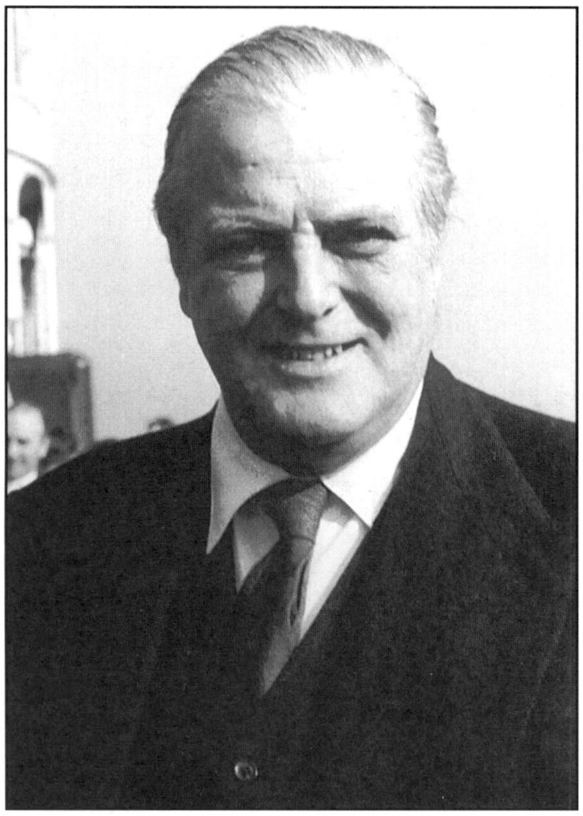

RANDOLPH CHURCHILL, WRITER & POLITICIAN

MR. RANDOLPH CHURCHILL, who has died aged 57, was Sir Winston's only son. A man of charm and a writer of talent, he gave full rein to a tempestuous nature which kept him well in the limelight. It also led him into endless controversy.

He suffered to the full the disadvantage of being the son of a notable father and shared with that father a Whig ancestry which precluded both from happy and uncomplaining association with any of the political parties of the last 75 years.

Mr. Churchill's career in no way paralleled his father's; he took part in seven elections and was only once returned, when unopposed.

Educated at Eton and at Christ Church, Oxford, he entered the political arena at the age of 24, when he contested two Liverpool divisions. Wavertree and West Toxteth, as an Independent Conservative in the same year.

PRESTON'S MP

Unopposed in 1940

As a Conservative, he contested Ross and Cromarty in 1936 before his return unopposed for Preston in 1940. He retained the seat until 1945.

In 1938 he was commissioned as a second lieutenant, Supplementary Reserve, in his father's old regiment, the 4th Queen's Own Hussars.

After the outbreak of war he served as a Commando at home and in the Middle East before joining GHQ Middle East as a GSO (Intelligence) in 1941.

In 1944 he parachuted into Jugoslavia to join the staff of the British Mission to Marshal Tito's army. He was one of the Allied officers who escaped with Tito to the mountains when their headquarters were raided by German parachutists and airborne troops a few months later.

How far Mr. Churchill's reports convinced his father that Tito should be backed by the Allies must remain uncertain. Both agreed that "politics is the art of the impossible," and the reputation of both must be judged accordingly.

Defeated at Preston in the 1945 General Election he stood unsuccessfully for Devonport in 1950 and again in the following year.

In recent years he had become a familiar, and not universally popular, figure on television screens. In mellow mood he was a polished and attractive broadcaster, but on occasions he irritated many viewers who telephoned their complaints to the BBC.

In America in 1958, he created a storm by rounding on his interviewer, John Wingate, after questions that he considered were too personal.

The suggestion in the play, "The Soldiers," by Rolf Hochhuth, that Sir Winston was responsible for the death of General Sikorski, the wartime Polish leader, was called "a bloody lie" by his son in an interview in "The Frost Programme" on ITV in October, 1967.

He featured in several court actions. In 1956 he was awarded £5,000 against the People newspaper for libel, and in 1960 £1,500 for slander by Sir Gerald Nabarro. In 1963 he secured perpetual injunctions against the magazine Private Eye.

In 1963, the News of the World to which he contributed, declined to print, without cuts, an article he had written about Mr. Wilson. Mr. Churchill later published it as a full-page advertisement in Tribune.

His was a strange career. The vast shadows of Blenheim Palace have sometimes inspired and sometimes defeated the members of this powerful family.

(June 8)

Wally Grout

WALLY GROUT, one of the greatest of Australian wicket-keepers, died last night in Brisbane at the age of 41. he played for his country 51 times.

Born at Mackay, Queensland, on March 30, 1927. Arthur Theodore Wallace Grout first played in state cricket in Australia for Queensland in 1946 but was not capped until 1957 against South Africa, when he succeeded Don Tallon.

He toured England, South Africa, India, West Indies and Pakistan and he claimed 187 victims (163 caught 24 stumped) in Test cricket, a total second only to that of T.G. Evans, Kent, who took 219 in 91 matches.

Grout twice made eight dismissals in a Test. and his six victims in an innings, all caught in the 1957-58 series in South Africa set a Test record.

He also holds the world record for catches in an innings, dismissing eight Western Australia batsmen in February, 1960, at Brisbane.

As well as being one of the finest wicketkeepers of modern times he possessed a sense of humour which made him one of the characters of the game.

(November 9)

Sir Donald Wolfit, actor and manager

SIR DONALD WOLFIT, the actor and manager, who died in the Royal Masonic Hospital, London on Saturday, aged 65, played many memorable parts on the stage. His stirring performance of King Lear was one of the highlights of his career.

He had been called "the last of the actor-managers" and he will be remembered for his work in taking Shakespeare to audiences all over the country and various places overseas.

In his autobiography, "First Interval," he showed himself as a schoolboy grimly determined against all odds to get himself on to the stage, as the young man joyously abandoning his job as a schoolmaster because a chance had presented itself to join a touring Shakespearean company.

He made his debut as Biondello in "The Taming of the Shrew" at the Theatre Royal, York, in 1920. His first London appearance was in 1924 as Phirous in "The Wandering Jew," with Matheson Lang. In 1927 he joined the Sheffield Repertory Theatre.

He later joined the Old Vic and the Stratford memorial Theatre. In 1937 he formed his own dramatic company and toured as Hamlet, Shylock, Macbeth and Malvolio.

After the war Wolfit made many overseas tours, including visits to Canada and the United States. He also gave distinguished performances in modern plays including those of Shaw and Ibsen.

"COSTUME" ACTOR

Born too late

W.A. DARLINGTON writes: Donald Wolfit was an actor of outstanding emotional power, who belonged in spirit to an earlier generation.

To my mind, he was the best King Lear we have seen; and to say that is indeed to say something, for it is a part in which we have seen many notable performances.

Also, he was the most striking Volpone that I have seen, bringing to the part a sardonic humour all his own. Solness in "The Master Builder" was notable also - the best thing I ever saw him do - in what may be loosely called modern dress.

(February 19)

WALTER H. SHIERS

Walter Henry (Wally) Shiers, sole remaining member of the first crew to fly from England to Australia, died in Adelaide yesterday. He was 79.

Mr. Shiers was one of two mechanics in the Vickers Vimy aircraft flown by the brothers, Sir Ross Smith and Sir Keith Smith, in 1919.

The aircraft left Hounslow on Nov. 12 and landed in Darwin on Dec. 10. The Vimy, still in perfect condition, is displayed in the Memorial Building at Adelaide Airport.

(June 3)

Hancock found dead in flat

SYDNEY, Tuesday.

TONY HANCOCK, 44, the comedian, was found dead by a friend today in a flat in the Sydney suburb of Bellevue Hill. The police said a post-mortem examination would be held.

Police said Hancock was found dead in bed in his pyjamas. There were no suspicious circumstances but a bottle of tablets was being examined.

Tony Hancock won wide popularity as a television, radio and screen comedian in Britain. He will be best remembered for his success on television, but had not appeared in any series of his own for some time.

In his radio programmes of the 1950's he created his hilarious world of distorted realism which centred on domestic strife at Railway Cuttings, East Cheam.

Later he scored a major success with Sid James in the television series "Hancock's Half-Hour."

(June 25)

PRINCESS MARINA

SORROW at the death of PRINCESS MARINA, Duchess of Kent, will be neither formal nor restricted. She herself, while never lacking the dignity expected of Royal persons, always preferred informality - indeed, she presented a rare combination of elegance, grace, humour and charm.

Those who knew her well, and this circle extended far beyond those in any way attached to the Court, greatly appreciated the breadth of her interests, the sincerity which she brought to personal friendship, her unfailing readiness to amuse and be amused.

When she married the late DUKE OF KENT in 1934, the sentimental public regarded her as a fairy princess. When the Duke was tragically killed in 1942, she again aroused in many hearts a kind of sad romance. She herself, with sterling courage, took over many of his tasks.

PRINCESS MARINA carried out her public duties with the devotion expected from one of her status. She did so, however, with a high degree of individuality which at once removed any hint of wooden formality.

It is rare indeed that a Royal Princess should exhibit so natural a talent for culture in such varied forms, and rarer still that she should so impeccably combine taste with public duty. "Rare" is probably the best description of PRINCESS MARINA. It goes without saying that she was much beloved throughout the Commonwealth and beyond. But, during her life, her rarity went largely unperceived because it was always unobtrusive. She will be sorely missed.

(August 28)

'VIAN OF THE COSSACK'

ADML. OF THE FLEET SIR PHILIP LOUIS VIAN, who will always be remembered as "Vian of the Cossack," has died at his home near Newbury, Berks, aged 73.

The famous cry "The Navy's here!" with which 299 British seamen were freed from the German supply ship Altmark in Jossing Fjord, Norway, in February, 1940, became a national catch phrase.

Sir Philip revealed in "Action This Day," his war memoirs, that the cry was made by the then Lieut. Bradwell Turner, who was the leader of the destroyer Cossack's boarding party.

The Altmark affair was a minor happening in the great pattern of Britain's war at sea, but it came at a time when the Royal Navy was suffering reverses and Allied shipping losses were mounting at a frightening rate.

Sir Philip, then Capt. Vian acted under Admiralty orders, notably those of Winston Churchill as First Lord.

He set out to intercept the Altmark after hearing from the Admiralty that the enemy supply ship had passed Bergen steaming eastwards, and after receiving a signal from Adml. Sir Charles Forbes, C-in-C, Home Fleet: "Altmark your objective, act accordingly."

The Altmark was said to have removed her guns and seemed to Norwegian observers an innocent tanker making for neutral waters. She was reported to have on board the crews of British merchantmen sunk by the German rocket battleship Graf Spee.

After assurances from the commander of Norwegian torpedo boats in the area that three searches of the Altmark had revealed no prisoners. Capt. Vian asked the Admiralty for further instructions. He was told to board the Altmark, free the prisoners and hold the ship.

Resistance was overcome, and the prisoners were found under locked hatches in the holds. When these had been broken open, Lt. Bradwell Turner called: "Any British down there?" He was greeted with a shout of: "Yes we're all British." "Come on up, then," the lieutenant said, "The Navy's here!"

In the Japanese war he took part in the operations off Sumatra as Commander of the British Pacific Fleet's Aircraft Carrier Squadron.

He was appointed KBE in 1942, KCB in 1944 and GCB in 1952. He received the DSO in 1940 and Bars in 1940 and 1941.

He was C-in-C., Home Fleet from 1950 until 1952, when it was announced that the Queen had approved, as a special case, his promotion to Admiral of the Fleet supernumerary to the establishment of Admirals of the Fleet, in recognition of his "distinguished and outstanding services during the last war."

(May 29)

FRANCHOT TONE

Franchot Tone, who died yesterday in New York, aged 65, was a brilliant actor in many outstanding Hollywood films in his "perfect gentlemen" roles.

He was equally known for his tempestuous marriages and love affairs, and feuds with gossip writers.

The older generation will remember his impressive performance in the original "Mutiny on the Bounty," with Charles Laughton, Clark Gable and Dorothy Lamour, shown in 1936, and with Gary Cooper in "The Lives of a Bengal Lancer," in 1935.

His career in Hollywood and on the Broadway stage spanned almost 40 years. Four times married, his wives were the actresses Joan Crawford, Jean Wallace, Barbara Payton and Dolores Dorn-Heft.

The most sensational real-life romance came in 1951 just before his third marriage. He was the loser in a fist fight with Tom Neal, another actor, for the affections of Barbara Payton, but he won the girl.

(September 19)

Mervyn Peake

Mervyn Peake, the author and artist, has died at Burcot, Oxfordshire, aged 57, after a long illness.

For more than 10 years he had been unable to write or paint as the result of a progressive brain disease.

Although he worked in many media, Peake's great talent lay within the pages of a book.

(November 19)

JIM CLARK

JIM CLARK, who has died, aged 32, after an accident in a car race at Hockenheim, Germany, was considered by many knowledgeable students of motor racing to be one of the greatest drivers of all time.

Twice he won the world championship. In four attempts at the classic Indianapolis 500 Miles Race he finished twice in second place and once in the lead - the first non-American ever to be placed, let alone win, the event.

There have been world champions to whom the title fell more than twice. Fangio was the holder no fewer than five times, and Brabham held the title on three occasions. But Jim Clark won his world championship crowns in the most decisive manner.

On the first occasion, 1963, he won no fewer than seven of the events which counted towards the championship, and became the youngest driver ever to win the world title. In that same year he finished a brilliant second, beaten by the cruellest luck, at Indianapolis, driving the smallest engined car in the race.

His victories in top class international events, in both Formula and grande tourisme categories, were legion, but it was not only his total of wins that impressed; the manner in which they were won - the apparently utterly relaxed, and polished style of his driving - helped to create the reputation of being "the greatest."

(April 8)

GAGARIN, FIRST SPACE PIONEER AND ENVOY

By Dr. ANTHONY MICHAELIS
Science Correspondent

COL. YURI GAGARIN, 34, the world's first spaceman, who was killed yesterday during a training flight, orbited the earth on April 12, 1961, in a Vostok spacecraft.

His one-orbit trip lasted 108 minutes. He never made a second space flight, although he played a leading role in training the Russian cosmonauts who followed him.

He was awarded the title of "Pilot Cosmonaut of the Soviet Union" and received the Order of Lenin from Mr. Khruschev in a triumphal ceremony in Red Square, Moscow, three days after his flight.

A funeral commission has been set up to arrange his burial in the Kremlin Wall, the most honoured burial place in Russia.

The full details of his space flight have never been revealed. Unlike all American space flights, the Russian flights end on land, instead of in the sea.

The day after his landing Col. Gagarin described how it felt to be in space. "Everything was easier to perform. Legs and arms weighed nothing."

Objects moved about inside Vostok's cabin and he sat suspended above his chair, gazing in admiration at the beauty of the earth while floating in a black sky.

"I ate and drank and everything was like on earth." He had no feeling of loneliness.

Col. Gagarin, a Communist party member and son of a collective farmer, was promoted from major to colonel after his flight. he was appointed Commander of the cosmonauts and played a key role in recruitment and training.

A stock, modest and friendly man, he travelled the world as a Russian goodwill ambassador and a propagandist for Russian space and scientific achievements. In December, he attended the opening night of a Moscow tour by the Royal Shakespeare Company.

Col. Gagarin and his wife, Valentina, a doctor, have two daughters, Yelena, 9, and Galya, 7.

(March 29)

Crazy Gang member Bud Flanagan

BUD FLANAGAN, who died in hospital at Kingston, Surrey, yesterday aged 72, was one of the original members of the London Palladium Crazy Gang, and was famous for the song "Underneath the Arches."

He was a favourite performer of the Royal family and appeared in many Royal Command performances.

In recent years he was in partnership with Mr. Jack Solomons in the betting shop business. His voice was heard recently on BBC television as the singer of the theme song, "Who are you kidding Mr. Hitler?" in the series "Dad's Army."

It was Bud who gave Britain its first two 1939-45 war hit songs, "Run, rabbit run" after an air raid on the Orkneys was said to have resulted in the death of only one rabbit, and "We'll Hang out our Washing on the Siegfried Line" during the "phoney war" period of 1939-40.

Business bad

Had Mr. Flanagan and his then partner, Chesney Allen, gone ahead with a plan they made in 1931 the public would not have known either as idols of the music hall. Business was so bad that they planned to become greyhound racecourse bookmakers.

They changed their minds, and their success in the Crazy Gang made them stars.

Flanagan was a Crazy Gang stalwart until he was more than 60. He appeared in the Gang's farewell show, "The Young in Heart," which opened at the Victoria Palace in December, 1960, and ran for 824 performances.

During the 1914-18 war he served in the Army in France, where he was wounded and gassed. In lean times after the war he took up taxi-driving and even boxing.

Author and composer of many popular songs, his biggest song hit, "Underneath the Arches," was dashed off in a Derby Hippodrome dressing room in 1926. It was not published until 1932.

(October 21)

Lise Meitner

Prof. Lise Meitner, who died in Cambridge yesterday, aged 89, was an Austrian Jewess whose brilliant mathematical brain helped to unveil the secret of the release of atomic energy.

At one time head of the physics department of the Kaiser Wilhelm Institute, Berlin, she was conducting research there when she discovered the tremendous energy which could be released when the uranium atom was split.

(October 28)

George Papandreou

MR. GEORGE PAPANDREOU, whose death at the age of 80 was reported in later editions of The Daily Telegraph yesterday, was former leader of Greece's Union of the Centre party and Prime Minister from February 1964 until July 1965.

He had been under house arrest on and off since the Army seized power in April, 1967.

His downfall as Prime Minister followed differences with King Constantine which started a chain of political crises ending in the coup. Outside politics there appeared to be a common regard between him and the King.

Political crisis

The discovery in 1965 of the clandestine organisation Aspida (Shield) led to a political crisis and the fall of Mr. Papandreou's Government. Mr. Papandreou resigned after the King had refused to give him the Defence Ministry, and his Centre Union party launched a campaign accusing the King of trying to rule rather than reign.

Mr. Papandreou had been harassed by rumours that his son, Andreas, was implicated in the Aspida plot.

Born at Kaledzi, Patras, he studied law at the University of Athens and political and economic science in Berlin.

Twice imprisoned

He was twice imprisoned and suffered exile. Following an article he wrote in 1921 calling on King Constantine's grandfather to abdicate he was sentenced to 18 months by court martial. After serving four months he was released, the conviction having been overruled by the Review Court.

In 1942 he was imprisoned by the Italians after taking an active part in the national resistance movement. He escaped to the Middle East in April, 1944, becoming Prime Minister in a two-man Government.

(November 2)

Sir Herbert Read, poet

Sir Herbert Read, who has died, aged 74, was the provocative, yet persuasive spokesman for the avant garde painters, sculptors, artists and writers of the 1930s.

His comments on men and affairs were sometimes scathing but he yet inspired an affection that found expression on his 70th birthday, when gifts valued at £10,000 were piled on a table at the Arts Club.

These included original works by Henry Moore, Ben Nicholson, Barbara Hepworth, Joan Miro and Maxwell Fry.

(June 13)

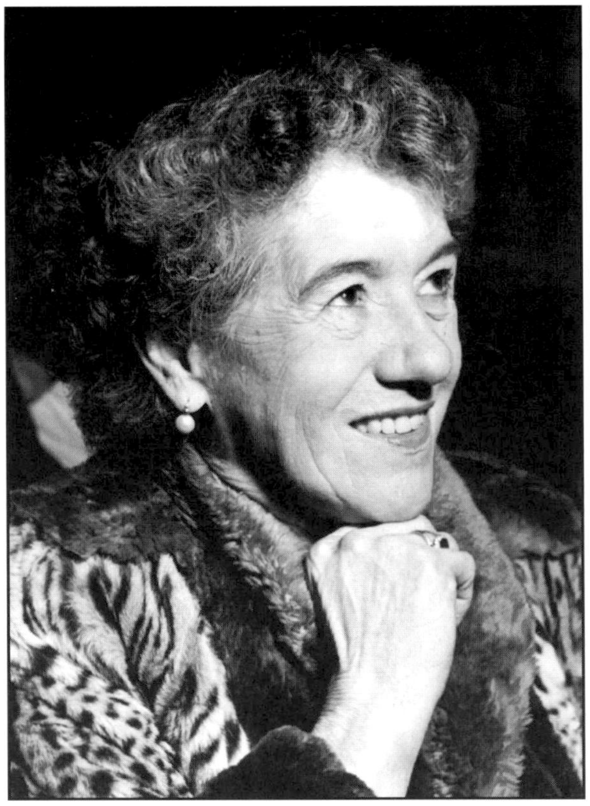

Enid Blyton, creator of Noddy

By DAVID HOLLOWAY

ENID BLYTON, the most prolific and successful of all children's writers, has died in a Hampstead nursing home after an illness of several months. Her age was uncertain. Although some reference books give it as 68, she was believed to be 70 or 71.

Half affectionately and half derisively, her two best-known creations, Noddy and Big Ears, have become as much part of the national myth as Winnie the Pooh, Peter Rabbit and Peter Pan.

The Noddy stories alone have sold more than 11 million copies and Miss Blyton stood third among British authors in the list compiled by UNESCO of most translated writers - only Agatha Christie and William Shakespeare stood higher.

Despite its immense popularity, Enid Blyton's writing was constantly at the centre of controversy in recent years.

Libraries' ban

Public libraries in various parts of Britain and in Australia, New Zealand and South Africa had banned her work as meretricious and trivial. School teachers also denounced it as educationally undesirable.

Yet she herself was much liked by anyone who met her, particularly children. It was indeed her very kindness, her spoiling of her readers that caused many adults to dislike her work.

She once said she liked to "take a child by the hand when he was three and walk with him all through his childhood."

The result was that although she wrote for children of different ages she was always firmly holding them by the hand, warning them of the dangers of difficult words and easing their way from full stop to full stop when they would have benefitted far more if they had been allowed to wander freely through books alone.

A great deal of nonsense has, however, been talked about the evil influence of Noddy, particularly the citing of Miss Blyton's characterisation of Gollywogs as being anti-Negro.

She did without doubt bring a great deal of pleasure. Hardly a child can have failed to go through an Enid Blyton phase when her writings seemed utterly riveting.

Happily most children leave this phase quite quickly and seek more solid reading fodder. Those who stay holding her hand start life shockingly ill-prepared for life or literature.

(November 29)

Ramon Novarro

RAMON NOVARRO, one of the great romantic stars of the early days of films, was found beaten to death today in bed at his Hollywood home. Police said there were signs of a desperate struggle, with bloodstains all over the bedroom and furniture broken.

His nude body was found by his male secretary when he reported for work at the house in Laurel Canyon.

Police said Novarro, aged 69, was apparently the victim of a robbery. The house had been ransacked. They thought Novarro had been reading or writing in bed when he was attacked. His spectacles were found smashed and near the body.

Born in Mexico, Novarro reached stardom shortly after he arrived in Hollywood in 1917. He started in the silent film version of "Ben Hur," and for the next 15 years anjoyed the adulation of women fans all over the world.

(November 1)

Steinbeck, winner of Nobel prize

JOHN STEINBECK, who has died, aged 66, was the American author of "Of Mice and Men," "The Grapes of Wrath" and "East of Eden." He was awarded the £17,700 Nobel Prize for Literature in 1962.

The citation announcing the award referred to his "realistic and imaginative writings, distinguished as they are by a sympathetic humour and a social perception."

He won the Pulitzer Prize in 1940 for "The Grapes of Wrath." It was about farm families who fled the dust bowls of Oklahoma and became migrant workers in California.

Steinbeck was acquainted personally with the under-privileged people he often wrote about.

He knew the Mexican and other foreign labourers in his native Monterey County, California, whom he wrote about in "Tortilla Flat," the labourers and strikers in "In Dubious Battle" and the itinerate ranch hands who figured in "Of Mice and Men," a controversial novel that was dramatised on stage and screen. The moral concerned the homeless lot of itinerant workers.

(December 21)

Anthony Asquith

ANTHONY ASQUITH, who has died in London, aged 65, was a Prime Minister's son who became one of Britain's most original film directors.

He directed Terence Rattigan's "The VIPs," which had its London premiere in 1963, with Richard Burton, Elizabeth Taylor, Orson Welles and other stars. He also directed "The Yellow Rolls-Royce," a very smooth vehicle, shown in the following year.

Mr. Asquith combined his film work with trade unionism. He was president of the Association of Cinematograph, Television and Allied Technicians and always anxious to improve the quality of television programmes. He was also a governor of the British Film Institute and a Fellow of the British Film Academy.

(February 22)

Mrs. Wallace

Mrs Lurleen Wallace, who has died from cancer in Montgomery, Alabama, aged 41, was elected Democratic Governor of Alabama in November, 1966, to succeed her husband, Mr. George Wallace, the arch-segregationalist.

Mrs. Wallace was as strong a believer in racial segregation as her husband.

(May 8)

Sir Harold Nicolson, writer & MP

By KENNETH ROSE

THE death of Sir Harold Nicolson at Sissinghurst Castle, Kent, yesterday aged 81, deprives English letters of a biographer and critic whose sympathy of judgment and grace of style endeared him to a wide reading public.

His life was also in turn devoted to diplomacy and politics. In both these fields he achieved some success mingled with much disappointment.

Perhaps the most enduring value of this buffeting experience was to enrich his writings with the humanity often denied the occupants of ivory towers.

Nicolson did not regret the abandonment of his first profession. Yet he was never to find a comfortable niche in the rigid framework of party politics. His conscience was too tender for him to join the pre-war Conservatives, while his experience of what was practicable in affairs of state made him shun the Socialists. In 1931 he unsuccessfully contested Combined Universities as a candidate for Sir Oswald Mosley's New party.

The loss of his Parliamentary seat in 1945 was a wound that never quite healed. Though he joined the Labour pary in 1947, he was found no place in either House.

What politics lost, literature gained. While still a diplomatist he had written works on Verlaine, Tennyson, Byron (dedicated of course to Venizelos) and Swinburne. He had also exploded "Some People," a seires of brilliant autobiographical essays, upon his startled colleagues.

He was now to produce during the next 20 years, several biographies and literary studies any one of which would alone have made a reputation.

He crowned them in 1952 with the greatest of his literary works, the official life of King George V. Later works - "Good Behaviour," "Journey to Java," "The Age of Reason" and "Monarchy" - did not add appreciably to his reputation. He was created a KCVO in 1953.

His family life was of sustained happiness. He was never separated from his wife for a single day without writing to her.

From the moment of her death in 1962 his health began to fail and his zest for life gave way to a resigned melancholy.

(May 2)

Virginia Maskell

Virginia Maskell, the actress, who has died aged 31, was well known on cinema and television screens. One of her film parts was as Peter Sellers's wife in "Only Two Can Play."

(January 30)

WAY OF THE WORLD

Revolutionary Trends

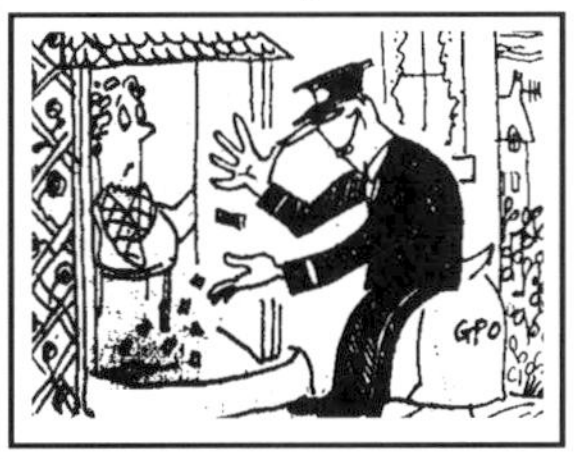

ONE of the leaders of the Leftist mob which demonstrated in London on Easter Monday, a young man wearing a military jacket and a red steel helmet, is said to be a fashion photographer by profession.

Is one more of my familiar nightmares coming true? Are such modish professions as acting, hairdressing and photography, which have long been getting more and more aggressive, hoping to take over the country altogether?

The violent sect of Leftist demonstrators seems to include many heterogeneous elements. There are Marxists of various brands, professional hooligans, military pacifists, anarchists (some of them neo-Luddites whose views on some things are not unlike my own). There are also elements of trendy smartness and of the Theatre of the Absurd.

Faced with this roaring, gaily-dressed mob, led by characters who look as if they came from unpublished passages of "Ubu Roi" or "Alice in Wonderland," the police, solid and sensible in their clean, old-fashioned uniforms, may well feel puzzled and at a disadvantage, and all the more angry for being so. Thus what might be kept on the level of rough farce turns too serious.

Would the authorities be wiser to oppose fantasy with fantasy? Shouldn't they form special squads of modish and fantastically dressed anti-riot policemen, waving their own nonsensical banners, rolling their own marbles and ball-bearing (much bigger ones, of course) beneath the demonstrators' heels, and hurling five shillings' worth of coins for every penny their opponents can muster?

(April 12)

Opportunity

AN article in Look magazine suggests that the way out of what it calls the "birth control and authority crises now raging throughout Roman Catholicism" is to elect a new Pope. He should not be an Italian, it adds.

Should he even be a Roman Catholic? Logically, the new Pope should not be white - he should be an African, perhaps, from one of the smaller "emergent" nations - with progressive humanist views on all subjects and for preference some kind of scientific training.

Such a choice would give almost unbearable satisfaction to progressive Catholics everywhere. It might even reconcile them to some of the encyclicals His Progressive Holiness would be churning out in due course.

(December 11)

True Blue

"WHEN I looked into the cloakroom today I counted 14 bags with airline tickets on them. They were for various countries - Rhodesia, South Africa, Greece, and mine is packed to go to East Germany" (Mr. R. Swain, Labour MP for North-East Derbyshire).

(April 10)

Peter Simple

RIOT STOPS PLAY IN TEST

COWDREY STRUCK BY BOTTLE

By E.W. SWANTON

KINGSTON, Jamaica, Monday.

POLICE used tear gas to break up a riot by spectators which halted play in the second Test match between England and the West Indies at Sabina Park, Kingston, today.

Trouble began when the West Indian batsman, Basil Butcher, was given out, to make the score 204 for 5 in the West Indies second innings with 29 runs needed to avoid an innings defeat.

There was uproar and bottles began to fly on to the pitch. Colin Cowdrey, the England captain was struck on the foot.

Cowdrey courageously walked to the boundary fence and appealed for calm. His move was in vain and bottles continued to fly.

Police carrying plastic shields to fend off the bottles moved into action. Gary Sobers, the West Indian captain, joined the appeals for peace and both he and Cowdrey had to retreat.

LOVELY CATCH
Behind wicket

Parks behind the wicket had just caught Butcher left-handed and low from a leg glance. It was a lovely catch that Butcher could see better than anyone. He walked before Sand Hue, the umpire, had given the decision.

Nothing happened until Holford, the next batsman got to the wicket. First a few bottles, then a larger number arrived from the popular side

Cowdrey at once appealed to the crowd. There were, perhaps, five minutes when with Sobers and the England players and police confronting the rowdy section, it seemed that the outburst would peter out.

Sobers shouted: "Butcher was out." But those bent on mischief were past hearing.

MORE BOTTLES
Crowd panic

Suddenly more bottles were thrown from another corner on the same eastern edge of the field. More police, first with shields and then with tear-gas, ran from their assembly point.

The order to throw the bombs was given and the crowd broke in panic and made off on to the field and out of the ground.

After a meeting between officers of the board, Cowdrey and Mr. Leslie Ames, MCC manager, and an inspection of the pitch and outfield by the captains, it was stated that the game would be resumed at four o'clock.

(February 13)

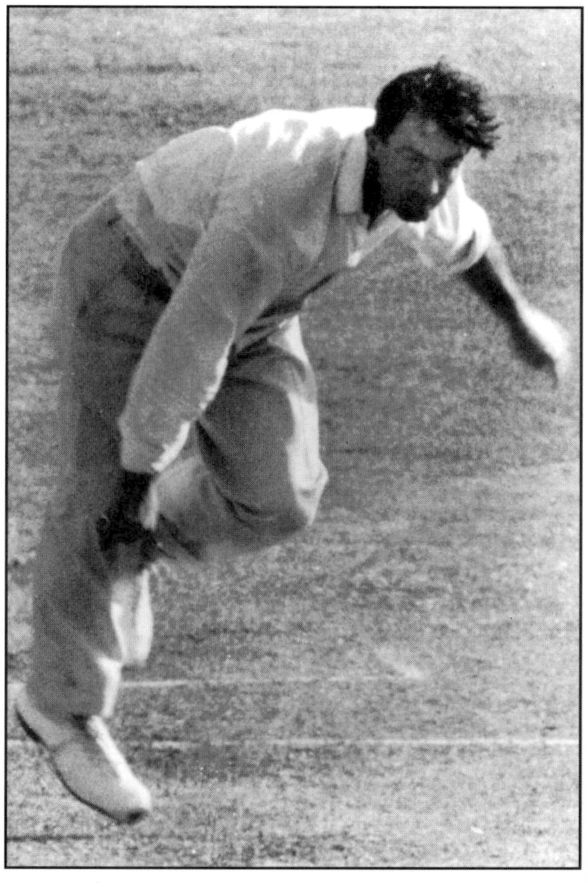

TRUEMAN'S RETIREMENT

THE END OF AN ERA

By E.W. SWANTON

THE Yorkshire chairman, Brian Sellers, yesterday annnounced the retirement from first-class cricket of F.S. Trueman, saying that: "Although it is with very great regret that we part with him, I am sure that in his own interests he has done the right thing."

So, within a few months of Brian Statham leaving the scene, cricket loses the other half of, perhaps, the most successful fast bowling partnership ever to have represented England.

"Freddie" Trueman will be 38 next February - a few months younger than Statham - and that is a ripe age for a truly fast bowler.

In terms of work done and results achieved, no one of comparable pace can match his figures: 2,301 wickets in all, a record 307 in his 67 Test matches.

Only 15 bowlers in history have a higher bag, and none was genuinely fast. Hence, the aptness of Trueman's remark when asked whether anyone will take more Test wickets. "Maybe" he said, "But whoever does will be bloody tired."

Not least, the personality of this rumbustious, explosive, unpredictable fellow, the extrovert of all extroverts, enlivened every game he ever played in, and sparked an answering warmth from the crowd.

One might well echo John Warr, who has written of him: "Cricket and the Anglo-Saxon tongue have been enriched by his presence."

(November 11)

MANCHESTER UNITED STORM PAST BENFICA

By DONALD SAUNDERS

Manchester United ..... 4 Benfica 1
(After extra time)

MANCHESTER UNITED hauled themselves up off their knees like true champions at Wembley last night, destroyed Benfica with three goals in the first 10 minutes of extra time and so became the first English club to win the European Cup.

Derby Day has produced many fine thoroughbreds over the years. None has been greater, I suspect, than the team that made manager Matt Busby's dream come true.

For 11 years Mr. Busby has been trying to get his hands on that elusive trophy. During the next 12 months he need only walk into the boardroom at Old Trafford to satisfy his wish whenever he chooses.

But, my goodness, I thought United were going to let the Cup slip from their eager grasp before their manager could get near it.

SAVAGE START
Graca equalises

After moving into control of a match, that began savagely and ended dramatically, they allowed Benfica to snatch the initiative towards the end of the second half.

With 10 minutes of normal time left, Graca equalised Charlton's 55th-minute goal. And the Portuguese champions began to play with the skill and rhythm that twice previously had earned them success in this great competition.

Twice Eusebio raced through a tired defence and let go shots that reminded us why he is Europe's ace marksman. But Stepney, who grew into a world-class goalkeeper last night, was there to save his colleagues from the defeat they did not deserve.

Despite our relief at United's escape, few of us were happy about their chances as they slumped wearily on the turf during the brief respite allowed them. Benfica looked like arrogant, storm-troopers eagerly awaiting battle, United like shipwrecked mariners.

How deceiving the eyes can be. Within three minutes of the restart, Busby's men had shown us just how great is the pride that has driven this club to the top through disappointment and even disaster.

Best, hacked and hustled out of the game for much of the previous 93 minutes, collected a header from Kidd, then slipped neatly past a desperate tackle. Calmly he strolled round Henrique, before placing the ball in the net with the nonchalance of a practised driver, parking the family car in the garage.

(May 30)

SOBERS AND HALL SAVE WEST INDIES

THE most exciting Test match played in the West Indies for more than 30 years ended here this evening in a draw. The West Indies saved their necks with a ninth wicket partnership of 63 by Sobers and Hall that lasted from tea until the close.

Needless to say the honours of the game belonged chiefly to England. But for the loss of an hour and a half's cricket last evening the high probability is that they would have won.

As it is much praise is due to all eleven and not least to Cowdrey, for his tactical handling in the field and for making the decision to let the first innings run its course.

Regrets England certainly had, notably for a missed catch offered by Hall when there was one and a quarter hours to go, which as it turned out was the first and last chance of breaking the stand. But the chief sentiment must be one of much thankfulness for a grand game which must, I think, "make" the series.

An hour after lunch when Butcher and Kanhai were batting fluently for the West Indies' third wicket with the difference between the sides only 40-odd the match looked as good as dead.

Kahhai then went, followed by Lloyd, Holford, Butcher, Murray and Griffith, while the score jerked uncertainly forward from 164 to 180. Six wickets indeed went for 16 runs.

It was one of the more extraordinary transformations in modern Test cricket, brought about in the first place by a very good catch on the part of Hobbs, in the second by some greathearted fast bowling by Jones and Brown.

Titmus played his part also with several teasing overs in the course of which he bowled Holford, who did not offer a stroke.

Brown, however, was the chief hero of the moment. In the last over before tea he had Butcher lbw with his second ball. Murray with his fifth and bowled Griffith with the sixth.

(January 25)

BOBBY CHARLTON SETS SCORING RECORD

By DONALD SAUNDERS

England ..... 3 Sweden 1

BOBBY CHARLTON scored his 45th goal in his 85th senior international at Wembley last night, as England swept to a comfortable victory in their final appearance before setting off in search of the European championship.

During the first half of a highly entertaining match that was marred by a late injury to the Swedish goalkeeper, Sven-Gunnar Larsson, Charlton put this much changed team into a commanding 2-0 lead and broke the England scoring record he held jointly with Greaves.

Then, when his colleagues came out for the second half, he remained behind in the dressing room on the orders of Sir Alf Ramsey.

Sir Alf, mindful of Manchester United's need of Charlton on this same pitch a week hence, decided this gifted forward should not risk further damage to a shin abrasion suffered in the first half.

England's manager sent on Hurst as substitute and saw enough during the next 45 minutes to decide that the West Ham marksman, troubled recently by injury, is fit enough to go to Europe next week.

(May 23)

LAVER AND MRS. KING JOIN ALL-TIME GREATS

By LANCE TINGAY

THE first Open Wimbledon was a stirring success.

Among the men the standard of play from first to last was never higher and its champion one of the all-time greats.

The influx of professionals did not change the pattern of the honours board, the men's events going to Australians, the women's to Americans. On Saturday the skill of Billie-Jean King gave her the women's singles title for the third successive year.

To take a Wimbledon singles three years running is no mean feat. Since the abolition of the challenge round in 1922, three other players have won three times in a row.

The feat was achieved by Helen Wills Moody, by Louise Brough and by Maureen Connolly - all Americans and, like Mrs. King, all Californians. Mrs. King placed herself in distinguished company which belongs exclusively to her State. She says she will come back to try for a fourth title.

The success of Wimbledon's first open was in spite of appalling weather in the first five days. The fall in attendance figures - 23,000 below last year's record 301,000 - was almost certainly due to the rail go-slow.

(July 8)

STEWART WINS U.S. GRAND PRIX

British drivers swept home first, second and third in the United States Grand Prix in Watkins Glen, New York, this afternoon. Jackie Stewart, in a Matra-Ford, took the winner's $20,000 (£8,300) purse and moved to second place in the world championship.

Stewart now has 36 points. Graham Hill, who won $10,000 (£4,100) for second place in his Lotus-Ford, remains in the championship lead with 39 points. The decision will come in the Mexico Grand Prix on Nov. 23.

Third was John Surtees in a Honda; Dan Gurney (United States) was fourth in a McLaren-Ford; Jo Siffert (Switzerland) fifth in a Lotus-Ford; and Bruce McLaren (New Zealand) sixth in a McLaren-Ford.

(October 7)

MATT BUSBY KNIGHTED

Matt Busby, 58, manager of Manchester United, receives a Knighthood in the Queen's Birthday Honours, published today. The award is for his long service to football.

(June 8)

ENGLISH PLAYERS FOR KNOCK-OUT

By Ray Robinson

SYDNEY, Wednesday.

Sixteen English, West Indian, Australian and South African cricketers will compete for $A20,000 (£9,330) prize money in a new world cricket championship in Australia next October. Four cricketers from each country will be invited to play in pairs in a knock-out double-wicket series as a prelude to the West Indies Test tour of Australia.

Promoter John Neary said tonight that he had formed a company with former Australian captain Bobby Simpson. They would fly English and South African players to Australia and pay all expenses during one-day knock-out contests in Brisbane, Oct. 5; Sydney, Oct. 6; Adelaide, Oct. 12; and a grand finale in Melbourne on Oct. 13; plus an exhibition contest in Perth the following day.

(April 14)

MCC tour officially cancelled

Daily Telegraph Reporter

THE MCC tour of South Africa was officially cancelled yesterday because of South Africa's refusal to accept Basil d'Oliveira, Worcestershire's Cape Coloured all-rounder, in the touring side.

The MCC committee spent four hours in session at Lord's during which Mr. Jack Cheetham, a former South African captain, and Mr. Arthur Coy, members of the South African Cricket Association Board, were invited into the meeting for 40 minutes. Later they were called back and told the MCC's decision.

Basil d'Oliveira, who had waited all day hoping for an 11th-hour reprieve for the tour, just shook his head, and said: "I'm sorry. I'm sorry."

Later he said: "I hope it will not be for always. I do not want to have to bear this cross for the rest of my life, to feel responsible for no more cricket between the two countries."

(September 25)

CROWD HELP MOP UP AUSTRALIA

IN one of the most exciting finishes to a Test match, England beat Australia at the Oval yesterday with six minutes to spare.

Just before lunch an England win looked a formality with Australia struggling at 86 for five. Then a thunderstorm swamped the ground and further play seemed out of the question.

But the rain stopped at 2.15. Eager volunteers from the crowd helped Ted Warn, the groundsman, mop up the water. By 4.45 the pitch was ready for play, but with a wet ball, England's chances of dismissing five Australians by 6 p.m. were slim.

With only 35 minutes to go Cowdrey - the England captain, brought on d'Oliveira. The last ball of his second over broke the stand between Jarman, Australia's vice-captain, and their batting hero, Inverarity.

Cowdrey immediately brought back Underwood, who completed a triumphant day's work by taking the last four wickets in 25 minutes. This is how the wickets fell:

4.45 - Play resumed. Australia 86 for 5.

5.24 - 110 for 6. Jarman, b d'Oliveira 21.

5.29 - 110 for 7. Mallett, c Brown, b Underwood 0.

5.33 - 110 for 8. McKenzie, c Brown, b Underwood 0.

5.47 - 120 for 9. Gleeson, b Underwood 5.

5.54 - 125 all out. Inverarity, lbw, b Underwood 56.

England's win, by 226 runs, squared the rubber, one match all.

(August 28)

SUPERB JACKLIN WINS BY TWO STROKES

AMERICAN STARS THRASHED

JACKSONVILLE, Florida, Sunday.

TONY JACKLIN, 23, the British Ryder Cup player, won the $100,000 (£41,000) Jacksonville Open golf tournament here today with a one-under-par final round of 71, giving him a total of 273. His rounds of 68,65,69 and 71 left him 15 under par for the tournament and earned him the first prize of £8,300.

Jacklin, a lorry driver's son from Scunthorpe, is the first British golfer to win a major tournament in America for 20 years.

After the third round Jacklin shared the lead with Doug Sanders on 202. One stroke behind was Arnold Palmer. Jacklin partnered Palmer in his final round, but did not let the fervour of "Arnie's Army" disturb him.

Jacklin's cool, controlled play enabled him to finish two strokes ahead of Sanders, Gardner Dickinson, Don January, Chi Chi Rodriguez and Dewitt Weaver.

His victory here has brought his prize money to £16,600 in the 10 weeks he has been playing on the American circuit.

Jacklin was 17 under par and four strokes ahead of the field with only five holes left to play but then had a shaky finish, driving into the woods once and twice playing his approach shots into bunkers. Jack Nicklaus finished on 280.

Jacklin's feats on the American circuit have impressed spectators here. During this tournament he has been signed as the playing professional by the Sea Island, Georgia Club. - Agencies.

(April 1)

WALES GIVES CAPTAINCY TO GARETH EDWARDS

By TONY LEWIS

THE Welsh selectors last night announced six changes in the team to meet Scotland at Cardiff on Feb. 3 - five at forward. The team includes a change of captaincy, Gareth Edwards taking over from Norman Gale, who is dropped. Wheeler, D. Williams, James, Mainwairing and Wanbon also lose their places.

Edwards, 20, a student at the Cardiff College of Education, is the youngest player ever to captain Wales. He recently led the East Wales side which drew with the New Zealand tourists.

With Gale's omission, a change comes in the leadership of the pack. Lloyd, of Bridgend, nine times capped, returns to lead from the loose head position.

The grave lack of possession against England has been given obvious attention. The front row now looks right, with O'Shea, Young and Lloyd providing a solid scrum and increased speed about the field.

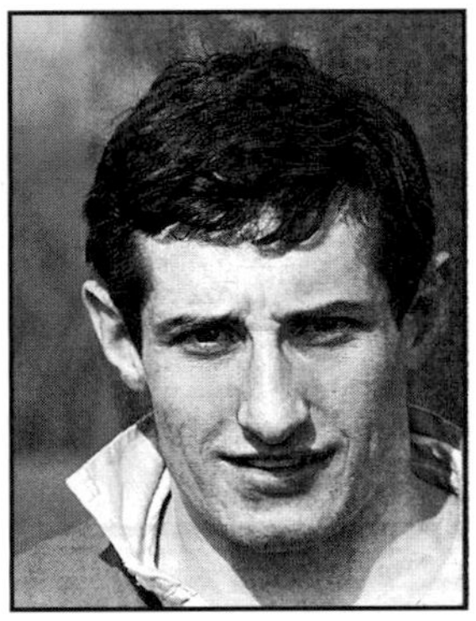

The cry for a line-out specialist has also been answered. The British Lion, Delme Thomas, who was capped against Australia in 1966, plays alongside Wiltshire. His claim was strong, especially as B.V. Price has only just returned to the game after an appendicitis operation.

With a further mind to the lineout, this time at the back, R. Jones replaces Wanbon - perhaps on the grounds of extra height.

Rees and Young are the new caps. Rees, 23, has not yet played a full season in first-class rugby. He is a model of steadiness and can, if Jarrett fails, turn to goal-kicking. He contributed 11 of 14 points for West Wales against the New Zealand tourists.

(January 26)

SIR IVOR'S BRILLIANT SPEED

By HOTSPUR (Peter Scott)

EPSOM, Wednesday.

SIR IVOR, with a turn of speed that puts him in the Sea Bird II class among post-war Derby winners, split open all defences when Lester Piggott set him alight here this afternoon and he beat Connaught running away.

Piggott, riding his fourth Derby winner, handled Sir Ivor with even more audacious confidence than he had done in the 2,000 Guineas, and was in no way flurried when Connaught opened up a lead that had his admirers counting their spoils.

Sixth as they entered the straight, Piggott did not shake up the favourite until a furlong and a half out.

Lengthening his stride - and what a picture he makes in full flow - Sir Ivor skimmed past Remand and slashed down Connaught's lead that had once been four lengths.

Sir Ivor's head was in front only 100yards from home yet he won by a length and a half.

The time of two minutes. 38.73 seconds testifies to a truly run race. Sir Ivor stayed the distance all right and will undoubtedly stay further if he is ever required to.

Mr. Guest bought Sir Ivor for $42,000 (£17,500) when the colt's breeder, Mrs. Alice Headley Bell, submitted him at the Keeneland yearling sales of 1966.

His value could be at least 40 times that amount now. Sir Ivor's stakes earnings in England, France and Ireland are just over £118,000. He is the 18th European-trained horse to top the six figure winnings mark and only Ragusa and Santa Claus of former Irish-trained champions stand above him in the list.

(May 30)

Nobby Stiles attacked by Madrid mob

Nobby Stiles, who was booked by the referee in tonight's European Cup semi-final between Manchester United and Real Madrid, was attacked as he left the football stadium.

Angry Spanish fans lay in wait outside the Bernabeu Stadium as Stiles left the dressing-rooms to board the team coach.

(May 16)

Port Vale re-elected

Port Vale, whose expulsion from the Football League was ordered by the Management Committee earlier this year, will play in the League next season. Vale were re-elected by 40 votes to nine at the League's annual meeting in London on Sunday.

(June 10)

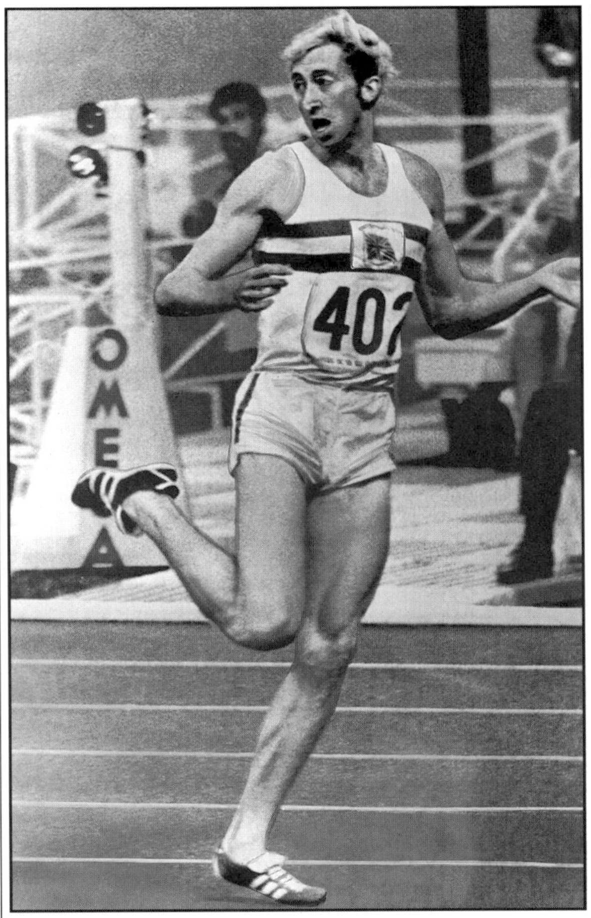

HEMERY WINS 'GOLD' WITH RECORD RUN

By JAMES COOTE

MEXICO CITY, Tuesday.

BRITAIN won her first Gold Medal of the Olympics today with a world-record run in the 400-metre hurdles by David Hemery, 24. Another Briton, John Sherwood, finished third to take the Bronze Medal.

Hemery's time was 48.1 sec. - exactly one second faster than the listed record of Gert Potgieter, the South African. Just a month ago, Potgieter's 49.1 was lowered to 48.8 sec by Geoff Vanderstock (America), one of the men in today's race. But Vanderstock's time has not yet been notified.

The Marquess of Exeter, who as Lord Burghley was the last Briton to win the event 40 years ago, said tonight that Hemery's race was a "magnificent performance."

"I retired at the right time didn't I?" he added when asked about the new record time.

Hemery, a lean, fair-haired, six-footer, with an American accent - the legacy of his education at Boston University - seemed to pause for a split second after the starting gun. But then it was so smooth that there appeared to be no hurdles at all.

Within two flights, he had overtaken Ron Whitney, the American, who once held the record. It seemed impossible that Hemery could continue to increase his lead - but he did.

John Sherwood crossed the line in 49.0 sec to win the Bronze Medal. He finished behind Gerhard Hennige (Germany) and ahead of Vanderstock.

(October 16)

ALLHUSEN AND JONES CLINCH FIRST PLACE

By A Special Correspondent

AVANDARO, Monday.

THE British team won the three-day event gold medal here this evening, with Major Derek Allhusen, 54, who led them, taking the individual "silver" on Lochinvar.

Sixth after the dressage, the British team went into the lead in yesterday's cross-country phase, when they were one of the few to surmount the terrible conditions which followed torrential rain.

They started today's show jumping with a lead of 49 points over the United States, and maintained this lead to the end.

Show jumping has always been considered Allhusen and Lochinvar's weakest point, but the veteran Norfolk farmer and his 10-year-old went round the course, still deep mud, without fault.

Richard Meade, who had led at Tokyo up to the show-jumping phase, rode his new mount, Cornishman. They had two fences down for a total of 20 faults, and Staff-Sgt, N. Jones, with The Poacher, needed a clear round to clinch the gold medal.

Jones had the crowd on their toes, but he is too experienced a horseman to be rattled in a situation like this, and he took The Poacher, which he was riding competitively for the first time here in Mexico, round without a semblance of a fault.

This is the first time Britain have won an Olympic Three-Day Event medal since taking the gold at Helsinki in 1952.

The fourth member of the British team in Mexico, student nurse Jane Bullen, 20, had the bad luck to slip up twice on the flat on her diminutive Our Nobby in the cross-country, and so finished out of the prizes.

(October 23)

ROBSON LOSES U.S. JOB

Bobby Robson, 33, the former Fulham and England wing-half has lost his job as chief coach to the Vancouver club with two years of his three-year contract still to run. He is a victim of the amalgamation of the two American leagues.

Robson was coach to the Vancouver Canadians who were merged with the San Francisco Golden Gate Gales last November. Ferenc Puskas, 41, the former Real Madrid star, was coach to the San Francisco club - and he has been preferred to Robson to coach the new Vancouver Royals.

Puskas also has a three-year contract and will begin his duties with the Royals later this month. The Royals will play in the North American Soccer League this year.

(January 18)

MISS BOARD KEPT OUT BY FRENCH GIRL

LILLIAN BOARD, 19, so widely tipped to win an Olympic gold medal, had to be content with second place in the women's 400 metres here. In a terrific finish she was beaten on the line by Colette Besson, of France.

So much had been expected from young Lillian that a silver medal will be considered a disappointment, but she did, after all, clock 52.1 sec, which is faster than Ann Brightwell ran four years ago when she too won the silver.

Miss Besson's time was 52 sec, equalling the Olympic record, and she was described to me by a French colleague as "the surprise of the Games."

Without making excuses for Miss Board, there is no doubt that the 20 min delay at the start of her race when she had to hang around, nervously taking off her track suit and putting it on again, did her no good at all.

When she started, there was a fractional pause before she clicked into motion, and when she did move, she went too fast. Within 30 yards she had caught up Aurelia Penton, of Cuba, and it was obvious that unless she was at her physical peak she would not be able to last.

She entered the last 100 yards with a five-yard advantage over the rest of her rivals, who were in a ragged line behind. She looked very tired, and would be lucky to hold on. By now her teammate, Janet Simpson, who this morning woke up with a streaming cold, was also moving through the field.

Suddely, there came from the pack the dark-blue-vested French girl, who was not even ranked number one in her country, and who came to Mexico with hopes only of making the final.

After the race, Lillian fell to the inside of the track, where television cameras descended on her, not even giving her the chance to recover or take off her shoes.

Lillian did not fail, for to get a silver medal, or a medal of any colour, is a great achievement. She had cut another four-tenths of a second off her fastest time, and had run herself to exhaustion. What more can you ask of a girl?

Dick Fosbury took the high jump title back to the United States after a long absence with his unique style, the Fosbury flop, in which he pivots on his right foot as he goes over the bar. He pulls his knees up and lands on his back facing the way he came.

Fosbury won with 7ft 4 1/4 in, a height beaten only by the world record holder, Valeriy Brumel, of Russia, and Ni Chih-Chin, of China.

(October 21)

FINNEGAN EARNS BOXING GOLD

By DONALD SAUNDERS

MEXICO CITY, Sunday.

CHRIS FINNEGAN, 24, of Iver, in Buckinghamshire, finds himself in the strange position today of being the amateur middleweight champion of the world, but not the holder of the British title.

An eye injury suffered in a divisional qualifying competition ended his chances of appearing in last spring's ABA Championships, but fortunately the selectors still decided to include him in the British Olympic team.

At the Arena Mexico last night, he upset odds that would have been around 100-1 a fortnight ago by outpointing Alexei Kiselov, of the Soviet Union, to win Britain's first boxing gold medal since 1956.

As he sat in the dressing room afterwards, Finnegan remarked: "Well, it's better than being just a silly old bricklayer," Silly is the one word I would never use to describe this young man. Sound commonsense and commendable maturity have been largely responsible for his unexpected but well-deserved success.

PUNCHING POWER

Weight advantage

In each of his five contests out here - all of them won on points - he has employed intelligence and tactical know-how that, alas, British amateurs seldom possess.

He knew he could not match the punching power of Kiselov, who was the light-heavyweight silver medalist in Tokyo and probably enjoyed an advantage of half-a-stone during last night's bout, the limit for which was 11st 11lb.

"My plan was to keep away from him make the best possible use of my right jab, and put some real beef behind it," Finnegan explained.

But during the first three minutes it did seem to me that Finnegan was rather overdoing things. He made few positive moves and I began to wonder if his only aim was to last the distance.

(October 28)

Graham Hill is world car champion

By COLIN DRYDEN

Motoring Correspondent

GRAHAM HILL, 39, of Britain, driving a Lotus-Ford, won the Mexican Grand Prix here today and with it the 1968 world driving championship. His time was 1 hr 56 min 43.95 sec, at a speed of 104 mph.

Hill began the race with 39 points towards the championship, three more than Jackie Stewart. But Stewart (Matra-Ford) had fuel pump trouble and finished seventh in the race.

Denis Hulme, last year's champion, who with 33 points was the only other contender for the title, crashed early in the race in his McLaren-Ford.

Second in the race was Bruce McLaren (McLaren-Ford) in 1 hr 58 min 3.27 sec. Third was Jackie Oliver (Lotus-Ford) 1 hr 58.24.6, 4th Pedro Rodriguez (BRM) of Mexico, 1-58-25.04, 5th Joe Bonnier (Honda) 1-57-44.95, and 6th Joe Siffert (Lotus-Ford) 1-57-56.26.

(November 4)

NIHILL WILTS IN THE SUN

MEXICO CITY, Friday.

Yesterday was not Britain's day, and this was epitomised by the collapse of Paul Nihill in the 50 kilometres walk. He set off at what appeared to be a one-man Charge of the Light Brigade with a result that was, alas, equally futile.

The race started in the heat of the day, and until about 37 kilometres Nihill was always either leading or lying second, but then he suddenly found he was walking on one side of the road, whereas he thought he was on the other. A classic case of sunstroke.

(October 19)

Virginia Wade overwhelms Mrs. King

Virginia Wade today played the finest lawn tennis of her career to become the first open champion of America, overwhelming the Wimbledon champion Billie Jean King 6-4, 6-2.

One can only make a comparison with American amateur championships of previous years. The last, and for that the only British woman to win that title, was Betty Nuthall way back in 1930.

This memorable achievement by Miss Wade, 23 last July, was accomplished before 14,000 spectators on the centre court at Forest Hills today in the cool of the evening.

(September 9)

Black Power protest mars Olympics medal ceremony

A BLACK POWER PROTEST being made on the Olympic rostrum by two American Negro sprinters after they had received their medals. Tommie Smith, who won the 200 metres in a world record time of 19.8 sec., and John Carlos, who came third, gave Nazi-style salutes with black-gloved fists as their national anthem was played. They refused to look up as the Stars and Stripes were hoisted. Spectators greeted their action with cat-calls.

Crowds at Martin Luther King's funeral

ABOVE: SEATED IN THE FRONT ROW AT SOUTH VIEW Cemetary in Atlanta for the burial of Dr. Martin Luther King Jr. are (from left) Bernice, Yolanda and Martin King III, Dr. King's children; Obadiah Scott of Marion County, Ala., Mrs King's father; Mrs King and singer Harry Belafonte.

RIGHT: MRS. CORETTA KING and her daughter Bernice, 5.

MRS MARGARET THATCHER, 43, who was appointed Shadow Transport Minister yesterday by Mr. Heath, reading a recent transport debate in Hansard at her Westminster home last night.

MR. ARISTOTLE ONASSIS and his bride, the former Mrs. Jacqueline Kennedy, during their wedding reception in the yacht Christina, 1,600 tons, at Skorpios, the Aegean island owned by Mr. Onassis. On the right is her daughter, Caroline, 10.

1969

The Daily Telegraph

"That's one small step for man but one giant leap for mankind." So said Neil Armstrong as he became the first man to walk on the Moon's surface on Monday, July 21st, 1969. As the decade drew to a close, it would be difficult to show that in terrestial matters there had been any similar giant advance. Too much unfinished business remained. The Vietnam war dragged on to the increasing disillusion of the troops on the ground who were only too conscious of the loudly expressed disagreement with the war of their friends and families at home.

In Britain the Labour government was battling against further economic problems and suffered a humiliating defeat when it was forced by its own back-benchers and the might of the trades unions to abandon the plans for curbing unofficial strikes that had been outlined in Mrs Barbara Castle's white paper, "In place of strife". In Ulster civil disorder became widespread and the situation was only momentarily quietened when troops were sent in. Both Bernadette Devlin, the newly elected republican MP, and the Rev. Ian Paisley, the extreme protestant leader, were sentenced to prison. The students of the London School of Economics once again took to the streets when the doors were closed against them. The occupation of the University Senate building by the LSE activists was ended by members of the rugby teams of other colleges.

The "Curse of the Kennedys" became apparent again when Senator Edward Kennedy was given a suspended jail sentence after Mary Jo Kopechne had drowned in a car he had driven into Chappaquiddick Sound. He swam to safety and did not report the accident for some time. Joseph Kennedy, the "father of the clan", died.

Having staked all on a referendum demanding an approval of his policies, President de Gaulle withdrew from politics when the vote went against him. In China the cultural revolution continued, though Anthony Grey, the Reuter's correspondent who had been held prisoner in his Peking flat, was released after more than a year in custody. The small Leeward island of Anguilla, having declared its independence, was occupied by a small force of British paratroopers before a handful of Metropolitan Policemen arrived to maintain order.

Robert Maxwell, having failed in his take-over battle with Rupert Murdoch for the *News of the World*, found that he had been ousted from the board of his original company, the Pergamon Press, in another take-over. The Kray Brothers, the gang leaders of the East End, were sent to prison for 30 years apiece. The world was horrified when the pregnant film actress Sharon Tate and seven others were butchered in Hollywood by a wandering band of hippies.

The death of President Eisenhower was announced as was that of one of his closest associates in command during the Second World War, Field Marshal Earl Alexander. Judy Garland committed suicide and the sex symbol of the 1930s, Robert Taylor, died. The yacht being navigated solo by Donald Crowhurst was found abandoned in the Atlantic. At the time he was thought to be leading the single-handed round-the-world race. It was not for years that it was discovered that he had never left Atlantic waters and had been sending faked messages of his position in other oceans.

With due pomp, her eldest son was invested as Prince of Wales by the Queen. In his first televised interview the Prince told his fellow countrymen of his hope that he would marry an English or Welsh girl. But, he added, there were difficulties.

Je Reviens

The Daily Telegraph
and Morning Post

5d.

No. 35412. LONDON, WEDNESDAY, MARCH 5, 1969   Printed in LONDON and MANCHESTER

BRC
Specialists in Reinforced Concrete Design
& Suppliers of Reinforcement

KRAY TWINS GUILTY OF MURDER

JURY OUT 7 HOURS: SENTENCES TODAY

By C.A. COUGHLIN, Old Bailey Correspondent

RONALD KRAY, 35, and his twin brother, Reginald, who terrorised East London, were both found guilty of murder at the Old Bailey yesterday. The jury was out for six hours and 54 minutes.

Four members of their "firm" were also found guilty of murder. Mr. Justice MELFORD STEVENSON will pass sentence today.

SPACEMEN PASS VITAL TESTS

By Dr. Anthony Michaelis, Science Correspondent, at Cape Kennedy

APOLLO nine passed the second critical test yesterday afternoon. Shortly after 3.0 p.m., BST, the main engine was fired to change the orbit of the linked command capsule, service module and Lunar Module, the space dinghy.

The minor troubles which cropped up yesterday – a faulty pressure gauge and a computer out of synchronisation with ground control in Houston, Texas – have been corrected. "There is nothing wrong" said one official "I am happy, very happy."

One purpose of the main-engine firings yesterday was to ensure that the delicate Lunar Module could stand up to the vibrations. It did, but the acceleration was so great that oxygen hoses inside the astronauts' cabin began flailing about – "like octopuses," said Russell Schweickart.

Col. David Scott described the incident as "like an attack by a pack of wild elephants." The two-minute firing was purposely made as tough as possible, testing the equipment beyond normal limits.

Testing time

The next testing time is today. Mr. Schweickart and Col. McDivitt, the mission commander, will enter the Lunar Module for the first time. It will be tested while attached to the mother ship before being detached on Friday. Tomorrow, Mr. Schweickart makes a two-hour space "walk" to test emergency transfers.

All these manoeuvres are necessary to a manned landing on the moon, which would actually be carried out in the Lunar Module. If the remaining checks are completed as successfully as the early ones, the landing could come this summer.

The Apollo 9 crew are standing up well to their ambitious and dangerous tasks. They slept for 9 ½ hours on Tuesday night, had a breakfast of cornflakes, and pronounced themselves "all vanilla" – a phrase eventually translated as doing very well.

CHINESE SHOT 34 RUSSIANS, SAYS MOSCOW

Chinese troops killed 34 Russian soldiers and wounded "several dozen" in Sunday's frontier clash, it was stated unofficially in Moscow last night. The Russians accused China of trying to "evade" responsibility for the incident.

Moscow Radio said Peking "is embarked on the way of dangerous and provocative actions." It accused Mao Tse-tung of "increasing nationalistic hysteria in the country by staging mass demonstrations."

The broadcast was the first Russian comment on the clash. The radio said Peking's reply to a Russian protest on Sunday was "another attempt to evade responsibility for the committed actions." – UPI.

The trial, which lasted 39 days, has been the longest murder hearing at the Central Criminal Court. Costs of the whole case, in which 23 counsel were engaged, are expected to exceed £200,000.

Court No. 1 was packed when the jury returned. Women relatives of the 10 accused men were crying.

But the father of the Kray brothers, Mr. Charles Kray senior, sat impassively in the same seat he has occupied throughout the trial.

Strict security precautions surrounded the court while the jury was out. Cars were towed away from parking meters outside the building. Extra uniformed police patrolled with two-way portable radios, with several police on the roof.

Verdicts unanimous

The defendants were summoned into the dock one by one and stood flanked by three prison officers as the jury foreman, gave the unanimous verdicts.

Ronald Kray, plump faced and bespectacled, blinked repeatedly while Mr. LESLIE BOYD, clerk of the court, recorded the verdicts.

Ronald was found guilty of murdering GEORGE CORNELL, 38, by shooting him through the head at the Blind Beggar public house, Whitechapel, on March 9, 1966, and guilty of murdering JACK "THE HAT" McVITIE, 38, at a basement flat at Evering Road, Stoke Newington, in October, 1967.

His brother, Reginald, was found guilty of murdering McVitie by stabbing him in the face, chest and throat nine times while Ronald held him from behind.

He was also found guilty of being an accessary after the murder of Cornell by harbouring his brother.

"See you later"

JOHN ALEXANDER BARRIE, 31, of no settled address, was found guilty of the murder of Cornell. The prosecution case against him was that he went armed with Ronald Kray to the Blind Beggar, and fired shots to distract customers.

CHRISTOPHER LAMBRIANOU, 29, of Queensbridge Road, Hackney, was found guilty of the murder of McVitie. Before going to the cells, he turned in the dock and called out to someone in the public gallery: "See you later."

The part he played in the McVitie murder was to get him drunk at the Regency Club, Stoke Newington, and lure him to the Evering Road flat.

His brother, ANTHONY LAMBRIANOU, 26, of Blythe Road, Bethnal Green, was also found guilty of murdering McVitie by luring him to the flat with his brother. As he left the dock, he made the "thumbs up" sign to someone in the public gallery.

RONALD ALBERT BENDER, 31, of Cubitt House, Millwall, Poplar, was found guilty of the murder of McVitie. He provided the carving knife with which Reginald Kray stabbed McVitie to death.

Elder brother guilty

The twins' elder brother, CHARLES JAMES KRAY, 42, of Rosefield Gardens, Birchfield Estate, Poplar was found guilty of being an accessary after the McVitie murder by organising some of the accused including his brothers, and assisting in arrangements for the disposal of McVitie's body.

Continued on Back Page, Col. 6

THE MURDER VICTIMS: Jack "The Hat" McVitie and George Cornell

HEALEY'S DEFENCE QUANDARY

By ANDREW ALEXANDER

THE first leg of a two-day debate on defence yesterday saw the House quickly splitting into its familiar trio of interests.

There are those who want more defence (the Tories), those who want defence on the cheap (the Government) and those who do not really want any defence (the Labour Left-wingers).

Yesterday that inveterate unilateral disarmer Mr. Allaun (Lab., Salford E.) had managed to whip up nearly 100 Labour MPs of various hues to support his amendment which declared that the level of defence spending was still far too high.

These signatories are apparently anxious for a transfer of funds which would ensure that Russian bombs rained down on a British Welfare State of impressive luxuriance.

"Some people," commented Mr. Donnelly (Ind. Lab., Pembroke), "never seem to realise the climate we are living in." He followed this with a bitter attack on the Government for its failure to maintain adequate defences.

Decision difficulties

Mr. Healey, Minister of Defence, opened the debate obviously in a quandary. He could not make up his mind which he was proudest of – the low level of defence spending he had achieved, or what he had provided with the money.

On the first point meaningless statistics were bandied around the House in a sadly uncritical way. The Minister was proud of the fact that defence spending would now be getting closer to the proportion of national income which was common in Western Europe.

That is all very well, but as these other nations use conscription and thus conceal many true costs the comparison seems unusually pointless.

Mr. Rippon, Shadow Minister of Defence, was in vigorous form when he opened for the Tories. He certainly makes a better defence spokesman for the Opposition than Mr. Enoch Powell.

Ford workers angry at dispute tactics

Most Dagenham Ford workers, two in every three, are opposed to the company's pay and productivity deal. Indeed, most not only object to the provisions aimed at blocking unofficial strikes, overtime bans and working to rule, but also believe the deal itself should be re-negotiated "to try to get better terms, including more money."

Nearly one in three, however, are in favour of accepting the present deal "as it stands." But, in the view of the Ford workers, the unions were wrong to go to the length of calling a strike to express their dislike of the deal.

These are the main findings of an inquiry by the Gallup Poll on behalf of The Daily Telegraph. Interviewing was carried out between Saturday, March 1, and Monday, March 3, with a cross-section of Ford employees living within three miles of the Dagenham works.

51 p.c. seek more

A total of 291 interviews were completed. Gallup put the question: *What do you think the unions and the workers ought to do about the pay and productivity deal offered by the Ford management?*

The answers, in percentages, recorded for the three choices posed, were:

Re-negotiate the pay and productivity deal to try to get better terms, including more money: 51 per cent.

Refuse to accept it until the provisions to try to stop unofficial strikes, overtime bans and working to rule are removed: 17 per cent.

Accept it as it stands, including these provisions: 31 per cent.

Don't know: one per cent.

Amalgamated Union of Engineering and Foundry Workers' members are particularly strong in opposition to the present deal — 63 per cent. want complete re-negotiation and a further 20 per cent. oppose the special provisions.

QE2 VOYAGE INQUIRIES FROM 57 COUNTRIES

Bookings and inquiries from prospective passengers in 57 countries were received by Cunard yesterday following the announcement that the QE2 will make her maiden voyage on May 2.

BP gains £170m in U.S. deal

By Our City Staff

Nearly £170 million was added to the market valuation of British Petroleum in the London Stock Exchange yesterday, following news from New York that the way had been cleared for BP to enter the American oil market.

Local demand for the shares was reinforced by American support and the final price was 151s, a gain of 9s 6d. Confirmation that the United States would allow the merger of the Atlantic Richfield and Sinclair oil companies came well after market hours.

Court clears way

Within hours of a New York court ruling permitting the deal BP yesterday bought for $400 million (£166 million) a major stake in the American oil market, Dominick Harrod cables from New York.

A Federal judge had sanctioned the purchase as part of the merger of two American oil companies, Atlantic Richfield and Sinclair oil, whose 9,000 petrol stations in 16 states and two oil refineries BP bought.

The two refineries will be capable of refining 185,000 barrels of crude oil a day, and the retail outlets, which will continue to operate under the "Sinclair" brand name for the moment, will give BP its first stake in the United States.

BP will pay for the deal in six equal installments, beginning in 1972. The company's aim is to earn enough dollars from its American operation to pay for the deal.

Income from the sale of Alaskan crude oil, for which the company is at present drilling, would, BP hopes, contribute to dollar earnings to pay for the refineries and petrol stations.

By making these arrangements, BP avoids any balance of payments effect.

Merger opposed

Last autumn, when the companies decided to couple they planned to sell 5,000 of Sinclair's East-coast petrol stations and two refineries to avoid opposition to the merger from the anti-trust division of the Justice Department.

TUC MOVE TO END DEADLOCK

By Blake Baker, Industrial Correspondent

A fresh attempt to secure a return-to-work in the eight-day Fords strike will be made by the Trade Union Congress today.

Mr. Victor Feather, the new general secretary, has called a meeting of the major unions involved at TUC headquarters. The move follows soundings of both management and unions by Mr. Leslie Cannon, president of the Electrical Trades Union.

Today Mr. Cannon will put forward his plan which provides for suspension of the whole £5 million pay and productivity deal, which led to the strike, withdrawal of the strike notices and a resumption of work and fresh negotiations on the whole package.

£10m loss for Fords

The latter course was also urged by Mr. Justice Geoffrey Lane during yesterday's hearing of Fords' application for continuation of their injunction against the Unions.

Should today's moves fail, there is every prospect of the stoppage, which has already cost Fords £10 million, having a catastrophic effect on the firm, exports workers and quite possibly—if legal action succeeds—for the unions also.

Production at Vauxhall's Luton plant stopped last night because of an official strike by 10 men in the firm's plating plant at Ellesmere Port, Cheshire. At Luton, 3,500 men were told not to report for work today and the number laid off is expected to rise to 7,000 by the end of the week.

Fords Case & Industrial News P26

The Daily Telegraph

5d.

No. 35529. LONDON, MONDAY, JULY 21, 1969 — and Morning Post — Printed in LONDON and MANCHESTER

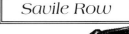

Lunarnauts' perfect landing

AMERICANS WALK ON THE MOON

'It has a soft beauty all its own'

By Dr. ANTHONY MICHAELIS and ADRIAN BERRY, Science Staff, at the Manned Spacecraft Centre, Houston

NEIL ARMSTRONG, 38-year-old American commander of the Apollo 11 mission, became the first man to set foot on the moon at 3.56 a.m. BST today. As he stood on the moon, he said the surface was "like a fine powder, a very fine grain surface" and it had "a soft beauty all its own like some desert of the United States."

Armstrong climbed slowly down the nine rungs of the Eagle ladder and placed his left foot on the lunar surface first. Television pictures of excellent quality were sent back live from a camera on Eagle.

Waiting inside Eagle to join him was Col. Edwin "Buzz" Aldrin, 39, lunar module pilot, who sent a message back to earth asking for people to give thanks for the events of the past few hours. Aldrin stepped on the moon at 4.15 a.m.

President Nixon, speaking to astronauts from the White House at 4.48 a.m., told them: "Because of what you have done the heavens have become part of man's world."

TENDENCY TO TOPPLE

"It's a very soft surface but here and there where I poke with the sample collector I run into a very hard surface," Armstrong reported, even though "it appears to be the same material. I'll try to get a rock here," he said.

Aldrin said: "There's a slight tendency, I can see now, to topple backwards due to the soft, very soft texture" of the lunar soil.

On reaching the surface, Aldrin did a three foot jump. His first words were: "Beautiful, beautiful." Armstrong replied: "Isn't it something."

The lunarnauts moved with a curious bouncing, floating motion, like someone walking under water. The Stars and Stripes was implanted at 4.41 a.m.

WE'RE BREATHING AGAIN

Earlier as the lunar module made a perfect landing on the Sea of Tranquillity. Armstrong reported: "The Eagle has landed. We are breathing again. Thanks a lot."

Almost immediately Mission Control began referring to Eagle with a new radio call-sign of "Tranquillity Base."

Aldrin said he took over manual control before touch-down and landed four miles away because the target "would have taken us right into a football pitch-sized crater with a large number of big boulders." They said the surface was "ashen grey."

Overhead at a height of less than 70 miles, Col. Michael Collins, 38, orbited the moon in the command module Columbia, to which Armstrong and Aldrin are due to return tonight.

A LOT OF ROCKS

Then Armstrong made a quick description of the touchdown scene, saying that Eagle was "surrounded by a lot of rocks about 10 feet high.

"We are in a relatively smooth plain with many craters five to 50ft in size. We see some ridges. And there are literally thousands of little one and two feet craters.

"We see some angular blocks some feet in front of us, about two-to-three ft. in size." He could see a hill about "half a mile away."

No description came until they had made sure Eagle was in a proper condition to stay.

At about midnight, they settled down to man's first meal on the moon. They had bacon squares, peaches, biscuits and fruit drink. Armstrong said: "There was no difficulty" in adapting to the lunar gravity.

(Continued on Back Page, Col. 4)

'One giant leap for mankind'

By Our Science Staff in Houston

"THAT'S one small step for man but one giant leap for mankind," said Neil Armstrong as he stepped on the lunar surface.

These were probably words that will be remembered for ages to come and be learned by schoolchildren a thousand years from now.

As he began walking with a somewhat jerky gait, Armstrong reported: "The surface is fine and powdery. I can pick it up loosely with my toe. It adheres like powdered charcoal to my boot. I only go in a fraction of an inch, an eighth of an inch.

"I can clearly see the footprint of my shoes in the fine sandy particles. It's quite dark here in the shadow and a bit difficult to see. But I have good footing. I'll work my way over into the sunlight here."

His voice shaking slightly, Armstrong added: "There seems to be no difficulty in walking around . . . The descent engine did not leave a crater of any size . . . We are on a very level site here."

That's our home

Then, as Aldrin began to climb down the ladder from Eagle to the moon's surface, Armstrong warned him: "You saw what difficulties I was having."

Aldrin took the descent slowly. "That's our home for the next couple of hours," he called down to Armstrong, "so we'll want to take good care of it."

As they moved across the surface, both astronauts appeared to television watchers to be leaping in slow motion.

Aldrin reported that the rocks were rather slippery with a powdery surface and the men tended to slide over them rather easily.

Aldrin exclaimed: "Isn't it something?"

'Very pretty'

Armstrong, after a reminder from Mission Control, scooped up a small sample of the lunar soil to put in a pocket of his space suit. This was a "contingency sample" collected immediately in case the men had to cut short their stay on the moon.

"It's very interesting. It's a very fine soft surface, but when I dig for the contingency sample it appears to be very hard cohesive material of the same sort," he said.

"It's much like the High Desert of the United States, but it has a beauty of its own. It's very pretty up here."

Aldrin reported: "You've got to be careful you lean in the direction you want to go, otherwise you seem inebriated." Then he reported that he found a purple rock.

'SAFE RETURN'

Mr. Wilson, speaking on ITV, expressed "our deep wish for a safe return at the end of what has been a most historic scientific achievement in the history of man." The first feeling of all in Britain was "that this very dangerous part of the mission has been safely accomplished."

When to see Apollo on TV

RECORDED pictures of the first steps on the moon will be shown every hour on the hour between 8 a.m. and 10.30 a.m.today on BBC-1. ITV will also show pictures from 8 a.m. to 10 a.m. with a progress report on Apollo.

Today's coverage will be:

BBC-1: 8 a.m.-10.30 a.m. moonwalk pictures with progress report. 1 p.m.-1.30 p.m., report on preparations to leave moon. 4.20 p.m.-4.40 p.m., report on preparations for blast-off from moon. 6.20 p.m.-7.05 p.m., report on blast-off with possible live pictures. 8 p.m.-8.50 p.m. Panorama report on Apollo. 10.25 p.m.-11 p.m. report in 24 Hours as luna module joins command module.

BBC-2: 9 a.m. onwards, moonwalk pictures every hour on the hour with possible colour pictures.

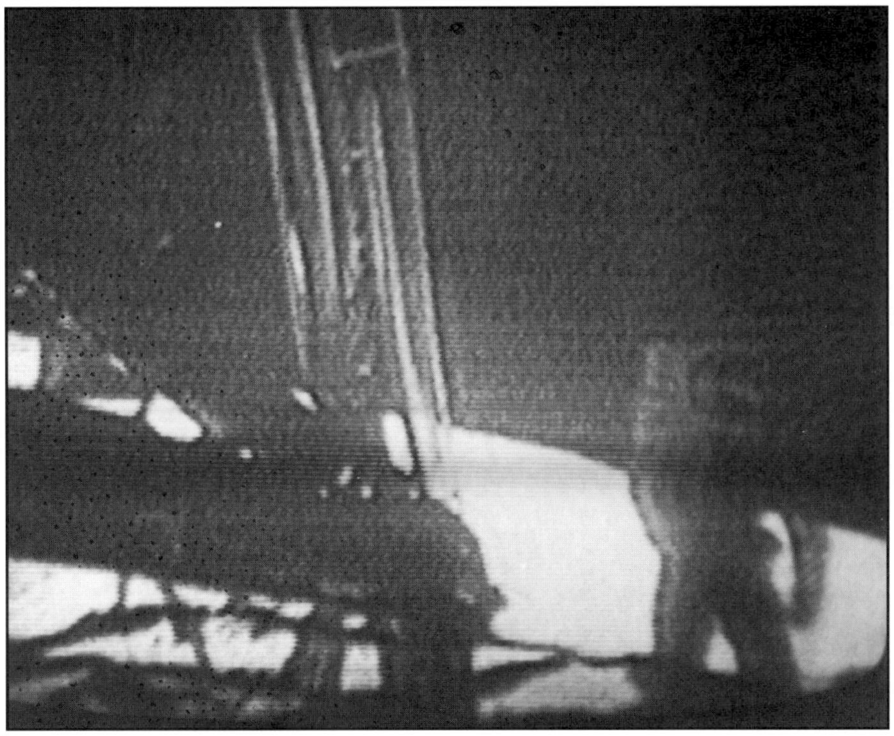

FIRST FOOTSTEPS . . Neil Armstrong standing near the lunar module as he prepared to collect his first sample of rock.

NEW YORK MAKES IT A PARTY

By JOHN MOSSMAN in New York

ONE single phrase by announcers on the major television networks – "Man is on the moon" – gave the go-ahead to New Yorkers and millions of other Americans to start the biggest celebration of the century.

Earlier yesterday in New York and other major cities streets were virtually deserted as people stayed close to their television sets. But last night, when the news came that "it was a success," the real celebrations began. People spilled out into Times Square waving and cheering.

Tens of thousands of New Yorkers wearing symbolic white dresses and suits flocked to Central Park for an all-night "moon in."

While history was being made and celebrated, Aldrin's wife, Joan, who followed the flight from her home near the Houston space centre, exclaimed: "I just can't believe it.

"I concentrated on the smallest thing – like the numbers on the screen. I cried ... it seemed like forever ... tears of relief."

Mrs. Armstrong sat on a bed with her youngest son, Ricky, 6, and monitored the final minutes before touchdown. She kept muttering, "Good, good, good," until the ship was safely down.

She disclosed her husband was carrying a memento to the moon for her. "But that's private, she said, and refused to disclose what it was.

Mrs. Pat Collins, wife of the command module pilot said "I thought it was positively beautiful. I wasn't nervous. I was excited. Very excited."

Luna 15 in lower orbit

By FRANK TAYLOR in Moscow

RUSSIA announced last night that Luna 15 had been put into an orbit bringing it down from 80 miles to within ten miles of the moon at its closest point.

Tass, the Soviet news agency, reported that the change in orbit of the unmanned spacecraft was made at 3.16 p.m. BST. Luna 15's maximum distance from the moon was 68 miles.

EMBASSY BLACKOUT

Disappointed American tourists were turned away last night from their embassy in London, where they had gone to watch the lunar landing. An internal power failure blacked out the screens.

Kennedy may face crash summons

By MABEL ELLIOTT in Edgartown

SENATOR EDWARD KENNEDY is expected to receive a summons today to appear in court for failing to report the accident in which his car plunged into Nantucket Sound, killing a woman passenger, Miss Mary Kopechne.

If an application is granted to the chief of police the summons will be presented personally to the senator, who is 37. If the senator is found guilty he faces a minimum sentence of two months' imprisonment and a maximum of two years.

The eight or so hours between the time his car plunged into Nantucket Sound from a bridge on Chappaquiddick island and Mr. Kennedy reporting distraught and shocked at the police station at Martha's Vineyard have not yet been officially accounted for by police or friends.

The body of Miss Kopechne, 28, attractive blonde secretary to the late Senator Robert Kennedy was found in the back seat of the submerged car.

Police chief dived in

The police chief, Mr. Dominic Arena, told me yesterday: "It was about 8 a.m. on Saturday morning we were told of the accident by two boys fishing off the bridge. They said they had spotted a car in the water.

"I put on swimming trunks and dived into about 8 ft of water. The girl's body was in the back of the car.

"Her face was upwards and she was wearing a white blouse, slacks and sandals. A pink hairbrush lay on the front passenger seat.

"I had been told this was the senator's car. I phoned my office and said "Get hold of Ted Kennedy at once." I was told he had just walked in. It was then about 8.30 a.m. A doctor said the girl had been dead 'some hours'."

The police chief added: "When I saw Mr. Kennedy he was extremely distressed. I told him he need not make a statement, but he said he wanted to co-operate fully.

"There will be no post mortem examination. The medical examiner said there was no doubt whatever that Miss Kopechne had died from drowning."

Samples of her blood are being analysed to discover whether there was any alcohol content. The senator, with the dead girl and six or seven other guests including four women, had been attending a party on the island at a house rented by his cousin Mr. Joseph Gargan.

The senator told police he could not remember how he escaped from the car after it hit the water. But he did remember "diving repeatedly" to try to save the girl.

The events of the next hours appear confusing to both Mr. Kennedy and the police. Wet through but uninjured, he said he returned to the party cottage and sat in the back of a friend's car.

On his way from the accident he must have passed at least two houses in which the occupants were up and burning lights.

The ferryman did not get a call during the early hours.

Continued on Back P., Col 6

LATE NEWS

MOON WALK
(See this page)

Scoop fulls of lunar surface picked up to be returned to earth in sealed aluminium casket.

Armstrong reported Eagle in good shape for take-off again and that legs, with circular pads, had only little penetration into lunar surface.

At 5.40 a.m. astronauts were given extra 15 minutes on moon's surface.

Today's Weather

(Midnight Forecast)

GENERAL SITUATION: S.W. airstream will be maintained across Britain.

LONDON, S.E., CENT. S., CENT. N. ENGLAND, E. ANGLIA, MIDLANDS: Dry, sunny intervals. Wind S.W. light to moderate. Max 79F (16c)

CHANNEL IS., S.W. ENGLAND, S. WALES: Mainly dry, cloudy, sunny intervals. Some hill or coast fog. 73F (23C)

N. WALES, N.W. ENGLAND, ISLE OF MAN, S.W.SCOTLAND, N. IRELAND: Mainly dry, cloudy, sunny intervals. Hill or coast fog. 68F (20C)

Weather Maps, Reports —P8.

Daily Telegraph and Morning Post, 1969

France votes 'Non'
DE GAULLE RESIGNS
By ANTHONY MANN in Paris

GENERAL DE GAULLE announced his resignation to the French people early today after being defeated in the referendum on which he had staked his political career. In a statement issued from his home at Colombey-les-deux-Eglises, he said: "I am ceasing the exercise of my functions as President of the Republic. This decision takes effect at noon."

The General's resignation will necessitate a Presidential election at a date not less than three weeks and not more than five weeks from today.

Gen. de Gaulle had twice announced in television speeches that if his proposals were defeated, he would "immediately lay down the functions of Head of State."

A grim-faced M. Couve de Murville warned the nation in a television broadcast that they must take the consequences of voting against the referendum.

"These consequences have been clearly announced. From tomorrow a new page will be turned in the history of France," the Prime Minister said.

The referendum was on the reform of the Senate and regional councils. With 29 million valid votes counted, the breakdown was:

YES: 47.13 per cent.
NO: 52.87 per cent.

Gen. de Gaulle, who is 78, resigned as first post-war Prime Minister after 17 months, but came back to power in June, 1958, when the settlers' revolt in Algeria had brought France to the brink of civil war. Six months later he became President, and retained his office in the 1965 election.

News that the General faced defeat had been flashed to waiting Frenchmen within 30 seconds of the last polling station closing. It was based on computer calculations.

M. Pleven, a former Gaullist Minister, said a few moments after these forecasts were known, "I warned the General against this ill-judged referendum."

Other political commentators declared that the triumph of the 'No' voters was due to "an accumulation of many different kinds of discontent in the country."

POMPIDOU READY

The most likely successor of the General appears at the moment to be M. Pompidou, for many years his Prime Minister.

M. Pompidou has already made it clear that he will be a candidate. M. Giscard d'Estaing, leader of the Independant Republicans, who broke with the General a fortnight before the referendum, announced last night that he will make a policy statement this afternoon.

APPEAL FOR CALM

The Gaullist youth movement issued a communiqué shortly after the trend of voting became known, urging its members to "refrain from all demonstrations and provocations," whatever the result.

The referendum was the first since Gen. de Gaulle was re-elected President in 1965.

At the height of the disturbances in France last year the General told the nation in a televised broadcast that he would offer them a referendum on industrial participation.

The speed of events proved this unpopular and under the pressure of M. Pompidou, then the Prime Minister, he did not go ahead with it.

Once the elections were over, Gen. de Gaulle repeatedly announced he would still have a referendum, and finally fixed the date and the new subject last February.

The previous referenda were:

SEPT. 28, 1958 on the Constitution of the Fifth Republic; won by 79 per cent. of votes cast, with 15 per cent. abstention.

JAN. 8, 1961, on independence for Algeria: won by 75 per cent. with 23 per cent. abstention.

APRIL 8, 1962, on independence agreements for Algeria: won by 90 per cent. with 24 per cent. abstention.

OCT. 28, 1962 on electing the President of France by universal suffrage: won by 61 per cent. with 22 per cent. abstention.

In December, 1965, after a second ballot, Gen. de Gaulle won the Presidential election with 55 per cent. of the votes against his Socialist opponent, M. Mitterrand, with 45 per cent. In this election there was a 15 per cent. abstentions.

(April 28)

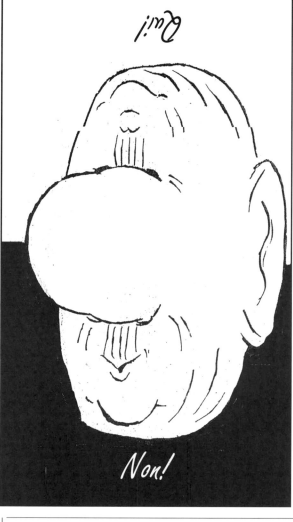

Oui! ... *Non!*

Want to hide thousands of kangeroos?

Who would - apart from the proud motheroos? But then, no marsupial ever had the sort of capacity WE can offer at Cumbernauld. We have, for more practical purposes, 100,000 sq. ft. of Warehouse READY NOW!

CUMBERNAULD

'HAMBURGER HILL' EMBITTERS U.S. VIETNAM TROOPS

A SCRAWLED notice stuck with a bayonet to a charred tree stump on a remote South Vietnamese peak read: "Hamburger Hill – was it worth it?"

Nearby lay a huge pile of discarded helmets, bullet proof jackets and blood-soaked rucksacks which belonged to the 55 Americans who died, or the 300 who were wounded in repeated ground assaults up the steep slopes.

Senior American officers speak of the strategic location of the 3,074ft mountain, and of the 619 North Vietnamese troops they say were killed defending it, and say "of course, it was worth it."

But the young American paratroopers, who hurled themselves against fierce machine gun and rocket grenade fire for a week before seizing the hill – two miles of the Laos border - on Tuesday, are not convinced.

Sgt. Butler Johnson, 26, described the final assault: "There were lots of guys, screaming guys, cries of agony, God, it was awful to see your buddies like that."

"1939-45 war" tactics

Many of the troops are puzzled over what they called "1939-45 war" tactics of ground attack used to capture the hill in an age of computerised bombing.

Senator Edward Kennedy said in Washington this week that the assault was "senseless."

Another question mark is why the North Vietnamese, estimated at 1,500-strong, clung to the slopes despite heavy artillery and air strikes which tore deep gashes in the mountain jungle.

Cut to pieces

Important or not, the operation drew caustic comments from the men who had to scramble up the mountain in face of heavy machine gun fire. Many felt that big B-52 bombers, or as one said, a "small nuke" (nuclear explosion) could have done the job.

There appears to have been no breakdown in American morale in the attack, although accounts of the troops' fighting spirit differ.

"They were a proud and happy bunch standing there at the top, mowing down the enemy as they retreated," said Col. Honeycutt.

But, Lt. Charles said, "This time they were not all happy and clapping each other on the back. They just wanted to get the hell out of there." – Reuter.

(May 24)

GIANT JET CAUSES PROBLEMS
By RICHARD BEESTON in Washington

THE Boeing 747, the £8 million 350-ton airliner capable of carrying 490 passengers, may prove a major headache to its owners and aviation authorities.

The 747, which cut short its maiden flight after wing-flap trouble on Sunday, is due to go into service at the end of the year.

Costly extensions are now being made at major American airports to deal with the new airliner but most are still far from ready. One of the biggest problems is the handling at arrival and departure of over 400 passengers and baggage at already congested air terminals.

Another major problem is the noise factor. There are doubts at present that the 747 can comply with noise abatement rules without coming up against safety regulations which prohibit power reductions below an altitude of 1,000 feet.

There is also the added responsibility for safety involved with such large numbers of passengers in one aircraft. As one Federal Aviation Agency spokesman said: "If one of these goes down it would be a disaster like the Titanic."

(February 11)

POLICE FIGHT PAISLEYITES IN ST. PAUL'S
By BRIAN SILK and A.J. McILROY

PLAIN clothes police struggled with Protestant demonstrators, some of them wearing clerical collars, in St. Paul's Cathedral last night. The congregation gasped at unprecedented scenes as Cardinal Heenan, Roman Catholic Archbishop of Westminster, rose to preach on Christian Unity.

About 20 men, including supporters of the Rev. Ian Paisley, were heaved from their pews by the officers, who pushed, dragged and carried them to a side door. As they went, resisting vigorously, the cathedral rang with cries of "You're a liar" and "Popery is hell itself." One man was arrested.

Mr. Paisley, Northern Ireland's militant Protestant leader, accused the Archbishop of Canterbury, Dr. Ramsey, of "betraying the Protestant Church."

Thirty officers formed a protective ring round Mr. Paisley, as angry Roman Catholics hurled abuse and ripe tomatoes at him and screamed "Adolph Paisley."

Cardinal jeered

Mr. Paisley, his head and shoulders splattered with burst tomatoes, said to his supporters: "The more they do that the better. They are proving that Popery is thuggery."

About 100 policemen sealed the cathedral entrance as Cardinal Heenan arrived to a chorus of boos and jeers.

Trouble began as soon as he entered the pulpit to become the first Roman Catholic primate to preach in St. Paul's. A man shouted: "I rebuke you in the name of Lord Jesus Christ."

It was 10 minutes before the Cardinal was able to start his sermon. One by one the Protestants stood and shouted anti-Catholic slogans, but before they could say more than a few words the police moved in.

Several men in dog collars, who appeared to be from Ulster, struggled furiously with the officers, who tried to gag them as they were dragged away, kicking and clawing at the seats.

Calm and patient

Cardinal Heenan took each outburst calmly and patiently. As one clergyman was half thrown through the exit shouting "Blasphemy," Cardinal Heenan said: "We ought to be grateful for these demonstrations, which show the need for the ecumenical movement."

A double line of 50 police held back a chanting crowd which had swelled as members of the congregation stayed behind to argue with Mr. Paisley and the demonstrators. Mr. Paisley and his supporters struggled through the crowd as tomatoes and eggs were hurled at him.

Later, as Cardinal Heenan's car drove off, onlookers shouted: "Well done your Eminence. You are a brave man."

(January 23)

PARTY NAME LIN PIAO AS MAO'S HEIR
By FRANK ROBERTSON in Hongkong

LIN PIAO, China's Defence Minister, was confirmed as the eventual successor to Chairman Mao Tse-tung by the Ninth Congress of the party in Peking yesterday.

The 1,500 delegates also approved a draft constitution hailing Mao – eight mentions by name – and pledging China "to fight to overthrow imperialism headed by the United States, the Soviet revisionist renegade clique and reactionaries in all countries."

The New China News Agency reported that the constitution, more a party polemic than a juridical document, "is the integration of the great leader Chairman Mao's wise leadership with the broad masses, and a vivid manifestation of the party's democratic centralism and the mass line."

The new committee is notable for the many former senior comrades now missing, a result of Mao's sweeping purges and the number of Army men represented – some 40 per cent. against 28 per cent. in the last Central Committee.

(April 15)

THREE BORN, TWO DIE, AT FESTIVAL
By Our New York Staff

A drowning, a stabbing death and three childbirths were among the incidents at a free "rock" music festival that featured the Rolling Stones and other groups and drew more than 200,000 to a car speedway arena at Tracy, California, at the weekend.

Hundreds of young people had to be treated by doctors, mainly for drug overdoses, but considering the size of the turnout, the behaviour of the fans was generally good.

Police and specially-hired security guards made few arrests and tried to be as tolerant as possible. They had to restrain a few people from trying to demonstrate their appreciation of the festival in the nude.

A young man drowned in a 13ft deep canal near the festival site while trying to escape arrest.

(December 8)

WOMEN TO GO TO KING'S CAMBRIDGE

KING'S COLLEGE, Cambridge, founded in 1441, is to admit women undergraduates from 1972 or 1973.

Churchill founded nine years ago as a national memorial to Sir Winston has already announced that it will accept women, but King's is the first of the old foundations to break the all-male rule.

The Provost of King's Dr. Edmund Leach, said the governing body had agreed in principle to admit women.

Their decision was based on the double conviction that Cambridge should be making a greater contribution to women's education and that an academic and social environment would be provided superior to that of single-sex institutions.

Dr. James Turner, admissions tutor, said: "It will mean a very slight reduction in the number of men undergraduates admitted each year.

"We have not yet finalised details about mixed living accommodation, but we do not foresee any difficulty."

(May 29)

NOBEL PRIZE PRESENTED TO BRITAIN
By Our Stockholm Staff

Prof. Derek Barton, 51, of the Imperial College of Science and Technology, London, who shared this year's £30,000 Nobel chemistry prize with Prof. Odd Hassel, Norway, was among those who received their Nobel diplomas and medals from the King of Sweden in Stockholm yesterday.

The £30,000 economics prize created last year by the Bank of Sweden, was shared by Prof. Jan Tibergen of Holland, and Prof. Ragnar Frisch of Norway. The Medicine prize was shared by three American professors. Profs. Max Delbruck, Alfred Hershey and Salvador Luria. Another American, Prof. Murray Gell-Mann, received the physics prize.

In Oslo, Mr. David A. Morse, Director-General of the International Labour Organisation, received the 1969 Nobel Peace Prize on behalf of the organisation.

(December 11)

FIVE KILLED IN ULSTER CLASHES

FIVE people, including a child of nine, were killed early today as renewed rioting flared across Ulster a few hours after 300 British troops had moved into Londonderry at the request of the Ulster Government to pacify the Roman Catholic Bogside area.

Three policemen were wounded in Belfast as a gun battle raged through the city. Sten guns and rifles were used against police in the Falls Road and Shanklin Road areas. Fires burned in many areas.

Trouble in Belfast began when fire bombs were thrown at the law courts and public houses in the Crumlin Road area were set on fire.

Police fired warning shots over the heads of the crowd in an attempt to disperse them.

The man killed in Armagh was named as John Gallagher, father of three children, who was 31. Police said early today that they were not using arms in Armagh.

The shot that killed Mr Gallagher was fired during a confrontation between Catholic and Protestants. "It was not a police bullet" said a spokesman at police headquarters in Belfast.

The Belfast victims were Mr Samuel McLarnon, 30, shot dead through the window of his kitchen, and Mr Herbert Roy, 26, who was shot in Shankill Road.

Patrick Rooney, 9, was killed when a bullet entered a window at his home in a tenement block, in Belfast, and a man's body was found on the roof of a nearby block. Police said he died from violence.

RING OF BARBED WIRE

Earlier yesterday British troops restored calm to the Bogside area of Londonderry, scene of this week's bitterest fighting. They surrounded the Roman Catholic district with a ring of barbed wire and machine guns.

The troops, from the 1st Bn. The Prince of Wales' Own Regiment, arrived from a nearby shore base as petrol bomb and riot gas fighting between besieged Roman Catholics and Royal Ulster Constabulary reached a climax of violence.

But as the troops took up their positions the tension which had gripped the city for more than two days began to evaporate. People behind the barricades cheered and sang as the police withdrew, to be replaced by soldiers.

And, as the town gained its first brief respite since a Protestant rally on Tuesday began the hours of fire-bomb terror, Major Hanson added: "Provided one is pleasant and polite, one can achieve an awful lot in this world."

The Ulster Government decided to ask for British troops yesterday "to prevent a breakdown of law and order."

The decision was greeted with widespread relief in Ulster. But the Eire Government last night repeated its view that the use of British troops was not acceptable.

The troops remain exclusively in the control of the GOC, Northern Ireland, and are to open fire only in order to save life. There is no intention of trying to force the Bogside barricades.

The British Government emphasised that the intervention of troops was a "limited operation" and that they would be withdrawn as soon as law and order was restored.

(August 15)

ASIANS' EXODUS TO BRITAIN

By Our Nairobi Correspondent

MANY Asian traders were making plans to wind up their businesses in Kenya yesterday and prepare for a mass exodus to Britain during the next few months.

They are the ones who under Kenya's new Trade Licensing Bill brought into force yesterday, have been warned that their trading licences will not be renewed in 1969. The Act aims to transfer Kenya's commerce into the hands of the Africans.

Mr. Mwai Kibaki, Kenyan Commerce and Industry Minister, says the Act will put more than 3,000 Asian traders out of business in Kenya within the next six months and with families send more than 15,000 clamouring for entry into Britain.

March exodus

An elderly trader, Mr. J. C. Patel, said: "The biggest exodus ever seen in Kenya is likely to take place at the end of March." Last March more than 10,000 Asians left Kenya for Britain in an effort to beat the Commonwealth Immigration Bill.

Like most of the Asians who will be forced from Kenya, Mr. Patel holds a British passport and will be allowed into Britain through a loophole in the Commonwealth Immigration Bill which allows free entry for Asian citizens who are unemployed or ordered to leave Kenya.

(January 2)

QE2 SAILS ON FIRST CRUISE

By ROBERT BEDLOW
Shipping Correspondent

THE Queen Elizabeth 2 began her first commercial voyage yesterday with 1,350 fare-paying passengers. She came into service four months later than planned.

She was given the traditional send-off as she slipped her moorings at the Ocean Terminal, Southampton, and moved out into the Solent on an eight-day cruise which includes calls at Las Palmas, Tenerife and Lisbon.

A brass band from the Royal Corps of Transport played "Oceans Away" and streamers from the ship and the quayside made it a ticker-tape farewell.

On board the QE2 Mr Jimmy Smith, the hotel manager, and Mr. Stuart Humphries, his second in command, had taken 400lb of caviar, 3,500 bottles of champagne, 75,000lb of steak, 280lb of pate de foie gras and 2,000lb of live lobsters. Champagne was selling at 75s a bottle and Havana cigars at 6s.

(April 23)

Sikh busmen win right to turban

Daily Telegraph Reporter

Sikh busmen in Wolverhampton have won their two-year battle for the right to wear turbans on duty.

The borough Transport Committee dropped the ban last bight. Mr. Sohan Singh Jolly, the Sikh's leader, had promised to burn himself to death on Sunday if the committee did not give way.

Ald. Ronald Gough, committee chairman, said after its meeting: "We honestly believe that Mr. Jolly would take his life and so in the interests of race relations we have taken the decision to relax the rule.

(April 10)

CONCORDE'S 715 mph

France's Concorde passed through the "sound barrier" for the first time yesterday. M. Andre Turcat, Sud Aviation's chief test pilot, flew it at 715 mph and at 36,000ft over Cahors some 80 miles north of its base at Toulouse.

(September 29)

MEN OF THE 1st Bn, The Prince of Wales's Own Regiment of Yorkshire, patrolling Derry's Bogside area after moving into the riot-torn city last night. Earlier, mobs of roaming youths engaged the weary Ulster police.

Guns & gas kill animals in rabies area

Daily Telegraph Reporter

ALL wildlife in an area of about 3,000 acres around Camberley, Surrey, where Fritz, a rabid mongrel died nine days ago after biting two people, is to be destroyed by order of Mr Hughes, Minister of Agriculture.

Extermination started yesterday at Old Dean Common, where cyanide powder was put into foxes' lairs, badgers' sets and rabbit warrens. The powder vapourises into gas when the holes are sealed, killing the animals.

The killing will continue on Thursday when 60 Ministry men with guns will shoot all animals on the surface, under the direction of Mr Harry Thompson, a Ministry principal scientific officer.

"It may take two days though we would like to do it in one," he said. "There will be some guns among the beaters in case animals, such as squirrels, try to get out of range.

"It may take a year or so for things to return to normal afterwards. it is not a thing that we like to do, but it is a necessity.

"The area is about 3,000 acres and if there are a few scrub areas which could hide a brace of foxes left over after the shoot these will be dealt with separately. Fritz was missing for about 30 minutes and it could be that he attacked a wild animal."

Mr Alan Joiner, deputy secretary of the RSPCA, said yesterday: "Much as we deplore and regret the killing of any creature, I can't see how we can reasonably object to this. Rabies is an awful disease."

(October 28)

DUBCEK OUSTED

By DAVID FLOYD, Communist Affairs Correspondent

THE end of Mr Dubcek's career as a political leader was announced in Prague yesterday. He has been dropped from the ruling Presidium of the Czechoslovak Communist party, and is to be removed soon from the chairmanship of the Federal Assembly.

The decision to remove Mr Dubcek, who led the Czechoslovak Communist party in the period of democratic reform in 1968, was taken at a two-day meeting of the Party's Central Committee last week. But the Committee stopped short of excluding Mr Dubcek from its membership or disgracing him publicly.

His close colleague, the popular liberal leader, Mr Josef Smrkovsky, however, was expelled from the Central Committee, and will be removed from chairmanship of the House of the People, one of the Chambers of Parliament.

The removal of Mr Dubcek and Mr Smrkovsky symbolises the victory of Dr Husak and the pro-Russian hard-line group in the Central Committee.

Mr Dubcek's place in the Presidium will be taken by Mr Josef Kempny, head of the party's ideological commission, and chief controller of the Czech Press. He is also to become a deputy Prime Minister.

(September 29)

GAS CHAMBER FOR SIRHAN

ALOS ANGELES jury decided yesterday that Sirhan Bishara Sirhan, the 25-year-old Jordanian immigrant who assassinated Senator Robert Kennedy last June, should die in the gas chamber at San Quentin Penitentiary, California.

The short, swarthy Arab, who said he shot Senator Kennedy because of his support for Israel, accepted the verdict silently and with no display of emotion.

(April 27)

THALIDOMIDE BOYS GET £33,000

Daily Telegraph Reporter

TWO boys, deformed at birth because their mothers took thalidomide during pregnancy, were awarded damages totalling £33,600 in the High Court yesterday.

The award is expected to lead to the settlement out of court of many, if not all, of 60 other actions initiated at the same time.

The boys, aged 7 and 8, are to receive £20,800 and £12,800 respectively. This is 40 per cent of the amount they would have received if the action had gone to trial and they had been wholly successful.

The agreement to accept 40 per cent. was made in February, 1968. Under it the Distillers Company, which made and marketed the German drug under licence in Britain, had all allegations of negligence against it withdrawn.

On the basis of yesterday's awards, the Distillers Company (Biochemicals) Ltd., may have to face damages of at least an additional £1 million.

Guide for future

Should any of the 60 pending actions go to trial, yesterday's decision would be taken as a guide to the amount of damages which might be expected to be awarded. Until yesterday, there was no such guide, a fact which was commented on by the judge, Mr. Justice Hinchcliffe.

He said mathematical accuracy was impossible and that there was no yardstick by which he could measure disability. The money, less certain payments that have already been made, is to be paid into court and is to be invested until trusts for the children are approved by the court.

(July 31)

SHEPPARD BISHOP OF WOOLWICH

Daily Telegraph Reporter

THE REV. DAVID SHEPPARD, 39, the former Test cricketer, who, it was announced yesterday, has been appointed Suffragan Bishop of Woolwich, said last night: "I do not want to be a Church bureaucrat."

The Queen's approval of the appointment was announced from 10, Downing Street yesterday. He succeeds the Rt. Rev. John Robinson, author of the controversial "Honest to God," and who will resign on Sept. 28 to become Dean of Trinity College, Cambridge. It is almost unprecedented for a man to become a suffragan bishop within 14 years of ordination.

Mr. Sheppard said at the Mayflower Family Centre, Canning Town, where he is at present warden: "I am nervous about the Establishment because I have grown as a man and a person through this job.

"We are close to our neighbours and this is why I want to go on living in a working class district."

Mr. Sheppard, who is married with one child, has been at the Mayflower Family Centre for 11 years. He was ordained deacon in 1955, and from 1955 to 1958 he was curate of Islington.

(February 24)

U.S. SOLDIERS WEAR BLACK ARMBANDS

By Our Saigon Correspondent

A number of American soldiers in Vietnam wore black armbands in the field yesterday in support of the anti-war Moratorium taking place in the United States, a spokesman for the American High Command said last night.

A further measure of support came from 20 young American volunteer workers in Saigon who presented an anti-war petition to Mr. Ellsworth Bunker, the American Ambassador. They asked him to forward it to President Nixon.

Meanwhile South Vietnam's President Nguyen Van Thieu has invited American anti-war leaders to come to Saigon and "see for themselves."

(October 16)

STRIKE SURRENDER BY WILSON

By H.B. BOYNE
Political Correspondent

AFTER all their brave words and cudgel-shaking, the Prime Minister and Mrs. Barbara Castle, First Secretary, have caved in to the TUC on curbing unofficial strikes.

This was the interpretation which Conservative MPs placed on last night's announcement that an agreed settlement on industrial relations policy has been reached with the TUC General Council.

It amounts not only to deleting the so-called "penal clauses" from the Bill which was intended to curb unofficial strikes, but dropping the entire Bill from this session's legislative programme.

Consultations will proceed at leisure with a view to introducing next session a Bill to implement the more agreeable and less controversial proposals in Mrs. Castle's White Paper, "In Place of Strife."

But Parliament will not be asked to enact penal clauses of any kind this side of the General Election. Indeed, Mrs. Castle said on "24 Hours" last night: "We have given a pledge that in the lifetime of this Government we will not interfere in this field with penal sanctions."

So the crisis in the Labour movement is resolved, in a manner that recalls the opening words of successive instalments in serial stories intended strictly for juveniles: "With one bound, Jack was free."

Empty posturing

The question remains whether this result could not have been achieved without "a hundred dynamic days of empty posturing," as a Conservative MP, Mr. Ronald Bell (Bucks S.), called it in a contemptuous statement last night.

But Labour MPs are undoubtedly relieved and delighted, so are the Cabinet, who had been standing by all day to find out whether the Wilson-Castle confrontation with the General Council at 10, Downing Street was to end in peace or war.

Meeting immediately after the talks had concluded in a warm glow of mutual congratulations, it took the Cabinet less than 15 minutes to endorse the settlement.

Five ministers were absent on duty, including Mr. Denis Healey, Defence Secretary, the only "hard-liner" who might have been liable to consider it an indefensible climb-down. Safely away in Canberra, there would be no point in his objecting on his return, even if he felt disposed to do so.

It is confidently asserted that there will be no resignations from the Cabinet, such as would probably have followed a decision to retain the Industrial Relations Bill with its penal clauses.

As recently as May 9 Mrs. Castle was reported as having told Labour backbenchers that the Government would lose all credibility if it climbed down on her legislation.

But last night she went on record with this statement about the settlement:

"I am extremely happy with it, of course. I have been in all the discussions with the Prime Minister, and we have acted as one."

Left-wing Labour MPs were quick to note, with undisguised satisfaction, that the TUC is committed to nothing it could not have accepted on April 16, when Mrs. Castle so boldly proclaimed that "our major proposals cannot wait."

In their view, the unions can carry on exactly as they have done in the past, with unimpaired sovereignty. They regarded this as a complete victory for themselves and the unions.

Right-wing Tories agree with them. "Abject total defeat" for the Government, Mr. Bell summed up.

(June 19)

MALTA LINK ENDS

Five British minesweepers left Valletta yesterday for Gibraltar, ending a British naval presence on the island which began in 1800. British warships will only return to Malta, once the home of the Mediterranean Fleet, for short visits and refits.

(April 1)

QUINS BORN IN LONDON

By A.J. McILROY

A 33-YEAR-OLD Essex woman, who has been taking a fertility drug, last night gave birth to quins – all girls — in Queen Charlotte's Maternity Hospital, London.

She is Mrs Irene Mary Hanson, wife of Mr John Hanson, 35, an engineer, who live in Rayleigh, Essex. The hospital said her condition was "excellent" and the babies were "satisfactory."

So far they have no names and as they were born tags numbering one to five were attached to them and they were taken to incubators. Mr Hanson was paying a routine visit to his wife when the matron told him his wife had had a premature Caesarean. The couple, who have no other children, celebrated with a kiss soon after the last arrival at 8.36 p.m.

The operation was begun at 8.32 p.m. and was completed by 9 p.m. All the babies were delivered within four minutes.

They weighed (in order of their birth) 2lb 7ozs, 2lb 13ozs, 2lb 15ozs, 3lb 7oz and 2lb 6 ½ozs. They were about two months premature.

Mrs Hanson who this week celebrated her birthday, thought she would never have a baby but in March she was put on the fertility drug gonadotrophin and almost immediately became pregnant.

(November 14)

CLINIC TO STERILISE MEN

Daily Telegraph Reporter

A STERILISATION clinic for men is due to open in Birmingham early next year. The clinic, operated by the Family Planning Association, will be only the second run by them in the country.

It will provide simple operations under local anaesthetic for a fee of about £16. Plans are also being considered for a second West Midlands clinic at West Bromwich.

A spokesman for Birmingham Family Planning Association said the clinic was being opened in response to a growing demand for the service among married couples in the area.

(December 20)

DR KING'S KILLER GETS 99 YEARS

By Henry Miller

MEMPHIS, Tennessee

James Earl Ray, 41, was gaoled for 99 years in Memphis, Tennessee, yesterday after admitting that he murdered Dr. Martin Luther King, the civil rights leader, on April 4 last year.

Though the prosecution and Ray's own lawyer Mr. Percy Foreman, insisted that no evidence of a conspiracy had been uncovered, Ray himself in a brief court statement hinted that there might have been some kind of plot and so the question of a possible conspiracy remains.

But Ray nevertheless agreed that he wanted to plead guilty to the first-degree (capital) murder of Dr King. He was doing so without any influence or pressure from anyone and was aware that he was waiving all rights to appeal.

(March 11)

CHARLES MANSON, 34, LEADER OF THE HIPPIE CULT, "Satan's Slaves," who with others, will face trial on murder conspiracy charges over the killing of Sharon Tate, the actress, and six other people, being escorted to the central jail in Los Angeles, California.

HIPPIES HELD IN SHARON TATE MURDERS CASE

By MABEL ELLIOTT in New York

LOS ANGELES police said yesterday they were confident that the Hollywood massacre, known as "the Sharon Tate murder case," had been solved with the arrest of members of a hippie tribe.

Their first real clue in an investigation that began when actress Sharon Tate, 26, and four friends were tortured and killed in grotesque circumstances last August, came two weeks ago.

Susan Atkins, 21, a member of the hippie group, who was known as "Sadie Glutz," told her story to a police informer. She is being held in protective custody.

Police said that the details she gave could have been known only to the murderers and witnesses. The girl said that seconds before she was killed Miss Tate pleaded: "Let me have my baby."

The actress, wife of Roman Polanski, the film director, was expecting her first child a month later. Her husband was in London when she was murdered.

All in custody

Los Angeles police believe that five members of the hippie tribe, two men and three women, took part in the murders. All are now in custody.

Among those held is Charles Manson, 34, leader of the "hate" tribe, who called himself both "Jesus" and "Satan." The Hippies at the time had settled in a desolate spot called the Barker Ranch, an abandoned mining camp in Death Valley, California.

Police believe the hippies murdered Miss Tate and her friends to "punish" them for their affluent way of life and to "liberate" them from it.

The hippie tribe lived in dilapidated outhouses, abandoned poultry runs and vegetable gardens.

The tribe was flushed when police inquiring about stolen cars and other property made a pre-dawn swoop in planes, and "dune buggies" – beach cars.

The victims in the Tate murders, in addition to the actress, were: Jay Sebring, 35, innovator of hair styling for men; Abigail Folger, 26, San Francisco heiress to the Folger coffee fortune; Voityck Frokowsky, 37, who worked with Miss Tate's husband in Polish films, and Steven Parent, 19, a friend of the estate caretaker.

(December 3)

MRS MEIR TO FOLLOW ESHKOL

By JOHN WALLIS
in Jerusalem

MRS. GOLDA MEIR, the "Grand Old Woman" of Israeli politics is to succeed her old friend, the late Mr. Levi Eskol, as Prime Minister of Israel.

This will be the inevitable result of her acceptance yesterday of the Labour party's candidature. She had received 287 votes with 47 abstentions in the party's Central Committee.

The abstentions were from the pro-Dayan group which claims that he is the only possible successor as Prime Minister.

Gen. Dayan, the Defence Minister, has not offered himself as a candidate.

Mrs. Meir told the Committee: "You impose this candidature on me and I will do all I can to preserve national unity."

On Sunday President Shazar will begin discussions with other parties to pave the way formally for her appointment.

Israel's next Prime Minister is 70 and a widowed grandmother. She will be the first woman to hold the post.

(March 8)

Students march to demand LSE reopening

By JAMES ALLAN and KENNETH CLARKE

A TORCHLIGHT procession of 2,000 students marched through London last night to demand the reopening of the London School of Economics.

They marched from the University of London building in Malet Street, Bloomsbury, to the LSE in Aldwych, down Fleet Street to the Financial Times building near St. Paul's University.

Their intention to stay for the night was foiled by the London University rugby players, who marched through the building cleaning them out.

Earlier at a meeting in the University of London Union building, about 400 students decided that the march would be "militant but peaceful."

Asked what this meant, an organiser explained: "There will be no provocation to the police and no attempt to take the school by force."

The march moved off at 6.45 p.m. with students chanting slogans and carrying banners that were as varied as the garb worn by many of the demonstrators.

The marchers had moved only a few yards when the occupant of a flat overlooking the route began to throw water at them, but it fell on Press reporters and cameramen.

Police kept the marchers in groups, but at frequent intervals the students, loudly chanting "Free, free the LSE," broke into a rhythmic trot to close the gaps.

Lecturers on march

Among the marchers were Mr. Robin Blackburn and Mr. Lawrence Harris, the two LSE lecturers who have been summoned to appear before an LSE disciplinary committee following last Friday's demonstration at the school which led to its closure.

Before the march began the students, and other older sympathisers, were told by one of the organisers, Mr. Chris Harman, that there should be no provocation and no arrests.

Their intention, however, was quickly thwarted by a couple of hundred moderate students, many of them members of the University of London rugby club.

They marched through the building chanting "LSE Out – Out!" and cleared the building of all LSE students.

The much-vaunted student solidarity finally crumbled outside the union building when, amid shouts of "Go home" a few LSE students who tried to make speeches were bundled away. Police watched but did not intervene.

As the march entered Aldwych, the chanting grew louder but the students found the entrance to Houghton Street, where the school building is situated, completely sealed off by policemen four deep, backed by six mounted officers.

Under the blaze of television lights they stood haranguing the police and the LSE authorities and demanding: "Free, free LSE – take it from the bourgeoisie," But there was no move to charge the police line.

There was a small skirmish on the pavement, however, when some of the students spotted Mr. Terence Morris, a senior lecturer at the School.

Someone hurled an object at him and the cry of "Fascist pig" was taken up. The militants have accused several members of the staff of informing on students to the police and the authorities.

Traffic, swelled by the late evening shopping in the West End, was seriously disrupted by the march.

Before the marchers dispersed, to a ragged rendering of the Internationale, Mr. Bateson announced a meeting today to discuss further action and to organise another demonstration on Monday.

Later a handful of LSE students returned to the University of London union building and took over the quarter which they are allowed to use during the day. When the building was being closed at 10.30 p.m., it appeared that they intended to stay for the night.

(January 31)

THE GIRL THAT I MARRY BY PRINCE CHARLES

By NORMAN HARE, Television Staff

PRINCE CHARLES, in a wide-ranging television interview, said last night that he often felt he would like to marry somebody English or perhaps, Welsh but it was "awfully difficult."

In his first television interview, recorded jointly by Harlech Television and the BBC and broadcast last night, he was asked by Brian Connell, for ITV, whether he thought the girl he should marry should be a royal or titled person.

The Prince replied: "You see this is awfully difficult because you've got to remember that when you marry in my position, you are going to marry somebody who perhaps one day is going to become Queen.

"You've got to choose somebody very carefully who could fulfil this particular role. It's got to be somebody pretty special and one advantage about marrying a princess for instance, or somebody from a royal family, is that they do know what happens".

Prince Charles also talked about the influence of his parents, his future as the Prince of Wales, the Investiture, Welsh nationalism and a possible career in the Services.

Also interviewed by Cliff Michelmore of the BBC, the Prince was completely at ease and answered personal questions without displaying any embarrassment or seeking to be evasive. He emerged as a young man of considerable charm and poise with keen wit.

(June 27)

KENNEDY ASKS VOTERS: SHOULD I GO?

TV appeal over girl's car death

By IAN BALL in New York and MABEL ELLIOTT in Edgartown, Massachussetts

THE Kennedy dynasty placed its future early today in the hands of the voters of its home state of Massachusetts when Senator Edward Kennedy gave on nationwide television his explanation of the incident a week ago that took the life of a pretty blonde secretary.

He was speaking a few hours after being given a two-month suspended prison sentence in the Distric Court of Dukes County, Edgartown, Massachusetts, where he pleaded guilty to leaving the scene of the accident in which Miss Mary Jo Kopechne was drowned.

Senator Kennedy, his voice occassionally breaking with emotion, made an oblique appeal for a plebiscite, a vote of confidence, to be taken among the voters of Massachusetts, to decide whether he should remain in the United States Senate.

He pointed out that after so much "publicity, innuendo" the question of whether he should step down from the Senate would arise.

He was ready to leave the settlement of that question in the hands of the people who had elected him.

Senator Kennedy, who is 37, spoke from the book-lined library of his father's house in Hyannis Port, Cape Cod, Massachusetts the hub of the so-called compound.

It was at times a remarkably frank statement from a troubled man. At one point he said that immediately after the accident he found himself wondering whether indeed some "curse did hang over the Kennedy's"

"No words can express the terrible pain and the agonising week," he said.

He declared that there was no truth whatever in any story of immoral conduct and there had never been a private relationship between Miss Kopechne and himself.

He added: "Nor was I driving under the influence of liquor."

Senator Kennedy had been under mounting pressure to explain the time lapse of more than eight hours between the accident and the time he reported it to the police.

Delay "indefensible"

"I regard as indefensible the fact that I did not report the accident to the police immediately," he said.

Senator Kennedy described how during his futile rescue attempt "Water entered my lungs and I felt the sensation of drowning."

He disclosed for the first time after the accident he had returned to the cottage and told two people, what had happened.

But he did not answer all of the many questions that had been lacking answers during the week of silence. The one point he did clear up conclusively was how he managed to make the crossing between Chappaquiddic island and Martha's Vineyard after the regular ferry service had ended at midnight.

He said that he "swam impulsively" across the water, and almost drowned for a second time that evening in the process.

Miss Kopechne, 28, drowned when the car driven by Senator Kennedy plunged into a sea water pond after a party on Chappaquiddick island early last Saturday. She was secretary to the late Senator Robert Kennedy.

Judge's comment

Judge James Boyle, passing sentence at the court hearing, said that the Senator "has been punished and will continue to be punished beyond anything this court can impose."

Senator Kennedy has been convicted for driving offences on at least four other occasions.

All four previous offences occurred while Senator Kennedy was studying law at the University of Virginia.

Senator Kennedy is now on probation for one year. If he had been ordered to serve his sentence he would have had to wear a grey prison uniform.

There is no hard labour at a house of correction which is for prisoners convicted of minor offences.

He would most likely have shared a cell with one other inmate and spent his time doing repair jobs such as painting, or scrubbing floors and kitchen duty. He would have had visiting privileges, mail, and reading matter.

(July 26)

SENATOR EDWARD KENNEDY LEAVING THE COURTHOUSE yesterday in Edgartown, Mass, with his wife Joan, after he had pleaded guilty to leaving the scene of the accident in which Miss Mary Jo Kopechne was killed.

10S ON TV BUT RADIO IS FREE

THE combined TV-radio licence is to go up 10s to £6 10s from April 1, 1971, when the separate sound and car radio fees of 25s will be abolished. About 1 ½ million householders will benefit from abolition of the sound licence.

Announcing these and other changes yesterday, Mr. Stonehouse, the Postmaster-General, said the increased revenue of £5.6 million would finance a general service of local revenue by the BBC.

(August 15)

£300m PLAN TO RETURN MIGRANTS

By H.B. BOYNE, Political Correspondent

MR. ENOCH POWELL urgently advocated last night a means of lifting from Britain's future the "dark and ever more menacing shadow" of the immigration problem.

His remedy, which he considers to be fully in accord with official Conservative policy, is a £300,000,000 scheme of organised repatriation and resettlement.

Commending it, he acquitted Mr. Heath, Conservative Leader, of "Humbug," but accused him of "something more alarming: sheer incomprehension of the very magnitude of the danger."

He also suggested that the party leadership had gone out of their way to "play down" the repatriation aspect of their policy, seeming "almost anxious to represent it as of no significant importance."

Mr. Powell, speaking at Wolverhampton, said the people of Britain were being misled if they imagined that net immigration had yet been reduced.

He quoted figures to show that it was running at 75,900 in 1968.

21 p.c. increase

At the beginning of last year the proportion of immigrant and immigrant-descended children in Wolverhampton infant schools was 17.1 per cent. Twelve months later it had jumped to almost 21 per cent.

In only two of London's 12 inner boroughs was the primary school proportion less than 13 per cent., and in Haringey it was as high as 30.8 per cent.

In Wolverhampton almost one birth in every four was immigrant, and the proportion had now been running steadily at that level for six years.

These figures, Mr. Powell argued, excused no one from forming a view as to what the future would be a generation or two ahead.

"Unless the proportion of births falls soon and sharply, and I see no reason for expecting that, at least one-quarter of the population of this borough will in course of time be Asian or West Indian.

"Such is the prospect which is taking shape before our eyes. In my opinion it is fraught with danger and disaster to all concerned, without exception, and we need only look across the Atlantic to discern the features of such a disaster."

The magnitude of the danger could be reduced decisively in two ways:

1 – Reduce admissions for settlement to "negligible proportions," and end the continuing inflow of dependants

2 – Facilitate the voluntary return to their own countries of as many as possible of the immigrants and their children already in Britain.

Whether the details of Mr. Powell's repatriation scheme will be incorporated in Conservative election policy remains to be seen.

What is certain is that once again, as at Birmingham in April, 1968, and at Eastbourne last November, he has pushed the immigration issue into the forefront of political controversy.

There are many Conservative MPs, and also some Labour ones from areas most affected, who believe he is perfectly right to do so.

(June 10)

BIRDS LOST IN FOG INVADE VILLAGE

Glinton village, near Peterborough, was "invaded" by a huge flock of birds at the weekend. Hundreds of birds apparently lost in thick fog, flopped against windows and doors.

The "siege" lasted almost two hours on Saturday night. A police spokesman said: "It was unbelievable. Literally hundreds of birds, mainly starlings, converged on the village."

(January 13)

GROWING PRESSURE TO RESTRICT USE OF DDT

By ADRIAN BERRY, Science Staff

PRESSURE to ban or curtail severely all use in Britain of the dangerous chemical insecticide DDT and its by-products, is building up following Canada's decision to restrict its use by 90 per cent.

An increasing number of national and local governments have forbidden its use. The State of California announced a ban on its sale in June. It is banned in Michigan and in Norway and Denmark. Its use is restricted in Arizona and Australia.

Most ironic of all, the first country to ban it was Sweden, which in 1930 awarded a Nobel Prize to its inventor, the Swiss chemist, Dr Paul Muller.

In Britain the Government's Advisory Committee on Pesticides is expected to announce its decision in December.

The Government decided in 1964 that there was "insufficient evidence to justify a complete ban," but the matter should be reviewed at the end of three years. Two years later this review is now imminent.

"Wonder chemical"

DDT is a prime example of a "wonder chemical" which at first seemed miraculous, but by degrees justly acquired a sinister reputation.

Short for dichloro-diphenyl-trichloro-ethane, DDT has the horrible characteristics of being almost indestructible. It can therefore be spread by wind and water to threaten all life far away from the place where it was first sprayed, and many years after the spraying occurred.

Because of this indestructibility, DDT builds up in the food-chain until in the higher mammals it has reached levels of contamination far above the maximim safety levels decreed by the most tolerant authorities.

Scientists are not agreed on the precise effect which heavy concentrations of DDT and DDD have on humans. One possibility is damage to the adrenal gland which can cause a rare kind of cancer.

Other poisonous pesticides at present being considered by the Advisory Committee include dieldrin, which can be up to 40 times more toxic than DDT.

It strikes at the nervous system and sends its victims into convulsions; and aldrin, which attacks the liver and kidneys. It has been found that a quantity of aldrin no bigger than an aspirin can kill up to 400 quail.

Other pesticides under consideration are camphochlor, chlordane, heptachlor, and TDE.

(November 5)

ITALIAN BOMBS KILL 13

By ERIC RORICH in Rome

ROME police detained four men last night after a series of bomb explosions in the city and Milan, causing the death of 13 people. Another 100 people were reported injured.

The 13 deaths and 78 of the injuries occurred in central Milan, where a bomb devastated the interior of a bank. Within an hour three further explosions shook two areas of Rome, injuring at least 14 people.

An Army bomb expert told reporters that the explosion at Milan's National Agricultural Bank was of a force equivalent to between 9lb and 11lb of TNT. The bomb was in a third floor waiting room occupied by more than 100 people.

Signor Michele Carlotto, 27, a clerk at the bank, said: "I was sitting at my desk beyond the bank counter. I heard a blast, a bolt which stunned me. In the smoke I saw a body flying from the public section above the counter and falling one yard away from me. I was shocked. I couldn't move."

Another unexploded bomb was found in a bank near Milan's La Scala Opera House. A performance of "The Barber of Seville" was cancelled, and Christmas illuminations were switched off.

(December 13)

POP SONGS HIDE LSD CODE

By Richard Beeston in Washington

Pop records convey hidden messages telling teenagers to take drugs, Mr. Art Linkletter, an American television personality, said in Washington yesterday. His daughter recently committed suicide after taking LSD.

"Every rock-n-roll radio station is sending out, 18 hours a day, messages to kids that are right over the heads of our generation," he told Mr. Nixon and a group of Congress leaders from both parties at a White House conference on improving drugs control.

"You don't realise it, but every time one of the Top 40 hit records is played, it is an advertisement for 'trips' (LSD experiences).

"They have words you've never heard of. When they are played, the kids are rapping (talking to each other).

(October 24)

LLOYD'S OPEN DOORS TO WOMEN

By GERDA PAUL

AFTER nearly 300 years women are to be admitted to membership of Lloyd's. From next January, any woman, British by birth or by naturalisation, with assets of £75,000, who has put down a deposit of about £15,000 and who has been passed by the committee, will be free to underwrite through an agent.

But she will not be allowed to conduct business personally in the Lloyd's market.

However, the full range of Lloyd's syndicates, covering marine, non-marine, aviation, and motor insurance will be open to her to invest in.

"I am delighted to welcome the ladies," said Mr. Henry Mance, 56, chairman, after the 16-strong Lloyd's Committee had announced its unanimous decision yesterday.

A spokesman agreed that the reason for allowing the ladies in was purely commercial. Their money would help Lloyd's expansion scheme.

He made clear they will be allowed to do so only at a distance. Although the day may come when women do the actual insurance business at present it is thought that they do not have the "necessary expertise."

From next January approved women will be allowed to wander through the "room" – the main hall where business is conducted – for the first time without escort. They may talk to the underwriters belonging to their syndicates who are conducting business to the "stalls."

No one has any idea how many women will apply. But at least one application went in yesterday – that of Mrs. Kenneth Alder, 55, of Chigwell, wife of a Lloyd's underwriter.

"I am very interested in the business," she said yesterday. "We have no family, and my only other interests are a little golf and a little racing. If I am accepted I shall come to Lloyd's quite a lot."

(February 21)

North Sea Oil Found

HIGH-GRADE oil has been discovered in the North Sea by the companies drilling for gas. There are "high-hopes" of it becoming a viable commercial prospect, an official of one of the companies said last night.

Geophysical experts were at present studying the north sea find because they believed it was so important.

If the find proved to be a viable proposition the oil would be pumped into Aberdeen.

(June 21)

MAXWELL IS OUSTED FROM PERGAMON

Daily Telegraph Reporter

MR ROBERT MAXWELL, the Labour MP, has been ousted as chairman and director of Pergamon Press. He and his fellow Pergamon directors were defeated by a share poll at a special meeting of shareholders yesterday.

When the result of the voting was announced at the Connaught Rooms, London, Mr Maxwell said: "The board of Pergamon has been sacked."

Resolutions for the removal of Mr Maxwell and his colleagues were put by Mr Saul Steinberg, head of the Leasco data group, which has been involved in the take-over struggle for Pergamon during the past few months.

Some 4,551,343 votes supported a resolution to keep the board in office pending a successful takeover, but 7,927,071 were cast against it.

Similar numbers also voted out of office the eight Pergamon directors including Mr Maxwell, the chairman, and replaced them with seven Leasco nominees.

Later Mr Steinberg and colleagues including Sir Henry d'Avigdor-Goldsmid, Conservative MP for Walsall S., the new independent chairman, met for about an hour. As they left a spokesman said: "The board has been reconstituted as promised and has met."

"Very, very sad"

Mr Maxwell commented: "You can't expect me to be other than very, very, sad."

Even before the votes had been counted Mr Maxwell mentioned the possibility of making a personal take-over bid for Pergamon, in conjunction with private Maxwell family companies, or of procuring a bid by an American company.

Mr Maxwell disclosed that the City institutions gave 20 per cent. of their votes against Pergamon to give Leasco a combined 61 per cent. majority against 33 1/3 per cent. for Pergamon.

He said: "My personal feelings are that Pergamon has been built up by me and my colleagues over 20 years, and having sacked the management in this way I am naturally a bit frightened for the future of Pergamon.

(October 11)

Round the world yacht found abandoned

By JOHN OWEN

MYSTERY surrounded the whereabouts of round-the-world yachtsman Donald Crowhurst when his trimaran, Teignmouth Electron, was found abandoned 700 miles west of the Azores yesterday.

The trimaran was found by the British vessel Picardy. There was no sign of Crowhurst, leader in the Sunday Times Golden Globe race, and no evidence as to why he left the craft.

Teignmouth Electron was drifting in much the same latitudes where fellow competitor, Lt.-Cdr. Nigel Tetley, was rescued recently when his trimaran broke up.

Personal papers and BBC tapes found on board indicated that Crowhurst had not intended to abandon ship. The life raft and dinghy were still on board.

The fact that the mainsail was set but the two foresails were lying on deck as if ready for hoisting suggested that Crowhurst slipped and fell overboard on going forward to hoist extra canvas.

Crowhurst, 36, from Bridgwater, Somerset, married with four children, hoped to reach Teignmouth in Devon next week and win the £5,000 prize for the fastest non-stop round the world voyage.

Search useless

His most recent messages indicated that he had hit light winds and was becalmed. But he still hoped to keep to his schedule.

Air-sea search and rescue authorities at Plymouth last night doubted whether search would be made by the Azores authorities.

"The chances of spotting a man out there are remote, and there is no indication when he left the trimaran," a spokesman said.

The news broke last night as the little Devon seaside resort, which contributed £1,500 to Crowhurst's costs in return for him taking its name around the world, was in the final stages of planning his welcome.

(July 11)

MR. ANTHONY GREY, the Reuter's correspondent who has returned to Britain after spending 26 months under house arrest in Peking, taking coffee in his London hotel yesterday with his mother, Mrs Agnes Grey, and elder sister, Mrs June Carter.

Grey tells how Red Guards hanged cat

ANTHONY GREY, Reuter correspondent, who flew back to London on Sunday, said yesterday that a terrible moment of his 26 months imprisonment in Peking was when Red Guards hanged his pet cat and then started to shout: "Hang Grey, Hang Grey."

Mr Grey, 31, was recovered enough from his journey from China following his release last week to talk about the night of Aug. 18, 1967, when at least 200 Red Guards swarmed into his house in Peking. This was about a month after he had been told that he was a prisoner in his house.

"There was a commotion in the street and I knew I was going to be invaded," Mr Grey said. Then they burst into my office and dragged me downstairs to the courtyard. It was a hot night. I was in shorts and a sweat shirt.

"They painted me with black paint and jet-planed me – forced my arms behind me so that my body was bent forward. Whenever I tried to straighten up one Red Guard at my side punched me in the stomach. They glued a poster to my back."

When Grey was frog-marched into the house again he found posters stuck up everywhere and black paint daubed even on his sheets.

The first month of his imprisonment had been fairly easy. He had the freedom of his entire house, and was allowed to write and play chess with a friend by telephone.

After the Red Guard invasion he was confined to a small room eight feet by eight feet that had been used by his driver between duties. It contained only a bed with the springs sticking up.

"This was my home for the next three months. I could walk only eight and a half paces to a small washroom. They had nailed boards across the window – and even daubed the bristles of my toothbrush with black paint.

Saved by Yoga

Grey said he had three books. One was about chess, another on the theory and practice of Communism and the third was a book describing yoga exercises which he had picked up by chance on his way to China.

"The Yoga book turned out to be my salvation, Grey said. In his confined space he did the exercises for two hours each day and found they kept him in physical health and brought him mental calm at times when he felt close to panic.

Later in the year he developed stomach trouble. "I could not walk even my eight and a half paces. I felt this very keenly."

His diet suddenly improved after a Chinese doctor had examined him. There was butter at last and fruit.

He was moved into a bigger room 12 feet by 12 feet. The floor was bare and a black board was propped up at eye level filled with the quotations of Mao Tse-tung.

From then until his release his life consisted of devising ways to occupy his mind and keep it balanced.

His guards never spoke to him, only stared at him with hostile eyes. He thought out nicknames for them,

composed insulting rhymes about them in his mind to the tune of popular songs. They kept singing revolutionary songs or chanting slogans.

"I thought of my past life, of course," Mr Grey said. "I thought of incidents, people, actions I had taken and analysed them all right back to my childhood. I felt after a while that I had scraped my memory clean.

"I refused to pass the time away by sleeping in the daytime. I knew that would be bad for me, that I had to maintain a proper rhythm of sleep so that I would not be awake in the long nights.

"So even on the hottest days I sat bolt upright in a chair keeping awake when even the guards were sleeping.

The letters he occasionally received from his mother and his friend, Shirley McGuinn, were high spots. "One letter would occupy me for a whole day. I would read it over and over again."

Mr Grey was remarkably relaxed yesterday and spoke quietly and unemotionally about his experiences, often laughing and joking.

Christmas present

On Christmas day, 1968, he received a crossword puzzle and looked upon it as a fine present. "Somehow I felt a quiet sort of joy on that day.

I put on my best suit – to the puzzlement of the guards – and I tried to make it a special day though I was so alone."

At the end of May this year Mr Grey suddenly found his conditions much improved. He was allowed to listen to the radio and this was his first contact with the outside world.

It was also the dawn of hope that at last freedom was nearing. – Reuter.

(October 14)

HOYLE REVEALS NEW GRAVITY THEORY

A new gravitational theory, taking account of both weak and strong gravity fields, was presented by Prof. Fred Hoyle, of Cambridge University, in a lecture to the Royal Institution of Great Britain last night.

He said weak gravity fields were those normally encountered in our solar system holding the planets and the sun together. Strong gravity fields were necessary to explain the events taking place inside quasars and pulsars.

The conventional nuclear forces which keep the sun and the other stars alight for millions of years were not enough to account for the fantastic output of light, radio waves and other radiation coming from quasars and pulsars.

(April 26)

Mrs Thatcher takes over

By Our Political Correspondent

MR HEATH, Leader of the Opposition sprang a surprise last night by announcing his appointment of Mrs Margaret Thatcher, 44, Conservative MP for Finchley, to succeed Sir Edward Boyle as Shadow Cabinet spokesman on Education.

Sir Edward, 46, resigned the post last week after his appointment as Vice-Chancellor of Leeds University. Mr Heath has kept to a minimum the consequent reshuffle of the Shadow Cabinet.

MR PETER WALKER, 37, takes over from Mrs Thatcher responsibility for transport, which has been her task since November last year. This will be in addition to his responsibilities for housing and local government.

SIR KEITH JOSEPH, 51, whom many had expected to become the education "Shadow" assumes overall responsibility for technology and power, in addition to trade.

As no newcomer has been brought in to replace Sir Edward, the size of the Shadow Cabinet is reduced from 17 to 16.

Mrs Thatcher has two children, twins aged 16, still at school. Mark is at Harrow, Carol at St Paul's girls. Her husband, Mr Denis Thatcher, whom she married in 1951, is a director of Castrol oil and other companies.

Mr Heath's choice of Mrs Thatcher will appeal to Conservative supporters who considered Sir Edward too far to the Left, without offending the so-called "progressives." It certainly does not indicate any change of policy.

(October 22)

John Lennon returns MBE in peace protest

By Philip Evans

Beatle John Lennon last night returned the MBE insignia he received in 1965. Letters explaining his action were delivered to the Queen and the Prime Minister.

Lennon said in the letters: "I am returning this MBE in protest against Britain's involvement in the Nigerian-Biafran thing, against our support of America in Vietnam, and because his record, "Cold Turkey," had slipped from 15 to 18 in the Top 20.

The insignia was delivered to Central Chancery of the Orders of Knighthood as the 29-year-old veteran of lie-ins for peace explained his latest crusade.

(November 26)

MURDOCH WINS NoW

MR RUPERT MURDOCH, 37, was appointed managing director of News of the World yesterday within an hour of a stormy shareholders' meeting which approved a link with News Ltd., of Australia and defeated a £35 million takeover bid by Mr. Robert Maxwell's Pergamon Press.

The decision signalled the end of one of the bitterest and most acrimonious takeover battles in the City's history.

(January 3)

Samuel Beckett wins Nobel prize

By Our Stockholm Correspondent

SAMUEL BECKETT, 63, who is acknowledged as one of the greatest living dramatists for his pioneering of new modes of theatrical expression, was yesterday awarded the 1969 Nobel Prize for literature.

A leading candidate for the award for many years, the controversial writer, who has lived in Paris since 1937, will receive about £30,000.

Last night Mr Beckett was not available and Mr Jerome Lindon, his publisher, said in Paris that he may be trying to avoid publicity by hiding under a false name in Tunisia.

"From what I know of him, Beckett left his hotel when the prize was announced to take refuge in another hotel under another name," said Mr. Lindon.

In its citation the Swedish Academy said Beckett was being honoured for writing which, in new forms for the novel and drama, acquired its elevation in the destitution of modern man.

Loneliness and despair are recurrent themes in Beckett's sombre works, particularly his plays, of which "Waiting for Godot" ("En Attendant Godot") – written in one month in 1952 – brought him instant recognition after more than 20 years as an obscure poet and novelist.

One major critic has described Beckett's characters as "solitaries, lonely men whom God has let down and from whom man has turned away in disgust."

Born in Dublin in April, 1906, of Protestant parents, Beckett was educated at Trinity College and later Portora Royal School in Ulster, where he was known as a brilliant scholar and an accomplished sportsman.

He received a lectorate in English at the Ecole Normale Superieure in Paris in 1928, where he first came under the influence of fellow-Irish author James Joyce and returned to Trinity College to teach English two years later, when his first publication, the poem "Whoroscope," was issued.

He wrote some essays for avante-garde literary reviews and published short stories and further poems before finally settling down in Paris in 1937.

At the outbreak of the 1939-45 war he was in Ireland but returned quickly to France and joined the Resistance, later moving to the unoccupied zone in the south where he wrote the novel "Watt."

The post-war years were his most creative. Turning to the French language, he produced the triology comprising "Molloy," "Malone Meurt" and "L'Innommable," and later the plays "Waiting for godot," "End Game," "All that Fall," "Play" and "Eh, Joe."

In the past decade, Beckett has continued to startle audiences with dramatic innovations such as "Play," in which only the heads of a man and two women are seen, chanting about their three-way relationship, and "Eh, Joe" in which a lone male character's thoughts are expressed in a woman's voice.

(October 24th)

SAMUEL BECKETT, 63, Dublin-born novelist, playwright and poet, who was awarded this year's £30,000 Nobel Prize for Literature in Stockholm yesterday.

PLAY'S BALEFUL HUMOUR OF HOSPITAL WARD

By JOHN BARBER

NO one has Peter Nichols's gift for wringing laughter out of suffering. His new play, "The National Health" at the Old Vic, turns a baleful eye on illness and death and discovers that every cloud has a jet-black lining.

The result – to be expected of the playwright who joked about a spastic child (in "A Day in the Death of Joe Egg) – is hilarious.

All comedy is about the troubles of others but here we reach rock-bottom. The scene is a hospital ward as grim as a hospital ward, where six desperate cases, all male and all ageing, grumble and gossip and tear at each other's nerves.

Abject, stripped of all dignity, the helpless sextet are thrust through the healing routine like grinning partners in a macabre jig. Breezy nurses call the figures. Have a bath, get up, get back to bed, lie down like a good boy. What about some bye-byes. Would you like a bottle? How are your waterworks? No personal remarks!

Life is worse than prison. A professional visitor whispers about Jesus. If you doze, someone yells you awake. You are always being asked if you are full of the joys of spring. People keep exclaiming "Well done!" and "That's the style!" and "Time marches on!"

As for why it is all so funny, I do not know: perhaps it is the appalling thoughtlessness of the cruelty to patients so pitiful. This is a play of revelatory wit and brutal compassion.

In a long cast Robert Lang is unforgettable as the frustrated Ash. Marry Lomax, Brian Oulton and Charles Kay among the patients and Cleo Sylvestre, Jim Dale and Paul Curran of the staff, contribute much to a disciplined team.

(October 17)

One-man satires on Australian life

By JOHN BARBER

THE one-man entertainment by the actor and cartoonist Barry Humphries at the Fortune Theatre is called, self-deprecatingly enough, "Just a Show." But there is nothing in the least modest or retiring about this aggressive Australian comedian.

He puts across his character-sketches of Antipodean types, all written by himself, with notable vigour and acerbity.

But besides being lustily rendered, they are clearly the work of a soured and sharp-eyed, sharp-eared observer who seems to have found only a little to recall with affection and plenty to hate in Australian life. It is his hatred that is Barry Humphries' greatest strength.

He appears first, looking like a younger Douglas Byng, in his famous characterisation (already seen on TV) of Edna Everage – the "Mrs Average" of the Melbourne suburbs. With thin lips, beak-nosed, pop-eyed, always smiling, her vowels hideous and a voice a squeaking falsetto, she speaks in sentimental clichés and has a half-pathetic, half-comic obsession with her native land and its too-abundant fruits.

From cruel gossip she switches to easy mawkishness, beaming at us vacuously through her spectacles as she damands: "What are crowsfeet but the dried-up beds of old smiles...?"

The other victims of the actor's satire are less original. There is the vulgarian father proposing a toast at the wedding-breakfast, bawling out his awareness of his daughter's contempt for him and leading up to his drunken refusal at the end to foot the catering bill.

The evening ends riotously with a parody of a modern "experimental" film and a return of the Edna Everage character, this time with armfuls of gladioli. These she hurls out into the auditorium, crying hysterically, "Gladdy time! Gladdy time!" When I left the theatre the audience were waving them delightedly and singing out loud.

If never very subtle, Barry Humphries is often extremely funny, and even though one misses many local allusions the savagery of his onslaught upon "the land where nothing happens" is to be relished.

(March 18)

Tynan's 'Erotic' fails to rouse critics

By HENRY MILLER in New York

THE "evening of erotica" promised by Kenneth Tynan in his off-Broadway production of "Oh! Calcutta!" which acquired an advanced reputation of being the dirtiest show in town, bored rather than stimulated most of the New York critics. The music was about the only thing they liked.

The nudity in the show, which had attracted capacity audiences to previews since May 11, failed to shock them or, evidently, most of the official first-nighters.

Clive Barnes, the New York Times critic, said: "There is no more innocent show in town – and certainly none more witless – than this silly little diversion.

"Innocent it is, completely. It is child-like when they strip and the stripping, dancing and staging are about the only tolerable parts of the evening for 'mature audiences' to whom the producers are somewhat foolhardily addressing their sales pitch."

He added: "This is the kind of show to give pornography a dirty name. What a nice dirtyminded boy like Kenneth Tynan is doing in a place like this I fail to understand."

Jerry Tallmer, reviewing the show for the New York Post, gave the director, Jacques Levy, credit for at least choosing good looking actors and actresses for the nude scenes. "It is a pleasure to watch them until the words come out," he said.

"The words, the skits that come between. I have seen better – and many much better – in plain old good burlesque. And I have been roused by better in good old burlesque, as not here."

(June 19)

TRENDSETTERS 'ROUNDABOUT

By Timothy Raison

The Neophiliacs.
By Christopher Booker.
(Collins 2gns)

IN a way, it was rash of Christopher Booker to reveal that he wrote part of his much-heralded "The Neophiliacs" while staying with Malcolm Muggeridge. It was even rasher to quote the immortal Ecclesiastes lament, "Vanity of vanities, saith the Preacher..."

For the message of "The Neophiliacs" is very much a Muggeridge-Ecclesiastes message, which exposes Mr Booker to the Preacher's own comments: "There is no new thing under the sun." Yet for all that the book was very well worth writing. And I would guess that it comes out at exactly the right moment, when the craze for novelty at all costs is dying away and people are beginning to weary of Pop-camp-colour-supplement culture.

Certainly its attack in this area is rollocking and highly successful. Booker – with Private Eye and "That Was the Week That Was" behind him – is very well qualified to demonstrate the dottinesses and trivialities of some of our recent arbiters of taste and fashion. The Tynans, Snowdons, Boxers, Quants, David Baileys, Terence Stamps and so on are skilfully put in perspective against the zany background of the age which they helped to shape, or at least epitomise.

But "The Neophiliacs" is not just a withering narrative of the clichés of the last few years. It is also an essay in social psychology. As such it seems to me very interesting, but ultimately not quite convincing.

(October 16)

THE 'ACID' WAY OF LIFE

By Roderick Junor

The Electric Kool-Aid Acid Test.
By Tom Wolfe
(Weidenfeld & Nicolson 2 gns)

THE scene is an old Wild West oasis, a "huge slimy kelpy pond," in the grey brown Arizona desert. The sun is shining. A girl goes running, kicking and screaming towards the pond, dives in, and comes up with her head covered in muck and great kelpy strands of green pond slime.

The beads of water on her slime stands are like diamonds to her. She keeps repeating: "Ooooooooh! It sparkles! Ooooooooh! It sparkles!" The explanation for the girl's behaviour is LSD. She has taken a dose of the drug in a glass of iced orange juice and is now letting her consciousness expand. It feels, she says, like an orgasm behind her eyeballs.

In "The Electric Kool-Aid Acid Test" by Tom Wolfe, we are taken into the world of drug-takers. We see how Ken Kesey, a writer who has turned to "acid" becomes the Pied Piper of the psychedelic way of life.

The book brilliantly portrays this life, takes us into the world of Kesey and his flower people, takes us through their "experiences" with drugs, and succeeds in transmitting the metabolic rhythm of their psychedelic existence.

(April 26)

THE DALES SAIL AWAY

By Norman Hare
Radio Staff

The BBC's most famous serial "The Dales," ended yesterday with Jim and Mary starting on a "second honeymoon," a cruise.

The last words of the radio serial which ran for over 21 years, were Mary's: "I'm afraid one thing is never going to change; I shall always worry about you Jim."

To tidy up loose ends, the scriptwriters had Gwen announcing that she was to marry Ian Trevelyan rather than Dr. Adam York, and Mrs. Freeman arranging for Franky the kitten and Titus the cat to go with her to Knightsbridge.

(April 26)

BRITAIN TIES FOR 1ST PLACE IN SONG CONTEST

Four countries, including Britain, shared first place in the Eurovision Song Contest in Madrid on Saturday, Spain, Holland, France and Britain each gained 18 points in the first tie since the contest began in 1956.

Britain's entry, "Boom Bang-A-Bang," which was sung by Lulu, was chosen by viewer's votes during the singer's recent television series.

(May 31)

SCRIPT MEN CLOWNS TOO

By NORMAN HARE

Described by the BBC as a nutty zany comedy show, "Monty Python's Flying Circus" came to town last night on BBC 1 television.

Occupying the late night spot, the show replaces the repeat of the religious programme, which has been moved to Tuesday afternoon at the request of tired clergymen, or so they say at the BBC. It could be that Messrs Cleese, Chapman, Jones, Paslin and Idle, the writer-performers involved, will prove less soporific than Mr Muggeridge, if not as intelligent.

The comedy was sophisticated and had much of the delightful absurdity which has not been on television since the Marty shows.

(October 6)

£5,000 fiction award for P.H. Newby

By SEAN DAY-LEWIS
Arts Reporter

P.H. NEWBY, 50, Controller of the Third Programme, was last night announced as the first winner of Britain's biggest literary award, the Booker Prize for fiction.

He received a £5,000 tax-free cheque and a trophy from Dame Rebecca West at a Drapers' Hall reception. His winning novel, "Something to Answer For," published by Faber and Faber, is set in Port Said at the time of the 1956 Anglo-French invasion.

It was praised last night by the chairman of the judges, Mr. W. L. Webb, for "its vision, its concreteness and its finely articulate energy."

Mr. Newby did not look unduly surprised at the announcement last night, as he had been told some time in advance so that he should be present at the reception. But he has still not worked out precisely how he will spend the money.

(April 23)

POP MEN CHARGED

Roger Daltrey, 25, and Peter Townsend, 24, of The Who pop group, yesterday pleaded not guilty in Manhattan Criminal Court to a charge of kicking a policemen on a New York theatre stage. Both were released on bail. – Reuter.

(May 28)

SPACE HERO REPLACING 'Dr. WHO'

By Our TV Staff

The BBC has bought an American space-adventure series to replace "Dr. Who," the children's serial. Called "Star Trek," it will be shown every Saturday evening on BBC-1 from July 12 until the end of the year.

The "Star Trek" adventures take place in the year 2069 aboard a spaceship called Enterprise, which carries a crew of 450 and is the pride of earth's space-ship fleet.

The second officer is a Mr. Spock, who is described as "half-human, half-Vulcanian." He has pointed ears and has become one of the "cult" characters on TV in the United States, where the series attracts a big audience.

(June 2)

BANNED RECORD'S TOP TEN SPOT

"Je t'aime... Moi Non Plus," the controversial record by Jane Birken and Serge Gainsbourg, which was withdrawn by Philips Records and banned by the BBC, is still third in the Melody Maker Top Ten list.

(September 30)

MALTINGS READY IN A YEAR

THE £176,000 Maltings concert hall at Snape, destroyed by fire on Saturday night, was fully insured and is to be rebuilt for the opening of the 1970 Aldeburgh Festival.

The festival organisers hope to raise an extra £20,000 to add to the insurance money, for the rebuilding, so that some improvements can be added.

(June 9)

POPS

Joseph and the Amazing Technicolor Dreamcoat.
Decca LK 4973.

THIS remarkable work was commissioned by the music master of Colet Court (junior section of the famous St. Paul's School) written by two hitherto unknown gentlemen, Andrew Lloyd Webber (music) and Tim Rice (lyrics), and performed by the school choir, an orchestra and a pop group, among others. It tells the story of the Biblical Joseph entirely in music and with words of startling modernity: "His astounding clothing took the biscuit/Quite the smoothest person in the district."

It is tuneful in a conventional way, funny, well-orchestrated, cohesive and very good-tempered.

What is more, it is a pioneer. The old concept of a pop LP as two sides each containing six songs of two or three minutes apiece has virtually died, and innumerable groups such as the Doors, the Nice and Love, have experimented with long tracks of, in some cases, over 10 minutes; yet, the imagination necessary to set in motion anything like a pop oratorio (as this has been called) has never quite been there. Ways are open now for a real pop opera.

HUGH PARRY

(January 25)

THE DAILY TELEGRAPH
AND
MORNING POST
DAILY TELEGRAPH - - - JUNE 29, 1855
MORNING POST - - - NOVEMBER 2, 1772
[Amalgamated October 1, 1937]
135, Fleet Street, London, E.C.4.
Telephone: 01-353 4242
CLASSIFIED ADVERTISING 01-583 3939
Telex 22874/5/6
INDEPENDENT OF ALL GROUPS

DE GAULLE'S LAST POST

NOT WITH A BANG, but a whimper. It is impossible not to feel a sense of anticlimax as President DE GAULLE finally withdraws from the control of France. And surely this time it is final. He has retired before, to be sure; but he is now 78. This must be it. What splendours and misery this great man has experienced – what bitterness, what defeats, what periods of impotence and humiliation, what vicissitudes; and on the other hand, what phoenix-like rebirth and triumph! What a career it has been to end in such a way!

He offered some paltry so-called reform to the French people. They looked at the packet they were offered; fingered and sniffed at the complex proposal which it contained; weighed the bogus concessions offered to regionalism against the real threat offered to the power of the Senate; and by the smallest possible majority turned up their noses.

What history will say of this extraordinary man is yet obscure. To France he gave back her self-confidence, even glory. Some might call it illusory; yet illusion well-sustained becomes a sort of reality. It would be idle to deny that he frustrated the legitimate and honourable aims of our own country. It is also desperately hard to see what he hopes to achieve by being so tiresome, by arousing such hopes in France's enemies, such fears and distrust in her friends. Whether Gaullism will survive his departure is doubtful; it will anyway be Hamlet without the Prince, easier to live with. One thing is clear, as M. COUVE DE MURVILLE put it: a page of French history has turned.

(April 28)

COOL HEADS FOR ULSTER

NO MYSTERY SURROUNDS the responsibity for the bloodshed in Belfast on Saturday night. At this moment it is the extremists in the Protestant camp who are the real enemies of the Union. These men or their dupes are prepared to kill policemen in the name of their affection for the Royal Ulster Constabulary and to attack the Queen's soldiers in the name of their loyalty to the Crown. Their conduct is contemptible, and the crimes they have encouraged or committed must be punished with exemplary severity. Those who try to put part of the blame for Saturday's riot on the Ulster Government's decision to publish the HUNT Report on a Friday (weekends are the most favourable times for riots in Ulster) misunderstand the calculated and sustained character of the agitation now going on. Moreover, Friday was the only possible publication date on the basis of the timetable agreed with Mr CALLAGHAN.

It is also important to remember that what gives the fanatics their chance is the genuine conviction of many even moderate Protestants that a conspiracy is going on in Britain (and being strongly encouraged from Dublin) to alter the status of Ulster. As far as the British Government is concerned, Mr CALLAGHAN has made it abundantly clear that this is a lie; he will have another opportunity of doing so in the Commons today. The removal of these fears is almost as essential now as strong government itself. The authorities are probably right, therefore, to forswear, at any rate for the moment, dramatic measures which might arouse or confirm suspicion. Governing Ulster today demands a cool head as well as a firm hand.

(October 13)

PRINCE OF WALES

MUCH HAS HAPPENED during the past few weeks to make today's Investiture of the Prince of WALES more interesting, more controversial and possibly more dangerous than that of his great-uncle in 1911. Bombs have been placed; one exploded in Cardiff yesterday. Let us pray that good sense and good feeling will prevail over criminal fanaticism. Much interest has also been aroused by the Prince's admirable confrontations with experienced interviewers on radio and television. It is certain that this young man has won many hearts and minds.

In an article which appears on this page today, Mr. CARADOG PRICHARD refers to "the silent ones and the non-heroes." This is significant, and not only for Wales. Great Britain has today many persons who are far from silent and who consider themselves, in loud terms, to be heroes. They can speak for themselves. It is for the Monarchy to represent, to understand, and to speak for the silent ones and the non-heroes, who after all constitute the great mass of the people. In a singularly able and unassuming manner, the Prince of WALES has shown that he can do precisely this. Let us hope that today's long, trying, but impressive ceremony will serve as a symbol of the great services which the Monarchy can still render to Great Britain and the Commonwealth. Let us hope too, that the people of Wales will be prepared, if not unanimously, then overwhelmingly, to greet their Prince with warmth and affection.

(July 1)

THE THALIDOMIDE CASE

Would you consent to the loss of both arms and both legs for £20,800, or to the loss of both arms for £12,800? Few indeed could honestly answer "yes." Few indeed can then think the damages awarded in the thalidomide case unduly generous. The damages are in fact only 40 per cent. of those which would have been awarded had allegations of negligence been pressed and proved. These were dropped in order to secure a relatively swift and certain settlement. Perhaps this was wise. In Germany the thalidomide case has turned into a "judicial orgy" which may deny all compensation to the victims for many years.

(July 31)

Fantasy World of Student Militants

By K.R. MINOGUE
Senior Lecturer in Political Science, London School of Economics

THE week before the student militants at the London School of Economics turned their attention to the gates, they brought out a pamphlet advocating a short-cut to revolution. The general theory was that capitalism could be brought to its knees by the strain of repairing the casual breakages of practically minded revolutionaries.

This was called " creative vandalism." Smash a bita stuffa day! Football vandals on this theory, might well be the vanguard of the new order.

This absurd fantasy is held by a tiny handful of militants, one sect among many. Before we become too indignant about such folly, however, we should try to understand how the student militants come to think as they do. It is not at all an easy task. The militants look like rather undisciplined Communists; certainly Marx supplies the words. But politically speaking student militancy is a new kind of thing, though the militants express a line of thought as old as the Orphic mysteries of classical Greece.

The militant's theory provides him will an all-purpose explanation of what is wrong with the world. Why the war in Vietnam? Why are some university lectures boring? Why are some people homeless? Why are there gates at LSE? Why are liberal writers on trial in Russia? All because of capitalism. (For, I have been solemnly told, Russia, too, is a capitalist country, in this quaintly theological sense of "capitalism.")

The beauty of this is that it puts all protest on the same level of moral grandeur. The flaw is that it cannot discriminate between the trivial and the important. Everything is connected with everything else and, when LSE militants contemplate Dr. Adams, a weird fantasmagoria, compounded of Ian Smith, napalm and a dollar sign, floats before the eyes.

Paradoxically, student militancy is a middle-class hobby, and few things reveal this more clearly than the overriding concern with an innocence which is beyond the reach of argument. This is why whatever the militant dislikes is called a "provocation." It is also why any punishment for militant acts is automatically stigmatised as "victimisation."

Student militancy is international. There is little doubt that the British movement has pretty shallow roots. Conditions in British universities are vastly better than those overseas. Besides, the world is to those who can build a bridge, transplant a heart, write a lucid report, bake a good cake or understand a theorem. The world is not transformed by verbosity, voting and vexation of shoeleather.

And most British students know this perfectly well. On a good day, and with their sense of student solidarity roused, they may turn out, but they are quickly bored, for they have other things to do. The result is that, for all but a few, student militancy has been little more than a passing phase.

Some, however, are so enchanted with the fantasy world of university revolution that they cannot bear to let go. That world enshrines for them all the romantic hopes of youth, and they resent the slow escalator of time which is carrying them so relentlessly away from it.

University students in the fifties were taught but not heard. Their successors in the sixties made of this situation a grievance. Led by the militants, they broke open the doors of committee rooms, and forced a reappraisal of university life. It has not so far been a profound reappraisal, but it has had a lot of administrative consequences. In the seventies, the innovations will shake down into a new pattern. What will it be like?

The keynote will be consultation, and the status of students, along with their freedom of action, will grow considerably. Bu the only serious result to be expected is a smoothing of administrative rough edges. Any real tampering with the academic side of university life, while it might be politically possible in some universities, would result in an immediate – and fatal – devaluing of the resulting degree. There are, in other words, built-in limits to the administrative role that students can play in a university, and no amount of militancy can shake them.

(February 1)

DIVORCE WITHOUT GUILT

IN A SENSE, THE DIVORCE REFORM BILL, which passed its final stages yesterday, represents a revolution in Britain's marriage customs. For the first time the divorce law is theoretically emptied of the concepts of guilt and innocence. The sponsors of the Bill have taken their stand on the proposition that the only case for ending a marriage is that it is irretrievably broken – a sociological rather than a legal decision. In reality, however, the new law will merely add two new grounds for divorce to those already existing. These will be mutual consent to the ending of a marriage after two years' separation, and determination on the part of one partner to end the marriage after five years' separation. The second of these grounds may be more offensive to traditional thought than the first, since it seems to violate the ideas of marriage as a contract no less than as a status. In practice, it will prove by far the less damaging to the institution itself.

The whole idea of removing guilt from the argument – attractive though it is to theologians – presents lawyers with extreme difficulties. Whether this Bill turns out to be a monstrosity or not will depend largely on the character of the new legislation which is to be introduced on the complex question of financial provision.

The sombre truth is that most men cannot afford to keep two wives. Adequate provision for a deserted wife may be enforced by the courts, but if so it will be a powerful deterrent to divorce save for the very rich. Unilateral dissolution after five years (more humane of the two new grounds) may, indeed, seldom be invoked – leaving divorce by mutual consent after two years (too short a period) as the only real effect of the change. Which would not make it a good law.

(October 18)

Consensus – or choice?

By MARGARET THATCHER, M.P.

IN politics, certain words suddenly become fashionable. Sometimes they are just words. Sometimes they reveal a whole attitude of mind and influence the development of thought. Then they can be dangerous and set us on a false trail. Consensus is one of these.

It isn't difficult to see how it has become popoular with some politicians. In the post-war years, all Governments in this country have tended to be more compromising in power than their policies in Opposition would have led an inexperienced observer to expect.

On the Left, Mr. Callaghan did not introduce the wealth tax he proclaimed as Shadow Chancellor, Mr. Wilson did not denegotiate the Nassau Agreement, the Health Minister had to bring back prescriptions charges, and the immigration laws have been strengthened although Mrs. Barbara Castle said they would be repealed.

On the Right, we were not as successful in controlling public expenditure as we ought to have been, we were slow to get on to trade union law reform, we left surtax too high and estate duty at confiscatory levels. On both sides performance seemed to fall short of political philosophy – why?

Economic realities and administrative difficulties are the two greatest modifiers of policies, but they are too readily used as an excuse. The reason why a particular policy has been delayed may be given as "No money"; but it is more likely that the Government has preferred to spend money elsewhere. And "administrative impossibility" so often turns out to be possible under another Minister or Government.

A democratic system of government rests in some measure on the consent of the governed. But consent will never be unanimous. There will be a majority for and a minority against.

Consent does not therefore require that the Government be the Government of one's own choice. But it does require that a periodic choice be made. This in turn necessitates the development and discussion of rival philosophies and policies, and the free play of conflicting opinions.

Now apply the consensus theory. If the parties between whom the choice is made become substantially similar the differences dwindle to insignificance and so there is no real choice. There could be no change of policy. Only a change of people responsible for those policies. But the majority reacts against policies as well as against politicians.

Democracy therefore contains within itself the means of orderly change through choice and consent. Clash of opinion is the stuff of which democracy is composed.

It therefore makes little sense to talk of taking the big issues "out of politics," or to imply that different approaches to the subject involve "playing politics" with it. They don't; they merely involve using the system for the purpose for which it was intended.

To adopt the consensus theory would be to do nothing. To adopt the alternative policy approach would be to set about making those changes which would gradually reduce the public sector, thus saving the taxpayers' money and giving greater consumer choice.

Certain things would need to be set in hand:

1 Before a buyer or buyers could be found, those parts of industries which could be denationalised would have to be reorganised into units that make them attractive and saleable.

2 Where utilities like electricity were concerned, we should investigate the possibility of increasing the amount of private generation.

We therefore come to the position that the Government of the day governs by consent of the majority on political issues, but may be without majority consent on certain specific matters

(March 17)

DECIMAL BLUES

At last the secret is out. Five new pennies will equal 12 old pennies and the Government, ever mindful of the interests of the housewife, has published a white paper to prove it. Moreover, to minimise confusion in that historic month two years' hence when we go decimal the banks are to be closed for several days during the change-over. So even the dimmest shopper has plenty of time to do his homework before the Sunshine Day.

(January 23)

MEN FOR NO SEASONS

While the Roman Catholic Church is engaged in so many agonising reappraisals, it seems rather sad that it should have taken time off to call in question the existence, or the comparative status, of some of its best known saints. St George and St Christopher may or may not have existed. Neither, certainly, is properly documented. But is not their dismissal, on that account, an example of the impudence of historiography? Is no weight to be given to tradition? Be Vatican scholarship ever so strict, will it persuade Englishmen to drop St. George or motorists St Christopher?

What, too, of the Roman Catholic faithful who have placed their children under the patronage of George, Christopher, Barbara, Susanna and the rest? Have they now to explain that the exercise has been misguided and that heavenly advocacy has to be sought elsewhere?

(May 12th)

LONDON DAY BY DAY

Miss Devlin's chance

IF Miss Bernadette Devlin so resolved, she could become not only the youngest MP to enter the House of Commons for half a century but the quickest ever to make a maiden speech.

She will take her seat at 3.30 p.m. today. By coincidence, one of her sponsors, Mr. Paul Rose, has secured the adjournment of the House for three hours immediately afterwards for a debate on Northern Ireland.

In so short a debate opening speeches are not likely to exceed 40 minutes. A maiden speaker would probably be called next. So Miss Devlin could be on her feet within an hour of taking her seat. No one has done that before.

How to woo France

Whatever embarrassments may await Mr. Nixon, he will at least be spared a repetition of the one at his first diplomatic reception in Washington the other day.

He provided what the Americans call French champagne – partly, it was said, as a friendly gesture towards Gen. de Gaulle. This upset Congress representatives of the States of California and New York, which call some of their sparkling wine champagne.

If Mr. Nixon is anxious to improve Franco-American relations nothing would please the French more than

"Its absolutely unforgiveable.I leaked it in confidence."

the application to the United States of the European laws limiting use of the word champagne to the product of Champagne.

Or die with

GOVERNOR REAGAN of California, who is in London for a few days does not think the Presidential Commission which has reported on the increasing risk of political assassination is exaggerating.

Most of the possible precautions, he said yesterday, have already been taken, but basically "it is just something that people in public life have to learn to live with."

The fatalistic Mr Reagan is here for the first time in over 20 years to meet exporters and address the Institute of Directors at the Albert Hall on Thursday. But most of his time will be spent on sightseeing.

As 58 he is wearing well despite the trials of political office. He was almost boyish in his excitement at the prospect of seeing London by night.

Dangerous journey

TO launch Europe Week in Britain Sir Geoffrey de Freitas, president of the Council of Europe's Parliamentary Assembly, is to release a white Strasbourg pigeon in Parliament Square on May 5. The idea is that it should fly home to symbolise Britain's determination to join a united Europe.

Fears are being expressed, however, that it will be shot down not far from Paris.

PETERBOROUGH

SPORTY CAPRI BY FORDS

By JOHN LANGLEY
Motoring Correspondent

FOR the family motorist who dreams of owning an E-type Jaguar or a Lamborghini, Ford today announces a new Capri – a family "fast back" saloon with room for four people and their luggage and at prices ranging from £890, including tax.

It is based on the philosophy that brought the American Ford Mustang record sales of more than 1,000,000 in its first year of production. The Capri is being produced at Ford plants in Britain and Germany but will use locally-designed engines.

"Selected drivers"

In addition a road version of the 16-valve 1600cc twin-cam Ford racing engine, developing more than 120 brake horsepower, will be available for "selected drivers." Claimed maximum speeds range from 86 mph for the standard 1,300cc version to 107 mph for the 2000 GT model.

I drove several versions of the Capri on varying types of road in Cyprus. Points which impressed included a combination of high speed, roll-free cornering and smooth ride from its conventional but well-tuned suspension.

(January 22)

Beachbuggy car goes on show

THE British public is being given its first chance to see an example of America's newest fun car, the Beachbuggy, in London over the next fortnight.

Thousands of American teenagers are buying or building these little open cars, which look like a cross between a home-made "special" and a racing dragster.

Like most of the American Beachbuggies, it is based on a Volkswagen frame. The glassfibre body was imported from one of the US specialists, Desert Fox Sand Buggies of Phoenix, Arizona, and the car is powered by a bored-out, second-hand Porsche engine.

(October 11)

Catch on to this code ...

THIS Christmas, many of us who were given electrical gadgets as gifts, saw for the first time the new colour coding on electrical wires, adopted by Britain to conform to an international colour coding.

To remind you: the new colours are brown for live (formerly red), blue for neutral (formerly black) and green and yellow stripes for earth (formerly green). I hope you, or the handyman of the house, wired them up correctly?

In a quick poll around my women friends the other day I was astonished to find how few knew how to wire up a plug or what to do when the iron flex burns out and a big pile of clothes lies waiting, or when some other electrical failure occurs.

It may be days before the ironing gets finished under circumstances like this. So surely a New Year resolution ought to be to learn how to wire up a plug.

(December 30)

SHIRTS HE CAN'T PUT HIS TIE ON

Is the tie becoming obsolete? Is it to be the great unloved article of the second half of this century, a museum artefact?

I hope not. Like many wives, I enjoy buying and giving them. But a fashion competition the other day—of shirts designed by the Royal College of Art Fashion School—yielded precisely one necktie and that one came with the shirt any way, press-studding on and off by means of a nifty white leather tab.

(April 29)

WHAT MINI-GIRLS SHOULD KNOW ABOUT MAXI-COATS

By Beryl Hartland

"YOU simply can't wear one, you will have no legs at all," cried all my friends when I hesitatingly confessed I longed (for warmth as much as anything) for a maxi-coat. "It will look for all the world like a dressing gown," jeered others.

But one day a couple of weeks ago, despite the ominous warnings, all foolhardy 5ft 2½ in of me, shrinking inwardly but outwardly, I prayed, brave as a lion, swept out to lunch in one.

Somehow I don't think the taxi driver mistook me for a legless female, while the cloakroom attendant – unless it was wishful thinking – viewed me with what I took for admiration in her eye. Lunch over, I was helped into my maxi by my male host with a solicitude I had almost forgotten existed. Since then two of my women friends, not much taller than I, have purred with delight as they tried on my coat, pirouetting before the mirror and vowing they'd be off shopping for one in the morning.

I am certain, now, that it's all a matter of proportion; a high belt and a tiny head. I happened to find this coat with almost a shoulder-blade-high black belt which made my legs look as if they went on for ever. On the other hand, Clive, the bright young London couturier, disagrees, and insists that "for a little woman a low belt gives a stretched-out look" and has made for Paul Newman's wife, actress Joanne Woodward (who is small, too) a check tweed with a tough leather belt slung just below the waist. So you can have it both ways. I'm sticking to my guns and my high waist. Here are a handful of Do's and Don'ts – if you are a maxi-minded mini-woman:

DON'T go for bright colours embellished with frogging, unless you want to look as if you're on your way either to or from bed.

DO wear high chunky-heeled shoes, or better still, those tiny delicious boots from Deliss or Ginny Brown.

DON'T choose a coat with wide lapels unless you want to look a complete square.

DO wear a neat hairdo or, much better, a fur or knitted cap, as then nobody will take it that you are dashing across the street for the breakfast milk. See that your handbag is small, too.

DON'T for heaven's sake, drop your chin and slouch or you WILL look as if you are walking in a trench. And try not to hurry: I had to learn to walk all over again.

DO put in some practice, in front of the mirror, on how to gracefully gather your skirts so that when you meet a flight of stairs you won't fall flat on your face, as I nearly did. Remember, none of these pavement-sweeping skirts for little women: ankle-bone length, or a little shorter is best.

(December 3)

Take away the world on a plate

"THE party was in full swing when the host nipped down the road and came back with 20 Indian curries – it couldn't have been easier," said one of the guests.

"We couldn't make up our minds whether or not to go out for a Chinese meal," said a father of two; "a good TV programme decided it. We went out and bought 42s worth of spare ribs, sweet and sour pork, chicken and pineapple, bean sprouts and rice and had our evening out at home." (Set menus are considerably cheaper).

Working wives are only too pleased to buy a meal on their way home; old people find it a boon, as do the bed-sitter brigade. Now harassed Christmas shoppers are carrying home a meal, too – anything from a pizza, a curry, an Irish stew, blanquette de veau or sole bonne femme.

The trend for restaurants of various nationalities, snack bars, delicatessen shops and food centres to provide meals to take away, is catching on all over the country.

"We do a lot with this service now," remarked one Chinese restaurant owner in Cardiff. "Welshmen have found that Chinese food is more interesting to take home than fish and chips."

The China Snack Bar in South Clark Street, Edinburgh, is setting the pace with its new sign advertising "Carry Home a China Hot Meal."

The Kentucky Fried Chicken establishments which offer take-away chicken meals only and have branches in and around London, Hove, Bournemouth, Westcliff-on-Sea, Birmingham, Leeds, Preston and a drive-in at Samlesbury on the main road between Blackburn and Blackpool, are planning to open another 100 branches round the country in the next four years.

Madame Prunier produces two booklets, spring-and-summer and autumn-and-winter for her service, "On Prendra." These give instructions on how to heat some of the dishes in a bain-marie and how to reset a sauce. What better tonic could there be, after a hard day's shopping, than to bring back some oysters (from 12s 6d half a dozen) or a delicate coquille St Jacques Prunier or croustade de fruits de mer?

Whereas most Indian (like Chinese) restaurants provide plastic or foil dishes for your take-away food, The Green Banana restaurant in soho, will only do so for a limited number of its dishes. For its special West Indian dishes, such as steamed red mullet with yams, bread fruit and sweet potatoes or mackerel, with green banana, you must bring your own containers.

Irish stew (6s 3d) is one of the most popular takeaway choices at the Midnight Shop in Brompton Road (open until midnight every night including Sundays).

Violet Johnstone

(December 23)

Opulence in the Biba manner

GERTRUDE LAWRENCE, I learn with awe, always slept between pale blue satin sheets, which accompanied her on overnight train journeys. Those who wish to emulate this prima-donna luxury should direct their chauffeurs forthwith to Biba's new Department Store in Kensington High Street.

Here they will find, in the bright, airy, elegant, two-storey store, a sort of boudoir/drawing-room satins-and-feather, gold-and-pearl-carving-knife opulence.

For this new Biba stocks household goods, considerately displayed just inside the door, so that you need neither mingle with, nor fight your way through, the dollies still catered for farther within, and downstairs.

Your sheets, in rayon satin, are available in all the soft, muted 15 household colours – including pinky mauve, deep purple, Air Force blue, oxblood red, cream, lime green and that Gertrude Lawrence pale blue – common to the Biba range of cushions, paints, lampshades, wallpapers (in 25in by 36in sheets, 1s 2d each), velvets and even lowly felts (for walls or floors).

A set of double sheets costs £17; a single-bed set (only one ruffled pillow) £12. A fringed satin tablecloth is £4 12s 6d.

The gold-on-nickel-silver cutlery, with mother-of-pearl handles, costs, variously; carving set £10 15s 6d; spoons 37s 2d each; pointed spoon 37s 5d; and fork, 32s 4d.

Silver-plated cutlery: ladle, £4 10s; table knife, with Georgian-inspired pistol handle, 32s 8d; fork, 22s 6d. Ostrich plumes (in 15 colours) are 12s apiece.

Dollies arriving on foot or by bus will also find satin cushions for only 18s 6d; ironstone china (thick and thin gold-banded, or white with blue floral band); from 2s 9d for an egg-cup (floral) and from 5s for a plate (white-gold).

JEAN SCROGGIE

(September 16)

UNDER THE CURLERS

I AM setting my hair in a hurry these days – with the unlikely co-operation of my iron.

The iron plugged in for the purpose, wears an ingenious enamelled metal plate, upon which six medium and six smaller rollers heat up to the point where a tiny red dot on each turns black. Whereupon I turn the iron off, pluck the rollers away and pinion them into my hair with the vast hooks supplied.

This "Valentine" variation of the hot-roller hairdo, sketched below, fits on any domestic iron. I spotted mine in Harrods, where it costs 59s 11d (postage 5s). Extra rollers, either size, 3s 6d each.

(October 1st)

Mrs Wilson's 'Desert Island' luxury

By L. MARSLAND GANDER

MRS. MARY WILSON, wife of the Prime Minister, would like to have a full make-up kit, Emily Bronte's novel "Wuthering Heights" and the record "I'll See You Again," if she was cast away on a desert island.

Mrs Wilson made her choice when she appeared on yesterday's broadcast of "Desert Island Discs" on Radio 4.

Mrs Wilson started by saying that she would choose her eight records to remind her of pleasant things.

Her first choice was the hymn "Hark Hark My Soul" because it reminded her of her father's Congregational church. She added: " I am fond of angels. I rather like Victorian angels."

She confessed that she had wanted to be a novelist but became a shorthand typist and met her future husband at a tennis Club when he was a promising academic with no sign of Downing Street on the Horizon.

Another choice was "I'll See You Again" from Noel Coward's "Bitter Sweet" by Peggy Wood and Georges Mexiaxa.

She liked it because "it is sung in that wonderfully refined way that we hear no longer" and it reminded her of when she first met Mr. Wilson.

(March 11)

Colour gives TV-watching social cachet

IT used to be the snob thing to say: "We don't have a television set, though Nanny has one in her room."

Now the pendulum has swung the other way. With the coming of colour, it is very much the "in" thing now to rent or to own a colour TV set, and if Nanny or the babysitter wants to watch, she comes into the living room instead of the family settling down in her quarters.

In fact, the demand for colour sets has now far exceeded expectations. When colour comes in on the two major channels on Nov. 15, production from the factories will be at the rate of 5,000 sets a week.

Most people, it seems, are renting their coloured TV sets, and the initial deposit of around £65 doesn't seem to deter them. The purchase price is from £230 to £300.

This explosion of colour in the ordinary homes of Britain is undoubtedly going to have a profound effect on our daily lives.

Apart from the impact of natural outdoor scenes, we shall, for the first time, see the colour and pattern of wallpapers, of carpets and curtains. We shall get the real beauty of fine pictures and be able to see the full effect of lighting. Even at the price, I reckon it's going to be value for money. A.H.

(November 4)

For the trendy

If the ambience counts as much, or even more, than the food then four-month-old Melita, 153, King's Road (FLA 0202) will not disappoint you.

Downstairs, against a gay decor of red and green giant herringbone walls, purple banquettes and candlelight, trouser suits, long silver cardigans and wide drooping hats, and long hair, you'll find a pretty fair gathering of the trendy people.

As for the food, the menu reads well, even if it caters for every conceivable taste from Italian and French to corn-on-the-cob and shrimp cocktail.

Ordering a sweet is a bit of a guessing game. My Grape Tart, with blithe disregard for the menu name, turned out to be a wedge of something remarkably like cake, but full of sultanas and grape juice (quite good), and my companion's Raspberry Mont Blanc would have been much happier called a raspberry Mousse.

Including cover charge and a carafe of good white chianti, 19s 6d, our bill was £4 17 6d. The ambience does much to cushion the blow.

(March 4)

From the first delightful pot of tea you just know your Swan teaset will always serve you right, never failing to grace your table.

Swan - just right

Eisenhower is dead

HOMESPUN HERO

EISENHOWER, THE SOLDIER, did not have the makings of a legend. His gifts – caution, precision and thoroughness – have no instant appeal to the British, and he had few of the irksome eccentricities about which we are fond, as a nation, or ever will obscure his greatest military achievement; the effective leadership of the most heterogeneous military force in history. His success in this was not only one of the greatest single ingredients in Allied victory; it also produced new conceptions about the possibilities of international co-operation in defence which have dominated strategic thinking in the years since the war.

The common sense, modesty and straightforward good nature which helped EISENHOWER to command the loyalty of a vast, polyglot army were also the distinguishing marks of his two terms as President. Both in their lives and in the circumstances of their deaths, other American Presidents have fired the imagination more. For sheer honesty, simplicity of aim and directness of method, however, EISENHOWER was incomparable. It was this, combined with the perfection with which he embodied the cherished concept of the "ordinary American," which enabled him to control a politically hostile Congress more effectively than many a President has controlled his own party supporters. By pure force of amiability and transparent trustworthiness, EISENHOWER sold to the Republican party policies, such as a serious attempt at conciliation with Russia, which in the fifties American opinion would never have tolerated from a Democrat. Yet he was no credulous "dove" as his last broadcast, in the context of the Republican Convention at Miami, made plain.

In the home affairs of the United States he was essentially the consolidator rather than the innovator. There had been more than two decades of innovation, however, under his predecessors, Presidents ROOSEVELT and TRUMAN. It was probably by its nature a time for consolidation and tranquillity, and EISENHOWER provided them. In the mouths of his critics tranquillity was complacency. Yet there was in the prosperous condition of the USA much to be complacent about. His philosophy was one of tolerance. He believed in being close to the people and keeping them free. A non-party man, he was slow to fight an opponent or a critic. His success was a success of personality rather than policy.

There were, of course, faults – the chief of them perhaps the almost childlike unworldliness which may explain his almost disastrous horror at EDEN'S apparent duplicity over Suez. His very tolerance led him to allow Senator MCCARTHY to develop, unimpeded, a campaign of which he disapproved. The mistakes of likeable and good men, however, are more easily repaired than those of controversial geniuses, and EISENHOWER weathered many a storm which would have proved too much for a better mind united to a worse character. When merits come to be accurately weighed, even on earthly scales, he will rank higher than he seems to now.

(March 29)

STEPHEN POTTER

STEPHEN POTTER, the biographer and humorist, who has died in London, aged 69, was one of those rare people who added a word to the English language.

His invention of "gamesmanship" indeed fathered a whole set of coinings by himself and other people.

"One-upmanship," "lifemanship", among others, became nearly as widely used in this country and the United States, where Adlai Stevenson added a further new word, "brinkmanship" for John Foster Dulles's foreign policy.

It was just before the austere Christmas of 1947 that Potter introduced "Gamesmanship" with its challenging subtitles "The Art of Winning Games Without Actually Cheating," to a delighted Britain that in times of severe rationing was trying to live in much the same way.

If the subsequent books did not have the same impact as "Gamesmanship" it was not that the humour was less good – some of the later inventions were quite as good as the original ones – but that the impact was blunted and Potter was persuaded to stretch the basic jest too far.

The sort of humour that he perfected in his books had its origins in the "How" programmes that he created with Joyce Grenfell and the "How" repertory company during the war with its gentle, but none the less pointed satire of modern life.

(December 3)

KENNETH HORNE

KENNETH HORNE, who died last night in a London hospital, aged 61, was acknowledged as one of radio's top mirth-makers for his "Beyond Our Ken" and "Round the Horne" programmes.

He had been broadcasting for more than 28 years. While serving in the RAF as a wing commander in the 1939-45 War he broadcast in a BBC feature "Ack-Ack, Beer Beer."

Later, he devised the comedy based on an RAF station "Much Binding in the Marsh," with Richard Murdoch, a fellow RAF officer at the Air Ministry.

Mr. Horne, educated at St. George's, Harpenden, and Magdalene College, Cambridge, was the son of the Rev. Sylvester Horne, a Congregationalist and a Liberal M.P. who ministered for years at the Whitefield's Tabernacle.

In February, 1958, he suffered a stroke which paralysed his left side and took away his speech. During the agonies of learning to walk and speak again, he decided to give up his business interests and concentrate on show business.

Later, using ideas worked out on his sick bed, he started the programme "Beyond Our Ken" which, after it became established, claimed 10 million listeners on Sunday afternoons. It was an immediate success with lovers of the sophisticated pun as well as those liking a good belly laugh.

(February 15)

BRIAN JONES

Brian Jones, 26, the pop star who left the Rolling Stones group three weeks ago after a policy disagreement, was found dead last night at his home in Hartfield, Sussex.

His body had been recovered from the swimming pool alongside the house by three friends who had been staying with him — a man and two women.

(July 3)

ROBERT PITMAN

The simplicity and vigour of his style showed Robert Pitman of the Express, who died on Thursday, as a good journalist. His patriotism and independence of mind showed him a good Englishman of a type still not common. His generosity and friendliness in private life showed him a good man.

Courage of one sort was shown by the rough but genial bluntness with which he expressed unpopular opinions.

(February 18)

FIELD MARSHALL EARL ALEXANDER OF TUNIS

EARL ALEXANDER, UNRUFFLED VICTOR OF TUNIS

By Lt.-Gen. H.G. MARTIN

FIELD MARSHAL EARL ALEXANDER OF TUNIS, who has died, aged 77, displayed throughout his long career as a soldier that supreme attribute of a leader: the capacity to meet triumph and disaster and treat these two impostors just the same. Few have fulfilled so fully Kipling's conception of a man.

Son of the fourth Earl of Caledon, who died when he was still an infant, Harold Rupert Alexander came from that great forcing-ground of soldiers, Northern Ireland. As a boy he ran wild on the family estate in Tyrone – a county famous for its snipe and its Sinn Feiners. That was no bad beginning for a soldier.

Going on to Harrow, young Alexander took five wickets for 40 runs in that most famous of Eton and Harrow games, "Fowler's Match," which Eton won by nine runs. Soon after he left Harrow he won the Irish mile.

"Charmed life"

Sir Winston Churchill wrote of him: "In the first Great War . . . he was reputed to bear a charmed life and under heavy fire men were glad to follow exactly in his footsteps."

After four years in the trenches, he went on to the newly-formed Baltic State of Latvia, where his command was a motley force of 10,000 levies – Baltic barons, White Russians, even a few Chinese.

By 1934 Alexander was a brigade commander in that nursery for high command, the North-West Frontier of India. In 1937 he was promoted major-general at 46, and soon after was appointed to command the 1st Division, spearhead of the BEF to be.

Almost on the beaches at Dunkirk he succeeded, first, to the command of the 1st Corps and then to that of the BEF after Lord Gort had been recalled to London. It was there that he first showed how to handle disaster.

Entirely unruffled, he refused to leave the beaches until the last British soldier had embarked on June 4. He then cruised along the shore in a motor-boat hailing in English and French for possible stragglers.

In February, 1942, Alexander now a general in command of Southern Command, received his next assignment with catastrophe: he was ordered to take over the Burma Command already in extremis. On March 5, he reached Rangoon, and by March 6 he had decided that Rangoon could not be held and had issued orders for the evacuation of our forces to Upper Burma.

Here again he demonstrated his concern for those under his command, and his own personal courage, by driving up and down the retreating column in a Jeep, steering with one hand and gripping a pistol with the other.

On Aug. 8, 1942, Alexander arrived in the Middle East to succeed Auchinleck as C-in-C. Here, too, the situation was critical.

Finding the Eighth Army, in Sir Winston Churchill's words, "brave but baffled," he supplemented the decision, already taken by Auchinleck, that the coming battle would be fought at El Alamein where the Eighth Army then stood, by flatly contradicting the prevailing impression that in the last resort, the Army would again withdraw.

Two days later, Montgomery arrived to take over the Eighth Army, and there began a fruitful partnership between two leaders of different character but identical conceptions. The battles of Alam el Halfa and El Alamein, and the victorious advance to Tripoli, followed.

By early February, 1943, Alexander could report to Churchill: "The orders you gave me on Aug. 10, 1942, have been fulfilled."

Less than a month later Alexander arrived in Algeria to take over command of the whole front in North Africa under Eisenhower. Again it was a time of great crisis; for Rommel was threatening the Allies' vital rearward areas.

With characteristic decision Alexander assumed command of the newly-formed 18th Army Group before the date appointed, and by prompt and forceful orders stemmed Rommel's onrush.

At Tunis, in the following spring, Alexander met with his greatest triumph. On May 13, 1943, he was able to signal to Churchill: "It is my duty to report that the Tunisian campaign is over. All enemy resistance has ceased. We are masters of the North African shores." He had put nearly a quarter of a million enemy soldiers in the bag.

Afterwards in the Italian campaign, Alexander was Supreme Allied Commander of the heterogeneous force comprising 26 nations.

(June 17)

DAME IVY COMPTON-BURNETT

By DAVID HOLLOWAY

DAME IVY COMPTON-BURNETT, who died, at her home in South Kensington yesterday, was one of the most brilliant and original novelists in the English language. Her age she kept a secret from all but her closest intimates, but it was certainly nearer 90 than 80.

Everyone could admire the immense skill with which she could contrive the long series of novels for which she is best known with the idiosyncratic linked titles – "A Family and a Fortune," "A House and its Head," "The Mighty and their Fall." But to enjoy them was another matter.

Her devotees would wait anxiously for the arrival of a new book, knowing that in background, in form, in style it would be almost exactly the same as the previous ones, but, at the same time, it would be entirely original.

All her novels from "Pastors and Masters" in 1925 to "A God and his Gifts" in 1963 take place in the same lost world of large country houses, adequately staffed, in an undated though clearly Edwardian, era.

Frustrated lives

And always these country houses were prisons frustrating the lives of their inhabitants. The frustration would often lead to violence, for in the background there lurked some terrible secret which would be revealed before the end of the book. It could be murder; it could be incest – it often was.

Yet for all this gloomy background, Dame Ivy was essentially a comic writer, commenting on a world of fools and their follies with a wealth of understanding.

Many readers were put off by the manner of her writing, which was almost entirely in dialogue. There were practically no descriptions of people or places. Although there were great emotions under the surface, on the surface there was a deadly calm.

(August 20)

TSHOMBE DIES AGED 49

MR. MOISE TSHOMBE, former Congo Prime Minister and President of the one-time breakaway State of Katanga, died of a heart attack in prison in Algeria yesterday, the official Algerian Press Service announced early today. He was 49 and had been detained in Algeria for two years.

Two years ago – June 30, 1967 – Mr. Tshombe's chartered British jet airliner was skyjacked while flying from Ibiza to Mallorca off the Spanish coast and forced to land at a military airfield near Algiers.

One of the most controversial figures in African politics, Mr. Tshombe was under sentence of death in Kinshasa for high treason at the time of his kidnapping.

His extradition to Congo-Kinshasa was requested by President Mobutu and was recommended by the Algerian supreme court last year.

But it was never sanctioned by the Algerian President, M. Boumedienne, on whom the final decision depended. – Reuter.

(June 30)

Boris Karloff

Boris Karloff, the actor who made millions of cinemagoers shudder with his portrayal of the cliff-browed monster in "Frankenstein," has died in hospital at Midhurst, Sussex. He was 81.

The "master of the macabre make-up," as he was known during the long series of horror films he made in the 1930s, was in private life the gentlest of men, sensitive and highly-strung. He had an abiding love of cricket, reading and gardening.

He tried hard to shake off his "horror" image. But the label stuck, even though in his later years he read bedtime stories for children on the radio.

(February 4)

ROBERT TAYLOR, FILM IDOL, DIES

ROBERT TAYLOR, the actor, who died yesterday, aged 57, set a Hollywood record by remaining with one studio, Metro-Goldwyn-Mayer, for 27 years.

In 60 films at MGM he was paired with such stars as Greta Garbo, Jean Halow, Ava Gardner, Elizabeth Taylor, Myrna Loy, Irene Dunne, Joan Crawford, Hedy Lamarr, Lana Turner, Katherine Hepburn and Greer Garson.

He was regarded at one time as the greatest romantic favourite since Valentino.

ROBERT TAYLOR

When he arrived in Britain in August, 1937, to appear in "A Yank at Oxford," Metro-Goldwyn-Mayer's first big British picture, he was mobbed by hundreds of girls.

Taylor made his film debut in "Handy Andy" in 1934 and went on to appear in many notable pictures.

These included "Waterloo Bridge," "Johnny Eager," "Bataan," "Song of Russia," "Undercurrent," "Quo Vadis," "Ivanhoe," "Knights of the Round Table," "A House is Not a Home," and the Western, "Return of the Gunfighter."

(June 9)

SIR OSBERT SITWELL

SIR OSBERT SITWELL, who has died at his home near Florence, aged 76, like his late sister, Dame Edith, and his brother Sacheverell, enriched English literature for many years.

He produced a stream of poems, essays, novels and short stories and a monumental, fascinating five-volume autobiography.

Son of the eccentric fourth baronet, whom he succeeded in 1943, he was a member of a family descended from the Saxon Earls of Northumberland. His mother was Lady Ida, daughter of the first Earl of Londesborough.

Educated, as he put it in the reference books, "during the holidays from Eton," he became a regular soldier. After a most unhappy spell in a cavalry regiment he transferred to the Grenadier Guards in 1912.

He fought in Flanders during the 1914-18 war; his bitter experiences were noticeably reflected in some of his writings.

His more recent publications included "The Four Continents," 1954, "On the Continent," 1958, "Fee Fi Fo Fum!", 1959, and "Tales My Father Taught Me," 1962.

He was made a Companion of Honour in 1958 and a Companion of Literature in 1967.

(May 6)

Sonja Henie

Sonja Henie, 56, the Norwegian ice-skating star who became one of the world's richest women, died yesterday on a plane taking her to Oslo from Paris for medical treatment.

Hers was a career without parallel. Trained as a dancer as a child, she became an ice-skater of such dazzling skill that she was Norwegian champion at the age of 11, in 1924, and competed in the Olympic Games of that year.

(October 13)

Success and tragedy of Judy Garland

By SEAN DAY-LEWIS Arts Reporter

JUDY GARLAND, who died at her London home yesterday, aged 47, was a classic example of an entertainer who did not have the resources to deal with her own success. The physical joy of her singing at its best was increasingly constrained by private agony.

In one of her last interviews she said: "The growing pains of a young girl are bad enough in private, when they're exposed to the public . . . well, it hardly makes for a smooth, easy life, does it?" This was one of her few under-statements.

Even in her increasingly difficult last years, when her voice had become something of a haunted ruin with a built-in ache, she still held an audience like nobody else. At one such performance 18,000 sat unflinching through a rainstorm in the open-air Hollywood Bowl right through to her traditional finale: "Somewhere over the Rainbow."

Recently her career became increasingly spattered with nervous upsets, law actions, marriage troubles and stage disasters.

Her final season at the Talk of the Town in London, beginning last Christmas, started with a law action in which two American businessmen, who claimed to have exclusive use of Miss Garland's services, sought to stop her appearance. The action was lost, but the season was full of incident.

Often late

She was often late and when she did appear was sometimes unsteady on her feet and asked for prompting with the words of songs. One night she walked off stage after being barracked by a dissatisfied audience and having biscuits, paper balls and other missiles thrown at her.

The promoter, Bernard Delfont, advised her to stay at home until she had entirely recovered from the "influenza" which was given as the reason for her difficulties. But against all expectation Miss Garland returned to complete the season and won applause as well as boos.

She was born in Grand Rapids, Minnesota, and named Frances Gumm. The Gumms were a stage family and Frances made her first appearance at 30 months singing "Jingle Bells."

Having changed her name to Judy Garland, she was signed by Metro-Goldwyn-Mayer in 1935. Later that year she made her first two-reel short, "Every Sunday Afternoon," with Deanna Durbin.

She achieve stardom with "Broadway Melody" in 1938, and particularly the song "Dear Mr. Gable" written for her by Roger Edens. Later that year she made the most famous of all her film appearances as the bright-eyed teenage Dorothy of "The Wizard of Oz."

Her performance won her a special Academy award and her song from the film "Over the Rainbow" gave her a hit from which she never really recovered. From then on it was both her signature tune and the never-never theme of her life of which she was constantly reminded.

(June 23)

JUDY GARLAND AS A CHILD STAR in "The Wizard of Oz," with Jack Haley as the Tin Man.

'Little Mo' ranked in first three women tennis players

By LANCE TINGAY

ON the eve of Wimbledon, an event she enriched both by her prowess and personality, Maureen Connolly-Brinker "Little Mo" died of cancer at the Baylor Medical Centre in Dallas, Texas, on Saturday. She was only 34.

She was 16 when she came from California to astonish the lawn tennis world by her prodigious skill. Between the autumn of 1951, when she won the American championship, and the late summer of 1954, when she won the United States clay courts championships, she was without a peer.

In three years she did everything it was possible for a woman to do in lawn tennis.

She won the Wimbledon singles three years running, 1952-4, and the American title three years running, 1951-53.

In 1953 she became the first woman to achieve the "grand slam" by becoming Australian, French, Wimbledon and American champion, a record that still has to be equalled.

I would unhestitatingly rank "Little Mo" as one of the three all-time "greats" of the women's game, alongside Suzanne Lenglen of France and Helen Wills Moody, another Californian.

She played "an old fashioned" women's game, in that her tremendous skill was based on impeccable driving power, especially on the backhand, from the back of the court. Her net game improved with experience but it was never more than an adjunct to her driving strength.

She was a natural left-hander who taught herself to play right-handed. Her unparallelled competitive career ended in 1954 when she broke her right leg in a riding accident. She was not then 20.

(June 23)

BILLY COTTON

Billy Cotton, the Cockney bandleader, whose career began as an army drummer boy at 14, died last night at Wembley while watching the Billy Walker-Jack Bodell fight. He was 69.

"Attempts made to resuscitate Mr. Cotton were made for half an hour," said a spokesman.

Mr. Cotton, whose full name was William Edward Cotton, was a household name, particulary for his cry of "Wakey, Wakey" at the beginning of radio and television programmes.

A former racing driver, he made his first stage appearance at Southport in 1926 after a sucession of dance hall engagements. At the age of 50, he was sixth in the British Grand Prix at Silverstone.

His son, Bill Cotton jun., is BBC Television's head of variety. In March, 1966, another son Edward, died in Poole, Dorset.

(March 26)

BARONESS ASQUITH

BARONESS ASQUITH of Yarnbury, the former Lady Violet Bonham Carter, one of the great names in the history of Liberalism, died shortly before midnight at her Hyde Park home in London last night. She was 81.

SIR COLIN COOTE writes: Lady Asquith of Yarnborough – her friends could never quite accustom themselves to recognise Violet Bonham Carter under that label. But she was an Asquith, the even more formidable daughter of a formidable Prime Minister, and by common consent the best woman politician who never sat in the House of Commons.

Indeed, while she was still in her teens, her father used to discuss with her every evening on his return from Westminster the events of the world. Right to the end her loyalty to him and to his brand of Liberalism was sensitive and unyielding.

Only a few years ago she won fame as an authoress with her book "WinstonChurchill As I Knew Him" – the best biography of Winston, worthy to rank with Winston's own biography of his father. For she knew him with an admiring and sometimes amused profundity which caused her to trust in his star without being dazzled by its glitter.

She greatly enjoyed her closing years in the House of Lords – an ambience which suited her. For she had an encyclopaedic knowledge and a tongue like a razor, both of which civilised audiences enjoy.

(February 20)

JACK KEROUAC

Jack Kerouac, who died in a hospital in St Petersburg, Florida, aged 47, yesterday was the author who coined the word "beat" and whose books ushered in the hippie era.

His most popular books were "On the Road," "The Dharma Burns," and "The Subterraneans." He was regarded as the founder of the "beat generation" after the 1939-45 war.

Jack Kerouac was the first and by far the most literate, prose voice of the "beat" movement of the 1950s, the predecessor of the more flamboyant hippie scene.

(October 22)

Joseph Kennedy, envoy who wrote off Britain

MR JOSEPH PATRICK KENNEDY, who has died, aged 81, was the patriarch of the "Kennedy clan." He was said to have planned for a long time the political success his family was to achieve.

He was the father of the assassinated President Kennedy and of Senator Robert Kennedy, who also died from a gunman's bullet, while campaigning for the 1968 Democratic Presidential nomination.

Joseph Kennedy will be remembered as a man who, while United States Ambassador in 1938-41, was one of the most popular after-dinner speakers in London, but whose criticisms after his return to the United States aroused resentment in Britain.

A self-made man, he was the son of a Boston saloon-keeper of substance who was active in local Democratic politics. He was born in Boston. His grandfather had emigrated from Ireland.

While at Harvard he made his first £1,000 running sight-seeing tours and then, as banker – he was a bank president at 25 – industrialist and Wall Street speculator, built up a fortune by the time he was 40.

The fortune was amassed from such widely diversified interests as banking, liquor, films, theatres and real estate. Unlike many who made fortunes in the 1920s he sold out before the 1929 stock market crash.

His money helped to finance the Presidential campaign of his son in 1960, although he kept deliberately in the background.

Roosevelt friend

In 1917 he was assistant general manager of a shipyard building warships when he met Mr Roosevelt, then Assistant Secretary of the Navy, and a firm friendship developed.

Throwing his energy and some of his money into Roosevelt's 1932 electoral campaign, he afterwards became one of the President's advisers and held several official posts. In 1937, as chairman of the Maritime Commission he was given the task of reorganising the American shipping industry.

He was still under 50 when he was chosen for the London Embassy. In Britain his love of sport, his zest for family – he had nine children – and social life and his unorthodox language in many speeches won him many friends.

Surprise and controversy were created by some of his remarks after his return to the United States late in 1940.

He was reported to have said that

MR. JOSPEH KENNEDY

"democracy is finished in England," and "England is virtually defeated." Despite his denials, he was accused by his fellow-countrymen of pessimism, defeatism and "unguarded talk."

Roosevelt disapproved of his opinions, and he resigned as Ambassador early in 1941.

(November 19)

MARCIANO - LION OF THE RING

By TERRY GODWIN

Rocky Marciano, who was killed in an air crash on Sunday night a few hours before his 46th birthday, had the punch, strength and unblemished streak of victories to be acknowledged as the greatest heavyweight champion of all time.

Marciano, born Rocco Marchegiano of Italian parentage in Brockton, Mass. became champion of the world in 1952 and retired four years later with a record of 49 wins in 49 contests.

Few fighters before him and none since gained such success in so short a time. For his career spanned only eight years and his earnings exceeded 1,750,000 dollars.

(September 2)

COMPOSER DIES

Frank Loesser, 59, the composer-producer, died in a New York hospital yesterday of lung cancer. He wrote the words and music for "Guys and Dolls," "The Most Happy Fella" and "How to Succeed in Business without Really Trying."

(July 29)

MISS MITZI GREEN

Miss Mitzi Green who has died in California, aged 48, played opposite Jackie Coogan as a Holywood child star in "Tom Sawyer."

Although she never attained the world fame of other young stars in the 1930s, such as Shirley Temple, she was the first child signed to a big contract by Paramount Studios.

(May 26)

HUGH WILLIAMS

Hugh Williams had been a successful and well liked actor for well over 40 years, and, in partnership with his second wife, Margaret Vyner, a popular dramatist for 13 of them.

The "Williamses" had made for themselves a considerable fame and an enthusiastic following as the last practitioners of a type of elegant drawing room comedy which to the dismay of a large section of the older or middle aged playgoing public has passed out of date.

(December 8)

KARL JASPERS

Karl Jaspers, who died in Basle, yesterday, aged 86, was the German philosopher whose works also ranged over psychology, religion and literature.

From 1948 to 1961 he was Professor of Philosophy at the University of Basle.

He became famous for his first book, on psychopathology, which he wrote in 1913. He wrote several books of philosophical content analysing the modern spirit and present-day concept of truth and history.

Most of these were translated into English and Spanish. In 1946 he published "The Question of Guilt" which dealt with Germany in the Nazi era.

His wife, formerly Gertrud Mayer, is 90 today.

(February 27)

WAY OF THE WORLD

New Borings

STUDENTS at Southampton have started a "sit-in" protest at the growing number of examination failures. A 20-year-old student leader, mouthing jargon with a fluency worthy of many a Leftist bore of twice his age, declares:

"We want to start a dialogue with the university authorities and get some kind of inquiry going into the relevance, validity and reliability of exams." Only "participation" and "meaningful relation" seem to be missing from this sentence.

At Nerdley University all examinations have been formally abolished. But they have crept back subtly in the form of practical tests in revolutionary rhetoric ("shout-ins"), wall defacement and anti-Establishment violence. The penalties for failure are as serious and much more painful than those at more backward universities.

(July 2)

Now Work This Out

ACCORDING to an article on the City Page of the Daily Mail, under the evocative title "Take the Pill and Get the Dollar," Mr Robert McNamara, of the World Bank, has again been telling the "under-developed countries" that their "immediate need is less for money than for experts in family planning."

How different from the "developed" countries! "Here" adds the article, "is a good trade for the young to go into . . . it also looks a good business to invest in. British shares in this business must have good prospects in world markets."

(October 3)

Nude Postman Drama

AT a performance of Dodie Smith's play "Autumn Crocus" by the Nerdley Amateur Dramatic Society (producer, Miss Joyce Minty-Smith) at Victoria Road Church Hall, a man in the audience, who claimed to be a policeman, suddenly stripped himself naked except for a pair of handcuffs. "I am trying to liberate mankind," he stated. "It is a gesture of world freedom, peace, love and that sort of thing."

A dentist at Bevindon has announced that in future he will be naked while treating patients, "as a gesture of liberation and world peace." Yesterday many of his patients were wearing full evening dress with medals, macintoshes and heavy tweed overcoats "as an assertion of National Health Service standards."

At a London conference of experimental theatre directors, members of Housewives for Peace and representatives of the League of Transmedia Activators, author Neville Dreadberg and his wife Pippa both appeared naked "as a gesture of world love, freedom and peace." In the rush for the doors a caretaker was knocked down, trampled on and slightly injured.

"I suppose it's all right for those that have the money," he commented later.

(June 12)

Among The Trends

POMPIDOU, reveals a gossip columnist, wears plain white braces, Poher prefers wine red or plain black. Gen. de Gaulle has a special pair for each of his suits, all in sober grey and made of very soft elastic. Alain Delon, the film actor, though normally wearing belts, has a fluorescent pair of braces adorned with nude female figures.

I, myself, personally, wear scarlet or lemon yellow braces (if you are at all interested). I have always wanted a pair in purple, but these can only be had, I believe, at ecclesiastical outfitters. When I last tried to buy a pair I was told by a suspicious shopman that they were supplied only to bishops in person or on production of a signed episcopal authorisation.

(July 2)

Peter Simple

GENIUS OF LAVER ENDS MEMORABLE WIMBLEDON

By LANCE TINGAY

THE Lawn Tennis Championships that ended at Wimbledon on Saturday were memorable on many counts, the prime one being the stature of the men's singles champion, the left-handed Australian, Rod Laver, with a standard of achievement that is unique.

From a patriotic viewpoint there never was such a meeting in more than three decades, for Ann Jones, as if taking the women's singles were not enough, won the mixed doubles as well with Fred Stolle.

The last British players to take two Wimbledon titles at the same meeting were Fred Perry in 1936 and Dorothy Round in 1934.

Laver and John Newcombe provided the best men's singles final, both in quality of play and in the excitement of an uncertain issue for many years. As it happened Newcombe won only the second set but he had a lead of 4-1 in the third.

This was the situation that provoked Laver to pull out his finest game and, as always at that level, it was of awesome quality. Newcombe himself, is a champion to his fingertips, but his high talent was as nothing when Laver exploded to his full potential.

No man player since 1919 has done what Laver achieved with his success at Wimbledon this year. With his victory in 1968 and those of 1962 and 1961, it means that he has gone through four successive Wimbledons (he was ineligible to play from 1963 to 1967) without being beaten.

In 1962 Laver won the "grand slam" of the four championships of Australia, France, Wimbledon and the United States, being the only man since Don Budge in 1938 to pull off such a feat. The possibility, perhaps the probability, of his doing this for the second time is now open. The pressure on him when he challenges for the United States Open title at Forest Hills in late August will be enormous.

No fewer than 298,808 spectators were at Wimbledon this year and the record attendance of 1967, when it topped 300,000, would certainly have been passed but for the rained-off opening day. As an open event Wimbledon has quickly grown up.

The champions
Seeded players in capitals

MEN'S SINGLES
R. LAVER (Australia, hldr.) (£3,000) bt J.D. NEWCOMBE (Australia) (£1,500) 6-4, 5-7, 6-4, 6-4

WOMEN'S SINGLES
MRS. F.F. JONES (£1,500) bt MRS. L.W. KING (US. holdr) (£750) 3-6, 6-3, 6-2

MEN'S DOUBLES
J.D. NEWCOMBE & A.D. ROCHE (Australia, hldrs) (£1,000) bt T.S. OKKER (Holland) & M.C. REISSEN (US) (£600) 7-5, 11-9, 6-3

WOMEN'S DOUBLES
MRS. B.M. COURT & MISS J.A.M. TEGART (Australia) (£600) bt MISS P.S.A. HOGAN & MISS M. MICHEL (US) (£400) 9-7, 6-2

MIXED DOUBLES
F.S. STOLLE (Australia) & MRS. P.F. JONES (£500) bt A.D. ROCHE & MISS J.A.M. TEGART (Australia) (£350) 6-2, 6-3

The prize money (totalling £33,370) rarely obtruded as a talking point and nor did the varying category of players, whether professional, registered or amateur – their capacity and personality were the only things that mattered.

The question of advertising on court was raised when Mrs. Jones was asked to be more discreet with a holdall bag designed for that effect. This came more from pressure by the BBC rather than the committee of management.

(July 7)

STEWART TRIUMPHS

By Colin Dryden at Monza

Jackie STEWART, of Scotland, driving a Matra-Ford, clinched the world championship at Monza yesterday after a wheel-to-wheel fight to the finishing line with Jochen Rindt in the Italian Grand Prix by inches. He now has an unassailable lead with 60 points.

It was one of the closest Grand Prix races – only just over a second separating the first five cars after 60 of the 68 laps of the terrifyingly fast Monza circuit.

Stewart completed the distance in his dark blue car in 1hr 39min 11.26sec at a record average of 146.97 m.p.h.

Rindt was timed at 1hr 39min 11.34sec in hundredths of a second. But the fastest lap, a record, was put in by Jean-Pierre Beltoise at 150.97 m.p.h. The French Matra-Ford driver finished third.

In the closing stages, Rindt was harrying Stewart every inch of the way with Beltoise close behind. The Scot and the Austrian took the finishing flag side-by-side, followed by Beltoise.

(September 8)

SPASSKY IS WORLD CHESS CHAMPION

BORIS SPASSKY, the 32-year-old Russian grand master, became the world chess champion in Moscow yesterday without moving a man.

Spassky, a Leningrad journalist drew with Tigran Petrosian, the reigning champion, in the adjourned 23rd game, and won the match for the world title with 12 ½ points against Petrosian's 10 ½ points.

Of the 23 games played Spassky won six, lost four, and drew thirteen.

(June 18)

ENGLAND RELY ON SPEED

By A Special Correspondent in Christchurch

England's team for the second Test against New Zealand at Hagley Park Oval, Christchurch, starting today, shows one change from the side that drew the first Test at Wellington three weeks ago. Carole Evans, the Glamorgan fast bowler, replaces the Middlesex all-rounder Anne Sanders.

Miss Evans was troubled by a back injury for much of the two-month Australian tour and played only in the first Test at Adelaide.

Three fast bowlers

Her inclusion means that the England attack will be spearheaded by three fast bowlers with Mary Pilling (Kent) and June Moorhouse (Yorkshire) completing the trio.

This Test will be played on the square where England beat Canterbury last week by 10 wickets - a match in which half the wickets fell to the fast bowlers.

(March 7)

UNDERWOOD'S £500

Derek Underwood found himself richer yesterday by £400 from the Horlicks's awards. He took £200 for being the "Man of the Series," £100 for his 12-101 in the Oval Test and £100 for the best bowling of the final Test. Underwood also won £100 at Lord's.

(August 27)

SAM SNEAD AND (RIGHT) ERIC BROWN, the rival captains, seem happy enough with the outcome as they jointly hold the Ryder Cup.

GALLACHER'S LION HEART TYPIFIES BRITISH SPIRIT

By LEONARD CRAWLEY

THE thrilling Ryder Cup matches which ended in a draw at Royal Birkdale on Saturday will have wide repercussions on the game of golf all over the world.

Ten thousand people breathless at the scene of the battle and countless millions watching on the small screen could neither have wished for, nor envisaged, a more palpitating or engrossing struggle in any field of sport.

A fresh wave of enthusiasm for this grand old game will sweep the country. On the other side of the Atlantic, whether they like it or not, they will have to take stock all over again.

The British amateurs came within an ace of beating the Americans on their own soil only a few weeks ago, and now the professionals have beaten them each morning for three days in succession and have competently held the most furious counter-attacks the old enemy could launch.

Jacklin inspired

Tony Jacklin, 25, the Open champion, was an infinitely more impressive player than when he won at Royal Lytham St Annes.

He used the inspiring occasion to step firmly into the top world class with a method that improves every month and will keep him at the helm for years.

Bernard Gallacher, 20, a Scot who has made an unparalleled impact on British professional golf and is the youngest player to take part in this great match, showed what we all knew already, namely, that he is genuinely afraid of no-one.

He withstood the tempest of Lee Trevino's opening attack and then took him, the best player on the American side, by the scruff of the neck.

The manner in which he shook him with successive birdies at the eighth and ninth, to turn one up with an outward half of 33 in a stiff westerly wind, was almost beyond belief.

If I add that Trevino impresses as one of the greatest golfers in the world today, and assert that he was a broken man by the time young Gallacher faced up to the final 6ft putt across the slope of the 15th green that was to finish the match at the first time of asking, I can say no more of either.

The occasion was also a great personal triumph for Eric Brown the British captain, with his own fine record behind him. He put a splendidly aggressive spirit into his men, and he deployed his forces superbly.

Brown never lost faith in them, nor they in themselves or their leader. And it must be remembered that he did not have quite the strength or depth of his opposite number, Sam Snead.

While Jacklin and Gallacher took most of the limelight, we must not overlook the invaluable contribution of two victories brought in by the steadfast Peter Butler on the final day. He has proved himself twice in the American Masters and I take my hat off to him.

The final scene will live a long time in the memories of all who saw it with the indomitable Brian Huggett holding off the great Billy Casper and then the two giants, Tony Jacklin and Jack Nicklaus, fighting out their titanic struggle.

Jacklin's long putt for an eagle three to square the match on the 17th green left the entire contest even, and although it is frustrating to have been pipped of victory on the post, a half in four at the last and an honourable division of the spoils was the fairest result.

They were heroes one and all.

(September 22)

Hats off to Lewis & Company

THE manner of Glamorgan's 1969 County Championship victory, makes it, I think, the most salutary and admirable thing that has happened in English cricket for several years.

After five championships in seven seasons Yorkshire, temporarily no doubt, have found themselves (apart from their Gillette Final appearance today) in unexpectedly complete eclipse. That was going to be for the general good only if their successors could match their habitual command of the basic virtues.

Glamorgan, under Tony Lewis, have done this with a vengeance and the vital quality of their cricket in recent weeks, particularly when spurred on by their fervid countrymen, has given a romantic touch to their success recalling that of Hampshire in '61 – and, of course, Glamorgan's own previous championship, won in '48.

While there is much individual merit in the Glamorgan side, those closest to them name a happy and relaxed approach to their cricket as the most important factor.

In 40 years Glamorgan have had only five captains, all in their way notable men, and the present incumbent is showing himself worthy of his predecessors: the late M.J. Turnbull, the maker of Glamorgan cricket, J.C. Clay, Wilfred Wooller and Lewis's friend and adviser, "Ossie" Wheatley.

E.W. SWANTON.

(September 8)

Bedford's record

By JAMES COOTE

DAVID BEDFORD, 19, a physical education student at Brighton, produced probably the most surprising result ever in British athletics when, in the Southern Counties championships at Crystal Palace on Saturday, he broke Mike Treacy's three-year-old national 10,000-metre record by 1.6 sec with a time of 28min 24.4sec. It was a world junior record by 40sec.

Bedford was not the only record-breaker on Saturday. Barbara Inkpen, another 19-year-old, jumped 5ft 9 ¼in to beat the previous national best of 5ft 9 ¼in set by Frances Slaap five years ago, in a club meeting at Ewell.

Bedford's performance was unexpected on many counts. First he is still a junior and bettered a record which is good even by top world-class standards. Jurgen Haase's European time is only 28min 4.4sec – not that much better considering the great athletes who have failed to lower the mark.

Second run

It was Bedford's second run over the distance. The last time he ran on the same track over the distance, in 1968, he attempted to stay with Ron Clarke. It proved a valuable, if chastening, experience – his time was 32min 16sec – but gave him an idea of the speed needed for a fast race.

A student at Brighton College of Further Education, Bedford, from Middlesex, has been hailed for two years as a prospect.

This winter he won the Middlesex cross-country title, and was 11th in the inter-counties. He was also second in the English junior and easily won the international junior championship at Clydebank.

(April 21)

PASCOE'S HURDLES WARNING

Alan Pascoe, 21, of Borough Road College warmed up for his Whitsun Games clash with David Hemery by equalling the British high hurdles record of 13.9 sec when he beat several good runners in Rome on Saturday, writes James Coote.

Eddy Ottoz, Italy's Mexico bronze medallist, was one of a number on 14.0 sec and he was only fourth. Strangely, Pascoe, who is one of three Britons who have a share in the record (Hemery and Mike Parker are the others), has never met Hemery over high hurdles.

(May 19)

Show-jump team's leader dropped

Show-jump team's leader dropped

MR PETER ROBESON, manager of the British show jumping team and international competitor, has been dropped from the team following renewed allegations that he used cruel methods to train his horses.

Mr Robeson, 39, was due to lead the British team at the Ostend Show in Belgium starting today and the Rotterdam Show next Wednesday. The British Show Jumping Association said yesterday that it had decided to stand Mr Robeson down pending a stewards' enquiry into the allegations.

On July 20th the News of the World alleged that a reporter and photographer had seen and photographed jumping poles studded with nails and a pole with hedgehog skins lashed to it at Mr Robeson's farm at Tyringham, near Newport Pagnell.

After the paper made the original allegations, Mr Robeson decided to resign from the team, while rejecting allegations of cruelty. Later he changed his mind.

Representatives of the paper later attended a show jumping association inquiry, but Mr Robeson rejected the newspaper's condition that if it provided a dossier of evidence he would undertake not to take legal action.

Earlier this month, Mr Robeson was reinstated as captain.

The inquiry will consider whether Mr Robeson has contravened Rule 5 of the association's regulations that deals with "unseemly conduct." Anyone found guilty under the rule can be suspended for 12 months, or be fined £100 and have their horses banned from shows affiliated to the association.

(August 29)

MILBURN HAS EYE OPERATION

Daily Telegraph Reporter

COLIN MILBURN, 27, the England and Northants cricketer, had an operation on his left eye at Northampton General Hospital following a multiple car crash near Moulton, Northants, just before midnight.

A hospital spokesman said Milburn had a "badly lacerated eye and a cut knee."

It was too early to tell whether or not he was in danger of losing his sight in one eye.

(May 24)

HARROW'S WINNING DEBUT

By Desmond Hill

A magnificent day's racing at the National School's Regatta at Pangbourne on Saturday was tragically overshadowed by the death by drowning of Jonathan Franklin, of the Norwich School eight.

He was thrown out of the boat after catching a crab and Jack Beresford, 71, the Olympic sculler who dived to his assistance, was also nearly drowned.

Harrow collected the Fours Cup on their first visit, and another successful debut by Bradford GS in the Colts Fours was foiled by less than a length by Pangbourne.

(June 16)

ILLINGWORTH LEADS ENGLAND AFTER DAY OF MYSTERY

By E.W. SWANTON

RAY ILLINGWORTH, recently of Yorkshire and the current captain of Leicestershire, was named last evening, after a day of mysterious uncertainty, as the captain of England in the first Test against the West Indies at Old Trafford tomorrow week.

The choice of the selectors, A.V. Bedser, D. Kenyon, A.C. Smith and W.H.H. Sutcliffe, is a surprise in the sense that Tom Graveney has acted as deputy to Colin Cowdrey over the 13 Tests that England have played since January, 1968. Graveney, furthermore, is the senior cricketer at all levels.

Illingworth, however, has the respect of all who have played with him, or have talked cricket with him, as a tactician and student of the game. The Yorkshire dressing room is a good and stern school. He has been, by repute, the right hand man to Brian Close these last few years, and I am sure will have the confidence of his side.

Illingworth's career as a Test cricketer has had its ups and downs, and has been in no sense parallel to his steady progress as an all-rounder for Yorkshire, whose service he left in favour of his new county at the end of last season after a disagreement as to terms.

In 30 Tests he has taken 71 wickets at the highest cost of 27 a time, and made 548 runs, averaging 16. But he has probably never been such a fine off-spinner as he is today. At 37 this coming Sunday, he is in his bowling prime.

Illingworth I make, by the way, the 17th England Test captain since the war. He is the fourth Yorkshireman and, incidentally, only the fifth bowler.

(June 4)

SUNDAY VICTORY

By HENRY CALTHORPE

The new Sunday League had a fine send-off at headquarters yesterday, when Middlesex beat Yorkshire by 43 runs in a very entertaining afternoon's cricket. Middlesex made 137 for eight in their 40 overs and Yorkshire, after four wickets for 10 runs were all out for 94 in 32.2 overs.

The match held the interest of the Lords crowd of about 5,000 right to the end - a good augury for the competition's future. In accordance with the rules, the game never stagnated and there was a lot of good cricket.

The overs were bowled quickly, the bowlers' 15 yard run-up limit playing its part; the running between wickets was good; the fielding excellent and there was a sense of urgency and purpose about every ball.

Two Spinners

Middlesex recovered from a bad start through some enterprising stroke play from Parfitt and Radley who added 55 for the third wicket.

Yorkshire made an even worse start, however. Sharpe was brilliantly caught at second slip by Parfitt in Connolly's first over. The score was only three when Price, following through, picked up and threw out Boycott going for a quick single.

In the fifth over Padgett drove at Price and was caught behind and three balls later Close was taken at first slip playing forward. When Hampshire drove Price into mid-on's hands and Balderstone was run out after a ghastly muddle with Wilson Yorkshire were in a hopeless position of being 26 for six.

(April 28)

BRUCE TULLOH, 33, THE BRITISH OLYMPIC ATHLETE, receiving the Freedom of New York City yesterday from Mr. Charles Willis, deputy Commissioner of Public Events, at the end of his 2,830-mile run across the United States from Los Angeles. During the 64 days and 22 hrs— nine days better than the previous record in 1964 — he was accompanied by his wife, Sue (background), and son, Clive, 7, in a car.

BLAKENEY'S TRIUMPH

By HOTSPUR (Peter Scott)

BLAKENEY'S bold run through on the inside gained him a well-deserved Derby success at Epsom yesterday and launched a new young international riding star in Ernie Johnson. Shoemaker beat the fast-finishing Prince Regent for second place.

Johnson had never before ridden in the Derby, and Shoemaker was only Brian Taylor's second mount, but their jockeyship put some of the established stars to shame. Yves Saint-Martin and Jean Deforge looked particularly at fault.

Their separate tactics on Countess de la Valden's two runners, Moon Mountain and Prince Regent, embodied rashness and over-caution.

Ribofilio, the 7-2 favourite, finished fifth. He never managed a really big threat and Lester Piggott said the colt handicapped himself by running too free early.

The well-backed Paddy's Progress ran prominently throughout but this big and still inexperienced colt became unbalanced when looking dangerous halfway up the straight.

Breeder, trainer and owner

Even more, perhaps, than for Ernie Johnson, Blakeney's win was a personal triumph for Arthur Budgett, who bred and trains Blakeney, besides owning a half-share in him.

That colourful little Italian Chevalier Ginistrelli played a rather similar part in the 1908 winner Signorinetta's career but he owned her outright. Blink Bonny (1857) and Blair Athol (1864) were both owned, trained and bred by William I'Anson, but these are the only other such cases in the Derby's 189-year history.

(June 3)

STAMINA AND FLAIR PAY OFF

By ROGER MALONE

SWINDON, after beating Arsenal 3-1 in the League Cup, for me are the greatest giant-killers of them all. And stamina, spiced with tactical enterprise, is their golden recipe.

There is in addition, of course, Don Rogers, a law unto himself – a big, fast dribbler with ice-cool, deadly finishing who soon surely must be England material.

The great contenders for the giant-killing crown are Millwall (1937), Port Vale (1954), York (1955) and Norwich (1959), who reached the F.A. Cup semi-finals as Third Division teams; Rochdale, who lost in the 1962 League Cup final as a Fourth Division side, and, above all, Queen's Park Rangers, who won the League Cup two years ago from the Third Division.

But West Bromwich, Rangers' Wembley victims, were not then such a power in the land as Arsenal have become this season. Nor did Rangers have to play for 12 matches, and come through extra time twice against First Division opponents – 19 hours' play in all – to win the trophy.

Danny Williams, the Swindon manager, has built up the stamina and nurtured the enterprise of his willing players.

In the dramatic moments of respite before extra time, he was able to give his men a mental lift by saying: "Look at Arsenal, they are tired out – one of them lying on the ground, another asking for the sponge You've still got plenty left. Now show them our stamina."

Arsenal could have won during the 90 minutes, but the longer extra time went on, the stronger Swindon looked – just as in extra time against Burnley in the semi-final.

(March 17)

MCC HOME AFTER PAKISTAN RIOTERS FORCE TOUR TO END

By MICHAEL MELFORD

AT lunchtime yesterday on what should have been the fourth day of the final Test in Karachi, MCC arrived back at Heathrow Airport. The most violent riot of all had caused the match to be abandoned 15 minutes before lunch on Saturday and MCC left for home that night.

This particular demonstration was directed against people watching cricket on a day set aside, only the night before, as one of protest on behalf of teachers.

The demonstrators assembled carrying banners outside the ground, broke into it, climbed the fence guarding the playing area with an ugly purposeful look which had not marked previous invasions and headed for the pitch.

England at this point had reached 502 for seven after some of the most adventurous batting of the series by Knott and Brown.

Knott was within four runs of his first test 100 but much of the success of the stand of 75 had come from Brown's swift appreciation of the quick single. He summed up the mood of the mob with the same swiftness and, summoning Knott, raced for the pavilion with the Pakistan players.

In a few seconds hundreds of youths were on the playing area. The stumps were pulled out and used to dig holes in the pitch – no easy feat for it would have lasted a fortnight. The mob then headed for the main stand which it wrecked.

After a few minutes armed police reinforcements arrived and quickly dispersed the demonstrators. This feat was greeted with loud applause from the honest cricket lovers in the main stands who also showed all signs of satisfaction when one of the banner-bearing ring-leaders was left unconscious and bleeding beside the Press box.

The teams had taken refuge in their dressing rooms and were driven away through an unruly throng before the abandonment of the match was announced.

The final decision was taken by Fida Hassan, President of the Pakistan Board of Control with the MCC manager's wholehearted agreement.

Perhaps the happiest feature of a sad tour was the harmony between the two sides. Much of this derived from the presence in the Pakistan side of three players from English counties. Mushtaq, Majid and Asif. For them and perhaps even more for the other Pakistan players whose cricket future looks even bleaker, the heart bleeds.

(March 10)

GREAVES: RAMSEY EXPLAINS

By DAVID MILLER

SIR ALF RAMSEY, who was pelted with fruit and rubbish as he walked out on the Wembley pitch before Wednesday's international against France, yesterday spoke bitterly about the campaign to restore Jimmy Greaves to the England team.

"I have been crucified by this campaign," he said. "Yet it was Greaves himself who asked to be left out of the team 15 months ago, before the match against Russia.

"There was no ill-feeling between us, but he also said that he did not want to spend time away from his business interests for England training and preparation if he was not going to be selected. How can I play any man whose heart and soul is not for England?"

The urbane and sometimes seemingly equivocal Ramsey which the public sees on TV is very different from the real man. That public image is merely protective. He has an intense, almost vehement side, which showed yesterday as he answered his critics.

"I'm only human. I cannot endure indefinitely without replying. But there's only one thing I ever have in mind. And that's to get my hands again on that World Cup trophy. How I set about it must be left to me."

(March 14)

'DOLLY' IS MADE AN OBE

BASIL D'OLIVEIRA, 34, the Cape-coloured cricketer whose ban by South Africa led to the cancellation of the MCC tour last winter, is made an OBE in the Birthday Honours List published today.

D'Oliveira, who joined Worcestershire after leaving his native South Africa, scored 57 for England against the West Indies at Old Trafford yesterday.

(July 24)

LEEDS EARN FIRST EVER TITLE

By DONALD SAUNDERS

Liverpool ...... 0 Leeds 0

LEEDS survived a passionate battle of the Roses at Anfield last night to break Lancashire's six-season monopoly of the League championship and make sure that the title will shortly cross the Pennines on its first visit to Yorkshire since Sheffield Wednesday held it in 1930.

You might think that in these days of violent partisanship on the terraces such effrontery would have caused a riot on the Kop. Far from it.

As Billy Bremner led his triumphant troops on a lap of honour the Kop rose to them in a spontaneous noisy gesture of acclamation. Soon the ground was resounding with full-throated Merseyside cheers, as though Liverpool were champions again.

What a joy it was to see sportsmanship return to an English football ground. But then, who could justly begrudge the dedicated, superbly efficient professionals from Elland Road their first success in this, the most demanding of all soccer competitions.

Twice in the past five years Leeds have suffered the heart-breaking disappointment of finishing as runners-up. But their determination to get there in the end has never wavered.

Now, having achieved their objective and earned nation-wide respect, perhaps they will begin to think about winning a lot more friends. That means a little more adventurous football, even at the expense of efficiency.

Commonsense returns

From the kick-off it was clearly going to be warfare, not football. In the first 20 minutes both sides might just as well have tossed the ball into the grandstand.

During that furious period, Cooper hurled himself recklessly at Smith, Jones badly fouled Lawrence, Sprake was badly shaken in a collision with Yeats and Jones was sent flying from a charge in the back by Smith.

Thereafter a little commonsense returned to the pitch, though he who foolishly tried to run five yards with the ball soon stretched his length on the turf.

Yet, for all the fury, both sides kept their tempers. Moreover, there was an amazing amount of method amid the madness.

But, for my money, the men who epitomised the type of footballer Liverpool and Leeds rely on so much were Smith and Hunter.

Smith was at the heart of Liverpool's defence and the springboard of the long determined assault they launched after the interval.

Hunter, never flustered, never in the wrong spot, was the strong man of a Leeds defence that stood so firmly under pressure that Liverpool must have despaired of ever getting through.

(April 29)

CLIVE LLOYD HITS OUT

By D.J. RUTNAGUR at Nuneaton

BEATING Warwickshire at Nuneaton by 51 runs for their 12th victory yesterday, Lancashire, who still have one match to play, became the first champions of the Player's Sunday League.

Batting first, Lancashire were given a speedy start by Engineer and David Lloyd.

There were two brief passages when headway was slow against Cartwright, Ibadulla and Gibbs, but once Clive Lloyd, after a hesitant start against Gibbs, had adjusted his sights, the Warwickshire attack came in for a period of devastation.

Lloyd made 59 with four sizes – all of them landing out of the ground – and three fours. Sullivan had nine fours in his unbeaten 60, and together he and Lloyd added 105 in 18 overs in the Lancashire total of 204 for five wickets.

Warwickshire scoring rate was, in the beginning, brisk enough to threaten Lancashire, but after they had reached 120 for three, wickets fell too frequently for the rate to be maintained. Their innings lasted only 36.5 overs when they were all out for 153.

(August 25)

SPACE LINK BY MOON MEN

IN VIETNAM the American nationwide anti-Vietnam war protest was observed by Lieut Jesse Rosen, of New York, who wore a black armband as he led his platoon on combat patrol south-west of Chu Lai. "It's just my way of silently protesting," he explained.

THE SYMBOLIC MOMENT as Neil Armstrong and Edwin Aldrin planted the Stars and Stripes on the lunar surface.

ABOVE: ROBIN-KNOX JOHNSON sets ashore.

LEFT: THE 32ft KETCH SUHAILI, with Robin Knox-Johnston at the helm, being escorted over the finishing line at Pendennis Point, Falmouth, Cornwall, yesterday at the end of a 312-day non-stop voyage round the world.

SQUATTERS PREPARING TO DEFEND 144, Piccadilly, yesterday after they had taken over the empty building. They hope to provide accommodation for homeless families.

THE QUEEN MAKING HER FIRST RIDE on the Underground since she was a child after she had opened the third stage of the £70 million Victoria Line yesterday.

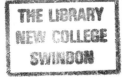